FAMILY LAW

CASES, COMMENTS AND QUESTIONS

Fourth Edition

By

Harry D. Krause
Max L. Rowe Professor of Law Emeritus
University of Illinois

Linda D. Elrod
Distinguished Professor of Law
Washburn Law School

Marsha Garrison
Professor of Law
Brooklyn Law School

J. Thomas Oldham
John H. Freeman Professor of Law
University of Houston Law Center

AMERICAN CASEBOOK SERIES®

WEST GROUP

ST. PAUL, MINN., 1998

610 Opperman Drive
P.O. Box 64526
St. Paul, MN 55164–0526
1–800–328–9352

Printed in the United States of America

Library of Congress Cataloging-in-Publication Data

Cases, comments, and questions on family law / by Harry D. Krause . . .
[et al.]. — 4th ed.
p. cm. — (American casebook series)
Rev. ed. of: Family law / by Harry D. Krause. 3rd ed. 1990.
Includes index.
ISBN 0–314–21123–3 (hardcover : alk. paper)
1. Domestic relations—United States—Cases. I. Krause, Harry D., 1932– . II. Krause, Harry D., 1932– Family law.
III. Series.
KF504.K7 1998
346.7301'5—dc21 98–20189
CIP

ISBN 0–314–21123–3

TEXT IS PRINTED ON 10% POST CONSUMER RECYCLED PAPER

2nd Reprint — 2001

This fourth edition is dedicated to:

Dr. Marion Llewellynn Drake,
who believed in his grandson.

J.T.O.

Harvey, Petey, and David

M.G.

Carson and Bree

L.D.E.

My splendid new coauthors—
Linda, Marsha and Tom

H.D.K.

*

Preface

With this edition, the Krause family law casebook has become the Krause/Elrod/Garrison/Oldham casebook. In this fourth edition, we have tried to carry on the tradition established in the earlier editions. That is, we have tried very hard to make this a book that considers family law issues from a comparative perspective, that emphasizes the connection between family law and family policy, and, while it addresses the many novel and interesting questions relating to family law (in vitro fertilization, abortion, minor's rights, etc.), a book that focuses on matters that are of the most practical importance to those who practice family law.

July 1998

*

Acknowledgments

The authors are indebted to Enrique Huerta for his word processing assistance and to Heather Peterson and Connie Kohler for proofreading. The authors also are grateful to family members for putting up with us while we were writing this edition.

*

Summary of Contents

	Page
PREFACE	v
ACKNOWLEDGMENTS	vii
TABLE OF CASES	xxv

Chapter

1.	American Family Law: Definitions, Policy and Trends	1
2.	The Regulation of Marriage	46
3.	The Legal Significance of Marriage—Rights and Obligations, Lost and Gained	110
4.	Marital Agreements	184
5.	Nonmarital Relationships—Rights and Obligations	225
6.	Becoming a Parent: Contraception, Abortion, and Paternity Establishment	266
7.	Adoption	307
8.	Assisted Reproduction	359
9.	Child, Parent, and State: Rights and Obligations	403
10.	The Lawyer's Role in Family Disputes	494
11.	Divorce and Divorce Substitutes	531
12.	Jurisdiction Over Family Disputes	571
13.	Child Custody on Divorce	628
14.	Property Division at Divorce	719
15.	Spousal Support	790
16.	Child Support	836
17.	Separation Agreements	898
18.	Alternative Dispute Resolution	925
19.	Legal Consequences of Child Support, Property Division and Alimony Distinguished: Taxation and Bankruptcy	947
20.	Modification and Enforcement of Support Awards	967

INDEX	1013

*

Table of Contents

		Page
Preface		v
Acknowledgments		vii
Table of Cases		xxv
Chapter 1. American Family Law: Definitions, Policy and Trends		**1**
Section 1.	The New Family and the New Family Law	1
A.	The New Family	1
	Mary Ann Glendon, The New Family and the New Property	1
	Notes and Questions	8
B.	The New Family Law	8
C.	A Family by Any Name?	9
	Moore v. City of East Cleveland, Ohio	10
	Notes and Questions	13
Section 2.	Constitutional Family Law: "Emanations and Penumbras"	19
	Griswold v. Connecticut	19
	Notes and Questions	23
	Doe v. Duling	24
	Notes and Questions	27
Section 3.	The Federal Tradition of Non–Involvement—The Tenth Amendment and More	30
	Ankenbrandt v. Richards	30
	Notes and Questions	35
Section 4.	The Future—and Inevitability—of Federal Involvement in Family Law	38
	Executive Order 12,606 of September 2, 1987	39
	Notes and Questions	40
	Notes and Questions	45
Chapter 2. The Regulation of Marriage		**46**
Section 1.	A Brief History of Marriage Regulation	46
Section 2.	Constitutional Limitations on State Marriage Regulation	48
	Zablocki v. Redhail	48
	Notes and Questions	57
Section 3.	Substantive Requirements for Entering Marriage	58
A.	Void and Voidable Marriages	58
B.	One at a Time	59
	Potter v. Murray City	60
	Notes and Questions	63
C.	Of Different Sexes	65

Page

Section 3. Substantive Requirements for Entering Marriage—Continued
Baehr v. Lewin 65
Baehr v. Miike 72
Notes and Questions 73
D. Unrelated by Blood 76
7 International Encyclopedia of the Social Sciences 76
Notes and Questions 80
Israel v. Allen 81
Notes and Questions 82
E. Of Sufficient Age 82
Uniform Marriage and Divorce Act § 205 83
Moe v. Dinkins 83
F. In Proper Health and With Good Genes? 86
William Vukowich, The Dawning of the Brave New World—Legal, Ethical, and Social Issues of Eugenics 86
Notes and Questions 86
Section 4. Procedures Relating to Entry Into Marriage 87
A. Consent to Marry 87
1. Capacity to Contract 87
Uniform Marriage and Divorce Act § 208 88
Larson v. Larson 88
Notes and Questions 90
2. Intent to Contract 90
Smith v. I.N.S. 91
B. Solemnization and Licensing 92
Uniform Marriage and Divorce Act 92
Carabetta v. Carabetta 93
Notes and Questions 94
Section 5. Exceptions to the Formal Requirements 96
A. Common Law Marriage 96
P. Bromley, Family Law 96
Estate of Keimig 98
Notes and Questions 102
Kelderhaus v. Kelderhaus 103
Notes and Questions 106
B. The Putative Spouse Doctrine 106
Uniform Marriage and Divorce Act § 209 107
In Re Estate of Vargas 107
Notes and Questions 109

Chapter 3. The Legal Significance of Marriage—Rights and Obligations, Lost and Gained **110**
Section 1. Marital Ideals: From Patriarchy to Equality 110
Beatrice Gottlieb, The Family in the Western World: From the Black Death to the Industrial Age 110
Section 2. Ownership and Control of Property During Marriage 114
A. Common Law States 114
Law Commission (London) 114
B. Community Property States 116
1. In General 116
Uniform Marital Property Act 117
Notes and Questions 118
2. Management of Community Property 119
Martin v. Martin 122

Page

Section 2. Ownership and Control of Property During Marriage—Continued
Notes and Questions 124
Andrews v. Andrews 124
Notes and Questions 125
C. "Til Death Us Do Part:" Spousal Property Rights at Death 127
D. Some Concluding Thoughts 130
Section 3. Spousal Support Obligations During Marriage 131
A. The Necessaries Doctrine 132
McGuire v. McGuire 132
Notes and Questions 136
Sharpe Furniture, Inc. v. Buckstaff 137
Notes and Questions 141
B. The Rights of Creditors 142
C. Private Support Obligations, Public Benefits 143
Septuagenarian v. Septuagenarian 143
Notes and Questions 146
Section 4. Names 147
Kruzel v. Podell 147
Notes and Questions 151
Section 5. Marriage and Tort Law 152
A. Tort Actions Between Husband and Wife 152
Notes and Questions 152
B. Heart Balm Actions 153
C. Spousal Consortium Claims 154
Section 6. Medical and Procreative Decision Making 155
A. Medical Decision Making for an Incompetent Spouse 155
Notes and Questions 156
B. The Affirmative Obligation to Obtain Medical Assistance 157
C. Procreative Decision Making 158
Planned Parenthood of Central Missouri v. Danforth 158
Planned Parenthood v. Casey 160
Notes and Questions 161
Section 7. Marriage and Crime 162
A. Crimes by One Spouse Against Another 162
162
1. Marital Rape 162
Warren v. State 162
Notes and Questions 163
2. Burglary and the Marital Home 165
Cladd v. State 165
Notes and Questions 167
3. The Battered Spouse 168
Developments in the Law—Legal Responses to Domestic Violence 168
State v. Hodges 173
Notes and Questions 177
B. Marriage and the Law of Evidence 178
Trammel v. United States 178
Notes and Questions 182

Page

Chapter 4. Marital Agreements **184**

Section 1. Marriage: Contract or Status? 184
Maynard v. Hill 184
Walton v. Walton 185
Notes and Questions 186

Section 2. Variability of the Marriage Status by Agreement Before Marriage 187
A. Validity of Premarital Agreements 187
1. Procedural Fairness 188
DeLorean v. DeLorean 189
Notes and Questions 193
2. Substantive Fairness 195
Restatement (Second) of Contracts (1981) 195
Gross v. Gross 196
Notes and Questions 202
Uniform Premarital Agreement Act 204
Notes and Questions 205
B. Conflicts Aspects of Premarital Agreements 211
C. Incorporating Noneconomic Provisions in a Premarital Agreement 212
Lenore J. Weitzman, The Marriage Contract 212
Notes and Questions 215

Section 3. Variability of the Marital Status by Agreement During Marriage 216
Borelli v. Brusseau 216
Notes and Questions 220
Curry v. Curry 222
Note and Questions 223

Chapter 5. Nonmarital Relationships—Rights and Obligations **225**

Section 1. Disputes Between Cohabitants 225
Marvin v. Marvin 226
Notes and Questions 234
Hewitt v. Hewitt 236
Notes and Questions 241
Connell v. Francisco 242
Notes and Questions 245

Section 2. Cohabitation Per Statute—The Future of the Cohabitation Alternative? 248
De Facto Relationships Act 248
Notes and Questions 252

Section 3. Disputes Between Dating Partners 254
A. Engagement Disputes 254
1. Breach of Promise to Marry 254
2. Engagement Gifts 254
In re Marriage of Heinzman 254
Notes and Questions 256
B. Disputes Between Dating Partners 256
Taylor v. Fields 256
Questions 260
Kathleen K. v. Robert B. 260
Notes and Questions 263

Page

Chapter 6. Becoming a Parent: Contraception, Abortion, and Paternity Establishment ---- **266**
Section 1. Contraception ---- 266
Notes and Questions ---- 267
Section 2. Abortion ---- 268
Roe v. Wade ---- 269
Notes and Questions ---- 272
Planned Parenthood v. Casey ---- 273
Notes and Questions ---- 279
Section 3. Paternity ---- 279
A. The Presumption of Legitimacy ---- 279
William Blackstone, Commentaries on the Laws of England, Book 1 ---- 279
Michael H. v. Gerald D. ---- 280
Notes and Questions ---- 288
B. Removing the Stigma of Illegitimacy ---- 293
Levy v. Louisiana ---- 293
Notes and Questions ---- 294
C. Establishing Paternity ---- 296
Hanson v. Hanson ---- 298
Notes and Questions ---- 298
G.E.B. v. S.R.W. ---- 300
Notes and Questions ---- 304

Chapter 7. Adoption ---- **307**
Section 1. The Changing Face of Adoption Practice ---- 307
Section 2. Consent to Adoption ---- 311
A. Consent by Birth Mothers ---- 311
In Re J.M.P. ---- 311
Notes and Questions ---- 318
B. The Unmarried Father ---- 319
Lehr v. Robertson Et Al. ---- 319
Adoption of Kelsey S. ---- 325
Notes and Questions ---- 331
Uniform Putative and Unknown Fathers Act ---- 332
Section 3. Who May Adopt Whom? ---- 336
A. Adoption in the Context of Nontraditional Relationships 336
In the Matter of Jacob, In the Matter of Dana, G.M. ---- 336
Notes and Questions ---- 343
B. Racial and Ethnic Matching in Adoption ---- 344
America's Waiting Children 29–30 ---- 345
Twila L. Perry, The Transracial Adoption Controversy: An Analysis of Discourse and Subordination ---- 346
Notes and Questions ---- 348
Section 4. The Effect of Adoption ---- 349
Michaud v. Wawruck Et Al. ---- 349
Notes and Questions ---- 352
Section 5. The Baby Market: Gray and Black ---- 353
In the Matter of the Adoption of a Child by N.P. & F.P. ---- 353
Notes and Questions ---- 355

Page

Chapter 8. Assisted Reproduction 359
Section 1. Artificial Insemination 360
Jhordan C. v. Mary K. 360
Notes and Questions 367
Section 2. In Vitro Fertilization and Ovum Transplantation 369
Davis v. Davis 369
Notes and Questions 377
Section 3. "Surrogate" Motherhood 379
Matter of Baby M 380
Notes and Questions 387
Johnson v. Calvert 390
Notes and Questions 397
Section 4. Toward a Legislative Framework 398
Harry Krause, Artificial Conception: Legislative Approaches 398

Chapter 9. Child, Parent, and State: Rights and Obligations 403
Section 1. Children's Rights and Legal Status 403
Kingsley v. Kingsley 404
Notes and Questions 408
William Blackstone, Commentaries on the Laws of England;Book I 411
Foster & Freed, A Bill of Rights for Children 413
Note and Questions 413
Section 2. Education 418
Wisconsin v. Yoder 419
Notes and Questions 424
Section 3. Medical Decision Making 427
Parham v. J. R. 428
Notes and Questions 433
In re Green 434
Notes and Questions 438
Maine Medical Center v. Houle 439
Robert & Peggy Stinson, On the Death of a Baby 441
Notes and Questions 443
Section 4. Contraception and Abortion: A Special Case of Medical Decision Making 447
Carey v. Population Services International Et Al. 447
Hodgson v. Minnesota 449
Notes and Questions 457
Section 5. Child Abuse and Neglect 459
A. An Overview of the Child Welfare System 459
Marsha Garrison, Child Welfare Decisionmaking: In Search of the Least Drastic Alternative 459
B. What Constitutes Neglect? 462
In re T.G., C.G., D.G., and D.G., D.F., and E.G. 462
Notes and Questions 468
Whitner v. State of South Carolina 471
Notes and Questions 477
C. Termination of Parental Rights 478
Kingsley v. Kingsley 478
In the Interest of M.M.L. 478
In the Matter of the Guardianship of J.C., J.C., and J.M.C., Minors 484
Notes and Questions 490

Page

Chapter 10. The Lawyer's Role in Family Disputes 494
Section 1. Family Law as a Specialty 494
Notes and Questions 497
Section 2. Regulating the Lawyer–Client Relationship 497
A. An Introduction 497
B. Avoiding Conflicts of Interest 498
1. Dual Representation 498
Klemm v. Superior Court 498
Notes and Questions 502
2. Prior Representation 503
3. The Unrepresented Litigant 503
C. Setting the Fee 504
Notes and Questions 504
V.W. v. J.B. 506
Notes and Questions 510
D. Duties to the Client 510
1. Competence and Diligence 510
2. Deference to the Client's Decisions 511
Florida Bar v. Susan K. Glant 511
Notes and Questions 514
3. Confidentiality 514
4. Sex with Clients 515
Notes and Questions 515
E. Duties to Opposing Parties and Counsel 516
1. Communication with Other Parties 516
2. Fair Bargaining 516
Section 3. Criticisms of Divorce Lawyers and the Divorce Process 516
A. The Process is Too Adversarial 517
Charles B. Craver, Negotiation Ethics: How to Be Deceptive Without Being Dishonest/How to Be Assertive Without Being Offensive 517
B. The Process is Too Expensive 520
C. The Process Takes Too Long 521
Section 4. Malpractice 521
A. Liability to the Client 522
Grayson v. Wofsey, Rosen, Kweskin and Kuriansky 522
Notes and Questions 528
B. Liability to Third Parties 528
Scholler v. Scholler 528
Notes and Questions 529

Chapter 11. Divorce and Divorce Substitutes 531
Section 1. A Brief History of Divorce 532
Section 2. Grounds for Divorce 537
A. Fault Divorce 537
Lynch v. Lynch 538
Capps v. Capps 539
Notes and Questions 541
B. Fault Divorce Defenses 542
Hollis v. Hollis 542
C. No–Fault Divorce 544

Page

Section 2. Grounds for Divorce—Continued
1. No–Fault Grounds 544
Notes and Questions 545
2. What Constitutes Irretrievable Breakdown 546
Hagerty v. Hagerty 546
Notes and Questions 548
3. What Constitutes Separation 548
Wife S. v. Husband S. 548
Notes and Questions 549
4. Summary Divorce Procedures 551
Section 3. The Current Debate: What Divorce Law Do We Want? 551
The Law Commission (London), Facing the Future: A Discussion Paper on the Ground for Divorce 551
Section 4. Alternatives to Divorce 560
A. Separate Maintenance and Divorce From Bed and Board 560
B. Annulment 560
Section 5. Access to Divorce 563
A. Is There a Constitutional Right to Divorce? 563
Boddie v. Connecticut 563
Notes and Questions 565
B. Residency Requirements 566
Sosna v. Iowa 566

Chapter 12. Jurisdiction Over Family Disputes 571
Section 1. Jurisdiction Over Divorce 571
P. Hay, Conflict of Laws 571
In re Estate of Steffke 575
Kazin v. Kazin 577
Notes and Questions 579
Section 2. Personal Jurisdiction 581
Kulko v. Superior Court of California 581
Notes and Questions 587
Section 3. Interstate Modification and Enforcement of Child Support Awards 588
Uniform Interstate Family Support Act 589
Department of Revenue v. Fleet 594
Section 4. Interstate Child Custody Jurisdiction 597
A. The Uniform Child Custody Jurisdiction Act 598
Uniform Child Custody Jurisdiction Act 598
Note 601
B. The Parental Kidnapping Prevention Act 601
Parental Kidnapping Prevention Act 601
Notes and Questions 603
C. Initial Custody Determinations Under the UCCJA and PKPA 605
In re Custody of Glanzner 605
Notes and Questions 610
D. Modification of Custody Decrees 611
Greenlaw v. Smith 611
Notes and Questions 616
Section 5. The Hague Convention 617
Friedrich v. Friedrich 617
Notes and Questions 625

Page

Chapter 13. Child Custody on Divorce **628**

Section 1. What Rights for Children? 629

The Law Commission (London), Facing the Future: A Discussion Paper on the Ground for Divorce 629

Notes and Questions 630

Miller v. Miller 632

Notes and Questions 636

Section 2. Parent v. Parent—Determining the Best Interests of the Child 638

Robert H. Mnookin, Child Custody Adjudication: Judicial Functions in the Face of Indeterminacy 639

Notes and Questions 640

A. Prohibited Factors: Gender and Race 640

Ex Parte Devine 640

Notes and Questions 643

Palmore v. Sidoti 645

Notes and Questions 647

B. The Role of Religion and Parental "Life-Style" 647

In Re Marriage of Wang 647

Notes and Questions 651

C. The Role of Domestic Violence 653

Owan v. Owan 653

Notes and Questions 657

D. The Role of the "Expert" 658

Jones v. Jones 660

Notes and Questions 662

Section 3. Alternatives to the Best Interests Standard—Solving or Compounding the Dilemma? 664

A. The Primary Caretaker Presumption 664

Garska v. McCoy 664

Notes and Questions 668

B. Joint Custody 670

Beck v. Beck 671

Martha A. Fineman, Dominant Discourse, Professional Language, and Legal Change in Child Custody Decisionmaking 675

Notes and Questions 676

Section 4. Access and Visitation Rights of the Nonresidential Parent 682

Schutz v. Schutz 682

Notes and Questions 684

Morgan v. Foretich 686

Notes and Questions 692

Section 5. Custody Disputes Between a Parent and Nonparent 693

Painter v. Bannister 694

Notes and Questions 700

Section 6. Nonparental Visitation Rights 705

Beagle v. Beagle 705

Notes and Questions 708

Section 7. Modifying a Custody Order 712

Levine v. Bacon 715

Notes and Questions 716

		Page
Chapter 14.	**Property Division at Divorce**	**719**
Section 1.	An Overview	719
Section 2.	Defining and Valuing Marital Property	721
A.	Separate v. Marital: When and How Was the Property Acquired?	721
	Giha v. Giha	721
	Notes and Questions	724
	Shea v. Shea	725
	O'Neill v. O'Neill	727
	Notes and Questions	728
B.	Separate v. Marital: Apportionment, Commingling, Tracing, and Transmutation	728
	Brown v. Brown	729
	Cockrill v. Cockrill	729
	Notes and Questions	730
	Friebel v. Friebel	731
	Notes and Questions	736
C.	Acquisitions Over Time	737
	Brandenburg v. Brandenburg	737
	Notes and Questions	739
D.	Insurance Proceeds and Tort Claims	740
	Trahan v. Trahan	740
	Andrle v. Andrle	741
	Notes and Questions	742
E.	Pension Benefits and Other Employee Compensation	743
	1. Basic Terminology	743
	2. Apportionment	744
	Taggart v. Taggart	744
	Notes and Questions	746
	3. Payment	748
	Johnson v. Johnson	748
	Notes and Questions	750
F.	Professional Degrees and Licenses	756
	O'Brien v. O'Brien	756
	Notes and Comments	762
G.	Business Goodwill	766
	Prahinski v. Prahinski	766
	Notes and Questions	773
H.	Debts	776
Section 3.	Dividing the Divisible Estate	778
	Gastineau v. Gastineau	781
	Notes and Questions	784
Chapter 15.	**Spousal Support**	**790**
Section 1.	An Introduction to Spousal Support: What Is It? Why Is It Awarded?	790
	Homer H. Clark, Jr., The Law of Domestic Relations in the United States	790
	Uniform Marriage and Divorce Act § 308. Maintenance	796
	Notes and Questions	798
Section 2.	Factors in Determining the Award of Alimony	798
A.	Need	798
	Morgan v. Morgan	798
	Notes and Questions	800

Page

Section 2. Factors in Determining the Award of Alimony—Continued
Marriage of Huntington 801
Notes and Questions 804
B. Marital Fault 805
Bender v. Bender 805
Notes and Questions 806
Section 3. The Duration and Value of Alimony 809
A. The Duration of Alimony 809
Otis v. Otis 809
Marriage of Baker 814
Notes and Questions 817
B. The Value of Alimony 819
Section 4. The Alimony Debate: Are Current Standards Fair? 821
Olsen v. Olsen 821
Richard Posner, Economic Analysis of Law 825
Notes and Questions 826
Ira M. Ellman, The Theory of Alimony 827
Jane Rutherford, Duty in Divorce: Shared Income as a Path to Equality 830
Notes and Questions 832

Chapter 16. Child Support **836**
Section 1. An Historical Perspective 836
William Blackstone, Commentaries on the Laws of England, Book I 836
Section 2. Support in the Intact Family 838
Roe v. Doe 838
Notes and Questions 841
Section 3. Support in the Separated Family: Who Pays? 842
A. Biological Parents 842
Straub v. B.M.T 842
Notes and Questions 846
B. Stepparents and Other Residential Adults 846
Wiese v. Wiese 846
Notes and Questions 850
C. Adult Children 852
William Blackstone, Commentaries on the Laws of England, Book I 852
Cannon v. Juras 853
Notes and Questions 854
Section 4. Support in the Separated Family 855
A. From Discretion to Bright–Line Rules 855
Uniform Marriage and Divorce Act § 309 855
National Center for State Courts, Development of Guidelines for Child Support Orders: Advisory Panel Recommendations and Final Report 856
Robert Williams, An Overview of Child Support Guidelines in the United States 859
Notes and Questions 862
B. Defining Income 865
William R.T. v. Bonnie R.T. 865
Notes and Questions 867
C. Applying the Guidelines: Recurring Special Cases 868
1. The Rich Obligor 868

Page

Section 4. Support in the Separated Family—Continued
McGinley v. Herman 868
Notes and Questions 872
2. The Poor Support Obligor 874
Notes and Questions 876
3. Joint and Split Custody; "Extra" Visitation 877
Bast v. Rossoff 877
Notes and Questions 880
D. The Duration of Child Support 882
1. Termination Due to the Child's Age 882
Neudecker v. Neudecker 882
Notes and Questions 884
2. Termination Due to the Death of the Obligor 886
William Blackstone, Commentaries on the Laws of England, Book I 886
Section 5. Evaluating Current Guidelines 887
A. Achieving Continuity–of–Expenditure 888
Burt Barnow, Economic Studies of Expenditures on Children and Their Relationship to Child Support Guidelines in Child Support Guidelines: The Next Generation 18 888
B. Raising Pre–Guideline Award Values: 891
C. Preventing Poverty and Standard of Living Disparity 892
D. Comparing the Models 894
Robert Williams, An Overview of Child Support Guidelines in the United States, in Child Support Guidelines: The Next Generation 894
American Law Institute, Principles of the Law of Family Dissolution: Analysis and Recommendations §§ 3.04, 3.05B 894

Chapter 17. Separation Agreements **898**
Section 1. Negotiating and Drafting the Agreement 898
A. Negotiating a Settlement 898
Robert Mnookin & Lewis Kornhauser, Bargaining in the Shadow of the Law: The Case of Divorce 899
B. Drafting the Agreement 902
Stewart v. Stewart 902
Notes and Questions 903
Section 2. Nondisclosure and Misrepresentation 904
Hresko v. Hresko 904
Notes and Questions 907
Section 3. What Terms Are Permissible? 908
A. Fairness 908
Jameson v. Jameson 910
Notes and Questions 911
B. Terms Encouraging Divorce 913
Restatement (Second) of Contracts § 190 (1981) 913
Section 4. Enforcement and Modification of the Agreement 915
A. Merger of the Agreement Into the Decree 915
Murphy v. Murphy 915
Notes and Questions 917
B. Enforcement by Contempt 919
Oedekoven v. Oedekoven 919
C. Waiver of the Right to Modify 920

Page

Section 4. Enforcement and Modification of the Agreement—Continued
Karon v. Karon 920
Notes and Questions 923

Chapter 18. Alternative Dispute Resolution **925**
Section 1. Introduction 925
Section 2. Mediation 927
A. Mediation 927
American Bar Association, American Arbitration Association, Society of Professionals in Dispute Resolution, Model Standards of Conduct of Mediators 927
B. The Mediation Process 928
Jay Folberg, Divorce Mediation: A Workable Alternative 928
Notes and Questions 929
C. Mediator Qualifications 931
Standards of Practice for Lawyer Mediators in Family Disputes 931
Notes and Questions 933
D. The Promise and Risks of Mediation 933
Stephen W. Schlissel, A Proposal for Final and Binding Arbitration of Initial Custody Determinations 933
Penelope E. Bryan, Killing Us Softly: Divorce Mediation and the Politics of Power 934
Martha Fineman, Dominant Discourse, Professional Language, and Legal Change In Child Custody Decision Making 935
Notes and Questions 937
Section 3. Arbitration 940
Allan R. Koritzinsky et al., The Benefits of Arbitration 940
Dick v. Dick 941
Notes and Questions 945

Chapter 19. Legal Consequences of Child Support, Property Division and Alimony Distinguished: Taxation and Bankruptcy **947**
Section 1. Basic Overview 947
A. During the Ongoing Marriage 948
Section 2. Taxation 948
A. During the Ongoing Marriage 949
Section 2. Taxation 950
B. At Divorce 950
1. Timing the Divorce Decree 950
2. Property Division (IRC § 1041) 950
3. Child Support and Alimony (IRC §§ 71 and 215) 951
4. Medical Expenses, Dependency Exemptions, Child Care and Earned Income Credits 953
Section 3. Bankruptcy 954
Huckfeldt v. Huckfeldt 954
Harrell v. Sharp 958
Notes and Questions 961
White v. White 962

Page

Chapter 20. Modification and Enforcement of Support Awards ---- **967**

Section 1. Modification: Some General Themes ---- 967

Section 2. Modification Based on a Shift in Income ---- 969

A. The Obligor's Income ---- 969

Marriage of Meegan ---- 969

Harvey v. Robinson ---- 972

Notes and Questions ---- 976

B. The Recipient's Income ---- 978

Carter v. Carter ---- 978

Notes and Questions ---- 979

Section 3. Modification Based on New Relationships ---- 980

A. Cohabitation by the Alimony Recipient ---- 980

Taake v. Taake ---- 980

Notes and Questions ---- 983

B. A Stepparent ---- 988

In Re Marriage of Nimmo ---- 988

Notes and Questions ---- 993

C. Subsequent Children ---- 994

Miller v. Tashie ---- 994

Notes and Questions ---- 995

Section 4. Enforcement of Support Obligations ---- 996

A. Incarceration ---- 997

American Law Institute, Model Penal Code and Commentaries 997

Commonwealth v. Pouliot ---- 998

Child Support Recovery Act of 1992 ---- 998

Notes and Questions ---- 999

B. Contempt ---- 999

Hicks on Behalf of Feiock v. Feiock ---- 999

Notes and Questions ---- 1006

C. Increasing Federal Involvement and Its Impact on Support Enforcement ---- 1006

Notes and Questions ---- 1008

Section 5. Defenses to the Obligation to Pay Support ---- 1011

A. Lack of Access ---- 1011

B. Estoppel ---- 1011

C. Laches ---- 1012

INDEX ---- 1013

Table of Cases

The principal cases are in bold type. Cases cited or discussed in the text are roman type. References are to pages. Cases cited in principal cases and within other quoted materials are not included.

A v. X, Y, and Z, 288
Aaby v. Strange, 717
Abbo v. Briskin, 652
A.C. v. C.B., 701
Adams, In re Marriage of, 785
Adams, Matter of Marriage of, 193
Adan, In re Marriage of, 743
Adoption of a Child by N. P., Matter of, 353
Adoption of A.M.B., Matter of, 331
Adoption of Baby Boy S., Matter of, 332
Adoption of B.L.V.B., In re, 343, 711
Adoption of Child by T.W.C., Matter of, 604
Adoption of H.M.G., Matter of, 318
Adoption of Kelsey S., 325, 331, 335, 336
Adoption of Michael, Matter of, 332
Adoption of Michael H., 331
Adoption of N.A.P., Matter of, 318
Adoption of Tammy, 343
Adoption of T.K.J., Matter of, 343
Adoption of Two Children by H.N.R., Matter of, 343
Ainsworth v. Ainsworth, 995
Akron, City of v. Akron Center for Reproductive Health, Inc., 272
Alderson v. Alderson, 235
Aleshire, In re Marriage of, 930
Alfonso v. Fernandez, 459
Alfree v. Alfree, 152
Alison D. v. Virginia M., 701, 710
Allee, State ex rel. v. Gocha, 863
Allen, In re, 246
Allen v. Farrow, 626 N.Y.S.2d 125, p. 686
Allen v. Farrow, 611 N.Y.S.2d 859, p. 686
Americana Healthcare Center, a Div. of Manor Healthcare Corp. v. Randall, 854
Anastasi v. Anastasi, 35
Anderson v. Anderson, 552 N.E.2d 546, p. 291
Anderson v. Anderson, 449 A.2d 334, p. 787
Andrews v. Andrews, 124, 125
Andrle v. Andrle, 741, 742
Anisimov v. Lake, 39, 178
Ankenbrandt v. Richards, 30, 35
Appeal in Maricopa County, Juvenile Action No. JS–8490, Matter of, 331
Application of (see name of party)
Archer v. Archer, 762
Aronow v. Silver, 256
Avitzur v. Avitzur, 208, 216

Baby Boy K., Matter of, 335
Baby Boy S., In re, 318
Baby Doe, In re, 368
Baby Girl, Matter of, 331
Baby M, Matter of, 542 A.2d 52, p. 387
Baby M, Matter of, 537 A.2d 1227, p. **380**
Baby M., Matter of, 525 A.2d 1128, pp. 380, 640
Baehr v. Lewin, 65
Baehr v. Miike, 72, 73
Bailey, United States v., 39, 999
Baird, People v., 510
Baker, In re Marriage of, 814, 817, 818
Baker v. Baker, 207
Baltimore City Dept. of Social Services v. Bouknight, 491
Barbarine v. Barbarine, 976
Barnes v. Barnes, 340 S.E.2d 803, p. 908
Barnes v. Barnes, 280 S.E.2d 538, p. 550
Bartsch v. Bartsch, 581
Bassler v. Bassler, 207
Bast v. Rossoff, 877, 880, 881
Batcheldor v. Boyd, 300
Bauder, Matter of Marriage of, 236
Bayley v. Bayley, 725
Beagle v. Beagle, 678 So.2d 1271, p. **705**
Beagle v. Beagle, 654 So.2d 1260, p. 709
Beal v. Doe, 273
Beam v. Bank of America, 731
Bechtold v. Bechtold, 587
Beck v. Beck, 671
Bell v. Bell, 206
Belle Terre, Village of v. Boraas, 9
Bellotti v. Baird, 438, 458
Belz v. Belz, 785
Benda v. Benda, 604

Bender v. Bender, 805, 809
Bennemon on Behalf of Williams v. Sullivan, 295
Bennett v. Jeffreys, 701
Bennett, People v., 426
Bentz v. Bentz, 818, 967
Berg, In re Marriage of, 725
Bergen v. Wood, 260
Berry v. Berry, 750
Bessette v. Saratoga County Com'r of Social Services, 705
Biddlecom v. Biddlecom, 756
Billington v. Billington, 516
Bilowit v. Dolitsky, 561
Bishop v. Bishop, 751
Bjorgen v. Kinsey, 503
Blackman v. Blackman, 784
Blackman, State ex rel. Hausner v., 298
Blanchard v. Blanchard, 953
Blisset v. Blisset, 1012
Blum v. Blum, 502
Bock v. Bock, 993, 995
Boddie v. Connecticut, 550, **563,** 565
Bodwell v. Brooks, 289, 292
Boehlje, In re Marriage of, 731
Bolger v. Youngs Drug Products Corp., 267
Bongiorno, United States v., 39, 999
Booth v. Booth, 784, 785
Borelli v. Brusseau, 216, 220, 221
Borgess Medical Center v. Smith, 141
Boris v. Blaisdell, 863
Borough of (see name of borough)
Boswell v. Boswell, 106
Boucher By and Through Boucher v. Dixie Medical Center, a Div. of IHC Hospitals, Inc., 154
Boulton v. Boulton, 788
Bowers v. Hardwick, 28, 29
Boyd v. Boyd, 765
Boynton v. Kusper, 95
Brady v. Brady, 541
Brandenburg v. Brandenburg, 737, 739
Brane, Matter of Marriage of, 753
Brantner, In re Marriage of, 792
Braschi v. Stahl Associates Co., 15
Brink v. Brink, 788
Brister, Ex parte, 692
Brister v. Brister, 983
Brock v. Cavanaugh, 1012
Brown v. Board of Ed. of Topeka, Shawnee County, Kan., 418
Brown v. Brown, 611 N.Y.S.2d 65, pp. **729,** 730
Brown v. Brown, 503 N.W.2d 280, p. 995
Brown v. Brown, 399 So.2d 1083, p. 1011
Browning v. Corbett, 95
Bruni v. Bruni, 885
Bryant v. Sullivan, 788
Bueche, In re Marriage of, 601
Bulicek v. Bulicek, 750
Burch v. Burch, 995
Burnham v. Superior Court of California, County of Marin, 587
Burns v. Burns, 776
Bu Roe v. I.N.S., 90
Burtoff v. Burtoff, 204, 206
Bush, In re Marriage of, 874
Button v. Button, 206, 207, 210

Caban v. Healey, 710
Caban v. Mohammed, 331
Cable v. Anthou, 299
Califano v. Boles, 246
Campas v. Campas, 147
Cannon v. Juras, 853, 855
Capazzoli v. Holzwasser, 915
Capps v. Capps, 539, 541
Carabetta v. Carabetta, 93, 95
Care and Protection of Charles, 426
Carey v. Population Services, Intern., 267, **447**
Carlson v. Olson, 234
Carnes v. Sheldon, 241
Carter v. Brodrick, 710
Carter v. Carter, 978
Carter, State v., 477
Cary v. Cary, 207
Casbar v. Dicanio, 292
Cassie M.D. v. Othmar D., 627
Catli, In re, 962
Chastain v. Chastain, 932 S.W.2d 396, p. 863
Chastain v. Chastain, 559 S.W.2d 933, p. 543
Cherradi v. Lavoie, 643
Childers v. Childers, 885
Ching v. Ching, 220
Chotiner v. Chotiner, 728
City of (see name of city)
Cladd v. State, 165
Clark v. Atkins, 718
Clark v. Jeter, 304
Clausen, In re, 604
Cleland v. Cleland, 503
C. M. v. C. C., 367
Cockrill v. Cockrill, 729, 730, 731
Coggins v. Coggins, 215
Cole, In re Marriage of, 718
Cole v. Cole, 35
Cole v. Roberts, 747
Colon v. Colon, 153
Combs v. Sherry–Combs, 215
Comiskey, In re Estate of, 1012
Commissioner v. ______ (see opposing party)
Commonwealth v. ______ (see opposing party)
Condore v. Prince George's County, 141
Conduct of Hockett, In re, 503
Coniglio v. Coniglio, 717
Connell v. Francisco, 898 P.2d 831, p. **242**
Connell v. Francisco, 872 P.2d 1150, pp. 245, 246, 252, 264, 265
Connin v. Bailey, 1012
Contino v. Contino, 785
Cooper v. Merkel, 710
Cooperman, Matter of, 504
Corbett v. Corbett, 75

Corrigan, State ex rel. T.A.B. v., 331
County of (see name of county)
Coviello v. Coviello, 725
Cramer v. Commonwealth, 95
Crawford, United States v., 39, 999
Cray, Matter of Marriage of, 724
Crites v. Smith, 420
Crutchley v. Crutchley, 945
Curry v. Curry, 222, 224
Curtis v. Curtis, 604
Curtis v. Kline, 885
Curtis v. School Committee of Falmouth, 459
Custody of C.C.R.S., In re, 318
Custody of C.C.R.S., Matter of, 701
Custody of H.S.H.-K., In re, 701, 710, 711
Czaplewski v. Czaplewski, 995

Daffin v. Daffin, 908
Daggett v. Neiman-Marcus Co., 141
Daghir v. Daghir, 717
Dahl v. Dahl, 784
Dallman's Estate, In re, 102
Damico, In re Marriage of, 1011
Danelson, In re, 510
Daniel v. Daniel, 208
Daniels v. Daniels, 776
Daniels on Behalf of Daniels v. Sullivan, 295
David M v. Lisa M, 711
Davis v. Davis, 643 So.2d 931, p. 241
Davis v. Davis, 842 S.W.2d 588, pp. **369,** 377, 378
Davis v. Davis, 749 P.2d 647, p. 668
Dawley, In re Marriage of, 850
Dean v. District of Columbia, 73
Debenham, Matter of Marriage of, 680
Deegan v. Deegan, 976
deElche v. Jacobsen, 143
DeHaan v. DeHaan, 725
DeJonge, People v., 426
Delconte v. State, 426
DeLorean v. DeLorean, 189, 193, 194, 195, 202, 205, 206, 207, 211, 913
Department of Human Resources v. Williams, 221
DeShurley, In re Marriage of, 756
Desrochers v. Desrochers, 548
Devine, Ex parte, 640, 643
Dewan v. Dewan, 751
Dick v. Dick, 941, 945
Dickens v. Ernesto, 348
Disciplinary Proceedings Against Kinast, Matter of, 516
Doe, In re, 680
Doe v. Attorney General, 390
Doe v. Clark, 318
Doe v. Doe, 39, 178
Doe v. Duling, 24, 29
Doe v. Hartz, 39, 178
Doe, Petition of, 331
Dora P., In re, 30
Dority v. Dority, 787
Doughty v. Engler, 297
Drapek v. Drapek, 762, 764
Dubroc v. Dubroc, 1011
Duell, State v., 177
Du Pont v. Du Pont, 561
Duro v. District Attorney, Second Judicial Dist. of North Carolina, 424, 426
Dyer v. Tsapis, 807, 809

Ebbert v. Ebbert, 546
Eberhardt, People v., 183
Eddy v. Eddy, 753
Edgerton v. Edgerton, 787
Edgett, Estate of, 246
Edwards v. Aguillard, 425
E.G., In re, 439
Eichelberger, In re, 961
Eisenstadt v. Baird, 23, 28, 267
Elden v. Sheldon, 155
Elizabeth Blackwell Health Center for Women v. Knoll, 273
Elkus v. Elkus, 765
Engel v. Vitale, 425
Estate of (see name of party)
Estevez v. Superior Court (Salley), 873
Evans v. Evans, 710
Evans v. Kelley, 279
Everette v. Everette, 747
Everhardt v. Everhardt, 743
Eversman v. Eversman, 548
Ex parte (see name of party)

Faherty v. Faherty, 945
Fall v. Eastin, 588
Fanning v. Fanning, 912
Fantanzo v. Decker, 995
Farrey v. Sanderfoot, 961, 962
Faustin v. Lewis, 90
Feliciano v. Feliciano, 930
Feliciano v. Rosemar Silver Co., 154
Fennell, In re Marriage of, 669
Fernandez v. Fernandez, 212
Fetters, In re Marriage of, 884
Figueiredo-Torres v. Nickel, 154
Finch, In re, 962
Fisher's Estate, In re, 98
Fitzgerald v. Fitzgerald, 863
Flanagan v. Flanagan, 993
Fleitz v. Fleitz, 742
Fletcher v. Fletcher, 193
Flockhart, In re Marriage of, 755
Flores v. Flores, 566
Flores v. Melo-Palacios, 587
Flynn v. Flynn, 725
Flynn v. Rogers, 753
Foley, Matter of Estate of, 300
Forristall v. Forristall, 764
Franks, In re Marriage of, 911
Franzen v. Borders, 977
Frazer v. Frazer, 867
Frederick, In re Marriage of, 784
Freehe v. Freehe, 787

Friebel v. Friebel, 731, 737
Friedrich v. Friedrich, 78 F.3d 1060, p. **617**
Friedrich v. Friedrich, 983 F.2d 1396, p. 625

GAF Corp. v. Diamond Carpet Corp., 142
Gainey v. Olivo, 604
Gammell v. Gammell, 985
Gant v. Gant, 194
Garcia v. Douglas Aircraft Co., 245
Gardner v. Gardner, 193
Garduno v. Garduno, 109
Garrett v. Garrett, 724
Garska v. McCoy, 664, 668, 669
Garvie v. Garvie, 678
Gastineau v. Gastineau, 781, 784
Gault, Application of, 412
Gayden, In re Marriage of, 710
G.E.B. v. S.R.W., 300, 304
Gehm v. Gehm, 908
Geitner By and Through First Nat. Bank of Catawba County v. Townsend, 90
Gelb v. Brown, 776
Gemma v. Gemma, 750
Gerber v. Gerber, 604
Gerth v. Gerth, 833
Gethers, State v., 477
G.F.C. v. S.G., 289
Gibbs v. Ernst, 353
Giha v. Giha, 721, 724
Gilbraith, In re, 292
Gilley v. Gilley, 224
Gimbel Bros., Inc. v. Pinto, 141
Glanzner v. State, Dept. of Social Services, Div. of Child Support Enforcement, 601, 604, **605,** 610
Glassboro, Borough of v. Vallorosi, 17
Glauber v. Glauber, 945
Glickman v. Collins, 915
Glona v. American Guarantee & Liability Ins. Co., 294
Gocha, State ex rel. Allee v., 863
Goldman, In re Marriage of, 216
Golub v. Golub, 765
Gomez v. Perez, 294
Goodwin v. Turner, 402
Gould, Matter of, 515
Gray, State v., 477
Grayson v. Wofsey, Rosen, Kweskin and Kuriansky, 522
Green, In re, 434
Green v. Commissioner, 236
Greenlaw, In re Marriage of, 611, 616
Greenspan v. Slate, 842
Greenwald v. Greenwald, 195
Greenwood, In re Estate of, 300
Gregory, Helvering v., 948
Gregory B., Matter of, 352
Gribble v. Gribble, 710
Griswold v. Connecticut, 19, 23, 24, 28, 29, 267
Gross v. Gross, 492 N.E.2d 476, pp. 202, 205, 207, 210, 211
Gross v. Gross, 464 N.E.2d 500, p. **196**
Grove, Matter of Marriage of, 984
Guardianship of (see name of party)
Guise v. Robinson, 292
Gulisano v. Gulisano, 541
Gursky v. Gursky, 360

Hagerty v. Hagerty, 546, 548
Hagshenas, In re Marriage of, 785
Hailey v. Holden, 1012
Hall, In re Marriage of, 773, 775, 776
Hall v. Fertility Institute of New Orleans, 368
Halvorson v. Halvorson, 785
Hambrick v. Prestwood, 886
Hampshire, United States v., 39, 999
Hann v. Housing Authority of City of Easton, 14
Hanson v. Hanson, 738 S.W.2d 429, p. 775
Hanson v. Hanson, 249 N.W.2d 452, p. **298**
Hardiman, Matter of Marriage of, 993
Hardy, People v., 477
Hare v. Hodgins, 750
Harrell, In re, 958, 961
Harris v. McRae, 273
Harsacky v. Harsacky, 627
Harvey v. Robinson, 972, 976
Hathaway v. Worcester City Hospital, 267
Hauge v. Hauge, 777
Hausner, State ex rel. v. Blackman, 298
Haviland v. Haviland, 787
Hawkins v. Commissioner, 752, 950
Hawkins v. Hawkins, 739
Heacock v. Heacock, 153, 786
Hecht v. Superior Court (Kane), 368
Heiman v. Parrish, 256
Heinzman, In re Marriage of, 254
Heist v. Heist, 153
Heistermann, In re Marriage of, 818
Helvering v. ______ (see opposing party)
Hendrickson, Matter of Estate of, 90
Henn v. Henn, 788, 908
Henriksen v. Cameron, 786
Henrikson v. Gable, 701
Herbert v. Herbert, 919
Hermanson v. State, 438
Hernandez, State v., 994
Hewitt v. Hewitt, 236, 241, 245, 246, 248, 265
Hicks on Behalf of Feiock v. Feiock, 999, 1006
Hildebrand v. Hildebrand, 678
Hill v. Hill, 398 N.E.2d 1048, p. 562
Hill v. Hill, 262 A.2d 661, p. 212
Hiner, In re Marriage of, 788, 908
Hitaffer v. Argonne Co., 154
Hodge v. Hodge, 763
Hodges, State v., 173
Hodgson v. Minnesota, 449
Hoefers v. Jones, 886
Hoffman v. Foley, 1011
Holler v. Holler, 753
Hollis v. Hollis, 542

Honore v. Honore, 924
Hood, In re, 712
Hoover v. Commissioner, 966
Horn, In re Marriage of, 755, 756
Hornbeck v. Hornbeck, 716
Howsden v. Rolenc, 787
Hresko v. Hresko, 904, 908
Hubbell (Gault) v. Hubbell, 643
Huckfeldt, In re, 954
Hudson v. Hudson, 747
Hug, In re Marriage of, 747
Hughes v. Creighton, 710
Hughes v. Hughes, 762
Hunt, In re Marriage of, 750
Hunter v. Christian, 306
Huntington, In re Marriage of, 801
Hurwitz v. Sher, 222
Hutchinson v. Hutchinson, 993
Hutto v. Kneipp, 976
Hylland v. Doe, 331

In Interest of A.E.H., 604
In Interest of Angel Lace M., 343
In Interest of B.G.C., 331
In Interest of J.M., 299
In Interest of J.W.T., 289
In Interest of M.M.L., 478, 490, 491
In Interest of N.M.W., 469
In Interest of R.C., 368
In re (see name of party)
International Shoe Co. v. State of Wash., Office of Unemployment Compensation and Placement, 587, 593
Ireland v. Smith, 670
Ismail v. Ismail, 787
Israel v. Allen, 81, 82

Jacob, Matter of, 336, 343
Jacobson, United States v., 402
J.A.L. v. E.P.H., 701
Jameson v. Jameson, 332 N.W.2d 721, p. 911
Jameson v. Jameson, 306 N.W.2d 240, p. 911
Jameson v. Jameson, 239 N.W.2d 5, pp. **910,** 912
Jane L. v. Rodney B., 297
Jaramillo v. Jaramillo, 717
Jaycee B. v. Superior Court (John B.), 397
J.C., Matter of Guardianship of, 484, 490, 491
Jennings v. Hurt, 106
Jersey Shore Medical Center–Fitkin Hospital v. Baum's Estate, 141
Jhordan C. v. Mary K., 360, 367
J.J., In re, 439
J.J.J., Matter of, 319
J.M.P., In re, 311, 318
John E. v. Doe, 336
Johnson v. Calvert, 390
Johnson v. Iowa Dist. Court for Mahaska County, 1006
Johnson v. Johnson, 468 N.W.2d 648, p. 993
Johnson v. Johnson, 638 P.2d 705, pp. **748,** 750, 751
Johnson v. State, 397, 477
Johnson, United States v., 39, 999
Joiner, Matter of Marriage of, 747
Jones, Matter of Marriage of, 924
Jones v. Daly, 235, 236
Jones v. Feiger, Collison & Killmer, 511
Jones v. Jones, 542 N.W.2d 119, pp. **660,** 662
Jones v. Jones, 450 S.E.2d 762, p. 886
Jordan v. Jordan, 562
Josic v. Josic, 924
Judd, In re Marriage of, 750
Juman v. Louise Wise Services, 353
Justus v. Justus, 207

Kaechele v. Kaechele, 820
Kamel v. Kamel, 752
Kane v. Superior Court (Hecht), 368
Kardokus, People v., 504
Karon v. Karon, 920, 923, 924
Kasinski v. Questel, 785
Kass v. Kass, 663 N.Y.S.2d 581, p. 378
Kass v. Kass, 1995 WL 110368, p. 378
Kathleen K. v. Robert B., 260, 263, 264
Katz, State ex rel. Oklahoma Bar Ass'n v., 503
Kazin v. Kazin, 577
Keimig's Estate, In re, 98, 102, 109
Kelderhaus v. Kelderhaus, 103, 109
Kelley v. Iowa Dept. of Social Services, 850
Kemp, Commonwealth v., 477
Kempf v. Kempf, 167
Kendall v. Kendall, 653
Kenik, In re Marriage of, 550
Ken R. on Behalf of C.R. v. Arthur Z., 711
Kiddie v. Kiddie, 565
Kiister, Matter of Marriage of, 712
Kingsley v. Kingsley, 404, 478, 490, 493
Kirchberg v. Feenstra, 119
Kirk, Matter of Marriage of, 911, 930
Kittleson, In re Marriage of, 742
K.J.B. v. C.M.B., 712
Klahold v. Kroh, 977
Klemm v. Superior Court of Fresno County, 498, 502
Klemme v. Schoneman, 962
Klipstein v. Zalewski, 711
Kober v. Kober, 561
Koss, State v., 177
Kozlowski v. Kozlowski, 234
Kristina L., In re, 491
Kruzel v. Podell, 147
Kujawinski v. Kujawinski, 885
Kulko v. Superior Court of California In and For City and County of San Francisco, 581
Kuzmiak, In re Marriage of, 755

L v. L, 850

Labine v. Vincent, 294, 295
Laird v. Laird, 194
Lalli v. Lalli, 295
Lane v. Lane, 368
Langone v. Coughlin, 58
Larson v. Larson, 88
LaShawn A. v. Dixon, 469
Lassiter v. Department of Social Services of Durham County, N. C., 491
Last Will and Testament of Blackwell, Matter of, 95
Laudig v. Laudig, 216
Lawrence, In re Marriage of, 912
Lawyer Disciplinary Bd. v. Printz, 503
Leckie and Voorhies, Matter of Marriage of, 368
LeClair v. LeClair, 885
Lee v. Savannah Guano Co., 221
Lee v. Weisman, 425
Lehr v. Robertson, 319, 331, 334
Lesko v. Lesko, 747
Levine v. Bacon, 715, 717
Levine v. Levine, 502
Levisen, People v., 426
Levy v. Louisiana, 293, 294
Lewis v. Lewis, 207, 212
Liebelt v. Liebelt, 194, 195
Liles v. Liles, 503
Little v. Streater, 299, 300
Little Rock Family Planning Services, P.A. v. Dalton, 273
Lizzio v. Jackson, 712
Locklin v. Duka, 701
Logan, In re Estate of, 747
Lombardo v. Lombardo, 680
Long, In re Marriage of, 868
Loughmiller's Estate, Matter of, 74
Lovelace v. Gross, 852
Loveridge v. Chartier, 263
Lucas v. Earl, 949
Ludwig v. Ludwig, 203
Lundman v. McKown, 438, 651
Luster, State v., 477
Lynch v. Lynch, 538, 538
Lynch, State v., 95
Lystad v. Lystad, 953

MacFarlane v. Rich, 207
Maharam v. Maharam, 153, 786
Maher v. Roe, 273
Mahoney v. Mahoney, 517 N.Y.S.2d 184, p. 587
Mahoney v. Mahoney, 453 A.2d 527, p. 763
Mahoney v. Mahoney, 442 A.2d 1062, p. 763
Malekos v. Chloe Ann Yin, 1011
Mallette v. Children's Friend and Service, 353
Mally, State v., 157
Maner v. Stephenson, 709
Mansell v. Mansell, 753
Marriage of (see name of party)
Marshall, In re Marriage of, 692
Marshfield Clinic v. Discher, 141
Martin v. Farber, 206
Martin v. Martin, 875 S.W.2d 819, p. 319
Martin v. Martin, 1 Civ.No. 52320, p. **122**
Martinez v. Martinez, 995
Marvin v. Marvin, 176 Cal.Rptr. 555, p. 233
Marvin v. Marvin, 134 Cal.Rptr. 815, pp. **226,** 234, 235, 236, 241, 245, 246, 247, 252, 264, 265
Maslen v. Maslen, 746
Mason, State ex rel. Torres v., 604
Massar v. Massar, 215
Matter of (see name of party)
Matthews v. Matthews, 220
May v. Anderson, 597
May v. Leneair, 90
May v. May, 652
May v. Sessums & Mason, P.A., 510
Maynard v. Hill, 46, **184,** 186
McAlpine v. McAlpine, 765
McCall v. Frampton, 226
McCann v. McCann, 786
McCarty v. McCarty, 30, 753
McCoy, In re Marriage of, 679
McDaniel v. Gile, 516
McDaniel v. McDaniel, 993
McDiarmid v. McDiarmid, 776
McDonald v. McDonald, 397
McDonald v. Wrigley, 701
McGhee, Matter of, 510
McGinley v. Herman, 868, 872, 873, 874
McGowan v. McGowan, 765
McGuffin v. Overton, 701
McGuire v. McGuire, 132, 136, 137, 167
McInnis v. Hyatt Legal Clinics, 514
McIntyre v. Crouch, 368
McKay v. McKay, 886
McKee–Johnson v. Johnson, 207
McKenna v. Steen, 977
McKinney v. McKinney, 977
McKown, State v., 438
McMahon v. Shea, 510
McMillan, Matter of, 425
McSparron v. McSparron, 764
Mead v. Batchlor, 1006
Meany v. Meany, 263
Medeiros v. Kiyosaki, 424
Meegan, In re Marriage of, 969, 976, 977
Meyer v. Nebraska, 693
Meyers v. Handlon, 510
M.H. v. Caritas Family Services, 353
M.H.B. v. H.T.B., 850
Michael H. v. Gerald D., 280, 288, 289, 292
Michael M. v. Superior Court of Sonoma County, 457
Michaud v. Wawruck, 349
Middleton v. Middleton, 611
Miller v. Christopher, 296
Miller v. Miller, 677 A.2d 64, pp. **632,** 636, 638
Miller v. Miller, 620 A.2d 1161, p. 945
Miller v. Miller, 491 N.W.2d 104, pp. 993, 995, 996
Miller v. Miller, 700 S.W.2d 941, pp. 516, 529
Miller v. Tashie, 994

Mills v. Habluetzel, 304
Mimkon v. Ford, 709
Minor v. Minor, 224
Mister v. A.R.K. Partnership, 28
Mitchell, In re Marriage of, 710
Mitchell v. Meisch, 788
M.L.B. v. S.L.J., 491
M.M.D., In re, 343
M.N.M., In re, 331
Mock v. Mock, 587
Moe v. Dinkins, 83
Moffat v. Moffat, 1011
Monslow, Matter of Marriage of, 724
Moore v. City of East Cleveland, Ohio, 10, 13, 15, 17, 18, 19
Morazan, In re Marriage of, 714
Morgan v. Foretich, 686
Morgan v. Morgan, 383 N.Y.S.2d 343, p. 801
Morgan v. Morgan, 366 N.Y.S.2d 977, pp. **798,** 801
Morimando v. Morimando, 765
Morone v. Morone, 234
Morris v. Morris, 819
Morrison, Matter of Marriage of, 984
Moseley v. Moseley, 976
Mosier, Matter of Marriage of, 616
Mosley v. Figliuzzi, 678
Mote v. Corser, 753
Mountain, Matter of, 355
Mozert v. Hawkins County Bd. of Educ., 424
M. T. v. J. T., 75
Mulford v. Mulford, 188
Murphy v. Murphy, 915, 917
Mussari, United States v., 39, 999
Myers, State v., 177

Nancy S. v. Michele G., 701
Nash, Matter of, 477
National Account Systems, Inc. v. Mercado, 142
Naydan v. Naydan, 752
Neilson v. Neilson, 203
Nelson, In re Marriage of, 747
Nelson v. Jacobsen, 153
Nelson v. Nelson, 910 P.2d 319, p. 616
Nelson v. Nelson, 548 A.2d 109, p. 884
Nelson v. Nelson, 736 P.2d 1145, p. 762
Neudecker v. Neudecker, 882
Newman v. Newman, 207
Newmark v. Williams, 438
Nichols Hills Bank v. McCool, 142
Nielsen v. Nielsen, 693
Nimmo, In re Marriage of, 988, 993
Nix v. Whiteside, 515
Noble v. Fisher, 918
Noghrey, In re Marriage of, 202
Norman v. Unemployment Ins. Appeals Bd., 246
North Carolina Baptist Hospitals, Inc. v. Harris, 141
Null v. Board of Educ. of County of Jackson, 426

Oberhansly v. Oberhansly, 725
O'Brien v. O'Brien, 756, 762, 763, 764, 765, 766
O'Connor Bros. Abalone Co. v. Brando, 986
Oedekoven v. Oedekoven, 918, **919**
O.G. v. Baum, 439
Oklahoma Bar Ass'n, State ex rel. v. Katz, 503
Oklahoma Bar Ass'n, State ex rel. v. Sopher, 515
Okocha v. Fehrenbacher, 505
Olar, In re Marriage of, 762
Oliverson v. West Valley City, 28
Olivier v. Doga, 510
Olsen v. Olsen, 821
O'Neil v. Schuckardt, 153
O'Neill v. O'Neill, 727, 728
Orlando F., Matter of, 408
Orr v. Bowen, 106
Orr v. Orr, 791
Osborne v. Osborne, 215
Osier v. Osier, 651
Otis v. Otis, 809, 817, 818, 819
Overstreet v. Merlos, 153
Owan v. Owan, 653, 657, 662
Owen v. Owen, 752

P., In re, 30
Pahlke, In re Marriage of, 785
Painter v. Bannister, 694, 700, 702, 703
Palmore v. Sidoti, 472 So.2d 843, p. 647
Palmore v. Sidoti, 466 U.S. 429, pp. **645,** 647
Panhorst v. Panhorst, 121
Paquette v. Paquette, 711
Parents United for Better Schools, Inc. v. School Dist. of Philadelphia Bd. of Educ., 459
Parham v. J. R., 428, 433
Parker v. Stage, 841
Parker, United States v., 39, 999
Pasqualone v. Pasqualone, 601
Patel v. Navitlal, 562
Paternity of C.A.S., In re, 289
Paternity of Tukker M.O., In re, 874
Peebles v. Disher, 1012
Pellegrini, Commonwealth v., 477
People v. ______ (see opposing party)
Percy v. State, Dept. of Corrections, 402
Pereira v. Pereira, 730
Perino, In re Marriage of, 725
Perry v. Atkinson, 264
Person v. Behnke, 528
Peters v. Peters, 152
Petersen v. Petersen, 763
Petition of (see name of party)
Pickett v. Brown, 304
Pickett v. Pickett, 1012
Pittman v. Pittman, 967
Planned Parenthood Ass'n of Kansas City, Mo., Inc. v. Ashcroft, 272
Planned Parenthood of Central Missouri v. Danforth, 158, 268

Planned Parenthood of Southeastern Pennsylvania v. Casey, 160, 273, 279
Pleasant v. Pleasant, 753
Plemel v. Walter, 299
Plyler v. Doe, 418
Pochop v. Pochop, 541
Poe v. Seaborn, 949
Pollock v. Pollock, 717
Pongonis v. Pongonis, 753
Ponter v. Ponter, 268
Poppe, In re Marriage of, 746
P.O.P.S. v. Gardner, 863
Potter v. Murray City, 60
Pouliot, Commonwealth v., 998
Prahinski v. Prahinski, 766, 773
Price v. Price, 731
Pride v. Baker, 224
Prill v. Hampton, 154
Prince v. Massachusetts, 693

Quilloin v. Walcott, 331

Randall, In re Marriage of, 785
Ranieri v. Ranieri, 95
Rankin v. Bobo, 885
Ranney v. Ranney, 194
Rathmell v. Morrison, 776
Ready v. Ready, 714
Reaney v. Reaney, 785
Rebecca R. & David R., In re Marriage of, 292
Renshaw v. Heckler, 102
Reyes v. Superior Court In and For San Bernardino County, 477
Reynolds v. Reynolds, 561
Ribner v. Ribner, 993
Rider v. Rider, 207
Riffenburg v. Riffenburg, 918
Rissberger v. Gorton, 235
Rivera v. Minnich, 304
Rivera, State v., 426
Robbins, People v., 157
Robert O. v. Russell K., 331
Roberts v. Roberts, 548
Robertson v. Robertson, 728
Robinson v. Trousdale County, 116
Robinson v. Tyson, 977
Rochelle G. v. Harold M.G., 764
Rock v. Rock, 785
Rockwell v. Rockwell, 917
Rodebaugh v. Sanks, 97
Rodgers v. Rodgers, 887 P.2d 269, p. 993
Rodgers v. Rodgers, 505 S.W.2d 138, p. 1011
Roe v. Catholic Charities of the Diocese of Springfield, Ill., 353
Roe v. Doe, 838, 841, 886
Roe v. Wade, 24, **269,** 269, 272, 279
Romer v. Evans, 29
R.S. v. R.S., 368
R.T. v. R.T., 865, 867
Ruben v. Ruben, 763
Rutgers Council of AAUP Chapters v. Rutgers, The State University, 73, 74
Ruzic v. Ruzic, 194
Ryan v. Ryan, 619 A.2d 692, pp. 747, 756
Ryan v. Ryan, 277 So.2d 266, p. 557
Ryman, In re Marriage of, 785

Sage, United States v., 39, 999
Sakovits v. Sakovits, 884
Sampsell v. Superior Court in and for Los Angeles County, 597
Sams v. Boston, 611
Sanders v. Sanders, 292
Sanderson v. Sanderson, 561
Sands v. Sands, 785
Sanjivini K., Matter of, 704
San Luis Obispo, County of v. Nathaniel J., 846
Santosky v. Kramer, 490
Sappington, In re Marriage of, 984
Sargent v. Buckley, 503
Saslow, In re Marriage of, 742
Sauer v. Sauer, 764
S.A.V. v. K.G.V., 787
Savelle v. Savelle, 787
Sawyer v. Bailey, 155
Scharringhaus v. Hazen, 254
Schenck v. Pro–Choice Network Of Western New York, 279
Schenek v. Schenek, 863
Scherer v. Scherer, 211
Schibi v. Schibi, 90
Schilling v. Bedford County Memorial Hosp., Inc., 142
Scholl v. Scholl, 216
Scholler v. Scholler, 528, 529
Schroeder, In re Marriage of, 984
Schult v. Schult, 636
Schumacher v. Sexton, 319
Schutz v. Schutz, 682
Schweiker v. Gray Panthers, 146
Seaton v. Seaton, 39, 178
Seifert v. Seifert, 750
Self v. Self, 818, 967
Septuagenarian v. Septuagenarian, 143, 146
Serrano v. Serrano, 953
Shaffer v. Heitner, 587
Sharma v. Sharma, 47
Sharpe Furniture, Inc. v. Buckstaff, 137, 842
Shaughnessy v. Shaughnessy, 976
Shea, In re Marriage of, 725, 728
Shelley v. Westbrooke, 638
Sheppard v. Sheppard, 693
Sherrer v. Sherrer, 581
Simeone v. Simeone, 188, 206
Simmons v. Simmons, 786
Simms v. Simms, 30
Simon, In re Marriage of, 743
Simpson v. Harper, 224
Simpson v. Simpson, 680 So.2d 1085, p. 881
Simpson v. Simpson, 473 So.2d 299, p. 787
Sinclair v. Sinclair, 881

Sinha v. Sinha, 550
Skaden, In re Marriage of, 754
Skomrock v. Skomrock, 669
Slagenweit v. Slagenweit, 626
Slawek v. Stroh, 297
Smiley, In re, 565
Smith, In re Marriage of, 976
Smith v. Board of School Com'rs of Mobile County, 827 F.2d 684, p. 425
Smith v. Board of School Com'rs of Mobile County, 655 F.Supp. 939, p. 425
Smith v. Dison, 292
Smith v. I.N.S., 91
Smith v. Organization of Foster Families For Equality and Reform, 19
Smith v. Ricci, 424
Smith v. Smith, 884
Smith v. Southern Farm Bureau Cas. Ins. Co., 152
Smith, State v., 157
Soderlund v. Alton, 528
Sogg v. Nevada State Bank, 194
Solomon L., In re, 477
Soos v. Superior Court in and for County of Maricopa, 390
Sopher, State ex rel. Oklahoma Bar Ass'n v., 515
Sorensen, People v., 360
Sorochan v. Sorochan, 245
Sosna v. Iowa, 566
Southwell, Matter of Marriage of, 881
Spencer v. Commonwealth, 299
Stakelum v. Terral, 90
Stallworth, Marriage of, 785
Stanard v. Bolin, 254
Stanley v. Georgia, 29
Stanley v. Illinois, 319, 657
Stanley v. Richmond, 502
Stanton v. Abbey, 977
Starck v. Nelson, 993
Stariha, In re Marriage of, 1006
Starzinger v. Starzinger, 1012
State v. ______ (see opposing party)
State Bar v. Cramer, 521
State, Dept. of Revenue By and on Behalf of Jorda v. Fleet, 594
State ex rel. v. ______ (see opposing party and relator)
Stefanel Tyesha C., Matter of, 477
Steffke's Estate, In re, 575, 579, 580
Stein–Sapir v. Stein–Sapir, 194
Stewart, In re Marriage of, 776
Stewart v. Stewart, 902
Stiver v. Parker, 402
Storrs v. Holcomb, 73
Strasen v. Strasen, 37
Straub v. B.M.T. by Todd, 842, 846
Streb v. Streb, 884
Strock v. Pressnell, 154
Stuart v. Stuart, 153
Sullivan, In re Marriage of, 794 P.2d 687, p. 867
Sullivan, In re Marriage of, 184 Cal.Rptr. 796, pp. 762, 766
Suter v. Artist M., 469
Swinney v. Mosher, 318
Swoap v. Superior Court of Sacramento County, 854

Taake v. Taake, 980, 984
T.A.B., State ex rel. v. Corrigan, 331
Taggart v. Taggart, 744, 746
Tahan v. Duquette, 626
Talent v. Talent, 776, 784
Talty, In re Marriage of, 776
Tapley v. Tapley, 234, 235
Tarry v. Stewart, 235
Tasker v. Tasker, 776
Tatham, In re Marriage of, 731
Taylor v. Fields, 256, 260
Taylor v. Taylor, 716
T.C.H. v. K.M.H., 652
T.E.P. v. Leavitt, 87
Tevis v. Tevis, 786
Texas Educ. Agency v. Leeper, 426
T.G., In re, 462, 468, 469, 470
The Florida Bar v. Furman, 521
The Florida Bar v. Glant, 511, 514
Thomas, State v., 177
Thomas S. v. Robin Y., 368
Thomasson v. Johnson, 977
Thompson v. Thompson, 604
Thornburgh v. American College of Obstetricians and Gynecologists, 272
Thrasher v. Wilburn, 885, 886
Titchenal v. Dexter, 712
Tobon v. Sanchez, 562
Toft on Behalf of Frisbie v. Frisbie, 841
Torres, State ex rel. v. Mason, 604
Trahan v. Trahan, 740, 742
Trammel v. United States, 178, 182, 183
Trimble v. Gordon, 294, 295
Tropea v. Tropea, 717
Trowbridge v. Trowbridge, 938
Troy D., In re, 477
Troy Sav. Bank v. Calacone, 903
Trump v. Trump, 216
Tsavaris v. Tsavaris, 511
Tucker v. Tucker, 652
Tucker v. Virginia State Bar, 510
Turner v. Safley, 58
Turner v. Turner, 586 A.2d 1182, p. 867
Turner v. Turner, 385 A.2d 1280, p. 792
Twitchell, Commonwealth v., 438
Twyman v. Twyman, 786, 787

Unander v. Unander, 207
Uniroyal Goodrich Tire Co. v. Martinez, 154
United States v. ______ (see opposing party)

Vallone v. Vallone, 731
Van Camp v. Van Camp, 730, 731
Vande Kop v. McGill, 528

Vandenburgh v. Vandenburgh, 502
Vargas' Estate, In re, 107
Veazey v. Veazey, 636
Verrilli v. Verrilli, 728
Village of (see name of village)
Viragh v. Foldes, 626
Virgil v. Haber, 256
Vryonis, In re Marriage of, 109
V.W. v. J.B., 506, 510

Wagner v. Wagner, 713
Walden v. Hoke, 502
Walker v. Chatfield, 718
Walker v. Superior Court (People), 438
Wallace v. Jaffree, 425
Wallace v. Rappleye, 226
Walther v. Walther, 657 N.E.2d 332, p. 911
Walther v. Walther, 709 P.2d 387, p. 786
Walton v. Lee, 753
Walton v. Walton, 565
Walton's Marriage, In re, 185, 186
Wang, In re Marriage of, 647
Ward v. Ward, 743
Warren v. State, 162
Wasserman v. Wasserman, 629 N.Y.S.2d 69, p. 911
Wasserman v. Wasserman, 671 F.2d 832, p. 35
Watson v. Watson, 785
Watts v. Watts, 405 N.W.2d 303, p. 234
Watts v. Watts, 337 A.2d 350, p. 292
Wawrykow v. Simonich, 300
Weber v. Aetna Cas. & Sur. Co., 294
Weber v. Coffey, 993
Weber v. Stony Brook Hosp., 447
Weber v. Weber, 911
Webster v. Reproductive Health Services, 273
Wehrkamp v. Wehrkamp, 763
Weil v. Lammon, 786
Weinschel v. Strople, 352
Weinstein, In re Marriage of, 762
Weintraub, In re Marriage of, 90
Weiss, In re Marriage of, 215
Weiss v. Weiss, 717
Welch, Commonwealth v., 477
Westrup v. Commonwealth, 157
Whelchel, In re Marriage of, 787
White, In re, 962
White v. White, 521 N.W.2d 874, p. 747
White v. White, 623 So.2d 31, p. 753
Whitner v. State, 471, 477
Whorrall v. Whorrall, 746
Whorton v. Dillingham, 235, 236
Wiese v. Wiese, 846, 850
Wife S. v. Husband S., 548, 549
Wilder v. Sugarman, 348
Williams v. Williams, 781 P.2d 1170, p. 1011
Williams v. Williams, 508 A.2d 985, pp. 911, 912
Williams v. Williams, 543 P.2d 1401, p. 47
Wilson v. Wilson, 291
Wilson, Commissioner v., 737
Wilson–Cunningham v. Meyer, 530
Windauer v. O'Connor, 786
Winfield v. Renfro, 106
Wing v. Wing, 1012
Wirth v. Wirth, 719
Wisconsin v. Yoder, 419, 424
Wisner v. Wisner, 762
Witbeck–Wildhagen, In re Marriage of, 368
Wolfe v. Wolfe, 521, 562
Woodruff v. Tomlin, 522
Wornkey v. Wornkey, 1012
Wright, In re Marriage of, 755
Wright v. Arnold, 504
Wright v. Wright, 528
Wulff v. Wulff, 408

Zablocki v. Redhail, 48, 57, 58, 95
Zack v. Fiebert, 701
Zecchin v. Zecchin, 776, 785
Zeigler v. Zeigler, 784
Zelnik v. Zelnik, 725, 731
Zern v. Zern, 724
Ziegelheim v. Apollo, 528
Zogby v. Zogby, 953
Zysk v. Zysk, 263

Chapter 1

AMERICAN FAMILY LAW: DEFINITIONS, POLICY AND TRENDS

Unfortunately, the American family is confronted with the problem whether it shall continue to exist, and the American people, whether they like it or not, should look the problems of their family life squarely in the face as the greatest of all their social problems.

Charles Ellwood, 1909

No matter how many communes anybody invents, the family always creeps back.

Margaret Mead

SECTION 1. THE NEW FAMILY AND THE NEW FAMILY LAW

A. THE NEW FAMILY

MARY ANN GLENDON, THE NEW FAMILY AND THE NEW PROPERTY

3–7, 11, 13–20, 28–38, 41–45, 245 (1981).

* * *

The "new family" is a convenient way of referring to that group of changes that characterizes 20th century Western marriage and family behavior, such as increasing fluidity, detachability and interchangeability of family relationships; the increasing appearance, or at least visibility, of family behavior outside formal legal categories, and to changing attitudes and behavior patterns in authority structure and economic relations within the family. It follows from these changes that the new family is *no* family in the sense of a single model that can be called typical for modern industrialized societies. The new family is a concept that represents a variety of co-existing family types.

As an example of the kinds of developments that can be illuminated by the analysis that will be set forth here, consider two pairs of interesting but at first sight unrelated legal events of the 1970s—one in family law, the other in the law of employment contracts. In 1973, Sweden and the American state of Washington changed their laws to permit one spouse unilaterally to terminate a marriage for any reason, or no reason. In 1974, Sweden extended protection against dismissal without cause to all employees in the labor force, and the Supreme Court of New Hampshire became the first in the nation to repudiate the time-honored common-law rule that an employer may terminate an at-will employment contract for any reason, or no reason. When viewed from a civilian, comparative, and historical perspective, and placed in the context of other private law developments, the American and Swedish innovations, while strikingly coincidental are seen to be neither isolated phenomena nor mere curiosities.

* * *

When comparative analysis is brought to bear on the two pairs of developments, it becomes clear that Sweden and the United States are not special or extreme cases. Comparison of the marriage and employment law of England, France, Sweden, West Germany and the United States ... shows that the once fundamental legal concepts that one spouse cannot repudiate the other at will and that an employer can fire an employee for any reason that suits him are legally moribund in fact in all those legal systems. Finally, from a historical perspective, the two legal trends are—to use characterizations employed by the French historian Braudel in another context—simultaneously "motors," "indicators," and "multipliers" of a vast reorganization of social relationships.

* * *

A. Circumscribing the Family Unit: The Law of Companionate Marriage

The husband-wife relationship has become the "central zone" of the modern family. This came about only gradually. The pre-modern family included a wide circle of people from different households related by blood ties and by a feeling that they belonged together in a different way from the way in which they belonged to a neighborhood, community or larger political entity. Lawrence Stone calls the pre-modern family the "open lineage" family to emphasize that its outer boundaries were relatively weak and permeable in contrast to what he perceives as the close-knit, inward-turning modern family. The strong sense of kinship did not exclude a wide range of connections with others through marriage or spiritual affinity (e.g., godparents and children) and with non-relatives. Over time, however, the feeling of being united by a common tie within the kinship group weakened, and the term "family" slowly came to be identified primarily with the household, conceived of as containing a husband, wife and minor children. * * *

The French Civil Code of 1804 appeared at just the right time to preserve the image of the older order, especially in the *conseil de famille,* to ensconce the conjugal household as the "family of the Civil Code," and to foreshadow the future in its short-lived introduction of divorce.

* * *

Comparing th[is] ... Code ... with the German Civil Code of 1896, one can observe the progress of the trends we have been following. In the "modern" German Civil Code, which went into effect in 1900, the family law sections were more decisively organized around the conjugal family of husband-wife and children. The kinship group had receded further into the background. Collaterals were dropped from the list of relatives entitled to a forced share in a decedent's estate, and the surviving spouse was added. English and American statutory and case law developments were following a similar general pattern.... By the turn of the 20th century, Western legal systems had come to share, generally speaking, a common set of assumptions. Marriage was an important support institution and a decisive determinant of the status of spouses and children. Marriage was in principle to last until the death of a spouse and should be terminable during the lives of the spouses, if at all, only for serious cause. The community aspect of marriage and the family was emphasized over the individual personalities of each member. Within the family, the standard pattern of authority and role allocation was that the husband-father was predominant in decision-making and was to provide for the material needs of the family, while the wife-mother fulfilled her role primarily by caring for the household and children. Procreation and child-rearing were assumed to be major purposes of marriage, and sexual relations within marriage were supposed to be exclusive, at least for the wife. Marriage and divorce were supposed to take place within legal categories. Underlying all these particular assumptions were general assumptions that "the" family was "a basic social institution" and that state regulation of its formation, organization and dissolution and even the conduct of its everyday affairs was proper.

* * *

B. The Bonding of the New Family

In the 20th century, as marriage and family both declined as focal points of security and standing, a family type has emerged that is characterized by, among other things, relatively loose bonding. In contrast to pre-modern, early modern and 19th century families, both kinship ties and marital ties are attenuated in the new family.

* * *

Outside the nuclear core the loosening of family ties is especially pronounced. While research in many countries has demonstrated that extensive kinship networks still exist and can be quite important even in modernized, urbanized industrial societies—more especially in some sectors than in others—it nevertheless seems generally true, as Konig says, that "one does not any more simply 'have' relatives; rather one decides with whom one will have contact, so that kin relationships can be compared to those among friends." It is common to hear people describe certain relatives approvingly as "not only my (mother, son, wife, brother, etc.) but also my friend." Konig's observation is neatly illustrated in the 1964 amendments to the French Civil Code provisions on the appointment of a family council when this becomes necessary to supervise the personal care of a child. Since 1964, little is presumed from the mere existence of a family tie, and the possibly greater significance of non-familial ties in individual cases is recognized. Article 408 of the Civil Code now requires the judge, in choosing the members of the council, to consider "before all else, the habitual relationships that the mother and father had with their various blood relatives and in-laws." Article 409, as amended, then goes on to introduce the possibility for the judge to appoint to the council "friends, neighbors, or any other persons who seem to him to have concern for the child."

* * *

2.a. *Fluidity, Detachability and Interchangeability*

1. *Marriage*

In historical perspective, two facts stand out that distinguish the modern couple relationship. They at first appear contradictory. One is that modern marriage, while it lasts, is companionate, its bonding seemingly close and intense; the other is that it is fragile, its close bonding seemingly unstable. This version of reality is faithfully reflected in modern marriage law which simultaneously expresses the closeness and intensity, yet the instability of the modern couple bonded more by emotional than economic ties.

This can best be observed by comparing the legal rights a spouse has in inheritance with those he or she has in divorce. The common thread running through the changes in the spouses' position in succession law stands out in contrast to the diversity of the responses of various legal systems to the problem of the increase in marriage termination by divorce. It is obvious why legal treatment of these two situations has become sharply differentiated in recent years. The surviving spouse has steadily gained against blood relations in inheritance, a natural consequence of the decline of kinship and the companionate nature of those marriages (still a majority) that last until death. The divorced spouse, on the other hand, is either increasingly required in principle to be self-sufficient, or the spousal support obligation is continued, but shifted over to a new utilitarian basis—the protection of the public purse. Both approaches are natural consequences of the perishability of the modern couple unit and the rise in successive marriages while the prior spouse is still alive. In the United States and England it has been estimated that 30 to 40 percent of marriages formed in the 1970s will end in divorce. Since most divorced persons remarry, the New Marriage is often a subsequent marriage, and the New Family a reconstituted family.

But what is modern about the New Marriage is not that it is perishable or that it is often a remarriage. * * * The information being assembled about marriage in the early modern period from 1500 to 1800 indicates that marriages then were dissolved by death almost as often as they are dissolved by divorce. * * * What is modern is that the doors do not revolve merely to the pearly gates. In close personal relationships today, impermanence, fluidity and interchangeability are mainly the result not of death, but of the exercise of choice, a choice made possible only by the opportunities which individuals have for finding economic subsistence outside the family.

The marriage bond seems to have been relatively durable when the conjugal family functioned as a productive unit. So long as this pattern prevailed, the husband was predominant in the legal authority structure of the family. But his superior legal authority was held in check in practice

> ... by a dependence on the productive labor force of his wife and her ability to bear children. Children are in this phase—in their quality as labour force—a considerable asset. Although the relationship between the partners was asymmetrical it was however at the same time characterized by an economic interdependence ...

When the productive work which formed the basis of the maintenance of the family was removed from the home through industrialization, women and children were vulnerable because the breadwinner upon whom they now depended entirely was released from his dependence on them. From being economic assets, women and children became a strain on resources in the marriage type where the husband worked outside the home and the wife was exclusively occupied with the household. This was the beginning of the end of marriage as a reliable support institution.

As women, too, entered the labor force, their economic vulnerability lessened somewhat, but at the same time it seems that the actual or potential participation of married women in the labor force makes it easier for men as well as women to leave marriages. * * *

Meanwhile, as marriage declined as a support institution, women decreasingly defined their social position with reference to their husbands or lack thereof. The notion, long taken for granted, that the "husband's occupation alone supposedly defines class and status for the family," and the assumption, attributed to Talcott Parsons, that "the family as a whole shares a status and that the man is the link with the economic system," have been undermined by the course of events in the 20th century. * * *

The fact that marriage in itself is no longer so important as a determinant of wealth, rank, and status has made it easy for "freedom to marry" to be established as a fundamental legal principle, coincidentally at about the same time, in France, West Germany and the United States. Ironically, marriage has become a basic human right just when it is losing much of its former economic importance. This is also why marriage is becoming freely terminable on the request of one party in countries where a century ago divorce was available, if at all, only for grave and serious cause, and why "legitimacy" is decreasingly tied to formal, legal marriage. In its encounter with informal marriage and family behavior, the law itself has become more fluid and informal.

* * *

b. Parents and Children

Like the bonds between husband and wife, those between parents and children have been reduced and relaxed in the modern family. Relationships between parent and child are said to have become looser, not only because the child upon reaching a certain age typically leaves the family, but because the child's psychological dependence on the family decreases even earlier. Surveying changes in American family life cycles over an 80–year period ending in the 1970s, Census Bureau senior demographer Paul Glick has stated that, contrary to what might be expected, the father and mother of today's smaller families are apparently not spending more time with their children than their great-grandparents did. In fact the period of child-rearing has been shortened by about three years. Those who believe that children today achieve emotional independence from their families earlier than in the recent past attribute this, variously, to the fact that children move in non-family milieus at an early age, and to the outside influences from television and the peer group that penetrate the family circle through the children.

Legally, these looser ties find expression in the decline of parental control over a child's marriage decision, the rise of "children's rights," the substitution of social for family responsibility for support of aged parents or more distant relatives and the near disappearance of patriarchal authority over wives and children. Laurence Tribe, in a perceptive analysis of recent Supreme Court cases affecting the parent-child relationship, observes that what the Court and commentators often characterize as " 'family rights' emerge as rights of individuals only." He reaches this conclusion by comparing cases "pitting the child against outside institutions" with cases where "the child seeks aid from outside institutions," finding that both lines of decisions "move in the parallel direction of reduced parental control."

Fluidity and interchangeability of relationships characterize many recent developments in child law just as they do marriage law. * * * [W]ith increasing acceptance of the notion that close attention should be paid in custody matters to the "psychological parent," neither the biological nor the legal tie is necessarily decisive for purposes of custody or termination of parental rights. In the area of post-divorce custody, wider kinship ties seem to reappear in the sprinkling of American cases that have begun to accord visitation rights to grandparents. But these cases do not represent a reinforcement of legal kinship ties so much as they do legal adaptation to the fluidity and shifting composition of families, a process in which grandparents are often lumped in with "significant others" who are not kinfolk, such as foster parents, cohabitants, step-parents and even babysitters. The step-relationship has begun to draw a number of legal incidents to itself, even in cases where it has not been formalized through legal adoption. At the same time, in the United States, the very theory of adoption is changing. While the aim of adoption was once to integrate the adopted child as fully as possible into the adoptive family, severing all other ties, the idea of "open adoption" has recently emerged to permit the adopted child to retain her old family ties while entering into new ones.

* * *

C. The Emergence of the Individual

* * *

It was to the declining influence of the family in determining an individual's security and standing that Sir Henry Maine was referring in his constantly quoted statement that "the movement of the progressive societies has hitherto been a movement *from Status to Contract.*"

* * *

Maine was more right than he knew and probably more right than he wanted to be. Particularly since the 1960s, the law in the countries discussed here has come increasingly to emphasize the individuality of the members of the conjugal family as well as to facilitate their independence from it and each other. For example, so far as the spouses are concerned, Rheinstein and Glendon's survey of the law of several countries on the personal and property relationships of husband and wife during marriage showed that legal and symbolic rules, which had captured and reinforced the trend toward viewing companionate marriage as a community of life between the spouses, are significantly affected by trends toward emphasizing the separateness and autonomy of the individual spouses.

* * *

The fact is that we may now carry Maine's analysis one step further: we have left a time when one's position in society was fixed by one's family, *not* for the reign of contract, but for a situation in which one's status is derived from one's occupation or fixed, in a negative way, by one's lack of occupation. Occupations are less and less governed by contract. The collective bargaining agreement is *sui generis*, with mixed elements of contract, statute and constitution, and with its terms, like other employment relationships and other aspects of work, increasingly fixed and regulated by law. The relationships which, unlike marriage and contract, are relatively hard to enter and leave today are the preferred sorts of New Property—good jobs with good fringe benefits.

* * *

Current changes in family behavior, property and law, and ways of thinking about them, contain bewildering possibilities for good and ill, for renewal or deterioration. It seems likely that, in the future, what we have here called the new family and the new property will be seen as transitional phenomena and identified with a period of extreme separation of man from man, and man from nature. * * *

Notes and Questions

1. What are the functions of the modern family? Which of its functions are most important to individual family members? to the public? How have these patterns shifted over the twentieth century?

2. Throughout the Western industrialized world, experts see a trend toward smaller families, more nonmarital cohabitation, more nonmarital births, more single-parent households, and more single-person households. The latter family form is the fastest growing household type. *See* Constance Sorrentino, *The Changing Family in International Perspective*, MONTHLY LABOR REVIEW 41–58 (1990); WILLIAM GOODE, WORLD CHANGES IN DIVORCE PATTERNS (1993). Between 1970 and the early 1990s in the United States, the number of unmarried heterosexual cohabitants rose from 523,000 to 3,661,000, an increase of more than 700%. During the same time period nonmarital births climbed from 11% of total births to 30%, the proportion of children living in single-parent households from 13% to 31%, and the proportion of all households with a single resident from 11% to 24%. U.S. DEPT. OF COMMERCE, BUREAU OF THE CENSUS, STATISTICAL ABSTRACT OF THE UNITED STATES: 1995 tbls. 60, 68, 71, 94, 1367.

3. In recent years, the history of the family has produced a voluminous literature. *See, e.g.,* ANDREW J. CHERLIN, MARRIAGE, DIVORCE, AND REMARRIAGE (1992); THE FAMILY: A SOCIAL HISTORY OF THE TWENTIETH CENTURY (John Harriss ed. 1991); J.E. Goldthorpe, FAMILY LIFE IN WESTERN SOCIETIES: A HISTORICAL SOCIOLOGY OF FAMILY RELATIONSHIPS IN BRITAIN AND NORTH AMERICA (1987); WILLIAM J. GOODE, WORLD REVOLUTION AND FAMILY PATTERNS 6 (2d ed. 1970); FAMILY HISTORY AT THE CROSSROADS: A JOURNAL OF THE FAMILY HISTORY READER (Tamara K. Hareven & Andrejs Plakans eds., 1987); Martha Minow, *Forming Underneath Everything That Grows—Toward A History of Family Law*, 1985 WIS. L. REV. 819; ROSEMARY O'DAY, THE FAMILY AND FAMILY RELATIONSHIPS, 1500–1900: ENGLAND, FRANCE AND THE UNITED STATES OF AMERICA (1994); LAWRENCE STONE, THE FAMILY, SEX AND MARRIAGE IN ENGLAND 1500–1800 (1977); Arland Thornton, *Comparative and Historical Perspectives on Marriage, Divorce and Family Life*, 1994 UTAH L. REV. 587; Martha Albertson Fineman, *Our Sacred Institution: The Ideal of the Family in American Law and Society*, 1993 Utah L. Rev. 387; Steven Mintz, *Children, Family, and the State: American Family Law in Historical Perspective*, 69 DENV. U. L. REV. 635 (1992).

B. THE NEW FAMILY LAW

Dramatic changes in family form and function have altered not only American family life, but also our family law. Today's family law must resolve disputes involving nonmarital cohabitants and participants in new forms of reproduction, such as surrogate parenting and in vitro fertilization. It must resolve challenges to traditional definitions of marriage, parenting, property, and the family itself.

Not surprisingly, the process of fashioning rules that are fair and workable for today's rapidly changing family has been far from smooth and uncontroversial. Family law is now central to many of the most difficult, and emotional, of social issues: Should same-sex couples be able to marry? Should couples who live together without marriage be entitled to benefits that have traditionally been available only to "family members"? Should a law degree be considered marital property to be "divided" at divorce? Who is the mother of a child born to one woman with genetic material from another? Should a lesbian "co-parent" be able to adopt her partner's child? Absent an adoption, should she have an entitlement to visitation when her relationship with the child's mother ends? These are some of the issues with which family law now contends, and which you will be studying.

Family law issues arouse controversy for a variety of reasons. Family relationships are intimate, generating strong, often conflicting, emotions. Family law often draws on other disciplines, such as sociology, psychology, mediation, medicine, and law enforcement, and thus becomes embroiled in debates within these other fields. Many issues of family law are also issues of morality, religious doctrine and cultural values; they can—and are—debated in these terms as well as in terms of law. Traditionally, much of family law has been based on widely accepted religious and cultural values. (Indeed, in England, ecclesiastical courts had exclusive jurisdiction over marriage and divorce until the 1850s.) But a more diverse populace challenges our ability to achieve consensus on many family law issues.

The one issue on which there is widespread consensus is the importance of the family as a cornerstone of our society. The United Nations in its Universal Declaration of Human Rights § 16(3) has recognized the family as "the natural and fundamental group unit of society and is entitled to protection by society and the State." The United States Supreme Court has held that the Constitution protects the sanctity of the family, noting "the institution of the family is deeply rooted in this Nation's history and tradition." Moore v. City of East Cleveland, [p. 10]. But exactly what makes a group of individuals a "family" remains unclear.

C. A FAMILY BY ANY NAME?

What entity—the state, the federal government, or the parties themselves—should determine what constitutes a family? Is a standardized definition preferable to a test that relies on the understanding of the individuals involved? If a standardized definition is employed, when is it appropriate to grant or withhold privileges based on that definition?

In Village of Belle Terre v. Boraas, 416 U.S. 1, 94 S.Ct. 1536, 39 L.Ed.2d 797 (1974), the Supreme Court upheld a zoning ordinance that defined a family as "one or more persons related by blood, adoption or marriage, living and cooking together as a single housekeeping unit, exclusive of household servants.... " In oft-quoted statements, Justices Douglas and Marshall eloquently disagreed about the effect of the ordinance. To Justice Douglas, the Village ordinance was a benign edict:

> A quiet place where yards are wide, people few, and motor vehicles restricted are legitimate guidelines in a land-use project addressed to family needs. This goal is a permissible one ... The police power is not confined to elimination of filth, stench, and unhealthy places. It is ample to lay out zones where family values, youth values, and the blessings of quiet seclusion and clean air make the area a sanctuary for people.

To Justice Marshall, on the other hand, the ordinance represented active discrimination against nonconformists:

> Belle Terre imposes upon those who deviate from the community norm in their choice of living companions significantly greater restrictions than are applied to residential groups who are related by blood or marriage, and compose the established order within the community. The village has, in effect, acted to fence out those individuals whose choice of lifestyle differs from that of its current residents.

When considering the definitions of "family" contained in the following cases, try to determine both whether the definition was drawn for benign or discriminatory reasons, and how much latitude government actors have to "fence out" certain lifestyles.

MOORE v. CITY OF EAST CLEVELAND, OHIO

Supreme Court of the United States, 1977.
431 U.S. 494, 97 S.Ct. 1932, 52 L.Ed.2d 531.

JUSTICE POWELL delivered the opinion of the Court.

East Cleveland's housing ordinance, like many throughout the country, limits occupancy of a dwelling unit to members of a single family.

But the ordinance contains an unusual and complicated definitional section that recognizes as a "family" only a few categories of related individuals. Section 1341.08 provides:

> " 'Family' means a number of individuals related to the nominal head of the household living as a single housekeeping unit in a single dwelling unit, but limited to the following:
>
> (a) Husband or wife of the nominal head of the household.
>
> (b) Unmarried children of the nominal head of the household or of the spouse of the nominal head of the household, provided, however, that such unmarried children have no children residing with them.
>
> (c) Father or mother of the nominal head of the household or of the spouse of the nominal head of the household.

(d) . . . a family may include not more than one dependent married or unmarried child of the nominal head of the household or of the spouse of the nominal head of the household and the spouse and dependent children of such dependent child. For the purpose of this subsection, a dependent person is one who has more than fifty percent of his total support furnished for him by the nominal head of the household and the spouse of the nominal head of the household.

(e) A family may consist of one individual."

Because her family, living together in her home, fits none of those categories, appellant stands convicted of a criminal offense. The question in this case is whether the ordinance violates the Due Process Clause of the Fourteenth Amendment.

* * *

Appellant, Mrs. Inez Moore, lives in her East Cleveland home together with her son, Dale Moore, Sr., and her two grandsons, Dale, Jr., and John Moore, Jr. The two boys are first cousins rather than brothers; we are told that John came to live with his grandmother and with the elder and younger Dale Moores after his mother's death.

In early 1973, Mrs. Moore received a notice of violation from the city, stating that John was an "illegal occupant" and directing her to comply with the ordinance. When she failed to remove him from her home, the city filed a criminal charge. Mrs. Moore moved to dismiss, claiming that the ordinance was constitutionally invalid on its face. Her motion was overruled, and upon conviction she was sentenced to five days in jail and a $25 fine. * * *

[An] overriding factor sets this case apart from Belle Terre v. Boraas, 416 U.S. 1, 94 S.Ct. 1536, 39 L.Ed.2d 797 (1974). The ordinance there affected only *unrelated* individuals. It expressly allowed all who were related by "blood, adoption, or marriage" to live together, and in sustaining the ordinance we were careful to note that it promoted "family needs" and "family values." East Cleveland, in contrast, has chosen to regulate the occupancy of its housing by slicing deeply into the family itself. This is no mere incidental result of the ordinance. On its face it selects certain categories of relatives who may live together and declares that others may not. In particular, it makes a crime of a grandmother's choice to live with her grandson in circumstances like those presented here.

When a city undertakes such intrusive regulation of the family, the usual judicial deference to the legislature is inappropriate. "This Court has long recognized that freedom of personal choice in matters of marriage and family life is one of the liberties protected by the Due Process Clause of the Fourteenth Amendment." Cleveland Board of Education v. LaFleur, 414 U.S. 632, 639–640, 94 S.Ct. 791, 796, 39 L.Ed.2d 52 (1974). A host of cases, * * * have consistently acknowledged a "private realm of family life which the state cannot enter." Of course, the family is not beyond regulation. But when the government intrudes on choices concerning family living arrangements, this Court must examine carefully the importance of the governmental interests advanced and the extent to which they are served by the challenged regulation.

When thus examined, this ordinance cannot survive. * * *

Appropriate limits on substantive due process come not from drawing arbitrary lines but rather from careful "respect for the teachings of history [and], solid recognition of the basic values that underlie our society". Our decisions establish that the Constitution protects the sanctity of the family precisely because the institution of the family is deeply rooted in this Nation's history and tradition. It is through the family that we inculcate and pass down many of our most cherished values, moral and cultural.

Ours is by no means a tradition limited to respect for the bonds uniting the members of the nuclear family. The tradition of uncles, aunts, cousins, and especially grandparents sharing a household along with parents and children has roots equally venerable and equally deserving of constitutional recognition. Over the years millions of our citizens have grown up in just such an environment, and most, surely, have profited from it. Even if conditions of modern society have brought about a decline in extended family households, they have not erased the accumulated wisdom of civilization, gained over the centuries and honored throughout our history, that supports a larger conception of the family. Out of choice, necessity, or a sense of family responsibility, it has been common for close relatives to draw together and participate in the duties and the satisfactions of a common home. Decisions concerning child rearing, which *Yoder, Meyer, Pierce* and other cases have recognized as entitled to constitutional protection, long have been shared with grandparents or other relatives who occupy the same household—indeed who may take on major responsibility for the rearing of the children. Especially in times of adversity, such as the death of a spouse or economic need, the broader family has tended to come together for mutual sustenance and to maintain or rebuild a secure home life. This is apparently what happened here.

Whether or not such a household is established because of personal tragedy, the choice of relatives in this degree of kinship to live together may not lightly be denied by the State. *Pierce* struck down an Oregon law requiring all children to attend the State's public schools, holding that the Constitution "excludes any general power of the State to standardize its children by forcing them to accept instruction from public teachers only." 268 U.S., at 535, 45 S.Ct., at 573. By the same token the Constitution prevents East Cleveland from standardizing its children—and its adults—by forcing all to live in certain narrowly defined family patterns.

MR. JUSTICE STEWART, with whom MR. JUSTICE REHNQUIST joins, dissenting.

* * * [T]he appellant contends that the importance of the "extended family" in American society requires us to hold that her decision to share her residence with her grandsons may not be interfered with by the State. This decision, like the decisions involved in bearing and raising children, is said to be an aspect of "family life" also entitled to substantive protection under the Constitution. Without pausing to inquire how far under this argument an "extended family" might extend, I cannot agree. When the Court has found that the Fourteenth Amendment placed a substantive limitation on a State's power to regulate, it has been in those rare cases in which the personal interests at issue have been deemed "implicit in the concept of ordered liberty." The interest that the appellant may have in permanently sharing a single kitchen and a suite of contiguous rooms with some of her relatives simply does not rise to that level. To equate this interest with the fundamental decisions to marry and to bear and raise children is to extend the limited substantive contours of the Due Process Clause beyond recognition.

* * *

MR. JUSTICE WHITE, dissenting.

That the Court has ample precedent for the creation of new constitutional rights should not lead it to repeat the process at will. The judiciary, including this Court is the most vulnerable and comes nearest to illegitimacy when it deals with judge-made constitutional law having little or no cognizable roots in the language or even the design of the Constitution. Realizing that the present construction of the Due Process Clause represents a major judicial gloss on its terms, as well as on the anticipation of the Framers, and that much of the underpinning for the broad, substantive application of the Clause disappeared in the conflict between the executive and the judiciary in the 1930's and 1940's, the Court should be extremely reluctant to breathe still further substantive content into the Due Process Clause so as to strike down legislation adopted by a State or city to promote its welfare. Whenever the judiciary does so, it unavoidably pre-empts for itself another part of the governance of the country without express constitutional authority.

Notes and Questions

1. What is the determining factor in the *Moore* decision? Is it tradition, current household residence patterns, economic and racial factors, or the court's reluctance to see a grandmother convicted of a crime for housing two grandsons?

2. Typical residence and family patterns vary significantly by race and ethnicity. Nonmarital births, for example, now comprise 68% of black births, 23% of white births, and 6% of Chinese-ancestry births; 82% of Asian and white, 68% of Hispanic, and 46% of black Americans now live in married-couple households. The same percentage of black and white Americans live in single-person households (12%) but the proportion of blacks living with relatives other than a spouse (48%) is double that of whites (24%). U.S. DEP'T OF COMMERCE, BUREAU OF THE

Census, Statistical Abstract of the United States 1995, tbls. 62, 70, 88. Family patterns also vary by socioeconomic status. Divorce is approximately twice as likely for couples with incomes below the poverty line as it is for the general population; nonmarital birth is also strongly associated with low income. U.S. Dep't of Commerce, Bureau of the Census, When Households Continue, Discontinue, and Form 18–21, tbl. I (Current Population Reports, Series P–23, No. 180) (1992); Elizabeth Phillips & Irwin Garfinkel, *Income Growth among Nonresident Fathers: Evidence from Wisconsin*, 30 Demography 227, 234–35 tbl. 2 (1993).

3. Because family forms vary widely by race, ethnicity, and socioeconomic status, family law may not be equally responsive to the needs and interests of all Americans:

> Class, race, and ethnic bias in family law and its administration have been widely documented in the legal literature. In its provisions regarding marriage, divorce, property, support, alimony and custody, the traditional model of universal legal marriage and universal legal divorce incorporate a white, middle-class ideal.
>
> ... "The financial obligations incurred as an incident to marriage may make it a luxury that the poor cannot afford." ... [R]esearch [also] carefully documents the "dual system" of family law for alimony, support, and property: the law for the poor is heavily political and measurably penal, whereas the law for the middle class is civil, nonpolitical, and less penal.* * *
>
> "Finally, the ideal family type assumed by traditional legal marriage may be less appropriate for some ethnic groups. While the conjugal family model that the law assumes is common among white Protestants, Jews and Italians are more likely to have extended families, and a single parent family is more common among blacks. Families in some ethnic groups might want a marriage contract which extended support obligations beyond the conjugal family unit to include grandparents, aunts, uncles and cousins among those who would provide or receive support. These families might also find it more appropriate and prefer to apportion financial, domestic, and child-care responsibilities along generational rather than sex-linked lines. However, by imposing the white middle-class ideal family type on all, traditional legal marriage often ignores and excludes the special concerns and needs of ethnic and racial minorities—as well as those of the poor."
>
> Lenore Weitzman, *Legal Regulation of Marriage: Tradition and Change*, 62 Cal. L. Rev. 1169, 1227 (1974).

4. In Hann v. Housing Authority of the City of Easton, 709 F.Supp. 605 (E.D.Pa.1989), a federal court had to interpret the meaning of the term "family" in the context of the U.S. Housing Act (USHA) and regulations promulgated by the U.S. Department of Housing and Urban Development (HUD). A local housing authority denied an application for low-income housing assistance on the sole basis that the applicants, who had three children, were unmarried. Based on the view that nonmarital

cohabitation is immoral, the housing authority (HACE) had interpreted the term "family" in USHA and HUD regulations to mean "two or more persons who live together in the dwelling and are related by blood, marriage or adoption." In reversing the housing authority's interpretation, the court reasoned that the purpose of the Act was to provide housing for low-income families and that the legislative history did not support a reading of the term "family" to mean "traditional" families only. The court also noted a number of other reasons for rejecting the HACE definition:

* * *

> First, HUD has recognized that couples with children can often create a positive family situation when unmarried * * * Second, it is clear that in some jurisdictions, such as New York and California, housing authorities now routinely allow couples who are cohabiting to participate in low-income housing. Third, the defendants' definition is so restrictive it would even exclude common-law relationships that are recognized under state law as the equivalent of more traditional marriages. Finally, empirical evidence demonstrates that it would be unreasonable to exclude unmarried couples from subsidized housing. According to the affidavit of an expert sociologist, there were 2.2 million couples living together in 1986. Approximately 30% or 666,000 of these couples lived with children. Cohabitation is also slightly more likely among those in the lower to lower middle economic classes. Allowing PHAs to exclude such a large group of people from rental assistance would be unconscionable. It could not have been the intent of Congress to deny these individuals and their innocent children access to the safe and sanitary housing promised by USHA.

* * *

> With respect to the plaintiffs in this action, it is clear that they are entitled to family status. The plaintiffs are unmarried but have three natural children.... The only thing missing is a marriage certificate....
>
> Defendants' moral vision of the world is hampered by their shortsightedness. While I, like the defendants, certainly endorse traditional concepts of marriage and family, the defendants have failed to consider the wider implications of their policy on the children of the poor. It would be a bizarre world where the refusal of the parents to get a marriage certificate condemns the children to a life of homelessness. Whether it is moral or immoral, wise or unwise, for the parents to spurn marriage, I cannot allow the sins of the parents to be visited upon their children.

Under *Moore*, could Congress have defined "family" in the USHA to exclude unmarried cohabitants from receipt of housing assistance?

5. In Braschi v. Stahl Associates Company, 74 N.Y.2d 201, 544 N.Y.S.2d 784, 543 N.E.2d 49 (1989), the New York Court of Appeals had

to interpret the term "family" in the context of New York City's Rent Control Code. Miguel Braschi and Leslie Blanchard were a gay couple who lived in Blanchard's rent-controlled apartment in New York city from the summer of 1975 until Blanchard's death in September of 1986. After Blanchard died, the property owner tried to evict Braschi based on the fact that Blanchard was the only tenant of record. Braschi argued that he was a member of Blanchard's "family," and thus protected from eviction under the rent control code. The rent control code did not define family. The owner argued that "family" under the code should be defined as it is for purposes of determining intestate succession, which would require a relationship based on blood, marriage, or adoption. Braschi argued that the code's purpose, protecting family members from the sudden loss of their home, required a more expansive definition. The Court agreed with Mr. Braschi:

> * * * [W]e conclude that the term family, as used in 9 NYCRR.6(d), should not be rigidly restricted to those people who have formalized their relationship by obtaining, for instance, a marriage certificate or an adoption order. The intended protection against sudden eviction should not rest on fictitious legal distinctions or genetic history, but instead should find its foundation in the reality of family life. In the context of eviction, a more realistic, and certainly equally valid, view of a family includes two adult lifetime partners whose relationship is long term and characterized by an emotional and financial commitment and interdependence. This view comports both with our society's traditional concept of "family" and with the expectations of individuals who live in such nuclear units ... In fact, Webster's Dictionary defines "family" first as "a group of people united by certain convictions or common affiliation" (Webster's Ninth New Collegiate Dictionary 448 (1984); see Ballantine's Law Dictionary 456 (3d ed. 1969) ("family" defined as "[p]rimarily, the collective body of persons who live in one house and under one head or management"); Black's Law Dictionary 543 (Special Deluxe 5th ed. 1979)). Hence, it is reasonable to conclude that, in using the term "family," the Legislature intended to extend protection to those who reside in households having all of the normal familial characteristics. Appellant Braschi should therefore be afforded the opportunity to prove that he and Blanchard had such a household.
>
> This definition of "family" is consistent with both of the competing purposes of the rent-control laws: the protection of individuals from sudden dislocation and the gradual transition to a free market system. Family members, whether or not related by blood, or law who have always treated the apartment as their family home will be protected against the hardship of eviction following the death of the named tenant, thereby furthering the Legislature's goals of preventing dislocation and preserving family units which might otherwise be broken apart upon eviction. This approach will foster the transition from rent control to rent stabilization by drawing a

> distinction between those individuals who are, in fact, genuine family members, and those who are mere roommates ... or newly discovered relatives hoping to inherit the rent-controlled apartment after the existing tenant's death.
>
> The determination as to whether an individual is entitled to noneviction protection should be based upon an objective examination of the relationship of the parties. In making this assessment, the lower courts of this State have looked to a number of factors, including the exclusivity and longevity of the relationship, the level of emotional and financial commitment, the manner in which the parties have conducted their everyday lives and held themselves out to society, and the reliance placed upon one another for daily family services.... These factors are most helpful, although it should be emphasized that the presence or absence of one or more of them is not dispositive since it is the totality of the relationship as evidenced by the dedication, caring and self-sacrifice of the parties which should in the final analysis, control.

Under *Moore*, could the City have defined "family" in the Rent Control Code to exclude all relationships except those based on blood, marriage, or consanguinity?

6. Can a group of college students be a "family"? In Borough of Glassboro v. Vallorosi, 117 N.J. 421, 568 A.2d 888 (1990), a New Jersey court interpreted another zoning ordinance. The Borough had amended its city ordinance in 1986 after a particularly rowdy weekend college celebration; the amendment defined a family as "[o]ne or more persons occupying a dwelling unit as a single non-profit housekeeping unit, who are living together as a stable and permanent living unit, being a traditional family unit or the functional equivalency [sic] thereof." The amendment contained a statement of purpose specifying that the Borough's intention was to confine college students either to college dormitories or to other zoning districts that permitted apartments and townhouses. The defendants had purchased a house in an area zoned for families for use by a college student (who was the brother of a defendant) and his friends. After ten unrelated students moved into the house, the Borough sought an injunction against their continued occupancy, arguing that they did not constitute a family. The court stated that:

> [t]he uncontradicted testimony reflects a plan by ten sophomore college students to live together for three years under conditions that correspond substantially to the ordinance's requirement of a "stable and permanent living unit." To facilitate the plan, the house had been purchased by relatives of one of the students. The students ate together, shared household chores, and paid expenses from a common fund. Although the students signed four-month leases, the leases were renewable if the house was "in order" at the end of the term. Moreover, the students testified to their intention to remain in the house throughout college.

> * * * It is a matter of common experience that the costs of college and the variables characteristic of college life and student relationships do not readily lead to the formation of a household as stable and potentially durable as the one described in this record. On these facts, however, we cannot quarrel with the Law Division's conclusion that the occupancy at issue here "shows stability, permanency, and can be described as the functional equivalent of a family."

Could (and should) a group of students be defined as a "family" for any purpose other than zoning? *See* Geoffrey R. Scott, *A Psycho–Social Analysis of the Concept of Family as Used in Zoning Laws*, 88 DICK. L. REV. 368 (1984).

7. During the Reagan administration, officials at the U.S. Department of Education characterized the *Moore* decision as follows:

"In *Moore,* the Court denied to the citizens of that predominately black community the power to zone their town to limit occupancy of dwelling units to members of a single family, in order to protect residents from the downward drag of the welfare culture. In so doing, *Moore* in effect forbade any community in America to define 'family' in a traditional way."

U.S. DEP'T OF EDUCATION, THE FAMILY: PRESERVING AMERICA'S FUTURE (transmitted to Pres. Reagan Dec. 2, 1986).

Is the Department of Education correct in its interpretation of *Moore*?

8. Does *Moore* mean that, "[i]n the end, the family is defined by the heart, not by the law?" Jennifer Jaff, *Wedding Bell Blues: The Position of Unmarried People in American Law*, 30 ARIZ. L. REV. 207, 242 (1988).

Problem 1–1:

a) The City's zoning ordinance defines "family" as "a group of individuals living as a single housekeeping unit in a single dwelling unit. A group of three or more individuals will not be considered a family unless each individual is related to the nominal household head(s) by ties of consanguinity, affinity, or adoption. A family may also consist of one individual." Based on the zoning ordinance, John and Jane Jones, who have contracted with the State Department of Social Services to accept up to eight adolescent children in state foster care for a per-child monthly fee, recently received a notice of violation from the City. Mr. and Mrs. Jones have appealed the determination, arguing that the ordinance is unconstitutional under *Moore*. You are the City Attorney and have been asked to evaluate the merits of their claim.

b) Mr. and Mrs. Jones have received notice that Jimmy Pitts, a foster child who has been in their care for five years, will be moved by the State to another foster home closer to his biological mother next month. Mr. and Mrs. Jones believe that such a move will be damaging to the child, who is well-integrated into their home and his current school; they want to contest the state's determination. They were told by state officials that "parents and grandparents are entitled to a hearing, but foster parents aren't." Mr. and Mrs. Jones have consulted you about the viability of an appeal from the State's determination. According to Mr. and Mrs. Jones, Jimmy sees his mother approximately once every two months and has not seen another biological relative for three years; as far as the Joneses and Jimmy are concerned, *they* are Jimmy's family. Based on *Moore*, evaluate the strength of the Joneses' claim. *See* Smith v. Organization of Foster Families for Equality and Reform (OFFER), 431 U.S. 816, 97 S.Ct. 2094, 53 L.Ed.2d 14 (1977).

SECTION 2. CONSTITUTIONAL FAMILY LAW: "EMANATIONS AND PENUMBRAS"

GRISWOLD v. CONNECTICUT

Supreme Court of the United States, 1965.
381 U.S. 479, 85 S.Ct. 1678, 14 L.Ed.2d 510.

JUSTICE DOUGLAS delivered the opinion of the Court.

Appellant Griswold is Executive Director of the Planned Parenthood League of Connecticut. Appellant Buxton is a licensed physician and a professor at the Yale Medical School who served as Medical Director for the league at its Center in New Haven—a center open and operating from November 1 to November 10, 1961, when appellants were arrested. They gave information, instruction, and medical advice to married persons as to the means of preventing conception. They examined the wife and prescribed the best contraceptive device or material for her use. Fees were usually charged, although some couples were serviced free.

The statutes whose constitutionality is involved in this appeal are §§ 53–22 and 54–196 of the General Statutes of Connecticut (1958 rev.). The former provides:

> Any person who uses any drug, medicinal article or instrument for the purpose of preventing conception shall be fined not less than fifty dollars or imprisoned not less than sixty days nor more than one year or be both fined and imprisoned.
>
> Section 54–196 provides:
>
> Any person who assists, abets, counsels, causes, hires or commands another to commit any offense may be prosecuted and punished as if he were the principal offender.

The appellants were found guilty as accessories and fined $100 each, against the claim that the accessory statute as so applied violated the Fourteenth Amendment . . .

* * *

Coming to the merits, we are met with a wide range of questions that implicate the Due Process Clause of the Fourteenth Amendment . . .

We do not sit as a super-legislature to determine the wisdom, need, and propriety of laws that touch economic problems, business affairs, or social conditions. This law, however, operates directly on an intimate relation of husband and wife and their physician's role is one aspect of that relation.

The association of people is not mentioned in the Constitution nor in the Bill of Rights. The right to educate a child in a school of the parent's choice—whether public or private or parochial—is also not mentioned. Nor is the right to study any particular subject or any foreign language. Yet the First Amendment has been construed to include certain of those rights.

By *Pierce v. Society of Sisters*, 268 U.S. 510, the right to educate one's children as one chooses is made applicable to the States by the force of the First and Fourteenth Amendments. By *Meyer v. State of Nebraska*, 262 U.S. 390, the same dignity is given the right to study the German language in a private school. In other words, the State may not, consistently with the spirit of the First Amendment, contract the spectrum of available knowledge. The right of freedom of speech and press includes not only the right to utter or to print, but the right to distribute, the right to receive, the right to read and freedom of inquiry, freedom of thought, and freedom to teach—indeed the freedom of the entire university community.... Without those peripheral rights the specific rights would be less secure. And so we reaffirm the principle of the *Pierce* and *Meyer* cases.

In *NAACP v. State of Alabama*, 357 U.S. 449, 462, we protected the "freedom to associate and privacy in one's associations," noting that freedom of association was a peripheral First Amendment right. Disclosure of membership lists of a constitutionally valid association, we held, was invalid "as entailing the likelihood of a substantial restraint upon the exercise by petitioner's members of the right to freedom of association." *Id.* In other words, the First Amendment has a penumbra where privacy is protected from governmental intrusion. In like context, we have protected forms of "association" that are not political in the customary sense but pertain to the social, legal, and economic benefit of the members. *NAACP v. Button*, 371 U.S. 415, 430–431 ...

Those cases involved more than the "right of assembly"—a right that extends to all irrespective of their race or ideology. De Jonge v. State of Oregon, 299 U.S. 353. The right of "association," like the right of belief, is more than the right to attend a meeting; it includes the right to express one's attitudes or philosophies by membership in a group by affiliation with it or by other lawful means. Association in that context is a form of expression of opinion; and while it is not expressly included in the First Amendment its existence is necessary in making the express guarantees fully meaningful.

The foregoing cases suggest that specific guarantees in the Bill of Rights have penumbras, formed by emanations from those guarantees that help give them life and substance. ... Various guarantees create zones of privacy. The right of association contained in the penumbra of the First Amendment is one, as we have seen. The Third Amendment in its prohibition against the quartering of soldiers "in any house" in time of peace without the consent of the owner is another facet of that privacy. The Fourth Amendment explicitly affirms the "right of the people to be secure in their persons, houses, papers, and effects, against unreasonable searches and seizures." The Fifth Amendment in its Self-Incrimination Clause enables the citizen to create a zone of privacy which government may not force him to surrender to his detriment. The Ninth Amendment provides: "The enumeration in the Constitution, of certain rights, shall not be construed to deny or disparage others retained by the people."

* * *

The present case, then, concerns a relationship lying within the zone of privacy created by several fundamental constitutional guarantees. And it concerns a law which, in forbidding the use of contraceptives rather than regulating their manufacture or sale, seeks to achieve its goals by means of having a maximum destructive impact upon that relationship. Such a law cannot stand in light of the familiar principle, so often applied by this Court, that a "government purpose to control or prevent activities constitutionally subject to state regulation may not be achieved by means which sweep unnecessarily broadly and thereby invade the area of protected freedoms." *NAACP v. Alabama*, 377 U.S. 288, 307. Would we allow the police to search the sacred precincts of marital bedrooms for telltale signs of the use of contraceptives? The very idea is repulsive to the notions of privacy surrounding the marriage relationship.

We deal with a right of privacy older than the Bill of Rights—older than our political parties, older than our school system. Marriage is a coming together for better or worse, hopefully enduring, and intimate to the degree of being sacred. It is an association that promotes a way of life, not causes; a harmony in living, not political faiths; a bilateral loyalty, not commercial or social projects. Yet it is an association for as noble a purpose as any involved in our prior decisions.

Reversed.

JUSTICE GOLDBERG, THE CHIEF JUSTICE AND JUSTICE BRENNAN, concurring.

* * *

The language and history of the Ninth Amendment reveal that the Framers of the Constitution believed that there are additional fundamental rights, protected from governmental rights, protected from governmental infringement, which exist alongside those fundamental rights specifically mentioned in the first eight constitutional amendments.

The Ninth Amendment reads, "The enumeration in the Constitution, of certain rights, shall not be construed to deny or disparage others retained by the people." The Amendment is almost entirely the work of

James Madison. It was introduced in Congress by him and passed the House and Senate with little or no debate and virtually no change in language. It was proffered to quiet expressed fears that a bill of specifically enumerated rights could not be sufficiently broad to cover all essential rights and that the specific mention of certain rights would be interpreted as a denial that others were protected . . .

The Connecticut statutes here involved deal with a particularly important and sensitive area of privacy—that of the marital relation and the marital home. This Court recognized in *Meyer v. Nebraska, supra*, that the right "to marry, establish a home and bring up children" was an essential part of the liberty guaranteed by the Fourteenth Amendment. In *Pierce v. Society of Sisters*, the Court held unconstitutional an Oregon Act which forbade parents from sending their children to private schools because such an act "unreasonably interferes with the liberty of parents and guardians to direct the upbringing and education of children under their control." As this Court said in *Prince v. Massachusetts*, 321 U.S. 158, at 166, the *Meyer* and *Pierce* decisions "have respected the private realm of family life which the state cannot enter."

I agree with Mr. Justice Harlan's statement in his dissenting opinion in *Poe v. Ullman*, 367 U.S. 497, 551–552: "Certainly the safeguarding of the home does not follow merely from the sanctity of property rights. The home derives its pre-eminence as the seat of family life. And the integrity of that life is something so fundamental that it has been found to draw to its protection the principles of more than one explicitly granted Constitutional right . . . Of this whole 'private realm of family life' it is difficult to imagine what is more private or more intimate than a husband and wife's marital relations."

The entire fabric of the Constitution and the purposes that clearly underlie its specific guarantees demonstrate that the rights to marital privacy and to marry and raise a family are of similar order and magnitude as the fundamental rights specifically protected.

Although the Constitution does not speak in so many words of the right of privacy in marriage, I cannot believe that it offers these fundamental rights no protection . . .

Finally, it should be said of the Court's holding today that it in no way interferes with a State's proper regulation of sexual promiscuity or misconduct. As my Brother Harlan so well states in his dissenting opinion in *Poe v. Ullman*,

> Adultery, homosexuality and the like are sexual intimacies which the State forbids . . . but the intimacy of husband and wife is necessarily an essential and accepted feature of the institution of marriage, an institution which the State not only must allow, but which always and in every age it has fostered and protected. It is one thing when the State exerts its power either to forbid extra-marital sexuality . . . or to say who may marry, but it is quite another when, having acknowledged a marriage and the intimacies inherent in it, it

undertakes to regulate by means of the criminal law the details of that intimacy.

In sum, I believe that the right of privacy in the marital relation is fundamental and basic—a personal right "retained by the people" within the meaning of the Ninth Amendment. Connecticut cannot constitutionally abridge this fundamental right, which is protected by the Fourteenth Amendment from infringement by the States. I agree with the Court that petitioners' convictions must therefore be reversed.

JUSTICE BLACK, with whom JUSTICE STEWART joins, dissenting.

* * *

One of the most effective ways of diluting or expanding a [constitutional] ... right is to substitute for the crucial word or words of a constitutional guarantee another word or words ... This fact is well illustrated by the use of the term "right of privacy" as a comprehensive substitute for the Fourth Amendment's guarantee against "unreasonable searches and seizures." ...

This brings me to [the due process clause and Ninth Amendment arguments.] [On] analysis they turn out to be the same thing—merely using different words to claim for this Court ... power to invalidate any legislative act which the judges find irrational, unreasonable or offensive.

... The Due Process Clause ... was liberally used by this Court to strike down economic legislation in the early decade of this century, threatening, many people thought, the tranquility and stability of the Nation. That formula, based on subjective considerations of "natural justice," is no less dangerous when used to enforce this Court's views about personal rights than those about economic rights....

Notes and Questions

1. How much emphasis is there in the welter of *Griswold* opinions on the right of *family* privacy as distinguished from *individual* privacy? Try a headcount.

2. Where does the court find a constitutional right to privacy limiting the state's authority to regulate family life? What *are* penumbras of the Constitution? What other means were available to interpret the text: express language? overall structure? the framers' intent? implicit values in the document?

3. The *Griswold* court relates its holding to "the notions of privacy surrounding the marriage relationship." In Eisenstadt v. Baird, 405 U.S. 438, 92 S.Ct. 1029, 31 L.Ed.2d 349 (1972), the Court was faced with a statute criminalizing the dispensing of contraceptives to anyone other than a married person. Noting that "the question for our determination ... is whether there is some ground of difference that rationally explains the different treatment accorded married and unmarried persons under [the statute]," the Court "conclude[d] that no such ground exists."

4. The privacy right enunciated in *Griswold* also provided the basis for later Supreme Court decisions on abortion rights. *See* Roe v. Wade [p. 269] (holding that "[t]his right of privacy, whether it be founded in the Fourteenth Amendment's concept of personal liberty and restrictions upon state action, as we feel it is, or, as the District Court determined, in the Ninth Amendment's reservation of rights to the people, is broad enough to encompass a woman's decision whether or not to terminate her pregnancy.").

DOE v. DULING

United States District Court, Eastern District of Virginia, 1985.
603 F.Supp. 960.

MERHIGE, DISTRICT JUDGE.

* * *

Plaintiffs are proceeding in this action under the pseudonyms of James Doe and Jane Doe. They are unmarried adults who reside in the City of Richmond, Virginia and allege to have engaged in sexual intercourse in Richmond with unmarried members of the opposite sex. They both express the desire to engage in such activity in the future and to cohabit with a member of the opposite sex "under conditions normally associated with living as husband and wife." In their depositions, both plaintiffs testified that they have not engaged in sexual intercourse since the filing of this action partly because of their fear of prosecution.

Defendant Frank Duling is the Chief of the Richmond Bureau of Police, and his co-defendant, Aubrey Davis, is the Commonwealth's Attorney for the City of Richmond.

* * *

The fundamental substantive issue before the Court is whether the State, consistent with the Constitution, may restrict the non-prostitutional, heterosexual activities of two unmarried, consenting adults when such activities occur in the privacy of one's home. Plaintiffs contend such intimate, sexual activity is protected by the constitutional right of privacy; any attempt by the state to regulate this activity is unconstitutional. Defendants contend the right of privacy only extends to sexual conduct between two people who are married to each other; heterosexual conduct between unmarried adults does not fall within the scope of the right of privacy.

* * *

Since its seminal decision of *Griswold v. Connecticut*, [p. 19] the Supreme Court has clarified the nature of the right of privacy as related to decisions of whether to bear or beget a child. The right of privacy expressed in *Griswold* was argued by some to extend only to marital privacy. *See, e.g., Doe*, 403 F.Supp. at 1201. The case of *Eisenstadt v. Baird*, [p. 23] held that there was no rational, articulated reason for limiting the access to contraceptives of single adults when married adults are afforded a right to contraceptives. "[W]hatever the rights of the individual to access to contraceptives may be, the rights must be the same for the unmarried and the married alike." The case of *Roe v. Wade*, [p. 269] decided one year later, extended the right of privacy to first trimester abortions.

Although the full extent of the right of privacy has not been determined, it is clear that the "decision whether or not to beget or bear a child is at the very heart of [the] cluster of constitutionally protected choices." *Carey v. Population Services International*, [p. 447].

* * *

Necessarily implicit in the right to make decisions regarding child-bearing is the right to engage in sexual intercourse. To hold otherwise would result in the constitutional right to decide whether to bear or beget a child [being] contingent on one's marital status. *Carey* makes it clear that such a limitation is not valid. "If the right of privacy means anything, it is the right of the *individual*, married or single, to be free from unwarranted governmental intrusion into matters so fundamentally affecting a person as the decision whether to bear or beget a child." *Eisenstadt*, [p. 23, n. 3] (emphasis in original). The decision to engage in sexual intercourse, just as the decision to use contraceptives, is a matter fundamental to the decision whether to bear or beget a child. In the view of this Court, the constitutional right of privacy extends to a single adult's decision whether to engage in sexual intercourse.

The inquiry, however, does not end here. Even fundamental constitutional rights are not absolute; the state's regulation of these rights may be justified if the statute infringing on them is shown to be narrowly tailored to further a *compelling state interest*. *Roe*, *supra*. The Court has great difficulty accepting an argument that the state's purpose for the fornication statute is anything other than preventing sexual intercourse among unmarried individuals. Clearly, such a purpose would not be constitutionally permissible. Nevertheless, defendants have articulated other reasons for passing the fornication statute. None of these reasons, in the Court's view, justify the fornication statute.

The defendants, in this instance, argue that the compelling reason for the fornication statute is to further the State's interest in "encouraging, promoting and regulating traditional marital and family relationships as well as traditional moral values." Defendants add that the fornication statute is designed to protect the State's citizens from sexual diseases and to minimize illegitimate births. As laudable as these state goals are, they do not justify an absolute prohibition of the exercise of a constitutionally protected activity.

The Court cannot accept the contention that sexual abstention, forced through criminal sanctions, will encourage or regulate marriage. Just as the decision whether to bear or beget a child, a decision to marry is a personal choice protected by the right of privacy. *Loving v. Virginia*,

388 U.S. 1 (1967). Such a decision cannot be coerced through infringement on other constitutional rights. Moreover, this state purpose, an attempt to regulate public morals, cannot extend into the privacy of one's home. There is no showing that fornication in private has any detrimental effect on society. * * * The Court appreciates the state goals of encouraging and regulating marital relationships and moral values. Such goals may be, and indeed are, generally accepted as desirable. Nevertheless, when an individual's constitutional rights are restricted in an effort to attain those goals, the state's interest must be more than merely desirable—it must be *compelling*. Our Constitution preserves for the individual the right to decide whether to procreate or marry. The state interest of promoting healthy and conforming social values is not a compelling interest which justifies deprivation of these fundamental constitutional rights.

The State's desire to prevent sexual diseases, although legitimate, does not justify prohibiting the exercise of a constitutional right. The fornication statute, involving, as it does, a fundamental right, "must be narrowly drawn to express only the legitimate state interests at stake." *Roe, supra*. The fornication statute is not narrowly drawn. All single people who engage in sexual intercourse do not pose a threat of spreading sexual diseases. Yet the statute prohibits single people under all circumstances and in any state of health from engaging in sexual intercourse. In short, the fornication statute is too broadly drawn to fulfill this stated purpose in light of the fundamental right implicated by the statute.

Finally, defendants argue that the fornication statute is designed to minimize illegitimate births. This argument is simply another way of saying that the statute is designed to prevent unmarried individuals from having children. That argument lacks viability. The decision whether to bear or beget a child is a personal one—a constitutional right. In the interest of encouraging family relationships, an attempt to minimize illegitimate births may be a justifiable exercise of state power. Though the interest be legitimate, it is not sufficiently compelling to outweigh an unmarried individual's right to procreate. If the state wishes to minimize illegitimate births, it will have to use alternative means. One alternative is to enact a statute ... which outlines procedures, short of forced marriage, that can be used to legitimate a child. The state may attempt to educate its citizens on the "immorality" of bearing or begetting a child out of wedlock. The state does not, however, have the power to impose criminal sanctions upon a person who engages in constitutionally protected conduct.

The focus of the Court changes some with regard to the cohabitation statute. Code § 18.2–345 punishes two types of behavior: all "open and gross lewdness and lasciviousness" and conduct between persons who are not married to each other and are cohabiting together which is lewd and lascivious.

* * *

It is the opinion of the Court that the portion of the statute criminalizing lewd and lascivious cohabitation between persons not married to each other cannot withstand constitutional scrutiny. The articulated state interests in having a cohabitation statute are identical to those state interests for the fornication statute. As discussed *supra*, all individuals have a constitutional right to decide whether to procreate. Implicit in this decision is the right to engage in private heterosexual intercourse. The state cannot absolutely proscribe such conduct. It is irrational to limit such conduct, if partners are not married to each other, only to those persons who are *not* living together. Such a limitation hardly furthers the marital relationship and may even frustrate a family relationship—unmarried parents of a child would be deterred from living together.

The Court concludes that, as they relate to the plaintiffs here, Virginia Code §§ 18.2–344 and 18.2–345 are too broad to withstand the searching scrutiny required when fundamental rights are restricted.[5] Plaintiffs have a fundamental constitutional right to decide whether to bear or beget children which can be infringed upon only in limited circumstances. Defendants have failed to articulate a compelling state interest which justifies the extensive intrusion into plaintiffs' constitutional rights.

An appropriate order will issue.

Notes and Questions

1. The Model Penal Code takes the position that fornication should not be subject to criminal penalties:

> Sexual intercourse out of wedlock is a crime in several American jurisdictions. The prohibition derives from Biblical sources and long fell within the exclusive jurisdiction of the ecclesiastical authorities. In England, secular punishment began under Cromwell's theocracy and was abandoned after the Restoration. The Puritans of New England reinstituted punishment for sexual misbehavior. At one time or another, most American states extended their penal laws to reach such misconduct, but the trend in this century has been toward decriminalization or reduction of penalties. A survey prepared in 1954 showed that only 18 jurisdictions punished a single act of intercourse between unmarried persons as a criminal offense, and four punished such conduct by fine alone. Most states required a relationship that was continuous or "open and notorious" or both. Eleven states and most foreign countries did not have a fornication offense. As of the same date, simple adultery constituted a criminal

5. It is important to note that the Court necessarily limits its inquiry into the constitutionality of statutes proscribing non-prostitutional, consensual, heterosexual conduct between two adults. To what extent this right of privacy extends to minors is not an issue before the Court. Likewise, the issues of whether the state may regulate or prohibit the commercial sale of sexual services and whether an individual has a legitimate expectation of privacy in prostitutional activities are issues not before the Court and, consequently, not decided today.

offense in 30 states, four of which punished it only by a fine. Some provision against instances of aggravated adultery was found in virtually every state and in many foreign nations. At common law, an illicit sexual relation constituted a secular offense only if it became a public nuisance. At least two recently revised codes follow the same idea by restricting the crime of fornication to relations that are "open" or "notorious." Only one recent revision appears similarly to circumscribe liability for adultery. * * *

The essential resolution of the issue * * * ultimately depends on the propriety of maintaining criminal sanctions against fornication and adultery simply because such behavior is widely thought to be immoral. * * * [T]he Model Code takes the position that private immorality should be beyond the reach of the penal law. Article 213 therefore includes no provision on this subject. This judgment has been accepted in at least 25 recently drafted codes and proposals, although there are a number of recent revisions that have prohibited such conduct. American Law Institute, Model Penal Code and Commentary, Part II, Vol. 1, at 430.

2. While the majority of states have repealed their fornication statutes, in 1996, fornication was still a misdemeanor in six states; in several others fornication was a crime if "open and notorious." Adultery remained a crime in 25 states. *See* Richard Posner & Katharine Silbaugh, A Guide to America's Sex Laws 98–110 (1996).

3. In Mister v. A.R.K. Partnership, 197 Ill.App.3d 105, 143 Ill.Dec. 166, 553 N.E.2d 1152 (1990) the court held that a landlord could refuse to rent to an unmarried couple without violating an Illinois statute barring discrimination based on marital status. The court held that, in light of the "longstanding policy reflected by the [Illinois] fornication statute," the legislature could not have intended any other result. *See also* Oliverson v. West Valley City, 875 F.Supp. 1465 (D.Utah 1995) (upholding Utah adultery statute).

4. While the Supreme Court has not addressed the constitutionality of criminalizing fornication, it has reviewed a criminal sodomy law. In Bowers v. Hardwick, 478 U.S. 186, 106 S.Ct. 2841, 92 L.Ed.2d 140 (1986), the Supreme Court (5–4) refused to extend *Griswold* and *Eisenstadt* to homosexual relationships and upheld a statute criminalizing consensual sodomy (then on the books in about half of the states). Justice White, speaking for the Court, phrased the issue as:

> ... whether the Federal Constitution confers a fundamental right upon homosexuals to engage in sodomy and hence invalidates the laws of the many States that still make such conduct illegal and have done so for a very long time....
>
> We first register our disagreement with the Court of Appeals and with respondent that the Court's prior cases have construed the Constitution to confer a right to privacy that extends to homosexual sodomy ...

> Accepting the decisions in these cases and the above description of them, we think it evident that none of the rights announced in those cases bears any resemblance to the claimed constitutional right of homosexuals to engage in acts of sodomy that is asserted in this case. No connection between family, marriage, or procreation on the one hand and homosexual activity on the other has been demonstrated, either by the Court of Appeals or by respondent ...
>
> It is obvious to us that neither of these formulations would extend a fundamental right to homosexuals to engage in acts of consensual sodomy. Proscriptions against that conduct have ancient roots. Sodomy was a criminal offense at common law and was forbidden by the laws of the original thirteen states when they ratified the Bill of Rights. In 1868, when the Fourteenth Amendment was ratified, all but 5 of the 37 States in the Union had criminal sodomy laws. In fact, until 1961, all 50 States outlawed sodomy, and today, 24 States and the District of Columbia continue to provide criminal penalties for sodomy performed in private and between consenting adults. Against this background, to claim that a right to engage in such conduct is "deeply rooted in this Nation's history and tradition" or "implicit in the concept of ordered liberty" is, at best, facetious.

The dissenting justices, led by Justice Blackmun, stated:

> This case is no more about "a fundamental right to engage in homosexual sodomy" ... than *Stanley v. Georgia* ... was about a fundamental right to watch obscene movies, or *Katz v. United States* ... was about a fundamental right to place interstate bets from a phone booth. Rather, this case is about "the most comprehensive of rights and the right most valued by civilized men," namely, "the right to be let alone." *Olmstead v. United States* ... (Brandeis, J. dissenting).

Justices Stevens, Brennan and Marshall filed an additional dissent finding the statute overbroad because it applied to married as well as unmarried persons, to heterosexuals as well as homosexuals. They urged that the Court should have determined whether the state had the power to prohibit totally the described conduct, and only then considered whether the state may only enforce the law against homosexuals.

5. In Romer v. Evans, 517 U.S. 620, 116 S.Ct. 1620, 134 L.Ed.2d 855 (1996), United States Supreme Court (6–3) struck a Colorado law prohibiting government protection of homosexuals under the equal protection clause. Are *Bowers* and *Romer* consistent? *See Gay Rights Watershed?*, ABA JOURNAL, (July 1996) at p. 30. Based on *Griswold, Bowers,* and *Romer*, how would you expect the Supreme Court to rule on *Duling*?

6. If the *Duling* court is correct that the state *may not* criminalize consensual sexual activity between unmarried adults, may the state still:

a) refuse to grant benefits to unmarried cohabitants that are enjoyed by married people?

b) criminalize prostitution (as opposed to barring only public solicitation)? *Compare* In re P., 92 Misc.2d 62, 400 N.Y.S.2d 455 (Fam.Ct.1977) *with* In re Dora P., 418 N.Y.S.2d 597 (App.Div.1979).

7. If the state *may* criminalize fornication, could the state selectively prosecute pregnant unmarried teenagers only? Does it matter if enforcement is through civil or criminal proceedings? *See* Mark Hansen, *Miscarriage of Justice*?, ABA J. (Nov. 1996), at 26.

SECTION 3. THE FEDERAL TRADITION OF NON-INVOLVEMENT—THE TENTH AMENDMENT AND MORE

The 10th Amendment to the United States Constitution specifies that "[t]he powers not delegated to the United States by the Constitution, nor prohibited by it to the States, are reserved to the States respectively, or to the people." Unlike taxation and interstate commerce, family matters are not among the enumerated powers of the federal government. As a result, and in contrast to other federal systems (i.e., Australia, Canada, Germany, Switzerland) where family law is predominantly federal law, in the United States, state legislatures have traditionally defined the family and enacted the laws that regulated marriage, parentage, divorce, family support obligations, and family property rights.

While federal courts might, theoretically, exercise diversity jurisdiction over family matters, as a result of the so-called "domestic relations exception" to diversity jurisdiction and various abstention doctrines, federal courts have seldom entertained family law matters. Indeed, the United States Supreme Court has often repeated that "[t]he whole subject of the domestic relations of husband and wife, parent and child, belongs to the laws of the State, and not the laws of the United States." Simms v. Simms, 175 U.S. 162, 167, 20 S.Ct. 58, 44 L.Ed. 115 (1899); *accord*, McCarty v. McCarty, 453 U.S. 210, 101 S.Ct. 2728, 69 L.Ed.2d 589 (1981).

ANKENBRANDT v. RICHARDS

Supreme Court of the United States, 1992.
504 U.S. 689, 112 S.Ct. 2206, 119 L.Ed.2d 468.

JUSTICE WHITE delivered the opinion of the Court.

This case presents the issue whether the federal courts have jurisdiction or should abstain in a case involving alleged torts committed by the former husband of petitioner and his female companion against petitioner's children, when the sole basis for federal jurisdiction is the diversity-of-citizenship provision of 28 U.S.C. § 1332.

Petitioner Carol Ankenbrandt, a citizen of Missouri, brought this lawsuit on September 26, 1989, on behalf of her daughters L.R. and S.R.

against respondents Jon A. Richards and Debra Kesler, citizens of Louisiana, in the United States District Court for the Eastern District of Louisiana. . . . Ankenbrandt's complaint sought monetary damages for alleged sexual and physical abuse of the children committed by Richards and Kesler. Richards is the divorced father of the children and Kesler his female companion.

* * *

We granted certiorari limited to the following questions: "(1) Is there a domestic relations exception to federal jurisdiction? (2) If so, does it permit a district court to abstain from exercising diversity jurisdiction over a tort action for damages? and (3) Did the District Court in this case err in abstaining from exercising jurisdiction under the doctrine of Younger v. Harris?". . . . We address each of these issues in turn.

The domestic relations exception upon which the courts below relied to decline jurisdiction has been invoked often by the lower federal courts. The seeming authority for doing so originally stemmed from the announcement in *Barber v. Barber*, 21 How. 582, 16 L.Ed. 226 (1859), that the federal courts have no jurisdiction over suits for divorce or the allowance of alimony. In that case, the Court heard a suit in equity brought by a wife (by her next friend) in federal district court pursuant to diversity jurisdiction against her former husband. She sought to enforce a decree from a New York state court, which had granted a divorce and awarded her alimony. The former husband thereupon moved to Wisconsin to place himself beyond the New York court's jurisdiction so that the divorce decree there could not be enforced against him; he then sued for a divorce in a Wisconsin court, representing to that court that his wife had abandoned him and failing to disclose the existence of the New York decree. In a suit brought by the former wife in Wisconsin Federal District Court, the former husband alleged that the court lacked jurisdiction. The court accepted jurisdiction and gave judgment for the divorced wife.

* * *

Counsel argued in *Barber* that the Constitution prohibited federal courts from exercising jurisdiction over domestic relations cases. An examination of Article III, *Barber* itself, and our cases since *Barber* makes clear that the Constitution does not exclude domestic relations cases from the jurisdiction otherwise granted by statute to the federal courts.

Article III, § 2, of the Constitution * * * delineates the absolute limits on the federal courts' jurisdiction. But in articulating three different terms to define jurisdiction—"Cases in Law and Equity," "Cases," and "Controversies"—this provision contains no limitation on subjects of a domestic relations nature. Nor did *Barber* purport to ground the domestic relations exception in these constitutional limits on federal jurisdiction. The Court's discussion of federal judicial power to hear suits of a domestic relations nature contains no mention of the

Constitution, and it is logical to presume that the Court based its statement limiting such power on narrower statutory, rather than broader constitutional, grounds.

* * *

That Article III, § 2, does not mandate the exclusion of domestic relations cases from federal-court jurisdiction, however, does not mean that such courts necessarily must retain and exercise jurisdiction over such cases.

* * *

The Judiciary Act of 1789 provided that "the circuit courts shall have original cognizance, concurrent with the courts of the several States, of *all suits of a civil nature at common law or in equity, where the matter in dispute exceeds*, exclusive of costs, the sum or value of *five hundred dollars*, and * * * an alien is a party, or the suit is *between a citizen of the State where the suit is brought, and a citizen of another State.*" (Emphasis added.) The defining phrase, "all suits of a civil nature at common law or in equity," remained a key element of statutory provisions demarcating the terms of diversity jurisdiction until 1948, when Congress amended the diversity jurisdiction provision to eliminate this phrase and replace in its stead the term "all civil actions."

The *Barber* majority itself did not expressly refer to the diversity statute's use of the limitation on "suits of a civil nature at common law or in equity." The dissenters in *Barber*, however, implicitly made such a reference, for they suggested that the federal courts had no power over certain domestic relations actions because the court of chancery lacked authority to issue divorce and alimony decrees. Stating that "the origin and the extent of [the federal courts'] jurisdiction must be sought in the laws of the United States, and in the settled rules and principles by which those laws have bound them," the dissenters contended that "as the jurisdiction of the chancery in England does not extend to or embrace the subjects of divorce and alimony, and as the jurisdiction of the courts of the United States in chancery is bounded by that of the chancery in England, all power or cognizance with respect to those subjects by the courts of the United States in chancery is equally excluded." Hence, in the dissenters' view, a suit seeking such relief would not fall within the statutory language "all suits of a civil nature at common law or in equity." Because the *Barber* Court did not disagree with this reason for accepting the jurisdictional limitation over the issuance of divorce and alimony decrees, it may be inferred fairly that the jurisdictional limitation recognized by the Court rested on this statutory basis and that the disagreement between the Court and the dissenters thus centered only on the extent of the limitation.

We have no occasion here to join the historical debate over whether the English court of chancery had jurisdiction to handle certain domestic relations matters. * * * We thus are content to rest our conclusion that a domestic relations exception exists as a matter of statutory construction not on the accuracy of the historical justifications on which it was seemingly based, but rather on Congress' apparent acceptance of this construction of the diversity jurisdiction provisions in the years prior to 1948, when the statute limited jurisdiction to "suits of a civil nature at common law or in equity." As the court in *Phillips, Nizer, Benjamin, Krim & Ballon v. Rosenstiel*, 490 F.2d 509, 514 (2d Cir.1973) observed, "[m]ore than a century has elapsed since the *Barber* dictum without any intimation of Congressional grant." Considerations of *stare decisis* have particular strength in this context, where "the legislative power is implicated, and Congress remains free to alter what we have done."

When Congress amended the diversity statute in 1948 to replace the law/equity distinction with the phrase "all civil actions," we presume Congress did so with full cognizance of the Court's nearly century-long interpretation of the prior statutes, which had construed the statutory diversity jurisdiction to contain an exception for certain domestic relations matters. * * *

In the more than 100 years since this Court laid the seeds for the development of the domestic relations exception, the lower federal courts have applied it in a variety of circumstances. Many of these applications go well beyond the circumscribed situations posed by *Barber* and its progeny. *Barber* itself disclaimed federal jurisdiction over a narrow range of domestic relations issues involving the granting of a divorce and a decree of alimony * * *.

* * *

The holding of the case itself sanctioned the exercise of federal jurisdiction over the enforcement of an alimony decree that had been properly obtained in a state court of competent jurisdiction. Contrary to the *Barber* dissenters' position, the enforcement of such validly obtained orders does not "regulate the domestic relations of society" and produce an inquisitorial authority" in which federal tribunals "enter the habitations and even into the chambers and nurseries of private families, and inquire into and pronounce upon the morals and habits and affections or antipathies of the members of every household." And from the conclusion that the federal courts lacked jurisdiction to issue divorce and alimony decrees, there was no dissent.

* * *

Subsequently, this Court expanded the domestic relations exception to include decrees in child custody cases. In a child custody case brought pursuant to a writ of habeas corpus, for instance, the Court held void a writ issued by a Federal District Court to restore a child to the custody of the father. "As to the right to the control and possession of this child, as it is contested by its father and its grandfather, it is one in regard to which neither the Congress of the United States nor any authority of the United States has any special jurisdiction." *In re Burrus*, 136 U.S. 586, 594 (1890). * * * We conclude, therefore, that the domestic relations exception, as articulated by this Court since *Barber*, divests the federal courts of power to issue divorce, alimony, and child custody decrees. Given the long passage of time without any expression of congressional dissatisfaction, we have no trouble today reaffirming the validity of the exception as it pertains to divorce and alimony decrees and child custody orders.

Not only is our conclusion rooted in respect for this long-held understanding, it is also supported by sound policy considerations. Issuance of decrees of this type not infrequently involves retention of jurisdiction by the court and deployment of social workers to monitor compliance. As a matter of judicial economy, state courts are more eminently suited to work of this type than are federal courts, which lack the close association with state and local government organizations dedicated to handling issues that arise out of conflicts over divorce, alimony, and child custody decrees. Moreover, as a matter of judicial expertise, it makes far more sense to retain the rule that federal courts lack power to issue these types of decrees because of the special proficiency developed by state tribunals over the past century and a half in handling issues that arise in the granting of such decrees.

By concluding, as we do, that the domestic relations exception encompasses only cases involving the issuance of a divorce, alimony, or child custody decree, we necessarily find that the Court of Appeals erred by affirming the District Court's invocation of this exception. This lawsuit in no way seeks such a decree; rather, it alleges that respondents Richards and Kesler committed torts against L.R. and S.R., Ankenbrandt's children by Richards. Federal subject-matter jurisdiction pursuant to § 1332 thus is proper in this case. We now address whether, even though subject-matter jurisdiction might be proper, sufficient grounds exist to warrant abstention from the exercise of that jurisdiction.

The courts below cited *Younger v. Harris*, 401 U.S. 37 (1971), to support their holdings to abstain in this case. In so doing, the courts clearly erred. *Younger* itself held that, absent unusual circumstances, a federal court could not interfere with a pending state criminal prosecution. Though we have extended *Younger* abstention to the civil context, we have never applied the notions of comity so critical to *Younger's* "Our Federalism" when no state proceeding was pending nor any assertion of important state interests made. In this case, there is no allegation by respondents of any pending state proceedings, and Ankenbrandt contends that such proceedings ended prior to her filing this lawsuit. Absent any pending proceeding in state tribunals, therefore, application by the lower courts of *Younger* abstention was clearly erroneous.

It is not inconceivable, however, that in certain circumstances, the abstention principles . . . might be relevant in a case involving elements of the domestic relationship even when the parties do not seek divorce, alimony, or child custody. This would be so when a case presents "difficult questions of state law bearing on policy problems of substantial public import whose importance transcends the result in the case then at bar." Such might well be the case if a federal suit were filed prior to effectuation of a divorce, alimony, or child custody decree, and the suit depended on a determination of the status of the parties. Where, as here, the status of the domestic relationship has been determined as a matter of state law, and in any event has no bearing on the underlying torts alleged, we have no difficulty concluding that *Burford* abstention is inappropriate in this case.

We thus conclude that the Court of Appeals erred by affirming the District Court's rulings to decline jurisdiction based on the domestic relations exception to diversity jurisdiction and to abstain under the doctrine of *Younger v. Harris*.

* * *

JUSTICE BLACKMUN, concurring in the judgment.

I agree with the Court that the District Court had jurisdiction over petitioner's claims in tort. Moreover, I agree that the federal courts should not entertain claims for divorce, alimony, and child custody. I am unable to agree, however, that the diversity statute contains any "exception" for domestic relations matters. The Court goes to remarkable lengths to craft an exception that is simply not in the statute and is not supported by the case law. In my view, the longstanding, unbroken practice of the federal courts in refusing to hear domestic relations cases is precedent at most for continued discretionary abstention rather than mandatory limits on federal jurisdiction. For these reasons I concur only in the Court's judgment.

Notes and Questions

1. Congress has not amended the 28 U.S.C.A. § 1332(a) since the *Ankenbrandt* case.

2. After *Ankenbrandt*, what is the scope of the domestic relations exception? *See* Cole v. Cole, 633 F.2d 1083 (4th Cir.1980) (permitting action by former husband's claim against ex-wife for malicious prosecution, abuse of process, arson, conspiracy and conversion); Wasserman v. Wasserman, 671 F.2d 832 (4th Cir.1982) (permitting action for intentional infliction of emotional distress and civil conspiracy in child abduction case); Anastasi v. Anastasi, 532 F.Supp. 720, 725 (D.N.J.1982) (permitting action based on contractual support claim based on a cohabitation arrangement when New Jersey law was unsettled on dissolution of such a relationship).

3. Would the possibility of an action in federal court for compensatory and punitive damages encourage settlement in state divorce actions? *See Divorcing Wives are Suing in Federal Court for Abuse*, 96 LAW. WEEKLY, Aug. 12, 1996, at 1, 15.

4. If family issues are of national importance, then why shouldn't federal courts hear family law cases?

> * * * A first possibility is that federal court involvement in family life is bad, per se, at a structural level. This claim takes

seriously the arguments made in the many cases espousing (slight pun intended) state control over family life and fearing that the federal courts would become hopelessly "enmeshed" in family disputes. Under this vision, the states (and Indian tribes) as smaller units of government are closer to "the people", and thus a more appropriate level of government to determine matters affecting intimate life.

Possible justifications for this view exist. Contemporary innovations of the domestic relations exception discard arguments based on ecclesiastical authority, the alleged lack of jurisdictional diversity between married couples, that the claim that divorces lack monetary value—all in favor of a "modern view that state courts have historically decided these matters and have developed both a well-known expertise in these cases and a strong interest in disposing of them." * * * Holding aside the ever-present question of boundaries, doctrine might shift in a variety of ways when ideological claims about the relationship between federal courts and families are revised.

First, one could insist that, despite recognition of federal laws of the family, the claim of deference to state governance remains strong and, as a matter of doctrine, complete abstention (a form of reverse presumption) is desirable. To the extent recent federal law in bankruptcy, pensions, and benefits law points in the other direction, that erosion should be stopped—by legislation or judicial interpretation. But were one really to press this claim—that states are specially situated and should be controlling family life-one would not seek only to cabin the federal courts. This position would also require urging Congress and agencies to avoid defining families by rewriting statutes and regulations to incorporate state law, so as to permit state governance of interpersonal relations. An array of federal statutes would have to incorporate state definitions of families, and what would be lost in uniformity and national norms would be gained in recognition of the special relationship of states in defining family life.

Alternatively, one might instruct the federal courts to adopt a somewhat weaker form of deference, reminiscent of eleventh amendment doctrine and conscious of the many instances of congressional silence. * * * Yet a third alternative is to have selective federal court interpretation of congressional silence as a basis for federal law to override state law. * * *

Yet a problem remains. The current hierarchy stipulates the federal courts as most powerful; the supremacy clause confirms that sense of authority. Further, federal courts theorists might affirmatively argue that federal courts are needed in this area—either because of their special capacity to protect the politically disfavored or because federal sovereign and administrative interests are at stake. While neither the appeal to the community envisioned by the claim of closeness of the state to the family nor the concern about attitudes and knowledge of federal judges should be discounted, the "inevitability of federal involvement" in family life remains, as does a sense that the rejection of that role by federal courts reconfirms the marginalization of women and families from national life.

Federal involvement emerges here, as it does in torts, land use, health regulation, criminal law, and other areas, because of the wealth of interactions that make the imagined coherence of the very categories "federal" and "state" themselves problematic. Whether looking at the problem from the top down, and seeing "joint governance" or considering the issue from the perspective of individuals and speaking of "membership in multiple communities," the point is the same: an interlocking, enmeshed regulatory structure covers the host of human activity in the United States. There is not a priori line one can invoke to separate legal regulation into two bounded boxes "state" and "federal." Uniform state laws demonstrate the limits of state court borders and the need for regulatory structures that bridge them. State and federal court interpretation of "family" are unavoidable. * * *

Judith Resnick, *"Naturally" Without Gender: Women, Jurisdiction, and the Federal Courts*, 66 N.Y.U. L. REV. 1682, 1750–1757 (1991).

5. For further discussion of federal court jurisdiction in family law, *see* Naomi R. Cahn, *Family Law, Federalism and the Federal Courts*, 79 IOWA L. REV. 1073 (1994); Ann C. Dailey, *Federalism and Families*, 143 U. PA. L. REV. 1787 (1995).

Problem 1–2:

Herbert and Wilma separated and, approximately a year ago, Herbert obtained a divorce in Wisconsin based on a marital settlement agreement. Herbert then remarried and moved to Texas. Based on information she has recently acquired, Wilma has now brought an action against Herbert in federal court alleging that, during the pendency of the divorce proceedings, Herbert concealed assets, committed perjury, and misrepresented his financial dealings so as to intentionally deprive Wilma of her interest in the couple's marital property. Herbert has filed a motion to dismiss. What arguments are available to Wilma? to Herbert? What result? *See* Strasen v. Strasen, 897 F.Supp. 1179 (E.D.Wis. 1995).

Problem 1–3:

Harry lives in New York. His wife Wanda lives in California. Can Wanda sue in federal court in New York for both physical abuse and divorce? What if Wanda alleges that the divorce and abuse arise out of a common nucleus of operative fact?

SECTION 4. THE FUTURE—AND INEVITABILITY—OF FEDERAL INVOLVEMENT IN FAMILY LAW

Despite the tradition of federal noninvolvement, in recent years Congress has become involved in many aspects of family law. The lengthiest list of new federal laws is in the area of child support. Federal activism here has been spurred by rising rates of single-parenthood and children's poverty, coupled with the fact that, until the welfare reform legislation of 1996, children in single-parent households with incomes below state-established standards were entitled to federal assistance through the Aid to Families with Dependent Children (AFDC) program. Since 1974, the federal government has revolutionized the process for establishing and enforcing child support throughout the United States. Congress has mandated that states enact wage withholding provisions, child support guidelines, and expedited procedures for determining paternity and establishing and enforcing child support orders. *See* Chapter 20 and Child Support Enforcement Amendments of 1984, Pub. L. No. 98–378, 98 Stat. 1205 (1984); Family Support Act of 1988, Pub. L. No. 100–485m 102 Stat. 234 (1988); Personal Responsibility Work Opportunity Reconciliation Act of 1996, Pub. L. No. 104–193, 110 Stat. 2105 (1996); Linda D. Elrod, *The Federalization of Child Support Guidelines,* 6 J. Am. Acad. Matrimonial Lawyers 103 (1990). Congress has also provided for federal court jurisdiction over child support actions certified by the Secretary of the Department of Health and Human Services (*see* 42 U.S.C.A. § 660 (1976)) and directed all states to adopt the Uniform Interstate Family Support Act, as amended, by January 1, 1998. Prior to this directive, states were free to adopt or reject a uniform act promulgated by the National Conference of Commissioners on Uniform States Laws (NCCUSL). The Child Support Recovery Act of 1992 (CSRA), 18 U.S.C.A. § 228 (1995) also made it a federal crime for a parent to willfully refuse to make support payments to a parent who lives in another state. *See* Margaret Campbell Haynes, *Supporting Our Children: A Blueprint for Reform,* 27 Fam. L. Q. 7 (1993) (detailing the work of the Interstate Commission on Child Support); Paul K. Legler, *The Coming Revolution in Child Support Policy: Implications of the 1996 Welfare Act,* 30 Fam. L. Q. 519 (1996).

Other recent federal laws dealing with family matters are quite diverse. The Parental Kidnapping Prevention Act has federalized the rules governing interstate custody disputes, and new federal statutes to implement the Hague Convention on the Civil Aspects of Child Abduction give federal and state courts concurrent jurisdiction over international child abduction cases. The Family and Medical Leave Act of 1993, 29 U.S.C.A. § 2601 et. seq., effective August 5, 1993, requires employers of fifty or more employees to grant eligible employees up to twelve weeks of leave (unpaid) per year to care for a family member or for a serious health condition. (FMLA implementing regulations are at 60 Fed. Reg.

2180 (1995).) The Violence Against Women Act of 1994 (VAWA), 42 U.S.C.A. § 13981, Pub. L. 103–322, 108 Stat. 1796, 1902—1955, created a new federal private right of action for damages suffered in the course of "a crime of violence motivated by gender." Section 40302(e)(3) confers concurrent jurisdiction on state and federal courts, but § 40302(e)(4) limited the scope of supplemental jurisdiction to exclude "any State law claim seeking the establishment of a divorce, alimony, equitable distribution or child custody."

Federal appeals courts have uniformly rejected arguments that Congress has violated the Tenth Amendment or exceeded its power under the Commerce Clause in enacting the CSRA. *See* U.S. v. Bongiorno, 106 F.3d 1027 (1st Cir.1997); U.S. v. Sage, 92 F.3d 101 (2d Cir.1996), cert. denied ___ U.S. ___, 117 S.Ct. 784, 136 L.Ed.2d 727 (1997); U.S. v. Parker, 108 F.3d 28 (3d Cir.1997); U.S. v. Johnson, 114 F.3d 476 (4th Cir.1997); U.S. v. Bailey, 115 F.3d 1222 (5th Cir.1997); U.S. v. Crawford, 115 F.3d 1397 (8th Cir.1997); U.S. v. Mussari, 95 F.3d 787 (9th Cir. 1996); U.S. v. Hampshire, 95 F.3d 999 (10th Cir.1996). Although no federal appeals courts had ruled on VAWA by late 1997, most lower federal courts have held that Congress had authority to enact the legislation. *See, e.g.,* Doe v. Doe, 929 F.Supp. 608 (D.Conn.1996); Doe v. Hartz, 970 F.Supp. 1375 (D.Iowa 1997); Seaton v. Seaton, 971 F.Supp. 1188 (E.D.Tenn.1997); Anisimov v. Lake, 23 Fam.L.Rep. 1587 (BNA) (N.D.Ill.1997).

But despite the recent proliferation of family law enactments, family policy in the United States continues to lack more generalized goals. Legislation has been passed to meet particular perceived needs, not to further a larger policy agenda. Historian John Demos sees the United States as standing alone in its lack of a coherent family policy:

> ... [O]ur inherited habits and values—our constricted capacity for extrafamilial caring—partly explain public indifference to the blighted conditions in which many families even now are obliged to live. The results are especially tragic as they affect children, and they leave us with a terrible paradox. In this allegedly most child-centered of nations, we find it hard to care very much or very consistently about other people's children ...

JOHN DEMOS, IMAGES OF THE AMERICAN FAMILY, THEN AND NOW, CHANGING IMAGES OF THE FAMILY 43–60 (1978).

In 1987, President Reagan attempted to establish a national family policy through issuance of this Executive Order:

EXECUTIVE ORDER 12,606 OF SEPTEMBER 2, 1987

52 Fed. Reg. 34188 (Sept. 9, 1987).

THE FAMILY

Section 1. *Family Policymaking Criteria.* In formulating and implementing policies and regulations that may have significant impact on family formation, maintenance, and general well-being, executive departments and agencies shall, to the extent permitted by law, assess such measures in light of the following questions:

(a) Does this action by government strengthen or erode the stability of the family and, particularly, the marital commitment?

(b) Does this action strengthen or erode the authority and rights of parents in the education, nurture and supervision of their children?

(c) Does this action help the family perform its functions, or does it substitute governmental activity for the function?

(d) Does this action by government increase or decrease family earnings? Do the proposed benefits of this action justify the impact on the family budget?

(e) Can this activity be carried out by a lower level of government or by the family itself?

(f) What message, intended or otherwise, does this program send to the public concerning the status of the family?

(g) What message does it send to young people concerning the relationship between their behavior, their personal responsibility, and the norms of our society?

The Order remained in effect until April 21, 1997, when it was superseded by President Clinton's Executive Order 13045, directing federal agencies to assess environmental health risks that affect children. The new order appears to be much more limited in scope. In response, a bill was introduced in Congress in 1997 which would forbid enactment of new federal policies without study of how the policy would affect families; thus far the bill has not been enacted.

Notes and Questions

1. Is the Reagan Executive Order an adequate account of national family policy goals? What, if any, issues does the Executive Order fail to address?

2. There have been attempts, other than the Reagan Executive Order, to formulate a cohesive policy. The Child Support Recovery Act of 1992, Pub. L. No. 102–521, 106 Stat. 3403 (1992), created the Commission on Child and Family Welfare and assigned it the task of compiling information on a range of issues affecting children, including child custody and visitation, child and spouse abuse, family relations; the Commission was also directed to study systems affecting children, including the child welfare system, juvenile and family courts, and service agencies. Some hoped that the Commission would be instrumental in establishing a national family policy. Its 1996 report to Congress made recommendations for greater use of alternative dispute resolution proce-

dures and addressing family problems more "holistically," but failed to contain specific policy proposals. A minority report of the Commission, acclaimed by fathers' rights groups, did set out a legislative agenda. *See* Minority Report and Policy Recommendations to the President and Congress, July, 1996. It urged:

(1) A national commitment to the preservation and encouragement of the institution of marriage;

(2) A national commitment to the re-inclusion and re-involvement of fathers in family life, whether married or not;

(3) A national commitment to support more and better involvement of both mothers and fathers with raising a child, regardless of marital status;

(4) A national commitment to decreasing the number of children raised solely by single-parents;

(5) A national commitment to welfare reform that reverses prior policy and places father-inclusiveness as a cornerstone of all new policy.

How does this agenda differ from the Reagan policy statement? Is it a better or worse attempt to formulate a national policy? Why?

One of the most polarizing debates over family policy was ignited in 1992 when then Vice President Dan Quayle criticized the television show *Murphy Brown* for Murphy's decision to have a child out of wedlock. The debate highlighted the strong correlation between single parenthood and a wide variety of adverse childhood consequences. Children in single-parent households are more likely to experience poor health, behavioral problems, delinquency, and low educational attainment than are their peers in intact families; as adults they have higher rates of poverty, early childbearing, and divorce. *See, e.g.*, DONALD J. HERNANDEZ, AMERICA'S CHILDREN: RESOURCES FROM FAMILY, GOVERNMENT, AND THE ECONOMY 58–64 (1993); S. Wayne Duncan, *Economic Impact of Divorce on Children's Development: Current Findings and Policy Implications*, 23 J. CLIN. CHILD PSYCH. 444 (1994); Sara McLanahan et al., *The Role of Mother–Only Families in Reproducing Poverty* in CHILDREN OF POVERTY: CHILD DEVELOPMENT AND PUBLIC POLICY 51–78 (Aletha C. Huston ed., 1991).

But correlation does not equal causation. The poverty rate of children in single-mother households is more than five times that of children living in married-couple households. U.S. DEP'T OF COMMERCE, BUREAU OF THE CENSUS, STATISTICAL ABSTRACT OF THE UNITED STATES: 1993 tbls. 737, 740. The lower standard of living associated with single parenthood appears to explain half or more of the variation between single and two-parent households. Moreover, childhood poverty—whether or not coupled with single parenthood—is correlated with risks to childhood functioning and adult attainments much like those attributed to single parenthood. CHILDREN IN POVERTY, *supra*; *Children in Poverty: Special Issue*, 65 CHILD DEVELOPMENT 275–700; McLanahan et al., *supra* at 51–78 (summarizing research).

So should public policy focus on improving the living standard of children in single-parent households? Or on deterring single parenthood? Some commentators see the key problem as the decline of marriage and rise of fatherless households:

> . . . The public believes unwed motherhood, and the policies that encourage it, are disastrous for various reasons, each of which alone would be sufficient to justify discouraging childbirth out of wedlock. Those reasons include: (1) unwed mothers and their children are an ever increasing fiscal burden on society, (2) the sires of these children succeed in procreating without first becoming productive members of society; (3) the working poor and lower middle class generally are demoralized when they see no reward for their restraint (i.e., in financial terms, working poor who practice restraint do not live markedly better lives than those who choose not to take the traditional precautions to provide for themselves and their kin); and (4) it is socially and genetically corrosive to provide incentives for the least productive people in society to have more children than they otherwise would. But beyond all other harms, the most disastrous effect of unwed motherhood is that on children. Children do better and turn out better when raised in traditional families than when raised by unwed mothers, or even when raised in what used to be called broken homes. The children of unwed mothers live out their lives in a growing subculture consisting of state wards, like themselves, and are not socialized to be self-sufficient human beings. They grow up not merely without fathers, but without even a vigorous concept of fatherhood in their lives. As far as the rest of us are concerned this is not merely some transpersonal interest in how other people live. Those poorly raised children are much more likely to grow up to be troublesome teenagers and adults. The dispute amongst, and predicament for, those of us who hold these views is simply this: how does one strike the balance between a perceived need to provide ex post charity to illegitimate children and the desire to remove the ex ante incentive for women to have children out of wedlock? . . . .
>
> * * *
>
> . . . Marriage is the cultural creation that restricts and channels men's sexual access to women. For several thousand years, both in the West and the East, the stable life-long monogamous marriage has been the norm. . . . Marriage is a cultural invention. It is designed to harness men's energies to support the only offspring they may legitimately have, or are likely to have, legitimately or

otherwise, in a world in which marriage is the norm. We lose sight of this truth at our peril. * * *

* * *

... Western society ... in the very recent past understood marriage as an allocation of separate spheres of power to husbands and wives based on their cultural and biological specialization and accepted hierarchy. That as a formal matter in law, and, as a practical matter, in most marriages, men have been on top of the hierarchy may be a reflection of men's greater physical strength, women's greater front-end investment in marriage, or the symbolic meaning of the sexual act itself.... I ... want to point out to those women who truly find the remaining vestiges of hierarchy unacceptable that the metaphor of equality offers scant application or relief. Beyond that I note that in marriage each couple dances its own dance, and it is far from universal that men lead.

... [I]t is not my belief that consciousness has not changed nor that the change in consciousness has not generated changes in behavior. Rather, I believe that those changes have less to do with women per se and more to do with mankind generally, and that present marriage patterns are as much, if not more, a function of men's changed consciousness as of women's. Specifically, if men no longer recognize the same duty to adhere to their commitments as their great-great-grandfathers, and neither society nor the law holds them to those commitments, the security of marriage and of women's investment in marriage dissolves. * * *

Lloyd R. Cohen, *Rhetoric, the Unnatural Family, and Women's Work,* 81 VA. L. REV. 2275, 2282, 2287, 2290–95 (1996).

See also DAVID POPENOE, LIFE WITHOUT FATHER (1995) ("Until today, no known society ever thought of fathers as potentially unnecessary"); DAVID BLANKENHORN, FATHERLESS AMERICA: CONFRONTING OUR MOST SERIOUS SOCIAL PROBLEM (1995); HENRY B. BILLER & ROBERT J. TROTTER, THE FATHER FACTOR (1994); ROBERT L. GRISWOLD, FATHERHOOD IN AMERICA: A HISTORY (1994); Barbara Dafoe Whitehead, *Dan Quayle was Right*, ATLANTIC MONTHLY 47 (April, 1993).

Other experts see the real problem as economic: "[A]ll that we know about families," they urge, "demonstrates that family form simply does not correlate with family function or developmental health.... No single form of family is essential nor is it a guarantor of healthy, happy children.... The empirical evidence supports correlation but not causation between father absence and children's difficulties or lack of success, and much of that ... connects economics, not the absence of a developmentally required father." NANCY E. DOWD, IN DEFENSE OF SINGLE PARENT FAMILIES at xv, 29 (1997). *See also* Sara McLanahan, *The Consequences of Single Motherhood,* 18 THE AMERICAN PROSPECT 48–58 (1994). In the view of these critics, the attack on single motherhood is just another attempt to "fence out" nontraditional family forms:

. . . An examination of the current statistics on intimate associations reveals that domestic arrangements that do not conform to the traditional family unit are on the rise. More and more individuals are living alone than in decades past. Divorce rates hover around fifty percent, and never-married motherhood is on the rise, even among middle-class, educated women. Couples choose not to become parents in larger numbers than prior generations. Furthermore, even in conforming families (married with children), the traditional roles have broken down. Many women work outside of the home either in a full-or part-time capacity, and some are as deeply committed to career and job advancement as their husbands.

* * *

Our conception of the family as an entity is built around a core unit, the married couple. The basic family relationship is founded on the sexual affiliation or conjugation of two heterosexual adults. This heterosexual unit continues to be considered as presumptively appropriate and it retains viability as the essential family connection. Even contemporary critics of the institution are typically revisionists, viewing marriage to be merely in need of some updating and structural reformulation. In fact, arguments that other sexual affiliations—such as nonmarital cohabitation or same-sex relationships—deserve the same privileges afforded to marriage, far from challenging the privileged status of marriage, reinforce it by inscribing onto it the attributes of normalcy, desirability and privilege.

* * *

* * * The statistics indicate that the time has come to admit that the gendered notion of the role-defined and mutually dependent marital couple no longer serves as an adequate concept. We must begin to rethink the institution of the contemporary family in a way that is responsive to emerging realities. We must begin to think of family policy in terms of the functions we want the family to perform and to leave behind our obsession with form. We should establish a system of sanctions and rewards that reflects the functions society should protect and encourage through social and economic subsidies. Our meager and sporadic family policies fail to facilitate or to support families as they struggle to fulfill their expectations and responsibilities. Unlike other industrialized democracies we have no well-defined notion of collective responsibility for inevitable dependency—lacking are basic income guarantees, comprehensive publicly assisted day care, universal health care coverage, and other societal structures and institutions to help shoulder caretaking burdens. . . .

Martha L. A. Fineman, *Masking Dependency: The Political Role of Family Rhetoric*, 81 VA. L. REV. 2181 (1996).

The "marriage and fathering" camp recently scored a major victory with the Welfare Reform Act of 1996 aimed (among other goals) at deterring nonmarital births, particularly to teenage mothers. But the debate is far from over. It can be expected to figure prominently in future attempts to formulate both state and federal family policy.

Notes and Questions

1. On what facts do Professors Fineman and Cohen agree? Disagree? How would Professor Fineman alter the Reagan family policy? Professor Cohen?

2. What information do we need to resolve the debate over single parenthood? Is it possible to formulate a sensible policy in the absence of such information?

Chapter 2

THE REGULATION OF MARRIAGE

[Marriage is like a] cage; the birds without despair to get in and those in despair of getting out.

Michel de Montaigne, Essays

** * * Marriage, as creating the most important relation in life, as having more to do with the morals and civilization of a people than any other institution has always been subject to the control of the legislature. That body prescribes the age at which parties may contract to marry, the procedure or form essential to constitute marriage, the duties and obligations it creates, its effects upon the property rights of both, present and prospective, and the acts which may constitute grounds for its dissolution . . .*

Maynard v. Hill, 125 U.S. 190, 8 S.Ct. 723, 31 L.Ed. 654 (1888)

SECTION 1. A BRIEF HISTORY OF MARRIAGE REGULATION

From ancient times to modern, entry into and exit from marriage has been subject to legal regulation. The Babylonian Code of Hammurabi (2250 B.C.) provided that, "[i]f a man take a wife and does not arrange with her the proper contracts, that woman is not his legal wife." Roman law, although it proscribed bigamy, also viewed marriage as essentially contractual. A valid marriage required mutual consent but no particular ceremony; spouses themselves determined marital obligations and could obtain a divorce based on consent or unilateral withdrawal from the marriage relationship. Although the law recognized both secular and religious rules governing family relationships, the religious law applied only to its adherents. *See* Marriage, Divorce, and Children in Ancient Rome (Beryl Rawson ed., 1991).

The advent of Christianity profoundly affected both social attitudes toward marriage and marriage law. Between the fifth and sixteenth centuries, canon law gradually merged with local marriage laws and customs. In England, marriage was recognized as a sacrament during the twelfth century, and by the thirteenth century the ecclesiastical courts had gained exclusive jurisdiction over marriage and its incidents.

Under canon law, marriage represented a sexual union blessed and sanctified by God. (What God has joined together, let no man put asunder.) Thus sex outside of marriage was criminalized, divorce was forbidden, and husband and wife treated as one legal person. (See Chapter 3.) Based on Biblical prohibitions, the law forbade marriage between persons related by consanguinity or affinity. The law also invalidated marriages in cases of insanity, impotence, or nonage, based on the view that entry into the marriage relationship required capacity. Violations of the law produced civil and/or religious penalties.

The most famous "victim" of this inflexible marriage law was Henry VIII, who broke with the Roman Catholic Church in 1534 because of its refusal to invalidate his marriage to Catherine of Aragon. Thereafter Anglican, rather than Catholic, law prevailed. While the Anglican ecclesiastical courts continued to have jurisdiction over marriage and divorce until passage of the Matrimonial Causes Act of 1857, which transferred disputes over marriage and divorce to the civil courts, from the time of Henry VIII Parliament also played a substantial role in marriage regulation. *See* FRANCIS & JOSEPH GIES, MARRIAGE AND THE FAMILY IN THE MIDDLE AGES (1987); LAWRENCE STONE, THE FAMILY, SEX AND MARRIAGE 1500–1800 (1977).

In the United States, marriage and divorce have always been subject to the civil law, although many substantive and formal marriage requirements have their roots in ecclesiastical law and practice. But the Establishment Clause of the First Amendment forbids any "official" deference to the views of a particular religion. Thus, in dissolving a marriage over a wife's religious objection, one court noted that:

> We have no jurisdiction to regulate or enforce scriptural obligations. * * * The action of the trial court only dissolved the civil contract of marriage between the parties. No attempt was made to dissolve it ecclesiastically. Therefore, there is no infringement upon her constitutional right of freedom of religion. She still has her constitutional prerogative to believe that in the eyes of God, she and her estranged husband are ecclesiastically wedded as one * * * Any transgression by her husband of their ecclesiastical vows, is, in this instance, outside the jurisdiction of the court.
>
> Williams v. Williams, 543 P.2d 1401 (Okla.1975).

See also Sharma v. Sharma, 8 Kan.App.2d 726, 667 P.2d 395 (1983) (granting divorce over objections of Hindu wife who argued that her religion not only forbade divorce, but would treat her as legally dead if a divorce were to be granted); David E. Engdahl, *The Secularization of English Marriage Law*, 16 U. KAN. L. REV. 505 (1968).

The validity of a marriage has important legal and economic ramifications. Spousal status creates entitlements and obligations. For example, one is entitled to inherit property from the other under the laws of intestate succession, sue for wrongful death, receive social security benefits and workers' compensation benefits, and obtain insurance coverage. Spousal status also gives rise to support rights and obligations. (*See* Chapter 3.)

SECTION 2. CONSTITUTIONAL LIMITATIONS ON STATE MARRIAGE REGULATION

ZABLOCKI v. REDHAIL

Supreme Court of the United States, 1978.
434 U.S. 374, 98 S.Ct. 673, 54 L.Ed.2d 618.

JUSTICE MARSHALL delivered the opinion of the Court.

At issue ... is the constitutionality of a Wisconsin statute §§ 245.10(1), (4), (5) (1973), which provides that a certain class of Wisconsin residents may not marry within the State or elsewhere, without first obtaining a court order granting permission to marry. The class is defined by the statute to include any "Wisconsin resident having minor issue not in his custody and which he is under obligation to support by any court order or judgment." The Statute specifies that court permission cannot be granted unless the marriage applicant submits proof of compliance with the support obligation and, in addition, demonstrates that the children covered by the support order "are not then and are not likely thereafter to become public charges." No marriage license may lawfully be issued in Wisconsin to a person covered by the statute, except upon court order; any marriage entered into without compliance with § 245.10 is declared void; and persons acquiring marriage licenses in violation of the section are subject to criminal penalties ...

[In a 1972 paternity action, appellee has been found to be the father of a baby girl and ordered to pay child support. In 1974, after not having paid his child support for over two years, he sought a marriage license which was denied for failure to satisfy the statute. It was stipulated that the child, who was on welfare, would have been "a public charge even if appellee had been current in his support payments ..."]

[T]he three-judge panel analyzed the ... statute under the Equal Protection Clause and concluded that "strict scrutiny" was required because the classification created by the statute infringed upon a fundamental right to marry. The court then proceeded to evaluate the interests advanced by the State to justify the statute, and, finding that the classification was not necessary for the achievement of those interests, the court held the statute invalid ...

Appellant brought this direct appeal ... Appellee defends the lower court's equal protection holding and, in the alternative, urges affirmance

. . . on the ground that the statute does not satisfy the requirements of substantive due process. We agree with the District Court that the statute violates the Equal Protection Clause.

In evaluating [the statute] under the Equal Protection Clause, "we must first determine what burden of justification the classification created thereby must meet, by looking to the nature of the classification and the individual interests affected." *Memorial Hospital v. Maricopa County*, 415 U.S. 250, 253 (1974). Since our past decisions make clear that the right to marry is of fundamental importance, and since the classification of that right, we believe that "critical examination" of the state interests advanced in support of the classification is required.

The leading decision of this Court on the right to marry is *Loving v. Virginia*, 388 U.S. 1 (1967). In that case, an interracial couple who had been convicted of violating Virginia's miscegenation laws challenged the statutory scheme on both equal protection and due process grounds. The Court's opinion could have rested solely on the ground that the statutes discriminated on the basis of race in violation of the Equal Protection Clause. But the Court went on to hold that the laws arbitrarily deprived the couple of a fundamental liberty protected by the Due Process Clause, the freedom to marry. The Court's language on the latter point bears repeating:

> "The freedom to marry has long been recognized as one of the vital personal rights essential to the orderly pursuit of happiness by free men.
>
> Marriage is one of the 'basic civil rights of man,' fundamental to our very existence and survival."

Id., quoting *Skinner v. Oklahoma ex rel. Williamson*, 316 U.S. 535, 541 (1942).

More recent decisions have established that the right to marry is part of the fundamental "right of privacy" implicit in the Fourteenth Amendment's Due Process Clause. In *Griswold v. Connecticut* [p. 19], the Court observed:

> We deal with a right of privacy older than the Bill of Rights—older than our political parties, older than our school system. Marriage is a coming together for better or for worse, hopefully enduring, and intimate to the degree of being sacred. It is an association that promotes a way of life, not causes; a harmony in living, not political faiths; a bilateral loyalty, not commercial or social projects. Yet it is an association for as noble a purpose as any involved in our prior decisions.

Cases subsequent to *Griswold* and *Loving* have routinely categorized the decision to marry as among the personal decisions protected by the right of privacy.

* * *

It is not surprising that the decision to marry has been placed on the same level of importance as decisions relating to procreation, childbirth, child rearing, and family relationships. As the facts of this case illustrate, it would make little sense to recognize a right of privacy with respect to other matters of family life and not with respect to the decision to enter the relationship that is the foundation of the family in our society. The woman whom appellee desired to marry had a fundamental right to seek an abortion of their expected child, or to bring the child into life to suffer the myriad social, if not economic, disabilities that the status of illegitimacy brings. Surely, a decision to marry and raise a child in a traditional family setting must receive equivalent protection. And, if appellee's right to procreate means anything at all, it must imply some right to enter the only relationship in which the State of Wisconsin allows sexual relations legally to take place.

[W]e do not mean to suggest that every state regulation which relates in any way to the incidents of or prerequisites for marriage must be subjected to rigorous scrutiny. To the contrary, reasonable regulations that do not significantly interfere with decisions to enter into the marital relationship may legitimately be imposed. The statutory classification at issue here, however, clearly does interfere directly and substantially with the right to marry.

Under the challenged statute, no Wisconsin resident in the affected class may marry in Wisconsin or elsewhere without a court order, and marriages contracted in violation of the statute are both void and punishable as criminal offenses. Some of those in the affected class, like appellee, will never be able to obtain the necessary court order, because they either lack the financial means to meet their support obligations or cannot prove that their children will not become public charges. These persons are absolutely prevented from getting married. Many others, able in theory to satisfy the statute's requirements, will be sufficiently burdened by having to do so that they will in effect be coerced into foregoing their right to marry. And even those who can be persuaded to meet the statute's requirements suffer a serious intrusion into their freedom of choice in an area in which we have held such freedom to be fundamental.

When a statutory classification significantly interferes with the exercise of a fundamental right, it cannot be upheld unless it is supported by sufficiently important state interests and is closely tailored to effectuate only those interests. Appellant asserts that two interests are served by the challenged statute: the permission-to-marry proceeding furnishes an opportunity to counsel the applicant as to the necessity of fulfilling his prior support obligations; and the welfare of the out-of-custody children is protected. We may accept for present purposes that these are legitimate and substantial interests, but, since the means selected by the State for achieving these interests unnecessarily impinges on the right to marry, the statute cannot be sustained.

There is no evidence that the challenged statute, as originally introduced in the Wisconsin Legislature, was intended merely to establish a mechanism whereby persons with support obligations to children from prior marriages could be counseled before they entered into new marital relationships and incurred further support obligations. Court permission was automatically to be granted after counseling was completed. The statute actually enacted, however, does not expressly require or provide for any counseling whatsoever, nor for any automatic granting of permission to marry by the court, and thus it can hardly be justified as a means for ensuring counseling ... Even assuming that counseling does take place—a fact as to which there is no evidence in the record—this interest obviously cannot support the withholding of court permission to marry once counseling is completed.

With regard to safeguarding the welfare of the out-of-custody children, appellant's brief does not make clear the connection between the State's interest and the statute's requirements. At argument, appellant's counsel suggested that, since permission to marry cannot be granted unless the applicant shows that he has satisfied his court-determined support obligations to the prior children and that those children will not become public charges, the statute provides incentive for the applicant to make support payments to his children. This "collection device" rationale cannot justify the statute's broad infringement on the right to marry.

First, with respect to individuals who are unable to meet the statutory requirements, the statute merely prevents the applicant from getting married, without delivering any money at all into the hands of the applicant's prior children. More importantly, regardless of the applicant's ability or willingness to meet the statutory requirements, the State already has numerous other means for exacting compliance with support obligations, means that are at least as effective as the instant statutes and yet do not impinge upon the right to marry. Under Wisconsin law, whether the children are from a prior marriage or were born out of wedlock, court-determined support obligations may be enforced directly via wage assignments, civil contempt proceedings, and criminal penalties. And, if the State believes that parents of children out of their custody should be responsible for ensuring that those children do not become public charges, this interest can be achieved by adjusting the criteria used for determining the amounts to be paid under their support orders.

There is also some suggestion that ... [the statute] protects the ability of marriage applicants to meet support obligations to prior children by preventing the applicants from incurring new support obligations. But the challenged provisions of [the statute] are grossly underinclusive with respect to this purpose, since they do not limit in any way new financial commitments by the applicant other than those arising out of the contemplated marriage. The statutory classification is substantially overinclusive as well: Given the possibility that the new spouse will actually better the applicant's financial situation, by contributing income from a job or otherwise, the statute in many cases may prevent affected individuals from improving their ability to satisfy their prior support obligations. And, although it is true that the applicant will incur support obligations to any children born during the contemplated marriage, preventing the marriage may only result in the children being born out of wedlock, as in fact occurred in appellee's case. Since the support obligation is the same whether the child is born in or out of wedlock, the net result of preventing the marriage is simply more illegitimate children.

The statutory classification ... thus cannot be justified by the interests advanced in support of it. The judgment of the District Court is, accordingly, Affirmed.

JUSTICE STEWART, concurring in the judgment.

I cannot join the opinion of the Court. To hold, as the Court does, that the Wisconsin statute violates the Equal Protection Clause seems to me to misconceive the meaning of that constitutional guarantee. The Equal Protection Clause deals not with substantive rights or freedoms but with invidiously discriminatory classifications. The paradigm of its violation is, of course, classification by race.

Like almost any law, the Wisconsin statute now before us affects some people and does not affect others. But to say that it thereby creates "classifications" in the equal protection sense strikes me as little short of fantasy. The problem in this case is not one of discriminatory classifications, but of unwarranted encroachment upon a constitutionally protected freedom. I think that the Wisconsin statute is unconstitutional because it exceeds the bounds of permissible state regulation of marriage, and invades the sphere of liberty protected by the Due Process Clause of the Fourteenth Amendment.

I do not agree with the Court that there is a "right to marry" in the constitutional sense. That right, or more accurately, that privilege, is under our federal system peculiarly one to be defined and limited by state law. A State may not only "significantly interfere with the decision to enter into the marriage relationship," but may in many circumstances absolutely prohibit it. Surely, for example, a State may legitimately say that no one can marry his or her sibling, that no one can marry who is not at least 14 years old, that no one can marry without first passing an examination for venereal disease, or that no one can marry who has a living husband or wife. But, just as surely, in regulating the intimate human relationship of marriage, there is a limit beyond which a State may not constitutionally go.

* * *

On several occasions this Court has held that a person's inability to pay money demanded by the State does not justify the total deprivation of a constitutionally protected liberty. In *Boddie v. Connecticut* [p. 563], the Court held that the State's legitimate purposes in collecting filing fees for divorce actions were insufficient under the Due Process Clause to deprive the indigent of access to the courts where that access was necessary to dissolve the marital relationship.

* * *

The principle of those cases applies here as well. The Wisconsin law makes no allowance for the truly indigent. The State flatly denies a marriage license to anyone who cannot afford to fulfill his support obligations and keep his children from becoming wards of the State. We may assume that the State has legitimate interests in collecting delinquent support payments and in reducing its welfare load. We may also assume that as applied to those who can afford to meet the statute's financial requirements but choose not to do so, the law advances the State's objectives in ways superior to other means available to the State. The fact remains that some people simply cannot afford to meet the statute's financial requirements. To deny these people permission to marry penalizes them for failing to do that which they cannot do. Insofar as it applies to indigents, the state law is an irrational means of achieving these objectives of the State.

As directed against either the indigent or the delinquent parent, the law is substantially more rational if viewed as a means of assuring the financial viability of future marriages. In this context, it reflects a plausible judgment that those who have not fulfilled their financial obligations and have not kept their children off the welfare rolls in the past are likely to encounter similar difficulties in the future. But the State's legitimate concern with the financial soundness of prospective marriages must stop short of telling people they may not marry because they are too poor or because they might persist in their financial irresponsibility. The invasion of constitutionally protected liberty and the chance of erroneous prediction are simply too great. A legislative judgment so alien to our traditions and so offensive to our shared notions of fairness offends the Due Process Clause of the Fourteenth Amendment.

JUSTICE POWELL, concurring in the judgment.

I concur in the judgment of the Court that Wisconsin's restrictions on the exclusive means of creating the marital bond . . . cannot meet applicable constitutional standards. I write separately because the majority's rationale sweeps too broadly in an area which traditionally has been subject to pervasive state regulation. The Court apparently would subject all state regulation which "directly and substantially" interferes with the decision to marry in a traditional family setting to "critical examination" or "compelling state interest" analysis. Presumably, "reasonable regulations that do not significantly interfere with decisions to enter into the marital relationship may legitimately be imposed." The Court does not present, however, any principled means for distinguishing between the two types of regulations. Since state regulation in this area typically takes the form of a prerequisite or barrier to marriage or divorce, the degree of "direct" interference with the decision to marry or to divorce is unlikely to provide either guidance for state legislatures or a basis for judicial oversight . . .

* * *

In my view, analysis must start from the recognition of domestic relations as "an area that has long been regarded as a virtually exclusive province of the States." . . . The State, representing the collective expression of moral aspirations, has an undeniable interest in ensuring that its rules of domestic relations reflect the widely held values of its people . . . State regulation has included bans on incest, bigamy, and homosexuality, as well as various preconditions to marriage, such as blood tests. Likewise, a showing of fault on the part of one of the partners traditionally has been a prerequisite to the dissolution of an unsuccessful union. A "compelling state purpose" inquiry would cause doubt on the network of restrictions that the States have fashioned to govern marriage and divorce.

State power over domestic relations is not without constitutional limits. The Due Process Clause requires a showing of justification "when the government intrudes on choices concerning family living arrangements" in a manner which is contrary to deeply rooted traditions.... Due process constraints also limit the extent to which the State may monopolize the process of ordering certain human relationships while excluding the truly indigent from that process . . .

The Wisconsin measure in this case does not pass muster under either due process or equal protection standards. Appellant identifies three objectives which are supposedly furthered by the statute in question: (1) a counseling function; (2) an incentive to satisfy outstanding support obligations; and (3) a deterrent against incurring further obligations. The opinion of the Court amply demonstrates that the asserted counseling objective bears no relation to this statute....

The so-called "collection device" rationale presents a somewhat more difficult question. I do not agree with the suggestion in the Court's opinion that a State may never condition the right to marry on satisfaction of existing support obligations simply because the State has alternative methods of compelling such payments....

* * *

[But] the marriage applicant is required by the Wisconsin statute not only to submit proof of compliance with his support obligation, but also to demonstrate . . . that his children "are not then and are not likely thereafter to become public charges." This statute does more than simply "fail to alleviate the consequences of differences in economic circumstances that exist wholly apart from any state action." It tells the truly indigent, whether they have met their support obligations or not, that they may not marry so long as their children are public charges or there is a danger that their children might go on public assistance in the future. Apparently, no other jurisdiction has embraced this approach as a method of reducing the number of children on public assistance.

Because the State has not established a justification for this unprecedented foreclosures of marriage to many of its citizens solely because of their indigency, I concur in the judgment of the Court.

JUSTICE STEVENS, concurring in the judgment.

* * * When a State allocates benefits or burdens, it may have valid reasons for treating married and unmarried persons differently. Classification based on marital status has been an accepted characteristic of tax legislation, Selective Service rules, and Social Security regulations. As cases like *Jobst*, 434 U.S. 47 (1977), demonstrate, such laws may "significantly interfere with decisions to enter into the marital relationship."* That kind of interference, however, is not a sufficient reason for invalidating every law reflecting a legislative judgment that there are relevant differences between married persons as a class and unmarried persons as a class.

A classification based on marital status is fundamentally different from a classification which determines who may lawfully enter into the marriage relationship. The individual's interest in making the marriage decision independently is sufficiently important to merit special constitutional protection. It is not, however, an interest which is constitutionally immune from evenhanded regulation. Thus, laws prohibiting marriage to a child, a close relative, or a person afflicted with venereal disease, are unchallenged even though they "interfere directly and substantially with the right to marry." This Wisconsin statute has a different character.

Under this statute, a person's economic status may determine his eligibility to enter into a lawful marriage. A noncustodial parent whose children are "public charges" may not marry even if he has met his court-ordered obligations. Thus, within the class of parents who have fulfilled their court-ordered obligations, the rich may marry and the poor may not. This type of statutory discrimination is, I believe, totally unprecedented, as well as inconsistent with our tradition of administering justice equally to the rich and to the poor.

The statute appears to reflect a legislative judgment that persons who have demonstrated an inability to support their offspring should not be permitted to marry and thereafter to bring additional children into the world. Even putting to one side the growing number of childless marriages and the burgeoning number of children born out of wedlock, that sort of reasoning cannot justify this deliberate discrimination against the poor.

The statute prevents impoverished parents from marrying even though their intended spouses are economically independent. Presum-

* [Ed. note: *Jobst*, decided during the same term as *Zablocki*, upheld a section of the Social Security Act providing for termination of a dependent child's benefits upon marriage to an individual not entitled in his or her own right to benefits under the Act. Jobst married a person who was disabled but did not receive benefits under the Act. The Court, applying the rational relationship standard, upheld the Act, noting that it was "not rendered invalid simply because some persons who might otherwise have married were deterred by the rule or because some who did marry were burdened thereby." 434 U.S. at 54.]

ably, the Wisconsin Legislature assumed (a) that only fathers would be affected by the legislation, and (b) that they would never marry employed women. The first assumption ignores the fact that fathers are sometimes awarded custody, and the second ignores the composition of today's work force. To the extent that the statute denies a hardpressed parent any opportunity to prove that an intended marriage will ease rather than aggravate his financial straits, it not only rests on unreliable premises, but also defeats its own objectives.

These questionable assumptions also explain why this statutory blunderbuss is wide of the target in another respect. The prohibition on marriage applies to the noncustodial parent but allows the parent who has custody to marry without the State's leave. Yet the danger that new children will further strain an inadequate budget is equally great for custodial and noncustodial parents, unless one assumes (a) that only mothers will ever have custody and (b) that they will never marry unemployed men.

Characteristically, this law fails to regulate the marriages of those parents who are least likely to be able to afford another family, for it applies only to parents under a court order to support their children. The very poorest parents are unlikely to be the objects of support orders. If the State meant to prevent the marriage of those who have demonstrated their inability to provide for children, it overlooked the most obvious targets of legislative concern.

In sum, the public charge provision is either futile or perverse insofar as it applies to childless couples, couples who will have illegitimate children if they are forbidden to marry, couples whose economic status will be improved by marriage, and couples who are so poor that the marriage will have no impact on the welfare status of their children in any event. Even assuming that the right to marry may sometimes be denied on economic grounds, this clumsy and deliberate legislative discrimination between the rich and the poor is irrational in so many ways that it cannot withstand scrutiny under the Equal Protection Clause of the Fourteenth Amendment.

MR. JUSTICE REHNQUIST, dissenting.

I substantially agree with my Brother Powell's reasons for rejecting the Court's conclusion that marriage is the sort of "fundamental right" which must invariably trigger the strictest judicial scrutiny. I disagree with his imposition of an "intermediate" standard of review, which leads him to conclude that the statute, though generally valid as an "additional collection mechanism" offends the Constitution by its "failure to make provision for those without the means to comply with child support obligations." For similar reasons, I disagree with my Brother Stewart's conclusion that the statute is invalid for its failure to exempt those persons who "simply cannot afford to meet the statute's financial requirements." I would view this legislative judgment in the light of the traditional presumption of validity. I think that under the Equal Protection Clause the statute need pass only the "rational basis test," and that under the Due Process Clause it need only be shown that it bears a rational relation to a constitutionally permissible objective. The statute so viewed is a permissible exercise of the State's power to regulate family life and to assure the support of minor children, despite its possible imprecision in the extreme cases envisioned in the concurring opinions.

Notes and Questions

1. The majority subjects the Wisconsin statute to an equal protection analysis. Justice Stewart, by contrast, sees the case not as a problem of discriminatory classification, but of the state's invasion of "the sphere of liberty protected by the Due Process Clause of the Fourteenth Amendment." What is the difference?

2. Could Wisconsin replace the statute struck down in *Zablocki* with one mandating driver's license suspension for delinquent child support obligors whose children go on public assistance? Could the state require license suspension only when the delinquent support obligor marries, incurring new support obligations?

3. The Universal Declaration of Human Rights, article 16, provides that:

> 1. Men and women of full age, without any limitation due to race, nationality or religion, have the right to marry and to found a family. They are entitled to equal rights as to marriage, during marriage and its dissolution....
>
> 2. Marriage shall be entered into only with the free and full consent of the intending spouses. Adopted by the United National General Assembly on December 10, 1948, U.N. Doc. No. A/810, Gen. Ass. Off. Rec., 3d Sess. (I), Resolutions, at 71.

Problem 2–1:

The State Division of Corrections recently refused several inmates permission to marry, based on a state prison regulation that permits an inmate to marry only with the permission of the superintendent of the prison. The regulation also specifies that approval should be given only "when there are compelling reasons to do so." Although the term "compelling" is not defined, prison officials have historically considered pregnancy or the birth of an illegitimate child as a compelling reason for marriage. All of the prisoners who were recently denied permission to marry met their prospective spouses through classified ads and correspondence and thus could not meet the "compelling reasons" test.

You are a lawyer at the Prisoners' Legal Assistance Project (PLAP) and have been consulted by one of the prisoners, who wants to know if there is any basis for challenging the regulation. You have already corresponded with prison officials, who indicate that the basis for the regulation is "security and rehabilitation concerns." Officials indicate that "some inmates will marry simply to obtain conjugal visits—and through those visits may incur support obligations they cannot possibly meet in prison. Nor can the prisoner provide either financial or meaningful emotional support to his new family. Finally, any marriage based on a classified ad and brief correspondence holds a high possibility of failure."

What arguments are available to the prisoners and State under *Zablocki*? How do you expect the Supreme Court would rule? *See* Turner v. Safley, 482 U.S. 78, 107 S.Ct. 2254, 96 L.Ed.2d 64 (1987); Langone v. Coughlin, 712 F.Supp. 1061 (N.D.N.Y.1989).

SECTION 3. SUBSTANTIVE REQUIREMENTS FOR ENTERING MARRIAGE

The following generalization can be made about entry into marriage today: "A man and a woman, unmarried and unrelated within prohibited degree, of due age and competence, by exercising their mutual consent, may marry." Lynn D. Wardle, *International Marriage and Divorce Regulation and Recognition: A Survey*, 29 FAM. L. Q. 497, 500 (1995).

All restrictions and regulations have the effect of giving approval to some marriages and not to others. In reading the materials that follow, consider why legislatures have chosen to approve some marriages and not others. What policies underlie current restrictions on marriage? Can restrictions on marriage be justified in the face of a more flexible approach to defining the family?

A. VOID AND VOIDABLE MARRIAGES

An attempted marriage that does not comply with state regulations may be *void, voidable or partially valid.* Technically, a *void* marriage is non-existent and has never existed; no formal procedure is necessary to terminate it. (Nevertheless, a declaratory judgment to the effect that a void marriage is really void may sometimes be useful to prevent confusion, unexpected claims or a prosecution for bigamy.) A *voidable* marriage, on the other hand, is effective until it is formally voided, usually by means of a court order. Traditionally, once a *voidable* marriage was voided, the effect was retroactive and, as in the case of a *void* marriage, the law treated the marriage as nonexistent. Given the inequities that may result from this approach, modern marriage law takes a more flexible approach. *See* Chapter 11, § 4(B).

The classification of invalid marriages into void or voidable marriages usually is (or at least should be) related to the intensity of the state's interest in the particular regulation that has been violated. For example, generally considered "void" is an attempted incestuous marriage, or one involving a party below the absolute minimum age for marriage, or one between persons one or both of whom are currently married to someone else (bigamy). Generally considered "voidable" is an attempted marriage between partners above the minimum age who need, but lack, parental consent for marriage, or one procured through fraud or duress, or one entered into in violation of "collateral", formal requirements, such as absence of health checks.

To be distinguished further are situations best described as "non-marriages", involving, for instance, a failure to comply with "essential" formal requirements, such as an attempted common law marriage in a jurisdiction not recognizing common law marriage or (at least for the time being) an attempted marriage between partners of the same sex.

Another important complication is *who* may attack a void or voidable marriage. If a "void" marriage is truly void, then it may safely be ignored by all, without formal attack. The situation is less clear with respect to "voidable" marriages. For instance, what should be the rights of the parents of the underage child who married without parental consent? (The majority view (*not* shared by UMDA § 208(a)(3), (b)(3)) seems to go against permitting parents to interfere with a *fait accompli.*) Should, in these circumstances, the "child" be permitted to attack his or her own marriage for lack of parental consent? What should be the role of the public, i.e., the juvenile authorities or the state's attorney, in these cases?

B. ONE AT A TIME

Polygamy became a political issue in the United States when Utah, settled by the polygamous Mormons, aspired to statehood. In Reynolds v. United States, 98 U.S. (8 Otto) 145, 25 L.Ed. 244 (1878), a Mormon brought an Establishment Clause challenge to his conviction under a federal law criminalizing bigamy. In sustaining the conviction and the statute, the Supreme Court noted that:

> Polygamy has always been odious among the northern and western nations of Europe, and, until the establishment of the Mormon Church, was almost exclusively a feature of the life of Asiatic and of African people. At common law, the second marriage was always void (2 Kent, Com. 79), and from the earliest history of England polygamy has been treated as an offence against society. * * *
>
> * * * [W]e think it may safely be said there never has been a time in any State of the union when polygamy has not been an offence against society, cognizable by the civil courts and punishable with more or less severity. In the face of all this evidence, it is impossible to believe that the constitutional guaranty of religious freedom was intended to prohibit legislation in respect to this most important feature of social life. Marriage, while from its very nature a sacred obligation, is nevertheless, in most civilized nations, a civil contract, and usually regulated by law. Upon it society may be said to be built, and out of its fruits spring social relations and social obligations and duties, with which government is necessarily required to deal. In fact, according as monogamous or polygamous marriages are allowed, do we find the principles on which the government of the people, to a greater or less extent, rests. Professor Lieber says, polygamy leads to the patriarchal principle, and which, when applied to large communities, fetters the people in

stationary despotism, while that principle cannot long exist in connection with monogamy. Chancellor Kent observes that this remark is equally striking and profound. 2 Kent, Com. 81, note (e).

An exceptional colony of polygamists under an exceptional leadership may sometimes exist for a time without appearing to disturb the social condition of the people who surround it; but there cannot be a doubt that, unless restricted by some form of constitution, it is within the legitimate scope of the power of every civil government to determine whether polygamy or monogamy shall be the law of social life under its dominion.

* * *

In our opinion, the statute immediately under consideration is within the legislative power of Congress.... Laws are made for the government of actions, and while they cannot interfere with mere religious belief and opinions, they may with practices. Suppose one believed that human sacrifices were a necessary part of religious worship, would it be seriously contended that the civil government under which he lived could not interfere to prevent a sacrifice? Of if a wife religiously believed it was her duty to burn herself upon the funeral pile of her dead husband, would it be beyond the power of the civil government to prevent her carrying her belief into practice?

So here, as a law of the organization of society under the exclusive dominion of the United States, it is provided that plural marriages shall not be allowed. Can a man excuse his practices to the contrary because of his religious belief? To permit this would be to make the professed doctrines of religious belief superior to the law of the land, and in effect to permit every citizen to become a law unto himself. Government could exist only in name under such circumstances.

POTTER v. MURRAY CITY

United States Court of Appeals, Tenth Circuit, 1985.
760 F.2d 1065.

HOLLOWAY, CHIEF JUDGE.

In this suit the plaintiff-appellant Royston E. Potter (plaintiff) challenges Utah's proscription against polygamy or plural marriage. His principal claim is that the termination of his employment as a city police officer for the practice of plural marriage violated his right to the free exercise of his religion and his right to privacy.

* * *

Plaintiff is a former police officer of Murray City, Utah. The City terminated plaintiff's employment after it was learned that he practiced plural marriage. The basis for the discharge was that by his plural marriage plaintiff failed to support, obey and defend Article III of the Constitution of the State of Utah.

Plaintiff brought suit under 42 U.S.C. § 1983 and the First and Fourteenth Amendments. He sought monetary damages against the City, its Chief of Police, and the Murray City Civil Service Commission. 585 F.Supp. at 1128. He also sought declaratory and injunctive relief against the State of Utah and its Governor and Attorney General to determine that Utah's laws prohibiting plural marriage are invalid and to enjoin their enforcement. * * *

On appeal, plaintiff argues that: (1) the portion of Utah's enabling act requiring that Utah forever prohibit polygamy is void by reason of the equal footing doctrine; (2) plaintiff's termination for practicing plural marriage violated his First Amendment right to the free exercise of religion; (3) this termination infringed on his fundamental right of privacy; and (4) his termination violated the constitutional guarantees of due process and equal protection because Utah's laws prohibiting plural marriages have long been in desuetude. Defendants disagree and also assert a number of defenses. We need not reach any of these arguments because we conclude that plaintiff's constitutional claims lack merit.

* * *

B. The Free Exercise Clause

In *Reynolds v. United States*, 98 U.S. (8 Otto) 145, 25 L.Ed. 244 (1878), the Supreme Court affirmed a criminal conviction of a Mormon for practicing polygamy and rejected the argument that Congress' prohibition of polygamy violated the defendant's right to the free exercise of religion. Plaintiff argues that *Reynolds* is no longer controlling because later cases have "in effect" overturned the decision. We disagree.

Plaintiff principally relies on *Wisconsin v. Yoder*, [p. 419]. There, the Supreme Court held that the religious belief of the Amish that their salvation requires life in a church community apart from the world necessitated that they be exempted from a state law requirement that children attend public school beyond the eighth grade. *Yoder* explained that for a state to compel school attendance beyond the eighth grade when there is a claim that it "interferes with the practice of a legitimate religious belief, it must appear either that the State does not deny the free exercise of religious belief by its requirement, or that there is a state interest claiming protection under the Free Exercise Clause." As Chief Justice Burger stated, "[t]he essence of all that has been said and written on the subject [of the Free Exercise Clause] is that only those interests of the highest order and those not otherwise served can overbalance legitimate claims to the free exercise of religion."

The parties have stipulated here for the purpose of the motions for summary judgment that plaintiff's practice of plural marriage is the result of a good faith religious belief. The plaintiff has made an undisputed showing that his two wives consented to the plural marriage, and that the wives and five children of the marriage receive love and adequate care and attention and do not want for any necessity of life. Plaintiff points out that the State defendants have not presented any empirical evidence that monogamy is superior to polygamy, nor has the Utah legislature ever considered whether its anti-polygamy laws are wise. Hence plaintiff argues that, under *Yoder*, summary judgment should have been entered in his favor rather than for the defendants.

We cannot disregard *Reynolds*, however, because in *Yoder* and afterwards the Supreme Court has recognized the continued validity of *Reynolds*. In *Yoder*, *Reynolds* was one of four cases that the Court cited in support of the proposition that "[i]t is true that activities of individuals, even when religiously based, are often subject to regulation by the States in the exercise of their undoubted power to promote the health, safety, and general welfare, or the Federal Government in the exercise of its delegated powers." Since *Yoder*, the Court has said that "[s]tatutes making bigamy a crime surely cut into an individual's freedom to associate, but few today seriously claim such statutes violate the First Amendment or any other constitutional provision." *Paris Adult Theatre I v. Slaton*, 413 U.S. 49 . . .; *see also Zablocki v. Redhail*, [p. 48] (Stewart, J., concurring) (state may legitimately say that no one who has a living husband or wife can marry); . . . (Powell, J., concurring) (state has undeniable interest in insuring that its rules of domestic relations reflect widely held values of its people, and state regulation has included bans on incest, bigamy and homosexuality as well as various preconditions to marriage). Moreover, *Reynolds* has been cited with approval since *Yoder*.

* * *

Monogamy is inextricably woven into the fabric of our society. It is the bedrock upon which our culture is built. *Cf. Zablocki v. Redhail*, *supra*, (marriage is foundation of family and society; "a bilateral loyalty"). In light of these fundamental values, the State is justified by a compelling interest, in upholding and enforcing its ban on plural marriage to protect the monogamous marriage relationship.

C. The Right To Privacy

Plaintiff argues that his constitutional right to privacy prohibits the State of Utah from sanctioning him for entering into a polygamous marriage. Again we disagree.

We find no authority for extending the constitutional right of privacy so far that it would protect polygamous marriages. We decline to do so. *Cf. Paris Adult Theatre I v. Slaton, supra*, (few today seriously claim that making bigamy a crime violates the First Amendment or any other constitutional provision).

D. Laws In Desuetude

Plaintiff further argues that Utah's laws prohibiting polygamy have fallen into desuetude. He says that there have been fewer than 25 prosecutions in Utah since 1952 for such offenses, that there are at least 5,000 to 10,000 polygamist family members in the State, and that during Chief Gillen's thirty year tenure he had never arrested anyone nor seen anyone arrested or prosecuted for violating Utah's anti-bigamy statute. Thus, he says that invoking laws which have long been in disuse to sanction him is a violation of the constitutional guarantees of due process and equal protection. We disagree.

Polygamy has been prohibited in our society since its inception. *See Reynolds, supra*.... The prohibitions continue in full force today. We cannot agree that the discharge of plaintiff for engaging in bigamy violated any constitutional guarantee. The showing made did not establish the enforcement of a "basically obsolete or an empty law whose function has long since passed." The showing of minimal numbers of prosecutions does not establish an abandonment of the State's laws and an irrational revival of them here.

* * *

Notes and Questions

1. While bigamy is rarely prosecuted, it is a crime (typically a misdemeanor) in most states. The Alabama statute is fairly typical:

> (a) A person commits bigamy when he intentionally contracts ... marriage with another person when he has a living spouse. A person who contracts a marriage outside this state, which would be bigamous if contracted in this state, commits bigamy by cohabiting in the state with the other party to such a marriage.
>
> (b) A person does not commit an offense under this section if:
>
> (1) He reasonably believes that his previous marriage is void or was dissolved by death, divorce or annulment; or
>
> (2) He and the prior spouse have been living apart for five consecutive years next prior to the subsequent marriage, during which time the prior spouse was not known by him to be alive. ALA. CRIM. CODE § 13A–13–1 (1996).

2. The Islamic religion permits polygamy. According to the Koran, a man may have as many as four wives at one time if they are treated equally. Even in Islamic countries, however, there appears to be a trend toward monogamy. Islamic Tunisia and Turkey have outlawed polygamy; Sierra Leone and Malaysia permit the practice only among Muslims. *See Symposium on Marriage and Divorce Recognition in Sixteen Countries*, 29 FAM. L. Q. 497, 613, 655, 701 (1995).

3. Should a polygamous marriage valid where contracted be recognized? Although a polygamous marriage cannot be celebrated, § 1 of the Matrimonial Proceedings (Polygamous Marriages) Act of 1972 allows a court to grant matrimonial relief or a declaration concerning validity of the marriage notwithstanding that it is polygamous. *See* S.M. POULTER, ENGLISH LAW AND ETHNIC MINORITY CUSTOMS 53–55 (1986). French law recognizes only one spouse, however. Marlise Simons, *In France, African Women Are Now Fighting Polygamy*, N.Y. TIMES, Jan. 26, 1996, A1, col. 1.

4. Researchers estimate that there are 20,000 to 40,000 fundamentalist Mormons who live in polygamous relationships in the western United States. Irwin Altman, *Polygamous Family Life: The Case of Contemporary Mormon Fundamentalists*, 1996 Utah L. Rev. 367, 369. *See also* Irwin Altman & Joseph Ginat, Polygamous Families in Contemporary Society (1996). Many, as the New York Times recently put it, "are part of a quietly emerging American subculture: the polygamous bourgeoisie."

> Polygamy remains a felony in Utah, but it is no longer prosecuted, said Eric A. Ludlow, the Washington County Attorney, in southern Utah where a number of plural families live. Polygamists, he said, get around bigamy statutes by legally marrying only one wife; the others are recognized by religious leaders or simply by the individuals themselves. "They go under the table, and we don't track it," Mr. Ludlow said. "It's a consensual relationship between adults."
>
> Increasingly plural families find themselves entering the mainstream, and with it, the middle class. "Our parents had a harder time," said Mr. Baker, a successful builder who works on construction jobs all over the state. "No one would hire them. Now, people don't care about your personal life. They don't ask. How do you lock up a guy for having two wives when Wilt Chamberlain talks about sleeping with thousands of women? We feel tolerated now for the first time."
>
> With tolerance and a measure of new prosperity comes creativity. The first question always asked by a young family is, "How can we expand the design?" said Ray Timpson, a fundamentalist Mormon, a draftsman specializing in house plans. He has 65 siblings and half siblings and grew up in a 21,000 square-foot house built in three phases . . .
>
> * * *
>
> . . . Thomas Carter, an associate professor of architectural history at the University of Utah, pointed out that the houses reveal a major power imbalance, somewhat like a traditional harem, reinforcing the relative mobility of the man and the relative immobility of the women and their availability to him.
>
> * * *
>
> . . . The most opulent home visited was also the strictest in terms of mandating communal living. The 35,000 square foot house was designed and built by a financier and fundamentalist in his 40's . . . [It] has 37 bathrooms and 31 bedrooms, this for 10 wives and 28 children. "Think of it this way," he said. "It's just like having 10 families with a fairly typical average of 2.8 children each. The only

thing unusual is there's only one father." And some high dental bills.

* * *

"Believe me," the Man said, "there are cheaper ways to have sex."

Florence Williams, *A House, 10 Wives: Polygamy in Suburbia*, N.Y. Times, Dec. 11, 1997, at B1.

5. If the effect of bigamy laws is to invalidate purported "marriages", should the bigamy laws be repealed? What state interests support the prohibition on bigamy?

6. How is polygamy different from serial monogamy? *See* Mary Ann Glendon, *Marriage and the State: The Withering Away of Marriage*, 62 Va. L. Rev. 663, 673 (1976).

C. OF DIFFERENT SEXES

BAEHR v. LEWIN

Supreme Court of Hawaii, 1993.
74 Hawaii 530, 852 P.2d 44.

Moon, Acting C.J.

* * *

On May 1, 1991, the plaintiffs filed a complaint for injunctive and declaratory relief in the Circuit Court of the First Circuit, State of Hawaii, seeking, inter alia: (1) a declaration that Hawaii Revised Statutes (HRS) § 572–1 (1985)—the section of the Hawaii Marriage Law enumerating the [r]equisites of [a] valid marriage contract—is unconstitutional insofar as it is construed and applied by the DOH to justify refusing to issue a marriage license on the sole basis that the applicant couple is of the same sex; and (2) preliminary and permanent injunctions prohibiting the future withholding of marriage licenses on that sole basis.

* * *

... [T]he precise question facing this court is whether we will extend the present boundaries of the fundamental right of marriage to include same-sex couples, or, put another way, whether we will hold that same-sex couples possess a fundamental right to marry. In effect, as the applicant couples frankly admit, we are being asked to recognize a new fundamental right.... [W]e have also held that the privacy right found in article I, § 6 [of the Hawaii Constitution] is similar to the federal right and that no "purpose to lend talismanic effect" to abstract phrases such as "intimate decision" or "personal autonomy" can "be inferred from [article I, § 6], any more than ... from the federal decisions."

* * *

[W]e do not believe that a right to same-sex marriage is so rooted in the traditions and collective conscience of our people that failure to recognize it would violate the fundamental principles of liberty and justice that lie at the base of all our civil and political institutions. Neither do we believe that a right to same-sex marriage is implicit in the concept of ordered liberty, such that neither liberty nor justice would exist if it were sacrificed. Accordingly, we hold that the applicant couples do not have a fundamental constitutional right to same-sex marriage arising out of the right to privacy or otherwise.

Our holding, however, does not leave the applicant couples without a potential remedy in this case. * * * In addition to the alleged violation of their constitutional rights to privacy and due process of law, the applicant couples contend that they have been denied the equal protection of the laws as guaranteed by article I, § 5 of the Hawaii Constitution.

* * *

The applicant couples correctly contend that the DOH's refusal to allow them to marry on the basis that they are members of the same sex deprives them of access to a multiplicity of rights and benefits that are contingent upon that status. Although it is unnecessary in this opinion to engage in an encyclopedic recitation of all of them, a number of the most salient marital rights and benefits are worthy of note. They include: (1) a variety of state income tax advantages, including deductions, credits, rates, exemptions, and estimates; (2) public assistance from and exemptions relating to the Department of Human Services; (3) control, division, acquisition, and disposition of community property; (4) rights relating to dower, curtesy, and inheritance; (5) rights to notice, protection, benefits, and inheritance; (6) award of child custody and support payments in divorce proceedings; (7) the right to spousal support; (8) the right to enter into premarital agreements; (9) the right to change of name; (10) the right to file a nonsupport action; (11) post-divorce rights relating to support and property division; (12) the benefit of the spousal privilege and confidential marital communications; (13) the benefit of the exemption of real property from attachment or execution; and (14) the right to bring a wrongful death action. For present purposes, it is not disputed that the applicant couples would be entitled to all of these marital rights and benefits, but for the fact that they are denied access to the state-conferred legal status of marriage. HRS § 572–1, on its face, discriminates based on sex against the applicant couples in the exercise of the civil right of marriage, thereby implicating the equal protection clause of article I, § 5 of the Hawaii Constitution.

* * *

The equal protection clauses of the United States and Hawaii Constitutions are not mirror images of one another. The fourteenth amendment to the United States Constitution somewhat concisely provides, in relevant part, that a state may not "deny to any person within its jurisdiction the equal protection of the laws." Hawaii's counterpart is more elaborate. Article I, § 5 of the Hawaii Constitution provides in relevant part that "[n]o person shall ... be denied the equal protection of the laws, nor be denied the enjoyment of the person's civil rights or be discriminated against in the exercise thereof because of race, religion, sex, or ancestry." (Emphasis added.) Thus, by its plain language, the Hawaii Constitution prohibits state-sanctioned discrimination against any person in the exercise of his or her civil rights on the basis of sex.

"The freedom to marry has long been recognized as one of the vital personal rights essential to the orderly pursuit of happiness by free [people]." *Loving*.... So "fundamental" does the United States Supreme Court consider the institution of marriage that it has deemed marriage to be "one of the 'basic civil rights of [men and women.]' " Id. (quoting *Skinner*, 316 U.S. at 541).

* * *

Relying primarily on four decisions construing the law of other jurisdictions, Lewin contends that "the fact that homosexual [sic—actually, same-sex] partners cannot form a state-licensed marriage is not the product of impermissible discrimination" implicating equal protection considerations, but rather "a function of their biologic inability as a couple to satisfy the definition of the status to which they aspire." Lewin's answering brief at 21. Put differently, Lewin proposes that "the right of persons of the same sex to marry one another does not exist because marriage, by definition and usage, means a special relationship between a man and a woman." We believe Lewin's argument to be circular and unpersuasive.

Two of the decisions upon which Lewin relies are demonstrably inapposite to the appellant couples' claim. *Baker v. Nelson*, 291 Minn. 310, 191 N.W.2d 185 (1971) ...; *De Santo v. Barnsley*, 328 Pa.Super. 181, 476 A.2d 952 (1984). * * *

Jones v. Hallahan, 501 S.W.2d 588 (Ky.Ct.App.1973), and *Singer v. Hara*, 11 Wash.App. 247, 522 P.2d 1187, review denied, 84 Wash.2d 1008 (1974), warrant more in-depth analysis. In *Jones*, the appellants, both females, sought review of a judgment that held that they were not entitled to have a marriage license issued to them, contending that refusal to issue the license deprived them of the basic constitutional rights to marry, associate, and exercise religion freely. In an opinion acknowledged to be "a case of first impression in Kentucky," the Court of Appeals summarily affirmed, ruling as follows: "Marriage was a custom long before the state commenced to issue licenses for that purpose.... [M]arriage has always been considered as a union of a man and a woman.... It appears to us that appellants are prevented from marrying, not by the statutes of Kentucky or the refusal of the County Clerk ... to issue them a license, but rather by their own incapability of entering into a marriage as that term is defined.... In substance, the relationship proposed by the appellants does not authorize the issuance of a marriage license because what they propose is not a marriage."

Significantly, the appellants' equal protection rights—federal or state—were not asserted in *Jones*, and, accordingly, the appeals court was relieved of the necessity of addressing and attempting to distinguish the decision of the United States Supreme Court in *Loving*. *Loving* involved the appeal of a black woman and a caucasian man (the Lovings) who were married in the District of Columbia and thereafter returned to their home state of Virginia to establish their marital abode. The Lovings were duly indicted for and convicted of violating Virginia's miscegenation laws, which banned interracial marriages. * * *

In a landmark decision, the United States Supreme Court ... struck down the Virginia miscegenation laws on both equal protection and due process grounds. The court's holding as to the former is pertinent for present purposes:

> [T]he Equal Protection Clause requires the consideration of whether the classifications drawn by any statute constitute an arbitrary and invidious discrimination.... There can be no question but that Virginia's miscegenation statutes rest solely upon distinctions drawn according to race. The statutes proscribe generally accepted conduct if engaged in by members of different races.... At the very least, the Equal Protection Clause demands that racial classifications ... be subjected to the "most rigid scrutiny," ... and, if they are ever to be upheld, they must be shown to be necessary to the accomplishment of some permissible state objective, independent of the racial discrimination which it was the object of the Fourteenth Amendment to eliminate. Id. at 10–12.

The facts in *Loving* and the respective reasoning of the Virginia courts, on the one hand, and the United States Supreme Court, on the other, both discredit the reasoning of *Jones* and unmask the tautological and circular nature of Lewin's argument that HRS § 572–1 does not implicate article I, § 5 of the Hawaii Constitution because same sex marriage is an innate impossibility. Analogously to Lewin's argument and the rationale of the *Jones* court, the Virginia courts declared that interracial marriage simply could not exist because the Deity had deemed such a union intrinsically unnatural, and, in effect, because it had theretofore never been the "custom" of the state to recognize mixed marriages, marriage "always" having been construed to presuppose a different configuration. With all due respect to the Virginia courts of a bygone era, we do not believe that trial judges are the ultimate authorities on the subject of Divine Will, and, as *Loving* amply demonstrates, constitutional law may mandate, like it or not, that customs change with an evolving social order.

Singer v. Hara, 11 Wash.App. 247, 522 P.2d 1187, review denied, 84 Wash.2d 1008 (1974), suffers the same fate as does *Jones*. * * * Regarding the appellants' federal and state claims, the court specifically "[did] not take exception to the proposition that the Equal Protection Clause of the Fourteenth Amendment requires strict judicial scrutiny of legislative attempts at sexual discrimination." Nevertheless, the *Singer* court found no defect in the state's marriage laws, under either the United States Constitution or the state constitution's equal rights amendment, based upon the rationale of *Jones*: "[a]ppellants were not denied a marriage license because of their sex; rather, they were denied a marriage license because of the nature of marriage itself." As in *Jones*, we reject this exercise in tortured and conclusory sophistry.

* * *

... [W]e hold that sex is a "suspect category" for purposes of equal protection analysis under article I, § 5 of the Hawaii Constitution and that HRS § 572–1 is subject to the "strict scrutiny" test. It therefore follows, and we so hold, that (1) HRS § 572–1 is presumed to be unconstitutional (2) unless Lewin, as an agent of the State of Hawaii, can show that (a) the statute's sex-based classification is justified by compelling state interests and (b) the statute is narrowly drawn to avoid unnecessary abridgements of the applicant couples' constitutional rights.

* * *

We understand that Judge Heen disagrees with our view ... based on his belief that "HRS § 572–1 treats everyone alike and applies equally to both sexes[,]" with the result that "[n]either sex is being granted a right or benefit the other does not have, and neither sex is being denied a right or benefit that the other has." The rationale underlying Judge Heen's belief, however, was expressly considered and rejected in *Loving*:

> Thus, the State contends that, because its miscegenation statutes punish equally both the white and the Negro participants in an interracial marriage, these statutes, despite their reliance on racial classifications do not constitute an invidious discrimination based upon race.... [W]e reject the notion that the mere "equal application" of a statute containing racial classifications is enough to remove the classifications from the Fourteenth Amendment's proscriptions of all invidious discriminations.... In the case at bar, ... we deal with statutes containing racial classifications, and the fact of equal application does not immunize the statute from the very heavy burden of justification which the Fourteenth Amendment has traditionally required of state statutes drawn according to race.

388 U.S. at 8. Substitution of "sex" for "race" and article I, § 5 for the fourteenth amendment yields the precise case before us together with the conclusion that we have reached.

As a final matter, we are compelled to respond to Judge Heen's suggestion that denying the appellants access to the multitude of statutory benefits "conferred upon spouses in a legal marriage * * * is a matter for the legislature, which can express the will of the populace in deciding whether such benefits should be extended to persons in (the applicant couples') circumstances." In effect, we are being accused of engaging in judicial legislation. We are not. The result we reach today is in complete harmony with the *Loving* Court's observation that any state's powers to regulate marriage are subject to the constraints imposed by the constitutional right to the equal protection of the laws. If it should ultimately be determined that the marriage laws of Hawaii impermissibly discriminate against the appellants, based on the suspect category of sex, then that would be the result of the interrelation of existing legislation. [W]hether the legislation under review is wise or unwise is a matter with which we have nothing to do. Whether it * * * work[s] well or work[s] ill presents a question entirely irrelevant to the issue. The only legitimate inquiry we can make is whether it is constitutional. If it is not, its virtues, if it have any, cannot save it; if it is, its faults cannot be invoked to accomplish its destruction. If the provisions of the Constitution be not upheld when they pinch as well as when they comfort, they may as well be abandoned.

... On remand, in accordance with the "strict scrutiny" standard, the burden will rest on Lewin to overcome the presumption that HRS § 572–1 is unconstitutional by demonstrating that it furthers compelling state interests and is narrowly drawn to avoid unnecessary abridgements of constitutional rights.

Vacated and remanded.

BURNS, J., concurring.

* * *

As used in the Hawaii constitution, to what does the word "sex" refer? In my view, the Hawaii constitution's reference to "sex" includes all aspects of each person's "sex" that are "biologically fated." The decision whether a person when born will be a male or a female is "biologically fated." Thus, the word "sex" includes the male-female difference. Is there any other aspect of a person's "sex" that is "biologically fated"?

* * *

If heterosexuality, homosexuality, bisexuality, and asexuality are "biologically fated[,]" then the word "sex" also includes those differences. Therefore, the questions whether heterosexuality, homosexuality, bisexuality, and asexuality are "biologically fated" are relevant questions of fact which must be determined before the issue presented in this case can be answered. If the answers are yes, then each person's "sex" includes both the "biologically fated" male-female difference and the "biologically fated" sexual orientation difference, and the Hawaii constitution probably bars the State from discriminating against the sexual orientation difference by permitting opposite-sex Hawaii Civil Law Marriages and not permitting same-sex Hawaii Civil Law marriages. If the answers are no, then each person's "sex" does not include the sexual orientation difference, and the Hawaii constitution may permit the State to encourage heterosexuality and discourage homosexuality, bisexuality, and asexuality by permitting opposite-sex Hawaii Civil Law Marriages and not permitting same-sex Hawaii Civil Law Marriages.

HEEN, J., dissenting.

* * *

I agree with the plurality's holding that Appellants do not have a fundamental right to a same sex marriage protected by article I, § 6 of the Hawaii State Constitution.

However, I cannot agree with the plurality that (1) Appellants have a "civil right" to a same sex marriage; (2) Hawaii Revised Statutes (HRS) § 572–1 unconstitutionally discriminates against Appellants who seek a license to enter into a same sex marriage; (3) Appellants are entitled to an evidentiary hearing that applies a "strict scrutiny" standard of review to the statute; and (4) HRS § 572–1 is presumptively unconstitutional. Moreover, in my view, Appellants' claim that they are being discriminatorily denied statutory benefits accorded to spouses in a legalized marriage should be addressed to the legislature.

* * *

Loving and *Zablocki* neither establish the right to a same sex marriage nor limit a state's power to prohibit any person from entering into such a marriage. The plurality's conclusion here that Appellants have a right to a same sex marriage and, therefore, an evidentiary hearing is completely contrary to the clear import of *Zablocki* and *Loving*. Although appellants suggest an analogy between the racial classification involved in *Loving* * * * and the alleged sexual classification involved in the case at bar, we do not find such an analogy. The operative distinction lies in the relationship which is described by the term "marriage" itself, and that relationship is the legal union of one man and one woman. Washington statutes, specifically those relating to marriage * * * and marital (community) property * * *, are clearly founded upon the presumption that marriage, as a legal relationship, may exist only between one man and one woman who are otherwise qualified to enter that relationship.

* * *

[A]ppellants are not being denied entry into the marriage relationship because of their sex; rather, they are being denied entry into the marriage relationship because of the recognized definition of that relationship as one which may be entered into only by two persons who are members of the opposite sex. *Singer v. Hara*, 11 Wash.App. 247, 253–55, 522 P.2d 1187, 1191–92, review denied, 84 Wash.2d 1008 (1974) (footnotes omitted).

* * *

In my view, the statute's classification is clearly designed to promote the legislative purpose of fostering and protecting the propagation of the human race through heterosexual marriages and bears a reasonable relationship to that purpose. I find nothing unconstitutional in that.

* * *

Appellants complain that because they are not allowed to legalize their relationships, they are denied a multitude of statutory benefits conferred upon spouses in a legal marriage. However, redress for those deprivations is a matter for the legislature, which can express the will of the populace in deciding whether such benefits should be extended to persons in Appellants' circumstances. Those benefits can be conferred without rooting out the very essence of a legal marriage. This court should not manufacture a civil right which is unsupported by any precedent, and whose legal incidents—the entitlement to those statutory benefits—will reach beyond the right to enter into a legal marriage and overturn long standing public policy encompassing other areas of public concern. This decision will have far-reaching and grave repercussions on the finances and policies of the governments and industry of this state and all the other states in the country.

BAEHR v. MIIKE

Hawaii Circuit Court, 1996.
1996 WL 694235.

* * *

Defendant has failed to present sufficient credible evidence which demonstrates that the public interest in the well-being of children and families, or the optimal development of children would be adversely affected by same-sex marriage. Nor has Defendant demonstrated how same-sex marriage would adversely affect the public fisc, the state interest in assuring recognition of Hawaii marriages in other states, the institution of traditional marriage, or any other important public or governmental interest.

The evidentiary record presented in this case does not justify the sex-based classification of HRS § 572–1.

Therefore, the court specifically finds and concludes, as a matter of law, that Defendant has failed to sustain his burden to overcome the presumption that HRS § 572–1 is unconstitutional by demonstrating or proving that the statute furthers a compelling state interest.

Further, even assuming arguendo that Defendant was able to demonstrate that the sex-based classification of HRS § 572–1 is justified because it furthers a compelling state interest, Defendant has failed to establish that HRS § 572–1 is narrowly tailored to avoid unnecessary abridgments of constitutional rights.

* * *

IT IS HEREBY ORDERED, ADJUDGED, AND DECREED THAT:

1. The sex-based classification in HRS § 572–1, on its face and as applied, is unconstitutional and in violation of the equal protection clause of article I, § 5 of the Hawaii Constitution.

Notes and Questions

1. The day after the Circuit Court decision on December 3, 1996, the judge entered a stay. A constitutional amendment was offered. As a compromise, the Hawaii legislature in the summer of 1997 adopted a domestic partnership law. In the fall of 1997, that law was challenged by several corporations which would have had to provide benefits. The battle continues.

2. What state policies support a ban on same-sex marriage?

3. How, according to the *Baehr* court, does the statutory prohibition on same-sex marriage violate the state constitution's prohibition on sex-based classification conclusion? Does the Court's conclusion hinge, as Justice Burns suggests, on whether homosexuality is "biologically fated?"

4. The *Baehr* approach to same-sex marriage has not been followed by other courts. In addition to the cases cited in the *Baehr* opinion, *see, e.g.,* Dean v. District of Columbia, 653 A.2d 307 (D.C.App.1995) (rejecting equal protection claim based on U.S. Constitution); Storrs v. Holcomb, 168 Misc.2d 898, 645 N.Y.S.2d 286 (1996) (same). *See also* Lynn D. Wardle, *A Critical Analysis of Constitutional Claims for Same–Sex Marriage,* 1996 B.Y.U. L. Rev. 1. In Rutgers Council of AAUP Chapters v. Rutgers, 298 N.J.Super. 442, 689 A.2d 828 (1997), the court held that the denial of health benefits to the same-sex companion of a state employee based on the lack of a marriage relationship did not violate the 14th amendment, and that it was up to the legislature to change state law:

> What goes on in other people's bedrooms is a question that has intrigued me since reaching puberty, but it is none of my business. I thus find it distasteful to uphold the denial of health insurance to the dependents of a deserving segment of the workforce merely because of their sexual predilections. To be sure, the State Health Benefits Program Act (N.J.S.A. §§ 52:14–17.25 et seq.) is neutral both with respect to gender and sexual orientation. However, the statutory reference to "employee's spouse" in the Act's definition of "dependents," N.J.S.A. § 52:14–17.26(d), indirectly discriminates against homosexual domestic partners who, because they are unable to enter into lawful marriage, are denied health benefits routinely enjoyed by similarly situated heterosexuals. The State seeks to perpetuate this injustice essentially on the grounds of administrative convenience. But other states, cities and private institutions have extended employee benefits to same-sex domestic partners without the severe dislocations envisioned by the Attorney General. The short answer to the State's argument is that it can be done, but New Jersey chooses not to do it.
>
> Despite this evident unfairness, I join in the decision of the court ... It is not our function as judges to construe statutes in accordance with our privately held views of justice. Instead, we must apply the law as written. The statutory language is crystal clear.

There is no room for interpretation. We are obliged to enforce the clearly expressed legislative intent. Nor does the New Jersey Constitution afford a remedy. Appellants point to a lengthening line of decisions in which the courts have relied upon state constitutional provisions in creating new rights and remedies. They argue that good law is simply a matter of fairness, and what is just in a given case merely requires us to summon the state constitution to rationalize the appropriate result.

But we would be myopic were we to see only the case before us. When the people perceive that they are not justly governed, the rallying cry is to throw the rascals out. But we judicial rascals are not answerable to the electorate and, absent calumny, enjoy the powers of our office for life. We must take care not to read the constitution to embrace subjects never thought to be within its reach. The more the state constitution is found to be intolerant of disagreement, the deadlier becomes the grip upon the people's inventiveness. The price of such intolerance may be sterility.

The most cherished principle in our system is that government rests on the consent of the governed. The central idea is that in the meandering course of history, there is time for visions and revisions—for mistakes to be made by the people and rectified by the people. Democracy has its price. Good people are sometimes hurt, even destroyed, in the process. But, surely, the judiciary does not have a monopoly on justice. Appellants must seek redress in another forum. Rutgers Council of AAUP Chapters v. Rutgers, 298 N.J.Super. 442, at 463, 689 A.2d 828 (Beame, J.A.D., concurring).

5. Most states consider it to be against public policy for domiciliaries to leave one state for the purpose of evading the laws of the state of domicile. *See* In re Estate of Loughmiller, 229 Kan. 584, 629 P.2d 156 (1981). The Uniform Marriage Evasion Act, withdrawn in 1943, remains in effect in some thirteen states and provides that:

If any person residing and intending to continue to reside in this state who is disabled or prohibited from contracting marriage under the laws of this state goes into another state or country and there contracts a marriage prohibited or declared void under the laws of this state, such marriage shall be void for all purposes in this state with the same effect as though it had been entered into in this state. WIS. STAT. ANN. § 765.04 (West 1993).

6. Under the Restatement (Second), Conflict of Laws (1969) the validity of a marriage contracted in state A, which would be illegal in State B, is determined as follows:

§ 283. Validity of Marriage

(1) The validity of a marriage will be determined by the local law of the state which, with respect to the particular issue, has the most significant relationship to the spouses and the marriage under the principles stated in § 6.

(2) A marriage which satisfies the requirements of the state where the marriage was contracted will everywhere be recognized as valid unless it violates the strong public policy of another state which had the most significant relationship to the spouses and the marriage at the time of the marriage.

At least sixteen states have enacted laws declaring that same sex marriages are contrary to public policy. *See, e.g.*, KAN. STAT. ANN. §§ 23–101, 23–115 (Supp. 1996) ("It is the strong public policy of this state only to recognize as valid marriages from other states that are between a man and a woman.") *See also* Curt Pham, *Let's Get Married in Hawaii: A Story of Conflicting Laws, Same–Sex Couples, and Marriage,* 30 FAM. L. Q. 727 (1996).

7. Congress, anticipating the Hawaii decision and not wishing to rely on state legislatures and the Restatement of Conflicts, enacted 28 U.S.C.A. § 1738C, providing that "[n]o state, territory, or possession of the United States, or Indian tribe, shall be required to give effect to any public act, record, or judicial proceeding of any other State, territory, possession, or tribe respecting a relationship between persons of the same-sex that is treated as a marriage under the laws of such other State ... or a right or claim arising from such relationship." Congress also enacted The Defense of Marriage Act, which defines "marriage" in all federal laws to mean a legal union between one man and one woman as husband and wife and denying any federal benefits to same-sex couples. Letter Report, 01/31/97, GAO/OCG–97–16. The constitutionality of the Act has been questioned. *See* Arthur R. Landever, *The Constitutional Requirements for and Against the Defense of Marriage Act*, 11 AMER. J. FAM. L. 23 (Spring 1997).

8. In 1989 Denmark adopted a registered partnership law applicable to same-sex couples only. Section 3 provides that the registering of a partnership has, with a few exceptions, the same legal effect as entering a marriage. Does the Danish registration procedure constitute marriage? *See* Linda Nielsen, *Family Rights and the "Registered Partnership" in Denmark,* 4 INTERNATIONAL J. LAW & THE FAMILY 297 (1990) and Chapter 5. The Netherlands has also adopted a registration of partnership law, effective January 1, 1998. The law gives same-sex couples who register the same rights as married couples, except that they may not adopt. *See* Marcus Tanner, *Dutch Gay Couple Make History with First Same-sex "Marriage,"* THE INDEPENDENT (LONDON), January 7, 1998, p. 9.

9. Transsexuals complicate the picture on same-sex marriage. The English view is that a person's gender is determined at birth. *See* Corbett v. Corbett, 2 All E.R. 33 (P.1970). In M.T. v. J.T., 140 N.J.Super. 77, 355 A.2d 204 (1976), M.T., a postoperative transsexual, married, then sought support and maintenance. J.T. countered that the marriage was void because M.T. was born a male. The New Jersey court found:

> We accept—and it is not disputed—as the fundamental premise in this case that a lawful marriage requires the performance of a ceremonial marriage of two persons of the opposite sex, a male and

female. Despite winds of change, this understanding of a valid marriage is almost universal.... In the matrimonial field the heterosexual union is usually regarded as the only one entitled to legal recognition and public sanction.

The issue must then be confronted whether the marriage between a male and a postoperative transsexual, who has surgically changed her external sexual anatomy from male to female, is to be regarded as a lawful marriage between a man and a woman.

* * *

In sum, it has been established that an individual suffering from the condition of transsexualism is one with a disparity between his or her genitalia or anatomical sex and his or her gender, that is, the individual's strong and consistent emotional and psychological sense of sexual being. A transsexual in a proper case can be treated medically by certain supportive measures and through surgery to remove and replace existing genitalia with sex organs which will coincide with the person's gender. If such sex reassignment surgery is successful and the postoperative transsexual is, by virtue of medical treatment, thereby possessed of the full capacity to function sexually as a male or female, as the case may be, we perceive no legal barrier, cognizable social taboo, or reason grounded in public policy to prevent that person's identification at least for purposes of marriage of the sex finally indicated ...

In this case the transsexual's gender and genitalia are no longer discordant; they have been harmonized through medical treatment. Plaintiff has become physically and psychologically unified and fully capable of sexual attributes of gender and anatomy. Consequently, plaintiff should be considered a member of the female sex for marital purposes....

The European Court on Human Rights found no violation of Article 8 or Article 12 when England refused to allow a person born a man who became a woman to marry a man. *See* Cossey v. United Kingdom, [1991] Family Law 362, European Court of Human Rights.

D. UNRELATED BY BLOOD

7 INTERNATIONAL ENCYCLOPEDIA OF THE SOCIAL SCIENCES

120 (1968).

Incest taboos, as one aspect of the regulation of sex and marriage, are integral to all known forms of social organization. Their form and function have varied extremely from one culture to another, in small and large societies, and in simple and complex societies. There seem to be no grounds for attributing the formation of this sanctioning system, by which an equilibrium is maintained between close and wide social ties, to any single set of innate human characteristics or to any specific set of historical circumstances. The universality of the occurrence of incest regulations, whatever form they may take or particular functions they may serve in a specific culture, suggests that they are part of a very complex system with deep biological roots, a system that is both a condition and a consequence of human evolution. Variations in the form and function of incest taboos suggest also that the formation of human character and the functioning of social systems are so intricately related to specific historical forms that changes within a social system are necessarily accompanied by some breakdown in the previously recognized pattern of personal relationships. Widespread failure to observe incest regulations is an index of the disruption of a sociocultural system that may be even more significant than the more usual indexes of crime, suicide, and homicide. (Margaret Mead).

Incest prohibitions may have existed as long as written law. Leviticus 18:6–18 of the Bible sets out incest prohibitions. Roman Catholic canon law, which regulated marriage in Europe during the medieval period, prohibited marriages within the fourth degree of consanguinity; it also prohibited marriage in some cases of relationship by affinity (i.e., through marriage), as well as between godfather and godchild or godfather's daughter and godson.

Today, incestuous marriages are prohibited in all states, although the relationships defined as incestuous vary. For example, Uniform Marriage and Divorce Act (UMDA) § 207(a) (9A U. L. A. 168 (1987)) prohibits:

(2) a marriage between an ancestor and a descendant, or between a brother and a sister, whether the relationship is by the half or the whole blood, or by adoption;

(3) a marriage between an uncle and a niece or between an aunt and a nephew, whether the relationship is by the half or the whole blood, except as to marriages permitted by the established customs of aboriginal cultures.

All states and the District of Columbia prohibit marriages between parent and child, siblings, aunt and nephew, uncle and niece. Nearly thirty states ban first cousin marriages. Some states do not forbid marriages between relatives by adoption; some do forbid marriage between cousins in addition to those proscribed by the UMDA.

Most states have statutes criminalizing incest, sometimes drafted more broadly than the the marriage prohibitions. Do the following arguments in support of the *criminal* incest prohibition stand up under equal protection analysis? Are they transferable to the civil context?

(a) *Religion*. The incest law may represent simply the use of criminal sanctions to enforce a religious tenet. The Bible defines and prohibits incest, and the offense was the exclusive concern of the church courts until 1908, with one brief interruption. * * * The specification of the forbidden degrees of kinship in legislation that prevailed at the time the Model Code was drafted was also largely derived from the religious history of the offense.

(b) *Genetics*. The laws against incest may have a genetic justification in that they may serve the civil and utilitarian function of preventing such inbreeding as would result in defective offspring. Mating between consanguineous relatives is non-random in the sense that close kinsmen are more likely to be genetically similar than are persons randomly selected from the population. Inbreeding therefore yields an increased probability of homozygosity with respect to a particular trait—that is, a greater chance that the offspring will receive an identical genetic contribution from each parent. If the pedigree contains a recessive abnormality—a genetic defect that does not appear in an individual unless both parents transmit the appropriate determinant—the increased probability of homozygosity in the first generation of offspring may have tragic consequences.

There are, however, a number of problems with relying upon a genetic theory to justify a law of incest. It must be noted first that none of the incest laws in the United States, or in the English ecclesiastical history from which they are derived, is limited to childbearing. The prohibition typically relates to marriage and sexual intercourse and, particularly in a day when contraceptive techniques are widely employed, is thus overbroad. It is clear, moreover, that former laws do not reflect genetic considerations insofar as marriages are prohibited between persons not related by blood, as in the extension to persons related by affinity such as stepchildren or daughters-in-law. As one anthropologist [Murdock] noted, "incest taboos, in their application to persons outside of the nuclear family, fail strikingly to coincide with nearness of actual biological relationship. * * * Very commonly * * * [they] exempt certain close consanguineal kinsmen but apply to adoptive, affinal, or ceremonial relatives with whom no biological kinsmen can be traced."

Even with respect to consanguineous mating, the science of human genetics has less solid guidance to offer than might be supposed. Geneticists are not agreed in their assessments of the relative dangers posed by inbreeding, and the number of serious genetic disorders related to inbreeding is quite limited. More importantly, some have argued that any decrease in the number of first-generation defectives resulting from the prevention of consanguineous marriages will be balanced by an increase in later generations, as the dispersal of unfavorable genes among the general population through exogamous matings raises the frequency with which the marriage of unrelated persons produces the unfavorable characteristic. "Thus," as one authority [Stern] put it, "the exclusion of consanguinity in one generation transfers the load of affected individuals to later generations." There is also the point that technological advance [pre-birth diagnosis] coupled with the general availability of abortion may provide at least a partial response to the problem of producing defective offspring, whether or not they result from consanguineous relationships.

(c) *Protection of the Family Unit.* The incest taboo and its origins are frequent topics of discussion in sociological and anthropological literature. Scholars from these disciplines have suggested various social objectives that the incest prohibition might serve. Perhaps the most persuasive theory is that social strictures against incest promote the solidarity of the nuclear family. This theory explains the universality of the concept of incest by reference to the universality of the nuclear family and derives strength from the anthropological verification of the existence of both across a wide range of cultural traditions.

The essentials of a nuclear family are a man and a woman in a relation of sexual intimacy and bearing a responsibility for the upbringing of the woman's children. This institution is the principal context for socialization of the individual. A critical component of that process is the channeling of the individual's erotic impulses into socially acceptable patterns. The incest prohibition regulates erotic desire in two ways that contribute to preservation of the nuclear family. First, the prohibition controls sex rivalries and jealousies within the family unit. It inhibits competing relations of sexual intimacy that would disorganize the family structure and undermine the family's role as the unit of socialization and personality development. Second, by ensuring suitable role models, the incest restriction prepares the individual for assumption of familial responsibility as an adult. Eventually, it propels the individual toward creation of a new nuclear family by his own marriage. It is worth noting also that this theory of the relation of incest to the nuclear family is consistent with Freudian psychology, which posits intrafamily sexual attraction as one of the basic facts of mental life and attributes much psychic disturbance to failure of the personality to resolve the internal conflict between such desires and societal repression of them.

(d) *Reinforcing Community Norms.* Even if it were demonstrable that the incest laws promote no secular goal, it might nevertheless be desirable to have a penal law on the subject. Where there is a general and intense hostility to behavior, a penal law will neither be accepted nor respected if it does not seek to repress that which is universally regarded by the community as misbehavior.

(e) *Sexual Imposition.* The actual incidence of prosecution for incest suggests that such laws have operated primarily against a kind of imposition on young and dependent females. A study of 30 appellate decisions on incest in the United States from 1846 to 1954 disclosed that all prosecutions were against males and that in 28 of the 30 cases the other party was the daughter or stepdaughter of the defendant. In the 21 instances where the court noted the age of the female, 18 involved girls aged 16 or younger, and none concerned a woman older than 22. Other research suggests that incest between stepfathers and stepdaughters occurs far more frequently than does incest between the parallel natural relations. In this aspect, therefore, the crime of incest can be viewed as supplementing other offenses of sexual imposition and assault.

(f) *Conclusion.* In light of the foregoing, it would appear that a modern penal code can appropriately contain a prohibition of incest, although attention plainly should be focused upon the scope of the prohibition. * * * It would seem * * * that a modern incest statute, carrying felony penalties, should be confined to relationships that present a high likelihood of threatening the solidarity of the nuclear family, that provide the occasion for sexual imposition of the experienced upon the inexperienced, and that coincide most closely with the intensely felt mores of the community. It may be permissible for a jurisdiction to adopt broader civil restrictions upon marriages regarded as undesirable, but the violation of any such regulations should not carry the infamy or penalty commonly associated with the crime of incest. It seems clear, therefore, that the law of incest should be separated from the civil law regulating the institution of marriage and that it should be confined more narrowly than the history of the offense might otherwise suggest.

American Law Institute, Model Penal Code and Commentaries § 230.2, at 403–407 (1980).

For discussion of incest taboos and justifications, *see* Margaret Mead, *Anomalies in American Post–Divorce Relationships*, in Divorce and After 104 (Paul Bohannan, ed. 1970); William J. Goode, The Family 40 (2d ed. 1982); Claude Levi–Strauss, *The Family,* in Man, Culture and Society 261 (Shapiro ed. 1956).

Notes and Questions

1. What is the basis for the proscription on first cousin marriage? Twenty-one states allow first cousins to marry. Is that a reason for upholding such a marriage?

2. Harry and Wanda marry after a brief courtship, then discover that they are biological brother and sister who were adopted into different families at very young ages. Is their marriage valid? If no, would it matter if they cannot have children? At one time several states had statutes allowing "feeble minded" women over age 55 to marry based on the idea that they were beyond the age of procreation. (These statutes were enacted before the 63 year old woman gave birth in November, 1996).

ISRAEL v. ALLEN

Supreme Court of Colorado, 1978.
195 Colo. 263, 577 P.2d 762.

PRINGLE, CHIEF JUSTICE.

Plaintiffs, Martin Richard Israel and Tammy Lee Bannon Israel, are brother and sister related by adoption and are not related by either the half or the whole blood.

Raymond Israel (the natural father of Martin Richard Israel) and Sylvia Bannon (the natural mother of Tammy Lee Bannon Israel) were married on November 3, 1972. At the time of their marriage, Martin was 18 years of age and was living in the State of Washington; Tammy was 13 years of age and was living with her mother in Denver, Colorado. Raymond Israel adopted Tammy on January 7, 1975.

Plaintiffs desired to be married in the State of Colorado. Defendant, Clerk and Recorder of Jefferson County, however, denied plaintiffs a license to marry. * * *

While the practice of adoption is an ancient one, the legal regulation of adoptive relationships in our society is strictly statutory in nature. The legislative intent in promulgating statutes concerning adoption was, in part, to make the law affecting adopted children in respect to equality of inheritance and parental duties *in pari materia* with that affecting natural children. It is clear, however, that adopted children are not engrafted upon their adoptive families for all purposes. See e.g., the criminal incest statute, which does not include sexual relationships between adopted brother and sister.

Nonetheless, defendant argues that this marriage prohibition provision furthers a legitimate state interest in family harmony. *See*, § 14–2–102(2)(a), C.R.S. 1973. We do not agree. As the instant case illustrates, it is just as likely that prohibiting marriage between brother and sister related by adoption will result in family discord. While we are not, strictly speaking, dealing with an affinity based relationship in this case, we find the following analysis equally applicable to the situation presently before us:

> "According to the English law, relationship by affinity was an impediment to marriage to the same extent and in the same degree as consanguinity. While this principle, derived from the ecclesiastically administered canon law, still strongly persists , in the United States the statutory law governing the marriage relationship nowhere so sweeping condemns the marriage of persons related only by affinity. * * * The objections that exist against consanguineous marriages are not present where the relationship is merely by affinity. The physical detriment to the offspring of persons related to blood is totally absent. The natural repugnance of people toward marriages of blood relatives, that has resulted in well-nigh universal moral condemnation of such marriages, is quite generally lacking in

application to the union of those related only by affinity. It is difficult to construct any very logical case for the prohibition of marriage on grounds of affinity * * *." 1 Vernier, American Family Laws 183.

We hold that it is just as illogical to prohibit marriage between adopted brother and sister.

Notes and Questions

1. Is it so illogical not to allow adoptive siblings to marry? Would you distinguish the "step-parent adoption" involved in *Israel* from the typical adoption situation? What if the stepfather had been the residential parent of Martin and had adopted Tammy when she was three years old?

2. Was it crucial to the court's decision that, in contrast to the rule in many states, Colorado's criminal incest statute does not cover brothers and sisters related by adoption?

3. Is the court's near total reliance on the affinity analogy persuasive? A few states do prohibit marriages between persons related by affinity, i.e., CONN. GEN. STAT. ANN. § 46b–21, "No man may marry his ... stepmother or stepdaughter, and no woman may marry her ... stepfather or stepson. Any marriages within these degrees is void." In England relationships based on marriage or adoption are prohibited along with those based on consanguinity. Matrimonial Causes Act (MCA) 1973 § 11. What legitimate state interests uphold marriage impediments based on affinity, adoption, or a step-relationship? Is there a stronger case for impediments based on adoption or step-relationships than for impediments based on affinity? What type of law would have prevented Woody Allen from marrying the adopted daughter of Mia Farrow, with whom he had had an intimate relationship for years? Would such a law be a good idea?

E. OF SUFFICIENT AGE

"Citizens of Rome contract lawful matrimony when they unite according to the precepts of the law; the males having attained the age of puberty, and the females a marriageable age. And this whether the males are fathers or sons of a family; but, if the latter, they must first have the consent of the parents under whose power they are. For both natural reason and the law convinces us that this consent of parents should precede marriage."

Justinian's Institutes, Book I, Title X (A.D. 533)

After passage of the Twenty–Sixth Amendment to the United States Constitution, which lowered the voting age to eighteen, most states selected 18 as the minimum age at which a person can marry without parental or judicial consent.

UNIFORM MARRIAGE AND DIVORCE ACT § 205

9A U.L.A. 168 (1987).

"(a) The [______] court, after a reasonable effort has been made to notify the parents or guardian of each underaged party, may order the [marriage license] clerk to issue a marriage license and a marriage certificate form:

[(1)] to a party aged 16 or 17 years who has no parent capable of consenting to marriage, or whose parent or guardian has not consented to his marriage; [or (2) to a party under the age of 16 years who has the consent of both parents to his marriage, if capable of giving consent, or his guardian].

(b) A marriage license and a marriage certificate form may be issued under this section only if the court finds that the underaged party is capable of assuming the responsibilities of marriage and the marriage will serve his best interest. Pregnancy alone does not establish that the best interest of the party will be served."

MOE v. DINKINS

United States District Court, S.D. New York, 1981.
533 F.Supp. 623, aff'd 669 F.2d 67 (2d Cir.1982).

[Plaintiffs, Maria Moe, age 15, Raoul Roe, age 18, and Ricardo Roe, their one year old son born out of wedlock, seek to have New York's parental consent to marry laws declared unconstitutional as violating due process and equal protection. New York Domestic Relations Law § 15.2 provides that male applicants for a marriage license between ages 16 and 18 and females between ages 14 and 18 must obtain written consent to the marriage from both parents, if living. Section 15.3 requires that a woman between ages 14 and 16 must also obtain judicial approval.

The Court notes that marriage is a liberty interest protected by the Constitution.]

* * *

While it is true that a child, because of his minority, is not beyond the protection of the Constitution, the Court has recognized the State's power to make adjustments in the constitutional rights of minors. The power of the State to control the conduct of children reaches beyond the scope of authority over adults. This power to adjust minors' constitutional rights flows from the State's concern with the unique position of minors. In *Bellotti v. Baird*, the Court noted "three reasons justifying the conclusion that the constitutional rights of children cannot be equated with those of adults: the peculiar vulnerability of children; their inability to make critical decisions in an informed and mature manner; and the importance of the parental role in child-rearing."

Likewise, marriage occupies a unique position under the law. It has been the subject of extensive regulation and control, within constitutional limits, in its inception and termination and has "long been regarded as a virtually exclusive province of the State." *Sosna v. Iowa.*

While it is evident that the New York law before this court directly abridges the right of minors to marry, *in the absence of parental consent,* the question is whether the State interests that support the abridgement can overcome the substantive protection of the Constitution. The unique position of minors and marriage under the law leads this court to conclude that § 15 should not be subjected to strict scrutiny, the test which the Supreme Court has ruled must be applied whenever a state statute burdens the exercise of a fundamental liberty protected by the Constitution. Applying strict scrutiny would require determination of whether there was a compelling state interest and whether the statute had been closely tailored to achieve that state interest.... It is this court's view that § 15 should be looked at solely to determine whether there exists a rational relation between the means chosen by the New York legislature and the legitimate state interests advanced by the State. Section 15 clearly meets this test.

The State interests advanced to justify the parental consent requirement of § 15 include the protection of minors from immature decision-making and preventing unstable marriages. The State possesses paternalistic power to protect and promote the welfare of children who lack the capacity to act in their own best interest. The State interests in mature decision-making and in preventing unstable marriages are legitimate under its *parens patriae* power.

An age attainment requirement for marriage is established in every American jurisdiction. The requirement of parental consent ensures that at least one mature person will participate in the decision of a minor to marry. That the State has provided for such consent in § 15 is rationally related to the State's legitimate interest in light of the fact that minors often lack the "experience, perspective and judgment" necessary to make "important, affirmative choices with potentially serious consequences."

Yet, plaintiffs fault the parental consent requirement of § 15 as possibly arbitrary, suggesting that courts, as non-interested third parties, are in a better position to judge whether a minor is prepared for the responsibilities that attach to marriage. Although the possibility for parents to act in other than the best interest of their child exists, the law presumes that the parents "possess what the child lacks in maturity" and that "the natural bonds of affection lead parents to act in the best interest of their children." *Parham v. J.R.* [p. 428] "That the governmental power should supersede parental authority in all cases because some parents" may act in other than the best interest of their children is "repugnant to the American tradition."

Plaintiffs also contend that § 15 denied them the opportunity to make an individualized showing of maturity and denies them the only means by which they can legitimize their children and live in the traditional family unit sanctioned by law. On the other hand, New

York's § 15 merely delays plaintiffs' access to the institution of marriage. Moreover, the prohibition does not bar minors whose parents consent to their child's marriage. Assuming arguendo that the illegitimacy of plaintiff Moe's child ... is a harm, it is not a harm inflicted by § 15. It is merely an incidental consequence of the lawful exercise of State power. The illegitimacy of plaintiffs' children, like the denial of marriage without parental consent, is a temporary situation at worst. A subsequent marriage of the parents legitimatizes the child, thereby erasing the mark of illegitimacy. The rights or benefits flowing from the marriage of minors are only temporarily suspended by § 15. Any alleged harm to these rights and benefits is not inflicted by § 15, but is simply an incidental consequence of the valid exercise of State power.

The fact that the State has elected to use a simple criterion, age, to determine probable maturity in the absence of parental consent, instead of requiring proof of maturity on a case by case basis, is reasonable, even if the rule produces seemingly arbitrary results in individual cases. * * *

Plaintiffs' reliance on the abortion and contraception cases is misplaced.... These cases can be distinguished from the instant case in that

> a pregnant minor's options are much different than those facing a minor in other situations, *such as deciding whether to marry.* A minor not permitted to marry before the age of maturity is required simply to postpone her decision. She and her intended spouse may preserve the opportunity for a later marriage should they continue to desire it.

Bellotti v. Baird, *supra*, 443 U.S. at 642 (emphasis added). Giving birth to an unwanted child involves an irretrievable change in position for a minor as well as for an adult, whereas the temporary denial of the right to marry does not. Plaintiffs are not irretrievably foreclosed from marrying. The gravamen of the complaint, in the instant case, is not total deprivation but only delay.

This court concludes that § 15's requirement of parental consent is rationally related to the State's legitimate interests in mature decision-making with respect to marriage by minors and preventing unstable marriages. It is also rationally related to the State's legitimate interest in supporting the fundamental privacy right of a parent to act in what the parent perceives to be the best interest of the child free from state court scrutiny. Section 15, therefore, does not offend the constitutional rights of minors but represents a constitutionally valid exercise of state power.

Accordingly, plaintiffs' motion for summary judgment in their favor is denied and summary judgment is entered in favor of defendants.

F. IN PROPER HEALTH AND WITH GOOD GENES?

WILLIAM VUKOWICH, THE DAWNING OF THE BRAVE NEW WORLD—LEGAL, ETHICAL, AND SOCIAL ISSUES OF EUGENICS

1971 U. ILL. L. F. 189, 214 (1971).

In the early 1900's many states enacted laws that prohibited marriage by criminals, alcoholics, imbeciles, feebleminded persons, and the insane. Today most states prohibit marriage by persons with venereal disease, but only a few states have laws which are similar to those of the early 1900's.

* * *

In addition to the existing marital restrictions, Nobel prize winner Linus Pauling has suggested that legislation prohibit marriages between heterozygotes for the same recessive gene if the recessive gene can be detected in the heterozygous state. The suggestion was made in reference to sickle-cell anemia, but is equally applicable to other serious defects which are caused by recessive genes that can or will become detectable in heterozygotes. Professor Pauling would require that heterozygotes for serious defects be conspicuously marked so that two heterozygotes for the same defect would not fall in love. In any event, their marriage would be prohibited, although there is only a 25 percent chance for two heterozygotes to have a homozygous child. Professor Pauling believes that severe marital restrictions are warranted because of the grave suffering borne by children with the diseases that the restrictions would prevent.

If heterozygotes for the same deleterious gene never intermarry, however, there would be an *increase* in the incidence of the gene.

Notes and Questions

1. An example of an old-line eugenic statute is N.D. CENT. CODE § 14–03–07: "Marriage by a woman under the age of forty-five years or by a man of any age, unless he marries a woman over the age of forty-five years, is prohibited if such a man or woman is [a chronic alcoholic, an habitual criminal, a mentally deficient person, an insane person, a person who has been afflicted with hereditary insanity, or with any contagious venereal disease]". Overwhelmingly, when referring to "insanity", "imbecility", "idiocy" and the like, modern legislation deals with *capacity to consent to marriage*, not mental or emotional capability to function in a marriage or with genetic problems that may be passed on to the children.

2. Muster arguments for and against the constitutionality of Professor Pauling's (who did not get his Nobel prize for this) proposal.

3. If it is "genetic risk" that affords a legitimate basis for upholding incest prohibitions, can you justify a marriage law that does not

apply equally strong prohibitions to marriages between nonrelatives who have known genetic defects that pose a risk to their offspring?

4. UTAH CODE ANN. tit. 30 § 1–2 prohibited marriages "with a person afflicted with acquired immune deficiency syndrome, syphilis, or gonorrhea that is communicable or that may become communicable." In T.E.P. v. Leavitt, 840 F.Supp. 110 (D.Utah 1993), the court struck down the Utah statute on the grounds that it violated the Americans with Disabilities Act, 42 U.S.C.A. § 1201 et. seq.

5. While disease-based marriage *prohibitions* are rare, a number of states require premarital health *examinations* to detect venereal and/or other diseases, including rubella, Rh incompatibility, tuberculosis, and drug addiction. More recent statutes have targeted AIDS. For a brief period, Illinois required premarital AIDS testing:

> During the first 6 months of legislatively mandated premarital testing for human immunodeficiency virus in Illinois, 8 of 70, 846 applicants for marriage licenses were found to be seropositive, yielding a seroprevalence of 0.011%. The total cost of the testing program for 6 months is estimated at $2.5 million or $312,000 per seropositive individual identified. Half of the reported seropositive individuals reported a history of risk behavior. During the same period, the number of marriage licenses issued in Illinois decreased by 22.5%, while the number of licenses issued to Illinois residents in surrounding states increased significantly. We conclude that mandatory premarital testing is not a cost-effective method for the control of human immunodeficiency virus infection. Turnock & Kelly, *Mandatory Premarital Testing for Human Immunodeficiency Virus: The Illinois Experience*, 261 J.A.M.A. 3415 (June 16, 1989), Summary.

Is the Illinois experience relevant to other forms of premarital testing? How and why?

6. Today there are tests available for a wide variety of genetically linked disorders. Should premarital testing for these disorders be required?

SECTION 4. PROCEDURES RELATING TO ENTRY INTO MARRIAGE

In the last section we looked at the *substantive* requirements for marriage that are typically found in state statutes. We now turn to the *procedural* requirements for a valid marriage.

A. CONSENT TO MARRY

1. *Capacity to Contract*

To marry requires *the capacity to contract*. Although state statutes invariably require mental capacity, they provide no effective mechanism to ascertain a marriage applicant's mental condition. Typically, the matter lies entirely in the hands of the clerks authorized to issue marriage licenses, few of whom are qualified mental health diagnosticians. Appellate cases involving the refusal of a marriage license on grounds of mental capacity are scarce, indicating either that marriage licenses are rarely refused on that ground or that, when refused, couples go to more hospitable jurisdictions.

UNIFORM MARRIAGE AND DIVORCE ACT § 208

9A U.L.A. 170 (1987).

The [___] court shall enter its decree declaring the invalidity of a marriage entered into under the following circumstances:

(1) a party lacked capacity to consent to the marriage at the time the marriage was solemnized, either because of mental incapacity or infirmity or because of the influence of alcohol, drugs, or other incapacitating substances, or a party was induced to enter into a marriage by force or duress, or by fraud involving the essentials of marriage;

(2) a party lacks the physical capacity to consummate the marriage by sexual intercourse, and at the time the marriage was solemnized the other party did not know of the incapacity;

(3) a party [was under the age of 16 years and did not have the consent of his parents or guardian and judicial approval or] was aged 16 or 17 years and did not have the consent of his parents or guardian or judicial approval; or

(4) the marriage is prohibited. [See § 207].

LARSON v. LARSON

Illinois Court of Appeals, 1963.
42 Ill.App.2d 467, 192 N.E.2d 594.

CROW, PRESIDING JUSTICE.

* * * When the celebration of a marriage is shown, the contract of marriage, the capacity of the parties, and, in fact, everything necessary to the validity of the marriage, in the absence of proof to the contrary, will be presumed; the burden of proof was upon the plaintiff to show the marriage was invalid; to enable a party legally to contract a marriage he or she must be capable of understanding the nature of the act. When a marriage is shown the law raises a strong presumption in favor of its validity, and the burden is upon the party objecting thereto to prove such facts and circumstances as necessarily establish its invalidity; there is no clear dividing line between competency and incompetency, and each case must be judged by its own peculiar facts; the parties must have sufficient mental capacity to enter into the status, but proof of lack of mental capacity must be clear and definite; if the party possesses sufficient mental capacity to understand the nature, effect, duties, and obligations of the marriage contract into which he or she is entering, the marriage contract is binding, as long as they are otherwise legally competent to enter into the relation.

A marriage contract will be invalidated by the want of consent of capable persons; it requires the mutual consent of two persons of sound mind, and if at the time one is mentally incapable of giving an intelligent consent to what is done, with an understanding of the obligations assumed, the solemnization is a mere idle ceremony,—they must be capable of entering understandingly into the relation. It is impossible to prescribe a definite rule by which the mental condition as to sanity or insanity in regard to a marriage can in every case be tested; the question is not altogether of brain quantity or quality in the abstract, but whether the mind could and did act rationally regarding the precise thing in contemplation,—marriage,—and the particular marriage in dispute,—not whether his or her conduct was wise, but whether it proceeded from a mind sane as respects the particular thing done. The decree here [denying annulment] is not contrary to the manifest weight of the evidence or to the law. Prior to and at the time of the marriage the plaintiff noticed nothing abnormal about the defendant. There is no evidence that any of the unusual things she thought and did some months after the marriage had also occurred prior to and at the time of the marriage. Her first commitment to Elgin State Hospital was in 1952, more than two years after the marriage. In 1954 she was found to have recovered and was restored to all her civil rights. She got along good for awhile thereafter. Her second commitment was in 1956, more than four and one-half years after the marriage. The plaintiff continued to live regularly with the defendant as husband and wife except for such times as she was actually physically confined at the Hospital. The doctor who testified had never examined, or treated the defendant and his entire testimony is based, necessarily, on an hypothetical question. The ostensible diagnosis was evidently made by another or other doctors, who were not available or did not testify here. No doctor, nurse, or attendant at the Hospital who might have observed, examined, or treated her testified. In this doctor's opinion, even, a patient of that type may have lucid intervals for months or years—she may not have had any symptoms which a layman would recognize as insanity,—she might be all right for years,—and he would not say a patient of such type could never be cured. Even he said such a patient might be legally all right,—not legally insane,—though medically it may be very difficult to say. The other witness' testimony was either quite remote in point of time, or related to an incident eight years after the marriage, or had to do with matters having no great legal significance.

The plaintiff has not satisfied the burden of proving, clearly and definitely, that the defendant was an "insane person" at the particular time of this marriage, March 21, 1950,—that she was at that time incapable of understanding the nature of the act, that she had insufficient mental capacity to enter into the status and understand the nature, effect, duties, and obligations of the marriage contract, that she was mentally incapable of giving an intelligent, understanding consent, or that her mind could not and did not act rationally regarding the precise thing in contemplation, marriage, and this particular marriage in dispute. The decree is correct and it will be affirmed.

Notes and Questions

1. Is the court concerned with capacity to *make* the contract or to *perform* the contract?

2. Less capacity is required to consent to a marriage than is required to execute a will, sign a deed, or to make a business contract. The fact that a spouse has a guardian or conservator will not, by itself, invalidate a marriage based on lack of capacity. *See* Uniform Probate Code §§ 5–401, 5–309.

3. Incapacity may derive from disease, mental retardation, or the influence of alcohol or drugs. But the burden of proof is on the party attacking the marriage, who is often required to show lack of capacity by clear and convincing evidence. *See* In re Estate of Hendrickson, 248 Kan. 72, 805 P.2d 20 (1991). Would a prior adjudication of mental incompetence be conclusive on the issue of capacity to marry? *Compare* Geitner v. Townsend, 67 N.C.App. 159, 312 S.E.2d 236 (1984) (no) *with* May v. Leneair, 99 Mich.App. 209, 297 N.W.2d 882 (1980) (yes).

2. *Intent to Contract*

If consent to marry was obtained by force, duress, or fraud, the party with clean hands may be able to annul the marriage. *See* Chapter 10 and Marriage of Weintraub, 167 Cal.App.3d 420, 213 Cal.Rptr. 159 (1985); Stakelum v. Terral, 126 So.2d 689 (La.App.1961). *See also* Walter Wadlington, *Shotgun Marriage by Operation of Law*, 1 GA. L. REV. 183 (1967).

In contrast to a fraudulently obtained marriage, a "sham" marriage is a marriage for a limited purpose and with a limited intent, for example a marriage entered simply to "give the baby a name." Most courts have upheld such marriages. *See* Schibi v. Schibi, 136 Conn. 196, 69 A.2d 831 (1949) (husband was denied annulment where parties married to legitimize an unborn child but never intended to cohabit as husband and wife). *See generally* J.H. Wade, *Limited Purpose Marriages*, 45 MOD. L. REV. 159 (1982).

Until 1986, when Congress substantially tightened the immigration laws, the most typical sham marriage was one arranged for the sole purpose of obtaining a visa to enter the United States. Typically, the foreign national paid money to an American citizen whom he or she married without any intention of maintaining a marital relationship. The U.S. Immigration and Naturalization Service (INS) took the position that it could make an independent determination of a marriage's validity for immigration purposes, even if the marriage was valid under another country's laws. *See* Bu Roe v. Immigration & Naturalization Service, 771 F.2d 1328 (9th Cir.1985); Faustin v. Lewis, 85 N.J. 507, 427 A.2d 1105 (1981); Eileen P. Lynsky, Note, *Immigration Marriage Fraud Amend-*

ments of 1986: Till Congress Do Us Part, 41 U. MIAMI L. REV. 1087 (1987).

SMITH v. I.N.S.

United States District Court, District of Massachusetts, 1988.
684 F.Supp. 1113.

CAFFREY, SENIOR DISTRICT JUDGE.

To alleviate the incentive to enter into sham marriages, Congress enacted the Marriage Fraud Amendments of 1986. Prior to the amendments, when a citizen petitioned for an adjustment of status for an alien spouse, the Immigration and Naturalization Service ("INS") conducted an inquiry into each petition to determine whether the marriage was bona fide or merely a sham entered into for the purpose of obtaining immigration benefits. If the INS concluded that the marriage was sincere, it granted the alien spouse permanent resident status. Obviously, no adjustment was granted if the marriage was determined to be a fraud.

The Marriage Fraud Amendments were designed to tighten the statutory scheme in order to prevent marriage fraud. Under the amendments, an alien who marries a citizen receives only a conditional adjustment of status based on the fact of the marriage. 8 U.S.C. § 1186a(a)(1). Conditional status is granted only after the INS conducts an inquiry into the sincerity of the marriage. The alien's immigration status remains conditional for a two year period, after which, if the marriage is in fact bona fide, the condition is removed and the alien spouse obtains permanent resident status. 8 U.S.C. § 1186a(c)(3)(B).

If, at the time of the marriage, the alien is involved in deportation or exclusion proceedings, the procedures prescribed by the amendments are very different. When an alien who is involved in such proceedings marries a citizen, the alien spouse is required to leave the United States for a two year period before he or she may obtain an adjustment of status based on the marriage. 8 U.S.C. §§ 1154(h) and 1255(e). The two year non-residency requirement is applied whether or not the alien/citizen marriage is in fact bona fide or a sham. The INS conducts no individual inquiry into the bona fides of the marriage until the two year non-residency period is completed. It is these latter provisions of the amendments which are at issue in the present action.

* * *

Ordinarily, a statute which imposes such a heavy burden on the marital relationship would be subject to searching judicial review in order to determine whether it is carefully crafted to achieve important governmental goals. *Zablocki v. Redhail*, [p. 48]. The right to marry has been deemed of fundamental importance in our country and matters relating to marriage and family are accorded special protection under our constitutional scheme.

Although marriage is recognized as one of the fundamental rights protected by the Constitution, the statute at issue here involves an exercise of congressional power in the area of immigration and naturalization. The extraordinarily broad power of Congress over immigration matters is well established. * * *

Turning to the challenged statute, this Court rules that the distinction drawn by the Marriage Fraud Amendments between aliens who marry while involved in deportation proceedings and other alien spouses is rationally related to a legitimate governmental interest. * * * Since marriage to a United States citizen will no longer allow an alien engaged in deportation proceedings to remain in this country, it is rational to conclude that the two year non-residency requirement will have some effect in reducing the incidence of marriage fraud within this high-risk group.

B. SOLEMNIZATION AND LICENSING

All states regulate the process of obtaining a marriage license and solemnization of marriage. The Uniform Marriage and Divorce Act has served as the model for a number of state licensing and solemnization statutes:

UNIFORM MARRIAGE AND DIVORCE ACT

9A U.L.A. 163, 166 (1987).

Section 203.

(a) When a marriage application has been completed and signed by both parties to a prospective marriage and at least one party has appeared before the [marriage license] clerk and paid the marriage license fee of [______], the [marriage license] clerk shall issue a license to marry and a marriage certificate form upon being furnished:

(1) satisfactory proof that each party to the marriage will have attained the age of 18 years at the time the marriage license is effective, or will have attained the age of 16 years and has either the consent to the marriage of both parents or his guardian, or judicial approval; [or if under the age of 16 years, has both the consent of both parents or his guardian and judicial approval;] and

(2) satisfactory proof that the marriage is not prohibited; [and]

[(3) a certificate of the results of any medical examination required by the laws of this State].

Section 206. [Solemnization and Registration]

(a) A marriage may be solemnized by a judge of a court of record, by a public official whose powers include solemnization of marriages, or in accordance with any mode of solemnization recognized by any religious denomination, Indian Nation or Tribe, or Native Group. Either the person solemnizing the marriage, or, if no individual acting alone solemnized the marriage, a party to the marriage, shall complete the marriage certificate form and forward it to the [marriage license] clerk.

(b) If a party to a marriage is unable to be present at the solemnization, he may authorize in writing a third person to act as his proxy. If the person solemnizing the marriage is satisfied that the absent party is unable to be present and has consented to the marriage, he may solemnize the marriage by proxy. If he is not satisfied, the parties may petition the [______] court for an order permitting the marriage to be solemnized by proxy.

(c) Upon receipt of the marriage certificate, the [marriage license] clerk shall register the marriage.

(d) The solemnization of the marriage is not invalidated by the fact that the person solemnizing the marriage was not legally qualified to solemnize it, if either party to the marriage believed him to be so qualified.

CARABETTA v. CARABETTA

Supreme Court of Connecticut, 1980.
182 Conn. 344, 438 A.2d 109.

PETERS, J.

The plaintiff and the defendant exchanged marital vows before a priest in the rectory of Our Lady of Mt. Carmel Church of Meriden, on August 25, 1955, according to the rite of the Roman Catholic Church, although they had failed to obtain a marriage license. Thereafter they lived together as husband and wife, raising a family of four children, all of whose birth certificates listed the defendant as their father. Until the present action, the defendant had no memory or recollection of ever having denied that the plaintiff and the defendant were married.

The issue before us is whether, under Connecticut law, despite solemnization according to an appropriate religious ceremony, a marriage is void where there has been noncompliance with the statutory requirement of a marriage license. This is a question of first impression in this state.

* * *

The governing statutes at the time of the purported marriage between these parties contained two kinds of regulations concerning the requirements for a legally valid marriage. One kind of regulation concerned substantive requirements determining those eligible to be married. * * * The other kind of regulation concerns the formalities prescribed by the state for the effectuation of a legally valid marriage. These required formalities, in turn, are of two sorts: a marriage license and a solemnization. In *Hames v. Hames*, [163 Conn. 588, 316 A.2d 379 (1972)] we interpreted our statutes not to make void a marriage consummated after the issuance of a license but deficient for want of due solemnization. Today we examine the statutes in the reverse case, a marriage duly solemnized but deficient for want of a marriage license.

* * *

In the absence of express language in the governing statute declaring a marriage void for failure to observe a statutory requirement, this court has held in an unbroken line of cases that such a marriage, though imperfect, is dissoluble rather than void. We see no reason to import into the language "[n]o persons shall be joined in marriage until [they have applied for] a license," a meaning more drastic than that assigned in *Gould v. Gould*, [78 Conn. 242, 61 A. 604 (1905)] to the statute that * * * provided that "[n]o man and woman, either of whom is epileptic * * * shall intermarry." Although the state may well have a legitimate interest in the health of those who are about to marry, *Gould v. Gould* held that the legislature would not be deemed to have entirely invalidated a marriage contract in violation of such health requirements unless the statute itself expressly declared the marriage to be void. Then as now, the legislature had chosen to use the language of voidness selectively, applying it to some but not to all of the statutory requirements for the creation of a legal marriage. Now as then, the legislature has the competence to choose to sanction those who solemnize a marriage without a marriage license rather than those who marry without a marriage license. In sum, we conclude that the legislature's failure to expressly characterize as void a marriage properly celebrated without a license means that such a marriage is not invalid.

* * *

The conclusion that a ceremonial marriage contracted without a marriage license is not null and void finds support, furthermore, in the decisions in other jurisdictions. In the majority of states, unless the licensing statute plainly makes an unlicensed marriage invalid, "the cases find the policy favoring valid marriages sufficiently strong to justify upholding the unlicensed ceremony. This seems the correct result. Most such cases arise long after the parties have acted upon the assumption that they are married, and no useful purpose is served by avoiding the long-standing relationship. Compliance with the licensing laws can better be attained by safeguards operating before the license is issued, as by a more careful investigation by the issuing authority or the person marrying the parties." Clark, Domestic Relations, p. 41 (1968).

Since the marriage that the trial court was asked to dissolve was not void, the trial court erred in granting the motion to dismiss for lack of jurisdiction over the subject matter.

Notes and Questions

1. The Connecticut court concludes that a marriage without a license is not invalid nor "null and void" and finds that the trial court had jurisdiction over the subject matter. Does this fuzzy rhetoric mean that the marriage is valid?

2. Connecticut does not recognize common law marriage. Is this case a "near-revival"? Weigh state policies favoring and disfavoring upholding the marriage in this case.

3. Waiting periods between the issuance of a marriage license and solemnization of the marriage are imposed by approximately three quarters of the states and range from one to ten days, with three days the most common requirement. Why have waiting periods?

4. Lewanee County, Michigan, is the first U.S. jurisdiction to require mandatory premarital counseling. In June, 1997, in an attempt to lower the county's 68% divorce rate, the judge, 60 churchmen and the 12 other officials authorized to conduct marriages, decided not to marry couples without evidence of premarital counseling. Couples are required to fill out a 16 page questionnaire, composed of 165 multiple-choice questions asking about money matters, hopes for children, sex, and conflict resolution. The author of the test alleges that it can predict divorce with 85% accuracy. At least 11 other states are considering premarital "testing." *See Judge Pops 165 Questions So Molly Can Wed David*, LONDON TIMES, June 7, 1997. Could the state deny a marriage license to a prospective spouse who fails the test? See *Zablocki* [p. 48].

5. In some states a portion of the marriage license fee is designated for funding state programs for the victims of domestic violence. *See e.g.* KAN. STAT. ANN. 23–108a (Supp. 1996). The Illinois Supreme Court struck down such a law, ruling that the state had failed to show a rational "relationship between the purchase of the marriage license and domestic violence" that would justify such a "tax" on marriage. Boynton v. Kusper, 112 Ill.2d 356, 98 Ill.Dec. 208, 494 N.E.2d 135 (1986). *But see* Browning v. Corbett, 153 Ariz. 74, 734 P.2d 1030 (Ariz.App.1986) (rejecting Illinois approach and upholding a similar statute).

6. Problems occasionally arise over who is authorized to solemnize a marriage. For example, some courts and the Attorney General of Tennessee (Opinion No. U97–041) have found that "ordained" ministers of the Universal Life Church are not "ministers" within the meaning of state laws describing who can administer the rites of marriage. *See* State v. Lynch, 301 N.C. 479, 272 S.E.2d 349 (1980) (bigamy conviction reversed where first marriage was performed by person holding $10.00 mail order certificate from Universal Life Church). *Accord*, Cramer v. Commonwealth, 214 Va. 561, 202 S.E.2d 911 (1974); Ranieri v. Ranieri, 146 A.D.2d 34, 539 N.Y.S.2d 382 (1989). *But see* Matter of Blackwell, 531 So.2d 1193 (Miss.1988) (sustaining marriage performed by minister of Universal Life Church).

Would a marriage solemnized by a Universal Life Church minister be valid under *Carabetta*? under UMDA § 206(d)?

7. UMDA § 206(b) and many other state statutes permit a marriage to be solemnized by proxy. The usual reason for a proxy marriage is that the bride and groom are in different states (or countries). The parties may designate a "stand in" who appears for the absent party at

the ceremony. Some states require both parties to be present at the ceremony. Would an internet connection be sufficient (with video)?

SECTION 5. EXCEPTIONS TO THE FORMAL REQUIREMENTS

A. COMMON LAW MARRIAGE

P. BROMLEY, FAMILY LAW

27–29 (4th Ed. 1971).

In England, until the middle of the eighteenth century a marriage could be contracted in one of three ways:

(a) *In facie ecclesiae*, after the publishing of banns or upon a license, before witnesses, and with the consent of the parent or guardian of a party who was a minor. Such a marriage was obviously valid for all purposes.

(b) Clandestinely, *per verba de praesenti* before a clerk in holy orders, but not *in facie ecclesiae*. This * * * was as valid as if it had been solemnized *in facie ecclesiae*.

(c) *Per verba de praesenti* or *per verba de futuro* with subsequent sexual intercourse, but where the words were not spoken in the presence of an ordained priest or deacon. Whilst such a marriage would no longer produce all the legal effects of coverture at common law, it was nevertheless valid for many purposes. Such a union was indissoluble, so that, if either party to it subsequently married another, the later marriage could be annulled. Moreover, either party could obtain an order from an ecclesiastical court calling upon the other to solemnize the marriage *in facie ecclesiae*.

Lord Hardwicke's Act.—It needs little imagination to picture the social evils which resulted from such a state of law. A person who had believed himself to be validly married for years would suddenly find that his marriage was a nullity because of a previous clandestine or irregular union, the existence of which he had never before suspected. Children would marry without their parents' consent, and if the minor was a girl with a large fortune, the old common law rule that a wife's property vested in her husband on marriage made her a particularly attractive catch. The "Fleet" parsons thrived—profligate clergy who traded in clandestine marriages. By the middle of the eighteenth century matters had come to such a pass that there was a danger in certain sections of society that such marriages would become the rule rather than the exception.

It was to stop these abuses that Lord Hardwicke's Act was passed in 1753. The principle underlying this Act was to secure publicity by enacting that no marriage should be valid unless it was solemnized according to the rites of the Church of England in the parish church of one of the parties in the presence of a clergyman and two other witnesses. Unless a license had been obtained, banns had to be published in the parish churches of both parties for three Sundays. If either party was under the age of 21, parental consent had to be obtained as well, unless this was impossible to obtain or was unreasonably withheld, in which case the consent of the Lord Chancellor had to be obtained. If these stringent provisions were not observed, the marriage would in the vast majority of cases be void. Furthermore, the Act abolished the jurisdiction of the Ecclesiastical Courts to compel persons to celebrate the marriage *in facie ecclesiae* if they had contracted a marriage *per verba de praesenti* or *futuro* followed by consummation.

Marriage Act 1823.—Whilst Lord Hardwicke's Act effectively put a stop to clandestine marriages in England, it caused an almost greater social evil. For the new law was so stringent and the consequence of failing to observe it—the avoidance of the marriage—so harsh, that many couples deliberately evaded it by getting married in Scotland. This was particularly the case when one of the parties was a minor and parental consent was withheld; so that the 70 years following the passing of the Act saw an increasing number of "Gretna Green" marriages. It was in an attempt to prevent this that the Legislature in 1823 repealed Lord Hardwicke's Act and replaced it by a new Marriage Act. So far as the positive directions of the earlier Act were concerned, *viz.* the necessity of the solemnization of the marriage in the church of the parish in which one of the parties resided after the publication of banns or the grant of a license, they were reenacted with only a few minor alterations of detail; where the new Act differed largely was in the effect of non-compliance with these directions. A marriage was now to be void only if both parties *knowingly and wilfully* intermarried in any other place than the church wherein the banns might be published, or without the due publication of banns or the obtaining of a license, or if they *knowingly and wilfully* consented to the solemnization of the marriage by a person not in holy orders. In all other cases the marriage was to be valid notwithstanding any breach in the prescribed formalities.

At one time nearly two-thirds of the states recognized common law marriages. American acceptance of common law marriage reflected the vast expanses of the American frontier, where there were few clergymen or state officials to perform marriage ceremonies. "[A] rigid execution of [the laws requiring ceremonial marriage]," courts opined, "would bastardize a vast majority of the children which have been born within the state for half a century." Rodebaugh v. Sanks, 2 Watts 9, 11 (Pa.1833). *See also* Walter Otto Weyrauch, *Metamorphoses of Marriage*, 13 Fam. L. Q. 415 (1980); Stuart Stein, *Common Law Marriage: Its History and Certain Contemporary Problems,* 9 J. Fam. L. 271 (1969).

By 1997 only a handful of states—Alabama, Colorado, Iowa, Kansas, Montana, Oklahoma, Pennsylvania, Rhode Island, South Carolina, Texas and Utah—and the District of Columbia continued to recognize common law marriage. (Georgia, Idaho, and Ohio abolished common law marriage during the 1990s). But because (absent a serious public policy concern) a marriage valid where contracted is valid everywhere, common law marriage has broader application.

When established, a common law marriage is legally no different than a formal, ceremonial marriage. But the fact of the marriage must *be* established by showing:

(1) intent to marry on the part of both parties;

(2) cohabitation; and

(3) "holding out" to the public by the parties that they are husband and wife.

The burden of proof is on the party asserting the marriage:

> [T]he courts do not look on . . . [common law] marriages with favor, and . . . where a common-law marriage is claimed, the courts will carefully scrutinize the evidence and require that the marriage be established by clear and convincing evidence. C.J.S. Marriage § 6, p. 818. If any of the essentials of a common-law marriage are lacking, the relationship is illicit and meretricious and is not a marriage. C.J.S. Marriage p. 819. There is no presumption that persons are married. Accordingly, the burden of proving a marriage rests on the party who asserts it, particularly where a common-law marriage is asserted; and an allegation that a party was not married does not thereby require a pleader to assume the burden of proof of non-marriage. C.J.S. Marriage § 43a, p. 887. A claim of common-law marriage is regarded with suspicion, and will be closely scrutinized. Thus, in order to establish a common-law marriage, all of the essential elements of such a relationship must be shown by clear, consistent and convincing evidence, especially must all of the essential elements of such a relationship be shown when one of the parties is dead; and such marriage must be proved by a preponderance. C.J.S. Marriage § 45b, pp. 911, 912.

In re Estate of Fisher, 176 N.W.2d 801, 804–805 (Iowa 1970).

ESTATE OF KEIMIG

Supreme Court of Kansas, 1974.
215 Kan. 869, 528 P.2d 1228.

HARMAN, COMMISSIONER.

This is an appeal from a judgment denying the claim of an alleged common law wife to her purported husband's estate.

The plaintiff-appellant, Ruth Ann Huss, was first married in 1920 to Joseph Cavanaugh. A daughter was born as a result of this marriage. In 1922 appellant secured a divorce from Mr. Cavanaugh.

In 1925 appellant was married in Kansas City, Kansas to Walter A. Keimig, the decedent whose estate she now claims. Eventually marital difficulties developed between appellant and Walter and they started living apart. Appellant filed suit for divorce in Atchison, Kansas, and obtained it March 21, 1935. That evening Walter went to appellant to discuss their situation. They decided to forgive and forget and go back together again. The couple spent the night together at plaintiff's father's home. The next day they returned to the same home in which they had resided prior to the separation and divorce.

After the reconciliation the couple held each other out as man and wife for the next nine years. During this time they resided in Shannon in Atchison County, Kansas, where Walter farmed extensively and conducted a farm equipment business. Appellant helped in this latter business and also carried out domestic tasks including cooking for the hired help and caring for Walter's father who lived with them. She signed her name as Mrs. Keimig; Walter introduced her as Mrs. Walter Keimig or "my wife;" she was known by Walter's employees as Mrs. Keimig; when appellant's daughter married in 1938, the nuptial announcements were made by "Mr. and Mrs. Walter Keimig."

In the spring of 1944 appellant made out a check to herself for $500.00, cashed it, left decedent and went to Plainville, Kansas. There she joined Albert Huss, a former farm employee of Walter. A short while thereafter she returned to Walter at Shannon for about a week, then departed again and went to Great Bend, Kansas, where she commenced living with Albert Huss. Appellant worked for a while in Great Bend using the name Cavanaugh. She lived with Mr. Huss in several western Kansas towns and eventually began using the name Huss. As time passed she and Mr. Huss acquired real estate in the names of Albert and Ruth Huss, husband and wife; their insurance was carried in the same way; appellant was listed in the census record as Ruth Huss; she received her driver's license and was assessed for personal property under that name; Huss named her as his wife in a deed conveying to her his interest in realty; she signed mortgages under the name of Ruth Huss. In 1954 appellant filed suit in Barton County, Kansas, for divorce from Albert Huss. Later she had this action dismissed on the ground she and Albert had reconciled their marital differences. Upon reaching the requisite ages Huss and appellant applied for and received social security benefits as husband and wife. Appellant lived continuously with Mr. Huss and on January 13, 1972—which was subsequent to Walter Keimig's death—they were formally married in a ceremony at Stillwater, Oklahoma.

Meanwhile, Walter Keimig dated other women. In 1962 he and defendant-appellee Goldie Keimig, then Goldie Sherrer, started living together at the Keimig home in Doniphan County. On July 20, 1967, Walter and appellee Goldie were married in a civil ceremony at Miami, Oklahoma. Walter told appellee he was divorced, single and free to marry. Prior to his marriage to Goldie, Walter executed documents conveying interests in realty in which he was described as an unmarried man. On March 26, 1970, Walter executed his last will which provided:

"I give, devise and bequeath all of my property, real, personal and mixed, and wheresoever situated unto my beloved wife, Goldie Keimig."

In a prior will executed in 1946 in which he referred to himself as unmarried, he had directed that all his property should go to his brother Philip Keimig.

On June 21, 1971, Walter died in Ray County, Missouri, where he and appellee were then living. On June 29, 1971, upon appellee's petition the probate court of Doniphan County, Kansas, admitted Walter's last will to probate and appointed her as his executrix. On December 29, 1971, appellant, using the name of Ruth Ann Keimig, petitioned the probate court for an order extending the statutory period of time for a surviving spouse to file an election. The probate court granted a thirty day extension.

On January 25, 1972, twelve days after her ceremonial marriage to Albert Huss, appellant filed an election to take under the law, alleging she was Walter's surviving spouse and sole heir at law. An evidentiary hearing was held upon this election. The probate court ruled against appellant on the ground she was not Walter's legal wife at the time of his death. Appellant appealed to the district court of Doniphan County where the matter was heard anew. That court likewise ruled against appellant. After making certain factual findings it held:

> "17. That Claimant has failed to show the establishment of a common law marriage with Walter A. Keimig subsequent to their divorce, in that Claimant did not show a marriage agreement in addition to an agreement to cohabit.
>
> 18. The Claimant has failed to overcome the presumption of the validity of a subsequent marriage of Walter A. Keimig and Goldie Sherrer."

Appellant's motion for new trial was denied and the present appeal ensued ... appellant's points on appeal as to the trial court's first finding are embraced in the assertion the trial court erred under all the evidence in failing to find appellant was the common law wife of Walter Keimig at the time of his death. She urges that Walter was rendered incapable of contracting marriage with appellee by reason of the fact appellant remained his legal spouse.

Kansas has long recognized the validity of common law marriage, the essential elements of which are: (1) A capacity of the parties to marry; (2) a present marriage agreement between the parties; and (3) a holding out of each other as husband and wife to the public. Common law marriages between persons previously divorced from each other have been considered judicially in other states. It is generally held, and we think correctly so, that the same tests and standards used in determining whether persons with no previous matrimonial history have entered into a common law marriage are to be applied in determining whether a common law remarriage exists between divorced spouses. This does not mean the fact of the previous marriage and divorce is to be removed from consideration or placed in a vacuum apart from other facts in the case.

The district court here specifically found appellant had failed to show the establishment of a common law marriage with Keimig in that she did not show a marriage agreement in addition to consent to cohabit. * * *

[I]n *In re Estate of Freeman*, 171 Kan. 211, 231 P.2d 261, we said:

> "In order to constitute a valid common law marriage there must also be a present marriage agreement rather than an agreement to be married in the future and a holding out of each other to the public as husband and wife." (p. 213)

However, the present marriage agreement need not be in any particular form.

We have already summarized the testimony respecting the resumption of cohabitation between appellant and Walter following their divorce and there is no question a holding out as man and wife was shown. The whole evidence concerning what occurred when Walter went to see appellant at her father's home on the evening the divorce was granted is disclosed by the testimony of appellant as follows:

"Q. All right, during the course of the evening in connection with your discussion about your marriage problems, tell us please what you said and he said as nearly as you recall about this divorce and about the marriage?

A. Well, we decided we never had no divorce, we just went back as we always had been when we first got married.

Q. And during the course of that evening did you have any discussion forgiving one another about what had gone on?

A. Yes.

Q. You say yes?

A. Yes.

Q. And what were those discussions, what did you say and what did he say as near as you recall about the things that had been, that bothered you before?

A. We were going to forget them and go back and live as we should have lived."

Although the evidence revealed a considerable period of living together as man and wife we cannot say the trial court was compelled or required by it or by all the evidence to find that appellant and Walter actually contemplated or entered into a new agreement to become husband and wife at the critical time in question. They did not say so and, aside from holding out, their subsequent conduct belied the fact. They may have considered remarriage in the future if and when that became mutually agreeable. Each definitely considered himself single for a period of time after their twice repeated separation and each became interested in new marital partners to the extent of a long time holding out by appellant as the wife of another, of whom she sought formal riddance by divorce, and of a ceremonial marriage by Walter. It appears it was only some time after Walter's death that appellant perceived herself as his widow. By coincidence she was in Atchison, Kansas, visiting her granddaughter at the time of Walter's death. She learned of his death then but did nothing about the funeral nor did she attend it. At that time she made no inquiry about Walter's estate and did nothing until after her daughter contacted her. Her testimony was she did not want Walter's not inconsiderable estate for herself—she wanted to give it to her daughter and to Walter's brother Philip, who appeared as a witness in support of her cause. Appellant's inconsistency in her marital positions was such as to render her entire testimony suspect. The most that can be said in her favor is that a factual issue was presented by reason of differing interpretations which could be placed upon all the evidence and the trial court after hearing it resolved any conflict by finding there was no present marriage agreement when appellant and Walter resumed cohabitation. We simply cannot say there was no substantial evidence in support thereof and the finding must be approved.

Having reached the foregoing conclusion it becomes unnecessary to consider whether the trial court correctly found that appellant had failed to overcome the presumption of the validity of Walter's subsequent marriage to appellee. The judgment is affirmed.

Notes and Questions

1. If Walter Keimig had died in 1942, would the Kansas court have found Ruth to be the common law wife for purposes of inheritance?

2. One source of hostility to common law marriage is the fact that common law marriage claims are most typically made when one "spouse" dies and the other claims a right to inherit or obtain some other form of death benefit, such as worker's compensation or Social Security survivor's benefits; the court's determination is thus retrospective rather than prospective. *See Keimig*; In re Estate of Dallman, 228 N.W.2d 187 (1975); Renshaw v. Heckler, 787 F.2d 50 (2d Cir.1986). (Of course, a "spouse" might also seek to establish a common law marriage in order to obtain divorce entitlements, such as alimony and marital property distribution, at separation.) What problems does retrospective marriage determination create?

3. Compare two recent "modern" common law marriage statutes:

UTAH CODE ANN. § 30–1–4.5

(1) A marriage which is not solemnized according to this chapter shall be legal and valid if a court or administrative order establishes that it arises out of a contract between two consenting parties who:

(a) are capable of giving consent;

(b) are legally capable of entering a solemnized marriage under the provisions of this chapter;

(c) have cohabited;

(d) mutually assume marital rights, duties, and obligations; and

(e) hold themselves out as and have acquired a uniform and general reputation as husband and wife.

(2) The determination or establishment of a marriage under this section must occur during the relationship described in Subsection (1), or within one year following the termination of that relationship. Evidence of a marriage recognizable under this section may be manifested in any form, and may be proved under the same general rules of evidence as facts in other cases.

Tex. Fam. Code § 2.402

Declaration and Registration

(a) A declaration of informal marriage shall be executed on a form prescribed by the Bureau of Vital Statistics of the State Department of Health and provided by the county clerk. Each party to the declaration shall provide the information required in the form.

(b) The declaration form shall contain:

(5) a printed declaration and oath reading: "I SOLEMNLY SWEAR (OR AFFIRM) THAT WE, THE UNDERSIGNED, ARE MARRIED TO EACH OTHER BY VIRTUE OF THE FOLLOWING FACTS: ON OR ABOUT (DATE) WE AGREED TO BE MARRIED, AND AFTER THAT DATE WE LIVED TOGETHER AS HUSBAND AND WIFE AND IN THIS STATE WE REPRESENTED TO OTHERS THAT WE WERE MARRIED. SINCE THE DATE OF MARRIAGE TO THE OTHER PARTY I HAVE NOT BEEN MARRIED TO ANY OTHER PERSON. THIS DECLARATION IS TRUE AND THE INFORMATION IN IT WHICH I HAVE GIVEN IS CORRECT";

What, if any, problems with common law marriage do these statutes attempt to cure? How successful are they?

4. Does acceptance of common law marriage require the creation of common law divorce? If yes, is the Utah statute a good way to deal with the problem?

KELDERHAUS v. KELDERHAUS

Virginia Court of Appeals, 1996.
21 Va.App. 721, 467 S.E.2d 303.

Bray, Judge.

These proceedings were initiated upon the bill of complaint of Lena Victoria Kelderhaus (wife) praying for a divorce from Bruce Lynn

Kelderhaus (husband) and attendant relief, including spousal support. In response, husband challenged the validity of the marriage. Following an *ore tenus* hearing, the trial court concluded that the parties were not married and dismissed wife's bill. On appeal, wife complains that the trial court erroneously declined to recognize her common-law marriage to husband or, in the alternative, award her relief as a "putative spouse." We disagree and affirm the judgment of the trial court.

Bruce and Lena Kelderhaus obtained a marriage license in California on December 21, 1992. When applying for the license, husband knowingly misrepresented that his marriage to another had been previously dissolved. Several days later, the parties ostensibly married in California, then traveled to Flagstaff, Arizona, residing together there as husband and wife. On July 26, 1993, an Arizona decree divorced husband from his former wife and, on August 1, 1993, husband and wife participated in a second marriage "ceremony." The parties thereafter continued to reside together and represented themselves as husband and wife in Arizona until early August, 1993, when they relocated to Virginia. In driving from Arizona to Virginia, the parties "travers[ed] the country" as "husband and wife," stopping "overnight" in Texas and Oklahoma.

THE MARRIAGE

"A marriage's validity is to be determined by the law of the state where the marriage took place, unless the result would be repugnant to Virginia public policy."

"A marriage entered into prior to the dissolution of an earlier marriage of one of the parties is [bigamous, and consequently,] a void marriage in ... Virginia." Bigamous marriages "confer [ ] no legal rights" and are "contrary to the laws of Virginia and [its] public policy." Id. at 190, 372 S.E.2d at 411. Thus, when the parties purportedly married in California, the union was bigamous and void as a matter of law.[1] *See* Code § 20–43.

Wife, however, argues that this impediment to husband's remarriage was removed by the subsequent Arizona divorce decree, and, therefore, the ensuing relationship as husband and wife during their passage through Texas and Oklahoma, states which recognize common-law marriages, resulted in marriage. Although Virginia does not recognize domestic common-law marriages, it does extend comity to such unions "valid under the laws of the jurisdiction where the common-law relationship was created."

TEXAS

By statute, Texas provides that " ... the marriage of a man and woman may be proved by evidence that ... they agreed to be married,

1. We note that the marriage entered into by the parties in California would also be considered void ab initio under California law. See CAL. FAM. CODE § 2201 (West 1995) ("A subsequent marriage contracted by a person during the life of a former husband or wife of the person, with a person other than the former husband or wife, is illegal and void from the beginning.").

and after the agreement they lived together in this state as husband and wife and there represented to others that they were married." TEX. FAM. CODE ANN. § 1.91(a)(2) (West 1996). The parties must represent to others while in the state of Texas that they are husband and wife. Residing together as husband and wife in another state does not satisfy the Texas statute. "Strict compliance with these requirements is a necessity, and each one must be established by sufficient proof before [Texas] courts will lend judicial sanction to any assertion ... that ... a [marital] relationship exists." *Middlebrook v. Wideman*, 203 S.W.2d 686, 688 (Tex.Civ.App.1947).

Here, the record does not support the requisite finding that the parties "lived together ... as husband and wife" in Texas and "there represented to others that they were married." *See* TEX. FAM. CODE ANN. § 1.91(a)(92) (emphasis added). The limited testimony that they migrated through Texas as "husband and wife" establishes only a brief, transitory contact with the state which clearly does not constitute "strict compliance" with the statutory requirements. Hence, wife's claim to a valid common-law Texas marriage is without merit.

OKLAHOMA

A party asserting common-law marriage in Oklahoma must prove: (1) an actual and mutual agreement between spouses to be husband and wife, (2) a permanent relationship, (3) an exclusive relationship, accompanied by cohabitation as man and wife, and (4) a mutual representation to the public as husband and wife, all by clear and convincing evidence. Although Oklahoma courts have not determined that the requisite mutual representation must occur within the state, several jurisdictions have addressed the issue relative to other common-law jurisdictions, and we are persuaded by their conclusion that this element must be satisfied within the common-law state. *See Kennedy v. Damron*, 268 S.W.2d 22 (Ky.Ct.App.1954); *Laikola v. Engineered Concrete*, 277 N.W.2d 653 (Minn.1979); *Andrews v. Signal Auto Parts, Inc.*, 492 S.W.2d 222 (Tenn. 1972).

In *Kennedy*, the Kentucky court declined to recognize mere visits to Ohio, a common-law state, by persons as sufficient to support a common-law marriage in that jurisdiction. 268 S.W.2d at 24. The court found "[i]t ... obvious that if ... conduct and reputation of ... parties as man and wife are to be accepted as evidence of a contract of marriage entered into in a state which recognizes common-law marriages, the conduct must be carried on and the reputation acquired ... [as] established members of a community." Id. at 23–24. Citing *Kennedy* with approval, the Supreme Court of Minnesota reached a similar conclusion in reviewing a Montana relationship, noting that "[t]he general ... rule ... is that the ... holding out as husband and wife must be of sufficient duration in the common-law state to create a public reputation of husband and wife." *Laikola*, 277 N.W.2d at 658.

Here, the record reveals only minimal contact with Oklahoma and no evidence of specific conduct or representations by the parties, as husband and wife, in that jurisdiction. To sanction marriage arising from such an insignificant nexus with the common-law state would at once distort and trivialize the concept of common-law marriage and ignore the principles which govern such unions in Oklahoma. We, therefore, find the evidence insufficient to prove a common-law marriage in Oklahoma.

PUTATIVE SPOUSE

Lastly, wife claims that the trial court, after finding her marriage to husband either "void or voidable," should have awarded putative spousal support in accordance with California law. *See* CAL. FAM. CODE §§ 2251, 2254 (West 1995). Assuming, without deciding, that these provisions are relevant to the instant proceeding, relief as a putative spouse requires that he or she "believed in good faith that the marriage was valid." Id. at § 2251. Here, husband testified that wife was aware that he remained married to another at the time of the void California nuptials. Consequently, wife could not have entertained the requisite good faith belief that the California marriage was valid and, therefore, was not a putative spouse within the intendment of the California statute.

Accordingly, we find that the trial court correctly concluded that the parties were not married to one another and affirm the decree dismissing the bill of complaint.

Affirmed.

Notes and Questions

1. What is the purpose of the holding out requirement? Why are courts reluctant to accept secret common law marriages? How much holding out is required? Over how long a period must the holding out occur? Is signing a hotel register enough? *See* Winfield v. Renfro, 821 S.W.2d 640 (Tex.App.1991) (no). Should there be a minimum "holding out period"? *See* Boswell v. Boswell, 497 So.2d 479 (Ala.1986). If yes, what should it be?

2. Where couples have lived in several different states, the question may arise as to whether or not a common law marriage was contracted in one of them. *See* Jennings v. Hurt, 160 A.D.2d 576, 554 N.Y.S.2d 220 (1990) (finding that actor William Hurt and Sandra Jennings did not establish a common law marriage while in South Carolina filming "The Big Chill.") When should a court apply the law of a state other than the parties' domicile to determine their marital status? Should the issue be whether the visit was of substantial duration?

3. A common law marriage requires capacity to marry. If, as in *Keimig*, one spouse is married when cohabitation begins, when must the present agreement to marry be formed? For another case involving impediments to the marriage and three states, *see* Orr v. Bowen, 648 F.Supp. 1510 (D.Nev.1986).

B. THE PUTATIVE SPOUSE DOCTRINE

The putative spouse doctrine derives from the civil law and was first found in former French or Spanish colonies, including California, Louisiana, and Texas. The doctrine was recognized in the Uniform Marriage and Divorce Act, however, and has spread to a number of common law states.

UNIFORM MARRIAGE AND DIVORCE ACT § 209

9A U.L.A. 174 (1987).

Any person who has cohabited with another to whom he is not legally married in the good faith belief that he was married to that person is a putative spouse until knowledge of the fact that he is not legally married terminates his status and prevents acquisition of further rights. A putative spouse acquires the rights conferred upon a legal spouse, including the right to maintenance following termination of his status, whether or not the marriage is prohibited (§ 207 [p. 88]) or declared invalid (§ 208 [p. 77]). If there is a legal spouse or other putative spouses, rights acquired by a putative spouse do not supersede the rights of the legal spouse or those acquired by other putative spouses, but the court shall apportion property, maintenance, and support rights among the claimants as appropriate in the circumstances and in the interests of justice.

IN RE ESTATE OF VARGAS

California Court of Appeals, 1974.
36 Cal.App.3d 714, 111 Cal.Rptr. 779.

FLEMING, ASSOCIATE JUSTICE.

For 24 years Juan Vargas lived a double life as husband and father to two separate families, neither of which knew of the other's existence. This terrestrial paradise came to an end in 1969 when Juan died intestate in an automobile accident. In subsequent heirship proceedings the probate court divided his estate equally between the two wives. Juan's first wife Mildred appeals, contending that the evidence did not establish Juan's second wife Josephine as a putative spouse, and that even if Josephine were considered a putative spouse an equal division of the estate was erroneous.

Mildred presented evidence that she and Juan married in 1929, raised three children, and lived together continuously in Los Angeles until Juan's death in 1969. From 1945 until his death Juan never spent more than a week or 10 days away from home. They acquired no substantial assets until after 1945.

Josephine countered with evidence that she met Juan in 1942 while employed in his exporting business. They married in Las Vegas in February 1945 and went through a second marriage ceremony in Santa Ana in May 1945. Josephine knew Juan had been previously married, but Juan assured her he had acquired a divorce. In July 1945 they moved into a home in West Los Angeles and there raised a family of four children. After 1949 Juan no longer spent his nights at home, explaining to Josephine that he spent the nights in Long Beach in order to be close to his business, but he and Josephine continued to engage in sexual relations until his death in 1969. He visited Josephine and their children every weekday for dinner, spent time with them weekends, supported the family, and exercised control over its affairs as husband and father. Throughout the years Josephine continued to perform secretarial work for Juan's business at home without pay.

The foregoing evidence amply supports the court's finding that Josephine was a putative spouse. An innocent participant who has duly solemnized a matrimonial union which is void because of some legal infirmity acquires the status of putative spouse. Although Josephine's marriage was void because Juan was still married to Mildred, Josephine, according to her testimony, married Juan in the good-faith belief he was divorced from his first wife. Her testimony was not inherently improbable; her credibility was a question for determination by the trial court; and court appearance of her testimony established her status as a putative spouse.

The more difficult question involves the equal division of Juan's estate between Mildred and Josephine.

California courts have relied on at least two legal theories to justify the award of an interest in a decedent's estate to a putative spouse. The theory of "quasi-marital property" equates property rights acquired during a putative marriage with community property rights acquired during a legal marriage. Subsequent to the time of Juan's death this theory was codified in Civil Code § 4452.

A second legal theory treats the putative marriage as a partnership: "In effect, the innocent putative spouse was in partnership or a joint enterprise with her spouse, contributing her services—and in this case, her earnings—to the common enterprise. Thus, their accumulated property was held in effect in tenancy-in-common in equal shares. Upon death of the husband, only his half interest is considered as community property, to which the rights of the lawful spouse attach."

In practice, these sometimes-conflicting theories have proved no more than convenient explanations to justify reasonable results, for when the theories do not fit the facts, courts have customarily resorted to general principles of equity to effect a just disposition of property rights. For example, in *Brown v. Brown*, 274 Cal. App. 2d 178, 82 Cal. Rptr. 238, the court found that a legal wife's acquiescence in a putative wife's 28–year marriage equitably estopped the legal wife from claiming any interest in the community property.

The present case is complicated by the fact that the laws regulating succession and the disposition of marital property are not designed to cope with the extraordinary circumstance of purposeful bigamy at the expense of two innocent parties. The laws of marital succession assume compliance with basic law and do not provide for contingencies arising during the course of felonious activity. For this reason resort to equitable principles becomes particularly appropriate here . . . Equity acts "in order to meet the requirements of every case, and to satisfy the needs of a progressive social condition, in which the primary rights and duties are constantly arising, and new kinds of wrongs are constantly committed." Equity need not wait upon precedent "but will assert itself in those situations where right and justice would be defeated but for its intervention." . . . For example, in *Estate of Krone*, where the putative husband died intestate and there was no legal wife, the court awarded the entire quasi-marital estate to the putative wife, even though the putative wife had no legal claim to the husband's share of the quasi-marital estate.

In the present case, depending on which statute or legal theory is applied, both Mildred, as legal spouse, and Josephine, as putative spouse, have valid or plausible claims to at least half, perhaps three-quarters, possibly all, of Juan's estate. The court found that both wives contributed in indeterminable amounts and proportions to the accumulations of the community. Since statutes and judicial decisions provide no sure guidance for the resolution of the controversy, the probate court cut the Gordian knot of competing claims and divided the estate equally between the two wives, presumably on the theory that innocent wives of practicing bigamists are entitled to equal shares of property accumulated during the active phase of the bigamy. No injury has been visited upon third parties, and the wisdom of Solomon is not required to perceive the justice of the result. The judgment is affirmed.

Notes and Questions

1. Would either of the plaintiffs in *Keimig* and *Kelderhaus* be putative spouses? Are common law marriage and the putative spouse doctrine mutually exclusive categories, or can the concepts operate together, i.e., might a bona fide, but false, belief in the existence of a common law marriage make the "believer" a putative spouse? *See* Garduno v. Garduno, 760 S.W.2d 735 (Tex.App.1988).

2. What would have happened if Josephine had died before Juan? Could he have been a putative spouse? Did he have a "reasonable" belief in the validity of the marriage? *See* Vryonis v. Vryonis, 202 Cal.App.3d 712, 248 Cal.Rptr. 807 (1988) (holding that a woman who claimed to have believed herself married, based on participation in a private, at-home religious ceremony without any officiating church official, was not a putative spouse).

Chapter 3

THE LEGAL SIGNIFICANCE OF MARRIAGE—RIGHTS AND OBLIGATIONS, LOST AND GAINED

SECTION 1. MARITAL IDEALS: FROM PATRIARCHY TO EQUALITY

BEATRICE GOTTLIEB, THE FAMILY IN THE WESTERN WORLD: FROM THE BLACK DEATH TO THE INDUSTRIAL AGE

90–92 (Oxford University Press, 1993).

While it is probably no surprise that [marital] inequality was rife in earlier centuries, it is important to recognize that what we see as a blemish was for a long time considered to be positive.... Husband and wife each had an "authentic place." ...

The main elements of the theory appear in Paul's Epistle to the Ephesians, where they are treated as long-established ideas:

> Wives, submit yourselves unto your own husbands ... for the husband is the head of the wife, even as Christ is the head of the church.... Let the wives be to their own husbands in everything. Husbands, love your wives, even as Christ also loved the church.... So ought men to love their wives as their own bodies. He that loveth his wife loveth himself ... For this cause shall a man leave his father and mother, and shall be joined unto his wife, and they two shall be one flesh.... Let every one of you in particular so love his wife even as himself, and the wife see that she reverence her husband. (5:22–23)

This idea of a loving despotism was buttressed by the idea of the natural inferiority of women, an idea whose antiquity argued for its truth. It was stated clearly in Aristotle and obliquely but unmistakably in the Old Testament. Worshipers in Anglican churches were regularly reminded that the woman is "the weaker vessel, of a frail heart." Frailty justified control, but a control that should not be too harsh. "Although she is inferior," said a handbook for French confessors in the sixteenth century, "yet she is not a slave or a servant but the companion and flesh of the flesh of her husband." . . .

The legal systems of the Western world supported the theory. When a woman married, her identity was swallowed up in her husband's. As William Blackstone pithily put it in the eighteenth century, summing up the thrust of English common law, "The husband and wife are one, and the husband is that one." What this meant was that, with a few exceptions, a wife could not bring a legal action in a court, make a contract, or own property. If she technically had title to property, it was controlled by her husband. The commonest way of looking at the property of a married couple saw it as a community of pooled resources, to which the wife sometimes made a major contribution in the form of her dowry. As long as the marriage lasted she had next to no say in how it was managed or spent. . . .

The law assumed, furthermore, that the husband as the ruler of the household had the right to use discipline to enforce his rule. In this respect, wives were subjects of the same loving despotism as servants and children. There were laws all over Europe giving men the right to beat their wives. The appalling behavior of Petruchio in The Taming of the Shrew was at the very least legal, and it was apparently expected of those who wived it wealthily as well as those who wived it poorly, although this seemed to be changing in the eighteenth century. Abuse and cruelty were always frowned on, but a man was expected to do what he had to in order to be obeyed. . . .

The materials in this chapter deal with the modern law of marriage, which is premised on an egalitarian, rather than patriarchal, view of the spousal relationship. While the ideal of the common law was benevolent despotism by the family patriarch, the new ideal posits marriage as a partnership of equals.

The shift in marital ideals from patriarchy to equality has been gradual and uneven. In the United States, one of the first legal reforms marking the shift was the Married Women's Property Acts. State legislatures began enacting these laws in the 1850s and, by the end of the nineteenth century, every state had one in its statute books. The Acts removed many of the disabilities imposed on married women by the common law. In general, they restored to the married woman the rights she had had when unmarried, including the right to acquire, own, or transfer property, to make a will and enter contracts, to engage in business or be employed, to keep her own earnings, to sue and be sued, and to testify in civil and criminal trials (except when the spousal privilege was applicable).

The Acts did not succeed in conferring full legal capacity on married women without a lengthy struggle, however:

> "The general and sometimes inappropriate language which they contained was often used by the courts as an excuse for restrictive interpretation. Part of this judicial conservatism reflected a desire to protect the married woman and to preserve family institutions, but it nonetheless ran counter to the clear spirit and purpose of the statutes. The legislatures were thereby led, over a long period, to pass specific provisions correcting the courts' mistakes. The outcome ... was that most of the married women's disabilities were ultimately removed."

HOMER H. CLARK, JR., THE LAW OF DOMESTIC RELATIONS IN THE UNITED STATES 289–90 (2d ed. 1987).

The Acts' primary focus was on the married woman's legal relationships with persons outside the family. Thus they did not abolish spousal immunity, which prevented one spouse from maintaining a tort action against another, or a range of other legal principles that fostered continued male dominance within the family. It was not long ago that many state family law codes contained provisions like this one:

> N.D. CENT. CODE § 14–07–02: Head of Family—The husband is the head of the family. He may choose any reasonable place or mode of living and the wife must conform thereto. Repealed, March 3, 1979, Ch. 195, N.D. Sess. Laws, p. 426.

The second wave of reform, focusing on the marital relationship itself, did not really take off until the 1960s. Like the earlier reform movement, the progress of this one has been fitful and uneven. Writing in 1968, the author of a leading family law treatise reported that only seventeen states had abolished spousal immunity, and that while "one might suppose that other states would join the chorus and discard the immunity, this does not seem to be happening." HOMER H. CLARK, THE LAW OF DOMESTIC RELATIONS 254 (1st ed. 1968).

While the recent reforms have undeniably produced greater equality in the legal status of husband and wife, for many married couples the new egalitarianism represents an aspirational ideal more than a lived reality. Researchers continue to report that the typical American husband has more power within marriage than does his wife. Husbands are more likely to dominate spending decisions; they are less likely, even when the wife works full-time outside the home, to perform house work or child care. *See, e.g.*, PHILIP BLUMSTEIN & PEPPER SCHWARTZ, AMERICAN COUPLES 53–59, 62–64; 144–46 (1983); ARLIE HOCHSCHILD, THE SECOND SHIFT 216–20; 259–62 (1989); FRANCES K. GOLDSCHEIDER & LINDA J. WAITE, NEW FAMILIES, NO FAMILIES? (1991); JAN PAHL, MONEY AND MARRIAGE (1989); Carole B. Burgoyne & Alan Lewis, *Distributive Justice in Marriage: Equality or Equity?*, 4 J. COMM. & APP. SOC. PSYCH. 101 (1994). Wife beating is also still with us. Thirty percent of women murdered in the United States are killed by their male partners.

One reason for the continuance of inequality in marital relationships is inequality in men's and women's earnings. On average, women still earn less than men; the evidence suggests that the power of husband and wife is strongly influenced by their monetary contributions to the household. A pioneering study of American couples reported that, three-quarters of the time, it was money that established the balance of power in a relationship. Among both married couples and heterosexual cohabitants, women gained power when they earned more. BLUMSTEIN & SCHWARTZ, at 53–54, 309. Spousal power was also significantly affected by the extent to which husband and wife expressed belief in the "male provider" philosophy, with a husband's power enhanced both when he strongly adhered to such a view, and when his wife did.

Given the continued appeal of the male provider norm and widespread variation in spousal earnings and household contributions, it is unsurprising that many marriages fail to conform to the new egalitarian ideal. Nor is it entirely clear just what the new ideal means. One vision of egalitarianism emphasizes marital community; another emphasizes the individual autonomy of husband and wife. Changes in the law over the past few decades evidence the pull of both visions and demonstrate no consistent preference or ordering principle. The expansion of spousal inheritance rights, for example, emphasizes community: absent a premarital agreement, spouses must share whether they individually like it or not. Other reforms—like the repeal of spousal immunity and the "Head of Family" statute reprinted above—emphasize individual autonomy: spouses individually may determine whether to sue and where to live, whether the other likes it or not. The slogans "partnership" and "equality" do not tell us which of these visions should be preferred, or what balance between autonomy and community is best.

The choice between autonomy and community is complicated by the continuing inequality of men and women both within the family and without. For example, the autonomy-focused Married Women's Property Acts did very little to improve the position of married women without property or earnings. If the husband worked outside the home and the wife did not, the husband retained control of all property (except what the wife acquired by gift or inheritance) during the marriage. But other reforms emphasizing individual autonomy—the abolition of spousal immunity, for example—have undeniably enhanced the power of married women.

The choice is also complicated by the fact that the passing of the doctrine of marital unity has not substantially altered the long-standing view of the family as an entity with a legal identity apart from those of its individual members. Because of its "deep root[s] in this Nation's history and tradition," because "[i]t is through the family that we inculcate and pass down many of our most cherished values, moral and cultural," the Supreme Court has held that "the Constitution protects the sanctity of the *family* . . ." Moore v. City of East Cleveland, [p. 10 (emphasis added)]. But an emphasis on the individual rights of family members necessarily undermines the importance of the family as a transcending entity. Some commentators thus worry that the recent wave of reforms "has contributed to a climate in which individuals are permitted, and even encouraged, to pursue narrow self-interest at great cost to other family members and to the family itself.... By maintaining a stance of moral neutrality toward the choices that people make about intimate associations, the law undermines the shared values that define the family. In this environment, family relationships are weakened, and the long-term viability of the family itself is threatened."

Elizabeth Scott, *Rehabilitating Liberalism in Modern Divorce Law*, 1994 UTAH L. REV. 687, 710 (summarizing views of various commentators).

As you read the materials in this chapter, try to chart which rules enhance marital community and which individual autonomy. Ask yourself whether, and how, we can attain an egalitarian marital ideal in the face of spousal inequality both in the marketplace and in unpaid service to the household. And ask yourself how the claims of individual husbands and wives should be balanced against "the shared values that define the family."

SECTION 2. OWNERSHIP AND CONTROL OF PROPERTY DURING MARRIAGE

A. COMMON LAW STATES

After the adoption of the Married Women's Property Acts, in "common law" states each spouse managed all property he or she owned. The net result of the common law and Married Women's Property Acts is a regime of individual ownership and management of property acquired during marriage.

indiv. ownership of prop. @ C.L.

LAW COMMISSION (LONDON)

Published Working Paper No. 42, Family Property Law.
(1971) p. 5 et seq.

.... It is said that equality of power, which separation of property achieves, does not of itself lead to equal opportunity to exercise that power; it ignores the fact that a married woman, especially if she has young children, does not in practice have the same opportunity as her husband or as an unmarried woman to acquire property; it takes no account of the fact that marriage is a form of partnership to which both spouses contribute, each in a different way, and that the contribution of each is equally important to the family welfare and to society. * * *

0.15 Criticisms of the present law are not limited to its unfairness. It is complained that the law is uncertain. This has been graphically illustrated by reference to the Jones family: Mr. and Mrs. Jones have been married for ten years and have three children. When they married they bought a house on mortgage. The deposit was paid partly from Mrs. Jones' savings and partly from a loan from Mr. Jones' employer. The mortgage installments have usually been paid by Mr. Jones. At the beginning Mrs. Jones had a job; she went back to part-time work when the children were older. From her wages she paid a large part of the household expenses and bought some of the furniture. Occasionally she paid the mortgage instalments. A car and a washing machine were bought on hire-purchase in Mr. Jones' name, but the instalments were sometimes paid by him and sometimes by her. . . .

0.16 If, in the above situation, Mrs. Jones asks what her property rights are . . . she will receive no clear answer. . . . It is said that this is unsatisfactory, and that the law should give "a clear and definite ruling as to what belongs to whom."

* * *

Legal doctrines which muddy the answer to ownership of the Joneses' property include presumptions of gift, "resulting trust," and "constructive trust." For example,

> If a husband buys property out of his earnings and takes the title in the joint names of himself and his wife, he is presumed in law to have intended to make a gift to her of one-half of the value of the property. Similarly, if he buys property in her name, the law presumes that he has made a gift of the entire property to her. This is called the "presumption of advancement" and applies only in one direction: if a wife buys property from her earnings and takes the title in joint names or in her husband's name alone, the presumption is that she retains the full interest, and that he holds the property, or a share in it, as a trustee for her. This is the presumption of "resulting trust." Both presumptions can be rebutted by evidence showing that the intention of the purchaser was different from what is presumed, but in the absence of such evidence wives take property purchased by their husbands under these conditions as gifts, while they retain the full beneficial interest in property that they have purchased and placed in their husband's names.

LAW REFORM COMMISSION OF CANADA, WORKING PAPER NO. 8, FAMILY PROPERTY 10 (MARCH 1975).

Another doctrine that might apply to the Joneses' case is that of "constructive trust." Constructive trust is a flexible remedy imposed in a variety of situations to prevent unjust enrichment. In order to establish a constructive trust, the plaintiff typically must show: 1) a confidential relationship; 2) a promise, express or implied; 3) a transfer of property made in reliance on such promise; and 4) unjust enrichment. Sometimes courts interpret these requirements loosely, imposing a constructive trust simply to prevent unjust enrichment. *See* 5 AUSTIN W. SCOTT, TRUSTS §§ 461–552 (William F. Fratcher ed., 4th ed. 1987).

Finally, while the facts do not specify, some of the Joneses' assets may be held in a tenancy by the entireties or a joint tenancy with right of survivorship. Surveys suggest that the marital home, often the couple's most valuable asset, is typically held jointly. One divorce survey, for example, found that approximately 89% of couples who owned their own home held title jointly. Marsha Garrison, *Good Intentions Gone Awry: The Impact of New York's Equitable Distribution Law on Divorce Outcomes*, 57 Brooklyn L. Rev. 621, 655 (1991).

The tenancy by the entireties was, under the common law, the primary exception to the principle of individual spousal control. Such a tenancy was created when husband and wife took the subject property by name, by the same conveyance, to take effect at the same time. When property was so held, neither spouse could independently convey, encumber, or use the property to the exclusion of the other; the tenancy thus could not be severed as could a joint tenancy with right of survivorship. On the death of one spouse, title vested automatically in the survivor. At common law, property held in a tenancy by the entireties was subject to the husband's management. Some states have abolished this feature of the tenancy (*see, e.g.*, Robinson v. Trousdale County, 516 S.W.2d 626 (Tenn.1974)); the majority of states have abolished the tenancy by the entireties itself. While the tenancy by the entireties is now available in only twenty or so states, joint tenancy with right of survivorship is universally recognized. Joint tenancy establishes equal rights to the subject property; when one dies, the other automatically succeeds to his or her interest.

B. COMMUNITY PROPERTY STATES

1. *In General*

Nine states—Arizona, California, Idaho, Louisiana, New Mexico, Nevada, Texas, Washington, and Wisconsin—have adopted a community property system. Wisconsin's community property system is the most recent, deriving from its adoption of the Uniform Marital Property Act during the 1980s.

The community property concept is part of the civil law tradition of the European continent, and was first enacted in states which were former French or Spanish colonies. Community property reverses the individual ownership principle of the common law and treats earnings during marriage as owned equally by both husband and wife.

Although different types of community property systems have evolved, including "universal" community property, where all property owned by either spouse is treated as community property regardless of when or how the property was acquired, American systems all restrict application of the community property principle to a "community of acquests." Under this approach, only those accumulations that are viewed as acquisitions of the marital partnership are considered community property.

Community property states agree that accumulations by one spouse before marriage should not be included. This "separate" property is owned and managed by the spouse who brought it into the marriage. So, under American community property systems, a couple may hold three types of property: the wife's separate property (owned solely by her), the husband's separate property (owned solely by him), and community property (owned equally by each).

The various community property states do not agree, however, on how broadly the community of acquests should extend:

TEX. FAM. CODE

§ 3.001. A spouse's separate property consists of:

1) the property owned or claimed by the spouse before marriage;

2) the property acquired by the spouse during marriage by gift, devise, or descent; and

3) the recovery for personal injuries sustained by the spouse during the marriage, except any recovery for loss of earning capacity during marriage.

§ 3.002. Community property consists of the property other than separate property, acquired by either spouse during marriage.

ARIZ. REV. STAT.

§ 25–211. All property acquired by either husband or wife during the marriage, except that which is acquired by gift, devise or descent, is the community property of the husband and wife.

§ 25–213. All property real and personal, of each spouse, owned by such spouse before marriage, and that acquired afterward by gift, devise, or descent, and also the increase, rents, issues, and profits thereof, is the separate property of each spouse.

UNIFORM MARITAL PROPERTY ACT

9A U.L.A. 109 (1987).

§ 4. Classification of Property of Spouses

(a) All property of spouses is marital property except that which is classified otherwise by this [Act].

(b) All property of spouses is presumed to be marital property.

(c) Each spouse has a present undivided one-half interest in marital property.

(d) Income earned or accrued by a spouse or attributable to property of a spouse during marriage and after the determination date is marital property.

(e) Marital property transferred to a trust remains marital property.

(f) Property owned by a spouse at a marriage after the determination date is individual property.

(g) Property acquired by a spouse during marriage and after the determination date is individual property if acquired:

(1) by gift or a disposition at death made by a third person to the spouse and not to both spouses;

(2) in exchange for or with the proceeds of other individual property of the spouse;

(3) from appreciation of the spouse's individual property except to the extent that the appreciation is classified as marital property under § 14;

(4) by a decree, marital property agreement, written consent, or reclassification under § 7(b) designating it as the individual property of the spouse;

(5) as a recovery for damage to property under § 15, except as specifically provided otherwise in a decree, marital property agreement, or written consent; or

(6) as a recovery for personal injury except for the amount of that recovery attributable to expenses paid or otherwise satisfied from marital property.

Notes and Questions

1. What important differences do you see between a typical common law state's rules and those of (i) Texas; (ii) Arizona; (iii) the UMPA?

2. About what types of property are Texas, Arizona, and the UMPA in agreement? Disagreement? What are the sources of disagreement?

3. In an ideal marital property system, should we treat income from and appreciation of separate property the same way or differently? Should both be community property? Separate property? Or should we distinguish between the two?

a) The "dim" line of distinction between appreciation of and income from separate property is between gain that is "intrinsic" to the property and gain that is "detached." *See* UMPA §§ 4(d) & (4)(g)(3). *See also* Thomas Andrews, *Income from Separate Property: Toward a Theoretical Foundation*, 56 LAW & CONTEMP. PROB. 171 (1993).

b) On the question whether appreciation of separate property is to become marital property, should (or must) a distinction be made between a price increase that is due solely to inflation, a value increase, and appreciation that is due to successful speculation or spousal efforts during marriage? If yes, how would you determine the source(s) of the appreciation?

Problem 3–1:

In 1990, Bernie inherited a stock portfolio worth $75,000 and real estate worth $500,000. The real estate was an apartment building with sixteen rental units; the net monthly profits from the building were $6,000. In 1991, Bernie married Susan. Shortly after the marriage, Bernie began to use the rents to make improvements to the building. All work was performed by a local contractor, although Bernie decided what should be done. As a result of the improvements, the building is now worth $1,000,000 and produces net monthly profits of $12,000. Although Bernie has neither bought nor sold any of the securities in his stock portfolio, it, too, has increased in value to $250,000. What, if any, part of the value of Bernie's stock and real estate are community property in Arizona? Texas? a UMPA state?

2. *Management of Community Property*

Under traditional community property rules both spouses were equal owners in theory, but the husband was legally entitled to manage community assets. The Louisiana management statute, for example, provided that "[t]he husband is the head and master of the partnership or community of gains; he administers its effects, disposes of the revenues which they produce, and may alienate them by an onerous title, without the consent and permission of his wife." LA. CIV. CODE ANN. Art. 2404 (repealed). These rules were already on the way out when, in Kirchberg v. Feenstra, 450 U.S. 455, 101 S.Ct. 1195, 67 L.Ed.2d 428 (1981), the Supreme Court held that the Louisiana statute impermissibly discriminated on the basis of gender.

Today, all community property states have moved away from male management in favor of one or another combination of sole management, joint management, and equal management:

TEX. FAM. CODE

§ 3.101. Each spouse has the sole management, control, and disposition of his or her separate property.

§ 3.102. (a) During marriage, each spouse has the sole management, control, and disposition of the community property that he or she would have owned if single, including but not limited to:

(1) personal earnings;

(2) revenue from separate property;

(3) recoveries for personal injuries; and

(4) the increase and mutations of, and the revenue from, all property subject to his or her sole management, control, and disposition.

(b) If the community property subject to the sole management, control, and disposition of one spouse is mixed or combined with community property subject to the sole management, control, and disposition of the other spouse, then the mixed or combined community property is subject to the joint management, control, and disposition of the spouses, unless the spouses provide otherwise by power of attorney in writing or other agreement.

(c) Except as provided in Subsection (a) of this section, the community property is subject to the joint management, control, and disposition of the husband and wife, unless the spouses provide otherwise by power of attorney in writing or other agreement.

Ariz. Rev. Stat. § 25–214.

A. Each spouse has the sole management, control and disposition rights of his or her separate property.

B. The spouses have equal management, control and disposition rights over their community property, and have equal power to bind the community.

C. Either spouse separately may acquire, manage, control or dispose of community property, or bind the community, except that joinder of both spouses is required in any of the following cases:

1. Any transaction for the acquisition, disposition or encumbrance of an interest in real property other than an unpatented mining claim or a lease of less than one year.
2. Any transaction of guaranty, indemnity or suretyship.

Cal. Fam. Code § 1100—Fiduciary Duty in Management and Control of Community Personal Property

(a) Except as provided in subdivisions (b), (c), and (d) . . . either spouse has the management and control of the community personal property . . . with like absolute power of disposition, other than testamentary, as the spouse has of the separate estate of the spouse.

(b) A spouse may not make a gift of community personal property, or dispose of community personal property for less than fair and reasonable value, without the written consent of the other spouse. This subdivision does not apply to gifts mutually given by both spouses to third parties and to gifts given by one spouse to the other spouse.

(c) A spouse may not sell, convey, or encumber community personal property used as the family dwelling, or the furniture, furnishings, or fittings of the home, or the clothing or wearing apparel of the other spouse or minor children which is community personal property, without the written consent of the other spouse.

(d) Except as provided in subdivisions (b) and (c), and in § 1102, a spouse who is operating or managing a business or an interest in a business that is all or substantially all community personal property has the primary management and control of the business or interest. Primary management and control means that the managing spouse may act alone in all transactions but shall give prior written notice to the other spouse of any sale, lease, exchange, encumbrance, or other disposition of all or substantially all of the personal property used in the operation of the business (including personal property used for agricultural purposes), whether or not title to that property is held in the name of only one spouse. Written notice is not, however, required when prohibited by the law otherwise applicable to the transaction. Remedies for the failure by a managing spouse to give prior written notice as required by this subdivision are only as specified in § 1101. A failure to give prior written notice shall not adversely affect the validity of a transaction nor of any interest transferred.

(e) Each spouse shall act with respect to the other spouse in the management and control of the community assets and liabilities in accordance with the general rules governing fiduciary relationships which control the actions of persons having relationships of personal confidence.... , until such time as the assets and liabilities have been divided by the parties or by a court. This duty includes the obligation to make full disclosure to the other spouse of all material facts and information regarding the existence, characterization, and valuation of all assets in which the community has or may have an interest and debts for which the community is or may be liable, and to provide equal access to all information, records, and books that pertain to the value and character of those assets and debts, upon request.

CAL. FAM. CODE § 1102—Management and Control of Community Real Property

(a) ... [E]ither spouse has the management and control of the community real property, ... but both spouses, either personally or by a duly authorized agent, must join in executing any instrument by which that community real property or any interest therein is leased for a longer period than one year, or is sold, conveyed, or encumbered.

(b) Nothing in this section shall be construed to apply to a lease, mortgage, conveyance, or transfer of real property or of any interest in real property between husband and wife.

(c) Notwithstanding subdivision (b):

* * *

2) The sole lease, contract, mortgage, or deed of either spouse, holding the record title to community real property to a lessee, purchaser, or encumbrancer, in good faith without knowledge of the marriage relation, shall be presumed to be valid....

In a common law state, there are no limits on what a spouse with title may do with property: She may dissipate it; she may give it away. A unilateral transfer of marital property during marriage thus will not generally be taken into account at divorce unless the court finds that the transfer was made in contemplation of divorce. *See* Panhorst v. Panhorst, 301 S.C. 100, 390 S.E.2d 376 (App.1990). By contrast, community property states impose significant limits on a spouse's unilateral management power.

MARTIN v. MARTIN

California Court of Appeal, First District,
Division 1, 1984, (A012041), 1 Civ.No. 52320.
(Sup. Ct. No. 230798). Not published.

HOLMDAHL, J.

Husband Thomas J. Martin (hereafter, "Husband") and wife Jean Martin (hereafter, "Wife"), appellant here and the petitioner below, were married on June 27, 1948, and separated on February 28, 1979. There is no minor child. Wife abandoned a career as a professional dancer when she married Husband. Husband graduated from law school, but worked as a building contractor and developer during the marriage. Toward the later part of the marriage, Husband developed an intimate friendship with another woman. Over a period of about 15 years, Husband gave the woman money and other gifts and traveled with her extensively, paying all or most of her expenses.

The San Mateo County Superior Court found that, at the time of separation, there were assets of the community having a total value of $3,555,006 (not including funds already distributed to the parties). The court also found that Husband had, during marriage, misappropriated community funds in the amount of $67,604 in connection with his extramarital relationship. * * * It awarded that sum to Husband and awarded to Wife assets of equal value as an offset. In essence, the action required Husband to pay to Wife her one-half share of the assets he had misappropriated. Thus, Wife was restored to the position she would have occupied had the assets not been misappropriated (ignoring the loss of the use of the funds).

* * *

Wife contends the court should have awarded interest (preferably compound interest) on the misappropriated assets. She argues that a fiduciary relationship exists between a husband and wife, in the nature of a trustee-beneficiary relationship, and that allowance of interest is permitted in such circumstances pursuant to Civil Code §§ 2237 and 2238. * * * A misappropriated asset is one which, by definition, does not exist at the time of trial. In other words, it is an asset which was removed from the community's control at some time in the past. Given this fact, we think it is significant that the statute dealing with misappropriation makes no provision for interest but, rather, expressly refers only to the "sum [the court] determines to have been deliberately misappropriated." Had the Legislature intended that interest be awarded, it would have expressly so provided.

Husband contends that because he received some value in connection with his expenditure of funds relative to his extramarital affair, the expenditures do not constitute misappropriations. He cites *In re Mar-*

riage of Moore (1980) 28 Cal.3d 366, in which the husband was found to have disposed of various items of community property, evidently to finance his acquisition of large amounts of alcoholic beverages. The California Supreme Court made the following observation: "Lydie, however, has failed to prove that David made a gift of the missing items or disposed of them without valuable consideration. The only evidence presented on the question—Lydie's belief that he disposed of the items to buy alcoholic beverages—indicates to the contrary. David could not have purchased alcoholic beverages with the items if he had not received valuable consideration for them."

To the extent, then, that valuable consideration was received, the expenditures were not misappropriations. He then goes on to argue that he derived a great deal of benefit from the expenditures, that the stipend he paid to his illicit companion was offset by the amount he saved by avoiding, with her help, undue consumption of alcohol (the parties agree Husband had an alcohol problem), and that he was entitled to have some recreation given the fact he had made for the community so much money. He gives examples of gifts which should not be considered misappropriations, including, for example, a gift to the S.P.C.A. He also suggests that the amount of the gift compared to the wealth of the community should be considered in determining whether a misappropriation occurred.

Husband's arguments do not persuade us. A spouse cannot be allowed to defeat a claim of misappropriation by claiming he derived benefit from expending the community's assets. The test should be whether the expenditure benefitted the community or occurred with its express or implied consent. As for Husband's suggestion that he was responsible for amassing the wealth of the community, we decline to establish some sort of a test relative to misappropriation which permits a spouse to spend in whatever way he chooses some of the community's assets because he was responsible for accumulating the assets. To do so would create a second category of community property and run counter to the very foundation of our community property system. Neither are we tempted to create exceptions based on the recipient of a gift. A gift to the S.P.C.A. might very well constitute misappropriation, if it is made over the other spouse's objection. Nor can the wealth of the community be the basis of any sort of workable test, even ignoring the fact that this too would tend to create two categories of community property.

This leads us to the other significant point raised by Husband relative to this issue. Husband says it was error for the court to prevent him from introducing evidence to the effect that "the reason he started spending money on [his illicit companion] in the first place was that he and his wife had not had sexual relations since 1958 and that she had denied him the affection and companionship of a normal marriage. Husband offered this evidence in order to show the circumstances surrounding his relationship with [her]. In Husband's view, this evidence would have negated any deliberate misappropriation on his part." Husband's point is not well-taken. The relevant question is not whether there was a good reason for his relationship with his companion, but whether the relationship and the related expenditures benefitted the community or occurred with its consent.

The proffered evidence was not offered for a proper purpose and, therefore, the trial court did not abuse its discretion in excluding it. * * * Husband's motion to dismiss the appeal is denied. The judgment is affirmed in all respects.

Notes and Questions

1. In California, a spouse does not have the right to make a unilateral gift of community property; a unilateral gift may always be rescinded by the other spouse. Under the UMPA and Texas law, a spouse may make a "reasonable" gift of community property. Which is the better rule? If the Texas/UMPA approach is more sensible, how should a court determine whether a gift was "reasonable?"

2. The American Law Institute has proposed that one spouse should be able to successfully challenge a unilateral gift of marital property by the other only if the gift was substantial, relative to the amount of the marital estate, and the gift was made shortly before a divorce action was filed. *See* PRINCIPLES OF THE LAW OF FAMILY DISSOLUTION, PROPOSED FINAL DRAFT, PART I, § 4.16, AT 213 (February 14, 1997). What is the basis for this approach?

3. While the issue of whether a spouse has exceeded his or her management authority is often litigated, as in *Martin*, in the context of a divorce proceeding, California has provided remedies aimed at spouses who remain married. Under CAL. FAM. CODE § 1101, a court may order "an accounting of the property and obligations of the parties to a marriage;" it may, with exceptions for certain types of property, order "that the name of a spouse shall be added to community property held in the name of the other spouse."

ANDREWS v. ANDREWS

Texas Court of Appeals, 1984.
677 S.W.2d 171.

SHANNON, SMITH and GAMMAGE, JUSTICES.

[The husband had challenged the manner in which the trial court divided the community estate.] Cynthia Mae Andrews suggests that the unequal distribution of the community was warranted by her former husband's "waste, mismanagement, or outright conversion of community funds." As authority for such proposition, appellee relies upon *Grothe v. Grothe*, 590 S.W.2d 238 (Tex.Civ.App.) and *Reaney v. Reaney*, 505 S.W.2d 338 (Tex.Civ.App.)

In *Grothe v. Grothe, supra*, the judgment recited that the former spouse wrongfully and willfully converted substantial amounts of community funds for his own personal use with the intention of depriving the former wife of her community interest in those funds. The former spouse failed to challenge that finding. In the absence of an attack upon the finding of conversion of community funds, this Court held that the finding of conversion justified an unequal distribution of the remaining community estate. In *Reaney v. Reaney, supra*, the former husband admitted that he "squandered" $53,000.00 in community funds. He lost some of the money gambling, he gave some of it away, and he spent some of the money "very foolishly." As this Court understands *Reaney*, the husband's profligacy must have been viewed by the Court as a fraud on the community estate.

There are no facts or findings in this appeal which are similar to those in either *Grothe*, or *Reaney*. Without dispute John Andrews made some poor investments of community funds. Also without doubt, he used community income to purchase with his mother some of the parcels of real estate. Cynthia Mae knew that her husband made payments on notes executed in such transactions. In fact, in at least one of the real estate transactions she wrote many of the checks for the monthly payments. Neither *Grothe* nor *Reaney* is authority for the proposition that a spouse's good faith, but unwise, investment of community funds resulting in losses to the community estate justifies an unequal distribution of remaining community property. Absent a fraud on the community, the court may not order reimbursement for gifts of community property made during the marriage to a stranger. *See* Geer, *Gifts in Fraud of the Rights of the Wife*, 26 Baylor L. Rev. 85 (1974). There are no findings by the district court that Andrews' investment of community funds in the purchase of the real estate was tantamount to a fraud on the community.

[The court reversed and remanded the division of community property by the trial court.]

Notes and Questions

1. Why is the court reluctant to hold the husband liable for a bad investment made in good faith? Is it a persuasive answer that, if the investment had been profitable, his wife would have shared the profits?

2. Under the approach described in *Andrews*, what should occur if one spouse goes to Las Vegas and loses a large amount of community savings at the roulette wheel by consistently betting on black? Assume, for purposes of analysis, that there is a 45% chance, on any spin, that black will come up. Is the series of bets negligent? What is the difference between a bad bet and a bad stock investment?

3. Should the standard for investment decisions be good faith or negligence? For a proposal for a "gross negligence" test, *see* Janet Riley, *Women's Right in the Louisiana Matrimonial Regime*, 50 Tulane L. Rev. 557, 570 (1976).

4. Could the *Andrews* problem be prevented if a joint management principle were applicable to all expenditures of community funds? Why has no state adopted this system?

5. Is sole, joint, or equal management the best system?:

Each system has its drawbacks. Joint management ensures that both owners will have the opportunity to participate in management of the community, but this requirement could place a substantial burden upon commerce, particularly if it were applied to all transactions involving any amount of community property. Furthermore, some spouses might not want to manage; the joint management system would burden them, unless some way of opting out were created. Also, what should occur under such a system if only one spouse purports to transfer community property? . . .

The sole management system clearly specifies who will have management power over each item of community property. However, if each spouse does not accumulate (or in some states have record ownership of) the same amount of property during marriage, this system would grant one spouse power over more than half of the community estate, even though both spouses possess a present, vested fifty percent interest. If one spouse works outside the home and the other does not, in many instances the spouse working in the home would manage little or no community property.

The equal management system, like the joint management system, reflects a general norm of equality; it does present a problem, however, if the spouses disagree, and especially if they give contradictory instructions to a third party. In addition, even though either spouse in theory may exercise management power, one might argue that the system facilitates the usurpation of management of the community by the dominant spouse. Also, equal and sole management both permit one spouse to affect the property interests of the other without giving that spouse notice.

No state has accepted one of these management systems for all transactions involving community property. Each has adopted a combination of management rules, in which some transactions are governed by one set of rules, and others by another set. * * *

J. Thomas Oldham, *Management of the Community Estate During an Intact Marriage*, 56 LAW & CONTEMP. PROB. 99, 106–07 (1993).

Is the best management system, as Professor Oldham suggests, some combination of sole, joint, and equal management? If so, what is the best combination? What rule should govern household property? a community property business? real estate? Why do most community property states require both spouses to consent to the sale or encumbrance of community realty?

Problem 3–2:

Wanda would like to invest funds she has earned during her marriage to Harry in an oil well. Harry thinks this is a bad idea and would like to veto it. Is there a legal remedy available to Harry: a) in a common law state? b) in a community property state? Which state's management rules are most helpful to Harry? In which states, if any, will Wanda be liable to Harry if she makes the investment and loses the money?

Problem 3–3:

Hank works outside the home and Wilma stays at home with their three children. Hank deposits his salary check in an account in his own name. Wilma wants the power to manage these funds, too. Is there a legal remedy available to Wilma: a) in a common law state? b) in a community property state? Which state's management rules are most helpful to Wilma?

C. "TIL DEATH US DO PART:" SPOUSAL PROPERTY RIGHTS AT DEATH

Under a community property regime, each spouse holds an equal, undivided interest in all community assets. Each spouse thus may dispose of his or her half of community property by will without restriction; the survivor spouse has no inheritance entitlement either to the decedent spouse's separate property or his half interest in community assets.

The traditional common law approach, which held that all property was owned by the husband, granted the surviving wife a right to "dower," i.e., a life estate in one-third of any land of which the husband was seized in fee at any time during the marriage. As a result of the wife's dower right, the husband was unable to alienate his lands during his lifetime so as to bar the wife's right of dower unless the wife consented. But the husband's personalty was his to dispose of as he wished:

> "He can, even by his will, give all of it away from her except her necessary clothes, and with that exception his creditors can take all of it. A further exception, of which there is not much to be read, is made of jewels, trinkets, and ornaments of the person, under the name of *paraphernalia*. The husband may sell or give these away in his lifetime, and even after his death they may be taken for his debts; but he can not give them away by will. If the husband dies during the wife's life and dies intestate, she is entitled to a third, or if there be no living descendant of the husband, to one-half of his personalty. But this is a case of pure intestate succession; she only has a share of what is left after payment of her husband's debts."

2 F. POLLOCK & F. MAITLAND, THE HISTORY OF THE ENGLISH LAW 405 (1899)

Although many common law states continue to follow the traditional approach to inheritance rights and grant a survivor spouse only a third of the decedent's estate where there are children of the marriage, surveys conducted over the past twenty years have uniformly found that Americans overwhelmingly prefer to leave their entire estate to a surviving spouse. This preference is particularly strong among persons of moderate means—those least likely to dispose of their property under a will—who tend to believe that the survivor will need the entire estate for support.[1]

Legislatures are beginning to react. For example, in 1992, New York changed its inheritance law by raising a surviving spouse's minimum inheritance entitlement to $50,000 plus one-half of the decedent's probate estate, whether or not the decedent has issue. N.Y. E.P.T.L. § 4-1.1. 1990 amendments to the Uniform Probate Code (UPC) provide the surviving spouse with an inheritance entitlement equal to the entire probate estate, unless the survivor has children who are not children of the decedent, or vice versa. UPC § 2-102.

The wife's dower right, in most common law states, has been replaced or augmented by a spousal "right of election," that applies to both husband and wife and guarantees the surviving spouse a fixed fractional share (typically the dower fraction, one-third) of the decedent spouse's probate assets, regardless of the terms of the decedent's will. Although the details of right of election schemes vary substantially from state to state, only one of the common law states (Georgia) lacks an elective share statute altogether; most statutes grant an entitlement to *ownership*, not a life estate or income, of assets equal to the spousal share. *See* J. Thomas Oldham, *Should the Surviving Spouse's Forced Share Be Retained?*, 38 CASE W. RES. L. REV. 225 (1988).

In many common law states, the spousal right of election has been extended to assets, such as joint tenancy property, that are not part of the probate estate. This extension of the probate asset pool (under the UPC, the "augmented estate") has been made both to prevent the decedent spouse from rendering the right of election meaningless through illusory or fraudulent lifetime transfers and to ensure that the surviving spouse's entitlement is fairly based on all the decedent's assets and all the survivor's assets derived from the decedent. Some states have not adopted the augmented estate concept, however. And many have included in the augmented estate some types of probate assets but not others, with the result that a spouse who wants to defeat his or her spouse's right of election can, with some careful planning, still do so.

A third round of reform is just now underway, this one motivated by the discrepancy between elective share rules and the widely accepted view that marriage is an equal partnership. The elective share fraction—typically one-third of the decedent's estate—does not comport with the partnership model, which would mandate one-half of all property accu-

1. The one exception is where there are children from a prior marriage. *See, e.g.*, Contemporary Studies Project, *A Comparison of Iowans' Dispositive Preferences with Selected Provisions of the Iowa and [the Pre-1990] Uniform Probate Codes*, 63 IOWA L. REV. 1041 (1978); Mary L. Fellows et al., *Public Attitudes About Property Distribution at Death and Intestate Succession Laws in the United States*, 1978 A.B.F. RES. J. 391; Mary L. Fellows, et al., *An Empirical Study of the Illinois Statutory Estate Plan*, 1978 U. ILL. L. F. 717; John Price, *The Transmission of Wealth at Death in a Community Property Jurisdiction*, 50 WASH. L. REV. 277 (1975). Earlier studies are cited in these publications. A strong preference for the surviving spouse has also been reported in England. U.K. LAW COMM'N, FAMILY LAW: DISTRIBUTION ON INTESTACY (NO. 187), at app. C, 36-37, 40-45 (1989).

mulated during the marriage. Moreover, the elective share fraction applies to what would be separate assets in a community property system, and does so without regard to marital duration; the spouse married for one day to the multi-millionaire gets exactly the same share of his estate as the spouse married for thirty years.

The aim of the new reform movement has been to infuse elective share law with community property concepts. But this is not so easy in states that do not recognize community property. The ingenious, if complex, approach to the problem adopted by the 1990 Uniform Probate Code retains the common law approach of granting the survivor spouse a fractional share of the decedent's property, whether it would be classified as separate or community property. But the revised elective share expands with the duration of the marriage; a surviving spouse married to the decedent for one year is entitled to only 3% of the augmented estate, while a survivor married for fifteen years is entitled to 50%. UPC § 2–201.

If the decedent and the spouse were married to each other:	The elective-share percentage is:
Less than 1 year	Supplemental Amount Only
1 year but less than 2 years	3% of the augmented estate
2 years but less than 3 years	6% of the augmented estate
3 years but less than 4 years	9% of the augmented estate
. . .	
15 or more years	50% of the augmented estate

These varying percentages are coupled with a newly defined augmented estate, which includes the *surviving* spouse's assets as well as those of the decedent. UPC §§ 2–202, 2–203.

The UPC scheme is aimed at achieving community property type results in the context of a common law system (UPC Part 2, General Comment) and achieves a reasonable facsimile in many cases. But it is not clear that the UPC achieves its goals in the case of the short first marriage. Consider the five year marriage where all property was owned by the decedent and all was obtained during the marriage. Under a community property regime, the surviving spouse would take half; under the UPC, the surviving spouse would take 15%. In contrast, if two retired people are married for 15 years, in a community property system the survivor may well have no community property, but gets 50% of the decedent's estate under the UPC.

Problem 3–4:

Consider the following fact patterns and determine how much money each surviving spouse would be entitled to in a community property state, a common law state with a spousal right of election equal to one-third of the decedent's probate estate, and under the 1990 UPC. None of the spouses entered into a premarital agreement.

a) John and Marla married in February 1993. At the time of the marriage, each had assets worth $20,000. In 1994, they had a child. In

January, 1997, John and Marla separated. One month later John died, leaving his entire estate to the National Audubon Society. John's probate estate (which represented all of his assets) was worth $400,000; $380,000 represented money inherited from his mother in 1996. Marla owned assets worth $25,000.

b) Tom and Joanne married in 1960. At the time of the marriage, each had no debts. Tom died testate in 1995, leaving his entire estate to his disabled brother, Philip. Tom's probate estate (representing all of his assets) was worth $1 million; all assets were acquired with Tom's earnings during the marriage. Joanne owned assets worth $5,000.

c) Harry and Sally married in June, 1996. It was the third marriage for both; each had children from prior marriages. At the time of the marriage, Harry had assets worth $300,000; Sally had assets worth $1,900,000. Harry died testate in October, 1996, leaving his entire estate to his children, in equal shares. Harry's estate was worth $300,000; Sally had assets worth $2,000,000.

d) Harry and Sally married in June, 1996. It was the third marriage for both; each had children from prior marriages. At the time of the marriage, Harry had assets worth $300,000. Sally had assets worth $15,000; as a result of the marriage, she also lost her claim to alimony from her former husband, worth $2000 per month. Harry died testate in October, 1996, leaving his entire estate to his children, in equal shares. Harry's estate was worth $300,000; Sally had assets worth $15,000.

In what types of cases does the community property approach seem most fair? The common law right of election? The UPC approach? Is there some combination that seems preferable to any one approach alone?

D. SOME CONCLUDING THOUGHTS

So, is a community property system better than the common law approach? There does seem to be substantial resistance in common law states to the adoption of a community property system. In the decade since it was promulgated, the Uniform Marital Property Act (UMPA) has been adopted in only one state.

Is there some belated wisdom in the common law approach?

> "There is still one small fact that gives rise to a nagging doubt about our ... efforts [to reform the common law]. This is that in West Germany and Sweden, home of systems like those we are trying to establish, discontent is being registered with the deferred community. In Sweden, law reforms are in progress which seem likely to result in the curtailment or abolition of the deferred community and its replacement with another system, more responsible to current needs and desires. What is this ultra modern system? Separation of assets. O tempora, o mores!
>
> "Why should we be concerned with what is happening in West Germany and Sweden? Their societies and economies are not just

like ours. What are the reasons for their re-examination of deferred community and why are they casting their eyes toward our old system of the Married Women's Separate Property Acts? In both West Germany and Sweden, the feeling is being expressed in some quarters that legal devices developed for the situation where one spouse works outside and the other works inside the home are increasingly inappropriate. In Sweden, the exclusively housewife marriage is said now to be becoming uncommon. In West Germany, the two-earner marriage is said to have replaced *Hausfrauenehe* as the dominant pattern. The official family policy statement of the Social Democratic Party and government sponsored legislation are designed to reflect and respond to the changing social situation. Already, many West German couples are going to the trouble to contract out of the deferred community in favor of separation of assets."

Mary Ann Glendon, *Is There a Future for Separate Property?*, 8 FAM. L. Q. 315, 322–25 (1974).

Despite the developments described by Professor Glendon, women do, on average, earn substantially less than men and play a disproportionate role in child care activities that typically reduce long-term earning capacity. In these cases, the common law approach can produce results that seem unfair.

Perhaps we need a property rule that treats marriages differently. It is theoretically possible to impose a community property regime on traditional, role-divided marriages, and a separate property regime on dual earner/separate career marriages. It would also be possible, as in many civil law countries, to *require* spouses to opt into one regime or the other at the time of their marriage.

What advantages and disadvantages are there in a regime that imposes different property regimes on different marriage categories (i.e., traditional, two-earner, etc.). What advantages and disadvantages are there in a mandatory choice regime?

Problem 3–5:

You are counsel to the state legislature's Committee on Family Law. The legislature is considering marital property reform. Its goals are improvements in fairness and efficiency. Advise the Committee on how, if at all, your state's property classification and management scheme should be revised.

SECTION 3. SPOUSAL SUPPORT OBLIGATIONS DURING MARRIAGE

In common law states, we have seen that the spouse who accumulates property during the marriage is thought to "own" it; the other spouse has no interest in the property until dissolution. Courts and legislatures have had to decide when, if ever, to interfere with the management decisions of an owner spouse during an intact marriage.

A. THE NECESSARIES DOCTRINE

McGUIRE v. McGUIRE

Supreme Court of Nebraska, 1953.
157 Neb. 226, 59 N.W.2d 336.

MESSMORE, JUSTICE.

The plaintiff, Lydia McGuire, brought this action in equity in the district court for Wayne County against Charles W. McGuire, her husband, as defendant, to recover suitable maintenance and support money, and for costs and attorney's fees. Trial was had to the court and a decree was rendered in favor of the plaintiff.

* * *

The record shows that the plaintiff and defendant were married in Wayne, Nebraska, on August 11, 1919. At the time of the marriage the defendant was a bachelor 46 or 47 years of age and had a reputation for more than ordinary frugality, of which the plaintiff was aware. She had visited in his home and had known him for about 3 years prior to the marriage. After the marriage the couple went to live on a farm of 160 acres located in Leslie precinct, Wayne County, owned by the defendant and upon which he had lived and farmed since 1905. The parties have lived on this place ever since. The plaintiff had been previously married. Her first husband died in October 1914, leaving surviving him the plaintiff and two daughters. He died intestate, leaving 80 acres of land in Dixon County. The plaintiff and each of the daughters inherited a one-third interest therein. At the time of the marriage of the plaintiff and defendant the plaintiff's daughters were 9 and 11 years of age. By working and receiving financial assistance from the parties to this action, the daughters received a high school education in Pender. One daughter attended Wayne State Teachers College for 2 years and the other daughter attended a business college in Sioux City, Iowa, for 1 year. Both of these daughters are married and have families of their own.

On April 12, 1939, the plaintiff transferred her interest in the 80-acre farm to her two daughters. The defendant signed the deed.

At the time of trial plaintiff was 66 years of age and the defendant nearly 80 years of age. No children were born to these parties. The defendant had no dependents except the plaintiff.

The plaintiff testified that she was a dutiful and obedient wife, worked and saved, and cohabited with the defendant until the last 2 or 3 years. She worked in the fields, did outside chores, cooked, and attended to her household duties such as cleaning the house and doing the washing. For a number of years she raised as high as 300 chickens, sold poultry and eggs, and used the money to buy clothing, things she wanted, and for groceries. She further testified that the defendant was the boss of the house and his word was law; that he would not tolerate any charge accounts and would not inform her as to his finances or business; and that he was a poor companion. The defendant did not complain of her work, but left the impression to her that she had not done enough. On several occasions the plaintiff asked the defendant for money. He would give her very small amounts, and for the last 3 or 4 years he had not given her any money nor provided her with clothing, except a coat about 4 years previous. The defendant had purchased the groceries the last 3 or 4 years, and permitted her to buy groceries, but he paid for them by check. There is apparently no complaint about the groceries the defendant furnished. The defendant had not taken her to a motion picture show during the past 12 years. They did not belong to any organizations or charitable institutions, nor did he give her money to make contributions to any charitable institutions. The defendant belongs to the Pleasant Valley Church which occupies about 2 acres of his farm land. At the time of trial there was no minister for this church so there were no services. For the past 4 years or more, the defendant had not given the plaintiff money to purchase furniture or other household necessities. Three years ago he did purchase an electric, wood-and-cob combination stove which was installed in the kitchen, also linoleum floor covering for the kitchen. The plaintiff further testified that the house is not equipped with a bathroom, bathing facilities, or inside toilet. The kitchen is not modern. She does not have a kitchen sink. Hard and soft water is obtained from a well and cistern. She has a mechanical Servel refrigerator, and the house is equipped with electricity. There is a pipeless furnace which she testified had not been in good working order for 5 or 6 years, and she testified she was tired of scooping coal and ashes. She had requested a new furnace but the defendant believed the one they had to be satisfactory. She related that the furniture was old and she would like to replenish it, at least to be comparable with some of her neighbors; that her silverware and dishes were old and were primarily gifts, outside of what she purchased; that one of her daughters was good about furnishing her clothing, at least a dress a year, or sometimes two; that the defendant owns a 1929 Ford coupe equipped with a heater which is not efficient, and on the average of every 2 weeks he drives the plaintiff to Wayne to visit her mother; and that he also owns a 1927 Chevrolet pickup which is used for different purposes on the farm. The plaintiff has the privilege to use all of the rent money she wanted to from the 80–acre farm, and when she goes to see her daughters, which is not frequent, she uses part of the rent money for that purpose, the defendant providing no funds for such use. The defendant ordinarily raised hogs on his farm, but the last 4 or 5 years has leased the farm land to tenants, and he generally keeps up the fences and the buildings. At the present time the plaintiff is not able to raise chickens and sell eggs. She has about 25 chickens. The plaintiff has had three abdominal operations for which the defendant has paid. She selected her own doctor, and there were no restrictions placed in that respect. When she has requested various things for the home or personal effects, defendant has informed her on many occasions that he did not have the money to pay for the same. She would like to have a new car. She visited one daughter in Spokane, Washington, in March 1951 for 3 or 4 weeks, and visited the other daughter living in Fort Worth, Texas, on three occasions for 2 to 4 weeks at a time. She had visited one of her daughters when she was living in Sioux City some weekends. The plaintiff further testified that she had very little funds, possibly $1,500 in the bank which was chicken money and money which her father furnished her, he having departed this life a few years ago; and that use of the telephone was restricted, indicating that defendant did not desire that she make long distance calls, otherwise she had free access to the telephone.

It appears that the defendant owns 398 acres of land with 2 acres deeded to a church, the land being of the value of $83,960; that he has bank deposits in the sum of $12,786.81 and government bonds in the amount of $104,500; and that his income, including interest on the bonds and rental for his real estate, is $8,000 or $9,000 a year. There are apparently some Series E United States Savings Bonds listed and registered in the names of Charles W. McGuire or Lydia M. McGuire purchased in 1943, 1944, and 1945, in the amount of $2,500. Other bonds seem to be in the name of Charles W. McGuire, without a beneficiary or co-owner designated. The plaintiff has a bank account of $5,960.22. This account includes deposits of some $200 and $100 which the court required the defendant to pay his wife as temporary allowance during the pendency of these proceedings. One hundred dollars was withdrawn on the date of each deposit.

The facts are not in dispute.

* * *

. . . There are no cases cited by the plaintiff and relied upon by her from this jurisdiction or other jurisdictions that will sustain the action such as she has instituted in the instant case.

* * *

There are . . . several cases, under statutes of various states, in which separate maintenance was refused the wife, where the husband and wife were living in the same house. These cases are to the effect that it is indispensable requirement of a maintenance statute that the wife should be living separate and apart from her husband without her fault, and that therefore, a wife living in the same house with her husband, occupying a different room and eating at a different time, was not entitled to separate maintenance. *See Lowe v. Lowe*, 213 Ill.App. 607.

* * *

In the instant case the marital relation has continued for more than 33 years, and the wife has been supported in the same manner during this time without complaint on her part. The parties have not been separated or living apart from each other at any time. In the light of the cited cases it is clear, especially so in this jurisdiction, that to maintain an action such as the one at bar, the parties must be separated or living apart from each other.

The living standards of a family are a matter of concern to the household, and not for the courts to determine, even though the husband's attitude toward his wife, according to his wealth and circumstances, leaves little to be said in his behalf. As long as the home is maintained and the parties are living as husband and wife it may be said that the husband is legally supporting his wife and the purpose of the marriage relation is being carried out. Public policy requires such a holding. It appears that the plaintiff is not devoid of money in her own right. She has a fair-sized bank and is entitled to use the rent from the 80 acres of land left by her first husband, if she so chooses.

* * *

There being no legal basis for the plaintiff's action as required by the law of this jurisdiction, an allowance of attorney's fees is erroneous and not authorized.

For the reasons given in this opinion, the judgment rendered by the district court is reversed and the cause remanded with directions to dismiss the cause.

YEAGER, JUSTICE (dissenting).

I respectfully dissent. In doing so I do not question the correctness of the statement of facts set forth in the majority opinion. I, however, do not think some important considerations have received appropriate emphasis....

* * *

... [T]he district court decreed that plaintiff was legally entitled to use the credit of defendant and to obligate him to pay for a large number of items, some of which were in the nature of improvements and repairs to the house and some of which were furniture and appliances to be placed in the home. The total cost of these improvements and additions, as is apparent from the decree, would amount to several thousand dollars. As an alternative to a part of this defendant was permitted, in agreement with plaintiff, to purchase a modern house elsewhere. The defendant was ordered to purchase a new automobile with an effective heater within 30 days. He was ordered to pay traveling expenses of plaintiff for a visit to each of her daughters at least once each year. It was decreed that plaintiff was entitled in the future to pledge the credit of defendant for what may constitute necessaries of life. The plaintiff was awarded a personal allowance in the amount of $50 a month. An award of $800 was made for services for plaintiff's attorney.

* * *

It is true that in all cases examined which uphold the right of a wife to maintain an action in equity for maintenance the parties were living apart, but no case has been cited or found which says that separation is a condition precedent to the right to maintain action in equity for maintenance. Likewise none has been cited or found which says that it is not.

In primary essence the rule contemplates the enforcement of an obligation within and not without the full marriage relationship. The reasoning contained in the opinions sustaining this right declare the purpose....

> "The question is, whether or not the plaintiff shall be compelled to resort to a proceeding for a divorce, which she does not desire to do, and which probably she is unwilling to do, from conscientious convictions, or, in failing to do so, shall be deprived of that support which her husband is bound to give her."
>
> *Earle v. Earle.*

This reasoning has received the approval of this court in the later ... cases.

* * *

It is thought that the following from the same opinion should be regarded as controlling here: "It seems to us that a declaration of such a doctrine as the law of the land would place it within the power of every man, who, unrestrained by conscience, seeks to be freed from his obligations to his wife and family, by withholding the necessary comforts and support due them, to compel her to do that for him which the law would not do upon his own application."

I conclude therefore that the conclusion of the decree that the district court had the power to entertain the action was not contrary to law.

I think however that the court was without proper power to make any of the awards contained in the decree for the support and maintenance of the plaintiff except the one of $50 a month.

* * *

I am of the opinion that the power of the court in such instances as this should not be extended beyond the allowance of sufficient money to provide adequate support and maintenance. * * *

Notes and Questions

1. Commentators have disagreed over whether public policy requires the *McGuire* holding.

a. Dean Teitelbaum, for example, has argued that Mrs. McGuire should have been granted support, urging that "the practical consequence of ... the decision is to confer or ratify the power of one family member over others" and thus to "ratif[y] the naturally existing or socially created inequalities which have led to the victory of one over the other." Lee E. Teitelbaum, *Family History and Family Law*, 1985 Wis. L. Rev. 1135, 1145. In evaluating this claim, consider whether granting support to Mrs. McGuire wouldn't also have "conferred or ratified the power of one family member over others," in this case Mrs. McGuire's socially (i.e., legally) conferred power to demand support from her husband. Are there reasons for enhancing Mrs. McGuire's power rather than that of her husband? Why would you guess the court chose to enhance his power?

b. Professor Hafen, in support of *McGuire*, has argued that "constant legal intervention (or the threat of it) will destroy the continuity that is critically necessary for meaningful, ongoing relations and developmental nurturing" and "increas[ing] state intervention in an ongoing family to protect the autonomy of some family members ... may simply exchange one threat to autonomy for another." Bruce C. Hafen, *The Family as an Entity*, 22 U.C. Davis L. Rev. 865, 912 (1989). Is this argument in favor the *McGuire* result persuasive? Why or why not?

2. Although the case law is sparse, most American courts agree that a spouse in an intact marriage should not be able to obtain a support order unless separated. (Statutes in some other countries permit such an action during an intact marriage, however. *See* Quebec Civil Code, art. 400.) Why would American courts permit a separated spouse to sue for support when a Mrs. McGuire cannot?

3. Would a community property regime solve Mrs. McGuire's problem? What is the best system to deal with the financial disputes of spouses in an intact marriage?

SHARPE FURNITURE, INC. v. BUCKSTAFF

Supreme Court of Wisconsin, 1980.
99 Wis.2d 114, 299 N.W.2d 219.

Beilfuss, Chief Justice.

* * *

This controversy centers around the purchase of a sofa from Sharpe Furniture, Inc. (Sharpe). The purchase was made by Karen Buckstaff on August 15, 1973. On that date, Mrs. Buckstaff signed in her own name a special order for a "Henredon 6800 Sofa." Under the terms of the order she was to pay $621.50 within 60 days after the item was received from the factory. Interest at a rate of 1.5 percent per month was charged on the unpaid balance after that 60–day period. No representations were made to Sharpe at the time of the purchase that Mrs. Buckstaff was acting on behalf of her husband in purchasing the furniture. Indeed, John Buckstaff had previously written to the local credit bureau service to advise that office that he would not be responsible for any credit extended to his wife.

The Henredon sofa was received from the factory and delivered to the residence of the defendants on February 8, 1974. This piece of furniture has been a part of the Buckstaff home ever since its delivery. Despite this fact, neither John Buckstaff nor his wife have tendered payment for the sofa.

On November 20, 1975, Sharpe commenced this action against both Buckstaffs. The parties agreed to allow the trial court to decide the dispute on the basis of the undisputed facts as they appeared in the trial memoranda submitted by counsel. In addition to the facts already stated above, the informal stipulation of the parties reveals that John Buckstaff, Jr., is the president of Buckstaff Company of Oshkosh, Wisconsin. Mrs. Buckstaff is a housewife. Mr. Buckstaff earns a substantial income and the Buckstaff family is one of social and economic prominence in the Oshkosh area. It was further set forth that Mr. Buckstaff has always provided his wife with the necessaries of life and has never failed or refused to provide his wife with items which could be considered necessaries.

On the basis of these facts, the trial court found that Karen Buckstaff was liable on her contract and that John Buckstaff was also liable for the amount due on the sofa under the common law doctrine of necessaries. Judgment was entered accordingly. The court of appeals affirmed. John Buckstaff now seeks review of the decision of the court of appeals. Karen Buckstaff has not sought appellate relief from the entry of the judgment against her.

There are two issues which we must consider in reviewing the decision of the court of appeals:

1. Whether, under the common law doctrine of necessaries and in the absence of any contractual obligation on his part, a husband may be held liable for sums due as payment for necessary items purchased on credit by his wife.

2. Whether, in an action for recovery of the value of necessaries supplied on credit to a wife, it is essential for the plaintiff-creditor to prove either that the husband has failed, refused or neglected to provide the items which have been supplied by the plaintiff-creditor or that the items supplied were reasonably needed by the wife or the family.

Before proceeding to a discussion of the merits of this case, we examine the substance of the doctrine of necessaries.

The Wisconsin Supreme Court restated the common law rule of necessaries early on in the history of the jurisprudence of this state. In 1871, in the case of *Warner and Ryan v. Heiden*, 28 Wis. 517, 519 (1871), the court wrote:

> "The husband is under legal obligations to support his wife, and nothing but wrongful conduct on her part can free him from such obligation. If he fails to provide her with suitable and proper necessaries, any third person who does provide her therewith, may maintain an action against him for the same. 1 Bishop on Mar. and Div., § 553. The same learned author, in the next section (§ 554),

thus defines what are necessaries which the husband is bound to furnish to his wife: 'And, in general, we may say, that necessaries are such articles of food, or apparel, or medicine, or such medical attendance and nursing, or such provided means of locomotion, or provided habitation and furniture, *or such provision for her protection in society*, and the like, as the husband, considering his ability and standing, ought to furnish to his wife for her sustenance, and the preservation of her health and comfort.' "

This doctrine traditionally required the creditor to show that he supplied to the wife an item that was, in fact, a necessary and that the defendant had previously failed or refused to provide his wife with this item. When such a showing was made, the creditor was entitled to recovery as against the husband despite the fact that the husband had not contractually bound himself by his own act or by the act of an agent. The doctrine of necessaries is not imposed by the law of agency. This duty is placed upon a husband by virtue of the legal relationship of marriage. It arises as an obligation placed on him as a matter of public policy.

The appellant challenges the continued vitality of this common law rule. Mr. Buckstaff charges that the necessaries doctrine conflicts with contemporary trends toward equality of the sexes and a sex neutral society. He further argues that the doctrine is an outdated and inefficient means of compelling support. It is argued that various social welfare agencies and governmental institutions have replaced the doctrine of necessaries as a mechanism for the maintenance of the members of a household.

It is true that the necessaries rule has been justified in the past on the basis of a social view of the married woman as a person without legal capacity. However, the nature of the woman's obligations under the necessary rule in relation to the obligation of her husband is not at issue here. That question has been treated in our decision in *Estate of Stromsted*, 99 Wis.2d 136, 299 N.W.2d 226 (1980), wherein we concluded the husband was primarily liable for necessities and the wife secondarily liable. The question presented in this case involves a consideration of the nature of the husband's obligation. We must decide whether such a liability imposed upon the husband furthers a proper purpose in contemporary society.

We are of the opinion that the doctrine of necessaries serves a legitimate and proper purpose in our system of common law. The heart of this common law rule is a concern for the support and the sustenance of the family and the individual members thereof. The sustenance of the family unit is accorded a high order of importance in the scheme of Wisconsin law. It has been codified as a part of our statutes, and it has been recognized as a part of our case law. The necessaries rule encourages the extension of credit to those who in an individual capacity may not have the ability to make these basic purchases. In this manner it facilitates the support of the family unit and its function is in harmony with the purposes behind the support laws of this state. The rule retains a viable role in modern society.

We view the nature of the husband's liability as a contractual duty implied in law, i.e., a quasi-contractual obligation.

* * *

In light of the proper function of the necessaries rule in relation to the support of the family, in the absence of an express contract to the contrary, we hold that a husband incurs the primary obligation, implied as a matter of law, to assume liability for the necessaries which have been procured for the sustenance of his family.

Mr. Buckstaff's second argument is that, as a matter of law, he is not liable for the necessaries purchased by his wife because Sharpe did not plead or prove that he as a husband failed, refused or neglected to provide a sofa for his wife. It is also argued that liability cannot be found in the face of the parties' stipulation which states that Mr. Buckstaff has always provided his wife with the necessaries of life and has never failed or refused to provide her with items which would constitute necessaries.

* * *

The merchant's burden of proof was modified by the decision in *Simpson Garment Co. v. Schultz*, 182 Wis. 506, 196 N.W. 783 (1924). The *Simpson Garment Company* decision involved a defendant whose wife purchased a coat, a dress and a slip for her daughter. The daughter was about to graduate from high school and lacked the proper attire for the commencement exercises. The wife pledged the defendant's credit in order to purchase the items and when her husband refused to pay, a lawsuit was commenced. The defendant was found liable for the cost of the garments. In discussing the plaintiff's *prima facie* burden, the court said:

> "When a merchant sues a husband for necessaries sold to his wife or some member of his family, it is incumbent upon him to show, among other things, (1) that the articles purchased were such as are suitable for the wife or member of the family in view of the family's social position in the community in which they live and in view of the defendant's financial ability to pay for them; and (2) that the articles sold were reasonably needed by the wife or member of the family to whom they were sold at the time of the sale."

The *Simpson Garment Company* rule required only that the creditor show that the item was "reasonably needed" by the wife or family, and not that the husband wilfully refused to provide his wife with the necessary item as suggested by [earlier cases].

In applying the rule of the *Simpson Garment Company* decision to the case at bar, the creditor Sharpe must prevail over Mr. Buckstaff's two-pronged attack on the judgment. * * * Mr. Buckstaff's second contention is that the sofa should not be considered a necessary in view of the stipulation that he as a husband provided his wife with all necessaries. Whether or not, as a general matter, a man provides his wife with necessaries is irrelevant to a determination of whether a particular item is reasonably needed under the *Simpson Garment Company* rule. This stipulation, which is phrased in terms of the conclusion which it seeks to establish, is not probative of whether the sofa in issue was reasonably needed.

We have reviewed the stipulation of the parties in this matter and we are satisfied that ample evidence supported the trial court's conclusion that the Henredon sofa was a legally necessary item. The Buckstaffs are a prominent family and their socio-economic standing justifies a finding that the sofa at issue here was a suitable and proper item for their household. With reference to the element of reasonable need, we note that the sofa has been in use in the Buckstaff home since its delivery. Such continued use gives rise to an inference of reasonable need. This inference is not rebutted by the stipulation stating that Mr. Buckstaff provided his wife with "all necessaries."

. . . The decision of the court of appeals is affirmed.

Notes and Questions

1. Community property states also accept the necessaries doctrine. *See, e.g.*, TEX. FAM. CODE § 3.201; CAL. FAM. CODE § 914.

2. What should be considered a necessity? Medical care clearly qualifies, but why should a couch costing more than $600 in 1980 (more than $1100 in current dollars)? In fact, courts have tended to construe the necessaries doctrine expansively. For example, in Gimbel Bros. v. Pinto, 188 Pa.Super. 72, 145 A.2d 865 (Pa.Super.1958) the court found that a $3300 mink coat was a necessity. In Daggett v. Neiman–Marcus Co., 348 S.W.2d 796 (Tex.Civ.App.1961) the court reached the same conclusion regarding $2000 worth of clothes (in 1960!). *Should* the doctrine apply only to ensure a minimal standard of living, or encompass all expenditures that appear appropriate, given the income and resources of the couple? What are the pros and cons of each approach?

3. Why is an aggrieved spouse like Mrs. McGuire permitted to bind her husband's credit under the necessaries doctrine when she cannot sue him for increased support directly? Can you think of any reason why Mrs. McGuire didn't employ the necessaries doctrine?

4. The trend is toward gender-neutral application of the necessaries doctrine. Some jurisdictions have expanded the doctrine to apply equally to either gender. *See, e.g.*, Jersey Shore Medical Center–Fitkin Hospital v. Baum's Estate, 84 N.J. 137, 417 A.2d 1003 (1980); N.C. Baptist Hospitals, Inc. v. Harris, 319 N.C. 347, 354 S.E.2d 471 (1987). Other jurisdictions have imposed liability on the wife only where the husband is unable to pay for his own necessaries. *See, e.g.*, Borgess Medical Center v. Smith, 149 Mich.App. 796, 386 N.W.2d 684 (1986); Marshfield Clinic v. Discher, 105 Wis.2d 506, 314 N.W.2d 326 (1982). And some states have eliminated the doctrine from their common law altogether. *See, e.g.*, Condore v. Prince George's County, 289 Md. 516,

425 A.2d 1011 (1981); Schilling v. Bedford County Memorial Hospital, Inc., 225 Va. 539, 303 S.E.2d 905 (1983). *See generally* Margaret Mahoney, *Economic Sharing During Marriage: Equal Protection, Spousal Support, and the Doctrine of Necessaries*, 22 J. FAM. L. 221 (1983–84).

5. As the citations in note 4 suggest, today the necessaries doctrine is most often utilized by hospitals.

6. What is the effect of advertisements such as "responsible for my own debts and signature only, John Doe" as are frequently seen in newspapers? Can you explain why John Buckstaff was not exonerated from liability on the basis of his writing to the local credit bureau that he would not be responsible for any credit extended to his wife?

7. Some states have concluded that the necessaries doctrine should not apply after permanent separation. *See* VA. CODE § 55–37; National Account Systems v. Mercado, 196 N.J.Super. 133, 481 A.2d 835 (1984).

B. THE RIGHTS OF CREDITORS

In common law states marriage has little effect on the rights of creditors. A creditor of one spouse may not attach the property of the other to collect the debt, unless the doctrine of necessaries applies.

In community property states, the effect of marriage is more significant, but the rules are not uniform. Some states provide that a creditor of a spouse may attach all property over which that spouse has management power. In Texas, for example, a creditor may attach a debtor spouse's separate property as well as all property over which the spouse has sole or joint management power. *See* TEX. FAM. CODE §§ 3.201, 3.202. Other states base the creditor's rights on whether the debt is a separate or community debt (*see* GAF Corp. v. Diamond Carpet Corp., 117 Ariz. 297, 572 P.2d 125 (Ariz.App.1977); Nichols Hills Bank v. McCool, 104 Wash.2d 78, 701 P.2d 1114 (1985)). In these states, for a community debt, the creditor may attach all community property and the debtor spouse's separate property. *See* ARIZ. REV. STAT. § 25–215; N.M. STAT. ANN. § 40–3–11; WIS. STAT. ANN. § 766.55 For a separate debt, some of these states restrict the creditor's rights to separate property; the remainder permit the creditor to attach the debtor-spouse's interest in community assets as well. *See* N.M. STAT. ANN. § 40–3–10; WIS. STAT. ANN. § 766.55.

Many community property states also distinguish tort judgments from other debts. Most permit the tort judgment creditor to attach at least the tortfeasor's half of the community estate. Some distinguish between a "separate" and "community" tort. In California, for example, the tort judgment creditor must first exhaust community property before attaching the tortfeasor's separate property if the tort is a community tort; for a separate tort the creditor must first exhaust separate property before the tortfeasor's share of community assets may be attached. See CAL. FAM. CODE § 1000.

> "[T]oo often the determination of whether the tort is separate or community has been based on distinctions without a difference.

For example, ... [in] Newbury v. Remington, ... an assault was held to be separate although it arose out of driving the community automobile while returning from recreational activities ... on the ... rationale [that] the automobile was not used by respondent husband in striking and beating the appellant, nor was it in use at all by him at the time the assault and battery was inflicted by the respondent husband. He was away from the automobile at that time ...

Clearly, if defendant had struck plaintiff with the automobile, rather than with his fist, the community would have been held liable. The same result would have been reached had he stayed inside his auto rather than alighting ... An analogous case decided the opposite way is *Bensun v. Bush* ... There defendant broke up a dog fight between his community-owned dog and that of his neighbors by spraying a chemical in the face of the neighbors' dog. Thereafter defendant became angered by the neighbor and, when the latter started to walk away, sprayed some chemical in his face also. This was held to be a community tort since defendant had not "launched upon an individual enterprise of his own which had no relationship to the community ..."

de Elche v. Jacobsen, 95 Wash.2d 237, 622 P.2d 835, 837 (1980).

Problem 3–6:

Harvey is a homemaker and Willa works outside the home, where she earns a substantial amount of money. All savings accrued during the marriage are in accounts in Willa's name alone. If Harvey buys a piece of art on credit for the living room, may the art dealer attach Willa's property? Does it matter if they live in a common law or community property state?

C. PRIVATE SUPPORT OBLIGATIONS, PUBLIC BENEFITS

SEPTUAGENARIAN v. SEPTUAGENARIAN

Family Court, City of New York, Queens County, 1984.
126 Misc.2d 699, 483 N.Y.S.2d 932.

JEFFRY H. GALLET, JUDGE.

Petitioner requests support of $1,125 a month from her husband of 50 years. She convincingly supports her entitlement to that amount, in addition to her own monthly Social Security payment, by testimony and other evidence showing that it is the minimum amount required to maintain her modest standard of living.

This is not a normal adversarial support proceeding between estranged spouses. To the contrary, petitioner remains devoted to her husband and his care and visits him several times a week at the nursing home where he now resides. Respondent David Septuagenarian was not able to appear in court to participate in this proceeding due to his ill health and was represented by a guardian ad litem and court appointed counsel. On his behalf, apparently to avoid the possibility of his waiving medicaid benefits, they did not oppose the petition but stopped short of supporting it.

David Septuagenarian's income consists entirely of a pension of $375 and Social Security benefits of about $800 a month. Prior to his illness and confinement to a nursing home, those funds, combined with petitioner's Social Security benefits of less than $400 a month, paid their joint expenses. The Commissioner of Social Services, under contract with the federal government, pursuant to Social Services Law § 363–b, has determined that virtually all of respondent's income should be used to partially reimburse the state for its expenditures for his care, medical attention, housing and food. 18 N.Y.C.R.R. § 360.5.

Does an institutionalized spouse, receiving public assistance under the medicaid program, which requires that substantially all of his income be applied to his support and medical care, have sufficient means to support his or her spouse?

The Social Services Law sets forth the medicaid eligibility requirements and exemptions from the requirement that all of a medicaid recipient's income be applied to the cost of her or his care. SSL § 366. Section 366(2)(a)(7) of that statute exempts "payments for support of dependents required to be made pursuant to court order * * * ." The petitioner argues that the plain language of the statute specifically provides for the issuance of an order of support as she requests. The Commissioner counters that the statute applies to orders of support already issued at the time the medicaid recipient is found eligible for assistance. Although an interpretation of the statute is pivotal to the resolution of this controversy, there is neither case law nor legislative history upon which to rely for guidance.

* * *

There are two important public policy issues which must have faced the legislature when the statute was drafted. However, except for the words of the statute itself, we have no indication of the legislature's position on either.

The first stems from Mr. Septuagenarian's status as a public assistance recipient. Since the Commissioner intends to use Mr. Septuagenarian's assets to reduce the public's burden for his support, it can be argued that it is the public which pays any support granted petitioner. The medicaid rules now clearly provide for a portion of an institutionalized spouse's income equal to the difference between his or her spouse's actual income and the amount that spouse would receive on public assistance, if the spouse's income falls below the public assistance level, to be applied to the dependent spouse's support. Under that rule petitioner would, essentially, be granted public assistance at the same level as others requiring it. However, if she receives support based on her standard of living, it would be measured by her prior life style rather than the statutory guidelines applicable to those on public assistance. The net effect would be that the overall cost to the public for the support and care of both Mr. and Mrs. Septuagenarian will be more than it would be if both received maximum public assistance benefits.

On the other hand, to deprive women, and particularly women of petitioner's generation who, in many cases, were denied an equal opportunity to fulfill their potential in the employment market and are, therefore, dependent on their husbands for support, access to their husbands' pension and assets in their later years effectively sentences many of them to tremendous hardship and a complete disruption of their lives at a time when they are extremely vulnerable.

We must note that an overwhelming majority of married women are younger than their husbands. In addition, actuarial tables tell us that women live longer than men. (For example, a woman of 70 will outlive her 75 year old husband by more than eleven years.) From those facts, together with the common knowledge that medical costs for many illnesses of old age are beyond the financial means of most American families, we can reasonably draw the conclusion that husbands are more likely to require care which will deplete the marital assets than their wives, who are likely to be the economically weaker spouse. So in cases such as this, where the petitioner is 72 years old and infirm, women will be forced from their homes, deprived of even their modest life styles and relegated to a life of grinding poverty.

We must presume that the legislature considered both of these issues when it enacted the statute. We must presume as well that it considered the question of a spouse's interest in his or her spouse's pension. While they have not addressed the issue *sub judice*, our appellate courts have held spouses to have a proprietary interest in their spouses pension in matrimonial actions. * * * Accordingly, in interpreting the statute, we must consider petitioner's interest in her husband's pension. In coming to that conclusion, we are not unmindful of the seemingly contrary holding in *Granneman v. Myers*, 115 Cal.App.3d 846, 171 Cal.Rptr. 583, which the Commissioner urges should be persuasive here.

The *Granneman* facts differ from this case. In *Granneman*, the non-institutionalized spouse was attacking the validity of a California statute which provided, essentially, that the non-institutionalized spouse would receive support from the institutionalized spouse at the public assistance level, without exception for court orders of support. The California Court of Appeal, that state's intermediate appellate court, held that the legislature, in a community property state, could require a greater portion of the marital assets be applied to the support of an institutionalized spouse than would be available for his or her support if the parties had divorced. That same principle is probably applicable to an equitable distribution state such as New York, but we see no legislative intent to set such a requirement in this state.

Furthermore, the Commissioner's reliance on the *Granneman* case *supra*, for the principle that the legislature can give no greater benefit to public assistance recipients than the federal statute provides is also misplaced. Neither the rule in that case, nor in the federal law, prohibits a state from providing benefits in excess of those provided for by the federal statute, so long as federal funds are not used to fund them. It appears that the California legislature intended to limit that state to the maximum benefits under the federal statute. We see no evidence that the New York State legislature had the same intent.

Recently, the Appellate Division considered the question of whether basic Social Security benefits were public assistance or insurance and found them to be "akin to an annuity" and "not a form of public assistance." No other conclusion can be reached in this case and all of Mr. Septuagenarian's income will be treated as pension proceeds. Were Social Security benefits public assistance, the petitioner would not be able to consider them as a potential source for her support.

The plain language of Social Services Law § 366(2)(a)(7) permits the order for which petitioner prays. We find no legislative intent to the contrary and that to deny her the support she seeks would cause her and other spouses similarly situated great hardship. Significantly, the legislature placed with the courts, and not the Commissioner, the discretion to grant relief from the potentially draconian results of the medicaid rules on a case by case basis. Accordingly, petitioner is awarded support in the sum of $1,125 a month, retroactive to the date that she filed her petition.

Notes and Questions

1. What would have been the outcome in *Septuagenarian* if the partners had been (a) long-term, unmarried cohabitants [*see* Chapter 5]; (b) divorced; (c) married, but separated? (In *Septuagenarian* are they not separated?)

2. Assume that the jurisdiction in question has enacted the Uniform Premarital Agreement Act ("UPAA") [see Chapter 4] and that the Mr. and Mrs. Septuagenarian had entered into a premarital agreement relieving each other of all liability for medical support. As a judge, what effect would you give to such a stipulation?

3. Under the "Medicare Catastrophic Coverage Act" (Public Law 100–360), as of July 1, 1992, the spouse of a nursing home resident who receives Medicaid benefits may keep income equal to 150% of the federal poverty level for a couple, plus a shelter allowance, and at least $12,000 or one half of the couple's assets, whichever is greater, up to a maximum of $60,000. The monthly allowance is indexed for inflation. What are the advantages of this approach, as compared to that in *Septuagenarian*?

4. In Schweiker v. Gray Panthers, 453 U.S. 34, 101 S.Ct. 2633, 69 L.Ed.2d 460 (1981), the Supreme Court upheld federal regulations permitting the Social Security Administration to assume, or "deem," that a portion of the income of the Medicaid applicant's spouse is available to

the applicant, noting that the Senate Report on the legislation indicates that

> "the committee believes it is proper to expect spouses to support each other and parents to be held accountable for the support of their minor children.... Beyond such degree of relationship, however, requirements imposed are often destructive and harmful to the relations among members of the family group. Thus, States may not include in their plans provisions for requiring contributions from relatives *other than a spouse or the parent of a minor child.** * *"
>
> S.Rep.No. 404, 89th Cong., 1st Sess., 78 (1965) (emphasis added)

Is the Senate correct that there is a greater risk that deeming will prove destructive and harmful to family relations other than those of spouses and parents/children? Why didn't Congress treat long-term cohabitants the same way as spouses?

5. Many states have spousal support rules that limit defenses to a support action when the claimant spouse is a public assistance recipient. For example, in Campas v. Campas, 61 Misc.2d 49, 304 N.Y.S.2d 876 (N.Y.Fam.Ct.1969), the court interpreted New York's spousal responsibility law (N.Y. Soc. Serv. L. § 101(1)), to require spousal support even though the claimant spouse had abandoned her husband eight years earlier: "So long as the recipient of public assistance remains the respondent's lawful wife," the court held, "the burden of her support should fall upon him rather than the public." Is this fair?

SECTION 4. NAMES

KRUZEL v. PODELL

Supreme Court of Wisconsin, 1975.
67 Wis.2d 138, 226 N.W.2d 458..

Heffernan, Justice.

This case presents the question of whether upon marriage a woman is required by law to assume the surname of her husband. We conclude that a woman upon marriage adopts the surname of her husband by thereafter customarily using that name, but no law requires that she do so. If she continues to use her anti-nuptial [sic! Freud?] surname, her name is unchanged by the fact that marriage has occurred.

Kathleen Rose Harney married Joseph Michael Kruzel on July 31, 1971. She is an art teacher in the Milwaukee school system and was issued a teacher's certificate under her birth-given surname. She was employed by the Milwaukee school system under that name and exhibited works of art under the name Harney. She at all times used the name Harney and not Kruzel.

The Milwaukee School Board insisted, however, for group insurance purposes, that Kathleen either use her husband's surname or "legally" change her surname to Harney.

Kathleen accordingly petitioned the circuit court for Milwaukee county for an order "changing" her surname from Kruzel to Harney. At the hearing it was shown that at no time had the petitioner ever used the name Kruzel. The only time she had used Kruzel as her surname was in the petition for the instant proceeding, and then only for the purpose of "changing" that name to Harney.

The trial judge relied on 57 Am.Jur.2d, Name, § 9, page 281, which states: "It is well settled by common-law principles and immemorial custom that a woman upon marriage abandons her maiden name and assumes the husband's surname."

The trial judge also reasoned that § 247.20, Stats., which permits a woman, upon divorce, under some circumstances, to "resume" her maiden name, indicates that "a woman upon marriage assumes the surname of the husband * * *."

No one testified in opposition to the name change. However, the trial judge stated that to permit Kathleen to bear the surname Harney and her husband the name Kruzel would be contrary to the best interests of any children that might thereafter be born to the marriage. He said that it should be agreed at the time of marriage that all members of the family should bear the same name. "If they cannot at that time agree, it would be better for them, any children they may have, and society in general that they do not enter into the marriage relationship." He concluded that, upon marriage, her surname was changed to that of her husband, and the petition for change of name back to Harney was denied. The appeal is from the order dismissing the petition for change of name.

Although the petition brought by Kathleen was based upon her assumption that the marriage had compelled a change of name in law, the record shows, and counsel on appeal concedes, that the petitioner never used the surname of her husband but only her paternal surname. Accordingly, this case does not present the legal problems that might arise were a married woman, who had assumed and used her husband's surname, to seek to change that married name and resume her maiden name.

If it can be said that a marriage does not compel a woman to assume her husband's surname, in this case no name change took place at all, and Kathleen's last name remained Harney.

While counsel for the petitioner and for the trial judge have ably briefed the court on numerous other related aspects of the law of name change, the linchpin of either argument is whether a name change occurs automatically upon marriage. The respondent has argued that the trial judge correctly concluded that the common law compelled a marital name change. The petitioner's counsel argued that the common law does not require or cause a change in a woman's surname upon marriage, but rather that such change of name will occur only with the acquiescence of the woman and the use by her of her husband's surname, i.e., the change of name is one of custom and not of law.

There is, as counsel for respondent concedes, no Wisconsin statute that requires a married woman to take her husband's surname. The respondent argues that, because it is customary for a wife to take her husband's name on marriage, that custom has ripened into a rule of common law. While it is true that some customs of society have developed into rules of law, there is no evidence that in this jurisdiction the custom was ever accorded that effect. Our case law also is silent on this point.

* * *

It is undoubtedly true that the tendency of a wife to take her husband's surname was spawned by the common law theory of marriage. Under that theory, upon marriage, a man and a woman became one and that one was the husband. * * *

Obviously, the conditions that led to the practice of having women adopt their husbands' surnames no longer have their foundation in existing law. * * *

We conclude that the statutes of Wisconsin are consistent with the common law, which does not require a wife to assume her husband's surname and when the husband's surname was acquired, it was the result of usage and her holding out to the world that the surname is the same as the husband's.

Since we conclude in this case that Kathleen Rose Harney was never compelled to change her name, nor did she ever in fact adopt the surname Kruzel by usage, her petition, although ostensibly brought under § 296.36, Stats., amounted only to a request for judicial recognition that she had been correct in using her maiden surname in the past. The recognition of her right should have been given by the mandate of the court. Accordingly, the order is vacated and the cause remanded to the trial court for the entry of an order declaring her right to use the name of Kathleen Rose Harney.

ROBERT W. HANSEN, JUSTICE (dissenting).

* * *

The new "habitual user" test replaces the options granted to married women under *Lane*. For now the majority opinion makes clear that a married woman in this state acquires her husband's surname only if, as and when it is "* * * the result of usage and her holding out to the world that the surname is the same as the husband's." If she doesn't use it, she doesn't get it. If she blurs the situation by using both her maiden name and her married name, she will be hard put to qualify as an "habitual user" under the new test.

What does this new "habitual user" test do to the options granted to married women in this state by the *Lane* decision?

(1) *It ends the right of a married woman in this state to use either her married name, or her maiden name, or both.* For the "either-or", it substitutes "one-or-the-other." Since the petitioner here for a change-of-

name never did " * * * in fact adopt the surname Kruzel [her husband's name] by usage, * * * " her petition, the majority holds, was not really for change-of-name but " * * * a request for judicial recognition that she had been correct in using her maiden surname in the past." * * *

(2) *It finds unnecessary the existence of a legal name for the children unit, available to husband and wife, and prescribed for their children.* Under the *Lane* holding the married woman's use of her maiden name did not bar or affect her right to also use her married name, the court there holding that she could use her maiden name and that, nonetheless, "since her marriage she is entitled to the name of her husband, Zentner." However, now under the majority's rule, if the wife is an "habitual user" of her maiden name, she does not acquire her husband's name. She is not entitled to use the name of her husband and their children. Folks may differ on what that family name ought be. By law and custom it certainly has been the surname of the husband. But the legislature could as well make it the maiden name of the wife, or some combination of the names of the husband and the wife. That there be such single name available to spouses, and identifying their children, is inherent in the concept of marriage as a partnership. The roles of the partners may vary, but the identity of the partnership as a viable and functioning unit or entity is not served by its having no name. That idea should appeal only to those who see our society as a numerical aggregate of atomized particles rather than as a plurality of groupings, the family the most basic and significant among them.

(3) *It eliminates the married woman's prerogative to change her mind.* Under the *Lane* option a married woman in this state could, at her option, use either her maiden name or her married name. The right to use what the court then called her baptismal name was hers to exercise whenever "she chooses to give or take them in that form." Under the majority's "habitual user" test, it is only through usage that a married woman secures the right to use the family name, that of her husband. If there is "habitual use" of her married name, and only if there is, has she " * * * effected a common law change in her name." No such "habitual use," and her name remains her maiden name. There is an element of choice remaining but only as to whether the family name is to be acquired or the maiden name retained. Circumstances may change, but the choice, once made, appears final. If the bride, after the wedding, elects to retain her maiden name by not getting into the habit of using her husband's surname, she has made her decision. If, after the babies arrive, she would like to go to the PTA meeting as Mrs. So-and-So, that right has long ago been abandoned by her under the new test. For the free and continuing "either-or" alternatives of *Lane*, there has been substituted a "one-or-the-other" election, apparently irrevocable once exercised. Who gains by that?

The petitioner-schoolteacher here came to court seeking a change-of-name in order that she might teach her classes under her maiden name. The writer would affirm the trial court here and hold that the right she sought to secure was hers before she came to court. The majority vacates and remands, with directions to the trial court to enter an order that the petitioner never acquired her married name because she never was an "habitual user" of it. When she leaves the courtroom with that order she will have won only what was her right to do before she came to court. In the winning she will have lost for herself and others entitlement to the family name, the right to use either her maiden name or her married name or both, and the right to ever change her mind. The thought occurs that she might have been better off if she had never gone to that courthouse at all.

Notes and Questions

1. The married woman is nowhere *required* to take the husband's name. But, in several states, marriage may still effect a legal name change in one context or another.

2. Consider Harry Krause, Kinship Relations, 4 INTERNATIONAL ENCYCLOPEDIA OF COMPARATIVE LAW § 144 (1976):

> An interesting feature of Polish, Czechoslovakian and East German law is that the married woman, as a point of equality, does not necessarily adopt her husband's name. Thus, while East German spouses are required to have a common name, they may choose either the wife's or the husband's name (FC § 7). In consequence, even legitimate children may bear their mother's surname. In Poland, the wife has the option to keep her own name, adopt her husband's name or add the husband's name to her own (FC art. 25). Legitimate children bear their father's name, unless the mother has kept her own name or has added her husband's name to hers and the spouses declared at the time they married that their children would take the name of the wife (FC art. 88 par. I). In Czechoslovakia, spouses may adopt either the wife's or the husband's name as their common name or they may keep their separate names. In the latter case, they must declare which of their names their divorce will take (FC § 8).

3. At divorce, most states have established a procedure whereby a woman may change her surname to her maiden name if she wishes. *See* UMDA § 314(d). In the less common case where the divorced wife (having kept her ex-husband's name) remarries and, instead of taking the name of her new husband, keeps her ex-husband's name, does the ex-husband have a right to compel his remarried ex-wife to change her name? In Cook County (Illinois) Circuit Court, Mr. Brode testified that his name was loaned to Mrs. Brode as a "cattle brand" and that she should have given it up when she became "a part of another person's stable." "I'm not cattle, you can't brand me," testified Mrs. Brode. While the parties' reasoning may not be persuasive, the Court refused the husband's petition. *See* N. Y. TIMES, May 22, 1977, at p. 54, col. 4.

SECTION 5. MARRIAGE AND TORT LAW

A. TORT ACTIONS BETWEEN HUSBAND AND WIFE

Under the common law, a husband could not sue his wife in tort, nor could a wife sue her husband. One reason for this result was the doctrine that a husband and wife were one legal person; another was that the husband was liable for his wife's torts; another was that the wife could only sue by joining the husband as a plaintiff. Thus a suit by one spouse against the other would legally mean a lawsuit against oneself.

After the passage of the Married Women's Property Acts, these reasons no longer applied. But courts nonetheless continued to disallow tort actions between spouses, utilizing one or another of these public policy arguments:

> a) Such suits would disturb the harmony of the marital relation. b) They would involve the courts in endless litigation over trivial disputes between the spouses. c) They would encourage fraud and collusion between spouses where the conduct constituting the tort is covered by insurance. d) The criminal law provides an adequate remedy. e) Such suits would reward the defendant spouse for his own wrong, since, if the parties are living together, they both share in the benefits of the judgment.

HOMER H. CLARK, LAW OF DOMESTIC RELATIONS 253 (1st ed. 1968).

Although noting that "[t]he kindest thing to be said for the first four of these policy arguments is that they are frivolous," Professor Clark nonetheless reported, as late as 1968, that "[w]here the tort consists in harm to the person of a spouse, the majority of American courts persist in refusing relief." CLARK, *supra*, at 252–53.

Over the past thirty years, most courts have come to agree with Professor Clark. As of 1992, thirty-eight states and the District of Columbia had fully abrogated interspousal tort immunity either by judicial opinion or by statute. Nine states (Florida, Georgia, Idaho, Iowa, Massachusetts, Nevada, Rhode Island, Utah, and Vermont) had abolished the rule only in specific circumstances such as intentional or vehicular torts. *See* LEONARD KARP & CHERYL L. KARP, DOMESTIC TORTS 240 App. B (Supp. Dec. 1992). Only three jurisdictions still fully retained the doctrine. *See* Peters v. Peters, 63 Haw. 653, 634 P.2d 586, 590–91 (Haw.1981); Alfree v. Alfree, 410 A.2d 161, 163 (Del.1979), appeal dismissed, 446 U.S. 931, 100 S.Ct. 2145, 64 L.Ed.2d 783 (1980); Smith v. Southern Farm Bureau Casualty Ins. Co., 247 La. 695, 174 So.2d 122, 124 (La.1965).

Notes and Questions

1. In states that have abolished spousal immunity, courts have had to decide whether a tort action should, or may, be joined with a divorce

action. At this point, there is no agreement on this issue. *Compare* Maharam v. Maharam, 123 A.D.2d 165, 510 N.Y.S.2d 104 (1986) (joinder encouraged); *with* Heacock v. Heacock, 402 Mass. 21, 520 N.E.2d 151 (1988) (joinder barred); Stuart v. Stuart, 143 Wis.2d 347, 421 N.W.2d 505 (1988) (joinder permitted but discouraged). The issue is complicated by the fact that some states permit spousal fault to be taken into account in dividing marital property and awarding alimony, while others do not. *See* Chapters 14 and 15.

2. Should spouses be able to sue each other for intentional infliction of emotional distress? If so, when? In Colon v. Colon, 600 F.Supp. 814 (W.D.N.Y.1985), a prisoner brought a civil rights action under 42 U.S.C.A. § 1983 alleging a violation of his constitutional rights because his wife "refuses to write him while in prison or to communicate with him by telephone, visits, etc." The court held that "[a]lthough her conscience may one day compel Robin Colon to write to her husband, the constitution will never do so. On the contrary, the Constitution guarantees that defendant need never write or call anyone against her will." *See also* Ira M. Ellman & Stephen D. Sugarman, *Spousal Emotional Abuse as a Tort?*, 55 MD. L. REV. 1268 (1996) (suggesting that emotional distress claims be allowed only when the spousal conduct violates a criminal statute).

B. HEART BALM ACTIONS

The common law granted husbands whose wives' affections had strayed an action against the interloper. The action for "criminal conversation" required proof of the defendant's adulterous sexual intercourse with the plaintiff's wife and covered both rape and consensual sexual relations. The related tort of "alienation of affections" protected the husband's relational interest, permitting him to sue, as the name of the tort suggests, based on an interference with the marriage which resulted in a change in the wife's attitudes and affections. *See* KEETON, PROSSER, & KEETON ON TORTS 918–31 (5th ed. 1984).

In states where these torts survive, they are now available to both spouses. But instead of expanding the availability of the "heart balm" claims to aggrieved wives, most courts and legislatures have taken the opposite tack. At least twenty-eight states have either abolished or severely restricted these torts. *See* J. THOMAS OLDHAM, DIVORCE, SEPARATION AND DISTRIBUTION OF PROPERTY § 8.01[4]. But some states have recently reaffirmed their availability. For example, the Utah Supreme Court, upholding an action for alienation of affections, noted that it protected a spouse's "valuable interest in the marriage *relationship*, including its intimacy, companionship, support, duties, and affection." Nelson v. Jacobsen, 669 P.2d 1207 (Utah 1983) (emphasis in original). *Accord*, Overstreet v. Merlos, 570 So.2d 1196 (Miss.1990); Heist v. Heist, 46 N.C.App. 521, 265 S.E.2d 434 (1980).

Some courts have encouraged aggrieved spouses to utilize alternate remedies. For example, in O'Neil v. Schuckardt, 112 Idaho 472, 733 P.2d

693 (Idaho 1986), the Idaho Supreme Court held that an aggrieved husband could not maintain an action for alienation of affections against a religious sect and its officers for "converting" plaintiff's wife, but left open the possibility of recovery on the basis of invasion of privacy based on the same facts. *But see* Strock v. Pressnell, 38 Ohio St.3d 207, 527 N.E.2d 1235 (1988); Figuciredo–Torres v. Nickel, 584 A.2d 69 (Md.App. 1991) (denying recovery on any basis).

C. SPOUSAL CONSORTIUM CLAIMS

Under the common law, the husband was entitled to maintain an action against a tortfeasor who had intentionally injured his wife so as to deprive him of her services, society, and conjugal relations. As the negligence action developed during the nineteenth century, most courts extended the husband's consortium claim to negligent tortfeasors. A wife did not have a corresponding consortium claim; she could not sue in her own name, and was regarded as having an entitlement from her husband to support, but not to services.

While the Married Women's Property Acts might have been expected to result in extension of the consortium claim to wives, they did not. It was not until 1950, in Hitaffer v. Argonne Co., 183 F.2d 811 (D.C.Cir. 1950), cert. denied 340 U.S. 852, 71 S.Ct. 80, 95 L.Ed. 624 (1950), that an American court held that a wife could maintain a consortium action based on an injury to her husband. In the years since 1950, the vast majority of states have followed *Hitaffer* and extended the consortium claim to wives on the same basis as husbands; in a handful of others, the doctrine has been rejected for both spouses. *See* Boucher By Boucher v. Dixie Medical Center, 850 P.2d 1179 (Utah 1992) (rejecting action).

Under current law, both husband and wife may recover when a spouse has been injured by the negligence or intentional conduct of a third person. In order to avoid the risk of double recovery, many states require that the consortium claim be brought with the underlying tort action and permit the defendant to raise any defenses available against the victim against the victim's spouse as well.

Damage awards for loss of consortium generally reflect the value of damages awarded to the tort victim. Sometimes the awards are substantial. *See, e.g.*, Uniroyal Goodrich Tire Co. v. Martinez, 928 S.W.2d 64 (Tex.App.1995) (affirming $500,000 award for loss of spousal consortium and $1,000,000 award for consortium losses of each of two children). At least one court has rejected enhancement of consortium damages when the injury allegedly caused a divorce. Prill v. Hampton, 154 Wis.2d 667, 453 N.W.2d 909 (Wis.App.1990).

Over the past decade or so, several courts have addressed the question of whether cohabitants can also claim damages for loss of consortium. Feliciano v. Rosemar Silver Co., 401 Mass. 141, 514 N.E.2d 1095 (1987), for example, involved Marcial and Delores Feliciano, who had cohabited for approximately twenty years "as a de facto married couple." Delores had taken Marcial's surname, they held themselves out as husband and wife, had joint savings accounts, filed joint tax returns, jointly owned their home, "depended on each other for companionship, comfort, love and guidance, and maintained a sexual relationship to the exclusion of all others." [Massachusetts does not recognize common law marriage.] The Court followed the prevailing pattern in holding that:

> "Marriage is not merely a contract between the parties. It is the foundation of the family. It is a social institution of the highest importance. The Commonwealth has a deep interest that its integrity is not jeopardized. Our recognition of a right of recovery for the loss of a spouse's consortium promotes that value. Conversely, that value would be subverted by our recognition of a right to recover for loss of consortium by a person who has not accepted the correlative responsibilities of marriage. This we are unwilling to do.
>
> ... Distinguishing between the marriage relationship and the myriad relationships that may exist between mere cohabitants serves the purpose of limiting protection to interests and values that are reasonably ascertainable. That cohabitants must have a 'stable and significant' relationship to qualify for loss of consortium recovery, a standard relied on in the case of Butcher v. Superior Court, 139 Cal.App.3d 58, 70 (1983), is an unsatisfactorily vague and indefinite standard."
>
> 514 N.E.2d 1095 at 1097.

The court also noted that no other state courts of last resort had approved extension of the spousal consortium claim to unmarried cohabitants. *See also* Elden v. Sheldon, 46 Cal.3d 267, 250 Cal.Rptr. 254, 758 P.2d 582 (1988); Sawyer v. Bailey, 413 A.2d 165 (Me.1980).

Problem 3–7:

The state legislature is reviewing the whole area of spousal immunities and tort claims. Currently, consortium claims are available to either spouse, spousal immunity has been abolished for intentional torts but not for negligence actions, and "heart-balm" claims, while still available, are hemmed in by a one year statute of limitations and a requirement that the plaintiff show economic loss resulting from the tort. Tort actions may not be joined with a divorce action. There are no special rules relating to cohabitants. You have been asked to advise the legislature on the pros and cons of the current approach and to make suggestions for reform. The legislature's general goals are fairness and efficiency.

SECTION 6. MEDICAL AND PROCREATIVE DECISION MAKING

A. MEDICAL DECISION MAKING FOR AN INCOMPETENT SPOUSE

NEW YORK TIMES, Nov. 14, 1968, p. 36, col. 1. Hempstead, L. I., Nov. 13 (AP)—A 24–year-old mother of three children, who was injured in an automobile crash, died today after her husband had refused on religious grounds to allow doctors to give her a blood transfusion.

"The police said the victim, Betty Jackson, was pinned in her car when it struck a utility pole at Wellsley Street and Rumsen Avenue near her home. She was admitted to Hempstead General Hospital at about 11:30 a.m.

Doctors said examination showed Mrs. Jackson was suffering from multiple injuries and bleeding internally. They sought permission from her husband, Clemons Jackson, to administer a transfusion.

Mr. Jackson, a follower of Jehovah's Witnesses, refused. He remained adamant, despite the pleading of several doctors, and at 4:30 p.m. the hospital administrator appealed to State Supreme Court Judge William Sullivan.

'If I allow blood to be given into her and if she lived, she wouldn't be considered my wife,' the Nassau County police said Mr. Jackson had told the doctors.

Judge Sullivan refused to order the transfusion. Mrs. Jackson died at 6:30 P.M. Her three children, who were with her when the car struck the utility pole, were also in the hospital and reported in fair condition."

Notes and Questions

1. While there is no common law authority for the practice, when a patient is incompetent, it has become standard for doctors to seek consent to any medical procedure from a close family member; in the case of a married person, the spouse is invariably considered the closest relative. A Presidential Commission has listed five reasons for such deference to the patient's family:

> (a) The family is generally most concerned about the good of the patient.
>
> (b) The family will also usually be most knowledgeable about the patient's goals, preferences, and values.
>
> (c) The family deserves recognition as an important social unit that ought to be treated, within limits, as a responsible decision maker in matters that intimately affect its members.
>
> (d) Especially in a society in which many other traditional forms of community have eroded, participation in a family is often an important dimension of personal fulfillment.
>
> (e) Since a protected sphere of privacy and autonomy is required for the flourishing of this interpersonal union, institutions and the state should be reluctant to intrude, particularly regarding matters that are personal and on which there is a wide range of opinion in society.

PRESIDENT'S COMMISSION, DECIDING TO FORGO LIFE-SUSTAINING TREATMENT 127 (1983).

Based on this reasoning, can marital relationships be distinguished from nonmarital cohabitation? Should cohabitants be treated the same way as marriage partners for purposes of medical decision making, or differently?

2. Following the reasoning of the President's Commission, the Uniform Rights of the Terminally Ill Act grants to family members the right to make decisions about the withdrawal of life support in the case of a terminally ill patient who is "no longer able to make decisions regarding administration of life-sustaining treatment," and who has neither appointed an agent to make health care decisions on his or her behalf or expressed her preferences in a "living will." The authority to consent is to be exercised, in order of priority, by:

> 1) the spouse of the individual [patient];
>
> 2) an adult child . . . or, if there is more than one adult child, a majority of the adult children who are reasonably available for consultation;
>
> 3) the parents of the individual; . . .
>
> UNIFORM RIGHTS OF THE TERMINALLY ILL ACT § 7(B) (1989).

The Act makes no provision for cohabitants.

3. The newspaper story reports Mr. Jackson's religious beliefs but fails to mention those of Mrs. Jackson. If the judge knew nothing of her beliefs, what should he have done? Under the Uniform Act, "[a] decision to grant or withhold consent . . . is not valid if it conflicts with the expressed intention of the individual." § 7(d).

4. If Mrs. Jackson had given a power of attorney for health care decision making to her mother, and her mother approved the transfusion, what should the hospital have done?

B. THE AFFIRMATIVE OBLIGATION TO OBTAIN MEDICAL ASSISTANCE

Spouses have been held subject to an affirmative obligation to obtain medical assistance for each other. So, for example, in State v. Mally, 139 Mont. 599, 366 P.2d 868 (1961) the court upheld the husband's conviction for involuntary manslaughter when he left his wife without medical attention for two days when she was suffering from chronic hepatitis and kidney disease. Similarly, in State v. Smith, 65 Me. 257 (1876), the court upheld the husband's manslaughter conviction when he confined his wife, who was insane and crippled, in a drafty room where she died of exposure.

A spouse does not have a duty to overrule a reckless decision of the other spouse to refuse treatment. So, in Westrup v. Commonwealth, 123 Ky. 95, 93 S.W. 646 (Ky.1906) when a wife believed in natural childbirth and refused treatment or medicine, the husband was not held criminally responsible when she died after complications in child birth. In People v. Robbins, 83 A.D.2d 271, 443 N.Y.S.2d 1016 (App.Div.1981) the court reached the same conclusion when the wife, for religious reasons, decided to stop taking her medicine for epilepsy and diabetes and died.

C. PROCREATIVE DECISION MAKING

PLANNED PARENTHOOD OF CENTRAL MISSOURI v. DANFORTH

Supreme Court of the United States, 1976.
428 U.S. 52, 96 S.Ct. 2831, 49 L.Ed.2d 788.

JUSTICE BLACKMUN delivered the opinion of the Court.

* * * *The Spouse's Consent.* Section 3(3) requires the prior written consent of the spouse of the woman seeking an abortion during the first 12 weeks of pregnancy, unless "the abortion is certified by a licensed physician to be necessary in order to preserve the life of the mother."

The appellees defend § 3(3) on the ground that it was enacted in the light of the General Assembly's "perception of marriage as an institution," Brief for Appellees 34, and that any major change in family status is a decision to be made jointly by the marriage partners. Reference is made to an abortion's possible effect on the woman's childbearing potential. It is said that marriage always has entailed some legislatively imposed limitations: reference is made to adultery and bigamy as criminal offenses; to Missouri's general requirement, Mo.Rev.Stat. § 453.030.3 (1969), that for an adoption of a child born in wedlock the consent of both parents is necessary; to similar joint consent requirements imposed by a number of States with respect to artificial insemination and the legitimacy of children so conceived; to the laws of two States requiring spousal consent for voluntary sterilization; and to the long-established requirement of spousal consent for the effective disposition of an interest in real property. It is argued that "[r]ecognizing that the consent of both parties is generally necessary * * * to begin a family, the legislature has determined that a change in the family structure set in motion by mutual consent should be terminated only by mutual consent," Brief for Appellees 38, and that what the legislature did was to exercise its inherent policymaking power "for what was believed to be in the best interests of all people of Missouri."

The appellants on the other hand, contend that § 3(3) obviously is designed to afford the husband the right unilaterally to prevent or veto an abortion, whether or not he is the father of the fetus, and that this not only violates *Roe* and *Doe* but is also in conflict with other decided cases. They also refer to the situation where the husband's consent cannot be obtained because he cannot be located. And they assert that § 3(3) is vague and overbroad.

In *Roe* and *Doe* we specifically reserved decision on the question whether a requirement for consent by the father of the fetus, by the spouse, or by the parents, or a parent, of an unmarried minor, may be constitutionally imposed. We now hold that the State may not constitutionally require the consent of the spouse, as is specified under § 3(3) of the Missouri Act, as a condition for abortion during the first 12 weeks of pregnancy. We thus agree with the dissenting judge in the present case, and with the courts whose decisions are cited above, that the State cannot "delegate to a spouse a veto power which the state itself is absolutely and totally prohibited from exercising during the first trimester of pregnancy." Clearly, since the State cannot regulate or proscribe abortion during the first stage, when the physician and his patient make that decision, the State cannot delegate authority to any particular person, even the spouse, to prevent abortion during that same period.

We are not unaware of the deep and proper concern and interest that a devoted and protective husband has in his wife's pregnancy and in the growth and development of the fetus she is carrying. Neither has this Court failed to appreciate the importance of the marital relationship in our society. *See, e.g., Griswold v. Connecticut*, [p. 19]; *Maynard v. Hill*, [p. 184]. Moreover, we recognize that the decision whether to undergo or to forego an abortion may have profound effects on the future of any marriage, effects that are both physical and mental, and possibly deleterious. Notwithstanding these factors, we cannot hold that the State has the constitutional authority to give the spouse unilaterally the ability to prohibit the wife from terminating her pregnancy, when the State itself lacks that right. *See Eisenstadt v. Baird*, [p. 23, n. 3].

It seems manifest that, ideally, the decision to terminate a pregnancy should be one concurred in by both the wife and her husband. No marriage may be viewed as harmonious or successful if the marriage partners are fundamentally divided on so important and vital an issue. But it is difficult to believe that the goal of fostering mutuality and trust in a marriage, and of strengthening the marital relationship and the marriage institution, will be achieved by giving the husband a veto power exercisable for any reason whatsoever or for no reason at all. Even if the State had the ability to delegate to the husband a power it itself could not exercise, it is not at all likely that such action would further, as the District Court majority phrased it, the "interest of the state in protecting the mutuality of decisions vital to the marriage relationship."

We recognize, of course, that when a woman, with the approval of her physician but without the approval of her husband, decides to terminate her pregnancy, it could be said that she is acting unilaterally. The obvious fact is that when the wife and the husband disagree on this decision, the view of only one of the two marriage partners can prevail. Since it is the woman who physically bears the child and who is the more directly and immediately affected by the pregnancy, as between the two, the balance weighs in her favor.

We conclude that § 3(3) of the Missouri Act is inconsistent with the standards enunciated in *Roe v. Wade* and is unconstitutional. It is therefore unnecessary for us to consider the appellant's additional challenges to § 3(3) based on vagueness and overbreadth.

PLANNED PARENTHOOD v. CASEY

Supreme Court of the United States, 1992.
505 U.S. 833, 112 S.Ct. 2791, 120 L.Ed.2d 674.

JUSTICE O'CONNOR, JUSTICE KENNEDY, and JUSTICE SOUTER announced the judgment of the Court and delivered the opinion of the Court with respect to Parts I, II, III, V–A, V–C, and VI . . .

* * *

V

C

The District Court heard the testimony of numerous expert witnesses and made detailed findings of fact regarding the effect of [the statute's requirement that, with certain exceptions, a married woman must sign a statement indicating that she has notified her husband of her intended abortion before obtaining abortion services. It concluded that the requirement would deter women who were victims of domestic violence from obtaining abortions and that, although the statutes contained exemptions for some forms of domestic violence, these were insufficient.] "Because of the nature of the battering relationship, battered women are unlikely to avail themselves of the exceptions to . . . the Act, regardless of whether the section applies to them."....

These findings are supported by studies of domestic violence. The American Medical Association (AMA) has published a summary of the recent research in this field, which indicates that in an average 12–month period in this country, approximately two million women are the victims of severe assaults by their male partners. In a 1985 survey, women reported that nearly one of every eight husbands had assaulted their wives during the past year. The AMA views these figures as "marked underestimates" . . .

Other studies fill in the rest of this troubling picture. Physical violence is only the most visible form of abuse. Psychological abuse, particularly forced social and economic isolation of women is also common. Many victims of domestic violence remain with their abusers, perhaps because they perceive no superior alternative. Many abused women who find temporary refuge in a shelter return to their husbands in large part because they have no other source of income. Returning to one's abuser can be dangerous. Recent Federal Bureau of Investigation statistics disclose that 8.8% of all homicide victims in the United States are killed by their spouse. Mercy & Saltzman, Fatal Violence Among Spouses in the United States, 1976–85, 79 Am. J. Pub. Health 595 (1989). Thirty percent of female homicide victims are killed by their male partners....

This information and the District Court's findings reinforce what common sense would suggest. In well-functioning marriages, spouses discuss important intimate decisions such as whether to bear a child. But there are millions of women in this country who are the victims of regular physical and psychological abuse at the hands of their husbands ... The spousal notification requirement is thus likely to prevent a significant number of women from obtaining an abortion ...

[The Act] embodies a view of marriage consonant with the common-law status of married women but repugnant to our present understanding of marriage and of the nature of the rights secured by the Constitution. Women do not lose their constitutionally protected liberty when they marry. The constitution protects all individuals, male or female, married or unmarried, from the abuse of governmental power even where that power is employed for the supposed benefit of a member of the individual's family. These considerations confirm our conclusion that [the spousal notification rule] ... is invalid.

Notes and Questions

1. Would a statute requiring a physician who has performed an abortion to inform the patient's husband *after* the procedure survive constitutional attack?

2. SB 935, 92d General Assembly, Illinois, 1981 and 1982 (*not enacted*) provided that:

> "(Sec. 401) The court shall enter a judgment of dissolution of marriage (formerly known as divorce) if: * * * (2) the court finds that, without cause or provocation by the petitioner: either party * * * has obtained an abortion without first having secured the written consent of the other spouse, unless the court finds the abortion was necessary to preserve the maternal life or that the other spouse rendered an informed voluntary consent to the abortion.
>
> "(Sec. 504) * * * (e) Notwithstanding any contrary provision, the court shall not grant a maintenance order in favor of a spouse whom it finds to have obtained an abortion without first having secured the written consent of the other spouse, unless the court finds the abortion was medically necessary to preserve the maternal life or that the other spouse rendered an informed voluntary consent to the abortion."

Would the bill be constitutional if enacted?

3. After the abortion is performed, the physician finds out that the wife has no funds of her own. Could the physician recover his or her fee from the husband who was not aware of the abortion until he received the bill? On what theory?

SECTION 7. MARRIAGE AND CRIME

A. CRIMES BY ONE SPOUSE AGAINST ANOTHER

1. Marital Rape

WARREN v. STATE

Supreme Court of Georgia, 1985.
255 Ga. 151, 336 S.E.2d 221.

SMITH, JUSTICE.

"When a woman says I do, does she give up her right to say I won't?" This question does not pose the real question, because rape and aggravated sodomy are not sexual acts of an ardent husband performed upon an initially apathetic wife, they are acts of violence that are accompanied with physical and mental abuse and often leave the victim with physical and psychological damage that is almost always long lasting. Thus we find the more appropriate question: When a woman says "I do" in Georgia does she give up her right to State protection from the violent acts of rape and aggravated sodomy performed by her husband. The answer is no. We affirm.

The appellant, Daniel Steven Warren, was indicted by a Fulton County Grand Jury for the rape and aggravated sodomy of his wife. They were living together as husband and wife at the time. The appellant filed a pre-trial general demurrer and motion to dismiss the indictment.

* * *

The appellant asserts that there exists within the rape statute an implicit marital exclusion that makes it legally impossible for a husband to be guilty of raping his wife.

* * *

What is behind the theory and belief that a husband could not be guilty of raping his wife? There are various explanations for the rule and all of them flow from the common law attitude toward women, the status of women and marriage.

Perhaps the most often used basis for the marital rape exemption is the view set out by Lord Hale in 1 Hale P.C. 629. It is known as Lord Hale's contractual theory. The statement attributed to Lord Hale used to support the theory is: "but a husband cannot be guilty of a rape committed by himself upon his lawful wife, for by their mutual matrimonial consent and contract the wife hath given up herself in this kind unto her husband which she cannot retreat."

* * *

Another theory stemming from medieval times is that of a wife being the husband's chattel or property. Since a married woman was part of her husband's property, nothing more than a chattel, rape was nothing more than a man making use of his own property.

A third theory is the unity in marriage or unity of person theory that held the very being or legal existence of a woman was suspended during marriage, or at least was incorporated and consolidated into that of her husband. In view of the fact that there was only one legal being, the husband, he could not be convicted of raping himself.

These three theories have been used to support the marital rape exemption. Others have tried to fill the chasm between these three theories with justifications for continuing the exemption in the face of changes in the recognition of women, their status, and the status of marriage. Some of the justifications include: Prevention of fabricated charges; Preventing wives from using rape charges for revenge; Preventing state intervention into marriage so that possible reconciliation will not be thwarted. A closer examination of the theories and justifications indicates that they are no longer valid, if they ever had any validity.

Hale's implied consent theory was created at a time when marriages were irrevocable and when all wives promised to "love, honor, and obey" and all husbands promised to "love, cherish, and protect until death do us part." Wives were subservient to their husbands, her identity was merged into his, her property became his property, and she took his name for her own.

There have been dramatic changes in women's rights and the status of women and marriage. * * *

One would be hard pressed to argue that a husband can rape his wife because she is his chattel. Even in the darkest days of slavery when slaves were also considered chattel, rape was defined as "the carnal knowledge of a female whether free or slave, forcibly and against her will." Georgia Code, § 4248, p. 824 (1863). Both the chattel and unity of identity rationales have been cast aside. * * *

We find that none of the theories have any validity. The justifications likewise are without efficacy. There is no other crime we can think of in which *all of the victims are denied protection* simply because someone might fabricate a charge; there is no evidence that wives have flooded the district attorneys with revenge filled trumped-up charges, and once a marital relationship is at the point where a husband rapes his wife, state intervention is needed for the wife's protection.

Notes and Questions

1. Although most states have now abolished the marital rape exclusion, a number continue to make some distinction between marital and nonmarital rape. For example, in some states marital rape is punished less severely than stranger rape. *See* VA. CODE § 18.2–67.2:1. *See generally* Jaye Sitton, *Old Wine in New Bottles: The "Marital" Rape Allowance*, 72 N.C. L. REV. 261 (1993).

2. The Model Penal Code, drafted in 1980, continues to recognize the marital rape exclusion:

> "The major context of which those who would abandon the spousal exclusion are thinking, however, is the situation of rape by force or threat. The problem with abandoning the immunity in many such situations is that the law of rape, if applied to spouses, would thrust the prospect of criminal sanctions into the ongoing process of adjustment in the marital relationship. Section 213.1, for example, defines as gross sexual imposition intercourse coerced "by any threat that would prevent resistance by a woman of ordinary resolution." It may well be that a woman of ordinary resolution would be prevented from resisting by her husband's threat to expose a secret to her mother, for example. Behavior of this sort within the marital relationship is no doubt unattractive, but it is risky business for the law to intervene by threatening criminal sanctions. Retaining the spousal exclusion avoids this unwarranted intrusion of the penal law into the life of the family.
>
> Finally, there is the case of intercourse coerced by force or threat of physical harm. Here the law already authorizes a penalty for assault. If the actor causes serious bodily injury, the punishment is quite severe. The issue is whether the still more drastic sanctions of rape should apply. The answer depends on whether the injury caused by forcible intercourse by a husband is equivalent to that inflicted by someone else. The gravity of the crime of forcible rape derives not merely from its violent character but also from its achievement of a particularly degrading kind of unwanted intimacy. Where the attacker stands in an ongoing relation of sexual intimacy, that evil, as distinct from the force used to compel submission, may well be thought qualitatively different. The character of the voluntary association of husband and wife, in other words, may be thought to affect the nature of the harm involved in unwanted intercourse.

AMERICAN LAW INSTITUTE, MODEL PENAL CODE AND COMMENTARY PART II, VOL. 1, COMMENT TO § 213.1 (p. 341, 345–46) (1980).

3. In contrast to the ALI view, consider the following:

> "In reality, marital rape is often *more traumatic* than stranger rape. When you have been intimately violated by a person who is supposed to love and protect you, it can destroy your capacity for intimacy with anyone else. Moreover, many wife victims are trapped in a reign of terror and experience repeated sexual assaults over a period of years. When you are raped by a stranger you have to live with a frightening memory. *When you are raped by your husband, you have to live with your rapist.*"

(Testimony and Statement of the Judiciary Committee, New Hampshire State Legislature on March 25, 1981, in support of HB 516, bill to remove spousal exception to sexual assault offenses, reprinted in 15 CLEARINGHOUSE REV. 342 (1981)).

2. *Burglary and the Marital Home*

CLADD v. STATE

Supreme Court of Florida, 1981.
398 So.2d 442.

ALDERMAN, JUSTICE.

* * *

The factual situation is narrow. The defendant and his wife had been separated for approximately six months, although there was no formal separation agreement or restraining order. He had no ownership or possessory interest in his wife's apartment and had at no time lived there. One morning, he broke through the locked door of her apartment with a crowbar, struck her, and attempted to throw her over the second floor stair railing. The next morning, he again attempted to break into her apartment but left when the police arrived.

The defendant was charged with burglary and attempted burglary. Although conceding that his wife did not in fact consent to his entry into her apartment, he moved to dismiss the charges on the basis that since the victim was his wife, he was licensed or invited to enter her apartment as a matter of law. He then contended that, if he had the right to enter the apartment, he could not be guilty of burglary or attempted burglary.

* * *

We reject the defendant's contention that the marriage relationship and the right of consortium deriving therefrom preclude the State from ever establishing the nonconsensual entry requisite to the crime of burglary * * *. Since burglary is an invasion of the possessory property rights of another, where premises are in the sole possession of the wife, the husband can be guilty of burglary if he makes a nonconsensual entry into her premises with intent to commit an offense, the same as he can be guilty of larceny of his wife's separate property. * * * The defendant's consortium rights did not immunize him from burglary where he had no right to be on the premises possessed solely by his wife independent of an asserted right to consortium.

The defendant's estranged wife was in sole possession of the premises into which he broke with intent to assault her. The district court correctly reversed the trial court's dismissal of the burglary and attempted burglary charges.

ENGLAND, JUSTICE, dissenting.

Like an anxious Pandora endeavoring to stuff the ills of the world back into her box, the majority endeavors to confine interspousal crimes to the factual situation of this case. As Pandora and the world sadly learned however, once the box is opened there is no way to contain the ephemeral evils which escape.

The majority today holds that one spouse may commit burglary against another. This new common law doctrine has emanations which go far beyond this case. This becomes evident when the case is viewed preliminarily from the perspective of what is *not* here involved.

First, this is not a prosecution for assault. Any discussion with regard to the husband's physical abuse or intended physical abuse of his wife is extraneous to the legal question presented. Mr. Cladd may or may not be prosecuted for his violent acts toward his wife's person. Whether that occurs is beside the point.

Second, this case does not involve spouses who are divorced, legally separated, or already in court in a pending dissolution proceeding. The husband and wife here are married, and there is no objective, legal manifestation that their marriage or interpersonal relations are being unwound. That they live apart, it will be seen, is quite irrelevant to the legal issue posed.

Third, this case does not entail a situation where separately-owned property, purchased or inherited by the wife, was established as a residence apart from her husband's. The record here only shows that Mrs. Cladd's living accommodations were separate from her husband's. We do not know who purchased the furnishings and fixtures, whether they came from a residence which had been occupied jointly, or even whether the separate abode was a second or alternative home.

When these matters are removed from the *legal* considerations, this case boils down to a husband's uninvited entry onto premises which the wife occupies away from the marital home. This situation is legally indistinguishable from other situations in which a separate residence is maintained by one or both spouses and in which one is temporarily residing, such as a summer home, a winter ski lodge, a vacation cottage at the seashore, a temporary, rented, haven from marital incompatibility, a remote wing or separate building on jointly occupied property (such as a studio-garage in which one spouse alone works), or even a separate bedroom in which one spouse may be seeking a retreat in the marital home. The record of this proceeding nowhere indicates that the wife had a separate possessory interest in the property she placed in her separate facility. We do not know whether the six-month separation of these spouses was the result of estrangement, a mutually agreed-upon cooling off period, a segregated vacation plan, or some other reason. Mr. Cladd here, I submit, was simply charged with illegal entry into a place where his wife claimed sanctuary from their common residence. The manner of entry and the purpose for entry may prompt judicial concerns for the wife's welfare, but the parties' motives or state of mind will prove an unreliable touchstone for criminal prosecutions of this sort, I predict.

The effect of today's decision is to bring prosecuting attorneys into marital disputes in a way which is unprecedented in Florida or elsewhere. I confess I am not comfortable with the Third District's analysis of the basis for rejecting burglary prosecutions in these situations—a right of cohabitation or consortium. Those concepts connote marital harmony, and here we have obvious discord. I am quite comfortable, however, with the thought that our criminal courts should not be involved, in fact or as a threat, in domestic disputes which involve an invasion of one spouse's claim of separateness or privacy. Personal assaults, I repeat, are different, and in those cases perhaps different considerations should pertain.

Notes and Questions

1. Does Justice England have a point? Can a fair analogy be made to *McGuire*?

2. Would it matter to Justice England if the couple were cohabitants rather than married? Should the fact of marriage make a difference here?

3. Should the existence of a court order requiring one spouse to leave the other alone be relevant?

4. A number of federal courts have considered whether the Omnibus Crime Control and Safe Streets Act of 1968, 18 U.S.C.A. § 2510 et seq. (Title III), which proscribes wiretapping, is applicable when the wiretapping occurs in the marital home and is conducted by a spouse. For example, in Kempf v. Kempf, 677 F.Supp. 618 (E.D.Mo.1988), Mr. Kempf became suspicious that his wife was engaging in extra-marital affairs, based on the fact that he often answered the telephone, only to have the caller hang up or claim he had reached a wrong number. After this had gone on long enough that Mr. Kempf began to recognize some of the voices, he connected a cassette tape recorder, in full view, to one of the three telephones in the home. Mr. Kempf then filed a petition for divorce, and offered into evidence the tapes he had made of his wife's telephone conversations. The tapes were admitted over the objections of Mrs. Kempf's lawyer, and judgment entered in Mr. Kempf's favor. Mrs. Kempf thereafter filed suit in federal court under Title III, seeking money damages. After noting that the federal courts were divided on the applicability of Title III to domestic wiretapping, the trial court found that

> "Congress did not intend to give a remedy for interspousal wiretapping when the parties involved were sharing a home and living together as husband and wife at the time the wiretap was utilized. Extending federal law into such a purely domestic matter runs counter to the tradition federal courts have followed in leaving family matters to the discretion of the state courts. It is one thing to apply this law in the case of an estranged couple where the surveillor has no legal rights to begin with in entering the separate home of the surveilled spouse. It is quite another to forbid a person from attaching a wiretapping device on his or her own telephone within the marital home. This type of spouse-snooping might be morally reprehensible in some respects. Nonetheless, it is an inappropriate subject for federal litigation, and the Court does not believe, in view of the congressional testimony and the historical view that state

courts are better facilitated to handle domestic conflicts, that Congress meant for Title III to apply to the facts herein." 677 F.Supp. 618 (E.D.Mo.1988).

The Court of Appeals reversed, noting that the district court's conclusion was contrary to the interpretation of the statute made by the majority of Courts of Appeals:

> "Title III prohibits all wiretapping activities unless specifically excepted. There is no express exception for instances of willful, unconsented to electronic surveillance between spouses. Nor is there any indication in the statutory language or in the legislative history that Congress intended to imply an exception to facts involving interspousal wiretapping." 868 F.2d 970, 973 (8th Cir.1989), (quoting Pritchard v. Pritchard, 732 F.2d 372 (4th Cir.1984).

3. *The Battered Spouse*

DEVELOPMENTS IN THE LAW—LEGAL RESPONSES TO DOMESTIC VIOLENCE

106 Harv. L. Rev. 1501–04, 1528–29, 1534–43 (1993).

* * * The impact of domestic violence reaches far beyond its immediate victims. Domestic violence strains the resources of law enforcement agencies and the legal system in general. As many as forty percent of all calls to which police must respond involve domestic disturbances. In fact, domestic violence consumes more police time than all other major felonies involving physical violence combined. Judicial resources are similarly burdened. In Massachusetts, for example, the courts issued an estimated 60,000 civil restraining orders in 1992 alone. Domestic abuse also imposes significant indirect economic costs on communities in the form of increased health care expenditures and lost productivity from employee absenteeism.

* * *

In the late 1960s, the battered women's movement helped bring the problem of domestic violence to the public's attention, leading to a series of legal and social reforms on the national, state, and local levels. Despite efforts to increase protection for battered women, however, the continued reluctance of government at all levels to intervene in family conflicts minimized the practical effect of these reforms. This hesitance stemmed from beliefs that the legal system was ill-equipped to deal with the problem and that interference would only exacerbate the violence by further angering the batterer.

This history of limited legal response is largely the product of various stereotypes and misconceptions about domestic violence. In broad terms, the classic myths are that domestic violence is a family matter in which state officials should not interfere, that victims provoke incidents of domestic violence, and that victims can easily leave abusive relationships.

* * *

Today, legislators are beginning to recognize that, until these stereotypes are exorcized, the law cannot adequately address the problems raised by domestic violence. Yet, lawmakers are still faced with questions of how best to respond to battering. A commitment to eliminate historically-imbedded biases does not by itself provide a ready solution to the myriad problems that arise from domestic violence. * * *

Until the late nineteenth century, a man's right to use violence to manage his household was legally protected and socially condoned ... Indeed, until the 1970s, the only civil remedy available to a married woman battered by her husband was an injunction issued pursuant to a divorce or a legal separation. Spurred by the direct efforts of the women's movement beginning in the 1960s and the resulting heightened public awareness of domestic abuse, all fifty states and the District of Columbia eventually established battered women's shelters and passed legislation that criminalized domestic violence. Yet an estimated four million women continue to be battered each year. * * *

* * *

As a result, new responses to domestic violence have been developed that aim not only to protect victims, but also to end the violence by eliminating the social attitudes that sanction female subjugation.

Stalking Statutes.—Although one way to end the violence in an intimate relationship is to end the relationship itself, battered women are often afraid to do so. Some studies show that at least half of the women who leave violent relationships are subsequently followed and threatened by their abusers. This harassment, which is terrifying and threatening to a battered woman, frequently presages further violence. In fact, the most severe abuse is often committed when a batterer attempts to prevent his partner from leaving, to retaliate for her departure, or to forcibly end the separation. But until there is an actual assault, the police can do little to end the harassment or to protect the woman from further harm.

Recently, however, thirty-one states have enacted "stalking statutes" that criminalize behavior by which any person "willfully, maliciously, and repeatedly follows or harasses another person and ... makes a credible threat with the intent to place that person in reasonable fear of death or great bodily injury." Stalking statutes require courts to use a "reasonable person standard" in determining whether the actor's conduct created such a threat. These new laws could provide effective protection for abused women, especially if the courts employ a partially subjective "reasonable battered woman" standard sensitive to the fact that some acts not normally considered life-threatening to an average person may be terrifying to a woman who has been the victim of repeated abuse.

Arrest Policies.—The protection of battered women requires not only adequate laws but also effective enforcement. In the past, however, the police have responded poorly to domestic violence complaints.

* * *

A landmark study conducted in Minneapolis in 1984 compared the deterrent effects of three different police responses to domestic violence incidents: arrest plus a night in jail, mediation, and requiring the batterer to leave the house for at least eight hours. The researchers concluded that the arrest option was the most effective in deterring subsequent violence. Prompted by these findings, the U.S. Attorney General recommended arrest as the standard police response to domestic assault.

* * *

In response, many states enacted mandatory arrest statutes under which a police officer must arrest an abuser when the officer has probable cause to believe that a domestic assault has occurred or that a protection order has been violated.[1] * * *

Despite their benefits, mandatory arrest laws also impose costs on the victim, the police, and the entire criminal justice system. First, under mandatory arrest laws, a battered woman's call to the police is tantamount to a request for arrest. Although some women may be encouraged to summon help because they will be assured of at least temporary incarceration of their abuser, those women who do not want their batterer arrested may be discouraged from calling the police.

Second, women also risk being arrested along with their abusers. Because mandatory arrest statutes often require arrest when there is bodily harm, a victim who injures her abuser may be subject to arrest if an officer cannot or will not determine whether the batterer's injury resulted from self-defense. This problem of dual arrest may be alleviated by instructing officers to arrest the primary physical aggressor only, or by requiring them to document the probable cause for each arrest separately.

Third, mandatory arrest may backfire and lead to increased violence if it angers the batterer further. Five recent studies designed to replicate the Minneapolis study have questioned the wisdom of mandating arrest. Two of them confirmed the deterrent effect of arrest found in Minneapolis, but in three others, arrest correlated with an increase in subsequent violence. Although these studies were intended to be replications, generalization across and comparison between them is difficult because their experimental designs actually varied considerably. One consistent finding across all six studies that may explain the inconsistent results, however, was a robust correlation between the deterrent effect of arrest

1. Fifteen states currently mandate arrest for a domestic violence offense, and nineteen require that police arrest when the batterer has violated a protection order [citations omitted].

and the employment status of the batterer: arrest correlated with increased violence when the batterers were unemployed, but it correlated with decreased subsequent abuse by employed batterers. Another possible reason for the diverse findings may lie in differential prosecution or conviction rates. For example, in the Milwaukee study, only five percent of those arrested were prosecuted and only one percent were eventually convicted. The study's conclusion that arrest correlated with a subsequent increase in violence thus might suggest not that mandatory arrest is ineffective, but that the stakes need to be higher and prosecution more vigorous in order to achieve a substantial deterrent effect.

Prosecution Policies.—Like the police, prosecutors play an integral role in the implementation of state domestic violence laws. Faced with limited time, personnel, and resources, however, prosecutors often give domestic violence cases low priority and sometimes even try to persuade battered women not to prosecute. Frequently, prosecutors do not pursue domestic violence cases because they fear that the victim might not support the state's effort to punish the batterer.[2] The victim might drop charges for many reasons, including fear of reprisal, economic and emotional dependence on her batterer, mistrust or lack of information about the judicial system, or the desire to reconcile with her abuser. But because domestic violence is a crime against society as well as against the victim, some prosecutor's offices have instituted "no-drop" policies under which, absent danger to the abused woman, requests to drop charges are generally denied.

Although no-drop policies can ensure that the batterer is prosecuted, they cannot ensure victim cooperation. Sometimes, however, victim testimony will be unnecessary: "Once the [batterer] realizes, 'Hey, this is a crime, this is prosecutable,' he pleads guilty right there." Moreover, some reluctant witnesses will change their minds and eventually testify at trial. To increase victim cooperation, some prosecutor's offices have implemented advocacy programs to explain the judicial system, to provide emotional support, and to act as a liaison between the victim and the prosecutor. Other prosecutors use subpoenas to compel battered women to testify. This approach is most effective when subpoenas are used uniformly for both cooperative and uncooperative witnesses because the appearance of compulsion shields a woman from blame and pressure by the batterer to drop the case. Finally, if despite these efforts the victim still refuses to cooperate, a prosecutor may try the case without her testimony by using police reports, testimony from other witnesses, and other indirect evidence.

No-drop policies do have a number of drawbacks, however. They have been criticized as paternalistic and erosive of a battered woman's self-esteem because they take the decision of whether to prosecute away

2. Los Angeles Deputy City Attorney Susan Kaplan estimated that "[o]ut of 5,000 domestic-violence cases that cross our desk each year, half of the victims want to drop the charges." [citation omitted].

from her. In addition, these policies may not do much to prevent sheer retaliatory attacks by abusers. Taken to extremes, rigid enforcement of no-drop policies can further victimize a battered woman, as was the case in Alaska, where a victim who refused to testify against her abuser was jailed for contempt. If designed with these concerns in mind, however, these policies can clearly communicate social disapproval of domestic abuse and remove the "abuser's coercive strangle-hold over the victim."

Diversion to Counseling Programs.—If the prosecution does go forward, some state statutes provide the option of diverting the batterer to a counseling program. In many states, these procedures defer trial, conviction, or sentencing of a criminal defendant pending his voluntary participation in a treatment program designed to prevent further violence. Some states provide for diversion only at the sentencing phase—as an alternative to incarceration or as a condition of probation. In other states, diversion may occur before prosecution or an adjudication of guilt if the defendant consents. Usually, if a batterer diverted before trial successfully completes the program, the charges against him will be dismissed, but if he fails to finish the program, commits a crime, or violates a protection order, the criminal prosecution will be reinstated. If the seriousness of the abuse or the defendant's history indicates that counseling would be fruitless, diversion is generally unavailable. Most states also exclude from eligibility defendants who previously have been diverted to treatment programs and those who recently have been convicted of violent offenses.

Diversion to counseling programs can rehabilitate some batterers while remaining sensitive to the needs of women and reducing backlog in the courts. Because diversion is more expedient than full-scale criminal prosecution, it can better harness the batterer's feelings of guilt after the abusive incident. Counseling programs are also more responsive to women whose primary wish is to stop the violence rather than to punish the batterer. Finally, because diversion avoids incarceration, it allows the abuser to keep his job and maintain the relationship with his partner if that is what she wants.

Despite its benefits, diversion may not have a strong deterrent effect because it permits the batterer to avoid criminal punishment, and pre-trial diversion allows him to escape prosecution and trial as well. As such, diversion may communicate a message that domestic violence is not as serious as assault between strangers, especially if the jurisdiction does not employ diversion for other offenses. Moreover, the pre-trial diversion option may be abused by prosecutors who use these programs as "dumping grounds" for domestic violence cases.

* * *

STATE v. HODGES

Supreme Court of Kansas, 1986.
239 Kan. 63, 716 P.2d 563.

SCHROEDER, CHIEF JUSTICE.

This is a criminal action in which Joan Hodges (defendant-appellant) appeals from her conviction by a Wyandotte County jury of voluntary manslaughter (K.S.A. § 21–3403) in the shooting of her husband, Harvey Hodges. The defendant claims the trial court erred in refusing to permit expert testimony on the battered woman syndrome and erred in its instructions to the jury on self-defense by using the word "immediate" rather than "imminent."

At approximately 3:00 a.m. on July 19, 1983, the defendant shot and killed her husband with a 12–gauge shotgun. The defendant claims she shot him in self-defense. Around 2:00 a.m. that same morning, defendant's stomach was upset and she went to a convenience store to get some Di–Gel for herself and some Skoal for her husband. She returned, went into the bedroom where her husband was lying in bed watching TV, and handed him the Skoal. Before she was out of the bedroom doorway, he jumped off the bed, grabbed her by the back of the hair and slammed her head against the doorjamb of the bedroom door twenty times saying, "God damn you. It's all right if you've got Di–Gel [but] you don't care if my blood sugar is 264. I'm going to kill you." Defendant soiled her clothes and told Harvey she needed to go to the bathroom. Harvey shoved her; she sprawled onto the floor and he repeatedly kicked her toward the bathroom with his bare feet. While the defendant cleaned herself up in the bathroom, Harvey continued to yell and threaten her from the bedroom. After changing into a nightgown, the defendant left the bathroom, went into a smaller bedroom and threw her clothes down on the bed. When she heard Harvey say, "God damn you. Get in here now," she reached for the shotgun in the closet, ran into the open bedroom doorway, and fired twice. Without knowing whether she had hit Harvey, defendant ran out of the house and to her mother's, Mrs. Bushey, who lived next door. The defendant and her mother called the police from a neighbor's house because Mrs. Bushey had no telephone.

Harvey died from massive blood loss due to two wounds located near each armpit. At the time of the shooting, he was lying horizontally on the bed. Harvey was a strong, well-muscled man measuring 5′8″ and weighing 245 pounds. His liver was examined during the autopsy. The pathologist testified Harvey had been a drinker for a considerable length of time, and in significant amounts. Harvey also suffered from diabetes.

* * *

Although defendant and other members of her family related various incidents of abuse Harvey inflicted upon defendant, other witnesses testified Harvey was an easy-going man, quiet and never angry or violent towards anybody.

* * *

Dr. Ann Bristow, an assistant professor of psychology at Kansas State University, testified at the hearing on the motion as defendant's expert.

* * *

Dr. Bristow explained the battered woman syndrome is a post-traumatic stress disorder with the particular stressor being wife abuse. Symptoms manifested by a woman suffering from the syndrome include an attempt to minimize the violence and to live for the positive aspects of the relationship. She lives in a highly fearful state, becoming very sensitive to when the situation is becoming more violent and to those things that precede arguments. The batterer isolates the woman and will not allow her to go places, and she becomes more and more withdrawn. Few women will discuss their problems even with close family members because of their feeling that there is nothing that can be done about the situation. They have a "learned helplessness;" the more the repeated trauma occurs, the more the woman learns she has no control.

* * *

* * * First, to be admissible, expert testimony must be helpful to the jury. Second, before expert scientific opinion may be received into evidence at trial, the basis of that opinion must be shown to be generally acceptable within the expert's particular scientific field.

* * *

The State argues the above testimony is not helpful to the jury because the jury heard ample evidence concerning the alleged abuse, and defendant had explained why she stayed with Harvey. The defendant did testify at trial concerning her marriage to the victim. They were first married in 1950 when defendant was seventeen, and early on Harvey beat her and tried to strangle her. Although defendant left him many times, he would find her and she would return home with him. The defendant related one incident where, after Harvey found her, he took her to a wooded location where he beat her, broke her jaw, and said she was either going to live with him or she wasn't going to live. He left her there unconscious, but eventually returned, took her to the hospital, and told her to tell the hospital staff she fell down. She returned home with him because he had her children. The defendant didn't call the police after any beatings because Harvey had threatened her life if she did. They were divorced in 1957 and remarried in 1970. Harvey had explained he was hot-headed before and wanted to make up for the previous things he had done. The defendant left him again in 1974, but he found her and eventually she stopped trying to run from him. The beatings did not stop. On June 4, 1978, Harvey threw a Coke bottle at her, hitting her in the back near the left shoulder blade. Her mother took her to the emergency room and just as the defendant was ready to make a police report, Harvey walked in and said, "You tell the police that and you will never tell anybody anything again." A medical report dated August 15, 1979, reflected the defendant slipped and fell, but defendant testified Harvey beat her unconscious. Another medical report dated December 21, 1980, reflected the defendant was beaten by her husband. Harvey had beaten her and kicked her down the porch stairs. Finally, a medical report dated February 6, 1983, showed the defendant slipped on ice and lacerated her left knee on concrete. The defendant testified she was coming home from her mother's and Harvey pushed her down onto the icy concrete, causing a cut in her knee which required 63 stitches. The defendant's family members—her mother and daughter—testified that Harvey had threatened them if they ever called the police or helped the defendant to leave him.

We disagree with the State's contention the jury does not need help in addressing the foregoing evidence.

The Supreme Court recently recognized the dilemma of jurors understanding a battered woman's situation in *State v. Hundley*, 236 Kan. 461, 467, 693 P.2d 475 (1985):

> "[T]here is no easy answer to why battered women stay with their abusive husbands. Quite likely emotional and financial dependency and fear are the primary reasons for remaining in the household. They feel incapable of reaching out for help and justifiably fear reprisals from their angry husbands if they leave or call the police. The abuse is so severe, for so long a time, and the threat of great bodily harm so constant, it creates a standard mental attitude in its victims. Battered women are terror-stricken people whose mental state is distorted and bears a marked resemblance to that of a hostage or a prisoner of war. The horrible beatings they are subjected to brainwash them into believing there is nothing they can do. They live in constant fear of another eruption of violence. They become disturbed persons from the torture."

Expert testimony on the battered woman syndrome would help dispel the ordinary lay person's perception that a woman in a battering relationship is free to leave at any time. The expert evidence would counter any "common sense" conclusions by the jury that if the beatings were really that bad the woman would have left her husband much earlier. Popular misconceptions about battered women would be put to rest, including the beliefs the women are masochistic and enjoy the beatings and that they intentionally provoke their husbands into fits of rage. *See* Walker, The Battered Woman, 19–31 (1979).

Of the jurisdictions which have considered this question, the majority have ruled a battering relationship is a subject beyond the understanding of the average juror. We agree.

The second requirement to be met here before expert scientific opinion may be admitted into evidence is that the basis of that opinion must be shown to be generally acceptable within the expert's particular scientific field.

* * *

In *Buhrle v. State*, 627 P.2d 1374, 1378 (Wyo.1981), the court rejected the expert's testimony on the syndrome stating, "[W]e are not saying this type of expert testimony is not admissible; we are merely holding that the state of the art was not adequately demonstrated to the court, and because of inadequate foundation the proposed opinions would not aid the jury."

The Ohio court in *State v. Thomas*, 66 Ohio St.2d 518, 423 N.E.2d 137, rejected expert testimony on the battered woman syndrome, ruling the subject matter of the expert testimony was within the understanding of the jury and was not sufficiently developed, as a matter of commonly accepted scientific knowledge, to warrant expert testimony.

The court in *State v. Kelly*, 97 N.J. at 210–11, 478 A.2d 364, recognized three ways a proponent of scientific evidence can prove its general acceptance and thereby its reliability: (1) through the expert's testimony; (2) by authoritative scientific and legal writings; and (3) by judicial opinions indicating the expert's premises have been generally accepted. The court ruled the battered woman syndrome had a sufficient scientific basis to produce uniform and reasonably reliable results. The case was remanded, however, because the State had not been given a full opportunity to question the expert's methodology.

* * *

Dr. Bristow explained at the hearing on the motion that this field has been researched for ten years with extensive publications and articles, and four or five books written on the subject matter of the battered woman syndrome. When questioned whether there is a common acceptance within the scientific community, Dr. Bristow enumerated two ways to tell. One indication is the extent to which the battered woman syndrome is referred to in professional literature. She testified it is noted in the American Medical Association Journal, in social workers' journals, and in experimental and clinical psychologists' journals, and that papers from conferences on domestic violence cover the topic. Second, by looking at which professionals are involved in either intervention or research of battered women, one can determine the extent of its acceptance. Dr. Bristow testified psychiatrists and psychologists are doing research in this area.

As we stated in *State v. Washington*, 229 Kan. 47, 622 P.2d 986, it is the *basis* of the expert's opinion that must be shown to be generally accepted. The record before us reveals the theory underlying the battered woman syndrome has gained a substantial enough scientific acceptance to warrant admissibility. It also appears from the record Dr. Bristow is a qualified expert on the subject of the battered woman syndrome. Furthermore, she spent a total of seven and one-half hours with the defendant and found the defendant suffered from the syndrome. The State had an ample opportunity to question Dr. Bristow about the methodology testimony on the battered woman syndrome.

The State argues the testimony is not relevant to defendant's claim of self-defense, which in Kansas is determined by an objective standard of reasonableness, rather than a subjective standard.

* * *

In *State v. Hundley*, 236 Kan. at 467, 693 P.2d 475, we stated:

> "The objective test is how a reasonably prudent battered wife would perceive [the aggressor's] demeanor. Expert testimony is admissible to prove the nature and effect of wife-beating just as it is admissible to prove the standard mental state of hostages, prisoners of war, and others under long-term life-threatening conditions."

Actually, to ask how a reasonably prudent battered woman would have perceived the aggressor's demeanor results in applying a subjective standard of reasonableness, *i.e.*, from the viewpoint of defendant's mental state. The same facts perceived by a person who has been repeatedly abused in a relationship would certainly be perceived differently by an ordinary and prudent non-battered person.

Therefore, we hold where the battered women syndrome is in issue, the proper standard to determine whether the accused's belief in asserting self-defense was reasonable is a subjective standard. The jury must determine, from the viewpoint of the defendant's mental state, whether the defendant's belief in the need to defend herself was reasonable.

Evidence of the battered woman syndrome is not a defense to a murder charge. The evidence is introduced to help the jury understand why a battered woman is psychologically unable to leave the battering relationship and why she lives in a high anxiety of fear from the batterer. The evidence aids the jury in determining whether her fear and her claim of self-defense are reasonable. It was error for the trial court to exclude the expert testimony on the battered woman syndrome.

The trial court improperly excluded expert testimony on the battered woman syndrome and improperly instructed the jury on self-defense. The judgment of the trial court is reversed and the case is remanded for a new trial.

Notes and Questions

1. Although the Ohio Supreme Court reversed *Thomas* in State v. Koss, 49 Ohio St.3d 213, 551 N.E.2d 970 (1990), other courts continue to reject evidence of this syndrome. *See* Note, 72 Va. L. Rev. 619 (1986). Courts that have accepted the doctrine have applied it to both married and unmarried women.

2. Evidence of battered woman syndrome could be relevant to a plea of temporary insanity. *Compare* State v. Duell, 175 W.Va. 233, 332 S.E.2d 246 (W.Va.1985) *with* State v. Myers, 239 N.J.Super. 158, 570 A.2d 1260 (App.Div.1990).

3. Congress passed the Violence Against Women Act of 1994 (42 U.S.C.A. § 13981), an additional remedy for women who are victims of

violence. The Act does not distinguish on the basis of marital status. Although no federal appeals courts had ruled on VAWA by late 1997, most lower federal courts have held that Congress had authority to enact the legislation. *See, e.g.*, Doe v. Doe, 929 F.Supp. 608 (D.Conn.1996); Doe v. Hartz, 970 F.Supp. 1375 (D.Iowa 1997); Seaton v. Seaton, 971 F.Supp. 1188 (E.D.Tenn.1997); Anisimov v. Lake, 23 Fam. L. Rep. 1587 (BNA) (N.D. Ill. 1997).

4. Compare the "battered woman" plea with that of self-defense:

> As a general matter, the requirement [in self-defense] that the attack reasonably appear to be imminent in a sensible one. If the threatened violence is scheduled to arrivc in the more distant future, there may be avenues open to the defendant to prevent it other than to kill or injure the perspective attacker; but this is not so where the attack is imminent. But the application of this requirement in some contexts has been questioned. "Suppose A kidnaps and confines D with the announced intention of killing him one week later. D has an opportunity to kill A and escape each morning as A brings him his daily ration. Taken literally, the *imminent* requirement would prevent D from using deadly force in self-defense until A is standing over him with a knife, but that outcome seems inappropriate. * * * The proper inquiry is not the immediacy of the threat but the immediacy of the response necessary in defense. If a threatened harm is such that it cannot be avoided if the intended victim waits until the last moment, the principle of self-defense must permit him to act earlier—as early as is required to defend himself effectively." [2 P. Robinson, Criminal Law Defenses § 131 (c)(1) (1984)]. However, the question of whether there should be an imminence-of-attack requirement and, if so, how it should be characterized, is most dramatically presented in the context of a homicide by a battered wife.

WAYNE LAFAVE & A. SCOTT, SUBSTANTIVE CRIMINAL LAW 656–57 (1986).

B. MARRIAGE AND THE LAW OF EVIDENCE

TRAMMEL v. UNITED STATES

Supreme Court of the United States, 1980.
445 U.S. 40, 100 S.Ct. 906, 63 L.Ed.2d 186.

CHIEF JUSTICE BURGER delivered the opinion of the Court.

We granted certiorari to consider whether an accused may invoke the privilege against adverse spousal testimony so as to exclude the voluntary testimony of his wife.

* * *

According to the indictment, petitioner and his wife flew from the Philippines to California in August 1975, carrying with them a quantity of heroin. Freeman and Roberts assisted them in its distribution. Elizabeth Trammel then traveled to Thailand where she purchased another supply of the drug. On November 3, 1975, with four ounces of heroin on her person, she boarded a plane for the United States. During a routine customs search in Hawaii, she was searched, the heroin was discovered, and she was arrested. After discussions with Drug Enforcement Administration agents, she agreed to cooperate with the Government.

* * *

The privilege claimed by petitioner has ancient roots. Writing in 1628, Lord Coke observed that "it hath been resolved by the Justices that a wife cannot be produced either against or for her husband." 1 Coke, A Commentarie upon Littleton 6b (1628). *See generally*, 8 J. Wigmore, Evidence 2227, (McNaughton rev. 1961). This spousal disqualification sprang from two canons of medieval jurisprudence: first, the rule that an accused was not permitted to testify in his own behalf because of his interest in the proceeding; second, the concept that husband and wife were one, and that since the woman had no recognized separate legal existence, the husband was that one. From those two now long-abandoned doctrines, it followed that what was inadmissible from the lips of the defendant-husband was also inadmissible from his wife.

Despite its medieval origins, this rule of spousal disqualification remained intact in most common-law jurisdictions well into the 19th century. *See* 8 Wigmore, § 2333. It was applied by this Court * * *, where it was deemed so well established a proposition as to "hardly requir[e] mention." Indeed, it was not until 1933, in *Funk v. United States*, 290 U.S. 371, that this Court abolished the testimonial disqualification in the federal courts, so as to permit the spouse of a defendant to testify in the defendant's behalf. *Funk*, however, left undisturbed the rule that either spouse could prevent the other from giving adverse testimony. The rule thus evolved into one of privilege rather than one of absolute disqualification.

The modern justification for this privilege against adverse spousal testimony is its perceived role in fostering the harmony and sanctity of the marriage relationship. Notwithstanding this benign purpose, the rule was sharply criticized. Professor Wigmore termed it "the merest anachronism in legal theory and an indefensible obstruction to truth in practice." 8 Wigmore, § 2228, at 221. The Committee on the Improvement of the Law of Evidence of the American Bar Association called for its abolition. In its place, Wigmore and others suggested a privilege protecting only private marital communications, modeled on the privilege between priest and penitent, attorney and client, and physician and patient.

These criticisms influenced the American Law Institute, which, in its 1942 Model Code of Evidence advocated a privilege for marital confidences, but expressly rejected a rule vesting in the defendant the right to exclude all adverse testimony of his spouse. See American Law Institute, Model Code of Evidence, Rule 215 (1942). In 1953 the Uniform Rules of Evidence, drafted by the National Conference of Commissioners on Uniform State Laws, followed a similar course; it limited the privilege to confidential communications and "abolishe[d] the rule, still existing in some states, and largely a sentimental relic, of not requiring one spouse to testify against the other in a criminal action." See Rule 23(2) and comments. Several state legislatures enacted similarly patterned provisions into law.

In *Hawkins v. United States*, 358 U.S. 74 (1958), this Court considered the continued vitality of the privilege against adverse spousal testimony in the federal courts. There the District Court had permitted petitioner's wife, over his objection, to testify against him. With one questioning concurring opinion, the Court held the wife's testimony inadmissible; it took note of the critical comments that the common-law rule had engendered, but chose not to abandon it.

* * *

Since 1958, when *Hawkins* was decided, support for the privilege against adverse spousal testimony has been eroded further. Thirty-one jurisdictions, including Alaska and Hawaii, then allowed an accused a privilege to prevent adverse spousal testimony. The number has now declined to 24. In 1974, the National Conference on Uniform States Laws revised its Uniform Rules of Evidence, but again rejected the *Hawkins* rule in favor of a limited privilege for confidential communications. See Uniform Rules of Evidence, Rule 504. That proposed rule has been enacted in Arkansas, North Dakota, and Oklahoma—each of which in 1958 permitted an accused to exclude adverse spousal testimony. The trend in state law toward divesting the accused of the privilege to bar adverse spousal testimony has special relevance because the law of marriage and domestic relations are concerns traditionally reserved to the states. *See Sosna v. Iowa*, [p. 566]. Scholarly criticism of the *Hawkins* rule has also continued unabated.

* * *

It is essential to remember that the *Hawkins* privilege is not needed to protect information privately disclosed between husband and wife in the confidence of the marital relationship—once described by this Court as "the best solace of human existence." Those confidences are privileged under the independent rule protecting confidential marital communications. The *Hawkins* privilege is invoked, not to exclude private marital communications, but rather to exclude evidence of criminal acts and of communications made in the presence of third persons.

No other testimonial privilege sweeps so broadly. The privileges between priest and penitent, attorney and client, and physician and patient limit protection to private communications. These privileges are rooted in the imperative need for confidence and trust. The priest-penitent privilege recognizes the human need to disclose to a spiritual counselor, in total and absolute confidence, what are believed to be flawed acts or thoughts and to receive priestly consolation and guidance in return. The lawyer-client privilege rests on the need for the advocate and counsel to know all that relates to the client's reasons for seeking representation if the professional mission is to be carried out. Similarly, the physician must know all that a patient can articulate in order to identify and to treat disease; barriers to full disclosure would impair diagnosis and treatment.

The *Hawkins* rule stands in marked contrast to these three privileges. Its protection is not limited to confidential communications; rather it permits an accused to exclude all adverse spousal testimony. As Jeremy Bentham observed more than a century and a half ago, such a privilege goes far beyond making "every man's house his castle," and permits a person to convert his house into "a den of thieves." 5 Rationale of Judicial Evidence 340 (1827). It "secures, to every man, one safe and unquestionable and ever ready accomplice for every imaginable crime."

The ancient foundations for so sweeping a privilege have long since disappeared. Nowhere in the common-law world—indeed in any modern society—is a woman regarded as chattel or demeaned by denial of a separate legal identity and the dignity associated with recognition as a whole human being. Chip by chip, over the years those archaic notions have been cast aside. * * *

The contemporary justification for affording an accused such a privilege is also unpersuasive ... When one spouse is willing to testify against the other in a criminal proceeding—whatever the motivation—their relationship is almost certainly in disrepair; there is probably little in the way of marital harmony for the privilege to preserve. In these circumstances, a rule of evidence that permits an accused to prevent adverse spousal testimony seems far more likely to frustrate justice than to foster family peace. Indeed, there is reason to believe that vesting the privilege in the accused could actually undermine the marital relationship. For example, in a case such as this the Government is unlikely to offer a wife immunity and lenient treatment if it knows that her husband can prevent her from giving adverse testimony. If the Government is dissuaded from making such an offer, the privilege can have the untoward effect of permitting one spouse to escape justice at the expense of the other. It hardly seems conducive to the preservation of the marital relation to place a wife in jeopardy solely by virtue of her husband's control over her testimony.

Our consideration of the foundations for the privilege and its history satisfy us that "reason and experience" no longer justify so sweeping a rule as that found acceptable by the Court in *Hawkins*. Accordingly, we conclude that the existing rule should be modified so that the witness spouse alone has a privilege to refuse to testify adversely; the witness may be neither compelled to testify nor foreclosed from testifying. This modification—vesting the privilege in the witness spouse—furthers the important public interest in marital harmony without unduly burdening legitimate law enforcement needs.

Here, petitioner's spouse chose to testify against him. That she did so after a grant of immunity and assurances of lenient treatment does not render her testimony involuntary. Accordingly, the District Court and the Court of Appeals were correct in rejecting petitioner's claim of privilege, and the judgment of the Court of Appeals is affirmed.

Notes and Questions

1. As the Court points out, information "privately disclosed between husband and wife in the confidence of the marital relationship" remains fully protected.

> "The adverse testimony privilege permits witnesses to refuse to testify against their spouses and, in some jurisdictions, gives parties the power to prevent their spouses from testifying against them. The confidential communications privilege permits individuals to refuse to reveal, or empowers them to prevent their spouses from revealing, confidential marital communications. Although these two privileges often overlap in practice, they are doctrinally distinct and are supported by different justifications. * * * The privilege protecting confidential marital communications was not explicitly recognized until the 1850s. One reason for this late recognition may have been that the spousal disqualification rule and the adverse testimony privilege covered most attempts to introduce evidence based on confidential communications. Marital communications could be introduced only in the rare cases when they were material to an action to which neither spouse was a party. Once state and federal courts abolished the disqualification rule, many state legislatures recognized the need for distinct protection of confidential marital communications. Today, many state codes recognize both the marital communications privilege and the adverse testimony privilege." * * *
>
> Note, *Privileged Communications*, 98 HARV. L. REV. 1450, 1563–64 (1985).

2. Not all commentators agree that the marital privilege should be limited to confidential communications. *See* Milton C. Regan, Jr., *Spousal Privilege and the Meanings of Marriage*, 81 VA. L. REV. 2045 (1996).

3. Is the Court's analogy to the attorney-client, priest-penitent, physician-patient privileges appropriate?

4. Does the Court strike a reasonable balance in upholding the *witness* spouse's privilege to refuse to testify? While the Commissioners on Uniform State Laws have called the rule of not *requiring* one spouse to testify against the other in a criminal action "a sentimental relic," in fact the states remain seriously divided.

5. A different type of compromise, more limited than the one accepted in *Trammel*, is to give one spouse the right to testify adversely against the other over the objection of the other only when the defendant spouse has committed a "personal wrong" against the other. *See*

People v. Eberhardt, 205 Mich.App. 587, 518 N.W.2d 511 (Mich.App. 1994).

6. In a number of states, an exception to the spousal testimonial privilege has been made for spouse abuse charges. In these cases, the state may force a spouse to testify against the other, even if the spouse does not want to testify. *See* Verhovek, "*Athlete and Legal Issue on Trial*," NEW YORK TIMES, Feb. 19, 1996, at A6, col. 1 (discussing a case involving football player Warren Moon and his wife). Will this approach result in increased convictions? (Note that Mr. Moon was acquitted.) Will it help reduce the level of family violence?

7. In balancing the social interest in not losing possibly important (in *Trammel*, decisive) evidence of criminal activity against the social interest in discouraging undesirable official behavior, how does the marital privilege compare with the Fourth Amendment's exclusionary rule? *See* LAFAVE & SCOTT, *supra*. Consider the relative ease with which a wife might be confronted with a more or less spurious charge of conspiracy and her "voluntary" testimony obtained by a promise of immunity and remember that it was a promise of immunity that induced Mrs. Trammel to throw her husband overboard!

8. Should the privilege extend past divorce? Consider MARK GRAHAM, HANDBOOK OF FEDERAL EVIDENCE 335–336 (1981): "[U]nlike the testimonial privilege, the confidential communication privilege survives termination of the marriage by annulment, divorce or death. The husband-wife confidential communication privilege barring disclosure by either spouse belongs to both spouses and may be asserted by either in his or her own right."

9. On the following scale, where would you draw the line?

(a) Neither spouse is allowed to testify;

(b) Defendant is allowed to compel an unwilling spouse to testify for him/her;

(c) Defendant is allowed to prevent a spouse from testifying against him/her;

(d) The spouse is allowed to choose whether or not to testify for or against the defendant;

(e) The spouse is compelled to testify against the defendant;

(f) The spouse is "bribed" to testify against the defendant (*Trammel*).

Chapter 4

MARITAL AGREEMENTS

They are our enemies,
and so we marry them.
Zulu saying

SECTION 1. MARRIAGE: CONTRACT OR STATUS?

UMDA § 201: "Marriage is a personal relationship between a man and a woman arising out of a civil contract to which the consent of the parties is essential * * * "

MAYNARD v. HILL

Supreme Court of the United States, 1888.
125 U.S. 190, 8 S.Ct. 723, 31 L.Ed. 654.

JUSTICE FIELD.

* * * It is also to be observed that, while marriage is often termed by text writers and in decisions of courts as a civil contract, generally to indicate that it must be founded upon the agreement of the parties, and does not require any religious ceremony for its solemnization, it is something more than a mere contract. The consent of the parties is of course essential to its existence, but when the contract to marry is executed by the marriage, a relation between the parties is created which they cannot change. Other contracts may be modified, restricted, or enlarged, or entirely released upon the consent of the parties. Not so with marriage. The relation once formed, the law steps in and holds the parties to various obligations and liabilities. It is an institution, in the maintenance of which in its purity the public is deeply interested, for it is the foundation of the family and of society, without which there would be neither civilization nor progress. This view is well expressed by the supreme court of Maine in *Adams v. Palmer*, 51 Me. 480, 483: "It is not then a contract within the meaning of the clause of the constitution which prohibits the impairing the obligation of contracts. It is rather a

social relation like that of parent and child, the obligations of which arise not from the consent of concurring minds, but are the creation of the law itself, a relation the most important, as affecting the happiness of individuals, the first step from barbarism to incipient civilization, the purest tie of social life, and the true basis of human progress."

WALTON v. WALTON

California Court of Appeals, 1972.
28 Cal.App.3d 108, 104 Cal.Rptr. 472.

KAUFMAN, ACTING PRESIDING JUSTICE.

Wife appeals from an interlocutory judgment granting Husband's petition for dissolution of marriage and denying Wife's request for legal separation. * * *

Wife's contention that dissolution of her marriage on the ground of irreconcilable differences as prescribed in The Family Law Act constitutes an unconstitutional impairment of her rights is untenable. In the first place, marital rights and obligations are not contractual rights and obligations within the meaning of article I, § 10 of the United States Constitution or Article I, § 16 of the California Constitution. (*Maynard v. Hill*). Marriage is much more than a civil contract; it is a relationship that may be created and terminated only with consent of the state and in which the state has a vital interest. Secondly, even if marital obligations were treated as contractual obligations protected by the constitutional prohibitions, a statutory change in the grounds for divorce would not constitute an unconstitutional impairment thereof. * * * When persons enter into a contract or transaction creating a relationship infused with a substantial public interest, subject to plenary control by the state, such contract or transaction is deemed to incorporate and contemplate not only the existing law but the reserve power of the state to amend the law or enact additional laws for the public good and in pursuance of public policy, and such legislative amendments or enactments do not constitute an unconstitutional impairment of contractual obligations.

Similarly, Wife's contention that the dissolution of her marriage on the ground of irreconcilable differences under The Family Law Act unconstitutionally deprives her of a vested interest in her married status cannot be sustained. Certainly a wife has a legitimate interest in her status as a married woman, but, separate and apart from marital property and support rights as to which Wife makes no contention, we entertain some doubt whether her interest in her status as a married woman constitutes property within the purview of the due process clauses of article I, § 13 of the California Constitution and the Fourteenth Amendment to the United States Constitution. In any event, in view of the state's vital interest in the institution of marriage and the state's plenary power to fix the conditions under which the marital status may be created or terminated, it is clear that Wife could have no vested interest in the state's maintaining in force the grounds for divorce that existed at the time of her marriage. Her interest, however it be classified, was subject to the reserve power of the state to amend the law or enact additional laws for the public good and in pursuance of public policy. Even if Wife is said to have some constitutionally protected vested right, she has not been deprived thereof without due process of law. " 'Vested rights, of course, may be impaired "with due process of law" under many circumstances. The state's inherent sovereign power includes the so called "police power" right to interfere with vested property rights whenever reasonably necessary to the protection of the health, safety, morals, and general well being of the people.' " * * *

The public policy considerations felt by the Legislature to be compelling reasons for the enactment of The Family Law Act and the change in grounds for divorce from a fault standard to a marital breakdown standard are described in the Report of 1969 Divorce Reform Legislation of the Assembly Committee on Judiciary. * * *

Notes and Questions

1. UMDA § 201 defines marriage as a contract. *Maynard* states that marriage is something more than a contract. Does *Maynard* mean that the parties' expectations are irrelevant? Should the law generally try to uphold the parties' expectations? What about Mrs. Walton's expectations regarding the dissolution of her marriage? Is it enough to say that, by virtue of getting married, she is deemed to agree to be governed by both current marriage law and subsequent amendments?

2. *Walton* graphically raises the question whether marriage partners should be permitted to protect themselves against changes in the law (whether by action of the legislature or by change of domicile) through private contractual arrangements. Why might the court have reached the result it did in *Walton*? If the wife had prevailed, what effect would this have had on California divorces?

3. After New York expanded the grounds for divorce to include grounds that previously would have effected only a legal separation, N.Y. Dom. Rel. L. § 170 was added:

> "a. A spouse against whom a decree of divorce has been obtained [on the 'living apart' ground], where the decree, judgment or agreement of separation was obtained or entered into prior to [January 21st, 1970], may institute an action in which there shall be recoverable, in addition to any rights under this or any other provisions of law, an amount equivalent to the value of any economic and property rights of which the spouse was deprived by virtue of such decree, except where the grounds for the separation judgment would have excluded recovery of economic and property rights.
>
> b. In determining the value of the economic and property rights described in subdivision a hereof, the plaintiff's interest shall be calculated as though the defendant died intestate and as if the death of the defendant had immediately antedated the divorce."

Would this be a fairer way to deal with complaints like those of Mrs. Walton?

4. How should a substantial change in marital property law be applied? For example, in 1985 the New York Court of Appeals decided that a professional degree earned during marriage was property subject to division at divorce. Should this rule be applied to a spouse who obtained a degree before 1985 and divorces after 1985?

SECTION 2. VARIABILITY OF THE MARRIAGE STATUS BY AGREEMENT BEFORE MARRIAGE

Premarital agreements, also referred to as antenuptial agreements or contracts, may (try to) cover a great variety of subjects, including support, property rights, and issues related to the care of children; they may treat the spouses' rights during marriage, upon divorce, or after the death of a spouse.

Before "contaminating" your good sense with law, do you think that it would be appropriate to enforce a premarital agreement specifying: the religion in which the children of the marriage will be reared?; the number and type of vacations, visits to and by in-laws, or the number of children? [*See* Uniform Premarital Agreement Act § 3(a)(8); whether a spouse must agree to a religious divorce? [*see* note 2]; in a common law state, adopting community property rules to govern the spouses' economic relationship; in a community property state, adopting common law property rules to govern the spouses' economic relationship? What effect would (or should) such stipulations be given at the time of divorce?

A. VALIDITY OF PREMARITAL AGREEMENTS

If you have concluded that marriage is a contract rather than a status, you have moved too fast. Marriage is a contract and a status. Marriage is a contract in that it rests on an agreement between the marriage partners and, at least to some extent, the terms of the marriage may be modified by the parties. Marriage is a status because a large set of rules is thrust upon the spouses without their specific agreement. Now we shall see that the parties' freedom to contract is limited by policy considerations, and we may be tempted to compare marriage with a form contract. Some blank lines are left for the parties to complete, but most of the content is prescribed by the state.

In reviewing contracts relating to marriage, courts have traditionally been concerned with three issues: (1) the presence (or more likely the absence) of contractual "consideration;" (2) the parties' so-called "fiduciary" relationship, including the duty to disclose information material to the bargain and to deal fairly; and (3) "public policy." An invocation of public policy is the open signal that a particular contract will not stand, but a great deal of judicial "policy-mongering" also has been done under the seemingly objective guise of the first two headings.

Traditionally, premarital agreements regarding property rights at death were enforceable, but premarital agreements contemplating divorce were unenforceable. *See* Charles Gamble, *The Antenuptial Contract*, 26 U. MIAMI L. REV. 692 (1972). Thus, one spouse could waive his or her rights to a share of other's assets at death, but could not waive a right to alimony post-divorce. One source of this traditional approach was a concern that prospective spouses would not bargain fairly with each other regarding the financial ramifications of divorce. This fear may have stemmed both from a perception that women were less sophisticated than men and a belief that the parties' intimate relationship might undermine their ability to bargain. Another concern was that agreements fixing post-divorce obligations would encourage divorce. *See* Mulford v. Mulford, 211 Neb. 747, 320 N.W.2d 470, 471 (Neb.1982).

The materials which follow show that, over the past three decades, courts and legislatures have allowed couples much greater—although not yet complete—freedom in negotiating the terms of their marriage. The new view is that a couple may, with some limits, determine property rights and support obligations at divorce as well as death.

This new view reflects a variety of factors. First, the increased rate and social acceptability of divorce has increased the acceptability of contracts that take account of the divorce possibility. With approximately 50% of marriages ending in divorce (*see* Martin & Bumpass, *Recent Trends in Marital Disruption*, 26 DEMOGRAPHY 37, 49 (1989)), it seems sensible for a couple to think about and plan for the divorce possibility. Second, a higher divorce rate and increased longevity have expanded the number of remarriages where one or both spouses have children from a prior marriage; in these cases spouses often wish to ensure that their children are provided for. Third, perhaps as a result of the feminist movement and women's increased labor force participation, judges today exhibit less paternalism toward women. *See* J. Thomas Oldham, *Putting Asunder in the 1990s*, 80 CALIF. L. REV. 1091, 1106–1107 (1992); Simeone v. Simeone, 525 Pa. 392, 581 A.2d 162 (1990).

Today, all states agree that a premarital agreement is enforceable if it meets certain requirements. But no consensus has yet emerged on what those requirements should be. Nor is there consensus on whether *post*marital agreements should be enforced on the same, or different, terms.

1. *Procedural Fairness*

Under the original Statute of Frauds, 29 Car. II, ch. 3 (1677), and modern variants, promises made in consideration of marriage must be in writing and signed by the party to be charged. Courts also agree that a premarital agreement must be made freely and intelligently in order to be enforceable.

DeLOREAN v. DeLOREAN

Supreme Court of New Jersey, Chancery Division, 1986.
211 N.J.Super. 432, 511 A.2d 1257.

IMBRIANI, J.S.C.

This matrimonial case examines the circumstances under which an antenuptial agreement may be enforced and whether that issue may be resolved by arbitration. The intent of most marriages is to create an "indivisible union of one" in which both spouses generally contribute whatever they own prior to the marriage or acquire thereafter into a common marital fund. Upon death the survivor usually receives whatever has been accumulated but, if a divorce ensues, in the usual case they share all marital assets equally.

However, when parties enter into an antenuptial agreement their purpose is to alter that usual arrangement and enter into an economic partnership whereby many or all of the assets owned prior to the marriage or acquired thereafter are not contributed into a common marital fund but are kept segregated and, when the marriage ceases, whether by death or divorce, they are not shared equally but pursuant to a plan conceived and agreed upon before the marriage was consummated. It is important that we understand that normally the intent of most antenuptial agreements is to deny a spouse an interest in assets held in the sole name of the other which the former would ordinarily receive by operation of law when the marriage ceased.

These parties entered into an antenuptial agreement on May 8, 1973 (only a few hours before they married) which provided that: "any and all property, income and earnings acquired by each before and after the marriage shall be the separate property of the person acquiring same, without any rights, title or control vesting in the other person." The potential assets could exceed $20 million and practically all of them are in the sole name of the husband. Absent this agreement and considering that this is a thirteen-year marriage in which there are two minor children, under New Jersey law this wife could reasonably have anticipated receiving approximately 50% of the marital assets at the time of divorce. But if this agreement is upheld she will receive relatively little. She asserts that this agreement should not be enforced because: (1) she was not provided with a full and complete disclosure of her husband's financial affairs before she signed it and (2) undue influence was exerted upon her by her husband who possessed far greater financial knowledge and experience than she.

Initially, it is clear that "antenuptial agreements fixing post-divorce rights and obligations [are] ... valid and enforceable" and courts should "welcome and encourage such agreements 'to the extent that the parties have developed comprehensive and particularized agreements responsive to their peculiar circumstances.' " In determining whether to enforce an antenuptial agreement, there are at least three requirements that have to be met.

First, that there was no fraud or duress in the execution of the agreement or, to put it another way, that both parties signed voluntarily. The wife alleges she did not sign voluntarily because her husband presented the agreement to her only a few hours before the marriage ceremony was performed and threatened to cancel the marriage if she did not sign. In essence she asserts that she had no choice but to sign. While she did not have independent counsel of her own choosing, she did acknowledge that before she signed she did privately consult with an attorney selected by her husband who advised her not to sign the agreement. Yet, for whatever reasons, she rejected the attorney's advice and signed.

While her decision may not have been wise, it appears that she had sufficient time to consider the consequences of signing the agreement and, indeed, although she initially refused to sign it, after conferring with her intended spouse and an attorney, she reconsidered and decided to sign it. Concededly, the husband was 25 years older and a high powered senior executive with General Motors Corporation, but she was not a "babe in the woods." She was 23 years old with some business experience in the modeling and entertainment industry; she had experienced an earlier marriage and the problems wrought by a divorce; and she had advice from an attorney who, although not of her own choosing, did apparently give her competent advice and recommended that she not sign. While it may have been embarrassing to cancel the wedding only a few hours before it was to take place, she certainly was not compelled to go through with the ceremony. There was no fraud or misrepresentation committed by the husband. He made it perfectly clear that he did not want her to receive any portion of the marital assets that were in his name. At no time did she ever make an effort to void the agreement and, of course, it was never voided. Under those circumstances the court is satisfied that the wife entered into the agreement voluntarily and without any fraud or duress being exerted upon her.

Second, the agreement must not be "unconscionable." This is not to say that the agreement should be what a court would determine to be "fair and equitable." The fact that what a spouse receives under an antenuptial agreement is small, inadequate or disproportionate does not in itself render the agreement voidable if the spouse was not overreached and entered into the agreement voluntarily with full knowledge of the financial worth of the other person. So long as a spouse is not left destitute or as a public charge the parties can agree to divide marital assets in any manner they wish. Mrs. DeLorean presently enjoys substantial income from her employment as a talk-show television hostess and was given a life interest in a trust of unknown amount created by Mr. DeLorean, which he testified had assets of between $2 and $5 million dollars.[1] She will not be left destitute. The court is unaware of

1. Actually the testimony of the husband was vague, if not evasive, about the content and value of the trust fund and it appeared that the wife was unaware that she possessed a life interest in a trust fund until he disclosed that information during his testimony in court.

any public policy which requires that the division of marital assets be made in [a manner] the court believes to be fair and equitable if the parties freely and voluntarily agree otherwise. In the final analysis it is for the parties to decide for themselves what is fair and equitable, not the court. So long as a spouse had sufficient opportunity to reflect on her actions, was competent, informed, and had access to legal advice and that of any relevant experts, a court should not, except in the most unusual case, interject its own opinion of what is fair and equitable and reject the wishes of the parties. Since the wife voluntarily agreed to this division of the marital assets and she will not become destitute or a public charge, the agreement is not unconscionable.

Third, the spouse seeking to enforce the agreement made a full and complete disclosure of his or her financial wealth before the agreement was signed. Obviously, one cannot make a knowing and intelligent waiver of legal and financial rights unless fully informed of all the facts; otherwise one cannot know what is being waived. The husband asserts that the wife acknowledged that she received a full and complete disclosure of his financial wealth because the agreement states:

> Husband is the owner of substantial real and personal property and he has reasonable prospects of earning large sums of monies; these facts have been fully disclosed to Wife.

However, that statement is not very meaningful and is insufficient to satisfy his obligation to make a full and complete disclosure of his financial wealth. While several states hold that a full and complete disclosure is not synonymous with a detailed disclosure, *see e.g., Lopata v. Metzel*, 641 P.2d 952 (Colo.1982), those cases can be distinguished because they impose upon each spouse a duty to inquire and investigate into the financial condition of the other. However, as far as this court can ascertain, New Jersey imposes no such duty.

A conflict arose as to precisely what financial information was disclosed by Mr. DeLorean. However, the court is satisfied that even if it accepted as true the testimony of Mr. DeLorean he did not satisfy his legal obligation to make a full and complete disclosure. But we should address the question of how to avoid disputes of this nature in the future. It is clear that we can ascertain with complete certainty whether there was a full and complete disclosure only by requiring a written list of assets and income be attached to the antenuptial agreement. Anything less will encourage a plethora of plenary hearings which would frequently be contemplated by contradictory and conflicting testimony, often tainted by memory lapses. Research has disclosed, for reasons not clear to this court, several cases in which the suggestion of a written list has been rejected, *Roberts v. Estate of Roberts*, 664 S.W.2d 634 (Mo.App. 1984); *Hengel v. Hengel*, 122 Wis.2d 737, 365 N.W.2d 16 (App.1985).

Our purpose must be to fashion a rule which will avoid litigation. * * *

While the wife was aware that Mr. DeLorean was a person of substantial wealth, there was no way that she could have known with any substantial degree of certainty the extent of his wealth. This is important because one can appreciate that while a wife might waive her legal rights to share in marital assets of $1 million, she might not be willing to do so if she knew the marital assets were worth $20 million. And the suggestion that Mrs. DeLorean had a duty to investigate to ascertain the full nature and extent of his financial wealth is both unfair and unrealistic. How many people when about to marry would consider investigating the financial affairs of their intended spouse? How many people would appreciate or tolerate being investigated by an intended spouse? And how many marriages would be canceled when one of the parties is informed of an investigation being conducted by the other? Such a requirement would cause embarrassment and impose a difficult burden. The better rule is that the:

> burden is not on either party to inquire, but on each to inform, for it is only by requiring full disclosure of the amount, character, and value of the parties' respective assets that courts can ensure intelligent waiver of the statutory [and other] rights involved. [*Rosenberg v. Lipnick*, 377 Mass. 666, 389 N.E.2d 385, 388 (1979).]

When a spouse has a duty to fully and completely disclose his financial wealth we would eviscerate and render meaningless that duty if we imposed upon the other spouse a duty to investigate.

The only way that Mrs. DeLorean could knowingly and intelligently waive her legal rights in Mr. DeLorean's assets was if she was fully and completely informed what they were. And for Mr. DeLorean to merely state that he had an interest in a farm in California, a large tract of land in Montana, and a share in a major league baseball club fell far short of a full and complete disclosure. If this issue were decided under New Jersey law the court would conclude that Mr. DeLorean did not make a full and complete disclosure of his financial wealth before his spouse signed the antenuptial agreement and, therefore, it would not be valid and enforceable.

However, it is argued that California, not New Jersey, law should be applied. The parties married and executed the agreement in California. It is hornbook law that when an agreement is silent as to which law should be applied, the validity and construction of a contract shall be determined by the law of the place of contracting. But this agreement is not silent and expressly provides that it:

> shall be construed under the laws of the State of California and enforceable in the proper courts of jurisdiction of the State of California.

When the agreement was executed the parties had substantial contacts with California and reasonably expected to retain many of them which, indeed, has been the case. For these reasons the law of California must be applied in this case.

That being so, what duty does California law impose upon a party to an antenuptial agreement with regard to the disclosure of one's financial wealth? In both California and New Jersey fiduciaries are required to exercise a high degree of trust, good faith and candor in their dealings with each other.

* * *

Where California and New Jersey law part is in their determination of what constitutes a fiduciary because, unlike New Jersey, California does not treat a party to an antenuptial agreement as a fiduciary on the theory that "parties who are not yet married are not presumed to share a confidential relationship." *Marriage of Dawley*, 17 Cal. 3d 342, 355, 131 Cal. Rptr. 3, 551 P.2d 323 (1976). So long as the spouse seeking to set aside such an agreement has a general idea of the character and extent of the financial assets and income of the other, that apparently is sufficient in California. Indeed, absent fraud or misrepresentation, there appears to be a duty to make some inquiry to ascertain the full nature and extent of the financial resources of the other. As this court reads California law, the disclosures made by John DeLorean appear to be sufficient for purposes of enforcing this agreement.

Notes and Questions

1. Although courts agree that a premarital agreement must be signed voluntarily, they have not (as *DeLorean* shows) construed that requirement consistently. What policy goals underlie the voluntariness requirement? Would those goals be advanced by enforcing the agreement in *DeLorean*? What is the basis of the claim that Mrs. DeLorean did not sign the agreement voluntarily?

2. Most courts have found involuntariness when the agreement was presented on the day of the wedding and the party waiving rights had no time to confer with genuinely independent counsel. *See generally* J. Thomas Oldham, Divorce, Separation and the Distribution of Property, § 4.03[2][d]. One concern in these cases is simply the frenzy a wedding occasions; anyone who has experienced the hysteria produced by an imminent wedding might easily conclude that this time is not a good one for negotiating an important agreement. Another concern is the embarrassment occasioned by calling off the wedding at a late date. To the extent that a court is sensitive to these concerns, when is it "too late" to enter into a premarital agreement? Is the pivotal date when out-of-town guests begin to arrive? Should it matter if the couple have previously discussed and agreed upon the general terms of the agreement? What if they had begun negotiations long before the planned wedding date, but finalized the agreement only shortly before the wedding? *See* Gardner v. Gardner, 190 Wis.2d 216, 527 N.W.2d 701 (Wis.App.1994) (enforcing agreement signed five days before wedding, where the parties had been negotiating for two months); In re Marriage of Adams, 240 Kan. 315, 729 P.2d 1151 (1986). Is the size of the wedding party relevant? *See* Fletcher v. Fletcher, 68 Ohio St.3d 464, 628 N.E.2d 1343 (1994) (suggesting yes).

Would it be sensible to establish a rule, or at least a presumption, that a premarital contract signed within seven days of the wedding is invalid due to undue influence?

3. Circumstances other than timing may also affect the court's decision on voluntariness. For example, if previously married spouses are considering remarriage and one party presents an agreement to the other in front of the children, this could cause a court to find overreaching. *See* Ranney v. Ranney, 219 Kan. 428, 548 P.2d 734 (1976). What if the woman asked to waive her rights in a premarital agreement is pregnant? What if the prospective spouse asked to waive rights has already quit his or her job and moved to the planned marital domicile?

4. Perhaps not surprisingly, courts have not been receptive to the argument "I shouldn't be bound by the premarital agreement because I didn't read it." *See, e.g.*, Liebelt v. Liebelt, 118 Idaho 845, 801 P.2d 52 (Idaho App.1990). But what if the agreement was written in a language the prospective spouse can't understand? *See* Stein–Sapir v. Stein–Sapir, 52 A.D.2d 115, 382 N.Y.S.2d 799 (1976) (not a defense). What if one prospective spouse tells the other that the agreement only deals with property rights at death, when in fact the agreement also limits property rights at divorce? *See* Laird v. Laird, 597 P.2d 463 (Wyo.1979) (not a defense).

5. Whether the prospective spouse received independent legal advice is often taken into account in determining voluntariness. Some courts have held that an agreement signed without the opportunity to consult with independent counsel will be scrutinized more closely. *See* Gant v. Gant, 174 W.Va. 740, 329 S.E.2d 106 (1985); Sogg v. Nevada State Bank, 108 Nev. 308, 832 P.2d 781 (1992). In Ruzic v. Ruzic, 549 So.2d 72 (Ala.1989), the Alabama Supreme Court decided that a premarital agreement should be enforceable *only* if each party received independent counsel. Few courts have adopted this extreme view. What are its advantages and disadvantages?

6. Almost all courts consider the poorer prospective spouse's knowledge of the other's financial situation important to determining enforceability, but they do not agree on what constitutes adequate knowledge. *See* Col. Rev. Stat. § 14–2–307(1)(b). New Jersey requires disclosure in the form of a detailed schedule showing the prospective spouses' incomes and the net value of all their property interests. California does not. Which policy is more sensible? Should inadequate disclosure by itself void the agreement? (*See* Uniform Premarital Agreement Act, *infra* p. 204.)

7. Why did the *DeLorean* court apply California law instead of New Jersey law in resolving the disclosure issue?

Problem 4–1:

Biff and Buffy are engaged and have planned a relatively large wedding. One week before the wedding, Biff presents Buffy with a premarital contract which would substantially limit Buffy's marital property and support rights if the marriage ends in divorce. Biff has substantial assets; Buffy does not. Buffy is quite surprised and does not want to sign the agreement. Biff suggests that she talk about the marital contract with a lawyer he knows. She immediately does this; he advises her not to sign. Biff tells her that if she does not sign the agreement, he will not marry her. Five days before the wedding, she reluctantly agrees to sign the agreement. What arguments are available to both parties? What result under *DeLorean*? Is this the right result? *See Liebelt, supra* note 4; Greenwald v. Greenwald, 154 Wis.2d 767, 454 N.W.2d 34 (Wis. App.1990).

2. *Substantive Fairness*

If an agreement is freely and intelligently signed, is there any other reason not to enforce it? Must such agreements be fair? If yes, what does "fairness" mean? Should fairness be judged at the time of signing or at the time of divorce?

RESTATEMENT (SECOND) OF CONTRACTS (1981)

§ 190. Promise Detrimental to Marital Relationship

(1) A promise by a person contemplating marriage or by a married person, other than as part of an enforceable separation agreement, is unenforceable on grounds of public policy if it would change some essential incident of the marital relationship in a way detrimental to the public interest in the marriage relationship.[1] Here a separation agreement is unenforceable on grounds of public policy unless it is made after separation or in contemplation of an immediate separation and is fair in the circumstances.

(2) A promise that tends unreasonably to encourage divorce or separation is unenforceable on grounds of public policy.

1. a. *Change in essential incident of marital relationship.* Although marriage is sometimes loosely referred to as a "contract," the marital relationship has not been regarded by the common law as contractual in the usual sense. Many terms of the relationship are seen as largely fixed by the state and beyond the power of the parties to modify. Two reasons support this view. One is that there is a public interest in the relationship, and particularly in such matters as support and child custody, that makes it inappropriate to subject it to modification by the parties. Another is that the courts lack workable standards and are not an appropriate forum for the types of contract disputes that would arise if such promises were enforceable. The rule stated in Subsection (1) reflects this view by making a promise unenforceable if it changes an essential incident of marriage in a way detrimental to the public interest in the relationship. This rule, however, does not prevent persons contemplating marriage or married persons from making contracts between themselves for the disposition of property, since this is not ordinarily regarded as an essential incident of the marital relationship. Nor does it prevent their making contracts for services that are not an essential incident of the marital relationship within the rule stated here. But it does, for example, preclude them from changing in a way detrimental to the public interest in the relationship the duty imposed by law on one spouse to support the other. Whether a change in the duty of support is detrimental in this way will depend on the circumstances of each case. The presence of an unenforceable promise in an otherwise enforceable antenuptial or separation agreement does not, of course, necessarily entail the unenforceability of the entire agreement. * * *

GROSS v. GROSS

Supreme Court of Ohio, 1984.
11 Ohio St.3d 99, 464 N.E.2d 500.

HOLMES, JUDGE.

The agreement, which was in consideration of the marriage between the parties and their mutual promises, provided, in part, at § 13, that:

> "Jane shall after the consummation of the marriage between the parties hereto, in the event of the separation or divorce of the parties be entitled to receive as alimony or separate maintenance the maximum sum of $200.00 per month for a period of 10 years, from the time of such separation (either by legal action or by actually living apart) or from the date of a divorce action being filed, if a court of competent jurisdiction will award Jane any alimony. This shall be the maximum amount Jane shall be entitled to receive under any and all circumstances and conditions, and Jane shall not be entitled to any division of the property of Thomas nor to any expense money or counsel fees in connection with any separation or divorce, and Jane agrees to waive any and all such rights or claims. Further, Jane specifically releases all her rights of dower in the property of Thomas."

Additional provisions relating to a possible divorce between the parties were the following:

> "16. In the event of a divorce the personal residence of the parties shall be sold and the equity therein realized, shall be divided equally between the parties.
>
> "17. In the event of a divorce the personal property and possessions of the parties located in their residence shall be the property of Jane with the exception of Thomas' clothing, sports equipment and other purely personal items. Jane shall be entitled to the ownership of one automobile out of Thomas' property."

The antenuptial agreement also contained provisions relative to payments that would be disbursed from Thomas' estate to Ida Jane. Such provisions provided for the establishment of a trust in the principal sum of $200,000, or twenty percent of his net estate, whichever is lesser. The income derived from the trust was to be paid to Mrs. Gross for life and upon her death to provide education for her children by her previous marriage.

Attached, and made a part of the antenuptial agreement, was a statement of the assets owned by each party. At the date of the agreement, most of the appellant's assets were his interests in the family Pepsi–Cola bottling franchises located in a number of cities. There were additional stocks in other companies, as well as an interest in a real estate partnership. The value of Mr. Gross' assets at the time was listed in the proximity of $550,000. The appellee disclosed assets of household goods and effects, an automobile, and $1,000 cash for what is alleged to be a total of approximately $5,000.

The parties were married in September 1968. A son was born of the marriage in 1970. The marriage lasted nearly fourteen years when the appellant filed for divorce. However, this action was dismissed by the appellant. Subsequently, the appellee filed for a divorce which was granted on grounds of extreme cruelty being found attributable to appellant. At trial there was evidence adduced that Mr. Gross had increased his total assets to some $8,000,000 with a net equity of $6,000,000. His gross income for the year 1980 was approximately $250,000. The trial court found the antenuptial agreement to be valid and enforceable in that it had been fairly entered into since there was no evidence of fraud, duress, or misrepresentation, and there had been a full disclosure of assets. The court entered an order in accordance with the terms of the agreement.

The court of appeals by way of a majority opinion, opted for the position that antenuptial agreements were not void per se, but that such contracts were not enforceable by a party found to be at fault in a divorce proceeding. The court ruled that such fault was a breach of the terms of the antenuptial agreement. Thus, the court of appeals held that inasmuch as the divorce had been granted upon the trial court's finding that Mr. Gross has been guilty of gross neglect of duty, he had thereby breached the antenuptial agreement and could not enforce its provisions against Mrs. Gross. Mr. Gross subsequently appealed the decision.

* * *

HOLMES, JUDGE.

Historically, there has been a notable contrast between the views taken by courts in this country of provisions within antenuptial agreements setting forth the division of property and other rights and interests upon the death of one of the parties, contrasted to provisions in such agreements providing for, or affecting, property rights or conjugal and marital rights in the event of divorce. In the majority of jurisdictions, prospective spouses could contract as to the division of their property in the event of the death of one of the parties, and these agreements were generally enforced if the parties made a full disclosure of their assets and there was no showing of fraud, duress, or undue influence in the procurement of the agreement. Such provisions in an antenuptial agreement were generally recognized as being conducive to marital tranquility and thus in harmony with public policy.* * * [C]ourts throughout the country have historically taken a significantly different attitude toward provisions in antenuptial agreements providing for a division of property and sustenance alimony upon the divorce of the parties. The prevailing law in the United States was that such contracts were considered as being made in contemplation of divorce and were held to be void as against public policy.

Generally, two basic policy arguments were advanced for the invalidation of provisions in antenuptial agreements in reference to the divorce of the parties. First, provisions in such contracts which provide for one spouse to forfeit marital property or conjugal rights are potentially profitable to the other party, would encourage divorce, and, therefore, would be contrary to the state's interest in preserving the marriage. Second, the state is virtually a party to every marital contract in that it possesses a continuing concern in the financial security of divorced or separated persons.

In the last decade and a half many changes have taken place in the attitudes and mores surrounding marriage and marital relationships. These changes have altered the public policy view toward antenuptial agreements made in contemplation of a possible divorce. Some of the factors involved within this evolution of policy are the social changes which affect family law in general, such as the greater frequency of divorce and remarriage, the percentage drop in marriage generally among our citizens, the adoption by a number of states of all or a number of the provisions of the Uniform Marriage and Divorce Act and, most significantly, the widespread adoption of some manner of "no fault" divorce laws. * * *

Exemplary of this trend among the states to reconsider the common-law position or rule of law, which disfavors agreements providing for division of property and sustenance provisions under divorce, is the often cited case of *Posner v. Posner* (Fla.1970), 233 So.2d 381. The Florida Supreme Court held that antenuptial agreements settling alimony and property rights upon divorce should not be held *ab initio* as contrary to public policy. The court adopted the same tests which had previously been applied for the determination of the validity of antenuptial agreements containing provisions disposing of property at time of death, i.e., a showing of good faith in the entry into the agreement, and a full disclosure of assets. The court also held that upon evidence of changed circumstances, the contract would be subject to the same modification provisions that apply to all support orders in divorce proceedings.

A number of courts in other states followed the lead of *Posner* and held that this type of antenuptial agreement was valid if fairly negotiated upon a full disclosure of assets. * * *

We * * * join those other jurisdictions that have expressed the growing trend of legal thought in this country that provisions contained within antenuptial agreements providing for the disposition of property and awarding sustenance alimony upon a subsequent divorce of the parties are not void *per se* as being against public policy. We hold that such agreements are valid and enforceable if three basic conditions are met: one, if they have been entered into freely without fraud, duress, coercion, or overreaching; two, if there was a full disclosure, or full knowledge, and understanding, of the nature, value and extent of the prospective spouse's property; and, three, if the terms do not promote or encourage divorce or profiteering by divorce.

The elements of the first condition may be read with their generally accepted meaning being applicable. Accordingly, the term "overreaching" is used in the sense of one party by artifice or cunning, or by significant disparity to understand the nature of the transaction, to outwit or cheat the other.

The elements of the second condition would be satisfied either by the exhibiting of the attachment to the antenuptial agreement of a listing of the assets of the parties to the agreement, or alternatively a showing that there had been a full disclosure by other means.

A hypothetical example of the type of situation which condition three seeks to avoid is where the parties enter into an antenuptial agreement which provides a significant sum either by way of property settlement or alimony at the time of a divorce, and after the lapse of an undue short period of time one of the parties abandons the marriage or otherwise disregards the marriage vows.

We are called upon to answer other important questions in this case. One is whether fault on the part of one of the parties, which occasions a divorce, invalidates the agreement, or at least vitiates the terms of the contract as to the one at fault.

* * *

Upon our considered view and analysis of the very specialized purpose of these types of agreements, i.e., the disposition of property, and provision for support or sustenance alimony at the time that a divorce or separation might take place between the parties, we conclude that a strict application of the law of contracts would not be appropriate. The terms of the instrument are not the only important factors to be considered; the intent of the parties at the time of the execution of the agreement is also of prime importance. The parties here, and others who enter into such instruments, specifically provide for a possible "parting of the twain" by way of divorce or separation. It would seem that some misconduct was contemplated at that time. If there would be no basic circumstance present which would occasion a separation or divorce of the parties, how could the provisions in the contemplated contract ever be meaningful as to either party? Any other view taken of such agreements would undermine and render inane the basic purpose of such agreements. If the parties had intended that the subsequent marital misconduct would extinguish the mutual promises in the agreement, either voiding the provisions or permitting only the one not at fault to enforce such provisions, the parties could very well have made this clear within the terms of the agreement.

Although there seems to be a notable difference of positions across the country upon this issue, there are a number of jurisdictions which hold that antenuptial agreements containing provisions for property distribution or sustenance allowance are not abrogated, nor held to be unenforceable by the party found to be at fault in a divorce proceeding, unless the language of the contract contains an express provision against such conduct.

* * *

As to this issue, we conclude the better view to be, and so hold, that antenuptial agreements providing for division of property and containing provisions for sustenance alimony, if otherwise found to be valid, are not abrogated as to either party for marital misconduct arising after the marriage.

Having determined the general validity of antenuptial agreements providing for the disposition and division of property and allowing for sustenance or maintenance at the time of a divorce of the parties, we must now provide for the standards of judicial review of such agreements.

At the outset it must be restated that upon a judicial review of any such agreement, it must meet the general test of fairness as referred to previously, and must be construed within the context that by virtue of their anticipated marital status, the parties are in a fiduciary relationship to one another. The parties must act in good faith, with a high degree of fairness and disclosure of all circumstances which materially bear on the antenuptial agreement.

Upon the consideration of provisions relating to the division or allocation of *property* at the time of a divorce, the applicable standards must relate back to the time of the execution of the contract and not to the time of the divorce. As to these provisions, if it is found that the parties have freely entered into an antenuptial agreement, fixing the property rights of each, a court should not substitute its judgment and amend the contract. A perfect or equal division of the marital property is not required to withstand scrutiny under this standard. This is in keeping with this court's standard of review of provisions contained in antenuptial agreements providing for the devolution of property at the time of the death of one of the parties.

In the review of provisions in antenuptial agreements regarding *maintenance or sustenance* alimony, a further standard of review must be applied—one of conscionability of the provisions at the time of the divorce or separation. Although we have held herein that such provisions in an antenuptial agreement generally may be considered valid, and even though it is found in a given case upon review that the agreement had met all of the good faith tests, the provisions relating to maintenance or sustenance may lose their validity by reasons of changed circumstances which render the provisions unconscionable as to one or the other at the time of the divorce of the parties. Accordingly, such provisions may, upon a review of all of the circumstances, be found to have become voidable at the time of the divorce or dissolution.

We believe that the underlying state interest in the welfare of the divorced spouse, when measured against the rights of the parties to freely contract, weighs in favor of the court's jurisdiction to review, at the time of a subsequent divorce, the terms in an antenuptial agreement providing sustenance alimony for one of the parties. There is sound public policy rationale for not strictly enforcing such a provision which, even though entered into in good faith and reasonable at the time of execution, may have become unreasonable or unconscionable as to its application to the spouse upon divorce. It is a valid interest of the state to mitigate potential harm, hardship, or disadvantage to a spouse which would be occasioned by the breakup of the marriage, and a strict and literal interpretation of the provisions for maintenance of the spouse to be found in these agreements.

One who, by way of a motion for modification, claims the unconscionability of a provision for maintenance within an antenuptial agreement has the burden of showing the unconscionable effect of the provision at the time of divorce or dissolution.[11] The trial court, in the determination of the issue of conscionability and reasonableness of the provisions for sustenance or maintenance of a spouse at the time of the divorce, shall utilize the same factors that govern the allowance of alimony which are set forth in R.C. 3105.18.[12]

Applying the law to the facts and circumstances of this case, we find that there is accord that the antenuptial agreement was entered into with all of the factors of good faith and non-overreaching as previously set forth herein. There also is no question that there was in fact a full disclosure of the assets of the parties as evidenced by the list of such assets attached to the agreement. Further, we believe that the provisions of the contract did not promote or encourage divorce, or present a profiteering device for the parties. Here, we are reviewing an antenuptial agreement entered into by the parties who married and lived together as man and wife for fourteen years, which marriage must have been a harmonious one for a considerable period of time, and one which produced an offspring.

Therefore, the basic agreement in its totality was a valid one when entered into by the parties. In accord with the principles discussed

11. Unconscionability of a provision for maintenance and sustenance contained in an antenuptial agreement may be found in a number of circumstances, examples of which might be an extreme health problem requiring considerable care and expense; change in employability of the spouse; additional burdens placed upon a spouse by way of responsibility to children of the parties; marked changes in the cost of providing the necessary maintenance of the spouse; and changed circumstance of the standards of living occasioned by the marriage, where a return to the prior living standard would work a hardship upon a spouse.

12. R.C. 3105.18(B) provides:

"In determining whether alimony is necessary, and in determining the nature, amount, and manner of payment of alimony, the court shall consider all relevant factors, including:

"(1) The relative earning abilities of the parties;

"(2) The ages, and the physical and emotional conditions of the parties;

"(3) The retirement benefits of the parties;

"(4) The expectancies and inheritances of the parties;

"(5) The duration of the marriage;

"(6) The extent to which it would be inappropriate for a party, because he will be custodian of a minor child of the marriage, to seek employment outside the home;

"(7) The standard of living of the parties established during the marriage;

"(8) The relative extent of education of the parties;

"(9) The relative assets and liabilities of the parties;

"(10) The property brought to the marriage by either party;

"(11) The contribution of a spouse as homemaker."

previously, the fact that a divorce was granted to the wife upon the trial court's finding that the husband had been at fault does not abrogate the contract upon which he relies, and does not prevent the husband from enforcing the provisions other than those pertaining to sustenance or maintenance which might be held voidable on behalf of the wife.

Concerning the latter point, the facts would tend to show that, although a comparatively wealthy man at the time of the execution of the antenuptial agreement, Mr. Gross became a man of considerably greater means during the years of his second marriage. Not only did his stock holdings and value thereof increase markedly, but his net income also substantially increased. The wife's standard of living has changed quite dramatically from the time of the execution of the agreement until the time of the divorce. To require the wife to return from this opulent standard of living to that which would be required within the limitations of the property and sustenance provisions of this agreement, could well occasion a hardship or be significantly difficult for the former wife.

Under the facts here, and in light of the law pronounced in this opinion, we find the provisions for maintenance within this agreement to be unconscionable as a matter of law and voidable by Mrs. Gross. Accordingly, we hold that the provisions within this agreement for the maintenance of Mrs. Gross should be reviewed by the trial court, and alternative provisions be ordered by the court.

Accordingly, the judgment of the court of appeals is reversed, and this cause is remanded to the trial court for further proceedings in accordance with this opinion.

Notes and Questions

1. On remand, "[t]he plaintiff is awarded the sum of $2500.00 per month, not to be diminished or modified by what plaintiff may earn, so long as her earning is moderate. The alimony ordered herein is retroactive to the date of the Judgment Entry and is in addition to the child support previously referred to." Gross v. Gross, 23 Ohio App.3d 172, 492 N.E.2d 476 (1985), app. dismissed, Dec. 11, 1985.

2. How would *DeLorean* be resolved under *Gross*? How would *Gross* be resolved under *DeLorean*?

3. *Agreements "encouraging divorce:"* The *Gross* decision notes that an enforceable premarital agreement must not "promote or encourage divorce." Few cases analyze in detail what types of provisions violate this limit. Of course, *all* premarital agreements encourage divorce, in the sense that they facilitate the divorce process. Some courts analyze the "promote divorce" issue in terms of whether the contract provides one or the other spouse with an incentive to file for divorce. For example, in In re Marriage of Noghrey, 169 Cal.App.3d 326, 215 Cal.Rptr. 153 (1985):

> "* * * Kambiz and Farima were married for seven and one-half months when Farima filed for divorce. * * * [T]he trial court filed

> the following Memorandum of Decision: It is the opinion of the Court that the petitioner and respondent entered into a written antenuptial agreement, also known as 'Katuba' [sic], prior to their marriage. The terms of the agreement were as follows: 'I, Kambiz Noghrey, agree to settle on Farima Human the house in Sunnyvale and $500,000 or one-half of my assets, whichever is greater, in the event of a divorce.' The said agreement should be found to be a valid, binding, and enforceable agreement. * * * The agreement before us * * * is not of the type that seeks to define the character of property acquired after marriage nor does it seek to ensure the separate character of property acquired prior to marriage. This agreement is surely different and speaks to a wholly unrelated subject. It constitutes a promise by the husband to give the wife a very substantial amount of money and property, *but only upon the occurrence of a divorce.* No one could reasonably contend this agreement encourages the husband to seek a dissolution. Common sense and fiscal prudence dictate the opposite. Such is not the case with the wife. She, for her part, is encouraged by the very terms of the agreement to seek a dissolution, and with all deliberate speed, lest the husband suffer an untimely demise, nullifying the contract, and the wife's right to the money and property. * * * Farima did testify that neither she nor her parents possessed great wealth. The prospect of receiving a house and a minimum of $500,000 by obtaining the no-fault divorce available in California would menace the marriage of the best intentioned spouse."

See also Illustration 5, RESTATEMENT (SECOND) OF CONTRACTS § 190 ("A and B, who are about to be married, make an antenuptial agreement in which A promises that in case of divorce, he will settle $1,000,000 on B. A court may decide that, in view of the large sum promised, A's promise tends unreasonably to encourage divorce and is unenforceable on grounds of public policy."); Neilson v. Neilson, 780 P.2d 1264 (Utah App.1989) (denying enforcement when premarital agreement specified that, if the wealthy spouse filed for divorce, the other would receive 50% of that spouse's assets based on the conclusion that this provision encouraged the less wealthy spouse to goad the other to file for divorce).

The "encouraging" divorce issue can also arise if one party is married to another when the agreement is being negotiated. For example, in Ludwig v. Ludwig, 693 S.W.2d 816 (Mo.App.1985), one prospective spouse, as an inducement to the other to divorce her current husband and marry him, agreed to an equal division of his assets at divorce. The court refused to enforce this provision because it induced the woman to divorce her first husband.

Some premarital agreements provide for a property award that varies based on the duration of the marriage. For example, John F. Kennedy, Jr. reportedly signed a premarital agreement which provides his wife with $1 million if the couple divorce during the first year of marriage, $2 million if they divorce after three years of marriage but before ten years and $3 million if they divorce after more than ten years of marriage. *See Deal Protects $32 Million Man if Knot Breaks*, BOSTON HERALD, Oct. 14, 1996, p. 1. If Mr. Kennedy were to sue for divorce eight days before his first anniversary, would you enforce the agreement? *See* Burtoff v. Burtoff, 418 A.2d 1085 (D.C.App.1980) (yes, but not considering the encouraging divorce argument). If you wouldn't enforce the agreement, would you apply the state's normal marital property and spousal support rules to determine Mr. and Mrs. Kennedy's rights?

Is the "encouraging divorce" ground for denying enforcement a sensible one? If yes, how should it be construed?

UNIFORM PREMARITAL AGREEMENT ACT

9B U.L.A. 376 (1987).

§ 2. A premarital agreement must be in writing and signed by both parties. It is enforceable without consideration. (Editor's note: See § 4).

§ 3. (a) Parties to a premarital agreement may contract with respect to:

(1) the rights and obligations of each of the parties in any of the property of either or both of them whenever and wherever acquired or located;

(2) the right to buy, sell, use, transfer, exchange, abandon, lease, consume, expend, assign, create a security interest in, mortgage, encumber, dispose of, or otherwise manage and control property;

(3) the disposition of property upon separation, marital dissolution, death, or the occurrence or nonoccurrence of any other event;

(4) the modification or elimination of spousal support;

(5) the making of a will, trust, or other arrangement to carry out the provisions of this agreement;

(6) the ownership rights in and disposition of the death benefit from a life insurance policy;

(7) the choice of law governing the construction of the agreement, and

(8) any other matter, including their personal rights and obligations, not in violation of public policy or a statute imposing a criminal penalty.[1]

(b) The right of a child to support may not be adversely affected by a premarital agreement.

§ 4. A premarital agreement becomes effective upon marriage.

§ 5. After marriage, a premarital agreement may be amended or revoked only by a written agreement signed by the parties. The amended agreement or the revocation is enforceable without consideration.

1. OFFICIAL COMMENT: * * * [S]ubject to this limitation, an agreement may provide for such matters as the choice of abode, the freedom to pursue career opportunities, the upbringing of children, and so on.

§ 6. (a) A premarital agreement is not enforceable if the party against whom enforcement is sought proves that:

(1) that party did not execute the agreement voluntarily; or

(2) the agreement was unconscionable when it was executed and, before execution of the agreement, that party:

(i) was not provided a fair and reasonable disclosure of the property or financial obligations of the other party;

(ii) did not voluntarily and expressly waive, in writing, any right to disclosure of the property or financial obligations of the other party beyond the disclosure provided; and

(iii) did not have, or reasonably could not have had, an adequate knowledge of the property or financial obligations of the other party.

(b) If a provision of a premarital agreement modifies or eliminates spousal support and that modification or elimination causes one party to the agreement to be eligible for support under a program of public assistance at the time of separation or marital dissolution, *a court*, notwithstanding the terms of the agreement, may require the other party to provide support to the extent necessary to avoid that eligibility.

(c) An issue of unconscionability of a premarital agreement shall be decided by the court as a matter of law.

§ 7. If a marriage is determined to be void, an agreement that would otherwise have been a premarital agreement is enforceable only to the extent necessary to avoid an inequitable result.

§ 8. Any statute of limitations applicable to an action asserting a claim for relief under a premarital agreement is tolled during the marriage of the parties to the agreement. However, equitable defenses limiting the time for enforcement, including laches and estoppel, are available to either party.

Notes and Questions

1. How would *DeLorean* and *Gross* be resolved under the UPAA?

2. By 1997, the UPAA had been adopted (with some modifications) by a majority of all states, including Arizona, Arkansas, California, Connecticut, Hawaii, Idaho, Illinois, Iowa, Kansas, Maine, Montana, Nebraska, Nevada, New Jersey, North Carolina, North Dakota, Oregon, Rhode Island, South Dakota, Texas, Utah and Virginia.

3. The UPAA does not define "unconscionable," although the official comments to the UPAA do try to clarify the term's meaning.[1]

1. OFFICIAL COMMENT: The test of "unconscionability" is drawn from § 306 of the Uniform Marriage and Divorce Act (UMDA). The following discussion set forth in the Commissioner's Note to § 306 of the UMDA is equally appropriate here:

Subsection (b) undergirds the freedom allowed the parties by making clear that the

How might a court determine whether an agreement was unconscionable at the time of signing?

4. *Disclosure*: The UPAA provides for enforcement of an unconscionable agreement if there was adequate disclosure. *Accord*, Burtoff v. Burtoff, 418 A.2d 1085 (D.C.App.1980). A few states, such as North Dakota, have adopted the UPAA but amended it to provide that a court need not enforce an unconscionable agreement. *See* N.D. CENT. CODE § 14–03.1–06. Some courts have taken the approach that the issue of unconscionability in a prenuptial contract should be treated as it is under general contract rules. *See* Simeone v. Simeone, 525 Pa. 392, 581 A.2d 162 (1990) (court should not review the "reasonableness" of the agreement). These courts refuse enforcement only if a premarital contract is unconscionable when signed. *See* Arthur Leff, *Unconscionability and the Code*, 115 U. PA. L. REV. 485 (1967). Other courts and legislatures have required more. For example, under N.Y. DOM. REL. L. § 236B, a premarital agreement will not be enforced unless it is "fair and reasonable" when signed and "not unconscionable" at the time enforcement is sought. *Accord*, Button v. Button, 131 Wis.2d 84, 388 N.W.2d 546 (1986). While the difference between "unconscionable" and "unfair" may be somewhat vague, courts typically interpret unfairness so as to permit less deviation from the state's marital property and spousal support rules. (For example, in *DeLorean, supra*, the court decided that the agreement was not unconscionable because Mrs. DeLorean did not qualify for public assistance; in contrast, the *Button* court stated that the agreement "should in some manner appropriate to the circumstances of the parties take into account that each spouse contributes to the prosperity of the marriage.")

What values are promoted by the UPAA approach? the approach of *Button* and the New York Domestic Relations Law?

5. *Timing*: Under any fairness standard, timing is important. Some standards, such as the UPAA, look only to circumstances at the time of signing, the point at which courts normally determine whether a contract is unconscionable. *See* UPAA; Martin v. Farber, 68 Md.App. 137, 510 A.2d 608 (1986). Others take into account the facts at the time of

terms of the agreement respecting maintenance and property disposition are binding upon the court unless those terms are found to be unconscionable. The standard of unconscionability is used in commercial law, where its meaning includes protection against one-sidedness, oppression, or unfair surprise (see § 2–302, Uniform Commercial Code), and in contract law. It has been used in cases respecting divorce settlements or awards. Bell v. Bell, 150 Colo. 174, 371 P.2d 773 (1962)('this division of property is manifestly unfair, inequitable and unconscionable'). Hence the act does not introduce a novel standard unknown to the law. In the context of negotiations between spouses as to the financial incidents of their marriage, the standard includes protection against overreaching, concealment of assets, and sharp dealing not consistent with the obligations of marital partners to deal fairly with each other.

"In order to determine whether the agreement is unconscionable, the court may look to the economic circumstances of the parties resulting from the agreement, and any other relevant evidence such as the conditions under which the agreement was made, including the knowledge of the other party. If the court finds the agreement not unconscionable, its terms respecting property division and maintenance may not be altered by the court at the hearing."

enforcement. *See, e.g.*, N.Y. Dom. Rel. L. § 236B; *Button, supra*; Justus v. Justus, 581 N.E.2d 1265 (Ind.App.1991); Bassler v. Bassler, 156 Vt. 353, 593 A.2d 82 (Vt.1991); McKee–Johnson v. Johnson, 444 N.W.2d 259 (Minn.1989) (premarital agreement unenforceable if the premises upon which [the contract was] based have so drastically changed that enforcement would not comport with the [original] reasonable expectations of the parties to such an extent that enforcement would be unconscionable). Still others look to the time of signing for property rights and the time of divorce for spousal support. *See, e.g., Gross*; Lewis v. Lewis, 69 Haw. 497, 748 P.2d 1362 (Hawaii 1988); Newman v. Newman, 653 P.2d 728 (Colo.1982); Rider v. Rider, 669 N.E.2d 160 (Ind. 1996).

Under which, if any, of these approaches would the agreement in *DeLorean* be unenforceable? the agreement in *Gross*? What values are promoted by each approach? Is the important issue the parties' circumstance at the time of signing? their circumstances at divorce? the extent of change between signing and divorce?

6. *Spousal support waiver:* No consensus has yet evolved on the enforceability of a waiver of spousal support in a premarital agreement. A few courts have enforced unfair spousal support waivers, as long as the waiving spouse signed the agreement voluntarily and had the advice of independent counsel. *See* Baker v. Baker, 622 So.2d 541 (Fla.App.1993). The UPAA provides that such waivers are enforceable, but if a spouse qualifies for public assistance at the time of divorce, the court may require the other party to provide support to the extent necessary to avoid that eligibility. UPAA § 6(c); *accord* MacFarlane v. Rich, 132 N.H. 608, 567 A.2d 585 (N.H.1989); Cary v. Cary, 937 S.W.2d 777 (Tenn. 1996). Some states adopting the UPAA have eliminated the provision permitting spousal support waivers. See CAL. FAM. CODE § 1612; S. D. COD. LAWS § 25–2–18. And, in Illinois, the UPAA was modified to provide that a spousal support waiver will not be enforced if it causes the waiving spouse undue hardship in light of circumstances not reasonably foreseeable at the time of signing. *See* 750 ILL. COMPILED STAT. ANN., § 10/7. *See also* Unander v. Unander, 265 Or. 102, 506 P.2d 719 (1973) (accepting spousal support waivers, unless waiver deprives spouse of support he or she could not otherwise secure).

Are these hardship standards (such as *Unander*) simply another way of saying that a spousal support waiver is not enforceable?

7. *Post-agreement events:* In those jurisdictions willing to take account of events after the agreement is signed, a finding of unconscionability may be based on loss of spousal earning capacity due to child care responsibilities, health problems, etc., or an unexpected gain or career success. In *Newman* (*supra* n. 5), both parties had been previously married, the wife filed for divorce only thirty months after the wedding, and each party's circumstances had not changed since the wedding; although the parties' financial situations at divorce were very different, the maintenance waiver was enforced.

8. *Common law defenses*: Does the UPAA set forth all grounds available to challenge a premarital agreement? In *Daniel v. Daniel*, 779 S.W.2d 110 (Tex.App.1989), a Texas court held that the enactment of the UPAA did not do away with "common-law defenses." The Official Comment also states that, unless a specific common-law defense is barred (like lack of consideration), ordinary contract defenses remain available.

9. *Criticism*: A number of commentators have criticized policy judgments made by the drafters of the UPAA. Professor Judith Younger, for example, has proposed five amendments to the UPAA in *Perspectives on Antenuptial Agreements*, 40 RUTGERS L.REV. 1059, 1089–90 (1988):

> "The Uniform Act would be immeasurably improved by five amendments. First, the phrase 'including personal rights and obligations' should be eliminated from § 3(a)(8). The section would then read 'any other matter not in violation of public policy or a statute imposing a criminal penalty.' It would be broad enough to include the ruling in *Avitzur v. Avitzur* [p. 216], noted in the comment to the enforcement section, in which the New York Court of Appeals enforced the parties' antenuptial promise to appear before a religious divorce court. As amended, it would not permit agreements relating to daily domestic affairs. As it currently reads, it seems to permit such agreements without providing for their enforcement.
>
> "Second, the public policy and criminal statute limitation articulated in this section should be extended to the first seven listed subjects as well. The Act would thus recognize the fact that a court may invalidate any agreement on the ground that it violates public policy or a statute imposing a criminal penalty.
>
> "Third, in the enforcement section, 6(a)(1), the word 'and' should be substituted for 'or,' conforming the Act to the official comment and the evolving case law. This change was made by the Rhode Island Legislature in the version it adopted.
>
> "Fourth, a provision requiring a fairness review of all provisions of all agreements at enforcement should be added to the statute. The best standard is 'unconscionability' understood as protecting against 'one-sidedness, oppression or unfair surprise.' Indeed, this is the statutory standard in Colorado, New York and North Dakota for review at enforcement; it is one of the standards being employed by courts in states without statutes; and it is the statutory standard under the Uniform Act for review of agreements at the time of execution. * * *
>
> "Fifth, the Act should take a clear stand on the permissibility of agreements relating to children, prohibiting those which adversely affect their support or other rights, and conditioning enforcement of any such agreement upon compliance with the well-understood 'best interests' " standard.

In *Premarital Contracts Are Now Enforceable, Unless ...*, 21 HOUS. L.REV. 757, 780–81 (1984) Professor Thomas Oldham proposed a substitute test for determining whether to enforce a premarital agreement:

(a) A written premarital or postnuptial agreement is enforceable at divorce if it is freely and intelligently executed and, considering the property and support received pursuant thereto, both spouses have adequate support at divorce under the terms of the agreement in light of the length of marriage and the wealth, needs, health, and earning capacities of the parties.

(b) A written premarital or postnuptial agreement is enforceable at divorce if it is freely and intelligently executed, even if both spouses do not receive adequate support pursuant thereto, unless subsection (c) applies.

(c) If (i) the terms of a premarital or postnuptial agreement, considering the property and support received pursuant thereto, provide inadequate support for a spouse at divorce, in light of the length of marriage and the wealth, needs, health, and earning capacities of the parties, and (ii) there was a substantial and unforeseeable change in the parties' circumstances between the time of execution of the agreement (or the most recent amendment thereof) and divorce, the divorce court can, in its discretion, fashion a division of property and support award so that the financially dependent spouse will receive adequate support. The duration and amount of the support and property so awarded are to be based upon the length of the marriage and the wealth, needs, health, and earning capacities of the parties.[1]

(d) A premarital or postnuptial agreement may address the property division or spousal support, if any, that will result if divorce occurs.

Problem 4–2:

Jeremy and Jessica married fifteen years ago just after both graduated from law school. Before marriage, they signed a premarital agree-

1. Courts desirous of establishing safeguards to protect mothers against oppressive marital contracts might adopt the following guidelines as a second paragraph of "c" of the proposal set forth above in text:

If (i) the terms of a premarital or postnuptial agreement provide inadequate support for a spouse at divorce, in light of the length of the marriage and the wealth, needs, health, and earning capacities of the parties; (ii) the parties had one or more children together, (iii) the financially dependent spouse did not work outside the home at a full-time job for more than one-half of the duration of the marriage; (iv) the respective wealth and earning capacities of the parties are substantially different at divorce; and (v) either the marriage was of substantial duration or the financially dependent spouse will receive physical custody of one or more minor children at divorce, the court may, in its discretion, despite the agreement, fashion a division of property and support award so that the financially dependent spouse will receive adequate support, the duration and amount of which is to be based upon the length of the marriage and the wealth, needs, health, and earning capacities of the parties.

ment which provided that: 1) each spouse's earnings (including all professional partnership interests) would be separate property not subject to division at divorce; and 2) each spouse waives any right to post-divorce spousal support from the other. When Jeremy and Jessica married, both earned about the same amount of money and worked at comparable legal jobs at different law firms. Jessica had a child during her first year of work and quit her job to assume the role of primary caretaker for the child; thereafter she worked only sporadically and part-time as a lawyer. Jeremy continued to work full-time as a lawyer. Jeremy has now initiated a divorce action. He is a partner in a law firm earning $200,000 annually; Jessica is working part-time, earning approximately $20,000 per year. Jeremy and Jessica have agreed that Jessica will receive custody of their child and will receive monthly child support of $500 for three years, until the child is 18 years old. Would Jeremy and Jessica's premarital agreement be enforced under the UPAA? under the N.Y. Dom. Rel. Law and *Button* (note 4 *supra*)? under *Gross*? *Should* the agreement be enforced?

Problem 4–3:

Lois, a wealthy woman, is planning to marry Clark, a younger man with few assets and a small salary. Lois has consulted you about asking Clark to sign a premarital agreement whereby he would waive all rights to marital property and spousal support if the marriage ends in divorce. How would you structure the negotiations: 1) to maximize the likelihood that the agreement would be enforced; and 2) to minimize the likelihood that the contract negotiations would not undermine the relationship. If Lois were to ask whether you think she should ask Clark to sign the agreement, how would you respond?

Problem 4–4:

Premarital agreements generally provide that, if the parties divorce, each will have certain rights and obligations. (For example, that W will pay H $X.) You represent W. Opposing counsel has suggested that the agreement provide that W pay H $X if H gives W written notice that he desires a divorce. Would you agree to this suggestion? Why or why not?

Problem 4–5:

Two prospective spouses have asked you to draft a premarital agreement for them. What, if any, professional responsibility issues would this present?

Problem 4–6:

Helen and Walter signed a premarital agreement that complies with the UPAA. At a festive dinner on their first anniversary, they decided to revoke the agreement; to memorialize this intention they threw a copy of the agreement into the fire in the fireplace. Two years later, Helen and Walter divorce. Under the UPAA, is the agreement still valid?

Problem 4–7:

You are counsel to the state legislature's Committee on Family Law, which is considering the adoption of legislation governing premarital agreements. Case law had, by and large, followed the approach of the *Gross* decision until last year, when the state Supreme Court enforced a premarital agreement on facts similar to those in the *Gross* case. The Committee has concluded that legislation would be useful to ensure a predictable approach to the enforcement of premarital agreements.

At a public hearing, the Committee heard a number of family lawyers report anecdotal evidence that couples with a premarital agreement are more prone to divorce. The Committee also heard testimony from an expert on comparative law, who testified that, in many civil law countries, marriage partners must affirmatively elect a marital property regime (i.e, shared or separate property rights) and that a number of both civil and common law countries (including England and Australia) do not permit binding premarital agreements on divorce entitlements.

You have been asked to advise the Committee:

1. If marriages dissolve at a higher rate when there is a premarital agreement, is this a significant public concern?
2. Should the state permit bargaining over the financial consequences of divorce? Should it matter if the parties are already living together?
3. If bargaining is to be permitted, how (if at all) should the state protect the poor and/or unsophisticated prospective spouse?
4. Are there rules or entitlements so important that they should not be subject to bargaining? If yes, what are they and what limits should be imposed on bargaining?
5. What test for determining the enforceability of premarital agreements best balances all competing concerns?

B. CONFLICTS ASPECTS OF PREMARITAL AGREEMENTS

As you have seen, state laws on premarital agreements vary. If spouses have contacts with more than one state or country, a court must decide which law to apply.

Under current conflicts of law principles, most courts will apply the law of a state chosen by the parties, as long as the parties have some connection with that state and its law does not violate an important policy of the forum jurisdiction. *See, e.g.*, UPAA § 3 (7) (permitting parties to elect applicable law). So, in *DeLorean,* the New Jersey court applied the law of California, not New Jersey, to determine whether Mr. DeLorean's financial disclosure was adequate. But some courts have held that laws governing premarital agreements reflect state policies so important that party election should not be permitted. *See* Scherer v. Scherer, 249 Ga. 635, 292 S.E.2d 662 (1982). Aside from the issue of state policy, what problem would be presented if two Americans living in the U.S. were to choose Iranian law to govern their marital property rights?

If the parties to a premarital agreement do not specify which state's law will govern, some courts apply the law of the state where the contract was signed. *See* Hill v. Hill, 262 A.2d 661 (Del.Ch.1970). Others apply the law of the state with which the parties have the most significant relationship. *See* RESTATEMENT, SECOND, CONFLICT OF LAWS, §§ 187, 188. If a couple marries in one state, then moves to another and divorces there, the evidence suggests that (as long as both spouses move) the forum jurisdiction will typically find that it has the most significant relationship with the couple. *See* Lewis v. Lewis, 69 Haw. 497, 748 P.2d 1362 (Hawaii 1988). Is this unfair? If so, in what situations?

Premarital agreements made in another country raise even more difficult problems. What, for example, should a U.S. court do if foreign nationals comply with premarital agreement laws of their own country, move to the United States, and later divorce? Some civil law countries permit spouses to elect a community or separate property system to govern their rights at divorce. If the spouses elect a separate property regime, what should a court do if they later divorce in a community property state in the U.S.? *See* Fernandez v. Fernandez, 194 Cal.App.2d 782, 15 Cal.Rptr. 374 (1961). Should it matter if the election procedure complies with the forum's requirements for premarital agreements?

C. INCORPORATING NONECONOMIC PROVISIONS IN A PREMARITAL AGREEMENT

While premarital agreements often address property rights, some spouses (and psychotherapists) have urged that premarital agreements could usefully address a variety of other matters. Here is an example given by Professor Weitzman:

LENORE J. WEITZMAN, THE MARRIAGE CONTRACT

295 et seq. (1981).

A TRADITIONAL MARRIAGE BETWEEN A MEDICAL DOCTOR AND A HOUSEWIFE WITH FULL PARTNERSHIP RIGHTS FOR THE WIFE

Commitment to Ourselves

1. Absent truly extraordinary circumstances, we agree to spend at least one evening a week enjoying each other—alone together. An evening begins at 7 P.M.

2. Absent truly extraordinary circumstances, we agree to spend at least three weekend days a month together enjoying each other.

Sex

1. We recognize the central importance of sex in human relationships and commit ourselves to putting time and creative energy into realizing our sexual potential.

2. We do not intend that our love and commitment to each other shall exclude other relationships in work, friendship, or sex.

3. We do intend that our relationship with each other shall be a primary one and that each other's feelings and needs should be a major consideration in our other actions.

4. We will tell each other when we have sex with other people, and we will make an effort to communicate honestly about all other important relationships in our lives.

Other Responsibilities

1. Nancy agrees to further David's career by maintaining appropriate social relationships with other doctors and their wives.

2. Nancy agrees to participate actively in church and country club activities, to serve on medical auxiliary and hospital benefit committees, and to socialize with David's colleagues and other physicians.

3. Nancy promises to give a dinner party or to otherwise aid David's professional advancement by entertaining at least twice a week.

4. David agrees to accompany Nancy to the ballet at least once a month.

5. David also agrees to schedule at least two two-week vacations with her each year, at least one of them in Europe.

Children

1. Children will be postponed until David's education is completed.

2. If Nancy should become pregnant prior to that time, she will have an abortion.

3. Nancy will have full responsibility for the care of the children; financial responsibility will be fully met from the income from David's practice.

Conditions of Separation

1. We agree to stay together, absent intense pain, for four years or until our child is three years old, whichever is earlier.

2. After that time, we can separate at any time that we freely and mutually agree to do so.

3. In the event that one of us wants to separate and the other does not, we agree to:

a. Give explicit notice of the desire to separate.

b. Work to mend our relationship for a period of six months after such notice.

c. Make time for each other during that period, and seek professional assistance if either of us believes it would be useful.

4. We recognize that the process of growth is the process of change. We respect each other's freedom and separate character. We hope that we will always freely choose to grow together, but we recognize that we may not. We agree always to try to treat each other gently, politely, and with consideration. We agree that, even if we separate, we will do it in a loving way.

Termination

1. This partnership may be dissolved by either party, at will, upon six months notice to the other party.

2. If this partnership is terminated by either party prior to the completion of David's education, Nancy's obligation to support him will cease. Moreover, once David's career has begun, he will have the obligation of supporting Nancy at the rate of $50,000 a year (in 1979 dollars with built-in cost-of-living and inflation adjustments) for as many years as she supported him. If necessary, David will secure a loan to repay Nancy for her support. If Nancy prefers a lump-sum settlement equal to the value of this support, David will arrange a loan to provide it. Both parties agree to treat Nancy's original support of David as a loan of the value specified above. David's obligation to repay this loan has the standing of any other legal debt.

3. Once David finishes his residency, Nancy will acquire a one-quarter vested interest in his future earnings. If the partnership is terminated after this date, Nancy will be entitled to one-fourth of his net yearly income, to be paid quarterly, for as long as he continues to practice medicine. David will purchase insurance or a bond to guarantee this payment. It is agreed that this payment is not alimony, and that it shall be continued unmodified regardless of her earning capacity or remarriage. The parties consider this Nancy's reimbursement for investing in and helping to launch David's career. It is agreed that her efforts will have been crucial to any future success that he has, and that her vested interest in his career is the consideration for that support.

4. David agrees to pay Nancy the fixed sum of $50,000 if their marriage terminates within 15 years, as liquidated damages for the pain and suffering she will experience from the change in her expectations and life plans.

5. David also agrees [in the event of termination of the marriage] to pay for Nancy's medical expenses or to provide her with adequate insurance at the rate of one year of coverage for every year of marriage. It is explicitly agreed that psychiatric and dental bills be included in the above.

6. Community property will be divided equally upon termination.

7. If there are children, Nancy will have custody of the children. David will have full responsibility for their support, as well as the responsibility for compensating Nancy for her services in caring for them

(at the then current rate for private nurses). Suitable visiting arrangements will be made.

Notes and Questions

1. Would a court enforce all of these provisions? If not, is unenforceability a problem?

(a) Some of the provisions seem to reflect aspirational goals and may not be intended to be enforceable. For example, it seems unlikely that David and Nancy contemplate any legal consequences from their failure to spend at least three weekend days a month together or David's failure to attend the ballet. What purposes might such provisions have?

(b) Other provisions seem more significant. For example, what if Nancy doesn't have an abortion if she gets pregnant? A court would not order specific enforcement. Does this mean it is senseless to include such a provision in a premarital agreement?

(c) UPAA § 3(a)(8) seems to endorse provisions dealing with the day-to-day aspects of married life, like those included in the Weitzman contract, as long as they are "not in violation of public policy." This approach has been criticized by some, including Professor Younger [p. 208].

(d) Courts agree that provisions in a premarital agreement relating to children, including those governing child custody and support, are unenforceable. *See, e.g.*, Osborne v. Osborne, 384 Mass. 591, 428 N.E.2d 810 (1981) (custody); Combs v. Sherry–Combs, 865 P.2d 50 (Wyo.1993); (support); UPAA § 3(b). Should an agreement to raise the children in a particular church be enforced? *See* In re Weiss, 42 Cal.App.4th 106, 49 Cal. Rptr. 2d 339 (1996) (no).

(e) Should spouses be able to waive the right to divorce? If no, what about the more limited waiver in the Weitzman contract that the parties will not separate for four years, and will "work on the relationship" for six months before separating? *See* Coggins v. Coggins, 601 So.2d 109 (Ala.Civ.App.1992) Or a waiver of the right to initiate a divorce action on "no-fault" grounds, if the right to initiate a fault divorce is retained (but, of course, only if a "fault" ground is available)? Or a waiver of the right to initiate a divorce action on a "fault" ground, if the right to initiate a "no-fault" divorce is retained? *See* Massar v. Massar, 279 N.J.Super. 89, 652 A.2d 219 (App.Div.1995). If such a provision is valid, should it be specifically enforced or should the breaching party be required to pay damages to the other? Would recovery on a provision not to get a divorce be comparable to recovery for breach of the contract to marry? *See generally* Theodore Haas, *The Rationality and Enforceability of Contractual Restrictions on Divorce*, 66 N.C.L. Rev. 879 (1988). What policy issues are presented by this type of waiver?

2. Some religions have divorce requirements that differ from those of the secular law. For example, a Jewish wife may not remarry unless her husband obtains a bill of divorce ("get"). Sometimes divorcing Jewish husbands have refused to obtain a get, causing significant hardship to their wives. *See* Feldman, *Jewish Women and Secular Courts: Helping a Jewish Woman Obtain a Get*, 5 BERKELEY WOMEN'S L.J. 139 (1989–90). In recent cases, most courts have enforced agreements requiring the husband to cooperate in the get procedure. *See* Scholl v. Scholl, 621 A.2d 808 (Del.Fam.1992); Marriage of Goldman, 196 Ill.App.3d 785, 143 Ill.Dec. 944, 554 N.E.2d 1016 (1990); Avitzur v. Avitzur, 58 N.Y.2d 108, 459 N.Y.S.2d 572, 446 N.E.2d 136 (1983).

3. A celebrity may be concerned about the possibility that a former spouse may write about intimate details of their life together. Donald Trump included a provision in his premarital agreement that prohibited his wife Ivana from writing about their marriage without his consent. Should the provision be enforced? *See* Trump v. Trump, 179 A.D.2d 201, 582 N.Y.S.2d 1008 (1992).

4. What if the premarital agreement specifies that a spouse will lose all marital property rights if he or she is sexually unfaithful during marriage? *See* Laudig v. Laudig, 425 Pa.Super. 228, 624 A.2d 651 (1993).

SECTION 3. VARIABILITY OF THE MARITAL STATUS BY AGREEMENT DURING MARRIAGE

The UPAA only applies to premarital agreements. Should the rules be the same for agreements made during marriage, or are there different concerns?

BORELLI v. BRUSSEAU

California Court of Appeals, 1993.
12 Cal.App.4th 647, 16 Cal.Rptr.2d 16.

PERLEY, ASSOCIATE JUSTICE.

Plaintiff and appellant Hildegard L. Borelli (appellant) appeals from a judgment of dismissal after a demurrer was sustained without leave to amend her complaint against defendant and respondent Grace G. Brusseau, as executor of the estate of Michael J. Borelli (respondent). The complaint sought specific performance of a promise by appellant's deceased husband Michael J. Borelli (decedent) to transfer certain property to her in return for her promise to care for him at home after he had suffered a stroke.

On April 24, 1980, appellant and decedent entered into an antenuptial contract. On April 25, 1980, they were married. Appellant remained married to decedent until the death of the latter on January 25, 1989.

In March 1983, February 1984, and January 1987, decedent was admitted to a hospital due to heart problems. As a result, "decedent became concerned and frightened about his health and longevity." He discussed these fears and concerns with appellant and told her that he intended to "leave" the following property to her.

1. "An interest" in a lot in Sacramento, California.

2. A life estate for the use of a condominium in Hawaii.

3. A 25 percent interest in Borelli Meat Co.

4. All cash remaining in all existing bank accounts at the time of his death.

5. The costs of educating decedent's step-daughter, Monique Lee.

6. Decedent's entire interest in a residence in Kensington, California.

7. All furniture located in the residence.

8. Decedent's interest in a partnership.

9. Health insurance for appellant and Monique Lee.

In August 1988, decedent suffered a stroke while in the hospital. "Throughout the decedent's August, 1988 hospital stay and subsequent treatment at a rehabilitation center, he repeatedly told [appellant] that he was uncomfortable in the hospital and that he disliked being away from home. The decedent repeatedly told [appellant] that he did not want to be admitted to a nursing home, even though it meant he would need round-the-clock care, and rehabilitative modifications to the house, in order for him to live at home."

"In or about October, 1988, [appellant] and the decedent entered an oral agreement whereby the decedent promised to leave to [appellant] the property listed [above], including a one hundred percent interest in the Sacramento property.... In exchange for the decedent's promise to leave her the property ... [appellant] agreed to care for the decedent in his home, for the duration of his illness, thereby avoiding the need for him to move to a rest home or convalescent hospital as his doctors recommended. The agreement was based on the confidential relationship that existed between [appellant] and the decedent."

Appellant performed her promise but the decedent did not perform his. Instead his will bequeathed her the sum of $100,000 and his interest in the residence they owned as joint tenants. The bulk of decedent's estate passed to respondent, who is decedent's daughter.

Marriage is a matter of public concern. The public, through the state, has interest in both its formation and dissolution.... The regulation of marriage and divorce is solely within the province of the Legislature except as the same might be restricted by the Constitution.

In accordance with these concerns the following pertinent legislation has been enacted: Civil Code § 242—"Every individual shall support his or her spouse.... " Civil Code § 4802—"[A] husband and wife cannot, by any contract with each other, alter their legal relations, except as to property.... " Civil Code § 5100—"Husband and wife contract toward each other obligations of mutual respect, fidelity, and support." Civil Code § 5103—"[E]ither husband or wife may enter into any transaction with the other ... respecting property, which either might if unmarried." Civil Code § 5132—"[A] married person shall support the person's spouse while they are living together.... "

The courts have stringently enforced and explained the statutory language.

Estate of Sonnicksen (1937) 23 Cal.App.2d 475, 479, 73 P.2d 643, and *Brooks v. Brooks*, (1941) 48 Cal. App.2d 347, 349–50, 119 P.2d 970, each hold that under the above statutes and in accordance with the above policy a wife is obligated by the marriage contract to provide nursing type care to an ill husband. Therefore, contracts whereby the wife is to receive compensation for providing such services are void as against public policy and there is no consideration for the husband's promise.

Appellant argues that *Sonnicksen*, and *Brooks* are no longer valid precedents because they are based on outdated views of the role of women and marriage. She further argues that the rule of those cases denies her equal protection because husbands only have a financial obligation toward their wives, while wives have to provide actual nursing services for free. We disagree. The rule and policy of *Sonnicksen* and *Brooks* have been applied to both spouses in several recent cases arising in different areas of the law.

Webster's New Collegiate Dictionary (1981) p. 240, defines consortium as "The legal right of one spouse to the company, affection, and service of the other." Only married persons are allowed to recover damages for loss of consortium.

Rodriguez v. Bethlehem Steel Corp. (1974) 12 Cal.3d 382, 525 P.2d 669, held that a wife could recover consortium damages. The Supreme Court's reasoning was as follows. "But there is far more to the marriage relationship than financial support. The concept of consortium includes not only loss of support or services, it also embraces such elements as love, companionship, affection, society, sexual relations, solace and more." As to each, "the interest sought to be protected is personal to the wife." (*Rodriguez, supra*, at 404–405, 525 P.2d 669.) "The deprivation of a husband's physical assistance in operating and maintaining the family home is a compensable item of loss of consortium."

In *Krouse v. Graham* (1977) 19 Cal.3d 59, 66–67, 562 P.2d 1022, an action for the wrongful death of the wife, the husband was allowed to recover consortium damages "for the loss of his wife's 'love, companionship, comfort, affection, society, solace or moral support, any loss of enjoyment of sexual relations, or any loss of her physical assistance in the operation or maintenance of the home.' " The wife "had recently retired as a legal secretary in order to care for her husband, Benjamin, whose condition of emphysema, in turn, caused him to retire and necessitated considerable nursing services."

The principal holding of *Watkins v. Watkins* (1983) 143 Cal.App.3d 651, 192 Cal.Rptr. 54, was that a marriage did not extinguish a woman's right to recover the value of her homemaker services rendered prior to the marriage. Much of the opinion is devoted to a discussion of *Sonnicksen* and *Brooks*. Those cases are approved by the court but not expanded to cover the period before marriage.

Vincent v. State of California (1971) 22 Cal.App.3d 566, 99 Cal.Rptr. 410, held that for purposes of benefit payments spouses caring for each other must be treated identically under similar assistance programs. In reaching such conclusion the court held: "Appellants suggest that one reason justifying denial of payment for services rendered by ATD attendants who reside with their recipient spouses is that, by virtue of the marriage contract, one spouse is obligated to care for the other without remuneration. Such pre-existing duty provides a constitutionally sound basis for a classification which denies compensation for care rendered by a husband or wife to his spouse who is receiving welfare assistance.... But insofar as one spouse has a duty created by the marriage contract to care for the other without compensation when they are living together, recipients of aid to the aged, aid to the blind and aid to the disabled are similarly situated." *Vincent*, supra, at 572, 99 Cal.Rptr. 410.

These cases indicate that the marital duty of support under Civil Code §§ 242, 5100, and 5132 includes caring for a spouse who is ill. They also establish that support in a marriage means more than the physical care someone could be hired to provide. Such support also encompasses sympathy, love, companionship and affection. Thus, the duty of support can no more be "delegated" to a third party than the statutory duties of fidelity and mutual respect (Civ.Code, § 5100). Marital duties are owed by the spouses personally. This is implicit in the definition of marriage as "a personal relation arising out of a civil contract between a man and a woman." (Civ.Code, § 4100.)

We therefore adhere to the longstanding rule that a spouse is not entitled to compensation for support, apart from rights to community property and the like that arise from the marital relation itself. Personal performance of a personal duty created by the contract of marriage does not constitute a new consideration supporting the indebtedness alleged in this case.

We agree with the dissent that no rule of law becomes sacrosanct by virtue of its duration, but we are not persuaded that the well-established rule that governs this case deserves to be discarded. If the rule denying compensation for support originated from considerations peculiar to women, this has no bearing on the rule's gender-neutral application today. There is as much potential for fraud today as ever, and allegations like appellant's could be made every time any personal care is rendered. This concern may not entirely justify the rule, but it cannot be said that all rationales for the rule are outdated.

Speculating that appellant might have left her husband but for the agreement she alleges, the dissent suggests that marriages will break up if such agreements are not enforced. While we do not believe that marriages would be fostered by a rule that encouraged sickbed bargaining, the question is not whether such negotiations may be more useful than unseemly. The issue is whether such negotiations are antithetical to the institution of marriage as the Legislature has defined it. We believe that they are.

The dissent maintains that mores have changed to the point that spouses can be treated just like any other parties haggling at arm's length. Whether or not the modern marriage has become like a business, and regardless of whatever else it may have become, it continues to be defined by statute as a personal relationship of mutual support. Thus, even if few things are left that cannot command a price, marital support remains one of them.

The judgment is affirmed.

Notes and Questions

1. Getting married is sufficient consideration for a premarital agreement; no other consideration is required. *See* UPAA § 2; J. THOMAS OLDHAM, DIVORCE, SEPARATION AND THE DISTRIBUTION OF DISTRIBUTION OF PROPERTY, § 4.03[2][g]. But, as *Borelli* indicates, postnuptial agreements require consideration.

2. Some states have enacted statutes analogous to the UPAA to determine the enforceability of postnuptial agreements. *See* TEX. FAM. CODE §§ 4.101, 4.105. But even if one determines the enforceability of a postnuptial agreement under UPAA standards, different questions arise. Most courts agree that, if one prospective spouse presents a contract to the other a significant time before the wedding and says "sign this or I won't marry you," this does not constitute coercion or duress. But what if one spouse presents the other with a postnuptial agreement and says "sign this or I'll divorce you"? Should it matter whether the parties have had children together? *See* Matthews v. Matthews, 725 S.W.2d 275 (Tex.App.1986). Although the *Borelli* court frames the issue as consideration, isn't it really duress and overreaching?

3. Some courts have not applied UPAA standards to postnuptial agreements. For example, although Hawaii has adopted the UPAA, in Ching v. Ching, 7 Haw.App. 221, 751 P.2d 93 (1988), the court held that a postnuptial agreement should be enforced only if it was "equitable" at divorce. *See also* MINN. STAT. ANN. § 519.11 (postnuptial agreements enforceable only if (i) both spouses possess assets amounting to at least $1,200,000; (ii) both parties are represented by independent counsel; and (iii) a divorce action is not filed within two years of signing); Uniform Marital Property Act (UMPA) § 10(f) (employing UPAA standard for premarital agreements), but denying enforcement to postnuptial agreements if (i) the agreement was unconscionable when signed; (ii) the agreement was involuntarily signed; or (iii) there was inadequate disclo-

sure). Why would states adopt more substantial restrictions on the enforceability of postnuptial agreements?

4. Are you persuaded by *Borelli* that spouses should not be able to contract for payment for services? In Department of Human Resources v. Williams, 130 Ga.App. 149, 202 S.E.2d 504 (1973), the state's welfare regulations provided that disabled recipients were entitled to a specified dollar amount in order to pay someone to provide personal care. A recipient argued that he should be entitled to the same sum to pay for services provided by his wife. Not surprisingly, the state argued that the wife was obligated to provide these personal care services to the husband without compensation. In contrast to the *Borelli* court, the Georgia court proposed this compromise:

> "The report of the hearing officer contains as a conclusion of law, that 'Georgia law provides that a husband is entitled to the services of his wife.' This is not the law. The law is that a husband is entitled to receive the *domestic* services of his wife. *Lee v. Savannah Guano Co.*, 99 Ga. 572, 27 S.E. 159.
>
> The *Lee* case concerned a conveyance of land from husband to wife in satisfaction of the wife's claim for money due her under a contract with her husband for "her undertaking to perform * * * the *ordinary household duties* (emphasis supplied) devolving upon a wife in her position." The court, while finding nothing wrong with the agreement, refused to make it effectual against creditors of the husband who had become creditors prior to the conveyance of land. The court found the wife could not charge the husband "for cooking his meals, making or mending his garments, sweeping the floors of his house, milking the cow, or for *other services of a like kind*. Their duties are correlative, the performance of hers being no less obligatory than the performance of his. The husband is not legally bound to support his wife in luxurious idleness.
>
> The services undertaken by the wife, which were not sufficient consideration, were "ordinary household duties." As the husband's correlative legal duty of support does not legally bind him to support his wife in luxurious idleness, the wife's duty of performing ordinary household services can not legally bind her to render those extensive personal care services required by a husband who has suffered such brain damage that he must be tended as is a young child.
>
> A husband is entitled to the *domestic* service of his wife, rendered in and about the household, in the *general* work of keeping and maintaining the home.
>
> The authorized personal care expenditures include services other than domestic services. The trial court did not err in reversing the ruling of the agency and remanding for a finding of facts."

5. Should a court enforce an agreement by one spouse to pay the other for child care and housekeeping? If consideration is the issue, would such a promise in a premarital agreement be enforceable (because

the marriage is the consideration), or would it be considered a promise detrimental to the marital relationship in violation of *Restatement of Contracts § 190(1)*?

6. Some types of waivers may be enforceable only if made after the wedding. For example, some courts have concluded that prospective spouses may not waive certain private pension rights. *See* Hurwitz v. Sher, 982 F.2d 778 (2d Cir.1992); Note, 47 WASH. U.J. URB. & CONTEMP. L. 157 (1995).

CURRY v. CURRY

Supreme Court of Georgia, 1990.
260 Ga. 302, 392 S.E.2d 879.

WELTNER, JUSTICE.

The parties were married in 1975, divorced in 1977, and remarried "by the common law" later in 1977. The husband filed for divorce in 1981 and again in 1984. In 1984, the parties signed a reconciliation agreement that dismissed the pending action without prejudice; provided for certain payments by the husband to the wife; and barred the wife from future claims for alimony or equitable division of property. In 1989, the husband filed a new complaint for divorce, and sought an order enforcing the reconciliation agreement. A hearing was held and the trial court entered a final judgment to enforce the agreement. We granted the wife's application for discretionary appeal.

In *Scherer v. Scherer*, 249, Ga. 635, 641, 292 S.E.2d 662 (1982), we held:

> [T]he trial judge should employ basically three criteria in determining whether to enforce [an antenuptial agreement in contemplation of divorce] in a particular case: (1) was the agreement obtained through fraud, duress or mistake, or through misrepresentation or nondisclosure of material facts? (2) is the agreement unconscionable? (3) have the facts and circumstances changed since the agreement was executed, so as to make its enforcement unfair and unreasonable?

We know of no reason why a reconciliation agreement should stand on a different footing from an antenuptial agreement under *Scherer, supra*. *Scherer* specifies that the trial judge shall determine whether or not to enforce the agreement. There was no error.

The wife asserts that the trial court's conclusion (that the agreement was not unconscionable) is inconsistent with its findings that:

> "The terms and conditions of the reconciliation agreement were unfair and inequitable in that in any divorce proceeding in 1984, the wife had a substantial likelihood of receiving some equitable division of property despite any acts of adultery which could bar alimony....
>
> "When ... [the wife] entered into such agreement, while unfair as to specific economic benefits accruing at the time of the execution or within a reasonably foreseeable time thereafter, ... [it] did not constitute an unconscionable agreement."

Viewing the findings in toto, there was no error. The findings are, in part, as follows:

The substantial non-marital assets and the value of the total estate of the ... [husband] and continuing in a marriage relationship with a man who has a deteriorating health condition and a foreseeable shortened life expectancy in itself was a substantial legal benefit.

This marriage would have terminated in 1984 but for such reconciliation which ... [the wife] fully recognized.

There has been no change in circumstances that was not foreseeable at the time that the agreement was entered into, that the deteriorating disability of the ... [husband] was foreseeable, the increase in the value of the non-marital assets was foreseeable as well as her graduating from nursing school and having an independent source of earnings.

... [T]here has been a substantial performance under the reconciliation agreement as to the terms and conditions of said agreement such as to make the reconciliation agreement binding on the parties.

[U]nder the doctrine of equitable estoppel, since the major benefit sought by the ... [wife] was a continuation of a marriage which but for such agreement would have terminated in divorce in 1984, and because of her intent to enter into the agreement no matter what the terms as far as immediate economic benefit to her, she achieved and received the benefit of the bargain sought and caused a substantial change in condition on the part of the ... [husband].

... [Husband] had a right to rely on the agreement to his detriment.... [I]n entering into such agreement ... the [husband] did not do so fraudulently or to mislead or misrepresent the facts to the ... [wife] because he lived under said agreement from 1984 to the date of said hearing, which is a significant period of time.

... [S]ince the parties were represented by counsel and dealt at arm's length and bargained for what they received, this court is bound by the terms and conditions whether fair or unfair or contrary to what a court or jury would do upon a divorce proceeding.

... [A]bsent a showing of fraud, mistake, duress, misrepresentation of fact, unconscionability or substantial change in condition, the court does not have the authority to set aside or ignore such contract.... [T]he parties are both bound by those terms.

Note and Questions

1. Should premarital agreements and reconciliation agreements be treated identically? In the former context, the parties are negotiating an agreement when the relationship is going well; in the latter, substantial problems have arisen, and the probabilities have increased that the marriage will end in divorce. Should this difference matter?

2. Divorcing spouses sometimes sign a separation agreement, or "property settlement," setting forth their property rights and support obligations. These agreements will be discussed in Chapter 17, *infra*. In some states that subject premarital agreements to minimal require-

ments, separation agreements are subjected to a fairly rigorous fairness review. *See* TEX. FAM. CODE § 7.006. The rationale for this approach is that spouses are less likely to bargain fairly with each other after the relationship has broken down. Assuming the validity of the assumption, are reconciliation agreements more like premarital agreements or separation agreements?

3. Both Mr. Borelli and Mrs. Curry were at a substantial bargaining disadvantage. Are these disadvantages any different from those a poor person would experience when negotiating a premarital agreement with a rich person?

4. How did the *Curry* court determine whether the agreement was unconscionable? Under this view, could an agreement ever be unconscionable, absent a change in circumstances?

5. A reconciliation agreement is often made to induce one spouse to stay married. In this context, what would make the signing involuntary? In Gilley v. Gilley, 778 S.W.2d 862 (Tenn.App.1989) the parties signed a one-sided reconciliation agreement after the wife discovered that the husband was having an affair. When they divorced two years later, the husband challenged the agreement, arguing duress and lack of consideration. The court responded in this way:

> We find no merit to the assertion that the agreement was without consideration. Wife had several grounds upon which to prosecute a divorce, which she did not do at the husband's request, receiving promises of faithfulness secured by a property distribution, in the event of divorce, satisfactory to wife.
>
> Neither is there merit to the assertion that the agreement was obtained through coercion or duress. Duress is a condition of the mind produced by improper external pressure or influence that destroys the free will of a person causing him to make a contract not of his own volition. *Simpson v. Harper*, 21 Tenn.App. 431, 111 S.W.2d 882, 886 (1937); *Pride v. Baker*, 64 S.W. 329 (Tenn.Ch.App. 1901). Husband asks us to find duress in his "willingness to sign anything" to preserve his marriage. Perhaps husband was under duress due to the discovery of his own miscreant conduct, but in order for the agreement to be defeated, we must find legal duress. Whatever perceived pressures constrained him to sign the agreement against his free will were internal and of his own making, and whatever external pressures there may have been were not improper. The wife clearly had a legal basis and right to prosecute a divorce and did nothing improper in negotiating an agreement in consideration of forgoing her claim.

6. If a couple sign a reconciliation agreement, successfully reconcile for a substantial period, and then divorce, should the agreement be enforced? In Minor v. Minor, 863 S.W.2d 51 (Tenn.App.1993) the parties cohabited for twelve years after signing a reconciliation agreement and then filed for divorce. The court did not enforce the agreement, citing changes in the parties' circumstances since the signing of the agreement.

7. Did the agreement in *Curry* "encourage divorce?"

Chapter 5

NONMARITAL RELATIONSHIPS—RIGHTS AND OBLIGATIONS

> *Love and marriage, love and marriage,*
> *Go together like a horse and carriage,*
> *This I tell ya, brother,*
> *Ya can't have one without the other.*
>
> *Sammy Cahn, 1955*

> *Is Marriage Really Necessary? At one time only Bohemians and socialists—people like that—asked the question. Now it has become the property of the middle class: the people who twenty years ago talked about togetherness; the people who ten years ago thought once you had her orgasm straightened out, that was that; the people who faithfully kept saying that marriage has its ups and downs, and, you know, it's a compromise and you have to work at it but, taken all in all, it's still the best shot at happiness. These are the people who are now saying, "Marriage is hell"—and maybe the hell with it. * * * Suddenly priests seem to be the only people left who really want to get married. * * * Marriage has become one of those antiquated institutions—another dirty word—that bricks people in.*
>
> *Maddocks, Brave New Marriage*
> *Atlantic Monthly 230:66–69 (1972).*

SECTION 1. DISPUTES BETWEEN COHABITANTS

Marriage may or may not be an "antiquated institution," but it is undeniable that nonmarital cohabitation has increased dramatically. In 1994, the U.S. Census Bureau counted 3.7 million unmarried-couple households in the United States, up from 523,000 in 1970. Today there are seven unmarried couples for every 100 married couples, compared with only one for every 100 in 1970. U.S. DEP'T OF COMMERCE, BUREAU OF THE CENSUS, MARITAL STATUS AND LIVING ARRANGEMENTS: MARCH 1994 (Current Pop. Rep. P–20–484, February 1996). While we lack detailed information on the social characteristics of nonmarital cohabitants, we do know that two-thirds of unmarried-couple households have no children under fifteen at home. We also know that the ranks of nonmarital cohabitants are no longer populated exclusively by the poor and bohemian.

With the infiltration of nonmarital cohabitation into middle-class life has come increased social acceptability. But it was not so long ago that a nonmarital, or "meretricious" relationship was considered so outrageous and immoral that, even if the parties had an express written agreement, a court would not enforce it. *See* Wallace v. Rappleye, 103 Ill. 229, 249 (1882). The harshness of this rule was ameliorated in several ways, however. The doctrine of common-law marriage, more widely accepted than it is today, increased the percentage of couples who were considered legally married. Moreover, the "illegality" rule did not apply to all dealings between cohabitants; if their agreement had nothing to do with their domestic arrangements, it was considered to be "severable" and enforceable. So, for example, if a cohabitant's legal claim related solely to a separate business arrangement, it was not barred by illegality. *See* McCall v. Frampton, 81 A.D.2d 607, 438 N.Y.S.2d 11 (1981). Finally, courts were sometimes willing to provide an equitable remedy for cohabitants through the use of constructive or resulting trust.

While this summary still described the law in most states when the California Supreme Court considered Marvin v. Marvin (the next case), the increased rate and social acceptability of nonmarital cohabitation had substantially altered the context of such a dispute. Additionally, many states had abolished common-law marriage during the twentieth century, causing a gradual but substantial increase in the number of cohabiting couples who were considered unmarried. And, because the common law marriage doctrine requires the couple to hold themselves out to the community as married—and most of the new cohabitants did not do so—they could not be considered married even in jurisdictions that retained common-law marriage. *See* Chapter 2, § 5. It was in this context that the California Supreme Court had to decide whether or not to reaffirm the traditional rule regarding cohabitants' rights.

MARVIN v. MARVIN

Supreme Court of California, 1976.
18 Cal.3d 660, 134 Cal.Rptr. 815, 557 P.2d 106.

TOBRINER, J.

During the past 15 years, there has been a substantial increase in the number of couples living together without marrying. Such nonmarital relationships lead to legal controversy when one partner dies or the couple separates. Courts of Appeal, faced with the task of determining property rights in such cases, have arrived at conflicting positions: two cases have held that the Family Law Act requires division of the property according to community property principles, and one decision has rejected that holding. We take this opportunity to resolve that controversy and to declare the principles which should govern distribution of property acquired in a nonmarital relationship.

We conclude: (1) The provisions of the Family Law Act do not govern the distribution of property acquired during a nonmarital relationship; such a relationship remains subject solely to judicial decision. (2) The courts should enforce express contracts between nonmarital partners except to the extent that the contract is explicitly founded on the consideration of meretricious sexual services. (3) In the absence of an express contract, the courts should inquire into the conduct of the parties to determine whether that conduct demonstrates an implied contract, agreement of partnership or joint venture, or some other tacit understanding between the parties. The courts may also employ the doctrine of quantum meruit, or equitable remedies such as constructive or resulting trusts, when warranted by the facts of the case.

In the instant case plaintiff and defendant lived together for seven years without marrying; all property acquired during this period was taken in defendant's name. When plaintiff sued to enforce a contract under which she was entitled to half the property and to support payments, the trial court granted judgment on the pleadings for defendant, thus leaving him with all property accumulated by the couple during their relationship. Since the trial court denied plaintiff a trial on the merits of her claim, its decision conflicts with the principles stated above, and must be reversed.

* * *

Plaintiff avers that in October of 1964 she and defendant "entered into an oral agreement" that while "the parties lived together they would combine their efforts and earnings and would share equally any and all property accumulated as a result of their efforts whether individual or combined". Furthermore, they agreed to "hold themselves out to the general public as husband and wife" and that "plaintiff would further render her services as a companion, homemaker, housekeeper and cook to * * * defendant."

Shortly thereafter plaintiff agreed to "give up her lucrative career as an entertainer [and] singer" in order to "devote her full time to defendant * * * as a companion, homemaker, housekeeper and cook"; in return defendant agreed to "provide for all of plaintiff's financial support and needs for the rest of her life."

Plaintiff alleges that she lived with defendant from October of 1964 through May of 1970 and fulfilled her obligations under the agreement. During this period the parties as a result of their efforts and earnings acquired in defendant's name substantial real and personal property, including motion picture rights worth over $1 million. In May of 1970, however, defendant compelled plaintiff to leave his household. He continued to support plaintiff until November of 1971, but thereafter refused to provide further support.

* * *

In *Trutalli v. Meraviglia*, 215 Cal. 698, 12 P.2d 430 (1932), we established the principle that nonmarital partners may lawfully contract concerning the ownership of property acquired during the relationship. We reaffirmed this principle in *Vallera v. Vallera*, 21 Cal.2d 681, 685, 134 P.2d 761, 763, (1943), stating that "If a man and a woman [who are not married] live together as husband and wife under an agreement to pool their earnings and share equally in their joint accumulations, equity will protect the interests of each in such property".

In the case before us plaintiff, basing her cause of action in contract upon these precedents, maintains that the trial court erred in denying her a trial on the merits of her contention. Although that court did not specify the ground for its conclusion that plaintiff's contractual allegations stated no cause of action, defendant offers some four theories to sustain the ruling; we proceed to examine them.

Defendant first and principally relies on the contention that the alleged contract is so closely related to the supposed "immoral" character of the relationship between plaintiff and himself that the enforcement of the contract would violate public policy. He points to cases asserting that a contract between nonmarital partners is unenforceable if it is "involved in" an illicit relationship, or made in "contemplation" of such a relationship. A review of the numerous California decisions concerning contracts between nonmarital partners, however, reveals that the courts have not employed such broad and uncertain standards to strike down contracts. The decisions instead disclose a narrower and more precise standard: a contract between nonmarital partners is unenforceable only to the extent that it explicitly rests upon the immoral and illicit consideration of meretricious sexual services.

* * *

Although the past decisions hover over the issue in the somewhat wispy form of the figures of a Chagall painting, we can abstract from those decisions a clear and simple rule. The fact that a man and woman live together without marriage, and engage in a sexual relationship, does not in itself invalidate agreements between them relating to their earnings, property, or expenses. Neither is such an agreement invalid merely because the parties may have contemplated the creation or continuation of a nonmarital relationship when they entered into it. Agreements between nonmarital partners fail only to the extent that they rest upon a consideration of meretricious sexual services. Thus the rule asserted by defendant, that a contract fails if it is "involved in" or made "in contemplation" of a nonmarital relationship, cannot be reconciled with the decisions.

* * *

The principle that a contract between nonmarital partners will be enforced unless expressly and inseparably based upon an illicit consideration of sexual services not only represents the distillation of the decisional law, but also offers a far more precise and workable standard than that advocated by defendant. * * *

In the present case a standard which inquires whether an agreement is "involved" in or "contemplates" a nonmarital relationship is vague and unworkable. Virtually all agreements between nonmarital partners can be said to be "involved" in some sense in the fact of their mutual sexual relationship, or to "contemplate" the existence of that relationship. Thus defendant's proposed standards, if taken literally, might invalidate all agreements between nonmarital partners, a result no one favors. Moreover, those standards offer no basis to distinguish between valid and invalid agreements. By looking not to such uncertain tests, but only to the consideration underlying the agreement, we provide the parties and the courts with a practical guide to determine when an agreement between nonmarital partners should be enforced.

Defendant secondly relies upon the ground suggested by the trial court: that the 1964 contract violated public policy because it impaired the community property rights of Betty Marvin, defendant's lawful wife. Defendant points out that his earnings while living apart from his wife before rendition of the interlocutory decree were community property under 1964 statutory law and that defendant's agreement with plaintiff purported to transfer to her a half interest in that community property. But whether or not defendant's contract with plaintiff exceeded his authority as manager of the community property, defendant's argument fails for the reason that an improper transfer of community property is not void ab initio, but merely voidable at the instance of the aggrieved spouse.

In the present case Betty Marvin, the aggrieved spouse, had the opportunity to assert her community property rights in the divorce action. The interlocutory and final decrees in that action fix and limit her interest. Enforcement of the contract between plaintiff and defendant against property awarded to defendant by the divorce decree will not impair any right of Betty's, and thus is not on that account violative of public policy.[8]

Defendant's third contention is noteworthy for the lack of authority advanced in its support. He contends that enforcement of the oral agreement between plaintiff and himself is barred by Civil Code § 5134, which provides that "All contracts for marriage settlements must be in writing." A marriage settlement, however, is an agreement in contem-

8. Defendant also contends that the contract is invalid as an agreement to promote or encourage divorce. The contract between plaintiff and defendant did not, however, by its terms require defendant to divorce Betty, nor reward him for so doing. Moreover, the principle on which defendant relies does not apply when the marriage in question is beyond redemption, whether or not defendant's marriage to Betty was beyond redemption when defendant contracted with plaintiff is obviously a question of fact which cannot be resolved by judgment on the pleadings.

plation of marriage in which each party agrees to release or modify the property rights which would otherwise arise from the marriage. The contract at issue here does not conceivably fall within that definition, and thus is beyond the compass of § 5134.[9]

* * *

In summary, we base our opinion on the principle that adults who voluntarily live together and engage in sexual relations are nonetheless as competent as any other persons to contract respecting their earnings and property rights. Of course, they cannot lawfully contract to pay for the performance of sexual services, for such a contract is, in essence, an agreement for prostitution and unlawful for that reason. But they may agree to pool their earnings and to hold all property acquired during the relationship in accord with the law governing community property; conversely they may agree that each partner's earnings and the property acquired from those earnings remains the separate property of the earning partner. So long as the agreement does not rest upon illicit meretricious consideration, the parties may order their economic affairs as they choose, and no policy precludes the courts from enforcing such agreements.

* * *

As we have noted, both causes of action in plaintiff's complaint allege an express contract; neither assert any basis for relief independent from the contract. In *In re Marriage of Cary*, 34 Cal. App. 3d 345, 109 Cal.Rptr. 862, however, the Court of Appeals held that, in view of the policy of the Family Law Act, property accumulated by nonmarital partners in an actual family relationship should be divided equally. Upon examining the *Cary* opinion, the parties to the present case realized that plaintiff's alleged relationship with defendant might arguably support a cause of action independent of any express contract between the parties. The parties have therefore briefed and discussed the issue of the property rights of a nonmarital partner in the absence of an express contract. Although our conclusion that plaintiff's complaint states a cause of action based on an express contract alone compels us to reverse the judgment for defendant, resolution of the *Cary* issue will serve both to guide the parties upon retrial and to resolve a conflict presently manifest in published Court of Appeals decisions.

Both plaintiff and defendant stand in broad agreement that the law should be fashioned to carry out the reasonable expectations of the parties.

* * *

This failure of the courts to recognize an action by a nonmarital partner based upon implied contract, or to grant an equitable remedy,

9. Our review of the many cases enforcing agreements between nonmarital partners reveals that the majority of such agreements were oral. In two cases the court expressly rejected defenses grounded upon the statute of frauds.

contrasts with the judicial treatment of the putative spouse. Prior to the enactment of the Family Law Act, no statute granted rights to a putative spouse. The courts accordingly fashioned a variety of remedies by judicial decision. Some cases permitted the putative spouse to recover half of the property on a theory that the conduct of the parties implied an agreement of partnership or joint venture. Others permitted the spouse to recover the reasonable value of rendered services, less the value of support received. Finally, decisions affirmed the power of a court to employ equitable principles to achieve a fair division of property acquired during putative marriage.

* * *

The remaining arguments advanced from time to time to deny remedies to the nonmarital partners are of less moment. There is no more reason to presume that services are contributed as a gift than to presume that funds are contributed as a gift; in any event the better approach is to presume, as Justice Peters suggested, "that the parties intend to deal fairly with each other."

The argument that granting remedies to the nonmarital partners would discourage marriage must fail; as *Cary* pointed out, "with equal or greater force the point might be made that the pre–1970 rule was calculated to cause the income producing partner to avoid marriage and thus retain the benefit of all of his or her accumulated earnings." Although we recognize the well-established public policy to foster and promote the institution of marriage, perpetuation of judicial rules which result in an inequitable distribution of property accumulated during a nonmarital relationship is neither a just nor an effective way of carrying out that policy.

In summary, we believe that the prevalence of nonmarital relationships in modern society and the social acceptance of them marks this as a time when our courts should by no means apply the doctrine of the unlawfulness of the so-called meretricious relationship to the instant case. As we have explained, the nonenforceability of agreements expressly providing for meretricious conduct rested upon the fact that such conduct, as the word suggests, pertained to and encompassed prostitution. To equate the nonmarital relationship of today to such a subject matter is to do violence to an accepted and wholly different practice.

We are aware that many young couples live together without the solemnization of marriage, in order to make sure that they can successfully later undertake marriage. This trial period, preliminary to marriage, serves as some assurance that the marriage will not subsequently end in dissolution to the harm of both parties. We are aware, as we have stated, of the pervasiveness of nonmarital relationships in other situations.

The mores of the society have indeed changed so radically in regard to cohabitation that we cannot impose a standard based on alleged moral considerations that have apparently been so widely abandoned by so many. Lest we be misunderstood, however, we take this occasion to point out that the structure of society itself largely depends upon the institution of marriage, and nothing we have said in this opinion should be taken to derogate from that institution. The joining of the man and woman in marriage is at once the most socially productive and individually fulfilling relationship that one can enjoy in the course of a lifetime.

We conclude that the judicial barriers that may stand in the way of a policy based upon the fulfillment of the reasonable expectations of the parties to a nonmarital relationship should be removed. As we have explained, the courts now hold that express agreements will be enforced unless they rest on an unlawful meretricious consideration. We add that in the absence of an express agreement, the courts may look to a variety of other remedies in order to protect the parties' lawful expectations.[24] The courts may inquire into the conduct of the parties to determine whether that conduct demonstrates an implied contract or implied agreement of partnership or joint venture, or some other tacit understanding between the parties. The courts may, when appropriate, employ principles of constructive trust or resulting trust. Finally, a nonmarital partner may recover in quantum meruit for the reasonable value of household services rendered less the reasonable value of support received if he can show that he rendered services with the expectation of monetary reward.[25] * * *

The judgment is reversed and the cause remanded for further proceedings consistent with the views expressed herein.

CLARK, JUSTICE (concurring and dissenting).

The majority opinion properly permits recovery on the basis of either express or implied in fact agreement between the parties. These being the issues presented, their resolution requires reversal of the judgment. Here, the opinion should stop.

This court should not attempt to determine all anticipated rights, duties and remedies within every meretricious relationship—particularly in vague terms. Rather, these complex issues should be determined as each arises in a concrete case.

The majority broadly indicates that a party to a meretricious relationship may recover on the basis of equitable principles and in quantum meruit. However, the majority fails to advise us of the circumstances permitting recovery, limitations on recovery, or whether their numerous remedies are cumulative or exclusive. Conceivably, under the majority

24. We do not seek to resurrect the doctrine of common law marriage, which was abolished in California by statute in 1895. Thus we do not hold that plaintiff and defendant were "married," nor do we extend to plaintiff the rights which the Family Law Act grants valid or putative spouses; we hold only that she has the same rights to enforce contracts and to assert her equitable interest in property acquired through her effort as does any other unmarried person.

25. Our opinion does not preclude the evolution of additional equitable remedies to protect the expectations of the parties to a nonmarital relationship in cases in which existing remedies prove inadequate; the suitability of such remedies may be determined in later cases in light of the factual setting in which they arise.

opinion a party may recover half of the property acquired during the relationship on the basis of general equitable principles, recover a bonus based on specific equitable considerations, and recover a second bonus in quantum meruit.

* * *

By judicial overreach, the majority perform a nunc pro tunc marriage, dissolve it, and distribute its property on terms never contemplated by the parties, case law or the Legislature.

On April 18, 1979, the *Marvin* trial court, Case No. C23303, 5 Fam.L.Rep. (BNA) 3077 (1979), after remand decided that "no express contract was negotiated between the parties." As the court found that "the conduct of the parties * * * certainly does not reveal any implementation of any contract nor does such conduct give rise to an implied contract," the equitable remedy of resulting or constructive trust did not "in good conscience" apply, and dismissed the plaintiff's quantum meruit causes of action. It also found that there was no "mutual effort" that might support a recovery. Nevertheless, the trial court held that:

> "[t]he court is aware that Footnote 25 urges the trial court to employ whatever equitable remedy may be proper under the circumstances. The court is also aware of the recent resort of plaintiff to unemployment insurance benefits to support herself and of the fact that a return of plaintiff to a career as a singer is doubtful. Additionally, the court knows that the market value of defendant's property at time of separation exceeded $1,000,000. In view of these circumstances, the court in equity awards plaintiff $104,000 for rehabilitation purposes so that she may have the economic means to re-educate herself and to learn new, employable skills or to refurbish those utilized, for example, during her most recent employment and so that she may return from her status as companion of a motion picture star to a separate, independent but perhaps more prosaic existence."

On August 11, 1981, the California Appellate Court (Marvin v. Marvin, 122 Cal.App.3d 871, 176 Cal.Rptr. 555, 559 (1981)) reversed the trial court's $104,000 award, holding:

> " * * * the special findings in support of the challenged rehabilitative award merely established plaintiff's need therefor and defendant's ability to respond to that need. This is not enough. The award, being nonconsensual in nature, must be supported by some recognized underlying obligation in law or in equity. A court of equity admittedly has broad powers, but it may not create totally new substantive rights under the guise of doing equity. The trial court in its special conclusions of law addressed to this point attempted to state an underlying obligation by saying that plaintiff had a right to assistance from defendant until she became self-

supporting. But this special conclusion obviously conflicts with the earlier, more general, finding of the court that defendant has never had and did not then have any obligation to provide plaintiff with a reasonable sum for her support and maintenance and, in view of the already-mentioned findings of no damage (but benefit instead), no unjust enrichment and no wrongful act on the part of defendant with respect to either the relationship or its termination, it is clear that no basis whatsoever, either in equity or in law, exists for the challenged rehabilitative award. It therefore must be deleted from the judgment."

One day later, Michelle Marvin, 57, was fined $250 and placed on probation for shoplifting some bras and a sweater from a Beverly Hills store. TIME, Aug. 24, 1981, at p. 59; N.Y. TIMES, Aug. 13, 1981, at p. 8, col. 12.

The California Supreme Court refused Michelle's final appeal. N. Y. TIMES, Oct. 9, 1981, at p. 14, col. 4.

Notes and Questions

1. Is the *Marvin* result fair? Why or why not?

2. A number of states have adopted the *Marvin* approach toward cohabitants' disputes. *See* Carlson v. Olson, 256 N.W.2d 249 (Minn. 1977); Kozlowski v. Kozlowski, 80 N.J. 378, 403 A.2d 902 (1979). *See generally* J. THOMAS OLDHAM, DIVORCE, SEPARATION AND THE DISTRIBUTION OF PROPERTY § 1.02 (1998). Other states have accepted some, but not all, of the grounds for recovery sanctioned by *Marvin*. Some courts permit recovery based on an express contract (either oral or written), but not on an implied contract or quantum meruit. *See* Morone v. Morone, 50 N.Y.2d 481, 429 N.Y.S.2d 592, 413 N.E.2d 1154 (1980); Tapley v. Tapley, 122 N.H. 727, 449 A.2d 1218 (1982). Two states permit recovery based only on an express, written contract. *See* MINN. STAT. ANN. § 513.075; TEX. FAM. CODE § 1.108. As compared to the *Marvin* approach, what are the advantages and disadvantages of confining recovery to: i) express, written contracts; or ii) express (oral or written) contracts? (Note that researchers in Norway and Denmark found that only about 5% of all cohabitants had signed written agreements. *See* Bull, *Nonmarital Cohabitation in Norway*, 30 SCANDINAVIAN STUD. IN LAW 31 (1986)).

3. In states that permit recovery based on quantum meruit or unjust enrichment, the plaintiff typically must show that (i) the defendant received a benefit, (ii) the benefit was at the plaintiff's expense, and (iii) it would be unjust to permit the defendant to retain the benefit without compensating the plaintiff. *See* Watts v. Watts, 137 Wis.2d 506, 405 N.W.2d 303 (1987). *See generally* J. THOMAS OLDHAM, DIVORCE, SEPARATION AND THE DISTRIBUTION OF PROPERTY § 1.02[5][3] (1998); Robert C. Casad, *Unmarried Couples and Unjust Enrichment: From Status to Contract and Back Again*, 77 MICH. L. REV. 47 (1978). But quantum meruit claims are generally permitted only in those situations where it would be reasonable to expect compensation and any support received by

the claimant during the relationship is offset against such a claim. Thus, in Tarry v. Stewart, 98 Ohio App.3d 533, 649 N.E.2d 1 (1994), a court refused one cohabitant's claim to be reimbursed for contributions to improvements made to the other cohabitant's house, due to the benefit the claimant had received from living in the house during the relationship. *See also* Tapley v. Tapley, 122 N.H. 727, 449 A.2d 1218 (1982) (limiting quantum meruit cohabitant recovery to business services).

4. *Marvin* significantly changed the test for severability, an important concept under the traditional approach. Michelle Marvin's claim would not have been severable from the sexual relationship under the traditional approach, but the *Marvin* court concludes that it is severable, distinguishing agreements that merely "contemplate" a sexual relationship (valid), from those that "rest on an unlawful meretricious consideration" (invalid). Does this mean that any contract between cohabitants is enforceable unless it is simply a prostitution arrangement? Or does it mean that an invalid agreement is one that would not have been made but for the sexual relationship? (If so, didn't the *Marvin* agreement fall into this category?)

Courts have not agreed on this aspect of the *Marvin* opinion. In Jones v. Daly, 122 Cal.App.3d 500, 176 Cal.Rptr. 130 (1981) the plaintiff claimed that he had agreed to devote a substantial amount of time to the defendant as his lover, companion, homemaker, traveling companion, housekeeper and cook, and that the defendant had agreed to share with him all accumulations during the relationship. The court concluded that sex was the predominant consideration and that the sexual aspect of their relationship was not severable from their agreement. But in Whorton v. Dillingham, 202 Cal.App.3d 447, 248 Cal.Rptr. 405 (1988), the plaintiff and defendant agreed to have a sexual relationship, and the plaintiff agreed to act as the defendant's chauffeur, bodyguard, secretary, real estate counselor, confidant, and companion. The court distinguished *Jones* on the basis of the services provided. Because the Whorton plaintiff's services as a bodyguard, secretary, and real estate counselor would not normally be offered without payment, the court concluded that sexual services were severable. Is this a sensible construction of *Marvin*?

5. How would a court determine whether the parties had an implied agreement? Although a couple may take title jointly and consistently pool resources, (Alderson v. Alderson, 180 Cal.App.3d 450, 225 Cal.Rptr. 610 (1986)), in many cases the evidence will be conflicting, or will reflect the fact that one party wants to share and the other does not. *See* Rissberger v. Gorton, 41 Or.App. 65, 597 P.2d 366 (1979). What result would *Marvin* require in such a case?

Consider Carol Bruch, *Property Rights of De Facto Spouses Including Thoughts on the Value of Homemakers' Services*, 10 FAM. L.Q. 101, 136 (1976):

> Surely it is more sensible to place the burden upon individuals to state clearly their desire to bring about inequitable results, than

to impose such results upon large numbers of people who live together without marriage with no articulated division of financial responsibility. To do otherwise is to imply in law an unconscionable contract, one in which one party may render services for a period of years only to return to the job market upon the relationship's termination with no marketable skills or financial resources while the other retains the full measure of increased wealth and increased earning power that were acquired through participation in monetarily rewarded activity outside the home.

Is Professor Bruch suggesting a presumption of equal sharing, at least in those relationships of some duration where one partner does not work outside the home? If so, how could the presumption be rebutted? How does this approach differ from the implied agreement approach of *Marvin*?

6. *Marvin* claims have been made by gay as well as heterosexual cohabitants. *See* Jones v. Daly, *supra* note 4; Whorton v. Dillingham, *supra* note 4; N.Y. TIMES, July 9, 1981, at p. 7 col. 3 (describing claim by Marilyn Barnett against Billie Jean King); *Palimony Lawsuit Filed Against Pianist Cliburn*, HOUSTON CHRONICLE, Apr. 30, 1996, at 17A. It has been estimated that there are 1.6 million same-sex couples. *See* Victor F. Zonana, *Census Will Count "Unmarried Partners" for First Time*, L.A. TIMES, Feb. 15, 1990, at A39. Is there any reason to treat such cohabitants differently from those who are heterosexual? Does the fact that same-sex couples may not marry affect the analysis? If so, in what way? *See* Kristin Bullock, Comment, *Applying Marvin v. Marvin to Same–Sex Couples: a Proposal for a Sex–Preference Neutral Cohabitation Statute*, 25 U.C. DAVIS L. REV. 1029 (1992).

7. Should *Marvin* apply regardless of the length or type of cohabitation? For example, in Marriage of Bauder, 44 Or.App. 443, 605 P.2d 1374 (1980), a man cohabited with a married couple (apparently maintaining a sexual relationship with both) and alleged an agreement to share property. Should *Marvin* apply? Should *Marvin* apply to dating couples?

8. If Ms. Marvin had recovered something from Lee Marvin, would it have been taxable income? *See* Green v. C.I.R., 846 F.2d 870 (2d Cir.1988).

9. Is the *Marvin* court correct that its decision does not "resurrect the doctrine of common law marriage?"

HEWITT v. HEWITT

Supreme Court of Illinois, 1979.
77 Ill.2d 49, 31 Ill.Dec. 827,394 N.E.2d 1204.

UNDERWOOD, JUSTICE.

The issue in this case is whether plaintiff Victoria Hewitt, whose complaint alleges she lived with defendant Robert Hewitt from 1960 to 1975 in an unmarried, family-like relationship to which three children have been born, may recover from him "an equal share of the profits and properties accumulated by the parties" during that period.

Plaintiff initially filed a complaint for divorce, but at a hearing on defendant's motion to dismiss, admitted that no marriage ceremony had taken place and that the parties have never obtained a marriage license. In dismissing that complaint the trial court found that neither a ceremonial nor a common law marriage existed; that since defendant admitted the paternity of the minor children, plaintiff need not bring a separate action under the Paternity Act (Ill.Rev.Stat. 1975, ch. 106 3/4, par. 51 et seq.) to have the question of child support determined; and directed plaintiff to make her complaint more definite as to the nature of the property of which she was seeking division.

Plaintiff thereafter filed an amended complaint alleging the following bases for her claim: (1) that because defendant promised he would "share his life, his future, his earnings and his property" with her and all of defendant's property resulted from the parties' joint endeavors, plaintiff is entitled in equity to a one-half share; (2) that the conduct of the parties evinced an implied contract entitling plaintiff to one-half the property accumulated during their "family relationship"; (3) that because defendant fraudulently assured plaintiff she was his wife in order to secure her services, although he knew they were not legally married, defendant's property should be impressed with a trust for plaintiff's benefit; (4) that because plaintiff has relied to her detriment on defendant's promises and devoted her entire life to him, defendant has been unjustly enriched.

The factual background alleged or testified to is that in June 1960, when she and defendant were students at Grinnell College in Iowa, plaintiff became pregnant; that defendant thereafter told her that they were husband and wife and would live as such, no formal ceremony being necessary, and that he would "share his life, his future, his earnings and his property" with her; that the parties immediately announced to their respective parents that they were married and thereafter held themselves out as husband and wife; that in reliance on defendant's promises she devoted her efforts to his professional education and his establishment in the practice of pedodontia, obtaining financial assistance from her parents for this purpose; that she assisted defendant in his career with her own special skills and although she was given payroll checks for these services she placed them in a common fund; that defendant, who was without funds at the time of the marriage, as a result of her efforts now earns over $80,000 a year and has accumulated large amounts of property, owned either jointly with her or separately; that she has given him every assistance a wife and mother could give, including social activities designed to enhance his social and professional reputation.

The amended complaint was also dismissed, the trial court finding that Illinois law and public policy require such claims to be based on a valid marriage. The appellate court reversed, stating that because the parties had outwardly lived a conventional married life, plaintiff's conduct had not "so affronted public policy that she should be denied any and all relief," and that plaintiff's complaint stated a cause of action on an express oral contract. We granted leave to appeal. Defendant apparently does not contest his obligation to support the children, and that question is not before us.

The appellate court, in reversing, gave considerable weight to the fact that the parties had held themselves out as husband and wife for over 15 years. The court noted that they lived "a most conventional, respectable and ordinary family life" that did not openly flout accepted standards, the "single flaw" being the lack of a valid marriage. Indeed the appellate court went so far as to say that the parties had "lived within the legitimate boundaries of a marriage and family relationship of a most conventional sort," an assertion which that court cannot have intended to be taken literally. Noting that the Illinois Marriage and Dissolution of Marriage Act (Ill.Rev.Stat. 1977, ch. 40 par. 101 et seq.) does not prohibit nonmarital cohabitation and that the Criminal Code of 1961 (Ill.Rev.Stat. 1977, ch. 38, par. 11–8(a)) makes fornication an offense only if the behavior is open and notorious, the appellate court concluded that plaintiff should not be denied relief on public policy grounds.

In finding that plaintiff's complaint stated a cause of action on an express oral contract, the appellate court adopted the reasoning of the California Supreme Court in the widely publicized case of *Marvin v. Marvin* [p. 226] quoting extensively therefrom.

* * *

The issue of whether property rights accrue to unmarried cohabitants can not, however, be regarded realistically as merely a problem in the law of express contracts. Plaintiff argues that because her action is founded on an express contract, her recovery would in no way imply that unmarried cohabitants acquire property rights merely by cohabitation and subsequent separation. However, the *Marvin* court expressly recognized and the appellate court here seems to agree that if common law principles of express contract govern express agreements between unmarried cohabitants, common law principles of implied contract, equitable relief and constructive trust must govern the parties' relations in the absence of such an agreement. In all probability the latter case will be much the more common, since it is unlikely that most couples who live together will enter into express agreements regulating their property rights. (Carol Bruch, *Property Rights of De Facto Spouses, Including Thoughts on the Value of Homemakers' Services*, 10 FAM.L.Q. 101, 102 (1976).) The increasing incidence of nonmarital cohabitation referred to in *Marvin* and the variety of legal remedies therein sanctioned seem certain to result in substantial amounts of litigation, in which, whatever the allegations regarding an oral contract, the proof will necessarily involve details of the parties' living arrangements.

Apart, however, from the appellate court's reliance upon *Marvin* to reach what appears to us to be a significantly different result, we believe there is a more fundamental problem. We are aware, of course, of the increasing judicial attention given the individual claims of unmarried cohabitants to jointly accumulated property, and the fact that the majority of courts considering the question have recognized an equitable or contractual basis for implementing the reasonable expectations of the parties unless sexual services were the explicit consideration. The issue of unmarried cohabitants' mutual property rights, however, as we earlier noted, cannot appropriately be characterized solely in terms of contract law, nor is it limited to considerations of equity or fairness as between the parties to such relationships. There are major public policy questions involved in determining whether, under what circumstances, and to what extent it is desirable to accord some type of legal status to claims arising from such relationships. Of substantially greater importance than the rights of the immediate parties is the impact of such recognition upon our society and the institution of marriage. Will the fact that legal rights closely resembling those arising from conventional marriages can be acquired by those who deliberately choose to enter into what have heretofore been commonly referred to as "illicit" or "meretricious" relationships weaken marriage as the foundation of our family-based society? In the event of death shall the survivor have the status of a surviving spouse for purposes of inheritance, wrongful death actions, workmen's compensation, etc.? And still more importantly: what of the children born of such relationship? What are their support and inheritance rights and by what standards are custody questions resolved? What of the sociological and psychological effects upon them of that type of environment? Does not the recognition of legally enforceable property and custody rights emanating from nonmarital cohabitation in practical effect equate with the legalization of common law marriage—at least in the circumstances of this case? And, in summary, have the increasing numbers of unmarried cohabitants and changing mores of our society reached the point at which the general welfare of the citizens of this State is best served by a return to something resembling the judicially created common law marriage our legislature outlawed in 1905?

Illinois' public policy regarding agreements such as the one alleged here was implemented long ago in *Wallace v. Rappleye* (1882), 103 Ill. 229, 249, where this court said: "An agreement in consideration of future illicit cohabitation between the plaintiffs is void." This is the traditional rule, in force until recent years in all jurisdictions.

* * *

It is true, of course, that cohabitation by the parties may not prevent them from forming valid contracts about independent matters, for which it is said the sexual relations do not form part of the consideration. Those courts which allow recovery generally have relied on this principle to reduce the scope of the rule of illegality.

* * *

The real thrust of plaintiff's argument here is that we should abandon the rule of illegality because of certain changes in societal norms and attitudes. It is urged that social mores have changed radically in recent years, rendering this principle of law archaic. It is said that because there are so many unmarried cohabitants today the courts must confer a legal status on such relationships. This, of course, is the rationale underlying some of the decisions and commentaries. If this is to be the result, however, it would seem more candid to acknowledge the return of varying forms of common law marriage than to continue displaying the naivete we believe involved in the assertion that there are involved in these relationships contracts separate and independent from the sexual activity, and the assumption that those contracts would have been entered into or would continue without that activity.

The issue, realistically, is whether it is appropriate for this court to grant a legal status to a private arrangement substituting for the institution of marriage sanctioned by the State. The question whether change is needed in the law governing the rights of parties in this delicate area of marriage-like relationships involves evaluations of sociological data and alternatives we believe best suited to the superior investigative and fact-finding facilities of the legislative branch in the exercise of its traditional authority to declare public policy in the domestic relations field. [citations omitted]. That belief is reinforced by the fact that judicial recognition of mutual property rights between unmarried cohabitants would, in our opinion, clearly violate the policy of our recently enacted Illinois Marriage and Dissolution of Marriage Act. Although the Act does not specifically address the subject of nonmarital cohabitation, we think the legislative policy quite evident from the statutory scheme.

* * *

We cannot confidently say that judicial recognition of property rights between unmarried cohabitants will not make that alternative to marriage more attractive by allowing the parties to engage in such relationships with greater security. As one commentator has noted, it may make this alternative especially attractive to persons who seek a property arrangement that the law does not permit to marital partners. This court, for example, has held void agreements releasing husbands from their obligation to support their wives. In thus potentially enhancing the attractiveness of a private arrangement over marriage, we believe that the appellate court decision in this case contravenes the Act's policy of strengthening and preserving the integrity of marriage.

The Act also provides: "Common law marriages contracted in this State after June 30, 1905 are invalid."

* * *

While the appellate court denied that its decision here served to rehabilitate the doctrine of common law marriage, we are not persuaded. Plaintiff's allegations disclose a relationship that clearly would have constituted a valid common law marriage in this State prior to 1905. The parties expressly manifested their present intent to be husband and wife; immediately thereafter they assumed the marital status; and for many years they consistently held themselves out to their relatives and the public at large as husband and wife. Revealingly, the appellate court relied on the fact that the parties were, to the public, husband and wife in determining that the parties living arrangements did not flout Illinois public policy. It is of course true, as plaintiff argues, that unlike a common law spouse she would not have full marital rights in that she could not, for example, claim her statutory one-third share of defendant's property on his death. The distinction appears unimpressive, however, if she can claim one-half of his property on a theory of express or implied contract.

* * *

We do not intend to suggest that plaintiff's claims are totally devoid of merit. Rather, we believe that our statement in *Mogged v. Mogged* (1973), 55 Ill.2d 221, 225, 302 N.E.2d 293, 295, made in deciding whether to abolish a judicially created defense to divorce, is appropriate here:

> "Whether or not the defense of recrimination should be abolished or modified in Illinois is a question involving complex public-policy considerations as to which compelling arguments may be made on both sides. For the reasons stated hereafter, we believe that these questions are appropriately within the province of the legislature, and that, if there is to be a change in the law of this State on this matter, it is for the legislature and not the courts to bring about that change."

We accordingly hold that plaintiff's claims are unenforceable for the reason that they contravene the public policy, implicit in the statutory scheme of the Illinois Marriage and Dissolution of Marriage Act, disfavoring the grant of mutually enforceable property rights to knowingly unmarried cohabitants. The judgment of the appellate court is reversed and the judgment of the circuit court of Champaign County is affirmed.

Notes and Questions

1. How would Ms. Hewitt's claim be resolved under *Marvin*? How would Michelle Marvin's claim be resolved under *Hewitt*?

2. Is the *Hewitt* result fair? Why or why not?

3. For other decisions following the *Hewitt* approach, *see, e.g.*, Carnes v. Sheldon, 109 Mich.App. 204, 311 N.W.2d 747 (1981) (emphasizing need for legislative action); Davis v. Davis, 643 So.2d 931 (Miss. 1994) (emphasizing the illegality of nonmarital cohabitation under Mississippi's criminal law). But, among courts that have considered the issue, *Hewitt* has gained fewer adherents than *Marvin*. Why?

CONNELL v. FRANCISCO

Supreme Court of Washington, 1995.
127 Wash.2d 339, 898 P.2d 831.

GUY, JUSTICE.

This case requires us to decide how property acquired during a meretricious relationship is distributed.

BACKGROUND

[Richard Francisco and Shannon Connell met in 1983. They were both unmarried; Richard lived in Las Vegas and Shannon in New York. Richard's net worth in 1983 was $1,300,000 while Shannon owned little. At Richard's request, Shannon moved into Richard's home in November 1983. They lived together in Las Vegas for almost three years. She worked as a dancer and helped Richard some with his businesses. In 1986 she and Richard moved to Washington to manage an inn he had purchased. For more than two years, Shannon received no compensation for these management services; in 1989 and 1990 she received $400 weekly. Between 1986 and the end of 1990 Richard and a corporation controlled by him accumulated various pieces of realty. The parties separated in March 1990; all the property accumulated during their relationship was accumulated in the name of Richard or his corporation.]

Connell filed a lawsuit against Francisco in December 1990 seeking a just and equitable distribution of the property acquired during the relationship. The Island County Superior Court determined Connell and Francisco's relationship was sufficiently long term and stable to require a just and equitable distribution. The Superior Court limited the property subject to distribution to the property that would have been community in character had they been married. The trial court held property owned by each party prior to the relationship could not be distributed.

The only property characterized by the Superior Court as being property that would have been community in character had Connell and Francisco been married was the increased value of Francisco's pension plan. The increased value of the pension plan, $169,000, was divided equally, with $84,500 distributed to Connell. The Superior Court, concluding Connell did not satisfy her burden of proof with respect to the remaining property, distributed to Francisco the remainder of the pension plan and all real property.

The Court of Appeals reversed, holding both property owned by each prior to the relationship and property that would have been community in character had the parties been married may be distributed following a meretricious relationship. *Connell v. Francisco*, 74 Wash.App. 306, 317, 872 P.2d 1150 (1994).

Francisco petitioned this court for discretionary review. He argues property owned by each party prior to the relationship may not be distributed following a meretricious relationship, and a community-property-like presumption is inapplicable when a trial court distributes property following a meretricious relationship. We granted discretionary review.

ANALYSIS

A meretricious relationship is a stable, marital-like relationship where both parties cohabit with knowledge that a lawful marriage between them does not exist. *In re Marriage of Lindsey*, 101 Wash.2d 299, 678 P.2d 328 (1984). Relevant factors establishing a meretricious relationship include, but are not limited to: continuous cohabitation, duration of the relationship, purpose of the relationship, pooling of resources and services for joint projects, and the intent of the parties.

In *Lindsey*, this court ruled a relationship need not be "long term" to be characterized as a meretricious relationship. While a "long term" relationship is not a threshold requirement, duration is a significant factor. A "short term" relationship may be characterized as meretricious, but a number of significant and substantial factors must be present. *See*, *Lindsey* (a less than 2–year meretricious relationship preceded marriage).

The Superior Court found Connell and Francisco were parties to a meretricious relationship. This finding is not contested.

Historically, property acquired during a meretricious relationship was presumed to belong to the person in whose name title to the property was placed. *Creasman v. Boyle*, 31 Wash.2d 345, 356, 196 P.2d 835 (1948). This presumption is commonly referred to as "the *Creasman* presumption."

In 1984, this court overruled *Creasman*. *Lindsey, supra*. In its place, the court adopted a general rule requiring a just and equitable distribution of property following a meretricious relationship.

In *Lindsey*, the parties cohabited for less than 2 years prior to marriage. When they subsequently divorced, the wife argued the increase in value of property acquired during the meretricious portion of their relationship was also subject to an equitable distribution as if the property were community in character. We agreed, citing former RCW 26.09.080 [Ed.—The statute cited permits a divorce court to divide property acquired by a spouse before marriage.]

Francisco contends the Court of Appeals misinterpreted *Lindsey* when it applied all the principles contained in RCW 26.09.080 to meretricious relationships. We agree. A meretricious relationship is not the same as a marriage. * * * [The court cites many instances where cohabitants are not treated in the same manner as spouses.] As such, the laws involving the distribution of marital property do not directly apply to the division of property following a meretricious relationship. Washington courts may look toward those laws for guidance.

Once a trial court determines the existence of a meretricious relationship, the trial court then: (1) evaluates the interest each party has in the property acquired during the relationship, and (2) makes a just and equitable distribution of the property. *Lindsey, supra*. The critical focus is on property that would have been characterized as community property had the parties been married. This property is properly before a trial court and is subject to a just and equitable distribution.

While portions of RCW 26.09.080 may apply by analogy to meretricious relationships, not all provisions of the statute should be applied. The parties to such a relationship have chosen not to get married and therefore the property owned by each party prior to the relationship should not be before the court for distribution at the end of the relationship. However, the property acquired during the relationship should be before the trial court so that one party is not unjustly enriched at the end of such a relationship. We conclude a trial court may not distribute property acquired by each party prior to the relationship at the termination of a meretricious relationship. Until the Legislature, as a matter of public policy, concludes meretricious relationships are the legal equivalent to marriages, we limit the distribution of property following a meretricious relationship to property that would have been characterized as community property had the parties been married. This will allow the trial court to justly divide property the couple has earned during the relationship through their efforts without creating a common law marriage or making a decision for a couple which they have declined to make for themselves. Any other interpretation equates cohabitation with marriage; ignores the conscious decision by many couples not to marry; confers benefits when few, if any, economic risks or legal obligations are assumed; and disregards the explicit intent of the Legislature that RCW 26.09.080 apply to property distributions following a marriage.

CONCLUSION

In summary, we hold that property which would have been characterized as separate property had the couple been married is not before the trial court for division at the end of the relationship. The property that would have been characterized as community property had the couple been married is before the trial court for a just and equitable distribution. There is a rebuttable presumption that property acquired during the relationship is owned by both of the parties and is therefore before the court for a fair division.

We reverse the Court of Appeals in part, affirm in part, and remand the case to the Superior Court for a just and equitable distribution of property.

UTTER, JUSTICE (dissenting).

I disagree with the majority's conclusion that the Court of Appeals misinterpreted our decision in *In re Marriage of Lindsey*, when it applied the principles found in RCW 26.09.080 to meretricious relationships. By limiting the distribution of property following a meretricious relationship to property that would have been characterized as community property had the parties been married, the majority establishes a new rule that will be uncertain in application and will likely interfere with the ability of the courts to "make a just and equitable distribution of the property" as is required by *Lindsey*. Given the increasing number of these cases in our trial courts, what is needed in this context is a simple rule that is easy to apply. Our holding in *Lindsey*, as understood by the Court of Appeals, does just that.

The majority is correct in pointing out that a meretricious relationship is not the same as a marriage. In citing a number of cases in which this court has refused to treat them the same, however, the majority fails to realize that the question of how closely these two types of relationships are treated depends upon the context. We discussed *Lindsey* in *Davis v. Employment Sec. Dept.,* 108 Wash.2d 272, 737 P.2d 1262 (1987), a case in which we held that an unmarried cohabitant is not eligible for benefits triggered by a "marital status" provision under our state's unemployment compensation statutes. There we noted that while *Lindsey* treated meretricious relationships like marriages in the context of property distribution, "the extension of property distribution rights of spouses to partners in meretricious relationships does not elevate meretricious relationships themselves to the level of marriages for any and all purposes."

I, therefore, would affirm the opinion of the Court of Appeals in its entirety.

Notes and Questions

1. How would Ms. Hewitt's and Ms. Marvin's claims be resolved under *Connell*? How would Ms. Connell's claim be resolved under *Marvin* and *Hewitt*?

2. Is the *Connell* result fair? Why or why not?

3. To date, no other American jurisdiction has followed the *Connell* approach, although the Canadian Supreme Court has held that it might be appropriate to require cohabitants to share property accumulated while they lived together if the cohabitation was "lengthy." *See* Sorochan v. Sorochan, [1986] 2 S.C.R. 38, 29 D.L.R. (4th) 1; Nicholas Bala & Marlene Cano, *Unmarried Cohabitation in Canada: Common Law and Civil Approaches to Living Together*, 4 CAN. FAM. L. Q. 147 (1989).

4. The bright line rule used in *Connell*, which gives nonmarital cohabitants property rights less extensive than those of a married couple, relies on the fact that a Washington divorce court may divide property acquired by either spouse before marriage. In those states (a substantial majority) where a divorce court may only divide property acquired during marriage, what rule would be analogous to that in *Connell*?

5. *Public Benefits*: While *Connell* goes further than any other American decision in basing rights on status as a cohabitant, it is important to keep in mind that it confers rights only against the other cohabitant. It does not convey rights to public benefits. Even in Washington, cohabitants may not bring an action for loss of consortium if their partner is injured nor maintain a wrongful death action if the partner is killed. *See* Garcia v. Douglas Aircraft Co., 133 Cal.App.3d 890,

184 Cal.Rptr. 390 (1982). The surviving cohabitant will not receive Social Security benefits available to a surviving spouse (Califano v. Boles, 443 U.S. 282, 99 S.Ct. 2767, 61 L.Ed.2d 541 (1979)), nor inherit from the decedent cohabitant under the state's intestacy laws. Cohabitants do not enjoy the benefits of tax preferences such as the unlimited marital deduction from estate and gift tax (*see* Cory v. Edgett, 111 Cal.App.3d 230, 168 Cal.Rptr. 686 (1980)). If one cohabitant's employer provides health insurance to the other through its group health insurance plan, the value of the insurance will not be exempt from taxation as it would for a spouse. *See* Private Letter Ruling No. 9603011, 22 Fam. L. Rep. (BNA) 1144 (10/18/95). They may not jointly petition for bankruptcy. Bone v. Allen, 186 B.R. 769 (N.Ga.1995). If one cohabitant quits his job to follow the other to new employment in a different location, he may not be able to establish "good cause" for the move so as to obtain unemployment insurance benefits. *See* Norman v. Unemployment Insurance Appeals Board, 34 Cal.3d 1, 192 Cal.Rptr. 134, 663 P.2d 904 (Cal. 1983).

Problem 5–1:

Bill is a wealthy investor; Robin, an inspiring model, has few financial assets. Three years ago, Bill and Robin decided to live together and orally agreed that: (1) they would be lovers; (2) they would live in Bill's house; (3) Robin would postpone his modeling career to travel with Bill; and (4) Bill would share equally with Robin all property accumulated during the relationship, and support Robin for three years after the relationship ended. The relationship recently ended. Bill has accumulated $1,000,000 during the three years of the relationship. How would the *Marvin, Hewitt*, and *Connell* courts respond to a claim by Robin against Bill?

Problem 5–2:

Twenty years ago, Melissa and Adam decided to live together. Melissa was a wealthy performer and Adam a surfer. Adam asked Melissa to marry him, but Melissa refused. Two years later they had a child, who was cared for primarily by Adam. During the relationship, Adam frequently asked Melissa to pool assets with him, but she refused. Adam and Melissa have now separated. Melissa had saved $500,000 prior to entering the relationship with Adam and accumulated $1,000,000, in her own name, during the relationship. How would the *Marvin, Hewitt*, and *Connell* courts respond to a claim by Adam against Melissa?

Problem 5–3:

You are a law clerk for Justice Abel, a member of the State Supreme Court. The Court has agreed to hear appeals in two cases involving claims by unmarried cohabitants.

One case involves George Smith and Amanda Martin, an unmarried couple who cohabited for twenty years and had three children before separating. George is a successful businessman with assets totaling $2 million, all titled in his name alone. Amanda has been a homemaker throughout the relationship, although before the birth of the couple's children she occasionally helped out in George's office. George and Amanda did not hold themselves out as married and did not pool assets, although George did list Amanda and the children as dependents on his income tax return. Amanda has sued George for an equal share of property accumulated during the relationship based on: i) an alleged meretricious relationship, ii) an express contract (Amanda claims that George told her that "they would share everything;" George denies any such statement), iii) an implied contract, and iv) quantum meruit.

The other case involves Ann Jones and Amy Barnes, who cohabited for one year and have no children. The only substantial asset owned by either is a winning lottery ticket purchased by Ann during the year's cohabitation, entitling her to $5 million over the next twenty years. Amy has sued Ann for an equal share of the lottery winnings based on claims identical to those listed by Amanda. But she also has a handwritten document, dated shortly after Ann's and Amy's cohabitation began and signed by each in which both Ann and Amy promised "... to share equally in all fruits of our partnership."

The Supreme Court has not heard an appeal from a claim by an unmarried cohabitant for more than thirty years, when it reaffirmed the traditional meretricious relationship rule. (A. v. B.) conflicting lower court decisions have variously followed this approach, followed *Marvin*, or allowed claims based solely on an express agreement. The state also retains the doctrine of common law marriage.

Justice Abel has asked you to advise her on the merits of the various approaches open to the court. Specifically, she wants to know:

a) Is common law marriage an adequate basis for resolving claims between unmarried cohabitants? If not, what "deserving" claimants does it omit?

b) Which approach will produce the most litigation? the least?

c) Which approach will produce the most predictable outcomes? the least?

d) What public policy concerns are relevant to claims between cohabitants?

e) From a public policy perspective, what are the advantages and disadvantages of basing a cohabitant's recovery on an agreement? on his or her status as a cohabitant?

f) From a public policy perspective, should the length of the relationship be taken into account? If yes, which approach can best do so?

g) On balance, what approach should the court take?

SECTION 2. COHABITATION PER STATUTE—THE FUTURE OF THE COHABITATION ALTERNATIVE?

Legislators considering the regulation of cohabitation must address a number of issues:

(1) Should regulated couples be limited to heterosexuals, or should the rules apply also to same-sex couples?

(2) Should there be any limits on contractual freedom other than the general rules governing validity and enforcement of contracts? Should it be possible to contract expressly out of implied obligations that might arise from cohabitation? Should persons be permitted to contract into cohabitation relationships with legal effects that differ from standard marriage more than standard marriage may be modified by marital contracts?

(3) In the absence of an express contract, should a cohabitation arrangement carry (a) defined consequences imposed by law; (b) consequences depending on the parties' intent as implied in their conduct; (c) a mix of (a) and (b); or (d) no legal consequences at all?

(4) If the options remain limited to the legal status of marriage or no legal status at all, should an exception be made for the *Hewitt* type of case in which the retroactive imposition of something like common law marriage seems "equitable?"

(5) Should the rights and obligations at the end of a cohabitation relationship be affected by whether either cohabitant was married to someone else?

(6) Should cohabitants have the same public benefits as spouses? If yes, should they also shoulder spousal obligations? For example, should they be *required* to file jointly if that would be to the advantage of the IRS? Should they have support obligations to their partner?

DE FACTO RELATIONSHIPS ACT

New South Wales, 1984, No. 147.

Part I. 3. (1) * * * "de facto partner" means—(a) in relation to a man, a woman who is living or has lived with the man as his wife on a bona fide domestic basis although not married to him; and (b) in relation to a woman, a man who is living or has lived with the woman as her husband on a bona fide domestic basis although not married to her;

"de facto relationship" means the relationship between de facto partners, being the relationship of living or having lived together as husband and wife on a bona fide domestic basis although not married to each other;

* * *

Part II. * * * 14. (1) Subject to this Part, a de facto partner may apply to a court for an order under this Part for the adjustment of interests with respect to the property for the de facto partners or either of them or for the granting of maintenance, or both.

* * *

Part III. * * * 17. (1) Except as provided by subsection (2), a court shall not make an order under this Part unless it is satisfied that the parties to the application have lived together in a de facto relationship for a period of not less than 2 years.

(2) A court may make an order under this Part where it is satisfied—

(a) that there is a child of the parties to the application; or

(b) that the applicant—

(i) has made substantial contributions of the kind referred to in § 20(1)(a) or (b) for which the applicant would otherwise not be adequately compensated if the order were not made; or

(ii) has the care and control of a child of the respondent,— and that the failure to make the order would result in serious injustice to the applicant.

18. (1) Except as provided by subsections (2) and (3), where de facto partners have ceased to live together as husband and wife on a bona fide domestic basis, an application to a court for an order under this Part shall be made before the expiration of the period of 2 years after the day on which they ceased, or last ceased, as the case may require, to so live together.

(2) A court may, at any time after the expiration of the period referred to in subsection (1), grant leave to a de facto partner to apply to the court for an order under this Part (other than an order under § 27(1)) made where the court is satisfied as to the matters specified in § 27(1)(b) where the court is satisfied, having regard to such matters as it considers relevant, that greater hardship would be caused to the applicant if that leave were not granted than would be caused to the respondent if that leave were granted.

* * *

19. In proceedings for an order under this Part, a court shall, so far as is practicable, make such orders as will finally determine the financial relationships between the de facto partners and avoid further proceedings between them.

20. (1) On an application by a de facto partner for an order under this Part to adjust interests with respect to the property of the de facto partners or either of them, a court may make such order adjusting the interests of the partners in the property as to it seems just and equitable having regard to—

(a) the financial and non-financial contributions made directly or indirectly by or on behalf of the de facto partners to the acquisition, conservation or improvement of any of the property of the partners or either of them or to the financial resources of the partners or either of them; and

(b) the contributions, including any contributions made in the capacity of homemaker or parent, made by either of the de facto partners to the welfare of the other de facto partner or to the welfare of the family constituted by the partners and one or more of the following, namely:—

(i) a child of the partners;

(ii) a child accepted by the partners or either of them into the household of the partners, whether or not the child is a child of either of the partners.

* * *

27. (1) On an application by a de facto partner for an order under this Part for maintenance, a court may make an order for maintenance (whether for periodic maintenance or otherwise) where the court is satisfied as to either or both of the following:—

(a) that the applicant is unable to support himself or herself adequately by reason of having the care and control of a child of the de facto partners or a child of the respondent, being, in either case, a child who is, on the day on which the application is made—

(i) except in the case of a child referred to in subparagraph (ii)—under the age of 12 years; or

(ii) in the case of a physically handicapped child or mentally handicapped child—under the age of 16 years;

(b) that the applicant is unable to support himself or herself adequately because the applicant's earning capacity has been adversely affected by the circumstances of the relationship and, in the opinion of the court—

(i) an order for maintenance would increase the applicant's earning capacity by enabling the applicant to undertake a course or programme of training or education; and

(ii) it is, having regard to all the circumstances of the case, reasonable to make the order.

(2) In determining whether to make an order under this Part for maintenance and in fixing any amount to be paid pursuant to such an order, a court shall have regard to—(a) the income, property and financial resources of each de facto partner (including the rate of any pension, allowance or benefit paid to either partner or the eligibility of either partner for a pension, allowance or benefit) and the physical and mental capacity of each partner for appropriate gainful employment; (b) the financial needs and obligations of each de facto partner; (c) the responsibilities of either de facto partner to support any other person; (d) the terms of any order made or proposed to be made under § 20 with respect to the property of the de facto partners; and (e) any payments

made, pursuant to an order of a court or otherwise, in respect of the maintenance of a child or children in the care and control of the applicant.

28. Where, on an application by a de facto partner for an order under this Part for maintenance, it appears to a court that the applicant is in immediate need of financial assistance, but it is not practicable in the circumstances to determine immediately what order, if any, should be made, the court may order the payment by the respondent, pending the disposal of the application, of such periodic sum or other sums as the court considers reasonable.

29. Where de facto partners have ceased to live together as husband and wife on a bona fide domestic basis, an application to a court for an order under this Part for maintenance may not be made by a de facto partner who, at the time at which the application is made, has entered into a subsequent de facto relationship with another person or who, at that time, has married or remarried.

30. (1) An order under this Part for periodic maintenance, being an order made where a court is satisfied solely as to the matters specified in § 27(1)(a), may apply for such period as may be determined by the court, not exceeding the period expiring when the child to whom § 27(1)(a) applies, or the younger or youngest such child, as the case may require—(a) except in the case of a child referred to in paragraph (b)—attains the age of 12 years; or (c) in the case of a physically handicapped child or mentally handicapped child—attains the age of 16 years.

(2) An order under this Part for periodic maintenance, being an order made where a court is satisfied solely as to the matters specified in § 27(1)(b), may apply for such period as may be determined by the court, not exceeding—(a) 3 years after the day on which the order is made; or (b) 4 years after the day on which the de facto partners ceased, or last ceased, as the case may require, to live together,—whichever is the shorter.

32. (1) An order under this Part for maintenance shall cease to have effect—(a) on the death of the de facto partner in whose favour the order was made; (b) on the death of the de facto partner against whom the order was made; or (c) on the marriage or remarriage of the de facto partner in whose favour the order was made.

* * *

Part IV. * * * 45. (1) Notwithstanding any rule of public policy to the contrary, a man and a woman who are not married to each other may enter into a cohabitation agreement or separation agreement.

(2) Nothing in a cohabitation agreement or separation agreement affects the power of a court to make an order with respect to the right to custody of, maintenance of or access to or otherwise in relation to the children of the parties to the agreement.

* * *

46. Except as otherwise provided by this Part, a cohabitation agreement or separation agreement shall be subject to and enforceable in accordance with the law of contract, including, without limiting the generality of this section, the Contracts Review Act, 1980.

* * *

49. (1) On an application by a de facto partner for an order under Part III, a court may vary or set aside the provisions, or any one or more of the provisions, of a cohabitation agreement (but not a separation agreement) made between the de facto partners, being a cohabitation agreement which satisfies the matters referred to in § 47(1)(b), (c), (d) and (e) [Formalities] where, in the opinion of the court, the circumstances of the partners have so changed since the time at which the agreement was entered into that it would lead to serious injustice if the provisions of the agreement, or any one or more of them, were, whether on the application for the order under Part III or on any other application for any remedy or relief under any other Act or any other law, to be enforced.

(2) A court may, pursuant to subsection (1), vary or set aside the provisions, or any one or more of the provisions, of a cohabitation agreement notwithstanding any provision of the agreement to the contrary.

50. Without limiting or derogating from the provisions of § 46, on an application by a de facto partner for an order under Part III, a court is not required to give effect to the terms of any cohabitation agreement or separation agreement entered into by that partner where the court is of the opinion—(a) that the de facto partners have, by their words or conduct, revoked or consented to the revocation of the agreement; or (b) that the agreement has otherwise ceased to have effect.

* * *

Notes and Questions

1. How does the New South Wales statutory scheme differ from the *Marvin* approach? the *Connell* approach?

2. How would Ms. Marvin, Ms. Hewitt, and Ms. Connell fare in New South Wales?

3. Four other Australian jurisdictions have adopted statutes similar to the New South Wales statute. *See* Rebecca Bailey–Harris, *Financial Rights in Relationships Outside Marriage: A Decade of Reforms in Australia*, 9 INT. J. L. & FAM. 233 (1995). A number of other countries also have created some status-like rules that apply to cohabitants. *See* Wolfram Muller–Freienfels, *Cohabitation and Marriage Law—A Comparative Study*, 1 INT. J. L. & FAM. 259 (1987); Carol Bruch, *Cohabitation in the Common Law Countries a Decade after Marvin: Settled or Moving Ahead?*, 22 U.C. DAVIS L. REV. 717 (1989); Nicholas Bala & Marlene Cano, *Unmarried Cohabitation in Canada: Common Law and Civilian*

Approaches to Living Together, 4 CAN. FAM. L. Q. 147 (1989); Von Sachsen Gessaphe, *Concubinage in Mexico*, 3 INT. J. LAW & FAM. 40 (1989).

4. Sweden has taken a different statutory approach to cohabitants; post-separation support is not available and property rights arise only with respect to property acquired during the relationship with intent that it be for mutual use. *See* Matthew Fawcett, *Taking the Middle Path: Recent Swedish Legislation Grants Minimal Property Rights to Unmarried Cohabitants*, 24 FAM. L. Q. 179 (1990). While the Swedish cohabitation legislation covers gay as well as heterosexual couples, gay couples may also register as partners and obtain a marriage-like status; once a couple registers they are treated as if married for most purposes, including inheritance, post-separation support and property rights, and social benefits (but excluding adoption). Peter Nygh, *Homosexual Partnership in Sweden*, 11 AUST. J. FAM. L. 11 (1997). What are the pros and cons of this approach as compared to that of the New South Wales statute?

5. Some American localities have established "domestic partnership" ordinances. These ordinances often enable cohabitants of municipal employees to qualify for health insurance benefits under group health insurance plans, but do not confer property or support rights. *See* Note, *A More Perfect Union: A Legal and Social Analysis of Domestic Partnership Ordinances*, 92 COLUM. L. REV. 1164 (1992). (San Francisco went further and required companies doing business with the city to offer fringe benefits to domestic partners of employees. *See* Tim Golden, *San Francisco Near Domestic–Partner Rule*, N.Y. TIMES, Nov. 6, 1996, at A9, col. 1.)

These domestic partnership ordinances require both people to take some affirmative act, like registration, to establish partnership status. Should the New South Wales statute require some affirmative act by both parties as a precondition to statutory entitlements?

6. Does the New South Wales scheme establish a statutory variant of common law marriage?

7. Do the statute's highly discretionary provisions regulating cohabitation agreements (§§ 45–50) render such agreements illusory, or is this flexibility necessary? (Compare the discussion of premarital agreements in Chapter 4.)

8. Could the statute be improved? What particulars would you change, delete or add? As amended, would you favor enactment of the statute in your jurisdiction?

9. In the United States, common-law marriage has come under increasing attack. Less than one-third of all states now recognize these marriages. During the 1990s, Georgia, Idaho, and Ohio abolished common-law marriage. Does this trend suggest a lack of political support for statutory solutions to nonmarital cohabitation?

SECTION 3. DISPUTES BETWEEN DATING PARTNERS

A. ENGAGEMENT DISPUTES

1. *Breach of Promise to Marry*

In an earlier era, the period during which a woman was considered marriageable was quite limited and long engagements were common. If the man broke the engagement, the woman might not be able to find another marriage partner; the engagement thus was treated like a contract. If one party "breached" the contract, the innocent party could sue the other for damages. In addition to out-of-pocket losses, the innocent party could recover damages for humiliation and loss of the future economic benefit that would have resulted from the marriage. *See* Scharringhaus v. Hazen, 269 Ky. 425, 107 S.W.2d 329 (1937) (upholding award of $65,000 compensatory and $15,000 punitive damages in breach of promise action.)

Over the years, many commentators—including Gilbert and Sullivan in "Trial By Jury"—argued that the breach of promise action should be abolished. Critics have argued that loss of a proposed marriage no longer produces real economic losses, and that the availability of an action for breach thus encourages lawsuits based on spite and discourages withdrawal from "shaky" relationships.

About half of the states have now followed Gilbert & Sullivan's advice and abolished the action. *See* J. THOMAS OLDHAM, DIVORCE, SEPARATION AND THE DISTRIBUTION OF PROPERTY § 1.05 (1998). But some courts have been reluctant to abolish the cause of action. For example, in Stanard v. Bolin, 88 Wash.2d 614, 565 P.2d 94 (1977), the court argued that mental and emotional harm are foreseeable consequences of a broken engagement, and concluded that the action should be retained. (Mental anguish is typically *not* compensable in other family law disputes, such as divorce, unless the other spouse has behaved outrageously.) In at least one state, Illinois, the cause of action has been retained, but only to recover out-of-pocket losses (deposits, wedding clothing, wages, etc.) incurred as a result of a broken engagement. *See* 740 ILL. COMP. STAT. ANN. § 15/2. Is this approach a sensible compromise?

2. *Engagement Gifts*

IN RE MARRIAGE OF HEINZMAN

Supreme Court of Colorado, 1979.
198 Colo. 36, 596 P.2d 61.

GROVES, JUSTICE.

This case was commenced as an action for dissolution of a common-law marriage in the district court of Boulder County. For convenience the petitioner is referred to as "Beth" and the respondent as "William." The court found that there was no marriage, but with the consent of the parties proceeded to a determination of their respective rights in a residence property, the title to which was in their names in joint tenancy. It ordered Beth to convey her record interest to William. On review the ruling that there was no marriage was not raised. The court of appeals by a two to one majority affirmed as to the property disposition on grounds somewhat different from those of the trial court. We granted certiorari to the court of appeals and now affirm on the grounds used by the trial court.

In 1970 Beth had been occupying the residence property as a tenant. That summer it appeared that her tenancy would end as the owner intended to sell the property. William entered into a contract to purchase it in July 1970 and the real estate transaction thereunder was "closed" the following December. William moved into the residence in late September 1970, and he and Beth resided there until June 1973.

By deed executed by William on March 25, 1971 and recorded on April 16, 1971, the residence property was conveyed to William and Beth in joint tenancy. Beth was there designated as "Beth Lavato." In June 1973 Beth moved to Sparks, Nevada, and she and William did not live together thereafter. William married another on August 26, 1974. The case was tried on June 20, 1975.

At the conclusion of the trial the district court, in addition to ruling that there was no common-law marriage, found: that William intended and wished to marry Beth; that he gave her an engagement ring in the spring of 1971; that "from the acts of the parties in addition to their admitted cohabitation, it would seem to be a presumption on the side of engagement"; "that an engagement did in fact exist"; "that the gift of real estate ... was a gift conditioned upon the subsequent ceremonial marriage"; that Beth had abandoned the home and the engagement; and that the condition was not defeated by William's actions. The court ruled that the transfer of the real estate was a gift conditioned upon a subsequent ceremonial marriage, and it ordered Beth to transfer interest in the property to William.

The majority rule appears to be that B must transfer back to A a gift received and held under the following circumstances: A and B are engaged to be married to each other. In contemplation of the formal commencement of that life of bliss A makes a gift to B. Later, through no fault of A, B breaks the engagement. The majority of courts reason that such a gift was conditioned upon a subsequent ceremonial marriage. We adopt the majority rule as applied to the facts here and affirm the trial court's conclusion that the deed was conditioned upon a subsequent ceremonial marriage.

Beth contends that recovery of the property under these circumstances is proscribed by the Statute of Frauds and the Heart Balm Statute. The Statute of Frauds does not prevent the declaration of a constructive trust. By the same reasoning it does not prevent recovery of property delivered conditionally under the particular circumstances here.

The Heart Balm Statute reads:

> All civil causes of action for breach of promise to marry, alienation of affections, criminal conversation, and seduction are hereby abolished.
>
> No act done within this state shall operate to give rise, either within or without this state, to any of the rights of action abolished [herein]. No contract to marry made or entered into in this state shall operate to give rise, either within or without this state, to any cause or right of action for the breach thereof, nor shall any contract to marry made in any other state give rise to any cause of action within this state for the breach thereof.

We follow the rule that this statute bars actions for damages suffered from breach of promise to marry and other direct consequences of the breach, such as humiliation; but that it should not be extended to affect common-law principles governing a gift to a fiancee made on condition of marriage, with condition broken by the donee.

Judgment affirmed.

Notes and Questions

1. Today most courts permit a donor to recover an engagement gift only if the donee breaks the engagement, or if the engagement is broken by mutual consent. "Bad behavior" (violence, an affair, etc.) that causes the broken engagement may also be taken into account.

2. Some states permit recovery of engagement gifts regardless of who breaks the engagement. *See, e.g.*, Heiman v. Parrish, 262 Kan. 926, 942 P.2d 631 (1997); Aronow v. Silver, 223 N.J.Super. 344, 538 A.2d 851 (1987); Virgil v. Haber, 21 Fam. L. Rep. (BNA) 1154 (N.M. 1995).

B. DISPUTES BETWEEN DATING PARTNERS

If a married person has an affair, is an agreement between the married person and the third party enforceable? Are any equitable remedies available?

TAYLOR v. FIELDS

California Court of Appeals, 1986.
178 Cal.App.3d 653, 224 Cal. Rptr. 186.

KLEIN, PRESIDING JUSTICE.

Plaintiff and appellant Flossie Taylor (Taylor) appeals from the granting of a summary judgment in favor of defendant and respondent Jean B. Fields (Jean).

The papers in the summary judgment motion disclosed Leo D. Fields (Leo), a married man, and Taylor never lived together, and had a meretricious relationship. No existing case law supports a contract theory of recovery based on such a fact situation. Therefore, the summary judgment is affirmed.

Leo and Jean were married on April 20, 1930, in Alameda County, California. They lived together as husband and wife for more than 50 years, until Leo's death in September 1980.

Taylor met Leo in 1938 in connection with a job application, and went to work for him. They became lovers, and began what turned out to be a 42 year relationship. During the first 20 years, Taylor was married to and lived with her husband, Jack, and they had two children.

After her divorce from Jack, Taylor continued her relationship with Leo, but never lived with him. Taylor alleged in 1969 or 1970 Leo asked her to marry him and she accepted. However, Leo did not end his marriage to Jean, and instead, told Taylor that if she would continue their relationship, he would take care of her financially and see to it that she would live comfortably for the rest of her life. As part of this agreement, Taylor promised Leo that during the period of their relationship, she would not marry anyone else.

Taylor also claimed Leo promised to provide for her by giving her $3,000 a month starting in 1973. She never received any such payments, and instead, received only the sums of $200 or $500 occasionally. Leo allegedly gave Taylor approximately $10,000 worth of water bonds and deposited $20,000 in a joint checking account with Taylor.

In September 1981, after Leo's death, Taylor filed a complaint against Jean as the sole defendant for breach of contract arising out of the alleged intimate and "fiduciary" relationship of 42 years between herself and Leo.

The complaint alleged in three causes of action an oral contract, an implied contract, and breach of fiduciary duty and fraudulent transfer, and prayed for damages and a constructive trust. These causes of action were based on Leo's alleged promise to take care of Taylor financially, thus enabling her to live in comfort the rest of her life, in exchange for Taylor's continuing to be Leo's companion and confidante and devoting herself to his care, comfort and happiness.

Jean answered the complaint and discovery commenced.

On June 15, 1984, Jean filed a motion for summary judgment on the following grounds: no triable issues of material fact existed; the alleged contract was unlawful and against public policy; the action was barred by the statutes of frauds and limitations; and the complaint failed to name the trustee of the decedent's trust as an indispensable party. In support of this motion Jean filed a statement of undisputed facts.

Taylor filed an opposition motion and a statement of disputed facts, to which Jean filed a reply.

On August 27, 1984, the trial court heard and granted Jean's motion for summary judgment. In its minute order, the trial court stated the case did not come within *Marvin v. Marvin*, [p. 226] and to apply *Marvin* to these facts would require a "quantum leap." The trial court also held the contract which contemplated, *inter alia*, Taylor would not remarry until and unless she could marry Leo, was void as being in restraint of marriage and therefore against public policy.

Taylor appealed.

Taylor contends the granting of the summary judgment was in error because there are triable issues of fact as to the existence of a valid oral and/or implied contract between Taylor and Leo.

Jean counters the summary judgment was proper because: the alleged contracts are illegal; Taylor's causes of action are barred by the statutes of frauds and limitations; and an indispensable party was not joined.

Taylor boldly asserts *Marvin* enables her causes of action based on her relationship with Leo. However, neither *Marvin* nor any other case to date has allowed recovery to an unmarried partner without a showing of a stable and significant relationship evolving out of cohabitation. A further requirement is a showing the agreement relied upon does not rest on illicit meretricious consideration.

Here, admittedly Taylor and Leo never lived together, but were "intimate lovers." Taylor's deposition testimony clearly discloses sex formed an inseparable part of the consideration for any alleged agreement between them. Unfortunately for Taylor as the woman involved herein, her relationship with Leo was nothing more than that of a legally married man and his mistress, albeit a long term one.

The existing law does not afford any relief to Taylor in her fact situation, and even though she challenges us to do so, this court does not intend to carve out a cause of action for her.

Marvin negates recovery here.

Taylor contends her relationship is somehow sanctioned by the holding in *Marvin*; we find it is not.

In *Marvin*, Michelle brought an action against Lee with whom she had lived for over six years to enforce an alleged oral contract under which she was entitled to half the property acquired during that period in Lee's name, and to support payments.

In *Butcher v. Superior Court*, a case decided since *Marvin*, the court held a cohabitant may state a cause of action for loss of consortium for injury to her nonmarital partner, thus extending recovery rights beyond the enforcement of an agreement between cohabiting partners. In *Butcher*, the couple had lived together for 11 ½ years, had two children, filed joint tax returns and regarded each other as husband and wife. The court rejected the argument that a cause of action for loss of consortium should be limited to those named under the wrongful death statutes and workers' compensation, and held such rights should be accorded to nonmarital partners who engaged in "stable and significant" relationships.

In all these cases, whether successful or not, the plaintiffs at least alleged the parties lived together.

Here, to the contrary, the facts are vastly different. There is no evidence Taylor and Leo ever "lived together" or cohabited during their 42–year relationship. It was undisputed that Leo was married to Jean during the entire period of his relationship with Taylor, and there was no evidence Jean and Leo ever separated or lived apart. During the first 20 years of the relationship, Taylor admits being married to Jack and having two children.

While Taylor avers she and Leo occasionally spent weekends together and registered as husband and wife, such claims are inadequate to bring their relationship within *Marvin* principles. In *Marvin* and its progeny, the parties lived together in stable nonmarital relationships, and the alleged agreements were upheld so long as they were not based on meretricious consideration.

Taylor contends even if part of her consideration is illegal, *Marvin* allows for enforcement of a contract of parties living together in a sexual relationship, if any portion of the contract is severable and supported by independent consideration. But such a contract will be held invalid "if sexual acts form an inseparable part of the consideration for the agreement." *(Id.).*

In *Jones v. Daly*, [p. 235, n. 4], a surviving partner to a "cohabiter's agreement" brought suit for declaratory relief against the estate of the decedent partner to enforce an oral agreement. The trial court dismissed the action after sustaining defendants' demurrer to the complaint without leave to amend.

In the instant complaint and in her deposition, Taylor alleges she acted as Leo's confidante, friend, travel companion and lover in return for his promises of lifetime financial care. Leaving aside the lack of a claim of cohabitation for the purposes of discussing this point, here, as in *Jones*, Taylor's rendering of sexual services for Leo is inseparable from the rest of the contract. Nothing in the alleged oral agreement rests upon Taylor's acting as a friend, traveling companion or confidante as distinguished from her role as Leo's paramour. Hence, the latter service forms an inseparable part of the consideration for the agreement and renders it unenforceable in its entirety.

Thus, as a matter of law, the alleged oral contract was unenforceable as based on illegal meretricious consideration.

Taylor's complaint claimed she was entitled to a remedial constructive trust as to all of Leo's community and separate property which he transferred to the trustee of an *inter vivos* trust in 1968. The theory fails for the same reasons as the contract causes of action.

It is a basic principle of equity that one who seeks equity must have clean hands; therefore, a court will not aid the commission of fraud by enforcing a contract nor relieve one of the parties to a fraud from its consequences when both are in *pari delicto*.

As discussed *ante*, Taylor's contract with Leo is unenforceable because there is no showing of stable and significant cohabitation and it is based upon illicit meretricious consideration. Here, both parties are in *pari delicto* in an adulterous relationship as Leo was married to someone else, and Taylor knew that fact. Because Taylor cannot obtain any relief under the illegal agreement at law, no constructive trust theory is available to her.

Because Taylor and Leo, a married man, did not live together and their alleged agreement was grounded on meretricious consideration and was therefore illegal, the trial court did not err in granting the summary judgment.

Questions

Which fact is crucial to the holding in *Taylor*: that Leo and Flossie did not cohabit, or that Leo lived with his wife while having a relationship with Flossie? Which should be determinative? *See* Bergen v. Wood, 14 Cal.App.4th 854, 18 Cal.Rptr.2d 75 (1993) (applying the *Taylor* holding to two unmarried noncohabitants).

KATHLEEN K. v. ROBERT B.

California Court of Appeals, 1984.
150 Cal.App.3d 992, 198 Cal.Rptr. 273.

HASTINGS, ASSOCIATE JUSTICE.

In this action, plaintiff and appellant Kathleen K. seeks damages because she contracted genital herpes, allegedly by way of sexual intercourse with defendant and respondent Robert B. The trial court granted respondent's motion for judgment on the pleadings based upon failure to state a cause of action. We reverse the judgment.

The complaint sets forth four causes of action: (1) negligence (alleging that respondent inflicted injury upon appellant by having sexual intercourse with her at a time when he knew, or in the exercise of reasonable care should have known, that he was a carrier of venereal disease); (2) battery; (3) intentional infliction of emotional distress; and (4) fraud (alleging that respondent deliberately misrepresented to appellant that he was free from venereal disease, and that appellant, relying on such representations, had sexual intercourse with respondent, which she would not have done had she known the true state of affairs).

In granting respondent's motion for judgment on the pleadings, the trial court relied upon the case of *Stephen K. v. Roni L.*, 105 Cal.App.3d 640, 164 Cal.Rptr. 618. In *Stephen K.*, the father of a child filed a cross-complaint against the child's mother who had brought a paternity action, claiming that the mother had falsely represented to him that she was taking birth control pills. The father alleged that in reliance upon that misrepresentation, he engaged in sexual intercourse with the mother, resulting in the birth of a child which he did not want. He further alleged that as a proximate result of the misrepresentation, he had become obligated to support the child financially and had suffered emotional distress.

In affirming dismissal of the cross-complaint, the court held that the misrepresentation was not actionable:

> The claim of Stephen is phrased in the language of the tort of misrepresentation. Despite its legalism, it is nothing more than asking the court to supervise the promises made between two consenting adults as to the circumstances of their private sexual conduct. To do so would encourage unwarranted governmental intrusion into matters affecting the individual's right to privacy. We reject Stephen's contention that tortuous liability should be imposed against Roni, and conclude that as a matter of public policy the practice of birth control, if any, engaged in by two partners in a consensual sexual relationship is best left to the individuals involved, free from any governmental interference. *(Stephen K., supra)*

After the trial court entered its judgment, the First District Court of Appeal decided the case of *Barbara A. v. John G.*, 193 Cal. Rptr. 422, 145 Cal.App.3d 369 (1983). In *Barbara A.*, a woman who suffered an ectopic pregnancy and was forced to undergo surgery to save her life, which rendered her sterile, brought an action against the man who impregnated her (her former attorney), alleging that she consented to sexual intercourse in reliance on the man's knowingly false representation that he was sterile. The court reversed a judgment on the pleadings in favor of the defendant and held that the complaint stated causes of action for battery and for deceit.

The court distinguished *Stephen K.*, noting that: "In essence, Stephen was seeking damages for the 'wrongful birth' of his child resulting in support obligations and alleged damages for mental suffering. Here, no child is involved; appellant is seeking damages for severe injury to her own body." We conclude that these same factors distinguish this case from *Stephen K.*, and accordingly hold that *Barbara A.* is controlling here.

Respondent, urging us to follow *Stephen K.*, criticizes *Barbara A.* in several respects. First, he argues that the viability of appellant's cause of action should not depend upon whether the injury alleged is mental or physical. However, the *Barbara A.* court did not focus solely on the type of injury involved in *Stephen K.*, but upon the fact that Stephen was alleging an injury which had significant public policy overtones:

> To assess damages against the mother for false representations about birth control would have the practical effect of reducing or eliminating support from the father by way of offset. Erasing much or all of the father's financial support, to the detriment of the child, is clearly against public policy and the statutory mandate.
>
> Further, we think it is not sound social policy to allow one parent to sue the other over the wrongful birth of their child. Using the child as the damage element in a tortuous claim of one parent against the other could seldom, if ever, result in benefit to a child.

In the present case, as in *Barbara A.*, there is no child involved, and the public policy considerations with respect to parental obligations are absent.

Respondent also argues that it is not the business of courts to "supervise the promises made between two consenting adults as to the circumstances of their private sexual conduct." (*Stephen K. v. Roni L.*)

Respondent correctly focuses on the constitutional right of privacy as the crux of this case. Courts have long recognized the right of privacy in matters relating to marriage, family and sex and accordingly have frowned upon unwarranted governmental intrusion into matters affecting the individual's right of privacy. The key word here, however, is *unwarranted*. The right of privacy is not absolute, and in some cases is subordinate to the state's fundamental right to enact laws which promote public health, welfare and safety, even though such laws may invade the offender's right of privacy. Examples cited by the *Barbara A.* court were the penal statutes acts, registration of convicted sex offenders, the recently enacted criminal statute prohibiting spousal rape (Pen. Code, § 262), and the various laws relating to the paternity of children. In each of these cases, the right of privacy is outweighed by the right of the state to protect the health, welfare and safety of its citizens. The *Barbara A.* court concluded that the right of privacy "does not insulate a person from all judicial inquiry into his or her sexual relations," and expanded the exceptions to the right of privacy to impose liability upon "one sexual partner who by intentionally tortuous conduct causes physical injury to the other."

This is precisely the type of conduct alleged in appellant's complaint. Appellant has alleged that she sustained physical injury due to respondent's tortuous conduct in either negligently or deliberately failing to inform her that he was infected with venereal disease. The disease which appellant contracted is serious and (thus far) incurable. The tortuous nature of respondent's conduct, coupled with the interest of this state in the prevention and control of contagious and dangerous[1] diseases brings appellant's injury within the type of physical injury contemplated by the court in *Barbara A.* The constitutional right of privacy does not protect respondent here.

It should be noted that several out-of-state cases, cited by the court in *Barbara A.*, have held that a woman's consent to sexual intercourse was vitiated by the man's fraudulent concealment of the risk of infection with venereal disease. Respondent contends that these cases are old and, if decided today, would be dismissed under the public policy considerations outlined in *Stephen K., supra.* He distinguishes *Crowell* and *Lankford* (involving suits by a wife against her husband for damages

1. Respondent's argument that genital herpes is not a venereal disease is unpersuasive. Although herpes is not listed among the "venereal diseases" covered by the Health & Safety Code (specifically § 3001), that section was enacted in 1957, long before herpes achieved its present notoriety. We are not inclined to bar appellant's cause of action on the basis that genital herpes is not a venereal disease. It is a disease that can be propagated by sexual contact. Like AIDS it is now known by the public to be a contagious and dreadful disease. At the core of this action is the misrepresentation of defendant that he did not have a contagious disease that could be passed to his partner. If a person knowingly has genital herpes, AIDS or some other contagious and serious disease, a limited representation that he or she does not have a venereal disease is no defense to this type of action.

resulting from contraction of venereal disease) on the basis that a husband and wife occupy a confidential relationship of trust and confidence in one another which does not exist between non-married persons. However, a certain amount of trust and confidence exists in any intimate relationship, at least to the extent that one sexual partner represents to the other that he or she is free from venereal or other dangerous contagious disease. The basic premise underlying these old cases—consent to sexual intercourse vitiated by one partner's fraudulent concealment of the risk of infection with venereal disease—is equally applicable today, whether or not the partners involved are married to each other.

We are also unpersuaded by respondent's argument that this is really an action for seduction (which he calls "the use of deception to effect intercourse"), and is therefore barred by Civil Code § 43.5. "Seduction imports the idea of illicit intercourse accomplished by the use of arts, persuasions, or wiles to overcome the resistance of a female who is not disposed of her own volition to step aside from the paths of virtue." Appellant is not complaining that respondent induced her to "step aside from the paths of virtue," and in fact she willingly engaged in sexual intercourse with him. This is an action for damages based upon severe injury to appellant's body, which allegedly occurred because of respondent's misrepresentation that he was disease free. Such an action is not barred by Civil Code § 43.5

In summary, we conclude that *Stephen K. v. Roni L.*, on which the trial court relied, is inapplicable here, and that the reasoning of Barbara A. v. John G., in which a hearing was denied by our Supreme Court, is controlling.

The judgment is reversed.

Notes and Questions

1. Most courts have permitted recovery for misrepresentation leading to the contraction of a sexually transmitted disease. However, in Zysk v. Zysk, 239 Va. 32, 387 S.E.2d 466 (1990), republished 404 S.E.2d 721, the court denied recovery on a claim identical to that in *Kathleen K.*; because fornication violated Virginia's criminal law, the court held that "people who participate in immoral or illegal acts cannot recover damages from other participants for the consequence of the act."

2. When the disease transmitted is AIDS, damage awards could be quite large. Even in suits for herpes transmission, damages sometimes have been substantial. *See, e.g.*, Meany v. Meany, 639 So.2d 229 (La. 1994) ($93,000). Homeowner's insurance coverage may apply. *See* Loveridge v. Chartier, 161 Wis.2d 150, 468 N.W.2d 146 (1991).

3. There are no immunities that restrict tort actions between cohabitants or dating partners; a full range of tort claims and defenses is available. See Brooke Masters, *Marv Albert Sex Trial Could Set Precedent*, HOUSTON CHRONICLE, Sept. 22, 1997, at 3A, col. 5 (describing battery

action brought by Albert's girlfriend and consent defense alleged by Albert.)

Problem 5–4:

Lee and Richard met at a party. Although Richard was married, he and Lee began an intimate relationship which continued for more than a year. During that year, Lee learned she was pregnant with Richard's child. When Lee told Richard, he became upset and urged her to have an abortion. Lee did not want to have an abortion, but Richard persisted. He told Lee that, although he would like her to have this child, he wanted to postpone doing so for a year. He promised Lee that, even if they were not together in a year, he would conceive a child with her by artificial insemination. After the abortion, Lee discovered that Richard had never intended to keep his promise of another baby. As a result, Lee became depressed, requiring psychiatric treatment, incurring extensive medical bills and losing six months of earnings. Lee sued Richard for fraud, deceit, and intentional infliction of emotional distress. Under *Kathleen K.*, what arguments are available to each party? What result? *See* Perry v. Atkinson, 195 Cal.App.3d 14, 240 Cal.Rptr. 402 (1987).

Some Concluding Thoughts

In chapters 1 through 5, we have seen concrete evidence of the "increasing fluidity, detachability and interchangeability of family relationships" outlined by Professor Glendon in Chapter 1. Distinctions between nonmarital cohabitation and marriage are blurring. Loosened marriage laws have reduced or eliminated many substantive and most formal restrictions on entry into marriage. Entry into marriage is nearly unrestricted, and—as we will see in Chapter 11—exit from marriage is all but unlimited. Moreover, relaxation of restrictions that traditionally governed premarital contracts has made it increasingly possible for marriage partners to individualize the terms of their marriage, typically by contracting "down" from statutory marriage. On the other side of the spectrum, cohabitants are contracting "up" from no-consequences liaisons.

Has competition from new lifestyles forced the downgrading of marriage, or has the downgrading of marriage made nonmarital cohabitation a more competitive option? Or are the decline of traditional marriage and the increase in cohabitation simply parallel developments marking a general withdrawal from traditional standards and mores? Who knows? Ironically, marriage (or a modern variant) may gain strength from the "forced marriage" concept implicit in the *Marvin* and *Connell* doctrines. This raises a question of labels: Are *Marvin* and *Connell* "reactionary" or "progressive?" Do they discourage out-of-wedlock cohabitation by making a "free union" less free? Do they resurrect the time-honored (but in this day—one might have thought—outdated) legal institution of "concubinage," conferring on the "concubine" a legal status somewhere below that of a wife?

Consider MARY ANN GLENDON, STATE, LAW AND FAMILY 85, 91 (1977):

> The *union libre*, or free union, is a venerable institution in French law. Despite the fact that it is almost completely ignored by the Civil Code, and only discreetly alluded to in other legislation, it has acquired enough of a legal existence through the case law to be described in the leading treatises as comparable to the Roman *concubinatus*, a kind of qualitatively inferior marriage with legal attributes. The fact that a chapter on the *union libre* is a standard feature in French treatises on civil law is itself a sign of its established character. * * * [I]t seems to be distinctive of the French developments that the *union libre* has come to resemble legal marriage by drawing to itself many of the legal effects of marriage and by imitating others. Thus, it is possible to see the French situation as one in which the legitimate family prevails after all: "In appearance, it has certainly lost ground, but in fact it has imposed the matrimonial model on those who have declined to marry. No longer bothering to look down on its adversaries, it has transformed them in its own image."

No method of regulating nonmarital cohabitation is perfect. Cohabitation without marriage *and with Hewitt* permits separation without "divorce" and without financial consequences. But cohabitation without marriage *and with Connell or the New South Wales statute* will encroach (perhaps unduly) upon the personal freedom of the parties. And cohabitation without marriage *and with Marvin* may encourage frivolous litigation and lead to unpredictable, "hit-or-miss" results. *See* Ruth Deech, *The Case Against Legal Recognition of Cohabitation*, 29 INT. & COMP. L. Q. 480 (1980).

No matter what attitude a state adopts on the broad issues raised by nonmarital cohabitation, basic legal problems arising in such relationships will still have to be resolved. These inescapable problems include paternity of the unmarried woman's children [Chapter 6], the rights of the father to custody [Chapter 13] or to veto an adoption [Chapter 7] of the children, support duties to the children [Chapter 16], as well property rights in (joint?) acquisitions during the period of cohabitation.

Chapter 6

BECOMING A PARENT: CONTRACEPTION, ABORTION, AND PATERNITY ESTABLISHMENT

I regard sex as the central problem of life.

Havelock Ellis, Studies in the Psychology of Sex

In an earlier era, becoming a parent was a relatively simple, if often accidental, matter: A man and a woman engaged in sexual intercourse and conceived a child. If the woman was married, her husband was presumed to be the child's father; with no medical tests available to disprove parentage, the presumption was rarely rebutted. If the woman was unmarried, a "shotgun" marriage was hastily arranged, an illegal (and probably unsafe) abortion was obtained, or the pregnancy was concealed to the extent possible and the baby given up for adoption at birth. In the rare event that the unmarried woman gave birth to a child and kept it, she faced scandal and the problem of establishing paternity without modern medical technology.

Technological and social change have dramatically altered both the process of becoming a parent and the legal determination of parentage. With highly effective contraception techniques, procreation can be avoided; with access to legal abortion, pregnancy can be terminated at will; with sophisticated medical tests, paternity is relatively easy to establish or rebut. And, as a result of altered social mores, the unmarried woman who becomes pregnant no longer faces social opprobrium if she gives birth; indeed, approximately 30% of U.S. births now occur out of wedlock. From an evidentiary perspective, the legal determination of parentage is now simpler; from a normative perspective, it is perhaps more complex.

SECTION 1. CONTRACEPTION

Although contraceptives have been known for generations, modern science has made it easier, safer, and cheaper to prevent pregnancy. The first contraceptive pills were marketed in 1960, the first intrauterine devices (IUDs) in 1963.

At the time these new, highly effective means of contraception came on the market, many states and the federal government had laws, most dating from the late 19th century, that forbade their dissemination and/or use. The 1873 Comstock Law (18 U.S.C.A. §§ 1461–62), for example, outlawed both the importation and transmittal through the mails of all articles designed to prevent conception. Although the law was not enforced after the 1920s, it was not repealed until 1971.

The constitutionality of these laws was tested in Griswold v. Connecticut, [p. 19]; as you know, the Supreme Court ruled that the states could not forbid use of contraceptives by married couples, a holding extended in Eisenstadt v. Baird, 405 U.S. 438, 92 S.Ct. 1029, 31 L.Ed.2d 349 (1972) to unmarried individuals. In Carey v. Population Services International, 431 U.S. 678, 97 S.Ct. 2010, 52 L.Ed.2d 675 (1977), the Court addressed the sale of contraceptives. The New York law at issue in *Carey* forbade: i) the sale of all contraceptives by anyone other than a licensed pharmacist; and ii) all advertisement or display of contraceptives. Writing for the majority, Justice Brennan stated:

> . . . That the constitutionally protected right of privacy extends to an individual's liberty to make choices regarding contraception does not . . . automatically invalidate every state regulation in this area. The business of manufacturing and selling contraceptives may be regulated in ways that do not infringe protected individual choices. And even a burdensome regulation may be validated by a sufficiently compelling state interest.
>
> * * *
>
> Restrictions on the distribution of contraceptives clearly burden the freedom to make such decisions . . . This is so not because there is an independent fundamental "right of access to contraceptives," but because such access is essential to exercise of the constitutionally protected right of decision in matters of childbearing that is the underlying foundation of the holdings in *Griswold* [and] *Eisenstadt* . . .

The court found no compelling state interest in either limiting distribution of nonmedical contraceptives to licensed pharmacists or in prohibiting advertising. *See also* Bolger v. Youngs Drug Products Corp., 463 U.S. 60, 103 S.Ct. 2875, 77 L.Ed.2d 469 (1983) (invalidating federal law prohibiting use of the mails to send unsolicited advertisements for contraceptives on First Amendment grounds).

Notes and Questions

1. State laws barring voluntary sterilization have fallen along with restrictions on access to contraceptives. *See* Hathaway v. Worcester City Hospital, 475 F.2d 701 (1st Cir.1973) (city hospital's policy of barring use of facilities for consensual sterilization violated equal protection clause).

Could a state require spousal notification or consent before a surgeon performs a sterilization procedure? *See* Planned Parenthood v. Danforth [p. 17]; Ponter v. Ponter, 135 N.J.Super. 50, 342 A.2d 574 (1975).

2. A range of new contraceptives has given rise to new legal issues:

a. *Norplant*, approved for use in the United States in 1990, provides contraceptive protection that lasts up to five years. A doctor inserts six matchstick size silicone capsules containing the drug levonorgestrel in a woman's upper arm; fertility is restored when the capsules are removed. (Norplant 2, not yet approved as of late 1997, requires implantation of only two capsules and provides contraceptive protection for only three years.) May the state legally require Norplant use by women receiving public assistance benefits on behalf of minor children? by women who had previously been convicted of child abuse or neglect? *See* Note, *Norplant Bonuses and the Unconstitutional Conditions Doctrine*, 71 TEX. L. REV. 189 (1992); Stacey L. Arthur, *The Norplant Prescription Birth Control, Woman Control, or Crime Control?* 40 UCLA L. REV. 1 (1992); JOHN A. ROBERTSON, CHILDREN OF CHOICE (1994).

b. At least six types of oral contraceptives now being marketed are safe and effective "morning after" pills that, for up to seventy-two hours after unprotected sex, not only prevent ovulation and/or ovum fertilization, but also implantation of a fertilized egg (sometimes described as a pre-embryo) in the uterus, a step necessary to achieving a viable pregnancy. *See* 62 Fed. Reg. 8610 (1997); Lauran Neergaard, *'Morning-after Pill' Wins Government's Approval, AP,* TOPEKA CAPITAL JOURNAL, Feb. 25, 1997, p. 1–A, 2–A, col. 1. RU 486 (mifepristone), developed in France and tentatively approved by the FDA on September 18, 1996, takes these possibilities a step further by permitting the termination of an established pregnancy (i.e., a fertilized ovum has implanted in the uterus); pro-life activists had kept RU 486 out of the United States for several years. *See FDA close to approving nonsurgical abortion drug*, CNN INTERACTIVE, Sept. 18, 1996. Should these drugs be regarded (and regulated) as contraceptives or abortifacients?

SECTION 2. ABORTION

Abortion has long been controversial. Although Aristotle held that early abortion ("before sense and life have begun") should be available "when couples have children in excess" (ARISTOTLE, POLITICS, Book VII, Ch. 16), Roman Catholic canon law forbade abortion under all circumstances. The first U.S. abortion law, enacted in Connecticut in 1821 to protect pregnant women's health, prohibited abortion by use of poison. During the nineteenth century, the medical profession encouraged states to enact similar statutes because of the high mortality rate associated with abortion. Many of these laws permitted abortion by a licensed physician when necessary to preserve the life or health of the mother.

At the time these laws were adopted, there were in fact many indications for life-saving abortions, such as tuberculosis, cardiovas-

> cular and renal disease, and the so-called pernicious vomiting of pregnancy. By the 1960s, however, advances in medicine meant that it was only a rare case where the pregnant woman's life could be said to be at stake. Fewer and fewer abortions were being performed to preserve the woman's life or ... health. The numbers revealed how many had always been and were still being performed for other reasons. With its cover story gone, the medical profession began to be concerned about protecting its legal position and to become an active and powerful force for liberalization.
>
> MARY ANN GLENDON, ABORTION AND DIVORCE IN WESTERN LAW 11–12 (1987).

Public and legislative attitudes toward abortion were also affected by the liberalization of sexual mores during the 1960s and widespread publicity given the plight of severely deformed "thalidomide babies," whose mothers had taken the drug thalidomide while pregnant. The English Abortion Act was adopted in 1967; during the same period, several American states—including California, Colorado, Maryland and North Carolina—enacted laws permitting abortion under carefully defined and limited circumstances. While these laws generally required pre-abortion review by a committee of physicians, New York enacted legislation permitting abortion essentially on demand. For historical accounts of abortion law, *see* GLENDON, *supra*; LAURENCE H. TRIBE, ABORTION: THE CLASH OF ABSOLUTES (1990); ABORTION, MEDICINE AND THE LAW (J. Douglas Butler and David F. Walbert, eds., 4th rev. ed. 1992).

ROE v. WADE

Supreme Court of the United States, 1973.
410 U.S. 113, 93 S.Ct. 705, 35 L.Ed.2d 147.

JUSTICE BLACKMUN delivered the opinion of the Court.

* * *

The Texas statutes that concern us here are Arts. 1191–1194 and 1196 of the State's Penal Code, Vernon's Ann. P.C. These make it a crime to "procure an abortion," as therein defined, or to attempt one, except with respect to "an abortion procured or attempted by medical advice for the purpose of saving the life of the mother." Similar statutes are in existence in a majority of the states.

* * *

The Constitution does not explicitly mention any right of privacy. In a line of decisions, however, going back perhaps as far as *Union Pacific R.R. Co. v. Botsford*, 141 U.S. 250, 251, 11 S.Ct. 1000, 35 L.Ed. 734(1891), the Court has recognized that a right of personal privacy, or a guarantee of certain areas or zones of privacy, does exist under the Constitution. In varying contexts, the Court or individual have, indeed, found at least the roots of that right in the First Amendment, *Stanley v. Georgia*, 394 U.S. 557, 564 (1969); in the Fourth and Fifth Amendments,

Terry v. Ohio, 392 U.S. 1, 8–9; *Katz v. United States*, 389 U.S. 347, 350 (1967); *Boyd v. United States*, 116 U.S. 161 (1886); see *Olmstead v. United States*, 277 U.S. 438, 478 (1928); (Brandeis, J., dissenting); in the penumbras of the Bill of Rights, *Griswold v. Connecticut*, 381 U.S. 479 (1965), in the Ninth Amendment, *Id.*; or in the concept of liberty guaranteed by the first section of the Fourteenth Amendment, *see Meyer v. Nebraska*, 262 U.S. 390, 399 (1923). These decisions make it clear that only personal rights that can be deemed "fundamental" or "implicit in the concept of ordered liberty," are included in this guarantee of personal privacy. They also make it clear that the right has some extension to activities relating to marriage, *Loving v. Virginia*, 388 U.S. 1, 12 (1967); procreation, *Eisenstadt v. Baird*, 405 U.S. 438 (1972); (White, J., concurring in result); family relationships, *Prince v. Massachusetts*, 321 U.S. 158, 166 (1944); and child rearing and education, *Pierce v. Society of Sisters*, 268 U.S. 510, 535 (1925); *Meyer v. Nebraska, supra*.

This right of privacy, whether it be founded in the Fourteenth Amendment's concept of personal liberty and restriction upon a state action, as we feel it is, or, as the District Court determined, in the Ninth Amendment's reservation of rights to the people, is broad enough to encompass a woman's decision whether or not to terminate her pregnancy. The detriment that the State would impose upon the pregnant woman by denying this choice altogether is apparent. Specific and direct harm medically diagnosable even in early pregnancy may be involved. Maternity, or additional offspring, may force upon the woman a distressful life and future. Psychological harm may be imminent. Mental and physical health may be taxed * * * by child care. There is also the distress, for all concerned, associated with the unwanted child, and there is the problem of bringing a child into a family already unable, psychologically and otherwise, to care for it. In other cases, as in this one, the additional difficulties and continuing stigma of unwed motherhood may be involved. All these are factors the woman and her responsible physician necessarily will consider in consultation.

* * *

We therefore conclude that the right of personal privacy includes the abortion decision, but that this right is not unqualified and must be considered against important state interest in regulation. * * *

Where certain "fundamental rights" are involved, the Court has held that regulation limiting these rights may be justified only by a "compelling state interest." * * *

* * *

The appellee and certain *amici* argue that the fetus is a "person" within the language and meaning of the Fourteenth Amendment. In support of this they outline at length and in detail the well-known facts of fetal development. * * *

The Constitution does not define "person" in so many words. Section 1 of the Fourteenth Amendment contains three references to "person." The first, in defining "citizens" speaks of "persons born or naturalized in the United States." The word also appears both in the Due Process Clause and in the Equal Protection Clause. "Person" is used in other places in the Constitution ... [b]ut in nearly all these instances, the use of the word is such that it has application only post-natally. None indicates, with any assurance, that it has any possible pre-natal application.

All this, together with our observation, that throughout the major portion of the 19th century prevailing legal abortion practices were far freer than they are today, persuades us that the word "persons," as used in the Fourteenth Amendment, does not include the unborn. This is in accord with the results reached in those few cases where the issue has been squarely presented.

* * *

Texas urges that, apart from the Fourteenth Amendment, life begins at conception and is present throughout pregnancy, and that, therefore, the state has a compelling interest in protecting that life from and after conception. We need not resolve the difficult question of when life begins. When those trained in the respective disciplines of medicine, philosophy, and theology are unable to arrive at any consensus, the judiciary at this point in the development of man's knowledge, is not in a position to speculate as to the answer.

* * *

[We hold that:]

A state criminal abortion statute of the current Texas type, that excepts from criminality only a *life saving* procedure on behalf of the mother, without regard to pregnancy state and without recognition of the other interests involved, is violative of the Due Process Clause of the Fourteenth Amendment.

(a) For the stage prior to approximately the end of the first trimester, the abortion decision and its effectuation must be left to the medical judgment of the pregnant woman's attending physician.

(b) For the stage subsequent to approximately the end of the first trimester, the state, in promoting its interest in the health of the mother, may, if it chooses, regulate the abortion procedure in ways that are reasonably related to maternal health.

(c) For the stage subsequent to viability the state, in promoting its interest in the potentiality of human life, may, if it chooses, regulate, and even proscribe, abortion except where it is necessary in appropriate medical judgment, for the preservation of the life or health of the mother. * * *

JUSTICE REHNQUIST, dissenting.

* * *

The fact that a majority of the States reflecting, after all, the majority sentiment in those States, have had restrictions on abortions for at least a century is a strong indication, it seems to me, that the asserted right to an abortion is not "so rooted in the traditions and conscience of our people as to be ranked as fundamental." Even today, when society's views on abortion are changing, the very existence of the debate is evidence that the "right" to an abortion is not so universally accepted as the appellant would have us believe.

To reach its result, the Court necessarily has had to find within the scope of the Fourteenth Amendment a right that was apparently completely unknown to the drafters of the Amendment. As early as 1821, the first state law dealing directly with abortion was enacted by the Connecticut Legislature. By the time of the adoption of the Fourteenth Amendment in 1868, there were at least 36 laws enacted by state or territorial legislatures limiting abortion. While many States have amended or updated their laws, 21 of the laws on the books in 1868 remain in effect today. Indeed, the Texas statute struck down today was, as the majority notes, first enacted in 1857 and "has remained substantially unchanged to the present time."

There apparently was no question concerning the validity of this provision or of any of the other state statutes when the Fourteenth Amendment was adopted. The only conclusion possible from this history is that the drafters did not intend to have the Fourteenth Amendment withdraw from the States the power to legislate with respect to this matter.

* * *

Notes and Questions

1. Following its decision in *Roe*, the Supreme Court reviewed a series of state abortion restrictions. It rejected an Ohio requirement that after the first trimester all abortions be performed in an accredited hospital instead of an outpatient clinic as imposing "a heavy and unnecessary burden on women's access to a relatively inexpensive, otherwise accessible, and safe abortion procedure," as well as some of the statute's "informed" consent and waiting period provisions which, the court concluded, were designed to "persuade . . . [the woman seeking an abortion] to withhold [consent] altogether." Akron v. Akron Center for Reproductive Health, 462 U.S. 416, 103 S.Ct. 2481, 76 L.Ed.2d 687 (1983) (Akron I). In Thornburgh v. American College of Obstetricians & Gynecologists, 476 U.S. 747, 106 S.Ct. 2169, 90 L.Ed.2d 779 (1986), the Court struck down a Pennsylvania statute requiring doctors who performed abortions to provide a detailed report on the reason the fetus was not viable. But, in Planned Parenthood Ass'n v. Ashcroft, 462 U.S. 476, 103 S.Ct. 2517, 76 L.Ed.2d 733 (1983), the Court upheld Missouri statutes requiring a pathology report on fetal tissue removed during an abortion and the attendance of a second physician to try to preserve the life of the unborn child.

2. The Supreme Court has consistently upheld the right of states not to pay for abortion-related services. *See* Maher v. Roe, 432 U.S. 464, 97 S.Ct. 2376, 53 L.Ed.2d 484 (1977); Beal v. Doe et al., 432 U.S. 438, 97 S.Ct. 2366, 53 L.Ed.2d 464 (1977). Federal funding for abortions came to an abrupt halt with the 1976 Hyde Amendment, Pub. L. 94–439, 90 Stat. 1434 (1976), prohibiting the use of federal funds to reimburse states for the cost of abortion under Medicaid. The Court upheld both the Hyde amendment (Harris v. McRae, 448 U.S. 297, 100 S.Ct. 2671, 65 L.Ed.2d 784 (1980), rehearing denied 448 U.S. 917, 101 S.Ct. 39, 65 L.Ed.2d 1180) and a state law prohibiting the use of public employees and facilities in performing or assisting in abortions not necessary to save the life of the mother (Webster v. Reproductive Health Services, 492 U.S. 490, 109 S.Ct. 3040, 106 L.Ed.2d 410 (1989)). Since 1994, federal reimbursement has been available for abortion of pregnancies resulting from rape or incest (Pub. L. 103–112, 107 Stat. 1082); the states may no longer deny abortion to rape or incest victims and still claim federal reimbursement. *See* Elizabeth Blackwell Health Center for Women v. Knoll, 61 F.3d 170 (3d Cir.1995); Little Rock Fam. Planning Servs. v. Dalton, 60 F.3d 497 (8th Cir.1995). *See generally* Gayle Binion, *Reproductive Freedom and the Constitution: The Limits on Choice*, 4 Berkeley Women's L.J. 12 (1988).

3. Between 1970 and 1990, most European nations liberalized their abortion laws. By 1987, abortion was illegal only in Belgium and Ireland. In Spain, Portugal and Switzerland, abortion was made available based on one or another "hard ground" such as rape, incest, a danger to the mother's health, or a pregnancy resulting from rape or incest. In Austria, Denmark, Greece, Norway and Sweden, abortion was made elective early in pregnancy but was strictly regulated thereafter. In England, Finland, France, West Germany, Iceland, Italy, Luxembourg, and the Netherlands abortion was made available early in pregnancy based on a variety of "soft grounds" such as a pregnancy placing the woman "in a situation of distress." Typically these soft grounds were not tested by any review process. *See* Glendon, *supra*, at 13–15 & tbl. 1 (categorizing and explaining European abortion regimes). Since German reunification, abortion has been available during the first twelve weeks of pregnancy if the woman first receives counseling. *See* Alan Cowell, *Obeying Pope, German Bishops End Role in Abortion System*, N.Y. Times, Jan. 28, 1998, p. A3, col. 1.

PLANNED PARENTHOOD v. CASEY

Supreme Court of the United States, 1992.
505 U.S. 833, 112 S.Ct. 2791, 120 L.Ed.2d 674.

Justice O'Connor, Justice Kennedy, and Justice Souter announced the judgment of the Court and delivered the opinion of the Court with respect to Parts I, II, III, V–A, V–C, and VI, an opinion with respect to Part V–E, in which Justice Stevens joins, and an opinion with respect to Parts IV, V–B and V–D.

I

Liberty finds no refuge in a jurisprudence of doubt. Yet 19 years after our holding that the Constitution protects a woman's right to terminate her pregnancy in its early stages, Roe v. Wade, that definition of liberty is still questioned. Joining the respondents as *amicus curiae*, the United States, as it has done in five other cases in the last decade, again asks us to overrule *Roe*.

At issue in these cases are five provisions of the Pennsylvania Abortion Control Act of 1982 as amended in 1988 and 1989. The Act requires that a woman seeking an abortion give her informed consent prior to the abortion procedure, and specifies that she be provided with certain information at least 24 hours before the abortion is performed. § 3205. For a minor to obtain an abortion, the Act requires the informed consent of one of her parents, but provides for a judicial bypass option if the minor does not wish to or cannot obtain a parent's consent. § 3206. Another provision of the Act requires that, unless certain exceptions apply, a married woman seeking an abortion must sign a statement indicating that she has notified her husband of her intended abortion. § 3209. The Act exempts compliance with these three requirements in the event of a "medical emergency," which is defined in § 3203 of the Act. In addition to the above provisions regulating the performance of abortions, the Act imposes certain reporting requirements on facilities that provide abortion services. §§ 3207(b), 3214(a), 3214(f). Before any of these provisions took effect, the petitioners, who are five abortion clinics and one physician representing himself as well as a class of physicians who provide abortion services, brought this suit seeking declaratory and injunctive relief. Each provision was challenged as unconstitutional on its face. The District Court entered a preliminary injunction against the enforcement of the regulations, and, after a 3-day bench trial, held all the provisions at issue here unconstitutional, entering a permanent injunction against Pennsylvania's enforcement of them. The Court of Appeals for the Third Circuit affirmed in part and reversed in part, upholding all the regulations except for the husband notification requirement. We granted certiorari.

* * *

After considering the fundamental constitutional questions resolved by *Roe*, principles of institutional integrity, and the rule of stare decisis, we are led to conclude this: the essential holding of Roe v. Wade should be retained and once again reaffirmed.

It must be stated at the outset and with clarity that *Roe's* essential holding, the holding we reaffirm, has three parts. First is a recognition of the right of the woman to choose to have an abortion before viability and to obtain it without undue interference from the State. Before viability, the State's interests are not strong enough to support a prohibition of abortion or the imposition of substantial obstacles to the woman's effective right to elect the procedure. Second is a confirmation of the State's power to restrict abortions after fetal viability, if the law contains exceptions for pregnancies which endanger a woman's life or health. And third is the principle that the State has legitimate interests from the outset of the pregnancy in protecting the health of the woman and the life of the fetus that may become a child. These principles do not contradict one another; and we adhere to each.

* * *

III

A

The obligation to follow precedent begins with necessity, and a contrary necessity marks its outer limit. With Cardozo, we recognize that no judicial system could do society's work if it eyed each issue afresh in every case that raised it. Indeed, the very concept of the rule of law underlying our own Constitution requires such continuity over time that a respect for precedent is, by definition, indispensable. At the other extreme, a different necessity would make itself felt if a prior judicial ruling should come to be seen so clearly as error that its enforcement was for that very reason doomed.

* * *

So in this case we may inquire whether *Roe's* central rule has been found unworkable; whether the rule's limitation on state power could be removed without serious inequity to those who have relied upon it or significant damage to the stability of the society governed by the rule in question; whether the law's growth in the intervening years has left *Roe's* central rule a doctrinal anachronism discounted by society; and whether *Roe's* premises of fact have so far changed in the ensuing two decades as to render its central holding somehow irrelevant or unjustifiable in dealing with the issue it addressed.

Although *Roe* has engendered opposition, it has in no sense proven "unworkable," representing as it does a simple limitation beyond which a state law is unenforceable. While *Roe* has, of course, required judicial assessment of state laws affecting the exercise of the choice guaranteed against government infringement, and although the need for such review will remain as a consequence of today's decision, the required determinations fall within judicial competence.

* * *

IV

* * *

Yet it must be remembered that Roe v. Wade speaks with clarity in establishing not only the woman's liberty but also the State's "important and legitimate interest in potential life." That portion of the decision in *Roe* has been given too little acknowledgment and implementation by the Court in its subsequent cases. Those cases decided that any regulation touching upon the abortion decision must survive strict scrutiny, to be sustained only if drawn in narrow terms to further a compelling state interest. *See e.g., Akron I*, 462 U.S., at 427. Not all of the cases decided under that formulation can be reconciled with the holding in *Roe* itself that the State has legitimate interests in the health of the woman and in protecting the potential life within her. In resolving this tension, we choose to rely upon *Roe*, as against the later cases.

Roe established a trimester framework to govern abortion regulations. Under this elaborate but rigid construct, almost no regulation at all is permitted during the first trimester of pregnancy; regulations designed to protect the woman's health, but not to further the State's interest in potential life, are permitted during the second trimester; and during the third trimester, when the fetus is viable, prohibitions are permitted provided the life or health of the mother is not at stake. Most of our cases since *Roe* have involved the application of rules derived from the trimester framework.

* * *

We reject the trimester framework, which we do not consider to be part of the essential holding of *Roe*. Measures aimed at ensuring that a woman's choice contemplates the consequences for the fetus do not necessarily interfere with the right recognized in *Roe*, although those measures have been found to be inconsistent with the rigid trimester framework announced in that case. A logical reading of the central holding in *Roe* itself, and a necessary reconciliation of the liberty of the woman and the interest of the State in promoting prenatal life, require, in our view, that we abandon the trimester framework as a rigid prohibition on all previability regulation aimed at the protection of fetal life. The trimester framework suffers from these basic flaws: in its formulation it misconceives the nature of the pregnant woman's interest; and in practice it undervalues the State's interest in potential life, as recognized in *Roe*.

* * *

The very notion that the State has a substantial interest in potential life leads to the conclusion that not all regulations must be deemed unwarranted. Not all burdens on the right to decide whether to terminate a pregnancy will be undue. In our view, the undue burden standard is the appropriate means of reconciling the State's interest with the woman's constitutionally protected liberty.

* * *

Some guiding principles should emerge. What is at stake is the woman's right to make the ultimate decision, not a right to be insulated from all others in doing so. Regulations which do no more than create a structural mechanism by which the State, or the parent or guardian of a minor, may express profound respect for the life of the unborn are permitted, if they are not a substantial obstacle to the woman's exercise of the right to choose. Unless it has that effect on her right of choice, a state measure designed to persuade her to choose childbirth over abortion will be upheld if reasonably related to that goal. Regulations designed to foster the health of a woman seeking an abortion are valid if they do not constitute an undue burden.

Even when jurists reason from shared premises, some disagreement is inevitable. That is to be expected in the application of any legal standard which must accommodate life's complexity. We do not expect it to be otherwise with respect to the undue burden standard. We give this summary:

(a) To protect the central right recognized by Roe v. Wade while at the same time accommodating the State's profound interest in potential life, we will employ the undue burden analysis as explained in this opinion. An undue burden exists, and therefore a provision of law is invalid, if its purpose or effect is to place a substantial obstacle in the path of a woman seeking an abortion before the fetus attains viability.

(b) We reject the rigid trimester framework of Roe v. Wade. To promote the State's profound interest in potential life throughout pregnancy, the State may take measures to ensure that the woman's choice is informed, and measures designed to advance this interest will not be invalidated as long as their purpose is to persuade the woman to choose childbirth over abortion. These measures must not be an undue burden on the right.

(c) As with any medical procedure, the State may enact regulations to further the health or safety of a woman seeking an abortion. Unnecessary health regulations that have the purpose or effect of presenting a substantial obstacle to a woman seeking an abortion impose an undue burden on the right.

(d) Our adoption of the undue burden analysis does not disturb the central holding of Roe v. Wade, and we reaffirm that holding. Regardless of whether exceptions are made for particular circumstances, a State may not prohibit any woman from making the ultimate decision to terminate her pregnancy before viability.

(e) We also reaffirm *Roe's* holding that "subsequent to viability, the State in promoting its interest in the potentiality of human life may, if it chooses, regulate, and even proscribe, abortion except where it is necessary, in appropriate medical judgment, for the preservation of the life or health of the mother."

These principles control our assessment of the Pennsylvania statute, and we now turn to the issue of the validity of its challenged provisions.

V (A)

Because it is central to the operation of various other requirements, we begin with the statute's definition of medical emergency. Under the statute, a medical emergency is

> "[t]hat condition which, on the basis of the physician's good faith clinical judgment, so complicates the medical condition of a pregnant woman as to necessitate the immediate abortion of her

pregnancy to avert her death or for which a delay will create serious risk of substantial and irreversible impairment of a major bodily function." 18 Pa. Cons. Stat. (1990).

We * * * conclude that, as construed by the Court of Appeals, the medical emergency definition imposes no undue burden on a woman's abortion right.

B

We next consider the informed consent requirement. Except in a medical emergency, the statute requires that at least 24 hours before performing an abortion a physician inform the woman of the nature of the procedure, the health risks of the abortion and of childbirth, and the "probable gestational age of the unborn child." The physician or a qualified nonphysician must inform the woman of the availability of printed materials published by the State describing the fetus and providing information about medical assistance for childbirth, information about child support from the father, and a list of agencies which provide adoption and other services as alternatives to abortion. An abortion may not be performed unless the woman certifies in writing that she has been informed of the availability of these printed materials and has been provided them if she chooses to view them.

* * *

Our analysis of Pennsylvania's 24–hour waiting period between the provision of the information deemed necessary to informed consent and the performance of an abortion under the undue burden standard requires us to reconsider the premise behind the decision in *Akron I* invalidating a parallel requirement. In *Akron I* we said: "Nor are we convinced that the State's legitimate concern that the woman's decision be informed is reasonably served by requiring a 24–hour delay as a matter of course." We consider that conclusion to be wrong. The idea that important decisions will be more informed and deliberate if they follow some period of reflection does not strike us as unreasonable, particularly where the statute directs that important information become part of the background of the decision. The statute, as construed by the Court of Appeals, permits avoidance of the waiting period in the event of a medical emergency and the record evidence shows that in the vast majority of cases, a 24–hour delay does not create any appreciable health risk. In theory, at least, the waiting period is a reasonable measure to implement the State's interest in protecting the life of the unborn, a measure that does not amount to an undue burden.

* * *

Our Constitution is a covenant running from the first generation of Americans to us and then to future generations. It is a coherent succession. Each generation must learn anew that the Constitution's written terms embody ideas and aspirations that must survive more ages than one. We accept our responsibility not to retreat from interpreting the full meaning of the covenant in light of all of our precedents. We invoke it once again to define the freedom guaranteed by the Constitution's own promise, the promise of liberty.

* * *

Notes and Questions

1. Compare *Roe* and *Casey*. On what points do the two courts agree? Disagree? What are the merits of each approach?

2. Abortion opponents have become more visible, better organized, and more violent. In Schenck v. Pro–Choice Network of Western New York, ___ U.S. ___, 117 S.Ct. 855, 137 L.Ed.2d 1 (1997), the Supreme Court upheld a federal injunction against anti-abortion protestors demonstrating outside family planning clinics in so far as it established "fixed buffer zones" around the clinics but withheld its approval of "floating buffer zones." The Court held that there were sufficient government interests—ensuring public safety and order, promoting the free flow of traffic, protecting property rights, and protecting a woman's right to seek pregnancy-related services—to justify an appropriately tailored injunction but that the floating zones burdened speech more than the protection of these interests required.

3. Congress has passed several bans on "partial birth" abortion, but thus far none has survived a presidential veto. As of 1997, laws banning one or another form of partial birth abortion in some or all circumstances had been enacted in Michigan, Ohio, and Utah. *See* Comment, *Michigan's Ban on Partial–Birth Abortions: Balancing Competing Interests*, 75 U. Detroit Mercy L. Rev. 685, 695–97 (1997) (describing and comparing statutes). Michigan's law was declared unconstitutionally vague in Evans v. Kelley, 977 F.Supp. 1283 (E.D.Mich.1997).

4. Nationally, the number of abortions declined during the 1990–1995 period, although increases were registered in a few states. *See* Tamar Lewin, *Abortions Fell Again in 1995, U.S. Says, but Rose in Some Areas Last Year,* N.Y. Times, Dec. 5, 1997, at A10.

SECTION 3. PATERNITY

A. THE PRESUMPTION OF LEGITIMACY

WILLIAM BLACKSTONE, COMMENTARIES ON THE LAWS OF ENGLAND, BOOK 1

Ch. 16, 454–459 (1765).

* * * A bastard, by our English laws, is one that is not only begotten, but born, out of lawful matrimony. The civil and canon laws do not allow a child to remain a bastard, if the parents afterwards intermarry: and herein they differ most materially from our law; which, though not so strict as to require that the child shall be *begotten*, yet makes it an indispensable condition that it shall be *born,* after lawful wedlock * * *

The main end and design of marriage, therefore, being to ascertain and fix upon some certain person, to whom the care, the protection, the maintenance, and the education of the children should belong. * * *

* * * [C]hildren born during wedlock may in some circumstances be bastards. And if the husband be out of the kingdom of England (or, as the law somewhat loosely phrases it, *extra quatuor maria*) for above nine months, so that no access to his wife can be presumed, her issue during that period shall be bastard. But, generally, during the coverture access of the husband shall be presumed, unless the contrary can be shewn; which is such a negative as can only be proved by shewing him to be elsewhere: for the general rule is, *praesumitur pro legitimatione*. * * *

Let us next see the duty of parents to their bastard children, by our law; which principally that of maintenance. For, though bastards are not looked upon as children to any civil purposes, yet the ties of nature, of which maintenance is one, are not so easily dissolved: and they hold indeed as to many other intentions; as, particularly, that a man shall not marry his bastard sister or daughter * * *

The incapacity of a bastard consists principally in this, that he cannot be heir to any one, neither can he have heirs, but of his own body; for, being *nullius filius*, he is therefore of kin to nobody, and has no ancestor from whom any inheritable blood can be derived.

Under the common law, as Blackstone notes, it was possible for a married woman to have an illegitimate child. But, under Lord Mansfield's Rule, first enunciated in Goodright v. Moss, 2 Cowp. 291, 98 Eng. Rep. 1257 (1777), neither spouse could testify to nonaccess by the husband; the result, in a time before blood testing and DNA analysis, was that the marital presumption of legitimacy was almost impossible to rebut.

Today, legitimacy has little bearing on a child's rights [*see* Chapter 9] or his parent's obligations [*see* Chapter 16]. But the determination of paternity, i.e., biological fatherhood, remains important; paternity will typically (although not invariably) establish a legal father-child relationship. State rules governing, and restricting, paternity establishment, thus remain an important determinant of rights and obligations.

MICHAEL H. v. GERALD D.

Supreme Court of the United States, 1989.
491 U.S. 110, 109 S.Ct. 2333, 105 L.Ed.2d 91.

JUSTICE SCALIA announced the judgment of the Court and delivered an opinion, in which THE CHIEF JUSTICE joins, and in all but note 6 of which JUSTICE O'CONNOR and JUSTICE KENNEDY join.

Under California law, a child born to a married woman living with her husband is presumed to be a child of the marriage. Cal.Evid.Code

Ann. § 621 (West Supp. 1989). The presumption of legitimacy may be rebutted only by the husband or wife, and then only in limited circumstances. The instant appeal presents the claim that this presumption infringes upon the due process rights of a man who wishes to establish his paternity of a child born to the wife of another man, and the claim that it infringes upon the constitutional right of the child to maintain a relationship with her natural father.

I

The facts of this case are, we must hope, extraordinary. On May 9, 1976, in Las Vegas, Nevada, Carole D., an international model, and Gerald D., a top executive in a French oil company, were married. The couple established a home in Playa del Rey, California in which they resided as husband and wife when one or the other was not out of the country on business. In the summer of 1978, Carole became involved in an adulterous affair with a neighbor, Michael H. In September 1980, she conceived a child, Victoria D., who was born on May 11, 1981. Gerald was listed as father on the birth certificate and has always held Victoria out to the world as his daughter. Soon after delivery of the child, however, Carole informed Michael that she believed he might be the father.

In the first three years of her life, Victoria remained always with Carole, but found herself within a variety of quasi-family units. In October 1981, Gerald moved to New York City to pursue his business interests, but Carole chose to remain in California. The end of that month, Carole and Michael had blood tests of themselves and Victoria, which showed a 98.07% probability that Michael was Victoria's father. In January 1982, Carole visited Michael in St. Thomas, where his primary business interests were based. There Michael held Victoria out as his child. In March, however, Carole left Michael and returned to California, where she took up residence with yet another man, Scott K. Later that spring, and again in the summer, Carole and Victoria spent time with Gerald in New York City, as well as on vacation in Europe. In the fall, they returned to Scott in California.

In November 1982, rebuffed in his attempts to visit Victoria, Michael filed a filiation action in California Superior Court to establish his paternity and right to visitation. In March 1983, the court appointed an attorney and guardian ad litem to represent Victoria's interests. Victoria then filed a cross-complaint asserting that if she had more than one psychological or *de facto* father, she was entitled to maintain her filial relationship, with all of the attendant rights, duties, and obligations, with both. In May 1983, Carole filed a motion for summary judgment. During this period, from March through July of 1983, Carole was again living with Gerald in New York. In August, however, she returned to California, became involved once again with Michael, and instructed her attorneys to remove the summary judgment motion from the calendar.

For the ensuing eight months, when Michael was not in St. Thomas he lived with Carole and Victoria in Carole's apartment in Los Angeles, and held Victoria out as his daughter. In April 1984, Carole and Michael signed a stipulation that Michael was Victoria's natural father. Carole left Michael the next month, however, and instructed her attorneys not to file the stipulation. In June 1984, Carole reconciled with Gerald and joined him in New York, where they now live with Victoria and two other children since born into the marriage.

In May 1984, Michael and Victoria, through her guardian ad litem, sought visitation rights for Michael *pendente lite*. To assist in determining whether visitation would be in Victoria's best interests, the Superior Court appointed a psychologist to evaluate Victoria, Gerald, Michael, and Carole. The psychologist recommended that Carole retain sole custody, but that Michael be allowed continued contact with Victoria pursuant to a restricted visitation schedule. The court concurred and ordered that Michael be provided with limited visitation privileges *pendente lite*.

On October 19, 1984, Gerald, who had intervened in the action, moved for summary judgment on the ground that under Cal.Evid.Code § 621 there were no triable issues of fact as to Victoria's paternity. This law provides that "the issue of a wife cohabiting with her husband, who is not impotent or sterile, is conclusively presumed to be a child of the marriage." Cal.Evid.Code Ann. § 621(a) (Supp.1989). The presumption may be rebutted by blood tests, but only if a motion for such tests is made, within two years from the date of the child's birth, either by the husband or, if the natural father has filed an affidavit acknowledging paternity, by the wife. §§ 621(c) and (d).

On January 28, 1985, having found that affidavits submitted by Carole and Gerald sufficed to demonstrate that the two were cohabiting at conception and birth and that Gerald was neither sterile nor impotent, the Superior Court granted Gerald's motion for summary judgment, rejecting Michael's and Victoria's challenges to the constitutionality of § 621. The court also denied their motions for continued visitation pending the appeal under Cal.Civ.Code § 4601, which provides that a court may, in its discretion, grant "reasonable visitation rights * * * to any * * * person having an interest in the welfare of the child." Cal.Civ.Code Ann. § 4601 (West Supp.1989). It found that allowing such visitation would "violat[e] the intention of the Legislature by impugning the integrity of the family unit."

* * *

Before us, Michael and Victoria both raise equal protection and due process challenges. *We do not reach Michael's equal protection claim, however, as it was neither raised nor passed upon below* [emphasis added by editor].

II

The California statute that is the subject of this litigation is, in substance, more than a century old. * * * In their present form, the substantive provisions of the statute are as follows:

§ 621. Child of the marriage; notice of motion for blood tests

(a) Except as provided in subdivision (b), the issue of a wife cohabiting with her husband, who is not impotent or sterile, is conclusively presumed to be a child of the marriage.

(b) Notwithstanding the provisions of subdivision (a), if the court finds that the conclusions of all the experts, as disclosed by the evidence based upon blood tests performed pursuant to Chapter 2 (commencing with § 890) of Division 7 are that the husband is not the father of the child, the question of paternity of the husband shall be resolved accordingly.

(c) The notice of motion for blood tests under subdivision (b) may be raised by the husband not later than two years from the child's date of birth.

(d) The notice of motion for blood tests under subdivision (b) may be raised by the mother of the child not later than two years from the child's date of birth if the child's biological father has filed an affidavit with the court acknowledging paternity of the child.

(e) The provisions of subdivision (b) shall not apply to any case coming within the provisions of § 7005 of the Civil Code [dealing with artificial insemination] or to any case in which the wife, with the consent of the husband, conceived by means of a surgical procedure.

III

* * * Michael contends as a matter of substantive due process that because he has established a parental relationship with Victoria, protection of Gerald's and Carole's marital union is an insufficient state interest to support termination of that relationship. This argument is, of course, predicated on the assertion that Michael has a constitutionally protected liberty interest in his relationship with Victoria.

It is an established part of our constitutional jurisprudence that the term "liberty" in the Due Process Clause extends beyond freedom from physical restraint. * * * In an attempt to limit and guide interpretation of the Clause, we have insisted not merely that the interest denominated as a "liberty" be "fundamental" (a concept that, in isolation, is hard to objectify), but also that it be an interest traditionally protected by our society.

* * *

This insistence that the asserted liberty interest be rooted in history and tradition is evident, as elsewhere, in our cases according constitutional protection to certain parental rights. Michael reads the landmark case of *Stanley v. Illinois*, 405 U.S. 645 (1972), and the subsequent cases of *Quilloin v. Walcott*, 434 U.S. 246 (1978), *Caban v. Mohammed*, 441 U.S. 380 (1979) and *Lehr v. Robertson*, [p. 319], as establishing that a liberty interest is created by biological fatherhood plus an established parental relationship—factors that exist in the present case as well. We think that distorts the rationale of those cases. As we view them, they rest not upon such isolated factors but upon the historic respect—indeed, sanctity would not be too strong a term—traditionally accorded to the relationships that develop within the unitary family.[3] In *Stanley,* for example, we forbade the destruction of such a family when, upon the death of the mother, the state had sought to remove children from the custody of a father who had lived with and supported them and their mother for 18 years. As Justice Powell stated for the plurality in *Moore v. East Cleveland* [p. 10]: "Our decisions establish that the Constitution protects the sanctity of the family precisely because the institution of the family is deeply rooted in this Nation's history and tradition."

Thus, the legal issue in the present case reduces to whether the relationship between persons in the situation of Michael and Victoria has been treated as a protected family unit under the historic practices of our society, or whether on any other basis it has been accorded special protection. We think it impossible to find that it has. In fact, quite to the contrary, our traditions have protected the marital family (Gerald, Carole, and the child they acknowledge to be theirs) against the sort of claim Michael asserts.[4]

The presumption of legitimacy was a fundamental principle of the common law. Traditionally, that presumption could be rebutted only by proof that a husband was incapable of procreation or had had no access to his wife during the relevant period.

* * *

We have found nothing in the older sources, nor in the older cases, addressing specifically the power of the natural father to assert parental rights over a child born into a woman's existing marriage with another man. Since it is Michael's burden to establish that such a power (at least where the natural father has established a relationship with the child) is

3. Justice Brennan asserts that only "a pinched conception of 'the family'" would exclude Michael, Carole and Victoria from protection. We disagree. The family unit accorded traditional respect in our society, which we have referred to as the "unitary family," is typified, of course, by the marital family, but also includes the household of unmarried parents and their children. Perhaps the concept can be expanded even beyond this, but it will bear no resemblance to traditionally respected relationships—and will thus cease to have any constitutional significance—if it is stretched so far as to include the relationship established between a married woman, her lover and their child, during a three-month sojourn in St. Thomas, or during a subsequent 8-month period when, if he happened to be in Los Angeles, he stayed with her and the child.

4. Justice Brennan insists that in determining whether a liberty interest exists we must look at Michael's relationship with Victoria in isolation, without reference to the circumstance that Victoria's mother was married to someone else when the child was conceived, and that that woman and her husband wish to raise the child as their own. See *post*, at 2353. We cannot imagine what compels this strange procedure of looking at the act which is assertedly the subject of a liberty interest in isolation from its effect upon other people—rather like inquiring whether there is a liberty interest in firing a gun where the case at hand happens to involve its discharge into another person's body. The logic of Justice Brennan's position leads to the conclusion that if Michael had begotten Victoria by rape, that fact would in no way affect his possession of a liberty interest in his relationship with her.

so deeply embedded within our traditions as to be a fundamental right, the lack of evidence alone might defeat his case. But the evidence shows that even in modern times—when, as we have noted, the rigid protection of the marital family has in other respects been relaxed—the ability of a person in Michael's position to claim paternity has not been generally acknowledged. For example, a 1957 annotation on the subject: "Who may dispute presumption of legitimacy of child conceived or born during wedlock," 53 ALR2d 572, shows three States (including California) with statutes limiting standing to the husband or wife and their descendants, one State (Louisiana) with a statute limiting it to the husband, two States (Florida and Texas) with judicial decisions limiting standing to the husband, and two States (Illinois and New York) with judicial decisions denying standing even to the mother. Not a single decision is set forth specifically according standing to the natural father, and "express indications of the nonexistence of any * * * limitation" upon standing were found only "in a few jurisdictions."

Moreover, even if it were clear that one in Michael's position generally possesses, and has generally always possessed, standing to challenge the marital child's legitimacy, that would still not establish Michael's case. As noted earlier, what is at issue here is not entitlement to a state pronouncement that Victoria was begotten by Michael. It is no conceivable denial of constitutional right for a State to decline to declare facts unless some legal consequence hinges upon the requested declaration. What Michael asserts here is a right to have himself declared the natural father *and thereby to obtain parental prerogatives*.[5] What he must establish, therefore, is not that our society has traditionally allowed a natural father in his circumstances to establish paternity, but that it has traditionally accorded such a father parental rights, or at least has not traditionally denied them. Even if the law in all States had always been that the entire world could challenge the marital presumption and obtain a declaration as to who was the natural father, that would not advance Michael's claim. Thus, it is ultimately irrelevant, even for purposes of determining *current* social attitudes towards the alleged substantive right Michael asserts, that the present law in a number of States appears to allow the natural father—including the natural father who has not established a relationship with the child—the theoretical power to rebut the marital presumption, see Note, *Rebutting the Marital Presumption: A Developed Relationship Test*, 88 Col.L.Rev. 369, 373 (1988). What counts is whether the States in fact award substantive parental rights to the natural father of a child conceived within and born into an extant marital union that wishes to embrace the child. We are

5. According to Justice Brennan, Michael does not claim—and in order to prevail here need not claim-a substantive right to maintain a parental relationship with Victoria, but merely the right to "a hearing on the issue" of his paternity. "Michael's challenge * * * does not depend," we are told, "on his ability ultimately to obtain visitation rights." To be sure it does not depend upon his ability ultimately to *obtain* those rights, but it surely depends upon his *asserting a claim* to those rights, which is precisely what Justice Brennan denies. We cannot grasp the concept of a "right to a hearing" on the part of a person who claims no substantive entitlement that the hearing will assertedly vindicate.

not aware of a single case, old or new, that has done so. This is not the stuff of which fundamental rights qualifying as liberty interests are made.[6]

* * *

... [W]e [have] observed that "[t]he significance of the biological connection is that it offers the natural father an opportunity that no other male possesses to develop a relationship with his offspring," (*Lehr, supra)* and ... assumed that the Constitution might require some protection of that opportunity. Where, however, the child is born into an extant marital family, the natural father's unique opportunity conflicts

6. Justice Brennan criticizes our methodology in using historical traditions specifically relating to the rights of an adulterous natural father, rather that inquiring more generally "whether parenthood is an interest that historically has received our attention and protection." There seems to us no basis for the contention that this methodology is "nove[l]." For example, in *Bowers v. Hardwick*, 478 U.S. 186 (1986), we noted that at the time the Fourteenth Amendment was ratified all but 5 of the 37 States had criminal sodomy laws, that all 50 of the States had such laws prior to 1961, and that 24 States and the District of Columbia continued to have them: and we concluded from that record, regarding that very specific aspect of sexual conduct, that "to claim that a right to engage in such conduct is 'deeply rooted in this Nation's history and tradition' or 'implicit in the concept of ordered liberty' is, at best, facetious." In *Roe v. Wade*, 410 U.S. 113 (1973), we spent about a fifth of our opinion negating the proposition that there was a longstanding tradition of laws proscribing abortion.

We do not understand why, having rejected our focus upon the societal tradition regarding the natural father's rights vis-a-vis a child whose mother is married to another man, Justice Brennan would choose to focus instead upon "parenthood." Why should the relevant category not be even more general—perhaps "family relationships"; or "personal relationships"; or even "emotional attachments in general"? Though the dissent has no basis for the level of generality it would select, we do: We refer to the most specific level at which a relevant tradition protecting, or denying protection to, the asserted right can be identified. If, for example, there were no societal tradition, either way, regarding the rights of the natural father of a child adulterously conceived, we would have to consult, and (if possible) reason from, the traditions regarding natural fathers in general. But there is such a more specific tradition, and it unqualifiedly denies protection to such a parent.

One would think that Justice Brennan would appreciate the value of consulting the most specific tradition available, since he acknowledges that "[e]ven if we can agree * * * that 'family' and 'parenthood' are part of the good life, it is absurd to assume that we can agree on the content of those terms and destructive to pretend that we do." Because such general traditions provide such imprecise guidance, they permit judges to dictate rather than discern the society's views. The need, if arbitrary decision-making is to be avoided, to adopt the most specific tradition as the point of reference-or at least to announce, as Justice Brennan declines to do, some other criterion for selecting among the innumerable relevant traditions that could be consulted-is well enough exemplified by the fact that in the present case Justice Brennan's opinion and Justice O'Connor's opinion, which disapproves this footnote, *both* appeal to tradition, but on the basis of the tradition they select reach opposite results. Although assuredly having the virtue (if it be that) of leaving judges free to decide as they think best when the unanticipated occurs, a rule of law that binds neither by text nor by any particular, identifiable tradition, is no rule of law at all.

Finally, we may note that this analysis is not inconsistent with the result in cases such as *Griswold v. Connecticut* [p. 19], or *Eisenstadt v. Baird*, 405 U.S. 438 (1972). None of those cases acknowledged a longstanding and still extant societal tradition withholding the very right pronounced to be the subject of a liberty interest and then rejected it. Justice Brennan must do so here. In this case, the existence of such a tradition, continuing to the present day, refutes any possible contention that the alleged right is "so rooted in the traditions and conscience of our people as to be ranked as fundamental," or "implicit in the concept of ordered liberty."

with the similarly unique opportunity of the husband of the marriage; and it is not unconstitutional for the State to give categorical preference to the latter.... [A]lthough " '[i]n some circumstances the actual relationship between father and child may suffice to create in the unwed father parental interests comparable to those of the married father,' " " 'the absence of a legal tie with the mother may in such circumstances appropriately place a limit on whatever substantive constitutional claims might otherwise exist.' " *Caban, supra* at 397, (Stewart J., dissenting) In accord with our traditions, a limit is also imposed by the circumstance that the mother is, at the time of the child's conception and birth, married to and cohabitating with another man, both of whom wish to raise the child as the offspring of their union.[7] It is a question of legislative policy and not constitutional law whether California will allow the presumed parenthood of a couple desiring to retain a child conceived within and born into their marriage to be rebutted.

We do not accept Justice Brennan's criticism that this result "squashes" the liberty that consists of "the freedom not to conform." It seems to us that reflects the erroneous view that there is only one side to this controversy-that one disposition can expand a "liberty" of sorts without contracting an equivalent "liberty" on the other side. Such a happy choice is rarely available. Here, to *provide* protection to an adulterous natural father is to *deny* protection to a marital father, and vice versa. If Michael has a "freedom not to conform" (whatever that means), Gerald must equivalently have a "freedom to conform." One of them will pay a price for asserting that "freedom"—Michael by being unable to act as father of the child he has adulterously begotten, or Gerald by being unable to preserve the integrity of the traditional family unit he and Victoria have established. Our disposition does not choose between these two "freedoms," but leaves that to the people of California. Justice Brennan's approach chooses one of them as the constitutional imperative, on no apparent basis except that the unconventional is to be preferred.

IV

We have never had occasion to decide whether a child has a liberty interest, symmetrical with that of her parent, in maintaining her filial relationship. We need not do so here because, even assuming that such a

7. Justice Brennan chides us for thus limiting our holding to situations in which, as here, the husband and wife wish to raise her child jointly. The dissent believes that without this limitation we would be unable to "rely on the State's asserted interest in protecting the 'unitary family' in denying that Michael and Victoria have been deprived of liberty." As we have sought to make clear, however, and as the dissent elsewhere seems to understand, we rest our decision not upon our independent "balancing" of such interests, but upon the absence of any constitutionally protected right to legal parentage on the part of an adulterous natural father in Michael's situation, as evidenced by long tradition. That tradition reflects a "balancing" that has already been made by society itself. We limit our pronouncement to the relevant facts of this case because it is at least possible that our traditions lead to a different conclusion with regard to adulterous fathering of a child whom the marital parents do not wish to raise as their own. It seems unfair for those who disagree with our holding to include among their criticisms that we have not extended the holding more broadly.

right exists, Victoria's claim must fail. Victoria's due process challenge is, if anything, weaker than Michael's. Her basic claim is not that California has erred in preventing her from establishing that Michael, not Gerald, should stand as her legal father. Rather, she claims a due process right to maintain filial relationships with both Michael and Gerald. This assertion merits little discussion, for, whatever the merits of the guardian ad litem's belief that such an arrangement can be of great psychological benefit to a child, the claim that a State must recognize multiple fatherhood has no support in the history or traditions of this country. Moreover, even if we were to construe Victoria's argument as forwarding the lesser proposition that, whatever her status vis-a-vis Gerald, she has a liberty interest in maintaining a filial relationship with her natural father, Michael, we find that, at best, her claim is the obverse of Michael's and fails for the same reasons.

Victoria claims in addition that her equal protection rights have been violated because, unlike her mother and presumed father, she had no opportunity to rebut the presumption of her legitimacy. We find this argument wholly without merit. We reject, at the outset, Victoria's suggestion that her equal protection challenge must be assessed under a standard of strict scrutiny because, in denying her the right to maintain a filial relationship with Michael, the State is discriminating against her on the basis of her illegitimacy. See Gomez v. Perez, 409 U.S. 535, 538 (1973). Illegitimacy is a legal construct, not a natural trait. Under California law, Victoria is not illegitimate, and she is treated in the same manner as all other legitimate children: she is entitled to maintain a filial relationship with her legal parents.

We apply, therefore, the ordinary "rational relationship" test to Victoria's equal protection challenge. The primary rationale underlying § 621's limitation on those who may rebut the presumption of legitimacy is a concern that allowing persons other than the husband or wife to do so may undermine the integrity of the marital union. When the husband or wife contests the legitimacy of their child, the stability of the marriage has already been shaken. In contrast, allowing a claim of illegitimacy to be pressed by the child-or, more accurately, by a court-appointed guardian ad litem-may well disrupt an otherwise peaceful union. Since it pursues a legitimate end by rational means, California's decision to treat Victoria differently from her parents is not a denial of equal protection.

The judgment of the California Court of Appeal is Affirmed.

Notes and Questions

1. *Michael H.* is only one (but *the* one to reach the U.S. Supreme Court) of a line of cases in which unmarried fathers have challenged the presumption of legitimacy. Most of these challenges have been brought on equal protection grounds. Because the Supreme Court did not consider the equal protection argument, the precedential value of the plurality opinion in *Michael H.* is limited. The Supreme Court refused to grant cert. in A. v. X., Y., and Z., 641 P.2d 1222 (Wyo.1982), cert. denied 459

U.S. 1021, 103 S.Ct. 388, 74 L.Ed.2d 518 (1982), in which the equal protection issue was squarely presented to the Wyoming Supreme Court:

> * * * As reflected in its opinion letter, the trial court properly found that:
>
> * * * the State has an interest in protecting and preserving the integrity of the family unit. * * * It also has an interest in protecting the best interests of the child. Even in this era of no-fault divorce, frequent premarital sex and cohabitation and new attitudes toward child rearing, a child has a right to legitimacy and that right is one the State is bound to protect during minority.
>
> * * *
>
> The statute is a legitimate attempt by the legislature to protect the family unit and the children from external forces. A suit by one outside the marriage, such as in this case, could well destroy a marriage. * * * [Appellant] is concerned that the mother (actually those within the family unit-the child, the mother, and the presumed father) can bring a parentage action which would have the same deleterious effect on the marriage as would a suit by an outsider. But, the members of the family, not the outsider, are in the best position to judge whether the marriage can stand the trauma or has already failed. * * *

With *X.Y.Z.* and *Michael H.*, compare the decision in In re Paternity of C.A.S., 161 Wis.2d 1015, 468 N.W.2d 719 (1991):

> We do not . . . suggest that a putative father may never have a constitutionally protected right to establish his parentage of an illegitimate child. Rather, we conclude that if a putative father of a child born to the wife of another man has not established an actual relationship with that child, he does not have a constitutionally protected interest in establishing his parentage of the child, or in a relationship with that child. * * * An existing marital unit is not a per se bar to a blood test, however. Ultimately, it is the manner in which this unit contributes to the best interests of the children that renders it significant. The best interests of the children are the ultimate and paramount considerations in this case, and reflect a strong public policy of this state. * * *

Is the approach of *C.A.S.* likely to produce more or less litigation than that of *X.Y.Z.*? What values are served by each approach? *See also* In re J.W.T., 872 S.W.2d 189 (Tex.1994); G.F.C. v. S.G., 686 So.2d 1382 (Fla.App.1997); Bodwell v. Brooks, 141 N.H. 508, 686 A.2d 1179 (1996).

2. The Uniform Parentage Act (UPA), 9B U.L.A. 295, has been adopted in nearly half of the states. The Act provides:

§ 4.

(a) A man is presumed to be the natural father of a child if:

(1) he and the child's natural mother are or have been married to each other and the child is born during the marriage, or within

300 days after the marriage is terminated by death, annulment, declaration of invalidity, or divorce, or after a decree of separation is entered by the court;

(2) before the child's birth, he and the child's natural mother have attempted to marry each other by a marriage solemnized in apparent compliance with law, although the attempted marriage is or could be declared invalid, and,

(i) if the attempted marriage could be declared invalid only by a court, the child is born during the attempted marriage, or within 300 days after its termination by death, annulment, declaration of invalidity, or divorce; or

(ii) if the attempted marriage is invalid without a court order, the child is born within 300 days after the termination of cohabitation;

(3) after the child's birth, he and the child's natural mother have married, or attempted to marry, each other by a marriage solemnized in apparent compliance with law, although the attempted marriage is or could be declared invalid, and

(i) he has acknowledged his paternity of the child in writing filed with the [appropriate court or Vital Statistics Bureau],

(ii) with his consent, he is named as the child's father on the child's birth certificate, or

(iii) he is obligated to support the child under a written voluntary promise or by court order;

(4) while the child is under the age of majority, he receives the child into his home and openly holds out the child as his natural child; or

(5) he acknowledges his paternity of the child in a writing filed with the [appropriate court or Vital Statistics Bureau], which shall promptly inform the mother of the filing of the acknowledgment, and she does not dispute the acknowledgment within a reasonable time after being informed thereof, in a writing filed with the [appropriate court or Vital Statistics Bureau]. If another man is presumed under this section to be the child's father, acknowledgment may be effected only with the written consent of the presumed father or after the presumption has been rebutted.

(b) A presumption under this section may be rebutted in an appropriate action only by clear and convincing evidence. If two or more presumptions arise which conflict with each other, the presumption which on the facts is founded on the weightier considerations of policy and logic controls. The presumption is rebutted by a court decree establishing paternity of the child by another man.

§ 6.

(a) A child, his natural mother, or a man presumed to be his father under Paragraph (1), (2), or (3) of § 4(a), may bring an action

(1) at any time for the purpose of declaring the existence of the father and child relationship presumed under Paragraph (1), (2), or (3) of § 4(a); or

(2) for the purpose of declaring the non-existence of the father and child relationship presumed under Paragraph (1), (2), or (3) of § 4(a) only if the action is brought within a reasonable time after obtaining knowledge of relevant facts, but in no event later than [5] years after the child's birth. After the presumption has been rebutted, paternity of the child by another man may be determined in the same action, if he has been made a party.

(b) Any interested party may bring an action at any time for the purpose of determining the existence or non-existence of the father and child relationship presumed under Paragraph (4) or (5) of § 4(a).

(c) An action to determine the existence of the father and child relationship with respect to a child who has no presumed father under § 4 may be brought by the child, the mother or personal representative of the child, the [appropriate state agency], the personal representative or a parent of the mother if the mother has died, a man alleged or alleging himself to be the father, or the personal representative or a parent of the alleged father if the alleged father has died or is a minor.

(d) Regardless of its terms, an agreement, other than an agreement approved by the court in accordance with § 13(b), between an alleged or presumed father and the mother or child, does not bar an action under this section.

§ 7.

An action to determine the existence of the father and child relationship as to a child who has no presumed father under § 4 may not be brought later than [3] years after the birth of the child, or later than [3] years after the effective date of this Act, whichever is later. However, an action brought by or on behalf of a child whose paternity has not been determined is not barred until [3] years after the child reaches the age of majority. Sections 6 and 7 do not extend the time within which a right of inheritance or a right to a succession may be asserted beyond the time provided by law relating to distribution and closing of decedents' estates or to the determination of heirship, or otherwise.

3. A year after Tom was divorced from Jenny and agreed to pay child support pursuant to a marital separation agreement, he discovered that he is now and has always been sterile. Can Tom reopen the divorce judgment? What if he found out within a year of the divorce but did not mention it until six years later when the mother brought an action for increased child support for a sixteen-year-old? *See* Wilson v. Wilson, 16 Kan.App.2d 651, 827 P.2d 788 (1992); Anderson v. Anderson, 407 Mass. 251, 552 N.E.2d 546 (1990) (res judicata principles apply); Gilbraith v.

Hixson, 32 Ohio St.3d 127, 512 N.E.2d 956 (1987) (same); Watts v. Watts, 115 N.H. 186, 337 A.2d 350 (1975) (husband is estopped because of the prejudice to the children); Guise v. Robinson, 219 Mich.App. 139, 555 N.W.2d 887 (1996). How does the use of estoppel and res judicata principles differ from the conclusive presumption of legitimacy?

4. As an alternative to the identification of *one* legal father, in a case like *Michael H.* would it make sense to establish a legal relationship between the child and *both* her mother's husband and biological father? What are the pros and cons of this approach? *See* Bodwell v. Brooks, 141 N.H. 508, 686 A.2d 1179 (1996); Smith v. Dison, 662 So.2d 90, 94 (La.App.1995).

Problem 6–1:

When Ann and Robert divorced, they were granted joint custody of Susan, born during their marriage; Robert was also required to pay child support. Four years later, Ann filed a petition in which she alleged that Robert was not the biological father of Susan and sought blood tests to prove it. Under the UPA, does Ann have standing? Should the judge order blood tests? *See* Sanders v. Sanders, 384 Pa.Super. 311, 558 A.2d 556 (1989).

Problem 6–2:

Two children were born to Mary during her marriage to Tom. During a mediation session in connection with Tom and Mary's divorce, Mary mentioned that Larry was the biological father of both of her children. After blood tests confirmed Mary's assertion, Tom brought an action to establish Larry's paternity. Under state law, a child born to a married woman who cohabits with her husband is conclusively presumed to be a child of the marriage if the husband is not impotent or sterile. But state law also provides that the court *must* order blood tests to resolve an issue of paternity when a proper motion is filed within two years of the child's birth; Tom filed his motion before either of Mary's children reached the age of two. Does the presumption of legitimacy trump the blood test requirement, or vice versa? Would it make a difference if Tom wants to maintain his relationship with his children but avoid a support obligation? *See* In re Marriage of Rebecca R. & David R., 62 Cal.Rptr.2d 730, (Cal.1997) (not officially published), affirming 46 Cal.App.4th 431, 53 Cal.Rptr.2d 870 (1996).

Problem 6–3:

Ron and Sharon are in the process of obtaining a divorce. Sharon is pregnant and Ron is pretty sure it is not his child. Ron and Sharon enter into an agreement which specifies that Ron waives all parental rights to the child Sharon is carrying and is relieved of all obligations to pay support. The child is born two months later. Is the child (or the divorce court) bound by Ron and Sharon's agreement? *See* Casbar v. Dicanio, 666 So.2d 1028 (Fla.App.1996).

B. REMOVING THE STIGMA OF ILLEGITIMACY

Common law disabilities based on a child's illegitimacy were maintained well into the twentieth century. As late as the 1960s, in most states an illegitimate child had no right to inherit from his or her father, no right to bear the father's name, and no right to public benefits for wrongful death, workers' compensation, insurance and social security; some denied the illegitimate child paternal support. *See* Harry Krause, *Equal Protection for the Illegitimate*, 65 MICH. L. REV. 477 (1967).

In 1968, the Supreme Court initiated a sweeping revision of the law of illegitimacy. In more than thirty decisions issued since that time, the Court has utilized the Equal Protection and Due Process Clauses to invalidate nearly all forms of legal discrimination against nonmarital children.

LEVY v. LOUISIANA

Supreme Court of the United States, 1968.
391 U.S. 68, 88 S.Ct. 1509, 20 L.Ed.2d 436.

JUSTICE DOUGLAS delivered the opinion of the Court.

Appellant sued on behalf of five illegitimate children to recover, under a Louisiana statute for two kinds of damages as a result of the wrongful death of their mother: (1) the damages to them for the loss of their mother; and (2) those based on the survival of a cause of action which the mother had at the time of her death for pain and suffering. Appellees are the doctor who treated her and the insurance company.

We assume in the present state of the pleadings that the mother, Louise Levy, gave birth to these five illegitimate children and that they lived with her; that she treated them as a parent would treat any other child; that she worked as a domestic servant to support them, taking them to church every Sunday and enrolling them, at her own expense, in a parochial school. [The trial court's dismissal was affirmed by the Louisiana Court of Appeal which held that the "child" in Article 2315 meant "legitimate child." Denial of an action to illegitimate children was "based on morals and general welfare because it discourages bringing children into the world out of wedlock." 192 So.2d 193, 195. The Supreme Court of Louisiana denied certiorari.]

* * *

We start from the premise that illegitimate children are not "nonpersons." They are humans, live, and have their being. They are clearly "persons" within the meaning of the Equal Protection Clause of the Fourteenth Amendment.

While a State has broad power when it comes to making classifications it may not draw a line which constitutes an invidious discrimination against a particular class. Though the test has been variously stated, the end result is whether the line drawn is a rational one.

In applying the Equal Protection Clause to social and economic legislation, we give great latitude to the legislature in making classifications. Even so, would a corporation, which is a "person," for certain purposes, within the meaning of the Equal Protection Clause be required to forgo recovery for wrongs done its interest because its incorporators were all bastards? However that might be, we have been extremely sensitive when it comes to basic civil rights and have not hesitated to strike down an invidious classification even though it had history and tradition on its side. The rights asserted here involve the intimate, familial relationship between a child and his own mother. When the child's claim of damage for loss of his mother is in issue, why, in terms of "equal protection," should the tortfeasors go free merely because the child is illegitimate? Why should the illegitimate child be denied rights merely because of his birth out of wedlock? He certainly is subject to all the responsibilities of a citizen, including the payment of taxes and conscription under the Selective Service Act. How under our constitutional regime can he be denied correlative rights which other citizens enjoy?

Legitimacy or illegitimacy of birth has no relation to the nature of the wrong allegedly inflicted on the mother. These children, though illegitimate, were dependent on her; she cared for them and nurtured them; they were indeed hers in the biological and in the spiritual sense; in her death they suffered wrong in the sense that any dependent would.

We conclude that it is invidious to discriminate against them when no action, conduct, or demeanor of theirs is possibly relevant to the harm that was done the mother.

Notes and Questions

1. In Glona v. American Guarantee & Liability Ins. Co., 391 U.S. 73, 88 S.Ct. 1515, 20 L.Ed.2d 441 (1968), a companion case to *Levy*, the Court struck down Louisiana's wrongful death statute, which barred recovery of damages by the mother of an illegitimate child but allowed recovery by the parents of a legitimate child. In Weber v. Aetna Casualty & Surety Co., 406 U.S. 164, 92 S.Ct. 1400, 31 L.Ed.2d 768 (1972), the Court held that a state law which denied worker's compensation benefits to nonmarital dependent children violated both the Equal Protection and Due Process clauses of the Fourteenth Amendment. The right of a nonmarital child to be supported by his or her father was established in Gomez v. Perez, 409 U.S. 535, 93 S.Ct. 872, 35 L.Ed.2d 56 (1973).

2. Laws governing intestate succession have traditionally been a major source of discrimination against nonmarital children. On this issue, the Supreme Court has had more difficulty enunciating clear guidelines. In Labine v. Vincent, 401 U.S. 532, 91 S.Ct. 1017, 28 L.Ed.2d 288 (1971), the Court upheld a Louisiana law denying a right to intestate succession to a nonmarital child whose father had acknowledged her during his lifetime. But in Trimble v. Gordon, 430 U.S. 762, 97 S.Ct. 1459, 52 L.Ed.2d 31 (1977), the Court (5–4) utilized "intermediate

scrutiny" to strike down an Illinois statute which denied nonmarital children a right to intestate succession unless the child's parents married, essentially overruling *Labine*. The Supreme Court indicated that:

> * * * [f]or at least some significant categories of illegitimate children of intestate men, inheritance rights can be recognized without jeopardizing the orderly settlement of estates or the dependability of titles to property passing under intestacy laws. Because it excludes those categories of illegitimate children unnecessarily, § 12 is constitutionally flawed. * * *

A year later, Justice Powell, who wrote the opinion in *Trimble*, found himself allied with the dissenters. In Lalli v. Lalli, 439 U.S. 259, 99 S.Ct. 518, 58 L.Ed.2d 503 (1978), again using "intermediate scrutiny," the Court (5–4) upheld a New York statute which conditioned a nonmarital child's right to intestate succession on the judicial establishment of paternity during the father's lifetime. The court stated that:

> The primary state goal underlying the challenged aspects of § 4–1.2 is to provide for the just and orderly disposition of property at death. We long have recognized that this is an area with which the States have an interest of considerable magnitude ... This interest is directly implicated in paternal inheritance by illegitimate children because of the peculiar problems of proof that are involved. Establishing maternity is seldom difficult. * * * Proof of paternity, by contrast, frequently is difficult when the father is not part of a formal family unit* * *.

Unsurprisingly, the Court's "see-saw" jurisprudence on the inheritance rights of nonmarital children has been difficult for lower courts and state legislatures to apply. *See* HARRY KRAUSE, CHILD SUPPORT IN AMERICA: THE LEGAL PERSPECTIVE 119–62 (1981).

4. A dependent nonmarital child is entitled to Social Security survivor's benefits if he or she has been formally recognized (through a written acknowledgment, paternity proceeding, or court order of support) prior to the death of the alleged father. 42 U.S.C.A. § 416(h)(3)(C)(i)(1994). If there has been no formal recognition of the child prior to the death of the alleged father, the Secretary may determine paternity based on: 1) the evidentiary standard contained in the relevant state intestacy law (42 U.S.C.A. § 416(h)(2)(A)(1994)); or 2) evidence "satisfactory to the Secretary" that the deceased was the father of the applicant and lived with or contributed to the support of the child (42 U.S.C.A. § 416(h)(3)(C)(ii)(1994)). *See* Daniels, on Behalf of Daniels v. Sullivan, 979 F.2d 1516 (11th Cir.1992) (court refused to read Georgia intestacy law requiring paternity establishment during father's lifetime into federal law); Bennemon v. Sullivan, 914 F.2d 987 (7th Cir.1990) (no benefits where child had not been born when alleged father died and there was no proof of support).

Problem 6–4:

Under state law, a nonmarital child has no right to intestate succession unless paternity was established during the lifetime of the alleged father. Jane and John had a sexual relationship but did not live together. Jane became pregnant but did not get a chance to tell John before he was killed in a car accident. John, age 24, comes from a wealthy family and has left no heirs except his parents. What, if any, constitutional arguments are available to Jane on behalf of her child? to the State? What result?

Problem 6–5:

8 U.S.C.A. § 1409(a) confers U.S. citizenship on an illegitimate child born outside of the United States if child is born to a citizen mother and alien father but not if the child is born to a citizen father and alien mother. Ann, a Bosnian citizen, and Tom, a U.S. citizen stationed in Bosnia, had an affair leading to the birth of their child in Bosnia. What constitutional arguments are available to Ann on behalf of her child? to the federal government? What result? *See* Miller v. Christopher, 96 F.3d 1467 (D.C.Cir.1996), cert. granted 4/28/97.

C. ESTABLISHING PATERNITY

The paternity action evolved from the criminal law; from its inception the action was designed to assist welfare authorities, on whom the burden of supporting the child would fall if the father could not be held responsible:

> ... The first such statute was enacted in England in 1576 and labeled 'An Act for Setting the Poor on Work.' It provided as follows:
>
> "Concerning bastards begotten and born out of lawful matrimony (an offence against God's law and man's law) the said bastards being now left to be kept at the charges of the parish where they be born, to the great burden of the same parish, and in defrauding of the relief of the impotent and aged true poor of the same parish, and to the evil example and encouragement of the lewd life: (2) It is ordained and enacted by the authority aforesaid, That two Justices of the peace (whereof one to be of the *quorum*, in or next unto the limits where the parish church is, within which parish such bastard shall be born, upon examination of the cause and circumstance) shall and may by their discretion take order, as well for the punishment of the mother and reputed father of such bastard child, as also for the better relief of every such parish in part or in all; (3) and shall and may likewise by such discretion take order for the keeping of every such bastard child, by charging such mother or reputed father with the payment of money weekly or other sustentation for the relief of such child in such wise as they shall think meet and convenient." * * *
>
> The attitude that the paternity action is brought primarily for the benefit of the public persists. * * * Throughout most of the country, the action remains of limited scope, the primary and usually sole objective being to charge the father with a limited duty to support his illegitimate child. Only a few statutes allow the court to confer

> legitimate status on the child in the paternity proceeding or award inheritance rights in addition to support. * * *
>
> Paternity practice has suffered from the old saw to the effect that 'maternity is a matter of fact whereas paternity is a matter of opinion.' * * * Current paternity prosecution practice in many metropolitan areas is abhorrent. Blackmail and perjury flourish, accusation is often tantamount to conviction, decades of support obligation are decided upon in minutes of court time and indigent defendants usually go without counsel or a clear understanding of what is involved.
>
> HARRY KRAUSE, ILLEGITIMACY: LAW AND SOCIAL POLICY 105 (1971).

At the time Professor Krause wrote, state paternity laws were quite varied. A few states retained remnants of the common law bastardy action, which permitted a paternity claim to be made on behalf of the child throughout the child's minority. *See* Doughty v. Engler, 112 Kan. 583, 211 P. 619 (1923). Either in addition to or in lieu of the bastardy action, several states had laws which permitted the mother to bring an action to obtain child support and recover expenses related to pregnancy and child birth; these statutes usually had statutes of limitation that required initiation of such an action within one to two years of the child's birth. Few states made provision, other than a declaratory judgment action, to allow fathers to establish their paternity. *See* Slawek v. Stroh, 62 Wis.2d 295, 215 N.W.2d 9 (1974).

Paternity trials at this time typically turned on circumstantial evidence (dates of intercourse compared with date of birth) and the credibility of the parties. Because the defendant could escape liability by using the defense of *exception plurium concubenium* (i.e., that other men had had sexual relations with the mother during the period of conception), the mother's virtue was often a major focus of the litigation. *See* Jane L. v. Rodney B., 111 Misc.2d 761, 444 N.Y.S.2d 1012 (1981); Stephen Sass, *The Defense of Multiple Access (Exception Plurium Concubentium) in Paternity Suits: A Comparative Analysis*, 51 TULANE L. REV. 468 (1977). Some states allowed jury trials; some treated the paternity action as quasi-criminal and required the plaintiff to prove parentage by clear and convincing evidence.

With the advent of paternity blood testing, the focus of paternity litigation shifted dramatically. UPA § 11 provides that:

> (a) The court may, and upon request of a party shall, require the child, mother, or alleged father to submit to blood tests. The tests shall be performed by an expert qualified as an examiner of blood types, appointed by the court.
>
> (b) The court, upon reasonable request by a party, shall order that independent tests be performed by other experts qualified as examiners of blood types.
>
> (c) In all cases, the court shall determine the number and qualifications of the experts.

HANSON v. HANSON

Supreme Court of Minnesota, 1977.
311 Minn. 388, 249 N.W.2d 452.

TODD, JUSTICE.

Charles W. Hanson petitioned district court for dissolution of marriage from Joann B. Hanson. At trial, the husband presented evidence of blood grouping tests which established he was not the father of the minor child born to his wife during their marriage. This evidence was not rebutted, and based on the record before it, the trial court found the husband not to be the father and refused to grant to the wife support for the minor child. We affirm. * * *

This court in considering the legitimacy of children born during wedlock has held that there is a presumption of legitimacy, but that such presumption may be rebutted by the results of reliable blood tests, conducted by impartial physicians, which establish nonpaternity . . . In this case, the evidence presented by the husband was reliable, impartial, and not rebutted by another evidence.

Minnesota, unlike some states, has not adopted any statute specifying the amount of weight to be given exclusionary results of blood grouping tests. Some jurisdictions only allow blood tests indicating nonpaternity to be given the same weight as other evidence. Another group of jurisdictions holds that while test results excluding paternity are not conclusive, they should be given considerable weight in rebutting the presumption. A third group of jurisdictions has ruled that a blood grouping test, properly conducted, which excludes paternity is conclusive. * * *

The record in this case would compel a finding of nonpaternity under each of the above standards.

Notes and Questions

1. *Paternity testing:* The blood tests described in the *Hanson* opinion were so-called "exclusionary" blood tests. Both the ABO–MN and Rh–Hr tests, commonly known as the Lansteiner blood grouping tests, utilized factors found within red blood cells. Red blood cell groupings could conclusively eliminate the possibility of paternity; for example, two persons with type O blood could not produce a child with type A blood. But the tests were incapable of proving parentage because the probability of paternity based solely upon nonexclusion was not high. *See* Jack P. Abbott and Kenneth W. Sell, *Joint AMA–ABA Guidelines: Present Status of Serologic Testing in Problems of Disputed Parentage,* 10 FAM. L. Q. 247 (1976). Some courts were reluctant to permit the use of exclusionary blood tests as evidence of paternity unless the exclusion rate exceeded 90%. *See* State ex rel Hausner v. Blackman, 233 Kan. 223, 662 P.2d 1183 (1983).

Human leukocyte or lymphocyte antigen (HLA) tissue tests, developed in the late 1960s to match tissue types for organ transplant operations, began to come into use for paternity testing by the late 1970s. In contrast to the exclusionary tests, HLA testing can be used to affirmatively establish the probability that a particular man is the father of a particular child. *See* Ira Ellman & David Kaye, *Probabilities and Proof: Can HLA and Blood Group Testing Prove Paternity?*, 54 N.Y.U.L. Rev. 1131 (1979). *See also* American Association of Blood Banks, Inclusion Probabilities in Paternity Testing (1983). For discussions of the use and misuse of probabilistic evidence of paternity, *see* Plemel v. Walter, 303 Or. 262, 735 P.2d 1209 (1987); David H. Kaye, *Plemel as a Primer for Proving Paternity*, 24 Willamette L. Rev. 867 (1988).

DNA, or "genetic marker" testing now offers an even more certain method of establishing paternity. By matching DNA samples from the child and one parent, it is possible to determine which portion of the child's DNA came from the other parent. If the suspected parent's DNA matches the child's DNA and is not attributable to the known parent, there is a very high probability that the suspect is the child's parent. *See* David H. Kaye, *DNA Paternity Probabilities*, 24 Fam. L. Q. 268 (1990). Genetic marker testing can be done with many different types of specimens—blood, body tissue, fluid, sperm and bone—but buccal swab testing is most typical. *See* Cable v. Anthou, 449 Pa.Super. 553, 674 A.2d 732 (1996) (buccal swab DNA tests are accepted by scientific community and thus are admissible in paternity proceeding). Genetic marker testing technology continues to change and pose new legal issues. *See* Spencer v. Commonwealth, 240 Va. 78, 393 S.E.2d 609, cert. denied 498 U.S. 908, 111 S.Ct. 281, 112 L.Ed.2d 235 (1990) (analyzing admissibility of "PCR" genetic marker tests).

2. *Admissibility and Evidentiary Weight of Genetic Marker Tests:* Genetic marker tests to establish paternity are admissible in all states if the testing is performed by an accredited laboratory. *See* Kan. Stat. Ann. § 38–1118 (Supp. 1996) (verified written report of the experts is considered stipulated to unless written notice of intent to challenge is given not more than 20 days after receipt of the report but not less than 10 days before a hearing); N.C. Gen. Stat. § 8–50.1(b1). Some state laws allow the trier of fact to find against the paternity defendant who refuses to submit to blood testing; most courts have upheld these laws against constitutional challenges. *See* In re J.M., 590 So.2d 565 (La.1991) (discussing cases). Since 1993, the federal government has required the states to employ procedures in paternity actions that establish a rebuttable or conclusive presumption of paternity when the results of genetic marker tests meet or surpass a threshold probability of paternity. *See* 42 U.S.C.A. §§ 666(5)(F), 666(5)(G); Cal. Fam. Code § 7555; Fla. Stat. Ann. § 742.12(1); Ohio Rev. Code Ann. § 3111.03(6).

3. *Payment for genetic testing:* In Little v. Streater, 452 U.S. 1, 101 S.Ct. 2202, 68 L.Ed.2d 627 (1981), the Supreme Court held that the state must pay for blood tests requested by indigent civil paternity defendants in some instances. The *Little* case began when the child's mother, on

public assistance, was required to identify the father so that the state could initiate a paternity action to recoup some of its assistance payments to the child. Although such an action was, in form, a private civil action by the mother against the alleged father, a state attorney represented the mother and the state would be the primary beneficiary of any support ordered on behalf of the child. The *Little* court thus concluded that "state action . . . pervaded this case." But the precedential value of *Little* is limited by the fact that the action was tried under an unusual evidentiary rule that shifted the burden of persuasion to the paternity defendant, a fact relied on by the *Little* court in concluding that state payment was required.

The federal Family Support Act (42 U.S.C.A. § 466(a)(5)(B)) now requires states to provide for genetic testing of the child and all parties in a contested paternity proceeding when the child is a public assistance recipient.

4. *Post-mortem genetic marker testing:* Because genetic marker tests can be performed on cadavers, courts have recently been confronted with requests for exhumation of a deceased alleged parent. *See* Estate of Greenwood, 402 Pa.Super. 536, 587 A.2d 749 (1991), app. den'd 529 Pa. 634, 600 A.2d 953 (Pa. 1991) (ordering release of blood specimens from the coroner so that child could attempt to establish paternity); Wawrykow v. Simonich, 438 Pa.Super. 340, 652 A.2d 843 (1994) (ordering exhumation of alleged father's body); Batcheldor v. Boyd, 108 N.C.App. 275, 423 S.E.2d 810 (1992), rev. denied, 333 N.C. 254, 426 S.E.2d 700 (1993) (same). Should the court's response to such a petition depend on whether the child has a legal father or if the child has reached adulthood? *See* In re Estate of Foley, 22 Kan.App.2d 959, 925 P.2d 449 (1996) (no).

G.E.B. v. S.R.W.

Massachusetts Supreme Judicial Court, 1996.
422 Mass. 158, 661 N.E.2d 646.

ABRAMS, JUSTICE.

The child brought an action in the Probate and Family Court Department for a judgment of paternity under G.L. c. 209C. The complaint was amended to name the mother as a plaintiff in response to the defendant's claim that the child could not litigate on her own behalf but rather only through a next friend. The putative father (defendant) moved to dismiss the child's action on the ground that the action is barred by his previous action for declaratory relief brought in June, 1982, against the mother and by the settlement agreement that followed. * * *

On November 30, 1990, a Probate Court judge ordered that the issues of paternity and support be bifurcated and that the parties proceed first on the issue of paternity. On October 10, 1991, a judgment of paternity was entered in favor of the child and, in a separate ruling, temporary child support and counsel fees were ordered. The defendant appeals * * *[. W]e affirm.

* * *

Facts. The child was born on February 22, 1982, to the mother, who was not then married and had not been married within 300 days prior the child's birth. The mother asserts that the defendant, with whom she had a sexual relationship for approximately one decade, is the child's father. The defendant disputes this.

In June, 1982, the defendant sought a declaratory judgment against the mother that he was not the child's father. The child was not a party to that action nor was she represented by counsel. Neither a guardian nor next friend was appointed to safeguard the child's interests. That case was settled by an agreement for judgment signed by counsel for the defendant and counsel for the mother. The mother and the defendant also signed a settlement agreement under which the defendant was to pay the mother $25,000 in exchange for the mother's assent to a stipulation stating that the defendant was not the child's father. The agreement purported to be signed by the mother "acting on her own behalf and on behalf of a daughter born to her on February 22, 1982," and provided that neither party would bring any further action or claim arising out of the facts giving rise to the case being settled. The agreement specifically provided that it "shall be binding upon the successors, representatives, heirs and assigns of both parties including, without limitation, the child." The child did not sign the agreement and the agreement did not provide that the money be used for child support. The stipulation was not signed by a judge of the Superior Court nor filed with the Superior Court.

On August 2, 1990, the child brought an action under G.L. c. 209C against the defendant. Genetic marker tests were performed. The plaintiff's expert, Dr. David H. Bing, opined that these tests showed the statistical probability of the defendant's paternity to be 99.8%. The paternity tests performed would have excluded 98.63% of falsely accused men as the father. The trial judge also found a physical resemblance between the defendant and the child in facial bone structure and complexion.

Res judicata effect of 1982 Adjudication under G.L. c. 273. General Laws c. 209C, § 22(d), provides: "No proceeding hereunder shall be barred by a prior finding or adjudication under any repealed sections of [c. 273] or by the fact that a child was born prior to the effective date of this chapter." The parties dispute whether the 1982 action was an adjudication under a repealed section of c. 273. A Probate Court judge found that the subject matter of the prior proceeding was similar in nature to proceedings under G.L. c. 273, § 12, and did not bar a proceeding under c. 209C. We agree. The defendant, as plaintiff in the 1982 action, relied on G.L. c. 273, § 12A, in litigating his claim. The mother, as defendant, counterclaimed for "an adjudication under G.L. c. 273, § 12, that [the defendant] is the father of [the child]." It is clear that the parties, in signing the settlement agreement, were agreeing to a legal determination of the paternity of the child. We agree with the trial judge that, "[i]f, instead of a settlement agreement, there had been an adjudication on the merits of the 1982 action in [the defendant's] favor on the question of paternity, there is no doubt that the prior adjudication would *not* have been a bar to [the child's] claim under G.L. c. 209C in the Probate Court." That the stipulation as to paternity was entered by the agreement of the parties rather than by the court is immaterial in determining whether it can be attacked collaterally.

General Laws c. 209C, § 22(*d*), specifically erodes the common law policy on finality of judgments and allows readjudication of paternity where there has been a judgment in favor of the alleged father. * * * We conclude that the 1982 Superior Court action is not a bar to the current proceeding.

Preclusive effect of 1983 judgment and agreement on the child. Even if the 1982 action could operate as a bar to subsequent proceedings, it could not have preclusive effect on the child who was not a party to that action commenced by the defendant against the mother. As a nonparty, the child's rights could not have been prejudiced by the 1982 action. * * *

The child cannot be bound by the mother's settlement of the mother's claims. We cannot conclude that the child's interests were fully protected by the mother. The child has her own, independent, interests in determining the identity of her father. She has intangible interests independent of monetary support which cannot be equated completely with her mother's interests. * * * ("At some point, the law must recognize the fact that a child's interests in paternity litigation are much greater than the mother's interest in continued support. 'In addition to the right of the child to receive support many other present as well as future rights of the child are involved, depending on the facts and circumstances of a specific case' "). The mother also has independent interests that may prevent her from fully protecting the child's sometimes competing concerns.

The defendant argues that, even if the child were not in privity with her mother and thereby bound, she should be barred from proceeding in this action because her mother was acting as "procheine amie" or "next friend" on her behalf in the 1982 action and released her rights. The child disputes that the mother can bind the child when the mother was not legally the child's representative. *See Rudow v. Fogel*, 376 Mass. 587, 589, 382 N.E.2d 1046 (1978) (policy forbids assimilation of parent litigating on his own behalf with parent litigating as representative of child). The child cannot be bound by her mother's bare assertion that she was acting on behalf of the child without a formal recognition of her status as guardian or without the child's being joined as a party to the action. * * *

Other jurisdictions are in accord. * * *

Additionally, the child has unequivocally disaffirmed her mother's purported release in the settlement agreement by instigating the instant suit. "[A] release is a type of contract which a minor may disaffirm." "A minor, in order to avoid a contract, is not obliged to use any particular words or perform any specific acts. Any acts or words showing unequivocally a repudiation of the contract are sufficient to avoid it." * * *

Even if the mother had been properly acting on behalf of the child, the agreement was subject to disaffirmance by the child who effectively disaffirmed the agreement by filing the instant suit. There is no res judicata effect from the 1982 proceedings.

* * *

The defendant also claims that to allow this suit to proceed would be an unconstitutional impairment of contracts in violation of art. I, § 10, cl. 1, of the United States Constitution.... [but t]he defendant's contractual rights were only against the mother, not the child. There is no impairment of contract when a State law authorizes a party not bound by that contract to act.

Estoppel and laches. The defendant argues that the mother is estopped from pursuing this action by virtue of the 1983 judgment and agreement. This argument fails because the mother is not pursuing this action, the child is. The trial judge held that "[i]n equity I don't believe the child should be barred by her mother's actions." We agree. Because, as we have previously said, the mother was not legally a representative of the child, the child cannot be barred from pursuing her legal rights by her mother's representation that she was acting on the child's behalf. The child has done nothing to induce detrimental reliance on the part of the defendant. There is no estoppel.

The defense of laches is equally inapplicable. Laches is an equitable defense. "A judge may find as a fact that laches exists if there has been unjustified, unreasonable, and prejudicial delay in raising a claim." The burden of proving laches rests with the defendant.... The defendant offered no proof that the child knew or should have known of her rights under G.L. c. 209C or that she unreasonably delayed after having such knowledge. "[S]o long as there is no knowledge of the wrong committed and no refusal to embrace opportunity to ascertain facts, there can be no laches." The defendant's claim of laches must fail.

* * *

Admission of [evidence]. [The trial court ruled that genetic marker tests could be admitted into evidence based on the mother's affidavit alleging sexual intercourse with the putative father during the probable period of conception.] The [trial] judge ruled that the question of whether "there was intercourse between the parties on several dates ... is [judged] by a preponderance of the evidence." The defendant asserts that this ruling was erroneous. He contends that "sufficient evidence" required by G.L. c. 209C refers back to the burden [of proof] in G.L. c. 109C, § 7 to establish paternity by clear and convincing evidence. * * *

We decline to imply the clear and convincing standard into § 17 where it is not expressly required.... Evidence of intercourse between the defendant and the mother consisted of the mother's testimony. The trial judge found the mother's "testimony in this regard to be credible ..." ... This is legally sufficient.

[The court ruled that the trial judge had correctly excluded proffered evidence of the mother's alleged prostitution outside the period of probable conception.]

* * *

We conclude that the record was sufficient to support the judge's findings of fact and rulings of law. * * *

Notes and Questions

1. *Statutes of Limitation:* During the 1980s, the Supreme Court invalidated a number of paternity statutes of limitation on equal protection grounds, holding that short periods of limitation were not substantially related to the state's interest in avoiding stale or fraudulent claims. *See* Mills v. Habluetzel, 456 U.S. 91, 102 S.Ct. 1549, 71 L.Ed.2d 770 (1982) (one year); Pickett v. Brown, 462 U.S. 1, 103 S.Ct. 2199, 76 L.Ed.2d 372 (1983) (two years); Clark v. Jeter, 486 U.S. 456, 108 S.Ct. 1910, 100 L.Ed.2d 465 (1988) (six years). The statutes of limitation issue became moot when Congress passed the Child Support Enforcement Amendments of 1984, 42 U.S.C.A. § 666(a)(5)(A)(i) (West 1996), which requires each state to permit the paternity establishment at any time prior to a child's eighteenth birthday. The Family Support Act of 1988, Pub. L. No. 100–485, 102 Stat. 2343 (1988), extended the statute of limitations to pre–1984 paternity actions which had been dismissed because the statute of limitations did not allow establishment of paternity until the child's eighteenth birthday.

2. *Type of Action and Standard of Proof:* In most jurisdictions, the paternity action is now treated as a civil action. UPA § 14(a), for example, specifies that the paternity action will be "governed by the rules of civil procedure" and that "[t]he mother of the child and the alleged father are competent to testify and may be compelled to testify". It also provides that any trial shall be by the court without a jury. The Supreme Court has ruled that the standard of proof required in a paternity action is only a preponderance of the evidence. Rivera v. Minnich, 483 U.S. 574, 107 S.Ct. 3001, 97 L.Ed.2d 473 (1987).

3. *Admissible Evidence:* Like the *G.E.B.* court, UPA § 14 bars evidence of the mother's sexual activity during a time other than at the time of conception if offered by the alleged father. But such evidence is admissible if offered by the mother. What is the basis of such a distinction?

UPA § 12 sets out what evidence is admissible.

Section 12. Evidence relating to paternity may include:

(1) evidence of sexual intercourse between the mother and alleged father at any possible time of conception;

(2) an expert's opinion concerning the statistical probability of the alleged father's paternity based upon the duration of the mother's pregnancy;

(3) blood test results, weighted in accordance with evidence, if available, of the statistical probability of the alleged father's paternity;

(4) medical or anthropological evidence relating to the alleged father's paternity of the child based on tests performed by experts. If a man has been identified as a possible father of the child, the court may, and upon request of a party shall, require the child, the mother, and the man to submit to appropriate tests; and

(5) all other evidence relevant to the issue of paternity of the child.

4. Why couldn't the mother represent the child's interest? UPA § 9 provides that:

> [t]he child shall be made a party to the action. If he is a minor he shall be represented by his general guardian or a guardian ad litem appointed by the court. The child's mother or father may not represent the child as guardian or otherwise. The court may appoint the [appropriate state agency] as guardian ad litem for the child. The natural mother, each man presumed to be the father under § 4, and each man alleged to be the natural father, shall be made parties or, if not subject to the jurisdiction of the court shall be given notice of the action in a manner prescribed by the court and an opportunity to be heard. The court may align the parties.

How, if at all, will representation of the child by a guardian ad litem differ from representation by a parent?

5. The Personal Responsibility and Work Opportunity Reconciliation Act of 1996 (PRWORA), Pub. L. No. 104–193, 110 Stat. 2105 (1996), now imposes on the states a range of requirements aimed at early paternity establishment, including provision for voluntary acknowledgments of paternity, early genetic testing, and limitations on rebuttal of a presumption of paternity. Paul K. Legler summarizes the shift in paternity practice in *The Coming Revolution in Child Support Policy: Implications of the 1996 Welfare Act*, 30 Fam. L. Q. 519, 527–531 (1996):

> The changes in paternity establishment law mandated by PRWORA are the result of three developments that have occurred over the past decade: a change in social perspective, in-hospital paternity establishment, and advancement in genetic testing.
>
> Perhaps the major catalyst for change in paternity law has been the change in social perspective on the importance of paternity establishment. As policymakers began to pay attention to the mushrooming number of out-of-wedlock births during the 1980s, there was a growing focus on the poverty often associated with single parenthood. Establishing paternity was seen as a way to alleviate

some of the poverty because it opened the door to the possible receipt of child support. * * *

The second catalyst for change in paternity establishment law and procedure came out of the social sciences. Esther Wattenburg published a study in 1991 focusing on the relationship of young fathers and mothers at the time of out-of-wedlock births. The findings indicated that such births were often the result of established relationships, not casual ones, and that the mothers almost always knew who the father was and where he could be found. Significantly, Wattenburg found that two-thirds of fathers went to the hospital at the time of the out-of-wedlock birth . . .

Almost simultaneous with the release of the Wattenburg study, the State of Washington issued a report on a successful, innovative program it has started to obtain voluntary paternity acknowledgments at the time of the birth at the hospital . . .

The third catalyst for the change in the paternity establishment process was the advancement made in scientific testing for paternity, especially the use of DNA testing. DNA testing made the identification of fathers a new certainty and suggests the possibility that fathers could be readily and confidently identified, particularly if the legal processes were to be changed to make it easier to obtain genetic tests.

6. Susan had a child out of wedlock in 1980. She tried to get John to admit his paternity and help her with the child. John refused. When Susan went on public assistance a few years later, state welfare authorities attempted to get John to admit his paternity. (At that time the paternity statute of limitations was three years.) John continued to deny paternity and did not pay child support. At the age of nineteen, the child was killed in a car accident and Susan recovered a $350,000 wrongful death award. Can John prove his paternity and get half of the award? *See* Hunter v. Christian, 191 W.Va. 390, 446 S.E.2d 177, 181–82 (1994):

> Mr. McCoy's false representation that he was not Sharon's father enabled him to avoid the legal and moral responsibility of paying child support. Throughout Sharon's life, however, he was well aware that he was her father, as evidenced by his motion to intervene, filed almost immediately upon Sharon's death * * * A creature of equity, the doctrine of equitable estoppel is rooted in natural justice and good conscience. Therefore, for the reasons stated above, Mr. McCoy is equitably estopped from reaping the financial benefits of the death of his daughter, . . . when he disavowed paternity in order to escape legal and financial responsibility to her.

A similar case, in Rhode Island, involved a father of a fifteen year old child. The father was alleged to be $15,000 to $69,000 in arrears in paying child support and to have failed to visit the child for years but nonetheless sought to recover $175,000 in a wrongful death action. *See Father Returns to Claim Estate of Child He Left*, N.Y. TIMES, Jan. 17, 1994, A7, col. 1.

Chapter 7

ADOPTION

The beggarly question of parentage—what is it after all? What does it matter, when you come to think of it, whether a child is yours by blood or not? All the little ones of our time are collectively the children of us adults of the time, and entitled to our general care . . .

Thomas Hardy, Jude the Obscure (1896).

SECTION 1. THE CHANGING FACE OF ADOPTION PRACTICE

Adoption creates a legal parent-child relationship between a child and adults who are not the child's biological parents. Ordinarily, an adoption order terminates legal rights and obligations between the child and his or her biological family, replacing them with similar rights and obligations in the adoptive family.

Most ancient legal systems—including those of the Babylonians, Greeks, Egyptians and Romans—sanctioned adoption. The purpose of these early adoption laws was to meet the needs of would-be adoptive parents. For example, in ancient Greece and Rome, adoptions were often arranged to provide an heir to perpetuate the family line. *See* Stephen B. Presser, *The Historical Background of the American Law of Adoption*, 11 J. FAM. L. 443 (1971).

As the common law did not permit adoption, U.S. adoption laws are entirely statutory. *See* Louis Quarles, *The Law of Adoption—A Legal Anomaly,* 32 MARQUETTE L. REV. 237 (1949). The first American adoption statutes were enacted in Texas and Massachusetts in the mid-nineteenth century. The Massachusetts law became a model for many of the other state adoption laws passed during or shortly after the Civil War. To effect an adoption, it required the written consent of the child's biological parent, a joint petition by the adoptive mother and father, and a finding by the trial judge that the adoption was "fit and proper." *See*

ALFRED KADUSHIN & JUDITH A. MARTIN, CHILD WELFARE SERVICES 538 (4th ed. 1988).

By 1929, every state had passed adoption legislation. *Id.* In contrast to ancient adoption laws, these new statutes were thought to serve the interests of children. But the Massachusetts model, in which the propriety of the adoption order was determined based solely on a courtroom examination of the adoptive parents, was over time found inadequate to protect adoptive children. For example, a 1925 Commission appointed to study and revise Pennsylvania's adoption laws produced reports of cases like this one:

> Frances, aged thirteen recently made a personal application to a social agency stating that her foster father had been having sexual relations with her for the last two years. Upon investigation living conditions were found to be very bad. The foster mother corroborated the child's statements. Frances had been legally adopted in May 1918. She was sold to her foster parents by her mother for a quart of whisky.
>
> 2 CHILDREN AND YOUTH IN AMERICA: A DOCUMENTARY HISTORY 142 (Robert H. Bremner ed. 1971).

As a result of cases like Frances's, more and more states adopted procedures to investigate prospective adoptive parents before a judicial hearing. Minnesota passed the first law requiring a pre-hearing investigation and report by a local child welfare agency in 1917; by 1938, similar laws had been enacted in twenty-four states. State legislatures introduced other protections for the adoptive child as well, including, in some states, a trial period in the adoptive home before the adoption was legally finalized.

The Minnesota act is widely credited with having initiated sealed records in adoption proceedings, another innovation that soon became universal. The movement toward secrecy in adoption proceedings was apparently urged by social workers in child-placing agencies, who believed that assuring biological and adoptive parents' anonymity would both foster the integration of the child into the adoptive family and prevent the stigma of illegitimacy from tainting the child's future. *See* Burton Z. Sokoloff, *Antecedents of American Adoption*, 3 THE FUTURE OF CHILDREN: ADOPTION 17, 22 (Spring 1993).

The trend toward anonymity in adoption was facilitated by the development of specialized adoption agencies, where biological parents who wished to relinquish a child and would-be adoptive parents who wanted one could effect an exchange without personal contact. Although most states did not outlaw nonagency, or "independent" adoptions, by 1971 nearly eighty percent of nonrelative adoptions were arranged by specialized agencies. *See* VIVIANA A. ZELIZER, PRICING THE PRICELESS CHILD: THE CHANGING SOCIAL VALUE OF CHILDREN 263 (1981).

Adoption agencies often had strict requirements for adoptive parents. Many agencies refused adoption applications from would-be parents over a set age. All stressed a stable marital relationship as a requirement to adopt. And agencies with religious affiliations typically matched the religious preferences of the birth mother with the affiliations of the prospective adoptive parents.

Adoptive parents had their own preferences, of course. Nineteenth century adoptive parents typically wanted an older child who could work, but twentieth century adoptive parents (other than those who were adopting a stepchild or relative) typically sought an infant due to infertility. For this pool of adoptive parents, the ideal child was a healthy newborn whose appearance was not markedly different from their own.

Until the mid–1950s, the goals of adoption agencies, the pool of adoptive parents, and the supply of adoptable children were fairly well balanced. Most potential adoptive parents were infertile married couples in their child-bearing years; due to declining rates of orphanage, most of the children available for adoption were infants placed with adoption agencies by unmarried mothers.

Many of these biological mothers had backgrounds similar to those of the couples who sought to adopt. Unmarried motherhood was still seen as shameful and abortion was illegal, dangerous and often unavailable. The young woman who became pregnant out of marriage thus typically saw only two choices, marriage to the child's father or an adoption.

Although demand for adoptable infants began to exceed supply as early as the 1950s, the U.S. adoption rate moved consistently upward until 1970, when 175,000 children were adopted in the United States; about half (approximately 87,000) of these adoptions were by nonrelatives. Although the number of nonrelative adoptions thereafter dropped precipitously to 49,700 in 1974, the numbers have since levelled off. Kathy S. Stolley, *Statistics on Adoption in the United States*, 3 THE FUTURE OF CHILDREN: ADOPTION 26, 29 (Spring 1993). The decline in nonrelative adoptions derives largely from a reduced supply of adoptable infants resulting both from the Supreme Court's decision in Roe v. Wade [p. 269], which dramatically increased the availability of abortion, and a marked shift in social mores reducing the stigma associated with unwed motherhood. *See* KADUSHIN & MARTIN, *supra*, at 495.

While the supply of adoptable infants has declined, demand has moved in the opposite direction. While the estimates vary, some experts have estimated that more than a million couples seek to adopt the approximately 30,000 white infants available each year. *See* Sokoloff, *supra*, at 23; Cynthia Crossen, *Hard Choices: In Today's Adoptions, the Biological Parents Are Calling the Shots*, WALL ST. J., Sept. 14, 1989, at A1. The result of these changes in supply and demand has been a dramatic shift in the adoption "market."

First, the locus of adoption exchanges has shifted. Independent adoptions—where the birth parents either make the placement themselves or use an intermediary, such as a doctor or lawyer, to find adoptive parents—have increased and now occur in at least 30% of nonrelative adoptions. *See* Mark T. McDermott, *Agency versus Independent Adoption: The Case for Independent Adoption,* in 3 THE FUTURE OF CHILDREN: ADOPTION 146, 151 n. 3 (Spring 1993). International adoptions have also increased markedly, now comprising one-fifth to one-sixth of all nonrelative adoptions in the U.S. and a somewhat larger portion of infant adoptions. Elizabeth Bartholet, *International Adoption: Current Status and Future Prospects,* 3 THE FUTURE OF CHILDREN: ADOPTION 89, 90 (Spring 1993).

Second, the smaller supply of healthy white infants available for adoption has increased demand for transracial adoption, as well as the adoption of older and "special needs" children. One result of this shift has been a new emphasis on adoption for children who are in state foster care due to parental neglect, abuse, or incapacity. In an earlier era, these children had typically remained in state-paid foster care until the age of majority if they could not be returned home. *See* Chapter 9, § 5.

Third, the secrecy that traditionally characterized adoption proceedings has begun to give way. Many states now permit an adult adoptee to obtain information about his or her biological parents if those parents agree. "Open" adoption, where the biological parent(s) or family retain the right to continuing contact with the child, is permitted in a growing number of jurisdictions. *See* Annette Ruth Appell, *Blending Families Through Adoption: Implications for Collaborative Adoption Law and Practice,* 75 B.U. L. REV. 997, 1028–38 (1995) (describing and comparing statutes). These shifts have been fueled by pressure from adult adoptees who want information about their biological families, the increase in adoptions of older children who have often had ongoing relationships with their biological families, and the greater power of biological mothers resulting from the scarcity of adoptive infants and shift toward independent adoptions. The increase in divided families resulting from a higher rate of single parenthood may also have played a role. *Id.* at 1008–13.

State law has not always kept up with these various shifts in the adoption "market" and adoption practice. Nor have state adoption laws ever been uniform. The result is considerable variation in adoption law from one state to the next. Most states permit independent adoption, but some do not; some states recognize open adoption, but others do not. Standards governing the timing and revocability of parental consent also vary widely. While some experts worry that such diversity may produce both forum-shopping and unfairness, attempts to unify adoption laws have been unsuccessful to date. In 1994 the National Conference of Commissioners on Uniform State Laws made its latest attempt to facilitate state uniformity in adoption procedures by approving the Uniform Adoption Act, 9 U.L.A. Part 1 (West Supp. 1995). But, to date, only Vermont has used the Uniform Adoption Act as a model for changes to its adoption laws. VT. STAT. ANN. 15A § 1–101 et seq. (1996). For discussion of the Uniform Act, *see* Joan Heifetz Hollinger, *The Uniform Adoption Act: Reporter's Ruminations,* 30 FAM. L. Q. 345 (1996).

SECTION 2. CONSENT TO ADOPTION

A. CONSENT BY BIRTH MOTHERS

IN RE J.M.P.

Supreme Court of Louisiana, 1988.
528 So.2d 1002

DENNIS, JUSTICE.

* * *

The facts of this case follow a sadly familiar pattern. Dawn B., an eighteen year old unmarried woman, was employed in a grocery store but remained economically dependent on her mother and stepfather, Mr. & Mrs. B., with whom she resided. She became pregnant but concealed the fact from her mother for six months. At that time, with her mother's financial assistance, she traveled by bus from her home in Zachary to consult with a doctor at an abortion clinic in Metairie. The doctor informed her that her pregnancy was too far into its term to permit an abortion. Instead, he gave her the name and phone number of an anti-abortionist attorney, Perez, who would arrange for the placement of the child for private adoption free of charge. When she returned home Dawn placed a call to Perez but had to leave her number because he was out. When Perez returned the call, Dawn's mother, Mrs. B., answered and asked him to come to Zachary to discuss surrendering the expected child for private adoption. A few days later, Perez met with Dawn and Mr. and Mrs. B. in their home and explained what he was able to do: He could find a suitable couple to adopt the baby. He would have the couple pay the hospital, OBGYN, pediatrician, anesthesiologist, and drug bills. He explained that he would not charge a fee to them or the adoptive parents because his only interest was his personal cause of preventing abortions. Everything would be handled through him confidentially so that the identities of the two families would not be disclosed to each other. He told Dawn that she could change her mind and reclaim her child at any time up until the act of surrender was signed. Dawn, her mother and her stepfather agreed to the arrangement and asked him to proceed.

Between that meeting and the birth of the child Perez said he talked with Dawn on numerous occasions over the phone. On these occasions she called him to see if checks had been mailed for drug bills that she had sent him. During this period she gave him no indication of changing her mind with respect to the adoption.

After the birth of the child on November 30, 1985, Mr. Perez met with Dawn and Mr. & Mrs. B. at the hospital. Perez testified that he reminded them that his only interest was in seeing that the baby was born and told them that he would leave immediately if they wanted to keep the child. Dawn appeared to be sad about giving up the child, but this was not unusual, he said. At his request, she readily signed the hospital release form giving him permission to take the baby from the premises. Without any objection from Dawn he removed the baby from the hospital and took it to the prospective adoptive parents in Houma.

A week later, on December 7, 1985, Perez returned to Mr. & Mrs. B's house in Zachary to have Dawn execute the act of surrender. He brought along his law partner, Roberts, to act as Dawn's attorney and to advise her of her rights. Perez and the parents stepped out on the porch while Roberts and Dawn conferred in the house. Dawn testified that Roberts read the act of surrender to her, and that she did not ask any questions. She said that she told him to change the child's name in the act, and he said that he would do so later. The act of surrender which Dawn signed before a notary and two witnesses after conferring with Roberts, declares that it was fully explained to her by the attorney and that she understood she was surrendering the child for adoption and terminating her rights as a parent of the child. We cannot consider Roberts' testimony in this regard because he was not called as a witness.

While they were on the porch, Perez again informed Mrs. B. that Dawn could still change her mind and he offered to undertake the six hour round trip to fetch the child if Dawn did not want to sign the act of surrender. Mrs. B. replied that Dawn would like to keep the child but that the only way she could raise it would be on welfare and that, since she, Mrs. B., had already raised five children, she was not going to raise another. Perez testified that he did not interpret this remark as an indication that Dawn had changed her mind.

After the act of surrender was signed, Perez continued to receive medical bills and calls about their payment from Dawn. Sometime prior to December 30, 1985, however, he received a letter from her revoking her consent to the adoption.

The testimony of Dawn, Mrs. B. and Mr. B. reveals that the young natural mother signed the act and gave up her child although she knew that she had a right to refrain from doing so. Further, the record shows she surrendered the child not because of any improper act or omission by Perez or Roberts but primarily because she did not wish to undertake the hardship of caring for the child outside of her home and without her mother's assistance.

Dawn testified that early on the morning that the act of surrender was executed her mother and stepfather told her that if she refused to sign the instrument she could not bring the baby into their house. She expressed how this affected her decision to sign the act in several ways: She signed because it was what her mother wanted; her mother wanted her to start a new life. She couldn't bring the baby into the house and she had nowhere else to go with the baby. Although she could have gone to stay with her sister in Indiana, she would have had nowhere to go with the baby for the two days it would take for her to receive transportation fare from her sister or father in Indiana. This last explanation was inconsistent with other portions of her testimony in which she admitted that she had saved an unspecified sum of money before her child was born.

Dawn contradicted Perez on one point saying that he never told her that she had the right to refuse to surrender and reclaim her child. This disagreement is, however, without consequence because her testimony and that of her parents makes it clear that she fully understood her dilemma: she could either sign the act and lose her child or refuse to sign, keep her child, and lose her home and her mother's support.

Mr. & Mrs. B. admitted that they had caused Dawn to sign the act of surrender by telling her that she could not bring the child home. They testified that they had experienced a change of heart because of the suffering Dawn had endured, that they regretted their actions which had been intended only for her own welfare, and that they now stood ready to support Dawn financially and in every other way should she recover custody of the child.

* * *

At the conclusion of the hearing on the issue of the validity of the surrender, the trial judge ruled that because Perez was not acting as the adoptive parents' attorney, there was no conflict with his law partner's representation of Dawn; that Roberts was Dawn's attorney and that he provided her with adequate representation; that there was no coercion on the part of Perez or the adoptive parents; and that the pressure put on Dawn by her parents was not the type of coercion which would cause the act of surrender to be null and void. Therefore, the trial court concluded that the act of surrender was valid. Immediately after the trial judge's ruling, the hearing as to the best interests of the child was held.

James P., the adoptive father, testified that he had been married for approximately ten years to Laura P. and that they had a two and a half year old girl whom they had adopted. He further testified that he was a high school graduate, had attended trade school for two and a half years and had over the years attended schools in connection with his employment. In relation to his job, he said that he had been a mechanic for Halliburtion for nearly ten years, earned about $41,000 a year, had around $44,000 in a profit sharing plan with Halliburtion, that he rarely travels due to his work, and that he got three weeks of vacation every year. He also stated that he and his wife owned their four bedroom home, that they only had $5,000 left to pay on it, that he owned three automobiles, a small boat and a three wheel motorcycle. He added that he had recently borrowed $10,000 to build a barn type structure in his backyard. According to him, they have had the child since December 7, 1985, she sleeps with a heart and respiratory monitor because she has been identified as a candidate for crib death, his wife takes care of the child during the day, and the child had developed an attachment to them.

Mr. P. testified that the child "responds" well to him and is "close" to his wife. However, in his explanation of these terms he spoke only of "starting to turn over and goo and laugh" and of physical resemblances. On the other hand, he did testify that the child stops crying more readily when picked up by his wife than by him.

Laura P. testified that she is a thirty year old high school graduate with two semesters at Nicholls State University in accounting and that she was a homemaker. She additionally testified that the child was doing fine, that the child's medical problem was being taken care of, that the child slept in their room with them, and that they had decided to adopt no more children. She testified that the child is responding to her "real good," that the child recognizes her, and that the child is progressing as well as their older adopted daughter.

Dawn stated that she was an eighteen year old high school graduate and that she worked at Winn Dixie about thirty-six hours a week making $110 a week. In response to a question about how she intended to care for the child, she answered that her parents had agreed to help take care of the baby both financially and by babysitting when she was not there, that someone would always be with the child, and that she was prepared to continue the precautions taken due to the child's medical condition. She also testified that she intended to improve her job situation by continuing her education, that she intended to pay the P's back for the medical expenses they incurred, and that the father of the child, who was in Indiana, had agreed to help her out financially. She, however, admitted that she did not have any idea of how much day care, insurance, food or diapers for the baby would cost. In conclusion, Dawn said she loved the child very much and that she thought she would be able to raise the child responsibly.

Dawn's mother testified that she had raised five children, that she and her husband were willing and able to support Dawn and the baby financially, and that they would add Dawn and the child to their insurance. She added that she would do whatever was necessary to provide for the child's medical problems.

The trial court found that the adoption was in the child's best interest and entered an interlocutory decree of adoption. In his reasons for judgment the judge found it important that the P's owned a large home on which they owed only $5,000, that James P., the main wage earner, made over $40,000 a year and had substantial savings, and that the P's could provide the child a traditional family within which she could grow. He also thought it important that Dawn had originally sought an abortion, that she earned only minimum wage, that she was a single, working mother, who would have to rely on her parent's aid in raising the child and that the child would be raised in a trailer. In concluding that it would be in the best interests of the child to grant the adoption, the judge found that Dawn, as an unmarried eighteen year old, could not offer the child the stable and financially secure family unit the P's could, and that the P's were sincerely committed to providing for the welfare of the child and that they could offer the child a stable, supportive, and loving family unit. Dawn appealed the trial court's decision to the Court of Appeal, First Circuit, which affirmed for the reasons assigned by the trial court.

* * *

The Private Adoption Act of 1979 applicable to this case provides that a parent of either a natural or legitimate child may execute a voluntary surrender of custody of the child for private adoption. La.R.S. 9:422.3.... [T]he surrendering parent must sign the surrendering document freely and voluntarily, and the parent must be informed and understand that his or her rights to the child are to be terminated. The act of surrender may not be signed before the fifth day following the child's birthday, and the surrendering parent must be represented by an attorney at the execution of the act. However, to preserve anonymity, an attorney at law may be named in the act of surrender as representative of the adopting parents.

By an act of surrender, the surrendering parent transfers legal custody of the child to the adopting parents and grants consent to their adoption of the child. However, the surrendering parent may revoke her consent to the transfer and adoption by a written declaration within 30 days after executing the act of surrender. Nevertheless, the withdrawal of consent will not prevent the adoption if the adoption is found to be in the best interests of the child. Should an interlocutory decree have been entered without opposition, the child shall not be removed from the custody of the adopting parents nor adoption denied unless the department disapproves or the court finds the adopting parents unfit.

* * *

The evidence does not establish that the plaintiff was subject to the type of duress which justifies vitiation of her consent. Dawn's decision to surrender her child for adoption was induced principally by her own desire to do what was best for the child and by her mother's refusal to allow her to rear the child in her home. * * * Mr. & Mrs. B. had a legal right to refuse to allow the adult natural mother to rear the child in their home. Therefore, their refusal was an exercise or threat to exercise a right and did not constitute duress.

* * *

The natural parent in this case timely exercised her right to revoke her consent to the surrender and to oppose the adoption. However, her action does not bar a decree of adoption if the adoption is in "the best interests of the child." La.R.S. § 9:422.11(A).

* * *

The exact scope of the standard "best interest of the child" under the private adoption statute has not been detailed by the Legislature or this court. But the policy reflected in these words is firmly established in other statutes and in the law of virtually every American jurisdiction. The basic concept underlying this standard is nothing less than the dignity of the child as an individual human being. For this reason the words of the criterion cannot be precise and their scope cannot be static. "The best interests of the child" must draw its meaning from the evolving body of knowledge concerning child health, psychology and welfare that marks the progress of a maturing society.

* * *

[The best interests of the child require] [t]he court . . . [to] prefer a psychological parent (i.e., an adult who has a psychological relationship with the child from the child's perspective) over any claimant (including a natural parent) who, from the child's perspective, is not a psychological parent. To award custody to a person who is a "stranger" to the child would unnecessarily risk harming the child where the other claimant has, on a continuing, day-to-day basis, fulfilled the child's psychological needs for a parent as well as his physical need.

Whether any adult becomes the psychological parent of a child is based on day-to-day interaction, companionship, and shared experiences. The role can be fulfilled either by a biological parent or by any other caring adult—but never by an absent, inactive adult, whatever his biological or legal relationship to the child. J. GOLDSTEIN, A. FREUD & A. SOLNIT, BEYOND THE BEST INTEREST OF THE CHILD (2d ed. 1979) at 18. * * *

There is little disagreement within the profession of child psychology as to the existence of the phenomenon of the child-psychological parent relationship and its importance to the development of the child. A substantial and impressive consensus exists among psychologists and psychiatrists that disruption of the parent-child relationship carries significant risks. The only disagreement among the experts appears to be over how great the significant risks are in comparison with other factors influencing a child's mental and emotional growth.

When the natural parent poses no danger to the child's physical health, and the child has not yet formed an attachment to and begun to view one of the adoptive parents as his psychological parent, the natural parent should be preferred over others. Under broadly shared social values the general rule is that the responsibility and opportunity of custody is assigned to a child's natural parents. The high value placed on family autonomy reflects a consensus that the natural parent-child relationship should be disturbed only if necessary to protect the child from physical or psychological harm. Moreover, preservation of the child's sense of lineage and access to his extended biological family can be important psychologically, as evidenced by the felt need of some adoptive children to search out their natural parents.

These guidelines are consistent with the best interests of the child principle and should dispose of most private adoption cases. * * *

* * *

Applying the best interests guidelines we conclude that the trial court fell into error by omitting any consideration of two of the most important factors in a private adoption case, viz., the natural mother-child biological relationship and the possible psychological tie of the child to one or both of the adoptive parents. Instead, the trial court based its decision primarily on the relative wealth of the parties, a factor that can have little, if any, relevance in a case of this kind. If the natural mother is fit, the broad social policy of basing custody and responsibility on the biological relationship outweighs whatever material advantages might be provided by the adoptive parents, if neither of the adoptive parents is the child's psychological parent. On the other hand, if the adoptive parents are fit, and the child has formed a psychological attachment to one or both of them, the adoptive parents should be preferred so as to avoid the grave risk of mental and emotional harm to the child which would result from a change in custody, even if the natural parent is relatively affluent.

The record does not contain sufficient evidence from which we may determine whether the child had developed a substantial psychological relationship with one of the adoptive parents. There is no psychiatrist or psychologist testimony in the record and the adoptive parents' testimony is only sketchy on this subject. The child who was five months old at the time of the best interest hearing, is now approximately 2 ½ years old. We can only speculate as to the child's psychological development at the time of the hearing and as to what has occurred since. It is quite possible that the child by now has acquired a strong and healthy psychological attachment to her adoptive parents. There is also the possibility that the child tragically has no psychological parent. More happily, it is possible that the child has developed a psychological tie with her natural mother if there has been regular contact between the two. We cannot decide what is in the best interest of this child on the basis of these speculations.

Accordingly, in the interest of justice we will vacate the adoption decree and remand the case for a new hearing on the best interest of the child. * * * The best interest hearing under the private adoption statute should be scheduled and conducted expeditiously in order to afford the natural mother who timely revokes her consent a real opportunity to reclaim her child. * * *

The facts of this case, which unfortunately are not atypical, illustrate the problems caused by the law's ordinary delay in adoption cases. The child was born on November 30, 1985, and surrendered for adoption on December 7, 1985 when she was one week old. The natural mother revoked her consent within thirty days of this date, at which time the child could not have been over five weeks old. The adoptive parents filed a petition for adoption on January 30, 1986 when the child was two months old. The best interest hearing was not held until April 15, 1986 by which time the child was almost 5 months old. The trial court rendered a judgment that the surrender was valid and the adoption was in the child's best interest on June 20, 1986 when the child was almost seven months old. The court of appeal affirmed the trial court's judgment on December 22, 1987 by which time the child was over two years old.

Delays of this kind cannot be tolerated under an adoption statute which was intended to (1) grant the natural parent a brief but meaningful opportunity to change her mind and to reclaim the child, provided that this may be done without psychological harm to the child, and (2) ensure that the child will not be taken from the adoptive parents after one of them has become the psychological parent of the child.... The basic problem is with the statute which contains no provision for expedited hearings or machinery for calling the need therefor to the courts' attention....

Notes and Questions

1. On remand, what is the probability that Dawn will regain her child?

2. The facts of *J.M.P.* illustrate a fairly typical teenage pregnancy scenario. In view of the teenage parent's relative immaturity, should the state impose additional requirements to ensure that his or her consent to adoption is informed and has not been coerced? What rules would be helpful? *See* In re N.A.P., 23 Kan.App.2d 257, 930 P.2d 609 (1996); C.M.S. v. Goforth, 606 N.E.2d 874 (Ind.App.1993).

3. *Timing of Consent:* Rules governing the timing of parental consent are variable, but the trend has been toward prohibition of pre-birth consent. *See* UAA § 2–404(a). Some states additionally impose post-birth waiting periods ranging from twelve hours (KAN. STAT. ANN. § 59–2116) to several days. What is the purpose of these waiting periods? See Doe v. Clark, 318 S.C. 274, 457 S.E.2d 336 (1995) (mother allowed to revoke her consent where she signed consent five days before birth and attempted to revoke two days after birth). *See* Elizabeth Bartholet, *Beyond Biology: The Politics of Adoption and Reproduction*, 2 DUKE J. GENDER L. & POL'Y 5 (1995).

4. *Revocability of Consent:* Rules governing the revocability of parental consent also vary widely. In some states parental consent is irrevocable unless procured by fraud, undue influence or duress. *See* IDAHO CODE § 16–2005 (1995); MASS. ANN. LAWS ch. 210 § 2. In a few states, consent may be revoked with court approval. *See* ARK. STAT. ANN. § 9–9–220 (revocation to be granted if in the best interest of the child); HAWAII REV. STAT. § 578–2 (1992) (same). In others, consent may be revoked until the entry of an interlocutory adoption decree. Finally, in some states, consent may be revoked, with or without cause, until the adoption becomes final. *See* COLO. REV. STAT. § 19–5–104 (1995); PA. CONS. STAT. ANN. § 2711); In re Baby Boy S., 540 Pa. 302, 657 A.2d 484 (1995); Swinney v. Mosher, 830 S.W.2d 187 (Tex.App.1992). The UAA § 2–404(a) allows revocation within 192 hours after the child's birth.

Which of these approaches best serves the mother's interests? Which best serves the interests of the child? Which approach, on balance, is the best? *See* In re Custody of C.C.R.S., 872 P.2d 1337 (Colo.App.1993);

Schumacher v. Sexton, 216 Ga.App. 628, 455 S.E.2d 348 (1995); Annette R. Appell & Bruce A. Boyer, *Parental Rights vs. Best Interest of the Child: A False Dichotomy in the Context of Adoption,* 2 Duke J. Gender L. & Pol'y 63 (1995); Henry H. Foster, Jr., *Adoption and Child Custody: Best Interests of the Child,* 22 Buff. L. Rev. 1 (1972).

5. *Stepparent Adoptions:* Many states have special rules governing consent in stepparent adoptions, which terminate only the parental rights of the noncustodial parent. While consent of the noncustodial parent is typically required, in some states it may be waived in cases of abandonment or nonsupport. *See* In re J.J.J., 718 P.2d 948 (Alaska 1986) (statute waives consent of noncustodial parent who "failed significantly without justifiable cause ... to communicate meaningfully with the child or ... to provide ... support as required by law" for at least a year; fact that father made payments after the year pursuant to court order did not preclude finding).

6. *Technical defects:* State law varies with respect to technical defects in the execution of an adoption consent. In some states, a parent's consent is valid if there is substantial compliance with the statutory requirements. *See* Martin v. Martin, 316 Ark. 765, 875 S.W.2d 819 (1994) (where name and address of magistrate to whom revocation should be addressed was missing, consent valid).

B. THE UNMARRIED FATHER

While the rights of married fathers are identical to those of mothers, the unmarried father poses special problems. The "typical" case involves a mother who has consented to an adoption and a putative father who is seeking to prove his paternity and bar the adoption. Before 1972, based in part on the difficulty of definitively establishing the paternity of a nonmarital child, most states did not permit an unmarried father to block an adoption. But in Stanley v. Illinois, 405 U.S. 645, 92 S.Ct. 1208, 31 L.Ed.2d 551 (1972), the Supreme Court held that an unmarried father was entitled to a hearing on his fitness before his children could be placed in state custody. In a series of later cases, the Court has attempted to fashion an approach that protects the legitimate interests of unmarried fathers, but does not unduly delay or disrupt the adoption process.

LEHR v. ROBERTSON ET AL.

Supreme Court of the United States, 1983.
463 U.S. 248, 103 S.Ct. 2985, 77 L.Ed.2d 614.

Justice Stevens delivered the opinion of the Court.

The question presented is whether New York has sufficiently protected an unmarried father's inchoate relationship with a child whom he has never supported and rarely seen in the two years since her birth. The appellant, Jonathan Lehr, claims that the Due Process and Equal Protection Clauses of the Fourteenth Amendment, as interpreted in

Stanley v. Illinois, 405 U.S. 645 (1972), and *Caban v. Mohammed*, 441 U.S. 380 (1979), give him an absolute right to notice and an opportunity to be heard before the child may be adopted. We disagree.

Jessica M. was born out of wedlock on November 9, 1976. Her mother, Lorraine Robertson, married Richard Robertson eight months after Jessica's birth. On December 21, 1978, when Jessica was over two years old, the Robertsons filed an adoption petition in the Family Court of Ulster County, New York. The court heard their testimony and received a favorable report from the Ulster County Department of Social Services. On March 7, 1979, the court entered an order of adoption. In this proceeding, appellant contends that the adoption order is invalid because he, Jessica's putative father, was not given advance notice of the adoption proceeding.

The State of New York maintains a "putative father registry." A man who files with that registry demonstrates his intent to claim paternity of a child born out of wedlock and is therefore entitled to receive notice of any proceeding to adopt that child. Before entering Jessica's adoption order, the Ulster County Family Court had the putative father registry examined. Although appellant claims to be Jessica's natural father, he had not entered his name in the registry.

In addition to the persons whose names are listed on the putative father registry, New York law requires that notice of an adoption proceeding be given to several other classes of possible fathers of children born out of wedlock—those who have been adjudicated to be the father, those who have been identified as the father on the child's birth certificate, those who live openly with the child and the child's mother and who hold themselves out to be the father, those who have been identified as the father by the mother in a sworn written statement, and those who were married to the child's mother before the child was six months old. Appellant admittedly was not a member of any of those classes. He had lived with appellee prior to Jessica's birth and visited her in the hospital when Jessica was born, but his name does not appear on Jessica's birth certificate. He did not live with appellee or Jessica after Jessica's birth, he has never provided them with any financial support, and he has never offered to marry appellee. Nevertheless, he contends that the following special circumstances gave him a constitutional right to notice and a hearing before Jessica was adopted.

On January 30, 1979, one month after the adoption proceeding was commenced in Ulster County, appellant filed a "visitation and paternity petition" in the Westchester County Family Court. In that petition, he asked for a determination of paternity, an order of support, and reasonable visitation privileges with Jessica. Notice of that proceeding was served on appellee on February 22, 1979. Four days later appellee's attorney informed the Ulster County Court that appellant had commenced a paternity proceeding in Westchester County; the Ulster County judge then entered an order staying appellant's paternity proceeding until he could rule on a motion to change the venue of that proceeding to

Ulster County. On March 3, 1979, appellant received notice of the change of venue motion and, for the first time, learned that an adoption proceeding was pending in Ulster County.

On March 7, 1979, appellant's attorney telephoned the Ulster County judge to inform him that he planned to seek a stay of the adoption proceeding pending the determination of the paternity petition. In that telephone conversation, the judge advised the lawyer that he had already signed the adoption order earlier that day. According to appellant's attorney, the judge stated that he was aware of the pending paternity petition but did not believe he was required to give notice to appellant prior to the entry of the order of adoption.

Thereafter, the Family Court in Westchester County granted appellee's motion to dismiss the paternity petition, holding that the putative father's right to seek paternity "must be deemed severed so long as an order of adoption exists." Appellant did not appeal from that dismissal. On June 22, 1979, appellant filed a petition to vacate the order of adoption on the ground that it was obtained by fraud and in violation of his constitutional rights [which was denied by the trial and appellate courts] . . .

Appellant . . . [first] contends that a putative father's actual or potential relationship with a child born out of wedlock is an interest in liberty which may not be destroyed without due process of law; he argues therefore that he had a constitutional right to prior notice and an opportunity to be heard before he was deprived of that interest. Second, he contends that the gender-based classification in the statute, which both denied him the right to consent to Jessica's adoption and accorded him fewer procedural rights than her mother, violated the Equal Protection Clause.

* * *

. . . This Court has examined the extent to which a natural father's biological relationship with his child receives protection under the Due Process Clause in precisely three cases: *Stanley v. Illinois*, 405 U.S. 645 (1972), *Quilloin v. Walcott*, 434 U.S. 246 (1978), and *Caban v. Mohammed*, 441 U.S. 380 (1979).

Stanley involved the constitutionality of an Illinois statute that conclusively presumed every father of a child born out of wedlock to be an unfit person to have custody of his children. The father in that case had lived with his children all their lives and had lived with their mother for 18 years. There was nothing in the record to indicate that Stanley had been a neglectful father who had not cared for his children. Under the statute, however, the nature of the actual relationship between parent and child was completely irrelevant. Once the mother died, the children were automatically made wards of the State. . . . [T]he Court held that the Due Process Clause was violated by the automatic destruction of the custodial relationship without giving the father any opportunity to present evidence regarding his fitness as a parent.

Quilloin involved the constitutionality of a Georgia statute that authorized the adoption, over the objection of the natural father, of a child born out of wedlock. The father in that case had never legitimated the child. It was only after the mother had remarried and her new husband had filed an adoption petition that the natural father sought visitation rights and filed a petition for legitimation. The trial court found adoption by the new husband to be in the child's best interests, and we unanimously held that action to be consistent with the Due Process Clause.

Caban involved the conflicting claims of two natural parents who had maintained joint custody of their children from the time of their birth until they were respectively two and four years old. The father challenged the validity of an order authorizing the mother's new husband to adopt the children; he relied on both the Equal Protection Clause and the Due Process Clause. Because this Court upheld his equal protection claim, the majority did not address his due process challenge....

The difference between the developed parent-child relationship that was implicated in *Stanley* and *Caban*, and the potential relationship involved in *Quilloin* and this case, is both clear and significant. When an unwed father demonstrates a full commitment to the responsibilities of parenthood by "[coming] forward to participate in the rearing of his child," *Caban*, his interest in personal contact with his child acquires substantial protection under the Due Process Clause. At that point it may be said that he "[acts] as a father toward his children." But the mere existence of a biological link does not merit equivalent constitutional protection. The actions of judges neither create nor sever genetic bonds. "[The] importance of the familial relationship, to the individuals involved and to the society, stems from the emotional attachments that derive from the intimacy of daily association, and from the role it plays in '[promoting] a way of life' through the instruction of children ... as well as from the fact of blood relationship."

The significance of the biological connection is that it offers the natural father an opportunity that no other male possesses to develop a relationship with his offspring. If he grasps that opportunity and accepts some measure of responsibility for the child's future, he may enjoy the blessings of the parent-child relationship and make uniquely valuable contributions to the child's development. If he fails to do so, the Federal Constitution will not automatically compel a State to listen to his opinion of where the child's best interests lie.

... [A]s all of the New York courts that reviewed this matter observed, the right to receive notice was completely within appellant's control. By mailing a postcard to the putative father registry, he could have guaranteed that he would receive notice of any proceedings to adopt Jessica. The possibility that he may have failed to do so because of his ignorance of the law cannot be a sufficient reason for criticizing the law itself. The New York Legislature concluded that a more open-ended notice requirement would merely complicate the adoption process, threaten the privacy interests of unwed mothers, create the risk of unnecessary controversy, and impair the desired finality of adoption decrees. Regardless of whether we would have done likewise if we were legislators instead of judges, we surely cannot characterize the State's conclusion as arbitrary.

Appellant argues, however, that even if the putative father's opportunity to establish a relationship with an illegitimate child is adequately protected by the New York statutory scheme in the normal case, he was nevertheless entitled to special notice because the court and the mother knew that he had filed an affiliation proceeding in another court. This argument amounts to nothing more than an indirect attack on the notice provisions of the New York statute. The legitimate state interests in facilitating the adoption of young children and having the adoption proceeding completed expeditiously that underlie the entire statutory scheme also justify a trial judge's determination to require all interested parties to adhere precisely to the procedural requirements of the statute....

* * *

[The appellant also argues that the statute impermissibly discriminates on the basis of gender.] As we have already explained, the existence or nonexistence of a substantial relationship between parent and child is a relevant criterion in evaluating both the rights of the parent and the best interests of the child. In *Quilloin v. Walcott*, we noted that the putative father, like appellant, "[had] never shouldered any significant responsibility with respect to the daily supervision, education, protection, or care of the child. Appellant does not complain of his exemption from these responsibilities.... " We therefore found that a Georgia statute that always required a mother's consent to the adoption of a child born out of wedlock, but required the father's consent only if he had legitimated the child, did not violate the Equal Protection Clause. Because appellant, like the father in *Quilloin*, has never established a substantial relationship with his daughter, the New York statutes at issue in this case did not operate to deny appellant equal protection.

The judgment of the New York Court of Appeals is Affirmed.

JUSTICE WHITE, with whom JUSTICE MARSHALL and JUSTICE BLACKMUN join, dissenting.

* * *

According to Lehr, he and Jessica's mother met in 1971 and began living together in 1974. The couple cohabited for approximately two years, until Jessica's birth in 1976. Throughout the pregnancy and after the birth, Lorraine acknowledged to friends and relatives that Lehr was Jessica's father; Lorraine told Lehr that she had reported to the New York State Department of Social Services that he was the father. Lehr visited Lorraine and Jessica in the hospital every day during Lorraine's confinement. According to Lehr, from the time Lorraine was discharged from the hospital until August 1978, she concealed her whereabouts from him. During this time Lehr never ceased his efforts to locate Lorraine and Jessica and achieved sporadic success until August 1977, after which time he was unable to locate them at all. On those occasions when he did determine Lorraine's location, he visited with her and her children to the extent she was willing to permit it. When Lehr, with the aid of a detective agency, located Lorraine and Jessica in August 1978, Lorraine was already married to Mr. Robertson. Lehr asserts that at this time he offered to provide financial assistance and to set up a trust fund for Jessica, but that Lorraine refused. Lorraine threatened Lehr with arrest unless he stayed away and refused to permit him to see Jessica. Thereafter Lehr retained counsel who wrote to Lorraine in early December 1978, requesting that she permit Lehr to visit Jessica and threatening legal action on Lehr's behalf. On December 21, 1978, perhaps as a response to Lehr's threatened legal action, appellees commenced the adoption action at issue here. * * * Lehr's version of the "facts" paints a far different picture than that portrayed by the majority.... [We must] assume that Lehr's allegations are true—that but for the actions of the child's mother there would have been the kind of significant relationship that the majority concedes is entitled to the full panoply of procedural due process protections.

* * *

... It makes little sense to me to deny notice and hearing to a father who has not placed his name in the register but who has unmistakably identified himself by filing suit to establish his paternity and has notified the adoption court of his action and his interest. I thus need not question the statutory scheme on its face. Even assuming that Lehr would have been foreclosed if his failure to utilize the register had somehow disadvantaged the State, he effectively made himself known by other means, and it is the sheerest formalism to deny him a hearing because he informed the State in the wrong manner.

No state interest is substantially served by denying Lehr adequate notice and a hearing. The State no doubt has an interest in expediting adoption proceedings to prevent a child from remaining unduly long in the custody of the State or foster parents. But this is not an adoption involving a child in the custody of an authorized state agency. Here the child is in the custody of the mother and will remain in her custody. Moreover, had Lehr utilized the putative fathers' register, he would have been granted a prompt hearing, and there was no justifiable reason, in terms of delay, to refuse him a hearing in the circumstances of this case. * * * Respectfully, I dissent.

ADOPTION OF KELSEY S.

Supreme Court of California, 1992.
1 Cal.4th 816, 4 Cal.Rptr.2d 615, 823 P.2d 1216.

BAXTER, JUSTICE.

The primary question in this case is whether the father of a child born out of wedlock may properly be denied the right to withhold his consent to his child's adoption by third parties despite his diligent and legal attempts to obtain custody of his child and to rear it himself, and absent any showing of the father's unfitness as a parent. We conclude that, under these circumstances, the federal constitutional guarantees of equal protection and due process require that the father be allowed to withhold his consent to his child's adoption and therefore that his parental rights cannot be terminated absent a showing of his unfitness within the meaning of Civil Code § 221.20.

FACTS

Kari S. gave birth to Kelsey, a boy, on May 18, 1988. The child's undisputed natural father is petitioner Rickie M. He and Kari S. were not married to one another. At that time, he was married to another woman but was separated from her and apparently was in divorce proceedings. He was aware that Kari planned to place their child for adoption, and he objected to her decision because he wanted to rear the child.

Two days after the child's birth, petitioner filed an action in superior court under Civil Code § 7006 to establish his parental relationship with the child and to obtain custody of the child. (The petition erroneously stated that the child had not yet been born. His birth was earlier than expected, and petitioner had not been informed of it when he filed his action.) That same day, the court issued a restraining order that temporarily awarded care, custody, and control of the child to petitioner. The order also stayed all adoption proceedings and prohibited any contact between the child and the prospective adoptive parents.

Later that day, petitioner filed a copy of the order with law enforcement officials. He also personally attempted to serve it on the prospective adoptive parents at their home. He was unsuccessful.

On May 24, 1988, Steven and Suzanne A., the prospective adoptive parents, filed an adoption petition under Civil Code § 226. Their petition alleged that only the mother's consent to the adoption was required because there was no presumed father under § 7004, subdivision (a).

* * *

On August 26, 1988, the court found "by a bare preponderance" of the evidence that the child's best interest required termination of petitioner's parental rights.

* * *

Th[e] statutory scheme creates three classifications of parents: mothers, biological fathers who are presumed fathers, and biological fathers who are *not* presumed fathers (i.e., natural fathers). A natural father's consent to an adoption of his child by third parties is not required unless the father makes the required showing that retention of his parental rights is in the child's best interest. Consent, however, is required of a mother and a presumed father regardless of the child's best interest. The natural father is therefore treated differently from both mothers and presumed fathers. With this statutory framework in mind, we now examine petitioner's contentions.

A man becomes a "presumed father" under § 7004, subdivision (a)(4) (hereafter § 7004(a)(4)) if "*[h]e receives the child into his home* and openly holds out the child as his natural child." (Italics added.) It is undisputed in this case that petitioner openly held out the child as being his own. Petitioner, however, did not physically receive the child into his home. He was prevented from doing so by the mother, by court order, and allegedly also by the prospective adoptive parents.

* * *

The precise question before us has not been addressed by the United States Supreme Court. We are guided, however, by a series of high court decisions dealing with the rights of unwed fathers. From those decisions, we must attempt to distill the guiding constitutional principles.

In *Stanley v. Illinois* (1972) 405 U.S. 645 (*Stanley*), the court held that under the due process clause of the Fourteenth Amendment to the federal Constitution an unmarried father was entitled to a hearing on his fitness as a parent before his children were taken from him. *Stanley* is factually distinguishable because the father in that case had lived intermittently with his children and their mother for 18 years.... [But] the court seemed to indicate that a father's parental rights could not be terminated absent a showing of his unfitness, and that a showing of the child's best interest would be an insufficient basis for termination of the father's rights. "What is the state interest in separating children from fathers without a hearing designed to determine *whether the father is unfit* in a particular disputed case?" ...

If petitioner is not a presumed parent under § 7004(a)(4), his parental rights may be terminated under § 7017, subdivision (d)(2) merely by showing that termination would be in the child's best interest. No showing of petitioner's unfitness is required under the statutes. The statutory scheme therefore appears to conflict with the emphasis in *Stanley*, on the need for *a particularized finding of unfitness*. Petitioner was never found to be unfit.

In its next case dealing with unwed fathers, *Quilloin v. Walcott*, 434 U.S. 246 (*Quilloin*), ... [a] unanimous court ... found no denial of either due process or equal protection. As to due process, the court explained, "We have little doubt that the Due Process Clause would be offended '[i]f a State were to attempt to force the breakup of a natural family, over the objections of the parents and their children, *without some showing of unfitness* and for the sole reason that to do so was thought to be in the children's best interest.' But this is not a case in which the unwed father at any time had, or sought, actual or legal custody of his child. Nor is this a case in which the proposed adoption would place the child with a new set of parents with whom the child had never before lived. Rather, the result of the adoption in this case is to give full recognition to a family unit already in existence, a result desired by all concerned, except appellant [the father]. Whatever might be required in other situations, we cannot say that the State was required in this situation to find anything more than that the adoption, and denial of legitimation, were in the 'best interests of the child.' "

* * *

The present case has several of the earmarks the court found lacking in *Quilloin*, and which the court suggested might render invalid a termination of a father's rights based only on a showing of the child's best interest. Those factors are as follows:

(i) Unlike the father in *Quilloin*, petitioner asked the mother for custody of their child and, when rebuffed, immediately (as soon as the child was born) went to court seeking legal custody. He continues to seek legal recognition of his parental rights.

(ii) The mother does not seek to retain the child and have it adopted by a husband. As put by the *Quilloin* court, "the proposed adoption would place the child with a new set of parents with whom the child had never before lived." Of course, we recognize that as a result of the lower courts' decisions the child has now been living with the prospective adoptive parents for more than three years. This fact, however, is not relevant to the analysis of whether petitioner's rights were violated *ab initio*.

(iii) The parties disagree as to the amount of care and support that petitioner provided to the child and its mother. The record is unclear as to whether and to what extent, if any, this dispute affected the trial court's decision that the adoption was barely in the child's best interest. The record is clear, however, that petitioner is not like the natural father in *Quilloin*, who avoided contact with his child until several years after its birth and came forward only when another man tried to adopt it. More important for this part of our analysis, petitioner, also unlike the father in *Quilloin*, did attempt through legal channels to shoulder full responsibility for his child.

In short, the present case is the type of case the high court emphasized it was not deciding in *Quilloin*. By implication, however, the *Quilloin* decision strongly suggests that the parental rights of a father in petitioner's position may not properly be terminated absent a showing of his unfitness as a father. On the present facts, a showing of the child's best interest would appear to be insufficient under *Quilloin*. This conclusion is reinforced by the high court's ... decision [i]n *Caban v. Mo-*

hammed (1979) 441 U.S. 380 (*Caban*) . . . [where the court struck down an adoption consent statute that] "treats unmarried parents differently according to their sex." In this respect, California law is indistinguishable. . . .

* * *

The high court again considered the rights of biological fathers only four years later in *Lehr v. Robertson* (1983) 463 U.S. 248 (*Lehr*). * * * On its face, *Lehr*, does not resolve the dilemma before us. The stated premise of the court's holding was that the equal protection clause does not prevent a state from according a child's biological father fewer rights than the mother if he has "never established a relationship" with the child. The court did not purport to decide the legal question in the present case, that is, whether the mother may constitutionally prevent the father from establishing the relationship that gives rise to his right to equal protection. The *Lehr* court, however, recognized the uniqueness of the biological connection between parent and child. "The significance of the biological connection is that it offers the natural father an opportunity that no other male possesses to develop a relationship with his offspring. If he grasps that opportunity and accepts some measure of responsibility for the child's future, he may enjoy the blessings of the parent-child relationship and make uniquely valuable contributions to the child's development." *Lehr* can fairly be read to mean that a father need only make a reasonable and meaningful attempt to establish a relationship, not that he must be successful against all obstacles.

. . . [In] *Michael H. v. Gerald D.* [p. 280] (*Michael H.*)—a majority of the justices were [again] solicitous of the rights of unwed biological fathers. For them, the determinative factor was whether a biological father has attempted to establish a relationship with his child.

Although the foregoing high court decisions do not provide a comprehensive rule for all situations involving unwed fathers, one unifying and transcendent theme emerges. The biological connection between father and child is unique and worthy of constitutional protection if the father grasps the opportunity to develop that biological connection into a full and enduring relationship.

* * *

Petitioner asserts a violation of equal protection and due process under the federal Constitution; more specifically, that he should not be treated differently from his child's mother. In constitutional terms, the question is whether California's sex-based statutory distinction between biological mothers and fathers serves " '* * * important governmental objectives and [is] *substantially related* to achievement of those objectives.' "(*Caban*, supra, italics added.) * * *

There is no dispute that "The State's interest in providing for the well-being of illegitimate children is an important one." Although the legal concept of illegitimacy no longer exists in California, the problems and needs of children born out of wedlock are an undisputed reality. The state has an important and valid interest in their well-being.

* * *

Respondents do not adequately explain how an unwed mother's control over a biological father's rights furthers the state's interest in the well-being of the child. The linchpin of their position, however, is clear although largely implicit: Allowing the biological father to have the same rights as the mother would make adoptions more difficult because the consent of both parents is more difficult to obtain than the consent of the mother alone. This reasoning is flawed in several respects.

A. Respondents' view too narrowly assumes that the proper governmental objective is adoption. As we have explained, the constitutionally valid objective is the protection of the child's well-being. We cannot conclude in the abstract that *adoption* is itself a sufficient objective to allow the state to take whatever measures it deems appropriate. Nor can we merely assume, either as a policy or factual matter, that adoption is necessarily in a child's best interest. This assumption is especially untenable in light of the rapidly changing concept of family. As recently as only a few years ago, it *might* have been reasonable to assume that an adopted child would be placed into a two-parent home and thereby have a more stable environment than a child raised by a single father. The validity of that assumption is now highly suspect in light of modern adoption practice. Recent statistics show that a significant percentage of children placed for independent adoption—7.7 percent—are adopted by a single parent. The figure is even higher—21.9 percent—for children placed with agencies for adoption....

If the possible benefit of adoption were by itself sufficient to justify terminating a parent's rights, the state could terminate an unwed *mother*'s parental rights based on nothing more than a showing that her child's best interest would be served by adoption. Of course, that is not the law; nor do the parties advocate such a system. We simply do not in our society take children away from their mothers—married or otherwise—because a "better" adoptive parent can be found. We see no valid reason why we should be less solicitous of a father's efforts to establish a parental relationship with his child. Respondents seem to suggest that a child is inherently better served by adoptive parents than by a single, biological father but that the child is also inherently better served by a single, biological mother than by adoptive parents. The logic of this view is not apparent, and there is no evidence in the record to support such a counterintuitive view.

B. Nor is there evidence before us that the statutory provisions allowing the mother to determine the father's rights are, in general, *substantially* related to protecting the child's best interest. As a matter of cold efficiency, we cannot disagree that eliminating a natural father's rights would make adoption easier in some cases. That, however, begs the question because it assumes an unwed mother's decision to permit an immediate adoption of her newborn is always preferable to custody by the natural father, even when he is a demonstrably fit parent. We have no evidence to support that assumption. Moreover, the assumption has already been rejected by the United States Supreme Court: "It may be that, given the opportunity, some unwed fathers would prevent the adoption of their illegitimate children. This impediment to adoption usually is the result of a natural parental interest shared by both genders [sexes] alike; it is not a manifestation of any profound difference between the affection and concern of mothers and fathers for their children. Neither the State nor the appellees have argued that unwed fathers are more likely to object to the adoption of their children than are unwed mothers; nor is there any self-evident reason why as a class they would be." (*Caban*). * * *

* * *

Clearly, the father is treated unfairly under § 7004, subdivision (a), but equally important is the loss to the child. The child has a genetic bond with its natural parents that is unique among all relationships the child will have throughout its life. "The intangible fibers that connect parent and child have infinite variety. They are woven throughout the fabric of our society, providing it with strength, beauty, and flexibility." (*Lehr*). It therefore would be curious to conclude that the child's best interest is served by allowing the one parent (the mother) who wants to sever her legal ties to decide unilaterally that the only other such tie (the father's) will be cut as well. Absent a showing of a father's unfitness, his child is ill-served by allowing its mother effectively to preclude the child from ever having a meaningful relationship with its only other biological parent.

E. In summary, we hold that § 7004, subdivision (a) and the related statutory scheme violates the federal constitutional guarantees of equal protection and due process for unwed fathers *to the extent that* the statutes allow a mother unilaterally to preclude her child's biological father from becoming a presumed father and thereby allowing the state to terminate his parental rights on nothing more than a showing of the child's best interest. If an unwed father promptly comes forward and demonstrates a full commitment to his parental responsibilities—emotional, financial, and otherwise—his federal constitutional right to due process prohibits the termination of his parental relationship absent a showing of his unfitness as a parent. Absent such a showing, the child's well-being is presumptively best served by continuation of the father's parental relationship. Similarly, when the father has come forward to grasp his parental responsibilities, his parental rights are entitled to equal protection as those of the mother.

A court should consider all factors relevant to that determination. The father's conduct both *before and after* the child's birth must be considered. Once he knows or reasonably should know of the pregnancy, he must promptly attempt to assume his parental responsibilities as fully as the mother will allow and his circumstances permit. In particular, the father must demonstrate "a willingness himself to assume full custody of the child—not merely to block adoption by others." A court should also consider the father's public acknowledgment of paternity, payment of pregnancy and birth expenses commensurate with his ability to do so, and prompt legal action to seek custody of the child.

We reiterate and emphasize the narrowness of our decision. The statutory distinction between natural fathers and presumed fathers is constitutionally invalid *only to the extent* it is applied to an unwed father who has sufficiently and timely demonstrated a full commitment to his parental responsibilities. * * *

Notes and Questions

1. How does the California Supreme Court's interpretation of *Caban* and *Quilloin* compare with that of the *Lehr* court? Assume that the U.S. Supreme Court has agreed to hear *Kelsey S.* What arguments would you expect the State to make? The successful father? How would you expect the Supreme Court to rule?

2. Cases involving maternal concealment of the father's identity have proliferated. For others, *see, e.g.,* In re Petition of Doe, 159 Ill.2d 347, 202 Ill.Dec. 535, 638 N.E.2d 181 (1994), cert. denied, 513 U.S. 994, 115 S.Ct. 499, 130 L.Ed.2d 408 (1994); In re Adoption of A.M.B., 514 N.W.2d 670, 673 (N.D.1994); Hylland v. Doe, 126 Or.App. 86, 867 P.2d 551 (1994), review denied, 318 Or. 478, 871 P.2d 123 (Or.1994); In re Child Whose First Name is Baby Girl, 206 A.D.2d 932, 615 N.Y.S.2d 800, 801 (1994); State ex rel. T.A.B. v. Corrigan, 600 S.W.2d 87 (Mo.App. 1980); In re Juvenile Action No. JS–8490, 179 Ariz. 102, 876 P.2d 1137, 1141 (1994); In re Robert O., 80 N.Y.2d 254, 590 N.Y.S.2d 37, 604 N.E.2d 99 (1992); In re M.N.M., 605 A.2d 921 (D.C.App.1992); In re B.G.C., 496 N.W.2d 239 (Iowa 1992).

3. In In re Adoption of Michael H., 10 Cal.4th 1043, 43 Cal.Rptr.2d 445, 898 P.2d 891 (1995), the California Supreme Court distinguished *Kelsey S.* and held that the consent of Mark S., an unmarried father who had requested custody approximately one week after his baby's birth, was not required. Mark had concurred in the teenage mother's decision to give the baby up for adoption until their relationship ended approximately four months before the baby's birth. After the relationship ended, Mark attempted suicide and thereafter admitted himself into a rehabilitation hospital where he decided to stop using drugs, seek stable employment and residence, and continue counseling. He also decided that he did not want to give up his child for adoption and started looking for an attorney to help him obtain custody after the child was born. Mark and the mother had very little contact after his suicide attempt and the baby was released directly from the hospital into the adoptive parents' custody, where he remained during the four years in which it took the case to reach the California Supreme Court. The Court ruled that Mark's conduct did not satisfy the *Kelsey S.* requirement that "[o]nce . . . [the father] knows or reasonably should know of the pregnancy, he must promptly attempt to assume his parental responsibilities as fully as the

mother will allow and his circumstances permit." What else should Mark have done?

4. If Tom impregnates Mary in a state which permits an alleged father to block an adoption if he files a paternity claim within six months of a child's birth, can Mary alter the father's ability to block an adoption by moving during her pregnancy to a state which grants an alleged unmarried father fewer rights? *See* In re Baby Boy S., 22 Kan.App.2d 119, 912 P.2d 761 (1996), cert. denied, Allred v. A.L.L., ___ U.S. ___, 117 S.Ct. 185, 136 L.Ed.2d 123 (1996).

5. Mother, a single woman, bears a child conceived through artificial insemination at a medical facility. Mother subsequently marries and wants her husband to adopt the child. If the medical facility that performed the artificial insemination knows the donor's identity, must an attempt be made to notify him? *See* In the Matter of the Adoption of Michael, 166 Misc.2d 973, 636 N.Y.S.2d 608 (Sur.Ct.1996).

UNIFORM PUTATIVE AND UNKNOWN FATHERS ACT

9B U.L.A. 82 (Supp.1997).

§ 3.

(a) In an adoption or other judicial proceeding that may result in termination of any man's parental rights with respect to a child, the person seeking termination shall give notice to every putative father of the child known to that person.

(b) The notice must be given (i) at a time and place and in a manner appropriate under the [rules of civil procedure for the service of process in a civil action in this State] or (ii) as the court directs and which provides actual notice.

(c) A putative father may participate as a party in a proceeding described in subsection (a).

(d) If, at any time in the proceeding, it appears to the court that there is a putative father of the child who has not been given notice, the court shall require notice of the proceeding to be given to him in accordance with subsection (b).

(e) If, at any time in the proceeding, it appears to the court that an unknown father may not have been given notice, the court shall determine whether he can be identified. The determination must be based on evidence that includes inquiry of appropriate persons in an effort to identify him for the purpose of providing notice. The inquiry must include:

(1) whether the mother was married at the probable time of conception of the child or at a later time;

(2) whether the mother was cohabiting with a man at the probable time of conception of the child;

(3) whether the mother has received support payments or promises of support, other than from a governmental agency, with respect to the child or because of her pregnancy;

(4) whether the mother has named the biological father in connection with applying for or receiving public assistance; and

(5) whether any man has formally or informally acknowledged or claimed paternity of the child in a jurisdiction in which the mother resided at the time of or since conception of the child or in which the child has resided or resides at the time of the inquiry.

(f) If the inquiry required by subsection (e) identifies the unknown father, the court shall require notice of the proceeding to be given to him pursuant to subsection (b).

(g) If, after the inquiry required by subsection (e), it appears to the court that there may be an unknown father of the child, the court shall consider whether publication or public posting of notice of the proceeding is likely to lead to actual notice to him. The court may order publication or public posting of the notice only if, on the basis of all information available, the court determines that the publication or posting is likely to lead to actual notice to him.

§ 4.

(a) The petitioner in a judicial proceeding to change or establish legal or physical custody of or visitation rights with respect to a child shall give notice to every putative father of the child known to the petitioner, except a proceeding for annulment, declaration of invalidity, divorce, marital dissolution, legal separation, modification of child custody, or determination of paternity.

(b) The notice must be given (i) at a time and place and in a manner appropriate under the [rules of civil procedure for the service of process in a civil action in this State] or (ii) as the court determines will likely provide actual notice.

(c) If, at any time in the proceeding, it appears to the court that there is a putative father of the child who has not been given notice of the proceeding, the court shall require notice of the proceeding to be given to him pursuant to subsection (b).

(d) If, at any time in the proceeding, it appears to the court that there may be an unknown father who has not been given notice of the proceeding, the court, in the best interest of the child, may attempt to identify him pursuant to § 3(e) and require notice of the proceeding to be given to him pursuant to § 3(f) and (g).

(e) A putative father may participate as a party in a proceeding described in subsection (a).

How would *Lehr* be decided under the Uniform Act? Would the Act pass constitutional muster under *Lehr*?

Problem 7–1:

Mother, an unmarried woman, gave birth to Baby Boy K. on February 12 and, four days later, filed a petition for voluntary termination of parental rights in which she alleged that the child's father was unknown. The trial court ordered that notice of a hearing to terminate parental rights be served by publication in local newspapers not less than five days prior to the hearing. The notice was printed on February 19 and was addressed "TO: All Whom It May Concern/Daryl" and identified the child by Mother's last name (Baby Boy K___.).

At a hearing on February 24, the trial judge questioned the mother about the father's identity:

> The Court: What were the circumstances here? The father, you don't know him or—
>
> Mother: It was just a one-night drunken incident.
>
> The Court: And you didn't know his full name?
>
> Mother: No.
>
> The Court: The only reason is, we worry about this because sometimes they come back later and we want to make sure that we have done everything we can to make sure that he's been notified. So you are assured it isn't anybody that you know that may later show up and claim the child?
>
> Mother: Yep.
>
> The Court: You are comfortable with that as well?
>
> Social Worker: Yeah, we talked a lot about it.

At the conclusion of the hearing, the trial court terminated the parental rights of both parents. Notice of entry of the judgment was entered on April 8.

On July 26, W. L. filed a petition to vacate the termination order, to establish his paternity, and to obtain custody. In an affidavit included with his motion, W. L. stated that: i) he was unaware of Mother's pregnancy or Child's birth until he was told by a friend of Mother during the second week of March; ii) he immediately confronted Mother; and, iii) after initial denials, she admitted he was the father of Child and told him that the Child had been adopted. W. L. denied having any actual notice of the hearing to terminate his parental rights until this discussion with Mother. W. L.'s affidavit further stated that, on May 23, after he learned of his fatherhood, he filed, before another judge, a paternity action and requested a writ of habeas corpus. In another affidavit filed with the motion, the mother acknowledged that she and W. L. had had a sexual relationship for approximately two weeks during the period of the child's conception, that she had had no contact with him between then and March, that she had lied because "she just wanted to see the baby adopted quickly" and that she believed W. L. was the child's father and a proper person to have custody.

State law provides that "a father of an illegitimate child shall have no right to the service of process in adoption ... or termination of parental rights proceedings unless he is known and identified by the mother or unless he, prior to the entry of a final order in any of the three proceedings, shall have acknowledged the child as his own by affirmatively asserting paternity within sixty (60) days after the birth of the child."

What result under state law? Under the Uniform Act? What constitutional arguments are available to W.L.? Would the *Kelsey S.* court uphold the state statute? Would the U.S. Supreme Court? *See* In the Matter of Baby Boy K., 546 N.W.2d 86 (S.D.1996).

Problem 7–2:

During the fall, John E., age 48, became involved in an extramarital affair with a married woman. At some point during the following spring or summer, the woman learned that she had become pregnant. Initially, she and John E. intended to live together and raise the child, but that fall the woman left John E. and resumed living with her husband. The child, Daniel, was born on December 15 and was turned over to adoptive parents four days later.

John E. had been willing to see his child raised by its mother and her husband but, when he learned in mid-January of the proposed adoption, he commenced a proceeding in Family Court to establish his paternity and seek custody; he also sought to stay the pending adoption proceeding. A genetic marker test ordered by the Court indicated the probability of John E.'s paternity to be 99.93%.

At a hearing in May, John E. indicated that he had been raised by foster parents and, although he had no regrets about his upbringing, he believed that a certain "bonding" occurs between a biological parent and a child which is important to the child's well-being. He also told the court that, as he is divorced and employed full-time, he plans to leave Daniel during his work hours with an adult daughter, with whom he is currently living and who operates a day-care center from her home.

State law provides that the consent of the father of a child born out of wedlock who is under the age of six months at the time he or she is placed for adoption is required if: "(i) such father openly lived with the child or the child's mother for a continuous period of six months immediately preceding the placement of the child for adoption; and (ii) such father openly held himself out to be the father of such child during such period; and (iii) such father paid a fair and reasonable sum, in accordance with his means, for the medical, hospital and nursing expenses incurred in connection with the mother's pregnancy or with the birth of the child."

What result under state law? What constitutional arguments are available to John E.? Would the *Kelsey S.* court uphold the state statute? Would the U.S. Supreme Court? *See* In the Matter of John E. v. John Doe et al., 164 A.D.2d 375, 564 N.Y.S.2d 439 (1990).

Problem 7–3:

You are counsel to the California Legislature's Committee on Family Law. The legislature is aware of the California Supreme Court's decision in *Kelsey S.* and wants to enact new standards governing the rights of unmarried fathers. Its goal is a statute that meets constitutional standards, but does not unduly delay or burden the adoption process. Draft legislation responsive to this aim. How would *Kelsey S.* and problems 7–1 and 7–2 be resolved under your statute?

SECTION 3. WHO MAY ADOPT WHOM?

State restrictions on adoption vary substantially. The Uniform Adoption Act simply, and expansively, permits "any individual ... [to] adopt or be adopted by another individual for the purpose of creating the relationship of parent and child between them." UAA § 1–102. But many state statutes impose restrictions. *See, e.g.,* KAN. STAT. ANN. § 59–2113 (Any adult, or husband and wife jointly, may adopt any minor or adult as their child except that one spouse cannot do so without the consent of the other).

A. ADOPTION IN THE CONTEXT OF NONTRADITIONAL RELATIONSHIPS

IN THE MATTER OF JACOB, IN THE MATTER OF DANA, G.M.

Court of Appeals of New York, 1995.
86 N.Y.2d 651, 636 N.Y.S.2d 716, 660 N.E.2d 397.

KAYE, CHIEF JUDGE.

Under the New York adoption statute, a single person can adopt a child (Domestic Relations Law § 110). Equally clear is the right of a single homosexual to adopt (see, 18 NYCRR 421.16[h][2] [qualified adoption agencies "shall not * * * reject [adoption petitions] solely on the basis of homosexuality"]). These appeals call upon us to decide if the unmarried partner of a child's biological mother, whether heterosexual or homosexual, who is raising the child together with the biological parent, can become the child's second parent by means of adoption.

Because the two adoptions sought—one by an unmarried heterosexual couple, the other by the lesbian partner of the child's mother—are fully consistent with the adoption statute, we answer this question in the affirmative. To rule otherwise would mean that the thousands of New

York children actually being raised in homes headed by two unmarried persons could have only one legal parent, not the two who want them.

The Adoptions Sought

In *Matter of Jacob*, Roseanne M.A. and Jacob's biological father (from whom she is divorced) separated prior to the child's birth and Roseanne M.A. was awarded sole custody. Jacob was a year old when Stephen T.K. began living with him and his mother in early 1991. At the time of filing the joint petition for adoption three years later, Stephen T.K. was employed as a programmer/analyst with an annual income of $50,000, while Roseanne M.A. was a student at SUNY Health Center. Jacob's biological father consented to the adoption.

Though acknowledging that "the granting of an adoption in this matter may be beneficial to Jacob," Family Court dismissed the petition for lack of standing on the ground that Domestic Relations Law § 110 does not authorize adoptions by an unmarried couple. The Appellate Division affirmed, two Justices dissenting, and an appeal to this Court was taken as of right.

In Matter of Dana, appellants are G.M. and her lesbian partner, P.I., who have lived together in what is described as a long and close relationship for the past 19 years. G.M. works as a special education teacher in the public schools earning $38,000 annually and P.I., employed at an athletic club, has an annual income of $48,000. In 1989, the two women decided that P.I. would have a child they would raise together. P.I. was artificially inseminated by an anonymous donor, and on June 6, 1990, she gave birth to Dana. G.M. and P.I. have shared parenting responsibilities since Dana's birth and have arranged their separate work schedules around her needs. With P.I.'s consent, G.M. filed a petition to adopt Dana in April 1993.

In the court-ordered report recommending that G.M. be permitted to adopt, the disinterested investigator described Dana as an attractive, sturdy and articulate little girl with a "rich family life," which includes frequent visits with G.M.'s three grown children from a previous marriage "who all love Dana and accept her as their baby sister." Noting that G.M. "only has the best interest of Dana in mind," the report concluded that she "provides her with a family structure in which to grow and flourish."

As in *Matter of Jacob*, Family Court, while conceding the favorable results of the home study and "in no way disparaging the ability of [G.M.] to be a good, nurturing and loving parent," denied the petition for lack of standing. In addition, the court held that the adoption was further prohibited by Domestic Relations Law § 117 which it interpreted to require the automatic termination of P.I.'s relationship with Dana upon an adoption by G.M. Despite its conclusion that G.M. had standing to adopt, the Appellate Division nevertheless affirmed on the ground that Domestic Relations Law § 117 prohibits the adoption. We granted leave to appeal.

Limiting our analysis, as did the courts below, to the preserved statutory interpretation issues, we conclude that appellants have standing to adopt under Domestic Relations Law § 110 and are not foreclosed from doing so by Domestic Relations Law § 117. There being no statutory preclusion, we now reverse the order of the Appellate Division in each case and remit the matter to Family Court for a factual evaluation and determination as to whether these adoptions would be in the best interest of the children.

The Context of our Statutory Analysis

Two basic themes of overarching significance set the context of our statutory analysis.

First and foremost, since adoption in this State is "solely the creature of * * * statute," the adoption statute must be strictly construed. What is to be construed strictly and applied rigorously in this sensitive area of the law, however, is legislative purpose as well as legislative language. Thus, the adoption statute must be applied in harmony with the humanitarian principle that adoption is a means of securing the best possible home for a child.

Ten years ago, in *Matter of Robert Paul P.*, 63 N.Y.2d 233, we refused to allow the adoption of a 50–year-old man by his 57–year-old homosexual partner even though the statutory language permitted the adoption. Our refusal in *Robert Paul P.* rested solely on the fact that the adult adoption sought in that case would have been "wholly inconsistent with the underlying public policy of providing a parent-child relationship for the welfare of the child" (*id.*).

The very next year, in *Matter of Best*, 66 N.Y.2d 151, we again chose not to construe the words of the adoption statute strictly, declining to permit an adopted child to inherit under the will of his biological grandmother because "[p]owerful policy considerations militate against construing a class gift to include a child adopted out of the family." One commentator has characterized our decision in *Best* as "in defiance of * * * the text of the Domestic Relations Law * * * yet in accordance with current societal views of adoption and the adoptive relationship."

What *Matter of Robert Paul P.* and *Matter of Best* underscore is that in strictly construing the adoption statute, our primary loyalty must be to the statute's legislative purpose—the child's best interest ... This profound concern for the child's welfare is reflected in the statutory language itself: when "satisfied that the best interests of the * * * child will be promoted thereby," a court "shall make an order approving the adoption" (Domestic Relations Law § 114).

This policy would certainly be advanced in situations like those presented here by allowing the two adults who actually function as a child's parents to become the child's legal parents. The advantages which would result from such an adoption include Social Security and life insurance benefits in the event of a parent's death or disability, the right to sue for the wrongful death of a parent, the right to inherit under rules of intestacy and eligibility for coverage under both parents' health insurance policies. In addition, granting a second parent adoption further ensures that two adults are legally entitled to make medical decisions for the child in case of emergency and are under a legal obligation for the child's economic support (*see*, Domestic Relations Law § 32).

Even more important, however, is the emotional security of knowing that in the event of the biological parent's death or disability, the other parent will have presumptive custody, and the children's relationship with their parents, siblings and other relatives will continue should the coparents separate. Indeed, viewed from the children's perspective, permitting the adoptions allows the children to achieve a measure of permanency with both parent figures and avoids the sort of disruptive visitation battle we faced in *Matter of Alison D. v. Virginia M.* [where the biological mother's former lesbian "coparent," who had not adopted the child and from whom the mother had separated, sought visitation over the mother's objection; the Court ruled that she did not have standing to seek visitation].

A second, related point of overriding significance is that the various sections comprising New York's adoption statute today represent a complex and not entirely reconcilable patchwork. Amended innumerable times since its passage in 1873, the adoption statute was last consolidated nearly 60 years ago, in 1938. Thus, after decades of piecemeal amendment upon amendment, the statute today contains language from the 1870's alongside language from the 1990's.

Though courts surely must, and do, strive to give effect to every word of a statute, our analysis must recognize the difficulty—perhaps unique difficulty—of such an endeavor here. With its long, tortuous history, New York's adoption statute today is a far cry from a "methodical and meticulous" expression of legislative judgment. That the questions posed by these appeals are not readily answerable by reference to the words of a particular section of the law, but instead require the traditional and often close and difficult task of statutory interpretation is evident even in the length of today's opinions—whichever result is reached.

Against this backdrop, we turn to the particular provisions at issue.

Domestic Relations Law § 110: Despite ambiguity in other sections, one thing is clear: § 110 allows appellants to become adoptive parents. Domestic Relations Law § 110, entitled "Who May Adopt," provides that an "adult unmarried person or an adult husband and his adult wife together may adopt another person." Under this language, both appellant G.M. in *Matter of Dana* and appellant Stephen T.K. in *Matter of Jacob*, as adult unmarried persons, have standing to adopt and appellants are correct that the Court's analysis of § 110 could appropriately end here.

Endowing the word "together" as used in § 110 with the overpowering significance of enforcing a policy in favor of marriage (as the dissent does) would require us to rewrite the statute. The statute uses the word "together" only to describe married persons and thus does not preclude an unmarried person in a relationship with another unmarried person from adopting. Rather, by insisting on the joint consent of the married persons, the statutory term "together" simply insures that one spouse cannot adopt a child without the other spouse's knowledge or over the other's objection. Since each of the biological mothers here is not only aware of these proceedings, but has expressly consented to the adoptions, § 110 poses no statutory impediment.

* * *

Domestic Relations Law § 117: Appellants having standing to adopt pursuant to Domestic Relations Law § 110, the other statutory obstacle relied upon by the lower courts in denying the petitions is the provision that "[a]fter the making of an order of adoption the natural parents of the adoptive child shall be relieved of all parental duties toward and of all responsibilities for and shall have no rights over such adoptive child or to his property by descent or succession" (DOMESTIC RELATIONS LAW § 117[1][a]). Literal application of this language would effectively prevent these adoptions since it would require the termination of the biological mothers' rights upon adoption thereby placing appellants in the "Catch–22" of having to choose one of two coparents as the child's only legal parent.

As outlined below, however, neither the language nor policy underlying § 117 dictates that result.

The Language of § 117. Both the title of § 117 ("Effect of adoption") and its opening phrase ("After the making of an order of adoption") suggest that the section has nothing to do with the standing of an individual to adopt, an issue treated exclusively in § 110. Rather, § 117 addresses the legal effect of an adoption on the parties and their property.

Also plain on the face of § 117 is that it speaks principally of estate law. Words such as "succession," "inheritance," "decedent," "instrument" and "will" permeate the statute. Read contextually, it is clear that the Legislature's chief concern in § 117 was the resolution of property disputes upon the death of an adoptive parent or child. As we observed in *People ex rel. Sibley v. Sheppard*, *supra*, where we declined to read § 117's termination language "overbroadly * * * [to] interfere with the court's ability to protect the best interest of the child" and thereby prohibit visits with the child's biological grandparents, the "bulk of the statute refers to intestacy and succession." Thus, from the very beginning of what is now § 117, both the scholarly commentary about the section and its dozen or so amendments have centered on issues of property rights and inheritance . . .

* * *

Recent Statutory Amendments: Moving beyond the language and history of § 117 itself, our reading of the statute is further supported by recent amendments to other sections of the adoption law ... Social Services Law § 383–c, enacted in 1990, provides that biological parents willing to give their child up for adoption must execute a written instrument, known as a "surrender," stating "in conspicuous bold print on the first page" that "the parent is giving up all rights to have custody, visit with, write to or learn about the child, forever." [Independent adoption] is also regulated by a newly revised statute requiring the execution of a written "consent" stating that "no action * * * may be maintained * * * for the custody of the child." DOMESTIC RELATIONS LAW § 115–b. Both statutes ... require biological parents to execute a document that effectively terminates parental rights. Both provisions require a Judge or Surrogate (if the document is executed in court) to inform the biological parents of the consequences of their act, and advise them of their right to be represented by counsel. More importantly, both statutes provide generally that the biological parents' "surrender" or "consent" may be revoked within 45 days, and that an adoption proceeding may not be commenced until after the expiration of that period....

The procedural safeguards contained in Social Services Law § 383–c and Domestic Relations Law § 115–b—safeguards that reflect modern sensitivities as to the level of procedural protection required for waiver of parental rights—further indicate that § 117 does not invariably mandate termination in all circumstances. Under the language of § 117 alone, a biological mother's rights could theoretically be severed unilaterally, without notice as to the consequences or other procedural protections. Though arguably adequate in 1938 when the statute was enacted, such a summary procedure would be unlikely to pass muster today.

The above-described amendments to Social Services Law § 383–c and Domestic Relations Law § 115–b suggest that the Legislature in recent years has devised statutory vehicles other than § 117 to carefully regulate and restrict parental rights during the adoption process, again militating against a rigid application of subdivision (1)(a).

The Ambiguity Should Be Resolved in the Children's Favor:

* * *

"Where the language of a statute is susceptible of two constructions, the courts will adopt that which avoids injustice, hardship, constitutional doubts or other objectionable results." Given that § 117 is open to two differing interpretations as to whether it automatically terminates parental rights in all cases, a construction of the section that would deny children like Jacob and Dana the opportunity of having their two de facto parents become their legal parents, based solely on their biological mother's sexual orientation or marital status, would not only be unjust under the circumstances, but also might raise constitutional concerns in light of the adoption statute's historically consistent purpose—the best interests of the child.

These concerns are particularly weighty in *Matter of Dana*. Even if the Court were to rule against him on this appeal, the male petitioner in

Matter of Jacob could still adopt by marrying Jacob's mother. Dana, however, would be irrevocably deprived of the benefits and entitlements of having as her legal parents the two individuals who have already assumed that role in her life, simply as a consequence of her mother's sexual orientation.

Any proffered justification for rejecting these petitions based on a governmental policy disapproving of homosexuality or encouraging marriage would not apply. As noted above, New York has not adopted a policy disfavoring adoption by either single persons or homosexuals. In fact, the most recent legislative document relating to the subject urges courts to construe § 117 in precisely the manner we have as it cautions against discrimination against "nonmarital children" and "unwed parents." An interpretation of the statute that avoids such discrimination or hardship is all the more appropriate here where a contrary ruling could jeopardize the legal status of the many New York children whose adoptions by second parents have already taken place.

Conclusion: To be sure, the Legislature that last codified § 117 in 1938 may never have envisioned families that "include[ ] two adult lifetime partners whose relationship is * * * characterized by an emotional and financial commitment and interdependence." Nonetheless, it is clear that § 117, designed as a shield to protect new adoptive families, was never intended as a sword to prohibit otherwise beneficial intrafamily adoptions by second parents.

* * *

BELLACOSA, JUDGE (dissenting).

These appeals share a statutory construction issue under New York's adoption laws. While the results reached by the majority are intended to have a benevolent effect on the individuals involved in these two cases, the means to those ends transform the legislative adoption charter governing countless other individuals. Additionally, the dispositional methodology transcends institutional limitations on this Court's proper exercise of its authority, fixed by internal discipline and by the external distribution of powers among the branches of government.

The majority minimizes the at-will relationships of the appellant couples who would be combined biological-adoptive parents in each case, but the significant statutory and legally central relevancy is inescapable. Unlike married and single parent households, each couple here cohabits only day-to-day, no matter the depth or length of their voluntary arrangements. Their relationships lack legal permanency and the State has not endowed them with the benefits and enforceable protections that flow from relationships recognized under color of law. Nowhere do statutes, or any case law previously, recognize de facto, functional or second parent adoptions in joint circumstances as presented here.

* * *

Pointedly, this Court's unqualified utterance is that " ' "[t]he Legislature has supreme control of the subject" ' " A transcendent societal goal in the field of domestic relations is to stabilize family relationships, particularly parent-child bonds. That State interest promotes permanency planning and provides protection for an adopted child's legally secure familial placement. Therefore, statutory authorizations should not be substantively transformed under the guise of interpretation, and all facets of the adoption statutes should be harmonized.

* * *

... [T]he common issue here involves a subject on which the Legislature has expressed itself. These cases appear on a screen on which the Legislature has delineated its will and judgment methodically and meticulously to reflect its enactments. Ambiguity cannot directly or indirectly create or substitute for the lack of statutory authorization to adopt. These adoption statutes are luminously clear on one unassailable feature: no express legislative authorization is discernible for what is, nevertheless, permitted by the holdings today. Nor do the statutes anywhere speak of de facto, functional or second parent adoptions. Frankly, if the Legislature had intended to alter the definitions and interplay of its plenary, detailed adoption blueprint to cover the circumstances as presented here, it has had ample and repeated opportunities, means and words to effectuate such purpose plainly and definitively as a matter of notice, guidance, stability and reliability. It has done so before (*see, e.g.*, L. 1984, ch. 218 [permitting adoption by adults not yet divorced]; L. 1951, ch. 211 [permitting adoption by a minor].

Because the Legislature did not do so here, neither should this Court in this manner. * * *

Notes and Questions

1. How, if at all, would the court's decision be affected if Dana, who was in fact conceived with sperm obtained from a sperm bank, had been conceived with sperm donated by a friend?

2. A few states have barred all adoptions by homosexuals. *See, e.g.*, N.H. Rev. Stat. Ann. §§ 170–B:4,-F:6; Fla. Stat. Ann. § 63.042(3). In states without such a prohibition, courts have divided on the propriety of an adoption like that sought in Matter of Dana. For cases following the *Dana* approach, *see, e.g.,* In re Tammy, 416 Mass. 205, 619 N.E.2d 315 (1993); In re Adoptions of B.L.V.B. & E.L.V.B., 160 Vt. 368, 628 A.2d 1271 (Vt. 1993); In re Adoption by H.N.R., 285 N.J.Super. 1, 666 A.2d 535 (1995); In re M.M.D., 662 A.2d 837 (D.C.App.1995). For cases denying permission to adopt, *see, e.g.*, In re Angel Lace M., 184 Wis.2d 492, 516 N.W.2d 678 (1994); In re T.K.J. & K.A.K., 931 P.2d 488 (Colo.App.1996). *See also* Annot, 27 A.L.R.5th 54 (1995).

3. Is the New York Court of Appeals correct in equating gay and heterosexual cohabitants under the New York adoption laws? What are the pros and cons of treating these cases alike?

B. RACIAL AND ETHNIC MATCHING IN ADOPTION

Traditionally, adoption agencies attempted to place each child with adoptive parents who offered a close match with the child's biological and cultural heritage. Matching typically was based on race, religion, and physical features; it was done behind the scenes in order to protect the privacy of the biological mother.

Starting in the 1960s and 70s, as the gap between the supply of and demand for adoptable white infants mounted, agencies reassessed these practices; many began to permit transracial adoption. But the increased rate of transracial adoption produced organized opposition:

> Organized opposition to transracial adoption began in the early part of the 1970s, and by 1975 was formidable enough to bring about a reversal in policy on the part of major adoption agencies in various states throughout the country. The opposition was led and organized primarily by black social workers and leaders of black political organizations who saw in the practice an insidious scheme for depriving the black community of its most valuable future resource: its children. In essence, the leaders of black and Indian organizations argue that non-white children who are adopted by white parents are lost to the non-white community. The experience of growing up in a white world makes it impossible for them to ever take their rightful place among the non-white communities. And this they see as a double tragedy.
>
> * * *
>
> Some of the leaders of American Indian groups labeled transracial adoption "genocide" and accused white society of perpetuating its most malevolent scheme, that of seeking to deny the Indians their future by taking away their children.
>
> Both the blacks and the Indians who led and organized the opposition to transracial adoption agreed on one major point—that it is impossible for white parents to rear black or Indian children in such an environment as to permit them to retain or develop a black or Indian identity.

RITA J. SIMON & HOWARD ALTSTEIN, TRANSRACIAL ADOPTION 2–3 (1977)

Simon and Altstein noted that "[a]s we write in the beginning of 1976, it appears that we are witnessing the demise of transracial adoption as a significant alternative to homelessness," and for a while this appeared to be the case. In the Indian Child Welfare Act, Congress required the states to prefer a member of an Indian child's tribe or another Indian over other prospective adoptive parents. The justification for the Act was summarized by the Supreme Court:

> The Indian Child Welfare Act of 1978 (ICWA) was the product of rising concern in the mid-1970's over the consequences to Indian children, Indian families, and Indian tribes of abusive child welfare practices that resulted in the separation of large numbers of Indian

children from their families and tribes through adoption or foster care placement, usually in non-Indian homes.... Studies undertaken by the Association on American Indian Affairs in 1969 and 1974, and presented in the Senate hearings, showed that 25% to 35% of all Indian children had been separated from their families and placed in adoptive families, foster care, or institutions. Adoptive placements counted significantly in this total: in the State of Minnesota, for example, one in eight Indian children under the age of 18 was in an adoptive home, and during the year 1971–1972 nearly one in every four infants under one year of age was placed for adoption. The adoption rate of Indian children was eight times that of non-Indian children. Approximately 90% of the Indian placements were in non-Indian homes. A number of witnesses also testified to the serious adjustment problems encountered by such children during adolescence,[1] as well as the impact of the adoptions on Indian parents and the tribes themselves.

Mississippi Band of Choctaw Indians v. Holyfield, 109 S.Ct. 1597 (1989).

While Congress did not act to protect other ethnic and racial minorities, a number of states adopted or maintained race-matching requirements for adoptable children placed in foster care or waiting for adoption. Some maintained a time limit for a same-race search before a transracial placement could be considered.

But consensus on transracial adoption has not been reached. Some experts, armed with the results of studies finding no obvious adverse psychological effects from transracial adoption, argue that the result of racial matching policies is simply children without homes. Others disagree.

AMERICA'S WAITING CHILDREN 29–30

Interagency Task Force on Adoption (1988).

Nearly half of the children waiting to be adopted are minorities, with 43 percent being black and the remainder Hispanic, Indian, Orien-

1. For example, Dr. Joseph Westermeyer, a University of Minnesota social psychiatrist, testified about his research with Indian adolescents who experienced difficulty coping in white society, despite the fact that they had been raised in a purely white environment: "[T]hey were raised with a white cultural and social identity. They are raised in a white home. They attended predominantly white schools, and in almost all cases, attended a church that was predominantly white, and really came to understand very little about Indian culture, Indian behavior, and had virtually no viable Indian identity. They can recall such things as seeing cowboys and Indians on TV and feeling that Indians were a historical figure but were not a viable contemporary social group. Then during adolescence, they found that society was not to grant them the white identity that they had. They began to find this out in a number of ways. For example, a universal experience was that when they began to date white children, the parents of the white youngsters were against this, and there were pressures among white children from the parents not to date these Indian children. * * * The other experience was derogatory name calling in relation to their racial identity * * * [T]hey were finding that society was putting on them an identity which they didn't possess and taking from them an identity that they did possess."

tal or other. Black children remain in foster care longer than white children. As a result, they are disproportionately represented among the older and more severely disabled foster children. Black families are more difficult to recruit for adolescents or children with disabilities. In some areas of the country, finding black or Indian families willing to adopt same-race or biracial infants is time consuming, expensive, and often, futile.

* * *

The Task Force recommends . . . that . . . [,a]ll things being equal, it is preferable to place a child in a family of his own racial background. However, no child available for adoption should be deprived of the opportunity to have a permanent family of his own because of his age, religion, race, nationality, residence or handicaps that do not preclude his living in a family or community. Because of this, racial background in itself should not determine the selection of a family for a child. Transracial adoption is a valid method of providing a child with a home and family that will meet his needs. * * *

TWILA L. PERRY, THE TRANSRACIAL ADOPTION CONTROVERSY: AN ANALYSIS OF DISCOURSE AND SUBORDINATION

21 N.Y.U. Rev. Law & Soc. Change 33, 57–59, 82, 86–87, 107 (1993–94).

For some years, researchers have concluded that transracial parenting has not detrimentally affected the adopted children.... [T]hese conclusions have not compelled opponents of transracial adoption to change their views.

There are several reasons why the studies may not have swayed transracial adoption's opponents. First, opponents may believe that the results of the studies are overstated, particularly since the studies are not uniformly positive. At least one study found that the development of a positive racial identity seemed to be more difficult for transracial adoptees than for children adopted by adults of the same race. Another study, comparing white, Colombian, Korean, and African American transracial adoptees, found the latter group to be the least well-adjusted.

Second, a number of methodological concerns may cast doubt on the studies' findings. Many of the studies lack control groups and may be biased, either in favor of, or against transracial adoption, because of the source of their funding or their sponsorship. In some of the longitudinal studies, only a relatively small percentage of the families are still being followed years later. The families who were unsuccessful with transracial adoption may have dropped out of the studies at a greater rate than those who were successful. In addition, the objectivity of the children and their parents in assessing the transracial adoption relationship must be questioned. Furthermore the research to date has followed the children only into early adulthood. While it is true that a significant number of life patterns are usually established by this age, we still do not know how the transracial adoption experience will affect particular aspects of adulthood, such as marriage or long-term success in the workplace. These are also important in gauging the true effects of transracial adoption on Black children.

Finally, the conclusions of the studies are somewhat contradictory. Most of the researchers have concluded, despite their empirical findings that while Black children who are transracially adopted are not detrimentally affected, that Black children should still be placed with Black adoptive parents whenever possible. Apparently the researchers believe that racial considerations cannot be disaggregated from the "best interests" of the transracially adopted child.

* * *

One false impression ... [some advocates of transracial adoption convey] is that the policies preferring Black adoptive parents for Black children are primarily responsible for the number of Black children remaining in foster care on a long-term basis.* * * [But this] ... gloss[es] over the fact that the debate over transracial adoption is really a struggle over Black babies instead of a struggle over the full range of Black children available for adoption. It has been reported that "only 1% or less of the white families willing to adopt Black children request children who are most in need of families: children over eight years of age, sibling groups and emotionally and physically handicapped children." This statistic belies the fantasy world of the television sitcom, in which whites are shown adopting "cute" older Black children with growth disorders. The reality is that most white families that are willing to adopt transracially are not interested in these children. They want black newborns, not older children with emotional or physical disabilities.

Another fact glossed over by advocates of transracial adoption is that there are also plenty of white children available for adoption. These children, like most of the Black children available, are older, physically, or emotionally disabled, or are siblings in need of the same placement. If white families want to adopt children who are in need of homes, we must ask why they are not rushing to adopt these children.

Arguments that Black children are trapped in foster care because of agencies' antitransracial policies can easily become a type of rescue fantasy—a modern-day version of "white man's burden." Such arguments depict Black people as unwilling or unable to help themselves, while they let whites off the hook—permitting them to believe they are willing to do something significant to help Black people, while the systemic problems confronting the vast majority of Black children go unaddressed.... [Yet] research demonstrates that Black people do indeed adopt ... Indeed, middle income Black families adopt at a higher rate than their white counterparts. Furthermore, research has shown that Blacks adopt relatives at a higher rate than do whites.

One of the saddest facts of the transracial adoption controversy is that this is the context in which a significant debate over the welfare of Black children is taking place.... The energy spent on the issue of transracial adoption is not accompanied by energy directed toward improving the material circumstances that so profoundly affect the welfare of the vast majority of Black children who will continue to be raised in Black families in Black communities. This raises the question of whether the transracial adoption debate is really about the interests of Black children at all, or is instead about the right of white people to parent whichever children they choose.

In 1996, Congress enacted the Adoption Assistance Act of 1996, Pub. L. 104–188, § 1808, which prohibits racial matching in adoption (although it does create an exemption for the Indian Child Welfare Law). UAA § 2–104(c) also provides that an "... agency may not delay or deny a minor's placement for adoption solely on the basis of the minor's race, national origin, or ethnic background...." The National Association of Black Social Workers continues to favor racial matching as a means of protecting minority children from losing their identities.

Notes and Questions

1. For more on transracial adoption, *see, e.g.* Elizabeth Bartholet, *Where Do Black Children Belong? The Politics of Race Matching in Adoption,* 139 U. Pa. L. Rev. 1163 (1991); Margaret Howard, *Transracial Adoption: Analysis of the Best Interests Standard,* 59 Notre Dame L. Rev. 503, 517 (1984); Joan Mahoney, *The Black Baby Doll: Transracial Adoption and Cultural Preservation,* 59 UMKC L.Rev. 487 (1991). *See also* Kim Forde–Mazrui, Note, *Black Identity and Child Placement: The Best Interests of Black and Biracial Children,* 92 Mich. L. Rev. 925 (1994).

2. Would it be constitutional (or logical) to treat different racial groups differently? If so, on what basis?

3. Religious matching was once widely practiced along with racial and ethnic matching. For example, New York Const: Art. VI, § 32 states that a child "shall be committed or remanded or placed, when practicable, in an institution or agency governed by persons, or in the custody of a person, of the same religious persuasion as the child." *See* Dickens v. Ernesto, 30 N.Y.2d 61, 330 N.Y.S.2d 346, 281 N.E.2d 153 (N.Y. 1972); Wilder v. Sugarman, 385 F.Supp. 1013 (S.D.N.Y.1974). Religious matching policies derived in part from the fact that many adoption agencies were religiously affiliated. *See* Homer H. Clark, Jr., Domestic Relations in the United States 917 (2d ed. 1988); Martin Guggenheim, *State-Supported Foster Care: The Interplay Between the Prohibition of Establishing Religion and the Free Exercise Rights of Parents and Children: Wilder v. Bernstein*, 56 Brooklyn L. Rev. 603, 605 (1990); Laura J. Schwartz,

Religious Matching For Adoption: Unraveling the Interests Behind the "Best Interests" Standard, 25 Fam. L. Q. 171 (1991).

Problem 7–4:

Draft a policy on transracial adoption that is responsive both to the concerns raised by the Interagency Task Force and Professor Perry. Would you recommend this policy to Congress? Why or why not?

SECTION 4. THE EFFECT OF ADOPTION

MICHAUD v. WAWRUCK ET AL.

Supreme Court of Connecticut, 1988.
209 Conn. 407, 551 A.2d 738.

Peters, Chief Justice.

The sole issue in this case is whether a written visitation agreement between a genetic mother and adoptive parents violates the public policy of this state. The plaintiff, Jacqueline Michaud, filed a complaint seeking specific enforcement of an "Open Adoption and Visitation Agreement" between herself and the defendants, James Wawruck and Cynthia Wawruck. The defendants filed a motion to strike the complaint, which was granted by the trial court, Barall, J., and was the basis for the subsequent rendering of a judgment in favor of the defendants by the trial court ... We find error and remand the case for further proceedings.

* * *

We assume the following factual circumstances concerning the "Open Adoption and Visitation Agreement" negotiated by the parties. The Ellington Probate Court, on August 31, 1981, terminated the plaintiff's parental rights with respect to her child born on February 5, 1979. The same Probate Court terminated the father's parental rights on January 6, 1982. At some time thereafter, in 1982, the plaintiff filed a Superior Court action against the commissioner of children and youth services to set aside the Probate Court's decree terminating her parental rights, on the ground that her consent to that proceeding had been fraudulently procured by the child's father. The child's foster parents, who were then seeking to adopt the child, were permitted to intervene as defendants in the Superior Court action. The plaintiff agreed to withdraw her lawsuit, and to allow the adoption to go forward, in exchange for the defendants' agreement to permit regular visitation between the plaintiff and the child during the child's minor years.[2]

2. The "Open Adoption and Visitation Agreement" provides in relevant part: ... 3. Visitation. The adopting parents will cooperate fully with the natural-mother in the natural mother's visits with the child both now and after the adoption takes place until the child's 18th birthday. The parties agree to be guided in carrying out this provision by the present laws of Connecticut regarding reasonable visitation, which are partly embodied in Connecticut General Statutes § 46b–56, as they pertain to visitation rights of non-custodial parents in dissolutions of marriage. The tender age of the child and her high sensitivity to her, up to

The agreement between the parties was placed on record in the Superior Court on September 16, 1983. Acquiescence in the agreement was noted, in open court, by counsel for the plaintiff, for the defendants, for the commissioner, and for the minor child. The agreement was not, however, made part of the subsequent decree of the Probate Court permitting the defendants to adopt the child, although the parties to that proceeding, having all appeared in the Superior Court action, were fully aware of its terms. After the adoption had been finalized, the defendants terminated all visitation between the plaintiff and the child.

The trial court, after reviewing these facts, granted the defendants' motion to strike the plaintiff's complaint because, in its view, enforcement of the "Open Adoption and Visitation Agreement" would violate Connecticut's adoption statutes. According to the trial court, adoption, as a creature of statute, must comply strictly with statutory requirements, and the existing statutes governing adoption preclude private "side agreements" that would serve to perpetuate a relationship, after adoption, between a genetic parent and an adopted child. The court noted that termination of parental rights, under General Statutes § 45–61b(g), operates as a "complete severance by court order of the legal relationship ... between the child and his parent ..." Furthermore, under General Statutes § 45–64a, adoption creates new legal relationships in which the adopting parents are completely substituted for the genetic parents of an adopted person. Finally, the trial court observed that General Statutes § 45–63 requires agreements about adoption to be in writing and filed in the Probate Court. Relying on these statutory provisions, and a number of out-of-state cases, the court concluded that the contract between the parties could not confer upon the plaintiff a specifically enforceable right to visitation after completion of the adoption process.

... We disagree with the trial court's ruling.

The validity of an "open adoption" agreement is a matter of first impression for this court. Before we address the merits of this question, we should note that the title "open adoption," which has apparently become the standard characterization of such agreements, conveys a misleading impression of what such agreements intend to accomplish. The plaintiff does not seek to "open," to set aside or to diminish in any way the adoptive process that has substituted the defendants as the legal parents of the child. The plaintiff's rights are not premised on an ongoing genetic relationship that somehow survives a termination of parental rights and an adoption. Instead, the plaintiff is asking us to decide whether, as an adult who has had an ongoing personal relation-

the present, state of uncertainty shall be taken into account by the parties.

Each of the parties shall at all times in good faith endeavor to maintain in the child respect and affection for the other parties.

The rights of visitation shall not be exercised by the natural mother at any time or in such a manner as to interfere with the education and normal social and school activities of the child.

Visitation shall be twice a month for three (3) hours each visit at the Wawrucks' home."

ship with the child, she may contract with the adopting parents, prior to adoption, for the continued right to visit with the child, so long as that visitation continues to be in the best interest of the child.

Our statutes recognize that visitation encompasses considerations that differ from those that govern custody, guardianship or parental status. The plaintiff reminds us that, in the adoption statutes themselves, while an application for adoption must disclose pending proceedings "affecting the custody of the child to be adopted ... [f]or the purposes of [such disclosure], visitation rights granted by any court shall not be considered as affecting the custody of the child." General Statutes § 45–63(a)(2). The defendants maintain that this statutory distinction merely reflects the fact that Probate Court adoption proceedings necessarily must take outstanding custody orders into account, while visitation rights are not so implicated. This explanation for the distinction contained in § 45–63 may well be accurate but it does not eradicate the existence of the distinction and thus supports the plaintiff's position that the adoption statutes do not expressly make a visitation agreement void as against public policy.

Even more significantly, our visitation statute, permits the Superior Court, upon a proper application, to "grant the right of visitation with respect to any minor child ... to any person .... In making, modifying or terminating such an order, the court shall be guided by the best interest of the child ... Visitation rights granted in accordance with this section shall not be deemed to have created parental rights in the person ... to whom such visitation rights are granted. * * * The only criterion under § 46b–59 is the best interest of the child." All this plaintiff seeks is a court order consistent with the statutory constraints imposed on visitation by § 46b–59.

In light of these statutes, we are unpersuaded that the agreement between the parties in this case violates the public policy of Connecticut. * * * Case law in other jurisdictions does not persuade us that we should strike down the visitation agreement in this case. To a significant extent, the cases turn on legislative determinations that vary from state to state....

Traditional models of the nuclear family have come, in recent years, to be replaced by various configurations of parents, stepparents, adoptive parents and grandparents. We are not prepared to assume that the welfare of children is best served by a narrow definition of those whom we permit to continue to manifest their deep concern for a child's growth and development. The record of the 1982 Superior Court proceedings to set aside the termination of the plaintiff's parental rights demonstrates that, in the present case, the "Open Adoption and Visitation Agreement" was openly and lovingly negotiated, in good faith, in order to promote the best interest of the child. The attorney for the child reported that the child thought the agreement between her mother and her soon-to-be adoptive parents would be "the best world that she could imagine." This agreement did not violate public policy, either ab initio or upon the subsequent entry of a decree of adoption.

We therefore remand this case to the trial court for a hearing on the merits of the plaintiff's claim that visitation would now be in the best interest of the child. * * *

Notes and Questions

1. *The Availability of Open Adoption:* State court decisions on the availability of open adoption under traditional adoption statutes are not uniform. *Compare* Weinschel v. Strople, 56 Md.App. 252, 261, 466 A.2d 1301 (1983) (approving open adoption) *with* In re Gregory B., 73 N.Y.2d 704, 537 N.Y.S.2d 491, 534 N.E.2d 329 (1989) (disapproving open adoption). As of 1995, Indiana, Nebraska, New Mexico, New York, Oregon and Washington had enacted legislation specifically authorizing and governing this form of adoption. *See* Annette Ruth Appell, *Blending Families Through Adoption: Implications for Collaborative Adoption Law and Practice,* 75 B.U. L. REV. 997, 1028–38 (1995) (describing and comparing statutes).

2. *The Impact of Open Adoption:* Studies have found that some birth mothers are more willing to relinquish their children for adoption when they can receive information from the adoptive parents or maintain some form of contact after the relinquishment. *See* Marianne Berry, *Risks and Benefits of Open Adoption,* 3 THE FUTURE OF CHILDREN: ADOPTION 125, 129–30 (Spring 1993). Is this a risk or a benefit of open adoption? Why?

Research reports describing the impact of open adoption on the children are still sparse; none of these reports have followed children to adulthood. But in what is perhaps the largest study to date, which compared outcomes in almost 1400 adoptions of children from infants to sixteen year olds, the researchers found that children in open adoptions had significantly better behavior scores (as rated by their adoptive parents) than did children in adoptions with no access to birth parents; they also found that adoptive parents of children who were in contact with birth parents had more positive impressions of those birth parents than did adoptive parents who had no contact. But it is possible that adoptive parents with favorable impressions of birth parents were willing to undertake open adoption precisely for that reason; it is also possible that a willingness to undertake open adoption is related to a greater willingness to assess the adoptive child's behavior favorably. *See* Berry, *supra,* at 132–34 (describing and assessing research).

3. *Abrogation of Adoption:* While the traditional view has been that adoptive parents cannot annul an adoption, "failed" adoptions are on the increase. An important source of failed nonrelative adoptions is the increase in adoptions of older children with emotional or physical problems; a few states now have statutory provisions that allow an adoption to be set aside for a developmental or mental "deficiency" existing or unknown at the time of the adoption. *See, e.g.,* CAL. CIV. CODE § 228.10

(permitting action up to five years after adoption is final). For stepparent adoptions, divorce between the stepparent and biological parent is the typical reason for failure. *See* Kathleen M. Lynch, *Adoption: Can Adoptive Parents Change Their Minds?*, 26 FAM. L.Q. 257, 260 (1992).

4. *Wrongful Adoption:* A number of courts have recognized a tort of "wrongful adoption" when an adoption agency misrepresents or withholds information relating to the adoptive child's health or psychological background. *See, e.g.,* Juman v. Louise Wise Services, 211 A.D.2d 446, 620 N.Y.S.2d 371 (1995); M.H. & J.L.H. v. Caritas Family Serv., 475 N.W.2d 94 (Minn.App.1991); Mallette v. Children's Friend & Service, 661 A.2d 67 (R.I.1995); Gibbs v. Ernst, 538 Pa. 193, 647 A.2d 882 (1994); Roe v. Catholic Charities, 225 Ill.App.3d 519, 167 Ill.Dec. 713, 588 N.E.2d 354 (1992); Note, *When Love Is Not Enough: Toward A Unified Wrongful Adoption Tort,* 105 HARV. L. REV. 1761 (1992).

Problem 7–5:

The state's highest court has recently ruled that current state adoption law does not permit open adoption.

a) The legislature has scheduled hearings on whether the statute should be amended to permit open adoption. Representatives from adoption agencies, the state foster care system, Concerned United Birthmothers (CUB), and the state bar association have been invited to give testimony. A number of adoptive parents and hopeful adoptive parents will also speak. Which speakers will favor open adoption? On what basis? Which speakers will oppose open adoption? On what basis?

b) You are counsel to the Legislature's Family Law Committee and have been asked to draft a statute legalizing and regulating open adoption. The legislature's goals are: protecting the interests of children available for adoption, ensuring the fairness of the adoption process, minimizing litigation, and improving the adoption prospects of foster children who are available for adoption. Draft a statute that, to the extent possible, is responsive to these various concerns.

SECTION 5. THE BABY MARKET: GRAY AND BLACK

IN THE MATTER OF THE ADOPTION OF A CHILD BY N.P. & F.P.

New Jersey Superior Court, Probate Part, 1979.
165 N.J.Super. 591, 398 A.2d 937.

COLEMAN, J.

* * * The child herein was born on March 30, 1978 in Santiago, Chile, South America. On March 30, 1978 the natural mother delivered custody of the child for adoption to the Maternity Clinical Hospital, Social Services, Chile University. The prospective adoptive parents have no children born of their marriage. They read an article in the New York

Daily News concerning children who were available for adoption from Chile. The article referred them to Pat Quinlan . . . who recommended a lawyer in Santiago, Chile, by the name of Don Eugenio Donoso. Several days later Quinlan . . . called the prospective adoptive parents to advise that a child, born March 16, 1978, was available for adoption. The prospective adoptive parents forwarded to Donoso the necessary papers to obtain a visa to bring the child to the United States. On June 9, 1978 Donoso received approval from the Fourth Judge of Letters of Courts of Minor, Santiago, Chile, to have the child brought to the United States for the purpose of adoption by the prospective adoptive parents. On June 17, 1978 the child was brought into the United States by Maria Elena Ibarra, who was hired . . . to bring the child to Kennedy Airport in New York. The prospective adoptive parents met Maria Elena Ibarra at Kennedy Airport and took custody of the child.

The plaintiffs expended the following monies in connection with receiving the child into their home: (a) $3,000 to Don Eugenio Donoso, attorney in Santiago, Chile; (b) $1,169 to Maria Elena Ibarra for plane fare for herself and the child, clothing and passport; (c) $72 to the Consulate of Chile for legalization of documents; (d) $50 for translations; (e) $150 . . . for a home study; (f) $625 to a New Jersey attorney for services in the Union County Court, Probate Division, in connection with the instant adoption.

Donoso further itemized the disbursement of the $3,000 he received as follows: $238.79 for foster home care; $27.41 for medicine; $16.13 for doctor's bill; $9.67 for pictures; $158.85 for clothes . . . ; $18 for notary on the power of attorney; $12.58 for legalization of the power of attorney and decision of the judge; $16.13 for tips to employees of the hospital; $16.13 for miscellaneous expenses; $500 for a donation to the Chile University Clinical Hospital; and $2,000 for attorney's fees.

* * *

The essential provisions of N.J.S.A. § 9:3–54 . . . provide that no person shall pay, give, or agree to give any money in connection with a placement for adoption except for fees or services of an approved agency or reimbursement of medical, hospital or other similar expenses incurred in connection with the birth or any illness of the child. It appears unmistakably clear that the payments by plaintiffs of such items as air fare for the child and escort, attorney's fee to the foreign attorney and fees paid for the foreign court proceedings and passport, were all payments of money that should subject the plaintiffs to violations of the said Statute. These payments were mailed from New Jersey and intended to pay the incidental expenses necessary to have the child placed in the plaintiff's home. Where no approved agency is involved the Legislature intended to permit payment only for medical or hospital bills related to the birth or any illness of the child. Surely the payments of air fare and the foreign attorney's fee could not qualify under the Statute. The so-called attorney's fee was more like a broker's fee or finder's fee.

The facts present a prima facie showing that plaintiffs have used international agents and large sums of money to illegally obtain a child. They have used their financial means to jump to the head of the line of those couples waiting for a placement by an approved agency.

Even though the court has concluded that plaintiffs . . . violated N.J.S.A. § 9:3–54, the court has seen no evidence indicating that plaintiffs are unfit parents with the contemplation of N.J.S.A. § 9:3–48(c)(4). The evidence does not warrant the conclusion that the possible criminal conduct of plaintiffs make them unfit parents or that the adoption would not be in the best interest of the child. However, the matter will be referred to the Union County Prosecutor in accordance with N.J.S.A. § 9:3–55(b).

Notes and Questions

1. If the adoption was illegal, why didn't the court simply void it?

2. Although most states do not outlaw independent adoptions altogether, they remain controversial. Some experts argue that the practice of payment for prenatal expenses may "create a sense of obligation on the part of the birth parents to the adoptive parents which may unfairly influence the birth parents' decision . . . to surrender their infant . . ." They also note that the child is often placed in the adoptive home before a home study has been completed and the birth parents have signed consents, perhaps raising the risk of later disruption. L. Jean Emery, *Agency versus Independent Adoption: The Case for Agency Adoption*, 3 The Future of Children: Adoption 139, 144 (Spring 1993). But other experts point to evidence suggesting that birth parents often prefer independent adoption, in part because it offers them the opportunity to choose the home in which their child will reside. *See* Mark T. McDermott, *Agency versus Independent Adoption: The Case for Independent Adoption*, in 3 The Future of Children: Adoption 146 (Spring 1993).

3. Attorneys who facilitate independent adoptions cannot represent both the birth and adoptive parents and thus sometimes face difficult ethical dilemmas. *See* Paul K. Stom Amlung, *Conflicts of Interest in Independent Adoptions: Pitfalls for the Unwary*, 59 U. Cin. L. Rev. 169 (1990); In re Mountain, 239 Kan. 412, 721 P.2d 264 (1986).

4. For many prospective adoptive parents, independent adoption is attractive because of the lengthy waiting periods and application restrictions that characterize agency adoption. But, as independent adoptions often involve payment of the mother's medical and living expenses during pregnancy, they may find themselves competing for a baby in a nebulous "gray market" where outright baby sales are clearly outlawed, but the rules governing the extent and type of permissible inducements are often unclear. Some experts believe that there is also an active black market for healthy white infants with prices ranging up to $75,000. *See* E.R. Shipp, *Death Draws Public's Eye to Adoption*, N.Y. Times, Nov. 27, 1987, at B1. According to one recent report, American Embassy officials in Paraguay are sufficiently concerned about baby theft and sale that

they are requesting DNA tests to establish whether the adults who offer children for adoption are indeed the children's parents; Paraguay was the leading South American exporter of children for U.S. adoption in 1995, with 410 adoptions. Schemo, *Adoptions in Paraguay: Mothers Cry Theft,* N.Y. TIMES, Mar. 19, 1996, at A1.

5. In 1993, the Hague Conference on Private International Law completed a Convention on Intercountry Adoption. The Convention endorses intercountry adoption to provide permanent families for children for whom intracountry adoption is not available. Article 23 of the Convention provides that an adoption appropriately certified as made in accordance with the Convention "shall be recognized by operation of law in the other Contracting States." Under Article 24, a Contracting State may refuse recognition of a Convention adoption "... only if the adoption is manifestly contrary to its public policy, taking into account the best interests of the child." Articles 4 and 5 of the Convention set out adoption requirements. Competent authorities of the state of origin must establish that the child is adoptable and that an intercountry adoption is in the child's best interests. The state of origin must also ensure that the necessary consents have been given. The consents must be written and must not have been induced by payment or compensation of any kind; a birth mother's consent is valid only if given after birth of the child. The receiving state must establish that the prospective adoptive parents are suitable and legally eligible to adopt. For a more detailed discussion of the Convention, *see* Peter H. Pfund, *Intercountry Adoption: The 1993 Hague Convention: Its Purpose, Implementation, and Promise,* 28 FAM. L.Q. 53 (1994). The United States signed the Convention in 1994.

6. The existence of a gray and black market in babies led noted economists Elizabeth M. Landes and Richard A. Posner to advocate a legal baby market:

> ... [G]overnment restrictions on the fees that may be paid in an independent adoption artificially depress the net price of providing babies through this process. the result is to reduce the number of babies supplied below the free market level while simultaneously restricting the use of price to ration the existing, and inadequate, supply. * * * In these circumstances, the economist expects a black market to emerge. Some fraction—we do not know what—of ... independent adoptions are indeed black-market adoptions in the sense that the compensation paid either the natural parents or the middlemen, or both, exceeds the lawful limits. However, the potential criminal and professional sanctions for the individuals involved in babyselling not only drive up the costs and hence the price of babies (and so reduce demand) but necessarily imply a clandestine mode of operation. This imposes significant information costs on both buyers and sellers in the market, which further raise the (real) price of black-market babies to buyers and reduce the net price to sellers.

* * *

> . . . [T]here will be more fraud in a black market for babies than in a lawful market, so fear of being defrauded will further deter potential demanders. In lawful markets the incidence of fraud is limited not only by the existence of legal remedies against sellers but also by his desire to build a reputation for fair dealing. Both the clandestine mode of operation of current baby sellers and the lack of a continuing business relationship between seller and buyer reduce the seller's market incentives to behave reputably.
>
> * * *
>
> [Landes and Posner note that the cost of adoption would probably go down if a free market were established and that there is no evidence that such a market would harm children's interests, as children adopted through an independent adoption appear to do just as well as others and adoption agencies] . . . after determining the pool of fit, or eligible-to-adopt, couples . . . allocate available children among them on a first-come, first-served basis. The "fittest" parents are not placed at the head of the line . . .
>
> * * *
>
> [Given these facts, t]he antipathy to an explicit market in babies may be part of a broader wish to disguise facts that might be acutely uncomfortable if widely known. Were baby prices quoted as prices of soybean futures are quoted, a racial ranking of these prices would be evident, with white baby prices higher than nonwhite baby prices . . .
>
> Some people are also upset by the implications for the eugenic alteration of the human race that are presented by baby selling. Baby selling may seem logically and inevitably to lead to baby breeding, for any market will generate incentives to improve the product as well as to optimize the price and quantity of the current quality level of the product. . . . However, so long as the market for eugenically bred babies did not extend beyond infertile couples and those with serious genetic disorders, the impact of a free baby market on the genetic composition and distribution of the human race at large would be small.
>
> The emphasis placed by critics on the social costs of a free market in babies blurs what would probably be the greatest long-run effect of legalizing the baby market: inducing women who have unintentionally become pregnant to put up the child for adoption rather than raise it themselves or have an abortion.
>
> Elizabeth M. Landes & Richard A. Posner, *The Economics of the Baby Shortage*, 7 J. LEGAL STUD. 323 (1978).

Most of Landes and Posner's critics concur in their assessment of the ills associated with a black market, but nonetheless find their solution unpersuasive. *See, e.g., Forum: Adoption and Market Theory*, 67 B.U. L. REV. 59–175 (1987); J. Robert S. Prichard, *A Market for Babies*,

34 U. Toronto L.J. 341 (1984); Margaret Brinig, *The Effect of Transactions Costs on the Market for Babies*, 18 Seton Hall Legis. J. 553 (1994). *See also* Patricia Williams, *Spare Parts, Family Values, Old Children, Cheap*, 28 New Eng. L. Rev. 913 (1994). Are Landes and Posner right about the "greatest long-run effect" of legalizing baby sale? Are they right about the reasons most people object to such sales?

7. Short of legalizing baby sale, are there other steps that legislatures can take to minimize the problem of gray and black market adoptions?

Chapter 8

ASSISTED REPRODUCTION

Infertility affects as many as 4.9 million American couples, or ten to fifteen percent of those trying to conceive. *See* HARRISON'S PRINCIPLES OF INTERNAL MEDICINE 2029 (13th ed. 1994). Female infertility may account for approximately one-third of these cases, male infertility another third, with the remaining third due to shared or unknown factors.

Alternatives to traditional reproduction have been available for a long time. Hagar bore a child for Sarah and Abraham (*see* Genesis 16–17); artificial insemination was utilized by married couples as early as the 1950s. Newer alternatives include in vitro fertilization (with or without ovum donation), embryo transfer, and "surrogate" motherhood using either artificial insemination, in vitro fertilization, or both. These new means of reproduction raise a host of ethical, social and legal issues. *See* John A. Robertson, *Embryos, Families, and Procreative Liberty: The Legal Structure of the New Reproduction*, 59 S. CAL. L. REV. 939 (1986). Family law must: (1) regulate access to and use of these technologies; and (2) define the legal relationships of children conceived through assisted reproduction to the various actors involved. Depending on the facts of the case and the technique used, these actors may include: (1) a biological (sperm-supplying) father who: a) has donated sperm; or b) intends to become a parent himself; (2) a biological (ovum-supplying) mother who: a) has donated ova or; b) intends to become a parent herself; (3) a gestational mother who carries the child to term either (a) pursuant to a contract with a woman (and her husband) or a man (and his wife); or (b) who is using donated ova (and or sperm) to become a mother herself.

The possibilities and combinations are dizzying; the law, at least in the United States, has not yet caught up. In England, the Human Fertilization and Embryology Act of 1990 established a statutory authority to license and set standards for facilities offering assisted reproductive services. The Act sets out: (1) limits on the maximum number of preembryos that can be transferred in a cycle and the conditions under which oocyte donation and other procedures can be performed; (2) rules on consent, disclosure, and eligibility for treatment; and (3) rules defining the legal status of children born through assisted reproduction. *See* Elizabeth Ann Pitrolo, *The Birds, the Bees, and the Deep Freeze: Is There International Consensus in the Debate Over Assisted Reproductive Technologies?*, 19 HOUS. J. INTN'L L. 147 (1996). In the United States, there are as yet no federal laws dealing with assisted reproduction; state law is scattered and nonuniform. As you read the materials in this chapter, consider whether this area is more appropriate for federal or state regulation.

SECTION 1. ARTIFICIAL INSEMINATION

The simplest of assisted reproduction procedures is artificial insemination. Artificial insemination was first used by married couples when the husband was infertile. The early cases dealt with the issue of whether a child conceived by artificial insemination was legitimate. *Compare* Gursky v. Gursky, 39 Misc.2d 1083, 242 N.Y.S.2d 406 (Sup.Ct. 1963) (no) *with* People v. Sorensen, 68 Cal.2d 280, 66 Cal.Rptr. 7, 437 P.2d 495 (1968) (yes). Today all states have statutes regulating the status of children born through artificial insemination to a *married* woman whose husband consents to the procedure. But, because many of the statutes date from the time when unmarried women did not seek to become pregnant, they often provide unclear guidance when an unmarried woman makes use of artificial insemination.

JHORDAN C. v. MARY K.

California Court of Appeals, 1986.
179 Cal.App.3d 386, 224 Cal.Rptr. 530.

KING, ASSOCIATE JUSTICE.

By statute in California a "donor of semen *provided to a licensed physician* for use in artificial insemination of a woman other than the donor's wife is treated in law as if he were not the natural father of a child thereby conceived." (Civ.Code, § 7005, subd. (b); emphasis added.) In this case we hold that where impregnation takes place by artificial insemination, and the parties have failed to take advantage of this statutory basis for preclusion of paternity, the donor of semen can be determined to be the father of the child in a paternity action.

Mary K. and Victoria T. appeal from a judgment declaring Jhordan C. to be the legal father of Mary's child, Devin. The child was conceived by artificial insemination with semen donated personally to Mary by Jhordan. We affirm the judgment.

II. FACTS AND PROCEDURAL HISTORY

In late 1978 Mary decided to bear a child by artificial insemination and to raise the child jointly with Victoria, a close friend who lived in a nearby town.[1] Mary sought a semen donor by talking to friends and

1. As many as 20,000 women each year are artificially inseminated in the United

acquaintances. This led to three or four potential donors with whom Mary spoke directly. She and Victoria ultimately chose Jhordan after he had one personal interview with Mary and one dinner at Mary's home.

The parties' testimony was in conflict as to what agreement they had concerning the role, if any, Jhordan would play in the child's life. According to Mary, she told Jhordan she did not want a donor who desired ongoing involvement with the child, but she did agree to let him see the child to satisfy his curiosity as to how the child would look. Jhordan, in contrast, asserts they agreed he and Mary could have an ongoing friendship, he would have ongoing contact with the child, and he would care for the child as much as two or three times per week.

None of the parties sought legal advice until long after the child's birth. They were completely unaware of the existence of Civil Code section 7005. They did not attempt to draft a written agreement concerning Jhordan's status.

Jhordan provided semen to Mary on a number of occasions during a six month period commencing in late January 1979. On each occasion he came to her home, spoke briefly with her, produced the semen, and then left. The record is unclear, but Mary, who is a nurse, apparently performed the insemination by herself or with Victoria.

Contact between Mary and Jhordan continued after she became pregnant. Mary attended a Christmas party at Jhordan's home. Jhordan visited Mary several times at the health center where she worked. He took photographs of her. When he informed Mary by telephone that he had collected a crib, playpen, and high chair for the child, she told him to keep those items at his home. At one point Jhordan told Mary he had started a trust fund for the child and wanted legal guardianship in case she died; Mary vetoed the guardianship idea but did not disapprove the trust fund.

* * *

Mary gave birth to Devin on March 30, 1980. Victoria assisted in the delivery. Jhordan was listed as the father on Devin's birth certificate. Mary's roommate telephoned Jhordan that day to inform him of the birth. Jhordan visited Mary and Devin the next day and took photographs of the baby.

Five days later Jhordan telephoned Mary and said he wanted to visit Devin again. Mary initially resisted, but then allowed Jhordan to visit, although she told him she was angry. During the visit Jhordan claimed a right to see Devin, and Mary agreed to monthly visits.

Through August 1980 Jhordan visited Devin approximately five times. Mary then terminated the monthly visits. Jhordan said he would consult an attorney if Mary did not let him see Devin. Mary asked

States. (Note, Reproductive Technology and the Procreation Rights of the Unmarried (1985) 98 Harv.L.Rev. 669, fn. 1.) By one estimate some 1,500 of these women are unmarried. (Donovan, *The Uniform Parentage Act and Nonmarital Motherhood-by-Choice*, 11 N.Y.U.Rev. of Law & Soc. Change 193, 195 (1982–83)).

Jhordan to sign a contract indicating he would not seek to be Devin's father, but Jhordan refused.

In December 1980 Jhordan filed an action against Mary to establish paternity and visitation rights. In June 1982, by stipulated judgment in a separate action by the County of Sonoma, he was ordered to reimburse the county for public assistance paid for Devin's support. The judgment ordered him to commence payment, through the district attorney's office, of $900 in arrearages as well as future child support of $50 per month.[3]

Victoria had been closely involved with Devin since his birth. Devin spent at least two days each week in her home. On days when they did not see each other they spoke on the telephone. Victoria and Mary discussed Devin daily either in person or by telephone. They made joint decisions regarding his daily care and development. The three took vacations together. Devin and Victoria regarded each other as parent and child. Devin developed a brother-sister relationship with Victoria's 14–year old daughter, and came to regard Victoria's parents as his grandparents. Victoria made the necessary arrangements for Devin's visits with Jhordan.

In August 1983 Victoria moved successfully for an order joining her as a party to this litigation. Supported by Mary, she sought joint legal custody (with Mary) and requested specified visitation rights, asserting she was a de facto parent of Devin. Jhordan subsequently requested an award of joint custody to him and Mary.

After trial the court rendered judgment declaring Jhordan to be Devin's legal father. However, the court awarded sole legal and physical custody to Mary, and denied Jhordan any input into decisions regarding Devin's schooling, medical and dental care, and day-to-day maintenance. Jhordan received substantial visitation rights as recommended by a court-appointed psychologist. The court held Victoria was not a de facto parent, but awarded her visitation rights (not to impinge upon Jhordan's visitation schedule), which were also recommended by the psychologist.

Mary and Victoria filed a timely notice of appeal, specifying the portions of the judgment declaring Jhordan to be Devin's legal father and denying Victoria the status of de facto parent.[4]

III. Discussion

We begin with a discussion of Civil Code § 7005, which provides in pertinent part: "(a) If, under the supervision of a licensed physician and with the consent of her husband, a wife is inseminated artificially with semen donated by a man not her husband, the husband is treated in law

3. During the pendency of this appeal *Mary sought and obtained an increase* in Jhordan's support obligation.

4. The Sonoma County Public Defender has filed a brief on behalf of Devin which is *identical* to Jhordan's brief in both form and content, indicating the two briefs were produced in concert. We strongly disapprove of such conduct by counsel for a minor child in custody proceedings, as its substantially compromises counsel's independence.

as if he were the natural father of a child thereby conceived ... (b) The donor of semen provided to a licensed physician for use in artificial insemination of a woman other than the donor's wife is treated in law as if he were not the natural father of a child thereby conceived."

Civil Code § 7005 is part of the Uniform Parentage Act (UPA), which was approved in 1973 by the National Conference of Commissioners on Uniform State Laws. The UPA was adopted in California in 1975. Section 7005 is derived almost verbatim from the UPA as originally drafted, with one crucial exception. The original UPA restricts application of the nonpaternity provision of subdivision (b) to a *"married* woman other than the donor's wife." 9A West's U.Laws Ann. (1979) U.Par. Act, § 5, subd. (b), p. 593 (emphasis added). The word "married" is excluded from subdivision (b) of § 7005, so that in California, subdivision (b) applies to all women, married or not.[5]

Thus the California Legislature has afforded unmarried as well as married women a statutory vehicle for obtaining semen for artificial insemination without fear that the donor may claim paternity, and has likewise provided men with a statutory vehicle for donating semen to married and unmarried women alike without fear of liability for child support. Subdivision (b) states only one limitation on its application: the semen must be "provided to a licensed physician." Otherwise, whether impregnation occurs through artificial insemination or sexual intercourse, there can be a determination of paternity with the rights, duties and obligations such a determination entails.

A. Interpretation of the Statutory Nonpaternity Provision.

Mary and Victoria first contend that despite the requirement of physician involvement stated in Civil Code § 7005, subdivision (b), the Legislature did not intend to withhold application of the donor nonpaternity provision where semen used in artificial insemination was not provided to a licensed physician. They suggest that the element of physician involvement appears in the statute merely because the Legislature assumed (erroneously) that all artificial insemination would occur under the supervision of a physician. Alternatively, they argue the requirement of physician involvement is merely directive rather than mandatory.

We cannot presume, however, that the Legislature simply assumed or wanted to recommend physician involvement, for two reasons.

First, the history of the UPA (the source of § 7005) indicates conscious adoption of the physician requirement. The initial "discussion draft" submitted to the drafters of the UPA in 1971 did not mention the involvement of a physician in artificial insemination; the draft stated no requirement as to how semen was to be obtained or how the insemination procedure was to be performed. (H. KRAUSE, ILLEGITIMACY: LAW AND

5. This omission also occurs in the versions of the UPA adopted in Wyoming and Colorado.

SOCIAL POLICY (1971) pp. 240, 243.) The eventual inclusion of the physician requirement in the final version of the UPA suggests a conscious decision to require physician involvement.

Second, there are at least two sound justifications upon which the statutory requirement of physician involvement might have been based. One relates to health: a physician can obtain a complete medical history of the donor (which may be of crucial importance to the child during his or her lifetime) and screen the donor for any hereditary or communicable diseases. Indeed, the commissioners' comment to the section of the UPA on artificial insemination cites as a "useful reference" a law review article which argues that health considerations should require the involvement of a physician in statutorily authorized artificial insemination. This suggests that health considerations underlie the decision by the drafters of the UPA to include the physician requirement in the artificial insemination statute.

Another justification for physician involvement is that the presence of a professional third party such as a physician can serve to create a formal, documented structure for the donor-recipient relationship, without which, as this case illustrates, misunderstandings between the parties regarding the nature of their relationship and the donor's relationship to the child would be more likely to occur.

It is true that nothing inherent in artificial insemination requires the involvement of a physician. Artificial insemination is, as demonstrated here, a simple procedure easily performed by a woman in her home. Also, despite the reasons outlined above in favor of physician involvement, there are countervailing considerations against requiring it. A requirement of physician involvement, as Mary argues, might offend a woman's sense of privacy and reproductive autonomy, might result in burdensome costs to some women, and might interfere with a woman's desire to conduct the procedure in a comfortable environment such as her own home or to choose the donor herself.

However, because of the way § 7005 is phrased, a woman (married or unmarried) can perform home artificial insemination or choose her donor and still obtain the benefits of the statute. Subdivision (b) does not require that a physician independently obtain the semen and perform the insemination, but requires only that the semen be "provided" to a physician. Thus, a woman who prefers home artificial insemination or who wishes to choose her donor can still obtain statutory protection from a donor's paternity claim through the relatively simple expedient of obtaining the semen, whether for home insemination or from a chosen donor (or both), through a licensed physician.

Regardless of the various countervailing considerations for and against physician involvement, our Legislature has embraced the apparently conscious decision by the drafters of the UPA to limit application of the donor nonpaternity provision to instances in which semen is provided to a licensed physician. The existence of sound justifications for physician involvement further supports a determination the Legislature intended to require it. Accordingly, § 7005, subdivision (b), by its terms does not apply to the present case. The Legislature's apparent decision to require physician involvement in order to invoke the statute cannot be subject to judicial second-guessing and cannot be disturbed, absent constitutional infirmity.

B. Constitutional Considerations.

Mary and Victoria next contend that even if § 7005, subdivision (b), by its terms does not apply where semen for artificial insemination has not been provided to a licensed physician, application of the statute to the present case is required by constitutional principles of equal protection and privacy (encompassing rights to family autonomy and procreative choice).

1. *Equal protection.*

Mary and Victoria argue the failure to apply § 7005, subdivision (b) to unmarried women who conceive artificially with semen not provided to a licensed physician denies equal protection because the operation of other paternity statutes precludes a donor assertion of paternity where a *married* woman undergoes artificial insemination with semen not provided to a physician.

This characterization of the effect of the paternity statutes as applied to married women is correct. In the case of the married woman her husband is the presumed father (Civ.Code, § 7004, subd. (a)(1)), and *any* outsider—including a semen donor, regardless of physician involvement—is precluded from maintaining a paternity action unless the mother "relinquishes for, consents to, or proposes to relinquish for or consent to, the adoption of the child." (Civ.Code, § 7006, subd. (d).) An action to establish paternity by blood test can be brought only by the husband or mother. (Evid.Code, § 621, subds. (c) & (d); . . .).

But the statutory provision at issue here—Civil Code § 7005, subdivision (b)—treats married and unmarried women equally. Both are denied application of the statute where semen has not been provided to a licensed physician.

The true question presented is whether a completely different set of paternity statutes—affording protection to husband and wife from any claim of paternity by an outsider—denies equal protection by failing to provide similar protection to an unmarried woman. The simple answer is that, within the context of this question, a married woman and an unmarried woman are not similarly situated for purposes of equal protection analysis. In the case of a married woman, the marital relationship invokes a long-recognized social policy of preserving the integrity of the marriage. No such concerns arise where there is no marriage at all. Equal protection is not violated by providing that certain benefits or legal rights arise only out of the marital relationship. For example, spousal support may be awarded pursuant to Civil Code § 4801 upon the breakup of a marital relationship, but not upon the breakup of a nonmarital relationship.

2. *Family autonomy.*

Mary and Victoria contend that they and Devin compose a family unit and that the trial court's ruling constitutes an infringement upon a right they have to family autonomy, encompassed by the constitutional right to privacy. But this argument begs the question of which persons comprise the family in this case for purposes of judicial intervention. Characterization of the family unit must precede consideration of whether family autonomy has been infringed.

The semen donor here was permitted to develop a social relationship with Mary and Devin as the child's father. During Mary's pregnancy Jhordan maintained contact with her. They visited each other several times, and Mary did not object to Jhordan's collection of baby equipment or the creation of a trust fund for the child. Mary permitted Jhordan to visit Devin on the day after the child's birth and allowed monthly visits thereafter. The record demonstrates no clear understanding that Jhordan's role would be limited to provision of semen and that he would have no parental relationship with Devin; indeed, the parties' conduct indicates otherwise.

We do not purport to hold that an oral or written nonpaternity agreement between the parties would have been legally binding; that difficult question is not before us (and indeed is more appropriately addressed by the Legislature). We simply emphasize that for purposes of the family autonomy argument raised by Mary, Jhordan was not excluded as a member of Devin's family, either by anonymity, by agreement, or by the parties' conduct.

In short, the court's ruling did not infringe upon any right of Mary and Victoria to family autonomy, because under the peculiar facts of this case Jhordan was not excluded as a member of Devin's family for purposes of resolving this custody dispute.

3. *Procreative choice.*

Mary and Victoria argue that the physician requirement in Civil Code § 7005, subdivision (b), infringes a fundamental right to procreative choice, also encompassed by the constitutional right of privacy.

But the statute imposes no restriction on the right to bear a child. Unlike statutes in other jurisdictions proscribing artificial insemination other than by a physician, subdivision (b) of § 7005 does not forbid self-insemination; nor does the statute preclude personal selection of a donor or in any other way prevent women from artificially conceiving children under circumstances of their own choice. The statute simply addresses the perplexing question of the legal status of the semen donor, and provides a method of avoiding the legal consequences that might otherwise be dictated by traditional notions of paternity.

* * *

We wish to stress that our opinion in this case is not intended to express any judicial preference toward traditional notions of family structure or toward providing a father where a single woman has chosen to bear a child. Public policy in these areas is best determined by the legislative branch of government, not the judicial. Our Legislature has already spoken and has afforded to unmarried women a statutory right to bear children by artificial insemination (as well as right of men to donate semen) without fear of a paternity claim, through provision of the semen to a licensed physician. We simply hold that because Mary omitted to invoke Civil Code § 7005, subdivision (b), by obtaining Jhordan's semen through a licensed physician, and because the parties by all other conduct preserved Jhordan's status as a member of Devin's family, the trial court properly declared Jhordan to be Devin's legal father.

The judgment is affirmed.

Notes and Questions

1. *Statutory Standards:* In addition to the Uniform Parentage Act (UPA), described in *Jhordan C.*, two other uniform acts contain provisions on artificial insemination. The Uniform Putative and Unknown Fathers Act (UPUFA) § 1, 9B U.L.A. 16 (Supp. 1991) provides that:

> "Putative father" means a man who claims to be, or is named as, the biological father . . ., and whose paternity of the child has not been judicially determined, excluding . . . (ii) a donor of semen used in artificial insemination or in vitro fertilization whose identity is not known by the mother of the resulting child or whose semen was donated under circumstances indicating that the donor did not anticipate having an interest in the resulting child . . .

Under the Uniform Status of Children of Assisted Conception Act (USCACA) § 3, 9B Unif. L. Ann. 155 (Supp. 1994), the husband of a woman, other than a surrogate mother, who bears a child through assisted conception is deemed to be the father if he does not challenge his paternity in court within two years after discovering the child's birth. Section 4 provides that a sperm donor is not a parent of a child conceived through assisted conception. What result in *Jhordan C.* under the UPUFA and USCACA?

As of 1994, fifteen states had statutes similar to the UPA, providing that a donor is not the legal father of a child born through artificial insemination if the semen was provided to a licensed physician; fifteen provided that a donor is not the father if the mother is married and was inseminated with her husband's consent, regardless of whether a physician was involved. Many state statutes, like that of California, represent variations on one or another uniform act or a unique statutory standard; only a few explicitly address artificial insemination of an unmarried woman.

2. *The "Known" Semen Donor:* On either statutory or policy grounds, a number of state courts have ruled that a known semen donor, like Jhordan C., is the legal father of a child born to an unmarried woman through artificial insemination. *See, e.g.*, C.M. v. C.C., 152

N.J.Super. 160, 377 A.2d 821 (1977) ("[I]f an unmarried woman conceives a child through artificial insemination from semen from a known man, that man cannot be considered to be less a father because he is not married to the woman"). In resolving these cases, some courts have seen the donor's and mother's understanding about his status as an important factor; others have not. *See, e.g.*, In re Interest of R.C., 775 P.2d 27 (Colo.1989) (statute did not cut off a donor's rights where "the unmarried woman and the known donor at the time of insemination agree that the donor will be the natural father . . ."); Thomas S. v. Robin Y., 209 A.D.2d 298, 618 N.Y.S.2d 356, 361–363 (1994) (agreement between mother and donor that donor would have no parental status unenforceable on public policy grounds); In re Leckie & Voorhies, 128 Or.App. 289, 875 P.2d 521 (Or.App.1994) (granting summary judgment against sperm donor who had signed written contract providing that his visitation was at the convenience of lesbian couple and that he would not assert parental claims). *See also* McIntyre v. Crouch, 98 Or.App. 462, 780 P.2d 239 (Or.App.1989). Is it sensible to distinguish between situations where the semen donation is anonymous and situations where the donor is known?

3. *The Husband's Consent:* State statutory standards invariably hold that a child born through artificial insemination to a married woman *whose husband has consented to the procedure* is the child of the mother's husband, not the sperm donor. In cases where the husband's consent is at issue, courts have sometimes waived "technical" consent requirements in order to ensure the child's legitimacy, particularly when there is a basis to apply estoppel principles. *See* Lane v. Lane, 121 N.M. 414, 912 P.2d 290 (1996) (waiving requirement that husband consent in writing); R.S. v. R.S., 9 Kan.App.2d 39, 670 P.2d 923 (1983) (husband's consent presumed to continue until wife becomes pregnant unless there is clear and convincing evidence that consent was withdrawn). *See also* In re Baby Doe, 291 S.C. 389, 353 S.E.2d 877 (1987); In re Marriage of Witbeck–Wildhagen, 281 Ill.App.3d 502, 217 Ill.Dec. 329, 667 N.E.2d 122 (1996).

4. *Post-mortem conception:* This is the latest legal puzzle derived from the practice of artificial insemination. One case required the court to determine whether sperm was property that could be bequeathed under a will. The testator, who committed suicide, willed his sperm to his girlfriend; his adult children urged the court to rule that the bequest violated public policy. Ultimately, the girlfriend got the sperm. *See* Hecht v. Superior Ct. for L.A. County, 16 Cal.App.4th 836, 20 Cal.Rptr.2d 275 (1993); Kane v. Superior Court (Hecht), 37 Cal.App.4th 1577, 44 Cal. Rptr.2d 578 (1995). Another case involved the eligibility of a child conceived through post-mortem artificial insemination for Social Security Survivor's Benefits. The insured stored his sperm before undergoing cancer treatments and agreed with his wife that she would use it to conceive a child after his death. Because the child was not born within nine months of the insured's death, the Social Security Administration originally refused to grant the child benefits. *See* Hart v. Shalala,

No.94–3944 (Ed.La.1994). *See also* Gina Kolata, *Uncertain Area for Doctors: Saving Sperm of Dead Men, N.Y. Times,* May 30, 1997, at Al, col. 5.

SECTION 2. IN VITRO FERTILIZATION AND OVUM TRANSPLANTATION

In vitro fertilization involves the fertilization of one or more ova with sperm in a Petri dish—*not* the proverbial test tube. After fertilization, the ova are (1) reimplanted into the woman from whom they came with the hope of establishing a pregnancy, (2) implanted into another woman with the hope of establishing a pregnancy, or (3) frozen for later use. The technique enables a woman to bear a child if she has viable ova but cannot become pregnant naturally; it also enables a woman to "farm out" a pregnancy to another woman, whether because she cannot maintain a pregnancy, has a health problem exacerbated by pregnancy, or simply wishes to avoid pregnancy.

DAVIS v. DAVIS

Supreme Court of Tennessee, 1992.
842 S.W.2d 588.

Daughtrey, Justice.

This appeal presents a question of first impression, involving the disposition of the cryogenically-preserved product of *in vitro* fertilization (IVF), commonly referred to in the popular press and the legal journals as "frozen embryos." The case began as a divorce action, filed by the appellee, Junior Lewis Davis, against his then wife, appellant Mary Sue Davis. The parties were able to agree upon all terms of dissolution, except one: who was to have "custody" of the seven "frozen embryos" stored in a Knoxville fertility clinic that had attempted to assist the Davises in achieving a much-wanted pregnancy during a happier period in their relationship.

* * *

Mary Sue Davis originally asked for control of the "frozen embryos" with the intent to have them transferred to her own uterus, in a post-divorce effort to become pregnant. Junior Davis objected, saying that he preferred to leave the embryos in their frozen state until he decided whether or not he wanted to become a parent outside the bounds of marriage.

Based on its determination that the embryos were "human beings" from the moment of fertilization, the trial court awarded "custody" to Mary Sue Davis and directed that she "be permitted the opportunity to bring these children to term through implantation." The Court of Appeals reversed, finding that Junior Davis has a "constitutionally protected right not to beget a child where no pregnancy has taken place" and holding that "there is no compelling state interest to justify ordering implantation against the will of either party." The Court of Appeals further held that "the parties share an interest in the seven fertilized ova" and remanded the case to the trial court for entry of an order vesting them with "joint control * * * and equal voice over their disposition."

* * *

We note ... that their positions have already shifted: both have remarried and Mary Sue Davis (now Mary Sue Stowe) has moved out of state. She no longer wishes to utilize the "frozen embryos" herself, but wants authority to donate them to a childless couple. Junior Davis is adamantly opposed to such donation and would prefer to see the "frozen embryos" discarded. The result is, once again, an impasse, but the parties' current legal position does have an effect on the probable outcome of the case, as discussed below.

At the outset, it is important to note the absence of two critical factors that might otherwise influence or control the result of this litigation: When the Davises signed up for the IVF program at the Knoxville clinic, they did not execute a written agreement specifying what disposition should be made of any unused embryos that might result from the cryopreservation process. Moreover, there was at that time no Tennessee statute governing such disposition, nor has one been enacted in the meantime.[1]

In addition, because of the uniqueness of the question before us, we have no case law to guide us to a decision in this case. Despite the fact that over 5,000 IVF babies have been born in this country and the fact that some 20,000 or more "frozen embryos" remain in storage, there are apparently very few other litigated cases involving the disputed disposition of untransferred "frozen embryos," and none is on point with the facts in this case.[2]

But, if we have no statutory authority or common law precedents to guide us, we do have the benefit of extensive comment and analysis in the legal journals. In those articles, medical-legal scholars and ethicists have proposed various models for the disposition of "frozen embryos" when unanticipated contingencies arise, such as divorce, death of one or both of the parties, financial reversals, or simple disenchantment with the IVF process. Those models range from a rule requiring, at one extreme, that all embryos be used by the gamete-providers or donated

1. At the time of trial, only one state had enacted pertinent legislation. A Louisiana statute entitled "Human Embryos," among other things, forbids the intentional destruction of a cryopreserved IVF embryo and declares that disputes between parties should be resolved in the "best interest" of the embryo. 1986 La. Acts R.S. §§ 9:121 *et seq.* Under the Louisiana statute, unwanted embryos must be made available for "adoptive implantation."

2. The only reported decision is *York v. Jones*, 717 F. Supp. 421 (E.D.Va.1989). Another case, involving a California couple who underwent IVF in Australia and later died in an airplane crash, is noted in Smith, *Australia's Frozen "Orphan" Embryos*, 24 J. FAM. L. 27 (1985–86). Because the couple died intestate, their estates were distributed under California law without regard to the "frozen embryos" left in storage in Australia.

for uterine transfer, and, at the other extreme, that any unused embryos be automatically discarded. Other formulations would vest control in the female gamete-provider—in every case, because of her greater physical and emotional contribution to the IVF process, or perhaps only in the event that she wishes to use them herself. There are also two "implied contract" models: one would infer from enrollment in an IVF program that the IVF clinic has authority to decide in the event of an impasse whether to donate, discard, or use the "frozen embryos" for research; the other would infer from the parties' participation in the creation of the embryos that they had made an irrevocable commitment to reproduction and would require transfer either to the female provider or to a donee. There are also the so-called "equity models": one would avoid the conflict altogether by dividing the "frozen embryos" equally between the parties, to do with as they wish; the other would award veto power to the party wishing to avoid parenthood, whether it be the female or the male progenitor.

Each of these possible models has the virtue of ease of application. Adoption of any of them would establish a bright-line test that would dispose of disputes like the one we have before us in a clear and predictable manner. As appealing as that possibility might seem, we conclude that given the relevant principles of constitutional law, the existing public policy of Tennessee with regard to unborn life, the current state of scientific knowledge giving rise to the emerging reproductive technologies, and the ethical considerations that have developed in response to that scientific knowledge giving rise to the emerging reproductive technologies, and the ethical considerations that have developed in response to that scientific knowledge, there can be no easy answer to the question we now face. We conclude, instead, that we must weigh the interests of each party to the dispute, in terms of the facts and analysis set out below, in order to resolve that dispute in a fair and responsible manner.

* * *

In the record, and especially in the trial court's opinion, there is a great deal of discussion about the proper descriptive terminology to be used in this case. Although this discussion appears at first glance to be a matter simply of semantics, semantical distinctions are significant in this context, because language defines legal status and can limit legal rights. Obviously, an "adult" has a different legal status than does a "child." Likewise, "child" means something other than "fetus." A "fetus" differs from an "embryo." There was much dispute at trial about whether the four-to eight-cell entities in this case should properly be referred to as "embryos" or as "preembryos," with resulting differences in legal analysis.

One expert, a French geneticist named Dr. Jerome Lejeune, insisted that there was no recognized scientific distinction between the two terms. He referred to the four-to eight-cell entities at issue here as "early human beings," as "tiny persons," and as his "kin." Although he is an internationally recognized geneticist, Dr. Lejeune's background fails to reflect any degree of expertise in obstetrics or gynecology (specifically in the field of infertility) or in medical ethics. His testimony revealed a profound confusion between science and religion. For example, he was deeply moved that "Madame [Mary Sue], the mother, wants to rescue babies from this concentration can," and he concluded that Junior Davis has a moral duty to try to bring these "tiny human beings" to term.

Dr. Lejeune's opinion was disputed by Dr. Irving Ray King, the gynecologist who performed the IVF procedures in this case. Dr. King is a medical doctor who had practiced as a sub-speciality in the areas of infertility and reproductive endocrinology for 12 years. He established the Fertility Center of East Tennessee in Knoxville in 1984 and had worked extensively with IVF and Cryopreservation. He testified that the currently accepted term for the zygote immediately after division is "preembryo" and that this term applies up until 14 days after fertilization. He testified that this 14—day period defines the accepted period for preembryo research. At about 14 days, he testified, the group of cells begins to differentiate in a process that permits the eventual development of the different body parts which will become an individual.

Dr. King's testimony was corroborated by the other experts who testified at trial, with the exception of Dr. Lejeune. It is further supported by the American Fertility Society, an organization of 10,000 physicians and scientists who specialize in problems of human infertility. The Society's June 1990 report on Ethical Considerations of the New Reproductive Technologies indicates that from the point of fertilization, the resulting one-cell zygote contains "a new hereditary constitution (genome) contributed to by both parents through the union of sperm and egg."

* * *

* * * The trial court reasoned that if there is no distinction between embryos and preembryos, as Dr. Lejeune theorized, then Dr. Lejeune must also have been correct when he asserted that "human life begins at the moment of conception." From this proposition, the trial judge concluded that the eight-cell entities at issue were not preembryos but were "children *in vitro*." He then invoked the doctrine of *parens patriae* and held that it was "in the best interest of the children" to be born rather than destroyed. Finding that Mary Sue Davis was willing to provide such an opportunity, but that Junior Davis was not, the trial judge awarded her "custody" of the "children *in vitro*."

The Court of Appeals explicitly rejected the trial judge's reasoning, as well as the result. Indeed, the argument that "human life begins at the moment of conception" and that these four-to eight-cell entities therefore have a legal right to be born has apparently been abandoned by the appellant, despite her success with it in the trial court. We have nevertheless been asked by the American Fertility Society, joined by 19 other national organizations allied in this case as amici curiae, to respond to this issue because of its far-reaching implications in other cases of this kind. We find the request meritorious.

* * *

Left undisturbed, the trial court's ruling would have afforded preembryos the legal status of "persons" and vested them with legally cognizable interests separate from those of their progenitors. Such a decision would doubtless have had the effect of outlawing IVF programs in the state of Tennessee. But in setting aside the trial court's judgment, the Court of Appeals, at least by implication, may have swung too far in the opposite direction.

* * *

The provisions of T.C.A. §§ 68–30–101 et seq. on which the intermediate appellate court relied, codify the Uniform Anatomical Gift Act. T.C.A. § 39–15–208 prohibits experimentation or research using an aborted fetus in the absence of the woman's consent. These statutes address the question of who controls disposition of human organs and tissue with no further potential for autonomous human life; they are not precisely controlling on the question before us, because the "tissue" involved here does have the potential for developing into independent human life, even if it is not yet legally recognizable as human life itself.

The intermediate court's reliance on York v. Jones is even more troublesome. That case involved a dispute between a married couple undergoing IVF procedures at the Jones Institute for Reproductive Medicine in Virginia. When the Yorks decided to move to California, they asked the Institute to transfer the one remaining "frozen embryo" that they had produced to a fertility clinic in San Diego for later implantation. The Institute refused and the Yorks sued. The federal district court assumed without deciding that the subject matter of the dispute was "property." The *York* court held that the "cryopreservation agreement" between the Yorks and the Institute created a bailment relationship, obligating the Institute to return the subject of the bailment to the Yorks once the purpose of the bailment had terminated.

In this case, by citing to York v. Jones but failing to define precisely the "interest" that Mary Sue Davis and Junior Davis have in the preembryos, the Court of Appeals has left the implication that it is in the nature of property interest. For purposes of clarity in future cases, we conclude that this point must be further addressed.

* * *

We conclude that preembryos are not, strictly speaking, either "persons" or "property," but occupy an interim category that entitles them to special respect because of their potential for human life. It follows that any interest that Mary Sue Davis and Junior Davis have in the preembryos in this case is not a true property interest. However, they do have an interest in the nature of ownership, to the extent that they have decision-making authority concerning disposition of the preembryos, within the scope of policy set by law.

* * *

We believe, as a starting point, that an agreement regarding disposition of any untransferred preembryos in the event of contingencies (such as the death of one or more of the parties, divorce, financial reversals, or abandonment of the program) should be presumed valid and should be enforced as between the progenitors. This conclusion is in keeping with the proposition that the progenitors, having provided the gametic material giving rise to the preembryos, retain decisionmaking authority as to their disposition.[20]

At the same time, we recognize that life is not static, and that human emotions run particularly high when a married couple is attempting to overcome infertility problems. It follows that the parties' initial "informed consent" to IVF procedures will often not be truly informed because of the near impossibility of anticipating, emotionally and psychologically, all the turns that events may take as the IVF process unfolds. Providing that the initial agreements may later be modified *by agreement* will, we think, protect the parties against some of the risks they face in this regard. But, in the absence of such agreed modification, we conclude that their prior agreements should be considered binding.

It might be argued in this case that the parties had an implied contract to reproduce using *in vitro* fertilization, that Mary Sue Davis relied on that agreement in undergoing IVF procedures, and that the court should enforce an implied contract against Junior Davis, allowing Mary Sue to dispose of the preembryos in a manner calculated to result in reproduction. The problem with such an analysis is that there is no indication in the record that disposition in the event of contingencies other than Mary Sue Davis's pregnancy was ever considered by the parties, or that Junior Davis intended to pursue reproduction outside the confines of a continuing marital relationship with Mary Sue. We therefore decline to decide this case on the basis of implied contract or the reliance doctrine.[21]

We are therefore left with this situation: there was initially no agreement between the parties concerning disposition of the prembryos under the circumstances of this case; there has been no agreement since; and there is no formula in the Court of Appeals opinion for determining the outcome if the parties cannot reach an agreement in the future.

20. This situation is thus distinguishable from that in which a couple makes an agreement concerning abortion in the event of a future pregnancy. Such agreements are unenforceable because of the woman's right to privacy and autonomy.

21. We also point out that if the roles were reversed in this case, it is highly unlikely that Junior Davis could force transfer of the preembryos to Mary Sue over her objection. Because she has an absolute right to seek termination of any resulting pregnancy, at least within the first trimester, ordering her to undergo a uterine transfer would be a futility. * * *

In granting joint custody to the parties, the Court of Appeals must have anticipated that, in the absence of agreement, the preembryos would continue to be stored, as they now are, in the Knoxville fertility clinic. One problem with maintaining the status quo is that the viability of the preembryos cannot be guaranteed indefinitely. Experts in cryopreservation who testified in this case estimated the maximum length of preembryonic viability at two years. Thus, the true effect of the intermediate court's opinion is to confer on Junior Davis the inherent power to veto any transfer of the preembryos in this case and thus to insure their eventual discard or self-destruction.

As noted . . ., the recognition of such a veto power, as long as it applies equally to both parties, is theoretically one of the routes available to resolution of the dispute in this case. Moreover, because of the current state of law regarding the right of procreation, such a rule would probably be upheld as constitutional. Nevertheless, . . . we conclude that it is not the best route to take, under all the circumstances.

* * *

Here, the specific individual freedom in dispute is the right to procreate. In terms of the Tennessee state constitution, we hold that the right of procreation is a vital part of an individual's right to privacy. Federal law is to the same effect.

* * *

For the purposes of this litigation, it is sufficient to note that, whatever its ultimate constitutional boundaries, the right of procreational autonomy is composed of two rights of equal significance—the right to procreate and the right to avoid procreation. Undoubtedly, both are subject to protections and limitations.

The equivalence of and inherent tension between these two interests are nowhere more evident than in the context of *in vitro* fertilization. None of the concerns about a woman's bodily integrity that have previously precluded men from controlling abortion decisions is applicable here. We are not unmindful of the fact that the trauma (including both emotional stress and physical discomfort) to which women are subjected in the IVF process is more severe than is the impact of the procedure on men. In this sense, it is fair to say that women contribute more to the IVF process than men. Their experience, however, must be viewed in light of the joys of parenthood that is desired or the relative anguish of a lifetime of unwanted parenthood. As they stand on the brink of potential parenthood, Mary Sue Davis and Junior Lewis Davis must be seen as entirely equivalent gamete-providers.

It is further evident that, however far the protection of procreational autonomy extends, the existence of the right itself dictates that decisional authority rests in the gamete-providers alone, at least to the extent that their decisions have an impact upon their individual reproductive status.

* * *

Certainly, if the state's interests do not become sufficiently compelling in the abortion context until the end of the first trimester, after very significant developmental stages have passed, then surely there is no state interest in these preembryos which could suffice to overcome the interests of the gamete-providers. The abortion statute reveals that the increase in the state's interest is marked by each successive developmental stage such that, toward the end of a pregnancy, this interest is so compelling that abortion is almost strictly forbidden. This scheme supports the conclusion that the state's interest in the potential life embodied by these four-to eight-cell preembryos (which may or may not be able to achieve implantation in a uterine wall and which, if implanted, may or may not begin to develop into fetuses, subject to possible miscarriage) is at best slight. When weighed against the interests of the individuals and the burdens inherent in parenthood, the state's interest in the potential life of these preembryos is not sufficient to justify any infringement upon the freedom of these individuals to make their own decisions as to whether to allow a process to continue that may result in such a dramatic change in their lives as becoming parents.

The unique nature of this case requires us to note that the interests of these parties in parenthood are different in scope than the parental interest considered in other cases. Previously, courts have dealt with the child-bearing and child-rearing aspects of parenthood. Abortion cases have dealt with gestational parenthood. In this case, the Court must deal with the question of genetic parenthood. We conclude, moreover, that an interest in avoiding genetic parenthood can be significant enough to trigger the protections afforded to all other aspects of parenthood. * * *

Beginning with the burden imposed on Junior Davis, we note that the consequences are obvious. Any disposition which results in the gestation of the preembryos would impose unwanted parenthood on him, with all of its possible financial and psychological consequences.

* * *

Balanced against Junior Davis's interest in avoiding parenthood is Mary Sue Davis's interest in donating the preembryos to another couple for implantation. Refusal to permit donation of the preembryos would impose on her the burden of knowing that the lengthy IVF procedures she underwent were futile, and that the preembryos to which she contributed genetic material would never become children. While this is not an insubstantial emotional burden, we can only conclude that Mary Sue Davis's interest in donation is not as significant as the interest Junior Davis has in avoiding parenthood. If she were allowed to donate these preembryos, he would face a lifetime of either wondering about his parental status or knowing about his parental status but having no control over it. He testified quite clearly that if these preembryos were brought to term he would fight for custody of his child or children. Donation, if a child came of it, would rob him twice—his procreational autonomy would be defeated and his relationship with his offspring would be prohibited.

The case would be closer if Mary Sue Davis were seeking to use the preembryos herself, but only if she could not achieve parenthood by any other reasonable means. * * *

Further, we note that if Mary Sue Davis were unable to undergo another round of IVF, or opted not to try, she could still achieve the child-rearing aspects of parenthood through adoption. The fact that she and Junior Davis pursued adoption indicates that, at least at one time, she was willing to forego genetic parenthood and would have been satisfied by the child-rearing aspects of parenthood alone.

* * *

In summary, we hold that disputes involving the disposition of preembryos produced by in vitro fertilization should be resolved, first, by looking to the preferences of the progenitors. If their wishes cannot be ascertained, or if there is dispute, then their prior agreement concerning disposition should be carried out. If no prior agreement exists, then the relative interests of the parties in using or not using the preembryos must be weighed. Ordinarily, the party wishing to avoid procreation should prevail, assuming that the other party has a reasonable possibility of achieving parenthood by means other than use of the preembryos in question. If no other reasonable alternatives exist, then the argument in favor of using the preembryos to achieve pregnancy should be considered. However, if the party seeking control of the preembryos intends merely to donate them to another couple, the objecting party obviously has the greater interest and should prevail.

But the rule does not contemplate the creation of an automatic veto, and in affirming the judgment of the Court of Appeals, we would not wish to be interpreted as so holding.

For the reasons set out above, the judgment of the Court of Appeals is affirmed, in the appellee's favor. This ruling means that the Knoxville Fertility Clinic is free to follow its normal procedure in dealing with unused preembryos, as long as that procedure is not in conflict with this opinion. Costs on appeal will be taxed to the appellant.* * *

Notes and Questions

1. After its ruling in *Davis*, the Tennessee Supreme Court discovered that the clinic's "normal procedure in dealing with unused pre-embryos" was to "donate" them to other childless couples. Since that was an outcome the Court had precluded, the parties were ordered to return to court and agree on either donating the pre-embryos to an approved research project or destroying them. (Davis v. Davis, unpublished opinion). In the end, the pre-embryos were destroyed. *7 Embryos*

Contested in Divorce are Disposed of by Ex-husband, WASH. POST, June 16, 1993, at A18.

2. Kass v. Kass, 1995 WL 110368 (N.Y.Sup.) involved a dispute similar to that in *Davis*, but produced a different outcome. The trial judge awarded possession and control to the wife, holding that:

> . . . there is no legal, ethical or logical reason why an in vitro fertilization should give rise to additional rights on the part of the husband. From a propositional standpoint it matters little whether the ovum/sperm union takes place in the private darkness of a fallopian tube or the public glare of a petri dish. Fertilization is fertilization and fertilization of the ovum is the inception of the reproductive process. Biological life exists from that moment forward. The fact that an in vitro zygote does not seek to fulfill its biological destiny immediately upon such fertilization does not alter that fact. The rights of the parties are dependent upon the nature of the zygote not the stage of its development or its location. To deny a husband rights while an embryo develops in the womb and grant a right to destroy while it is in a hospital freezer is to favor situs over substance.
>
> Just as an in vivo husband's "right to avoid procreation" is waived and ceases to exist after intercourse in a coital reproduction, such right should be deemed waived and non-existent after his participation in an in vitro program. * * *

The appellate court ruled that where, as here, the parties had previously agreed that any unused cyropreserved pre-embryos would be destroyed, the agreement must be honored. Kass v. Kass, 235 A.D.2d 150, 663 N.Y.S.2d 581 (1997).

3. In November, 1997, the Family Law Section of the American Bar Association endorsed a policy resolution on the disposition of cryopreserved pre-embryos. The resolution provides that, where a divorcing couple has stored such pre-embroyos with the intent to procreate in the future and there is no clear agreement or contract, a spouse who wishes, in good faith and within a reasonable time, to achieve gestation to term should be given possession and control of the frozen pre-embryo or embryos. But, if a birth occurs, the nonconsenting parent has no parental rights or responsibilities. What are the pros and cons of this approach as compared to that in *Davis?*

4. What should be done with frozen pre-embryos which have been forgotten or abandoned? Under English law, they are destroyed after five years without contact from sperm and ovum providers; in August, 1996, 3000 embryos were destroyed. *See* Michael D. Lemonick, *Sorry, Your Time is Up,* TIME, August 12, 1996, at 41. What is the policy basis for destroying the embryos rather than donating them either to other couples who wish to conceive or to researchers?

5. On May 16, 1995, the University of California at Irvine filed a lawsuit against the three directors of its Center for Reproductive Health

alleging improprieties that included misappropriation of patient eggs and embryos. *See* Kathryn Wexler, *Egg-Swapping Scandal Still Unfolding: Infertility Client's Practices Put Doctors, University Under Scrutiny*, WASH. POST, Oct. 16, 1995, at A1. *See also* Karen T. Rogers, *Comment, Embryo Theft: The Misappropriation of Human Eggs at an Irvine Fertility Clinic Has Raised a Host of New Legal Concerns for Infertile Couples Using New Reproductive Technologies*, 26 SW. U. L. REV. 1133 (1997). In reaction to scandals such as this, some states are beginning to regulate in vitro fertilization practices. CAL. PENAL CODE § 367G, for example, makes it a felony to knowingly transfer gametic material from a gamete provider to a recipient without written authorization from both parties. MINN. STAT. § 145.422 prohibits the use of any living human conceptus for either research or experimentation.

SECTION 3. "SURROGATE" MOTHERHOOD

The term "surrogate" motherhood is something of a misnomer. Most surrogacy arrangements have involved artificial insemination of a woman with the sperm of a prospective "buyer" whose wife is infertile. If anything is clear here, it is that there is nothing "surrogate" about the motherhood of the woman who gives birth to the child in these circumstances. She is simply a mother who, in *advance* of her child's birth, has agreed to give up *her* child for a price. The chief difference between this case and that of the woman who engages in baby selling is that the child is the "buyer's" genetic child, if he furnished the sperm that led to conception, as well as the mother's.

Most disputes between "purchasers" and "sellers" in "surrogacy" arrangements occur when the mother refuses to give up her child in accordance with her contract. One notable disaster involved the opposite scenario. The case involved a baby who was rejected by the couple who had contracted for the child because it had been born with physical defects. Amid televised hype, the results of a blood test showing the *non*paternity of the contracting sperm donor were first announced on the Phil Donahue show. The would-have-been "purchasers" sued the "selling" couple for $30,000 for breach of their contract not to have intercourse during the insemination period, and the "surrogate" mother's husband had blood tests made "just in case." A court ultimately assumed jurisdiction over the child, who was placed in state care. NEW YORK TIMES, February 7, 1983, p. 8, col. 1; February 8, 1983, p. 26, col. 1.

No surrogacy case has received as much play as the saga of "Baby M," in which the trial court held that "[t]he biological father pays the surrogate for her willingness to be impregnated and carry his child to term. At birth, the father does not purchase the child. It is his own biological genetically related child. He cannot purchase what is already his.... [I]t must be reasoned that if one has a right to procreate coitally, then one has the right to reproduce noncoitally. If it is the reproduction that is protected, then the means of reproduction are also to be protected. The value and interests underlying the creation of family are the same by whatever means obtained. This court holds that the protected means extends to the use of surrogates." * * * "For the foregoing reasons, this court concludes and holds that the surrogate parenting agreement is a valid and enforceable contract pursuant to the Laws of New Jersey." (*In re* Baby M., 217 N.J.Super. 313, 525 A.2d 1128, 1157, 1164, 1166 (Ch.Div.1987). The surrogate mother appealed.

MATTER OF BABY M

Supreme Court of New Jersey, 1988.
109 N.J. 396, 537 A.2d 1227.

WILENTZ, C.J.

I. FACTS

In February 1985, William Stern and Mary Beth Whitehead entered into a surrogacy contract. * * * The contract provided that through artificial insemination using Mr. Stern's sperm, Mrs. Whitehead would become pregnant, carry the child to term, bear it, deliver it to the Sterns, and thereafter do whatever was necessary to terminate her maternal rights so that Mrs. Stern could thereafter adopt the child. Mrs. Whitehead's husband, Richard,[1] was also a party to the contract; Mrs. Stern was not. Mr. Whitehead promised to do all the acts necessary to rebut the presumption of paternity under the Parentage Act. Although Mrs. Stern was not a party to the surrogacy agreement, the contract gave her sole custody of the child in the event of Mr. Stern's death. Mrs. Stern's status as a nonparty to the surrogate parenting agreement presumably was to avoid the application of the baby-selling statute to this arrangement.

Mr. Stern, on his part, agreed to attempt the artificial insemination and to pay Mrs. Whitehead $10,000 after the child's birth, on its delivery to him. In a separate contract, Mr. Stern agreed to pay $7,500 to the Infertility Center of New York ("ICNY"). The Center's advertising campaigns solicit surrogate mothers and encourage infertile couples to consider surrogacy. ICNY arranged for the surrogacy contract by bringing the parties together, explaining the process to them, furnishing the contractual form, and providing legal counsel.

* * *

Mrs. Whitehead had reached her decision concerning surrogacy before the Sterns, and had actually been involved as a potential surrogate mother with another couple. After numerous unsuccessful artificial inseminations, the effort was abandoned. Thereafter, the Sterns learned of the Infertility Center, the possibilities of surrogacy, and of Mary Beth

1. Subsequent to the trial court proceedings, Mr. and Mrs. Whitehead were divorced, and soon thereafter Mrs. Whitehead remarried. Nevertheless, in the course of this opinion we will make reference almost exclusively to the facts as they existed at the time of trial, the facts on which the decision we now review was reached. We note moreover that Mr. Whitehead remains a party to this dispute. For these reasons, we continue to refer to appellants as Mr. and Mrs. Whitehead.

Whitehead. The two couples met to discuss the surrogacy arrangement and decided to go forward. On February 6, 1985, Mr. Stern and Mr. and Mrs. Whitehead executed the surrogate parenting agreement. After several artificial inseminations over a period of months, Mrs. Whitehead became pregnant. The pregnancy was uneventful and on March 27, 1986, Baby M was born.

* * *

Mrs. Whitehead realized, almost from the moment of birth, that she could not part with this child. She had felt a bond with it even during pregnancy. Some indication of the attachment was conveyed to the Sterns at the hospital when they told Mrs. Whitehead what they were going to name the baby. She apparently broke into tears and indicated that she did not know if she could give up the child. She talked about how the baby looked like her other daughter, and made it clear that she was experiencing great difficulty with the decision.

Nonetheless, Mrs. Whitehead was, for the moment, true to her word. Despite powerful inclinations to the contrary, she turned her child over to the Sterns on March 30 at the Whiteheads' home.

* * *

Later in the evening of March 30, Mrs. Whitehead became deeply disturbed, disconsolate, stricken with unbearable sadness. She had to have her child. She could not sleep, eat, or concentrate on anything other than her need for her baby. The next day she went to the Sterns' home and told them how much she was suffering.

The depth of Mrs. Whitehead's despair surprised and frightened the Sterns. She told them that she could not live without her baby, that she must have her, even if only for one week, that thereafter she would surrender the child. The Sterns, concerned that Mrs. Whitehead might indeed commit suicide, not wanting under any circumstances to risk that, and in any event believing that Mrs. Whitehead would keep her word, turned the child over to her.

* * *

The struggle over Baby M began when it became apparent that Mrs. Whitehead could not return the child to Mr. Stern. Due to Mrs. Whitehead's refusal to relinquish the baby, Mr. Stern filed a complaint seeking enforcement of the surrogacy contract. He alleged, accurately, that Mrs. Whitehead had not only refused to comply with the surrogacy contract but had threatened to flee from New Jersey with the child in order to avoid even the possibility of his obtaining custody. The court papers asserted that if Mrs. Whitehead were to be given notice of the application for an order requiring her to relinquish custody, she would, prior to the hearing, leave the state with the baby. And that is precisely what she did. After the order was entered, *ex parte*, the process server, aided by the police, in the presence of the Sterns, entered Mrs. Whitehead's home to execute the order. Mr. Whitehead fled with the child, who had been handed to him through a window while those who came to enforce the order were thrown off balance by a dispute over the child's current name.

The Whiteheads immediately fled to Florida with Baby M. They stayed initially with Mrs. Whitehead's parents, where one of Mrs. Whitehead's children had been living. For the next three months, the Whiteheads and Melissa lived at roughly twenty different hotels, motels, and homes in order to avoid apprehension. From time to time Mrs. Whitehead would call Mr. Stern to discuss the matter; the conversations, recorded by Mr. Stern on advice of counsel, show an escalating dispute about right, morality, and power accompanied by threats of Mrs. Whitehead to kill herself, to kill the child, and falsely to accuse Mr. Stern of sexually molesting Mrs. Whitehead's other daughter.

Eventually the Sterns discovered where the Whiteheads were staying, commenced supplementary proceedings in Florida, and obtained an order requiring the Whiteheads to turn over the child. Police in Florida enforced the order, forcibly removing the child from her grandparents' home. She was soon thereafter brought to New Jersey and turned over to the Sterns. The prior order of the court issued *ex parte*, awarding custody of the child to the Sterns *pendente lite*, was reaffirmed by the trial court after consideration of the certified representations of the parties (both represented by counsel) concerning the unusual sequence of events that had unfolded. Pending final judgment, Mrs. Whitehead was awarded limited visitation with Baby M.

The Sterns' complaint, in addition to seeking possession and ultimately custody of the child, sought enforcement of the surrogacy contract. Pursuant to the contract, it asked that the child be permanently placed in their custody, that Mrs. Whitehead's parental rights be terminated, and that Mrs. Stern be allowed to adopt the child, *i.e.*, that, for all purposes, Melissa become the Sterns' child.

The trial took thirty-two days over a period of more than two months. It included numerous interlocutory appeals and attempted interlocutory appeals. There were twenty-three witnesses to the facts recited above and fifteen expert witnesses, eleven testifying on the issue of custody and four on the subject of Mrs. Stern's multiple sclerosis; the bulk of the testimony was devoted to determining the parenting arrangement most compatible with the child's best interests. Soon after the conclusion of the trial, the trial court announced its opinion from the bench. 217 N.J. Super. 313, 525 A.2d 1128 (1987). It held that the surrogacy contract was valid; ordered that Mrs. Whitehead's parental rights be terminated and that sole custody of the child be granted to Mr. Stern; and after hearing brief testimony from Mrs. Stern, immediately entered an order allowing the adoption of Melissa by Mrs. Stern, all in accordance with the surrogacy contract. Pending the outcome of the appeal, we granted a continuation of visitation to Mrs. Whitehead, although slightly more limited than the visitation allowed during the trial.

* * *

II. INVALIDITY AND UNENFORCEABILITY OF SURROGACY CONTRACT

We have concluded that this surrogacy contract is invalid. Our conclusion has two bases: direct conflict with existing statutes and conflict with the public policies of this State, as expressed in its statutory and decisional law.

One of the surrogacy contract's basic purposes, to achieve the adoption of a child through private placement, though permitted in New Jersey "is very much disfavored." Its use of money for this purpose—and we have no doubt whatsoever that the money is being paid to obtain an adoption and not, as the Sterns argue, for the personal services of Mary Beth Whitehead—is illegal and perhaps criminal. N.J.S.A. § 9:3–54.[4] In addition to the inducement of money, there is the coercion of contract: the natural mother's irrevocable agreement, prior to birth, even prior to conception, to surrender the child to the adoptive couple. Such an agreement is totally unenforceable in private placement adoption. Even where the adoption is through an approved agency, the formal agreement to surrender occurs only *after* birth, and then, by regulation, only after the birth mother has been counseled. Integral to these invalid provisions of the surrogacy contract is the related agreement, equally invalid, on the part of the natural mother to cooperate with, and not to contest, proceedings to terminate her parental rights, as well as her contractual concession, in aid of the adoption, that the child's best interests would be served by awarding custody to the natural father and his wife—all of this before she has even conceived, and, in some cases, before she has the slightest idea of what the natural father and adoptive mother are like.

The foregoing provisions not only directly conflict with New Jersey statutes, but also offend long-established State policies. These critical terms, which are at the heart of the contract, are invalid and unenforceable; the conclusion therefore follows, without more, that the entire contract is unenforceable.

* * *

4. *N.J.S.A.* § 9:3–54 reads as follows:

a. No person, firm, partnership, corporation, association or agency shall make, offer to make or assist or participate in any placement for adoption and in connection therewith (1) Pay, give or agree to give any money or any valuable consideration, or assume or discharge any financial obligation; or (2) Take, receive, accept or agree to accept any money or any valuable consideration.

b. The prohibition of subsection a. shall not apply to the fees or services of any approved agency in connection with a placement for adoption, nor shall such prohibition apply to the payment or reimbursement of medical, hospital or other similar expenses incurred in connection with the birth or any illness of the child, or to the acceptance of such reimbursement by a parent of the child. . . .

The surrogacy contract creates, it is based upon, principles that are directly contrary to the objectives of our laws. It guarantees the separation of a child from its mother; it looks to adoption regardless of suitability; it totally ignores the child; it takes the child from the mother regardless of her wishes and her maternal fitness; and it does all of this, it accomplishes all of its goals, through the use of money.

Beyond that is the potential degradation of some women that may result from this arrangement. In many cases, of course, surrogacy may bring satisfaction, not only to the infertile couple, but to the surrogate mother herself. The fact, however, that many women may not perceive surrogacy negatively but rather see it as an opportunity does not diminish its potential for devastation to other women.

In sum, the harmful consequences of this surrogacy arrangement appear to us all to be palpable. In New Jersey the surrogate mother's agreement to sell her child is void. Its irrevocability infects the entire contract, as does the money that purports to buy it.

III. TERMINATION

We have already noted that under our laws termination of parental rights cannot be based on contract, but may be granted only on proof of the statutory requirements. That conclusion was one of the bases for invalidating the surrogacy contract. Although excluding the contract as a basis for parental termination, we did not explicitly deal with the question of whether the statutory bases for termination existed. We do so here.

* * *

Nothing in this record justifies a finding that would allow a court to terminate Mary Beth Whitehead's parental rights under the statutory standard. It is not simply that obviously there was no "intentional abandonment or very substantial neglect of parental duties without a reasonable expectation of reversal of that conduct in the future," N.J.S.A. § 9:3–48c(1), quite the contrary, but furthermore that the trial court never found Mrs. Whitehead an unfit mother and indeed affirmatively stated that Mary Beth Whitehead had been a good mother to her other children.

Although the best interests of the child is dispositive of the custody issue in a dispute between natural parents, it does not govern the question of termination. It has long been decided that the mere fact that a child would be better off with one set of parents than with another is an insufficient basis for terminating the natural parents' rights. Furthermore, it is equally well settled that surrender of a child and a consent to adoption through private placement do not alone warrant termination. It must be noted, despite some language to the contrary, that the interests of the child are not the only interests involved when termination issues are raised. The parent's rights, both constitutional and statutory, have their own independent vitality.

* * *

IV. Constitutional Issues

Both parties argue that the Constitutions—state and federal—mandate approval of their basic claims. The source of their constitutional arguments is essentially the same: the right of privacy, the right to procreate, the right to the companionship of one's child, those rights flowing either directly from the fourteenth amendment or by its incorporation of the Bill of Rights, or from the ninth amendment, or through the penumbra surrounding all of the Bill of Rights. They are the rights of personal intimacy, of marriage, of sex, of family, of procreation. Whatever their source, it is clear that they are fundamental rights protected by both the federal and state Constitutions. The right asserted by the Sterns is the right of procreation; that asserted by Mary Beth Whitehead is the right to the companionship of her child. We find that the right of procreation does not extend as far as claimed by the Sterns. As for the right asserted by Mrs. Whitehead, since we uphold it on other grounds (*i.e.*, we have restored her as mother and recognized her right, limited by the child's best interests, to her companionship), we need not decide that constitutional issue, and for reasons set forth below, we should not.

The right to procreate, as protected by the Constitution, has been ruled on directly only once by the United States Supreme Court. *See Skinner v. Oklahoma*, 316 U.S. 535 (forced sterilization of habitual criminals violates equal protection clause of fourteenth amendment). Although *Griswold v. Connecticut* [p. 19] is obviously of a similar class, strictly speaking it involves the right *not* to procreate. The right to procreate very simply is the right to have natural children, whether through sexual intercourse or artificial insemination. It is no more than that. Mr. Stern has not been deprived of that right. Through artificial insemination of Mrs. Whitehead, Baby M is the child. The custody, care, companionship, and nurturing that follow birth are not parts of the right to procreation; they are rights that may also be constitutionally protected, but that involve many considerations other than the right of procreation. To assert that Mr. Stern's right of procreation gives him the right to the custody of Baby M would be to assert that Mrs. Whitehead's right of procreation does *not* give her the right to the custody of Baby M; it would be to assert that the constitutional right of procreation included within it a constitutionally protected right to destroy someone else's right of procreation.

We conclude that the right of procreation is best understood and protected if confined to its essentials, and that when dealing with rights concerning the resulting child, different interests come into play. There is nothing in our culture or society that even begins to suggest a fundamental right on the part of the father to the custody of the child as part of his right to procreate when opposed by the claim of the mother to the same child. We therefore disagree with the trial court: there is no constitutional basis whatsoever requiring that Mr. Stern's claim to the custody of Baby M be sustained. Our conclusion may thus be understood as illustrating that a person's rights of privacy and self-determination are qualified by the effect on innocent third persons of the exercise of those rights.

Mr. Stern also contends that he has been denied equal protection of the laws by the State's statute granting full parental rights to a husband in relation to the child produced, with his consent, by the union of his wife with a sperm donor. N.J.S.A. § 9:17—44. The claim really is that of Mrs. Stern. It is that she is in precisely the same position as the husband in the statute; she is presumably infertile, as is the husband in the statute; her spouse by agreement with a third party procreates with the understanding that the child will be the couple's child. The alleged unequal protection is that the understanding is honored in the statute when the husband is the infertile party, but no similar understanding is honored when it is the wife who is infertile.

It is quite obvious that the situations are not parallel. A sperm donor simply cannot be equated with a surrogate mother. The State has more than a sufficient basis to distinguish the two situations—even if the only difference is between the time it takes to provide sperm for artificial insemination and the time invested in a nine-month pregnancy—so as to justify automatically divesting the sperm donor of his parental rights without automatically divesting a surrogate mother. Some basis for an equal protection argument might exist if Mary Beth Whitehead had contributed her egg to be implanted, fertilized or otherwise, in Mrs. Stern, resulting in the latter's pregnancy. That is not the case here, however.

Mrs. Whitehead, on the other hand, asserts a claim that falls within the scope of a recognized fundamental interest protected by the Constitution. As a mother, she claims the right to the companionship of her child. This is a fundamental interest, constitutionally protected. Furthermore, it was taken away from her by the action of the court below. Whether that action under these circumstances would constitute a constitutional deprivation, however, we need not and do not decide. By virtue of our decision Mrs. Whitehead's constitutional complaint—that her parental rights have been unconstitutionally terminated—is moot. We have decided that both the statutes and public policy of this state require that the termination be voided and that her parental rights be restored. It therefore becomes unnecessary to decide whether that same result would be required by virtue of the federal or state Constitutions. . . .

Having held the contract invalid and having found no other grounds for the termination of Mrs. Whitehead's parental rights, we find nothing remains of her constitutional claim. It seems obvious to us that since custody and visitation encompass practically all of what we call "parental rights," a total denial of both would be the equivalent of termination of parental rights. That, however, as will be seen below, has not occurred here. We express no opinion on whether a prolonged suspension of visitation would constitute a termination of parental rights, or whether, assuming it would, a showing of unfitness would be required.

V. Custody

Having decided that the surrogacy contract is illegal and unenforceable, we now must decide the custody question without regard to the provisions of the surrogacy contract that would give Mr. Stern sole and permanent custody. (That does not mean that the existence of the contract and the circumstances under which it was entered may not be considered to the extent deemed relevant to the child's best interests). With the surrogacy contract disposed of, the legal framework becomes a dispute between two couples over the custody of a child produced by the artificial insemination of one couple's wife by the other's husband. Under the Parentage Act the claims of the natural father and the natural mother are entitled to equal weight, *i.e.,* one is not preferred over the other solely because it is the father or the mother. The applicable rule given these circumstances is clear: the child's best interests determine custody.

* * *

Notes and Questions

1. On remand, the trial court held that Melissa's best interest would be served by giving custody to the Sterns and unsupervised, liberal visitation to Mary Beth Whitehead-Gould. In re Baby M., 225 N.J.Super. 267, 542 A.2d 52 (Ch.Div.1988). Melissa spends two days a week and every other weekend with her mother and four half siblings. She spends the rest of the time with the Sterns. *See* Susan Squire, *Whatever Happened to Baby M?*, Redbook, January, 1994, at 60. *See also* Mary Beth Whitehead, A Mother's Story: The Truth About the Baby M Case (1989).

2. The Uniform Status of Children of Assisted Conception Act (1988), 9B Unif. L. Ann. 155 (Supp. 1994) offers two alternative approaches to surrogacy contracts:

ALTERNATIVE A. § 5.

(a) A surrogate, her husband, if she is married, and intended parents may enter into a written agreement whereby the surrogate relinquishes all her rights and duties as a parent of a child to be conceived through assisted conception, and the intended parents may become the parents of the child pursuant to § 8.

(b) If the agreement is not approved by the court under § 6 before conception, the agreement is void and the surrogate is the mother of a resulting child and the surrogate's husband, if a party to the agreement, is the father of the child. If the surrogate's husband is not a party to the agreement or the surrogate is unmarried, paternity of the child is governed by [the Uniform Parentage Act].

§ 6. Petition and Hearing for Approval of Surrogacy Agreement

(a) The intended parents and the surrogate may file a petition in the [appropriate court] to approve a surrogacy agreement if one of them is a resident of this State. The surrogate's husband, if she is married; must join in the petition. A copy of the agreement must be attached to the petition. The court shall name a [guardian ad litem] to represent the interests of a child to be conceived by the surrogate through assisted conception and [shall] [may] appoint counsel to represent the surrogate.

(b) The court shall hold a hearing on the petition and shall enter an order approving the surrogacy agreement, authorizing assisted conception for a period of 12 months after the date of the order, declaring the intended parents to be the parents of a child to be conceived through assisted conception pursuant to the agreement and discharging the guardian ad litem and attorney for the surrogate, upon finding that:

(1) the court has jurisdiction and all parties have submitted to its jurisdiction under subsection (e) and have agreed that the law of this State governs all matters arising under this [Act] and the agreement;

(2) the intended mother is unable to bear a child or is unable to do so without unreasonable risk to an unborn child or to the physical or mental health of the intended mother or child, and the finding is supported by medical evidence;

(3) the [relevant child-welfare agency] has made a home study of the intended parents and the surrogate and a copy of the report of the home study has been filed with the court;

(4) the intended parents, the surrogate, and the surrogate's husband, if she is married, meet the standards of fitness applicable to adoptive parents in this State;

(5) all parties have voluntarily entered into the agreement and understand its terms, nature, and meaning, and the effect of the proceeding;

(6) the surrogate has had at least one pregnancy and delivery and bearing another child will not pose an unreasonable risk to the unborn child or to the physical or mental health of the surrogate or the child, and this finding is supported by medical evidence;

(7) all parties have received counseling concerning the effect of the surrogacy by [a qualified health-care professional or social worker] and a report containing conclusions about the capacity of the parties to enter into and fulfill the agreement has been filed with the court;

(8) a report of the results of any medical or psychological examination or genetic screening agreed to by the parties or required by law has been filed with the court and made available to the parties.

(9) adequate provision has been made for all reasonable health-care costs associated with the surrogacy until the child's birth including responsibility for those costs if the agreement is terminated . . .

§ 7. Termination of Surrogacy Agreement

* * *

(b) A surrogate who has provided an egg for the assisted conception pursuant to an agreement approved under § 6 may terminate the agreement by filing written notice with the court within 180 days after the last insemination pursuant to the agreement. Upon finding, after notice to the parties to the agreement and hearing, that the surrogate has voluntarily terminated the agreement and understands the nature, meaning and effect of the termination, the court shall vacate the order entered under § 6.

§ 8. Parentage Under Approved Surrogacy Agreement

(a) The following rules of parentage apply to surrogacy agreements approved under § 6:

(1) Upon birth of a child to the surrogate, the intended parents are the parents of the child and the surrogate and her husband, if she is married, are not parents of the child unless the court vacates the order pursuant to § 7(b).

(2) If, after notice of termination by the surrogate, the court vacates the order under § 7(b) the surrogate is the mother of a resulting child, and her husband, if a party to the agreement, is the father. If the surrogate's husband is not a party to the agreement or the surrogate is unmarried, paternity of the child is governed by [the Uniform Parentage Act].

* * *

(b) Upon birth of the child, the intended parents shall file a written notice with the court that a child has been born to the surrogate within 300 days after assisted conception. Thereupon, the court shall enter an order directing the [Department of Vital Statistics] to issue a new birth certificate naming the intended parents as parents and to seal the original birth certificate in the records of the [Department of Vital Statistics]. * * *

§ 9. Surrogacy: Miscellaneous Provisions

* * *

(d) A child born to a surrogate within 300 days after assisted conception pursuant to an order under § 6 is presumed to result from the assisted conception. The presumption is conclusive as to all persons who have notice of the birth and who do not commence within 180 days after notice, an action to assert the contrary in which the child and the parties to the agreement are named as parties. The action must be commenced in the court that issued the order under § 6.

ALTERNATIVE B. § 5.

An agreement in which a woman agrees to become a surrogate or to relinquish her rights and duties as parent of a child thereafter conceived through assisted conception is void. However, she is the mother of a resulting child, and her husband, if a party to the agreement, is the father of the child. If her husband is not a party to the agreement or the surrogate is unmarried, paternity of the child is governed by [the Uniform Parentage Act].

3. At least nineteen states now have statutes governing surrogacy contracts. Most, like Alternative B, declare surrogacy contracts void. *See* D.C. CODE ANN. § 16–401, 402; KY. REV. STAT. ANN. § 199.590; MICH. COMP. LAWS § 722.851–722.863; NEB. REV. STAT. § 25–21,200; N.D. GEN. CODE ANN. § 14–18–01; N.Y. DOM. REL. LAWS §§ 122–124. Some permit gratuitous surrogacy contracts. *See, e.g.,* N.Y. DOM. REL. LAWS §§ 122–124; WASH. REV. CODE ANN. § 26.26.210-.260. In a few states, statutes have been adopted legalizing and regulating surrogacy. *See, e.g.,* N.H. REV. STAT. ANN. ch. 168–B:30; VA. CODE § 20–156.

4. Should legislatures distinguish between paid and unpaid surrogacy? If any payments are allowed, should payment be permitted for (1) maternity expenses (are lost earnings allowable?); (2) the services of the surrogate; (3) the services of a commercial surrogacy agency; (4) a lawyer's legal services or role as an intermediary; or (5) payment for the child? *See Ethics Committee of the American Fertility Society, Ethical Considerations of Assisted Reproductive Technologies*, 62 FERTILITY & STERILITY (1994).

5. Are statutes regulating surrogacy constitutional? *Compare* Doe v. Attorney General, 194 Mich.App. 432, 487 N.W.2d 484 (1992) *with* Soos v. Superior Court, 182 Ariz. 470, 897 P.2d 1356 (Ariz.App.1994).

6. There is now a voluminous literature on the legal, moral, and ethical dimensions of surrogacy contracts. *See, e.g.,* LORI B. ANDREWS, BETWEEN STRANGERS: SURROGATE MOTHERS, EXPECTANT FATHERS, & BRAVE NEW BABIES (1989); MARTHA F. FIELD, SURROGATE MOTHERHOOD: THE LEGAL AND HUMAN ISSUES (1990); SCOTT B. RAE, THE ETHICS OF COMMERCIAL SURROGATE MOTHERHOOD: BRAVE NEW FAMILIES? (1994); Richard A. Epstein, *Surrogacy: The Case for Full Contractual Enforcement*, 81 VA. L. REV. 2305 (1995): J. Robert S. Prichard, *A Market for Babies*, U. TORONTO L.J. 34 (1984); Lori B. Andrews, *Beyond Doctrinal Boundaries: A Legal Framework for Surrogate Motherhood*, 81 VA. L. REV. 2343 (1995).

JOHNSON v. CALVERT

Supreme Court of California, 1993.
5 Cal.4th 84, 19 Cal.Rptr.2d 494, 851 P.2d 776.

PANELLI, J.

In this case we address several of the legal questions raised by recent advances in reproductive technology. When, pursuant to a surrogacy agreement, a zygote formed of the gametes of a husband and wife is implanted in the uterus of another woman, who carries the resulting fetus to term and gives birth to a child not genetically related to her, who is the child's "natural mother" under California law? Does a determination that the wife is the child's natural mother work a deprivation of the gestating woman's constitutional rights? And is such an agreement barred by any public policy of this state?

We conclude that the husband and wife are the child's natural parents, and that this result does not offend the state or federal Constitution or public policy.

FACTS

Mark and Crispina Calvert are a married couple who desired to have a child. Crispina was forced to undergo a hysterectomy in 1984. Her ovaries remained capable of producing eggs, however, and the couple eventually considered surrogacy. In 1989 Anna Johnson heard about Crispina's plight from a coworker and offered to serve as a surrogate for the Calverts.

On January 15, 1990, Mark, Crispina, and Anna signed a contract providing that an embryo created by the sperm of Mark and the egg of Crispina would be implanted in Anna and the child born would be taken into Mark and Crispina's home "as their child." Anna agreed she would relinquish "all parental rights" to the child in favor of Mark and Crispina. In return, Mark and Crispina would pay Anna $10,000 in a series of installments, the last to be paid six weeks after the child's birth. Mark and Crispina were also to pay for a $200,000 life insurance policy on Anna's life.

The zygote was implanted on January 19, 1990. Less than a month later, an ultrasound test confirmed Anna was pregnant.

Unfortunately, relations deteriorated between the two sides. Mark learned that Anna had not disclosed she had suffered several stillbirths and miscarriages. Anna felt Mark and Crispina did not do enough to obtain the required insurance policy. She also felt abandoned during an onset of premature labor in June.

In July 1990, Anna sent Mark and Crispina a letter demanding the balance of the payments due her or else she would refuse to give up the child. The following month, Mark and Crispina responded with a lawsuit, seeking a declaration they were the legal parents of the unborn child. Anna filed her own action to be declared the mother of the child, and the two cases were eventually consolidated. The parties agreed to an independent guardian ad litem for the purposes of the suit.

The child was born on September 19, 1990, and blood samples were obtained from both Anna and the child for analysis. The blood test results excluded Anna as the genetic mother. The parties agreed to a court order providing that the child would remain with Mark and Crispina on a temporary basis with visits by Anna.

* * *

Anna, of course, predicates her claim of maternity on the fact that she gave birth to the child. The Calverts contend that Crispina's genetic relationship to the child establishes that she is his mother. Counsel for the minor joins in that contention and argues, in addition, that several of the presumptions created by the Act dictate the same result. As will appear, we conclude that presentation of blood test evidence is one means of establishing maternity, as is proof of having given birth, but that the presumptions cited by minor's counsel do not apply to this case.

* * *

We see no clear legislative preference in Civil Code § 7003 as between blood testing evidence and proof of having given birth.[8] * * * It is arguable that, while gestation may demonstrate maternal status, it is not the *sine qua non* of motherhood. Rather, it is possible that the common law viewed genetic consanguinity as the basis for maternal rights. Under this latter interpretation, gestation simply would be irrefutable evidence of the more fundamental genetic relationship. This ambiguity, highlighted by the problems arising from the use of artificial reproductive techniques, is nowhere explicitly resolved in the Act.

Because two women each have presented acceptable proof of maternity, we do not believe this case can be decided without enquiring into the parties' intentions as manifested in the surrogacy agreement. Mark and Crispina are a couple who desired to have a child of their own genes but are physically unable to do so without the help of reproductive technology. They affirmatively intended the birth of the child, and took the steps necessary to effect in vitro fertilization. But for their acted-on intention, the child would not exist. Anna agreed to facilitate the procreation of Mark's and Crispina's child. The parties' aim was to bring Mark's and Crispina's child into the world, not for Mark and Crispina to donate a zygote to Anna. Crispina from the outset intended to be the child's mother. Although the gestative function Anna performed was necessary to bring about the child's birth, it is safe to say that Anna would not have been given the opportunity to gestate or deliver the child had she, prior to implantation of the zygote, manifested her own intent to be the child's mother. No reason appears why Anna's later change of heart should vitiate the determination that Crispina is the child's natural mother.

8. We decline to accept the contention of amicus curiae the American Civil Liberties Union (ACLU) that we should find the child has two mothers. Even though rising divorce rates have made multiple parent arrangements common in our society, we see no compelling reason to recognize such a situation here. The Calverts are the genetic and intending parents of their son and have provided him, by all accounts, with a stable, intact, and nurturing home. To recognize parental rights in a third party with whom the Calvert family has had little contact since shortly after the child's birth would diminish Crispina's role as mother.

We conclude that although the Act recognizes both genetic consanguinity and giving birth as means of establishing a mother and child relationship, when the two means do not coincide in one woman, she who intended to procreate the child—that is, she who intended to bring about the birth of a child that she intended to raise as her own—is the natural mother under California law.

* * *

In deciding the issue of maternity under the Act we have felt free to take into account the parties' intentions, as expressed in the surrogacy contract, because in our view the agreement is not, on its face, inconsistent with public policy.

Preliminarily, Mark and Crispina urge us to interpret the Legislature's 1992 passage of a bill that would have regulated surrogacy as an expression of this state's public policy despite the fact that Governor Wilson's veto prevented the bill from becoming law. Senate Bill No. 937 contained a finding that surrogate contracts are not against sound public and social policy. Had Senate Bill No. 937 become law, there would be no room for argument to the contrary. The veto, however, raises a question whether the legislative declaration truly expresses California's public policy.

In the Governor's veto message we find no unequivocal agreement with the Legislature's public policy assessment, but rather reservations about the practice of surrogate parenting. "Surrogacy is a relatively recent phenomenon. The full moral and psychological dimensions of this practice are not yet clear. In fact, they are just beginning to emerge. Only two published court opinions in California have treated this nettlesome subject * * *. Comprehensive regulation of this difficult moral issue is premature * * * To the extent surrogacy continues to be practical, it can be governed by the legal framework already established in the family law area." Given this less than ringing endorsement of surrogate parenting, we conclude that the passage of Senate Bill No. 937, in and of itself, does not establish that surrogacy contracts are consistent with public policy. (Of course, neither do we draw the opposite conclusion from the fact of the Governor's veto.)

Anna urges that surrogacy contracts violate several social policies. Relying on her contention that she is the child's legal, natural mother, she cites the public policy embodied in Penal Code § 273, prohibiting the payment for consent to adoption of a child. She argues further that the policies underlying the adoption laws of this state are violated by the surrogacy contract because it in effect constitutes a prebirth waiver of her parental rights.

We disagree. Gestational surrogacy differs in crucial respects from adoption and so is not subject to the adoption statutes. The parties voluntarily agreed to participate in *in vitro* fertilization and related medical procedures before the child was conceived; at the time when Anna entered into the contract, therefore, she was not vulnerable to financial inducements to part with her own expected offspring. As discussed above, Anna was not the genetic mother of the child. The payments to Anna under the contract were meant to compensate her for her services in gestating the fetus and undergoing labor, rather than for giving up "parental" rights to the child. Payments were due both during the pregnancy and after the child's birth. We are, accordingly, unpersuaded that the contract used in this case violates the public policies embodied in Penal Code § 273 and the adoption statutes. For the same reasons, we conclude these contracts do not implicate the policies underlying the statutes governing termination of parental rights.

* * *

Finally, Anna and some commentators have expressed concern that surrogacy contracts tend to exploit or dehumanize women, especially women of lower economic status. Anna's objections center around the psychological harm she asserts may result from the gestator's relinquishing the child to whom she has given birth. Some have also cautioned that the practice of surrogacy may encourage society to view children as commodities, subject to trade at their parents' will.

We are all too aware that the proper forum for resolution of this issue is the Legislature, where empirical data, largely lacking from this record, can be studied and rules of general applicability developed. However, in light of our responsibility to decide this case, we have considered as best we can its possible consequences.

We are unpersuaded that gestational surrogacy arrangements are so likely to cause the untoward results Anna cites as to demand their invalidation on public policy grounds. Although common sense suggests that women of lesser means serve as surrogate mothers more often than do wealthy women, there has been no proof that surrogacy contracts exploit poor women to any greater degree than economic necessity in general exploits them by inducing them to accept lower-paid or otherwise undesirable employment. We are likewise unpersuaded by the claim that surrogacy will foster the attitude that children are mere commodities; no evidence is offered to support it. The limited data available seems to reflect an absence of significant adverse effects of surrogacy on all participants.

The argument that a woman cannot knowingly and intelligently agree to gestate and deliver a baby for intending parents carries overtones of the reasoning that for centuries prevented women from attaining equal economic rights and professional status under the law. To resurrect this view is both to foreclose a personal and economic choice on the part of the surrogate mother, and to deny intending parents what may be their only means of procreating a child of their own genes. Certainly in the present case it cannot seriously be argued that Anna, a licensed vocational nurse who had done well in school and who had previously borne a child, lacked the intellectual wherewithal or life experience necessary to make an informed decision to enter into the surrogacy contract.

CONSTITUTIONALITY OF THE DETERMINATION THAT ANNA JOHNSON IS NOT THE NATURAL MOTHER

Anna argues at length that her right to continued companionship of the child is protected under the federal Constitution. * * * Anna relies mainly on theories of substantive due process, privacy, and procreative freedom, citing a number of decisions recognizing the fundamental liberty interest of natural parents in the custody and care of their children. Most of the cases Anna cites deal with the rights of unwed fathers in the face of attempts to terminate their parental relationship to their children. These cases do not support recognition of parental rights for a gestational surrogate. Although Anna quotes language stressing the primacy of a developed parent-child relationship in assessing unwed fathers' rights, certain language in the cases reinforces the importance of genetic parents' rights.

* * *

Anna relies principally on the decision of the United States Supreme Court in *Michael H. v. Gerald D.* [p. 280] to support her claim to a constitutionally protected liberty interest in the companionship of the child, based on her status as "birth mother." In that case, a plurality of the Court held that a state may constitutionally deny a man parental rights with respect to a child he fathered during a liaison with the wife of another man, since it is the marital family that traditionally has been accorded a protected liberty interest, as reflected in the historic presumption of legitimacy of a child born into such a family. The reasoning of the plurality in *Michael H.* does not assist Anna. Society has not traditionally protected the right of a woman who gestates and delivers a baby pursuant to an agreement with a couple who supply the zygote from which the baby develops and who intend to raise the child as their own; such arrangements are of too recent an origin to claim the protection of tradition. To the extent that tradition has a bearing on the present case, we believe it supports the claim of the couple who exercise their right to procreate in order to form a family of their own, albeit through novel medical procedures.

Moreover, if we were to conclude that Anna enjoys some sort of liberty interest in the companionship of the child, then the liberty interests of Mark and Crispina, the child's natural parents, in their procreative choices and their relationship with the child would perforce be infringed. Any parental rights Anna might successfully assert could come only at Crispina's expense. As we have seen, Anna has no parental rights to the child under California law, and she fails to persuade us that sufficiently strong policy reasons exist to accord her a protected liberty interest in the companionship of the child when such an interest would necessarily detract from or impair the parental bond enjoyed by Mark and Crispina.

Amicus curiae ACLU urges that Anna's rights of privacy embodied in the California Constitution (Cal. Const., art. I, § 1), requires recognition and protection of her status as "birth mother." We cannot agree.

* * * *Amicus curiae* appears to assume that the choice to gestate and deliver a baby to its genetic parents pursuant to a surrogacy agreement is the equivalent, in constitutional weight, of the decision whether to bear a child of one's own. We disagree. A woman who enters into a gestational surrogacy arrangement is not exercising her own right to make procreative choices; she is agreeing to provide a necessary and profoundly important service without (by definition) any expectation that she will raise the resulting child as her own.

Drawing an analogy to artificial insemination, Anna argues that Mark and Crispina were mere genetic donors who are entitled to no constitutional protection. That characterization of the facts is, however, inaccurate. Mark and Crispina never intended to "donate" genetic material to anyone. Rather, they intended to procreate a child genetically related to them by the only available means. Civil Code § 7005, governing artificial insemination, has no application here.

Finally, Anna argues that the Act's failure to address novel, reproductive techniques such as in vitro fertilization indicates legislative disapproval of such practices. Given that the Act was drafted long before such techniques were developed, we cannot agree. Moreover, we may not arrogate to ourselves the power to disapprove them. It is not the role of the judiciary to inhibit the use of reproductive technology when the Legislature has not seen fit to do so; any such effort would raise serious questions in light of the fundamental nature of the rights of procreation and privacy. Rather, our task has been to resolve the dispute before us, interpreting the Act's use of the term "natural mother" when the biological functions essential to bringing a child into the world have been allocated between two women.

The judgment of the Court of Appeal is affirmed.

ARABIAN, JUDGE, concurring.

I concur in the decision to find under the Uniform Parentage Act that Crispina Calvert is the natural mother of the child she at all times intended to parent and raise as her own with her husband Mark, the child's natural father. That determination answers the question on which this court granted review, and in my view sufficiently resolves the controversy between the parties to warrant no further analysis. I therefore decline to subscribe to the dictum in which the majority find surrogacy contracts "not * * * inconsistent with public policy." * * *

Clearly, this court should not avoid proper resolution of the issue before it. * * * Nevertheless, I would not move beyond the available legal mechanism into such socially and morally uncharted waters. The implications of addressing the general soundness of surrogacy contracts are vast and profound. To date, the legislative process has failed to produce a satisfactory answer. This court should be chastened and not emboldened by that failure.

Notes and Questions

1. Under *Johnson*, what result if the ova had been donated by a third party? If Anna had used IVF to become pregnant with ova donated by Crispina? *See* McDonald v. McDonald, 196 A.D.2d 7, 608 N.Y.S.2d 477 (1994).

2. Under the English Human Fertilization and Embryology Act of 1990 § 27, a woman who carries a child to term is the legal mother. But § 30 of the Act permits a court to issue an order recognizing that a child born of a gestational surrogate mother is the legal child of the genetic parents when there was an agreement to that effect. *See* Gillian Douglas, *The Human Fertilization and Embryology Act 1990*, [March 1991] Fam. Law 330.

3. Jack and Sarah, a married couple, had trouble conceiving a baby; using sperm and ova from anonymous donors, they employed in vitro fertilization to create pre-embryos which were implanted in Mary, whom they hired to carry the baby to term. During Mary's pregnancy, Jack and Sarah initiated divorce proceedings; Sarah sought custody and child support for the as yet unborn child. The trial court ruled that:

> * * * While this case is obviously one of first impression, it involves a "Catch 22" or chicken-and-egg problem which *is* familiar to the courts, and which our Supreme Court has already solved, albeit in decisions more resembling *Sense and Sensibility* than *Cells and Surrogacy*.
>
> The present case is the functional equivalent of a paternity action, where a mother who is the caretaker of a child seeks court-ordered support from a man *but for whose actions* the child would never have come into existence. As in a classic paternity action, this case involves the conundrum of a court's authority to order a man to pay child support before it is authoritatively adjudicated that he is the child's father: If jurisdiction depends on first establishing the fact of parentage by final decree, then there can be no jurisdiction to award support prior to such an adjudication. (And, of course, if the paternity defendant really is the father of the child, it means that he escapes his duty to support the child for the duration of the litigation over the parentage issue.)
>
> Jaycee B. v. Superior Ct., 42 Cal.App.4th 718, 49 Cal.Rptr.2d 694 (1996).

After the baby was born, the court denied the wife's request for child support from the husband based on its finding that the baby had no known parents. The result appeared to be that five humans contributed to the creation of a child for whom no one had legal responsibility. On appeal, the court held that the intended parents, the former husband and wife, were the legal parents. Ann Davis, *Artificial Reproduction Arrangers Are Ruled Child's Legal Parents,* Wall St. J., March 11, 1998, at B2.

SECTION 4. TOWARD A LEGISLATIVE FRAMEWORK

HARRY KRAUSE, ARTIFICIAL CONCEPTION: LEGISLATIVE APPROACHES

19 FAM. L. Q. 185, 192–96 (1985).

* * *

Throughout this area, the overriding social concern—in my view—is to safeguard the best interests of children. Our law emphasizes that point of view wherever children are in the picture, even in derogation of parental rights, once there is a clear conflict.

I am not troubled here about the metaphysical point, that we are talking about the interests of a child who is not yet in existence, or worse, about the interests of a child in not being brought into existence.

* * *

. . . In terms of law, the most important question goes to the child's legal status. What is to be the child's status (1) vis-à-vis the married mother's husband where it was conceived by its mother's artificial insemination with semen donated by a third party; (2) vis-à-vis the woman who carried it to term and gave birth to it where the pregnancy resulted from an ovum or embryo transplant from another woman and the ovum was fertilized with sperm provided by the "birth mother's husband or by another man; (3) vis-à-vis the donor of the semen; (4) vis-à-vis the donor of the ovum or embryo?" * * *

Take the . . . case of the husband's absolute sterility, to be alleviated by AID provided to his wife. The only sensible legal response is obvious: If the husband has consented to his wife's artificial insemination by donor, he is to be deemed the legal father of the child and the donor must be legally out of the picture. This does no more than reflect the age-old common law presumption that (1) holds legitimate any child born to a married mother, (2) presumes her husband's paternity, and (3) disallows strangers to the marriage—even the actual biological father himself—to challenge that presumption. Such a provision is included in the Uniform Parentage Act I drafted a dozen years ago. Many states now have that provision or equivalent legislation, and the various commissions agree.

If it is the wife who is infertile, the newer technique of egg donation and embryo transfer will alleviate the problem. Legally, the obvious answer is to provide the mirror-image of the response to AID. If the husband's sperm has fertilized a donated ovum that is then implanted in his wife, the wife should legally be the mother of the resulting child and the ovum donor should be out of the picture. The husband, of course, is the genetic and legal father.

If, finally, both husband and wife are infertile and both sperm and ovum are donated (or a donated, fertilized embryo is used), I still see no reason to vary the response: Both should be the child's legal parents and the donors should not.

* * *

Let us look now at lower-level regulatory issues such as (1) the question whether artificial insemination (or fertilized egg donation) should be available to single women, and (2) whether sperm donors, banks and physicians should be regulated?

(1) Having worked for the rights of the child to have two parents [in the area of child support and paternity] . . ., I am strongly opposed to single mother fertilization—and I have good company. Each child is entitled to the social and financial support of two parents—and so is the taxpayer who has quite enough single mothers and one-parent children to support. It seems ironic that the illegitimacy battle—waged and won on the idea that each child is entitled to two legal parents—may have to be refought so soon on this new territory.

The analogy to the reality of single, divorced, or widowed mothers is—by the way—wholly inappropriate. These are real-life tragedies. It is not good practice to manufacture tragedies.

* * *

(2) Regarding the regulation of sperm and ovum donors, and physicians, much could be said and should be done. Again, rather than encumber this legislative proposal with potential and, for now, avoidable controversy from this direction, I think we should trust the self-regulation of our medical profession as reinforced by their healthy respect for—or fear of—our tort and malpractice laws, to ensure their adherence to good practice. To fail to screen donors for disease or genetic defects, to fail to keep relevant records, to fail to safeguard anonymity in either direction, may well subject the physician to potential professional liability to the child, the parents or the donor, quite out of proportion to the income to be derived from a "fertility practice." In short, rudimentary and reasonably adequate regulation will tend to be automatic, if indirect.

What then is left of the basic issues? The very controversial problem of surrogate motherhood! * * * Today, commercial surrogacy is practiced quite openly in many states. Advertisements are carried by respectable publications. Women willing to carry a child for another are paid handsomely, although—given not only their relative efforts, but also the fact that the surrogate mother is "occupied" with just one child for nine to twelve months—it is the middleman who profits most, such as the Michigan attorney who is reported to have netted $184,000 from his practice in 1983.

* * *

I would prefer to see *commercial* surrogate motherhood being declared illegal. Justification for such a prohibition can be found by the analogy to the widespread illegality of receiving compensation ("baby selling") in adoption, as well as by more remote and even less pleasant analogy to the continuing illegality of prostitution. If illegal and sanctioned criminally, the sanction should focus on the intermediary, the lawyer, physician, and whoever is instrumental in arranging the surrogacy, and probably not on the intending purchasers, and certainly not on the woman who is persuaded to rent her womb. If the practice is illegal, any surrogacy agreement would of course be automatically unenforceable.

* * *

In several American states, a variety of laws are currently being proposed. The range includes stamping surrogate motherhood a crime, but the great majority of proposals would regulate commercial surrogate motherhood and, as regulated, allow it. While I again would discount some of these latter proposals as commercially inspired, and probably all of them as not having had the benefit of careful analysis, I also have to consider the reality of fifty American states making autonomous decisions in this area. There is more than just a chance that, somewhere, surrogate motherhood will be legalized. If so, people will travel there and an export business will develop from that state.

If that be so, sound rules need to govern the practice. It may be hoped that socially responsible, non-profit agencies along the lines of adoption agencies will be developed and put in charge of assuring some decency in the process, and to guard against exploitation of surrogate mothers as well as of purchasing couples, not to mention again the children.

* * *

Good reasons for prohibiting surrogacy range from the esthetic to the moral—but let us leave them aside. It is my goal to emphasize the pragmatic. And once we look to seek how the law would have to proceed to allow surrogate motherhood, we shall see that not allowing it really is the only practical approach.

Let me ask just one question—granting that money damages would be an obviously inadequate remedy—is there anyone here who would grant "specific performance" against a "carrier mother" prohibiting her from having an abortion, or taking away from her a child she carried and to whom she gave birth, whether her own or even one resulting from a donated embryo? I think not. At the opposite extreme, how could—or should?—"purchasers" be forced to go through with their bargain if the child did not turn out as expected?

There also is the risk that, without specific enforceability, surrogacy contracts would become a blackmail tool. Many a money-conscious surrogate (who, we must remember, is in this for money) would be tempted to seek to extract further payments from the purchasers, either by threatening to have an abortion or by threatening to keep the child. That prospect alone may justify prohibition!

* * *

If unenforceable, the parties to a surrogacy arrangement that might (and probably will) nevertheless be entered into, will be subject to the controls of the adoption laws. Those are reasonably adequate to deal with most cases, especially when they include a prohibition—as many do—against giving consent to the adoption of a child prior to its birth, and—as most do—prohibit paying compensation to mother or middleman (lawyer, physician, etc.) and as, I think, all do, allow the court to have an appropriate investigation made of the prospective adopts' home. The case is slightly different if the purchaser-husband's sperm was used to inseminate the surrogate mother, so that he may be able to establish himself as the legal father by operation of the paternity laws. However, paternity does not equal custody, and various courts have dealt quite effectively with just these facts.

* * *

Let me focus—as an afterthought—on two aspects of the new techniques that are more immediate than the perhaps unanswerable ultimate question "when does life begin?" Specifically, even in the narrow, family-law limits which I have set for myself, I do worry about:

(1) The specter of possibly inevitable eugenic manipulation. Who would deny that sperm and ovum donors should be screened for genetic defects? Precisely what is a genetic defect? Color? Gender? Ugliness? Low IQ? What is a "low IQ"—50—80—100? Beyond screening out, that is to say, applying "negative" eugenics, inevitably there will be some "positive" eugenics, *i.e.,* screening *in.* Would-be parents would be matched for race and size and body build and hair and eye color—as indeed adoptive parents and children are matched now. The next steps will be sex selection and the professional couple who only want to have a smart kid!

(2) While I already have pointed to various concerns about surrogate motherhood, the further problem I see there is the use of surrogate gestation for the mere convenience of the genetic mother (and father).

But granting the enormity of these concerns, I shall nevertheless try to end on an optimistic note. Both concerns would largely be dealt with if the new techniques were to remain as what they started: an exceptional remedy for a married couple's infertility, and would not become the usual way to bring children into this world. If we adhere to this limitation, we face no great threat. And why should that be so difficult—conscientious doctors do not now give us pills and operations for our asking, but require a medical indication. Let us hope also that they will keep in mind that a child is not "medication" to be prescribed lightly to frustrated, would-be parents, but that the greatest responsibility is owed directly to the child!

There is a wide range of assisted reproduction issues that might be regulated. Consider these sundry examples and decide which are appropriate for regulation. If you decide that regulation is appropriate, determine whether it should be imposed at the federal or state level.

1. A sperm bank in California specializes in the sperm of Nobel prize winners. *See Repository for Germinal Choice Announces "First Birth,"* N.Y. TIMES, May 25, 1982, p. 21, col. 6.
2. A fertility doctor uses his own semen to impregnate several women patients. Robert F. Howe, *Citing Cruel Lies by Jacobson, Judge Gives Him 5 Years, Fine,* WASH. POST, May 9, 1992, at D1 (Doctor Jacobson was convicted of 52 counts of fraud and perjury for telling patients they were pregnant when they were not and for using his own sperm to impregnate women—he may have fathered over 70 children). *See* United States v. Jacobson, 785 F.Supp. 563 (E.D.Va.1992).
3. A prison inmate wants to artificially inseminate his wife. *See* Goodwin v. Turner, 908 F.2d 1395 (8th Cir.1990); Percy v. New Jersey, 278 N.J.Super. 543, 651 A.2d 1044 (N.J. Super. 1995).
4. A 63 year old postmenopausal woman wants to utilize in vitro fertilization to bear a child, using her husband's sperm and the egg of a younger woman. *See* Scott Lindlaw, *Late Life Pregnancy is Raising Many Ethical, Practical Questions*, TOPEKA CAP. J., Apr. 25, 1997, at 9A.
5. Roger, a single man, banked his sperm before he underwent chemotherapy treatment. Roger is now dead; his parents advertise for a woman to bear Roger's child for them to rear. *Quest for Grandchild Unique*, TOPEKA CAPITAL JOURNAL (AP), March 9, 1997; AP, *Parentless embryo is implanted*, SAN DIEGO UNION TRIBUNE, December 6, 1997, A–3.
6. A fertility clinic advertises that it will give your money back if you do not conceive. *See* Ann Wozencraft, *It's a Baby or It's Your Money Back*, N.Y. TIMES, Aug. 25, 1996, at p. 1.
7. The attorney who arranged a surrogacy contract is sued for damages based on the birth of a child with serious physical defects. *See* Stiver v. Parker, 975 F.2d 261 (6th Cir.1992).
8. "Dolly," a "cloned" Scottish sheep, is born. Using a cell from an adult ewe's mammary gland, scientists created Dolly, "a laboratory counterfeit so exact that she is in essence her mother's identical twin." *See* J. Madelieine Nash, *The Age of Cloning*, TIME, March 10, 1997, at 62. (Nineteen European nations have banned human cloning; *see* Robert Davis, *19 Countries Ban Human Cloning*, USA Today, January 13, 1998, page 1D, col. 4.)

Chapter 9

CHILD, PARENT, AND STATE: RIGHTS AND OBLIGATIONS

> *The Power, then, that Parents have over their Children, arises from that Duty which is incumbent on them, to take care of their Off-spring, during the imperfect state of Childhood. To inform the Mind, and govern the Actions of their yet ignorant Nonage, till reason shall take its place, and ease them of that Trouble, is what the Children want, and the Parents are bound to.*
>
> *John Locke, The Second Treatise on Government § 58*
>
> *I'm a goddamned minor.*
>
> *Holden Caulfield*
>
> *J.D. Salinger, The Catcher in the Rye*

SECTION 1. CHILDREN'S RIGHTS AND LEGAL STATUS

Consider the case of Gregory Kingsley, twelve years of age, the oldest child of Ralph and Rachel Kingsley. Gregory's parents separated when he was four. For most of the next five years, Gregory lived with his father, who suffered from a severe substance abuse problem. After investigation led the State Department of Health and Human Resources (HRS) to conclude that Gregory was being neglected, he was removed from his father's care and placed with his mother. But only five months later, when Gregory was still nine, his mother voluntarily placed him and his brother Jeremiah in foster care. Gregory remained in foster care for almost a year, then was returned to his mother. Less than three months later, Gregory was returned to foster care after Mrs. Kingsley told state authorities that she could no longer cope with her children. Mrs. Kingsley, like her husband, suffered from a substance abuse problem; she was also involved in abusive adult relationships and paid little attention to her children.

After returning to foster care, HRS placed Gregory at the Lake County Boys Ranch. His mother executed a performance agreement requiring her to take steps to cure the problems that had led to Gregory's placement. But Mrs. Kingsley failed to comply with the agreement and requested that her visits with Gregory cease. Accordingly, HRS transferred the case to its adoption unit. Later that year, Gregory, now eleven, was placed with the Russ family. Mr. Russ was an attorney who specialized in the representation of children; Mrs. Russ was a homemaker. They had several children of their own.

Three months later, HRS informed Mr. and Mrs. Russ that it would soon file a petition to terminate Gregory's parents' rights so that they could adopt him. Gregory was elated. But six weeks later, without explanation, HRS reversed its decision and decided to attempt another reunification with Gregory's parents. Gregory reacted to the new plan by threatening to run away. Mr. Russ suggested to Gregory that he might have "certain legal and Constitutional rights which, although not fully recognized presently under the law, may be obtainable for children."[1] Gregory then consulted Jerri Blair, an attorney and acquaintance of Mr. Russ, who agreed to sue on Gregory's behalf to terminate his parents' rights; Mr. Russ agreed to serve as co-counsel.

Shortly after Ms. Blair filed an action on behalf of Gregory and Mr. Russ seeking termination of Mr. and Mrs. Kingsley's parental rights, Gregory's father agreed to voluntarily relinquish his rights. Gregory's mother did not. HRS entered the case and argued that Gregory had no right either to select his own attorney or to file an action to terminate his parents' rights.

The decision that follows indicates how the court ruled, and why. As you read it, consider the larger questions: What are the rights of parents and children? What is the source of these rights and when are they forfeited? When should the state intervene on behalf of the child or to support parental authority? These are the questions with which this chapter is concerned.

KINGSLEY v. KINGSLEY

Florida Court of Appeals, 1993.
623 So.2d 780.

DIAMANTIS, JUDGE.

Rachel Kingsley, the natural mother of Gregory, a minor child, appeals the trial court's final orders terminating her parental rights based upon findings of abandonment and neglect, and granting the

1. Both the facts about Gregory K. and the quotation are drawn from an account of the litigation written by Mr. Russ. George H. Russ, *Through the Eyes of a Child, "Gregory K.": A Child's Right to Be Heard*, 27 FAM. L.Q. 365, 368 (1993).

petition for adoption filed by Gregory's foster parents, George and Elizabeth Russ.

* * *

1. Capacity: Rachel contends that the trial court erred in holding that Gregory has the capacity to bring a termination of parental rights proceeding in his own right. Specifically, Rachel argues that the disability of nonage prevents a minor from initiating or maintaining an action for termination of parental rights. We agree.

Capacity to sue means the absence of a legal disability which would deprive a party of the right to come into court.... Courts historically have recognized that unemancipated minors do not have the legal capacity to initiate legal proceedings in their own names. This historic concept is incorporated into Florida Rule of Civil Procedure 1.210(b), which provides as follows:

> * * * (b) Infants or Incompetent Persons. When an infant or incompetent person has a representative, such as a guardian or other like fiduciary, the representative may sue or defend on behalf of the infant or incompetent person. An infant or incompetent person who does not have a duly appointed representative may sue by next friend or by a guardian ad litem. The court shall appoint a guardian ad litem for an infant or incompetent person not otherwise represented in an action or shall make such other order as it deems proper for the protection of the infant or incompetent person. * * *

The necessity of a guardian ad litem or next friend, the alter ego of a guardian ad litem, to represent a minor is required by the orderly administration of justice and the procedural protection of a minor's welfare and interest by the court and, in this regard, the fact that a minor is represented by counsel, in and of itself, is not sufficient.

... Unless a child has a guardian or other like fiduciary, a child must sue by his next friend: however, the next friend does not become a party to the suit. Where the next friend brings the suit, the minor is the real party in interest.

This disability of nonage has been described as procedural, rather than jurisdictional, in character because if a minor mistakenly brings an action in his own name such defect can be cured by the subsequent appointment of a next friend or guardian ad litem. Thus, the concept of capacity determines the procedure which a minor must invoke in order to pursue a cause of action.

Section 39.461(1), Florida Statutes (Supp. 1992), provides that petitions for termination of parental rights may be initiated either by an attorney for [HRS], or by any other person who has knowledge of the facts alleged or is informed of them and believes that they are true.

> This court has construed the term "any other person who has knowledge" to mean someone who is in a peculiar position so that such knowledge can be reasonably inferred; for example, the judge

familiar with the file, the guardian or attorney for the children, neighbors or friends of the parties who, because of their proximity, would be expected to have such knowledge. This construction contemplates the situation which arose here—that Jerri Blair, an attorney, would file a termination petition on Gregory's behalf. She must do so, however, as his next friend. The next friend may be an attorney, but need not be one. Under this long-recognized and well-tested procedure, the child is the real party in interest, but the courts require that an adult person of reasonable judgment and integrity conduct the litigation for the minor as the latter's next friend. This procedural burden on the conduct of litigation on behalf of a child is only marginally greater than the burden on an adult and is necessary for the orderly conduct of judicial proceedings.

As a general rule, states "may require a minor to wait until the age of majority before being permitted to exercise legal rights independently." *Bellotti v. Baird*, 443 U.S. 622, 650, (1979). Objective criteria, such as age limits, although inevitably arbitrary, are not unconstitutional unless they unduly burden the minor's pursuit of a fundamental right. Gregory's lack of capacity due to nonage is a procedural, not substantive, impediment which minimally restricts his right to participate as a party in proceedings brought to terminate the parental rights of his natural parents; therefore, we conclude that this procedural requirement does not unduly burden a child's fundamental liberty interest to be "free of physical and emotional violence at the hands of his ... most trusted caretaker."

Although we conclude that the trial court erred in allowing Gregory to file the petition in his own name because Gregory lacked the requisite legal capacity, this error was rendered harmless by the fact that separate petitions for termination of parental rights were filed on behalf of Gregory by the foster father, the guardian ad litem, HRS, and the foster mother. * * *

HARRIS C.J., concurring in part, dissenting in part.

This rather ordinary termination of parental rights case was transformed into a cause celebre by artful representation and the glare of klieg lights. It is the judge's obligation, however, to look beyond the images created by light and shadow and concentrate on the real-life drama being played out on center stage. Florida recognizes no cause of action that permits a child to divorce his parents.

I concur with the majority holding that so long as the parents do nothing to forfeit their fundamental liberty interest in the care, custody and management of their child, no one (including the child) can interfere with that interest. While the child has the right not to be abused, neglected or abandoned, there is no right to change parents simply because the child finds substitutes that he or she likes better or who can provide a better standard of living.[2]

2. Because I was impressed with the general high quality of the amicus brief

Florida does not recognize "no-fault" termination of parental rights. That is why the focus in a termination case is (and must be), at least in the first analysis, on the alleged misconduct of the biological parent or parents which would authorize termination of parental rights. Termination of parental rights requires a two step analysis. First, did the parents do something that the State has determined to be sufficiently egregious to permit forfeiture of their right to continue as parents (abuse, neglect, abandonment, voluntary consent to adoption). Unless the answer to this first question is affirmative, the second step in the analysis (the best interest of the child) is unnecessary. Because of the trial strategy employed by the attorneys for the child in this case, the trial court failed to keep these steps separated.

One artful maneuver which attracted the attention of the media (and distracted the court) was the filing of this cause as a declaratory action ... in the name of the child (as opposed to next friend, etc.) and joining the proposed adoptive parents as parties in interest in the action for declaratory relief.... [T]he focus was shifted to a comparison of this troubled biological mother (a single parent) with the prospective adoptive parents (a lawyer and his wife) to determine which could provide the child a better life. The mother could not win this contest. The alleged misconduct of the biological mother ceased to be an issue independent of (except as a condition precedent to) any consideration of the best interest of the child; instead it became an issue inextricably intertwined with the best interest of the child—and even this issue was improperly influenced by the presence and active participation of the proposed adoptive parents as parties—and with the proposed adoptive father acting as one of the child's attorneys.

I concur with the majority that there is sufficient evidence in the record to support the court's finding of abandonment. But I also urge that there is sufficient evidence in the record (and precedent) to support the court had it found no abandonment. That is why I am unable to agree that the numerous errors in this case, and the cumulative effect of them, can be disregarded as merely harmless error.... [T]he "best interest" factors ... should not have been considered by the court until after the court first determined that there was abandonment.... Was the mother prejudiced by the manner in which this trial was conducted? It is possible that the court might have given more consideration to the mother's belated showing of interest in her son, her strong desire to accept her parenting obligations as evidenced by her willingness to expose all her blemishes to full media scrutiny, her apparent successful substantial completion of her HRS performance agreement and the

filed by Children First, I was surprised to read the following comment:

> The decision not to use drugs, not to bear a child or to go to work is no less momentous for a child than the decision as to whom he wants to raise him.

Is Children First suggesting that an eleven year old has the same right (not to mention the requisite maturity and insight) to change parents as he does to apply to become a newspaper boy?

recommendation by the Missouri[3] counterpart of our HRS to return the child to his mother, if it had not been subjected to the confusion and pressures caused by the procedural irregularities of this case. It is not clear what the court would have done if the case had been presented in the proper manner. Because the procedural errors may well have affected the outcome of this case, I submit that the mother is entitled to a new hearing on the issue of abandonment under proper pleadings and confronted only by the proper parties.

The mother might lose again. But even if she did, she (and all those who have closely followed this case) would at least know that she lost on a level playing field.

Notes and Questions

1. Would you classify Gregory's claimed rights as procedural or substantive? How would granting Gregory the right to bring an action in his own name affect his relationship with his biological parents? his foster parents?

2. If Gregory were granted the right to party status and to choose his own attorney, who would have the obligation to pay the attorney fees and court costs he incurs?

3. Legal capacity to sue or to retain an attorney is now based on a child's emancipation. Emancipation has two aspects: It removes a minor from parental authority and ends parental obligations; it may make the minor capable of transacting business with outsiders. Under the Restatement of Contracts, for example, "[u]nless a statute provides otherwise, a natural person has the capacity to incur only voidable contractual duties until the beginning of the day before the person's eighteenth birthday." RESTATEMENT OF CONTRACTS § 14. The most common emancipating event is attaining the age of majority (eighteen in most states). A child may also become emancipated before attaining the age of majority; getting married, enlisting in the armed forces, or becoming self-supporting are typically sufficient to effect emancipation. The issue of emancipation arises most often in cases where a parent's support obligation is at issue. *See* Wulff v. Wulff, 243 Neb. 616, 500 N.W.2d 845 (Neb. 1993) and Chapter 16. For further discussion of emancipation, *see* Sanger and Willemsen, *Minor Changes: Emancipating Children in Modern Times*, 25 MICH. J.L. REF. 239 (1992).

4. Although courts and legislatures have been loathe to declare that children have a right to counsel of their own choosing in child protection proceedings, in many states lawyers or "law guardians" are routinely appointed to represent their interests. In some states, the courts have held that such an appointment is constitutionally required. *See, e.g.*, In re Orlando F., 40 N.Y.2d 103, 386 N.Y.S.2d 64, 351 N.E.2d 711 (1976). There is also a trend toward the appointment of counsel for

3. The mother lived in Missouri and was under the supervision of its "HRS" during much of the time that the child was in foster care. It was shortly after Missouri had recommended returning the child to his mother that this action was commenced.

children in contested custody cases. The spotty empirical data suggests that lawyers for children play a powerful role in determining the outcome of both child protective and custody litigation. *See, e.g.*, Patricia S. Curley & Gregg Herman, *Representing the Best Interests of Children: The Wisconsin Experience*, J. AM. ACAD. MATRIMONIAL L. (1996) (finding that the recommendation of the child's representative is "commonly the eventual order of the court" both in settled and litigated cases and that representatives' recommendations in emergency hearings almost always determine the outcome).

5. The appropriate role of the child's lawyer in child protective and custody proceedings is controversial. Commentators do not agree that the lawyer should simply advocate the child's views:

> ... [C]ounsel for young children should maximize the possibility that the case will impose the least harm possible on the child. This goal is not necessarily advanced at all when counsel advocates a particular result. It is likely to be advanced, however, when lawyers shield their clients from harm, reduce tension between the parties, expedite the proceedings, and see to it that cases are most likely to be decided on the basis of what is best for children.
>
> * * *
>
> Given the importance to the determination of counsel's role of carefully identifying a child's substantive rights in the particular subject matter area in question, we begin by clarifying those rights in the area of child protection. As we shall see, that is not a simple task. One thing, however, is undeniable. As in custody cases, child protective proceedings have virtually nothing to do with empowering children. Children have no more right to insist that the state intervene to protect them from inadequate parents than to insist that the state stay out of their lives.... Child protective proceedings accord children special rights to protection from harm imposed by their caregivers. But these idiosyncratic rights require careful study before applying them to determine the role of counsel for young children. Children have distinctive protective rights. Their primary right is to remain in their parents' custody unless their parents have been inadequate. However, children also have the right to be protected from their parents when their parents fall below the minimal standard of care established by law. Their right to state protection, in other words, is conditional. If, and only if, a parent is inadequate, should the state interfere with the parents' and child's right to familial integrity.
>
> It is possible to define a child's substantive rights in this area in one of two ways. We might say that children have a right to live with their parents unless a court finds the parents unfit. Under such a definition, lawyers for children should regard intervention, even to protect children from harm, as an intrusion into their clients' rights to be raised by their parents. This definition of a child's rights, and the corollary role of counsel for young children, I recognize, will

trouble many children's advocates. These advocates will assert that this definition of a child's rights is inaccurate. For them, children have the right to be separated from their parents whenever their parents are actually unfit, not just when a judge enters a determination of unfitness. That is, children have the right to be free from harm, not merely to have a judge decide whether they are endangered.

There is much force to this alternative definition. Even when we accept it, however, the challenge still remains to clarify counsel's role.... [D]angers are created when lawyers are allowed to reach conclusions about facts that are preconditional to arguing an outcome in the case. In the real world, judges rely on the advocacy of a child's lawyer. It is impossible to know, however, whether the lawyer's views advance or hinder the child's rights. Because the child's right to secure state protection is conditional, that right is wrongfully invoked when the predicate facts justifying it do not exist. If a parent abused her child, the child has the right to be protected. But if a parent has not, the child has the right to have the case dismissed without additional intervention. When a young child's lawyer argues that the court should remove the child from her home based on the lawyer's incorrect conclusion that the parent is unfit, the lawyer has breached the child's right not to be removed.

In addition, ... the lawyer's views on the proper result unavoidably will be the product of a host of factors that will never be the subject of review by anybody. Finally, liberating lawyers for children to advocate results they believe are best for their clients will ensure the randomness and chaos that a rational legal system would avoid whenever possible. It is eminently possible to avoid such chaos in child protective proceedings by the simple device of barring lawyers from advocating an outcome. We should be particularly willing to impose this restriction precisely because there is no assurance in the first place that the lawyer will seek the correct result. * * *

Martin Guggenheim, *A Paradigm for Determining the Role of Counsel for Children*, 64 FORDHAM L. REV. 1399, 1428–31 (1996).

Had Gregory K.'s lawyer followed Professor Guggenheim's advice, what role would she have played in the termination of parental rights proceeding?

Under the English common law—as well as the traditional laws of most other legal systems—unemancipated minors had no rights whatsoever; parents were accorded virtually unlimited power over their child's care, education, and well-being. Blackstone, writing in the late eighteenth century, describes the rationale for parental power and its extent.

WILLIAM BLACKSTONE, COMMENTARIES ON THE LAWS OF ENGLAND;

Book I Ch. 16 (1765).

2. The *power* of parents over their children is derived from the former consideration, their duty; this authority being given them, partly to enable the parent more effectually to perform his duty, and partly as a recompence for his care and trouble in the faithful discharge of it. And upon this score the municipal laws of some nations have given a much larger authority to the parents, than others. The antient Roman laws gave the father a power of life and death over his children; upon this principle, that he who gave had also the power of taking away. * * * The power of a parent by our English laws is much more moderate; but still sufficient to keep the child in order and obedience. He may lawfully correct his child, being under age, in a reasonable manner; for this is for the benefit of his education. The consent or concurrence of the parent to the marriage of his child under age, was also *directed* by our ancient law to be obtained; but now it is absolutely *necessary*; for without it the contract is void. And this also is another means, which the law has put into the parent's hands, in order the better to discharge his duty; first, of protecting his children from the snares of artful and designing persons; and, next, of settling them properly in life, by preventing the ill consequences of too early and precipitate marriages. A father has no other power over his son's *estate*, than as his trustee or guardian; for, though he may receive the profits during the child's minority, yet he must account for them when he comes of age. He may indeed have the benefit of his children's labour while they live with him, and are maintained by him; but this is no more than he is entitled to from his apprentices or servants. The legal power of a father (for a mother, as such, is entitled to no power, but only to reverence and respect) the power of a father, I say, over the persons of his children ceases at the age of twenty one: for they are then enfranchised by arriving at years of discretion, or that point which the law has established (as some must necessarily be established) when the empire of the father, or other guardian, gives place to the empire of reason. Yet, till that age arrives, this empire of the father continues even after his death; for he may by his will appoint a guardian to his children. He may also delegate part of his parental authority, during his life, to the tutor or schoolmaster of his child: who is then *in loco parentis*, and has such a portion of the power of the parent committed to his charge, viz. that of restraint and correction, as may be necessary to answer the purposes for which he is employed.

The policies expressed by Blackstone were successfully challenged during the late nineteenth century by the child protection movement. As the movement's name suggests, child protectionists were concerned with ensuring that children received care, not rights. Their efforts led to the first White House Conference on Children, which proclaimed that, in order to ensure a productive economy and citizenry, government should ensure each child "humane treatment, adequate care, and proper education." Proceedings of the White House Conference on the Care of Dependent Children, S. Doc. 721, 60th Cong. 2d Sess. 192 (1909). The protection movement ultimately succeeded in altering many of the legal systems and rules that affect children; child labor laws, compulsory schooling, the juvenile court, and the modern child welfare system are all a product of protectionists' advocacy.

The child protection movement was linked with a bold new optimism about both the human condition and state intervention. Protectionists believed that the state could—and should—play the role of a beneficent parent toward wayward children and wayward parents. Allied with the new social work profession, protectionists argued that, when parents did not properly care for their children, the state should intervene with temporary out-of-home placement for the child and rehabilitative services for the parent; the goal of these services was return of the child to its parents' care. When children misbehaved, the state was again to intervene for the purpose of rehabilitation; the goal was to help the child, not to punish him.

Children's advocates did not talk in terms of rights for children until the 1960s, a period when distrust of legal authority was high and the civil rights movement had begun to achieve some improvements in the legal status of Afro-Americans. By this point, a growing body of evidence had also established that the reality of state intervention was often far removed from the rehabilitative ideal. For example, the landmark *Gault* decision (387 U.S. 1, 87 S.Ct. 1428, 18 L.Ed.2d 527 (1967)), in which the Supreme Court required juvenile courts to accord minors various due process protections, involved a fifteen year old boy who had been sentenced to an indefinite stay in a state "school" (i.e. kiddie prison), for having made a couple of phone calls "of the irritatingly offensive, adolescent, sex variety" to a neighbor. And a landmark study of the foster care system revealed that, once placed in foster care, children frequently remained there throughout their minority without any serious effort either to cure the parental problems that had led to placement or to sever parental rights. *See* HENRY S. MAAS & RICHARD E. ENGLER, JR, CHILDREN IN NEED OF PARENTS (1959).

Like their protectionist predecessors, children's rights advocates were initially bold and optimistic. Educator A.S. Neill argued that "children should be free to do exactly as they like as long as they don't interfere with the freedom of others" and that such "self-regulated" children would "not [be] haters; they could not possibly be anti-Semitic or racialists." A.S. Neill, *Freedom Works*, in CHILDREN'S RIGHTS: TOWARD THE LIBERATION OF THE CHILD 127, 137–38 (1971). The Bill of Rights for Children set out by Henry Foster and Doris Jonas Freed in 1972 evidences a similar spirit.

FOSTER & FREED, A BILL OF RIGHTS FOR CHILDREN

6 Fam L.Q. 343, 347 (1972).

A child has a moral right and should have a legal right:

1. To receive parental love and affection, discipline and guidance, and to grow to maturity in a home environment which enables him to develop into a mature and responsible adult;

2. To be supported, maintained, and educated to the best of parental ability, in return for which he has the moral duty to honor his father and mother;

3. To be regarded as a *person*, within the family, at school, and before the law.

4. To receive fair treatment from all in authority;

5. To be heard and listened to;

6. To earn and keep his own earnings;

7. To seek and obtain medical care and treatment and counseling;

8. To emancipation from the parent-child relationship when that relationship has broken down and the child has left home due to abuse, neglect, serious family conflict, or other sufficient cause, and his best interests would be served by the termination of parental authority;

9. To be free of legal disabilities or incapacities save where such are convincingly shown to be necessary and protective of the actual best interests of the child; and

10. To receive special care, consideration, and protection in the administration of law or justice so that his best interests always are a paramount factor.

Note and Questions

1. Legal rights may be either negative or affirmative; they may apply against one or many duty-bearers. Thus, according to one classic formulation:

> If B owes A a thousand dollars, A has an *affirmative* right *in personam* . . . that B shall do what is necessary to transfer to A the legal ownership of that amount of money . . . If A owns and occupies Whiteacre, not only B but also a great many other persons—not necessarily all persons—are under a duty, e.g., not to enter on A's land. The latter right is a multital one, for it is one of A's class of similar, though separate rights, actual and potential, against very many persons. The same points apply as regards A's right that B shall not commit a battery on him, and A's right that B shall not manufacture a certain article as to which A has a so-called patent. Wesley N. Hohfeld, Fundamental Legal Conceptions as Applied in

JUDICIAL REASONING AND OTHER ESSAYS 73–74 (Walter W. Cook ed. 1923).

What do the Foster and Freed mean when they say the child "should have a legal right"? Affirmative or negative? In personam or multital? Against whom? In tort, contract, equity or through the criminal law? Keep these questions in mind!

2. In 1989 the U.N. General Assembly adopted the U.N. Convention on the Rights of the Child, Part I of which sets out 41 articles providing rights for a child. U.N.Doc. A/Res/44/25, 28 I.L.M. 1456 (1989). One—like the tenth right in Foster and Freed's list—provides that the child's best interests are the primary consideration in any legal action. The Convention

> seeks to define a worldwide consensus on what society expects from and for its own future—even if there is disagreement on specific substantive mandates of the Convention, as well as on the manner in which it was adopted by the General Assembly or influenced by various social and political interest groups. The Convention asks society, the State, to recognize the child as an independent actor, breaking with a past that put children under the sole control of their parents. In that sense, the Convention mirrors developments in social programmes, tax policies and protective legislation of leading countries. * * *
>
> Ironically, the high rate of international acclaim that has accompanied the Convention may be due to the acceptability in many countries of a wide gulf between public, especially international, pronouncements and their realization in practical terms. In the United States, by contrast, a ratification of the Convention would force real change because a federal treaty would supersede state laws in an area traditionally reserved to the latter. Since that would strike at the heart US federalism, chances for ratification are not great.
>
> Harry D. Krause, *Child Law*, in 13 INT. LIBRARY OF ESSAYS IN LAW AND LEGAL THEORY XIX-XX (1992).

The United States has not yet ratified the Convention and does not seem to be in a hurry to do so. The 1995 attempt failed. S.Res. 133, 104th Cong. Rec. S8400–01 (1995).

3. Recent commentators do not agree on the utility of seeking more rights for children. Compare the following views:

> A friend who lived in New York could not see the sky from her windows. To discover the day's weather she had to peer at a glass-fronted building opposite, which offered a blurred reflection of part of the sky above her own building. I shall argue that when we take rights as fundamental in looking at ethical issues in children's lives we also get an indirect, partial and blurred picture . . .
>
> * * *

If the powerless gain recognition for the rights they claim, those on whom the counterpart obligations fall must acknowledge and fulfill them. Sometimes these obligations will be fulfilled with little urging from those whose rights are acknowledged; sometimes enormous "pressure from below" is needed before there is change. The political point of the rhetoric of rights is therefore evident: rhetoric has to be one of the main weapons of those who lack power. This also explains the easy and frequent misuse of that rhetoric to claim spurious rights even when no corresponding obligations can be justified. Many of the rights promulgated in international documents, including the International Declaration of the Rights of the Child, are perhaps not spurious, but they are patently no more than "manifesto" rights that cannot be claimed unless or until practices and institutions are established that determine against whom claims on behalf of a particular child may be lodged. Mere insistence that certain ideals or goals are rights cannot make them into rights . . . [although a] rhetoric of rights may be politically useful . . .

Appeals to children's rights might have political and rhetorical importance if children's dependence on others is like that of oppressed social groups whom the rhetoric of rights has served well. However, the analogy between children's dependence and that of oppressed groups is suspect. When colonial peoples, or the working classes or religious and racial minorities or women have demanded their rights, they have sought recognition and respect for capacities for rational and independent life and action that are demonstrably there and thwarted by the denial of rights. No doubt oppression takes its toll, and those who have been treated as dependent all their adult lives often lack confidence and are more subservient and less autonomous than they may become: . . . But the dependence of children is very different from the dependence of oppressed social groups on those who exercise power over them.

* * *

The crucial difference between (early) childhood dependence and the dependence of oppressed social groups is that childhood is a stage of life, from which children normally emerge and are helped and urged to emerge by those who have most power over them. Those with power over children's lives usually have some interest in ending childish dependence. Oppressors usually have an interest in maintaining the oppression of social groups. Children have both less need and less capacity to exert "pressure from below," and less potential for using the rhetoric of rights as a political instrument. Those who urge respect for children's rights must address not children but those whose action may affect children; they have reason to prefer the rhetoric of obligations to that of rights, both because its scope is wider and because it addresses the relevant audience more directly.

* * *

If we care about children's lives, we will have a number of good reasons not to base our arguments on appeals to children's fundamental rights.... To look at rights is to look at what is ethically required indirectly by looking at what should be received.... The view we get from the perspective of rights is not merely indirect, but blurred and incomplete.... The rhetoric of rights is mainly useful to agents who are largely powerless but able to exert at least rhetorical pressure from below. Children are more fundamentally but less permanently powerless; their main remedy is to grow up.... The great disanalogies between children's dependence and that of members of oppressed social groups suggest that the rhetoric of rights can rarely empower children.... Nothing is lost in debates about the allocation of obligations to children between families and public institutions if we do not suppose that fundamental rights are the basis of those obligations.

Onora O'Neill, *Children's Rights and Children's Lives*, 98 ETHICS 455, 460–63 (1988)

... Rights play an important role within our social, legal, and political institutions and it is difficult to see why we should exclude children from our rights rhetoric if we reconceive our notions of rights. Rights also offer the possibility of improving children's experiences by recognizing and remedying their powerlessness. Moreover, a rights-based approach provides greater protections for those who lack power than one in which the good will or good faith of others is offered as an alternative to rights. The latter approach actually disadvantages children; certainly, there is evidence to suggest that when we try to act on behalf of children, our efforts seldom have neutral consequences and, in fact, cause greater harm.

Rights have an empowering effect for they limit what we may do to others and what others may do to and for us. By empowering children, rights have the potential to minimize the victimization of the youngest members of society, even when that harm occurs privately within the family. There is a fundamental difference between respecting children because they are powerful and protecting children because they are vulnerable. Although it would be naive to think that if children had such rights they would no longer experience victimization, it is nevertheless realistic to believe that the nature and frequency of the harms inflicted upon children would change substantially if we envision children as powerful beings. Rethinking the construct of child as dependent and disabled through a coherent account of rights would enable us to see the ways in which we have disempowered and harmed children.

Two principles of an empowerment rights perspective are thus intertwined. The power principle acknowledges that power is a fundamental aspect of human relationships and pervades our personal and institutional interactions. Additionally, the power principle recognizes that power may collect within certain institutional frameworks to disadvantage particular groups within a society. By tying an account of rights to power, an empowerment rights perspective grounds the value of rights in a more realistic assessment of human nature and interpersonal relationship while illustrating the need for and intrinsic worth of a rights-based approach. The value of rights, therefore, relates not only to its practical worth but also to its empowering effects.

* * *

The experiences of children within the child welfare system ... reflect the disadvantaging effects of an impoverished rights theory. Because prevention and early intervention programs are virtually nonexistent in most jurisdictions, a typical case begins with an allegations that neglect has already occurred. If the allegation is substantiated, the child can be removed from her home and placed in foster care. However, financial constraints and programmatic limitations created by policy decisions limit the nature and kind of services available to the child and her family as well as the quality of the personnel in the child welfare system. The child, therefore, is likely to experience a number of foster care placements over a period of years and may never be reunited with her parents. Her views and preferences as to her placement also are unlikely to be heard because the child is seldom represented by independent counsel. From an empowerment rights perspective, however, the child would be a respected and powerful participant in the child welfare system. Under this view, one would expect the victimization of children to decrease as they come to be seen as powerful, rights-bearing individuals. Moreover, the emphasis would be on the vindication of children's rights rather than on their vulnerabilities and dependence. This would require a commitment to improving the economic conditions of children and their families through a reallocation of our financial resources. In turn, this may reduce opportunities for the neglect and abuse of children....

Katherine Hunt Federle, *Looking Ahead: An Empowerment Perspective on the Rights of Children*, 68 TEMPLE L. REV. 1585, 1596–97 (1995)

Reconsider the case of Gregory Kingsley. Gregory confronted parental abandonment and neglect, ineffectual attempts by state child welfare officials to cure the problems that led to his placement in foster care, and refusal by those officials to initiate parental rights termination proceedings at the point when Gregory wished. With respect to which problems are Professor O'Neill's views more persuasive? Professor Federle's? Why?

4. How, if at all, would you alter the Foster & Freed's Bill of Rights?

SECTION 2. EDUCATION

Education has the power to shape social development, moral values, and political participation; it is also a prime determinant of future employment. Although the state has a strong interest in ensuring that its future citizens have a minimum level of competency (sometimes defined as ability to read a ballot and to add and subtract numbers in a checkbook), parents have traditionally exercised substantial control over their child's education. The United State Supreme Court has made a number of pronouncements about the importance of education.

> "Today, education is perhaps the most important function of state and local governments. Compulsory school attendance laws and the great expenditures for education both demonstrate our recognition of the importance of education to our democratic society. It is required in the performance of our most basic public responsibilities, even service in the armed forces. It is the very foundation of good citizenship. Today it is a principal instrument in awakening the child to cultural values, in preparing him for later professional training, and in helping him to adjust normally to his environment."

Brown v. Board of Education, 347 U.S. 483, 493, 74 S.Ct. 686, 691, 98 L.Ed. 873 (1954).

> "Public education is not a 'right' granted to individuals by the Constitution. But neither is it merely some governmental 'benefit' indistinguishable from other forms of social welfare legislation. * * * But more is involved in this case than the abstract question whether § 21.031 discriminates against a suspect class of whether education is a fundamental right. Section 21.031 imposes a lifetime hardship on a discrete class of children [illegal aliens] not accountable for their disabling status. The stigma of illiteracy will mark them for the rest of their lives. By denying these children a basic education, we deny them the ability to live within the structure of our civic institutions, and foreclose any realistic possibility that they will contribute in even the smallest way to the progress of our Nation. In determining the rationality of § 21.031, we may appropriately take into account its costs to the Nation and to the innocent children who are its victims. In light of these countervailing costs, the discrimination contained in § 21.031 can hardly be considered rational * * *."
>
> *Plyler v. Doe*, 457 U.S. 202, 220–24, 102 S.Ct. 2382, 2396–98, 72 L.Ed.2d 786 (1982).

Can you reconcile these pronouncements with the holding of the following case?

WISCONSIN v. YODER

Supreme Court of the United States, 1972.
406 U.S. 205, 92 S.Ct. 1526, 32 L.Ed.2d 15.

CHIEF JUSTICE BURGER delivered the opinion of the Court.

* * *

Respondents Jonas Yoder and Adin Yutzy are members of the Old Order Amish Religion, and respondent Wallace Miller is a member of the Conservative Amish Mennonite Church. They and their families are residents of Green County, Wisconsin. Wisconsin's compulsory school attendance law required them to cause their children to attend public or private school until reaching age 16 but the respondents declined to send their children, ages 14 and 15, to public school after completing the eighth grade. The children were not enrolled in any private school, or within any recognized exception to the compulsory attendance law, and they are conceded to be subject to the Wisconsin statute.

On complaint of the school district administrator for the public schools, respondents were charged, tried and convicted of violating the compulsory attendance law in Green County Court and were fined the sum of $5 each. Respondents defended on the ground that the application of the compulsory attendance law violated their rights under the First and Fourteenth Amendments. The trial testimony showed that respondents believed, in accordance with the tenets of Old Order Amish communities generally, that their children's attendance at high school, public or private, was contrary to the Amish religion and way of life. They believed that by sending their children to high school, they would not only expose themselves to the danger of the censure of the church community, but, as found by the county court, endanger their own salvation and that of their children. The State stipulated that respondents' religious beliefs were sincere.

In support of their position, respondents presented as expert witnesses scholars on religion and education whose testimony is uncontradicted. They expressed their opinions on the relationship of the Amish belief concerning school attendance to the more general tenets of their religion, and described the impact that compulsory high school attendance could have on the continued survival of the Amish communities as they exist in the United States today.... Old Order Amish communities today are characterized by a fundamental belief that salvation requires life in a church community separate and apart from the world and worldly influence. This concept of life aloof from the world and its values is central to their faith....

Formal high school education beyond the eighth grade is contrary to Amish beliefs, not only because it places Amish children in an environment hostile to Amish beliefs with increasing emphasis on competition in class work and sports and with pressure to conform to the styles, manners, and ways of the peer group, but also because it takes them away from their community, physically and emotionally, during the crucial and formative adolescent period of life. During this period, the children must acquire Amish attitudes favoring manual work and self-reliance and the specific skills needed to perform the adult role of an Amish farmer or housewife. They must learn to enjoy physical labor.... And, at this time in life, the Amish child must also grow in his faith and his relationship to the Amish community if he is to be prepared to accept the heavy obligations imposed by adult baptism. In short, high school attendance with teachers who are not of the Amish faith—and may even be hostile to it—interposes a serious barrier to the integration of the Amish child into the Amish religious community. Dr. John Hostetler, one of the experts on Amish society, testified that the modern high school is not equipped, in curriculum or social environment, to impart the values promoted by Amish society....

On the basis of such considerations, Dr. Hostetler testified that compulsory high school attendance could not only result in great psychological harm to Amish children, because of the conflicts it would produce, but would also, in his opinion, ultimately result in the destruction of the Old Order Amish church community as it exists in the United States today ...

There is no doubt as to the power of a State, having a high responsibility for education of its citizens, to impose reasonable regulations for the control and duration of basic education. *See e.g., Pierce v. Society of Sisters,* 268 U.S. 510, 534 (1925). Providing public schools ranks at the very apex of the function of a State. Yet even this paramount responsibility was, in *Pierce,* made to yield to the right of parents to provide an equivalent education in a privately operated system. There the Court held that Oregon's statute compelling attendance in a public school from age eight to age 16 unreasonably interfered with the interest of parents in directing the rearing of their offspring including their education in church-operated schools. As that case suggests the values of parental direction of the religious upbringing and education of their children in their early and formative years have a high place in our society. Thus, a State's interest in universal education, however highly we rank it, is not totally free from a balancing process when it impinges on other fundamental rights and interests, such as those specifically protected by the Free Exercise Clause of the First Amendment and the traditional interest of parents with respect to the religious upbringing of their children so long as they, in the words of *Pierce,* "prepare [them] for additional obligations." * * *

The impact of the compulsory attendance law on respondents' practice of the Amish religion is not only severe, but inescapable, for the Wisconsin law affirmatively compels them, under threat of criminal sanction, to perform acts undeniably at odds with fundamental tenets of their religious beliefs. Nor is the impact of the compulsory attendance law confined to grave interference with important Amish religious tenets from a subjective point of view. It carries with it precisely the kind of objective danger to the free exercise of religion which the First Amendment was designed to prevent. As the record shows, compulsory school attendance to age 16 for Amish children carries with it a very real threat of undermining the Amish community and religious practice as it exists today; they must either abandon belief and be assimilated into society at large, or be forced to migrate to some other and more tolerant region. In sum, the unchallenged testimony of acknowledged experts in education and religious history, almost 300 years of consistent practice, and strong evidence of a sustained faith pervading and regulating respondents' entire mode of life support the claim that enforcement of the State's requirement of compulsory formal education after the eighth grade would gravely endanger if not destroy the free exercise of respondents' religious beliefs.

* * *

We turn, then to the State's broader contention that its interest in its system of compulsory education is so compelling that even the established religious practices of the Amish must give way. Where fundamental claims of religious freedom are at stake, however, we cannot accept such a sweeping claim; despite its admitted validity in the generality of cases, we must searchingly examine the interests which the State seeks to promote by its requirement for compulsory education to age 16, and the impediment to those objectives that would flow from recognizing the claimed Amish exemption.

The State advances two primary arguments in support of its system of compulsory education. It notes, as Thomas Jefferson pointed out early in our history, that some degree of education is necessary to prepare citizens to participate effectively and intelligently in our open political system if we are to preserve freedom and independence. Further, education prepares individuals to be self-reliant and self-sufficient participants in society. We accept these propositions.

However, the evidence adduced by the Amish in this case is persuasively to the effect that an additional one or two years of formal high school for Amish children in place of their long established program of informal vocational education would do little to serve those interests. Respondents' experts testified at trial, without challenge, that the value of all education must be assessed in terms of its capacity to prepare the child for life. It is one thing to say that compulsory education for a year or two beyond the eighth grade may be necessary when its goal is the preparation of the child for life in modern society as the majority live, but it is quite another if the goal of education be viewed as the preparation of the child for life in the separated agrarian community that is the keystone of the Amish faith.

The State attacks respondents' position as one fostering "ignorance" from which the child must be protected by the State. No one can question the State's duty to protect children from ignorance but this argument does not square with the facts disclosed in the record. Whatever their idiosyncrasies as seen by the majority, this record strongly shows that the Amish community has been a highly successful social unit within our society even if apart from the conventional "mainstream." Its members are productive and very law-abiding members of society; they reject public welfare in any of its usual modern forms. The Congress itself recognized their self-sufficiency by authorizing exemption of such groups as the Amish from the obligation to pay social security taxes.

* * *

Contrary to the suggestion of the dissenting opinion of Mr. Justice Douglas, our holding today in no degree depends on the assertion of the religious interest of the child as contrasted with that of the parents. It is the parents who are subject to prosecution here for failing to cause their children to attend school, and it is their right to free exercise, not that of their children, that must determine Wisconsin's power to impose criminal penalties on the parent. The dissent argues that a child who expresses a desire to attend public high school in conflict with the wishes of his parents should not be prevented from doing so. There is no reason for the Court to consider that point since it is not an issue in the case. The children are not parties to this litigation. The State has at no point tried this case on the theory that respondents were preventing their children from attending school against their expressed desires, and indeed the record is to the contrary. The State's position from the outset has been that it is empowered to apply its compulsory attendance law to Amish parents in the same manner as to other parents—that is, without regard to the wishes of the child. That is the claim we reject today.

Our holding in no way determines the proper resolution of possible competing interests of parents, children, and the State in an appropriate state court proceeding in which the power of the State is asserted on the theory that Amish parents are preventing their minor children from attending high school despite their expressed desires to the contrary. Recognition of the claim of the State in such a proceeding would, of course, call into question traditional concepts of parental control over the religious upbringing and education of their minor children recognized in this Court's past decisions. It is clear that such an intrusion by a State into family decisions in the area of religious training would give rise to grave questions of religious freedom comparable to those raised here and those presented in *Pierce v. Society of Sisters*. On this record we neither reach nor decide those issues.

* * *

For the reasons stated we hold, with the Supreme Court of Wisconsin, that the First and Fourteenth Amendments prevent the State from compelling respondents to cause their children to attend formal high school to age 16. Our disposition of this case, however, in no way alters our recognition of the obvious fact that courts are not school boards or legislatures, and are ill-equipped to determine the "necessity" of discrete aspects of a State's program of compulsory education. This should suggest that courts must move with great circumspection in performing the sensitive and delicate task of weighing a State's legitimate social concern when faced with religious claims for exemption from generally applicable educational requirements. It cannot be over-emphasized that we are not dealing with a way of life and mode of education by a group claiming to have recently discovered some "progressive" or more enlightened process for rearing children for modern life. * * *

JUSTICE DOUGLAS, dissenting in part.

* * * If the parents in this case are allowed a religious exemption, the inevitable effect is to impose the parents' notions of religious duty upon their children. When the child is mature enough to express potentially conflicting desires, it would be an invasion of the child's rights to permit such an imposition without canvassing his views.... As the child has no other effective forum, it is in this litigation that his rights should be considered. And, if an Amish child desires to attend high school, and is mature enough to have that desire respected, the State may well be able to override the parents' religiously motivated objections.

Religion is an individual experience. It is not necessary, nor even appropriate, for every Amish child to express his views on the subject in a prosecution of a single adult. Crucial, however, are the views of the child whose parent is the subject of the suit. Frieda Yoder has in fact testified that her own religious views are opposed to high-school education. I therefore join the judgment of the Court as to respondent Jonas Yoder. But Frieda Yoder's views may not be those of Vernon Yutzy or Barbara Miller. I must dissent, therefore, as to respondents Adin Yutzy and Wallace Miller as their motion to dismiss also raised the question of their children's religious liberty.

* * *

These children are "persons" within the meaning of the Bill of Rights. We have so held over and over again. In *Haley v. Ohio*, 332 U.S. 596, we extended the protection of the Fourteenth Amendment in a state trial of a 15–year-old boy. In *In re Gault*, 387 U.S. 1, 13, we held that "neither the Fourteenth Amendment nor the Bill of Rights is for adults alone." In *In re Winship*, 397 U.S. 358, we held that a 12–year-old boy, when charged with an act which would be a crime if committed by an adult, was entitled to procedural safeguards contained in the Sixth Amendment. * * * On this important and vital matter of education, I think the children should be entitled to be heard. While the parents, absent dissent, normally speak for the entire family, the education of the child is a matter on which the child will often have decided views. He may want to be a pianist or an astronaut or an ocean geographer. To do so he will have to break from the Amish tradition. * * * The views of the two children in question were not canvassed by the Wisconsin courts. The matter should be explicitly reserved so that new hearings can be held on remand of the case.

Notes and Questions

1. The trend has been to raise the age of required school attendance. The Wisconsin statute now requires school attendance until eighteen or high school graduation.

2. In a concurring opinion in *Yoder*, Justice White wrote that the state has a legitimate interest in "seeking to prepare ... [its children] for a lifestyle which they may later choose." Can this viewpoint be reconciled with the result in *Yoder*? Is it consistent with the Court's statement that "[i]t is one thing to say that compulsory education for a year or two beyond the eighth grade may be necessary when its goal is the preparation of the child for life in modern society as the majority live, but it is quite another if the goal of education be viewed as the preparation of the child for life in the separated agrarian community that is the keystone of the Amish faith?"

3. Douglas in his dissent suggests that someone should ask the children. What factors might color the children's expressed preference? How much weight should their statements receive?

4. Was the *Yoder* decision more influenced by the fact that the Amish are law-abiding, productive citizens (one of the goals of education) or by the free exercise claims that they raised? In Duro v. District Attorney, 712 F.2d 96 (4th Cir.1983), a federal appeals court upheld North Carolina's compulsory education law against a challenge by Pentecostalist parents who objected to the use of physicians and opposed "the unisex movement where you can't tell the difference between boys and girls and the promotion of secular humanism ..." Because of these beliefs, the parents wished to educate their children at home, using the Alpha Omega Christian Curriculum; instruction was to be offered by the mother, who lacked both a teaching certificate and teacher training. In upholding the law, the Court stressed that

> "[t]he Duros, unlike their Amish counterparts, are not members of a community which has existed for three centuries and has a long history of being a successful, self-sufficient, segment of American society. Furthermore, in *Yoder*, the Amish children attended public school through the eighth grade and then obtained information vocational training to enable them to assimilate into the self-contained Amish community. However, ... Duro refuses to enroll his children in a public or nonpublic school for any length of time, but still expects them to ... live normally in the modern world upon reaching the age of 18."

4. Do parents have a right to withdraw their children from classes of which they do not approve? Sex education classes? *See* Medeiros v. Kiyosaki, 52 Haw. 436, 478 P.2d 314 (1970); Smith v. Ricci, 89 N.J. 514, 446 A.2d 501 (1982). Reading classes using a particular series of books? *See* Mozert v. Hawkins County Board of Education, 827 F.2d 1058 (6th Cir.1987). AIDS instruction?

5. In a series of decisions the Supreme Court has held that the Establishment Clause forbids the state from introducing religion into its educational curriculum. *See* Engel v. Vitale, 370 U.S. 421, 82 S.Ct. 1261, 8 L.Ed.2d 601 (1962) (finding that the establishment clause prohibits a state from authorizing prayer in the public schools); Edwards v. Aguillard, 482 U.S. 578, 107 S.Ct. 2573, 96 L.Ed.2d 510 (1987) (invalidating Louisiana law requiring equal time for creation science); Wallace v. Jaffree, 472 U.S. 38, 105 S.Ct. 2479, 86 L.Ed.2d 29 (1985) (invalidating Alabama's period of silence for meditation or voluntary prayer); Lee v. Weisman, 505 U.S. 577, 112 S.Ct. 2649, 120 L.Ed.2d 467 (1992) (banning nonsectarian benedictions and prayers in public school graduation ceremonies).

Suppose that parents were to mount an Establishment Clause challenge to the school curriculum based on the claim that, because God is omitted from discussion and the curriculum approves the view that there are no moral absolutes, it constitutes the establishment of the religion of "secular humanism." What arguments would you expect from parents and the state? What result is likely? *See* Smith v. Board of School Comm'rs of Mobile Cty., 655 F.Supp. 939 (S.D.Ala.1987) What would be the result of a decision in favor of the parents? If revision of the curriculum is required, who would determine content? *See* Smith v. Board of School Comm'rs of Mobile Cty., 827 F.2d 684 (11th Cir.1987).

5. Article 28 of the U.N. Convention on the Rights of the Child recognizes a right to primary education that is "free and compulsory."

Traditionally, parents who refused to send their children to school could be subject to a state's abuse and neglect laws. For example, in In re McMillan, 30 N.C.App. 235, 237, 226 S.E.2d 693, 694 (1976), the court held that:

> It is fundamental that a child who receives proper care and supervision in modern times is provided a basic education. A child does not receive "proper care" and lives in an "environment injurious to his welfare" when he is deliberately refused this education, and he is "neglected" within the meaning of [the statute]. Most states have either enacted statutes allowing for home based education or interpreted their compulsory education laws to allow home schooling under certain conditions.

In recent years many states have enacted statutes or interpreted their compulsory education laws to allow home schooling under certain conditions. Standards vary widely. For example, N.Y. EDUCATION LAW § 3204(2) provides that private or home education must be "equivalent" to that received in the public schools while Mississippi exempts from the compulsory education law all "legitimate home instruction programs," defined as "those not operated or instituted for the purpose of avoiding or circumventing the compulsory attendance law." MISS. STAT. § 37–13–91.

These new laws reflect a new interest in home schooling and intensive lobbying efforts by religious groups. The number of parents educating their children at home has risen dramatically, from approximately 15,000 students taught at home in the 1970s to an estimated million plus students today. In response to the growing demand, a wide variety of home schooling materials and tests are now available. *See* THE HOME SCHOOL MANUAL (Theodore E. Wade, Jr., et al. 1995).

Courts in states without specific authorization have had to make constitutional and statutory interpretations to determine whether home schooling is allowed under their compulsory education laws. Some state courts have refused to sanction home schooling (*see, e.g.*, Duro v. District Attorney, p. 424) while others have held that home instruction may qualify as a private school. *See, e.g.*, People v. Levisen, 404 Ill. 574, 90 N.E.2d 213 (1950); Delconte v. State, 313 N.C. 384, 329 S.E.2d 636 (1985). And at least one state court has held that the allowability of home schooling may vary based on the reason for the parental request. *Compare* People v. DeJonge, 442 Mich. 266, 501 N.W.2d 127 (Mich. 1993) (state did not show compelling state interest in teacher certification requirement that infringed on parents ability to home school for religious reasons) *with* People v. Bennett, 442 Mich. 316, 501 N.W.2d 106 (Mich. 1993) (parents applying to home school for nonreligious reasons had to follow the statute).

Among states that permit home schooling, there is no consensus on the type of requirements the state should—or legally can—impose on home school programs. While courts have recognized the authority of the state to take steps to ensure that home schooling meets minimum standards, the Supreme Court has not ruled on any aspect of home schooling and the state case law is both sparse and nonuniform. *See* Texas Education Agency v. Leeper et al., 893 S.W.2d 432 (Tex.1994) (standardized achievement tests); Crites v. Smith, 826 S.W.2d 459 (Tenn.App.1991) (qualifications of teachers for high school age students); State v. Rivera, 497 N.W.2d 878 (Iowa 1993) (annual reports); Null v. Board of Education of County of Jackson, 815 F.Supp. 937 (S.D.W.Va. 1993) (minimum test scores); Care and Protection of Charles, 399 Mass. 324, 504 N.E.2d 592 (1987) (approval of instruction plan by local school committee). *See also* Jack MacMullan, *The Constitutionality of State Home Schooling Statutes*, 39 VILL. L. REV. 1309 (1994).

Finally, commentators disagree on whether home schooling is good or bad. According to some experts, home schooling interferes with the goal of ensuring that children develop the capacity to become responsible, deliberative citizens who both understand the values of our society and have the capacity to engage in critical thinking. *See* AMY GUTMANN, DEMOCRATIC EDUCATION 1–70 (1987); Ira C. Lupu, *Home Education, Religious Liberty, and the Separation of Powers*, 67 B.U.L. REV. 971 (1987) (arguing that home education is not constitutionally protected and should be discouraged). Under this view, home schooling should be outlawed or restricted. Others contend that allowing parents to reject schooling that promotes values contrary to their own fosters the democratic aim of achieving a diverse and pluralistic society. *See* Stephen G. Gilles, *On Educating Children: A Parentalist Manifesto*, 63 U. Chi. L. Rev. 937 (1996); Stephen Macedo, *Liberal Civic Education and Religious Fundamentalism: The Case of God v. John Rawls*, 105 Ethics 468 (1995).

Problem 9–1: Home Schooling

You are counsel to the State Senate Education Committee, which is currently considering the issue of home schooling. The state Education Law currently requires all children to attend either a public school or "a state-certified private educational institution." The Committee is considering changing the law to permit home schooling; if home schooling is allowed, the Committee must decide what conditions and requirements to impose on home schooling families. You have been asked to advise the Committee:

A. Whether a constitutional challenge to the current statute by parents who want to home school their children would likely succeed and why.

B. If the state authorizes home schooling in some circumstances, may it legally require that: parents who home school pass a state competency test? students who are home schooled pass standardized state achievement tests? May the state mandate some aspects of the curriculum?

C. Whether home schooling would comport with the stated goals of the Education Law, "to ensure that each child is literate and competent to participate meaningfully in public life and in productive employment."

The Committee has already heard testimony from a number of religious organizations that urge their members to engage in home schooling as well as a range of parents who want to engage in home schooling. Many of these parents are fundamentalist Christians who wish to shield their children from teaching that conflicts with their religious values. But others wish to withdraw their children from public school because of the perceived inadequacy of the curriculum or because of their child's special needs; the Committee has heard, for example, from parents of children who are particularly gifted, who have learning disabilities, who have been subject to bullying, or who have developed a school phobia.

SECTION 3. MEDICAL DECISION MAKING

Parents typically must consent to their child's medical treatment. But if a parent refuses to consent to treatment that medical professionals believe is necessary to protect the child's health, can a court overrule the parent? If yes, when and on what basis? Should the court's decision vary depending on whether the parents' refusal is based on their religious beliefs? On the child's views? What is the role of criminal law, child protection laws and tort law?

PARHAM v. J. R.

Supreme Court of the United States, 1979.
442 U.S. 584, 99 S.Ct. 2493, 61 L.Ed.2d 101.

CHIEF JUSTICE BURGER delivered the opinion of the Court.

The question presented in this appeal is what process is constitutionally due a minor child whose parents or guardian seek state administered institutional mental health care for the child and specifically whether an adversary proceeding is required prior to or after the commitment.

* * * For purposes of this decision, we assume that a child has a protectible interest not only in being free of unnecessary bodily restraints but also in not being labeled erroneously by some because of an improper decision by the state hospital superintendent.

We next deal with the interests of the parents who have decided, on the basis of their observations and independent professional recommendations, that their child needs institutional care. Appellees argue that the constitutional rights of the child are of such magnitude and the likelihood of parental abuse is so great that the parents' traditional interests in and responsibility for the upbringing of their child must be subordinated at least to the extent of providing a formal adversary hearing prior to a voluntary commitment.

Our jurisprudence historically has reflected Western Civilization concepts of the family as a unit with broad parental authority over minor children. Our cases have consistently followed that course; our constitutional system long ago rejected any notion that a child is "the mere creature of the State" and, on the contrary, asserted that parents generally "have the right, coupled with the high duty, to recognize and prepare [their children] for additional obligations." *Pierce v. Society of Sisters*, 268 U.S. 510, 535 (1924). *See also Wisconsin v. Yoder* [p. 419]; *Prince v. Massachusetts*, 321 U.S. 158, 166 (1944); *Meyer v. Nebraska*, 262 U.S. 390, 400 (1923). Surely, this includes a "high duty" to recognize symptoms of illness and to seek and follow medical advice. The law's concept of the family rests on a presumption that parents possess what a child lacks in maturity, experience, and capacity for judgment required for making life's difficult decisions. More important, historically it has recognized that natural bonds of affection lead parents to act in the best interests of their children. 1 W. Blackstone, Commentaries 447; 2 Kent. Commentaries on American Law 190.

As with so many other legal presumptions, experience and reality may rebut what the law accepts as a starting point; the incidence of child neglect and abuse cases attests to this. That some parents "may at times be acting against the interests of their child" . . . creates a basis for caution, but is hardly a reason to discard wholesale those pages of human experience that teach that parents generally do act in the child's best interests. The statist notion that governmental power should supersede parental authority in *all* cases because *some* parents abuse and neglect children is repugnant to American tradition.

Nonetheless, we have recognized that a state is not without constitutional control over parental discretion in dealing with children when their physical or mental health is jeopardized. Moreover, the Court recently declared unconstitutional a state statute that granted parents an absolute veto over a minor child's decision to have an abortion. *Planned Parenthood of Central Missouri v. Danforth*, 428 U.S. 52 (1976). Appellees urge that these precedents limiting the traditional rights of parents, if viewed in the context of the liberty interest of the child and the likelihood of parental abuse require us to hold that the parents' decision to have a child admitted to a mental hospital must be subjected to an exacting constitutional scrutiny, including a formal, adversary, preadmission hearing.

Appellees' argument, however, sweeps too broadly. Simply because the decision of a parent is not agreeable to a child or because it involves risks does not automatically transfer the power to make that decision from the parents to some agency or officer of the state. The same characterizations can be made for a tonsillectomy, appendectomy or other medical procedure. Most children, even in adolescence, simply are not able to make sound judgments concerning many decisions, including their need for medical care or treatment. Parents can and must make those judgments. Here there is no finding by the District Court of even a single instance of bad faith by any parent of any member of appellees' class. We cannot assume that the result in *Meyer, supra* and *Pierce, supra*, would have been different if the children there had announced a preference to learn only English or a preference to go to a public, rather than a church, school. The fact that a child may balk at hospitalization or complain about a parental refusal to provide cosmetic surgery does not diminish the parents' authority to decide what is best for the child. Neither state officials nor federal courts are equipped to review such parental decisions.

* * *

In defining the respective rights and prerogatives of the child and parent in the voluntary commitment setting, we conclude that our precedents permit the parents to retain a substantial, if not the dominant, role in the decision, absent a finding of neglect or abuse, and that the traditional presumption that the parents act in the best interests of their child should apply. We also conclude, however, that the child's rights and the nature of the commitment decision are such that parents cannot always have absolute and unreviewable discretion to decide whether to have a child institutionalized. They, of course, retain plenary authority to seek such care for their children, subject to a physician's independent examination and medical judgment.

The state obviously has a significant interest in confining the use of its costly mental health facilities to cases of genuine need. The Georgia program seeks first to determine whether the patient seeking admission has an illness that calls for in-patient treatment. To accomplish this purpose, the State has charged the superintendents of each regional hospital with the responsibility for determining, before authorizing an admission, whether a prospective patient is mentally ill and whether the patient will likely benefit from hospital care. In addition, the State has imposed a continuing duty on hospital superintendents to release any patient who has recovered to the point where hospitalization is no longer needed.

The State in performing its voluntarily assumed mission also has a significant interest in not imposing unnecessary procedural obstacles that may discourage the mentally ill or their families from seeking needed psychiatric assistance. The *parens patriae* interest in helping parents care for the mental health for their children cannot be fulfilled if the parents are unwilling to take advantage of the opportunities because the admission process is too onerous, too embarrassing or too contentious. It is surely not idle to speculate as to how many parents who believe they are acting in good faith would forego state-provided hospital care if such care is contingent on participation in an adversary proceeding designed to probe their motives and other private family matters in seeking the voluntary admission.

The State also has a genuine interest in allocating priority to the diagnosis and treatment of patients as soon as they are admitted to a hospital rather than to time-consuming procedural minutes before the admission. One factor that must be considered is the utilization of the time of psychiatrists, psychologists and other behavioral specialists in preparing for and participating in hearings rather than performing the task for which their special training has fitted them. Behavioral experts in courtrooms and hearings are of little help to patients.

* * *

We now turn to consideration of what process protects adequately the child's constitutional rights by reducing risks of error without unduly trenching on traditional parental authority and without undercutting "efforts to further the legitimate interests of both the state and the patient that are served by" voluntary commitments. We conclude that the risk of error inherent in the parental decision to have a child institutionalized for mental health care is sufficiently great that some kind of inquiry should be made by a "neutral factfinder" to determine whether the statutory requirements for admission are satisfied. That inquiry must carefully probe the child's background using all available sources, including, but not limited to, parents, schools and other social agencies. Of course, the review must also include an interview with the child. It is necessary that the decisionmaker have the authority to refuse to admit any child who does not satisfy the medical standards for admission. Finally, it is necessary that the child's continuing need for commitment be reviewed periodically by a similarly independent procedure.

We are satisfied that such procedures will protect the child from an erroneous admission decision in a way that neither unduly burdens the states nor inhibits parental decisions to seek state help.

Due process has never been thought to require that the neutral and detached trier of fact be law-trained or a judicial or administrative officer. Surely, this is the case as to medical decisions for "neither judges nor administrative hearing officers are better qualified than psychiatrists to render psychiatric judgments." Thus, a staff physician will suffice, so long as he or she is free to evaluate independently the child's mental and emotional condition and need for treatment.

It is not necessary that the deciding physician conduct a formal or quasi-formal hearing. A state is free to require such a hearing, but due process is not violated by use of informal traditional medical investigative techniques. Since well-established medical procedures already exist, we do not undertake to outline with specificity precisely what this investigation must involve. The mode and procedure of medical diagnostic procedures is not the business of judges. What is best for a child is an individual medical decision that must be left to the judgment of physicians in each case. We do no more than emphasize that the decision should represent an independent judgment of what the child requires and that all sources of information that are traditionally relied on by physicians and behavioral specialists should be consulted.

* * *

Another problem with requiring a formalized, factfinding hearing lies in the danger it poses for significant intrusion into the parent-child relationship. Pitting the parents and child as adversaries often will be at odds with the presumption that parents act in the best interests of their child. It is one thing to require a neutral physician to make a careful review of the parents' decision in order to make sure it is proper from a medical standpoint; it is a wholly different matter to employ an adversary contest to ascertain whether the parents' motivation is consistent with the child's interests.

Moreover, it is appropriate to inquire into how such a hearing would contribute to the long range successful treatment of the patient. Surely, there is a risk that it would exacerbate whatever tensions already existed between the child and the parents. Since the parents can and usually do play a significant role in the treatment while the child is hospitalized and even more so after release, there is a serious risk that an adversary confrontation will adversely affect the ability of the parents to assist the child while in the hospital. Moreover, it will make his subsequent return home more difficult. These unfortunate results are especially critical with an emotionally disturbed child; they seem likely to occur in the context of an adversary hearing in which the parents testify. A confrontation over such intimate family relationships would distress the normal adult parents and the impact on a disturbed child almost certainly would be significantly greater.

It has been suggested that a hearing conducted by someone other than the admitting physician is necessary in order to detect instances where parents are "guilty of railroading their children into asylums" or are using "voluntary commitment procedures in order to sanction behavior of which they disapprove." Ellis, *Volunteering Children: Parental Commitment of Minors to Mental Institutions*, 62 CALIF. L. REV. 840, 850–851 (1974). Curiously it seems to be taken for granted that parents who seek to "dump" their children on the state will inevitably be able to conceal their motives and thus deceive the admitting psychiatrists and the other mental health professionals who make and review the admission decision. It is elementary that one early diagnostic inquiry into the cause of an emotional disturbance of a child is an examination into the environment of the child. It is unlikely if not inconceivable that a decision to abandon an emotionally normal, healthy child and thrust him into an institution will be a discrete act leaving no trail of circumstances. Evidence of such conflicts will emerge either in the interviews or from secondary sources. It is unrealistic to believe that trained psychiatrists, skilled in eliciting responses, sorting medically relevant facts and sensitive to motivational nuances will often be deceived about the family situation surrounding a child's emotional disturbance. Surely a lay, or even law-trained factfinder, would be no more skilled in this process than the professional.

* * *

On this record we are satisfied that Georgia's medical factfinding processes are reasonable and consistent with constitutional guarantees. Accordingly, it was error to hold unconstitutional the State's procedures for admitting a child for treatment to a state mental hospital. The judgment is therefore reversed and the case is remanded to the District Court for further proceedings consistent with this opinion.

Reversed and remanded.

JUSTICE BRENNAN, with whom JUSTICE MARSHALL and JUSTICE STEVENS join, concurring in part and dissenting in part.

* * *

In our society, parental rights are limited by the legitimate rights and interests of their children.... This principle is reflected in the variety of statutes and cases that authorize state intervention on behalf of neglected or abused children and that, *inter alia*, curtail parental authority to alienate their children's property, to withhold necessary medical treatment, and to deny children exposure to ideas and experiences they may later need as independent and autonomous adults.

* * * Numerous studies reveal that parental decisions to institutionalize their children often are the results of dislocation in the family unrelated to the children's mental condition. Moreover, even well-mean-

ing parents lack the expertise necessary to evaluate the relative advantages and disadvantages of in-patient as opposed to out-patient psychiatric treatment. Parental decisions to waive hearings in which such questions could be explored, therefore, cannot be conclusively deemed either informed or intelligent. In these circumstances, I respectfully suggest, it ignores reality to assume blindly that parents act in their children's best interests when making commitment decisions and when waiving their children's due process rights.

This does not mean States are obliged to treat children who are committed at the behest of their parents in precisely the same manner as other persons who are involuntarily committed. The demands of due process are flexible and the parental commitment decision carries with it practical implications that States may legitimately take into account.... I believe that States may legitimately postpone formal commitment proceedings when parents seek in-patient psychiatric treatment for their children. Such children may be admitted, for a limited period, without prior hearing, so long as the admitting psychiatrist first interviews parent and child and concludes that short term in-patient treatment would be appropriate.

* * * The informal postadmission procedures that Georgia now follows are simply not enough to qualify as hearings—let alone reasonably prompt hearings. The procedures lack all the traditional due process safeguards. Commitment decisions are made *ex parte*. Georgia's institutionalized juveniles are not informed of the reasons for their commitment; nor do they enjoy the right to be present at the commitment determination, nor the right to representation, the right to be heard, the right to be confronted with adverse witnesses, the right to cross-examine, or the right to offer evidence of their own. By any standard of due process, these procedures are deficient. I cannot understand why the Court pretermits condemnation of these *ex parte* procedures which operate to deny Georgia's institutionalized juveniles even "some form of hearing," before they are condemned to suffer the rigors of long term institutional confinement.

Notes and Questions

1. Is the *Parham* decision based on parental rights or on the belief that parents will act in the best interest of their child? Put somewhat differently, could the state adopt more formal commitment procedures without infringing parents' constitutional rights?

2. How, if at all, would *Parham* apply to a parent's decision to institutionalize his or her child in a private mental hospital?

3. How does *Parham* bear on parental decisions regarding the child's physical health?

IN RE GREEN

Supreme Court of Pennsylvania, 1972.
448 Pa. 338, 292 A.2d 387.

JONES, CHIEF JUSTICE.

The Director of the State Hospital for Crippled Children at Elizabethtown, Pennsylvania, filed a "petition to initiate juvenile proceedings" under the Juvenile Court Law which sought a judicial declaration that Ricky Ricardo Green (hereinafter "Ricky") was a "neglected child" within the meaning of the Act and the appointment of a guardian. After an evidentiary hearing, the Court of Common Pleas, Family Division, Juvenile Branch, of Philadelphia dismissed the petition. On appeal, the Superior Court unanimously reversed and remanded the matter for the appointment of a guardian. We granted allocatur.

Ricky was born on September 10, 1955, to Nathaniel and Ruth Green. He lives with his mother as his parents are separated and the father pays support pursuant to a court order. Ricky has had two attacks of poliomyelitis which have generated problems of obesity and, in addition, Ricky now suffers from paralytic scoliosis (94% curvature of the spine).

Due to this curvature of the spine, Ricky is presently a "sitter," unable to stand or ambulate due to the collapse of his spine; if nothing is done, Ricky could become a bed patient. Doctors have recommended a "spinal fusion" to relieve Ricky's bent position, which would involve moving bone from Ricky's pelvis to his spine. Although an orthopedic specialist testified, "there is no question that there is danger in this type of operation," the mother did consent conditionally to the surgery. The condition is that, since the mother is a Jehovah's Witness who believes that the Bible proscribes any blood transfusions which would be necessary for this surgery, she would not consent to any blood transfusions. Initially, we must recognize that, while the operation would be beneficial, there is no evidence that Ricky's life is in danger or that the operation must be performed immediately. Accordingly, we are faced with the situation of a parent who will not consent to a dangerous operation on her minor son requiring blood transfusions solely because of her religious beliefs.

By statute, a "neglected child"—"a child whose parent * * * neglects or refuses to provide proper or necessary * * * medical or surgical care"—may be committed "to the care, guidance and control of some respectable citizen of good moral character * * * ' appointed by the court. The guardian appointed by the court may, with the court's approval, commit the child to a "crippled children's home or orthopaedic hospital or other institution" for treatment. Thus, it has been held that a child whose parent views smallpox vaccination as "harmful and injurious" may be considered a "neglected child." On the other hand, *In re Tuttendario*, 21 Pa.Dist. 561 (Q.S. Phila. 1912), held that surgery on a seven-year-old male to cure rachitis would not be ordered over the parents' refusal due to fear of the operation. While these statutes could be construed to cover the facts of this appeal, we cannot accept the Commonwealth's construction if it abridges the Free Exercise clause of the First Amendment.

Almost a century ago, the United States Supreme Court enunciated the twofold concept of the Free Exercise clause: "Laws are made for the government of actions, and while they cannot interfere with mere religious belief and opinions, they may with practices." *Reynolds v. United States*, 98 U.S. 145 (1878).

Turning to the situation where an adult refuses to consent to blood transfusions necessary to save the life of his infant son or daughter, other jurisdictions have uniformly held that the state can order such blood transfusions over the parents' religious objections. * * *

In our view, the penultimate question presented by this appeal is whether the state may interfere with a parent's control over his or her child in order to enhance the child's physical well-being when the child's life is in no immediate danger and when the state's intrusion conflicts with the parents' religious beliefs. Stated differently, does the State have an interest of sufficient magnitude to warrant the abridgment of a parent's right to freely practice his or her religion when those beliefs preclude medical treatment of a son or daughter whose life is not in immediate danger? We are not confronted with a life or death situation as in the cases cited earlier in this opinion. Nor is there any question in the case at bar of a parent's omission or neglect for non-religious reasons. * * *

Our research disclosed only two opinions on point; both are from the New York Court of Appeals but the results differ. In *Matter of Seiferth*, 309 N.Y. 80, 127 N.E.2d 820 (1955), the State of New York sought the appointment of a guardian for a "neglected child", a fourteen-year-old boy with a cleft palate and harelip. The father's purely personal philosophy, "not classified as religion," precluded any and all surgery as he believed in mental healing; moreover, the father had "inculcated a distrust and dread of surgery in the boy since childhood." The boy was medically advised and the Children's Court judge interviewed both the boy and his father in chambers. The trial judge concluded that the operation should not be performed until the boy agreed. After reversal by the Appellate Division, Fourth Department, the Court of Appeals, by a four-to-three vote, reinstated the order of the Children's Court. The primary thrust of the opinion was the child's antagonism to the operation and the need for the boy's cooperation for treatment; since the Children's Court judge saw and heard the parties involved and was aware of this aspect, the Court of Appeals decided that the discretion of the Children's Court judge should be affirmed.

On facts virtually identical to this appeal, the Family Court of Ulster County ordered a blood transfusion *In re Sampson*, 65 Misc.2d 658, 317 N.Y.S.2d 641 (1970). Kevin Sampson, fifteen years old, suffered from

Von Recklinghausen's disease which caused a massive disfigurement of the right side of his face and neck. While the incurable disease posed no immediate threat to his life, the dangerous surgery requiring blood transfusions would improve "not only the function but the appearance" of his face and neck. It should also be noted that all physicians involved counseled delay until the boy was old enough to decide since the surgical risk would decrease as the boy grew older. The Family Court judge ruled in an extensive opinion that the State's interest in the child's health was paramount to the mother's religious beliefs. That court further decided not to place this difficult decision on the boy and to order an immediate operation, thereby preventing psychological problems. On appeal, the Appellate Division, Third Department, unanimously affirmed the order in a memorandum decision. *In re Sampson*, 37 A.D.2d 668, 323 N.Y.S.2d 253 (1971). That court rejected the argument that "State intervention is permitted only where the life of the child is in danger by a failure to act [as] a much too restricted approach." When the matter reached the Court of Appeals, *In re Sampson*, 29 N.Y.2d 900, 328 N.Y.S.2d 686, 278 N.E.2d 918 (1972), that Court affirmed per curiam the opinion of the Family Court but added two observations: (1) the *Seiferth* opinion turned upon the question of a court's discretion and not the existence of its power to order surgery in a non-fatal case, and (2) religious objections to blood transfusions do not "present a bar at least where the transfusion is necessary to the success of the required surgery."

With all deference to the New York Court of Appeals, we disagree with the second observation in a non-fatal situation and express no view of the propriety of that statement in a life or death situation. If we were to describe this surgery as "required," like the Court of Appeals, our decision would conflict with the mother's religious beliefs. Aside from religious considerations, one can also question the use of that adjective on medical grounds since an orthopedic specialist testified that the operation itself was dangerous. Indeed, one can question who, other than the Creator, has the right to term certain surgery as "required." This fatal/non-fatal distinction also steers the courts of this Commonwealth away from a medical and philosophical morass: if spinal surgery can be ordered, what about a hernia or gall bladder operation or a hysterectomy? The problems created by *Sampson* are endless. We are of the opinion that as between a parent and the state, the state does not have an interest of sufficient magnitude outweighing a parent's religious beliefs when the child's life is *not immediately imperiled* by his physical condition.

Unlike *Yoder* and *Sampson*, our inquiry does not end at this point since we believe the wishes of this sixteen-year-old boy should be ascertained; the ultimate question, in our view, is whether a parent's religious beliefs are paramount to the possibly adverse decision of the child. * * * While the record before us gives no indication of Ricky's thinking, it is the child rather than the parent in this appeal who is directly involved which thereby distinguishes *Yoder's* decision not to discuss the beliefs of the parents vis-a-vis the children. In *Sampson*, the

Family Court judge decided not to "evade the responsibility for a decision now by the simple expedient of foisting upon this boy the responsibility for making a decision at some later day." While we are cognizant of the realistic problems of this approach enunciated by Judge (now Chief Judge) Fuld in his *Seiferth* dissent, we believe that Ricky should be heard.

It would be most anomalous to ignore Ricky in this situation when we consider the preference of an intelligent child of sufficient maturity in determining custody. Moreover, we have held that a child of the same age can waive constitutional rights and receive a life sentence. Indeed, minors can now bring a personal injury action in Pennsylvania against their parents. We need not extend this litany of the rights of children any further to support the proposition that Ricky should be heard. The record before us does not even note whether Ricky is a Jehovah's Witness or plans to become one. We shall, therefore, reserve any decision regarding a possible parent-child conflict and remand the matter for an evidentiary hearing similar to the one conducted in *Seiferth* in order to determine Ricky's wishes.

The order of the Superior Court is reversed and the matter remanded to the Court of Common Pleas of Philadelphia, Family Division, Juvenile Branch, for proceedings consistent with the views expressed in this opinion. In the meantime, awaiting the evidentiary hearing and result thereof, we will retain our jurisdiction in this matter.

EAGEN, JUSTICE (dissenting).

With all due deference to the majority of this Court, I am compelled to dissent. I would affirm the order of the Superior Court. * * *

I also do not agree with the emphasis the majority places on the fact this is not a life or death situation. The statute with which we are dealing does not contain any such language, nor do I find support for this position in the case law (note the use of the word health in the *Yoder* and *Prince* opinions). The statute in pertinent part states:

> "A child whose parent * * * neglects or refuses to provide *proper or necessary* subsistence, education, *medical or surgical care, or other care necessary for his or her health* * * * ."

The statute only speaks in terms of "health", not life or death. If there is a substantial threat to health, then I believe the courts can and should intervene to protect Ricky. By the decision of this Court today, this boy may never enjoy any semblance of a normal life which the vast majority of our society has come to enjoy and cherish.

Lastly, I must take issue with the manner in which the majority finally disposes of the case. I do not believe that sending the case back to allow Ricky to be heard is an adequate solution. We are herein dealing with a young boy who has been crippled most of his life, consequently, he has been under the direct control and guidance of his parents for that time. To now presume that he could make an independent decision as to what is best for his welfare and health is not reasonable. Moreover, the mandate of the Court presents this youth with a most painful choice between the wishes of his parents and their religious convictions on the one hand, and his chance for a normal healthy life on the other hand. We should not confront him with this dilemma.

On the basis of the foregoing, I would affirm the Order of the Superior Court.

Notes and Questions

1. What weight should be given to the child's wishes? What if Ricky had been twelve years of age instead of seventeen? What if he had been six? In formulating your answers, take into account the views expressed by dissenting Justice Eagen. *Compare* Bellotti v. Baird, 443 U.S. 622, 99 S.Ct. 3035, 61 L.Ed.2d 797 (1979) (holding that minors seeking an abortion are entitled to a hearing to determine whether they are sufficiently mature to make a decision themselves or whether an abortion would be in their interests).

2. Should a parent's objection based on religious beliefs be treated differently than an objection based on the risks and benefits of the proposed treatment? The issue often arises with Christian Scientist parents who withhold conventional medical treatment from their critically ill children; it is complicated by "religious accommodation" statutes that, in many states, establish a defense to a neglect action and/or criminal prosecution for parental failure to provide medical treatment based on a good-faith religious objection. *See, e.g.*, Walker v. Superior Court, 47 Cal.3d 112, 253 Cal.Rptr. 1, 763 P.2d 852, cert. denied 491 U.S. 905, 109 S.Ct. 3186, 105 L.Ed.2d 695 (1989) (upholding prosecution for involuntary manslaughter and rejecting challenge based on language of religious accommodation statute and 1st Amendment); Hermanson v. State, 604 So.2d 775 (Fla.1992) (setting aside child abuse conviction based on finding that religious accommodation statutes are "ambiguous and result in a denial of due process" due to lack of notice of prohibited conduct); Commonwealth v. Twitchell, 416 Mass. 114, 617 N.E.2d 609 (1993) (setting aside involuntary manslaughter conviction of Christian Scientist parents based on finding that statute failed to give fair notice of prohibited conduct). In some states, courts have held that, while the parent may not be subject to criminal liability, the parent may be civilly liable in damages. *Compare* State v. McKown, 461 N.W.2d 720 (Minn. App.1990) (dismissing manslaughter charge) *with* Lundman v. McKown, 530 N.W.2d 807 (Minn.App.1995) (allowing wrongful death action by father against mother, stepfather, and Christian Science nurse). For an argument that religious exemptions to child welfare laws violate the equal protection clause, *see* James G. Dwyer, *The Children We Abandon: Religious Exemptions to Child Welfare and Education Laws as Denials of Equal Protection to Children of Religious Objectors*, 74 N.C. L. Rev. 1321 (1996).

3. When may parents refuse a treatment that has less than certain prospects of success? In Newmark v. Williams, 588 A.2d 1108 (Del.1991),

the Court held that parents could refuse conventional medical treatment for their son's cancer, where the treatment offered only a 40% chance of success. Should it make a difference of the treatment were 51% likely to succeed? What factors should a court consider in reaching a decision?

4. What if the child does not want the treatment but the parent does?

Problem 9–2:

O.G., age 16, was struck by a train and severely injured. Unless O.G. undergoes surgery to repair damage to his right arm, it will be necessary to amputate it. Surgery to save the arm will necessitate blood transfusions. Amputation will not necessarily require transfusion. O.G. and his parents, all Jehovah's Witnesses, are willing to consent to surgery but not to a blood transfusion. The hospital seeks an order appointing a guardian ad litem to consent to both surgery and a blood transfusion on O.G.'s behalf. O.G. argues that he is mature and should be permitted to make his own decision. What arguments are available to O.G. and his parents? the hospital? What decision should the court make? *See* O.G. v. Baum, 790 S.W.2d 839 (Tex.App.1990); In re E.G., 133 Ill.2d 98, 139 Ill.Dec. 810, 549 N.E.2d 322 (1989); In the Matter of J.J., 64 Ohio App.3d 806, 582 N.E.2d 1138 (1990).

MAINE MEDICAL CENTER v. HOULE

Maine Superior Court, Cumberland, Docket No. 74–145, February 14, 1974.

ROBERTS, J.

The testimony herein indicates that a male child was born to the defendants on February 9, 1974 at the Maine Medical Center. Medical examination by the hospital staff revealed the absence of a left eye, a rudimentary left ear with no ear canal, a malformed left thumb and a tracheal esophageal fistula. The latter condition prevented the ingestion of nourishment, necessitated intravenous feeding and allowed the entry of fluids into the infant's lungs leading to the development of pneumonia and other complications. The recommended medical treatment was surgical repair of the tracheal esophageal fistula to allow normal feeding and respiration. Prior to February 11, 1974, the child's father directed the attending physician not to conduct surgical repair of the fistula and to cease intravenous feeding.

By Temporary Restraining Order issued ex parte on February 11, 1974, this court authorized the continuance of such measures as might be medically dictated to maintain said child in a stable and viable condition and restrained the defendants from issuing any order, which, in the opinion of the attending physician,would be injurious to the current medical situation of said child.

In the interim the child's condition has deteriorated. Periods of apnea have necessitated the use of a bag breathing device to artificially sustain respiration. Several convulsive seizures of unknown cause have occurred. Medications administered include gentimycin for the treatment of pneumonia and phenobarbitol to control convulsive seizures. Further medical evaluation indicates the lack of response of the right eye to light stimuli, the existence of some nonfused vertebrae and the virtual certainty of some brain damage resulting from anoxia. The most recent developments have caused the attending physician to form the opinion that all life supporting measures should be withdrawn. The doctor is further of the opinion that without surgical correction of the tracheal esophageal fistula the child will certainly die and that with surgical correction the child can survive but with some degree of permanent brain damage.

The court heard further testimony concerning the present posture of the mother's emotional condition and attitude toward the future survival of the child. Without disparaging the seriousness of the emotional impact upon the parents and without ignoring the difficulties which this court's decision may cause in the future, it is the firm opinion of this court that questions of permanent custody, maintenance and further care of the child are for the moment legally irrelevant.

Quite literally the court must make a decision concerning the life or death of a new-born infant. Recent decisions concerning the right of the state to intervene with the medical and moral judgments of a prospective parent and attending physician may have cast doubts upon the legal rights of an unborn child; but at the moment of live birth there does exist a human being entitled to the fullest protection of the law. The most basic right enjoyed by every human being is the right to life itself.

Where the condition of a child does not involve serious risk of life and where treatment involves a considerable risk, parents as the natural guardians have a considerable degree of discretion and the courts ought not to intervene. The measures proposed in this case are not in any sense heroic measures except for the doctor's opinion that probable brain damage has rendered life not worth preserving. Were it his opinion that life itself could not be preserved, heroic measures ought not be required. However, the doctor's qualitative evaluation of the value of the life to be preserved is not legally within the scope of his expertise.

In the court's opinion the issue before the court is not the prospective quality of the life to be preserved, but the medical feasibility of the proposed treatment compared with the almost certain risk of death should treatment be withheld. Being satisfied that corrective surgery is medically necessary and medically feasible, the court finds that the defendants herein have no right to withhold such treatment and that to do so constitutes neglect in the legal sense. Therefore, the court will authorize the guardian ad litem to consent to the surgical correction of the tracheal esophageal fistula and such other normal life supportive measures as may be medically required in the immediate future. It is further ordered that Respondents are hereby enjoined until further order of this court from issuing any orders to Petitioners or their employees which, in the opinion of the attending physicians or surgeons would be injurious to the medical condition of the child.

The court will retain jurisdiction for the purpose of determining any further measures that may be required to be taken and eventually for the purpose of determining the future custody of the child should the court determine that it is appropriate to do so.

ROBERT & PEGGY STINSON, ON THE DEATH OF A BABY

244 THE ATLANTIC MONTHLY, July 1979, at 64.

[Andrew was a baby born 15½ weeks prematurely weighing only 1 lb. 12 oz., who was placed on a respirator without parental consent, and remained dependent on it until his death five months later. During his hospitalization Andrew suffered a month-long case of bronchopulmonary dysplasia (sometimes known as "respirator lung syndrome"), retrolental fibroplasia, a pulmonary hemorrhage, demineralized and fractured bones, and numerous infections, including a prolonged case of E. coli septicemia, related abscesses at the arterial line sites which necessitated surgical removal of gangrene and necrotic muscle, several urinary tract infections, and multiple courses of pneumonia. Over time, perhaps as side effects from long-term respirator dependence, he developed cortical atrophy and microcephaly (i.e., shrinkage of the brain and skull), enlarged ventricles, chronic encephalopathy, pulmonary artery hypertension and brain seizures. After his death, his parents sent a letter to hospital authorities describing their experience. The letter, edited, abridged, and with names altered, is reprinted below.]

Dear Mr. Clark:

This letter concerns the case of Andrew Stinson, who was a patient in the Infant Intensive Care Unit (IICU) of Pediatric Hospital from December 24, 1976, to June 14, 1977. . . .

It was our position at the beginning of this case the medical knowledge was not sufficient to justify the no-holds-barred, heroic attempt to simulate the last 15½ weeks of pregnancy. It is hard to feel now that our pessimism was unreasonable. We can only hope that Andrew's case has been, for the doctors involved, an object lesson in humility—a reminder of how pathetically doctors can still fail and how much suffering that failure can inflict on other human beings, on tiny patients and on their families.

We think the question must be raised as to whose interests were really served by this six months of imposed hospitalization. Certainly not Andrew's. He had the misfortune of being declared "salvageable" (the IICU's word) by people who know neither how to "salvage" him nor when or how to stop. Certainly not ours. Those six months were for us a nightmare of anguish, frustration, and despair. It seems clear to us that all the benefits in this case went to Pediatric Hospital and its staff. The medical residents got a chance to broaden their education by working with a baby with malfunctions of virtually every system of this body, the specialists took part in some "interesting consults" and gathered some data, and the hospital collected the mind-boggling sum of $102,303.20 from our insurance company.

Although we signed a general consent form when Andrew was admitted to the hospital, we did not know that we were signing away control over the events of the next months or, until later, that we could withdraw our consent. However, in our opinion, the hospital did not accord us, Andrew's parents and legal guardians, our rights of informed consent in decisions about his care. From the very first, we were treated as wholly external to the case. Our wishes, judgments, and thoughts were rarely of interest to the IICU's medical staff, who arrogated decisions to themselves as though we did not exist.

* * *

We recognize that there are very real legal and ethical problems in the area of consent of remedial treatment when children are involved. We were told repeatedly that "someone must be the child's advocate." But how is it possible to be sure in a case like Andrew's just what that means? Who can determine whether or at what point the child's true advocate is the person proclaiming his right to life or the person proclaiming his right to death?. . . .

The medical record contains the following brief summary of Andrew's case, dated only June: "6 months bronchopulmonary dysplasia, pulmonary artery hypertension, cerebral atrophy now with seizures—? current status. Difficult parents as per chart." We asked ourselves again and again what the staff at PHC could have expected people in our situation to do. Did they think we didn't really mean it when we said we believed it was morally wrong to keep Andrew alive? Did anyone consider the impossible psychological position we were put into when we were systematically and casually overruled?

* * *

When this nightmare began, we had a small savings account, but this spring we saw it dwindle to nothing. An annual salary of $13,600 was enough in normal times to maintain a modest living for our family. Since December, when Andrew entered PHC, we have not been able to make ends meet and will do no better in the foreseeable future.

None of this seemed intelligible to the personnel of PHC. It was a problem, perhaps, but it was, again, someone else's problem ... Someone else will pay.

What happened at Pediatric Hospital has had a final bitter psychological cost: we have been robbed of the opportunity to grieve at the death of our child. We have friends whose baby son, brain-damaged and unable to breath on his own, died a day after birth in a community hospital. No respirators were available to prolong the suffering of everyone concerned, and the family was able to grieve for the baby in a normal way. The baby is buried in an old country cemetery where the parents, their older child, and their year-old normal, healthy son gather now and then to think of the child who might have been.

There can be no such scene for Andrew. By the time he was finally permitted to die, the death itself could bring only feelings of profound relief: relief that Andrew's pain, as well as our own, was finished at last; relief that we had all escaped the clutches of Pediatric Hospital at last.

We have taken the money that might have gone under different circumstances for a graveside marker and committed it to the only memorial which can have any meaning for us now: to the sponsorship of a living child, an impoverished child whose only problem at birth was that he was born into an affluent society that does not choose to put his well-being at very high priority. For we believe Andrew's case raises broad and difficult questions which the medical profession in particular and society as a whole must face up to.

What sort of memories or thoughts could we have of Andrew? By the time he was allowed to die, the technology being used to "salvage" him had produced not so much a human life as a grotesque caricature of a human life, a "person" with a stunted, deteriorating brain and scarcely an undamaged vital organ in his body, who existed only as an extension of a machine. This is the image left to us for the rest of our lives of our son, Andrew.

Sincerely yours....

Notes and Questions

1. In a famous article published in the New England Journal of Medicine in 1973 (Duff & Campbell, *Moral and Ethical Dilemmas in the Special Care Nursery*, 289 N. Eng. J. Med. 890), two physicians reported that 43 of 299 infants who died at the special-care nursery at Yale–New Haven Hospital over a 2½ year period did so after parents and doctors jointly decided to discontinue medical treatment.

> Duff and Campbell present the argument for granting parents and physicians final discretion to decide whether a defective infant should be treated, and hence live or die: 'We believe the burdens of decisionmaking must be borne by families and their professional advisers because they are most familiar with the respective situations. Since families primarily must live with and are most affected by the decisions, it therefore appears that society and the health professions should provide only general guidelines for decision making. Moreover, since variations between situations are so great, and the situations themselves so complex, it follows that much latitude in decisionmaking should be expected and tolerated.'
>
> The logic of this argument, however is unpersuasive. It rests on the assumption that parents have but two options—to withhold care or to be burdened with the care of the child throughout their lives. But a third option exists—termination of parental rights and obli-

gations. However, while parental discretion to terminate the parental relationship may be justified, it does not follow that parents should also have the right to decide whether the child lives or dies. Clearly, discretion to terminate a relationship of dependency does not mandate that one have the power to impose death on the terminated party. Furthermore, a central element of procedural justice is impartial decisionmaking after full consideration of relevant information. Yet, neither parents nor physicians are impartial or disinterested; both have a strong personal interest in the outcome of their decision. Parents face the decision with the guilt, grief, and damaged image that birth of a defective child brings. They have a strong interest in maintaining previous life plans, and adjustment patterns, and in avoiding the psychic and financial costs of adjusting to care of a defective infant. Moreover, the treatment decision arises in highly emotional circumstances, when their rational faculties are weakest and full information concerning the defect and prognosis is wanting. In addition, the physician's objectivity may be compromised. The obstetrician, for example, may feel guilt or responsibility for the defect, and prefer that the problem be eliminated as soon as possible. He may think that the least he can do for the parents is to relieve them of a potential lifelong burden. Similarly, though less involved, the advice of a pediatrician or consultant is likely to be influenced by his own values concerning care for defective infants. In short, since parents and physicians face the treatment decision with conflicting interests and the pressure of strong emotions, giving them final, unguided discretion to decide whether defective infants live will often lead to hasty, biased choices.

A glaring example of this danger is the 1971 Johns Hopkins case in which doctors did not operate on a Down's syndrome baby with duodenal atresia who died 15 days later of starvation. The parents decided that they did not want to be burdened with a child who would be retarded and incapable of full human development, and rejected surgery. The physicians acquiesced in their decision, even though allowing the baby to starve to death created great consternation among the staff. The death of this child appears particularly unnecessary since mongols can interact, be trained, and lead a reasonably comfortable or happy existence. Moreover, the child was otherwise healthy and would not have required constant medical care. The absence of a convincing case for death in this case illustrates the dangers of Duff's and Campbell's suggestion of having 'only general guidelines' and allowing 'much latitude' in this type of decisionmaking.

John A. Robertson, *Involuntary Euthanasia of Defective Newborns: A Legal Analysis*, 27 STAN. L. REV. 213, 262 et seq. (1975).

2. As a result of publicity surrounding the Johns Hopkins case and others like it, Congress amended the Child Abuse Prevention and Treatment Act (CAPTA) in 1984. It provides, in pertinent part, that:

> 3) the term "withholding of medically indicated treatment" means the failure to respond to the infant's life threatening conditions by providing treatment (including appropriate nutrition, hydration, and medication) which, in the treating physician's or physicians' reasonable medical judgment, will be most likely to be effective in ameliorating or correcting all such conditions, except that the term does not include the failure to provide treatment (other than appropriate nutrition, hydration, or medication) to an infant when, in the treating physician's or physicians' reasonable medical judgment, (A) the infant is chronically ill and irreversibly comatose, (B) the provision of such treatment would (i) merely prolong dying, (ii) not be effective in ameliorating or correcting all of the infant's life-threatening conditions, or (iii) otherwise be futile in terms of survival of the infant; or (C) the provision of such treatment would be virtually futile in terms of the survival of the infant and the treatment itself under such circumstances would be inhumane. 42 U.S.C.A. § 5102(3).

In order the comply with CAPTA, the states must establish programs for responding to reported cases, including those of "withholding of medically indicated treatment." 42 U.S.C.A. § 5103(b)(2)(K). Implementing regulations issued in 1985 by the federal Dept. of Health and Human Services require state programs to be in writing and to include an independent medical examination of the infant. What result would the federal statute require in *Houle*? the *Stinson* case? On what bases can these results be criticized? On balance, does the statute strike a reasonable accommodation between parental rights and children's interests?

3. Physician surveys suggest that CAPTA has had an effect on medical decision making. A 1988 survey of Massachusetts pediatricians, for example, indicated that doctors were more inclined to treat babies with problematic prognoses and were paying less heed to parents' wishes than they did when surveyed in 1977. *See* Gina Kolata, *Parents of Tiny Infants Find Care Choices Are Not Theirs*, N. Y. Times, Sept. 30, 1991, at A1. But the U.S. Commission on Civil Rights nonetheless reported in 1989 that the CAPTA requirements were not having their intended effect. According to the Commission, state child welfare authorities tend to defer to hospitals rather than conducting independent evaluations. While hospitals are encouraged under the federal regulations to set up infant care review committees to make recommendations in specific cases, the Commission did not find them effective. *See* U.S. Commission on Civil Rights, Medical Discrimination Against Children with Disabilities (1989).

Problem 9–3:

Linda Ames is 23; her husband Dan is 30. Linda entered St. Charles Hospital last week, three weeks past due with her first child. The baby was born by Caesarian section. When Linda awakened in the recovery room, Dan told her that their child was seriously handicapped.

The baby's handicaps are multiple: She has a damaged kidney, microcephaly (an abnormally small head), a cleft palate, spina bifida with meningomyelocele (a defect of skin, vertebral arches and neural tube evident at birth as a skin defect over the back, bordered laterally by bony prominences of the unfused neural arches of the vertebrae), and hydrocephalus (a disorder in which fluid fails to drain from the cranial areas).

Doctors told Mr. and Mrs. Ames that, with her combination of birth defects, chances that the baby could lead a relatively normal life were "a long shot." According to the doctors, it is fairly certain that the baby will be unable to walk, incontinent, incapable of normal speech, and mentally retarded. It is possible that she will also be bedridden and sufficiently retarded that she will be unable even to experience emotions such as sadness or joy. But it is also possible that she would be able to sit in a wheelchair, communicate, and learn at some level. At this point, doctors simply cannot predict the exact degree of impairment.

Doctors have also told Mr. and Mrs. Ames that the most common treatment for spina bifida and hydrocephalus is surgery to insert a "shunt" and repair the spinal lesion. Although surgery entails risks, there are also risks from nontreatment. Untreated, hydrocephalus results in grossly distorted skull growth and mental retardation. Where a baby shows evidence of hydrocephalus at birth, some mental retardation is ensured, but insertion of a shunt, which provides a drain for the excess fluid, can minimize skull distortion and reduce the level of future retardation. Untreated, spina bifida entails a serious danger of infection, such as spinal meningitis, and death. It is possible to treat the condition with sterile dressings and antibiotics until the skin grows over the opening, but this treatment entails higher risks of infection. According to Dr. Albert Butler, the hospital's chief neurosurgeon, "surgery is preferable because of the lower risk of infection, but in a case like this one, both procedures are medically acceptable."

Mr. and Mrs. Ames were asked if they would consent to surgery to insert a shunt and repair the spinal lesion. Mr. and Mrs. Ames spent the next few hours consulting with more neurological experts, family members, a hospital social worker, and their priest. In the end, they refused to consent to the operation.

While doctors and hospital officials were willing to abide by Mr. and Mrs. Ames' treatment decision, an aide in the pediatric intensive care unit was not. Believing that Baby Ames was not receiving the best possible treatment, she called Larry Washburn, an attorney and children's advocate, about Baby Ames. Washburn immediately brought an action against St. Charles Hospital and Mr. and Mrs. Ames alleging medical neglect and requesting the appointment of a guardian ad litem to consent to surgery for Baby Ames.

You are the law clerk of Judge Smith, to whom the case has been assigned, and have been asked to determine: 1. whether Baby Ames is a neglected child within the meaning of the state's neglect law, which specifies that a child is neglected if its "parent * * * neglects or refuses to provide necessary, medically appropriate, health or surgical care;" 2. what result is required under CAPTA; and 3. what, if any, weight federal law should receive in this proceeding. *See* Weber v. Stony Brook Hospital, 95 A.D.2d 587, 467 N.Y.S.2d 685, *aff'd*, 60 N.Y.2d 208, 469 N.Y.S.2d 63, 456 N.E.2d 1186 (1983), cert. denied 464 U.S. 1026, 104 S.Ct. 560, 78 L.Ed.2d 732 (1983).

SECTION 4. CONTRACEPTION AND ABORTION: A SPECIAL CASE OF MEDICAL DECISION MAKING

CAREY v. POPULATION SERVICES INTERNATIONAL ET AL.

Supreme Court of the United States, 1977.
431 U.S. 678, 97 S.Ct. 2010, 52 L.Ed.2d 675.

JUSTICE BRENNAN delivered the opinion of the Court (Parts I, II, III, and V), together with an opinion (Part IV), in which JUSTICE STEWART, JUSTICE MARSHALL, and JUSTICE BLACKMUN joined.

Under New York Educ. Law § 6811(8) it is a crime (1) for any person to sell or distribute any contraceptive of any kind to a minor under the age of 16 years; (2) for anyone other than a licensed pharmacist to distribute contraceptives to persons 16 or over; and (3) for anyone, including licensed pharmacists, to advertise or display contraceptives. A three-judge District Court ... declared § 6811(8) unconstitutional in its entirety under the First and Fourteenth Amendments of the Federal Constitution insofar as it applies to nonprescription contraceptives, and enjoined its enforcement as so applied.... We affirm.

* * *

IV

The District Court also held unconstitutional, as applied to nonprescription contraceptives, the provision of § 6811(8) prohibiting the distribution of contraceptives to those under 16 years of age. Appellants contend that this provision of the statute is constitutionally permissible as a regulation of the morality of minors, in furtherance of the State's policy against promiscuous sexual intercourse among the young.

The question of the extent of state power to regulate conduct of minors not constitutionally regulable when committed by adults is a vexing one, perhaps not susceptible of precise answer. We have been reluctant to attempt to define "the totality of the relationship of the juvenile and the state." *In re Gault,* 387 U.S. 1, 13 (1967). * * *

Of particular significance to the decision of this case, the right to privacy in connection with decisions affecting procreation extends to minors as well as to adults. *Planned Parenthood of Central Missouri v. Danforth,* held that a State "may not impose a blanket provision ... requiring the consent of a parent or person in loco parentis as a condition for abortion of an unmarried minor during the first 12 weeks of her pregnancy." 428 U.S., at 74. As in the case of the spousal-consent requirement struck down in the same case, "the State does not have the constitutional authority to give a third party an absolute, and possibly arbitrary, veto," " 'which the state itself is absolutely and totally prohibited from exercising.' " State restrictions inhibiting privacy rights of minors are valid only if they serve "any significant state interest ... that is not present in the case of an adult." *Planned Parenthood* found that no such interest justified a state requirement of parental consent.

Since the State may not impose a blanket prohibition, or even a blanket requirement of parental consent, on the choice of a minor to terminate her pregnancy, the constitutionality of a blanket prohibition on the distribution of contraceptives to minors is a fortiori foreclosed. The State's interests in protection of the mental and physical health of the pregnant minor, and in protection of potential life are clearly more implicated by the abortion decision than by the decision to use a nonhazardous contraceptive.

Appellants argue, however, that significant state interests are served by restricting minors' access to contraceptives, because free availability to minors of contraceptives would lead to increased sexual activity among the young, in violation of the policy of New York to discourage such behavior. The argument is that minors' sexual activity may be deterred by increasing the hazards attendant on it. The same argument, however, would support a ban on abortions for minors, or indeed support a prohibition on abortions, or access to contraceptives, for the unmarried, whose sexual activity is also against the public policy of many States. Yet, in each of these areas, the Court has rejected the argument, noting in *Roe v. Wade*, that "no court or commentator has taken the argument seriously." 410 U.S., at 148. * * *

Moreover, there is substantial reason for doubt whether limiting access to contraceptives will in fact substantially discourage early sexual behavior. Appellants themselves conceded in the District Court that "there is no evidence that teenage extramarital sexual activity increases in proportion to the availability of contraceptives," and accordingly offered none, in the District Court or here. Appellees, on the other hand, cite a considerable body of evidence and opinion indicating that there is no such deterrent effect. Although we take judicial notice, as did the District Court, that with or without access to contraceptives, the incidence of sexual activity among minors is high, and the consequences of such activity are frequently devastating, the studies cited by appellees play no part in our decision. It is enough that we again confirm the principle that when a State, as here, burdens the exercise of a fundamental right, its attempt to justify that burden as a rational means for the accomplishment of some significant state policy requires more than a bare assertion, based on a conceded complete absence of supporting evidence, that the burden is connected to such a policy. * * *

Affirmed.

JUSTICE WHITE, concurring in part and concurring in the result.

* * * I concur in the result in Part IV primarily because the State has not demonstrated that the prohibition against distribution of contraceptives to minors measurably contributes to the deterrent purposes which the State advances as justification for the restriction. Again, however, the legality of state laws forbidding premarital intercourse is not at issue here; and, with Justice Stevens, "I would describe as 'frivolous' appellees' argument that a minor has the constitutional right to put contraceptives to their intended use, notwithstanding the combined objection of both parents and the State". * * *

JUSTICE REHNQUIST, dissenting.

* * * The post-Civil War Congresses which drafted the Civil War Amendments to the Constitution could not have accomplished their task without the blood of brave men on both sides which was shed at Shiloh, Gettysburg, and Cold Harbor. If those responsible for these Amendments, by feats of valor or efforts of draftsmanship, could have lived to know that their efforts had enshrined in the Constitution the right of commercial vendors of contraceptives to peddle them to unmarried minors through such means as window displays and vending machines located in the men's room of truck stops, notwithstanding the considered judgment of the New York Legislature to the contrary, it is not difficult to imagine their reaction.

* * *

* * * The majority of New York's citizens are in effect told that however deeply they may be concerned about the problem of promiscuous sex and intercourse among unmarried teenagers, they may not adopt this means of dealing with it. The Court holds that New York may not use its police power to legislate in the interests of its concept of the public morality as it pertains to minors. The Court's denial of a power so fundamental to self-government must, in the long run, prove to be but a temporary departure from a wise and heretofore settled course of adjudication to the contrary. I would reverse the judgment of the District Court.

HODGSON v. MINNESOTA

Supreme Court of the United States, 1990.
497 U.S. 417, 110 S.Ct. 2926, 111 L.Ed.2d 344.

JUSTICE STEVENS announced the judgment of the Court and delivered the opinion of the Court with respect to Parts I, II, IV, and VII, an opinion with respect to Part III in which JUSTICE BRENNAN joins, an opinion with respect to Parts V and VI in which JUSTICE O'CONNOR joins, and a dissenting opinion with respect to Part VIII.

A Minnesota statute, Minn. Stat. §§ 144.343(2)–(7) (1988), provides, with certain exceptions, that no abortion shall be performed on a woman under 18 years of age until at least 48 hours after both of her parents have been notified. In subdivisions 2–4 of the statute the notice is mandatory unless (1) the attending physician certifies that an immediate abortion is necessary to prevent the woman's death and there is insufficient time to provide the required notice; (2) both of her parents have consented in writing; or (3) the woman declares that she is a victim of parental abuse or neglect, in which event notice of her declaration must be given to the proper authorities. The United States Court of Appeals for the Eighth Circuit, sitting en banc, unanimously held these provisions unconstitutional. * * *

II

This litigation was commenced on July 30, 1981, two days before the effective date of the parental notification statute. The plaintiffs include two Minnesota doctors who specialize in obstetrics and gynecology, four clinics providing abortion and contraceptive services in metropolitan areas in Minnesota, six pregnant minors representing a class of pregnant minors, and the mother of a pregnant minor. Plaintiffs alleged that the statute violated the Due Process and Equal Protection Clauses of the Fourteenth Amendment and various provisions of the Minnesota Constitution. * * *

III

* * * Th[is] Court has considered the constitutionality of statutes providing for parental consent or parental notification in six abortion cases decided during the last 14 years. Although the Massachusetts statute reviewed in *Bellotti v. Baird,* 428 U.S. 132 (1976) *(Bellotti I)*, and *Bellotti II* required the consent of both parents, and the Utah statute reviewed in *H. L. v. Matheson,* 450 U.S. 398 (1981), required notice to "the parents," none of the opinions in any of those cases focused on the possible significance of making the consent or the notice requirement applicable to both parents instead of just one. In contrast, the arguments in these cases, as well as the extensive findings of the District Court, are directed primarily at that distinction. It is therefore appropriate to summarize these findings before addressing the constitutionality of the 48-hour waiting period or the two-parent notification requirement, particularly since none of the findings has been challenged in either this Court or the Court of Appeals.

The District Court found—on the basis of extensive testimony at trial—that the two-parent notification requirement had particularly harmful effects on both the minor and the custodial parent when the parents were divorced or separated. Relations between the minor and absent parent were not reestablished as a result of the forced notification, thereby often producing disappointment in the minor "when an anticipated reestablishment of her relationship with the absent parent did not occur." Moreover, "the reaction of the custodial parent to the requirement of forced notification is often one of anger, resentment and frustration at the intrusion of the absent parent," and fear that notification will threaten the custody rights of the parent or otherwise promote intrafamily violence. Tragically, those fears were often realized.... The District Court further found:

> "Twenty to twenty-five percent of the minors who go to court either are accompanied by one parent who knows and consents to the abortion or have already told one parent of their intent to terminate their pregnancy. The vast majority of these voluntarily informed parents are women who are divorced or separated from spouses whom they have not seen in years. Going to court to avoid notifying the other parent burdens the privacy of both the minor and the accompanying parent. The custodial parents are angry that their consent is not sufficient and fear that notification will bring the absent parent back into the family in an intrusive and abusive way."

The District Court also found that the two-parent notification requirement had adverse effects in families in which the minor lives with both parents. These effects were particularly pronounced in the distressingly large number of cases in which family violence is a serious problem. The court found that many minors in Minnesota "live in fear of violence by family members" and "are, in fact, victims of rape, incest, neglect and violence." The District Court found that few minors can take advantage of the exception for a minor who declares that she is a victim of sexual or physical abuse because of the obligation to report the information to the authorities and the attendant loss of privacy.

This concern about family violence helps to explain why the District Court found that in many instances the requirement that both parents be notified actually impairs family communication. Minors who otherwise would inform one parent were unwilling to do so when such notification likely would also involve the parent in the torturous ordeal of explaining to a court why the second parent should not be notified. * * *

During the period between August 1, 1981, and March 1, 1986, 3,573 judicial bypass petitions were filed in Minnesota courts. All but 15 were granted. The judges who adjudicated over 90% of these petitions testified; none of them identified any positive effects of the law. The court experience produced fear, tension, anxiety, and shame among minors, causing some who were mature, and some whose best interests would have been served by an abortion, to "forego [sic] the bypass option and either notify their parents or carry to term." Among parents who supported their daughters in the bypass proceedings, the court experience evoked similar reactions. * * * At least 37 witnesses testified to the issue whether the statute furthered the State's interest in protecting pregnant minors. Only two witnesses testified that a two-parent notification statute did minors more good than harm; neither of these witnesses had direct experience with the Minnesota statute. * * *

V

Three separate but related interests—the interest in the welfare of the pregnant minor, the interest of the parents, and the interest of the family unit—are relevant to our consideration of the constitutionality of the 48–hour waiting period and the two-parent notification requirement.

The State has a strong and legitimate interest in the welfare of its young citizens, whose immaturity, inexperience, and lack of judgment may sometimes impair their ability to exercise their rights wisely. *See Bellotti II*, 443 U.S. at 634–639 (opinion of Powell, J.); *Prince v. Massachusetts*, 321 U.S. 158, 166–167 (1944). That interest, which justifies state-imposed requirements that a minor obtain his or her parent's consent before undergoing an operation, marrying, or entering military service, extends also to the minor's decision to terminate her pregnancy. Although the Court has held that parents may not exercise "an absolute, and possibly arbitrary, veto" over that decision, *Danforth,* 428 U.S. at 74, it has never challenged a State's reasonable judgment that the decision should be made after notification to and consultation with a parent. * * *

A natural parent who has demonstrated sufficient commitment to his or her children is thereafter entitled to raise the children free from undue state interference. "The Court has frequently emphasized the importance of the family. The rights to conceive and to raise one's children have been deemed 'essential,' 'basic civil rights of man,' and 'rights far more precious . . . than property rights.' " . . . The integrity of the family unit has found protection in the Due Process Clause of the Fourteenth Amendment, the Equal Protection Clause of the Fourteenth Amendment, and the Ninth Amendment. *Griswold v. Connecticut*, [p. 19].

VI

We think it is clear that a requirement that a minor wait 48 hours after notifying a single parent of her intention to get an abortion would reasonably further the legitimate state interest in ensuring that the minor's decision is knowing and intelligent. We have held that when a parent or another person has assumed "primary responsibility" for a minor's well-being, the State may properly enact "laws designed to aid discharge of that responsibility." To the extent that subdivision 2 of the Minnesota statute requires notification of only one parent, it does just that. The brief waiting period provides the parent the opportunity to consult with his or her spouse and a family physician, and it permits the parent to inquire into the competency of the doctor performing the abortion, discuss the religious or moral implications of the abortion decision, and provide the daughter needed guidance and counsel in evaluating the impact of the decision on her future. * * *

The 48–hour delay imposes only a minimal burden on the right of the minor to decide whether or not to terminate her pregnancy. Although the District Court found that scheduling factors, weather, and the minor's school and work commitments may combine, in many cases, to create a delay of a week or longer between the initiation of notification and the abortion, there is no evidence that the 48–hour period itself is unreasonable or longer than appropriate for adequate consultation between parent and child. * * *

VII

It is equally clear that the requirement that both parents be notified, whether or not both wish to be notified or have assumed responsibility for the upbringing of the child, does not reasonably further any legitimate state interest. The usual justification for a parental consent or notification provision is that it supports the authority of a parent who is presumed to act in the minor's best interest and thereby assures that the minor's decision to terminate her pregnancy is knowing, intelligent, and deliberate. To the extent that such an interest is legitimate, it would be fully served by a requirement that the minor notify one parent who can then seek the counsel of his or her mate or any other party, when such advice and support is deemed necessary to help the child make a difficult decision. In the ideal family setting, of course, notice to either parent would normally constitute notice to both. A statute requiring two-parent notification would not further any state interest in those instances. In many families, however, the parent notified by the child would not notify the other parent. In those cases the State has no legitimate interest in questioning one parent's judgment that notice to the other parent would not assist the minor or in presuming that the parent who has assumed parental duties is incompetent to make decisions regarding the health and welfare of the child.

Not only does two-parent notification fail to serve any state interest with respect to functioning families, it disserves the state interest in protecting and assisting the minor with respect to dysfunctional families. The record reveals that in the thousands of dysfunctional families affected by this statute, the two-parent notice requirement proved positively harmful to the minor and her family. The testimony at trial established that this requirement, ostensibly designed for the benefit of the minor, resulted in major trauma to the child, and often to a parent as well. In some cases, the parents were divorced and the second parent did not have custody or otherwise participate in the child's upbringing. In these circumstances, the privacy of the parent and child was violated, even when they suffered no other physical or psychological harm. In other instances, however, the second parent had either deserted or abused the child, had died under tragic circumstances, or was not notified because of the considered judgment that notification would inflict unnecessary stress on a parent who was ill. In these circumstances, the statute was not merely ineffectual in achieving the State's goals but actually counterproductive. The focus on notifying the second parent distracted both the parent and minor from the minor's imminent abortion decision.

The State does not rely primarily on the best interests of the minor in defending this statute. Rather, it argues that, in the ideal family, the minor should make her decision only after consultation with both parents who should naturally be concerned with the child's welfare and that the State has an interest in protecting the independent right of the parents "to determine and strive for what they believe to be best for their children." Minn. Br. 26. Neither of these reasons can justify the two-parent notification requirement. The second parent may well have an interest in the minor's abortion decision, making full communication among all members of a family desirable in some cases, but such communication may not be decreed by the State. The State has no more interest in requiring all family members to talk with one another than it has in requiring certain of them to live together. In *Moore v. East Cleveland* [p. 10], we invalidated a zoning ordinance which "sliced deeply into the family itself," permitting the city to "standardize its children—and its adults—by forcing all to live in certain narrowly defined family patterns." Although the ordinance was supported by state interests other than the State's interest in substituting its conception of family life for the family's own view, the ordinance's relation to those state interests was too "tenuous" to satisfy constitutional standards. By implication, a state interest in standardizing its children and adults, making the "private realm of family life" conform to some state-designed ideal, is not a legitimate state interest at all. Nor can any state interest in protecting a parent's interest in shaping a child's values and lifestyle overcome the liberty interests of a minor acting with the consent of a single parent or court. * * *

Unsurprisingly, the Minnesota two-parent notification requirement is an oddity among state and federal consent provisions governing the health, welfare, and education of children. A minor desiring to enlist in the armed services or the Reserve Officers' Training Corps (ROTC) need only obtain the consent of "his parent or guardian." 10 U.S.C. §§ 505(a), 2104(b)(4), 2107(b)(4). The consent of "a parent or guardian" is also sufficient to obtain a passport for foreign travel from the United States Department of State, 22 C.F.R. § 51.27 (1989) (emphasis added), and to participate as a subject in most forms of medical research, 45 CFR §§ 46.404, 46.405 (1988). In virtually every State, the consent of one parent is enough to obtain a driver's license or operator's permit. The same may be said with respect to the decision to submit to any medical or surgical procedure other than an abortion. Indeed, the only other Minnesota statute that the State has identified which requires two-parent consent is that authorizing the minor to change his name. These statutes provide testimony to the unreasonableness of the Minnesota two-parent notification requirement and to the ease with which the State can adopt less burdensome means to protect the minor's welfare. We therefore hold that this requirement violates the Constitution.

JUSTICE O'CONNOR, concurring in part and concurring in the judgment in part.

I join all but Parts III and VIII of JUSTICE STEVENS' opinion. * * *

I agree with Justice Stevens that Minnesota has offered no sufficient justification for its interference with the family's decisionmaking processes created by subdivision 2 of Minn. Stat. § 144.343 (1988)—two-parent notification. * * * Subdivision 6 passes constitutional muster because the interference with the internal operation of the family required by subdivision 2 simply does not exist where the minor can avoid notifying one or both parents by use of the bypass procedure.

JUSTICE STEVENS delivered a dissenting opinion in Part VIII.

VIII

The Court holds that the constitutional objection to the two-parent notice requirement is removed by the judicial bypass option provided in subdivision 6 of the Minnesota statute. I respectfully dissent from that holding.

A majority of the Court has previously held that a statute requiring one parent's consent to a minor's abortion will be upheld if the State provides an " 'alternative procedure whereby a pregnant minor may demonstrate that she is sufficiently mature to make the abortion decision herself or that, despite her immaturity, an abortion would be in her best interests.' " *Planned Parenthood Assn. of Kansas City, Mo., Inc. v. Ashcroft*, 462 U.S. 476, 491 (opinion of Powell, J.); id., at 505 (opinion of O'Connor, J.). Indeed, in *Bellotti II*, four Members of the Court expressed the same opinion about a statute requiring the consent of both parents. Neither of those precedents should control our decision today.

In *Bellotti II*, eight Members of the Court joined the judgment holding the Massachusetts statute unconstitutional. Thus, the Court did not hold that the judicial bypass set forth in that statute was valid; it held just the opposite. * * * The significance of the distinction between a statute requiring the consent of one parent and a statute requiring notice to both parents must be tested by the relationship of the respective requirements to legitimate state interests. We have concluded that the State has a strong and legitimate interest in providing a pregnant minor with the advice and support of a parent during the decisional period. A general rule requiring the minor to obtain the consent of one parent reasonably furthers that interest. An exception from the general rule is necessary to protect the minor from an arbitrary veto that is motivated by the separate concerns of the parent rather than the best interest of the child. *Cf. Parham v. J. R.*, 442 U.S. 584, 604–608. But the need for an exception does not undermine the conclusion that the general rule is perfectly reasonable—just as a rule requiring the consent of either parent for any other medical procedure would surely be reasonable if an exception were made for those emergencies in which, for example, a parent might deny lifesaving treatment to a child on religious grounds.

For reasons already set forth at length, a rule requiring consent or notification of both parents is not reasonably related to the state interest in giving the pregnant minor the benefit of parental advice. * * * A judicial bypass that is designed to handle exceptions from a reasonable general rule, and thereby preserve the constitutionality of that rule, is quite different from a requirement that a minor—or a minor and one of her parents—must apply to a court for permission to avoid the application of a rule that is not reasonably related to legitimate state goals. * * * As the Court of Appeals panel originally concluded, the "minor and custodial parent, ... by virtue of their major interest and superior position, should alone have the opportunity to decide to whom, if anyone, notice of the minor's abortion decision should be given." I agree with that conclusion. * * *

JUSTICE MARSHALL, with whom JUSTICE BRENNAN and JUSTICE BLACKMUN join, concurring in part, concurring in the judgment in part, and dissenting in part.

A majority of the Court today strikes down an unreasonable and vastly overbroad requirement that a pregnant minor notify both her parents of her decision to obtain an abortion. With that decision I agree. At the same time, though, a different majority holds that a State may require a young woman to notify one or even both parents and then wait 48 hours before having an abortion, as long as the State provides a judicial bypass procedure. From that decision I vehemently dissent. This scheme forces a young woman in an already dire situation to choose between two fundamentally unacceptable alternatives: notifying a possibly dictatorial or even abusive parent and justifying her profoundly personal decision in an intimidating judicial proceeding to a blackrobed stranger. For such a woman, this dilemma is more likely to result in trauma and pain than in an informed and voluntary decision.

JUSTICE SCALIA, concurring in the judgment in part and dissenting in part.

As I understand the various opinions today: One Justice holds that two-parent notification is unconstitutional (at least in the present circumstances) without judicial bypass, but constitutional with bypass, (O'Connor, J,, concurring in part and concurring in judgment in part); four Justices would hold that two-parent notification is constitutional with or without bypass, (Kennedy, J., concurring in judgment in part and dissenting in part); four Justices would hold that two-parent notification is unconstitutional with or without bypass, though the four apply two different standards, (opinion of Stevens, J.), (Marshall, J., concurring in part, concurring in judgment in part and dissenting in part); six Justices hold that one-parent notification with bypass is constitutional, though for two different sets of reasons, *Ohio v. Akron Center for Reproductive Health*, 497 U.S. at 510–517; 497 U.S. at 522–524 (Stevens, J., concurring in part and concurring in judgment); and three Justices would hold that one-parent notification with bypass is unconstitutional, (Blackmun, J., dissenting). One will search in vain the document we are supposed to be construing for text that provides the basis for the argument over these distinctions; and will find in our society's tradition regarding abortion no hint that the distinctions are constitutionally relevant, much less any indication how a constitutional argument about them ought to be resolved. The random and unpredictable results of our consequently unchanneled individual views make it increasingly evident, Term after Term, that the tools for this job are not to be found in the lawyer's—and hence not in the judge's—workbox. I continue to dissent from this enterprise of devising an Abortion Code, and from the illusion that we have authority to do so.

Justice Kennedy, with whom The Chief Justice, Justice White, and Justice Scalia join, concurring in the judgment in part and dissenting in part.

* * * I dissent from the portion of the Court's judgment affirming the Court of Appeals' conclusion that the Minnesota two-parent notice statute is unconstitutional. * * * Minnesota has done no more than act upon the commonsense proposition that, in assisting their daughter in deciding whether to have an abortion, parents can best fulfill their roles if they have the same information about their own child's medical condition and medical choices as the child's doctor does; and that to deny parents this knowledge is to risk, or perpetuate, estrangement or alienation from the child when she is in the greatest need of parental guidance and support. The Court does the State, and our constitutional tradition, sad disservice by impugning the legitimacy of these elemental objectives. * * *

In this case, the Court rejects a legislature's judgment that parents should at least be aware of their daughter's intention to seek an abortion, even if the State does not empower the parents to control the child's decision. That judgment is rejected although it rests upon a tradition of a parental role in the care and upbringing of children that is as old as civilization itself. Our precedents do not permit this result.

It is true that for all too many young women the prospect of two parents, perhaps even one parent, sustaining her with support that is compassionate and committed is an illusion. Statistics on drug and alcohol abuse by parents and documentations of child neglect and mistreatment are but fragments of the evidence showing the tragic reality that becomes day-to-day life for thousands of minors. But the Court errs in serious degree when it commands its own solution to the cruel consequences of individual misconduct, parental failure, and social ills. The legislative authority is entitled to attempt to meet these wrongs by taking reasonable measures to recognize and promote the primacy of the family tie, a concept which this Court now seems intent on declaring a constitutional irrelevance.

Notes and Questions

1. What significant difference justifies the constitutional requirement of individualized determination of a minor's maturity in the case of abortion, and the rigid age limits the law prescribes for other important events, such as the achievement of majority, drinking alcoholic beverages, driving, and marriage?

2. Could the state criminalize sexual activity by minors? *Cf.* Michael M. v. Superior Court, 450 U.S. 464, 101 S.Ct. 1200, 67 L.Ed.2d 437 (1981). Why?

3. Could the state require parental consent before an abortion is performed on a minor under the age of 13 (i.e., presume such a minor not to be mature)? Why?

4. Under the judicial "bypass" procedure required by the Supreme Court in *Bellotti II*, a judge must grant a minor's petition for permission to obtain an abortion without parental consent if: 1) he finds that the minor is sufficiently mature to make an abortion decision independently of her parents; or 2) even if she is too immature to make the decision independently, the desired abortion would be in her best interests. Research in Massachusetts on the impact of the new procedure revealed that, during the first twenty-two months the bypass procedure was available, approximately 1300 pregnant minors sought judicial authorization. In about 90% of the cases, the Court found that the minor was mature and allowed her to decide for herself. In the cases where the minor was found to be immature, the judge decided that an abortion would be in her best interests in all but five cases. Even in these cases, all of the girls obtained abortions. Four did so on appeal or through another judge; one went out of state rather than appeal the decision. The researchers concluded that "[t]he explanation for this result is that the superior court judges realize that it would be impossible as a legal proposition to justify a finding that a pregnant minor was too immature to decide whether to have an abortion for herself, but that it was in her best interests to bear a child. 'There is no way you could substantiate such a decision,' John J. Irwin, Jr., a judge who strongly opposes abortion, told the Boston Globe. 'I can't see any abortion that wouldn't be ordered or sanctioned by the courts under this law.' In the words of another Superior Court judge who indicated that he once gave permission for an abortion to an eleven year-old, '[t]he law puts judges in the ridiculous position of being rubber stamps.' " Robert H. Mnookin, *Bellotti v. Baird: A Hard Case*, in IN THE INTEREST OF CHILDREN: ADVOCACY, LAW REFORM, AND PUBLIC POLICY 150, 240 (Robert H. Mnookin ed. 1985).

Problem 9–4: Condom Distribution in Public Schools

Last month, following numerous public meetings at which the problems of teenage sexuality, venereal disease, and AIDS were discussed and debated, the local School Committee voted to make condoms available in the district's junior and senior high schools. Under the plan, junior high school students can obtain free condoms from the school nurse after receiving counseling and informational pamphlets on AIDS and other sexually transmitted diseases. Students at the high school can request free condoms from the nurse or buy them for $.75 from vending machines in the restrooms; counseling for high school students is optional. The plan does not allow parents to exclude their children from the program, nor does it provide for parental notification after a child requests condoms.

A group of parents has brought an action in which they allege that the condom availability program violates their rights to direct the upbringing of their children and infringes on their free exercise of religion. You are the law clerk to the trial court judge to which the case has been assigned. What Supreme Court precedents are relevant? What arguments can be expected from the parents? the state? How should the Court rule? *See* Alfonso v. Fernandez, 195 A.D.2d 46, 606 N.Y.S.2d 259, 260–61 (1993), app. dismissed, 83 N.Y.2d 906, 614 N.Y.S.2d 388, 637 N.E.2d 279 (1994); Curtis v. School Committee, 420 Mass. 749, 652 N.E.2d 580 (1995); Parents United for Better Schools v. Philadelphia Bd. of Educ., 978 F.Supp. 197 (E.D.Pa.1997). *See also* Comment, 109 HARV. L. REV. 687 (1996); Eugene C. Bjorklun, *Condom Distribution in the Public Schools: Is Parental Consent Required?*, 91 EDUC. L. REP. (West) 11 (1994); Karl J. Sanders, Comment, *Kids and Condoms: Constitutional Challenges to the Distribution of Condoms in Public Schools*, 61 U. CIN. L. REV. 1479 (1993).

SECTION 5. CHILD ABUSE AND NEGLECT

What circumstances justify state intervention to overrule a parent's child-rearing decisions? When is removal of the child from a parent's custody appropriate? How long should the parent have to cure the problems that necessitated placement before his or her rights are terminated?

A. AN OVERVIEW OF THE CHILD WELFARE SYSTEM

MARSHA GARRISON, CHILD WELFARE DECISION-MAKING: IN SEARCH OF THE LEAST DRASTIC ALTERNATIVE

75 GEO. L. J. 1745, 1750–58 (1987).

* * * The American child welfare system traces its descent from an early public assistance scheme, the Elizabeth Poor Laws. Under the Poor Laws, destitute children were placed in apprenticeship until the age of majority. Such placements could be accomplished without parental consent and divested the parent of both legal custody and the right to obtain the child's return. The Poor Laws aided only the destitute, however; except for the potential reach of the criminal law, abuse and neglect did not provoke state intervention.

The Poor Laws were transported to the American colonies along with other English legal institutions. During the colonial era, child welfare administration remained largely synonymous with public assistance administration, and apprenticeship until the age of majority remained the preferred form of aid. During the nineteenth century, as changing economic and social conditions made the indenture of young children increasingly difficult to arrange, the poorhouse, specialized children's institutions, foster care, and adoption came to supplement apprenticeship as methods of relieving childhood destitution. It was not until the latter half of the century, however, that the jurisdiction of child welfare authorities was redefined to include the prevention of harm due to parental abuse or neglect as well as poverty. Even then, abuse and neglect were poorly differentiated from mere need, and permanent placement was almost invariably the only service made available to children and their parents.

Not until the dawn of this century did enlightened opinion conclude that financial aid, rather than placement, was the most appropriate service for children of poor but competent parents. Only incompetents should lose their children to the state, reformers argued, and even then should not lose their children permanently. With proper diagnosis and individualized treatment by trained child welfare workers, the reformers claimed, parental inadequacies could be rectified so as to rehabilitate the family and save the state the cost of permanent placement. * * * The enactment of state and federal welfare programs for needy children, along with the introduction of social work techniques and personnel into child welfare administration, seemed to ensure that the[se] new goals could be met. * * *

By mid-century it was apparent that the goals of the new child welfare system had not been realized. * * * The system continued to serve substantial public assistance functions in addition to protecting children from parental incompetence. The most comprehensive study of foster care undertaken during this period determined that only 14.6% of the children surveyed were in foster care due to abuse or neglect, while problems associated with poverty—poor health, inadequate housing, and insufficient resources—were still responsible for many placements. * * * Poor families could seldom obtain the kind of help—daycare, for example, or temporary placement with a boarding school, friend or relative—that enabled wealthier families to cope with their children when an emergency occurred and were thus disproportionately forced to turn to the child welfare system. Moreover, as a result of the high stress levels and substandard living conditions associated with long-term indigence, poor parents were more likely to confront childcare crises, and more prone to other serious problems that impeded their ability to cope with them.

The system had also been less than totally successful in its goal of rehabilitating families and thus reducing the length of time children were wards of the state. Although most children did go home within a year or two, long-term placement continued to be fairly common, and some children still stayed in placement until the age of majority. Those parents who did regain their children apparently did so, in most cases, through their own efforts; rehabilitative services to parents were seldom provided, and many agencies did not even stay in touch with parents. During placement, children frequently lost touch with their own parents altogether. A few also suffered frequent shifts from one home to the next, thus depriving them of any meaningful familial relationships. * * *

In analyzing what had gone wrong, researchers discovered a system in which discretion was largely unbounded and frequently abused. * * * Although the rationale for . . . [officials'] broad discretionary powers was the need for individualized treatment in accordance with the specific needs of the child and his family, agencies tended instead to follow uniform practices based on bureaucratic convenience, custom, and funding priorities. Discretion was seldom exercised to meet the individual needs of the child or family. Many parents, for example, reported that daycare or housekeeping assistance could have averted foster care placement, but that agencies seldom offered such alternatives. Foster homes were typically selected with little attempt to match a child with adults who would be sensitive to the child's particular needs, or who lived in a location conducive to retaining ties with the child's natural parents, family, and friends. Frequently, foster parents were not even advised of a child's special problems prior to receiving the child. Rehabilitative efforts were also standardized, with little or no individualized treatment of the parental and family problems that had occasioned placement.

Moreover, agency practices had the effect of systematically discouraging parent-child contact or reunion. Visiting privileges, for example, were usually inflexible and infrequent. Parents were also given no role in the selection of the foster family and were not involved in decisions about the child's discipline or daily care.

Many factors contributed to the child welfare system's failure to exercise its discretion in accordance with the therapeutic ideal. Legislatures frequently failed to give adequate funding to services other than foster care and thus limited agency options. Agencies themselves also suffered from poor funding and from massive personnel problems. Bureaucratic inertia—unchecked by any review mechanisms—also kept alive the rigid, placement-oriented practices of the poor law era. The net result of these varied problems was that some poor children were unnecessarily placed in foster care and some stayed in foster care too long. The hopes of the turn of the century reformers had not been realized.

Mounting evidence of the inadequacies of the child welfare system produced a range of state initiatives aimed at foster care "permanency planning," as well as the federal Adoption Assistance and Child Welfare Act of 1980 (AACWA), Pub. L. 96–272, which set out a range of requirements that state child welfare agencies must meet as a condition of receiving federal foster care funds. More specifically, the Act requires a judicial finding that the state child welfare agency has made "reasonable efforts" to solve the problem in the home, the institution of case planning, periodic case review, and the provision of services to reunite children with their parents or ensure that they are placed in another permanent home. 42 U.S.C.A. §§ 671(a)(15), 671(a)(16), 672(a)(1), 627(a)(2)(B), 675(5)(B). As you read the following cases, assess the success of the AACWA in remedying the deficiencies in child welfare practice at which it was aimed.

B. WHAT CONSTITUTES NEGLECT?

IN RE T.G., C.G., D.G., and D.G., D.F., and E.G.

District of Columbia Court of Appeals, 1996.
684 A.2d 786.

MACK, SENIOR JUDGE.

The mother and father of four young children challenge, in separate appeals, the findings of a trial court that the children were "neglected" within the meaning of D.C. Code §§ 16–2301(9)(B) and (F) as well as the court's order committing the children to the Department of Human Services (DHS) for placement in foster homes. Basically, the parents attack the sufficiency of the evidence to support a finding of neglect. In the circumstances of this case, viewing, as we must, the evidence in the light most favorable to the government, we agree with the parents that the evidence supporting the finding that the children were "neglected" was insufficient as a matter of law. The government did not meet its burden of proof . . . of showing that any failure of proper care was not due to the parents' lack of financial means. On this record, we are disturbed at the rush to judgment exhibited by DHS, which on September 13, 1992, took the children into protective custody (and the following day sought the finding of neglect) based on a single visit to the home of the children. Finally, on the basis of a transcript of an October 1993, dispositional hearing which was requested, but not made a part of this record until after oral argument in this court, we conclude that DHS has not acted adequately to further the basic aim of society's interest in reunification of the family.

I. This family came to the attention of city officials for the first time on September 13, 1992. On that morning, the children's maternal grandmother died at her residence. An officer, responding to the report of death, found the two older children, T.G. and D.G., in their grandmother's house. The officer later described the house as being in a deplorable state and the children dirty and in need of clean clothes and baths. Shortly thereafter, the children's mother arrived with the two younger children. The officer drove the mother and the four children to the residence of the mother and father; he found that house likewise to be in a deplorable state. The two younger children were also dirty and in need of baths. The officer took all four children into protective custody and carried them to DHS. A social worker visited the two houses the same afternoon and thereafter corroborated the officer's description of the children and their living conditions. The next day, September 14, 1992, DHS filed neglect petitions. The court ordered that all four children be placed in the custody of DHS, pending further action, basing its finding on the inadequacy of the children's living arrangements and their then ages (approximately eight, four, two, and one).

The following year, on September 8, 1993, the trial court conducted a factfinding hearing with regard to the neglect petitions, heard and credited the testimony of the officer and social worker who discovered the family on September 13, 1992, and based its finding of neglect ... on the deplorable living conditions. The court did not adopt the reasoning of DHS that the mother and father were unable to discharge their parental responsibilities because of physical or mental disabilities, specifically stating that it did not find respondents to be neglected children pursuant to D.C. Code § 16–2301(9)(C). The mother and father were present at the hearing, did not testify, but moved through counsel for dismissal on the ground that a finding of neglect could not be based upon a lack of financial means ..., and that, therefore, DHS had failed to meet its burden. The trial court rejected the argument of DHS that the burden of showing that the deplorable living conditions resulted from the lack of financial means shifted to respondents; it nevertheless denied the motion to dismiss, holding that DHS had met its burden of proof. On October 26, 1993, the court held a dispositional hearing, indicated its intent to order a home-study and continued the placement of the children under the custody of DHS (with the boys remaining at St. Ann's Infant Home and the girls in foster care of a paternal aunt).

II. The term "neglect," warranting the protective intervention of the state, is by its very nature the equivalent of "negligence"—i.e., implying habits or omissions of duty, patterns of neglect, etc. Thus, we have held that a trial court's inquiry in neglect proceedings must go beyond "simply examining the most recent episode ... The judge must be apprised of the entire mosaic." Quite obviously, the "entire mosaic" includes an examination of any history of, but also the reasons for, neglect—i.e., chronic indifference, carelessness, dereliction, inability to perform, etc.

We have also held that "The purpose of the child neglect statute is to promote the best interests of allegedly neglected children." These "interests are presumptively served by being with a parent, provided that the parent is not unfit." Viewed against this backdrop, the circumstances of the instant case give us cause for concern. All four children were taken into protective custody on the same day (September 13, 1992), that their ailing grandmother died, and that their living quarters were first observed. They were taken into protective custody because they were dirty and their living quarters were dirty. All of the evidence as to parental housekeeping or child care was gathered on that one day in September 1992, and a neglect petition was filed on the following day. It was not until the following year, on October 12, 1993, that the children, on this evidence, were found to be neglected. Meanwhile, it appears that it was not until 1993 that DHS, in preparing for an October 26 disposition hearing, sought to contact these parents to inquire about reunification. At this time, no assessment of the parents' current living conditions had been made and no case plan had been developed. During this period, the parents had visited the two boys at St. Ann's Infant Home on a regular basis (and, presumably, the two girls who were in the care of a paternal aunt).

We are dealing here with parents who have not been found to be "unfit." While the neglect petition alleged incapacity because of physical or mental disabilities, the trial court did not find neglect on these grounds. Moreover, we have recognized that the "relevant focus" for the court in neglect proceedings is the children's condition, not parental culpability. State intervention is justified only after it is demonstrated that the need arises from some act or failure to act on the part of the parent "which endangers the welfare of the child." * * *

The problem in this case arises as a result of DHS's immediate focus on the conditions in two residences on a particular day. One could find empathy for the plight of social workers who, charged with the protection of children, must face the stark realities of poverty in an urban dwelling. One could also argue that constant exposure to filthy living conditions creates the risk of physical deterioration. Not enough focus, however, was centered on the physical or emotional condition of the children overall. There was testimony about some skin rash, but also the testimony of a social worker that she had seen many dirty children. There was testimony that there was no edible food in the residences, and that at the time the children appeared to be hungry. Yet, the children bore no signs of malnourishment or abuse requiring medical attention. In fact, there was testimony that the mother had explained that the father used borrowed funds to bring home food every day. There was testimony that the only family income came from a social security check, payable to the mother's father, who in turn gave the mother a certain amount of the funds for her use.

It may well be, as counsel for DHS argued (in opposing the motion to dismiss on the ground that a finding of neglect could not be based upon a lack of financial means), that society cannot bear the burden of funneling massive or minor amounts of money into deplorable housing to permit children to live there. True, also, as counsel argued, "you don't need a lot of money to clean up." It also may well be that overburdened service agencies and court systems are ill-equipped to meet certain problems of society. Nevertheless, here a sympathetic trial court, aware of the problems of substandard housing, rejecting the argument that the father and mother had the burden of proving the lack of financial means, but drawing inferences (on a "close issue") from the government's evidence of filthy conditions, found neglect, noting:

> We're talking about a bar of soap, we're talking about a washing of clothes, we're talking about changing of clothes, and even if there is one pair of clothes, these clothes can be washed out overnight.

There is a point, however, when decision-makers may be called upon to draw a balance between a bar of soap and love, and although we are loathe to second-guess the trial court's findings on this score, we nevertheless feel compelled to reverse the finding of neglect because of the failure of the government to meet its burden of proof.

We are also here disturbed by how little DHS did in seeking reunification of this family. It is beyond dispute that even if the parents were less than perfect, DHS has not lived up to its obligations in these proceedings. Although the allegations were made that the mother was learning disabled, and that the father had some substance abuse problems, the trial court's order of neglect made no findings as to unfitness. The court's findings reflected mostly the almost unspeakable poverty in which the family subsisted without the assistance of aid payments from the District. But DHS did not immediately seek to help the parents do what they had to do to reunite their family, according to the record before us. Indeed, in a report prepared in connection with the dispositional hearing scheduled for October 26, 1993, more than a year after the children were removed, DHS noted that it had not called the parents until recently. Although it may have been the parents' failings that brought DHS into the matter in the first place, DHS should not have been satisfied to document that the parents were imperfect. Instead, DHS should have taken an active role in spurring repair of the family by, for example, calling the parents immediately—and repeatedly, if necessary—to develop a strategy for reunification.

That the parents desired to be reunited with their children is evident from a reading of the transcript of the 1993 dispositional hearing. The father, mother, paternal grandparents, and paternal aunt (caretaker of the two girls) were present. Indeed, the father requested a short delay in proceedings to make certain that his wife, who walked slowly because of a weight problem, would arrive in time. The father sought custody of the boys because "it was better for children to be with relatives than [in an institution]." He told the court that the parents had a home available, but that no one from DHS had come to inspect it. Counsel explained that the mother was living at her father's house and was in the process of "fixing that home up" but had not been contacted by DHS. The children's father spoke of having to stop work in order to help his wife apply for public assistance and his desire to return to work. He indicated that he and his wife customarily visited the boys at St. Ann's twice a week. The trial court, in setting a date for further review, indicated that it would order a home-study before releasing the boys and it ordered that the continued visitation be preserved. In view of our holding that the evidence was not sufficient to support the drastic separation of parent from child in the first instance, it follows that (at least as to the DHS commitment) the question of disposition may be a moot one....

Because of the failure of the government to meet its burden of proof that any neglect was not due to the lack of financial needs, we are required to reverse the order with respect to neglect. In so doing, we recognize that the Superior Court, in the ordinary course of events, would order the release of the children from custody. In view of the intervening lapse of time since the children were taken into custody, however, we reverse the order of neglect, but stay the mandate of termination, to permit the court to review "the need for detention or shelter care" or to allow time for the parties to effect the children's transition to the parents' home or for the District to take such other action as the family's current circumstances and the children's best interest may require. * * * So ordered.

KING, ASSOCIATE JUDGE, dissenting.

Because I disagree with the majority's conclusion that the trial court erred in finding neglect ..., for each of the four children with respect to both the mother and father, I respectfully dissent. * * *

In my view, the majority has ... ma[de] its own findings of fact based on its interpretation of the evidence. At the evidentiary hearing the court heard from two witnesses presented by the government, a police officer and a social worker. Neither the father nor the mother testified. The trial judge made the following findings of fact:

1. After hearing the testimony, the Court credits the testimony of the two government witnesses. Based upon this persuasive testimony, this Court finds that the children were residing in deplorable living conditions, which were not the function or product of the parents' lack of financial means. 2. Officer Mathis testified that the grandparent's home was in a deplorable condition. Upon entering the house, he noticed a powerful stench which burned his nose with every breath. This odor emanated around the entire house. He observed piles of clothes and trash strewn about the home. The rug was filthy. There were holes in the floor and ceiling, and there were electrical wires hanging from the ceiling and walls. The officer stated that the entire kitchen was cluttered with trash, and there was the sound of mice in the corner. 3. Officer Mathis further testified that the children were unkempt. The children were not washed and one child's hair was completely matted. Both children were wearing clothes that had the appearance of not being washed for over a period of time. Their bodies emitted a foul odor. The children's room was filled with trash and scattered clothing. There was also one double-sized mattress on which all of the children slept. 4. Officer Mathis proceeded to visit the home of the parents. This house was found to be in the same deplorable condition as the grandmother's house. Two of the children found in this house suffered from skin rashes, which are consistent with dirt irritation. Furthermore, all of the children were hungry. Upon inspection of the kitchen, Officer Mathis noted only one item in the freezer and one half-gallon of sour milk in the refrigerator. 5. The Court heard the testimony of Joan Mallory, Department of Human Services Social Worker, who accompanied Officer Mathis into the grandparent's home. Ms. Mallory also had the opportunity to observe the clothing and hygiene of the children. She too stated that each child emitted a strong foul odor. The children slept on a single mattress, which smelled of urine and had no sheets. Upon examination of the home, she observed spoiled food, dirty utensils and stagnant water in the tub. She further stated that the carpeting and floor were so dirty that it was difficult to distinguish one from the other. The house was in a complete unsanitary condition. 6. The Court also concludes that the condition of the children and the home in which they were living was not caused by parents' lack of financial means. The evidence demonstrated that the family received Social Security Income benefits. The fact that the children were not malnourished further indicated that sufficient food was provided to the children. Whether the family lived in substandard

housing is of no significance because it is not the cause of the aforementioned deplorable conditions. The cost of cleaning the home, washing the children, and bathing a child is minimal. Therefore, the filthy conditions of the children and the home were the result of neglect, rather than lack of financial means.

I submit that these findings of fact are supported by the record and this court has no basis for concluding otherwise.

The majority faults the social worker, and inferentially, the trial judge for focusing on conditions on a particular day, i.e., the day that Officer Mathis took the children into protective custody, rather than examining the circumstances "beyond . . . the most recent episode." The majority seems to be saying that neglect was not established because it was only shown that the children and their homes were filthy on a single day in their lives. Setting aside the point that no such argument was ever made to the trial judge, it would not be unreasonable to infer, as the trial judge undoubtedly could and did, that the conditions described had existed for some time before the day they were observed. For example, the social worker testified that the children's clothes were so filthy that they had to be thrown away, and the trial court found that the clothing of at least two of the children "had the appearance of not being washed over a period of time." The social worker also testified that the odor given off by the children was so overwhelming that she had to air-out the office where the children had been taken. Finally, there was testimony that trash was strewn around the homes, the stove and utensils in one of the kitchens were "very very dirty," and both homes emitted a foul odor. This evidence strongly suggests that the condition of the children and the homes was a problem of long standing.

Moreover, the finding on financial ability is supportable based on the testimony regarding the mother's access to the proceeds of a Social Security Income ("SSI") benefits check. The majority places reliance on testimony that the proceeds of the check went to the mother's father who "gave [the mother] a certain amount of money to [take] care of herself," thus implying that the mother only received that portion of the proceeds that her father chose to give her. * * * There was also testimony, however, that the beneficiary of the SSI check was the mother, and that her father was the designated payee on her behalf and the proceeds were "solely for her."[4] From this testimony the trial court could conclude that all of the funds from the SSI check went to the mother, a conclusion bolstered by the mother's attorney who, during the course of her argument seeking dismissal of the petition, stated that "the income of that family is the Social Security Income check which is designated for the use of the mother alone," and the absence of any evidence (neither parent testified) that the proceeds of that check were

4. Whether such an arrangement formally existed cannot be determined from this record; however, the disposition report indicates that the mother was "unable to discharge her parental responsibilities . . . because of mental incapacity." Whether the mother's mental condition was such that it was necessary to designate someone to receive the benefits check on her behalf also cannot be determined from this record.

insufficient to allow the parents to purchase minimal cleaning supplies. Indeed the evidence that the children's rooms were filled with trash and their clothing strewn about, problems that could be corrected without any financial cost, supports a conclusion that the condition of the children and their homes were the product of the parents' long-term failure to provide even minimal care for their children rather than from the lack of financial means to correct it. Therefore, because the findings of the trial court are supported by the record, I would affirm its ruling that the government had met its burden of proof in establishing neglect.* * *

I take no position with respect to the majority's decision to stay the mandate. In light of the majority's opinion that neglect was not established, it is not clear to me exactly what action the trial court can take. I note, however, that on this record it is safe to say that the children's future can only be described as precarious. For example, at the disposition hearing on October 26, 1993, the trial judge had before him a disposition report that stated that the "mother is unable to discharge her parental responsibilities to and for the children. The father is unable to discharge his responsibilities to and for the children because of a physical incapacity [and] drug use. . . . " At the time of the hearing, the two daughters were placed with their paternal aunt and the two sons were in St. Anne's home. The father had no objection to the continued placement of the two girls with the aunt, but sought reunification with the two boys. Counsel for the mother represented that the mother "thought" she was capable of caring for two of the children. The trial judge committed all of the children to the custody of DHS, ordering that the two girls remain with the aunt and the two boys be placed in foster care. Because the majority has reversed the finding of neglect, however, that commitment must be set aside.

Notes and Questions

1. Why, according the majority, has the state failed to show neglect? What additional facts would be required? What should child welfare officials have done?

2. The *T.G.* decision offers a vivid portrayal of the familial circumstances which child welfare workers typically confront. Children who enter foster care have typically lived in extreme poverty, in inadequate housing, with inadequate social and community supports. *See* Garrison, *supra* at 1790–91 (surveying reports). Their parents are seldom employed and are poorly educated. *See, e.g.,* Mary Ann Jones, A Second Chance for Families (1985) (83% of biological mothers and 85% of fathers never went past eighth grade; only 8% of mothers and 44% of legal fathers could report "having had steady employment at the same job or consistent, though not steady employment"). Their families are overwhelmed with problems. In one often-cited survey, for example, 33% of the children's main caretakers suffered from "severe" mental or emotional problems, 60% of families included an adult member who used alcohol excessively, 20% had at least one member who had been a heroin

user, 53% of main caretakers had a severe physical illness or condition, and 76% of families had at least one child with a serious health problem. Horowitz & Wolock, *Material Deprivation, Child Maltreatment and Agency Interventions Among Poor Families, in* THE SOCIAL CONTEXT OF CHILD ABUSE AND NEGLECT 137, 146 (Leonard Pelton ed. 1981).

3. *T.G.* also offers a vivid portrait of a large, urban child welfare system. Before 1992, a number of federal courts held that the various provisions of the federal Adoption Assistance and Child Welfare Act of 1990 were enforceable through a private action brought under 42 U.S.C. § 1983; law reform actions based on the law were brought in many parts of the country—including the District of Columbia. In 1991, a federal district court ruled that the District of Columbia Department of Human Services had consistently evaded its responsibilities under local and federal law. Among the agency's failures were the "failure ... to initiate timely investigations into reports of abuse or neglect, the failure to provide services to families to prevent the placement of children in foster care, the failure to place those who may not safely remain at home in appropriate foster homes and institutions, the failure to develop case plans for children in foster care, and the failure to move children into a situation of permanency, whether by returning them to their homes or freeing them for adoption." LaShawn A. v. Dixon, 762 F.Supp. 959, 960 (D.D.C.1991). After the District Court's findings were upheld on appeal (990 F.2d 1319 (D.C.Cir.1993)), the district court judge, as part of a settlement, took control of a large part of the District's foster care system and announced that he was appointing the Center for the Study of Social Policy as a monitor to ensure that the District complied with strict deadlines concerning improved staffing and procedures, reducing the backlog of children in foster care, and establishing a procedure for reviewing the deaths of children in its care. In a later order, the judge extended the receivership order to child protective services as well as foster care. *See* Toni Lacy, *District's Foster Care Role Cut: Judge to Appoint Receiver, Threatens to Jail Officials*, WASHINGTON POST, Sept. 17, 1994, at A1; Tony Lacy, *Court Tightens Grip on D.C. Foster Care*, WASHINGTON POST, Nov. 19, 1994, at B1. To what extent does the Court's decision in *T.G.* appear to be influenced by the systemic inadequacies of the District's child welfare system?

4. In Suter et al. v. Artist M. et al., 503 U.S. 347, 112 S.Ct. 1360, 118 L.Ed.2d 1 (1992), an action brought on behalf of children against the director of the Illinois child abuse and neglect agency based on the agency's alleged failure to comply with the Adoption Assistance and Child Welfare Act of 1980, the Supreme Court held that the Act does *not* confer on its intended beneficiaries a private right that is enforceable in a 42 U.S.C.A. § 1983 action. As a result of *Suter*, plaintiffs may no longer rely on federal law when challenging local child welfare policies and practices.

5. Not all courts have agreed that facts like those in *T.G.* are inadequate to justify state intervention. *See, e.g.*, In re Interest of N.M.W., 461 N.W.2d 478 (Iowa App.1990) (upholding neglect determina-

tion based on "chronic unsanitary conditions" of home despite lack of evidence of adverse health effects). What are the arguments in favor of intervention on these facts? Against?

6. While the D.C. neglect statute is a fairly typical one, during the 1970s and early 80s, a number of commissions and panels recommended that state neglect statutes be redrawn so as to specify the grounds for state intervention with greater particularity and thus prevent unwarranted state intervention. Standards drafted under the auspices of the Institute for Judicial Administration and American Bar Association (IJA–ABA), for example, authorize state intervention for neglect only when:

> A. a child has suffered, or there is a substantial risk that a child will imminently suffer, a physical harm, inflicted nonaccidentally upon him/her by his/her parents, which causes, or creates a substantial risk of causing disfigurement, impairment of bodily functioning, or other serious physical injury;
>
> B. a child has suffered, or there is a substantial risk that a child will imminently suffer, physical harm causing disfigurement, impairment of bodily functioning, or other serious physical injury as a result of conditions created by his/her parents or by the failure of the parents to adequately supervise or protect him/her;
>
> C. a child is suffering serious emotional damage, evidenced by severe anxiety, depression, or withdrawal, or untoward aggressive behavior toward self or others, and the child's parents are not willing to provide treatment for him/her;
>
> D. a child has been sexually abused by his/her parent or a member of his/her household . . . where the parent know or should have known and failed to take appropriate action . . .
>
> E. a child is in need of medical treatment [for a serious medical condition] . . . and his/her parents are unwilling to provide or consent to the medical treatment;
>
> F. a child is committing delinquent acts as a result of parental encouragement, guidance, or approval.
>
> JOINT COMM'N ON JUVENILE JUSTICE STANDARDS, INST. OF JUDICIAL ADMIN., ABA STANDARDS RELATING TO ABUSE AND NEGLECT, STANDARD 2.1 (1981).

Would the Standards permit intervention in *T.G.*?

7. The philosophy of minimal state intervention that underlies the IJA–ABA standards rests in part on the "psychological parenting" theory described briefly in In re J.M.P. [p. 311]. In a pair of influential books that employ psychological parenting theory to develop legal standards for child custody and child protection cases, law professor Joseph Goldstein, psychoanalyst Anna Freud, and psychiatrist Albert Solnit have argued that the risks inherent in state intervention are sufficiently grave that only the most serious harms justify either removing the child from his parents or even providing services in the home. They explicitly

argue against intervention for "minor assaults" and serious emotional or intellectual harm.[5]

Their primary rationale for this position is that state intervention itself poses serious risks to children, risks so substantial that only the most serious harms justify removing the child from his parents or even providing services in the house. Removal from the home, they argue, disrupts "[c]ontinuity of relationships, surroundings and environmental influences [that] are essential for a child's normal development." The shared authority between parents and agency creates "insecurity caused by the constant need to find a balance between the competing demands of fostering parents and external authorities." The multiple placements some children encounter while in care interfere with the "attachments that are essential for an individual's growth." And the child's return to his parents when he has formed attachments elsewhere "causes distress and harm[s] ... his psychological development." Even intervention without removal, Goldstein, Freud, and Solnit opine, poses risks: "When family integrity is broken or weakened by state intrusion, [the child's] ... needs are thwarted and his belief that his parents are omniscient and all-powerful is shaken prematurely. The effect on the child's developmental progress is invariably detrimental." JOSEPH GOLDSTEIN ET AL., BEYOND THE BEST INTERESTS OF THE CHILD 31–32 (2d ed. 1979); JOSEPH GOLDSTEIN ET AL., BEFORE THE BEST INTERESTS OF THE CHILD 46, 49, 136 (1979).

Although the minimum intervention philosophy influenced the federal Adoption Assistance and Child Welfare Act of 1980, state legislatures have not heeded the call to narrow the grounds for state intervention. Can you think of any reasons why?

WHITNER v. STATE OF SOUTH CAROLINA

Supreme Court of South Carolina, 1997.
328 S.C. 1, 492 S.E.2d 777.

TOAL, A.J.

This case concerns the scope of the child abuse and endangerment statute in the South Carolina Children's Code (the Code), S.C. Code Ann. § 20–7–50 (1985). We hold the word "child" as used in that statute includes viable fetuses.

On April 20, 1992, Cornelia Whitner (Whitner) pled guilty to criminal child neglect, S.C. Code Ann. § 20–7–50, for causing her baby to be born with cocaine metabolites in its system by reason of Whitner's

5. They propose that intervention by child welfare authorities be limited to cases of "[s]erious bodily injury inflicted by parents upon their child, or an attempt to inflict such harms, or repeated failure of the parents to prevent the child from suffering such injury"; conviction of a sexual offense against the child; or abandonment. Other grounds for intervention include parental failure to abide by labor, education, and immunization laws affecting the child, the commission of acts by the child criminal under the adult penal system, and certain instances of medical treatment denial. JOSEPH GOLDSTEIN ET AL., BEFORE THE BEST INTERESTS OF THE CHILD 193–95 (1979).

ingestion of crack cocaine during the third trimester of her pregnancy. The circuit court judge sentenced Whitner to eight years in prison.... Thereafter, Whitner filed a petition for Post Conviction Relief (PCR), pleading the circuit court's lack of subject matter jurisdiction to accept her guilty plea ... The petition was granted on both grounds. The State appeals.

The State ... argues the PCR court erred in finding the sentencing circuit court lacked subject matter jurisdiction to accept Whitner's guilty plea. We agree. Under South Carolina law, a circuit court lacks subject matter jurisdiction to accept a guilty plea to a nonexistent offense. For the sentencing court to have had subject matter jurisdiction to accept Whitner's plea, criminal child neglect under § 20–7–50 would have to include an expectant mother's use of crack.[5]

The State contends this section encompasses maternal acts endangering or likely to endanger the life, comfort, or health of a viable fetus. Under the Children's Code, "child" means a "person under the age of eighteen." S.C. Code Ann. § 20–7–30(1). The question for this Court, therefore, is whether a viable fetus is a "person" for purposes of the Children's Code.

* * *

South Carolina law has long recognized that viable fetuses are persons holding certain legal rights and privileges. In 1960, this Court decided *Hall v. Murphy*, 236 S.C. 257, 113 S.E.2d 790 (1960). That case concerned the application of South Carolina's wrongful death statute to an infant who died four hours after her birth as a result of injuries sustained prenatally during viability. The Appellants argued that a viable fetus was not a person within the purview of the wrongful death statute [but] ... this Court unanimously held ... [that] a fetus having reached that period of prenatal maturity where it is capable of independent life apart from its mother is a person. Four years later, in *Fowler v. Woodward*, 244 S.C. 608, 138 S.E.2d 42 (1964), we interpreted *Hall* as supporting a finding that a viable fetus injured while still in the womb need not be born alive for another to maintain an action for the wrongful death of the fetus. * * * More recently, we held the word "person" as used in a criminal statute includes viable fetuses. *State v. Horne*, 282 S.C. 444, 319 S.E.2d 703 (1984), concerned South Carolina's murder statute. The defendant in that case stabbed his wife, who was nine months' pregnant, in the neck, arms, and abdomen. Although doctors performed an emergency caesarean section to deliver the child, the child died while still in the womb. The defendant ... appealed his conviction on the ground South Carolina did not recognize the crime of feticide.

5. S.C. Code Ann. § 20–7–50 (1985) provides:

Any person having the legal custody of any child or helpless person, who shall, without lawful excuse, refuse or neglect to provide, as defined in § 20–7–490, the proper care and attention for such child or helpless person, so that the life, health or comfort of such child or helpless person is endangered or is likely to be endangered, shall be guilty of a misdemeanor and shall be punished within the discretion of the circuit court.

This Court disagreed. In a unanimous decision, we held it would be "grossly inconsistent . . . to construe a viable fetus as a 'person' for the purposes of imposing civil liability while refusing to give it a similar classification in the criminal context." Accordingly, the Court recognized the crime of feticide with respect to viable fetuses.

Similarly, we do not see any rational basis for finding a viable fetus is not a "person" in the present context. Indeed, it would be absurd to recognize the viable fetus as a person for purposes of homicide laws and wrongful death statutes but not for purposes of statutes proscribing child abuse. Our holding in *Hall* that a viable fetus is a person rested primarily on the plain meaning of the word "person" in light of existing medical knowledge concerning fetal development. We do not believe that the plain and ordinary meaning of the word "person" has changed in any way that would now deny viable fetuses status as persons.

The policies enunciated in the Children's Code also support our plain meaning reading of "person." S.C. Code Ann. § 20–7–20(C), which describes South Carolina's policy concerning children, expressly states: "It shall be the policy of this State to concentrate on the prevention of children's problems as the most important strategy which can be planned and implemented on behalf of children and their families." The abuse or neglect of a child at any time during childhood can exact a profound toll on the child herself as well as on society as a whole. However, the consequences of abuse or neglect which takes place after birth often pale in comparison to those resulting from abuse suffered by the viable fetus before birth. This policy of prevention supports a reading of the word "person" to include viable fetuses. Furthermore, the scope of the Children's Code is quite broad. It applies "to all children who have need of services." S.C. Code Ann. § 20–7–20(B) (1985). When coupled with the comprehensive remedial purposes of the Code, this language supports the inference that the legislature intended to include viable fetuses within the scope of the Code's protection.

Whitner advances several arguments against an interpretation of "person" as used in the Children's Code to include viable fetuses. . . .

Whitner's first argument concerns the number of bills introduced in the South Carolina General Assembly in the past five years addressing substance abuse by pregnant women. . . . Whitner suggests that the introduction of several bills touching the specific issue at hand evinces a belief by legislators that prior legislation had not addressed the issue. Whitner argues the introduction of the bills proves that § 20–7–50 was not intended to encompass abuse or neglect of a viable fetus.

We disagree with Whitner's conclusion about the significance of the proposed legislation. Generally, the legislature's subsequent acts "cast no light on the intent of the legislature which enacted the statute being construed." Rather, this Court will look first to the language of the statute to discern legislative intent, because the language itself is the best guide to legislative intent. Here, we see no reason to look beyond the statutory language. Additionally, our existing case law strongly supports our conclusion about the meaning of the statute's language.

Whitner also argues an interpretation of the statute that includes viable fetuses would lead to absurd results obviously not intended by the legislature. Specifically, she claims if we interpret "child" to include viable fetuses, every action by a pregnant woman that endangers or is likely to endanger a fetus, whether otherwise legal or illegal, would constitute unlawful neglect under the statute. For example, a woman might be prosecuted under § 20–7–50 for smoking or drinking during pregnancy. Whitner asserts these "absurd" results could not have been intended by the legislature and, therefore, the statute should not be construed to include viable fetuses.

We disagree for a number of reasons. First, the same arguments against the statute can be made whether or not the child has been born. After the birth of a child, a parent can be prosecuted under § 20–7–50 for an action that is likely to endanger the child without regard to whether the action is illegal in itself. For example, a parent who drinks excessively could, under certain circumstances, be guilty of child neglect or endangerment even though the underlying act—consuming alcoholic beverages—is itself legal. Obviously, the legislature did not think it "absurd" to allow prosecution of parents for such otherwise legal acts when the acts actually or potentially endanger the "life, health or comfort" of the parents born children. We see no reason such a result should be rendered absurd by the mere fact the child at issue is a viable fetus.

Moreover, we need not address this potential parade of horribles advanced by Whitner. In this case, which is the only case we are called upon to decide here, certain facts are clear. Whitner admits to having ingested crack cocaine during the third trimester of her pregnancy, which caused her child to be born with cocaine in its system. Although the precise effects of maternal crack use during pregnancy are somewhat unclear, it is well documented and within the realm of public knowledge that such use can cause serious harm to the viable unborn child. *See, e.g.*, Joseph J. Volpe, M.D., *Effect of Cocaine Use on the Fetus*, 327 New Eng. J. Med. 399 (1992); Ira J. Chasnoff, M.D., et al., *Cocaine Use in Pregnancy*, 313 New Eng. J. Med. 666 (1985). There can be no question here Whitner endangered the life, health, and comfort of her child. We need not decide any cases other than the one before us.

We are well aware of the many decisions from other states' courts throughout the country holding maternal conduct before the birth of the child does not give rise to criminal prosecution under state child abuse/endangerment or drug distribution statutes. Many of these cases were prosecuted under statutes forbidding delivery or distribution of illicit substances and depended on statutory construction of the terms "delivery" and "distribution." Obviously, such cases are inapplicable to the present situation. The cases concerning child endangerment statutes or construing the terms "child" and "person" are also distinguishable, because the states in which these cases were decided have entirely different bodies of case law from South Carolina. For example, in *Commonwealth v. Welch,* the Kentucky Supreme Court specifically noted Kentucky law has not construed the word "person" in the criminal homicide statute to include a fetus (viable or not). *Welch,* 864 S.W.2d at 281....

Massachusetts, however, has a body of case law substantially similar to South Carolina's, yet a Massachusetts trial court has held that a mother pregnant with a viable fetus is not criminally liable for transmission of cocaine to the fetus. *See Commonwealth v. Pellegrini,* No. 87970, slip op. (Mass. Super. Ct. Oct. 15, 1990).... The Massachusetts trial court found [that state case law] ... "accord[s] legal rights to the unborn only where the mother's or parents' interest in the potentiality of life, not the state's interest, are sought to be vindicated." In other words, a viable fetus should only be accorded the rights of a person for the sake of its mother or both its parents. Under this rationale, the viable fetus lacks rights of its own that deserve vindication.... We do not think *Hall, Fowler,* and *Horne* can be interpreted so narrowly.... If, as Whitner suggests we should, we read *Horne* only as a vindication of the mother's interest in the life of her unborn child, there would be no basis for prosecuting a mother who kills her viable fetus by stabbing it, by shooting it, or by other such means, yet a third party could be prosecuted for the very same acts. We decline to read *Horne* in a way that insulates the mother from all culpability for harm to her viable child....

* * *

Whitner [also] argues that prosecuting her for using crack cocaine after her fetus attains viability unconstitutionally burdens her right of privacy, or, more specifically, her right to carry her pregnancy to term. We disagree.

Whitner argues that § 20–7–50 burdens her right of privacy, a right long recognized by the United States Supreme Court.... [H]owever, we do not think any fundamental right of Whitner's—or any right at all, for that matter—is implicated under the present scenario. It strains belief for Whitner to argue that using crack cocaine during pregnancy is encompassed within the constitutionally recognized right of privacy. Use of crack cocaine is illegal, period. No one here argues that laws criminalizing the use of crack cocaine are themselves unconstitutional. If the State wishes to impose additional criminal penalties on pregnant women who engage in this already illegal conduct because of the effect the conduct has on the viable fetus, it may do so. We do not see how the fact of pregnancy elevates the use of crack cocaine to the lofty status of a fundamental right.

Moreover, as a practical matter, we do not see how our interpretation of § 20–7–50 imposes a burden on Whitner's right to carry her child to term.... [D]uring her pregnancy after the fetus attained viability, Whitner enjoyed the same freedom to use cocaine that she enjoyed earlier in and predating her pregnancy—none whatsoever. Simply put, South Carolina's child abuse and endangerment statute as applied to this case does not restrict Whitner's freedom in any way that it was not already restricted. The State's imposition of an additional penalty when a pregnant woman with a viable fetus engages in the already proscribed behavior does not burden a woman's right to carry her pregnancy to term; rather, the additional penalty simply recognizes that a third party (the viable fetus or newborn child) is harmed by the behavior.

For the foregoing reasons, the decision of the PCR Court is REVERSED.

MOORE, A.J., dissenting.

In my view, the repeated failure of the legislature to pass proposed bills addressing the problem of drug use during pregnancy is evidence the child abuse and neglect statute is not intended to apply in this instance. This Court should not invade what is clearly the sole province of the legislative branch.... With today's decision, the majority not only ignores legislative intent but embarks on a course of judicial activism rejected by every other court to address the issue....

I cannot accept the majority's assertion that the child abuse and neglect statute unambiguously includes a "viable fetus." If that is the case, then why is the majority compelled to go to such great lengths to ascertain that a "viable fetus" is a "child?" ... In construing this statute to include conduct not contemplated by the legislature, the majority has rendered the statute vague and set for itself the task of determining what conduct is unlawful. Is a pregnant woman's failure to obtain prenatal care unlawful? Failure to quit smoking or drinking? Although the majority dismisses this issue as not before it, the impact of today's decision is to render a pregnant woman potentially criminally liable for myriad acts which the legislature has not seen fit to criminalize. To ignore this "down-the-road" consequence in a case of this import is unrealistic. The majority insists that parents may already be held liable for drinking after a child is born. This is untrue, however, without some further act on the part of the parent. A parent who drinks and then hits her child or fails to come home may be guilty of criminal neglect. The mere fact of drinking, however, does not constitute neglect of a child in being.

The majority attempts to support an overinclusive construction of the child abuse and neglect statute by citing other legal protections extended equally to a viable fetus and a child in being. The only law, however, that specifically regulates the conduct of a mother toward her unborn child is our abortion statute under which a viable fetus is in fact treated differently from a child in being.

The majority argues for equal treatment of viable fetuses and children, yet its construction of the statute results in even greater inequities. If the statute applies only when a fetus is "viable," a pregnant woman can use cocaine for the first twenty-four weeks [defined as the point of viability under S.C. law] of her pregnancy, the most dangerous period for the fetus, and be immune from prosecution under the statute so long as she quits drug use before the fetus becomes viable. Further, a pregnant woman now faces up to ten years in prison for ingesting drugs during pregnancy but can have an illegal abortion and receive only a two-year sentence for killing her viable fetus.

Notes and Questions

1. As *Whitner* notes, most other courts that have considered whether prenatal substance abuse provides a basis for criminal liability have disagreed with its conclusions. *See, e.g.*, Johnson v. State, 602 So.2d 1288 (Fla.1992); Commonwealth v. Welch, 864 S.W.2d 280 (Ky.1993); State v. Gray, 62 Ohio St.3d 514, 584 N.E.2d 710 (1992); Reyes v. Superior Court, 75 Cal.App.3d 214, 141 Cal.Rptr. 912 (1977); State v. Carter, 602 So.2d 995 (Fla.App.1992); State v. Gethers, 585 So.2d 1140 (Fla.App.1991); State v. Luster, 204 Ga.App. 156, 419 S.E.2d 32 (1992), cert. denied (Ga. 1992); Commonwealth v. Pellegrini, No. 87970, slip op. (Mass. Super. Oct. 15, 1990); People v. Hardy, 188 Mich.App. 305, 469 N.W.2d 50, app. denied, 437 Mich. 1046, 471 N.W.2d 619 (1991); Commonwealth v. Kemp, 434 Pa.Super. 719, 643 A.2d 705 (1994).

2. Some courts have approved commitment petitions to confine drug-abusing mothers for the purpose of protecting their viable fetuses. *See* In re Troy D., 215 Cal.App.3d 889, 263 Cal.Rptr. 869 (1989); In re Solomon L., 190 Cal.App.3d 1106, 236 Cal.Rptr. 2 (1987); In re Nash, 165 Mich.App. 450, 419 N.W.2d 1 (1987). *But see* In re Tyesha C., 157 App.Div.2d 322, 556 N.Y.S.2d 280 (1990) (denying commitment petition).

3. Jan C. is an alcoholic whose three year old child has been diagnosed with fetal alcohol syndrome, an incurable condition resulting from heavy prenatal alcohol use that causes mental retardation and minor physical deformity. Jan is now six months pregnant and is drinking heavily. Under *Whitner*, could she be convicted of child abuse and endangerment?

Problem 9–5:

To avoid a problem with statutory interpretation like that in *Whitner*, the legislature is considering the following bill:

> (A) As used in this section: (1) "Schedule I," "Schedule II," "controlled substance," and "prescription" have the same meanings as in § 3719.01 of the Revised Code. (2) "Drug exposed at birth" means exposed prenatally to a schedule I or II controlled substance, as evidence by at least one of the following: (a) Symptoms of withdrawal from the schedule I or II controlled substance at birth; (b) Results of tests of the child's blood, urine, stool, hair, chromosomes, or other bodily fluids or components that indicate the presence of the schedule I or II controlled substance in the child's body; (c) Medical effects or developmental delays that are apparent during the first three months after the child's birth. (3) "Use," as it relates to a controlled substance, means injecting, ingesting, inhaling, or

> otherwise introducing into the human body a schedule I or II controlled substance. (B) No woman shall knowingly use a schedule I or II controlled substance at a time when she knows or reasonably should know that she is pregnant if the use of the schedule I or II controlled substance results in the child with whom she is pregnant being drug-exposed at birth. (C) Division (B) of this section does not apply to a woman if the woman was prescribed the schedule I or II controlled substance by a physician licensed under Chapter 4731. of the Revised Code and the woman used the controlled substance in a manner substantially consistent with the instructions of the prescribing physician, or of any pharmacist licensed under Chapter 4729. of the Revised Code, who provided instructions for the use of the medication.

Should the legislation be amended to include cigarette and alcohol abuse? With or without such an amendment, would the legislation be constitutional if enacted? What benefits would flow from classifying prenatal drug abuse as neglect? What are the disadvantages of this approach? What alternatives to a neglect proceeding are available?

C. TERMINATION OF PARENTAL RIGHTS

KINGSLEY v. KINGSLEY

623 So.2d 780 (Fla. App. 1993).
[p. 404].

IN THE INTEREST OF M.M.L.

Supreme Court of Kansas, 1995.
258 Kan. 254, 900 P.2d 813.

HOLMES, C.J.

[Michael,] [t]he natural father of M.M.L., a minor, appeals in a child in need of care case from an order of the district court placing M.M.L. in long-term foster care. He argues the best interests of the child standard in K.S.A. § 38–1563(d) violates his constitutional right to custody of his child absent a finding of unfitness....

This case ... has had a long and tortured history. Despite extensive efforts by Michael, the courts, counsel, various social and professional workers, and others involved in this case, the results have been far from satisfactory. * * *

Michael and [M.M.L.'s mother] J.C. were married in 1974, and one son, now an adult, was born to the marriage. The couple was divorced in 1979; however, they reestablished a relationship and lived together until sometime in 1984, apparently as residents of the Kansas City, Missouri, area. M.M.L. was born during this period on January 4, 1981. In mid–1984 M.M.L. and her mother left the home, and at some later date J.C. married M.C., whose name is also Michael. The coincidence of both the father and stepfather having the same first name, Michael, creates some confusion in attempting to get a clear picture of some of the events described in the record. In an attempt to avoid further confusion, we will refer to the father of M.M.L. as Michael and the stepfather as M.C.

In 1985 Michael filed a proceeding in Missouri to obtain custody of both children. Soon thereafter M.M.L. alleged she had been sexually abused by "Michael" or by one of her mother's boyfriends. As it eventually turned out, Michael, the father, was absolved of any sexual abuse of M.M.L., although expert testimony did establish that she had, in all probability, been abused by someone, either M.C. or one of the other friends of J.C. Sometime in 1985 Michael moved to the state of Washington and lost track of his children. His custody suit was dismissed when he failed to show up for the hearing. Thereafter M.M.L. and her mother moved to Great Bend. Despite his efforts to obtain information about M.M.L from her maternal grandmother, Michael was unable to obtain any information about her whereabouts or about her welfare. Michael moved back to Kansas City in 1988 or 1989, to Georgia in 1989, and back to Kansas City in late 1991 or 1992. In late 1990 or early 1991 Michael learned by chance that J.C. and M.M.L. were in Great Bend. He has been attempting to gain custody ever since.

On September 6, 1990, M.M.L. was placed in the temporary custody of the Department of Social and Rehabilitation Services (SRS) based on allegations that she had been sexually abused by M.C. She was placed by SRS in a foster home in Great Bend, where she has remained since. On January 17, 1991, the trial court found by clear and convincing evidence that M.M.L. had been sexually abused by her stepfather and adjudicated her a child in need of care. At that point Michael had not had contact or a relationship with M.M.L. for approximately five years. At a dispositional hearing held March 12, 1991, the court found that placing M.M.L. with her father was not a viable option at that time and denied him visitation rights so that M.M.L.'s therapist could prepare her for future visitation. It was at about this time that J.C. moved to Texas and apparently abandoned any interest in M.M.L. or in any further court proceedings in her behalf.

As the case progressed, review hearings were held and, in early 1992 Michael was granted visitation rights. Initially the visits were limited to supervised visits in Great Bend, but eventually Michael was granted unsupervised visits at his home in Kansas City for several days at a time. Throughout the proceedings, Michael did everything requested of him by the court. Various examinations indicated (1) he does not portray sexual offender characteristics; (2) he has never sexually abused M.M.L.; (3) he exhibits no psychological problems impairing his ability to care for his daughter; and (4) he shows no signs of alcoholism or drug abuse. He has attended alcohol information school, effective parenting classes, anger-control counseling, counseling for parents of sexually abused children, individual counseling, and joint counseling with M.M.L. Home studies have been performed and the latest done in July 1994 recommended M.M.L. be placed in Michael's home with supervision.

Despite Michael's efforts, M.M.L. maintained throughout the proceedings that she did not want to live with him. Although she was initially excited and hopeful about a relationship with her father, she became frightened and disillusioned as the visits progressed. From the outset of the case, M.M.L. saw a psychologist, Dr. Kohrs. M.M.L. repeatedly expressed two concerns about her father's behavior to Dr. Kohrs, which Dr. Kohrs believed were based on M.M.L.'s observations and not on any "predictions" given to M.M.L. as a child by her mother. First, M.M.L. described "a pattern of arbitrary and provocative hostility" by her father, such as verbally abusing and continually provoking arguments with his mother to whom M.M.L. is attached, making exaggerated and hostile complaints in public places, teasing her cousins unnecessarily, and having conflicts with her aunts and foster mother. Michael's mother and his sisters (the aunts) deny these allegations. M.M.L. does not trust him and is afraid he will sexually abuse her because he gets so " 'pushy and mad.' " . . . M.M.L. was [also] concerned with her father's use of alcohol. Although he acknowledges occasional use of alcohol, he denies any problem, and various psychological tests and counseling bear that out. M.M.L.'s emotional and psychological concerns about sexual abuse and excessive use of alcohol appear to be a result of her early childhood experiences with her stepfather and one or more of her mother's other male companions.

M.M.L. seems to have established a good relationship with her paternal grandmother and her aunts, all of whom reside near Michael in the Kansas City area. The grandmother lives next door to Michael, and she and Michael's sisters are supportive of his efforts to obtain custody of M.M.L. They are also available to assist Michael in caring for M.M.L. Dr. Kohrs believed M.M.L. tried to focus on the positive aspects of the relationship, and M.M.L. likes it when Michael is nice to her and takes her bowling. She feels good about herself when she cooks meals for him and has appreciated getting to know her relatives in the Kansas City area. However, based on M.M.L.'s concerns, Dr. Kohrs recommended that M.M.L. remain in the foster home in Great Bend and continue visitation with her father and relatives in Kansas City. She was concerned "that if the situation is this problematic while being monitored by SRS and the Court, what the quality of home life would be if there were no scrutiny by the Court."

In contrast, M.M.L. was firmly attached to the foster care home, describing it as a place where she was safe, secure, and part of a family. At an earlier hearing, a counselor testified M.M.L. would suffer grief, loss, and confusion about her identity if she had to move away from the foster home and that moving her would add to the confusion and chaos in her life. Also, at this hearing, Dr. Kohrs testified the optimum placement was in the foster home because the children were involved in school and community activities and the relationship was not filled with conflict like the one with Michael.

On the other hand, professionals in the Kansas City area who have counseled with Michael over the years of these proceedings and with both Michael and M.M.L. on the occasions when she visits in Kansas City reach a diametrically opposite conclusion. They recommend that M.M.L. be placed in her father's custody. From their reports and the testimony of Michael, M.M.L. seems to be happy and well adjusted when with her father. She voiced no serious complaints to the Kansas City counselors and professionals. However, upon returning to Great Bend she apparently tells a totally different story and has consistently maintained she will not live with her father. The record includes several letters written by M.M.L. to the court in which she voices her desire to stay with her foster parents and complains bitterly about her father's actions and appearance.

* * * Michael moved for an order placing M.M.L. in his custody. He alleged that despite his compliance with all court orders, SRS had refused to prepare a reintegration plan with measurable objectives and time schedules and the only reason articulated for not placing M.M.L. with him was her desire not to live with him.... At a dispositional hearing on August 15, 1994, the district court concluded ... that although Michael was not an unfit parent, no close bond existed between Michael and M.M.L. despite his tremendous efforts. While reasonable efforts had been made to reintegrate M.M.L., the efforts had not been successful largely due to M.M.L.'s attitude and fears. The court believed forcing M.M.L. to live with her father could cause more emotional damage. Because a close bond existed between M.M.L. and her foster family, the court continued placement in long-term foster care with visitation to be worked out by the parties. At the August 15, 1994, hearing the court ... [heard] conflicting testimony of the various therapists, counselors, psychologists, and other professionals ... [and] made the following findings.

1. That the natural father is not an unfit parent.

2. That the Court recognizes that a parent has a fundamental right to have custody of his or her child. * * *

5. That the Court finds that reasonable efforts have been made to reintegrate the child into the home of the natural father.

6. That said efforts have not been successful due mainly to the attitude of the minor child.

7. That a close daughter-father bond does not exist despite the efforts of the father to re-establish that bond.

8. That placement of the child with the natural father could cause more emotional damage to the minor child.

9. That a close bond between the foster family and the child exists.

10. That placement therefore should continue in long term foster care with continuing visitation as agreed to by the parties between the father and the minor child."

There have been literally dozens of hearings held by the court and hundreds of hours devoted to this case by dedicated judges, counsel, and professional workers in an attempt to arrive at an acceptable solution to the apparent legal and emotional conflict between Michael and M.M.L. and/or SRS. While the legal principles, applicable statutes, and constitutional arguments are not extremely difficult to resolve, it is doubtful any good solution to the dilemma facing the trial court and this court exists.

* * *

Michael argues [that] K.S.A. § 38–1563(d), either on its face or as applied, violates his "fundamental right protected by the 14th Amendment." * * * K.S.A. § 38–1563 provides [that]

> (d) If the court finds that placing the child in the custody of a parent will not assure protection from physical, mental or emotional abuse or neglect or sexual abuse or will not be in the best interests of the child, the court shall enter an order awarding custody of the child, until the further order of the court, to one of the following:
>
> (1) A relative of the child or a person with whom the child has close emotional ties;
>
> (2) any other suitable person;
>
> (3) a shelter facility; or
>
> (4) the secretary."

* * * In the instant case all parties concede that Michael is not unfit to have the care and custody of M.M.L. It is also apparent that he has gone to great lengths to improve his parenting capabilities and educate himself in the skills necessary to raise his daughter. He has adequate physical and residential facilities for her care and also has the support of his sisters and mother, who are available to furnish family support....

Michael contends that K.S.A. § 38–1563(d) is either unconstitutional on its face or unconstitutional as applied to the facts of this case because the best interests of the child test, contained in the statute, violates his right to due process under the Fourteenth Amendment to the United States Constitution. He asserts that the parental preference rule is the proper test and that failure to apply it denies his fundamental right to custody of M.M.L.

* * * The United States Supreme Court [has] ... recognized the fundamental nature of the relationship between parent and child ... The State argues at length that Michael's fundamental constitutional rights must give way to the best interests of the child test set forth in the statute because actions under the Code are deemed to be taken and done under the parens patriae doctrine or parental power of the State. It also argues that because M.M.L. was found to be a child in need of care by clear and convincing evidence, Michael's due process rights were adequately protected.... A review of the numerous Kansas and United States Supreme Court cases involving the powers of the State under the

parens patriae doctrine clearly indicates that the courts must assert a balancing test between the fundamental constitutional right of parents to the care, custody, and control of their children and the power of the State to ensure the protection and welfare of children. In balancing the interests of all parties, the best interests of the child is a factor to be considered and must be given appropriate weight. However, absent a showing that the parent is unfit or that there are highly unusual or extraordinary circumstances mandating the State's exercise of its parens patriae powers, the rights of the parent must prevail.

* * * We therefore construe the best interests of the child language contained in K.S.A. § 38–1563(d) to be constitutional when applied in a child in need of care case in which the court has found by clear and convincing evidence that the parent or parents are unfit or that highly unusual or extraordinary circumstances exist which substantially endanger the child's welfare. Absent such findings the long-standing parental preference doctrine controls.

Here ... the primary basis of the trial court's holding was that M.M.L. does not want to leave her friends and comfortable foster home surroundings in Great Bend, coupled with her professed dislike of her father. Such feelings are not unusual in children who have become attached to, and feel comfortable with, their peers, school, and other surroundings. Such feelings and wishes do not, in our opinion, constitute the highly unusual or extraordinary circumstances necessary to deprive a parent, who is not unfit and who is capable and desirous of providing the necessary care, control, and guidance of his or her child, of the custody of the child. We conclude that under the facts of this case, K.S.A. § 38–1563(d), as applied, violated Michael's constitutional rights.... The welfare of M.M.L. and the best interests of the State mandate that Michael be given the opportunity to assume his parental duties and obligations. We recognize that M.M.L. will need continued counseling and Michael must make such provisions for further counseling with qualified personnel in the Kansas City area as may be directed by the trial court.

In conclusion, we hold that the best interests of the child test contained in K.S.A. § 38–1563(d) is constitutional when the court has determined by clear and convincing evidence that the parent is unfit or that highly unusual or extraordinary circumstances exist which substantially endanger the child's welfare. Absent such evidence and findings, the statute is unconstitutional, and the rights of the parent or parents under the parental preference doctrine are paramount and control over the parental power of the State. We further order that the custody of M.M.L. be placed with her father, Michael, subject to appropriate continued counseling in the father's residential area and under such conditions of reporting and monitoring as may be directed by the court.* * *

IN THE MATTER OF THE GUARDIANSHIP OF J.C., J.C., and J.M.C., MINORS

Supreme Court of New Jersey, 1992.
129 N.J. 1, 608 A.2d 1312.

HANDLER, J.

* * * The Court in this case ... is required to determine whether the parental rights of a natural mother should be terminated based on the need to protect children from potential harm that may result from being separated from foster parents with whom the children may have formed parental bonds. * * *

A.C., who was born in Colombia and came to this country as a teenager, is the natural mother of three children. Two girls, J.C. and J.M.C., were born in July 1983 and in January 1985, respectively, and J.C., a boy, was born in August 1986. A.C. voluntarily placed her two girls in foster care with the Division of Youth and Family Services (DYFS, Division, or agency) in August 1985. The children were returned to her after three months. Almost a year later, in October 1986, A.C. again placed the two girls, along with her new child, J.C., in foster care, where they have remained for the past five and a half years. A.C. began unsupervised weekend visits with her children soon after their placement in foster care, seeing them regularly twice a month during the following year. Although DYFS had intended to reunite the family, in November 1987 the agency stopped unsupervised visits out of concern that the children were not being properly cared for. DYFS also came to believe that A.C. was addicted to drugs and was being abused by her husband (who, she claims, was not the father of any of the children). However, bi-monthly visits at the DYFS office continued. In April of the following year, A.C. entered drug treatment. By November 1988 the agency concluded that the children could not be returned successfully and that preparation should be initiated for their permanent placement and adoption. The agency transferred the case to its Adoption Resources Center (A.R.C.), which subsequently terminated visitation.

DYFS filed a petition for guardianship over the three children on July 7, 1989. It sought the termination of A.C.'s parental rights on the grounds that A.C. was unable and unwilling to stop causing the children harm and that to delay permanent placement would add to the harm facing the children.

At the time that DYFS moved for guardianship, the oldest child, J.C., had lived with at least two foster families. She was moved to her current pre-adoptive parents a week later, on July 13, 1989. J.M.C. had been living with her current foster parents since October or November 1988. A.C. has since consented to the adoption of her youngest child, J.C., and his status is not an issue in the case.

The case was initially tried on November 9, 1989, and December 15, 1989. Following a remand and additional hearings held in March 1991, the trial court concluded that termination of A.C.'s parental rights was necessary in the best interests of the children. It determined that A.C. had not, as a matter of law, abandoned her children even though she had placed them in foster care and had failed to achieve the requisite fitness to secure their return. However, it did find that the children would suffer serious psychological harm if they were removed from their foster or pre-adoptive homes and returned to A.C., and that the harm in part was attributable to A.C.'s own inability to plan for their future and her failure to rehabilitate herself. The Appellate Division affirmed.

* * *

The Court in *New Jersey Division of Youth and Family Services v. A. W.*, 103 N.J. 591, 512 A.2d 438 (1986) . . . set out four specific findings that a trial court should make before it terminates parental rights. The first finding is that the child's health and development have been or will be seriously impaired by the parental relationship. . . . Secondly, the court must conclude that the parents are unable or unwilling to eliminate the harm and that a delay in permanent placement will add to the harm. . . . Third, the court should be convinced that alternatives to terminating parental rights have been thoroughly explored and exhausted, including sufficient efforts made to help the parents cure the problems that led to the placement. . . . Fourth, all of those considerations must inform the determination that termination of parental rights will not do more harm than good. [In 1991, the Legislature codified the *A.W.* requirements.]

* * *

Termination of parental rights permanently cuts off the relationship between children and their biological parents. * * * The burden falls on the State to demonstrate by clear and convincing evidence that the natural parent has not cured the initial cause of harm and will continue to cause serious and lasting harm to the child. * * *

In this case both parties presented evidence relating generally to the harm that would befall the children if they were removed from the custody and care of foster parents and returned to their natural parent. DYFS also presented evidence that addressed the conduct of A.C. as indicative of her own responsibility for having caused the harm to the children and her parental fitness as a factor in determining whether that harm could be remediated if the children were returned to her custody.

The evidence strongly indicated that A.C. showed an interest in her children while they were in foster care, visiting them regularly and frequently. DYFS recognized that interest but stopped short of returning the children to A.C. on several occasions due to concerns about her housing situation and drug and alcohol addiction. Toward the end of 1987, after the two girls had been in foster care for more than a year, DYFS made plans to return the children, one by one, to A.C. Those plans were cancelled after reports of domestic violence in A.C.'s home, as well as renewed concerns over her continuing drug and alcohol abuse.

* * * Based on the trial testimony and the subsequent report the trial court on May 22, 1990, ordered that parental rights be terminated and guardianship transferred to DYFS. * * * The Appellate Division remanded [and] ... [o]n remand, beginning in March 1991, the court heard six days of ... testimony from Ms. Johnson as well as from other experts. First, the parties stipulated to several facts about A.C.'s rehabilitation. With respect to her housing situation, they agreed that she was living in the same apartment in which she had been living since December 1989. Concerning her work, they agreed that she had a steady job, that she had been working there for the previous two years, and that there was on-site after school child care at her workplace. Finally the parties "stipulated" that A.C. asserted that she was drug and alcohol free and that DYFS had no evidence to suggest otherwise.

In addition to the testimony of Ms. Johnson, the court-appointed counselor, DYFS produced its own expert, Dr. Martha Page. Dr. Page testified only with respect to J.C., with whom she had a counseling relationship. Dr. Page stated that when she met with J.C. in November 1990, she "was having a great deal of difficulty in school" and "[h]er behavior was very uneven" and "she was extremely hard to handle." She described J.C. as an "emotionally disturbed child" with special needs and a low resiliency to change, one who "needs stability ... [and] a sense of identity." According to Dr. Page, separating J.C. from her foster parents would "reinforce her notion that she's somehow failed again." She mentioned J.C.'s fear of being rejected and emphasized her need for consistent care and permanency in planning for placement. Dr. Page also believed that if the child were returned to A.C. and the placement did not work out, the result would be particularly damaging to the emotional health of the child. She also concluded that any visitation with A.C. and delay in J.C.'s permanent placement would be "disastrous" and result in "transplant shock."

Dr. Matthew Johnson testified on behalf of A.C. He found a strong and enduring bonded relationship between J.C. and A.C. He believed "erasing" the biological mother from the child's life would cause the child serious emotional harm, particularly regarding the child's identity and development in adolescence. Thus, although he recognized potential danger in moving J.C. out of her current foster home, he also felt that terminating her relationship with her natural mother could also cause serious long-term harm. Dr. Johnson expressed concerns about A.C.'s ability to care for the children, mentioning among other things that she might have "residual emotional difficulty" in caring for the children and that she appeared to lack social networks necessary to support her in times of crisis. On the other hand, he noted that she had a number of strengths, that she was intelligent, had largely cleaned up her life, and had maintained contact with the children. Nevertheless, when asked on direct examination whether he believed A.C. could "assume custodial care of [J.C.]," Dr. Johnson again said that "to be frank there are concerns," and emphasized that "this child [J.C.] had emotional disturbance."

There was much less focus during the second trial on the younger child, J.M.C. Dr. Johnson found that she had significant relationships with both her foster mother and her natural mother. However, he was not able to say conclusively that there was bonding in either case.... Dr. Johnson made no recommendation on who should have final custody over the two children, but suggested continued visitation and, at least at that time, the preservation of parental rights in A.C.

* * * The trial court found that the children had bonded to their foster parents, and that this bonding had been caused by or exacerbated by A.C.'s conduct.... It based its decision to terminate parental rights on the substantial psychological harm to J.M.C. that would result from severing her relationship with her pre-adoptive mother. * * *

Without disparaging the reasoning and determinations made by the courts below, we are compelled by the record as it currently stands to conclude that there is not clear and convincing evidence to support the findings necessary to terminate parental rights. Although a significant amount of testimony has been taken in this case, much of the evidence was either flawed or insufficient to answer the central question of serious psychological harm. * * *

In cases in which DYFS seeks termination of parental rights, not on grounds of current unfitness but because of potential harm to the child based on separation from a foster parent with whom the child has bonded, the quality of the proof adduced must be consistent with the interests at stake. To the extent that the quality of the child's relationship with foster parents may be relevant to termination of the natural parents' status, that relationship must be viewed not in isolation but in a broader context that includes as well the quality of the child's relationship with his or her natural parents.... [P]rolonged inattention by natural parents that permits the development of disproportionately stronger ties between a child and foster parents may lead to a bonding relationship the severing of which would cause profound harm—a harm attributable to the natural parents.... To show that the child has a strong relationship with the foster parents or might be better off if left in their custody is not enough. DYFS must prove by clear and convincing evidence that separating the child from his or her foster parents would cause serious and enduring emotional or psychological harm. *Santosky v. Kramer*, 455 U.S. at 768. * * * Such proof should include the testimony of a well qualified expert who has had full opportunity to make a comprehensive, objective, and informed evaluation of the child's relationship with the foster parent. In hearing a petition for termination in which the fitness of natural parents is neither relied on nor disputed by the agency, the trial court must also consider parallel proof relating to the child's relationship with his or her natural parents in assessing the existence, nature, and extent of the harm facing the child.

As the contrasting opinions of the experts in this case illustrate, there are competing psychological theories of the effects of parental bonding. In large measure, the variances in their recommendations derive from different assumptions concerning the fragility versus resiliency of the child psyche. *Compare* JOSEPH GOLDSTEIN, ANNA FREUD, & ALBERT SOLNIT, BEYOND THE BEST INTERESTS OF THE CHILD (1973) *with* Everett Waters & Donna Noyes, *Psychological Parenting vs. Attachment Theory: The Child's Best Interests and the Risks of Doing the Right Things for the Wrong Reasons*, 12 N.Y.U.REV.L. & SOC. CHANGE 505, 513 (1983–84). Those who, like Dr. Page, urge the wider use of psychological parenting theory see children as highly vulnerable and fragile. Their psyches are easily injured by traumatic events and those injuries can adversely shape their subsequent development. *See* GOLDSTEIN, FREUD & SOLNIT, *supra*, at 33. In contrast, others, presumably like Dr. Johnson, posit more flexibility in children, arguing that attachments "support[ ] the development of independence." Waters & Noyes, *supra*, at 509–10. Change under the right circumstances can play a positive role in children's development. Indeed, a good deal of recent literature on the subject argues that psychological parenting theory overestimates the importance of continuity in care in relation to other factors that affect child development, such as the quality of care children receive. In addition, experts and commentators differ over the importance of ongoing relationships between children and their natural parents. Although natural parents can be a disruptive influence for children who have been adopted, some commentators and psychologists believe that trying to eliminate the natural parents from the children's lives and memory is impossible, and therefore wrong. * * * Scholars and some courts suggest that theories of parental bonding may be relied on too often to keep children in foster care rather than return them to their parents. Parents with few resources rely on foster care to protect their children during difficult periods, including but not limited to experiences of homelessness and domestic violence. A single-minded focus on continuity in care can result in parents who rely temporarily on foster care for needed assistance, finding it impossible to regain custody over their children. Parents, particularly those with limited incomes and unstable housing and work experiences, should be able to turn to the foster-care system without fear of losing their children.... Further, ... [t]ermination of parental rights does not always result in permanent placement of the child. Much of the literature on foster children makes clear that too many children "freed up" for adoption do not in the end find permanent homes.

* * * The tangles and snares that surround bonding theory are evident in this case. Important testimony was presented by DYFS employees and valuable information by the guardian.... The primary support for the trial court's decision came from Ms. Regina Johnson, whose report was initially requested by the trial court. Aside from the expert offered by A.C., Johnson was the only expert who testified to the children's relationships with their foster parents. However, her testimony revealed that she had little or no formal training in conducting bonding evaluations or comprehensive knowledge of the relevant scientific literature. Nor did she have an opportunity to evaluate A.C. or her relationship with the children. Her conclusion that bonding had occurred

and that harm would result if those bonds were severed lacked the support and cogency that should surround an expert's opinion in this kind of case.

A.C.'s expert, Dr. Johnson was qualified ... [but] we are unable to say here that Dr. Johnson's conclusion that there was a strong relationship between the children and their adoptive parents demonstrated that serious harm would ensue if the children were returned to their mother. That is particularly so in light of the expert's own inability to reach a firm conclusion with respect to custody.

* * *

Consequently, we remand to the trial court in order that additional evidence may be adduced directly addressing whether the two children have bonded with their foster parents and if so whether breaking such bonds would cause the children serious psychological or emotional harm. To determine these questions the trial court should conduct hearings and direct any of the witnesses to undertake any necessary investigations and examinations.... [W]e recognize that A.C.'s parental rights may ultimately be terminated even though her contact with the children, in contrast to her custody over them, exposes them to no harm. The risk to children stemming from the deprivation of the custody of their natural parent is one that inheres in the termination of parental rights and is based on the paramount need the children have for permanent and defined parent-child relationships.... In this case there is expert testimony indicating a significant relationship between A.C. and J.C. and a potential for harm to J.C. if contact does not continue. This evidence raises the question of whether the welfare of children under certain circumstances reasonably requires continued contact with natural parents subsequent to guardianship being granted to DYFS or an adoption. We note that this question may arise at some future time but do not address it here.

* * *

CLIFFORD, J., concurring in judgment.

* * * In addressing the intricate and painful issue before us, one can be forgiven for seeing ghosts; but I have a nagging concern that absent strict enforcement of the Child Placement Review Act, DYFS can unilaterally abandon plans for reunifying biological families in favor of pre-adoptive placement. Once that decision is implemented and the child is placed in the pre-adoptive home, bonding with that family begins. Until that time, bonding with the foster family, although ultimately relevant in the trial court's termination proceeding under N.J.S.A. § 30:4C–20, is an inevitable side effect of a temporary plan whose purpose is to promote stability in the relationship between biological parent and child. * * *

[T]he dearth of adequate and safe rehabilitation residences and the premium placed on stability in a child's home life force troubled parents to confront a harrowing choice between two alternatives, each of which equally damages the child and therefore compromises parental rights. A.C. could have chosen to forego seeking invaluable professional help in order to continue to live and bond with J.M.C., although she might thereby have risked exposing the child to an unrehabilitated lifestyle; or she could have attempted to avail herself of one of the scarce spots in a State rehabilitation facility, thereby assuming the very real risk that bonding during her rehabilitation would thwart reunification with her offspring. Notwithstanding its conclusion that A.C.'s temporary placement of J.M.C. with DYFS had averted damage to that child, the trial court terminated her parental rights to J.M.C. based solely on the bonding that had occurred during the pendency of that placement. A more graphic illustration of the parent's Catch–22 bind is difficult to imagine.

* * * Neither fundamental notions of justice nor the Constitution permits termination based solely on the psychological bonding that takes place while the mother complies with the visitation provisions of a plan that purportedly has been designed—by DYFS—to foster eventual reunification.... I would disallow termination of A.C.'s parental rights in respect of both J.C. and J.M.C. if the trial court concludes on remand that DYFS has not produced clear and convincing evidence of full compliance with the Child Placement Review Act. * * *

Notes and Questions

1. In *J.C.*, dissenting Judge Clifford notes his "nagging concern" that, once the agency has decided to proceed with termination and placed the child in a pre-adoptive home, "bonding with that family begins. Until that time, bonding with the foster family, although ultimately relevant in the trial court's termination proceeding under N.J.S.A. § 30:4C–20, is an inevitable side effect of a temporary plan whose purpose is to promote stability in the relationship between biological parent and child." Do the facts of *J.C.* support Judge Clifford's concern? If so, how (if at all) should the court take account of it?

2. How would the Kansas Supreme Court have decided *J.C.*? How would the New Jersey Supreme Court have decided *M.M.L.*? How would each court have decided the case of Gregory Kingsley? What are the pros and cons of each approach: from the child's perspective? the agency's? the parent's?

3. Is the holding in *J.C.* constitutional? What arguments would you expect from each side?

4. The Supreme Court has not yet ruled on the minimum circumstances that justify termination of parental rights, although it has ruled on a variety of procedural issues. The Court has held that the importance of the interests at stake mandate clear and convincing evidence as a basis for parental rights termination (Santosky v. Kramer, 455 U.S. 745, 102 S.Ct. 1388, 71 L.Ed.2d 599 (1982)), and that the state may not constitutionally condition appeal from a trial court's termination of parental rights order on advance payment of record preparation fees

(M.L.B. v. S.L.J., ___ U.S. ___, 117 S.Ct. 555, 136 L.Ed.2d 473 (1996)). But, in Lassiter v. Department of Social Services, 452 U.S. 18, 101 S.Ct. 2153, 68 L.Ed.2d 640 (1981) the Court held that the Due Process Clause did not require the appointment of counsel for indigent parents in every parental termination case; in Baltimore City Dept. of Social Serv. v. Bouknight, 493 U.S. 549, 110 S.Ct. 900, 107 L.Ed.2d 992 (1990), it held that the Fifth Amendment privilege against self-incrimination did not apply to a Juvenile Court order requiring a mother to produce a child under the supervision of state child welfare authorities.

5. The *J.C.* court notes the possibility of maintaining the child's relationship with her biological parent after termination of parental rights. Another state supreme court refused to terminate the biological parents' rights based on the child's bonds with her foster parents, with whom she had lived for all but six months of her life, holding that "[r]eunification will be difficult, at best, for all involved, and provisions must be made to ease the transition for everyone concerned. The foster family has earned a special place in Kristina's life, and its role cannot be forgotten. It should continue to be a part of the child's life." In re Kristina L., 520 A.2d 574 (R.I.1987). What are the advantages and disadvantages of the approaches in *M.M.L., Kristina L.*, and *J.C.*?

Problem 9–6: Termination of Parental Rights Legislation

Responding to the problem of long-term, "revolving door" foster care like that evident in the case of Gregory Kingsley, the state legislature is considering adoption of legislation that would alter the standards for and legal effect of parental rights termination. The new legislation would sever custody from visitation rights. If the legislation is enacted, a court could terminate the parent's right to regain custody based on a showing that the child has been in the care of the Department for at least two years, and cannot currently be returned to her parent(s)' care due to the continuance of conditions that led to placement.

A parent whose custody rights had been severed under the legislation would continue to be able to visit his or her child, with visitation frequency and restrictions to be determined on the basis of the "best interests of the child" standard utilized in divorce visitation cases. The parent would not, however, be able to regain the child's custody. Severance of custody rights thus would preserve visitation rights with the child's biological family, but free the child for adoption by another family.

The current termination standard requires a showing that "1) the parent has abandoned the child for a period of one year or more;" or "2) the parent has engaged in conduct which seriously endangers the welfare of the child and has substantially and continuously or repeatedly failed to maintain contact with or plan for the future of the child, although physically and financially able to do so; and the Dept. [of Child Welfare] has made diligent efforts to encourage and strengthen the parental relationship." Like the vast majority of other state termination statutes, it authorizes total severance of parental rights, but does not clearly permit severance of custody rights alone.

Sponsors of the legislation argue that it is necessary to "move children out of foster care at the point when they are still adoptable and can enjoy a normal childhood. We need to focus on the child's needs, rather than the parent's rights. Under the legislation the child's needs can be met whether or not overburdened child welfare workers are able to document a history of services to her parents." The sponsors also argue that the legislation meets constitutional standards, as it "preserves the child's relationship with her parent, as in a divorce proceeding, and thus is subject a different level of review."

You have been asked to determine whether: 1) the sponsors are correct that the proposed legislation would meet constitutional standards; 2) it would, in fact, serve children's interests; and 3) it would negatively affect the administration of child welfare services. You have also been asked to determine whether passage of the legislation is, on balance, a good idea and what alternatives to the proposal are available. As you answer these questions, you have also been told to keep these facts in mind:

A. As many as 40% of children who are released from foster care to their parent's custody simply wind up in foster care again. *See, e.g.,* TRUDY FESTINGER, RETURNING TO CARE: DISCHARGE AND REENTRY IN FOSTER CARE 1–2 (1994) (surveying reports).

B. The state's foster care case load has been rising (as it has nationwide). By one estimate, the U.S. foster care population increased 53% between 1987 and 1992. Judith K. McKenzie, *Adoption of Children with Special Needs*, 3 THE FUTURE OF CHILDREN: ADOPTION 63 (Spring 1993).

C. Foster care costs thousands of dollars of year per child, while adoption costs the state nothing; even subsidized adoption is much less costly than foster care. *See, e.g.,* N.Y.C. MAYOR'S COMM. FOR THE FOSTER CARE OF CHILDREN, CHILD WELFARE AT A CROSSROADS 65 (1993) (estimating one year savings to New York City of $18 million from approximately 2400 foster child adoptions).

D. There is a growing "backlog" of older foster children waiting for adoptive placements. *See* Martin Guggenheim, *The Effects of Recent Trends to Accelerate the Termination of Parental Rights of Children in Foster Care—An Empirical Analysis in Two States,* 29 FAM. L.Q. 121, 127, 130 (1995) (reporting that, between 1986 and 1992, number of children free for adoption increased 73% in Michigan and 86% in New York). Many of these children are members of minority groups and have special needs. *See* Kathy S. Stolley, *Statistics on Adoption in the United States*, 3 THE FUTURE OF CHILDREN: ADOPTION 26, 34 (Spring 1993) (median age of children awaiting adoptive placement was 8.3 years, 39.1% were black, 63.5% had one or more special needs, and almost 55% had been waiting two or more years to be placed for adoption).

Now that you are familiar with some of the constitutional doctrine relating to the rights of parents and children, as well as the context in which cases like *Kingsley* are played out, reconsider Foster and Freed's Bill of Rights for Children [p. 413]. Would you recommend legislative enactment of any of its provisions? Why or why not?

Chapter 10

THE LAWYER'S ROLE IN FAMILY DISPUTES

Divorce is the most difficult experience a person goes through alive. I often think that neurosurgeons have it easier because their patients are anesthetized. I have to keep clients not only conscious, but functioning.

Ira Lurvey, Attorney, quoted in *Emily Couric, The Divorce Lawyers* 39, 291 (1992)

SECTION 1. FAMILY LAW AS A SPECIALTY

Over the past thirty years, family law cases have become both more numerous and more complex. As a result, family law is now a recognized legal specialty encompassing adoption, custody, divorce, paternity, support, and visitation matters. The family law specialist engages in a wide range of "lawyering" activities, including counseling, drafting agreements (premarital, cohabitation or separation), negotiating, and litigating. This chapter examines the tasks that family lawyers perform, common criticisms of family lawyer behavior, the ethical rules governing lawyer conduct, and malpractice issues.

Family law litigants differ from litigants in other areas of law in that plaintiff and defendant have often had an intimate relationship; in a divorce action, for example, they will have lived and slept together, sometimes for a long time. Because they involve important personal relationships, family disputes are also emotionally charged and highly stressful.

The family lawyer will often meet the client at one of the worst times in the client's life, and will need to request personal, possibly embarrassing, information. In such a delicate situation, the family lawyer must combine the skills of a technician, a negotiator, and a counselor. Family lawyers typically have adequate legal training, but often lack adequate training in counseling and communication. Misunderstandings can arise when the lawyer wants to get the facts necessary to develop a case strategy, while the client simply wants to tell his or her story. Many criticisms of the legal profession (and most grievance complaints) result from poor lawyer-client communication or office management rather than incompetence.

The lawyer can best serve the client if he or she understands that divorce—for perhaps the majority of family law practitioners, their largest case category—and other family disputes involve social, moral, emotional, and economic issues as well as a legal claim. To help clients resolve these nonlegal issues, some lawyers recommend that prospective clients see a counselor before the first legal interview or during the divorce process. Geoffrey Hamilton and Thomas S. Merrill have developed these charts describing the stages of divorce in "*Why Is My Client Nuts? An Inquiry into the Psychodynamics of Divorce,*" in ABA Section of Family Law Compendium C–1 (1993):

DECISION	DIVORCE DECISION COMMUNICATED; CONFRONTATION, UPHEAVAL; SEPARATION (PHYSICAL, EMOTIONAL OR BOTH)		
	"Honeymoon" Relief/Euphoria Anger Depression Low self-esteem	Someone starts litigation ?	Denial/Disbelief/ Shock (typically the husband who says "I had no idea!!") Violence? Grief/Guilt/Failure Depression Low self-esteem
TRANSITION	Extreme Anger Love (or lust) affair Severe disorganization Mourning Relief of repressed anger Ambivalence (moves) into nostalgia) Sadness	Honeymoon settlement? or Escalation; Inflammatory behavior Anger, leads to abuse of legal process Litigation ?	Extreme anger Love (or lust) affair Severe disorganization Mourning Release of repressed anger Ambivalence Sadness "Rewrite" marital history Resignation
HEALING	Let go of past	Settlement more likely here – the longer it goes Not the end; possible chronic litigator.	Transition to new life; often recognition that divorce in hindsight was for the best.

See also Thomas H. Holmes & Richard H. Rakke, *The Social Readjustment Rating Scale*, 11 J. Psychosomatic Res. 213 (1967) (divorce second most stressful life event among 42 ranked events); Sheila Kessler, The American Way of Divorce: Prescription for Change (1975) (describing stages as disillusionment or disenchantment; erosion or disengagement;

disinterest or detachment; physical separation; mourning; second adolescence; hard work and resolution); JOHN HAYNES, DIVORCE MEDIATION: A PRACTICAL GUIDE FOR THERAPISTS AND COUNSELORS (1981) (describing stages as deliberation, litigation, transition, and redirection).

At the initial interview, the lawyer must determine the nature of the problem that has led the client to seek legal assistance. Some clients consult an attorney simply to obtain information; some present problems that have not "matured" into a legal claim; some present problems that the law cannot resolve. If the client needs legal assistance, the lawyer must also decide whether he or she is qualified to handle the case and wants to take it on.

Clients sometimes decide to divorce without significant deliberation or after a recent argument with a spouse. In such an instance it is normally desirable to encourage marriage counseling, or even to wait a short period, to be sure that the client has reached a final decision to initiate a divorce.

The lawyer should also obtain basic case information. Because that information will often be personal and embarrassing, the lawyer should carefully explain the confidential nature of the lawyer/client relationship. The client should not feel ignored, hurried, or subjected to "assembly-line" case processing. *See* James R. Elkins, *A Counseling Model for Lawyering in Divorce Cases*, 53 NOTRE DAME L. REV. 229 (1977); Ira C. Ellman, *Lawyers and Clients*, 34 UCLA L. REV. 717 (1987).

Finally, the lawyer should give the client information on the law and procedure applicable to the case. A lawyer and a client may have different conceptions of the lawyer's role:

> [Clients] expect the legal process to take their problems seriously, and they usually seek vindication of the positions that they have adopted. They expect the legal process to follow its own rules, to proceed in an orderly manner, and to be fair and error-free.... [M]ost litigants begin with a fairly strong belief in 'formal justice.' By the time a problem has become serious enough to warrant bringing it to a lawyer and mobilizing the legal process," the grievant wants vindication, protection of his or her rights, an advocate to help in the battle or a third party who will uncover the "truth" and declare the other party wrong. Observations suggest that courts rarely provide this ... but inexperienced plaintiffs do not know this.
>
> Lawyers believe that part of their job is to bring these expectations and images of law and legal justice closer to the "reality" that they experience daily by constructing new meanings and new understandings. The legal process provides an arena where compromises are explored, settlements are reached, and, if money is at issue, assets are divided. Because lawyers' experience is so much more extensive than that of clients, lawyers attempt to "teach" their clients about the requirements of the legal process and to socialize them into the role of the client. As a result, some of the client's

problems and needs will be translated into legal categories and many more will have legal labels attached to them. Yet, in the end, the fit between the legal categories through which lawyers see the world of divorce and the social and personal meanings that divorce holds for most clients is rarely very good.

AUSTIN SARAT & WILLIAM L.R. FELSTINER, DIVORCE LAWYERS AND THEIR CLIENTS: POWER AND MEANING IN THE LEGAL PROCESS (1995).

As clients typically do not remember all that they hear, the lawyer should provide a handout that repeats the essentials, including office procedures and hours, fee arrangements, phone call procedure, and "homework" such as property questionnaires or forms to fill out. A reading list is also useful. Information provided by the lawyer will enable the client to evaluate the lawyer's personal and litigation style; if, for example, the client wants a "hired gun," then a lawyer who believes in cooperative negotiation will not be a good match.

Notes and Questions

1. A lawyer can avoid many difficulties by screening for "problem" clients with unreasonable expectations before accepting a case. Why do clients have unreasonable expectations? What can the lawyer do to establish realistic goals? What are some of the warning signs for a potential problem client? *See* Lynne Z. Gold–Bikin, *Stress Test: Avoiding Troublesome Clients Can Make a Lawyer's Life Easier*, ABA JOURNAL 107 (Oct. 1993).

2. How far can lawyers go in selecting their clients?

> BOSTON, Feb. 26 (UPI) A Massachusetts man [has been] awarded $5,000 in "emotional distress" damages because a feminist lawyer [Judith L. Nathanson] refused to handle his divorce case ... Nathanson has not been available for comment since a ruling late Tuesday by the Massachusetts Commission Against Discrimination, believed to be one of the first of its kind in the nation.
>
> The state agency said the Lawrence, Mass., attorney violated the state's public accommodation law when she refused to take the Beverly man's divorce case in 1991. The MCAD said an attorney holding herself out as open to the public "may not reject a potential client solely on the basis of gender." During earlier hearings, Nathanson argued she specialized in helping women with family and abuse matters ...

SECTION 2. REGULATING THE LAWYER–CLIENT RELATIONSHIP

A. AN INTRODUCTION

Each state has a formal code regulating lawyer conduct. The majority of states (35) have adopted the American Bar Association (ABA) Model Rules of Professional Conduct (Model Rules), approved by the

ABA in 1983. Other states have adopted one or another variation of the ABA Model Code of Professional Responsibility (Model Code), which was first adopted in 1970. The Model Code consists of "Canons" under which are found "Ethical Considerations" and "Disciplinary Rules." The ABA, state, and local bar association ethics committees also issue opinions on ethical questions.

A lawyer's failure to follow applicable rules and ethical considerations can lead to public censure, license suspension, or disbarment. It may also lead to a malpractice claim. *See* Section 4.

Both the Model Rules and the Model Code are slanted toward litigation. Given the desirability of settling family law disputes without a trial, many family lawyers have felt that the Model Code and Model Rules provide inadequate guidance. To fill this gap, in 1992, the American Academy of Matrimonial Lawyers (AAML) published standards (AAML Standards) specifically tailored to family law practice. *See* American Academy of Matrimonial Lawyers, Bounds of Advocacy: American Academy of Matrimonial Lawyers Standards of Conduct (1991). The AAML Standards provide more guidance than either the Model Code or Model Rules, but they are aspirational rather than obligatory; they also apply only to members of the Academy. A few states have supplemented the Model Code or Rules in family law cases. States with specialty certification in family law also typically have additional ethical rules applicable to the specialty and, in 1993, the New York Court of Appeals issued binding rules to supplement the Model Code in divorce actions. *See* 22 N.Y.C.R.R. § 1200.1.

B. AVOIDING CONFLICTS OF INTEREST

1. *Dual Representation*

Many divorcing couples ask one lawyer to represent both husband and wife or to draft an agreement they have already made. Some of these couples feel that they cannot afford, or do not want, to pay for separate legal representation; others feel that they can resolve the dispute amicably and that two lawyers are unnecessary. Is this type of representation permissible?

KLEMM v. SUPERIOR COURT

California Court of Appeals, 1977.
75 Cal.App.3d 893, 142 Cal.Rptr. 509.

Brown, J.

The ultimate issue herein is to what extent one attorney may represent both husband and wife in a noncontested dissolution proceeding where the written consent of each to such representation has been filed with the court. * * *

At the dissolution hearing Attorney Catherine Bailey appeared for the wife. It developed that Bailey is a friend of the husband and wife and because they could not afford an attorney she was acting without compensation. The attorney had consulted with both the husband and wife and had worked out an oral agreement whereby the custody of the minor children would be joint, that is, each would have the children for a period of two weeks out of each month, and the wife waived child support.

The trial judge granted an interlocutory decree and awarded joint custody in accord with the agreement. However, because the wife was receiving aid for dependent children payments from the county, he referred the matter of child support to the Family Support Division of the Fresno County District Attorney's office for investigation and report.

The subsequent report from the family support division recommended that the husband be ordered to pay $25 per month per child (total $50) child support and that this amount be paid to the county as reimbursement for past and present A.F.D.C. payments made and being made to the wife. Bailey, on behalf of the wife, filed a written objection to the recommendation that the husband be required to pay child support.

At the hearing on the report and issue of child support on April 25, 1977, Bailey announced she was appearing on behalf of the husband. She said the parties were "in agreement on this matter, so there is in reality no conflict between them." No written consents to joint representation were filed. On questioning by the court the wife evinced uncertainty as to her position in the litigation. The wife said, "She [Bailey] asked me to come here just as a witness, so I don't feel like I'm taking any action against Dale." The judge pointed out that she (the wife) was still a party. When first asked if she wanted Bailey to continue as her attorney she answered "No." Later she said she would consent to Bailey's being relieved as her counsel. She then said she didn't believe she could act as her own attorney but that she consented to Bailey's representing the husband. After this confusing and conflicting testimony and a request for permission to talk to Bailey about it, the judge ordered, over Bailey's objection, that he would not permit Bailey to appear for either the husband or the wife because of a present conflict of interest and ordered the matter continued for one week.

At the continued hearing on May 2, 1977, Bailey appeared by counsel, who filed written consents to joint representation signed by the husband and wife and requested that Bailey be allowed to appear for the husband and wife (who were present in court). The consents, which were identical in form, stated:

> I have been advised by my attorney that a potential conflict of interest exists by reason of her advising and representing my ex-spouse as well as myself. I feel this conflict is purely technical and I request Catherine Bailey to represent me.

The court denied the motion, and the husband and wife have petitioned this court for a writ of mandate to direct the trial court to permit such representation.

Rule 5–102 of the State Bar Rules of Professional Conduct states:

> (A) A member of the State Bar shall not accept professional employment without first disclosing his relation, if any, with the adverse party, and his interest, if any, in the subject matter of the employment. A member of the State Bar who accepts employment under this rule shall first obtain the client's written consent to such employment.
>
> (B) A member of the State Bar shall not represent conflicting interests, except with the written consent of all parties concerned.

The California cases are generally consistent with rule 5–102 permitting dual representation where there is a full disclosure and informed consent by all the parties, at least insofar as a representation pertains to agreements and negotiations prior to a trial or hearing. Where, however, a fully informed consent is not obtained, the duty of loyalty to different clients renders it impossible for an attorney, consistent with ethics and the fidelity owed to clients, to advise one client as to a disputed claim against the other.

Though an informed consent be obtained, no case we have been able to find sanctions dual representation of conflicting interests if that representation is in conjunction with a trial or hearing where there is an actual, present, existing conflict and the discharge of duty to one client conflicts with the duty to another. As a matter of law a purported consent to dual representation of litigants with adverse interests at a contested hearing would be neither intelligent nor informed. Such representation would be per se inconsistent with the adversary position of an attorney in litigation, and common sense dictates that it would be unthinkable to permit an attorney to assume a position at a trial or hearing where he could not advocate the interests of one client without adversely injuring those of the other.

However, if the conflict is merely potential, there being no existing dispute or contest between the parties represented as to any point in litigation, then with full disclosure to and informed consent of both clients there may be dual representation at a hearing or trial.

In our view the case at bench clearly falls within the latter category. The conflict of interest was strictly potential and not present. The parties had settled their differences by agreement. There was no point of difference to be litigated. The position of each inter se was totally consistent throughout the proceedings. The wife did not want child support from the husband and the husband did not want to pay support for the children. The actual conflict that existed on the issue of support was between the county on the one hand, which argued that support should be ordered, and the husband and wife on the other who consistently maintained the husband should not be ordered to pay support.

While on the face of the matter it may appear foolhardy for the wife to waive child support, other values could very well have been more important to her than such support—such as maintaining a good relationship between the husband and the children and between the husband and herself despite the marital problems—thus avoiding the backbiting, acrimony and ill will which the Family Relations Act of 1970 was, insofar as possible, designed to eliminate. It could well have been if the wife was forced to choose between A.F.D.C. payments to be reimbursed to the county by the husband and no A.F.D.C. payments she would have made the latter choice.

Of course, if the wife at some future date should change her mind and seek child support and if the husband should desire to avoid the payment of such support, Bailey would be disqualified from representing either in a contested hearing on the issue. There would then exist an actual conflict between them, and an attorney's duty to maintain the confidence of each would preclude such representation.

The conclusion we arrive at is particularly congruent with dissolution proceedings under the Family Law Act of 1970, the purpose of which was to discard the concept of fault in dissolution of marriage actions, to minimize the adversary nature of such proceedings and to eliminate conflicts created only to secure a divorce. It is contrary to the philosophy of that act to create controversy between the parties where none exists in reality.

We hold on the facts of this case, wherein the conflict was only potential, that if the written consents were knowing and informed and given after full disclosure by the attorney, the attorney can appear for both of the parties on issues concerning which they fully agree. * * *

A word as to procedure. Initially, the trial court is entitled to accept properly executed written consents to joint representation at their face value. The judge is entitled to presume the attorney is familiar with the law and code of professional ethics and has complied with the proper standards. However, if the judge has any question regarding whether the proper standards have been observed, it is his duty to either require counsel to inquire further or inquire himself regarding the circumstances of the execution of the written consents and the state of mind of the clients for the purpose of making the necessary factual determination in this regard.

Finally, as a caveat, we hasten to sound a note of warning. Attorneys who undertake to represent parties with divergent interests owe the highest duty to each to make a full disclosure of all facts and circumstances which are necessary to enable the parties to make a fully informed decision regarding the subject matter of the litigation, including the areas of potential conflict and the possibility and desirability of seeking independent legal advice. Failing such disclosure, the attorney is civilly liable to the client who suffers loss caused by lack of disclosure. In addition, the lawyer lays himself open to charges, whether well founded or not, of unethical and unprofessional conduct. Moreover, the validity of any agreement negotiated without independent representation of each of the parties is vulnerable to easy attack as having been procured by misrepresentation, fraud and overreaching. It thus behooves counsel to cogitate carefully and proceed cautiously before placing himself/herself in such a position.

Notes and Questions

1. *Klemm* was decided under the Model Code. Is Model Rule 1.7 more precise?

> (a) A lawyer shall not represent a client if the representation of that client will be directly adverse to another client, unless:
>
> (1) The lawyer reasonably believes the representation will not adversely affect the relationship with the other client; and,
>
> (2) Each client consents after consultation.
>
> (b) A lawyer shall not represent a client if the representation of that client may be materially limited by the lawyer's responsibilities to another client or to a third person, or by the lawyer's own interests, unless (1) the lawyer reasonably believes the representation will not be adversely affected; and (2) the client consents after consultation. When representation of multiple clients in a single matter is undertaken, the consultation shall include explanation of the implications of the common representation and the advantages and risks involved.

For an article proposing a reexamination of the conflicts rules, *see* Russell G. Pearce, *Family Values and Legal Ethics: Competing Approaches To Conflicts in Representing Spouses*, 62 FORDHAM L. REV. 1253 (1994).

2. AAML Standard 2.20 provides that "[a]n attorney should not represent both husband and wife even if they do not wish to obtain independent representation." Some state ethics codes provide that a lawyer should never "represent" both parties to a divorce. *See* Utah State Bar Opinion 116 (6/25/92). In states that permit joint representation, the lawyer is required to withdraw if joint representation becomes "objectively unreasonable." *See* Model Rule 2.2(c); Comment 5 to Model Rule 1.7 (lawyer may not seek the client's consent if the common representation is not "objectively reasonable.")

3. Can a lawyer ever be a mere scrivener of a marital agreement? If yes, will the fact of joint representation affect the level or type of review a court will undertake? *See* Vandenburgh v. Vandenburgh, 194 A.D.2d 957, 599 N.Y.S.2d 328 (1993); Blum v. Blum, 59 Md.App. 584, 477 A.2d 289 (1984); Levine v. Levine, 56 N.Y.2d 42, 451 N.Y.S.2d 26, 436 N.E.2d 476 (1982).

4. Under the UPAA [p. 204], could Mrs. Klemm have waived child support in a premarital agreement without independent legal advice? Should the same standards apply to premarital and divorce negotiations?

5. Representation involving a conflict of interest may lead to disciplinary action, fees forfeiture, or a malpractice action. *See* Walden v. Hoke, 189 W.Va. 222, 429 S.E.2d 504 (1993); Stanley v. Richmond, 35

Cal.App.4th 1070, 41 Cal.Rptr.2d 768 (1995). On appropriate facts, the agreement negotiated by the attorney may also be set aside. *See* Liles v. Liles, 289 Ark. 159, 711 S.W.2d 447 (1986).

2. *Prior Representation*

Under what circumstances, if any, may a lawyer represent the spouse of a prior client? Model Rule 1.9 provides that:

> A lawyer who has formerly represented a client in a manner shall not thereafter:
>
> (a) represent another person in the same or a substantially related matter in which that person's interests are materially adverse to the interests of the former client unless the former client consents after consultation; or
>
> (b) use information relative to the representation to the disadvantage of the former client except as Rule 1.6 would permit ...

The basic question is whether the scope of representation is such that information pertinent to the present representation was also pertinent in the prior representation. In one case, a lawyer represented two business partners in a bankruptcy action in which he listed both wives as creditors; he also represented the wives in their divorce actions. In a disciplinary action, the court found that the clients could not give valid consent to such conflict-ridden representation and suspended him for 63 days. In re Hockett, 303 Or. 150, 734 P.2d 877 (1987). *See also* Bjorgen v. Kinsey, 466 N.W.2d 553 (N.D.1991); State ex rel. Oklahoma Bar Assoc. v. Katz, 733 P.2d 406 (Okl.1987). To avoid conflict problems, the lawyer should screen clients carefully. *See* ABA/BNA LAWYERS' MANUAL ON PROFESSIONAL CONDUCT, at 51:207—51:224.

Problem 10–1:

In 1990, Lara Lawyer represented Wanda in a custody, visitation and support action against Harry and drafted her will. In 1996 Harry hired Lara Lawyer to bring a partition action against Wanda. Is Lara's representation of Harry permissible? *See* Lawyer Disciplinary Board v. Printz, 192 W.Va. 404, 452 S.E.2d 720 (1994); Cleland v. Cleland, 35 Conn.Sup. 215, 404 A.2d 905 (1979).

Problem 10–2:

In 1986, Larry Lawyer represented Mary in negotiating a premarital agreement with Tom. In 1996, Tom asked Larry to represent him in a divorce action against Mary. Is the representation permissible? *See* Sargent v. Buckley, 697 A.2d 1272 (Me.1997).

3. *The Unrepresented Litigant*

What is the lawyer's duty to an unrepresented party? Model Rule 4.3 requires the attorney to "make reasonable efforts" to correct any misunderstanding an unrepresented party may have about the role of the opposing party's lawyer; the Comment to this rule also provides that, "[d]uring the course of a lawyer's representation of a client, the lawyer should not give advice to an unrepresented person other than the advice to obtain counsel." DR 7–104(A)(2) essentially repeats this admonition. AAML Standard 2.21 goes farther, recommending that the lawyer inform the opposing party, in writing that:

1. I am your spouse's lawyer.
2. I do not and will not represent you.
3. I will at all times look out for your spouse's interests, not yours.
4. Any statements I make to you about this case should be taken by you as negotiation or argument on behalf of your spouse and not as advice to you as to your best interest.
5. I urge you to obtain your own lawyer.

C. SETTING THE FEE

The cost of a divorce lawyer ranges from less than $100 per hour in smaller towns to over $300 per hour in some large cities; the "average" divorce may cost as much as $2000. Lawyers charge either by the hour or task. Some lawyers charge an up-front retainer fee to offset the initial costs of filing the petition, the initial interview and other expenses. *See* Leonard Loeb, *Hourly Charges in Divorce Cases are Archaic*, 1 AMER. J. FAM. L. 1 (1987). Among lawyers who charge a retainer fee, some deposit the fee in a trust account and utilize it to pay the client's bills; others do not utilize the retainer unless the client fails to pay monthly bills. In some states lawyers may charge a nonrefundable retainer fee to compensate the lawyer for forgoing other cases and establishing a case plan, and/or to prevent the client from "attorney shopping." The nonrefundable retainer was found unethical by the New York Court of Appeals and may no longer be utilized in that state. *In re* Cooperman, 83 N.Y.2d 465, 611 N.Y.S.2d 465, 633 N.E.2d 1069 (1994). *See also* People v. Kardokus, 881 P.2d 1202 (Colo.1994) (a $500 retainer was unreasonable where lawyer did not provide any services); Wright v. Arnold, 877 P.2d 616 (Okl.App.1994) ($4000 "nonrefundable" retainer contract provision was unenforceable and lawyer could recover only the reasonable value of services actually performed).

Many fee disputes arise because the lawyer and client did not have a clear agreement on how the fee would be determined. Neither the Model Rules nor the Model Code mandate a written fee agreement *(see* Model Rule 1.5(b)); the AAML Standards do. Is a written fee agreement desirable? Why?

Notes and Questions

1. Alex retains Larry Lawyer for an "uncontested" divorce. Larry explains that an uncontested divorce will cost $700. After Larry files the action and obtains temporary orders, opposing counsel enters an appearance, moves to set aside the orders, propounds interrogatories, and notices Alex for deposition. Three and a half months later, Larry submits

a bill calculated at a reasonable hourly rate. Alex refuses to pay, fires Larry, and reports him for unethical billing practices. What should Larry have done to avoid this situation? *See* AAML Standard 2.1, 2.2, 2.3.

2. Divorce lawyers have sometimes been criticized for charging excessive fees. *See* John Elson, *Divorce Bar Needs an Added Level of Checks*, NAT. LAW J., June 20, 1994, at A19–20; Ellen Joan Pollock, *Divorce Lawyers Often Shortchange, Overcharge Women Clients, Study Finds,* WALL STREET JOURNAL, March 13, 1992, p. B3. The Model Code set out standards for judging reasonableness of a fee:

> DR 2–106(B) A fee is clearly excessive when, after a review of the facts, a lawyer of ordinary prudence would be left with a definite and firm conviction that the fee is in excess of a reasonable fee. Factors to be considered as guides in determining the reasonableness of a fee include the following:
>
> (1) The time and labor required, the novelty and difficulty of the questions involved, and the skill requisite to perform the legal service properly.
>
> (2) The likelihood, if apparent to the client, that the acceptance of the particular employment will preclude other employment by the lawyer.
>
> (3) The fee customarily charged in the locality for similar legal services.
>
> (4) The amount involved and the results obtained.
>
> (5) The time limitations imposed by the client or by the circumstances.
>
> (6) The nature and length of the professional relationship with the client.
>
> (7) The experience, reputation, and ability of the lawyer or lawyers performing the services.
>
> (8) Whether the fee is fixed or contingent." * * *

What remedies are available to the client if the lawyer overcharges? *See* Okocha v. Fehrenbacher, 101 Ohio App.3d 309, 655 N.E.2d 744 (1995).

3. In response to a 1992 New York City Department of Consumer Affairs study of divorce lawyer conduct (WOMEN IN DIVORCE: LAWYERS, ETHICS, FEES AND FAIRNESS), the New York Court of Appeals imposed statewide rules applicable to divorce actions. The rules related to fees forbid nonrefundable retainer fees, require written explanations of any retainer fee, and mandate itemized bills issued at least every two months. If a lawyer and client cannot resolve a fee disagreement, the client can request binding arbitration by a panel, run by a local bar association, that includes both lawyers and nonlawyers. 22 NYCRR § 1200.12; Jan Hoffman, *New York's Chief Judge Imposes Strict Rules for Divorce Lawyers,* THE NEW YORK TIMES, Aug. 17, 1993, at A1, A9.

4. In 1996, the ABA adopted Model Rules for Fee Arbitration and recommended that all states adopt mandatory, nonbinding fee arbitration. California, New Jersey, and New York now follow this approach. *See* NYCRR §§ 1400.2, 1400.7.

V.W. v. J.B.

Supreme Court, New York County, 1995.
165 Misc.2d 767, 629 N.Y.S.2d 971.

LEWIS R. FRIEDMAN, JUSTICE.

Plaintiff seeks summary judgment on the fifth cause of action, for recision. The application raises serious questions under the Code of Professional Responsibility ("CPR"), not previously addressed in the New York cases, concerning retainer agreements and "bonuses" in matrimonial cases.

In July 1992 plaintiff retained defendant to represent her in a matrimonial matter. The written retainer called for plaintiff to pay a fee determined solely by multiplying the number of hours expended on the case times the hourly rate charged for the service. Negotiations proceeded for over two years until a settlement was reached. Plaintiff's Husband ultimately agreed to pay her more than 20 times his original offer. Plaintiff has stated in her pleadings that defendant's legal work was "fabulous." On August 18, 1994 plaintiff, in New York, executed the separation agreement. The document was shipped by Federal Express to plaintiff's husband who was in California; he executed it on August 19. The parties were divorced by judgment entered August 30, 1994.

Defendant and her former firm were paid about $300,000 based on their time charges. On August 18, allegedly after plaintiff had executed the Separation Agreement, plaintiff and defendant executed the Performance Fee Agreement ("PFA") which is at issue here. In the PFA, plaintiff "in light of the results achieved by [defendant] * * * has graciously and generously agreed to pay a performance fee of $2,000,000" in three installments. Defendant agreed to waive her outstanding bill for $41,000 in fees and expenses. The first installment of the performance fee $1,000,000, was due "upon transfer to [plaintiff] of the equitable distribution payment" in the separation agreement. That part of the fee was paid on August 29, 1994. Plaintiff retained new counsel in early January 1995, refused to pay the second installment, due January 15, and demanded repayment of the $1,000,000 already paid. This action for rescission and restitution followed. Defendant counterclaimed for the balance of her fee.

In the fifth cause of action plaintiff contends that the PFA violated the CPR. There is no doubt that a retainer agreement with counsel is invalid if it violates the CPR. Specifically plaintiff alleges a violation of DR 2–106[C][2] (22 NYCRR § 1200.11[C][2]) which at the relevant time provided that an attorney "shall not enter into an arrangement for, charge or collect: [2] any fee in a domestic relations matter (i) the payment or amount of which is contingent upon the securing of a divorce or upon the amount of maintenance, support, equitable distribution or property settlement * * *."

The rule against contingent fees in domestic relations cases in this state is deep-seated and well established. * * *

When New York adopted the CPR it modified the Model Code of Professional Responsibility promulgated by the American Bar Association to adopt the clear prohibition on contingent fees in domestic relations cases contained in DR 2-106[C][2]. The original ABA Ethical Consideration [EC 2020] as adopted in 1970 by the New York State Bar Association did not contain a flat prohibition on contingent fees in matrimonial cases but noted that "because of the human relationships involved and the unique character of the proceedings contingent fee arrangements in domestic relations cases are rarely justified."

The policy reasons for the restrictions in matrimonial cases on the use of fees which are contingent on the outcome has been that this kind of fee might induce lawyers to discourage reconciliation and encourage bitter and wounding court battles. Another often expressed policy reason to preclude contingent fees in matrimonial actions is that they are not necessary. Since the court may award attorney's fees to a non-monied spouse, any party should be able to retain counsel.

The question whether the PFA violates the CPR requires analysis of whether the payment or amount was "contingent" on the result. Plaintiff correctly notes that DR 2-106[C][2] does not use the term "contingent fee," which is used in DR 2-106[C][1] banning those fees in criminal cases. Clearly the fee here could not be called a "contingent fee" in its traditional sense. The CPR does not define "contingent." One common definition of a "contingent fee" between attorney and client is an agreement express, or implied, for legal services ... under which compensation, contingent in whole or in part upon the successful accomplishment or disposition of the subject matter of the agreement, is to be in an amount which either is fixed or is to be determined under a formula ...

That is consistent with the definition in Black's Law Dictionary, 553 [5th ed. 1979]. The usual meaning of a "contingent fee" is that the attorney will be paid only if the case is won. There is no doubt that by its terms the PFA was a fixed, binding agreement that did not turn on the outcome of the case or on the amount received by plaintiff. The attorney had no risk that the fee would not be paid if the case was lost.

Plaintiff suggests that because the first payment of the fee was to be paid from a specified equitable distribution payment it was "contingent" for payment on the completion of the case. In *Shanks v. Kilgore*, 589 S.W.2d 318, 321 [Mo. Ct. App. 1979] the court found that since the $60,000 fee was to be paid partially from each equitable distribution installment it was based on a prohibited contingency, the receipt of payment. This court rejects that analysis; once the fee has been firmly fixed the uncertainty of actual payment does not make it invalid. It has long been an accepted practice in this jurisdiction, even where the entire fee is fixed at an hourly rate, for counsel to agree to await payment until the ultimate resolution of the case. Neither the fee nor the obligation to pay it turn on the outcome. Only the timing of the payment is uncertain. Bar Ethics Committees appear to support that view. The court cannot conclude that such a provision makes a fixed fee into a "contingent fee."

A more troubling question is presented because the language of DR6–102[C][2] uses the term "contingent * * * upon the amount of * * * equitable distribution." "Contingent" means "possible, but not assured; doubtful or uncertain; conditional upon the occurrence of some future event which is itself uncertain, or questionable." (Black's Law Dictionary, 290 [5th ed. 1979]). The PFA based the fee on "the results achieved." The CPR, following well established New York law provides that one of the "factors to be considered as guides in determining the reasonableness of a fee * * * [is] the amount involved and the results obtained." (DR 2–106[B][4]; 22 NYCRR § 1200.11 [b][4]). Thus the question before this court becomes whether the use of the "results obtained" to set the final fee necessarily makes the fee "contingent" on the ultimate amount. The answer to that question has divided the courts which have considered it.

In *Head v. Head*, 66 Md. App. 655, 668, 505 A.2d 868, 874–5 [1986] the court found no violation of DR 2–106[C][2]. In that case there had been a judicial determination by the lower court of a legal fee which included a "bonus" based on the result. The fee was held not to be contingent because "the fee was not directly related by percentage or formula to the amount recovered or protected." The court supported its conclusion by noting that the fee did not serve the usual purpose of a contingent fee since the parties could afford counsel and no res was created since the party involved was the monied spouse. In *In re Marriage of Malec* [205 Ill. App.3d 273, 562 N.E.2d 1010 (1990)], the court simply agreed with Head's conclusion and observed that a fee to be determined based on performance would not be contingent. However, in *Malec* the fee arrangement was actually invalidated as "contingent" because a $1 million bonus was tied to counsel's achievement of a specific result. The court in *Eckell v. Wilson* [409 Pa. Super. 132, 597 A.2d 696 (1991] after reviewing the cases, concluded that a fee based on a minimum hourly rate with the final fee to be based on the reasonable value of the services, including whether a favorable result was reached, is not a fee grounded on a prohibited contingency. The court reasoned that since the attorney would be paid regardless of the outcome, the risk of nonpayment in case of an unfavorable result, characteristic of a contingent fee, was missing. The court found that the agreement was the equivalent of a quantum meruit fee based on the factors permitted by the Rules of Practice.

On the other hand a number of courts have found "result" based fees to be prohibited contingencies. In *Salerno v. Salerno*, 241 N.J.Super. 536, 575 A.2d 532 [1990], the retainer provided for hourly billing and a final fee "premium" based, inter alia, on "the result accomplished." The court held that a charge based on a percentage of the equitable distribution to the client clearly has all the aspects of a contingent fee. Although a fee contingent on the amount of equitable distribution was held valid under the New Jersey Rules, which are based on the Model Rules, the fee was invalidated for violation of Rule 1.5[c] which requires that the agreement be in writing and set the exact percentage of recovery which the attorney sought as a fee.

* * *

This court concludes that where the parties enter into a fee agreement prior to the completion of the matter where a legal fee turns on the "result obtained," that of necessity is a fee based on a prohibited contingency of the amount of the award. * * *

Defendant argues that this case differs from those where "bonuses" or "tips" have been invalidated because the PFA was not referred to in the retainer but was only agreed to after the case was "completed" and there was a "final resolution of the matrimonial matter." Defendant notes that plaintiff had also executed the documents necessary for an uncontested divorce prior to signing the PFA. Plaintiff, however, relies on the undisputed fact that on August 18, when the settlement agreement, other documents and the PFA were signed by her, her husband had not yet executed the settlement agreement, nor had Husband's counsel concluded that the other documents were "in acceptable form" as was required....

This court's experience is that, despite the sense of counsel that a deal has been struck and that a separation agreement is final, there are often last minute disagreements and proposed changes by the client. This matter was obviously not final, at least until signed by plaintiff's then husband. That uncertainty meant that, at the time of its execution, the PFA was contingent; it was contingent on the husband's execution of the separation agreement and his counsel's approval of certain documents. If the husband had raised any issues, defendant's self interest in the result would have created the conflicted loyalty to the client that DR 2–106[C][2] was designed to prevent. Defendant counters by claiming that the PFA is for a fixed "unconditional" fee, final and binding on plaintiff. Yet that position is belied by the use of the phrase "results achieved" in the PFA. If the husband did not sign or had demanded substantive changes there would have been no "results." Defendant's papers continuously justify the fee by the size of the equitable distribution settlement. Of course, a $2,000,000 "bonus" for an unexecuted separation agreement, with no results, would be patently excessive (see DR 2–106[A]; 22 NYCRR § 1200.11[A]) warranting invalidation of the PFA for that reason alone. Thus, this court concludes that the PFA when executed by plaintiff was invalid pursuant to DR 2–106[C][2]. Of course, this decision does not express any view on the propriety of a truly voluntary agreement for a "bonus" to counsel entered into after completion of the entire proceeding.

Plaintiff concedes that in light of the invalidity of the PFA defendant would be entitled to the $41,000 of her time charges which she waived. This court agrees.

Plaintiff's motion for summary judgment on the fifth cause of action is granted. The counterclaim is dismissed.

Notes and Questions

1. The bonus in *V.W.* was large. Is it appropriate to ban all bonus billing? Would a ban simply lead to higher quoted fees at the beginning of the representation? *See* May v. Sessums & Mason, 700 So.2d 22 (Fla.App.1997) (invalidating a $1,000,000 bonus based on vague language in the fee agreement). For a discussion of "results" billing, *see* Barbara A. Stark, *Value Billing–Matrimonial Attorney's Fees in the 90s*, 7 J. ACAD. MATRIMONIAL LAWYERS 83 (1991).

2. Although contingency fees are not allowed in family law matters in most states, they are common in tort cases. Should the family law prohibition apply if tort litigation is also involved? What is the basis of the family law prohibition? *See* Model Rule 1.5(d); Meyers v. Handlon, 479 N.E.2d 106 (Ind.App.1985); Olivier v. Doga, 384 So.2d 330 (La.1979).

D. DUTIES TO THE CLIENT

1. Competence and Diligence

Model Rule 1.1 requires that lawyers possess the "skill, knowledge, and diligence" necessary to the representation undertaken; a client is entitled to demand the same level of skill, knowledge and diligence in settlement of a matter as in litigation. *See* LOUIS PARLEY, THE ETHICAL FAMILY LAWYER: A PRACTICAL GUIDE TO AVOIDING PROFESSIONAL DILEMMAS chs. 3 & 5 (1995); In re Danelson, 142 B.R. 932 (Bkrtcy.D.Mont.1992); McMahon v. Shea, 441 Pa.Super. 304, 657 A.2d 938 (1995).

Model Rule 1.3 mandates that a lawyer act with reasonable diligence and promptness. *See* People v. Baird, 772 P.2d 110 (Colo.1989); In re McGhee, 248 Kan. 988, 811 P.2d 884 (1991) (attorney accepted three divorce referrals, two were never filed and the third was dismissed for lack of prosecution). A client's agreement or instruction to limit the scope of representation to save money does not excuse the lawyer from the responsibility to be competent and diligent. *See* Anita Bolanos Ward, *Cutting Costs Doesn't Mean Cutting Corners: How to Minimize Malpractice Risks*, 17 FAMILY ADVOCATE 38 (1994). Model Rule 1.4 also requires a lawyer to keep a client reasonably informed about the status of the case; AAML Standard 2.6 requires a lawyer to "keep the client informed of developments in the representation and promptly respond to letters and telephone calls." For example, in Tucker v. Virginia State Bar, 233 Va. 526, 357 S.E.2d 525 (1987), a lawyer was disbarred where he failed to return his clients' phone calls, closed his office and disconnected his phone without notifying clients.

2. *Deference to the Client's Decisions*

Model Rule 1.2 requires that a lawyer abide by the client's objectives in the representation. The client, not the lawyer, has the right to accept or reject a settlement offer. *See* Tsavaris v. Tsavaris, 244 So.2d 450 (Fla.App.1971); Jones v. Feiger, Collison & Killmer, 903 P.2d 27 (Colo. App.1994).

FLORIDA BAR v. SUSAN K. GLANT

Supreme Court of Florida, 1994.
645 So.2d 962.

PER CURIAM.

Attorney Susan K. Glant petitions this Court for review of the referee's recommendation that she receive a public reprimand for her handling of a child custody case. * * *

We agree that Glant violated Florida Rule of Professional Conduct 4–1.2(a), which requires a lawyer to abide by a client's decision regarding the objectives of representation,[1] and find that a public reprimand is the appropriate sanction.

The Bar filed a complaint against Glant over her handling of a child custody case at Central Florida Legal Services (CFLS). Glant was asked to resign from CFLS because of her actions.

The referee made these findings of fact: When Glant began working at CFLS in 1991, she was assigned to represent a mother with four minor children (two boys and two girls) in a custody action against the father. The mother wanted to end the Department of Health and Rehabilitative Services' (HRS) supervision of the children and to retain custody of her two girls. At one point, all four children had been removed from the father's home after allegations of sexual abuse. The record reflects that HRS did not litigate those allegations because of insufficient evidence.

Glant knew the mother did not want custody of all four children. She was to attend a hearing in June 1991 and present the court with a recommendation that HRS terminate its supervision and retain the current custody status (two girls living with the mother and two boys living with the father). After the hearing, based on her belief that the father was sexually abusing the girls, Glant sent a letter to HRS in Tallahassee requesting further investigation.[2] She included a copy of an

1. Florida Rule of Professional Conduct 4–1.2(a) provides in relevant part:

> A lawyer shall abide by a client's decisions concerning the objectives of representation, subject to subdivisions (c), (d), and (e), and shall consult with the client as to the means by which they are to be pursued.

Paragraph (c) allows a lawyer to limit the objectives of representation if the client consents. Paragraph (d) prohibits a lawyer from counseling a client to engage, or assisting a client, in conduct the lawyer knows or reasonably should know is criminal or fraudulent. Paragraph (e) requires a lawyer to consult with a client about limitations if the client expects assistance not permitted by law or the Rules of Professional Conduct.

2. Glant also mailed the letter to the U.S. Attorney General's office in Washington, Governor Lawton Chiles and the State

unfiled motion for custody modification which asked that the mother be given custody of all four children.

Glant testified that she felt obligated to send the letter and unfiled motion to HRS because of rule 4–1.2(d), which prohibits a lawyer from assisting a client in criminal or fraudulent conduct.[3] She also relied on rule 4–1.6(b).[4]

Glant challenges the referee's recommendations, arguing that: (1) there is no substantial, competent evidence in the record to support the referee's finding that she violated rule 4–1.2; (2) the referee erred as a matter of fact and law in refusing to direct a verdict in her favor; (3) the referee erred as a matter of law in finding Glant guilty of violating rule 4–1.2. * * *

Initially, we address the three issues dealing with rule 4–1.2(a). A referee's findings of fact are presumed correct and will be upheld unless "clearly erroneous or lacking in evidentiary support." *The Florida Bar v. Hayden*, 583 So.2d 1016, 1017 (Fla.1991). The record is undisputed that Glant sent the letter and documents to Bob Williams, who was then the Secretary of HRS, even though she knew her client did not want custody of all four children. Glant testified:

> In my opinion, there's really only two things an attorney can do when a client says the children are being sexually molested and you're faced with this type—with this type of, what I consider, solid evidence.... If I withdrew, those children would have been buried—been buried in paperwork, so I did the best thing that I thought in my opinion as an attorney—the next thing was that I wrote HRS whose [sic] got access to all those documents. I said, you better take a look at this case. You better take a look at what the local HRS attorney is doing to those children. Okay? I sent the Motion to—to Bob Williams. He knew, according to my letter, that I had not filed that Motion, and that's basically why I sent the letter.... The mother would have said no, and Jonathan Hewett would have told me no, and why would they have told me no. The mother would have told me no because she did not care that the children were being sexually molested by her ex-husband.
>
> Glant also testified that she did the right thing in sending the letter.
>
> THE COURT: Do you believe you should have disclosed to your client what you were going to do?
>
> MS. GLANT: No
>
> THE COURT: Why not?
>
> MS. GLANT: She would have said no.

Attorney's office for the Eight Judicial District.

3. A lawyer shall not counsel a client to engage, or assist a client, in conduct that the lawyer knows or reasonably should know is criminal or fraudulent.

4. A lawyer shall reveal such information to the extent the lawyer believes necessary: (1) to prevent a client from committing a crime; or (2) to prevent a death or substantial bodily harm to another.

THE COURT: No—in that you had made a decision—my understanding is that you made a decision regardless of what your client said to send the letter.

MS. GLANT: That's right.

THE COURT: My question is—you said—my question is do you believe you should have disclosed what you're about to do, that is, in the letter and the Motion to HRS and to the Governor, you believe you should not have disclosed—

MS. GLANT: Her opinion meant nothing to me at that point in time because this is a mother who knows that sexual abuse is happening to her children and is not doing a single thing to prevent it. I don't care if she said yes or no, Your Honor. I would have sent the letter anyway.

THE COURT: All right. And in sending the letter, you realized it could have subjected you to a violation or alleged violation—

MS. GLANT: Certainly.

THE COURT:—of the Code of Conduct for Attorneys.

MS. GLANT: Certainly.

THE COURT: All right.

MS. GLANT: But Your Honor, you know, I still—today, I still would have done it. I still would have done the same thing as I did then.

Glant was the only person who testified that the father had abused his children. The mother never testified that she knew her daughters were being molested; she told the grievance committee it was possible, but "I can't say that I know because I don't know, you know." It was Glant's opinion that the mother was engaging in criminal conduct, but the referee did not accept this opinion—or Glant's reliance on rule 4–1.2(a). We rely on the referee, as the fact-finder, to resolve any conflicts in the evidence. The record supports the referee's finding that Glant violated rule 4–1.2(a). Thus, the referee did not err in refusing to grant Glant's motion for a directed verdict, and we approve the finding that Glant violated rule 4–1.2(a).

We find that a public reprimand is the appropriate sanction for Glant. Florida Standard for Imposing Lawyer Sanctions 7.3 says a public reprimand is appropriate when a lawyer negligently engages in conduct that violates a duty owed as a professional and causes injury or potential injury to the client, the public, or the legal system. In deciding the appropriate sanction, a bar disciplinary action must serve three purposes: the judgment must be fair to society, it must be fair to the attorney, and it must sufficiently deter other attorneys from similar misconduct. Glant was admitted to the Bar in 1984 and has no disciplinary history. A public reprimand, followed by six months on probation, serves the purposes of attorney disciplinary action.

Notes and Questions

1. At what point did the lawyer err? Could she have corrected the error? (Perhaps she should have read Steve Cominsky's Secrets A Good Lawyer [and their best clients'] Already Know (1997) http://www.agood-lawyer.com.: "Know who your client is; Remember who your client is; Only represent your client; Don't surprise your client.")

2. How, if at all, would the outcome in *Glant* be affected if state law required lawyers to report sexual abuse of children? *See, e.g.* North Carolina Op. 120, at ABA/BNA 1001:6603 (no obligation to report but can report to stop future abuse). *See also* Robin A. Rosencrantz, *Rejecting "Hear No Evil Speak No Evil": Expanding the Attorney's Role in Child Abuse Reporting*, 8 Geo. J. Legal Ethics 327 (1995).

3. What is the lawyer's role in assisting the client to make decisions on case strategy? What should the lawyer do if he or she feels that the client's decisions are improvident?

4. Although a lawyer must generally defer to the client's decisions on case strategy, Model Rule 3.1 prohibits a lawyer from bringing or defending a proceeding or controverting an issue without a nonfrivolous basis. AAML Standard 2.25 also provides that "[a]n attorney should not contest child custody or visitation for either financial advantage or vindictiveness."

5. Jane hired Larry Lawyer to represent her in a divorce action and told him that she does not want any notice to appear in the paper. Larry used publication notice which appeared in the paper. Does Jane have a cause of action? *See* McInnis v. Hyatt Legal Clinics, 10 Ohio St.3d 112, 461 N.E.2d 1295 (1984).

3. *Confidentiality*

Except as specifically provided under the Model Rules or Code, a lawyer may not reveal any client confidences. Under Model Rule 1.6:

> (a) A lawyer shall not reveal information relating to representation of a client unless the client consents after consultation, except for disclosures that are impliedly authorized in order to carry out the representation . . .
>
> (b) A lawyer may reveal the following information to the extent the lawyer reasonably believes necessary:
>
> > (1) The intention of his client to commit a crime and the information necessary to prevent the crime;
>
> * * *
>
> (c) A lawyer shall reveal such information when required by law or Court Order.

Unsurprisingly, Model Rule 1.2(d) prohibits a lawyer from counseling a client to engage in or assist a client in conduct that the lawyer knows is criminal or fraudulent. Model Rule 3.3(a)(4) also provides that "[i]f a lawyer has offered material evidence and comes to know its falsity, the lawyer shall take reasonable remedial measures." Some states impose more stringent reporting requirements than do the Model Rules and require an attorney to reveal a client's intention to commit a crime. *See* Opinion No. 87–9, Ill. State Bar Comm. on Prof. Resp., 14 FAM. L. REP. (BNA) 1363 (1988). *See also* Nix v. Whiteside, 475 U.S. 157, 106 S.Ct. 988, 89 L.Ed.2d 123 (1986).

4. Sex with Clients

Nothing in the Model Code or Model Rules prohibits a lawyer from engaging in sexual relations with a client. ABA Formal Opinion 92–364, Sexual Relations With Clients (July 6, 1992), 1992 WL 348069 discourages, but does not forbid, a lawyer/client sexual relationship:

> It is apparent that a sexual relationship during the course of representation can seriously harm the client's interests. Therefore, the Committee concludes that because of the danger of impairment to the lawyer's representation associated with a sexual relationship between lawyer and client, the lawyer would be well advised to refrain from such a relationship. If such a sexual relationship occurs and the impairment is not avoided, the lawyer will have violated ethical obligations to the client. The client's consent to sexual relations alone will rarely be sufficient to eliminate this danger. In many cases, the client's ability to give meaningful consent is vitiated by the lawyer's potential undue influence and/or the emotional vulnerability of the client. The lawyer may therefore, be called upon in a disciplinary or other proceeding to show that the client consented, that the consent was freely given based on full and reasonable disclosure of the risks involved, and that any ensuing sexual relationship did not in any way disadvantage the client in the representation; that is, the attorney's judgment remained independent, the representation proceeded free of conflicts, the privilege was not compromised and the other ethical obligations to the client were fulfilled.

AAML Standard 2.16 goes further, providing that "an attorney should never have a sexual relationship with a client or opposing counsel during the time of representation." New York's rules relating to divorce representation similarly forbid "a sexual relationship with a client during the course of the lawyer's representation of the client." A violation will result in disciplinary action. *See* 22 NYCRR § 1200.3(A)(7); In re Gould, 207 A.D.2d 98, 620 N.Y.S.2d 491 (1995). In other states there are ethical opinions or case law imposing sanctions on lawyers who have engaged in sexual relations with clients. *See* State ex rel. Oklahoma Bar Association v. Sopher, 852 P.2d 707 (Okla.1993); Rhoda Feinberg & James Tom Greene, *Transference and Countertransference Issues in Professional Relationships*, 29 FAM. L. Q. 111 (1995).

Notes and Questions

1. Al is an attorney with a firm. Sue, a client, tells Al's partner John that she is having an affair with Al. What, if any, obligation does

John have? *See* Kansas Bar Association Ethics Advisory Services Comm. Op. 94–13, at ABA/BNA Manual, Current Reports, Vol. 12, p. 86.

2. What, if any, remedies are available to a client who has had a sexual relationship with his or her lawyer? What facts are relevant? *See* McDaniel v. Gile, 230 Cal.App.3d 363, 281 Cal.Rptr. 242 (1991); *Woman Wins Suit on Coerced Affair with Lawyer,* N.Y. Times, Nov. 29, 1992, at p. 38 (reporting award of $20,000 compensatory and $200,000 punitive damages in action against male lawyer alleged to have coerced his female client into having sex 200 times over 18 month period).

E. DUTIES TO OPPOSING PARTIES AND COUNSEL

1. *Communication with Other Parties*

A lawyer may not communicate with a person known to be represented by counsel unless the other lawyer consents. Model Rule 4.2. Some courts have also held that a lawyer may not communicate with children for whom a guardian ad litem has been appointed. *See* In re Disciplinary Proceedings Against Frank X. Kinast, 192 Wis.2d 36, 530 N.W.2d 387 (1995); *ABA Standards of Conduct for Lawyers Who Represent Children in Abuse and Neglect Cases,* 29 Fam. L. Q. 175 (1995). Can an attorney handle his own divorce case and talk to his wife who is represented by counsel? *See* Louis Parley, *Lawyers, Their Divorces and Legal Ethics*, 30 Fam. L. Q. 661 (1996).

2. *Fair Bargaining*

Model Rule 4.1 and D.R. 7–102(A)(3) prohibit a lawyer from making a false statement of a material fact. *See also* AAML Standard 3.2 ("An attorney should never deceive or intentionally mislead opposing counsel"); AAML Standard 2.13 (attorney should not encourage the client to hide or dissipate assets); AAML Standard 3.3 (attorney should not rely on a mistake by opposing counsel to obtain an unfair benefit for the client).

Although there is no duty to volunteer information which opposing counsel has not requested except to prevent fraud, many courts require counsel to provide information on property valuation changes occurring between pre-trial discovery and trial. Some courts have also held that the spousal relationship entails fiduciary obligations. *See* Cal. Fam. Code § 2100(c); Billington v. Billington, 220 Conn. 212, 595 A.2d 1377 (1991); Miller v. Miller, 700 S.W.2d 941 (Tex.App.1985).

SECTION 3. CRITICISMS OF DIVORCE LAWYERS AND THE DIVORCE PROCESS

"Are Divorce Lawyers Really the Sleaziest?" asks a recent headline. *See* Stephen Labation, N.Y. Times, Sept. 5, 1993, at E3. Some say yes. Karen Winner, for example, recently wrote a good-sized book (Divorced From Justice: The Abuse of Women and Children by Divorce Lawyers and

JUDGES (1996)), devoted entirely to lambasting divorce lawyers (and the judicial system in which they operate) for delay, secrecy, ineptitude, and high cost—among other things! While the stereotype of the divorce lawyer as a low-paid, sleazy practitioner has shifted toward the slicker, BMW-driving Arnie Becker of L.A. Law, Becker, too, is portrayed as engaging in every dirty trick imaginable, including sleeping with his client's wife.

What is the reality? And how did divorce lawyers get such a negative image? Here are some of the most common complaints:

A. THE PROCESS IS TOO ADVERSARIAL

Many critics argue that the divorce process is too adversarial. One complaint centers on "bombers," i.e., lawyers who engage in "dirty tricks" such as prolonging discovery by taking depositions of unneeded witnesses, excessively interfering with questioning of witnesses, making burdensome requests for unnecessary documents, denying allegations everyone knows are true, filing tons of unnecessary paperwork, failing to return phone calls, making personal attacks on opposing counsel, and generally using delay or nasty tactics to drag the case along and make it unpleasant for all involved. AAML Standard 3 specifies that "overzealous, discourteous, abrasive, 'hard ball' conduct by matrimonial lawyers is inconsistent with both their obligation to effectively represent their clients and their duty to improve the process of dispute resolution."

How should a lawyer respond to dirty tricks by the other side? The two predominant means of disciplining bombers are through sanctions and an attorney fees award. A court may also impose nonmonetary sanctions, such as requiring the attorney to attend educational seminars.

CHARLES B. CRAVER, NEGOTIATION ETHICS: HOW TO BE DECEPTIVE WITHOUT BEING DISHONEST/HOW TO BE ASSERTIVE WITHOUT BEING OFFENSIVE

38 S. Tex. L. Rev. 713 (1997).

* * *

Many practicing attorneys seem to think that competitive/adversarial negotiators—who use highly competitive tactics to maximize their own client returns—achieve more beneficial results for their clients than their cooperative/problem-solving colleagues—who employ more cooperative techniques designed to maximize the joint return to the parties involved. An empirical study, conducted by Professor Gerald Williams, of legal practitioners in Denver and Phoenix contradicts this notion. Professor Williams found that sixty-five percent of negotiators are considered cooperative/problem-solvers by their peers, twenty-four percent are viewed as competitive/adversarial, and eleven percent did not fit in either category. When the respondents were asked to indicate which attorneys were "effective," "average," and "ineffective" negotiators, the results were striking. While fifty-nine percent of the cooperative/problem-solving lawyers were rated "effective," only twenty-five percent of competitive/adversarial attorneys were rated effective. On the other hand, while a mere three percent of cooperative/problem-solvers were considered "ineffective," thirty-three percent of competitive/adversarial bargainers were rated "ineffective."

In this study, Professor Williams found that certain traits were shared by both effective cooperative/problem-solving negotiators and effective competitive/adversarial bargainers. Successful negotiators from both groups are thoroughly prepared, behave in an honest and ethical manner, are perceptive readers of opponent cues, are analytical, realistic, and convincing, and observe the courtesies of the bar. The proficient negotiators from both groups also sought to *maximize* their *own client's* return. Since this is the quintessential characteristic of competitive/adversarial bargainers, it would suggest that a number of successful negotiators may be adroitly masquerading as sheep in wolves' clothing. They exude a cooperative style, but seek competitive objectives.

Most successful negotiators are able to combine the most salient traits associated with the cooperative/problem-solving and the competitive/adversarial styles. They endeavor to maximize client returns, but attempt to accomplish this objective in a congenial and seemingly ingenuous manner. They look for shared values in recognition of the fact that by maximizing joint returns, they are more likely to obtain the best settlements for their own clients. Although successful negotiators try to manipulate opponent perceptions, they rarely resort to truly deceitful tactics. They know that a loss of credibility will undermine their ability to achieve beneficial results. Despite the fact successful negotiators want as much as possible for their own clients, they are not "win-lose" negotiators who judge their results, not by how well they have done, but by how poorly they think their opponents have done. They realize that the imposition of poor terms on opponents does not necessarily benefit their own clients. All factors being equal, they want to maximize opponent satisfaction. So long as it does not require significant concessions on their part, they acknowledge the benefits to be derived from this approach. The more satisfied opponents are, the more likely those parties will accept proposed terms and honor the resulting agreements.

These eclectic negotiators employ a composite style. They may be characterized as competitive/problem-solvers. They seek competitive goals (maximum client returns), but endeavor to accomplish these objectives through problem-solving strategies. They exude a cooperative approach and follow the courtesies of the legal profession. They avoid rude or inconsiderate behavior, recognizing that such openly adversarial conduct is likely to generate competitive/adversarial responses from their opponents. They appreciate the fact that individuals who employ wholly inappropriate tactics almost always induce opposing counsel to work harder to avoid exploitation by these openly opportunistic bargainers. Legal negotiators who are contemplating the use of offensive techniques should simply ask themselves how they would react if similar tactics were employed against them.

* * *

Despite the contrary impression of some members of the general public, I have generally found attorneys to be conscientious and honorable people. I have encountered few instances of questionable behavior. I would thus like to conclude with the admonitions I impart to my Legal Negotiating students as they prepare to enter the legal profession. Lawyers must remember that they have to live with their own consciences, and not those of their clients or their partners. They must employ tactics they are comfortable using, even in those situations in which other people encourage them to employ less reputable behavior. If they adopt techniques they do not consider appropriate, not only will they experience personal discomfort, but they will also fail to achieve their intended objective due to the fact they will not appear credible when using those tactics. Attorneys must also acknowledge that they are members of a special profession and owe certain duties to the public that transcend those that may be owed by people engaged in other businesses. Even though ABA Model Rule 1.3 states that "[a] lawyer shall act with reasonable diligence," Comment One expressly recognizes that "a lawyer is not bound to press for every advantage that might be realized for a client. A lawyer has professional discretion in determining the means by which a matter [shall] be pursued."

Popular negotiation books occasionally recount the successful use of questionable techniques to obtain short-term benefits. The authors glibly describe the way they have employed highly aggressive, deliberately deceptive, or equally opprobrious bargaining tactics to achieve their objectives. They usually conclude these stories with parenthetical admissions that their bilked adversaries would probably be reluctant to interact with them in the future. When negotiators engage in such questionable behavior such that they would find it difficult, if not impossible, to transact future business with their adversaries, they have usually transcended the bounds of propriety. No legal representatives should be willing to jeopardize long-term professional relationships for the narrow interests of particular clients. Zealous representation should never be thought to require the employment of personally compromising techniques.

Lawyers must acknowledge that they are not guarantors—they arc only legal advocates. They are not supposed to guarantee client victory no matter how disreputably they must act to do so. They should never countenance witness perjury or the withholding of subpoenaed documents. While they should zealously endeavor to advance client interests, they should recognize their moral obligation to follow the ethical rules applicable to all attorneys.

Untrustworthy advocates encounter substantial difficulty when they negotiate with others. Their oral representations must be verified and reduced to writing, and many opponents distrust their written documents. Their negotiations become especially problematic and cumbersome. If nothing else moves practitioners to behave in an ethical and dignified manner, their hope for long and successful legal careers should induce them to avoid conduct that may undermine their future effectiveness.

Attorneys should diligently strive to advance client objectives while simultaneously maintaining their personal integrity. This philosophy will enable them to optimally serve the interests of both their clients and society. Legal practitioners who are asked about their insistence on ethical behavior may take refuge in an aphorism of Mark Twain: "Always do right. This will gratify some people, and astonish the rest[!]"

B. THE PROCESS IS TOO EXPENSIVE

The lawyer's fee is not the only divorce expense. The client may also be billed for court costs, such as filing fees and court reporter charges; photocopying, faxing, and mailing costs; fees for investigation, discovery, and travel; expert fees, including accountants, investigators, appraisers for real estate, business, art or antiques, pension actuaries, psychologists or psychiatrists, and business or tax experts. The divorce will also entail hidden costs, including the time the client has to take off from work to attend depositions, hearings and to meet with his or her lawyer.

The perception that divorce lawyers are expensive is one reason that many divorces involve one (or even two) unrepresented parties. In many areas, a minority of divorces involves two-party representation; for example, a 1993 ABA report found that, in Maricopa County, Arizona, 88% of divorces involved one party unrepresented by counsel and 62% involved no lawyers. *See* ABA Standing Committee on Delivery of Legal Services, Self Representation in Divorce Cases 34 (Bruce D. Sales et al. 1993). See also Jessica Pearson, *Ten Myths About Family Law*, 27 Fam. L. Q. 279, 281–282 (1994) (finding that only 32% of divorce cases involved two attorneys and that 35–40% of cases involved no lawyer); Robert B. Yegge, *Divorce Litigants Without Lawyers*, 28 Fam. L.Q. 407 (1994); Forrest S. Mosten, *Unbundling of Legal Services*, 28 Fam. L. Q. 421, 427 (1994). The couples most likely to forgo legal representation are those "without children, who are not homeowners, have limited personal property, have household incomes less than $50,000 and/or have marriages of less than 10 years. . . ." American Bar Association, Responding to the Needs of the Self-Represented Divorce Litigant 3–6 (1994).

While nonrepresentation thus is concentrated among those with the fewest legal problems, "most pro se litigants report problems with forms or procedures, many of which are not resolved by the available written instructions. * * * " *Id.* Approximately 32% of all requests for services from low-income persons are in the area of family law. *See* ABA, Natural Civil Legal Needs Survey: A Graphical Overview (1989).

Increased rates of pro se representation in divorce have led some states to enact simplified divorce procedures. Others have adopted standard forms and pleadings, or provide some form of assistance (self help packets, clinics) for unrepresented litigants. Maricopa County, Arizona, for example, has initiated a range of reforms, including guidelines and printed forms, model pleadings, court-house assistance, night court, client libraries, and child care. Do-it-yourself divorce kits have also become popular in some areas. *See Project, The Unauthorized Practice of Law and Pro Se Divorce: An Empirical Analysis*, 86 YALE L. J. 104 (1976). Many lawyers feel that these kits mislead the lay public and result in serious problems that may not be recognized for several years.

Nonlawyers who provide legal advice in connection with a divorce, even if that advice is confined to help in filling out forms, may be subject to prosecution for the unauthorized practice of law. *See* State Bar v. Cramer, 399 Mich. 116, 249 N.W.2d 1 (1976); The Florida Bar v. Furman, 451 So.2d 808 (Fla.1984). The proliferation of divorce kits has led some states, like Arkansas and Ohio, to strengthen their unauthorized practice of law provisions; others, such as California and Oregon, are considering allowing nonlawyers ("legal technicians") who meet state-established educational and ethical requirements to sell legal forms or help clients in certain situations.

C. THE PROCESS TAKES TOO LONG

Divorce cases can take literally years to resolve. The case of Wolfe v. Wolfe, 76 Ill.2d 92, 27 Ill.Dec. 735, 389 N.E.2d 1143 (1979), for example, consumed eight years, cost more than $100,000, required 113 hearings, and involved 35 judges and 25 lawyers before concluding in an annulment. The vast majority of divorce cases are resolved in less than eight years but, in some urban courts, delays of nine to ten months are not uncommon in uncontested divorces and it may take years to resolve a contested divorce.

What, if anything, can be done to minimize delay? Would a speedy trial requirement, like that applicable to criminal cases, be desirable?

SECTION 4. MALPRACTICE

Family law claims comprise close to 10% of total malpractice claims. *See* ABA STANDING COMMITTEE ON LAWYERS' PROFESSIONAL LIABILITY AND THE NATIONAL ASSOCIATION OF BAR-RELATED INSURANCE COMPANIES, NATIONAL LEGAL MALPRACTICE DATA STUDY (1996) (family law cases comprised 9.13% of all claims); CHARACTERISTICS OF LEGAL MALPRACTICE: REPORT OF THE NATIONAL LEGAL MALPRACTICE DATA CENTER (ABA 1989) (family law cases comprised 7.88% of total claims).

In a malpractice action, the plaintiff must establish an attorney-client relationship giving rise to a duty of care, a breach of the attorney's duty that was the proximate cause of injury to the client, and actual damages. An attorney must exercise that degree of learning, skill and experience which is ordinarily possessed by other attorneys in the community practicing in the relevant area of law. *See* RONALD E. MALLEN AND JEFFREY M. SMITH, LEGAL MALPRACTICE, (4th ed. 1996). Expert testimony is generally required to establish the standard of care applicable to the attorney's conduct; an attorney is not answerable for every error or mistake based upon an honest exercise of professional judgment. Woodruff v. Tomlin, 616 F.2d 924, 930 (6th Cir.1980), *cert. denied*, 449 U.S. 888, 101 S.Ct. 246, 66 L.Ed.2d 114 (1980).

A. LIABILITY TO THE CLIENT

GRAYSON v. WOFSEY, ROSEN, KWESKIN AND KURIANSKY

Supreme Court of Connecticut, 1994.
231 Conn. 168, 646 A.2d 195.

PALMER, ASSOCIATE JUSTICE.

The principal issue raised by this appeal is whether a client who has agreed to the settlement of a marital dissolution action on the advice of his or her attorney may then recover against the attorney for the negligent handling of her case. The plaintiff, Elyn K. Grayson, brought this action against the defendants, Edward M. Kweskin, Emanuel Margolis, and their law firm, Wofsey, Rosen, Kweskin and Kuriansky, alleging that they had committed legal malpractice in the preparation and settlement of her dissolution action. After trial, a jury returned a verdict in the amount of $1,500,000 against the defendants. The trial court, Ballen, J., rendered judgment for the plaintiff in accordance with the jury verdict, and this appeal followed. The defendants claim that: (1) the plaintiff failed to establish, as a matter of law, that she was entitled to a recovery against them; (2) the evidence was insufficient to support the jury's verdict; (3) the trial court's rulings on certain evidentiary issues constituted an abuse of discretion; and (4) the trial court's instructions to the jury were improper. We affirm the judgment of the trial court.

The relevant facts and procedural history are as follows. In 1981, Arthur I. Grayson (husband) brought an action against the plaintiff for the dissolution of their marriage. On May 28, 1981, the third day of the dissolution trial before Hon. William L. Tierney, Jr., state trial referee, the plaintiff, on the advice of the defendants, agreed to a settlement of the case that had been negotiated by the defendants and counsel for her husband. The agreement provided, inter alia, that the plaintiff would receive lump sum alimony of $159,000 and periodic alimony of $12,000 per year. Judge Tierney found that the agreement was fair and reasonable and, accordingly, rendered a judgment of dissolution incorporating the agreement.[5]

5. "The stipulated judgment ordered the [husband] to pay to the [plaintiff] lump sum alimony of $150,000, payable in installments of $50,000 by June 28, 1981, $50,000 by August 28, 1981 ... and $50,000 by February 28, 1982 ... together with non-modifiable periodic alimony of $12,000 per year. The [husband] was also ordered to pay $15,000 as part of the [plaintiff's] attorney's fees and to maintain a $50,000 life insurance policy on his life owned by the [plaintiff] and payable to her. The [plaintiff]

On September 23, 1981, the plaintiff moved to open the judgment on the ground that the settlement agreement had been based on a fraudulent affidavit submitted to the court and to the plaintiff by her husband. The trial court, Jacobson, Jr. denied the plaintiff's motion to open the judgment and the plaintiff appealed to the Appellate Court, which affirmed the judgment. . . .

The plaintiff also brought this legal malpractice action against the defendants. Her complaint alleged that she had agreed to the settlement of the dissolution action on the advice of the defendants who, she claimed, had failed properly to prepare her case. The plaintiff further alleged that as a result of the defendants' negligence, she had agreed to a settlement that "was not reflective of her legal entitlement" and that she had "thereby sustained an actual economic loss."

At trial, the plaintiff introduced evidence concerning her thirty year marriage, its breakdown due to her husband's affair with another woman, and the couple's financial circumstances. After a detailed recounting of the history of the divorce litigation, the plaintiff presented the testimony of two expert witnesses, Thomas Hupp, a certified public accountant, and Donald Cantor, an attorney who specialized in the practice of family law.

Hupp testified that the defendants had failed properly to value the marital estate and, in particular, the husband's various business interests. Cantor gave his opinion that the defendants' representation of the plaintiff fell below the standard of care required of attorneys in marital dissolution cases. Specifically, Cantor testified that: (1) the defendants had not conducted an adequate investigation and evaluation of the husband's business interests and assets; (2) they had not properly prepared for trial; (3) as a result of the defendants' negligence, the plaintiff had agreed to a distribution of the marital estate and an alimony award that were not fair and equitable under the law; (4) the plaintiff would have received a greater distribution of the marital estate and additional alimony had she been competently represented. The trial court, Ballen, J., denied the defendants' motion for a directed verdict at the close of the plaintiff's case.

In their case in defense, the defendants testified concerning their handling of the plaintiff's case, and they also presented the expert testimony of two attorneys, James Stapleton and James Greenfield.

was ordered to transfer her one half interest in a business building at 636 Kings Highway, Fairfield, to the [husband], the equity in which he claimed was $50,000. The [plaintiff] was required to relinquish her claim in the amount of $27,000 to a certificate of deposit managed by the [husband]. The [plaintiff] was awarded full ownership of Daniel Oil [Company], which the [husband's] affidavit claimed produced an income of $18,000 per year. Works of art valued by the [husband] at $64,700 were ordered divided between the parties. Otherwise, each was to retain substantial other assets shown on their affidavits. The principal asset shown by the [husband's] affidavit [was] the valuation, after taxes due on liquidation, of his pension plan in Grayson Associates, Inc., at $340,152 and the principal asset shown by the [plaintiff's] affidavit [was] the former family residence at 15 Berkeley Road, Westport, in which the claimed equity was $167,000." *Grayson v. Grayson*, 4 Conn.App. 275, 277–78, 494 A.2d 576 (1985).

These experts expressed the opinion that the defendants' representation of the plaintiff comported with the standard of care required of attorneys conducting dissolution litigation.

The jury returned a verdict for the plaintiff in the amount of $1,500,000. The defendants thereafter filed motions to set aside the verdict and for judgment notwithstanding the verdict. The trial court denied those motions and rendered judgment in accordance with the verdict. Additional facts are set forth as relevant.

I

The defendants first claim that the trial court improperly denied their motions for a directed verdict and for judgment notwithstanding the verdict on the ground that the plaintiff was barred from recovering against them, as a matter of law, due to her agreement to settle the marital dissolution action. We conclude that the plaintiff was not so barred.

The defendants urge us to adopt a common law rule whereby an attorney may not be held liable for negligently advising a client to enter into a settlement agreement. They argue that, as a matter of public policy, an attorney should not be held accountable for improperly advising a client to settle a case unless that advice is the product of fraudulent or egregious misconduct by the attorney. The defendants contend that the adoption of such a rule is necessary in order to promote settlements, to protect the integrity of stipulated judgments, and to avoid the inevitable flood of litigation that they claim will otherwise result. They claim that such a rule is particularly appropriate if, as here, the court has reviewed and approved the settlement agreement.

* * * At a time when our courts confront an unprecedented volume of litigation, we reaffirm our strong support for the implementation of policies and procedures that encourage fair and amicable pretrial settlements.

We reject the invitation of the defendants, however, to adopt a rule that promotes the finality of settlements and judgments at the expense of a client who, in reasonable reliance on the advice of his or her attorney, agrees to a settlement only to discover that the attorney had failed to exercise the degree of skill and learning required of attorneys in the circumstances. "Although we encourage settlements, we recognize that litigants rely heavily on the professional advice of counsel when they decide whether to accept or reject offers of settlement, and we insist that the lawyers of our state advise clients with respect to settlements with the same skill, knowledge, and diligence with which they pursue all other legal tasks." Therefore, when it has been established that an attorney, in advising a client concerning the settlement of an action, has failed to "exercise that degree of skill and learning commonly applied under all the circumstances in the community by the average prudent reputable member of the [legal] profession . . . [and that conduct has] result[ed in] injury, loss, or damage to the [client]"; the client is entitled to a recovery against the attorney. Accordingly, like the majority of courts that have addressed this issue, we decline to adopt a rule that insulates attorneys from exposure to malpractice claims arising from their negligence in settled cases if the attorney's conduct has damaged the client....

Furthermore, we do not believe that a different result is required because a judge had approved the settlement of the plaintiff's marital dissolution action. Although in dissolution cases "[t]he presiding judge has the obligation to conduct a searching inquiry to make sure that the settlement agreement is substantively fair and has been knowingly negotiated"; the court's inquiry does not serve as a substitute for the diligent investigation and preparation for which counsel is responsible. Indeed, the dissolution court may be unable to elicit the information necessary to make a fully informed evaluation of the settlement agreement if counsel for either of the parties has failed properly to discover and analyze the facts that are relevant to a fair and equitable settlement.

Finally, we do not share the concern expressed by the defendants about the impact that our resolution of this issue will have on settlements, stipulated judgments, and the volume of litigation. Indeed, the defendants do not suggest that attorneys have heretofore been unwilling to recommend settlements out of concern over possible malpractice suits, for attorneys in this state have never been insulated from negligence claims by the protectional rule urged by the defendants. Because settlements will often be in their clients' best interests, we harbor no doubt that attorneys will continue to give advice concerning the resolution of cases in a manner consistent with their professional and ethical responsibilities.

The defendants contend that the evidence does not support a determination that they were deficient in their representation of the plaintiff. They also claim that the plaintiff's evidence was so speculative that a jury reasonably could not have concluded that the defendants' conduct was the proximate cause of any economic harm to the plaintiff. We disagree.

The following evidence, which the jury could have credited, is relevant to these claims. At the time of the trial of the marital dissolution action, the plaintiff and her husband had been married for thirty years. The plaintiff, fifty-three years old, was a graduate of Simmons College, and for eight years had owned and operated her own real estate business. Prior to opening her real estate office, the plaintiff had remained at home to raise the couple's three daughters. Her husband, a fifty-six year old graduate of Wharton School of Finance and Columbia Law School, was a successful entrepreneur.

Among her husband's business interests were several bowling alleys. He held a 20 percent general partnership interest in Nutmeg Bowl, Colonial Lanes and Laurel Lanes, and was in charge of their management. In addition, he owned 100 percent of the stock in three lounges that served food and beverages to patrons of the bowling alleys. The husband also had a beneficial interest in the Grayson Associate Pension and Profit Sharing Plan, which in turn was a limited partner in the three bowling alleys.

Grayson Associates, Inc., a management company in which the husband was the sole shareholder, received management fees from the three bowling alleys. Although Grayson Associates had a fair market value of $487,000, the husband's financial affidavit listed only its book value of $14,951. The husband's financial affidavit also listed a $46,080 limited partnership interest in Georgetown at Enfield Associates (Georgetown partnership), and a future general partnership interest in that partnership of $959.76. The husband's affidavit failed to disclose, however, that he intended to take a $165,000 partnership distribution from the Georgetown partnership and that he was entitled to $45,000 in management fees from that partnership. To the contrary, the affidavit affirmatively represented that the husband would receive no future income from the Georgetown partnership. Finally, the husband's affidavit indicated an annual income of approximately $62,000.

The plaintiff's financial affidavit, which was prepared by the defendants in consultation with the plaintiff, indicated that she had no income. The plaintiff had testified at her deposition prior to the dissolution trial, however, that she earned approximately $25,000 annually from her real estate business, and that she expected to receive commissions in excess of $34,000 in 1981.

The plaintiff's expert witness Cantor expressed his opinion that the defendants had been negligent in failing properly to discover and evaluate certain assets of the marital estate. Specifically, Cantor testified that the defendants had improperly failed to: (1) ascertain the full value of the Georgetown partnership; (2) discover the $165,000 anticipated distribution to the husband by that partnership; and (3) discover the $45,000 management fee owed to the husband by the partnership. Cantor also testified that because the defendants had failed to obtain appraisals for several of the assets, including 636 Kings Highway and Grayson Associates, Inc., the defendants were unable to challenge various inconsistencies in the husband's financial affidavit. Cantor further testified that the defendants had failed properly to establish the husband's "residual interest in the bowling alleys ... as a general partner," an asset not expressly valued in the husband's affidavit.

Cantor also explained that, in his opinion, the defendants had failed to exercise due care in the preparation of the plaintiff's financial affidavit. In Cantor's judgment, the plaintiff's credibility had been seriously and unnecessarily compromised because her financial affidavit did not include the income from her real estate business. Cantor also noted that the plaintiff's credibility may have been further undermined by virtue of the defendants' submission of three separate documents containing three different valuations of another marital asset, the Daniel Oil Company.

Cantor expressed his opinion that at the end of the two days of trial, there was not enough financial information available to the lawyers to permit them to responsibly recommend settlement to the plaintiff. He further concluded that the defendants' failure to satisfy the standard of skill and care required of attorneys in such cases was the cause of economic damage to the plaintiff because, in his view, she would have received a larger distribution of the marital estate had the defendants represented her competently.

Finally, Cantor testified to his opinion that the plaintiff reasonably could have anticipated receiving 40 to 60 percent of the total marital estate, which, according to the plaintiff's witnesses, had a value of approximately $2,400,000. Cantor also opined that the plaintiff reasonably could have anticipated receiving periodic modifiable alimony of approximately 35 to 50 percent of the parties' combined incomes.

We conclude that the evidence adduced at trial was sufficient to support the jury's determination that the defendants were negligent in their representation of the plaintiff. The jury reasonably could have determined, on the basis of the testimony of the plaintiff's expert, that the defendants had negligently failed to discover and value the husband's business interests and related assets, and that the terms of the settlement agreement did not represent a fair and equitable distribution of the true marital estate. Moreover, the jury was entitled to credit Cantor's testimony that the defendants' advice to accept the settlement agreement was the product of their inadequate investigation and preparation.

We further conclude that the evidence supported the jury's determination that the defendants' negligence was the proximate cause of economic damage to the plaintiff.

The defendants further claim that the jury's verdict was excessive as a matter of law. We do not agree.

The jury could have credited the testimony of the plaintiff's witnesses that the value of the marital estate, at the time of the divorce, was approximately $2,400,000, and that the value of the plaintiff's distribution, under the terms of the stipulated judgment, was approximately $450,000. Because the jury could have concluded, as Cantor testified, that the plaintiff reasonably could have expected to receive up to 60 percent of the value of the marital estate, namely, $1,400,000, the jury also could have determined that the plaintiff, had she been competently represented, would have received approximately $1,000,000 more of the estate's assets than she had been awarded pursuant to the stipulated judgment. In addition, on the basis of Cantor's testimony that the plaintiff could have expected to receive alimony of between 35 and 50 percent of the parties' combined annual income, the jury reasonably could have concluded that the plaintiff would have received alimony of up to $35,000 more per year than she had agreed to in settlement of the marital dissolution action. Furthermore, the jury was free to have calculated the economic damage to the plaintiff in lost alimony from the date of the marital dissolution action in 1981 indefinitely into the plaintiff's future. Viewed in the light most favorable to the plaintiff, therefore, the evidence supported the jury's verdict of $1,500,000.

Notes and Questions

1. Must an attorney obtain appraisals in every case, regardless of their cost and the value of the marital estate? *See* William C. Lhotka, *Woman Wins $6.8 Million From Her Divorce Attorney*, St. Louis Post Dispatch, March 9, 1993, at 1.

2. In giving advice about a proposed settlement, a lawyer must act with the same level of skill, knowledge, and diligence applicable to litigation. *See* Ziegelheim v. Apollo, 128 N.J. 250, 607 A.2d 1298 (1992).

a. Larry Lawyer represented Tom in drafting a premarital agreement which did not include an "alimony waiver" because, at the time the agreement was drafted, such a waiver was contrary to public policy. A few years later, a statute is enacted specifically allowing such a waiver. Does Tom have a viable malpractice against Larry if, following a divorce, he is ordered to pay his ex-wife alimony? *See* Vande Kop v. McGill, 528 N.W. 2d 609 (Iowa 1995).

b. Larry Lawyer failed to advise Sara that $228,000 in periodic alimony payments were taxable income. Does Sara have a viable malpractice against Larry? *See* Wright v. Wright, 92 Wis.2d 246, 284 N.W.2d 894, cert. denied 445 U.S. 951, 100 S.Ct. 1600, 63 L.Ed.2d 786 (1980).

c. Larry Lawyer failed to file a copy of his client Sally's Wisconsin child custody decree in Florida, the home state of Sally's former husband. Unaware of the Wisconsin order, the Florida court issued a conflicting custody order. Does Sally have a viable malpractice against Larry? What if Larry is not licensed to practice in Florida? *See* Person v. Behnke, 242 Ill.App.3d 933, 183 Ill.Dec. 702, 611 N.E.2d 1350 (1993); Soderlund v. Alton, 160 Wis.2d 825, 467 N.W.2d 144 (1991).

3. Herman has requested that you memorialize an agreement he has reached with his wife Wynette. No discovery has been initiated; Herman and Wynette have exchanged minimal information regarding their assets. Will you take the case? Why?

B. LIABILITY TO THIRD PARTIES

SCHOLLER v. SCHOLLER

Supreme Court of Ohio, 1984.
10 Ohio St.3d 98, 462 N.E.2d 158.

Frank D. Celebrezze, Chief Justice.

* * *

The ... issue is whether Alyce Scholler on behalf of Philip Scholler may maintain an action against Willoughby in malpractice even though Philip is a third party to the attorney-client relationship that existed between Willoughby and Alyce Scholler. The general rule was stated in the dissent in *Petrey v. Simon* (1983), 4 Ohio St.3d 154, 157, 158–159, 447 N.E.2d 1285, as follows:

> "* * * [A]n attorney is immune from liability to third persons arising from his performance as an attorney in good faith on behalf of, and with the knowledge of his client, unless such third person is in privity with the client or the attorney acts maliciously."

In the case at bar, Alyce Scholler on behalf of Philip Scholler makes no allegations that Willoughby acted maliciously. Thus, if Philip, as a third party, may maintain an action in legal malpractice against Willoughby, it must be established that Philip was in privity with Alyce Scholler, Willoughby's client.

* * *

[T]he husband's duty to support his minor children is independent from the other obligations attendant to the dissolution of a marriage. The court must be satisfied that the child support provision in the separation agreement represents compliance with the husband's duty of support. As a result, it cannot be said that the interests of the wife in negotiating a separation agreement to achieve a fair division of marital assets are concurrent with the interests of the child to receive support. It is not the wife's responsibility alone to see that a proper amount of child support is provided for in the separation agreement. That responsibility ultimately lies in the court upon consideration of the factors enumerated in R.C. 3109.05(A).

Moreover, the trial court, pursuant to R.C. § 3105.65(B), retains jurisdiction to modify the payment of child support when the circumstances would indicate.

* * *

Consequently, the interests of a spouse in a separation agreement leading to the dissolution of marriage are not the same as those of a minor child of a marriage. As such, an attorney who represents a spouse in the negotiation of a separation agreement does not simultaneously, automatically represent the interests of a minor child of the marriage.

Accordingly, the judgment of the court of appeals upholding summary judgment in favor of Willoughby in the malpractice action brought by Alyce Scholler on behalf of Philip is affirmed.

Notes and Questions

1. Does *Scholler* mean that children need their own lawyer(s) in every divorce action? *See* Miller v. Miller [p. 632].

2. Privity bars are falling in malpractice actions against attorneys. In the estate planning area (where third party claims are probably most common), only five states (Nebraska, New York, Ohio, Texas, and Virginia)—retained the privity barrier in 1990. Martin Begleiter, *Attor-*

ney Malpractice in Estate Planning—You've Got to Know When to Hold Up, Know When to Fold Up, 38 U. KAN. L. REV. 193 (1990).

3. Larry Lawyer represented Mary in a divorce action against Tom. The divorce was granted on November 4. Because of some delays and vacations, Larry did not get the divorce journal entry filed until December 1st at 8:00 a.m. Tom, however, had died at 3:00 a.m. that morning. Because the journal entry was not filed, the divorce was not final and Mary inherited Tom's property as a surviving spouse. Do Tom's children have a cause of action against Larry for failure to file the journal entry? *See* Wilson–Cunningham v. Meyer, 16 Kan.App.2d 197, 820 P.2d 725 (1991); Stephen Gillers, *Ethics That Bite: Lawyer's Liability to Third Parties*, 18 LITIGATION 8 (1987).

Chapter 11

DIVORCE AND DIVORCE SUBSTITUTES

[Divorce probably originated at nearly] the same date as marriage. I believe, however, that marriage is some weeks more ancient.

Voltaire

Why do people expect to be happily married when they are not individually happy? You go on so in America about marital contentment. Every magazine has an article with Nine Keys to it, or Seven Steps, as though the quest had any more sense to do it, or any more hope of fulfillment, that the search for El Dorado. In no other country is this juvenile ideal so naively held out—and with what failure! How do you expect mankind to be happy in pairs when it is so miserable separately?

Peter De Vries, Reuben, Reuben

We have examined the requirements our society imposes on those who want to marry, as well as the entitlements and disabilities with which it endows those who enter the married state. Now we must examine the rules applicable when one or both spouses want to terminate the relationship.

In modern America, marital termination is a frequent event. In 1994, there were 1,191,000 U.S. divorces. Domestic relations cases represented about one-third of all civil cases filed in U.S. courts of general jurisdiction in 1990. Paula M. DeWitt, *Breaking Up Is Hard to Do*, AMERICAN DEMOGRAPHICS, Oct. 1992, at 53.

Divorce is highly concentrated in the early years of marriage. In 1990, half of all divorces involved marriages of seven or fewer years. Half of divorcing men were age 35 or younger; half of divorcing women were age 33 or younger. U.S. DEP'T OF COMMERCE, BUREAU OF THE CENSUS,

STATISTICAL ABSTRACT OF THE UNITED STATES: 1995 tbl. 146. Many of these marriages appear to have been doomed from the start. "Almost 40% of divorced respondents to a Gallup poll reported that problems were present when they married or early in marriage." DeWitt, *supra*.

While the sources of today's high divorce rate are controversial, unprecedented prosperity and a remarkable increase in women's paid employment has reduced the likelihood that a dissatisfied spouse will remain married for purely economic reasons. Longer life expectancies have also dramatically increased the amount of time a married couple may expect to spend in the "bonds of matrimony." At the same time (whether as cause or effect or both), popular opinion on divorce has shifted dramatically. Many Americans do not remember—and cannot imagine—the time when a durable marriage was seen as a virtue per se, divorce was considered a disgraceful event, and divorce law was aimed at fettering the inclination to stray from the married state:

> [I]t must be carefully remembered that the general happiness of the married life is secured by its indissolubility. When people understand that they must live together, except for a very few reasons known to the law, they learn to soften by mutual accommodation that yoke which they know they cannot shake off; they become good husbands and good wives from the necessity of remaining husbands and wives; for necessity is a powerful master in teaching the duties which it imposes. If it were once understood that upon mutual disgust married persons might be legally separated, many couples who now pass through the world with mutual comfort, with attention to their common offspring and to the moral order of civil society, might have been at this moment living in a state of mutual unkindness, in a state of estrangement from their common offspring, and in a state of the most licentious and unreserved immorality. In this case, as in many others, the happiness of some individuals must be sacrificed to the greater and more general good.
>
> *Evans v. Evans*, 161 Eng.Rep. 466, 1 Hag.Con. 35 (1790).

Today, there is skepticism that "mutual disgust" can be transformed by indissolubility into "mutual comfort," and that restrictions on the legal termination of a marriage can play a meaningful role in preventing the factual termination of a relationship through abandonment or consensual separation. Nor is there widespread agreement that "the happiness of some . . . must be sacrificed to the greater good." This shift is linked (but without a clear causal relationship) to our relatively high divorce rate and relatively "lax" divorce laws.

SECTION 1. A BRIEF HISTORY OF DIVORCE

Most cultures have established procedures to terminate marital relationships. In Europe during the early Christian era, both Roman and Jewish law permitted divorce; somewhat later, Germanic and Anglo–Saxon law permitted either unilateral or mutual consent divorce. But, as we saw in Chapter 2, to the Roman Catholic Church marriage represented a sexual union blessed and sanctified by God. Under Roman Catholic canon law, "what God has joined together, let no man put asunder." In 1563, the Council of Trent officially reaffirmed the Church's prohibition on divorce, a prohibition maintained to the present day.

Canon law had a "safety valve," however, in annulment, which voided the marriage *ab initio*. The evidence suggests that annulment was freely obtainable for the right inducement:

> Practically speaking, it cannot be doubted that there existed a very wide liberty of divorce in the Middle Ages, though it existed mainly for those who were able to pay the ecclesiastical judge for finding a way through the tortuous maze of forbidden degrees [of consanguinity]. In a divorce procedure masquerading under the guise of an action for nullifying spurious marriages lurked the germs of perjury and fraud. When both persons were willing to separate, the matter must have been easy enough by collusion; and when one consort was tired of the other, the ecclesiastical court for money would be able to find good reasons for effecting his release. Spouses who had quarreled began to investigate their pedigrees and were unlucky if they could discover no "impedimentum dirimens" or cause which would have prevented the contraction of a valid marriage. The canons prescribing the prohibited degrees of relationship were marvels of ingenuity. Spiritual relationships, those gained in baptism, were recognized no less than natural relationships, and equally with them served as barriers to legal marriage. Marriage was prohibited within seven degrees of relationship and affinity; and none but the astutest students of the law were able to unravel so complicated a system. The annulling of marriages, which has been contracted within the prohibited degrees, became a flourishing business of the Church. No exercise of its power yielded more money, or caused more scandal. So tangled was the casuistry respecting marriage, at the beginning of the sixteenth century, that it might be said that, for a sufficient consideration, a canonical flaw could be found in almost any marriage.

G. Howard, II A History of Matrimonial Institutions 56–60 (1904).

Martin Luther and John Calvin criticized the Catholic Church's brisk business in annulments, as well as its views on marital indissolubility; both took the position that divorce should be permitted, at least for adultery. Their views influenced sixteenth-century marriage law in Scandinavia, Switzerland, the Netherlands, Scotland, and parts of Germany. *See generally* Roderick Phillips, Putting Asunder: A History of Divorce in Western Society (1988).

Other European nations, particularly those where most of the population was Catholic, continued to forbid divorce up to the modern era. Spain, Italy, and Ireland did not permit divorce until the twentieth century; in France, divorce was briefly available during the Revolution and Napoleonic era, then forbidden until 1884. Despite Henry VIII's break with the Catholic church over its unwillingness to annul his first marriage, in England absolute divorce was unobtainable except by a special act of Parliament until 1857. (The Church of England's ecclesiastical courts did grant divorces "*a mensa et thoro*" (from bed and board), that authorized legal separation but not remarriage.)

In keeping with the diverse geographic origins and religious views of the American colonists, colonial divorce laws were quite varied. In New England, many Puritans believed that divorce was preferable to a highly dysfunctional marriage. The Massachusetts divorce law dates from 1692 and, as early as 1620, Plymouth's officials declared marriage to be a civil rather than an ecclesiastical matter. Southern states typically agreed that marriage was a civil matter but refused to countenance divorce; South Carolina had no divorce law until the 1940s. *See* GLENDA RILEY, DIVORCE: AN AMERICAN TRADITION 8–29 (1991).

Any discussion of divorce history must, of course, acknowledge the possibly huge gulf between law and behavior. Even without divorce, desertion and separation were facts of life. Nor was it uncommon for a separated spouse to resettle, and remarry, in a new locale. (This option was, however, probably more open to men than women.)

During the nineteenth century, the demand for divorce increased. A system of legislative divorce was incapable of processing divorce petitions in quantity. As a delegate to the Kentucky Constitutional Convention of 1849 put it:

> "[Y]ear after year a great portion of the time of the general Assembly has been consumed with the passage of [private divorce] acts, [which] gave rise to 'universal complaint' because of the 'unnecessary' consumption of time and ... expense." The remedy, of course, was to abolish legislative divorce.
>
> The statutes were never simple, facilitative laws. To begin with, the law recognized no such thing as consensual divorce, Divorce was a privilege granted to an innocent spouse. It was in form an adversary lawsuit: plaintiff had to allege and prove "grounds" for divorce against defendant. In some states, only innocent plaintiffs were allowed to marry again. Guilty parties were left to stew in their juices.
>
> In other words, legislatures recognized the need for an efficient way to dissolve a marriage, but the enacted statutory schemes were never *too* efficient. There were, in short, compromises between two genuine social demands, which were in hopeless conflict. One was a demand that the law lend moral and physical force to the sanctity and stability of marriage. The other was a demand that the law permit people to choose and change their legal relations.
>
> The moral goals of divorce law were reflected in the statutory lists of "grounds." Adultery was always on the list. A few strict states, such as New York, hardly went further. Other states had longer lists. Desertion was commonly included. Other grounds in-

cluded fraud, impotence, conviction of a felony, or habitual drunkenness.

Lawrence Friedman, *Rights of Passage: Divorce Law in Historical Perspective*, 63 OR. L. REV. 649, 652 (1984).

By the dawn of the twentieth century, judicial divorce laws had been enacted by almost all American states and the vast majority of European nations.

The enactment of judicial divorce laws was accompanied by a rapid increase in the divorce rate. Between 1885 to 1910 the number of French divorces tripled; between 1867 and 1910, the number of English divorces increased fivefold. The same trend was seen in the United States.

Immediately following both World War I and World War II, the divorce rate climbed rapidly. The trend was widespread, but was most evident among young people directly affected by the War. In both instances, the abrupt post-war increase in the divorce rate was succeeded by a period of relative stability. In the 1960s, however, the divorce rate again began to rise sharply. In the U.S. and most European countries, the divorce rate doubled during the period from about 1960 to 1985. In the brief period since 1985, the divorce rate has, again, been relatively stable.

Across the "up and down" pattern in divorce rates, two trends, both evident in the graph reprinted below, are consistent. One, applicable to each country represented, is a higher divorce rate over time; while in all nations the divorce rate has gone up and down, overall the ups outweigh the downs. The other, applicable across nations, is in favor of a comparatively high U.S. divorce rate. In 1910, there were four times as many divorces in the U.S. as in England, Scotland, France, the Netherlands, Belgium and the Scandinavian countries combined, despite the fact that the U.S. population was smaller than the total population of these other nations. In 1980, at 5 divorces per 1000 population, the U.S. divorce rate was about twice that of England and Canada.

Comparative Divorce Rates—1865 to 1985

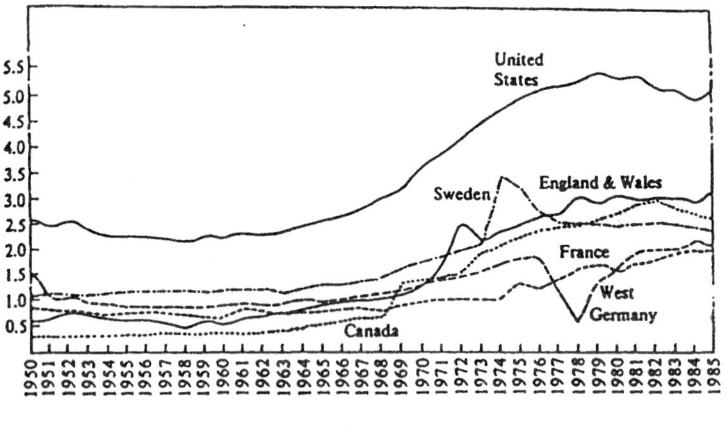

Divorces per 1,000 population

Source: RODERICK PHILLIPS, UNTYING THE KNOT 213 (1991).

The judicial divorce laws enacted during the nineteenth century made divorce available to a victimized spouse who could show, in a judicial proceeding, that the defendant spouse was guilty of one or another form of statutorily defined wrongdoing. While these laws were written with the idea that divorce would be denied if the plaintiff spouse could not show that the defendant spouse was guilty of conduct constituting a ground for divorce, the fact that the statutes permitted judgments on default opened the possibility of spousal collusion. The evidence suggests that collusion was common throughout the fault era. The proportion of divorce actions that were contested was 15.4 percent for the 1887–1906 period, 14.8 in 1922, declining to 11.9 in 1929, and increasing to 14.1 after the Depression began. U.S. DEP'T OF H.E.W., 100 YEARS OF MARRIAGE AND DIVORCE STATISTICS, UNITED STATES, 1867–1967 p. 19 (DHEW Publication No. (HRA) 74–1902 (1973)). In 1969, the Illinois Family Commission found that, in Cook County, Illinois, 97% of the 16,068 divorce decrees entered were uncontested. STATE OF ILLINOIS, FAMILY STUDY COMMISSION, REPORT AND RECOMMENDATIONS TO THE MEMBERS OF THE 76TH GENERAL ASSEMBLY 12 (1969). The evidence also suggests that divorce lawyers were sometimes knowing participants in sham proceedings. For example, in New York, where until 1966 adultery was the sole ground for divorce, researchers discovered that "the other woman" named in a number of cases was the secretary of a prominent divorce lawyer. *See, e.g.*, Richard H. Wels, *New York: The Poor Man's Reno*, 35 CORNELL L.Q. 303 (1950); *Note, Collusive and Consensual Divorce and the New York Anomaly*, 36 COLUM. L. REV. 1121 (1936).

Despite widespread acknowledgment of collusion and the law's inability to control it, the fault-based system of divorce survived, more or less intact, until the 1960s.

> Then, suddenly, the dam seemed to burst in divorce law.... The old system collapsed completely; no-fault rushed into the vacu-

um. California was a pioneer state, but no-fault is now the rule almost everywhere.... Why did this happen? With regard to this legal change, it certainly makes sense to note changing attitudes and ideologies about family, sex, and marriage, and push economic motives into the background. Many people have an economic interest in cheap divorce; but they always did. What stood in the way was an ethical opposition, which has gradually but definitely crumbled.

Lawrence Friedman, *Rights of Passage: Divorce Law in Historical Perspective*, 63 OR. L. REV. 649, 666–67 (1984).

Like the first wave of judicial divorce laws, "no-fault" divorce spread rapidly across the Western industrialized world; consistently, states and nations have moved from divorce based on fault toward at least limited acceptance of divorce based on demand. But today, no-fault divorce is also under attack. Some state legislatures have recently considered limiting or abolishing no-fault divorce; it is thus possible that fault divorce may become more important in the near future.

SECTION 2. GROUNDS FOR DIVORCE

A. FAULT DIVORCE

Although all states have accepted some form of no-fault divorce, fault-based divorce remains significant. First, most states merely added no-fault divorce as an additional divorce ground; a spouse may elect a "fault" or "no-fault" divorce process. Second, because many no-fault divorce statutes require a minimum period of separation but fault grounds do not, a fault divorce is often quicker to obtain. Third, divorce entitlements to spousal support and property may be affected by whether the divorce is obtained on fault grounds. In a number of states, a court may consider the relative fault of both spouses when dividing marital property (*see* Chapter 14); in some states spousal support may not be awarded to a spouse whose marital fault provided the basis of the divorce (*see* Chapter 15). Finally, in a few states no-fault divorce is available only if both spouses agree; absent such consent, divorce requires a showing of fault. N.Y. DOM. REL. L. § 170; MISS. CODE § 93–5–2; TENN. CODE § 36–4–103; OHIO REV. CODE §§ 3105.01, 3105.63.

Fault divorce grounds typically include adultery, desertion or abandonment, and cruelty. Adultery has been a basis for divorce in all American fault-based divorce statutes; while proof is not always easy, courts have interpreted adultery in a fairly consistent manner. Desertion invariably means a separation to which one spouse does not consent. But, in some courts, one spouse's departure will not be considered desertion if it was necessitated by the other's misconduct. Some courts have also held that, even if both spouses remain within the marital household, unjustified refusal to have sexual relations constitutes "constructive" desertion. *See* HOMER H. CLARK, JR., THE LAW OF DOMESTIC RELATIONS IN THE UNITED STATES 496–527 (2d ed. 1988); HARRY KRAUSE, FAMILY LAW IN A NUTSHELL 339–44 (3d ed. 1995).

As you can see from the chart below, adultery, cruelty and desertion were consistently the most common grounds for divorce during the period between the 1860s and 1960s. But the proportion of cases falling into each category changed dramatically over this period, with allegations of adultery declining from 25% of the total to 1.4% and allegations of cruelty rising from 16% to 42%. Can you think of any reasons for such a shift?

U.S. DEPT. OF H.E.W. 100 YEARS OF MARRIAGE AND DIVORCE STATISTICS, UNITED STATES, 1867–1967

DHEW Publication No. (HRA) 74–1902 (1973), p. 49

Table 20
DIVORCES AND PERCENT DISTRIBUTION BY LEGAL GROUNDS: UNITED STATES, SELECTED YEARS 1867–1965—Con.

Legal grounds	1965 [1]	1960 [2]	1950 [3]	1930	1916	1887–1906	1867–1886
	Percent distribution						
All grounds	100.0	100.0	100.0	100.0	100.0	100.0	100.0
Adultery	1.4	1.8	1.7	8.5	11.5	18.8	24.6
Bigamy and fraud	0.5	(4)	0.5	0.2	(4)	0.2	0.5
Conviction of crime	0.5	(4)	0.5	0.8	(4)	0.9	0.9
Cruelty	41.7	60.7	57.5	43.4	28.3	21.2	16.3
Desertion or abandonment	13.8	28.0	23.9	31.3	36.8	43.3	44.1
Drunkenness	0.3	(4)	2.5	2.5	3.4	5.7	7.8
Incompatibility	0.7	0.8	0.0	1.6	(4)	0.0	0.5
Indignities	15.5	(5)	9.9	(4)	(5)	1.2	(5)
Neglect or nonsupport	18.0	5.6	2.2	12.4	4.7	8.3	4.6
Separation or absence	3.5	0.6	0.2	0.5	(6)	0.1	0.0
Other grounds	4.1	2.5	1.1	0.4	15.3 [7]	0.4	0.6

1. Total of 22 reporting States.
2. Total of 18 reporting States.
3. Total of 20 reporting States.
4. Included with "other grounds."
5. Decrees granted for indignities included with decrees granted for cruelty.
6. Decrees granted for separations or absence included with decrees granted for desertion or abandonment.
7. Including 9,332 decrees granted for combinations of listed grounds—8.3 percent of the total.

LYNCH v. LYNCH

Massachusetts Court of Appeals, 1973.
1 Mass.App.Ct. 589, 304 N.E.2d 445.

KEVILLE, JUDGE.

This is an appeal by the libellant from a decree dismissing his libel for divorce brought on grounds of cruel and abusive treatment and desertion.

* * *

The parties have been married for fifty years and have not lived together since 1931. After finding that there was no evidence that the libellant had been deserted, the judge found, on admissions of the libellee, whose testimony he stated was "entirely credible," two isolated instances of her alleged cruel and abusive treatment toward the libellant. The first was an exchange of epithets between the parties in the libellant's barber shop in 1965 where the libellee had gone to ask him for money for her support. The second occurred in 1967 when she called him "a faker" after a court hearing to which he had been summoned for failure to obey an order of ten dollars a week for her support. There are instances in which verbal abuse may constitute cruel and abusive treatment. However, the facts found here do not as a matter of law require a different decree from that which had been entered.

The libellant has also appealed from the judge's order that he pay $100 as an allowance to the libellee to defend the libel. We find nothing on this record from which we conclude that the amount of the allowance granted by the judge was unreasonable. The order for an allowance and the decree dismissing the libel must be affirmed.

CAPPS v. CAPPS

Supreme Court of Virginia, 1975.
216 Va. 382, 219 S.E.2d 898.

PER CURIAM.

* * * The only questions properly presented on this appeal are whether the chancellor erred in awarding the wife a divorce on the ground of the physical cruelty alleged in her cross-bill and in denying the husband a divorce on the ground of desertion.

The parties were married on October 9, 1969. One child was born to them, and the husband adopted the wife's daughter by a former marriage. Prior to the marriage the husband had been seriously wounded while serving in the armed forces in Vietnam and, as a result, his left arm is paralyzed, he is forced to wear a leg brace for support, and he has a plate in his head.

The husband testified that his wife willfully deserted him on October 23, 1973. He admitted that he argued with her on the date of the alleged desertion and that, when she remarked that he "wasn't half the man Gary was," he became angry and struck her one time. He testified, however, that he immediately attempted to apologize to his wife, but was rebuffed. She then left their home, taking the two children with her, and they have not lived together as husband and wife since the date of the desertion. The husband admitted that there had been numerous separations and arguments in the past, but denied that he had ever been cruel to his wife.

The husband's father testified that the wife left his son on October 23, 1973, and that the parties have not lived together as husband and wife since that date.

The wife testified that on October 23, 1973, she had been physically abused by her husband. On that occasion, she said that an argument arose because he refused help from Child Protective Services to save their marriage. During the argument her husband struck her and choked her "in the bend of his arm." She testified that after she broke free from his hold, he said, "You and your bastard get out of here." She stated that immediately thereafter she left the home, taking with her the two children.

The wife's mother testified that on the evening of October 23, 1973, her daughter came to her home "hurting" and "crying." She noticed a "big knot" behind her daughter's ear, and she drove her to a hospital for x-rays.

* * *

In her cross-bill and proof, the wife relied on a single instance of physical abuse by her husband to support her claim of cruelty. Her testimony tended to show that during the October 23rd argument her husband struck and choked her, and ordered her to leave their home. There was no corroboration of the wife's testimony that her husband told her to "get out." Code § 20–99. While her testimony of physical injury is sufficiently corroborated by her mother's observation of a "big knot" on her head following the incident, we hold that this one instance of physical cruelty is insufficient to establish a ground for divorce.

In *DeMott v. DeMott*, 198 Va. 22, 92 S.E.2d 342 (1956), the wife established that during an argument her husband grabbed her, threw her against the wall, and threatened her with a knife. We held there that a divorce grounded on cruelty was properly denied the wife in that:

> "* * * [A] single act of physical cruelty does not constitute ground for divorce, unless it is so severe and atrocious as to endanger life, or unless the act indicates an intention to do serious bodily harm or causes reasonable apprehension of serious danger in the future, or the precedent or attendant circumstances show that the acts are likely to be repeated." 198 Va. at 28, 92 S.E.2d at 346.

* * *

Although we hold that the wife is not entitled to a divorce, it does not necessarily follow that the husband must be granted a divorce on the ground of desertion. * * *

Here the wife proved, by corroborated testimony, that her husband physically abused her and that this conduct was the provoking cause for her leaving the marital abode. Under these circumstances, we find that the husband's conduct did not entitle him to a divorce on the ground of willful desertion since his wife left the home without legal fault. Therefore the husband's prayer for a divorce was properly denied by the chancellor.

For the reasons stated the decree appealed from, insofar as it awarded the wife a divorce, is reversed.

Notes and Questions

1. The courts in *Lynch* and *Capps* attempted to articulate a distinction between relatively trivial marital misbehavior, insufficient to justify a divorce, from serious misbehavior, sufficient to justify a divorce. Can you articulate a better test? Under your rule, how, if at all, would the results change?

2. Should the test for cruelty justifying a divorce vary based upon the gender, race, class and cultural background of the petitioner? Consider Pochop v. Pochop, 89 S.D. 466, 233 N.W.2d 806, 807 (1975):

> Any definition of extreme cruelty in a marital setting must necessarily differ according to the personalities of the parties involved. What might be acceptable and even commonplace in the relationship between rather stolid individuals could well be extraordinary and highly unacceptable in the lives of more sensitive or high-strung husbands and wives. Family traditions, ethnic and religious backgrounds, local customs and standards and other cultural differences all come into play when trying to determine what should fall within the parameters of a workable marital relationship and what will not.

3. New York's highest court has consistently held that a stronger showing of cruelty is necessary in a lengthy marriage. *See* Brady v. Brady, 64 N.Y.2d 339, 486 N.Y.S.2d 891, 476 N.E.2d 290 (1985) Lower New York courts have taken this directive seriously. For example, in Gulisano v. Gulisano, 214 A.D.2d 999, 626 N.Y.S.2d 644 (1995), the court refused to grant a dissolve an eighteen year marital relationship that was "acrimonious, unhappy and incompatible." What policy concerns would motivate such a rule? (Remember that New York does not permit unilateral no-fault divorce.)

4. During the 1950s a highly respected sociologist conducted a survey and asked divorced wives to describe the cause of the divorce. He found that:

> [s]ome sophisticated respondents attempted to present a personality diagnosis of their husbands in superficially objective terms. Others felt that the husband personally betrayed them, or suddenly became a drunkard. A few never guessed that a divorce was impending until it happened, while others felt from an early period in the marriage that it would not last. It was not possible to classify each answer on several levels of meaning, as we wanted to do, because each respondent varied in her grasp of these levels. * * *
>
> The answers were varied, but almost all responses fell into these categories: *1. Personality, 2. Authority, or Cruelty, 3. "Complex," 4. Desertion, 5. Triangle, 6. Home Life, 7. Consumption, 8. Value, 9. Nonsupport, 10. Drinking, 11. Relatives.*

William J. Goode, Women in Divorce 115–116 (1969) (originally titled After Divorce (1956))

5. Does fault-based divorce encourage or discourage marriage? What, if any, effect is fault-based divorce likely to have on marital behavior?

B. FAULT DIVORCE DEFENSES

HOLLIS v. HOLLIS

Virginia Court of Appeals, 1993.
16 Va.App. 74, 427 S.E.2d 233.

BARROW, JUDGE.

In this appeal from a final decree of divorce, we ... hold that a finding of connivance, the prior consent of one spouse to the misconduct of another, was sufficiently supported by the evidence. We further hold that the defense of connivance need not be expressly asserted in the pleadings.

Responding to the wife's allegation of the husband's adultery, the husband admitted that he was engaged in an adulterous relationship with another woman before the husband and wife separated. The wife asserted in her cross-bill for divorce that the husband's adultery began "on or about May 24, 1990." The husband acknowledged that he had lived together with another woman since March 22, 1990, and had had sexual relations with the other woman. The nature of the relationship was corroborated by the testimony of the other woman and the testimony of a private investigator.

The husband, however, asserted that his wife had urged him to date the other woman and that he had entered into a relationship only after his wife encouraged it. He introduced into evidence a handwritten letter from the wife dated February 4, 1990, which he received before an intimate relationship with the other woman began. The wife wrote that she wished to be free from her marriage but was afraid that the husband would "marry some bimbo." She wrote that she had seen the husband talking to the other woman at a Christmas party and hoped that the husband would fall in love with the other woman so that the wife could get out of her marriage. She said, "I want so badly for [the husband] to fall in love and share the rest of his life with someone who really loves him; someone like [the other woman], or even [the other woman]."

The husband and the other woman testified that they first had sexual relations at the Greenbrier Hotel the third weekend in February, 1990. While there, they received flowers and a card from the wife. The card said, "My very best wishes to you both today, to your new beginning."

Finally, the husband and wife signed a document dated May 23, 1990, stating that the wife "consent[ed] to [the husband] moving out of our home." In it she also said that she was "aware that this could entail his moving in and living with another female." She agreed that she would not "use this against him as grounds for divorce or punitive action."

The trial court found that the husband's adultery resulted from the wife's "connivance and procurement" and granted the husband a divorce on no-fault grounds. The wife contends that the evidence does not support this finding and that the husband's failure to plead connivance barred his assertion of it.

Connivance has been defined as "the plaintiff's consent, express or implied, to the misconduct alleged as a ground for divorce." *Greene v. Greene*, 15 N.C.App. 314, 316, 190 S.E.2d 258, 260 (1972). Connivance denotes "direction, influence, personal exertion, or other action with knowledge and belief that such action would produce certain results and which results are produced." *Id.* The defense of connivance is based on "the maxim 'volenti non fit injuria,' or that one is not legally injured if he has consented to the act complained of or was willing that it should occur." *Id.* Other courts have similarly defined connivance.

Condonation, on the other hand, is one spouse's forgiveness of the other spouse's adulterous misconduct, usually evidenced by resumption and continuation of apparently normal matrimonial relations. Knowledge of the misconduct is necessary before condonation may occur. Condonation, it follows, may only occur after the occurrence of the misconduct and differs from connivance in when the act of consent or, in the case of connivance, influence occurs. While condonation occurs after the misconduct, connivance occurs before the misconduct.

* * *

The evidence supported the trial court's finding of the wife's connivance in the husband's misconduct. Her letters and the note accompanying the flowers amply support the finding that she encouraged, as well as consented to, the husband's adulterous relationship.

Another traditional defense to a fault divorce is *recrimination*, applicable when the misconduct of the plaintiff spouse constitutes a justification for the defendant spouse's misconduct. *See* Chastain v. Chastain, 559 S.W.2d 933 (1977). Even during the fault era, the defense was widely criticized:

> When both parties have committed material offenses it is generally obvious that the marriage is beyond salvage; yet the rule that recrimination is an absolute defense leaves the parties legally bound to each other. This situation produces many evils: it promotes adulterous relationships; it increases the danger of giving birth to illegitimate children; it encourages collusive and uncontested divorces; it exerts a corrupting influence on the negotiations that precede a default divorce case, including the exaction of an unfair property settlement or alimony arrangement; and in community

property states it leaves the management of the community property in the hands of the husband.

24 Am. Jur. 2d Divorce and Separation § 226 (1966).

In many states today, the recrimination defense has been expressly abolished by statute. *See* HOMER H. CLARK, JR., THE LAW OF DOMESTIC RELATIONS IN THE UNITED STATES 527–28 (2d ed. 1988).

C. NO–FAULT DIVORCE

1. *No–Fault Grounds*

UNIFORM MARRIAGE AND DIVORCE ACT

9A U.L.A. 147 (1987).

SECTION **302.**

(a) The [______] court shall enter a decree of dissolution of marriage if:

(1) the court finds that one of the parties, at the time the action was commenced, was domiciled in this State, or was stationed in this State while a member of the armed services, and that the domicil or military presence has been maintained for 90 days next preceding the making of the findings;

(2) the court finds that the marriage is irretrievably broken, if the finding is supported by evidence that (i) the parties have lived separate and apart for a period of more than 180 days next preceding the commencement of the proceeding, or (ii) there is serious marital discord adversely affecting the attitude of one or both of the parties toward the marriage;

(3) the court finds that the conciliation provisions of Section 305 either do not apply or have been met;

(4) to the extent it has jurisdiction to do so, the court has considered, approved, or provided for child custody, the support of any child entitled to support, the maintenance of either spouse, and the disposition of property; or has provided for a separate later hearing to complete these matters.

(b) If a party requests a decree of legal separation rather than a decree of dissolution of marriage, the court shall grant the decree in that form unless the other party objects.

SECTION **303.**

* * *

(e) Previously existing defenses to divorce and legal separation, including but not limited to condonation, connivance, collusion, recrimination, insanity, and lapse of time, are abolished.

SECTION **305.**

(a) If both of the parties by petition or otherwise have stated under oath or affirmation that the marriage is irretrievably broken, or one of the parties has so stated and the other has not denied it, the court, after hearing, shall make a finding whether the marriage is irretrievably broken.

(b) If one of the parties has denied under oath or affirmation that the marriage is irretrievably broken, the court shall consider all relevant factors, including the circumstances that gave rise to filing the petition and the prospect of reconciliation, and shall:

(1) make a finding whether the marriage is irretrievably broken; or

(2) continue the matter for further hearing not fewer than 30 nor more than 60 days later, or as soon thereafter as the matter may be reached on the court's calendar, and may suggest to the parties that they seek counseling. The court, at the request of either party shall, or on its own motion may, order a conciliation conference. At the adjourned hearing the court shall make a finding whether the marriage is irretrievably broken.

(c) A finding of irretrievable breakdown is a determination that there is no reasonable prospect of reconciliation.

* * *

Notes and Questions

1. After prolonged discussion with the Family Law Section of the American Bar Association (ABA), the new subsection (2) of § 302(a) was substituted for an earlier version which had simply read "the court finds that the marriage is irretrievably broken." The Family Law Section, however, was not satisfied and, in February 1974, recommended that the American Bar Association (ABA) House of Delegates withhold approval of the UMDA:

> [T]he grounds of objection include, but are not necessarily limited to, the fact that the alternative provision for divorce in § (a)(2) of the amended act 'or (ii) there is serious marital discord adversely affecting the attitude of one or both of the parties toward the marriage' makes possible a dissolution of marriage of however long duration by the whim of one party and, in practical effect, vitiates the 180 days separation period provided for in § 302(a)(2)(i). * * *

The Family Law Section recommended the following language:

> (2) * * * [A] marriage is irretrievably broken, which finding shall be established by proof (a) that the parties have lived separate and apart for a period of more than one year * * * (b) that such serious marital misconduct has occurred which has so adversely affected the physical or mental health of the petitioning party as to make it impossible for the parties to continue the marital relation, and that reconciliation is improbable * * * (3) The court finds that the conciliation provisions of § 305 have been met and that past

efforts at reconciliation have failed or that further attempts at reconciliation would be impracticable or not in the best interests of the family.

What are the pros and cons of (1) the original UMDA; (2) the ABA proposal; and (3) the amended UMDA?

2. Only a minority of states have followed the UMDA approach and adopted irretrievable breakdown (or irreconcilable differences or some other similar term) as the sole ground for divorce. *See* Linda D. Elrod & Robert Spector, *Family Law in the Fifty States*, 29 FAM. L.Q. 741, tbl. 4 (1996). Some have added an irretrievable breakdown ground to fault grounds for divorce (*see, e.g.*, TEX. FAM. CODE § 6.001; GA. CODE § 19–5–3). The majority have added to their fault grounds a provision permitting no-fault divorce after a minimum period of separation. *See, e.g.*, Elrod & Spector, *supra*. In three states (New York, Mississippi, Tennessee) no-fault divorce requires, in some or all cases, both a minimum period of separation and the consent of both spouses.

3. Germany, the Netherlands, England, and all of the Scandinavian countries except Denmark now accept unilateral no-fault divorce; a number of other European nations permit no-fault divorce based only on consent. *See* JEAN MILLAR & ANDREA WARMAN, FAMILY OBLIGATIONS IN EUROPE 14 (1996).

Problem 11–1:

You represent Henry in a divorce action against his wife Wendy. Henry initiated the divorce action alleging adultery by Wendy. Wendy has counterclaimed for divorce based on irreconcilable differences; she has also requested permanent maintenance and equitable property distribution. Would it make sense to consent to the entry of a divorce decree on a no-fault basis? What facts will be relevant to your determination? *See* Ebbert v. Ebbert, 123 N.H. 252, 459 A.2d 282 (1983).

2. *What Constitutes Irretrievable Breakdown*

HAGERTY v. HAGERTY

Supreme Court of Minnesota, 1979.
281 N.W.2d 386.

MAXWELL, JUSTICE.

* * * Claire, after unsuccessfully urging William to seek treatment for alcoholism, asked him in the summer of 1976 to leave the home. William moved out in August and filed for divorce in September. He made several unsuccessful attempts at reconciliation, but testified that no hope of reconciliation remained at the time of the proceedings. Claire claimed the marriage could be saved if William were treated for alcoholism, but she had not otherwise been willing to take him back.

Prior to the hearing on the dissolution petition, Claire had unsuccessfully sought a court order dismissing the petition unless her husband completed treatment for his alcoholism within 6 months and agreed to a one-year after-care program; if thereafter he wanted the dissolution she would not resist.

On April 6, 1978, the trial court dissolved the marriage after finding, among other things, that William suffered from alcoholism, a treatable disease; that it was a principal cause of marital discord which adversely affected his attitude towards the marriage; and that the marriage was irretrievably broken.

The pithy statement in appellant's brief that she "simply suggests that the alcoholism is the culprit and that Petitioner's assessment of the marriage is deluded," sets the scene. She then asks (1) how lucid are the perceptions of an alcoholic about the marriage; (2) whether the same perception would exist after recovery from alcoholism; and (3) whether the petitioner proved that the marriage was irretrievable broken.

The record amply supports the finding of serious marital discord, and Minn.St.1976, § 518.06, subd. 2, expressly permits a finding of irretrievable breakdown upon such evidence.

Since the record also amply supports the findings of alcoholism as a principal cause of the discord and as a treatable disease, the issue is whether the petitioner's untreated alcoholism can or should defeat findings of discord and breakdown. The "can" issue is one of statutory construction; the "should" issue is one of public policy.

Statutory Construction: Although irretrievable breakdown was the only ground for dissolution in the 1976 statute, several former grounds were retained in altered form in Minn.St.1976, § 518.06, subd. 2, as evidentiary guidelines for establishing that ground, and the guideline of serious marital discord was added. There was no requirement for reconciliation attempts or stay of dissolution for any specified, limited period. Without requirements indicating a legislative policy of affirmatively encouraging a possibility of reconciliation, the statute contemplates that the likelihood of reconciliation be considered in the determination of irretrievable breakdown along with the evidentiary guidelines.

Commentators and cases in other jurisdictions which have interpreted the grounds in no-fault dissolution statutes generally agree that the underlying concern is whether a meaningful marriage exists or can be rehabilitated. With that concern as the central issue, irretrievable breakdown is a fact which can be shown where both parties acknowledge that a breakdown exists at the time of the proceedings and one sees no reconciliation possibility. It can also be shown by evidence of only one party's belief that it is the existing state, particularly where the parties have been living apart.

Where one party urged that the marriage situation was remediable but the other refused to pursue counseling or reconciliation, the subjective factor proving irretrievable breakdown was established and dissolution was granted. In situations where statutes authorize counseling or continuance and the testimony of the party alleging breakdown might be impeachable or doubtful, a continuance is favored over a denial, with dissolution following in the event reconciliation is not accomplished.

Because the courts look at the existing subjective attitude, evidence of cause is no more determinative than evidence of fault. * * *

Upon the evidence introduced, . . . and under the prevailing view of the single ground for dissolution in no-fault statutes, the husband's untreated alcoholism cannot defeat findings of serious marital discord and irretrievable breakdown.

Notes and Questions

1. Most courts have followed the *Hagerty* approach, finding irretrievable breakdown even if one spouse wants to continue the marriage. *See* Desrochers v. Desrochers, 115 N.H. 591, 347 A.2d 150 (1975); Eversman v. Eversman, 4 Conn.App. 611, 496 A.2d 210 (1985); Note, 7 LOYOLA L. A. L. REV. 453 (1974).

2. Most courts have been reluctant to order a petitioner to do more than attend counselling in an attempt to save the marriage. In Roberts v. Roberts, 200 Neb. 256, 263 N.W.2d 449 (1978), for example, the court denied the defendant wife's request for an order requiring the plaintiff husband to stop living with his mistress. Why such reluctance? Would it make more sense for courts to require a showing of efforts to preserve the marriage as a precondition to a breakdown finding?

3. *What Constitutes Separation*

WIFE S. v. HUSBAND S.

Supreme Court of Delaware, 1977.
375 A.2d 451.

PER CURIAM.

* * * At the time the complaint was filed § 1505 provided as follows:

> "(a) The Court shall enter a decree of divorce when it finds that the marriage is irretrievably broken.
>
> (b) A marriage is irretrievably broken where it is characterized by (1) voluntary separation, * * *."

* * *

Defendant tacitly concedes that the Court correctly determined that the marriage was "irretrievably broken," so there is no dispute as to that aspect of the statute. The controversy centers on whether plaintiff proved that the parties were "voluntarily separated."

To be voluntary within the meaning of the statute, a separation must be with the consent of both parties. This is to say that a plaintiff must prove that the "separation was mutually voluntary." And a "consent" by one spouse which results from misconduct by the other is not voluntary. Mutuality is the essence of the statute.

Here, plaintiff made out a *prima facie* case when he offered evidence that his wife agreed to separate. But it is undisputed that during the year before the separation the husband, according to his own testimony, had engaged in sexual affairs with "possibly three" different women and that his wife was aware "at any rate" that he was "seeing" at least one of them. Thus the evidence as to the wife's "consent" must be viewed in light of these circumstances.

On this state of the evidence the Superior Court concluded that defendant, "having presented a defense, has not established it." In our view, the Court erroneously placed such a burden upon the wife. She was not obliged to prove any defense. The obligation was upon her husband to prove, by a preponderance of the evidence, that she had voluntarily agreed to separate from him. Given the husband's admitted infidelities and the wife's undisputed testimony as to *why* she was agreeable to a separation, there is not sufficient evidence to support a finding of voluntariness. In short, plaintiff's evidence showed a separation and expressions of consent thereto by the wife, but the evidence does not support a finding of mutuality which is the fundamental requirement of the statute.

It follows, therefore, that the judgment of the Superior Court [granting the husband a divorce] must be reversed.

Notes and Questions

1. In most states where no-fault divorce is available based on a period of separation, consensual separation is not required. *See* Homer H. Clark, The Law of Domestic Relations in the United States 517–18 (2d ed. 1988). In 1996, no-fault divorce separation periods ranged from six months (Montana, Vermont) to three years (Rhode Island, Texas, Utah). Irish law requires a four-year separation. Until 1996, English law required a two-year separation for consensual divorce and a five-year separation if one spouse resisted the divorce; in 1996, the law was changed to require a maximum waiting period of eighteen months. *See* Gibb, Sherman and Pierce, *Mackay Accepts Concessions to Save Divorce Bill*, London Times, June 12, 1996, Home News Section.

2. Why did the court construe the statute as it did in *Wife S.*? What type of no-fault divorce does the case sanction? *Compare* N.Y. Dom. Rel. L. § 170:

> An action for divorce may be maintained by a husband or wife . . . on . . . the . . . grounds [that]:
>
> * * *
>
> (6) The husband and wife have lived separate and apart pursuant to a written agreement of separation, subscribed by the parties thereto and acknowledged or proved in the form required to entitle a deed to be recorded, for a period of one or more years after the

execution of such agreement and satisfactory proof has been submitted by the plaintiff that he or she has substantially performed all the terms and conditions of such agreement. Such agreement shall be filed in the office of the clerk of the county wherein either party resides....

3. Some courts have held that the separation must be coupled with the intention of dissolving the marital relationship. For example, in Sinha v. Sinha, 515 Pa. 14, 526 A.2d 765 (1987) the husband moved from India to New Jersey to begin a graduate program. Due to visa problems, the wife stayed in India. The husband did not communicate to his wife that there were marital problems until he filed for divorce in Pennsylvania three years after he moved to the U.S. The Pennsylvania Supreme Court concluded that, to satisfy the statutory requirement that the spouses have lived separately for three years, at least one spouse must have "a clear intent ... to dissolve the marital ties at the beginning of the three-year period." Because the husband did not prove such intent, the divorce was not granted.

4. Most courts have held that separation entails residence in separate dwellings. Thus, in Barnes v. Barnes, 276 S.C. 519, 280 S.E.2d 538 (1981), the court denied a divorce petition when the parties claimed that they had lived in separate rooms of the marital home and had had no sexual relations during the required separation period. The court held that "[t]his situation encourages collusion between the dissatisfied partners of the marriage." *But see* In re Marriage of Kenik, 181 Ill.App.3d 266, 129 Ill.Dec. 932, 536 N.E.2d 982 (1989). What if people cannot afford two separate households? Would they effectively be barred from getting a divorce? Would that be constitutional? *Cf.* Boddie v. Connecticut, [p. 563].

5. The utility of a minimum separation period to deter hasty divorce will depend, in large part, on whether other divorce grounds that do not require such a separation are available. For example, until 1996 England retained fault grounds in addition to no-fault divorce based on separation; in 1986, three-fourths of all divorces were granted on fault grounds. *See* Law Commission, "Facing the Future: A Discussion Paper on the Ground for Divorce," Law. Com. 170 (1988). An Ohio study reports an even larger percentage of divorcing couples choosing fault divorce rather than utilizing no-fault divorce, which required a two-year separation. *See* Robert E. McGraw et al., *A Case Study in Divorce Law Reform and Its Aftermath*, 20 J. FAM. L. 443, 464 (1982).

The new English system (which also abolishes fault grounds for divorce) requires one spouse to file a statement of marital breakdown and then requires a waiting period of a maximum of eighteen months. What advantages does this approach offer as compared with the traditional one? Are there other policy bases for a minimum period of separation as a precondition for a no-fault divorce? If yes, what is a "reasonable" waiting period?

4. *Summary Divorce Procedures*

A few states have adopted summary dissolution (i.e., nonjudicial) divorce procedures for cases in which public policy concerns are minimal. For example, in California summary dissolution is available if the parties have not had a child (and the wife is not pregnant), the marriage has lasted fewer than five years, neither party owns realty other than a leasehold interest, the community estate does not exceed $25,000 and the family debts do not exceed $4,000, the parties have signed a settlement agreement regarding their rights and liabilities, and no spousal support is sought. *See* CAL. FAM. CODE § 2400. The Oregon provision is similar. *See* ORE. REV. STATS. § 107.485. These summary divorce procedures are significant, because a substantial number of divorcing couples fit the California criteria.

SECTION 3. THE CURRENT DEBATE: WHAT DIVORCE LAW DO WE WANT?

THE LAW COMMISSION (LONDON), FACING THE FUTURE: A DISCUSSION PAPER ON THE GROUND FOR DIVORCE

29–30, 32, 45 (Law Com. No. 170, 1988).

4.3 The move away from pure fault systems seems to reflect an almost universal recognition by legislators that restricting divorce to cases where a particular fault-based ground has been satisfied does not buttress the stability of marriage and does not ensure justice between the spouses, as was originally thought. Thus, provision is made for divorce either on the ground of breakdown or separation in addition to fault-based grounds. The retention of fault-based grounds in the mixed systems would seem to reflect the view that the law must provide a moral framework for marriage. Principally, it is thought that an innocent spouse must always be able to obtain an immediate divorce against a guilty one on the basis of the offence. The fault-based grounds define what behaviour is acceptable and what is not. However, as has been shown above, this view is based on the dubious assumptions that commission of a particular marital offence causes breakdown of marriage and that the victim of that offence is completely innocent. It is recognition that neither assumption is necessarily correct, * * * that has prompted a number of legal systems to remove the element of fault from their divorce laws entirely.

4.7 * * * [I]t would seem that although breakdown is a widely accepted *principle*, experience elsewhere bears out the Commission's earlier view that it is not a justiciable issue. Any attempt at adjudication is likely to reintroduce an element of fault or at least of bitter recrimination. A logical application of the breakdown principle requires divorce on unilateral demand, at least if that demand is persisted in for any length of time. * * *

* * *

4.14 There are two main criticisms [of unilateral divorce on demand]. The first is that it represents the abdication of the State from any responsibility for determining whether a divorce should be granted. Yet, as we have seen, this may be the only logical application of the breakdown principle, which has been so widely accepted as the basis of modern divorce law. If breakdown is not justiciable and any fact chosen to prove breakdown is arbitrary, the only true judges of whether the marriage can continue are the parties themselves. This criticism also fails to address the difficult question of the nature of the State's interest. Once breakdown is accepted as the proper rationale for divorce, it is difficult to devise any logical basis for protecting a spouse who does not wish to be divorced even though the marriage has clearly broken down. The State's real interest may then be in protecting that spouse's financial position (and with it that of the State itself) and the interests of any minor children.

4.15 A second criticism is that if divorce is available immediately on unilateral demand then parties may be tempted to divorce without having considered the implications thoroughly. The mere fact of requiring a court hearing does not necessarily solve this problem, as the court will not always be able to identify a possibility of reconciliation. The Swedish requirement that in cases involving minor children or lack of consent, the divorce is delayed for a six month "reconsideration period" (unless there has been a two years' separation) is clearly designed to meet the problem of precipitate divorce, although it may be thought too limited. It may, however, be more effective to use the divorce *process*, rather than the ground for divorce, as a means of identifying cases where there is a realistic possibility of reconciliation.

* * *

5.36 Under the present system, in.... [contested] cases a decree can be refused altogether if this would result in grave financial or other hardship to the respondent and it would in all the circumstances be wrong to dissolve the marriage. This has been restrictively applied, partly because any hardship has usually already resulted from five years' separation [required to obtain a contested no-fault divorce] and will not be materially increased by the divorce itself, save where substantial widows' benefits are at stake, and partly because a liberal application of the provision would circumvent the very policy which led to the 1969 reforms.

5.37 The rationale for this provision was to safeguard the position of the innocent spouse who did not wish to be divorced.... [but] the implication that only respondents in these cases are wholly innocent and worthy of protection whereas respondents in other cases are not, is unfounded.... If we were to move to a wholly no-fault divorce law, there would obviously be a case for extending the protection of a hardship bar to all who wished to invoke it.

5.38 There are considerable attractions in doing so. There is still a substantial economic imbalance between the spouses in most marriages which have lasted for any length of time, particularly where there are children. We cannot conclude from the fact that the hardship bar is hardly ever invoked at present that it is totally ineffective. The ... hardship bar at the end may well have an effect upon the bargaining of couples ... To remove all the obstacles to divorce by the economically more powerful spouse, without giving any protection to the weak, might well be thought objectionable.

5.39 However, there are objections to using a hardship bar to supply that protection. If divorce were impossible in cases where hardship could not be avoided, it would defeat the object of enabling dead marriages to be dissolved in due course.... [I]t would deny divorce to the poor or not-so-poor who were unable to make proper provision. It might well be necessary to reintroduce notions of fault in order to ensure that divorces were not denied to deserving spouses in such cases. There clearly will be cases in which to deny one spouse a divorce on the ground that it will cause hardship to the other will be to cause as much if not more hardship to the first.

* * *

6.2 We suggest that the principle that divorce should be available when, but only when, a marriage has irretrievably broken down should be retained. Several methods of establishing this are discussed. * * *

6.3 Two proposals ... emerge as the most realistic. These are:

(a) divorce after a period of separation; and

(b) divorce after a period of transition in which the parties are given time and encouragement to reflect and make the necessary arrangements for the future.

In its final report (The Ground for Divorce (Law Com. No. 192)), the Commission compared the pros and cons of the two proposals deemed "most realistic" in its 1988 report:

> [*Divorce after a period of separation*] would be beneficial for several reasons: for example, it would provide solid evidence of marital breakdown, prevent hasty or rash petitioning and ensure that the couple has experience of living apart. However, most respondents rejected this option. One reason for this was that it was felt it would discriminate against needy petitioners (such as dependent mothers with young children who are victims of domestic violence or other abuse) who could not afford to finance two properties and two households. Furthermore, there would be a very strong possibility that incidents of perjury would arise as there would be no method of checking the truth of the statement that the parties had been living apart for the required period of time. Perhaps one of the main disadvantages of such a system would be that it would drive couples

> further apart rather than encouraging them to explore the possibility of reconciliation.
>
> [*Divorce after a period of transition*] ... received the most support from respondents and from the public opinion survey which was undertaken by the Law Commission. Under this model, divorce would only be granted after a fixed minimum period of time which, as explained later, should be one year; in this period, the couple would have to consider the practical consequences resulting from the divorce (such as arrangements for the children and financial matters), and to decide whether the breakdown in their relationship was, indeed, irreparable. This proposal would avoid the defects contained in both the present law and the separation model, while providing solid evidence of marital breakdown. The beginning of the period would be officially recorded, thus minimising the chance of perjury. Although the couple would not be obliged to separate, the court would be able to deal with the practical consequences of the divorce before granting the order.
>
> ... A particular advantage of this option was said to be an increased potential for the use of conciliation, counseling and mediation in the resolution of disputes relating to practical issues. Thus, the cumulative effect of all these advantages would be that there would be a less hostile and more co-operative atmosphere created between the parties which should reduce the damage caused to any children involved.
>
> However, ... the objection was made that the 'process over time' model does not allow one spouse to contest the other spouse's allegation that marital breakdown has occurred, and thus it amounts to divorce by unilateral demand. However, this is the inevitable result of any system based on irretrievable breakdown, including the present one. A contest in court cannot be the best way to save those marriages where the breakdown is not irretrievable, as it places far too many emotional and financial demands on the parties and can only harm the children. A fairly long period of reflection, together with the availability of counselling, should result in saving the marriages which are capable of being saved....
>
> Jacqueline Brown & Clair Lydon, in FAMILY LAW 462–63 (Dec. 1990).

Perhaps ironically given the high U.S. divorce rate, American critics of no-fault divorce have been more willing than their British counterparts to abandon no-fault divorce in at least some situations. Their criticisms of no-fault divorce fall into several diverse categories.

1. *Divorce Bargaining under Fault and No-fault Divorce*: Some critics have focused on the divorce bargaining process. Fault divorce provided the virtuous spouse a very large bargaining chip; he or she could block the guilty spouse's ability to obtain a divorce. Professor Allen Parkman has argued that, because of the loss of the fault bargaining chip, unilateral divorce enables one spouse to obtain a divorce without adequately compensating the other for sacrifices made during marriage; mutual consent divorce, he asserts, would enhance the bargaining power

of the spouse who is not seeking a divorce, increasing the probability that he or she would receive adequate compensation in the divorce. *See* ALLEN PARKMAN, NO FAULT DIVORCE: WHAT WENT WRONG? (1992). Alternatively, Professor Mary Ann Glendon has suggested that the potential for economic hardship occasioned by unilateral no-fault divorce could be lessened by granting judges the power to deny a divorce based on a showing of exceptional hardship. *See* MARY ANN GLENDON, ABORTION AND DIVORCE IN WESTERN LAW 74 (1987); MARY ANN GLENDON, THE TRANSFORMATION OF FAMILY LAW 192 (1989).

Similar criticisms of no-fault divorce were made earlier by Professor Lenore Weitzman, who undertook a pioneering study of California's no-fault divorce law. Weitzman found that the likelihood of receiving alimony, the duration of alimony awards, and the proportion of marital property awarded women all decreased following the introduction of no-fault and thus argued that "[t]he major economic result of the divorce law revolution is the systematic impoverishment of divorced women and their children." *See* LENORE J. WEITZMAN, THE DIVORCE REVOLUTION, 74, 164–67 (1985).

The available data fail to support Weitzman's claims. First, Weitzman's assertion assumes that the spouse who will typically wish to resist divorce is the wife. While that assertion may well have been true in 1970 when women had fewer economic opportunities outside marriage, by the early 1990s more than half of the divorced women interviewed by the Gallup Organization said that it was their idea to separate, as compared with only 44 per cent of men. Paul M. DeWitt, *Breaking Up is Hard to Do*, AMERICAN DEMOGRAPHICS, Oct. 1992, at 53. *See also* Sanford L. Braver et al., *Who Divorced Whom? Methodological and Theoretical Issues*, 20 J. DIVORCE & REMARRIAGE 1 (1993); Marygold Melli, *Constructing a Social Problem: The Post–Divorce Plight of Women and Children*, 1986 AM. B. FOUND. RES. J. 759, 77–71.

Weitzman's assertion also neglects the fact that California, like many other states that adopted no-fault divorce, contemporaniously overhauled its rules governing alimony and property distribution. Professor Marsha Garrison reviewed research on divorce outcomes in a number of states before and after no-fault divorce was adopted and compared them to her own research results in New York, which changed its alimony and property distribution rules but did not adopt unilateral no-fault divorce. She found that divorced wives in New York who retained their fault bargaining chips were no more likely to receive an alimony award than were divorced wives in no-fault states. *See* Marsha Garrison, *The Economics of Divorce: Changing Rules, Changing Results,* in DIVORCE REFORM AT THE CROSSROADS 90–100 (Stephen D. Sugarman & Herma H. Kay eds. 1990).

2. *The "Message" of No–Fault*: Other critics of no-fault divorce have been less troubled by bargaining endowments than by no-fault's message about marital commitment:

The error of treating romantic love as the necessary condition for entering into marriage, and, more importantly, for continuing marriage has been by far the more harmful ... As a social matter ... the problem is not that love drives us only temporarily insane and that we eventually discover that our mate is not whom or what we thought. It is, rather, that we accept the belief that taking on, and adhering to, the life-long responsibility of marriage and children should be tied to the continuance of so ephemeral a thing as romantic love. This flawed notion has enticed millions of people to abandon marriage when romantic love faded, and, perhaps more importantly, it has led the rest of society to assent and to treat the absence of romantic love as an excuse, even a justification, for abandoning a marriage. Societal acceptance in turn encourages people to act toward their spouses without love, honor or respect, knowing that they can leave should they discover that they have "grown apart." That the law has assented to this cultural change by permitting divorce willy-nilly is independently harmful. But the liberalization of divorce laws was less the cause, and more the effect, of a widespread cultural acceptance of men and women renouncing their marriage vows.

Lloyd Cohen, *Rhetoric, The Unnatural Family, and Women's Work*, 81 VA. L. REV. 2275, 2291 (1995). *See also* Lynn Wardle, *No-Fault Divorce and the Divorce Conundrum*, 1991 B.Y.U. L. REV. 79.

A related claim relates to marriage incentives:

[Unilateral no-fault divorce] creates [incentives] for marriages designed from the outset to end in divorce. A poor young woman marries a rich old man, knowing that every year his income exceeds his expenses and produces substantial savings. At the end of five years, pursuant to her original intention, she dissolves the marriage and claims one half of the savings built up during it. Unilateral divorce ... fosters the symmetrical incentive for unscrupulous poor women to marry rich men.

RICHARD POSNER, ECONOMIC ANALYSIS OF LAW 134 (3rd ed. 1986).

Finally, some commentators argue that divorce *should* be about fault:

Under ... [no-fault] a wrongdoing husband can come home every Saturday night for five years, drunk and penniless because of skirt-chasing, gambling, or some other misdeeds; then, he may beat, bruise and abuse his wife because he is unhappy with himself, and then he will be permitted to go down and get a divorce on printed forms purchased at a department store and tell the trial judge that the marriage is "irretrievably broken." Or, the offending wife, after jumping from bed to bed with her new found paramours, chronically drunk, and when at home nagging, brawling and quarreling, all against the wishes of a faithful husband who remains at home nurturing the children, is permitted to divorce her husband who does not desire a divorce, but rather, has one forced upon him, not because of anything he has done, but because the offending wife tells the trial court that her marriage is "irretrievably broken." In my opinion, the offending spouse should not have standing to obtain a divorce if the innocent one invokes the doctrine that, "He who comes into equity must come with clean hands."

Ryan v. Ryan, 277 So.2d 266, 278 (Fla.1973) (Roberts, J., dissenting).

These claims are difficult to evaluate. Undeniably, no-fault divorce sends a different message about marital commitment than does fault divorce. But there is evidence to suggest that a shift in public attitudes toward marital commitment set the stage for no-fault divorce, rather than the reverse. And it is quite unclear what role, if any, divorce grounds play in determining divorce behavior; certainly the message of fault divorce did not suffice to prevent widespread fraud and collusion. Finally, the message of fault may hinder reconciliation and make it more difficult for a couple to work together after divorce. *See* Gwynn Davis & Mervyn Murch, Grounds for Divorce (1988) (arguing in favor of no-fault divorce).

3. *The Impact of No–Fault Divorce on the Divorce Rate*: Some commentators see no-fault divorce not just as a source of casual commitment to marriage, but also of a higher divorce rate. *See* Wardle, *supra* note 2, at 116–19. Support for this proposition comes from two studies. One reported a significant link between the introduction of no-fault divorce and a rise in the divorce rate. Nakonezny et al., *The Effect of No–Fault Divorce Law on the Divorce Rate Across the Fifty States*, 57 J. Marr. & Fam. 477 (1995). The other found evidence for a relationship between no-fault reforms and divorce rates in some states but not others, as well as regional differences in the impact of no-fault laws and differences associated with the way the various no-fault laws were classified. The latter researcher concluded that no-fault laws "had a significant impact on divorce rates" but, because he could explain none of the regional or classification differences, also suggested that methodological problems precluded a definitive answer to the debate. Thomas Marvell, *Divorce Rates and the Fault Requirement*, 23 Law & Soc. Rev. 543 (1989).

Other researchers have failed to find a link between the introduction of no-fault divorce and the divorce rate. The Nakonezny et al. results may also derive from methodological flaws in the study design. The study was based on a comparison of divorce rates during the three years preceding no-fault divorce and the three years following it. Critics argue that one would expect a temporary surge in divorces following the introduction of no-fault divorce both because its introduction would naturally lead some couples to postpone their divorce to take advantage of no-fault's lesser evidentiary requirements and because no-fault divorce tended to speed up the divorce process, producing a marked reduction in the fault era divorce backlog. Moreover, divorce rates in the United States and in Europe had been increasing for almost a century before the introduction of no-fault. *See* Ira M. Ellman, *The Misguided Movement to Revive Fault Divorce, and Why Reformers Should Look Instead to the American Law Institute*, 11 INTL. J. L. POLICY & FAM. 216, 219–20 & n.23 (1997) (summarizing studies).

4. *The Impact of No–Fault Divorce on Children*: Some critics of no-fault divorce see its use as particularly problematic in the case of couples with young children:

> . . . I propose the legislative creation of a special marital status: the marriage for minor children. It would be accorded to all couples upon the birth of their first child and would continue until their last child reached eighteen. Its legal incidents would differ from those of other marriages in two ways: the grounds for divorce and the governing marital property rules.
>
> Divorce to terminate a marriage for minor children would be hard to get. In addition to establishing the usual grounds for divorce, couples with minor children would have to establish that continuing the marriage would cause either or both spouses exceptional hardship and would harm their minor children more than the divorce. The more stringent ground would encourage parents to compromise their differences in the interests of their children, yet it would not perpetuate marriages in which parental discord damages the children more than divorce. It would enable the courts to explore the possible effects of the divorce on the children, an inquiry they do not make under current law. Children's interests would become a crucial factor not only in deciding custody, but also in deciding their parents' rights to divorce.
>
> Similarly, marital property rules governing the marriage for minor children would differ from those governing other types of marriage. Like the current laws prescribing divorce grounds, laws imposing economic rules upon married couples make no distinction between marriages with minor children and others. Yet parents of minor children have special needs. Their marriages call for economic incidents that reinforce the idea that they are partners in the joint endeavor of raising their children, and that the continuing efforts of both parents are necessary for optimum performance of the task.
>
> Existing judicial powers to grant alimony and child support to dependent family members would be expanded for marriages with minor children to allow the courts to order continuation of the economic partnership between ex-spouses in the children's interest. A divorcing court could thus delay ultimate property division between parents until all the children reached eighteen. The more difficult divorce standard and the immutable partnership rules would apply during the minority of all children. Thereafter, the couple could divorce as easily as couples without minor children and alter their economic relations by agreement if they chose.

Judith Younger, *Marital Regimes: A Story of Compromise and Democratization*, 67 CORNELL L. REV. 45, 90–91 (1981).

See also Galston, *Needed: A Not–So–Fast Divorce Law*, N.Y. TIMES, December 27, 1995 at A11 (proposing that divorce during children's minority be permitted only for fault or after a five-year waiting period).

The claims in favor of a special divorce regime for couples with minor children are also hard to evaluate. Younger's proposal contemplates extensive changes in the economic entitlements of divorce as well as divorce grounds. It is unclear whether judges are more capable of determining whether divorce is preferable to a continued unhappy marriage than they are of determining whether a marriage is irretrievably broken. And whether altered divorce grounds would in fact "encourage parents to compromise their differences in the interests of their children, yet . . . not perpetuate marriages in which parental discord damages the children more than divorce" is certainly speculative.

Whatever the merits of the arguments against no-fault divorce, within the past few years, legislators have paid them increasing heed. Laws making divorce more difficult for couples with minor children have been introduced in several states. *See* Vobejda, *Breaking Up Called Far Too Easy To Do*, HOUSTON CHRONICLE, March 12, 1996 at 7A. col. 1. Some states have considered the abolition of no-fault divorce across the board. *See* Milbank, *No–Fault Divorce Law Is Assailed in Michigan, and Debate Heats Up,* WALL STREET JOURNAL, January 5, 1995, at A1, col. 1. Thus far, none of these proposed changes in the law have been enacted. But, in 1997, Louisiana enacted a divorce law which allows a couple to choose at the time of marriage what grounds for divorce will be available. If both spouses sign, before marriage, an affidavit that their marriage is a "covenant marriage" it may be dissolved only if a fault ground is proved or if the parties have been separated for two years (three and a half years in the case of minor children). LA. REV. STAT. §§ 9: 273, 9: 307. For recent evaluations of challenges to no-fault divorce, *see* Ellman, *supra* note 3; Ira M. Ellman, *The Place of Fault in Modern Divorce Law*, 28 ARIZ. ST. L. J. 773 (1996); Comment, 49 STAN. L. REV. 607 (1997).

Problem 11–2:

Evaluate the merits of the following divorce regimes:

1. Pure fault-based divorce;
2. Fault-based divorce plus divorce based on mutual consent;
3. Fault-based divorce plus divorce based on a period of separation;
4. Divorce based solely on mutual consent;
5. Divorce based solely on a period of separation;
6. Divorce based either on mutual consent or a period of separation;
7. Divorce based on a period of separation, with a "hardship" exception;

8. Pure no-fault divorce (i.e., divorce at the request of either spouse);

9. A "private choice" divorce rule, like that adopted in Louisiana.

What are the advantages of each approach in terms of fairness, judicial economy, and promoting marital stability? the disadvantages? Which approach, on balance, should the legislature adopt?

SECTION 4. ALTERNATIVES TO DIVORCE

A. SEPARATE MAINTENANCE AND DIVORCE FROM BED AND BOARD

When judicial divorce became available, many states continued to permit courts to grant divorces *a mensa et thoro* (i.e., from bed and board)—legal separation without the right to remarry. Other states abolished divorce *a mensa et thoro* and enacted "separate maintenance" statutes that permitted a judge to compel support for a spouse living separately.

Technically, divorce *a mensa et thoro* requires the spouses to live apart and nullifies the marital obligation of cohabitation, while separate maintenance enforces the spouse's support obligation and favors a resumption of cohabitation. Under a decree of divorce *a mensa et thoro*, the court may settle the property interests of the parties; under a separate maintenance decree, marital property rights may continue to accrue. Divorce *a mensa et thoro* thus provides a potentially valuable alternative to full divorce where the parties (1) want to settle the full range of their economic affairs, (2) do not intend to remarry, (3) want to preserve entitlements available to spouses under public or private benefit plans, such as social security insurance, survivors' benefits or state or private pensions, worker's compensation or health care plans or (4) are religiously or emotionally opposed to full divorce. Under these circumstances, a separate maintenance order is an inferior remedy.

The two remedies have different tax consequences. Under the Internal Revenue Code, a divorce *a mensa et thoro* is treated as a dissolution of the marital status, while a separate maintenance decree is interpreted as maintaining it. While Internal Revenue Code § 143(a) (*cf.* § 71) specifies that an individual "shall not be considered as married" if "legally separated from his spouse under a decree of divorce or of separate maintenance," court decisions have interpreted this language to mandate a decree that *requires* the parties to live apart. Under a separate maintenance decree, one spouse thus may demand that the other participate in filing a joint return. Separate maintenance also does not allow filing separately under the "singles" tax tables, not is the payor entitled to deduct support paid as alimony.

B. ANNULMENT

In the strict sense, an annulment is a judicial declaration that, by reason of a defect in its inception, a purported marriage does not now and has never existed. As noted earlier, annulment stems from the same canonical roots that gave us divorce and separate maintenance. Typical grounds for annulment—reflecting the restrictions on marriage described in Chapter 2—include incest, bigamy, non-age, mental incapacity, impotence, insanity, and lack of consent. A ground for annulment must have existed at the time of marriage; a ground arising later might serve as the basis for a divorce, but not an annulment. In the absence of an applicable annulment statute (Illinois, for example, did not have one until 1977), courts have asserted jurisdiction in equity to annul a marriage.

Equitable doctrines, including variants of the clean hands doctrine, estoppel, ratification and laches, are often defenses to an annulment action, especially where the defect is primarily of interest to the partners. For instance, the underage "defrauder" of the adult spouse may be estopped from attacking the marriage; or the adult "victim" may be held to have ratified the marriage (but only after obtaining knowledge of the fraud or after the proper age for marriage has been reached). Of course, the partners may not ratify a marriage that offends an important policy, such as the prohibition on incest. In the case of bigamy, however, UMDA § 207(b), where adopted, validates a void marriage upon divorce from or the death of the "surplus" spouse, but only as of the time the impediment is removed.

Although some case law permits annulment based on a "material misrepresentation," (*see* Kober v. Kober, 16 N.Y.2d 191, 264 N.Y.S.2d 364, 211 N.E.2d 817 (1965) (annulment granted where husband concealed his Nazi past and fanatical anti-Semitism)), traditionally courts required fraud going to the "essentials of the marriage." *See* Reynolds v. Reynolds, 85 Mass. (3 Allen) 605 (1862); Bilowit v. Dolitsky, 124 N.J.Super. 101, 304 A.2d 774 (Ch.Div.1973) (husband misrepresented that he was a practicing Orthodox Jew). The line of distinctive between fraud going to the "essentials" and lesser misrepresentation in not always easy to discern. Nor is the case law necessarily consistent. States with narrow divorce grounds (New York, New Jersey) often tended toward a liberal view of fraud; some courts have taken the position that an unconsummated marriage should be annulled more readily. But try your hand at determining whether these forms of fraud go to the essentials of a marriage:

a. the spouse has been married and divorced five times but reveals only one prior marriage (Sanderson v. Sanderson, 212 Va. 537, 186 S.E.2d 84 (1972));

b. the wife misrepresents her chastity (DuPont v. DuPont, 90 A.2d 468 (Del.1952));

c. the spouse fails to disclose that four former spouses had died under mysterious circumstances;

d. the spouse fails to reveal his or her infection with herpes, AIDS, or another venereal disease;

e. the wife fails to disclose her pregnancy (Hill v. Hill, 79 Ill.App.3d 809, 35 Ill.Dec. 98, 398 N.E.2d 1048 (1979));

f. the husband fails to disclose a prior vasectomy or his determination not to have children; (Tobon v. Sanchez, 213 N.J.Super. 472, 517 A.2d 885 (Ch.Div.1986));

g. the wife misrepresents her family caste in India (Patel v. Navitlal, 265 N.J.Super. 402, 627 A.2d 683 (Ch.Div.1992)).

In deciding these cases, should it matter if the misrepresentation did not come to light for ten years? that the couple now has a child? *See* Wolfe v. Wolfe, 76 Ill.2d 92, 27 Ill.Dec. 735, 389 N.E.2d 1143 (1979); Jordan v. Jordan, 115 N.H. 545, 345 A.2d 168 (1975).

In some cases the litigant will have a choice between annulment and divorce. Depending on the litigant's circumstances and state law, the weight of advantages may lie with either choice. Annulment traditionally did not permit the grant of alimony or property rights but did revive the alimony obligation of an earlier marriage. This result flowed from the fact that an annulment voids the marriage from its inception. Carried to its logical conclusion, children born during the annulled marriage are illegitimate, and rights based on marital status (for example, a divorced wife's entitlement to Social Security benefits based on her husband's Social Security contributions) must be cancelled.

Because this "logical" approach would often produce inequitable results, today children of an annulled marriage are considered legitimate; alimony and property rights may be granted after an annulment; alimony is not revived after the nullification of any attempted later marriage; and government benefits typically do not hinge on whether the marriage was annulled or terminated through divorce. (However, while joint income tax returns filed during a voidable marriage survive an annulment, this is *not* so in the case of a void marriage.)

The UMDA goes further and treats void and voidable marriages alike in terms of (1) legal consequences, (2) limiting the circle of persons permitted to attack a defective marriage, and (3) the need for a formal "declaration of invalidity." The UMDA also provides flexibility on the question of retroactivity. Declarations of invalidity are retroactive "unless the court finds, after a consideration of all relevant circumstances, including the effect of a retroactive decree on third parties, that the interests of justice would be served by making the decree not retroactive." In that case, "the provisions * * * relating to property rights of the spouses, maintenance, support, and custody of children on dissolution of marriage are applicable" (UMDA § 208(e)). In terms of outcome, the non-retroactive declaration of invalidity turns into the equivalent of divorce.

SECTION 5. ACCESS TO DIVORCE

A. IS THERE A CONSTITUTIONAL RIGHT TO DIVORCE?

BODDIE v. CONNECTICUT

Supreme Court of the United States, 1971.
401 U.S. 371, 91 S.Ct. 780, 28 L.Ed.2d 113.

JUSTICE HARLAN delivered the opinion of the Court.

Appellants, welfare recipients residing in the State of Connecticut, brought this action in the Federal District Court for the District of Connecticut on behalf of themselves and others similarly situated, challenging, as applied to them, certain state procedures for the commencement of litigation, including requirements for payment of court fees and costs for service of process, that restrict their access to the courts in their effort to bring an action for divorce. * * *

As this Court on more than one occasion has recognized, marriage involves interests of basic importance in our society. See, e.g., *Loving v. Virginia*, 388 U.S. 1 (1967); *Skinner v. Oklahoma*, 316 U.S. 535; *Meyer v. Nebraska*, 262 U.S. 390 (1923). It is not surprising, then, that the States have seen fit to oversee many aspects of that institution. Without a prior judicial imprimatur, individuals may freely enter into and rescind commercial contracts, for example, but we are unaware of any jurisdiction where private citizens may covenant for or dissolve marriages without state approval. Even where all substantive requirements are concededly met, we know of no instance where two consenting adults may divorce and mutually liberate themselves from the constraints of legal obligations that go with marriage, and more fundamentally the prohibition against remarriage, without invoking the State's judicial machinery. * * *

Prior cases establish, first, that due process requires, at a minimum, that absent a countervailing state interest of overriding significance, persons forced to settle their claims of right and duty through the judicial process must be given a meaningful opportunity to be heard.

* * *

Our cases further establish that a statute or a rule may be held constitutionally invalid as applied when it operates to deprive an individual of a protected right although its general validity as a measure enacted in the legitimate exercise of state power is beyond question. Thus, in cases involving religious freedom, free speech or assembly, this Court has often held that a valid statute was unconstitutionally applied in particular circumstances because it interfered with an individual's exercise of those rights. * * *

Just as a generally valid notice procedure may fail to satisfy due process because of the circumstances of the defendant, so too a cost requirement, valid on its face, may offend due process because it operates to foreclose a particular party's opportunity to be heard. The State's obligations under the Fourteenth Amendment are not simply generalized ones; rather, the State owes to each individual that process which, in light of the values of a free society, can be characterized as due.

Drawing upon the principles established by the cases just canvassed, we conclude that the State's refusal to admit these appellants to its courts, the sole means in Connecticut for obtaining a divorce, must be regarded as the equivalent of denying them an opportunity to be heard upon their claimed right to a dissolution of their marriages, and, in the absence of a sufficient countervailing justification for the State's action, a denial of due process.

The arguments for this kind of fee and cost requirement are that the State's interest in the prevention of frivolous litigation is substantial, its use of court fees and process costs to allocate scarce resources is rational, and its balance between the defendant's right to notice and the plaintiff's right to access is reasonable.

In our opinion, none of these considerations is sufficient to override the interest of these plaintiff-appellants in having access to the only avenue open for dissolving their allegedly untenable marriages. Not only is there no necessary connection between a litigant's assets and the seriousness of his motives in bringing suit, but it is here beyond present dispute that appellants bring these actions in good faith. Moreover, other alternatives exist to fees and cost requirements as a means for conserving the time of courts and protecting parties from frivolous litigation, such as penalties for false pleadings or affidavits, and actions for malicious prosecution or abuse of process, to mention only a few. In the same vein we think that reliable alternatives exist to service of process by a state-paid sheriff if the State is unwilling to assume the cost of official service. This is perforce true of service by publication which is the method of notice least calculated to bring to a potential defendant's attention the pendency of judicial proceedings. We think in this case service at defendant's last known address by mail and posted notice is equally effective as publication in a newspaper.

We are thus left to evaluate the State's asserted interest in its fee and cost requirements as a mechanism of resource allocation or cost recoupment. Such a justification was offered and rejected in *Griffin v. Illinois*, 351 U.S. 12 (1956). In *Griffin* it was the requirement of a transcript beyond the means of the indigent that blocked access to the judicial process. While in *Griffin* the transcript could be waived as a convenient but not necessary predicate to court access, here the State invariably imposes the costs as a measure of allocating its judicial resources. Surely, then, the rationale of *Griffin* covers this case.

In concluding that the Due Process Clause of the Fourteenth Amendment requires that these appellants be afforded an opportunity to go into court to obtain a divorce, we wish to re-emphasize that we go no further than necessary to dispose of the case before us, a case where the *bona fides* of both appellants' indigency and desire for divorce are here beyond dispute. We do not decide that access for all individuals to the courts is a right that is, in all circumstances, guaranteed by the Due Process Clause of the Fourteenth Amendment so that its exercise may not be placed beyond the reach of any individual, for, as we have already noted, in the case before us this right is the exclusive precondition to the adjustment of a fundamental human relationship. The requirement that these appellants resort to the judicial process is entirely a state-created matter. Thus we hold only that a State may not, consistent with the obligations imposed on it by the Due Process Clause of the Fourteenth Amendment, preempt the right to dissolve this legal relationship without affording all citizens access to the means it has prescribed for doing so.

Reversed.

JUSTICE DOUGLAS, concurring in the result.

* * * The power of the States over marriage and divorce is, of course, complete except as limited by specific constitutional provisions. But could a State deny divorces to domiciliaries who were Negroes and grant them to whites? Deny them to resident aliens and grant them to citizens? Deny them to Catholics and grant them to Protestants? Deny them to those convicted of larceny and grant them to those convicted of embezzlement?

* * * While Connecticut has provided a procedure for severing the bonds of marriage, a person can meet every requirement save court fees or the cost of service of process and be denied a divorce. * * *

Thus, under Connecticut law divorces may be denied or granted solely on the basis of wealth. * * * Affluence does not pass muster under the Equal Protection Clause for determining who must remain married and who shall be allowed to separate.

Notes and Questions

1. Does *Boddie* imply that there is a constitutional right to divorce? Could a state prohibit absolute divorce if it permitted legal separation? Could it bar divorce based on hardship? Could it allow divorce based only on fault?

2. Is there a constitutional right *not* to be divorced? *Compare* Walton v. Walton [p. 185].

3. If there is a right to divorce (or at least a right not to be excluded from obtaining a divorce due to poverty), is there also a right to counsel in a divorce case? Most courts have not thought so. *See* In re Smiley, 36 N.Y.2d 433, 369 N.Y.S.2d 87, 330 N.E.2d 53 (1975) (legal counsel is not required to obtain a divorce, so court-ordered counsel is not required by *Boddie*). *See also* Kiddie v. Kiddie, 563 P.2d 139 (Okla.1977). *Cf.*, Peter Van Runkle, *Lassiter v. Dept. of Social Services: What It Means for the Indigent Divorce Litigant*, 43 OHIO ST. L. J. 969 (1982). The Alaska Supreme Court has held that there is a right to court-appointed counsel for an indigent party in a child custody dispute

where the other parent is represented by counsel provided by a public agency. *See* Flores v. Flores, 598 P.2d 893 (Alaska 1979).

B. RESIDENCY REQUIREMENTS

SOSNA v. IOWA

Supreme Court of the United States, 1975.
419 U.S. 393, 95 S.Ct. 553, 42 L.Ed.2d 532.

JUSTICE REHNQUIST delivered the opinion of the Court.

Appellant Carol Sosna married Michael Sosna on September 5, 1964, in Michigan. They lived together in New York between October 1967 and August 1971, after which date they separated but continued to live in New York. In August 1972, appellant moved to Iowa with her three children, and the following month she petitioned the District Court of Jackson County, Iowa, for a dissolution of her marriage. Michael Sosna, who had been personally served with notice of the action when he came to Iowa to visit his children, made a special appearance to contest the jurisdiction of the Iowa court. The Iowa court dismissed the petition for lack of jurisdiction, finding that Michael Sosna was not a resident of Iowa and appellant had not been a resident of the State of Iowa for one year preceding the filing of her petition. In so doing the Iowa court applied the provisions of Iowa Code § 598.6 requiring that the petitioner in such an action be "for the last year a resident of the state."

* * *

The durational residency requirement under attack in this case is a part of Iowa's comprehensive statutory regulation of domestic relations, an area that has long been regarded as a virtually exclusive province of the States. Cases decided by this Court over a period of more than a century bear witness to this historical fact. In *Barber v. Barber*, 62 U.S. (21 How.) 582, 584 (1859), the Court said that "[w]e disclaim altogether any jurisdiction in the courts of the United States upon the subject of divorce * * *." In *Pennoyer v. Neff*, 95 U.S. 714, 734–735 (1877), the Court said: "The State * * * has absolute right to prescribe the conditions upon which the marriage relation between its own citizens shall be created, and the causes for which it may be dissolved," and the same view was reaffirmed in *Simms v. Simms*, 175 U.S. 162, 167 (1899).

The statutory scheme in Iowa, like those in other States, sets forth in considerable detail the grounds upon which a marriage may be dissolved and the circumstances in which a divorce may be obtained. Jurisdiction over a petition for dissolution is established by statute in "the county where either party resides," * * * and the Iowa courts have construed the term "resident" to have much the same meaning as is ordinarily associated with the concept of domicile. * * * Iowa has recently revised its divorce statutes, incorporating the no-fault concept, but it retained the one-year durational residency requirement.

The imposition of a durational residency requirement for divorce is scarcely unique to Iowa, since 48 States impose such a requirement as a condition for maintaining an action for divorce. As might be expected, the periods vary among the States and range from six weeks to two years. The one-year period selected by Iowa is the most common length of time prescribed.

Appellant contends that the Iowa requirement of one year's residence is unconstitutional for two separate reasons: *first*, because it establishes two classes of persons and discriminates against those who have recently exercised their right to travel to Iowa, thereby contravening the Court's holdings in *Shapiro v. Thompson*, 394 U.S. 618 (1969), *Dunn v. Blumstein*, 405 U.S. 330 (1972), and *Memorial Hospital v. Maricopa County*, 415 U.S. 250 (1974); and *second*, because it denies a litigant the opportunity to make an individualized showing of bona fide residence and therefore denies such residents access to the only method of legally dissolving their marriage. *Vlandis v. Kline*, 412 U.S. 441 (1973); *Boddie v. Connecticut*, [p. 563].

State statutes imposing durational residency requirements were of course invalidated when imposed by States as a qualification for welfare payments, *Shapiro*, supra, for voting, *Dunn*, supra, and for medical care, *Maricopa County*, supra. But none of those cases intimated that the States might never impose durational residency requirements, and such a proposition was in fact expressly disclaimed. What those cases had in common was that the durational residency requirements they struck down were justified on the basis of budgetary or record-keeping considerations which were held insufficient to outweigh the constitutional claims of the individuals. * * *

Iowa's residency requirement may reasonably be justified on grounds other than purely budgetary considerations or administrative convenience. A decree of divorce is not a matter in which the only interested parties are the State as a sort of "grantor," and a plaintiff such as appellant in the role of "grantee." Both spouses are obviously interested in the proceedings, since it will affect their marital status and very likely their property rights. Where a married couple has minor children, a decree of divorce would usually include provisions for their custody and support. With consequences of such moment riding on a divorce decree issued by its courts, Iowa may insist that one seeking to initiate such a proceeding have the modicum of attachment to the State required here.

Such a requirement additionally furthers the State's parallel interests in both avoiding officious intermeddling in matters in which another State has a paramount interest, and in minimizing the susceptibility of its own divorce decrees to collateral attack. A State such as Iowa may quite reasonably decide that it does not wish to become a divorce mill for unhappy spouses who have lived there as short a time as appellant had when she commenced her action in the state court after having long resided elsewhere. Until such time as Iowa is convinced that appellant intends to remain in the State, it lacks the "nexus between person and place of such permanence as to control the creation of legal relations and responsibilities of the utmost significance." *Williams v. North Carolina*, 325 U.S. 226, 229 (1945). Perhaps even more importantly, Iowa's interest extend beyond its borders and include the recognition of its divorce decrees by other States under the Full Faith and Credit Clause of the Constitution, Art. IV, § 1. For that purpose, this Court has often stated that "judicial power to grant a divorce—jurisdiction, strictly speaking—is founded on domicile." *Williams, supra.* Where a divorce decree is entered after a finding of domicile in *ex parte* proceedings, this Court has held that the finding of domicile is not binding upon another State and may be disregarded in the face of "cogent evidence" to the contrary. *Williams*, supra, at 236. For that reason, the State asked to enter such a decree is entitled to insist that the putative divorce plaintiff satisfy something more than the bare minimum of constitutional requirements before a divorce may be granted. The State's decision to exact a one-year residency requirement as a matter of policy is therefore buttressed by a quite permissible inference like this requirement not only effectuates state substantive policy but likewise provides a greater safeguard against successful collateral attack than would a requirement of bona fide residence alone. This is precisely the sort of determination that a State in the exercise of its domestic relations jurisdiction is entitled to make.

We therefore hold that the state interest in requiring that those who seek a divorce from its courts be genuinely attached to the State, as well as a desire to insulate divorce decrees from the likelihood of collateral attack, requires a different resolution of the constitutional issue presented than was the case in *Shapiro*, supra, *Dunn*, supra, and *Maricopa County*, supra.

Nor are we of the view that the failure to provide an individualized determination of residency violates the Due Process Clause of the Fourteenth Amendment. *Vlandis v. Kline*, 412 U.S. 441 (1973), relied upon by appellant, held that Connecticut might not arbitrarily invoke a permanent and irrebuttable presumption of non-residence against students who sought to obtain in-state tuition rates when that presumption was not necessarily or universally true in fact. But in *Vlandis* the Court warned that its decision should not "be construed to deny a State the right to impose on a student, as one element in demonstrating bona fide residence, a reasonable durational residency requirement." 412 U.S., at 452. An individualized determination of physical presence plus the intent to remain, which appellant apparently seeks, would not entitle her to a divorce even if she could have made such a showing. For Iowa requires not merely "domicile" in that sense, but residence in the State for a year in order for its courts to exercise their divorce jurisdiction.

In *Boddie v. Connecticut*, [p. 563] this Court held that Connecticut might not deny access to divorce courts to those persons who could not afford to pay the required fee. Because of the exclusive role played by the State in the termination of marriages, it was held that indigents could not be denied an opportunity to be heard "absent a countervailing state interest of overriding significance." But the gravamen of appellant Sosna's claim is not total deprivation, as in *Boddie*, but only delay.

* * *

Affirmed.

JUSTICE MARSHALL, with whom JUSTICE BRENNAN joins, dissenting.

* * *

The Court omits altogether what should be the first inquiry: whether the right to obtain a divorce is of sufficient importance that its denial to recent immigrants constitutes a penalty on interstate travel. In my view, it clearly meets that standard. The previous decisions of this Court make it plain that the right of marital association is one of the most basic rights conferred on the individual by the State. The interests associated with marriage and divorce have repeatedly been accorded particular deference, and the right to marry has been termed "one of the vital personal rights essential to the orderly pursuit of happiness by free men." *Loving, supra.* In *Boddie v. Connecticut*, [p. 563], we recognized that the right to seek dissolution of the marital relationship was closely related to the right to marry, as both involve the voluntary adjustment of the same fundamental human relationship. Without further laboring the point, I think it is clear beyond cavil that the right to seek dissolution of the marital relationship is of such fundamental importance that denial of this right to the class of recent interstate travelers penalizes interstate travel within the meaning of *Shapiro, Dunn,* and *Maricopa County*.

Having determined that the interest in obtaining a divorce is of substantial social importance, I would scrutinize Iowa's durational residency requirement to determine whether it constitutes a reasonable means of furthering important interests asserted by the State. The Court, however, has not only declined to apply the "compelling interest" test to this case, it has conjured up possible justifications for the State's restriction in a manner much more akin to the lenient standard we have in the past applied in analyzing equal protection challenges to business regulations. I continue to be of the view that the "rational basis" test has no place in equal protection analysis when important individual interests with constitutional implications are at stake. But whatever the ultimate resting point of the current readjustments in equal protection analysis, the Court has clearly directed that the proper standard to apply to cases in which state statutes have penalized the exercise of the right to interstate travel is the "compelling interest" test. * * *

I conclude that the course Iowa has chosen in restricting access to its divorce courts unduly interferes with the right to "migrate, resettle, find a new job, and start a new life." *Shapiro v. Thompson*, 394 U.S. at 629. I would reverse the judgment of the District Court and remand for entry of an order granting relief if the court finds that there is a continuing controversy in this case.

* * *

Problem 11–3:

Hilda and Walter married in Louisiana in in 1998, satisfying the requirements for creating a "covenant marriage" [p. 559]. The following year, they moved to California, where Hilda filed for a no-fault divorce. Walter argues that he and Hilda may be divorced only for reasons permitted under the Louisiana code provisions governing a covenant marriage. What arguments are available to Hilda? What should the California court do?

Problem 11–4:

Before Helen and William married, they signed a premarital agreement including a waiver of the right to obtain a no-fault divorce. William later filed for divorce based on a no-fault ground permitted under state law. The state has adopted the UPAA [p. 204]. What arguments are available to William? to Helen? What result should the court reach?

Problem 11–5:

Heinrich and Wilhelmina, who are citizens of a country in which divorce is only permitted based on mutual consent, established a legal residence in the United States. Wilhelmina filed for divorce on a no-fault ground permitted under the divorce code of their state of residence. Heinrich argues that the marriage may be terminated only based on consent. What arguments are available to Wilhelmina? What should the court do?

Chapter 12

JURISDICTION OVER FAMILY DISPUTES

Jurisdictional rules play a significant role in family law disputes. A family lawyer must always ask "what court has the power to grant the relief my client wants?" Jurisdictional rules in family law are sometimes simple and sometimes complex. This chapter will give you the basis for mastering them.

SECTION 1. JURISDICTION OVER DIVORCE

P. HAY, CONFLICT OF LAWS

127–31 (West Blackletter Series, 1989).

An *"ex parte"* divorce is one in which *only the petitioner* was before and was subject to the jurisdiction of the divorce court.

THE *WILLIAMS* CASES

The early case law was restrictive (and uncertain) concerning a court's power to grant a divorce in the absence of personal jurisdiction (presence or domicile) over both spouses. The landmark decisions in *Williams v. North Carolina* addressed this problem but did not resolve it completely. 317 U.S. 287 (1942) ("Williams I"); 325 U.S. 226 (1945) ("Williams II").

In *Williams* the husband and the wife of two different marriages had gone to Nevada, complied with that state's six-weeks' residence requirement, divorced their respective spouses, married each other, and returned to North Carolina. The Nevada court did not have personal jurisdiction over the North Carolina stay-at-home spouses, but they had received notice in North Carolina of the Nevada divorce proceedings. Upon their return to North Carolina, the Nevada newlyweds faced criminal charges for bigamous cohabitation, on the ground that their Nevada divorces were invalid and that their subsequent marriage to each other was therefore bigamous.

The United States Supreme Court held in the first *Williams* decision that the *domicile of the plaintiff* suffices for divorce jurisdiction. The

Court likened an ex parte divorce proceeding (i.e., a proceeding in which the plaintiff who is before the court seeks divorce from a spouse who is not) to a proceeding *in rem*. The *res* before the court is the *marital status* of the parties, and that *status is localized at the domicile of each spouse*. With jurisdiction over the *res*, the court then has power to affect the marital status, for instance to dissolve the marriage.

Williams I thus established that the state of the plaintiff's domicile has jurisdiction to grant a divorce. Whether it was the state of domicile, however, is a *question of fact*. Since the absent spouse, by definition, did not have an opportunity to litigate this jurisdictional fact, he or she cannot be precluded by the F–1 decision with respect to this issue. The Supreme Court therefore held in the second *Williams* decision that F–2 may reexamine the existence of the plaintiff's domicile in F–1 and, with it, F–2's jurisdiction. In *Williams II*, the Supreme Court upheld North Carolina's finding that the parties had not established proper domicile, that their divorces were therefore invalid, and that their subsequent marriage was bigamous.

The *Williams* decisions raise a number of problems. They are outlined in the following subsections.

THE DEFINITION OF DOMICILE FOR DIVORCE JURISDICTION

The Supreme Court said in *Williams II* that the definition of domicile for divorce jurisdiction raises a federal question. This is so because *Williams I* proceeded on the assumption that due process requires the localization of the marital status in F–1 at the plaintiff-spouse's domicile. If domicile is required to satisfy due process, it follows that a state cannot define domicile by itself. Otherwise it could decide for itself whether it has complied with the due process requirement. Nevertheless, the Court concluded in *Williams II* that North Carolina's view with respect to the defendants' Nevada domicile was not unreasonable. Thus, rather than providing a federal definition, the Court merely reviewed the reasonableness of the state court's determination.

A few states have adopted the *Uniform Divorce Recognition Act*, which contains the presumption that a person, domiciled in the enacting state, who obtains a divorce in another state and returns to the enacting state thereafter, will be presumed to have been domiciled in the enacting state at the time of the divorce. Applying the *Williams* decisions, the out-of-state divorce would therefore be invalid. The constitutional validity of the presumption in the Uniform Act, in light of due process considerations, has not been tested.

In *Shaffer v. Heitner*, 433 U.S. 186 (1977), the U.S. Supreme Court said that all assertions of state court jurisdiction, including those based on *in rem* jurisdiction, must satisfy the "minimum contacts" test of *International Shoe*. The question is: are minimum contacts an additional requirement for *ex parte* divorce jurisdiction?

The answer is probably "no" if *ex parte* divorce jurisdiction is based on the plaintiff's domicile. By definition, domicile is the closest connection a person can have to a state; it therefore far exceeds any required "minimum" contacts. The Court also noted in *Shaffer* that its decision in that case was not meant to address traditional bases for jurisdiction in status matters.

The answer is of course less clear whether it should be permissible for a court to assert ex parte divorce jurisdiction on a basis *short* of the plaintiff's domicile.

PARTIES TO COLLATERAL ATTACK

The defendant spouse may collaterally attack the *ex parte* divorce on jurisdictional grounds because he or she is not bound by the determination of the underlying jurisdictional facts in an action to which he or she was not a party. Similarly, any other interested party, for instance an heir, may collaterally attack the F–1 decree.

IS DOMICILE REALLY NEEDED?

Several authorities, including the Restatement 2d § 72, suggest that a state may exercise ex parte divorce jurisdiction when the plaintiff has a close connection with the state but does not maintain his or her domicile there. In order to meet the needs of military personnel who may lack the capacity to establish a local domicile, several states have enacted statutes providing for divorce jurisdiction on the basis of specified periods of residence. The court in *Lauterbach v. Lauterbach*, 392 P.2d 24 (Alaska 1964) upheld such a statute on the ground that "domicile is not the sole jurisdictional basis for divorce." More broadly, Arkansas law bases divorce jurisdiction solely on residence and not on domicile. *Wheat v. Wheat*, 229 Ark. 842, 318 S.W.2d 793 (1958).

The *Williams* decisions are not necessarily inconsistent with a wider view of *ex parte* divorce jurisdiction. In *Williams*, Nevada law itself had equated six weeks' residence in Nevada with Nevada domicile. Nevada law therefore required domicile, and the question before the Supreme Court was only whether domicile was a sufficient basis, not whether it was the *only* basis for ex parte divorce jurisdiction.

* * *

DIVISIBLE DIVORCE

In *ex parte* divorces, the granting court's jurisdiction extends only to the status of the parties' marriage. Absent personal jurisdiction over the defendant, *the court lacks power to affect the incidents of the marriage, such as support and custody rights.* Its decree will be entitled to recognition in so far as it had jurisdiction (dissolution of the marriage) but not in so far as it attempted to affect the incidents of marriage without proper jurisdiction to do so. The divorce decree is thus "divisible." *Estin v. Estin*, 334 U.S. 541 (1948). When the divorcing court lacks jurisdiction to deal with the incidents of marriage, these must be litigated in a subsequent proceeding in which there is personal jurisdiction over the defendant.

The *Sherrer* Doctrine

When both parties participated in the divorce, ordinary principles of preclusion apply: unless raised by appeal, defects underlying the F–1 decree (except perhaps for certain species of fraud), *including an erroneous finding of jurisdiction*, are lost when that decree becomes final; they cannot be raised collaterally. Thus, even though a party's domicile may be required for the court's jurisdiction to grant a divorce, the absence of domicile cannot be raised collaterally: since it could have been raised in the F–1 proceeding, it has now become res judicata. *Sherrer v. Sherrer*, 334 U.S. 343 (1948). "Participation" in this context means that the defendant has entered an appearance which afforded him or her an opportunity to be heard, *Cook v. Cook*, 342 U.S. 126 (1951), or was subject to personal jurisdiction in the forum state by long arm statute or otherwise. Note that the Uniform Divorce Recognition Act, which establishes a presumption against domicile in the divorcing state, *cannot* be invoked by parties who, as a result of *Sherrer*, are bound by the F–1 determination.

Third Parties

Parties who are in privity with a former spouse are bound by the decree, such as children will be barred from a collateral attack the same as the spouses themselves. *Johnson v. Muelberger*, 340 U.S. 581 (1951) (daughter). Persons not in privity with the former spouse(s) have sometimes also been barred from a collateral attack. See *Cook v. Cook*, 342 U.S. 126 (1951) (second husband). The Supreme Court has not addressed the question whether the former home state of the parties, such as in *Williams*, may collaterally attack the divorce when it was procured bilaterally and not *ex parte* (as in *Williams*). Since it was not in privity, the home state technically is not precluded. The suggested answer, however, is that the home state is not a "third party to the marriage relationship" and thus has *no standing* to raise jurisdictional defects. Decisions like *Williams* must therefore be restricted to their context: the home state protecting the societal interest of the home state in and on behalf of the resident spouse.

Effect of Collateral Determinations of Invalidity

Assume that F–1 has granted an *ex parte* divorce, and has even done so upon the express jurisdictional finding that the plaintiff spouse was domiciled there. Since the absent spouse was not bound by the jurisdictional determination in the *ex parte* proceeding, she collaterally attacked the F–1 decree in F–2 in a proceeding with personal jurisdiction over the F–1 plaintiff. F–2 finds that F–1 lacked jurisdiction and holds the F–1 divorce to be invalid. What is the effect of the F–2 determination on the validity of the F–1 decree in F–1? The F–1 decree is invalid *everywhere* including in F–1.

IN RE ESTATE OF STEFFKE

Supreme Court of Wisconsin, 1974.
65 Wis.2d 199, 222 N.W.2d 628.

HEFFERNAN, JUSTICE.

The order of the trial judge concluded that Priscilla Baker Lane Steffke was not, for the purposes of heirship proceedings, the legal wife of Wesley A. Steffke, because her prior marriage to Crockett Warren Lane was not effectively terminated, for the reason that a Mexican divorce in 1966 granted to Priscilla Baker Lane was invalid under the law of the State of Wisconsin. Priscilla Baker Lane was the principal named beneficiary of the will of Wesley A. Steffke. Hence, her right to take from the estate of Steffke is unquestioned. * * * The practical effect of the order of the probate court was to require that the inheritance tax be computed at the rates applicable to beneficiaries who are strangers to the deceased, rather than at the rates applicable to the widows. * * *

Priscilla Baker Lane was married to Crockett Warren Lane on November 11, 1944. In October of 1963, Priscilla Baker Lane and Crockett Warren Lane entered into a property settlement agreement and at the same time Lane signed a waiver submitting to the jurisdiction of the Civil Court in the City of Juarez, State of Chihuahua, Republic of Mexico. He also executed an entry of appearance and power of attorney in order that a divorce might be granted in accordance with the applicable laws of Chihuahua, Mexico. Wesley A. Steffke was divorced from his first wife in Wisconsin in 1965. Subsequently, in June of 1966, Priscilla Lane and Wesley Steffke went to Mexico together to secure Priscilla's divorce. * * * [Priscilla Lane married Wesley Steffke on July 3, 1967].

The Mexican court granted the divorce for "incompatibility of temperaments," a ground not recognized by Wisconsin law. It is undisputed that the divorce was technically bilateral and that the Mexican court had jurisdiction over both the parties. The validity of that divorce in Mexico is unquestioned. Accordingly, had the divorce been granted under the same circumstances in the United States, the decree would be entitled to "full faith and credit" and would be enforceable anywhere in this country. The constitutional mandate of "full faith and credit" is not applicable, however, where a decree or judgment is obtained in a jurisdiction outside of the United States. Leflar, American Conflicts Law, § 74, page 172, points out: "* * * there is no compulsion on any American state to recognize or enforce judgments from foreign countries. An American court can deny effect to a foreign judgment because it does not like the kind of service employed even though the service was valid, or because the foreign judgment is on a kind of cause of action that the forum court for any reason dislikes." On page 202, Leflar writes: "When a court is not bound by constitutional compulsions, it may properly employ local public policy as a reason for refusing to entertain suits on objectionable foreign causes of action. Since the full faith and credit clause does not apply to the judgments of other nations, the states are left free to refuse enforcement of them on the local public policy ground."

Essentially then, since there is no compulsion constitutionally for the state of Wisconsin to recognize the Mexican decree, it will be recognized only on the principles of comity. * * * § 247.22, Stats., provides:

> "247.22 Uniform Divorce Recognition Act. (1) A divorce obtained in another jurisdiction shall be of no force or effect in this state, if both parties to the marriage were domiciled in this state at the time the proceeding for the divorce was commenced.
>
> "(2) Proof that a person obtaining a divorce in another jurisdiction was (a) domiciled in this state within 12 months prior to the commencement of the proceeding therefor, and resumed residence in this state within 18 months after the date of his departure therefrom, or (b) at all times after his departure from this state, and until his return maintained a place of residence within this state, shall be prima facie evidence that the person was domiciled in this state when the divorce proceeding was commenced."

The unequivocal declaration of legislative policy in § 247.21, Stats., is that no judgment of divorce is of effect in this state when a person domiciled in this state goes into another country for the purpose of obtaining a divorce for a cause which occurred in Wisconsin or for a cause which is not a ground for divorce under the laws of this state. "Incompatibility of temperaments" is not a ground recognized in Wisconsin. * * *

There is no constitutional requirement that Wisconsin give recognition to a Mexican decree affecting the marital status of Wisconsin domiciliaries. The appellants in this case argue, however, that § 247.21, Stats., does not bar the application of a doctrine of comity to a divorce decree. They are correct in that assertion. This court, under the common law and under the rules of comity, may give recognition to a decree even though it is not compelled to do so by the "full faith and credit" clause of the United States Constitution. However, the Wisconsin statute (§ 247.21) provides that such recognition can be accorded if "justified by the rules of international comity." As pointed out above, rules of comity prohibit according effect to a foreign decree when to do so would be to approve a policy contrary to the laws of this state, prejudicial to the interests of its citizens, or against good morals. The policy and moral determination has been made by the legislature, and this court is obliged to adhere to that policy. * * *

Appellants urge that we adopt the doctrine of comity recognized by the Court of Appeals of the State of New York in *Rosenstiel v. Rosenstiel* and *Wood v. Wood* (1965), 16 N.Y.2d 64, 262 N.Y.S.2d 86, 209 N.E.2d 709, cert. den. (1966), 384 U.S. 971, and 383 U.S. 943. Whatever the sociological wisdom of the policy adopted in *Rosenstiel*, the policy of Wisconsin is specifically expressed by our statutes. New York is not a signatory to the Uniform Divorce Recognition Act and stands alone in its position as stated in *Rosenstiel*.

In the absence of a revised legislative declaration of public policy, this court declines to extend comity to a divorce obtained in Mexico under the circumstances of this case.

It should be noted, however, that § 245.24, Stats., provides that, even where a subsequent marriage was invalid because of a prior defective divorce, a subsequent living together as husband and wife in good faith after the death of a party from whom a divorce was not validly obtained will be validated in the event of the death of that other party. The record is silent, however, in respect to the present whereabouts or vitality of Crockett Lane. In the event that he predeceased Wesley Steffke, the disability to the marriage of Wesley Steffke and Priscilla Lane would have been removed, and the marriage under those circumstances would be valid. There is, however, no evidence of such subsequent validation.

The Mexican divorce granted to Priscilla Lane in 1966 is of no effect in the State of Wisconsin. She was not the wife of Wesley Steffke under the laws of the State of Wisconsin and is not entitled to the benefit of inheritance tax rates applicable to a widow of a decedent.

KAZIN v. KAZIN

Supreme Court of New Jersey, 1979.
81 N.J. 85, 405 A.2d 360.

HANDLER, J.

This case presents the question whether the plaintiff, who obtained a presumably void or voidable Mexican divorce from her first husband, should be allowed to maintain a matrimonial action against her present husband for divorce, alimony and equitable distribution or, alternatively, for separate maintenance. The circumstances reveal that defendant participated in plaintiff's decision to obtain a Mexican divorce from her former husband, and, following that divorce, defendant and plaintiff married and lived together for seven years, apparently believing themselves to be husband and wife.

* * *

In October 1976 plaintiff instituted an action for divorce on grounds of extreme cruelty and desertion and, by later amendment, adultery, seeking alimony and equitable distribution; in the alternative, she sought separate maintenance. Defendant filed an answer in which he denied that the parties were validly married to each other. He also counter-claimed for a judgment that the purported marriage between the parties was null and void on grounds that plaintiff's Mexican divorce was invalid and that her prior marriage was still in force.

* * *

The equitable principle of estoppel has been applied broadly and in a wide variety of matrimonial cases. It has been recognized that "in cases involving foreign divorce decrees, as in other situations, * * * the application of the principles of equitable estoppel cannot be subjected to fixed and settled rules of universal application, but rests largely on the facts and circumstances of each particular case." *Weber v. Weber*, 200 Neb. 659, 666, 265 N.W.2d 436, 441 (Sup.Ct. 1978). The equitable rule precluding individuals from attacking foreign divorce decrees "[has] not [been] limited to situations of what might be termed 'true estoppel' where one party induces another to rely on his damage upon certain representations * * *", Restatement, Second, Conflict of Laws § 74, Comment b (1971), but has also encompassed situations sometimes termed "quasi-estoppel" where an individual is not permitted to "blow both hot and cold," taking a position inconsistent with prior conduct, if this would injure another, regardless of whether that person has actually relied thereon.

In the overwhelming majority of cases, estoppel has been applied to thwart a spouse from attacking his or her own divorce. Estoppel has also been applied, however, in situations analogous to that presented in this case, to prevent an individual from attacking his spouse's prior divorce.

In a number of cases, courts have forbidden a husband from attacking the prior divorce decree of his wife, where he took an active role in helping her to procure that decree. Estoppel has also been applied, however, where the second husband's involvement in his spouse's prior divorce was relatively passive but, in marrying her, he himself relied on that divorce. The doctrine estopping a party who marries in reliance upon a prior divorce from subsequently attacking that divorce has been widely endorsed. In cases in which several of these factors coalesce, as, for example, where the party seeking to attack the prior foreign divorce of a current spouse was not only aware of that decree but also assisted or helped in its procurement and, further, relied upon it by marrying that person, the claim for an estoppel is especially strong. Akin to the doctrine of estoppel as applied where there is a second marriage is the strong presumption in favor of the validity of the latest of two or more marriages, as well as the corollary presumption that a prior marriage has been lawfully terminated by death or divorce. These presumptions cast a heavy burden on the person objecting to the legality of the last marriage to prove its invalidity by clear and convincing evidence.

Not all courts have been persuaded that the estoppel doctrine is an appropriate judicial tool where there has been a remarriage. Some decisions have condemned application of the doctrine to uphold an invalid foreign divorce decree as tantamount to countenancing bigamy or conferring upon the parties the right to self-help in securing a divorce contrary to the laws of the jurisdiction. These approaches have in turn invited criticism. The State's concern over bigamous conduct need not be undermined by the estoppel doctrine invoked by private parties in civil matrimonial litigations. Many courts have expressed the view that it would be even more unseemly and inimical to a sound public policy to permit the spouse of a second marriage to act inconsistently with prior conduct in entering into that marriage. They have stressed that a spouse who has received the benefits of a second marriage should not be able to escape its obligations.

These views comport closely with our current matrimonial policies. Full weight should be given the legislative objectives governing divorce, which reflect a genuine concern for the realities of the marital relationship and allow the expeditious, orderly and fair dissolution of destroyed marriages and call for the protection, financial and otherwise, of the survivors of such marriages, including children. There remains little, if any, interest in encouraging the resurrection of deceased marriages, even if pronounced dead by other tribunals whose processes are not completely consistent with our own. In this context, the estoppel doctrine itself should be a reflection of that public policy and be applied, or not, in accordance with its demands in the circumstances of the given case.

Although the parties here offered different versions of the events which culminated in the Mexican divorce decree, certain matters are not disputed or contested and their differences do not militate against the application of the doctrine of estoppel. Defendant was hardly an ignorant or innocent bystander. He participated in some degree in the decision to obtain the divorce and admitted accompanying plaintiff on her trip to Mexico, at least as far as the border at El Paso. The parties married a month after the divorce and undertook the normal responsibilities of marriage, including the acquisition of a marital home and other assets and the mutual care of plaintiff's children by her first husband. Their married life together lasted for seven years. Additionally, defendant presumably knew that plaintiff's former husband, also in reliance upon the Mexican divorce, remarried and had two children from this second union. Thus, several factors, knowledge, participation, acceptance of benefits and subsequent marriage, establish defendant's nexus with plaintiff's foreign divorce. It would, in our view, be contrary to the public policy reflected in our current laws to permit defendant under these circumstances to attack the validity of his wife's prior Mexican divorce and to repudiate the obligations which he assumed in marrying plaintiff. To that end, he is estopped to assert these particular defenses to plaintiff's marital claims.

Notes and Questions

1. If Steffke's will had disinherited Priscilla, would she be entitled to claim the widow's indefeasible share? Argue her case! Would the case lie differently if Steffke (rather than Priscilla) had obtained a Mexican divorce from his first spouse?

2. Assume that Steffke had named Priscilla his sole heir, but that *he* had obtained an invalid Mexican divorce from his first wife (rather than the unchallenged Wisconsin divorce he did obtain in 1965) and that Steffke's first wife now claims her widow's share. Defend the estate.

3. Assume that Steffke is alive and Priscilla is seeking a divorce from him in a Wisconsin court. Steffke defends, arguing they are not married. What result?

4. The financial risk of a new marriage following a questionable or invalid divorce applies to tax benefits as well as to entitlements hinging on marital status:

> "In *Estate of Goldwater v. Commissioner*, 64 T.C. 540 (1975), appealed 539 F.2d 878 No. 75–4277 (2d Cir.), the Tax Court refused to recognize a Mexican divorce in the face of a declaratory judgment entered in favor of decedent's first wife, holding that she remained his lawful wife. The court allowed the marital deduction to the extent property passed to his first wife by reason of her elective share under state law but denied the deduction to the extent property passed under decedent's will to the person who purported to be his wife at the time of his death. In *Estate of Spaulding v. Commissioner*, 34 CCH Tax Ct Mem ¶ 33,360 (1975), appealed No. 75–4248 (2d Cir.), the Tax Court followed its decision in *Goldwater* and in the case at bar to deny the marital deduction to the estate of the purported wife of a New York resident who had been divorced in Nevada but which divorce had been declared invalid by a New York court. At the time of decedent's death, she was a resident of California; but the court ruled that this did not change the result, because since all relevant parties had participated in the New York proceedings which resulted in the declaration that the divorce was invalid, California was required by *Sutton v. Leib*, 342 U.S. 402 (1952), to give the New York judgment full faith and credit and under California precedent would do so. The Tax Court has consistently maintained the view that marital status is defined by state law.
>
> * * *
>
> In the construction of tax statutes, neither the Tax Court, nor this court in review, is sitting in the capacity of balancing the equities of a particular situation.
>
> * * *
>
> Perhaps the mores of the times do not place the high value on the sanctity of the continuance of the marital status as in previous years; but no matter how easily the status may now be discontinued, we are not presently persuaded when the state having the primary jurisdiction over a decedent's estate has specifically determined that a divorce elsewhere has provided no basis for a legal marriage, we can nevertheless say a marriage exists which would permit a spouse to survive upon the death of one."
>
> Steffke v. Commissioner of Internal Revenue, 538 F.2d 730 (7th Cir.1976).

5. In Bartsch v. Bartsch, 204 Va. 462, 132 S.E.2d 416 (1963), a man had obtained a divorce in Nevada and then married another woman. The first wife was served but did not appear in the Nevada proceeding. When the man died more than 20 years after the Nevada divorce, the first wife filed an action for declaratory judgment in Virginia challenging the jurisdiction of the Nevada court. The trial court concluded that the husband was not domiciled in Nevada at the time the court rendered the divorce, so the court lacked jurisdiction to enter a divorce decree. Therefore the first wife was the surviving spouse, entitled to a forced share of the decedent's estate. The Virginia Supreme Court reversed, holding that the first wife's challenge to the Nevada divorce was barred by laches. Is the first wife's claim also barred by *Sherrer* [p. 574]?

6. With the prevalence of no-fault divorce, there is little reason today either for a spouse to seek out a traditional divorce "haven," or for the spouse's home state to apply strict rules that would discourage doing so. But, because we are a highly mobile society, jurisdictional rules remain important. Today, few spouses move to Nevada for a few weeks to establish a (sham) domicile, but many spouses move from their home state before or after the home state issues a divorce decree. In these cases, it is still essential to determine which state(s) may divide the couple's property, award (or modify) custody of their children, and determine (or modify) the appropriate level of spousal and child support. These issues are addressed in the balance of this chapter.

SECTION 2. PERSONAL JURISDICTION

KULKO v. SUPERIOR COURT OF CALIFORNIA

Supreme Court of the United States, 1978.
436 U.S. 84, 98 S.Ct. 1690, 56 L.Ed.2d 132.

JUSTICE MARSHALL delivered the opinion of the Court.

The issue before us is whether, in this action for child support, the California state courts may exercise *in personam* jurisdiction over a nonresident, nondomiciliary parent of minor children domiciled within the State. For reasons set forth below, we hold that the exercise of such jurisdiction would violate the Due Process Clause of the Fourteenth Amendment.

Appellant Ezra Kulko married appellee Sharon Kulko Horn in 1959, during appellant's three-day stopover in California en route from a military base in Texas to a tour of duty in Korea At the time of this marriage, both parties were domiciled in and residents of New York State. Immediately following the marriage, Sharon Kulko returned to New York, as did appellant after his tour of duty. Their first child, Darwin, was born to the Kulkos in New York in 1961, and a year later their second child, Ilsa was born, also in New York. The Kulkos and their two children resided together as a family in New York City continuously until March 1972, when the Kulkos separated.

Following the separation, Sharon Kulko moved to San Francisco, California. A written separation agreement was drawn up in New York; in September 1972, Sharon Kulko flew to New York City in order to sign this agreement. The agreement provided that the children would remain with their father during the school year but would spend their Christmas, Easter and summer vacations with their mother. While Sharon Kulko waived any claim for her own support or maintenance, Ezra Kulko agreed to pay his wife $3,000 per year in child support for the periods when the children were in her care, custody and control. Immediately after execution of the separation agreement, Sharon Kulko flew to Haiti and procured a divorce there; the divorce decree incorporated the terms of the agreement. She then returned to California, where she remarried and took the name Horn.

The children resided with appellant during the school year and with their mother on vacations, as provided by the separation agreement, until December 1973. At this time, just before Ilsa was to leave New York to spend Christmas vacation with her mother, she told her father that she wanted to remain in California after her vacation. Appellant bought his daughter a one-way plane ticket, and Ilsa left, taking her clothing with her. Ilsa then commenced living in California with her mother during the school year and spending vacations with her father. In January 1976, appellant's other child, Darwin, called his mother from New York and advised her that he wanted to live with her in California. Unbeknownst to appellant, appellee Horn sent a plane ticket to her son, which he used to fly to California where he took up residence with his mother and sister.

Less than one month after Darwin's arrival in California, appellee Horn commenced this action against appellant in the California Superior Court. She sought to establish the Haitian divorce decree as a California judgment; to modify the judgment so as to award her full custody of the children; and to increase appellant's child support obligations. Appellant appeared specially and moved to quash service of the summons on the ground that he was not a resident of California and lacked sufficient "minimum contacts" with the State under *International Shoe Co. v. Washington*, 326 U.S. 310, 316 (1945), to warrant the State's assertion of personal jurisdiction over him.

The trial court summarily denied the motion to quash, and appellant sought review in the California Court of Appeal by petition for a writ of mandate. Appellant did not contest the court's jurisdiction for purposes of the custody determination, but, with respect to the claim for increased support, he renewed his argument that the California courts lacked personal jurisdiction over him. The appellate court affirmed the denial of appellant's motion to quash, reasoning that, by consenting to his children's living in California, appellant had "caused an effect in th[e] state" warranting the exercise of jurisdiction over him. 133 Cal. Rptr. 627, 628 (1976).

The California Supreme Court granted appellant's petition for review, and in a 4–2 decision sustained the rulings of the lower state courts. 19 Cal.3d 514, 138 Cal.Rptr. 586, 564 P.2d 353 (1977). (It noted first that the California Code of Civil Procedure demonstrated an intent that the courts of California utilize all bases of *in personam* jurisdiction "not inconsistent with the Constitution.") Agreeing with the court below, the Supreme Court stated that, where a nonresident defendant has caused an effect in the State by an act or omission outside the State, personal jurisdiction over the defendant in causes arising from that effect may be exercised whenever "reasonable." It went on to hold that such an exercise was "reasonable" in this case because appellant had "purposely availed himself of the benefits and protections of the laws of California" by sending Ilsa to live with her mother in California. While noting that appellant had not, "with respect to his other child, Darwin, caused an effect in [California]"—since it was appellee Horn who had arranged for Darwin to fly to California in January 1976—the court concluded that it was "fair and reasonable for defendant to be subject to personal jurisdiction for the support of both children, where he has committed acts with respect to one child which confers personal jurisdiction and has consented to the permanent residence of the other child in California."

We have concluded that jurisdiction by appeal does not lie, but, treating the papers as a petition for a writ of certiorari, we hereby grant the petition and reverse the judgment below.

The Due Process Clause of the Fourteenth Amendment operates as a limitation on the jurisdiction of state courts to enter judgments affecting rights or interests of nonresident defendants. See *Shaffer v. Heitner,* 433 U.S. 186, 198–200, (1977). It has long been the rule that a valid judgment imposing a personal obligation or duty in favor of the plaintiff may be entered only by a court having jurisdiction over the person of the defendant. *Pennoyer v. Neff,* 95 U.S. 714, 732–733 (1878); *International Shoe Co. v. Washington, supra,* 326 U.S., at 316, at 158. The existence of personal jurisdiction, in turn, depends upon the presence of reasonable notice to the defendant that an action has been brought. *Mullane v. Central Hanover Trust Co.*, 339 U.S. 306, 313–314 (1950), and a sufficient connection between the defendant and the forum State as to make it fair to require defense of the action in the forum. In this case, appellant does not dispute the adequacy of the notice that he received, but contends that his connection with the State of California is too attenuated, under the standards implicit in the Due Process Clause of the Constitution, to justify imposing upon him the burden and inconvenience of defense in California.

The parties are in agreement that the constitutional standard for determining whether the State may enter a binding judgment against appellant here is that set forth in this Court's opinion in *International Shoe Co. v. Washington, supra*: that a defendant "have certain minimum contacts with [the forum state] such that the maintenance of the suit does not offend 'traditional notions of fair play and substantial justice.' "

Like any standard that requires a determination of "reasonableness," the "minimum contacts" test of *International Shoe* is not susceptible of mechanical application; rather, the facts of each case must be weighed to determine whether the requisite "affiliating circumstances" are present. *Hanson v. Denckla*, 357 U.S. 235, 246 (1958). We recognize that this determination is one in which few answers will be written "in black and white. The greys are dominant and even among them the shades are innumerable." *Estin v. Estin*, 334 U.S. 541, 545 (1948). But we believe that the California Supreme Court's application of the minimum contacts test in this case represents an unwarranted extension of *International Shoe* and would, if sustained, sanction a result that is neither fair, just, nor reasonable.

In reaching its result, the California Supreme Court did not rely on appellant's glancing presence in the State some 13 years before the events that led to this controversy, nor could it have. Appellant has been in California on only two occasions, once in 1959 for a three-day military stopover on his way to Korea, and again in 1960 for a 24–hour stopover on his return from Korean service. To hold such temporary visits to a State a basis for the assertion of *in personam* jurisdiction over unrelated actions arising in the future would make a mockery of the limitations on state jurisdiction imposed by the Fourteenth Amendment. Nor did the California court rely on the fact that appellant was actually married in California on one of his two brief visits. We agree that where two New York domiciliaries, for reasons of convenience, marry in the State of California and thereafter spend their entire married life in New York, the fact of their California marriage by itself cannot support a California court's exercise of jurisdiction over a spouse who remains a New York resident in an action relating to child support.

Finally, in holding that personal jurisdiction existed, the court below carefully disclaimed reliance on the fact that appellant had agreed at the time of separation to allow his children to live with their mother three months a year and that he had sent them to California each year pursuant to this agreement. As was noted below, to find personal jurisdiction in a State on this basis, merely because the mother was residing there, would discourage parents from entering into reasonable visitation agreements. Moreover, it could arbitrarily subject one parent to suit in any State of the Union where the other parent chose to spend time while having custody of their offspring pursuant to a separation agreement. As we have emphasized,

> "The unilateral activity of those who claim some relationship with a nonresident defendant cannot satisfy the requirement of contact with the forum State.... [I]t is essential in each case that there be some act by which the defendant purposefully avails [him-]self of the privilege of conducting activities within the forum State...." *Hanson v. Denckla*, *supra*, 357 U.S., at 253.

The "purposeful act" that the California Supreme Court believed did warrant the exercise of personal jurisdiction over appellant in California was his "actively and fully consent[ing] to Ilsa living in California for the school year ... and ... sen[ding] her to California for that purpose." We cannot accept the proposition that appellant's acquiescence in Ilsa's desire to live with her mother conferred jurisdiction over appellant in the California courts in this action. A father who agrees, in the interests of family harmony and his children's preferences, to allow them to spend more time in California than was required under a separation agreement can hardly be said to have "purposefully availed himself" of the "benefits and protection" of California's laws. See *Shaffer v. Heitner*, *supra*, 433 U.S., at 216.[1]

Nor can we agree with the assertion of the court below that the exercise of *in personam* jurisdiction here was warranted by the financial benefit appellant derived from his daughter's presence in California for nine months of the year. This argument rests on the premise that, while appellant's liability for support payments remained unchanged, his yearly expenses for supporting the child in New York decreased. But this circumstance, even if true, does not support California's assertion of jurisdiction here. Any diminution in appellant's household costs resulted, not from the child's presence in California, but rather from her absence from appellant's home. Moreover, an action by appellee Horn to increase support payments could now be brought, and could have been brought when Ilsa first moved to California, in the State of New York; a New York court would clearly have personal jurisdiction over appellant and, if a judgment were entered by a New York court increasing appellant's child support obligations, it could properly be enforced against him in both New York and California. Any ultimate financial advantage to appellant thus results not from the child's presence in California but from appellee's failure earlier to seek an increase in payments under the separation agreement. The argument below to the contrary, in our view, confuses the question of appellant's liability with that of the proper forum in which to determine that liability.

In light of our conclusion that appellant did not purposefully derive benefit from any activities relating to the State of California, it is apparent that the California Supreme Court's reliance on appellant's having caused an "effect" in California was misplaced. This "effects" test is derived from the American Law Institute's Restatement (Second) of Conflicts § 37 (1971), which provides:

> "A state has power to exercise judicial jurisdiction over an individual who causes effects in the state by an act done elsewhere with respect to any cause of action arising from these effects unless

1. The court below stated that the presence in California of appellant's daughter gave appellant the benefit of California's "police and fire protection, its school system, its hospital services, its recreational facilities, its libraries and museums.... " 19 Cal.3d, at 522, 138 Cal.Rptr., at 589, 564 P.2d, at 356. But, in the circumstances presented here, these services provided by the State were essentially benefits to the child, not the father, and in any event were not benefits that appellant purposefully sought for himself.

the nature of the effects and of the individual's relationship to the state make the exercise of such jurisdiction unreasonable."

While this provision is not binding on this Court, it does not in any event support the decision below. As is apparent from the examples accompanying § 37 in the Restatement, this section was intended to reach wrongful activity outside of the State causing injury within the State, *see, e.g.* Comment a, p. 157 (shooting bullet from one State into another), or commercial activity affecting state residents, ibid. Even in such situations, moreover, the Restatement recognizes that there might be circumstances that would render "unreasonable" the assertion of jurisdiction over the nonresident defendant.

The circumstances in this case clearly render "unreasonable" California's assertion of personal jurisdiction. There is no claim that appellant has visited physical injury on either property or persons within the State of California. Compare *Hess v. Pawloski*, 274 U.S. 352, (1927). The cause of action herein asserted arises, not from the defendant's commercial transactions in interstate commerce, but rather from his personal, domestic relations.... Furthermore, the controversy between the parties arises from a separation that occurred in the State of New York; appellee Horn seeks modification of a contract that was negotiated in New York and that she flew to New York to sign....

Finally, basic considerations of fairness point decisively in favor of appellant's State of domicile as the proper forum for adjudication of this case, whatever the merits of appellee's underlying claim. It is appellant who has remained in the State of the marital domicile, whereas it is appellee who has moved across the continent.

In seeking to justify the burden that would be imposed on appellant were the exercise of *in personam* jurisdiction in California sustained, appellee argues that California has substantial interests in protecting the welfare of its minor residents and in promoting to the fullest extent possible a healthy and supportive family environment in which the children of the State are to be raised. These interests are unquestionably important. But while the presence of the children and one parent in California arguably might favor application of California law in a lawsuit in New York, the fact that California may be the "center of gravity" for choice of law purposes does not mean that California has personal jurisdiction over the defendant. And California has not attempted to assert any particularized interest in trying such cases in its courts by, e.g., enacting a special jurisdictional statute.

California's legitimate interest in ensuring the support of children resident in California without unduly disrupting the children's lives, moreover, is already being served by the State's participation in the Uniform Reciprocal Enforcement of Support Act of 1968. This statute provides a mechanism for communication between court systems in different States, in order to facilitate the procurement and enforcement of child-support decrees where the dependent children reside in a State that cannot obtain personal jurisdiction over the defendant. California's version of the Act essentially permits a California resident claiming support from a nonresident to file a petition in California and have its merits adjudicated in the State of the alleged obligor's residence, without either party having to leave his or her own State. Cal.Code Civ.Proc. § 1650 et seq. New York State is a signatory to a similar act. Thus, not only may plaintiff-appellee here vindicate her claimed right to additional child support from her former husband in a New York court, but the uniform acts will facilitate both her prosecution of a claim for additional support and collection of any support payments found to be owed by appellant.[2]

It cannot be disputed that California has substantial interests in protecting resident children and in facilitating child-support actions on behalf of those children. But these interests simply do not make California a "fair forum," *Shaffer v. Heitner, supra,* 433 U.S., at 215, in which to require appellant, who derives no personal or commercial benefit from his child's presence in California and who lacks any other relevant contact with the State, either to defend a child-support suit or to suffer liability by default.

* * *

Accordingly, we conclude that the appellant's motion to quash service, on the ground of lack of personal jurisdiction, was erroneously denied by the California courts. The judgment of the California Supreme Court is, therefore,

Reversed.

Notes and Questions

1. In Burnham v. Superior Court, 495 U.S. 604, 110 S.Ct. 2105, 109 L.Ed.2d 631 (1990) the Supreme Court held that a state may exercise personal jurisdiction over a party if the party was personally served in the state, even though the party does not have sufficient contacts with the forum to satisfy the *International Shoe* requirements. *See also* Flores v. Melo–Palacios, 921 S.W.2d 399 (Tex.App.1996) (holding that, because state court had personal jurisdiction over nonresident child support obligor based on personal service within state, court did not need subject matter jurisdiction as well).

2. To divide property outside the forum state, the court must have personal jurisdiction over both spouses. *See* Mock v. Mock, 11 Va.App. 616, 400 S.E.2d 543 (1991). But most courts agree that a court may divide property located in the forum state without personal jurisdiction over both spouses. *See, e.g.,* Shaffer v. Heitner, 433 U.S. 186, 97 S.Ct. 2569, 53 L.Ed.2d 683 (1977); Bechtold v. Bechtold, 588 So.2d 321 (Fla.App.1991); Mahoney v. Mahoney, 131 A.D.2d 822, 517 N.Y.S.2d 184 (1987). *Cf.* Dawson–Austin v. Austin, 41 Tex.Sup.Ct.J. 400 (1998) (hold-

2. Thus, it cannot here be concluded, as it was in *McGee v. International Life Insurance Co.*, 355 U.S., at 223–224, with respect to actions on insurance contracts, that resident plaintiffs would be at a "severe disadvantage" if *in personam* jurisdiction over out-of-state defendants were sometimes unavailable.

ing that the court did *not* have jurisdiction to divide the property in the forum where the forum did not have personal jurisdiction over both spouses and the spouse who filed for divorce moved the property to the forum after the spouses separated, apparently without the consent of the other spouse). There is some question whether a court in State A must enforce a divorce decree from State B that purports to affect title to realty in A. *See* Fall v. Eastin, 215 U.S. 1, 30 S.Ct. 3, 54 L.Ed. 65 (1909). The safest practice is to have the State A court order the title-holding spouse to sign the appropriate title instrument (quitclaim deed, grant deed, etc.), and then record that instrument in the appropriate office in State B. *See* William Dorsaneo, *Due Process, Full Faith and Credit, and Family Law Litigation*, 36 Sw. L. J. 1085 (1983).

3. Most courts agree that a court need not have personal jurisdiction over both parents to render a custody decree. *See* § 4, this chapter.

SECTION 3. INTERSTATE MODIFICATION AND ENFORCEMENT OF CHILD SUPPORT AWARDS

Separated parents frequently live in different states. The result, all too frequently, has been conflicting support orders. The typical pattern involves a divorce and support order entered in State A, a move by the noncustodial parent to State B, a modification proceeding in State B, and a new State B order. Which order controls? The first legislation that aimed to resolve the problem of conflicting support decrees was the 1950 Uniform Reciprocal Enforcement of Support Act (URESA). Under URESA, a custodial parent could initiate a support action in her own state, to be "forwarded" to another state where the obligor lived or owned property. A government attorney—usually a local prosecutor—appeared on behalf of the custodial parent in the distant forum, avoiding the necessity of an expensive personal appearance. If the court in the distant forum concluded that the obligor had a support obligation, it would enter a support order and forward payments to the obligee. All states enacted one or another version of URESA (it was amended in 1952 and 1956). *See* 9B U.L.A. 553 (1987). URESA's inadequacies produced the 1968 Revised Uniform Reciprocal Enforcement of Support Act (RURESA) (*see* 9B U.L.A. 393 (1987)); its inadequacies led the federal government to mandate state adoption, by January 1, 1998, of yet another interstate act, the Uniform Interstate Family Support Act (UIFSA). *See* 9 U.L.A. 316 (1997 Supp.). The federal government also enacted the Full Faith and Credit for Child Support Orders Act (FCCSOA), 28 U.S.C.A. § 1738B(a).

The central problem under both URESA and RURESA was that all proceedings were de novo; support orders entered under the statute had no effect on, and did not affect, other support orders. UIFSA was designed, in part, to cure this problem. To do so, it adopts the concept of continuing, exclusive jurisdiction to establish and modify a support order; once a court or administrative agency with jurisdiction over support enters a support decree, it is the *only* body which may modify that decree as long as it retains continuing jurisdiction under UIFSA. Other states may not modify the original decree or enter a new support order. UIFSA also contains long-arm jurisdiction provisions designed to ensure that the forum state will maximize its jurisdiction over out-of-state obligors, in addition to provisions designed to speed up interstate case processing, transmission of information and documents, interstate telephone conferencing, and standardized forms. UIFSA deals solely with child support; visitation issues may not be raised in a UIFSA proceeding. *See* § 305(a). For summaries of UIFSA, *see* Patricia Wick Hatamyar, *Critical Applications and Proposals for Improvement of the Uniform Interstate Family Support Act and the Full Faith and Credit for Child Support Orders Act*, 71 ST. JOHN'S L. REV. 1 (1997); John J. Sampson & Paul M. Kurtz, *UIFSA: An Interstate Support Act for the 21st Century*, 27 FAM. L.Q. 85 (1993).

UNIFORM INTERSTATE FAMILY SUPPORT ACT

9 U.L.A. 121 (1994).

Section 101. Definitions

(4) "Home state" means the state in which a child lived with a parent or a person acting as parent for at least six consecutive months immediately preceding the time of filing of a [petition] or comparable pleading for support and, if a child is less than six months old, the state in which the child lived from birth with any of them. A period of temporary absence of any of them is counted as part of the six-month or other period.

Section 205. Continuing, Exclusive Jurisdiction

(a) A tribunal of this State issuing a support order consistent with the law of this State has continuing, exclusive jurisdiction over a child support order:

(1) as long as this State remains the residence of the obligor, the individual obligee, or the child for whose benefit the support order is issued; or

(2) until each individual party has filed written consent with the tribunal of this State for a tribunal of another state to modify the order and assume continuing, exclusive jurisdiction.

(b) A tribunal of this State issuing a child support order consistent with the law of this State may not exercise its continuing jurisdiction to modify the order if the order has been modified by a tribunal of another state pursuant to a law substantially similar to this [act].

(c) If a child support order of this State is modified by a tribunal of another state pursuant to a law substantially similar to this [act], a tribunal of this State loses its continuing, exclusive jurisdiction with regard to prospective enforcement of the order issued in this State, and may only:

(1) enforce the order that was modified as to amounts accruing before the modification;

(2) enforce nonmodifiable aspects of that order; and

(3) provide other appropriate relief for violations of that order which occurred before the effective date of the modification.

(d) A tribunal of this State shall recognize the continuing, exclusive jurisdiction of a tribunal of another state which has issued a child support order pursuant to a law substantially similar to this [act].

(e) A temporary support order issued ex parte or pending resolution of a jurisdictional conflict does not create continuing, exclusive jurisdiction in the issuing tribunal.

(f) A tribunal of this State issuing a support order consistent with the law of this State has continuing, exclusive jurisdiction over a spousal support order throughout the existence of the support obligation. A tribunal of this State may not modify a spousal support order issued by a tribunal of another state having continuing, exclusive jurisdiction over that order under the law of that state.

Section 206. Enforcement and Modification of Support Order by Tribunal Having Continuing Jurisdiction

(a) A tribunal of this State may serve as an initiating tribunal to request a tribunal of another state to enforce or modify a support order issued in that state.

(b) A tribunal of this State having continuing, exclusive jurisdiction over a support order may act as a responding tribunal to enforce or modify the order. If a party subject to the continuing,exclusive jurisdiction of the tribunal no longer resides in the issuing state, in subsequent proceedings the tribunal may apply § 316 (Special Rules of Evidence and Procedure) to receive evidence from another state and § 318 (Assistance with Discovery) to obtain discovery through a tribunal of another state.

(c) A tribunal of this State which lacks continuing, exclusive jurisdiction over a spousal support order may not serve as a responding tribunal to modify a spousal support order of another state.

Section 601. Registration of Order for Enforcement.

A support order or an income-withholding order issued by a tribunal of another state may be registered in this State for enforcement.

Section 603. Effect of Registration for Enforcement.

(a) A support order or income-withholding order issued in another state is registered when the order is filed in the registering tribunal of this State.

(b) A registered order issued in another state is enforceable in the same manner and is subject to the same procedures as an order issued by a tribunal of this State.

(c) Except as otherwise provided in this article, a tribunal of this State shall recognize and enforce, but may not modify, a registered order if the issuing tribunal had jurisdiction.

Section 604. Choice of Law.

(a) The law of the issuing state governs the nature, extent, amount, and duration of current payments and other obligations of support and the payment of arrearages under the order.

(b) In a proceeding for arrearages, the Statute of limitation under the laws of this State or of the issuing state, whichever is longer, applies.

Section 605. Notice of Registration Order.

(a) When a support order or income-withholding order issued in another state is registered, the registering tribunal shall notify the nonregistering party. Notice must be given by first class, certified, or registered mail or by any means of personal service authorized by the law of this State. The notice must be accompanied by a copy of the registered order and the documents and relevant information accompanying the order.

(b) The notice must inform the nonregistering party:

(1) that a registered order is enforceable as of the date of registration in the same manner as an order issued by a tribunal of this State;

(2) that a hearing to contest the validity or enforcement of the registered order must be requested within [20] days after the date of mailing or personal service of the notice;

(3) that failure to contest the validity or enforcement of the registered order in a timely manner will result in confirmation of the order and enforcement of the order and the alleged arrearages and precludes further contest of that order with respect to any matter that could have been asserted; and

(4) of the amount of any alleged arrearages.

(c) Upon registration of an income-withholding order for enforcement, the registering tribunal shall notify the obligor's employer pursuant to [the income-withholding law of this State].

[§ 606 spells out the procedure for contesting the validity or enforcement of registered orders.]

Section 607. Contest of Registration or Enforcement.

(a) A party contesting the validity or enforcement of a registered order or seeking to vacate the registration has the burden of proving one or more of the following defenses:

(1) the issuing tribunal lacked personal jurisdiction over the contesting party;

(2) the order was obtained by fraud;

(3) the order has been vacated, suspended, or modified by a later order;

(4) the issuing tribunal has stayed the order pending appeal;

(5) there is a defense under the law of this State to the remedy sought;

(6) full or partial payment has been made; or

(7) the statute of limitation under § 604 (Choice of Law) precludes enforcement of some or all of the arrearages.

(b) If a party presents evidence establishing a full or partial defense under subsection (a), a tribunal may stay enforcement of the registered order, continue the proceeding to permit production of additional relevant evidence, and issue other appropriate orders. An uncontested portion of the registered order may be enforced by all remedies available under the law of this State.

(c) If the contesting party does not establish a defense under subsection (a) to the validity or enforcement of the order, the registering tribunal shall issue an order confirming the order.

Section 611. Modification of Child Support Order of Another State.

(a) After a child support order issued in another state has been registered in this State, the responding tribunal of this State may modify that order only if, after notice and hear, it finds that:

(1) the following requirements are met:

(i) the child, the individual obligee, and the obligor do not reside in the issuing state;

(ii) a [petitioner] who is a nonresident of this State seeks modification; and

(iii) the [respondent] is subject to the personal jurisdiction of the tribunal of this State; or

(2) an individual party or the child is subject to the personal jurisdiction of the tribunal and all of the individual parties have filed a written consent in the issuing tribunal providing that a tribunal of this State may modify the support order and assume continuing, exclusive jurisdiction over the order.

(b) Modification of a registered child support order is subject to the same requirements, procedures, and defenses that apply to the modification of an order issued by a tribunal of this State and the order may be enforced and satisfied in the same manner.

(c) A tribunal of this State may not modify any aspect of a child support order that may not be modified under the law of the issuing state.

(d) On issuance of an order modifying a child support order issued in another state, a tribunal of this State becomes the tribunal of continuing, exclusive jurisdiction.

(e) Within [30] days after issuance of a modified child support order, the party obtaining the modification shall file a certified copy of the order with the issuing tribunal which had continuing, exclusive jurisdiction over the earlier order, and in each tribunal in which the party knows that earlier order has been registered.

These examples summarize how UIFSA handles some common child support problems:

1. Henry and Winnie live in State A with their child, Carl. After their separation but before Winnie has obtained a child support order, Henry moves to State B. Under UIFSA, Winnie may obtain a support order in State A, based on the law of State A, or in State B, based on the law of State B, or she may initiate a two-state procedure that would result in an order in state B, based on the law of State B. The State in which she obtained the original order will have exclusive continuing jurisdiction.

2. Harold and Wanda live in State A with their child, Carla. Harold and Carla go to State B. Harold cannot initiate a support action in State B unless Wanda has sufficient B contacts to satisfy the *International Shoe* standard, or unless Wanda is served there. He may initiate a support action in State A, based on the law of State A or initiate a two-state procedure that would result in an order in State A, based on State A's law.

Problem 12–1:

Mary and Al Jones were married in California and have lived their throughout their marriage; both of their children were born in California and have lived there at all times.

a. Mary and Al decide to divorce. Mary moves to Kansas and files for divorce, custody, and support in Kansas. Does Kansas have jurisdiction over the divorce? over child support under UIFSA?

b. Mary and Al obtain a divorce in California; Mary is awarded custody and child support. Al moves to New Mexico and files a petition to modify his support obligation. Mary also moves to New Mexico. Under UIFSA, does New Mexico have jurisdiction to modify the support order?

c. Mary and Al obtain a divorce in California; Mary is awarded custody and child support. Al moves to New Mexico; Mary and the two children move to Florida. Mary files a petition to modify the support order. Under UIFSA, does Florida have jurisdiction to modify? If not, how should Mary proceed?

Problem 12–2:

George and Karen live in State A and obtain a divorce there; the divorce decree requires Karen to pay support for their child Eric until he turns 21. George moves to State B, where the obligation to support a child ends at age 18. Under UIFSA, if Karen stops paying support when the child turns 18 and George registers the order in State B for enforcement, will Karen be ordered to continue to pay support?

DEPARTMENT OF REVENUE v. FLEET

Florida Court of Appeals, 1996.
679 So.2d 326.

JOANOS, J.

This cause is before the court by a petition for writ of prohibition, seeking to preclude the circuit court from exercising subject matter jurisdiction over a motion for modification of a Georgia child support order. We conclude that enactment of the federal act requiring full faith and credit for child support orders of other states has limited the authority of the courts of this state to modify the amount of a child support award ordered by a court of another state. Therefore, we grant the writ.

In August 1992, a final divorce decree was entered in Cobb County, Georgia, dissolving the marriage of Roseann Jorda (mother) and Michael Jorda (father). The final judgment placed custody of the parties' two minor children with the mother, and ordered the father to pay monthly child support in the amount of $175.00 for each child. In March 1994, the mother filed a petition under the Georgia Uniform Reciprocal Enforcement of Support Act (URESA) to establish the Georgia child support obligation in Florida where the father now resides, and to enforce payment and arrearage of the support previously ordered. The father filed a pro se response to the petition in which he acknowledged the obligation to pay, and the amount of, the child support obligation, but alleged he was unable to pay the amount of support ordered.

In April 1995, the father filed a motion to modify the final judgment. The mother filed a motion to strike, alleging the father's motion violated the provisions of Florida Rule of Civil Procedure 1.110(h). The trial court granted the motion to strike, and directed the father to file a proper pleading. On July 25, 1995, the father filed a supplemental petition to modify the final judgment of dissolution of marriage. Before a hearing was held on the father's petition, a hearing was held on the mother's URESA petition. On September 29, 1995, the trial court issued an order directing the father to pay the $350.00 monthly child support obligation established in the Georgia decree, and reserving jurisdiction to address the child support arrearage. The order granted the mother ten days to file an answer to the father's supplemental complaint for modification.

After a hearing on the father's supplemental complaint for modification, the trial court issued an order granting the father fifteen days to file an amended supplemental complaint for modification addressed to the trial court's September 29, 1995, enforcement order. On December 6, 1995, the father served his amended supplemental petition to modify the child support obligation established in the Georgia decree. In response, the mother served motions to strike and to dismiss. The mother maintained that pursuant to the Full Faith and Credit for Child Support Orders Act, 28 U.S.C. § 1738B (1994), the trial court did not have jurisdiction to modify the Georgia support order. The trial court disagreed with this interpretation of the federal act, and issued an order denying the motions to strike and to dismiss.

The Full Faith and Credit for Child Support Orders Act was enacted October 22, 1994. Pub. L. No. 103–383, § 3(a), 108 Stat. 4064 (codified at 28 U.S.C. § 1738B (1994)). The provision states in part:

a) General rule. The appropriate authorities of each State

(1) shall enforce according to its terms a child support order made consistently with this section by a court of another State; and

(2) shall not seek or make a modification of such an order except in accordance with subsection (e).

* * *

e) Authority to modify orders. A court of a State may make a modification of a child support order with respect to a child that is made by a court of another State if—

(1) the court has jurisdiction to make such a child support order; and

(2)(A) the court of the other State no longer has continuing, exclusive jurisdiction of the child support order because that State no longer is the child's State or the residence of any contestant; or

(B) each contestant has filed written consent to that court's making the modification and assuming continuing, exclusive jurisdiction over the order.

The Child Support Act was designed to rectify the problems caused by the lack of uniformity among state law provisions dealing with child support orders. Among other things, Congress perceived that the lack of uniformity encouraged noncustodial parents to relocate to other states to avoid the jurisdiction of the courts of the home state, "resulting in an increase in the amount of interstate travel and communication required to establish and collect on child support orders and a burden on custodial parents that is expensive, time consuming, and disruptive of occupations and commercial activity." Pub. L. 103–383, § 2, 108 Stat. 4064 (1994), Congressional Findings and Declaration of Purpose. The stated purposes of the Act are:

(1) to facilitate the enforcement of child support orders among the States;

(2) to discourage continuing interstate controversies over child support in the interest of greater financial stability and secure family relationships for the child; and

(3) to avoid jurisdictional competition and conflict among State courts in the establishment of child support orders.

The parties have not cited, and our independent research has not disclosed, a decision of a Florida appellate court addressing application of the 1994 federal Child Support Orders Act to a request for modification of child support ordered by a court of another state. However, the petitioner has directed our attention to an Ohio opinion which raises essentially the same issue on similar facts. In *Paton v. Brill*, 104 Ohio App. 3d 826, 663 N.E.2d 421 (10 Dist. 1995), pursuant to a Maryland divorce decree, the former husband was ordered to pay support for the parties' two minor children. The husband moved to Ohio. The former wife filed a URESA petition, for enforcement of the Maryland child support order. In July 1994, the Ohio court entered a child support order which conformed to the initial Maryland order. Subsequently, the former wife filed a motion for contempt due to the former husband's failure to pay child support, whereupon the former husband filed a motion for reduction of the child support obligation. The referee recommended dismissal of the motion to modify, finding the Ohio court lacked authority to modify the initial Maryland order. The trial court overruled the objections to the referee's report and recommendation, and adopted the report of the referee. The former husband appealed, alleging a violation of his due process and equal protection rights, and contending the ruling discriminated against the class of noncustodial parents by denying access to the court.

* * * The Ohio court concluded that in view of the inapplicability of the exceptions set forth in subsection (e) of the Act, "the federal legislation clearly prohibits modification by the responding Ohio court and requires appellant to return to Maryland to seek modification of his child support obligation." 663 N.E.2d at 425. The court further found the distinctions resulting from operation of the statute are reasonable and directly related to solving a critical national problem concerning the failure of a significant number of parents to fulfill their responsibilities to support their children. We see no due process or equal protection problems with the statute. We also see no impermissible burden on the freedom of travel. Id. at 425. After rejecting arguments similar to those presented by respondents in this case, the Ohio court affirmed the judgment of the trial court dismissing the motion for modification. 663 N.E.2d at 425.

The trial court in this case reasoned that prior decisions of the Florida Supreme Court authorized modification of the child support ordered in the Florida URESA enforcement order. * * * [But] [w]e conclude the 1994 federal legislation has preempted Florida law with respect to modification of child support orders in a URESA enforcement action. Under the act, modifications are prohibited unless the exceptions set forth in subsection (e) are satisfied. This case does not fall within the restrictive exceptions, because the Georgia court has continuing, exclusive jurisdiction of the child support order. The minor children and custodial parent continue to reside in Georgia, and there is nothing in the record which indicates that each contestant has filed written consent to the Florida court's making the modification and assuming continuing, exclusive jurisdiction over the order. *See* 28 U.S.C. § 1738B(e)(2) (1994). Given the inapplicability of the exceptions, the federal legislation prohibits modification by the responding Florida court. Therefore, the father is required to seek modification of the child support obligation in the Georgia court.

Accordingly, we grant the petition for writ of prohibition, and remand this cause to the trial court with directions to grant petitioner's motion to dismiss the father's motion for modification of the child support enforcement order.

SECTION 4. INTERSTATE CHILD CUSTODY JURISDICTION

In order to make a decision regarding adoption, custody, child abuse/neglect, or termination of parental rights, the court must have jurisdiction over the child. Most jurisdictional disputes arise in the context of a child custody dispute. Prior to the Uniform Child Custody Jurisdiction Act (UCCJA), states exercised jurisdiction over custody disputes based either on personal jurisdiction over the parents or the child's physical presence in the state. Under the latter approach, the court exercised jurisdiction even if it lacked jurisdiction over the respondent parent. However, the Supreme Court has never expressly ruled that a child's physical presence in a state is constitutionally sufficient to confer jurisdiction. In a concurring opinion in May v. Anderson, 345 U.S. 528, 73 S.Ct. 840, 97 L.Ed. 1221 (1953), Justice Frankfurter did state that, while personal jurisdiction was necessary for application of the Full Faith and Credit Clause to a custody decree, the due process clause did not bar a state from adjudicating a custody dispute when it lacked personal jurisdiction; no other member of the *May* court addressed the issue and the Supreme Court has not revisited it. *See also* Sampsell v. Superior Court, 32 Cal.2d 763, 197 P.2d 739 (1948).

Under the traditional approach to child custody jurisdiction, the Full Faith and Credit issue was of marginal importance because, given that a child custody decree is always subject to modification (*see* chapter 13, no custody decree was final; even a decree clearly entitled to full faith and credit was subject to relitigation in another forum state. If a custodial parent, resident in State A, allowed the child to visit the other parent in State B, he or she thus risked the possibility that the noncustodial parent would bring another custody proceeding based on the child's presence in State B, and that the State B court would award custody to the (formerly) noncustodial parent. In this situation, State B courts, typically without the presence of the custodial parent and perhaps biased toward their own residents, did often award custody to the home litigant parent; even parents who kidnapped their children were sometimes able to find a friendly forum.

A. THE UNIFORM CHILD CUSTODY JURISDICTION ACT

The National Conference of Commissioners on Uniform State Laws (NCCUSL) proposed the Uniform Child Custody Jurisdiction Act (UCCJA) in 1968. With the Act, the Commissioners hoped to discourage continued controversies over child custody, to deter child abductions, to promote interstate cooperation and communication in adjudicating child custody matters, and to facilitate the enforcement of custody decrees of sister states. The UCCJA defined the bases for subject matter jurisdiction in a child custody action. (Subject matter jurisdiction, derived from a statute or the constitution, cannot be based on consent of the parties.) The drafters' comments are a good source of interpretive material. *See* 9, Part I, U.L.A. 115 (1988) and Brigitte Bodenheimer, *Interstate Custody: Initial Jurisdiction and Continuing Jurisdiction Under the UCCJA*, 14 FAM. L. Q. 203 (1981).

UNIFORM CHILD CUSTODY JURISDICTION ACT

9, Part I, U.L.A. 123 et seq. (1988)

§ 1. [Purposes]

(a) The general purposes of this Act are to

(1) avoid jurisdictional competition and conflict with courts of other states in matters of child custody which have in the past resulted in the shifting of children from state to state with harmful effects on their well-being;

* * *

(3) assure that litigation concerning the custody of a child take place ordinarily in the state with which the child and his family have the closest connection and where significant evidence concerning his care, protection, training, and personal relationships is most readily available, and that courts of this state decline the exercise of jurisdiction when the child and his family have a closer connection with another state.

§ 2. [Definitions]

As used in this Act: * * *

(5) "home state" means the state in which the child immediately preceding the time involved lived with his parents, a parent, or a person acting as parent, for at least 6 consecutive months, and in the case of a child less than 6 months old the state in which the child lived from birth with any of the persons mentioned. Periods of

temporary absence of any of the named persons are counted as part of the 6–month or other period;

* * *

§ 3. [Jurisdiction]

(a) A court of this State which is competent to decide child custody matters has jurisdiction to make a child custody determination by initial or modification decree if:

(1) This State (i) is the home state of the child at the time of commencement of the proceeding, or (ii) had been the child's home state within 6 months before commencement of the proceeding and the child is absent from this State because of his removal or retention by a person claiming his custody or for other reasons, and a parent or person acting as parent continues to live in this State; *or*

(2) it is in the best interest of the child that a court of this State assume jurisdiction because (i) the child and his parents, or the child and at least one contestant, have a significant connection with this State, and (ii) there is available in this State substantial evidence concerning the child's present or future care, protection, training, and personal relationships; or

(3) the child is physically present in this State and (i) the child has been abandoned or (ii) it is necessary in an emergency to protect the child because he has been subjected to or threatened with mistreatment or abuse or is otherwise neglected [or dependent]; or

(4)(i) it appears that no other state would have jurisdiction under prerequisites substantially in accordance with paragraphs (1), (2), or (3), or another state has declined to exercise jurisdiction on the ground that this State is the more appropriate forum to determine the custody of the child, and (ii) it is in the best interest of the child that this court assume jurisdiction.

(b) Except under paragraphs (3) and (4) of subsection (a), physical presence in this State of the child, or of the child and one of the contestants, is not alone sufficient to confer jurisdiction on a court of this State to make a child custody determination.

(c) Physical presence of the child, while desirable, is not a prerequisite for jurisdiction to determine his custody.

[Section 4 of the Act requires reasonable notice and an opportunity to be heard to parents and those having custody of a child and specifies the methods of giving notice in a manner reasonably calculated to give actual notice, including personal delivery outside the state, or by mail, or by publication where other methods are ineffective.]

§ 6. [Simultaneous Proceedings in Other States]

(a) A court of this State shall not exercise its jurisdiction under this Act if at the time of filing the petition a proceeding concerning the custody of the child was pending in a court of another state exercising jurisdiction substantially in conformity with this Act, unless the proceeding is stayed by the court of the other state because this State is a more appropriate forum or for other reasons.

(b) Before hearing the petition in a custody proceeding the court shall examine the pleadings and other information supplied by the parties under § 9 and shall consult the child custody registry established under § 16 concerning the pendency of proceedings with respect to the child in other states. If the court has reason to believe that proceedings may be pending in another state it shall direct an inquiry to the state court administrator or other appropriate official of the other state.

(c) If the court is informed during the course of the proceeding that a proceeding concerning the custody of the child was pending in another state before the court assumed jurisdiction it shall stay the proceeding and communicate with the court in which the other proceeding is pending to the end that the issue may be litigated in the more appropriate forum and that information be exchanged in accordance with §§ 19 through 22. If a court of this State has made a custody decree before being informed of a pending proceeding in a court of another state it shall immediately inform that court of the fact. If the court is informed that a proceeding was commenced in another state after it assumed jurisdiction it shall likewise inform the other court to the end that the issues may be litigated in the more appropriate forum.

[Section 7 provides that a court may decline to exercise jurisdiction if it finds that it is an inconvenient forum; § 8 provides that a court may decline to exercise jurisdiction if "the petitioner for an initial decree has wrongfully taken the child from another state or has engaged in similar reprehensible conduct," and that "[u]nless required in the interest of the child, the court shall not exercise its jurisdiction to modify a custody decree of another state if the petitioner, without consent of the person entitled to custody, has improperly removed the child from the physical custody of the person entitled to custody or has improperly retained the child after a visit or other temporary relinquishment of physical custody."]

§ 13. [Recognition of Out-of-State Custody Decrees]

The courts of this State shall recognize and enforce an initial or modification decree of a court of another state which had assumed jurisdiction under statutory provisions substantially in accordance with this Act or which was made under factual circumstances meeting the jurisdictional standards of the Act, so long as this decree has not been modified in accordance with jurisdictional standards substantially similar to those of this Act.

§ 14. [Modification of Custody Decree of Another State]

(a) If a court of another state has made a custody decree, a court of this State shall not modify that decree unless (1) it appears to the court of this State that the court which rendered the decree does not now have jurisdiction under jurisdictional prerequisites substantially in accordance with this Act or has declined to assume jurisdiction to modify the decree and (2) the court of this State has jurisdiction.

(b) If a court of this State is authorized under subsection (a) and § 8 to modify a custody decree of another state it shall give due consideration to the transcript of the record and other documents of all previous proceedings submitted to it in accordance with § 22.

Note

While the UCCJA has been enacted in all states, some states have modified the statute. These variations may affect both the outcome of custody litigation in the state with a modified UCCJA and in other states asked to honor decrees from states using a modified UCCJA. *See, e.g.,* In re Bueche, 193 Ill.App.3d 594, 140 Ill.Dec. 566, 550 N.E.2d 48 (1990) (Illinois court may entertain modification of Michigan decree despite Michigan's assertion of continuing jurisdiction because Illinois UCCJA permits such modification); Pasqualone v. Pasqualone, 63 Ohio St.2d 96, 406 N.E.2d 1121 (1980) (Ohio not required to honor Illinois custody decree because Illinois had omitted "important" sections of the UCCJA).

B. THE PARENTAL KIDNAPPING PREVENTION ACT

Under § 3 of the UCCJA, the home state is given no priority, a court may render an initial custody decree under any ground. Thus, one state could assume "home state" jurisdiction and another "substantial connection" jurisdiction. As *Glanzner* [p. 605] shows, this has occurred with disturbing frequency.

Because the UCCJA permitted concurrent jurisdiction, it did not resolve the problem of protracted, multistate custody litigation. The problem was exacerbated because most states treated interference with parental custody as a misdemeanor, with the result that extradition was not allowed.

In 1980, Congress sought to resolve these problems with the Parental Kidnapping Prevention Act (PKPA), 28 U.S.C.A. § 1738A. As a federal statute, the PKPA preempts state law, including the UCCJA, if there is a conflict. It applies to custody disputes even if there has been no kidnapping or other wrongdoing, and provides that a state *must* give full faith and credit to a sister state's custody order if it meets PKPA requirements.

PARENTAL KIDNAPPING PREVENTION ACT

§ 1738A. Full faith and credit given to child custody determinations

(a) The appropriate authorities of every State shall enforce according to its terms, and shall not modify except as provided in subsection (f) of this section, any child custody determination made consistently with the provisions of this section by a court of another State.

(b) As used in this section, the term—

(1) "child" means a person under the age of eighteen;

(2) "contestant" means a person, including a parent, who claims a right to custody of visitation of a child;

(3) "custody determination" means a judgment, decree, or other order of a court providing for the custody or visitation of a child, and includes permanent and temporary orders, and initial orders and modifications;

(4) "home State" means the State in which, immediately preceding the time involved, the child lived with his parents, a parent, or a person acting as parent, for at least six consecutive months, and in the case of a child less than six months old, the State in which the child lived from birth with any of such persons. Periods of temporary absence of any of such persons are counted as part of the six-month or other period;

(5) "modification" and "modify" refer to a custody determination which modifies, replaces, supersedes, or otherwise is made subsequent to, a prior custody determination concerning the same child, whether made by the same court or not;

(6) "person acting as a parent" means a person, other than a parent, who has physical custody of a child and who has either been awarded custody by a court or claims a right to custody;

(7) "physical custody" means actual possession and control of a child; and

(8) "State" means a State of the United States, the District of Columbia, the Commonwealth of Puerto Rico, or a territory or possession of the United States.

(c) A child custody determination made by a court of a State is consistent with the provisions of this section only if—

(1) such court has jurisdiction under the law of such State; and

(2) one of the following conditions is met:

(A) such State (i) is the home State of the child on the date of the commencement of the proceeding, or (ii) had been the child's home State within six months before the date of the commencement of the proceeding and the child is absent from such State because of his removal or retention by a contestant or for other reasons, and a contestant continues to live in such State;

(B)(i) it appears that no other State would have jurisdiction under subparagraph (A), and (ii) it is in the best interest of the child that a court of such State assume jurisdiction because (I) the child and his parents, or the child and at least one contestant, have a significant connection with such State other than mere physical presence in such State, and (II) there is available in such State substantial evidence concerning the child's present or future care, protection, training, and personal relationships;

(C) the child is physically present in such State and (i) the child has been abandoned, or (ii) it is necessary in an emergency to protect the child because he has been subjected to or threatened with mistreatment or abuse;

(D)(i) it appears that no other State would have jurisdiction under subparagraph (A), (B), (C), or (E), or another State has declined to exercise jurisdiction on the ground that the State whose jurisdiction is in issue is the more appropriate forum to determine the custody of the child, and (ii) it is in the best interest of the child that such court assume jurisdiction; or

(E) the court has continuing jurisdiction pursuant to subsection (d) of this section.

(d) The jurisdiction of a court of a State which has made a child custody determination consistently with the provisions of this section continues as long as the requirement of subsection (c)(1) of this section continues to be met and such State remains the residence of the child or of any contestant.

(e) Before a child custody determination is made, reasonable notice and opportunity to be heard shall be given to the contestants, any parent whose parental rights have not been previously terminated and any person who has physical custody of a child.

(f) A court of a State may modify a determination of the custody of the same child made by a court of another State, if—

(1) it has jurisdiction to make such a child custody determination; and

(2) the court of the other State no longer has jurisdiction, or it has declined to exercise such jurisdiction to modify such determination.

(g) A court of a State shall not exercise jurisdiction in any proceeding for a custody determination commenced during the pendency of a proceeding in a court of another State where such court of that other State is exercising jurisdiction consistently with the provisions of this section to make a custody determination.

Notes and Questions

1. Under the PKPA a state may not exercise "significant connection" jurisdiction unless no state has "home state" jurisdiction. 28 U.S.C.A. § 1738A(c)(2)(A–D). As *Glanzner* [p. 605] shows, this does not

bar a state from exercising jurisdiction in an initial decree proceeding in such an instance, but it may limit the enforceability of the decree in other states. *A state thus may have jurisdiction under the UCCJA, but not under the PKPA.* For a discussion of the PKPA, *see* Russell Coombs, *Interstate Child Custody: Jurisdiction, Recognition, Enforcement*, 66 MINN. L. REV. 711 (1982).

2. In Thompson v. Thompson, 484 U.S. 174, 108 S.Ct. 513, 98 L.Ed.2d 512 (1988), the Supreme Court held that the PKPA did not create a private right of action in federal court:

> Because Congress' chief aim in enacting the PKPA was to extend the requirements of the Full Faith and Credit Clause to custody determinations, the Act is most naturally construed to furnish a rule of decision for courts to use in adjudicating custody disputes and not to create an entirely new cause of action. It thus is not compatible with the purpose and context of the legislative scheme to infer a private cause of action.

Bills seeking to establish a private right of action under the PKPA have been introduced in almost every Congress since the *Thompson* decision, but none has been enacted.

3. Both the UCCJA and the PKPA provide for "emergency jurisdiction" to protect a child physically present in the state. Most, but not all, courts have held that emergency jurisdiction is only temporary jurisdiction, preserving the jurisdiction of the home or significant connection state to determine a permanent custodial arrangement. *See, e.g.*, Curtis v. Curtis, 574 So.2d 24 (Miss.1990); Gerber v. Gerber, 468 So.2d 1061 (Fla.App.1985). (The 1997 Uniform Child Custody Jurisdiction Enforcement Act (UCCJEA), specifies that emergency jurisdiction is only temporary jurisdiction.) Some courts have required a showing that the emergency cannot be effectively addressed in the home state or significant connection state as a precondition to the exercise of jurisdiction in the physical presence state. *See, e.g.*, Benda v. Benda, 236 N.J.Super. 365, 565 A.2d 1121 (App.Div.1989).

4. Most courts have held that the UCCJA and PKPA apply to adoption and termination of parental rights proceedings as well as custody litigation. *See, e.g.*, In re Baby Girl Clausen, 502 N.W.2d 649 (Mich. 1993); In re Adoption of Child by T.W.C., 270 N.J.Super. 225, 636 A.2d 1083 (1994); State ex rel. Torres v. Mason, 315 Or. 386, 848 P.2d 592 (1993); In re A.E.H., 161 Wis.2d 277, 468 N.W.2d 190 (1991). *But see* Gainey v. Olivo, 258 Ga. 640, 373 S.E.2d 4 (1988). But courts have had difficulty in adapting the UCCJA and PKPA to the adoption context. For a description of the issues, *see, e.g.*, Melanie T. Sloan, *No More Baby Jessicas: Proposed Revisions of the Parental Kidnapping Prevention Act*, 12 YALE L. & POL. REV. 355 (1994).

C. INITIAL CUSTODY DETERMINATIONS UNDER THE UCCJA AND PKPA

IN RE CUSTODY OF GLANZNER

Missouri Court of Appeals, 1992.
835 S.W.2d 386.

GRIMM, J.

In this case of first impression, we are called upon to resolve conflicting child custody decrees from California and Missouri. The California decree granted custody to mother; a later Missouri decree granted custody to father. Under the federal Parental Kidnapping Prevention Act (PKPA), we are required to hold that the California decree is not entitled to interstate enforcement because Missouri was the child's "home state." We therefore deny mother's petition for writ of habeas corpus and quash our temporary order.

* * *

I. BACKGROUND

Suzanne E. Glanzner and Keith W. Glanzner are the mother and father of Bradley Carl Glanzner. Mother and father were married in Illinois on September 5, 1981. Father was then in military service and the parties lived in Tennessee. Bradley was born in St. Louis on August 13, 1982. Mother and, after his birth, child, lived with paternal grandparents in St. Louis from June, 1982, to November, 1983; father was stationed in Okinawa during that time. From November, 1983, to January, 1985, mother, father, and child all lived in California where father was stationed. Mother had lived in California for seven years prior to her marriage. In January, 1985, mother, father, and child came to Missouri. All three of them resided in Missouri until mother and child returned to California on October 29, 1985.

On December 18, 1985, mother filed a petition for legal separation and custody in California. Father was personally served January 13, 1986. He filed a motion to quash service on the grounds that California should not exercise jurisdiction over the child custody issue.

In the meantime, on January 10, 1986, father filed a petition for dissolution in St. Louis County. Mother was apparently served on July 17, 1986. Proceedings continued in California. On June 4, 1986, the California court conducted a hearing on father's motion to quash. The hearing included a phone consultation with a judge in St. Louis County.

On June 18, 1986, the California court found that "the state in which the minor child resided for 6 consecutive months prior to the filing of the petition was Missouri." However, the court noted the child had now resided in California for 7 months. Although child had family members in both states, the court found "California has the most significant contacts with the minor child." As a result, the court held that under the Uniform Child Custody Jurisdiction Act (UCCJA), California was the proper jurisdiction in which to adjudicate the claim. A formal order incorporating that finding was entered July 2, 1986.

On August 12, 1986, following a hearing, the California court granted [the mother temporary custody.] On November 3, 1986, the California court dissolved the marriage of the parties. Mother was granted custody of the child, and father was granted reasonable visitation rights in California. In addition, father was ordered to pay child support and spousal support.

In the St. Louis County action filed January 10, 1986, mother filed a special appearance and objection to jurisdiction about August 15, 1986. She attached a copy of the June 4, 1986 order wherein the California court assumed jurisdiction over the child custody issue. On September 5, 1986, the St. Louis County court overruled mother's objections to jurisdiction. A default decree of dissolution was granted on September 26, 1986; the decree gave custody of child to father, and reasonable visitation rights to mother.

From October 29, 1985, until the summer of 1991, mother had continuous physical custody of child. Father admits he has not visited the child since that date. However, he claims he has attempted to exercise his rights, but mother has interfered with his efforts by "frequently moving, changing her address and not apprising [him] as to the whereabouts of the minor child."

In the spring of 1991, paternal grandparents visited mother and child in California. After returning to Missouri, grandmother phoned mother and asked if child could come to Missouri for a visit during the summer vacation. After receiving assurances from grandparents they would return the child, mother consented. Grandparents purchased a round trip airline ticket for child and sent it to mother. Child flew from California to St. Louis on July 27, 1991; he was to return on September 1, 1991.

Child did not return on September 1. On September 13, mother filed a petition for writ of habeas corpus with this court. Following a brief hearing, this court ordered custody of child returned to mother until further order. Our order was conditioned on mother filing a bond, which she filed. * * *

II. Dissolution Proceedings

In his answer to the petition for writ of habeas corpus, father claims he is entitled to custody of child pursuant to the St. Louis County decree of dissolution granted September 26, 1986. He contends the California orders "were contrary to the Uniform Child Custody Jurisdiction Act (§ 452.440, R.S.Mo. 1986 et seq.) and the Parental Kidnapping Prevention Act (28 U.S.C. § 1738A)."

* * *

Under the California and Missouri versions of the UCCJA, a court has jurisdiction to make a child custody determination if two conditions are met. First, the child and at least one parent has a significant connection with the state; second, substantial evidence concerning the child's present or future care, protection, training, and personal relationships is available in the state. In the summer of 1986, the California court determined it had jurisdiction because mother, child, and maternal grandmother were in California, as well as "neutral third parties from the school" who could testify.

The PKPA does not grant or deny initial jurisdiction to a state. Rather, it governs only the enforcement and modification of foreign decrees and the treatment of concurrent proceedings. Coombs, *Interstate Child Custody: Jurisdiction, Recognition, and Enforcement* 66 MINN. L.REV. 711, 765 (1982). Thus, the PKPA did not prevent California from exercising jurisdiction.

Further, the prohibition against simultaneous proceedings applies only to the state in which proceedings are subsequently commenced; the petition in California was filed before the petition in Missouri. Thus, California was not prohibited from hearing mother's case.

[F]ather contends the California court did not have personal jurisdiction over him.... [F]ather was personally served and he does not contest that fact.... Father made an appearance in the California court and nothing before us indicates father's appearance was a "special or limited" appearance or that he challenged personal jurisdiction.

Under California procedure, ... [i]f a defendant wishes to object that the court does not have "jurisdiction over his person, he must specially appear for that purpose only;" otherwise, he waives any objection to jurisdiction. Thus, from the record, it appears that father waived any objections to jurisdiction.

However, as we explain below, under the PKPA, it is immaterial to the child custody question whether California had personal jurisdiction over father. This is because Missouri was the child's home state under both the California and Missouri versions of the UCCJA, as well as the PKPA.

Missouri defines "home state" as "the state in which, immediately preceding the filing of custody proceeding, the child lived with his parents, [or] a parent ... for at least six consecutive months; ..." § 452.445(4), RSMo 1986. California has a similar definition. Cal. Civil Code § 5151(5) (West 1983). A Missouri court has jurisdiction if Missouri is the child's home state or had been the child's home state within six months before the commencement of the proceeding. § 452.450.1(1)(a) and (b), RSMo 1986.

Mother, father, and child lived in Missouri for approximately nine months from January, 1985, until mother and child moved to California on October 29, 1985. Since child had been in California approximately 51 days when mother filed her petition December 18, 1985, California was not the child's home state. Cal. Civil Code §§ 5151(5) and 5152(1) (West 1983). Father filed his petition on January 10, 1986. Since child had been in Missouri for approximately nine months and was absent from the state only for approximately 74 days before father filed, Missouri "had been the child's home state within six months before commencement of the proceeding." § 452.450.1(1)(b), RSMo 1986; *see also* 28 U.S.C.A. § 1738A (b)(4) (West Supp. 1992). Thus, the Missouri court had jurisdiction.

Mother contends the Missouri court was without jurisdiction because (1) only personal service on her was attempted, (2) the return of service was defective, and (3) the only appearance mother made was a "special appearance and objection to jurisdiction." Father admits because the return of service was defective, "such service was not sufficient to confer personal jurisdiction."

However, the parties agree that in personam jurisdiction is not necessary to dissolve a marriage or determine child custody. Mother was served with the summons and petition on July 17, 1986. Although she entered a special appearance, she did not object that the service or return of service was insufficient. The notice given mother was sufficient to satisfy the requirements of § 452.460, RSMo 1986.

The question then becomes which decree is entitled to be enforced. Under the PKPA, any decree "made consistently with the provisions of [the PKPA shall be enforced] by a court of another State." § 1738A(a). [The court quotes the provisions of PKPA §§ 1738(d) and 1738(d).]

Section 1738A(c) imposes two conditions in order to make a court's child custody determination consistent with the PKPA, and therefore entitled to full faith and credit. First, the court must have jurisdiction under the law of the state. The California court explicitly and the Missouri court implicitly held it met this condition under the UCCJA; California reached this conclusion through the "significant connection" test, Missouri through the "home state" test.

Second, one of the conditions enumerated in § 1738A(c)(2) must be met. If the petition is filed in the child's home state, the second condition is satisfied. Because Missouri had been child's home state within six months of filing, the Missouri petition satisfied § 1738A(c)(2)(A).

As previously noted, California did not meet the home state requirements. Thus, we consider whether California met any other requirements for acting consistently with the PKPA as enumerated in § 1738A(c)(2). § 1738A(c) provides that a state's child custody determination is consistent with this section if "it appears that no other State would have jurisdiction under [the home state provisions of paragraph (A)]." § 1738A(c)(2)(B). California did not meet this requirement because the child had a home state—Missouri. Thus, § 1738A(c)(2)(B) is not applicable.

The third condition in this section of the PKPA applies only if the child has been (1) abandoned or (2) subjected to or threatened with mistreatment or abuse. § 1738A(c)(2)(C). Neither is applicable here.

Likewise, the fourth and fifth conditions do not apply. The fourth condition applies if "it appears that no other State would have jurisdiction under [the other subparagraphs] or another State has declined to exercise jurisdiction." § 1738A(c)(2)(D). Missouri had jurisdiction and did not decline to exercise it.

The fifth condition applies if "the court has continuing jurisdiction pursuant to subsection (d)." § 1738A(c)(2)(E). Subsection (d) applies only if the child custody determination was made consistently with the PKPA. § 1738A(d). Here, the California court had not entered a decree consistently with the requirements of the PKPA.

The PKPA requires a state to give full faith and credit only to those child custody determinations made consistently with its provisions. § 1738A(a). Under the PKPA, California would be required to give full faith and credit to the Missouri decree because the Missouri proceedings comply with the PKPA. On the other hand, the PKPA precludes Missouri and other states from giving full faith and credit to the California decree because it did not meet any of the enumerated conditions in § 1738A(c)(2).

Our conclusion is supported by decisions in other jurisdictions. In *Mancusi,* 136 Misc. 2d 898, 519 N.Y.S.2d 476, father filed an action for child custody in New York. Thereafter, mother filed a similar action in Arizona. Arizona was the children's "home state." The New York court observed that "the PKPA makes it judicially imprudent for one state court to exercise jurisdiction when another state court fulfills the requirements and wishes to exercise 'home state' jurisdiction. If conflicting custody decrees were issued, only the custody decree of the 'home state' court would be entitled to full faith and credit under federal law." Id. at 479. The New York court vacated its custody order. Id. at 480; *accord* Sams v. Boston, 384 S.E.2d 151, 157 (W.Va.1989). * * * *[S]ee also Wachter v. Wachter,* 439 So.2d 1260 (La.App.1983).

Implicit in our holding is recognition that the PKPA preempts conflicting state law in interstate custody matters. "Congressional enactments which do not expressly exclude state legislation in the field nevertheless override state laws with which they conflict. U.S.Const. art. 1, § 8. In deciding whether state and federal laws are so inconsistent that state law must give way, we must 'determine whether, under the circumstances of this particular case [the state's] law stands as an obstacle to the accomplishment and execution of the full purposes and objectives of Congress.' " (citation omitted).

Section 1738A does not expressly exclude state legislation. However, Congress enacted the PKPA in part to avoid jurisdictional competition and to facilitate the enforcement of custody decrees in sister states. Both exist under the UCCJA. As a result, numerous states have recognized that the PKPA preempts conflicting portions of the UCCJA.

We recognize the preemption of the PKPA where it conflicts with our state law. To do otherwise would frustrate the sound purposes of the PKPA. Here, Missouri was the only state which could enter a decree consistent with the PKPA unless Missouri declined to exercise jurisdiction. Missouri did not decline and its decree is enforceable throughout the United States. No other state's decree would be. To hold otherwise would result in a decree which was subject to the same problems as those entered pre-PKPA, a system Congress found was inadequate.

Mother contends, however, that § 452.465.1, RSMo 1986, precluded the Missouri court from exercising jurisdiction. This section directs Missouri courts not to exercise jurisdiction "if, at the time of filing the petition, a proceeding concerning the custody of the child was pending in a court of another state exercising jurisdiction substantially in conformity" with the UCCJA. As a result, mother argues that Missouri was required to recognize and enforce the California decree.

Mother's contention might be tenable if we looked only at the California and Missouri UCCJA provisions, and not at the PKPA. However, some would argue that even under the UCCJA, preference to home state jurisdiction should be given. *See Hattoum v. Hattoum*, 295 Pa. Super. 169, 441 A.2d 403, 405 (1982) ("The Act treats as preferable the 'home' jurisdiction"); *Prickett v. Prickett*, 498 So.2d 1060, 1061 (Fla.App.1986) ("The general rule is that the 'home state' of the child should have jurisdiction."). Under this interpretation, California may not have been exercising jurisdiction substantially in conformity with the UCCJA.

More importantly, one of the reasons Congress adopted the PKPA was "to establish national standards under which the courts of such jurisdictions will determine ... the effect to be given by each such jurisdiction to such decisions by the courts of other such jurisdictions." § 1738A historical and statutory notes. The national standard which Congress established requires states to give full faith and credit to child custody orders which are "consistent with the provisions" of the PKPA. § 1738A (a) and (c). The California order is not.

... [T]he issue before us is not whether the initial California decree violated the UCCJA or PKPA when entered. Rather, the question is whether that decree is entitled to be enforced. Under the PKPA, it is not....

Mother's petition for a writ of habeas corpus is denied, and we quash our temporary order.

Notes and Questions

1. As *Glanzner* suggests, most courts agree that a court need not have personal jurisdiction over both parents to issue a custody decree.

2. If the father had filed his action in Missouri before mother filed in California, would he have had any additional arguments in the California proceeding?

3. The Uniform Child Custody Jurisdiction Act (UCCJEA), approved by the National Commissioners on Uniform State Laws in 1997 and envisioned as the successor to the UCCJA, provides that a state may

not issue an initial custody decree based on "substantial connections" jurisdiction unless the child has no "home state."

4. Harry and Wanda live in Maine with their child Sam. Harry takes Sam without Wanda's permission and absconds; Wanda does not know where they are. If Wanda files an action in Maine, can the court determine custody while Sam and Harry are out of state? *See* Lyons v. Lyons, 227 Va. 82, 314 S.E.2d 362 (1984). If she does not file an action, does the state to which Harry has taken Sam become the home state after six months? *See Sams v. Boston*, 181 W.Va. 706, 384 S.E.2d 151 (1989).

Problem 12–3:

Mary and Tom Smith have always lived in Florida with their two children, ages 6 and 9.

a. Mary and Tom decide to divorce. Mary moves to Kansas with the children in June, 1997. In October, 1997, she files for divorce and custody in Kansas. In November, 1997, Tom files for divorce and custody in Florida. Does Kansas have jurisdiction over the divorce? over child custody under the UCCJA? the PKPA?

b. Tom leaves Florida with the children and without Mary's consent. Mary does not know where he and the children are. Mary consults you about how to secure legal custody of the children. What advice will you give her?

c. In January, 1997, Mary moves, with the children, to Georgia. Mary has an excellent job; the children are enrolled in school and doing well. Tom files for divorce and custody in Florida in August, 1997. Mary files an action for divorce and custody in Georgia in September, 1997. Does Florida have jurisdiction over child custody under the UCCJA? the PKPA? Does Georgia have jurisdiction over child custody under the UCCJA? the PKPA?

D. MODIFICATION OF CUSTODY DECREES

GREENLAW v. SMITH

Supreme Court of Washington, 1994.
123 Wash.2d 593, 869 P.2d 1024.

ANDERSEN, CHIEF JUSTICE.

This is a child custody dispute. The mother, who is custodian of the child, challenges the subject matter jurisdiction of a Washington trial court to modify its own custody decree once the child and custodian have moved from the state of Washington and established a new "home state" under the Uniform Child Custody Jurisdiction Act, RCW 26.27.

Rosemary B. Greenlaw (the mother) and David Smith, III (the father) were married in January 1978. Their son, Alexander Geoffrey Smith (Alex), the child who is the subject of this proceeding, was born

October 14, 1978. He is now 15 years old. The marriage was dissolved on March 11, 1982, when Alex was 3 ½ years old. Under the decree of dissolution, the mother was granted custody of the child and the father apparently was granted reasonable visitation.

In May of 1985, the mother accepted a 3–year job assignment with the United States Army in Frankfurt, Germany. The mother's job required her to travel frequently and she placed Alex in a German-speaking boarding school for 3 years, from approximately age 7 to age 10. During this time Alex saw his mother only irregularly on weekends and on holidays.

In 1988, Alex and his mother returned to the United States and began living in California, and Alex resumed regular visitation with his father in Tacoma. From 1988 to 1990, Alex and his mother moved four times; Alex attended three different schools during that 2–year period. In 1990, the mother began attending law school in San Jose and Alex spent the school year living with his mother's former boyfriend in Berkeley, California. During the 1990–91 school year, Alex apparently saw his mother on weekends and saw his father during school vacation periods.

While Alex was in Tacoma with his father during visits in 1990 and 1991, the child began seeing a counselor who ultimately recommended a change in custody from the mother to the father. The counselor concluded:

> In summary, the emotional and mental needs of Alex, including needs of warmth, love, nurturing, caring and involvement in the social, cultural and family development have not been met or provided by his mother in the years that she has been charged with the custodial relationship of Alex. Similarly, these needs have not been met by the surrogate caretakers which Alex's mother has placed him with during several of these years. Alex has inappropriately been put in the position of self-parenting as a result of the neglect and virtual parental abandonment by his mother, his custodial parent. This situation is injurious to Alex and in my opinion there is an immediate need for corrective intervention to avoid additional injury and to assist Alex in a program of normal childhood development.

The mother denies the allegations of neglect and abandonment.

In July of 1991, the father filed a petition in the Pierce County Superior Court, asking that he be granted custody of Alex.

The mother responded by asking the court to decline jurisdiction over the matter and to transfer the case to the State of California, claiming California more properly had jurisdiction to determine the issues.

The superior court commissioner set the matter for hearing and appointed a guardian ad litem to investigate the request for modification. The hearing on the mother's motion was held after the guardian ad litem had filed his initial report and after the commissioner had interviewed the child in chambers. The commissioner, in an order entered September 20, 1991: (1) determined that it had jurisdiction to hear the case because Washington had significant contacts with the child and because an emergency existed; and (2) changed the residential placement of the child pending a final hearing on the father's petition.

Following entry of the commissioner's order, the mother moved to revise the decision with respect to the jurisdictional issues. The motion for revision was denied by the Superior Court on December 13, 1991, and the mother appealed. The Court of Appeals reversed, holding that Washington did not have subject matter jurisdiction. We reverse the Court of Appeals.

Two issues are determinative of the appeal.

ISSUES

ISSUE ONE. Does Washington have continuing jurisdiction to modify its own custody orders after the child and custodial parent have established residence in another state, if the noncustodial parent continues to reside in Washington and the child continues to have some connection with Washington?

ISSUE TWO. If so, did the trial court abuse its discretion in refusing to decline to exercise jurisdiction on the ground that California is a more convenient forum?

DECISION

ISSUE ONE.

CONCLUSION. A Washington court which enters a child custody decree continues to have jurisdiction to modify that decree so long as one of the parties remains in the state and so long as the child's contact with the state continues to be more than slight.

* * *

The PKPA requires states to give full faith and credit to the custody decrees of other states which are consistent with the federal law. The PKPA also attempts to more clearly limit the circumstances under which a court may modify the custody decree of another state. In addition to the jurisdictional bases set forth in § 3 of the UCCJA, the federal law includes the following basis:

> The jurisdiction of a court of a State which has made a child custody determination consistently with the provisions of this section continues as long as the requirement of subsection (c)(1) of this section continues to be met and such State remains the residence of the child or of any contestant.

28 U.S.C. § 1738A(d). Subsection (c)(1), which is referred to, requires that a state have jurisdiction to modify a custody decree under that state's own laws.

The PKPA should be considered whenever the court is asked to determine which of two or more states has jurisdiction to decide a custody dispute.

Much of the confusion generated by the language of the ... [UCCJA and PKPA] can be eliminated if a trial court which is asked to determine custody clearly distinguishes between jurisdiction to determine the *initial* custody of a child and jurisdiction to *modify* a prior custody order.

In the present case that distinction was not made. The trial court and the Court of Appeals both failed to consider the presumption created by the UCCJA and the PKPA that the decree state—Washington—had continuing jurisdiction to modify its own order and other states must decline to modify until the decree state loses or declines jurisdiction.

It appears that the majority of appellate courts which have addressed the issue presented here told that the state in which the initial decree was entered has *exclusive* continuing jurisdiction to modify the initial decree if: (1) one of the parents continues to reside in the decree state; and (2) the child continues to have some connection with the decree state, such as visitation.

We agree that this approach best advances the purposes of the law and provides the most security for children who are subject to these decrees.

We now apply this law to the present case. Washington is the decree state and the father continues to reside in Washington. There is no dispute that Washington had jurisdiction to enter the initial decree. Washington law provides that a custody decree may be modified under certain circumstances.

The remaining question is whether Alex has continued to have a sufficient connection with the State of Washington to result in continuing jurisdiction over his welfare. We conclude that he has. First, the Pierce County Superior Court file reflects the correspondence between the parents for a number of years, and reflects the history of this litigation. Second, the child has had consistent visits with his father when the child has been in the United States. Third, the child's extended family on both the mother's side and the father's side, live in Washington in the Tacoma area. Fourth, the child's counselor at the time the petition was filed is in Washington. Fifth, Alex, at age 15, is mature enough to have an opinion about his custody and has expressed that he wants to live with his father. Substantial evidence regarding the child's future care, education, social development and family and other personal relationships exists in the state of Washington. Thus the child's contact with the state of Washington continues to be more than slight.

* * *

In the present case the child has established a home state in California. Under California law this fact, alone, would not be a sufficient basis for determining that Washington had lost jurisdiction and that California was the appropriate forum for deciding the modification action. In *Kumar v. Superior Court*, 32 Cal.3d 689, 652 P.2d 1003, 186 Cal. Rptr. 772 (1982), the California Supreme Court held that under § 14 of the UCCJA

> the strong presumption is that the decree state will continue to have modification jurisdiction until it loses all or almost all connection with the child.

Kumar, 32 Cal.3d at 699, 652 P.2d at 1009, 186 Cal. Rptr. at 778.

Consistency and clarity are important to this area of law and the UCCJA was "designed to bring some semblance of order into the existing chaos" of pre-UCCJA decisions.

Interpreting the UCCJA to allow an automatic shift in modification jurisdiction simply because a child establishes a new home state would not further the purposes of the Act as it would permit forum shopping and instability of custody decrees.

We thus interpret the UCCJA and PKPA to mean that jurisdiction to modify a custody decree continues with the decree state so long as: (1) that state's decree is entered in compliance with the UCCJA and PKPA; (2) one of the parents or other contestants continues to reside in the decree state; and (3) the child continues to have more than slight contact with the decree state.

The trial court did not abuse its discretion in denying the mother's request that it decline to exercise jurisdiction on the basis that California is the more convenient forum.

Even though a decree state has jurisdiction to modify its own decree, that state is not required to retain jurisdiction if another state appears to be a more appropriate, more convenient forum. However, the fact that another jurisdiction may be *as* appropriate a forum as the decree state does not give that second state concurrent jurisdiction to decide the case.

RCW § 26.27.070 provides that a court which has jurisdiction to determine custody or to modify a custody order *may* decline to exercise its jurisdiction if it is an inconvenient forum to make a custody determination under the circumstances of the case and the court of another state is a more appropriate forum.

In determining if it is an inconvenient forum, the court shall consider if it is in the interest of the child that another state assume jurisdiction. For this purpose it may take into account the following factors, among others:

(a) If another state is or recently was the child's home state;

(b) If another state has a closer connection with the child and his family or with the child and one or more of the contestants;

(c) If substantial evidence concerning the child's present or future care, protection, training, and personal relationships is more readily available in another state;

(d) If the parties have agreed on another forum which is no less appropriate; and

(e) If the exercise of jurisdiction by a court of this state would contravene any of the purposes stated in RCW § 26.27.010.

RCW § 26.27.070(3).

Such a ruling is discretionary. A trial court abuses its discretion when its decision is manifestly unreasonable or based on untenable grounds.

In this case, based on the record on review, the trial court would have been justified in ruling either way on the motion to decline jurisdiction. Although California was the home state of the child and had some information about the child, Washington also had substantial evidence, including the court file discussed above, the child's counselor, and Alex's extended family, available within its jurisdiction. On the record before us, the trial court did not abuse its discretion in denying the motion to decline jurisdiction.

The Court of Appeals is reversed and the case is remanded for trial on the merits.

Notes and Questions

1. With increased mobility, the most frequent disputes arise over continuing, rather than initial, jurisdiction. As *Greenlaw* indicates, under the PKPA the initial decree state retains exclusive jurisdiction as long as one contestant remains in the state, there is "a" basis for jurisdiction under the state's law, and that state has not declined jurisdiction. *See also* In re Marriage of Mosier, 251 Kan. 490, 836 P.2d 1158 (1992).

2. Under the version of the UCCJA enacted in most states, even if a court exercises "home state" jurisdiction to render an initial decree, it may retain "substantial connection" continuing jurisdiction, even if the child has established a new home state. This is not true in Texas; jurisdiction to modify custody is lost when the child establishes a new home state. *See* Tex. Fam. Code § 155.003. Which approach is better? Why?

3. When Mary and Tom divorced in 1991, both lived in California. After the divorce, Mary and their child Ann moved to New Mexico. Tom later moved to New Mexico. If Tom wants to modify the existing custody order, is California or New Mexico the appropriate forum? Why? *See* Nelson v. Nelson, 121 N.M. 243, 910 P.2d 319 (1995).

Problem 12–4:

Mary and Tom Smith have lived in Florida throughout their marriage; both of their two children, now ages 6 and 9, have lived there throughout their lives. Mary moves to Kansas in June, 1997. In October, 1997 she files for divorce and custody in Kansas; one month later, a Kansas court awards Mary a divorce and custody of the two children. The court grants visitation to Tom. The children go to visit Tom in June,

1998; he refuses to return them and files a petition to modify the Kansas custody decree in Florida. Under the PKPA, must the Florida court enforce the Kansas decree? Must it *not* enforce the decree?

SECTION 5. THE HAGUE CONVENTION

FRIEDRICH v. FRIEDRICH

United States Court of Appeals, Sixth Circuit, 1996.
78 F.3d 1060.

BOGGS, CIRCUIT JUDGE.

For the second time, we address the application of the Hague Convention on the Civil Aspects of International Child Abduction ("the Convention") and its implementing legislation, the International Child Abduction Remedies Act ("the Act"), 42 U.S.C. §§ 11601–11610, to the life of Thomas Friedrich, now age six. We affirm the district court's order that Thomas was wrongfully removed from Germany and should be returned.

I

Thomas was born in Bad Aibling, Germany, to Jeana Friedrich, an American service-woman stationed there, and her husband, Emanuel Friedrich, a German citizen. When Thomas was two years old, his parents separated after an argument on July 27, 1991. Less than a week later, in the early morning of August 2, 1991, Mrs. Friedrich took Thomas from Germany to her family home in Ironton, Ohio, without informing Mr. Friedrich. Mr. Friedrich sought return of the child in German Family Court, obtaining an order awarding him custody on August 22. He then filed this action for the return of his son in the United States District Court for the Southern District of Ohio on September 23.

We first heard this case three years ago. *Friedrich v. Friedrich*, 983 F.2d 1396 (6th Cir.1993) ("*Friedrich I*"). At that time, we reversed the district court's denial of Mr. Friedrich's claim for the return of his son to Germany pursuant to the Convention. We outlined the relevant law on what was then an issue of first impression in the federal appellate courts, and remanded with instructions that the district court determine whether, as a matter of German law, Mr. Friedrich was exercising custody rights to Thomas at the time of removal. We also asked the district court to decide if Mrs. Friedrich could prove any of the four affirmative defenses provided by the Convention and the Act. Thomas, meanwhile, remained with his mother and his mother's parents in Ohio.

On remand, the district court allowed additional discovery and held a new hearing. The court eventually determined that, at the time of Thomas's removal on August 1, 1991, Mr. Friedrich was exercising custody rights to Thomas under German law, or would have been exercising such rights but for the removal. The court then held that Mrs. Friedrich had not established any of the affirmative defenses available to her under the Convention. The court ordered Mrs. Friedrich to return Thomas to Germany "forthwith," but later stayed the order, upon the posting of a bond by Mrs. Friedrich, pending the resolution of this appeal.

Mrs. Friedrich's appeal raises two issues that are central to the young jurisprudence of the Hague Convention. First, what does it mean to "exercise" custody rights? Second, when can a court refuse to return a child who has been wrongfully removed from a country because return of the abducted child would result in a "grave" risk of harm?

In answering both these questions, we keep in mind two general principles inherent in the Convention and the Act, expressed in *Friedrich I*, and subsequently embraced by unanimous federal authority. First, a court in the abducted-to nation has jurisdiction to decide the merits of an abduction claim, but not the merits of the underlying custody dispute. Hague Convention, Article 19; 42 U.S.C. § 11601(b)(4); *Friedrich I*, 983 F.2d at 1400; *Rydder v. Rydder*, 49 F.3d 369, 372 (8th Cir.1995); *Feder v. Evans–Feder*, 63 F.3d 217, 221 (3d Cir.1995); *Journe v. Journe*, 911 F.Supp. 43 (D.P.R.1995). Second, the Hague Convention is generally intended to restore the pre-abduction status quo and to deter parents from crossing borders in search of a more sympathetic court. Pub. Notice 957, 51 Fed.Reg. 10494, 10505 (1986); *Friedrich I*, 983 F.2d at 1400; *Rydder*, 49 F.3d at 372; *Feder*, 63 F.3d at 221; *Wanninger v. Wanninger*, 850 F.Supp. 78, 80 (D.Mass.1994).

II

The removal of a child from the country of its habitual residence is "wrongful" under the Hague Convention if a person in that country is, or would otherwise be, exercising custody rights to the child under that country's law at the moment of removal. Hague Convention, Article 3. The plaintiff in an action for return of the child has the burden of proving the exercise of custody rights by a preponderance of the evidence. 42 U.S.C. § 11603(e)(1)(A). We review the district court's findings of fact for clear error and review its conclusions about American, foreign, and international law *de novo*.

The district court held that a preponderance of the evidence in the record established that Mr. Friedrich was exercising custody rights over Thomas at the time of Thomas's removal. Mrs. Friedrich alleges that the district court improperly applied German law. Reviewing *de novo*, we find no error in the court's legal analysis. Custody rights "may arise in particular by operation of law or by reason of a judicial or administrative decision, or by reason of an agreement having legal effect under the law of the State." Hague Convention, Article 3. German law gives both parents equal *de jure* custody of the child, German Civil Code 1626(1), and, with a few exceptions, this *de jure* custody continues until a competent court says otherwise. *See Currier v. Currier*, 845 F.Supp. 916, 920 (D.N.H.1994) ("under German law both parents retain joint rights of custody until a decree has been entered limiting one parent's rights"); *Wanninger*, 850 F.Supp. at 78 (D.Mass.1994).

Mrs. Friedrich argues that Mr. Friedrich "terminated" his custody rights under German law because, during the argument on the evening of July 27, 1991, he placed Thomas's belongings and hers in the hallway outside of their apartment. The district court properly rejected the claim that these actions could end parental rights as a matter of German law. We agree. After examining the record, we are uncertain as to exactly what happened on the evening of July 27, but we do know that the events of that night were not a judicial abrogation of custody rights. Nor are we persuaded by Mrs. Friedrich's attempts to read the German Civil Code provisions stipulated to by the parties in such a way as to create the ability of one parent to terminate his or her custody rights extrajudicially.

Mrs. Friedrich also argues that, even if Mr. Friedrich had custody rights under German law, he was not *exercising* those custody rights as contemplated by the Hague Convention. She argues that, since custody rights include the care for the person and property of the child, Mr. Friedrich was not exercising custody rights because he was not paying for or taking care of the child during the brief period of separation in Germany.

The Hague Convention does not define "exercise." As judges in a common law country, we can easily imagine doing so ourselves. One might look to the law of the foreign country to determine if custody rights existed *de jure*, and then develop a test under the general principles of the Hague Convention to determine what activities—financial support, visitation—constitute sufficient exercise of *de jure* rights. The question in our immediate case would then be: "was Mr. Friedrich's single visit with Thomas and plans for future visits with Thomas sufficient exercise of custodial rights for us to justify calling the removal of Thomas wrongful?" One might even approach a distinction between the exercise of "custody" rights and the exercise of "access" or "visitation" rights. If Mr. Friedrich, who has *de jure* custody, was, not exercising sufficient *de facto* custody, Thomas's removal would not be wrongful.

We think it unwise to attempt any such project. Enforcement of the Convention should not to be made dependent on the creation of a common law definition of "exercise." The only acceptable solution, in the absence of a ruling from a court in the country of habitual residence, is to liberally find "exercise" whenever a parent with *de jure* custody rights keeps, or seeks to keep, any sort of regular contact with his or her child.

We see three reasons for this broad definition of "exercise." First, American courts are not well suited to determine the consequences of parental behavior under the law of a foreign country. It is fairly easy for the courts of one country to determine whether a person has custody rights under the law of another country. It is also quite possible for a court to determine if an order by a foreign court awards someone "custody" rights, as opposed to rights of "access." Far more difficult is the task of deciding, prior to a ruling by a court in the abducted-from country, if a parent's custody rights should be ignored because he or she was not acting sufficiently like a custodial parent. A foreign court, if at all possible, should refrain from making such policy-oriented decisions concerning the application of German law to a child whose habitual residence is, or was, Germany.

Second, an American decision about the adequacy of one parent's exercise of custody rights is dangerously close to forbidden territory: the merits of the custody dispute. The German court in this case is perfectly capable of taking into account Mr. Friedrich's behavior during the August 1991 separation, and the German court presumably will tailor its custody order accordingly. A decision by an American court to deny return to Germany because Mr. Friedrich did not show sufficient attention or concern for Thomas's welfare would preclude the German court from addressing these issues—and the German court may well resolve them differently.

Third, the confusing dynamics of quarrels and informal separations make it difficult to assess adequately the acts and motivations of a parent. An occasional visit may be all that is available to someone left, by the vagaries of marital discord, temporarily without the child. Often the child may be avoided, not out of a desire to relinquish custody, but out of anger, pride, embarrassment, or fear, vis a vis the other parent. Reading too much into a parent's behavior during these difficult times could be inaccurate and unfair. Although there may be situations when a long period of unexplainable neglect of the child could constitute non-exercise of otherwise valid custody rights under the Convention, as a general rule, any attempt to maintain a somewhat regular relationship with the child should constitute "exercise." This rule leaves the full resolution of custody issues, as the Convention and common sense indicate, to the courts of the country of habitual residence.

We are well aware that our approach requires a parent, in the event of a separation or custody dispute, to seek permission from the other parent or from the courts before taking a child out of the country of its habitual residence. Any other approach allows a parent to pick a "home court" for the custody dispute *ex parte*, defeating a primary purpose of the Convention. We believe that, where the reason for removal is legitimate, it will not usually be difficult to obtain approval from either the other parent or a foreign court. Furthermore, as the case for removal of the child in the custody of one parent becomes more compelling, approval (at least the approval of a foreign court) should become easier to secure.

Mrs. Friedrich argues that our approach cannot adequately cope with emergency situations that require the child and parent to leave the country. In her case, for example, Mrs. Friedrich claims that removal of Thomas to Ohio was necessary because she could no longer afford to have the child stay at the army base, and Mr. Friedrich refused to provide shelter. Examining the record, we seriously doubt that Mr. Friedrich would have refused to lodge Thomas at his expense in Germany. In any event, even if an emergency forces a parent to take a child to a foreign country, any such emergency cannot excuse the parent from returning the child to the jurisdiction once return of the child becomes safe. Nor can an emergency justify a parent's refusal to submit the child to the authority of the foreign court for resolution of custody matters, including the question of the appropriate temporary residence of the child. *See Viragh v. Foldes*, 415 Mass. 96, 612 N.E.2d 241 (1993) (child removed to America by one parent without notification to other parent may remain in America in light of decision by Hungarian court in parallel proceeding that best interests of the child require exercise of sole custody by parent in America).

We therefore hold that, if a person has valid custody rights to a child under the law of the country of the child's habitual residence, that person cannot fail to "exercise" those custody rights under the Hague Convention short of acts that constitute clear and unequivocal abandonment of the child. Once it determines that the parent exercised custody rights in any manner, the court should stop—completely avoiding the question whether the parent exercised the custody rights well or badly. These matters go to the merits of the custody dispute and are, therefore, beyond the subject matter jurisdiction of the federal courts. 42 U.S.C. § 11601(b)(4).

In this case, German law gave Mr. Friedrich custody rights to Thomas. The facts before us clearly indicate that he attempted to exercise these rights during the separation from his wife. Mr. and Mrs. Friedrich argued during the evening of July 27, 1991, and separated on the morning of July 28. Mrs. Friedrich left with her belongings and Thomas. She stayed on the army base with the child four days. Mr. Friedrich telephoned Mrs. Friedrich on July 29 to arrange a visit with Thomas, and spent the afternoon of that day with his son. Mr. and Mrs. Friedrich met on August 1 to talk about Thomas and their separation. The parties dispute the upshot of this conversation. Mrs. Friedrich says that Mr. Friedrich expressed a general willingness that Thomas move to America with his mother. Mr. Friedrich denies this. It is clear, however, that the parties did agree to immediate visitations of Thomas by Mr. Friedrich, scheduling the first such visit for August 3. Shortly after midnight on August 2, Mrs. Friedrich took her son and, without informing her husband, left for America by airplane.

Because Mr. Friedrich had custody rights to Thomas as a matter of German law, and did not clearly abandon those rights prior to August 1, the removal of Thomas without his consent was wrongful under the Convention, regardless of any other considerations about Mr. Friedrich's behavior during the family's separation in Germany.

III

Once a plaintiff establishes that removal was wrongful, the child must be returned unless the defendant can establish one of four defenses. Two of these defenses can be established by a preponderance of the evidence, 42 U.S.C. § 11603(e)(2)(B): the proceeding was commenced more than one year after the removal of the child and the child has become settled in his or her new environment, Hague Convention, Article 12; or, the person seeking return of the child consented to or subsequently acquiesced in the removal or retention, Hague Convention, Article 13a. The other two defenses must be shown by clear and convincing evidence, 42 U.S.C. § 11603(e)(2)(A): there is a grave risk that the return of the child would expose it to physical or psychological harm, Hague Convention, Article 13b; or, the return of the child "would not be permitted by the fundamental principles of the requested State relating to the protection of human rights and fundamental freedoms," Hague Convention, Article 20.

All four of these exceptions are "narrow," 42 U.S.C. § 11601(a)(4). They are not a basis for avoiding return of a child merely because an American court believes it can better or more quickly resolve a dispute. *See Rydder*, 49 F.3d at 372 (citing *Friedrich I*, 983 F.2d at 1400). In fact, a federal court retains, and should use when appropriate, the discretion to return a child, despite the existence of a defense, if return would further the aims of the Convention. *Feder*, 63 F.3d at 226 (citing Pub. Notice 957, 51 Fed. Reg. 10494, 10509 (1986)).

Mrs. Friedrich alleges that she proved by clear and convincing evidence in the proceedings below that the return of Thomas to Germany would cause him grave psychological harm. Mrs. Friedrich testified that Thomas has grown attached to family and friends in Ohio. She also hired an expert psychologist who testified that returning Thomas to Germany would be traumatic and difficult for the child, who was currently happy and healthy in America with his mother.

> [Thomas] definitely would experience the loss of his mother . . . if he were to be removed to Germany. That would be a considerable loss.
>
> And there then would be the probabilities of anger both towards his mother, who it might appear that she has abandoned him [sic], and towards the father for creating that abandonment. [These feelings] could be plenty enough springboard for other developmental or emotional restrictions which could include nightmares, antisocial behavior, a whole host of anxious-type behavior. Blaske Deposition at 28–29.

If we are to take the international obligations of American courts with any degree of seriousness, the exception to the Hague Convention for grave harm to the child requires far more than the evidence that Mrs. Friedrich provides. Mrs. Friedrich alleges nothing more than *adjustment* problems that would attend the relocation of most children. There is no allegation that Mr. Friedrich has ever abused Thomas. The district court found that the home that Mr. Friedrich has prepared for Thomas in Germany appears adequate to the needs of any young child. The father does not work long hours, and the child's German grandmother is ready to care for the child when the father cannot. There is nothing in the record to indicate that life in Germany would result in any permanent harm or unhappiness.

Furthermore, even *if* the home of Mr. Friedrich were a grim place to raise a child in comparison to the pretty, peaceful streets of Ironton, Ohio, that fact would be irrelevant to a federal court's obligation under the Convention. We are not to debate the relevant virtues of Batman and *Max und Mortiz,* Wheaties and *Milchreis*. The exception for grave harm to the child is not license for a court in the abducted-to country to speculate on where the child would be happiest. That decision is a custody matter, and reserved to the court in the country of habitual residence.

Mrs. Friedrich advocates a wide interpretation of the grave risk of harm exception that would reward her for violating the Convention. A removing parent must not be allowed to abduct a child and then—when brought to court—complaint that the child has grown used to the surroundings to which they were abducted. Under the logic of the Convention, it is the *abduction* that causes the pangs of subsequent return. The disruption of the usual sense of attachment that arises during most long stays in a single place with a single parent should not be a "grave" risk of harm for the purposes of the Convention.

In thinking about these problems, we acknowledge that courts in the abducted-from country are as ready and able as we are to protect children. If return to a country, or to the custody of a parent in that country, is dangerous, we can expect that country's courts to respond accordingly. And if Germany really is a poor place for young Thomas to grow up, as Mrs. Friedrich contends, we can expect the German courts to recognize that and award her custody in America. When we trust the court system in the abducted-from country, the vast majority of claims of harm—those that do not rise to the level of gravity required by the Convention—evaporate.

The international precedent available supports our restrictive reading of the grave harm exception. In *Thomson v. Thomson*, 119 D.L.R.4th 253 (Can.1994), the Supreme Court of Canada held that the exception applies only to harm "that also amounts to an intolerable situation." *Id.* at 286. The Court of Appeal of the United Kingdom has held that the harm required is "something greater than would normally be expected on taking a child away from one parent and passing him to another." *In re A*, 1 F.L.R. 365, 372 (Eng.C.A.1988). And other circuit courts in America have followed this reasoning in cases decided since *Friedrich I*. Finally, we are instructed by the following observation by the United States Department of State concerning the grave risk of harm exception.

> This provision was not intended to be used by defendants as a vehicle to litigate (or relitigate) the child's best interests. Only evidence directly establishing the existence of a grave risk that would expose the child to physical or emotional harm or otherwise place the child in an *intolerable* situation is material to the court's determination. The person opposing the child's return must show that the risk to the child is grave, not merely serious.

> A review of deliberations on the Convention reveals that "intolerable situation" was not intended to encompass return to a home where money is in short support, or where educational or other opportunities are more limited than in the requested State. An example of an "intolerable situation" is one in which a custodial parent sexually abuses the child. If the other parent removes or retains the child to safeguard it against further victimization and the abusive parent then petitions for the child's return under the Convention, the court may deny the petition. Such action would protect the child from being returned to an "intolerable situation" and subjected to a grave risk of psychological harm.

Public Notice 957, 51 FR 10494, 10510 (March 26, 1986) (emphasis added).

For all of these reasons, we hold that the district court did not err by holding that "[t]he record in the instant case does not demonstrate by clear and convincing evidence that Thomas will be exposed to a grave risk of harm." Although it is not necessary to resolve the present appeal, we believe that a grave risk of harm for the purposes of the Convention can exist in only two situations. First, there is a grave risk of harm when return of the child puts the child in imminent danger *prior* to the resolution of the custody dispute—*e.g.*, returning the child to a zone of war, famine, or disease. Second, there is a grave risk of harm in cases of serious abuse or neglect, or extraordinary emotional dependence, when the court in the country of habitual residence, for whatever reason, may be incapable or unwilling to give the child adequate protection. Psychological evidence of the sort Mrs. Friedrich introduced in the proceeding below is only relevant if it helps prove the existence of one of these two situations.

IV

Mrs. Friedrich also claims that the district court erred in ordering Thomas's return because Mrs. Friedrich proved by a preponderance of the evidence that Mr. Friedrich (i) consented to, and (ii) subsequently acquiesced in, the removal of Thomas to America.

Mrs. Friedrich bases her claim of consent to removal on statements that she claims Mr. Friedrich made to her during their separation. Mr. Friedrich flatly denies that he made these statements. The district court was faced with a choice as to whom it found more believable in a factual dispute. There is nothing in the record to suggest that the court's decision to believe Mr. Friedrich, and hold that he "did not exhibit an intention or a willingness to terminate his parental rights," was clearly erroneous. In fact, Mr. Friedrich's testimony is strongly supported by the circumstances of the removal of Thomas—most notably the fact that Mrs. Friedrich did not inform Mr. Friedrich that she was departing. *Supra* n. 7. The deliberately secretive nature of her actions is extremely strong evidence that Mr. Friedrich would not have consented to the removal of Thomas. For these reasons, we hold that the district court did not abuse its discretion in finding that Mrs. Friedrich took Thomas to America without Mr. Friedrich's consent.

Mrs. Friedrich bases her claim of subsequent acquiescence on a statement made by Mr. Friedrich to one of her commanding officers, Captain Michael Farley, at a cocktail party on the military base after Mrs. Friedrich had left with Thomas. Captain Farley, who cannot date the conversation exactly, testified that:

> During the conversation, Mr. Friedrich indicated that he was not seeking custody of the child, because he didn't have the means to take care of the child.

Farley Deposition at 13. Mr. Friedrich denies that he made this statement. The district court made no specific finding regarding this fact.

We believe that the statement to Captain Farley, even if it was made, is insufficient evidence of subsequent acquiescence. Subsequent acquiescence requires more than an isolated statement to a third-party. Each of the words and actions of a parent during the separation are not to be scrutinized for a possible waiver of custody rights. *See Wanninger*, 850 F.Supp. at 81–82 (refusing to construe father's personal letters to wife and priest as sufficient evidence of acquiescence where father consistently attempted to keep in contact with child). Although we must decide the matter without guidance from previous appellate court decisions, we believe that acquiescence under the Convention requires either: an act or statement with the requisite formality, such as testimony in a judicial proceeding, a convincing written renunciation of rights; or a consistent attitude of acquiescence over a significant period of time.

By August 22, 1991, twenty-one days after the abduction, Mr. Friedrich had secured a German court order awarding him custody of Thomas. He has resolutely sought custody of his son since that time. It is by these acts, not his casual statements to third parties, that we will determine whether or not he acquiesced to the retention of his son in America. Since Mrs. Friedrich has not introduced evidence of a formal renunciation or a consistent attitude of acquiescence over a significant period of time, the judgment of the district court on this matter was not erroneous.

V

The district court's order that Thomas be immediately returned to Germany, is AFFIRMED, and the district court's stay of that order pending appeal is VACATED. Because Thomas's return to Germany is already long-overdue, we order, pursuant to Fed.R.App.P. 41(a), that our mandate issue forthwith.

Notes and Questions

1. As the *Friedrich* case demonstrates, the Hague Convention and the U.S. implementing legislation (ICARA) are proving themselves to be powerful weapons in the orderly resolution of international child custody disputes. *See* 51 Fed. Reg. 10494 (March 26, 1986) (providing legal

analysis of the Convention by the State Department). By 1997, the treaty was in effect between the United States and Argentina, Australia, Austria, Bahamas, Belize, Bosnia–Herzegovina, Burkina Faso, Canada, Chile, Columbia, Croatia, Cypress, Denmark, Ecuador, Finland, France, Georgia, Germany, Greece, Honduras, Hong Kong, Hungary, Iceland, Ireland, Israel, Italy, Luxembourg, Macedonia, Mauritius, Mexico, Monaco, the Netherlands, New Zealand, Norway, Panama, Poland, Portugal, Romania, St. Kitts and Nevis, Slovenia, Spain, Sweden, Switzerland, the United Kingdom, Venezuela, and Zimbabwe.

2. Under the Convention, both federal and state courts in the jurisdiction where the child is located have concurrent jurisdiction to hear actions for return or visitation. Notice is given pursuant to the UCCJA and the PKPA. How would you determine whether to file in state or federal court?

3. If an action under the Convention is brought within one year of a wrongful taking or retention, the court must return the child unless a defense to return under article 13 or 20 is found. These defenses are: 1) parental consent or subsequent acquiescence to the removal; 2) a "grave risk" that return of the child will lead to physical or psychological harm or place the child in an intolerable situation; or 3) an objection to return by a child of "suitable age." *See* Tahan v. Duquette, 259 N.J.Super. 328, 613 A.2d 486 (App.Div.1992) (analyzing "grave risk" defense).

4. "Habitual residence" is not defined in the Hague Convention nor in the implementing legislation. One view, cited in Slagenweit v. Slagenweit, 841 F.Supp. 264, 268–269 (N.D.Iowa 1993), holds that to establish a "habitual residence"

> there must be a degree of settled purpose.... That is not to say that the propositus intends to stay where he is indefinitely. Indeed his purpose while settled may be for a limited period. Education, business or profession, employment, health, family or merely love of the place spring to mind as common reasons for a choice of regular abode ... All that is necessary is that the purpose of living where one does has a sufficient degree of continuity to be properly described as settled.

5. Does the Hague Convention protect visitation rights? *See* Viragh v. Foldes, 415 Mass. 96, 612 N.E.2d 241 (1993) (ordering mother to pay airfare for father to fly from Hungary for two visits a year).

6. The International Parental Kidnapping Crime Act of 1993 (IPKCA), 18 U.S.C.A. § 1204, makes it a crime to remove or retain outside of the United States a child with intent to obstruct the lawful exercise of parental rights. The three defenses are that: the defendant acted pursuant to a lawful court order under the Uniform Child Custody Jurisdiction Act; the defendant was fleeing an incident of domestic violence; or the defendant was unable to return the child for circumstances beyond the defendant's control and defendant tried to notify the person entitled to custody and did return the child as quickly as possible.

7. For further discussion of the Hague Convention, *see* Linda Silberman, *Hague Convention on International Child Abduction: A Brief Overview and Case Law Analysis*, 28 FAM. L. Q. 9 (1994); Carol S. Bruch, *The Central Authority's Role Under the Hague Child Abduction Convention: A Friend in Deed*, 28 FAM. L. Q. 35 (1994).

Problem 12-5:

Tuulikki, a citizen of Finland, and Frank, a citizen of the United States, were married in California in 1989. Their two children were also born (in 1990 and 1991) in California. In April, 1992 the family moved to Kentucky where Frank hoped to find work. But Tuulikki did not like Kentucky and, in June of 1992, the family moved to Finland, where they remained until April, 1995, when they returned to the United States. This time the family located in the Houston area, where Tuulikki had lived when she first came to the U.S. Prior to their arrival, they investigated job opportunities in South Texas, obtained information from the local Chamber of Commerce, and contacted a realtor; upon arrival, they leased two automobiles and rented a condominium; Frank prepared a resume. But in late May, 1995, Frank and Tuulikki had a violent argument that culminated in Tuulikki's arrest; thereafter, Frank took the two children and left for northern Kentucky to stay with his sister. On May 30, 1995 Frank filed a custody petition in Kentucky; on the same date, Tuulikki filed a custody petition in Texas, alleging that she was a Texas resident. At the same time, Tuulikki filed a custody petition in Finland. On June 13, the Finnish court issued an order granting custody to Tuulikki; neither Tuulikki nor Frank appeared in the Finnish court. Shortly thereafter, Tuulikki sought to enforce the Finnish order in Kentucky.

What, if any, U.S.court(s) have jurisdiction under the UCCJA? the PKPA? Under the Hague Convention, is the Kentucky court required to enforce the Finnish decree? *See* Harsacky v. Harsacky, 930 S.W.2d 410 (Ky.App.1996); Cassie M.D. v. Othmar D., 22 Fam.L.Rep. (BNA) 1313 (N.Y. Fam. 1996).

Chapter 13

CHILD CUSTODY ON DIVORCE

We are allowing our children to bear the psychological, economic, and moral brunt of divorce.
Judith S. Wallerstein & Sandra Blakeslee

What's done to children, they will do to society.
Karl Menninger

VENTURA, Calif. (UPI)—The only California condor egg known to have been laid this breeding season was knocked off a cliff by the parents, who were fighting. A team of specialists trying to save the huge endangered birds, watched from half a mile away as the four-inch egg smashed on the rocks below the condors' cave and the embryo was eaten by ravens. The condors, the specialists said, were apparently battling over which of them should take care of the egg. * * * "One of them would sit down on the egg and the other would come in and try to push the first one off. They would jab each other in the face and really get physical. This went on for hours. They were so absorbed, no one was incubating." NEW YORK TIMES, March 6, 1982, at 6, col. 13.

GRAND RAPIDS, Mich. (UPI)—In a ruling reminiscent of Solomon, a judge says a divorced couple should have the body of their son cremated and each claim half the ashes unless they can agree who has the right to bury him. * * * "I just want to take him home," a weeping Mrs. Simmons said when the judgment was delivered Wednesday. "We didn't want him to be alone." [Judge] Cook said Thursday his opinion was one of the most difficult he ever had to make. "We are asked to play God, a role we are neither trained nor prepared for." * * * Cook said he saw no other solution to the dilemma unless the parents could decide out of court which of them should have custody of Greg's body. CHICAGO DAILY LAW BULLETIN, July 21, 1978, at 1, col. 7.

This chapter explores child custody law. Custody is the term used to denote the right to decide where and how a child will be raised. More than one person may have custody of a particular child; in an intact family, the child's father and mother (either biological or adoptive) both have custody rights. In a separated family, parents may share *legal custody*, the right to make decisions about the child's care, education, health and religion; they may also share *physical custody* if the child spends a substantial amount of time living in each parent's household. Even if one parent obtains sole legal and physical custody, the other will typically retain the right to visitation and contact with the child.

Most divorcing parents settle custody arrangements for their children without the need for judicial intervention. But when a custody dispute does go to court, it is often bitterly fought. In the midst of battling over their own rights, it is easy for parents to lose track of their children's needs and interests.

SECTION 1. WHAT RIGHTS FOR CHILDREN?

THE LAW COMMISSION (LONDON), FACING THE FUTURE: A DISCUSSION PAPER ON THE GROUND FOR DIVORCE

24–26 (Law. Com. No. 170, May 1988).

3.37 The need for the law to protect the interests of children whose security and stability is threatened by their parents' divorce has long been recognized. This was one of the reasons why the Morton Commission did not recommend relaxation of divorce laws. However, by the 1960s, the "general orthodoxy" among social scientists was that "a bad marriage was worse for children than a divorce." The Law Commission in The Field of Choice was careful to reject any generalization on this point and to conclude that in some cases it would be better for the children if their parents were to stay together and in other cases if they were to divorce. It was recognized, however, that restrictive divorce laws did not make the parents stay together and that it was the separation rather than the divorce which was usually damaging to the children. So to prohibit or make divorce more difficult for those with children would serve little purpose and would cause resentment in the parents who would see the children as the obstacle to their divorce. More recently, in two working papers, the Commission has mentioned this question again but there is clearly little support for the idea that the availability of divorce should depend upon whether or not there are children. There must always be some cases, perhaps where physical or sexual abuse has occurred, when it will be better for the children if their parents are divorced and others in which it is impossible to tell which course will be best. Thus, restrictive grounds for divorce do not necessarily safeguard the interests of the children of the parties.

* * *

3.39 Several studies have indicated that most children whose parents have separated would have preferred them to have stayed together. Children of parents who have separated are more likely to suffer from at least temporary social and behavioural problems during and in the aftermath of the separation. Although the findings are less clear, research has also linked marital separation with various longer-term problems. As marital separation frequently leads to downward social mobility and economic hardship such findings are not surprising, but once again may be attributed to the consequences of separation rather than divorce as such. Perhaps the most significant research finding is that adjustment to separation depends on the quality of the relationships with and between both parents *after* the separation. Thus good continuing relationships with both parents seem to be protective against the problems associated with children from broken marriages. Conversely, post-divorce conflict between the parents is more damaging than marital conflict.

3.40 The implications from this research are that, although divorce law is powerless to prevent prejudice to the children caused by marital breakdown, it can help to minimise that prejudice in two ways. First, since the children are most vulnerable in the immediate aftermath of the separation which often coincides with the timing of the divorce process, nothing should be involved in that process which makes it more difficult for the children to cope with the separation. Secondly, every effort should be made to encourage good post-divorce relationships with both parents and between the parents themselves. The Booth Committee, expressing the view that divorcing or separating parents should be encouraged and advised to maintain their joint responsibility for the children and to co-operate in this respect, recommended that provision should be made for joint statement of arrangements to be filed. Such co-operation may only be possible where there has not been irretrievable harm to the spouses' own relationship.

Notes and Questions

1. Many researchers have investigated the effects of divorce on children. As a result of that research, "[t]he earlier view of divorce as a short lived crisis ... has given way to a more sober appraisal, accompanied by rising concern that a significant number of children suffer long-term, perhaps permanent detrimental effects from divorce, and that others experience submerged effects that may appear years later." Judith Wallerstein, *The Long–Term Effects of Divorce on Children: A Review*, 30 J. Child Adolescence & Psychiatry 349, 358 (1991). Today, experts agree that divorce poses serious risks to long-term childhood development:

> Overall, most children of divorce experience dramatic declines in their economic circumstances, abandonment (or the fear of abandonment) by one or both of their parents, the diminished capacity of both parents to attend meaningfully and constructively to their children's needs (because they are preoccupied with their own

psychological, social, and economic distress as well as stresses related to the legal divorce), and diminished contact with familial or potential sources of psychosocial support (friends, neighbors, teachers, schoolmates, etc.), as well as familiar living settings. As a consequence, the experience of divorce is a psychological stressor and a significant life transition for most children, with long-term repercussions for many. Some children from divorced homes show long-term behavior problems, depression, poor school performance, acting out, low self-esteem, and (in adolescence and young adulthood) difficulties with intimate heterosexual relationships.

Michael E. Lamb et al., *The Effects of Divorce and Custody Arrangements on Children's Behavior, Development, and Adjustment,* 35 FAM. & CONCIL. CTS. REV. 393, 395–396 (1997).

Experts also agree that the long-term effects of divorce are highly variable and those effects are mediated by psychological, social and economic factors:

Children who experience parental divorce, compared with children in continuously intact two-parent families, exhibit more conduct problems, more symptoms of psychological maladjustment, lower academic achievement, more social difficulties, and poorer self-concepts. Similarly, adults who experienced parental divorce as children, compared with adults raised in continuously intact two-parent families, score lower on a variety of indicators of psychological, interpersonal, and socioeconomic well-being.

However, the overall group differences between offspring from divorced and intact families are small, with considerable diversity existing in children's reactions to divorce. Children's adjustment to divorce depends on several factors, including the amount and quality of contact with noncustodial parents, the custodial parents' psychological adjustment and parenting skills, the level of interparental conflict that precedes and follows divorce, the degree of economic hardship to which children are exposed, and the number of stressful life events that accompany and follow divorce. These factors can be used as guides to assess the probable impact of various legal and therapeutic interventions to improve the well-being of children of divorce.

Paul R. Amato, *Life-Span Adjustment of Children to Their Parents' Divorce*, in THE FUTURE OF CHILDREN: CHILDREN AND DIVORCE 143 (1994).

2. In recent years, some courts have mandated parental attendance at one or another educational program in an attempt to reduce the risks to children posed by a parental divorce. *See, e.g.,* Andrew Schepard, *War and P.E.A.C.E.: A Preliminary Report and A Model Statute on an Interdisciplinary Educational Program for Divorcing and Separating Parents*, 27 U. MICH. J. LAW REFORM 131 (1993) (describing one such program in New York). *See also* Junda Woo, *More Courts Are Forcing Couples to Take Divorce–Education Class,* WALL STREET J., Oct. 1, 1993, at B8; Marcy L. Wachtel, *Divorce Counseling: For the Sake of the Child,*

LEGAL TIMES, May 24, 1993, at 29 (listing California, Connecticut, Florida, Georgia, Indiana, Minnesota and Texas as having mandatory parent education programs). Participation in a parent education program typically involves attendance at one or two lectures or films. *See, e.g.*, Margie J. Geasler & Karen R. Blaisure, *Court-Connected Programs for Divorcing Parents in Michigan: A Status Report*, 33 FAM. & CONCILIATION CTS. REV. 484, 487 (1995) (reporting that 85% of Michigan parent education programs consisted of one session varying in length from 90 minutes to three hours, with two hours the most popular option.) There are few formal evaluations of parent education. One group of researchers found that parents who attended a parent education program had significantly lower rates of relitigation than a control group 2¼ years after divorce. Jack Arbuthnot et al., *Pattterns of Relitigation Following Divorce Education*, 35 FAM. & CONCILIATION CTS. REV. 269 (1997). Others have failed to find significant effects.

MILLER v. MILLER

Supreme Judicial Court of Maine, 1996.
677 A.2d 64.

LIPEZ, Justice.

This case is before us on report ... of an interlocutory order entered in the Superior Court, granting the motion of three minor children to intervene as parties in the divorce action between their parents and be represented by legal counsel independently of the guardian ad litem appointed previously to represent their interests. We vacate the order of the Superior Court.

Eileen and Clark Miller were married on October 25, 1975. In December 1992, Eileen filed a complaint for a divorce ... Both parties ... [sought physical custody of] their three children: Carissa Noel Miller, age 14; Nicholas Russell Miller, age 11; and Dylan Patrick Miller, age 9. Following a contested hearing in June 1993, the court issued its order pending divorce and awarded the primary residence of all three children to Eileen.

Prior to its order pending the divorce, and by an agreement of the parties, the court appointed a guardian ad litem for the three children.[1]

1. The terms of the court's order provided, in relevant part: ORDERED that the guardian *ad litem* shall act in pursuit of the best interest of the children and shall investigate the circumstances concerning the childrens' welfare as it relates to the disposition of parental rights and responsibilities under 19 M.R.S.A. § 752. The guardian *ad litem* shall have the authority to undertake any or all of the following action [sic] which the guardian, in her discretion, deems appropriate including: (1) Review of relevant mental health records and materials of the parents and children; (2) Review of relevant medical records of the parents and children; (3) Review of relevant school records and other pertinent materials of the parents and children; (4) Interviews with the children with or without other persons present; (5) Interviews with parents, grandparents, teachers, daycare providers, psychologists and other persons who have been involved in caring for or treating the children or parents, or who may have knowledge of the children or family; (6) Request and arrange for psychological evaluations and/or counseling for the parents and/or children; (7) Appearance at any and all future proceed-

Pursuant to the terms of the order appointing the guardian, Charles L. Robinson, a psychologist, prepared a psychological evaluation of the parties and the children. In preparing his evaluation, Robinson had a joint ninety minute meeting with Clark and Eileen; one-time individual meetings with Clark and Eileen; one visit each at the homes of Clark and Eileen when the children were present; and finally, two meetings with each of the children individually, in the presence of the guardian. All three children rejected the opportunity to speak with Robinson or the guardian alone. In January 1994, Robinson submitted a report recommending that all three children's primary residence be with Clark. Robinson noted in his report Eileen's stated intention to move to Connecticut. He also noted that Nicholas had expressed a preference to live with his mother.

Less than one month after Robinson submitted his report, the guardian submitted her report, which also recommended that all three children maintain their primary residence with Clark. The guardian's investigation consisted of one interview separately with Clark and Eileen, and two interviews with each of the children in the presence of either Dr. Robinson or Clark. The guardian also accompanied Robinson on each of the home visits mentioned above. The guardian noted in her report Eileen's stated intention to move to Connecticut, and Nicholas's expressed desire to move to Connecticut with his mother. According to the guardian's report, Dylan did not express a discernible preference about where he wished to reside.

Subsequent to the recommendations of Robinson and the guardian, Clark filed a motion to alter and amend the order pending the divorce to provide that the children's primary residence be with him. The motion was based primarily on his belief that Eileen was considering moving from Maine to Connecticut. At the hearing on Clark's motion, Eileen admitted that she was planning to move to Connecticut, and Carissa expressed a clear preference to live with Eileen.

In May 1994, attorney Margaret Semple received a phone call from Nicholas Miller seeking legal representation for himself and his siblings in his parents' pending divorce. Semple agreed to represent all three children on a pro bono basis. In July 1994, the Miller children filed a motion to intervene in their own names and to be represented by legal counsel. Clark opposed the children's motion, as did the guardian.

In August 1994, the court granted Clark's motion to amend the order pending divorce by providing that the children's primary residence be with him. In September 1994, the children's motion to intervene [and to be represented by attorney Semple] was granted. * * *

The claim of the children pursuant to the common law.

ings, including pretrial conferences and trial; (8) Submission to the Court of a report in writing summarizing her position on behalf of the children with regard to the issues before the Court, provided that the guardian *ad litem* furnish copies to all parties reasonably in advance of hearing; and (9) Any other further and necessary authority as may be required to carry out her responsibilities.

There is no basis in the common law for the intervention of minor children as parties in the divorce action of their parents with an attorney of their choice. Although at common law minor children have a right to sue and be sued, children do not possess the requisite legal capacity to participate in litigation in their own names. This incapacity is premised on age, inexperience, and immaturity. Due to their incapacity, children must bring or defend a legal proceeding through an adult representative, such as a next friend or a guardian ad litem. 43 C.J.S. *Infants* § 215. Similarly, intervention of minor children in an action may only be commenced by a guardian ad litem or a next friend. A person acting as either a next friend or a guardian ad litem is only a nominal party to the litigation; the child is the real party in interest. The next friend or guardian ad litem brings the minor child's claim or interest to the attention of a court.

The Maine Rules of Civil Procedure reflect this common law tradition. * * * Pursuant to Rule 17(b), a minor child may only sue if the child has a representative, next friend, or guardian ad litem. The court is empowered to appoint such a representative for a child whenever protection of the child's interests demands it. * * *

There is another obstacle to the claim of the Miller children that they have a right to intervene as parties in this divorce action with an attorney of their choice. Pursuant to Maine law, children have "no authority to appoint an attorney." * * * "Even should the infant employ counsel, who procures the suit dismissed, the entry would be void, because the infant could not appear by attorney as the employment would be null." * * *

Although the law imposes procedural imitations on children, it does so to protect their interests. In the realm of divorce and other family litigation, this protective purpose finds expression in the best interest standard. In Maine, as in the multitude of other states which have adopted the best interest standard, courts faced with the task of rearranging parental rights and responsibilities must strive for an outcome that will maximize the best interest of children. This standard protects children who lack the ability because of youth, inexperience, and immaturity to protect themselves. The protective purpose of this standard is also important in analyzing the constitutional claim of the Miller children.

The constitutional claim of the children.

The remaining issue is whether the intervention of the children as parties in the divorce action of their parents with an attorney of their choice is constitutionally required. Relying on the procedural due process guarantees of the Fourteenth Amendment of the United States Constitution, the Miller children contend that they have a significant liberty interest in the outcome of their parents' divorce because of the custodial issues involved. Assuming, *arguendo*, that the Miller children have a liberty interest in the outcome of their parents' divorce, we must determine whether representation by a court-appointed guardian ad litem responsible for advocating for their best interests satisfies the requirements of procedural due process.

The test we use for evaluating procedural due process claims was set forth by the United States Supreme Court in *Mathews v. Eldridge*, 424 U.S. 319 (1976). It consists of three factors which must be balanced against each other: (1) the private interests affected by the chosen procedure; (2) the risk of erroneous deprivation of those interests by the chosen procedure and the probable value, if any, of additional or substitute procedural safeguards; and (3) the countervailing state interest(s) supporting use of the challenged procedure.

The interests involved in a divorce case include those of the divorcing parties and, if they have children, those of the children. The interests of the divorcing parents are financial, custodial, and emotional. As a result of divorce, financial and custodial rights and obligations are reconfigured. In addition, divorce terminates a legal partnership. For the children, there is an emotional fallout from the divorce, and an interest in the financial bargain struck by the divorcing parties, especially on child support. The most immediate interest of the children, however, is in the custodial outcome. The position of the Miller children confirms this immediacy. They do not want to intervene in their parents' divorce because of the potential impact on them of the property, alimony, or child support bargains that will be struck. Rather, the Miller children wish to participate in the reconfiguration of their family and advocate their preferences because their custody is at stake. They argue that this interest is not and cannot be met by the guardian ad litem, who is duty-bound to represent their best interests as *she* sees them. They emphasize that the guardian ad litem's recommendations on custody are directly contrary to their wishes.

In making this point, the Miller children link their custodial interest in the outcome of the divorce to forceful advocacy of their preference by independent counsel representing them as parties, and cite the absence of such advocacy as increasing the likelihood of an erroneous deprivation of their custodial interest. Implicit in that argument is the further contention that the preference of the children should have primacy when the court makes its custody determination. We reject that proposition. The best interest standard set forth in 19 M.R.S.A. § 752(5) appropriately makes the preference of the child only one of many factors that the court must consider. The exclusion of children as parties in the divorce of their parents, and the related possibility that there will be no forceful advocacy for the custodial preference of the children, does not increase the risk of erroneous custody determinations that deserve the best interests of children. The guardian ad litem is already an advocate for the best interest of the children in all of its complex dimensions. The narrow focus of an attorney for the children, who would be obligated to carry out their preferences regardless of the wisdom of such a course, might well increase the likelihood of a custody determination that is not in the best interest of the children.

Finally, the State has a substantial interest in divorce proceedings that do not include children as parties represented by counsel. Divorce litigation would be complicated exponentially by the involvement of children as parties. Children could object to any settlement offer. They would have the right to participate in discovery and at hearings to present witnesses on their own behalf and cross-examine witnesses called by the other parties. Multiple children could insist on multiple representation. The occurrence of any or all of these probabilities would protract divorce litigation beyond current bounds, and result in a substantial additional financial burden on both the parties and our court system.

In our view, the use of guardians ad litem to protect the best interests of children in divorce proceedings fully satisfies any federal constitutional requirements. Accordingly, the Miller children are not entitled to intervene in the divorce action of their parents and be represented by independent legal counsel.

Notes and Questions

1. Consult footnote 1 in *Miller* and determine how, if at all, the role of a guardian ad litem would differ from that of an attorney. Why does the *Miller* court believe that appointment of a guardian ad litem for the children is preferable to appointment of an attorney? Do you agree? *See also* Schult v. Schult, 241 Conn. 767, 699 A.2d 134 (1997) (child's attorney could advocate a position different from that of child's guardian ad litem).

2. Under UMDA § 310, "[t]he court may appoint an attorney to represent the interests of a minor or dependent child with respect to his support, custody, and visitation." Commissioners' Note. *See also* CONN. GEN. STAT. § 46b–54(a)-(b) ([in any marriage dissolution proceeding], the judge may "... appoint counsel for any minor child ... if the court deems it to be in the best interests of the child ... [or] when the court finds that the custody, care, education, visitation or support of a minor child is in actual controversy.") Even in states that lack statutory law specifically authorizing appointment of an attorney for children who are the subject of a support or custody dispute, the appointment of counsel or a guardian ad litem to represent the children's interest appears to be on the increase.

3. The arguments for and against appointment of counsel for children in a divorce action between their parents were summarized by the court in Veazey v. Veazey, 560 P.2d 382 (Alaska 1977):

> Appellee here urges that advocacy of the child's interest be left to the attorney for one or the other of the competing claimants, because there is only one ultimate issue in a custody case—the custody of the child—and ... adding an additional advocate [will merely increase] the cost and complexity of custody litigation without shedding any additional light on the facts and issues.

The attorney for a claimant has a professional duty to exercise his judgment "solely for the benefit of his client and free of compromising influences and loyalties. * * * [T]he desires of third persons should [not] be permitted to dilute his loyalty to his client." Code of Prof. Responsibility, EC 5–1. In a number of instances, that attorney cannot assert the interests of the child without creating a conflict of interest.

* * *

Furthermore, to say there is only one ultimate issue in a custody case oversimplifies the matter. The terms of custody, visitation, and support may vary greatly. None of those issues is of an "either-or" nature, and they are all of interest to the child. Shared or joint custody is sometimes awarded.

* * *

Unfortunately the custody of children is often merely another bargaining point between the divorcing parents, along with the questions of property division, spousal support, child support, and visitation. Divorcing parents seek, or decide not to seek, custody of their children for many different reasons, many of which may have little correlation with the best interests of the child.

4. Commentators do not agree on the circumstances that should trigger appointment of an attorney for children who are the subject of a custody dispute. *Compare* Linda D. Elrod, *Counsel for the Child in Custody Disputes: The Time is Now*, 26 Fam. L. Q. 53 (1992) (any time there is a dispute over custody) *with* American Academy of Matrimonial Lawyers, Representing Children: Standards for Attorneys and Guardians ad Litem in Custody or Visitation Proceedings 11 ("Appointment of counsel or guardians should be reserved for those cases in which both parties request the appointment or the court finds after a hearing that appointment is necessary in light of the particular circumstances of the case.") What are the pros and cons of these approaches?

If a lawyer is appointed for the children, must the parents pay his or her fees? If yes, must the state pay if the parents are financially unable to do so?

5. When counsel is appointed for the child, what role should he or she play? The AAML Standards take the position that the child's counsel should be a "full participant" in the proceedings. *See* A. Luie, *Representing the Child–Client: Kids are People Too*, 11 N.Y.L.Sch. J. Hum. Rts. 205 (1993). They also specify that the child should determine the goals of representation if he or she has the capacity to do so; under the Standards, the child's attorney should advocate the child's position. *See also* Model Rules 1.2, 1.14; ABA, *Standards for Lawyers Representing Children in Abuse and Neglect Case*, 29 Fam. L.Q. 375 (1995) (same approach in context of abuse and neglect proceedings). For an argument to the contrary, *see* Guggenheim, *supra* p. 409 note 5.

Assuming that a lawyer was appointed in *Miller* and the AAML Standards govern his role in the proceedings, could the lawyer jointly represent all of the children? Why or why not?

SECTION 2. PARENT v. PARENT—DETERMINING THE BEST INTERESTS OF THE CHILD

Under the common law, the child's father was entitled to custody. According to Blackstone, the mother was "entitled to no power [over her children], but only to reverence and respect." 1 WILLIAM BLACKSTONE, COMMENTARIES ON THE LAW OF ENGLAND 453 (1765). The paternal custody entitlement was not absolute—the poet Percy Bysshe Shelley, for example, was denied custody of his children based on his immorality, atheism, and denial of the Christian religion (Shelley v. Westbrooke, 37 Eng. Rep. 850 (Ch. 1817))—but absent unusual circumstances, the father's rights were paramount.

Over the course of the nineteenth century, "growing concern with child nurture and the acceptance of women as more legally distinct individuals, ones with a special capacity for moral and religious leadership and for child rearing, undermined the primacy of paternal custody rights ..." MICHAEL GROSSBERG, GOVERNING THE HEARTH: LAW AND THE FAMILY IN NINETEENTH CENTURY AMERICA 239 (1985). By the late nineteenth century, American courts universally awarded custody based on the "best interests of the child." The best interests standard was augmented by the "tender years doctrine," which established a rebuttable presumption that a young child belonged with its mother. *See generally* MARY ANN MASON, FROM FATHER'S PROPERTY TO CHILDREN'S RIGHTS (1994).

While the tender years doctrine survived in all jurisdictions until the 1960s and in some until considerably later, courts and legislatures have now universally moved toward gender-neutral application of the best interests standard. If the parents agree on a custody arrangement, the court will typically presume that the agreement is in the child's best interests. *See, e.g.*, Kan. Stat. Ann. § 60–1610(a)(3)(A) (court shall order the custodial terms agreed on by the parents unless it finds on the record by clear and convincing evidence that the parenting time terms are not in the best interests of the child.). But if the parents cannot agree, the trial judge must make a decision on the child's best interests. Without a presumption to simplify the process of determining a child's best interests, a court must assess information on a wide range of issues. The Uniform Marriage and Divorce Act § 402, 9A U.L.A. 561 (1987), for example, provides that judges should consider "all relevant factors," including:

§ 402. [Best Interest of Child]

* * *

(1) the wishes of the child's parent or parents as to his custody;

(2) the wishes of the child as to his custodian;

(3) the interaction and interrelationship of the child with his parent or parents, his siblings, and any other person who may significantly affect the child's best interest;

(4) the child's adjustment to his home, school, and community; and

(5) the mental and physical health of all individuals involved.

The court shall not consider conduct of a proposed custodian that does not affect his relationship to the child.

Several states have adopted modified versions of the UMDA custody standard; some of these contain an even larger number of factors to be taken into account. COLO. REV. STAT. § 14–10–124(1.5), for example, augments the UMDA factor list with "the economic situation of the parents; educational needs and opportunities; necessities; stable, consistent supervision; ability of each parent to promote a continuing relationship between the child and the other parent; age and sex of parent and child; religious needs; presence of domestic violence; and recommendations of professionals." Whether the statutory factor list is short or long, however, the aim of the best interests inquiry is to determine "... what combination of factors this child needs in a custody and/or access arrangement that will sustain his or her adjustment and development." Joan B. Kelly, *The Best Interests of the Child: A Concept in Search of a Meaning,* 35 FAM. & CONCIL. CTS. REV. 377, 378 (1997).

ROBERT H. MNOOKIN, CHILD CUSTODY ADJUDICATION: JUDICIAL FUNCTIONS IN THE FACE OF INDETERMINACY

39 LAW & CONTEMPORARY PROBLEMS 227 (1975).

* * * Custody disputes under the best-interests principle require "person-oriented," not "act-oriented," determinations. Most legal rules require determination of some event and are thus "act-oriented." A "person-oriented" rule, on the other hand, requires an evaluation of the "whole person viewed as a social being." * * *

... In a divorce custody fight, a court must evaluate the attitudes, dispositions, capacities, and shortcomings of each parent to apply the best-interest standard. * * * Adjudication usually requires the determination of past acts and facts, not a prediction of future events. Applying the best-interests standard requires an individualized prediction: with whom will this child be better off in the years to come? Proof of what happened in the past is relevant only insofar as it enables the court to decide what is likely to happen in the future.

* * *

Because custody disputes involve relationships between people, a decision affecting any one of the parties will often necessarily have an effect on the others. The resolution of a custody dispute may permanently affect—or even end—the parties' legal relationship; but the social and psychological relationships will usually continue. The best-interests principle requires a prediction of what will happen in the future, which, of course, depends in part on the future behavior of the parties. * * *

A determination that is person-oriented and requires predictions necessarily involves an evaluation of the parties who have appeared in court. This has important consequences for the roles of both precedent and appellate review in custody cases. The result of an earlier case involving different people has limited relevance to a subsequent case requiring individualized evaluations of a particular child and the litigants. * * * All of this makes the scope of appellate review extremely limited. Because the trial court's decision involves an assessment of the personality, character, and relationship of people the judge has seen in court, appellate courts are extremely loath to upset the trial court's determination on the basis of a transcript. * * *

Notes and Questions

1. Before your views have been "corrupted" by the remainder of this chapter, evaluate the UMDA factor list. Are there additional factors that should be added? Are there factors that should be subtracted? Should some factors receive more weight than others? If yes, which factors should receive more weight? How much weight should they receive?

2. Reconsider the *Baby M.* case [p. 380]. At the time the trial judge awarded temporary custody of Baby M. to the Sterns, she was only a few months old. What factors, would you guess, led the judge to decide in favor of the Sterns? How should a judge assess the best interests of a newborn?

A. PROHIBITED FACTORS: GENDER AND RACE

EX PARTE DEVINE

Supreme Court of Alabama, 1981.
398 So.2d 686.

MADDOX, JUSTICE.

* * * By the middle of the 19th century, the courts of England began to question and qualify the paternal preference rule. This was due, in part, to the "hardships, not to say cruelty, inflicted upon unoffending mothers by a state of law which took little account of their claims or feelings." W. FORSYTH, A TREATISE ON THE LAW RELATING TO THE CUSTODY OF INFANTS IN CASES OF DIFFERENCE BETWEEN PARENTS OR GUARDIANS 66 (1850). Courts reacted by taking a more moderate stance concerning child custody, a stance which conditioned a father's absolute custodial rights upon his fitness as a parent. Ultimately, by a series of statutes culminating with Justice Talfourd's Act, 2 and 3 Vict. c. 54 (1839), Parliament affirmatively extended the rights of mothers, especially as concerned the custody of young children. Justice Talfourd's Act expressly provided that

the chancery courts, in cases of divorce and separation, could award the custody of minor children to the mother *if the children were less than seven years old*. This statute marks the origin of the tender years presumption in England.

In the United States the origin of the tender years presumption is attributed to the 1830 Maryland decision of *Helms v. Franciscus*, 2 Bland Ch. (Md.) 544 (1830). In *Helms*, the court, while recognizing the general rights of the father, stated that it would violate the laws of nature to "snatch" an infant from the care of its mother:

> The father is the rightful and legal guardian of all his infant children; and in general, no court can take from him the custody and control of them, thrown upon him by the law, not for his gratification, but on account of his duties, and place them against his will in the hands even of his wife. * * * Yet even a court of common law will not go so far as to hold nature in contempt, and snatch helpless, puling infancy from the bosom of an affectionate mother, and place it in the coarse hands of the father. The mother is the softest and safest nurse of infancy, and with her it will be left in opposition to this general right of the father.

Thus began a "process of evolution, perhaps reflecting a change in social attitudes, [whereby] the mother came to be the preferred custodian of young children and daughter. * * * " Foster, *Life with Father: 1978*, 11 FAM.L.Q. 327 (1978).

* * *

At the present time, the tender years presumption is recognized in Alabama as a rebuttable factual presumption based upon the inherent suitability of the mother to care for and nurture young children. All things being equal, the mother is presumed to be best fitted to guide and care for children of tender years. To rebut this presumption the father must present clear and convincing evidence of the mother's positive unfitness. Thus, the tender years presumption affects the resolution of child custody disputes on both a substantive and procedural level. Substantively, it requires the court to award custody of young children to the mother when the parties, as in the present case, are equally fit parents. Procedurally, it imposes an evidentiary burden on the father to prove the positive unfitness of the mother.

In recent years, the tender years doctrine has been severely criticized by legal commentators as an outmoded means of resolving child custody disputes. Several state courts have chosen to abandon or abolish the doctrine, noting that the presumption "facilitates error in an arena in which there is little room for error." *Bazemore v. Davis*, 394 A.2d 1377 (D.C.App.1978). Only one court has expressly declared the presumption unconstitutional. State ex rel. *Watts v. Watts*, 77 Misc.2d 178, 350 N.Y.S.2d 285 (1973). Nevertheless, some form of the presumption remains in effect in at least twenty-two states. In twenty states the doctrine has been expressly abolished by statute or court decision, and in four other states its existence is extremely questionable. In four states the presumption remains in effect despite a state's equal rights amendment or statutory language to the contrary. As far as Alabama is concerned, the trial court correctly noted that the presumption, "while perhaps weaker now than in the past, remains quite viable today."

It is safe to say that the courts of this state, like the courts of sister states, have come full circle in resolving the difficult questions surrounding child custody. At common law, courts spoke of the natural rights of the father. Now they speak of the instinctive role of the mother.

The question we are confronted with is not dissimilar to the question confronting the English courts over 150 years ago: Is it proper to deny a parent the custody of his or her children on the basis of a presumption concerning the relative parental suitability of the parties? More specifically, can the tender years presumption withstand judicial scrutiny under the Fourteenth Amendment to the United States Constitution as construed in recent decisions by the Supreme Court of the United States? * * *

Having reviewed the historical development of the presumption as well as its modern status, and having examined the presumption in view of . . . [recent Supreme Court decisions], we conclude that the tender years presumption represents an unconstitutional gender-based classification which discriminates between fathers and mothers in child custody proceedings solely on the basis of sex. * * *

The trial court's custody decree conclusively shows that the tender years presumption was a significant factor underlying the court's decision. Confronted with two individuals who were equally fit (i.e., all things being equal), the trial court awarded custody to the mother.

Accordingly, the judgment of the Court of Civil Appeals affirming the lower court decree and affirming the constitutionality of the tender years presumption is hereby reversed. The cause is due to be remanded to the trial court with directions that the court consider the individual facts of the case. The sex and age of the children are indeed very important considerations; however, the court must go beyond these to consider the characteristics and needs of each child, including their emotional, social, moral, material and educational needs; the respective home environments offered by the parties; the characteristics of those seeking custody, including age, character, stability, mental and physical health; the capacity and interest of each parent to provide for the emotional, social, moral, material and educational needs of the children; the interpersonal relationship between each child and each parent; the interpersonal relationship between the children; the effect on the child of disrupting or continuing an existing custodial status; the preference of each child, if the child is of sufficient age and maturity; the report and recommendation of any expert witnesses or other independent investigator; available alternatives; and any other relevant matter the evidence may disclose. Only in this way will the court truly consider the best interests of the Devine children.

TORBERT, CHIEF JUSTICE (dissenting).

* * * The well-being of the child is the paramount consideration in determining its custody. The focus in a child custody hearing is on the child's welfare and best interest, not on the parents or their personal rights. Custody of one's child is not a prize to be fought for; rather it is a responsibility imposed by the court under appropriate conditions or restrictions the court sees fit to impose. Therefore, *Orr v. Orr,* 440 U.S. 268 (1979) [holding that a statute restricting alimony eligibility to women, and other cases involving gender-based eligibility barriers] ... [and other gender discrimination cases cited by the majority] have no relevance in the field of child custody. Gender may be an inappropriate factor to consider in bestowing a benefit, but it should be a factor in determining which parent will have primary custody of a very small child.

We are not faced here with ... a rule by which one gender was given absolute preference over the other. The tender years doctrine, as the majority correctly stated, has evolved over the years into a factor to be considered in child custody determinations, rather than a compelling presumption. I believe it is valid as such, and should be retained in its present form. I therefore respectfully dissent.

Notes and Questions

1. Gender-based classifications are now subject to so-called "intermediate" scrutiny. Using that approach, is the *Devine* court's holding sound?

2. Even if impermissible as a generalized presumption, may the tender years doctrine be used as a tie breaker? *See* FLA. STAT. § 61.13(2)(b)1 ("tender years doctrine is not a relevant fact, but an impermissible gender-based preference favoring the mother as custodian of a young child"); Cherradi v. Lavoie, 662 So.2d 751 (Fla.App.1995) (remanding for reconsideration where trial court found both parents equally fit and awarded custody of two-year-old child to mother when father had been the child's primary caregiver during the marriage); Hubbell (Gault) v. Hubbell, 702 A.2d 129 (Vt.1997) (remanding for reconsideration where judge awarded custody of 2½ year old to the father because he was the same sex parent even though mother had been the child's primary caregiver).

3. Some feminist scholars have argued for a return to a maternal preference standard. Consider Mary Becker, *Maternal Feelings: Myth, Taboo and Child Custody,* 1 S. CAL. REV. L. & WOMEN'S STUDIES 133, 223–24 (1992):

> I assess custody standards against their ability to protect the greater emotional commitments of women to children. I reject the best interest standard, joint custody, and deference to the mature child because they do not protect adequately the strong emotional bonds

between children and their mothers. * * * At divorce, judges should defer to the fit mother's decision with respect to custody.

6. Has the demise of the tender years doctrine made a difference in custody outcomes? Researchers who reviewed a hundred appellate opinions in each of three time periods—the 1920s, the 1960s and the 1990s—recently reported that

> ... in spite of ... outward change, mothers and fathers in 1920, 1960, and 1990–95 are each still favored close to half the time. This remarkable continuity in the face of what appears to be massive discontinuity, both in rhetoric and procedure, is not easily explained. One possible explanation is that mothers, not fathers, want custody in the vast majority of cases, but when fathers fight for custody they have always had about a 50 percent chance of winning, no matter what arguments or what experts they employ.... Mothers' preference and moral fitness have given way to gender-neutral criteria, such as stability and time spent with the child. There are those who argue that such criteria ... translates to maternal preference. That ... [is another possible] explanation of why fathers have not gained more. [But] others have claimed that judges consider mothers more critically today.... Seen in ... historical context, however, it is apparent that rhetoric alone cannot predict custody outcomes. It is not clear that the factors judges claim are most important in determining custody have much to do with the ultimate result.... The continuity of decision making may mean that divorcing families look much as they always have, and judges exercise the same judicial discretion to achieve similar results.
>
> Mary Ann Mason & Ann Quirk, *Are Mothers Losing Custody? Read My Lips: Trends in Judicial Decision–Making in Custody Disputes—1920, 1960, 1990, and 1995*, 31 FAM. L. Q. 215 (1997).

See also Stephen J. Bahr et al., *Trends in Child Custody Awards: Has the Removal of Maternal Preference Made a Difference?*, 28 FAM. L. Q. 247 (1994) (Utah fathers were no more likely to obtain sole custody in 1993 than in 1970, although joint custody awards increased significantly over this period); ELEANOR MACCOBY AND ROBERT MNOOKIN, DIVIDING THE CHILD: SOCIAL AND LEGAL DILEMMAS OF CUSTODY 273 (1992) (in surveyed cases from two northern California counties during the 1980s, fathers won custody about half the time where the conflict was resolved after court-appointed evaluation, negotiations on the courthouse steps, or through adjudication); LENORE WEITZMAN, THE DIVORCE REVOLUTION 231–235 (1985) (in 63% of surveyed California cases from late 1970s, fathers who requested physical and legal custody received it); Richard A. Warshak, *Gender Bias in Child Custody Decisions*, 34 FAM. & CONCILIATION CTS. REV. 396 (1996) (arguing that custody decision making is gender biased because, when uncontested cases are included in the pool, mothers obtain custody approximately 90% of the time).

PALMORE v. SIDOTI

Supreme Court of the United States, 1984.
466 U.S. 429, 104 S.Ct. 1879, 80 L.Ed.2d 421.

CHIEF JUSTICE BURGER delivered the opinion of the Court.

* * *

When petitioner Linda Sidoti Palmore and respondent Anthony J. Sidoti, both Caucasians, were divorced in May 1980 in Florida, the mother was awarded custody of their three-year old daughter.

In September 1981 the father sought custody of the child by filing a petition to modify the prior judgment because of changed conditions. The change was that the child's mother was then cohabiting with a Negro. Clarence Palmore, Jr., whom she married two months later. Additionally, the father made several allegations of instances in which the mother had not properly cared for the child.

After hearing testimony from both parties and considering a court counselor's investigative report, the court noted that the father had made allegations about the child's care, but the court made no findings with respect to these allegations. On the contrary, the court made a finding that "there is no issue as to either party's devotion to the child, adequacy of housing facilities, or respect[a]bility of the new spouse of either parent."

The court then addressed the recommendations of the court counselor, who had made an earlier report "in [another] case coming out of this circuit also involving the social consequences of an interracial marriage." From this vague reference to that earlier case, the court turned to the present case and noted the counselor's recommendation for a change in custody because "[t]he wife [petitioner] has chosen for herself and for her child, a life-style unacceptable to her father *and to society*. * * * The child * * * is, or at school age will be, subject to environmental pressures not of choice."

The court then concluded that the best interests of the child would be served by awarding custody to the father. The court's rationale is contained in the following:

> "The father's evident resentment of the mother's choice of a black partner is not sufficient to wrest custody from the mother. It is of some significance, however, that the mother did see fit to bring a man into her home and carry on a sexual relationship with him without being married to him. Such action tended to place gratification of her own desires ahead of her concern for the child's future welfare. *This Court feels that despite the strides that have been made in bettering relations between the races in this country, it is inevitable that Melanie will, if allowed to remain in her present situation and attains school age and thus more vulnerable to peer pressures, suffer*

from the social stigmatization that is sure to come." App. to Pet. for Cert. 26–27 (emphasis added)....

* * *

The judgment of a state court determining or reviewing a child custody decision is not ordinarily a likely candidate for review by this Court. However, the court's opinion, after stating that the "father's evident resentment of the mother's choice of a black partner is not sufficient" to deprive her of custody, then turns to what it regarded as the damaging impact on the child from remaining in a racially-mixed household. This raises important federal concerns arising from the Constitution's commitment to eradicating discrimination based on race.

The Florida court did not focus directly on the parental qualifications of the natural mother of her present husband, or indeed on the father's qualifications to have custody of the child. The court found that "there is no issue as to either party's devotion to the child, adequacy of housing facilities, or respectability of the new spouse of either parent." Id., at 24. This, taken with the absence of any negative finding as to the quality of the care provided by the mother, constitutes a rejection of any claim of petitioner's unfitness to continue the custody of her child.

The court correctly stated that the child's welfare was the controlling factor. But that court was entirely candid and made no effort to place its holding on any ground other than race. Taking the court's findings and rationale at face value, it is clear that the outcome would have been different had petitioner married a Caucasian male of similar respectability.

A core purpose of the Fourteenth Amendment was to do away with all governmentally-imposed discrimination based on race. * * *

The State, of course, has a duty of the highest order to protect the interests of minor children, particularly those of tender years. In common with most states, Florida law mandates that custody determinations be made in the best interests of the children involved. The goal of granting custody based on the best interests of the child is indisputably a substantial governmental interest for purposes of the Equal Protection Clause.

It would ignore reality to suggest that racial and ethnic prejudices do not exist or that all manifestations of those prejudices have been eliminated. There is a risk that a child living with a step-parent of a different race may be subject to a variety of pressures and stresses not present if the child were living with parents of the same racial or ethnic origin.

The question, however, is whether the reality of private biases and the possible injury they might inflict are permissible considerations for removal of an infant child from the custody of its natural mother. We have little difficulty concluding that they are not. The Constitution cannot control such prejudices but neither can it tolerate them. Private biases may be outside the reach of the law, but the law cannot, directly or indirectly, give them effect. "Public officials sworn to uphold the Constitution may not avoid a constitutional duty by bowing to the hypothetical effects of private racial prejudice that they assume to be both widely and deeply held." *Palmer v. Thompson,* 403 U.S. 217, 260–261 (1971) (WHITE, J., dissenting).

* * *

Whatever problems racially-mixed households may pose for children in 1984 can no more support a denial of constitutional rights than could the stresses that residential integration was thought to entail in 1917. The effects of racial prejudice, however real, cannot justify a racial classification removing an infant child from the custody of its natural mother found to be an appropriate person to have such custody.

The judgment of the District Court of Appeal is reversed.

Notes and Questions

1. On remand in *Palmore,* the trial court relinquished jurisdiction to the Texas courts, citing the child's 2½ year residence in Texas with her father and stepmother. The appellate court affirmed. Palmore v. Sidoti, 472 So.2d 843 (Fla.App.1985).

2. Does *Palmore* preclude all consideration of race? Reconsider the issue of transracial adoption. *See* Chapter 7, § 3(B).

B. THE ROLE OF RELIGION AND PARENTAL "LIFE-STYLE"

IN RE MARRIAGE OF WANG

Supreme Court of Montana, 1995.
271 Mont. 291, 896 P.2d 450.

TURNAGE, CHIEF JUSTICE.

Laurie April Wang (Laurie) appeals the decision of the Thirteenth Judicial District Court, Yellowstone County, appointing Michael W. Wang (Michael) primary residential custodial of their son Jesse. We affirm.

* * *

Michael and Laurie were married in 1989, and had one child, Jesse, who was born in 1990. In 1993 the couple separated and Michael filed for divorce. While Michael and Laurie agreed that joint custody would be in Jesse's best interest, they disagreed as to who should be the primary residential custodian. Both requested custody of Jesse during the school year, with the other having Jesse during the summers and alternating holidays.

Social workers conducted home evaluations of Michael and Laurie and concluded that both were suitable to be primary caretakers of Jesse. The District Court held a hearing in which Michael and Laurie presented evidence and arguments to support their respective positions. Laurie presented testimony that Michael was a member of the Cornerstone Community Church. She argued that the practices of this church, including the performance of exorcisms and the belief that a wife should be subservient to her husband, would be harmful to Jesse.

Following the hearing, the District Court issued its findings of fact, conclusions of law and order. The court granted Michael physical custody of Jesse during the school year. Laurie was granted physical custody of Jesse during the summer and alternating holidays. Laurie appeals the decision of the District Court.

ISSUE 1

Did the District Court err in failing to address Michael's religious beliefs and the effect those beliefs would have on Jesse when it determined what was in Jesse's best interests?

Laurie argues that the District Court should have made specific findings in relationship to Michael's involvement with the Cornerstone Community Church and how this involvement affected the best interest of Jesse. We disagree.

* * *

The District Court heard Laurie's allegations concerning Michael's religious practices. Applying the statutory factors, the court found that there were no adequate challenges to Michael's ability to care for Jesse. The court set forth the essential and determining facts upon which it based its conclusion. It is not bound to make a specific finding regarding every allegation by a party.

* * *

A review of the entire record, not merely Laurie's allegations concerning Michael's religious beliefs, reveals that the District Court's findings were supported by substantial credible evidence. While both parties presented testimony that reflected negatively on the other's parenting abilities, independent home evaluations found both Laurie and Michael to be suitable parents.

Sarah Seiler, the court-appointed social worker, performed a home evaluation of Michael. Seiler questioned Ken McCallum, the pastor of the Cornerstone Community Church. Seiler also made several home visits and observed Michael's interaction with Jesse. Following her evaluation, she determined that there were no "bizarre activities going on" at the Cornerstone Community Church but rather it was merely a fundamentalist church. Seiler concluded that Michael was a suitable residential custodian for Jesse.

After a thorough review of the record, we conclude that the court did not err in its application of § 40–4–212, MCA, and that there is substantial credible evidence to support its findings. * * *

LEAPHART, JUSTICE, dissenting.

I dissent. I would reverse and remand for specific findings on Laurie's allegations that Michael's religious beliefs adversely affect Laurie's relationship with Jesse.... [T]he district court must address the allegations which are at the heart of the dispute. In the case at bar, Laurie's main contention is that if Michael exposes Jesse to the teachings of the Cornerstone Community Church, that exposure will adversely impact on Jesse's relationship with his mother. Michael, on the other hand, contends that Laurie should not be designated the residential parent because she, in the past, restricted Michael's access to visitation. The District Court chose to specifically make findings as to Michael's contention but not to address Laurie's contentions about religious upbringing.

It appears from the transcript that the District Court, although listening to Laurie's testimony and proof on the question of religious teachings, took the position that religion is beyond the pale of the court's scrutiny. I disagree. Considerable psychological and/or physical harm can be inflicted in the name of religion. When sufficient evidence is produced to raise questions as to whether particular religious practices are adversely affecting a child's relationship with a parent, it is incumbent upon the district court to address those issues and make findings as to the allegations.

Montana law provides that the custodial parent may determine the child's religious training "unless the court after hearing finds, upon motion by the noncustodial parent, that in the absence of a specific limitation of the custodian's authority, the child's physical health would be endangered or his emotional development significantly impaired." § 40–4–218(1), MCA. This Court has recognized the right of parents to direct the religious upbringing of their children. * * * [It has also] noted that "courts will examine religious practices which interfere with the child's general welfare." * * *

The Supreme Court of North Dakota recently addressed a similar situation in *Leppert v. Leppert* (N.D.1994), 519 N.W.2d 287, in which the mother belonged to a small religious sect run by her father, Winrod. Her husband, (the father of the children) was once a follower of Winrod but had ceased following his teachings.... Holding that religious conduct which may harm the child, physically or emotionally, is subject to judicial scrutiny, the North Dakota court said:

> Although we agree with the district court that Quinta [the mother] must not be discounted from consideration as a custodial parent simply because of her religious *beliefs*, this does not mean her religiously motivated *actions*, which are emotionally and physically harmful to the children, should be ignored when determining the children's best interests. Such a holding would immunize from consideration all religiously motivated acts, no matter what their impact on the children. * * *

Leppert, 519 N.W.2d at 290.

* * *

In the same vein, the Colorado Supreme Court has held: "While courts must remain sensitive to first amendment concerns, a court in a custody proceeding must not blind itself to evidence of religious beliefs or practices of a party seeking custody which may impair or endanger the child's welfare." *In re Marriage of Short* (Colo.1985), 698 P.2d 1310, 1313.

Religious upbringing is clearly not beyond the scope of judicial scrutiny. Rather, it is a matter which the courts will (and should) examine to determine whether the religious practices interfere with the child's welfare or significantly impair his/her emotional development.

Other than what I have read in this record, I have no knowledge of the beliefs and teachings of the Cornerstone Community Church. Furthermore, it is not my function to debate the merits of different religions or show preference to any particular faith. However, there is testimony in the record indicating that the church teaches that women are not allowed any authority, and that men must be allowed to make all the decisions. One witness, a ten-year member of the church, had to undergo an exorcism to rid herself of the "evil unsubmissive spirits"—the spirits which caused her to speak up for herself and to exercise authority rather than completely submit to her husband. Further, there is testimony that the church believed that Laurie Wang was possessed by demons and therefore subjected her to an exorcising ritual. The District Court did not determine whether, in its judgment, there was any truth or significance to this testimony. The court did, however, enter Findings of Fact and Conclusions of Law which provide:

> Neither [parent] shall either directly or indirectly cause Jesse to lose respect for or alienate his affection to either parent. The parents shall cast each other in the most favorable light before the child and shall recognize the great importance of the parents/child relationship. Additionally, both parents shall:
>
> * * *
>
> c. Encourage the free and natural development of love and respect for both parents and do nothing which may estrange Jesse from the other parent, or injure the opinion of the child to the other parent;. . . .

If there is any validity to Laurie's allegations that Michael is taking Jesse to a church which teaches Jesse that his mother is possessed by demons and that she, in contrast to the male of the species, is a lesser, subservient human being, then there is a very serious question as to whether those teachings are in direct contravention of the court's directive that both parents will foster love and respect for the other parent and will do nothing which will estrange Jesse from the other parent or injure the child's opinion of the other parent.

Whether under the guise of religion or not, any indoctrination of a minor child which undermines a child's respect for his/her mother because she is a woman, subverts the child's interaction and interrelationship with that parent, contrary to § 40–4–212(1)(c), MCA, and the best interests of the child.

In response to Michael's allegations about Laurie's uncooperativeness, the District Court did find that Michael shows a greater ability to cooperate in his parental role "particularly as it relates to his ability to allow Jesse frequent and continuing contact with his Mother." Having addressed the issue of frequency of Jesse's contacts wit his mother, it is incongruous to then avoid the more substantive issue of whether Jesse, despite frequent contact with his mother, is being taught to disrespect and fear his mother as a subservient and demon-possessed person. Given that the trial court required the parties to foster the child's love and respect for the other parent, the court should have made specific findings as to whether the religious upbringing at the Cornerstone Community Church would be consistent with that directive.

Notes and Questions

1. Most authorities agree that a parent's religious practices are relevant to the custody determination if the practices are illegal, immoral, or pose a substantial threat of imminent harm to the child as a direct result of exposure to the practice. *See* Carolyn Wah, *Religion in Child Custody and Visitation Cases: Presenting the Advantage of Religious Participation*, 28 Fam. L. Q. 269 (1994); Carl E. Schneider, *Religion and Child Custody*, 25 U. Mich.J. L. Ref. 879 (1992). *See also* Lundman v. McKown, 530 N.W.2d 807 (Minn.App.1995), rev. denied, cert. denied 516 U.S. 1092, 116 S.Ct. 814, 133 L.Ed.2d 759 (1996).

2. In Osier v. Osier, 410 A.2d 1027 (Me.1980), the court proposed a two-pronged process for review of custody claims related to a parent's religious practices:

> Because of the sensitivity of the constitutional rights involved, however, any such inquiry must proceed along a two-stage analysis, designed to protect those rights against unwarranted infringement. To summarize that analysis briefly: first, in order to assure itself that there exists a factual situation necessitating such infringement, the court must make a threshold factual determination that the child's temporal well-being is immediately and substantially endangered by the religious practice in question and, if that threshold determination is made, second, the court must engage in a deliberate and articulated balancing of the conflicting interests involved, to the end that its custody order makes the least possible infringement upon the parent's liberty interests consistent with the child's well-being....

How would the *Osier* analysis apply to a case in which one parent's religious belief requires "shunning" the non-believer parent?

3. Is a premarital agreement regarding future children's religious upbringing enforceable during marriage? at divorce? *See* Abbo v. Briskin, 660 So.2d 1157 (Fla.App.1995).

4. Does the child have First Amendment rights that must be balanced against those of its parent(s)? *See* Susan Higginbotham, *"Mom, Do I Have to Go to Church?"—The Noncustodial Parent's Obligation to Carry Out the Custodial Parent's Religious Plans*, 31 FAM. L. Q. 585, 594–595 (1997).

5. *Parental Morality:* While in an earlier era, custody contests often turned on issues of parental morality, the approach followed by most courts today is to ignore parental conduct that does not adversely affect the child. Forms of parental misconduct that might influence a judge include excessive drinking, use of illegal drugs, maintaining an ongoing sexual relationship in the child's presence, promiscuity, or serious criminal misconduct; if the parent's immoral conduct is unrelated to the parent/child relationship, the court may exclude, or place little weight, on evidence of it.

> [T]o deprive a parent of custody [based on allegation of sale of drugs in the home], the evidence must support a logical inference that some specific, identifiable behavior or conduct of the parent will probably cause significant physical or emotional harm to the child. This link between parent's conduct and harm to the child, moreover, may not be based on evidence which raises a mere surmise or speculation of harm.

May v. May, 829 S.W.2d 373, 377 (Tex.App.1992).

Based on this child-centered approach to parental "morals," most appellate courts which have recently considered the issue have ruled that a parent's homosexuality is not by itself sufficient to deny a parent custody. *See, e.g.*, T.C.H. v. K.M.H., 784 S.W.2d 281, 284 (Mo.App.1989) ("the rule appears to be that there must be a nexus between harm to the child and the parent's homosexuality," before the parent's homosexuality is a relevant factor). *But see* Tucker v. Tucker, 910 P.2d 1209 (Utah 1996) (upholding award of custody to father based on trial court's finding that mother's maintenance of a "relationship with a woman companion involving cohabitation without benefit of marriage in the same home with a minor child . . . demonstrates a lack of moral example to the child and a lack of moral fitness.")

Problem 13–1:

Harry and Wilma married in 1988. Harry was a member of the Roman Catholic Church; Wilma was a member of a Jewish synagogue. At the time of their marriage, Harry and Wilma agreed that their children would be raised in the Jewish faith and attend a Jewish school; Harry and Wilma were married in a traditional Jewish ceremony. Ariel was born in 1989; he was circumcised in a traditional Jewish ceremony. His two sisters (born in 1991 and 1993) had Jewish naming ceremonies. In 1991, Harry joined the Boston Church of Christ, a fundamentalist

Christian organization; he is a regular participant in a range of church activities. In 1994, Wilma joined an Orthodox synagogue. (Orthodox Judaism is the branch of the Jewish religion which demands the strictest adherence to traditional Jewish religious laws related to diet, the Sabbath, etc.) Unsurprisingly, later that year Harry and Wilma decided to obtain a divorce; each of them has requested sole custody. At the time the divorce action was filed, all three of the children attended Jewish religious schools in accordance with the parents' premarital agreement. At trial, Harry testified that: i) he believes that those who don't accept Jesus Christ are "damned to go to hell," ii) he would like his children to accept Jesus Christ; and iii) "he will never stop trying to save his children." Wilma testified that she does not accept Jesus Christ, that she does not want her children to believe in Jesus Christ, and that she does want them to grow up in the Jewish religion as she and Harry originally agreed. She also expressed her fear that Harry will try to undermine not only the children's religious education but also their feelings about her. A court-appointed psychiatrist testified that all three children thought of themselves as Jewish, were deeply troubled by the conflict between their parents, and were deeply attached to both parents. The psychiatrist also testified that both parents were sincere, loving, and capable. You are the trial court judge; what custody decision will you make? How will you justify it? *See* Kendall v. Kendall, 426 Mass. 238, 687 N.E.2d 1228 (1997).

C. THE ROLE OF DOMESTIC VIOLENCE

OWAN v. OWAN

Supreme Court of North Dakota, 1996.
541 N.W.2d 719.

MESCHKE, JUSTICE.

Rayann Owan appeals from a divorce decree placing custody of her daughter Danika with Stephen Owan. We reverse and remand for findings about domestic violence and for reconsideration of custody accordingly.

Rayann and Stephen lived together for two years before their marriage in 1990. Their daughter Danika was born in 1991. They moved several times, going from Williston to Minnesota, back to Williston, to Arizona, and again back to Williston. The relationship between Rayann and Stephen was often turbulent.

Rayann testified that Stephen had kicked through a locked bathroom door in their apartment, had thrown a cordless phone into a wall near her, and often would put Rayann "up against the wall and hit the wall above me and scare me," while calling her names: "tramp, bitch, whore.... " Rayann testified about other controlling and domineering behavior by Stephen: "he'd go through my purse and rip my purse open and take all my credit cards, and take all my money." According to Rayann, Stephen threatened to kill her if she left him, and several times threatened suicide. There was also evidence that Rayann had slapped and scratched Stephen sometimes.

Rayann sued for divorce in February 1994 and received temporary custody of Danika. Before trial in December 1994, Stephen had moved back to Arizona to be close to his family, and Rayann was pregnant by a man she intended to marry. The trial court granted the divorce, divided the marital property, and placed custody of Danika with Stephen, with Rayann to pay child support. Rayann appealed.

We conclude that the dispositive aspect of this appeal is the lack of adequate attention to the statutory presumption against placing custody with a parent who has committed domestic violence. Part of NDCC § 14–09–06.2(1)(j) directs:

> The court shall cite specific findings of fact to show that the custody or visitation arrangement best protects the child and the parent or other family or household member who is the victim of domestic violence.... The fact that the abused parent suffers from the effects of the abuse may not be grounds for denying that parent custody.

"Domestic violence" is defined in NDCC § 14–07.1–01(2):

> "Domestic violence" includes physical harm, bodily injury, sexual activity compelled by physical force, assault, or the infliction of fear of imminent physical harm, not committed in self-defense, on the complaining family or household members.

* * * The effect of the statutory presumption makes domestic violence the paramount factor in a custodial placement when there is credible evidence of it. To rebut the presumption, the violent parent must prove by clear and convincing evidence that other circumstances require that the child be placed with the violent parent rather than the non-violent parent. * * * [W]hen there is evidence of domestic violence, the trial court must make specific findings about it.

On this record, the trial court made only a single finding from the opinion of Stephen's social-worker witness to minimize Stephen's violent conduct:

> The Court gives [Stephen's social-worker witness's] testimony and opinion a great deal of credibility. The Court has reviewed North Dakota Century Code § 14–09–06.2 and does concur with Mr. Yockim's findings as follows: the allegations of Stephen's physical altercations appear to be minor. In most cases, [Rayann] has acted and [Stephen] has reacted.

This finding is unsatisfactory for several reasons.

First, the trial court improperly relied upon Stephen's social-worker witness to assess trial testimony as an expert on Stephen's violent conduct. To justify the trial court's abbreviated analysis about violence, Stephen's brief in this court also relied on testimony by that witness, Jim Yockim:

> I was aware of the allegation, the verbal allegations, the abuse, the breaking the door in, the whole thing. Again it seemed to be situational in nature, situational in terms of the marital discord rather than a pattern, I guess, in Stephen's life. There were allegations on the other side in terms of scratching and those kinds of things, too, and I did not think that—again, I dealt with him in terms of being situational in the marital discord.
>
> * * *
>
> Q. Did you analyze that violence behavior in light of the presumption in the Century Code that absent other factors, the non-violent party is given a nod so to speak under the categories that are analyzed? how did you weigh that, if at all?
>
> A. I guess I did not feel that it met the same level of violent behavior that I would, I guess I—
>
> Q. You didn't apply the presumption basically, is that fair?
>
> A. I don't think that I held that what had happened in that case as meeting that standard that the Court is looking for as a determining factor.

Stephen principally urges here that we affirm the trial court's finding because Mr. Yockim's written home study makes no finding or suggestion of credible evidence of domestic violence by either party.

Rayann responds, "If one ... *assumes* the Court intended by its statement as to Yockim's credibility to *adopt* the findings of Stephen's expert, more is required." We agree.

The trial court cannot delegate its specific statutory responsibility to weigh the evidence and make findings on domestic violence. Generally, a "court cannot make the report of an independent investigator the conclusive basis of its decision regarding the custody of the children. The reason for this rule is usually expressed by the phrase that the trial court cannot delegate to anyone the power to decide questions of child custody." That concept is particularly important for domestic violence. Here, the statute directs the trial court itself to weigh the testimony about domestic violence, to make specific findings about it, and to "show" that the custodial arrangement "protects the child and the parent ... who is the victim of domestic violence." NDCC § 14–09–06.2(1)(j). Those duties cannot be delegated by the trial court.

Nor does the trial court's finding permit adequate review of the reason for minimizing the extensive evidence of Stephen's violent conduct in this record.... [T]he extent of the evidence of physical abuse in a case like this must be specifically addressed and dealt with in the findings.

The trial court also failed to make findings about the slapping and scratching that Stephen alleged Rayann did....

> [I]f domestic violence has been committed by both parents, the trial court [must] measure the amount and extent of domestic violence

> inflicted by both parents. If the amount and extent of domestic violence inflicted by one parent is significantly greater than that inflicted by the other, the statutory presumption against awarding custody to the perpetrator will apply only to the parent who has inflicted the greater domestic violence, and will not apply to the parent who has inflicted the lesser. However, if the trial court finds that the amount and extent of the violence inflicted by one parent is roughly proportional to the violence inflicted by the other parent, and both parents are otherwise found to be fit parents, the presumption against awarding custody to either perpetrating parent ceases to exist. In such a case, the trial court is not bound by any presumption, but may consider the remaining customary best-interests factors in making its custody decision.

Krank v. Krank, 529 N.W.2d at 850. If the violence between parents is proportional, the trial court should also consider, together with the other usual factors for custody, which parent is least likely to continue to expose the child to violence. Here, though, the trial court failed to measure or weigh the violent conduct described in the testimony, nor did it measure the propensity of each of these parents for continued violence.

The trial court's findings on domestic violence are insufficient for us to review its decision to place custody with Stephen. Accordingly, we reverse and remand for further findings and reconsideration of the custodial placement.

SANDSTROM, JUSTICE, dissenting.

* * *

This is a child custody case. Yet, nowhere does the majority even discuss "the best interests of the child." * * * Domestic violence is unacceptable. The goal of punishing perpetrators of domestic violence, however, cannot justify a child-custody award that is, in fact, not in the best interests of the child. Certainly domestic violence should be considered as it affects the best interests of the child. To the extent the majority analysis fails to limit child-custody-case consideration of domestic violence to the extent it in fact affects the best interests of the child, it is constitutionally infirm.

If the majority is saying, under the current law, a finding of domestic violence preempts consideration of all other factors relating to the best interests of the child, the legislation is remarkably parallel to that struck down as unconstitutional in *Stanley v. Illinois,* 405 U.S. 645 (1972). * * *

> "Procedure by presumption is always cheaper and easier than individualized determination. But when, as here, the procedure forecloses the determinative issues of competence and care, when it explicitly disdains present realities in deference to past formalities, it needlessly risks running roughshod over the important interests of both parent and child. It therefore cannot stand."
>
> *Stanley* at 656–57, 92 S.Ct. at 1215.

Because the majority ignores the fundamental need to determine the best interests of the child *in fact*, I dissent.

Notes and Questions

1. How, if at all, does the North Dakota domestic violence presumption at issue in *Owan* differ from the presumption at issue in *Stanley*? (Review Chapter 7, § 2(B) to refresh your recollection of *Stanley*.) Is the dissent correct that the presumption fails to meet constitutional standards?

2. Researchers have uniformly found that a child's exposure to domestic violence is associated with a range of harmful consequences. First, child abuse is far more common in homes where domestic violence is present. *See, e.g.*, M.A. Straus, *Ordinary Violence, Child Abuse, and Wife Beating: What Do They Have in Common?* in THE DARK SIDE OF FAMILIES: CURRENT FAMILY VIOLENCE RESEARCH 213–34 (David Finkelhor et al. eds., 1990) (fathers who were violent toward their child's mother were seven times more likely to be violent toward their children as compared to fathers who did not abuse child's mother); Mary M. McKay, *Domestic Violence and Child Abuse: Assessment and Treatment Considerations*, 63 CHILD WELFARE 29 (1994) (summarizing research and reporting that from 45% to 70% of battered women in shelters report child abuse by the batterer). Second, children exposed to domestic violence typically exhibit emotional and physical symptoms similar to those of abused children, as well as decreased empathy, increased aggression, tolerance of the use of violence, and victim blaming. *See, e.g.* PETER JAFFE ET AL., CHILDREN OF BATTERED WOMEN (1990); Mildred D. Pagelow, *Effects of Domestic Violence on Children and Their Consequences for Custody and Visitation Agreements*, 4 MEDIATION QTRLY. 7 (1990). Finally, exposure to parental violence has been found to vastly increase the risk of becoming violent—or victimized—in adult relationships. Indeed, one study found that almost half of the children from abusive families repeated the pattern themselves, becoming either abusive or victimized in early adulthood. *See* JUDITH S. WALLERSTEIN & SANDRA BLAKESLEE, SECOND CHANCES: MEN, WOMEN & CHILDREN A DECADE AFTER DIVORCE 117 (1989). For useful summaries of the research, *see, e.g.*, Naomi R. Cahn, *Civil Images of Battered Women: The Impact of Domestic Violence on Child Custody Decisions*, 44 VANDERBILT L. REV. 1041, 1055–58 (1991); Bonnie E. Rabin, *Violence Against Mothers Equals Violence Against Children: Understanding the Connections*, 58 ALBANY L. REV. 1109 (1995); Howard A. Davidson, *Child Abuse and Domestic Violence: Legal Connections and Controversies*, 29 FAM. L. Q. 357 (1995).

3. As evidence of the effects of domestic violence on children has mounted, lawmakers have reacted. In 1990, Congress adopted a joint resolution stating that "[it] is the sense of the Congress that, for purposes of determining child custody, credible evidence of physical abuse of a spouse would create a statutory presumption that it is detrimental to the child to be placed in the custody of the abusive spouse." H. Res. 172, 136 Cong. Rec. House at H8280 (September 27,

1990). More than 80% of the states and the District of Columbia now have custody provisions concerning domestic violence, almost triple the number in 1990. The Family Violence Project of the National Council of Juvenile and Family Court Judges, *Family Violence in Child Custody Statutes: An Analysis of State Codes and Legal Practice*, 29 FAM L. Q. 197, 199, 225–27 (1995) (analyzing and categorizing state laws). At least thirty-five states require courts to consider evidence of domestic violence or spouse abuse when making a custody or visitation determination. *Id.* at 208. At least ten states have established a rebuttable presumption against the award of custody and/or unsupervised visitation with the perpetrator of domestic violence. *See, e.g.,* DEL. CODE ANN. tit. 13, § 705A; FLA. STAT. ANN. § 61.13(2)(b)(2). Other states have created custody preclusions. *See, e.g.,* TEXAS FAM. CODE ANN. § 153.004 (precluding joint custody in context of domestic violence); 23 PA. CONS. STAT. ANN. § 5303 (1994) (precluding custody or visitation award to parent convicted of designated domestic violence or child abuse crimes unless qualified professional testifies that parent has participated in specialized counseling and does not pose risk of harm to child).

4. While custody statutes seldom address the issue, courts and commentators agree that there should be a strong presumption against the award of custody to a parent who has physically abused his or her child. Pointing to a seeming increase in allegations of child sexual abuse in custody litigation, in recent years some commentators have alleged that many of these allegations are made falsely in order to obtain a litigation advantage. Research to date fails to bear out the allegation. *See* Kathleen Coulborn Faller & Ellen DeVoe, *Allegations of Sexual Abuse in Divorce*, 4 J. CHILD SEXUAL ABUSE (1996) (reporting that 72.6% of allegations are substantiated).

D. THE ROLE OF THE "EXPERT"

In most litigated custody contests, the court cannot rely on a presumption. Instead, it must weigh and measure the advantages to the child of conferring custody on each parent. Almost invariably, each parent will offer a combination of strengths and weaknesses. Because both parents are typically "fit," the custody award will hinge on the court's decision as to which parent is better able to meet the child's needs.

If the parents can afford to do so, each will typically obtain and present expert testimony regarding his or her parenting skills and relationship with the children. This phase of the custody trial will closely resemble any other "battle of experts" in civil litigation. In about a third of the states, however, the court is authorized to order its own investigation and report, either by a guardian ad litem, a social services agency, or a private organization. These court-appointed investigators typically have, or may obtain from the court, the authority to obtain records, talk to witnesses, consult with other experts, and have the child evaluated. Here is an example of an authorizing statute:

KAN. STAT. ANN. § 60–1615. Information relating to custody of children.

(1) *Investigation and report.* In contested custody proceedings, the court may order an investigation and report concerning custodial arrangements for the child. The investigation and report may be made by court services officers or any consenting person or agency employed by the court for that purpose . . . The costs for making the investigation and report may be assessed as court costs in the case . . .

* * *

> (b) *Consultation.* In preparing the report concerning a child, the investigator may consult any person who may have information about the child and the potential custodial arrangements. Upon order of the court, the investigator may refer the child to professional personnel for diagnosis. The investigator may consult with and obtain information from medical, psychiatric or other expert persons who have served the child in the past. If the requirements of subsection (c) are fulfilled, the investigator's report may be received in evidence at the hearing.
>
> (c) *Use of report and investigator's testimony.* The court shall make the investigator's report available prior to the hearing to counsel or to any party not represented by counsel. Any party to the proceeding may call the investigator and any person whom the investigator has consulted for cross-examination. In consideration of the mental health or best interests of the child, the court may approve a stipulation that the interview records not be divulged to the parties.

The evidence suggests that the use of custody investigations has mushroomed in recent years. Judges have

> enthusiastically relied upon out-of-court caseworker custody investigations in divorce cases for a complex of reasons . . . : custody decisions are too important to be treated in the same fashion as ordinary adversary litigation—in which the parties have uncontrolled discretion as to what testimony is presented to the decision maker; a neutral expert, removed from the emotional turmoil of the dispute and the partisan advocacy of the lawyers, can provide more reliable information to the judge than the embattled spouses are likely to provide; the information essential to custody decision making tends to be more psychological than in other litigation contexts and therefore more suited to written reports by psychological experts than to testimony in a courtroom.

Robert J. Levy, *Custody Investigations as Evidence*, 21 FAM. L.Q. 149, 150–51 (1987).

JONES v. JONES

Supreme Court of South Dakota, 1996.
542 N.W.2d 119.

JOHNS, CIRCUIT JUDGE.

Dawn R. Jones (Dawn) appeals from a decree of divorce awarding custody of the parties' three minor children to Kevin Mark Jones (Kevin). We affirm.

FACTS

Dawn and Kevin Jones were married on March 11, 1989 in Britton, South Dakota. Kevin was thirty years old at time of trial and is an enrolled member of the Sisseton–Wahpeton Dakota Nation. He was adopted at age seven by Maurice and Dorothy Jones. Dawn was twenty-five years old at time of trial and is Caucasian. The parties have three children, Lyndra, Elias and Desiree. Lyndra was born to Dawn prior to her marriage to Kevin. She was subsequently adopted by Kevin.

During the marriage, the parties resided in a trailer house on the farm of Kevin's parents. Kevin is a minority shareholder in and works for Penrhos Farms. Penrhos is a close family farm corporation, owned primarily by Kevin's father and his three uncles. The Joneses are an extremely close-knit and supportive family. In fact, Kevin often takes the children to work with him, as this is a family tradition. However, farm safety is very important and is stressed by all members of the family.

Kevin works predominantly in construction and in the feeding of the cattle on the Penrhos Farms. His net earnings for child support purposes are approximately $1,880.00 a month. During the marriage, Dawn was a homemaker for a time and also held various jobs. She is currently enrolled in a nursing program at the Sisseton–Wahpeton Community College

Kevin is a recovering alcoholic who, while drinking, exhibited a behavior of violence towards Dawn and a somewhat casual indifference to the children. He has been sober since December 1992 and regularly attends and presents Alcoholics Anonymous meetings. Dawn suffers from depression and low self-esteem but is seeking counseling at this time.

Deterioration of the marriage is attributed to Kevin's alcoholism, Dawn's depression, financial problems and a lack of communication. Both parties were granted a divorce based upon mental cruelty. They were also granted joint legal custody of the children with primary physical custody being awarded to Kevin. * * *

Dawn contends that the trial court erred in finding as a matter of fact that Kevin is a fit person to have care, custody and control of his children. She also contends that even if the trial court did not err in finding that Kevin is fit to parent the children, the trial court abused its discretion when it chose Kevin over herself as the parent who would have primary physical custody of the children.

The paramount consideration for the trial court in deciding the issue of child custody is the temporal, mental and moral welfare of the child. The trial court exercises broad discretion in awarding custody and its discretion will be reversed only upon a clear showing of an abuse of that discretion. *Jones v. Jones*, 423 N.W.2d 517, 519 (S.D.1988); *Anderson v. Anderson*, 472 N.W.2d 519, 520 (S.D.1991). In determining whether there has been an abuse of discretion, this court does not decide whether it would have made the same ruling, but must determine if a judicial mind could have made a similar decision in view of the law and that particular case's circumstances.

Dawn contends that because Kevin sometimes verbally and physically abused her when he was drinking, he is not a fit person to have charge of the care and education of his children. The trial court's finding that Kevin is fit is based, in part, on a home study completed by Mr. Thomas L. Price, a licensed psychologist. His home study included clinical interviews with the parties, meetings with the children, and his observations of the parents and children together at the respective homes of the parties and his office. Mr. Price also administered to both parties the Minnesota Multiphasic Personality Inventory, the Millon Clinical Multiphasic Inventory—II, The Custody Quotient, the Child Access to Parental Strength Questionnaire, and the Access to Adult Strength: Parental Self–Report Data. After considering the effect of Kevin's alcoholism and domestic violence on his parental capacity, Mr. Price rendered the following conclusions and recommendations:

> Both Kevin and Dawn Jones were found to demonstrate adequate parental capacities. Dawn Jones obtained a higher score on the Custody Quotient. [Kevin obtained a CQ score of 112 which is in the High Average Parent Classification Range. Dawn obtained a CQ score of 120 which is at the low end of the Superior Parent Classification Range.] Her personality test findings were less suggestive of psychological difficulties and Lyndra's rating on the BPS [Bricklin Perceptual Scales: Child Perception of Parent] tended to favor her mother. Parent-child interactions and home visitations failed to reveal significant difference between the parents.
>
> The preponderance of information gathered by this examiner favors Dawn Jones as the custodial parent. The court is encouraged to afford liberal visitation rights to Kevin Jones, however.

Based on the home study of Mr. Price along with his testimony and all of the other evidence in the record, we are unable to say that the trial court's finding of Kevin's fitness is clearly erroneous. Thus, we affirm the trial court on this issue.

Contrary to the recommendations of Mr. Price and his associate, Ms. Judi Muessigmann, a clinical social worker, that primary custody of the children be placed with Dawn, the trial court determined that it should go to Kevin. In its findings of fact and conclusions of law, the court relied heavily upon the stability and continuity that Kevin could provide through his relationship with the Jones family. Specifically, the court stated in finding of fact number 52 that "the children have always known Penrhos Farms as their home, and granting primary physical custody to Father will allow the children to remain on the farm, and give them access to the numerous family support systems of the large and close Jones family." The trial court also stressed that, while Dawn may well be the preferable custodial parent at the immediate time, he was of the opinion that Kevin was the preferable parent over the "long haul." In doing so, he recognized our holding in *Jasper v. Jasper,* 351 N.W.2d 114 (S.D.1984) that stability is a very desirable factor in child rearing.

The trial court made its custody decision after hearing the testimony of the parties at the interim custody hearing and after nearly three days of trial testimony. It is apparent that the trial court wrestled long and hard with its decision as evidenced by the 20–page memorandum opinion, 15 pages of which dealt with the custody issue. After reviewing the testimony, along with the trial court's findings of fact and conclusions of law, we cannot say that its decision to award Kevin primary custody was an abuse of discretion. We affirm the trial court on this issue.

* * *

Notes and Questions

1. Would the *Owan* court uphold the trial court's decision in *Jones*? Why?

2. A recent survey analyzed current custody evaluation practices:

> 1. Child custody evaluators still prefer to serve in an impartial capacity, with almost 100 percent indicating they prefer to be retained by both parents or the court.
>
> 2. The average child custody evaluation, with report writing, takes 26.4 hours, 7.6 hours greater than in the 1986 study. Almost all of this difference comes from the increased amount of time spent reviewing materials and report writing.
>
> 3. Psychologists spend an additional three to four hours consulting with attorneys and testifying in court.
>
> 4. The average fee for a custody evaluation is $2,646; almost triple ten years ago.
>
> 5. Each child generally receives an intelligence test, personality tests, such as, the CAT, TAT, or Rorschach, an achievement test, Sentence Completion Test, and the Bricklin Perceptual Scales (BPS).
>
> 6. Each adult generally receives the MMPI/MMPI–2, MCMI–II/MCMI–III, Rorschach, intelligence test, and the TAT.
>
> 7. The ASPECT is the most frequently used custody test for adults, and the BPS is the most frequently used custody test for children.

8. Ninety-five percent of psychologists require some or all of the testing fee to be paid in advance, with 50 percent requiring it be paid totally in advance.

9. Eighty-three percent of psychologists require full payment of fees prior to testifying in court.

10. When making sole custody recommendations, active substance abuse, parental alienation, parenting skills, psychological stability, and emotional bonding with parents are considered most important when a forced choice is presented. When an open-ended choice is presented, geographical distance between parents and evidence of physical and sexual abuse are added.

11. Joint custody is preferred on a forced choice based on parents' ability to separate interpersonal difficulties from their parenting decisions, quality of relationship with child, problems with substance abuse, psychological stability of parents, the amount of anger and bitterness between parents, and the parents' willingness to enter into joint custody arrangements. On an open-ended basis, joint custody is preferred based on the parents' ability to cooperate, the child's attachment with both parents, psychological health of parents, ability to engage in more child rearing, and the desire of the parents.

12. Parental cooperation is the most frequently noted factor on open-ended choices of sole versus joint custody.

13. Joint custody is more preferred now than ten years ago.

14. Mediation is recommended by almost 50 percent [of surveyed evaluators].

15. The mean age at which children should be allowed to select the residential parent is 15.1 years.

16. Evaluators are less likely to make a recommendation based on a single issue.

17. Evaluators today rely more on psychological testing than they did ten years ago.

18. Alcoholism is a major negative factor, while being in recovery is not.

Marc. J. Ackerman & Melissa C. Ackerman, *Child Custody Evaluation Practices: A 1996 Survey of Psychologists*, 30 Fam. L. Q. 565 (1996).

For custody evaluation guidelines, *see* American Psychological Association, *Guidelines for Child Custody Evaluation in Divorce Proceedings*, 49 Am. Psychol. 677 (1994); Association of Family and Conciliation Courts, *Model Standards of Practice for Child Custody Evaluation*, 32 Fam. Conciliation Cts. 504 (1994).

3. A number of commentators have raised concerns about court-ordered child custody evaluations, including issues of confidentiality,

hearsay, and bias. An evaluation of custody investigations in Minnesota, for example, concluded that "[s]ome of the reports ... were modest, thoughtful and, insofar as it was possible to check their facts, careful and accurate. But such conclusions could not be drawn about all, or even most, of the reports." Levy, *supra* p. 659 at 160. The researcher found some instances in which facts about one or another parent were suppressed. In other cases there was clear evidence that the caseworker had "shaped" the report to produce a work product favorable to a judge or referee who had already made up his mind. *Id.* at 163. And "[i]n some of the cases, the investigators obviously imposed upon the divorcing spouses their own personal and idiosyncratic child care and personal behavioral values in making custodial recommendations." *Id. See also* Alison R. McBurney, *Bitter Battles: The Use of Psychological Evaluations in Child Custody Disputes in West Virginia*, 97 W. VA. L. REV. 773 (1995).

4. Some commentators have questioned the utility of all expert testimony in custody cases.

> Testifying about how the best interests of a particular child will be served by a particular custodial arrangement entails making a prediction, as contrasted with providing the court with information about the parties that would otherwise be unavailable. * * * While there is much well-grounded ... research relevant to family law decisions, there is often an inverse correlation between its legal relevance and scientific grounding. The best research is likely to be of general application and is unlikely to be useful in predicting outcomes in particular cases. Nonetheless, there is an understandable natural inclination for lawyers and judges to want mental health professionals to go beyond the data to predict outcomes in particular cases. And a natural belief on the part of mental health professionals that because of their qualifications they are capable of doing so, even when they can point to no research to support that belief."

Daniel W. Sherman, *What Should We Permit Mental Health Professionals to Say About "The Best Interests of the Child"? An Essay on Common Sense, Daubert and the Rules of Evidence*, 31 FAM. L.Q. 551 (1997).

SECTION 3. ALTERNATIVES TO THE BEST INTERESTS STANDARD—SOLVING OR COMPOUNDING THE DILEMMA?

A. THE PRIMARY CARETAKER PRESUMPTION

GARSKA v. McCOY

Supreme Court of West Virginia, 1981.
167 W.Va. 59, 278 S.E.2d 357.

NEELY, JUSTICE.

The appellant, Gwendolyn McCoy, appeals from an order of the Circuit Court of Logan County which gave the custody of her son,

Jonathan Conway McCoy, to the appellee, Michael Garska, the natural father. * * *

[The trial court's award of custody was] based on the following findings of fact: * * *

> (b) ... Michael Garska is better educated than the natural mother and her alleged fiance;
>
> (c) ... Michael Garska is more intelligent than the natural mother;
>
> (d) ... Michael Garska is better able to provide financial support and maintenance than the natural mother;
>
> (e) ... Michael Garska can provide a better social and economic environment than the natural mother;
>
> (f) ... Michael Garska has a somewhat better command of the English language than the natural mother;
>
> (g) ... Michael Garska has a better appearance and demeanor than the natural mother;
>
> (h) ... Michael Garska is very highly motivated in his desire to have custody of the infant child, and the natural mother had previously executed an adoption consent for said child.

* * * The final order was entered after the operative date of the 1980 Amendment to W.Va.Code, § 48–2–15, the relevant part of which provides:

> In making any such order respecting custody of minor children, there shall be no legal presumption that, as between the natural parents, either the father or the mother should be awarded custody of said children, but the court shall make an award of custody solely for the best interest of the children based upon the merits of each case.

Furthermore, the case was tried below on the theory that W. Va. Code 48–2–15 [1980] applies to this case to the extent that it obliterates the presumption ... that children of tender years should be awarded to the mother. * * *

* * *

In setting the child custody law in domestic relations cases we are concerned with three practical considerations. First, we are concerned to prevent the issue of custody from being used in an abusive way as a coercive weapon to affect the level of support payments and the outcome of other issues in the underlying divorce proceeding. Where a custody fight emanates from this reprehensible motive the children inevitably become pawns to be sacrificed in what ultimately becomes a very cynical game. Second, in the average divorce proceeding intelligent determination of relative degrees of fitness requires a precision of measurement which is not possible given the tools available to judges. Certainly it is no more reprehensible for judges to admit that they cannot measure minute gradations of psychological capacity between two fit parents than it is for a physicist to concede that it is impossible for him to measure the speed of an electron. Third, there is an urgent need in contemporary divorce law for a legal structure upon which a divorcing couple may rely in reaching a settlement.

While recent statutory changes encourage private ordering of divorce upon the "no-fault" ground of "irreconcilable differences," our legal structure has not simultaneously been tightened to provide a reliable framework within which the divorcing couple can bargain intelligently. Nowhere is the lack of certainty greater than in child custody. Not very long ago, the courts were often intimately involved with all aspects of a divorce. Even an estranged couple who had reached an amicable settlement had to undergo "play-acting" before the court in order to obtain a divorce. Now, however, when divorces are numerous, easy, and routinely concluded out of court intelligible, reliable rules upon which out-of-court bargaining can be based must be an important consideration in the formulation of our rules.

Since the Legislature has concluded that private ordering by divorcing couples is preferable to judicial ordering, we must insure that each spouse is adequately protected during the out-of-court bargaining. Uncertainty of outcome is very destructive of the position of the primary caretaker parent because he or she will be willing to sacrifice everything else in order to avoid the terrible prospect of losing the child in the unpredictable process of litigation.

This phenomenon may be denominated the "Solomon syndrome", that is that the parent who is most attached to the child will be most willing to accept an inferior bargain. In the court of Solomon, the "harlot" who was willing to give up her child in order to save him from being cleaved in half so that he could be equally divided was rewarded for her sacrifice, but in the big world out there the sacrificing parent generally loses necessary support or alimony payments. This then must also be compensated for "in the best interests of the children." Moreover, it is likely that the primary caretaker will have less financial security than the nonprimary caretaker and, consequently, will be unable to sustain the expense of custody litigation, requiring as is so often the case these days, the payments for expert psychological witnesses.

Therefore, in the interest of removing the issue of child custody from the type of acrimonious and counter-productive litigation which a procedure inviting exhaustive evidence will inevitably create, we hold today that there is a presumption in favor of the primary caretaker parent, if he or she meets the minimum, objective standard for being a fit parent . . . regardless of sex. Therefore, in any custody dispute involving children of tender years it is incumbent upon the circuit court to determine as a threshold question which parent was the primary caretaker parent before the domestic strife giving rise to the proceeding began.

While it is difficult to enumerate all of the factors which will contribute to a conclusion that one or the other parent was the primary caretaker parent, nonetheless, there are certain obvious criteria to which a court must initially look. In establishing which natural or adoptive parent is the primary caretaker, the trial court shall determine which parent has taken primary responsibility for, inter alia, the performance of the following caring and nurturing duties of a parent: (1) preparing and planning of meals; (2) bathing, grooming and dressing; (3) purchasing, cleaning, and care of clothes; (4) medical care, including nursing and trips to physicians; (5) arranging for social interaction among peers after school, i.e. transporting to friends' houses or, for example, to girl or boy scout meetings; (6) arranging alternative care, i.e. babysitting, day-care, etc.; (7) putting the child to bed at night, attending to child in the middle of the night, waking child in the morning; (8) disciplining, i.e. teaching general manners and toilet training; (9) educating, i.e. religious, cultural, social, etc.; and, (10) teaching elementary skills, i.e., reading, writing and arithmetic.

In those custody disputes where the facts demonstrate that child care and custody were shared in an entirely equal way, then indeed no presumption arises and the court must proceed to inquire further into relative degrees of parental competence. However, where one parent can demonstrate with regard to a child of tender years that he or she is clearly the primary caretaker parent, then the court must further determine only whether the primary caretaker parent is a fit parent. Where the primary caretaker parent achieves the minimum, objective standard of behavior which qualifies him or her as a fit parent, the trial court must award the child to the primary caretaker parent.

Consequently, all of the principles enunciated in [the tender years doctrine] are reaffirmed today except that wherever the words "mother," "maternal," or "maternal preference" are used in that case, some variation of the term "primary caretaker parent," as defined by this case should be substituted. In this regard we should point out that the absolute presumption in favor of a fit primary caretaker parent applies only to children of tender years. Where a child is old enough to formulate an opinion about his or her own custody the trial court is entitled to receive such opinion and accord it such weight as he feels appropriate. When, in the opinion of the trial court, a child old enough to formulate an opinion but under the age of 14 has indicated a justified desire to live with the parent who is not the primary caretaker, the court may award the child to such parent.

In the case before us it is obvious that the petitioner was the primary caretaker parent before the proceedings under consideration in this case arose, and there is no finding on the part of the trial court judge that she is an unfit parent. In fact, all of the evidence indicates that she mobilized all of the resources at her command, namely the solicitous regard of her grandparents, in the interest of this child and that she went to extraordinary lengths to provide for him adequate medical attention and financial support. While, as the trial court found, the educational and economic position of the father is superior to that of the mother, nonetheless, those factors alone pale in comparison to love, affection, concern, tolerance, and the willingness to sacrifice—factors about which conclusions can be made for the future most intelligently upon a course of conduct in the past. At least with regard to the primary caretaker parent there is a track record to which a court can look and where that parent is fit he or she should be awarded continued custody.

Certainly the record in the case before us does not demonstrate any intent by the mother to abandon the child through permitting him to be adopted by the grandparents; it is well recognized that mothers in penurious circumstances often resort to adoption in order to make the child eligible for social security or union welfare benefits, all of which significantly enhance the child's opportunities in life. Absent an explicit finding of intent to abandon we cannot construe manipulation of the welfare system to direct maximum benefits towards this child as anything other than solicitous concern for his welfare.... the judgment of the Circuit Court of Logan County is reversed and remanded with directions to enter an order in favor of the petitioner.

Notes and Questions

1. Is the primary caretaker presumption simply another version of the maternal preference? Justice Neely, author of the *Garska* opinion, has noted that "West Virginia law does not permit a maternal preference. But it does accord an explicit and almost absolute preference to the 'primary caretaker parent,' ... This list of criteria usually, but not necessarily, spells 'mother.' That fact reflects social reality; the rule itself is neutral on its face and in its application." Richard Neely, *The Primary Caretaker Parent Rule: Child Custody and the Dynamics of Greed*, 3 YALE LAW & POL'Y REV. 167 (1984).

2. *The Role of Caretaking Activities:* Many state statutes now explicitly require *consideration* of past caretaking roles in a custody determination. *See, e.g.*, LA. CIV. CODE ANN. art. 1334(12) (requiring consideration of "[t]he responsibility for the care and rearing of the child previously exercised by each party"); N.J. STAT. ANN § 9:2–4(c) (court must consider the "extent and quality of time spent with the child prior to or subsequent to the separation"). Several states, either under the relevant custody statute or case law, require the court to give *priority* to past caretaking roles. *See, e.g.*, WASH. REV. CODE ANN. § 26.09.187(3)(a)(i) (requiring court to give "greatest weight" to "[t]he relative strength, nature, and stability of the child's relationship with each parent, including whether a parent has taken greater responsibility for performing caretaking functions related to the daily needs of the child"); Davis v. Davis, 749 P.2d 647, 648 (Utah 1988) ("considerable weight" should be given to the identity of the primary caretaker). But only two states have established a *presumption* in favor of the primary caretaker. West Virginia continues to employ the presumption first enunciated in *Garska*; Montana adopted a statutory presumption in 1995. *See* MONT. CODE

ANN. § 40–4–212(3)(a). What are the pros and cons of these various methods of taking parental caretaking into account?

3. *What Caretaking Activities Are Relevant?* There is no judicial consensus evident on the weight to be given time spent on child care, as compared to the level of responsibility, or the allocation of particular tasks. In In re Marriage of Fennell, 485 N.W.2d 863 (Iowa App.1992), for example, the mother worked outside the home from 5:30 a.m. to 2:00 p.m. and assumed care of the children when she came home. The father, who did not work outside the home, was treated as the primary caretaker because he "relieved [the mother] of numerous childraising problems that occurred during her working hours." *Id.* at 864. By contrast, in Skomrock v. Skomrock, 1992 WL 15238 (Ohio App.), the court treated the mother as the primary caretaker because, even though she was a full-time student, she was "most often the one who supervised to make sure that the children were provided the essentials."

4. *Custody Bargaining:* The *Garska* court describes the need to "insure that each spouse is adequately protected during the out-of-court bargaining" as one basis for a primary caretaker presumption. Some family law experts have theorized that the indeterminacy of the best interests standard encourages fathers who are in reality uninterested in obtaining custody to threaten a custody fight in order to obtain economic concessions from mothers. *See, e.g.* LENORE J. WEITZMAN, THE DIVORCE REVOLUTION: THE UNEXPECTED SOCIAL AND ECONOMIC CONSEQUENCES FOR WOMEN AND CHILDREN IN AMERICA 242–43 (1985); ELEANOR E. MACCOBY & ROBERT H. MNOOKIN, DIVIDING THE CHILD: SOCIAL AND LEGAL DILEMMAS OF CUSTODY 44–56 (1992); Robert H. Mnookin & Lewis Kornhauser, *Bargaining in the Shadlow of the Law: The Case of Divorce*, 88 YALE L. J. 950, 963–66 (1979). Thus far researchers have failed to find any evidence of such strategic bargaining. *See, e.g.*, MACCOBY & MNOOKIN, *supra* at 154–57 (finding no relationship between parental conflict ratings and support outcomes); Marsha Garrison, *How Do Judges Decide Divorce Cases: An Empirical Analysis of Discretionary Decision Making*, 74 N.C. L. REV. 401, 461–62, 481–82, 492, 513 (1996) (finding no significant correlation between property and support awards and either case duration (an indicator of conflict level) or an unrealized custody claim by husband). *See also* Judith A. Seltzer & Irwin Garfinkel, *Inequality in Divorce Settlements: An Investigation of Property Settlements and Child Support Awards, in* CHILD SUPPORT ASSURANCE: DESIGN ISSUES, EXPECTED IMPACTS, AND POLITICAL BARRIERS AS SEEN FROM WISCONSIN 79, 105–107 (Irwin Garfinkel et al. eds., 1992) (reporting evidence of property for support trade-offs only when husband and wife had relatively equal incomes and theorizing that, in the more typical divorce negotiation characterized by income inequality, the more powerful spouse does not need to engage in strategic bargaining).

5. What if the primary caretaker parent will be placing the child in day care? In one such case, when an unmarried college student sought child support, the father countered with a custody petition. The father lived with *his* parents and argued that care by the child's grandparents

would better serve the child's interests than would day care. While the trial court granted the father custody, its order was reversed on appeal. The state supreme court affirmed the reversal:

* * *

... [W]e ... confirm that actual and proposed child-care arrangements—whether in the custodial home or elsewhere—are a proper consideration in a custody case. Many children spend a significant amount of time in such settings, and no reasonable person would doubt the importance of child-care decisions.

* * *

Having said that child-care arrangements are a proper consideration, we then encounter the issue that brought sixty-one amici curiae to the Court of Appeals (all in support of ... [the mother]): *How* are such arrangements to be considered? Does a parent seeking custody lose ground by proposing to place a child in a day-care center while the parent works or goes to school? Is in-home care from parents and other relatives better than day care with other children under the supervision of licensed care givers? Is day care better?

Such questions are not susceptible of a broad answer. Certainly, placement of a child in a good day-care setting can have many benefits and is in no sense a sign of parental neglect. Both single and married parents have many obligations, and day care generally is an entirely appropriate manner of balancing those obligations.

At the same time, it requires no stretch of imagination to produce hypothetical situations in which a parent's unwise choices in this regard would reflect poorly on the parent's judgment. More fundamentally, every child, every adult, and every custody case is unique. There can be no broad rules that dictate a preference for one manner of child care over another. The circuit court must look at each situation and determine what is in the best interests of the child. * * *

Ireland v. Smith, 451 Mich. 457, 547 N.W.2d 686 (1996).

Following the Supreme Court's decision, the parents agreed on a joint parenting schedule.

B. JOINT CUSTODY

A "joint custody" award preserves each parent's rights to make decisions regarding their child's care and may establish a residence pattern in which the child spends substantial periods of time in each parent's household. Joint custody emerged as an option during the 1970s; by the end of the 1980s, more than two-thirds of the states had statutes specifically authorizing an award of joint custody. Even without explicit statutory authorization, most courts have held that they have inherent authority to grant joint custody.

BECK v. BECK

Supreme Court of New Jersey, 1981.
86 N.J. 480, 432 A.2d 63

CLIFFORD, J.

The parties to this matrimonial action have been granted joint legal and physical custody of their two adopted female children. Although neither party requested joint custody, the trial court nevertheless found such an arrangement to be in the best interests of the children.

* * *

In recent years the concept of joint custody has become topical, due largely to the perceived inadequacies of sole custody awards and in recognition of the modern trend toward shared parenting in marriage. Sole custody tends both to isolate children from the noncustodial parent and to place heavy financial and emotional burdens on the sole caretaker, usually the mother, although awards of custody to the father, especially in households where both parents are employed outside the home, are more common now than in years past. Moreover, because of the absolute nature of sole custody determinations, in which one parent "wins" and the other "loses," the children are likely to become the subject of bitter custody contests and post-decree tension. The upshot is that the best interests of the child are disserved by many aspects of sole custody.

Joint custody attempts to solve some of the problems of sole custody by providing the child with access to both parents and granting parents equal rights and responsibilities regarding their children. Properly analyzed, joint custody is comprised of two elements—legal custody and physical custody. Under a joint custody arrangement legal custody—the legal authority and responsibility for making "major" decisions regarding the child's welfare—is shared at all times by both parents. Physical custody, the logistical arrangement whereby the parents share the companionship of the child and are responsible for "minor" day-to-day decisions, may be alternated in accordance with the needs of the parties and the children.

At the root of the joint custody arrangement is the assumption that children in a unified family setting develop attachments to both parents and the severance of either of these attachments is contrary to the child's best interest. Through its legal custody component joint custody seeks to maintain these attachments by permitting both parents to remain decision-makers in the lives of their children. Alternating physical custody enables the children to share with both parents the intimate day-to-day contact necessary to strengthen a true parent-child relationship.

Joint custody, however, is not without its critics. The objections most frequently voiced include contentions that such an arrangement creates instability for children, causes loyalty conflicts, makes maintaining parental authority difficult, and aggravates the already stressful divorce situation by requiring interaction between hostile ex-spouses. * * * Although these same problems are already present in sole custody situations, some courts have used these objectives either to reject or strictly limit the use of joint custody.

Because we are persuaded that joint custody is likely to foster the best interests of the child in the proper case, we endorse its use as an alternative to sole custody in matrimonial actions. We recognize, however, that such an arrangement will prove acceptable in only a limited class of cases.

* * *

At the conclusion of the plenary hearing the trial court reiterated its prior findings and modified its original decision. Viewing the issue in terms of the importance of fatherhood in the lives of the two girls, it concluded that the lack of real contact with the father would have negative developmental effects, particularly because the girls are adopted.

* * *

The trial court stressed that although defendant's care of the girls was more than adequate, she is limited by an inability to be both a mother and a father. It found Mrs. Beck to be a "sensible" person, but also somewhat bitter and "stiff lipped" and more partisan than plaintiff, whom he described as "a rather * * * relaxed type of man." Noting that Mrs. Beck "honestly objects to the plan because she contends she cannot cooperate with her former husband," the court concluded, based on the testimony of Dr. Greif, that an amicable relationship between the parties is "comparatively unimportant and not essential" as long as the parties "are looking out for the best interests of the children."

Referring to this state's policy of seeking maximum visitation by the non-custodial parent in sole custody cases and to N.J.S.A. § 9:2–4, which gives both parents equal rights to custody, the trial court concluded that "there is a real purpose of fatherhood as well as motherhood." Furthermore, it distinguished between custodial time and visitation, describing the former as "meaningful contact" and the latter as "entertainment time." It saw the contact and involvement of the girls with two fit, concerned parents as "going to be what's good for the girls." Finally, it reiterated that this case is uniquely suitable to joint custody and ordered that the parents share "joint control and supervision" of the children with alternating physical custody for four month periods. It also provided for counselling services for the family.

The Appellate Division reversed, ruling that Mr. Beck, as the party seeking to change the status quo, had failed to satisfy the burden of proving that "the potentiality for serious psychological harm accompanying [implementation of the plan] will not become a reality."

* * *

We find the determination of the Appellate Division to be fundamentally flawed. * * * The question of whether a trial court may make a *sua sponte* custody determination need not long detain us. The paramount consideration in child custody cases is to foster the best interests of the child. This standard has been described as one that protects the "safety, happiness, physical, mental and moral welfare of the child." It would be incongruous and counterproductive to restrict application of this standard to the relief requested by the parties to a custody dispute. Accordingly, a *sua sponte* custody determination is properly within the discretion of the trial court provided it is supported by the record. However, we emphasize again the desirability of the trial court giving the parties an opportunity to address any new issues raised by the court.

The factors to be considered by a trial court contemplating an award of joint custody require some elaboration. * * *

First, before embarking on a full-blown inquiry into the practicability of a joint custody arrangement, the court must determine whether the children have established such relationships with both parents that they would benefit from joint custody. For such bonds to exist the parents need not have been equally involved in the child rearing process. Rather, from the child's point of view it is necessary only that the child recognize both parents as sources of security and love and wish to continue both relationships.

Having established the joint custody arrangement's potential benefit to the children, the court must focus on the parents in order to determine whether they qualify for such an arrangement. At a minimum both parents must be "fit"—that is, physically and psychologically capable of fulfilling the role of parent. In addition, they must each be willing to accept custody, although their opposition to *joint* custody does not preclude the court from ordering that arrangement. Rather, even if neither parent seeks joint custody, as long as both are willing to care for the children joint custody is a possibility.

The most troublesome aspect of a joint custody decree is the additional requirement that the parent exhibit a potential for cooperation in matters of child rearing. This feature does not translate into a requirement that the parents have an amicable relationship. Although such a positive relationship is preferable, a successful joint custody arrangement requires only that the parents be able to isolate their personal conflicts from their roles as parents and that the children be spared whatever resentment and rancor the parents may harbor. Moreover, the potential for cooperation should not be assessed in the "emotional heat" of the divorce.

If the parents outside of the divorce setting, have each demonstrated that they are reasonable and are willing to give priority to the best interest of their child, then the judge need only determine if the parents can separate and put aside any conflicts between them to cooperate for the benefit of the child. The judge must look for the parents' ability to cooperate and if the potential exists, encourage its activation by instructing the parents on what is expected of them.

The necessity for at least minimal parental cooperation in a joint custody arrangement presents a thorny problem of judicial enforcement in a case such as the present one, wherein despite the trial court's determination that joint custody is in the best interests of the child, one parent (here, the mother) nevertheless contends that cooperation is impossible and refuses to abide by the decree. Traditional enforcement techniques are singularly inappropriate in a child custody proceeding for which the best interests of the child is our polestar. Despite the obvious unfairness of allowing an uncooperative parent to flout a court decree, we are unwilling to sanction punishment of a recalcitrant parent if the welfare of the child will also suffer. However, when the actions of such a parent deprive the child of the kind of relationship with the other parent that is deemed to be in the child's best interests, removing the child from the custody of the uncooperative parent may well be appropriate as a remedy of last resort. * * * Although an award of sole custody to Mr. Beck in this case may be a closer question, * * * it cannot be ruled out as a potential enforcement tool, albeit one to be considered only after all other measures have failed.

In addition to the factors set forth above, the physical custody element of a joint custody award requires examination of practical considerations such as the financial status of the parents, the proximity of their respective homes, the demands of parental employment, and the age and number of the children. Joint physical custody necessarily places an additional financial burden on the family. Although exact duplication of facilities and furnishings is not necessary, the trial court should insure that the children can be adequately cared for in two homes. The geographical proximity of the two homes is an important factor to the extent that it impinges on school arrangements, the children's access to relatives and friends (including visitation by the non-custodial parent), and the ease of travel between the two homes. Parental employment is significant for its effect on a parent's ability properly to care for the children and maintain a relationship with them. The significance of the ages and number of the children is somewhat unclear at present, and will probably vary from case to case, requiring expert testimony as to their impact on the custody arrangement.

If joint custody is feasible except for one or more of these practical considerations, the court should consider awarding legal custody to both parents with physical custody to only one and liberal visitation rights to the other. Such an award will preserve the decision-making role of both parents and should approximate, to the extent practicable, the shared companionship of the child and non-custodial that is provided in joint physical custody.

Finally, as in all custody determinations, the preference of the children of "sufficient age and capacity" must be accorded "due weight." This standard gives the trial court wide discretion regarding the probative value of a child's custody preference.

Our review of the record indicates that the trial court gave proper consideration to the preference expressed by the children, eight and ten years old at the time of trial. After interviewing them privately, the court stated for the record that the children were sincere and honest in their desire to remain with their mother. However, observing that they expressed love for both parents and wanted to continue visitation with their father, the court concluded that they had been "persuaded" to make their statements of preference and that the defendant's negative attitude toward joint custody had "consciously or unconsciously spilled over" to the children. Given this conclusion that the tender years of the children, a determination that did not fully accommodate their express wishes was not unreasonable.

Having found the decision of the trial court to be based on sufficient credible evidence, we would ordinarily reinstate it. However, in child custody cases we are always mindful that our task is to act in the best interests of the child as presently situated. Over two years have elapsed since the original decree of joint custody. Although we uphold that decree as originally made, we recognize that the facts and relationships upon which it was based may have changed dramatically. Therefore, we remand this case to the trial court for further fact-finding and a determination consonant with this opinion. We admonish the court to make a speedy but thorough investigation into the present circumstances of the parties and their children—using whatever procedural mechanism and hearing what further testimony, if any, is deemed necessary—so that this matter may be expeditiously and properly laid to rest.

The judgment of the Appellate Division is reversed and the case remanded to the trial court. We do not retain jurisdiction.

MARTHA A. FINEMAN, *DOMINANT DISCOURSE, PROFESSIONAL LANGUAGE, AND LEGAL CHANGE IN CHILD CUSTODY DECISIONMAKING*

101 HARV. L. REV. 727, 734–735, 768–769 (1988).

The helping professions' discourse has presented shared parenting as the only truly acceptable custody policy. This is because they view joint custody as the only "fair" result. Ironically, although they might question the capacity of legal processes and institutions to resolve custody disputes in accordance with this ideal, they view law itself as possessing vast power to transform people's behavior. The helping professions therefore have little hesitation in resorting to law for the implementation of their social policies.

The merits of shared parenting as a legal and social ideal have not been critically debated in political and legal forums in any meaningful way. Although there has been limited criticism of the feasibility of the ideal, these criticisms do not challenge the degree to which presumptive shared parenting actually reflects pre-or post-divorce family structures. Similarly, there has been uncritical acceptance of the empirical proposition that women and men make undifferentiated, exchangeable contributions to parenting. By focusing on the importance of the father/child relationship, the helping professions' discourse undervalues a mother's real life role, assuming it to be no different than a father's. The extreme presentation of this view is that at times a mother's "mothering" may be characterized as pathological and harmful to children. The creation of such a stereotype has gone largely unchallenged.

* * *

In focusing on ideal sex roles and equalitarian marriage, the helping professions' literature emphasized that traditional custody policy discriminated against men by unjustifiably favoring sole maternal custody. Not unlike the emerging fathers' rights discourse, their rhetoric asserted that there was no basis for maternal preference, which was grounded in the sexist assumption that men could not nurture but that women could. In real life, according to the helping profession, parents shared parenting and "parents are forever." * * * [But] [i]n most marriages, one parent, normally the mother, assumes day-to-day primary care. Shared parenting in these situations seldom means equally divided responsibility and control; typically one parent sacrifices more than the other in order to care for the child. The sense of sharing in this context is not based on the actual assumption of divided responsibilities by the parents. Rather, the shared parenting can be viewed as based on the relationship between the parents who, because of the intimacy of their situation, share the potential for jointly exercising important decisionmaking responsibility for their children. Yet an unrealistic and idealized vision of shared parenting *independent* of the relationship (or lack thereof) between parents is now imposed on couples after divorce. This vision assumes that they will work out their relationship to make shared parenting successful. It is one thing for divorcing parents voluntarily to choose the shared parenting ideal, but quite another to impose it on parents who do not or cannot live up to its demands. There may be substantial costs to treating the deviant as the norm and fashioning rights outside the context of responsibility. In the divorce context, this amounts to furthering the interests of non-caretaking fathers over the objections and, in many instances, against the interests of caretaking mothers.

Notes and Questions

1. Why, from a judge's perspective, is joint custody an attractive option? Does a joint custody award represent an abdication of judicial responsibility to determine the child's best interests?

2. *The Benefits of Joint Custody:* Researchers have reported that joint physical custody is associated with greater father contact, involvement, and payment of child support than is traditional mother custody.

See, e.g., J.A. Arditti, *Differences between Fathers with Joint Custody and Noncustodial Fathers,* 62 Am. J. Orthopsychiatry 186 (1992); M. Bowman & C.R. Ahrons, *Impact of Legal Custody Status on Fathers' Parenting Postdivorce*, 47 J. Marr. & Fam. 482 (1985); J.R. Dudley, *Exploring Ways to Get Divorced Fathers to Comply Willingly with Child Support Agreements,* 13 J. Divorce 1 (1986); Judith Seltzer, *Legal Custody Arrangements and Children's Economic Welfare*, 96 Amer. J. Sociology 895 (1991). Some studies also show that children in joint physical custody are more satisfied than those in the custody of one parent, while none demonstrates that children in joint custody are worse off. One comparative longitudinal study found that children in father-custody, mother-custody, and joint custody households "were quite similar in their self-reported levels of adjustment ... and most appeared to be functioning well within the normal range." The researchers also found that child satisfaction was highest with dual residence custodial arrangements. Eleanor E. Maccoby et al., *Postdivorce Roles of Mothers and Fathers in the Lives of Their Children*, 7 J. Fam. Psych. 24, 25–27, 34 (1993). *See also* Marsha Kline et al., *Children's Adjustment in Joint and Sole Physical Custody Families*, 23 Developmental Psych. 430 (1989) (no evidence that joint physical custody arrangements are different from sole physical custody arrangements with regard to post divorce adjustment of children).

3. *The Dangers of Joint Custody:* Joint physical custody is strongly associated with high income, education, and past cooperative parenting. Recent research suggests that the positive outcomes associated with joint custody may result, in large part, from preexisting attributes of the parents who make joint custody arrangements. When joint physical custody is imposed on unwilling parents, researchers have found that the typical results are a high level of parental conflict and a high likelihood of relitigation. The largest and most thorough evaluation of joint custody to date was conducted in California, where joint custody may be imposed. The researchers found that, among the group in which both parents had initially sought sole custody and ultimately obtained joint custody, only 6% were cooperative. By contrast, when both parents wanted joint custody, 45% were cooperative. Eleanor Maccoby & Robert Mnookin, Dividing the Child: Social and Legal Dilemmas of Custody 242–43 (1992). The researchers also found that, "[i]f parents were initially conflicted, there was little chance that they would become cooperative with time." *Id.* at 248. *See also* J.A. Arditti, *Joint and Sole Custody Mothers: Implications for Research and Practice*, 78 J. Contemporary Human Services 36 (1997) (joint physical custody associated with lower levels of custodial parental satisfaction); Susan Steinman et al., *A Study of Parents Who Sought Joint Custody Following Divorce: Who Reaches Agreement and Sustains Joint Custody and Who Returns to Court*, 24 J. Am. Acad. Child Psychiat. 545 (1985). Even the imposition of joint *legal* custody can enhance conflict and produce post-divorce relitigation; one researcher found that couples with joint legal custody relitigated custody and visitation more than twice as often as couples with sole legal

custody. Amy Koel et al., *Patterns of Relitigation in the Postdivorce Family*, 56 J. MARR. & FAM. 265, 273 tbl. 4 (1994). Even when relitigation does not occur, a substantial percentage of imposed joint custody arrangements simply break down, typically resulting in de facto mother custody. In the California study, for example, in about half of high-conflict joint physical custody cases, children in fact resided with their mother. Maccoby & Mnookin, *supra*, at 159. *See also* Carol Bohmer & Marilyn L. Ray, *Effects of Different Dispute Resolution Methods on Women and Children After Divorce*, 28 FAM. L. Q. 223 (1994) .

The California researchers also found that joint custody was often used as a means of compromise, even when parents exhibited little capacity for cooperative behavior. Indeed, the researchers found that when both parents had initially sought sole custody, the likelihood of joint custody increased along with the level of parental conflict. 36% of joint physical custody cases involved "substantial or intense legal conflict." MACCOBY & MNOOKIN, *supra*, at 150–51, tbl. 7.6 & 159. *See also* Janet R. Johnston, *High Conflict Divorce*, 4 FUTURE OF CHILDREN 165, 174 (Spring, 1994) (children who had more shared access to both parents in joint custody arrangements and those who had more frequent visitation with a noncustodial [parent] in sole custody situations were more emotionally and behaviorally disturbed).

4. All states now permit an award of joint custody, but not all favor it. *See, e.g.*, Hildebrand v. Hildebrand, 239 Neb. 605, 477 N.W.2d 1 (Neb. 1991) (court must conduct a hearing to determine if joint custody is in the best interests of the child even if parents have agreed to it). By contrast, a few states have enacted some type of presumption or preference in favor of joint physical custody. In some of these states, the presumption is a narrow one that operates only when the parents agree to joint custody. *See, e.g.*, CONN. GEN. STAT. ANN. § 46b–56a(b); CAL. FAM. CODE § 3080. In others, the preference in favor of joint custody may be overcome based on the child's best interests. *See, e.g.*, KAN. STAT. ANN. § 60–1610(a)(4)(A); MICH. COMP. LAWS ANN. § 40–4–224(1). Only Florida's presumption in favor of joint custody applies even when parents do not agree and the best interests of the child do not support joint custody. *See* FLA. STAT. ANN. § 61.13(3)(b). Florida courts, applying the test, have developed an expansive definition of joint custody and established a presumption against equal time sharing. *See* Garvie v. Garvie, 659 So.2d 394 (Fla.App.1995).

5. In most states, the trial judge may not impose joint physical custody on unwilling parents. *See* OR. REV. STAT. § 107.169(3) (joint custody prohibited "unless both parents agree to the terms and conditions of the order"); VT. STAT. ANN. tit. 15, § 665(a) (*accord*). But not all courts agree. For example, in Mosley v. Figliuzzi, 113 Nev. 51, 930 P.2d 1110 (1997), the Nevada Supreme Court upheld an intermediate appellate decision reversing the trial court's modification of a custody decree awarding the parents joint custody. The mother had sought modification based on the claim that she and the child's father were unable to

cooperate, communicate, or support each other as parents of their four year old child:

> * * * Although other reasons have been suggested by the mother in her efforts to "win" custody in this case, it is quite clear that all of her claims get down to the simple assertion that Michael's parents are at such odds with each other that the father must be cut out of the child's life. A basic question that must be answered in this case is, then, whether Michael should be denied the custodial care of one of his parents because of the parents' mutual fault in being unable to make suitable arrangements for joint physical custody.
>
> * * * The danger that arises in situations involving two, equally-competent but chronically conflicting parents is seen in cases in which a father might come in and say, in effect, "I cannot get along with the mother of my child; therefore, the court must award sole custody to me, the father." The court's accepting this kind of argument has the effect of permitting one uncooperative parent to deprive a child of either his mother or his father, merely by establishing that the parents are in conflict. Proving the existence of a conflict between parents could, thus, allow the complaining party to "win" a custody "battle." The prize should not automatically go to the parent who comes before the court and tells the court, as did the mother in this case, something to this effect: "I told the court before; we cannot get along and are not going to get along in the future—therefore, the best interests of the child requires that you give *me* the sole custody." Parental conflict almost always involves some fault on the part of each parent. To permit one non-cooperative parent to come in and get sole custody just because of a mutual conflict not only rewards uncooperative conduct but also, as said before, unnecessarily deprives the child of the company of one or the other of his or her parents.
>
> * * * What should the court do, then, when two parents want to have equal custody of their child but are unable to agree about what to do with respect to making arrangements for the equal sharing of custody? Quite obviously the courts should not grant custody to the first parent who comes in and claims that the child should be awarded to the complaining party because he or she cannot get along with the other parent.... In this kind of scenario the more aggressive and hostile parent is more likely to "win" and thus become the sole custodian of the child, while the more cooperative parent who did not have the presence of mind to seek sole custody on the ground that the parents were warring, becomes a marginal, no-real-contact parent.

See also FLA. STAT. ANN. § 61.13(3)(b) (presumption in favor of joint custody applies even when the parents do not agree). *But see* In re Marriage of McCoy, 272 Ill.App.3d 125, 208 Ill.Dec. 732, 650 N.E.2d 3 (1995) (upholding award of sole custody to mother even though parents had been using an alternate-week custody schedule for more than two years prior to award, based on mother's contention that that the father had a violent temper and that they could not agree on many child care issues).

6. What if the parents have joint custody and cannot agree on a major child care issue, such as where the child will go to school? Consider Lombardo v. Lombardo, 202 Mich.App. 151, 507 N.W.2d 788 (1993):

> Parties to a divorce judgment cannot by agreement usurp the courts authority to determine suitable provisions for the child's best interest. Similarly, the court should not relinquish its authority to determine the best interests of the child to the primary physical custodian. Accordingly, we conclude that a trial court must determine the best interests of the child in resolving disputes concerning "important decisions affecting the welfare of the child" that arise between joint custodial parents.

See also In re Marriage of Debenham, 21 Kan.App.2d 121, 896 P.2d 1098 (1995) (schools); *In re* Doe, 262 Ga. 389, 418 S.E.2d 3 (1992) (medical treatment).

Problem 13–2:

You are counsel to the state legislature's joint Committee on Family Law. The Committee has scheduled public hearings on whether current state custody standards (identical to UMDA § 402) should be revised. Various women's organizations have proposed that current law be replaced with a primary caretaker presumption; various father's groups have proposed that current law be replaced with a presumption in favor of joint custody. The chair of the Committee has suggested standards recently proposed by the American Law Institute (ALI) as a model for reform. The ALI proposal requires a court to make a custody decision based on the child's best interests, subject to certain limiting factors. Under § 2.14, the court is required to *disregard*

> 1) the race or ethnicity of a parent or of the child, except as necessary to meet the child's special needs relating to the child's race or ethnicity;
>
> 2) the sex of a parent or of the child, except as necessary to meet special developmental needs relating to the child's gender identity;
>
> 3) the religion of a parent or of the child, except to the minimum degree necessary to protect a child from manifest harm or to protect the child's ability to practice a religion to which the child has made a substantial and meaningful commitment;
>
> 4) the sexual conduct or sexual orientation of a parent, except as necessary to protect a child from demonstrated harm; and
>
> 5) the parents' relative earning capacities or financial circumstances, except insofar as the combined financial resources of the parents set practical limits on the feasible residential arrangements.

Under § 2.13, the court is required to "*limit or deny access* ... of a parent ... to the extent required to secure the safety and welfare of the child or of a child's parent," where it finds that the best interests of the child would be served by such limit or denial, in light of credible evidence that the parent to be limited

a) has abused, neglected, or abandoned a child ...

b) has inflicted domestic abuse, or allowed another to inflict domestic abuse

c) has an impairment resulting from drug, alcohol, or other substance abuse that interferes with the parent's ability to perform caretaking functions; or

d) has interfered persistently with the other parent's access to the child, except in the case of actions taken in the good faith belief that they are necessary to protect the safety of the child or the interfering parent or another family member.

Finally, the court is directed to assess the child's best interests in light of:

a) the caretaking functions each parent performed for the child before their separation or, if the child never lived with both parents, before the filing of the action;

b) the amount of residential time that will allow the child to maintain a meaningful relationship with each parent;

c) the quality of the emotional attachments of each parent to the child;

d) each parent's attitudes and abilities with respect to the child, including the ability to provide for the child's special needs;

e) the child's preference, taking into account the child's age and level of maturity and the reasonableness of the preference;

f) significant relationships of the child, including those with siblings and other relatives;

g) the proximity of the parents' residences, their schedules, and other factors relating to the child's need for stability at home, school, and in the community; and

h) the conflict level between the parents and their willingness to cooperate with one another.

In considering factors (a) through (h), the court is to "give greatest weight to factor (a), except that it shall allocate to a legal parent who has exercised a reasonable share of parenting functions for the child, sufficient residential responsibility to satisfy factor (b)." Factors (c) through (h) are not to "override factors (a) and (b) unless shown to be necessary to the child's welfare."

You have been asked to determine:

1. How, if at all, does the ALI approach differ the "traditional" best interests test? To the extent that there are differences, in what type(s) of cases would adoption of the ALI standard alter the case outcome?

2. What are the advantages and disadvantages of each approach to custody decision making?

3. Which approach is most likely to promote settlement of custody disputes?

4. Which approach is most likely to produce consistent and predictable case outcomes?

5. Which approach, on balance, is most likely to advance children's interests post-divorce?

SECTION 4. ACCESS AND VISITATION RIGHTS OF THE NONRESIDENTIAL PARENT

Most state laws provide that a nonresidential parent is entitled to continuing contact and visitation with his or her child except in unusual circumstances. UMDA § 407(a), for example, provides that "[a] parent not granted custody of the child is entitled to reasonable visitation rights unless the court finds, after a hearing, that visitation endangers seriously the child's physical, mental, moral, or emotional health."

SCHUTZ v. SCHUTZ

Supreme Court of Florida, 1991.
581 So.2d 1290.

KOGAN, JUSTICE.

* * * A final judgment dissolving the six-year marriage of petitioner, Laurel Schutz (mother) and respondent, Richard R. Schutz (father) was entered by the trial court on November 13, 1978. Although custody of the parties' minor children was originally granted to the father, the final judgment was later modified in 1979. Under the modified judgment, the mother was awarded sole custody of the children, and the father was both granted visitation rights and ordered to pay child support.

As noted by the trial court, the ongoing "acrimony and animosity between the adult parties" is clear from the record. The trial court found that in February 1981 the mother moved with the children from Miami to Georgia without notifying the father. After moving, the mother advised the father of their new address and phone number. Although the father and children corresponded after the move, he found an empty house on the three occasions when he traveled to Georgia to visit the children. The father was not notified that after only seven months in Georgia the mother and children had returned to Miami. Four years later in 1985, upon discovering the children's whereabouts, the father visited the children only to find that they "hated, despised, and feared" him due to his failure to support or visit them. After this visit, numerous motions concerning visitation, custody and support were filed by the parties.

After a final hearing on the motions, the trial court found that "the cause of the blind, brainwashed, bigoted belligerence of the children toward the father grew from the soil nurtured, watered and tilled by the mother." The court further found that "the mother breached every duty she owed as the custodial parent to the noncustodial parent of instilling love, respect and feeling in the children for their father." The trial court's findings are supported by substantial competent evidence.

Based on these findings, the trial court ordered the mother "to do everything in her power to create in the minds of [the children] a loving, caring feeling toward the father * * * [and] to convince the children that it is the mother's desire that they see their father and love their father." The court further ordered that breach of the obligation imposed "either in words, actions, demeanor, implication or otherwise" would result in the "severest penalties * * *, including contempt, imprisonment, loss of residential custody or any combination thereof."

Although the district court construed the above quoted portions of the order to require the mother to "instruct the children to love and respect their father," it concluded that she was not " 'protected' by the first amendment from a requirement that she fulfill her legal obligation to undo the harm she had already caused."

We begin our analysis by noting our agreement with the district courts of appeal that have found a custodial parent has an affirmative obligation to encourage and nurture the relationship between the child and the noncustodial parent. This duty is owed to both the noncustodial parent and the child. This obligation may be met by encouraging the child to interact with the noncustodial parent, taking good faith measures to ensure that the child visit and otherwise have frequent and continuing contact with the noncustodial parent and refraining from doing anything likely to undermine the relationship naturally fostered by such interaction.

Consistent with this obligation, we read the challenged portion of the order at issue to require nothing more of the mother than a good faith effort to take those measures necessary to restore and promote the frequent and continuing positive interaction (e.g., visitation, phone calls, letters) between the children and their father and to refrain from doing or saying anything likely to defeat that end. There is no requirement that petitioner express opinions that she does not hold, a practice disallowed by the first amendment.

Under this construction of the order, any burden on the mother's first amendment rights is merely "incidental." Therefore, the order may be sustained against a first amendment challenge if "it furthers an important or substantial governmental interest * * * and if the incidental restriction on alleged First Amendment freedoms is no greater than is essential to the furtherance of that interest." *United States v. O'Brien,* 391 U.S. 367, 377, (1968). Accordingly, we must balance the mother's right of free expression against the state's parens patriae interest in assuring the well-being of the parties' minor children. However, as with all matters involving custody of minor children, the interests of the father and of the children, which here happen to parallel those of the state, must also factor into the equation.

* * *

There is no question that the state's interest in restoring a meaningful relationship between the parties' children and their father, thereby promoting the best interests of the children, is at the very least substantial. Likewise, any restriction placed on the mother's freedom of expression is essential to the furtherance of the state's interests because affirmative measures taken by the mother to encourage meaningful interaction between the children and their father would be for naught if she were allowed to contradict those measures by word or deed.

Moreover, as evinced by this record, the mother as custodial parent has the ability to undermine the association to which both the father and the parties' children are entitled. * * * Therefore, not only is the incidental burden placed on her right of free expression essential to the furtherance of the state's interests * * * but also it is necessary to protect the rights of the children and their father to the meaningful relationship that the order seeks to restore.

Accordingly, construing the order as we do, we find no abuse of discretion by the trial court, nor impermissible burden on the petitioner's first amendment rights. Although we do not approve the district court's construction of that portion of the order under review, nor the analysis employed below, the result reached is approved.

Notes and Questions

1. Assess the likelihood that the court order requiring Mrs. Schutz "to do everything in her power to create in the minds of [the children] a loving, caring feeling toward the father * * * [and] to convince the children that it is the mother's desire that they see their father and love their father" will be effective in altering her behavior. Are there any other approaches to the problem that the court might have considered?

2. Psychoanalyst Anna Freud, law professor Joseph Goldstein, and psychiatrist Albert J. Solnit have urged that "the noncustodial parent should have no legally enforceable right to visit the child, and the custodial parent should have the right to decide whether it is desirable for the child to have such visits." JOSEPH GOLDSTEIN ET AL., THE BEST INTERESTS OF THE CHILD 24 (1996). The basis of Goldstein, Freud and Solnit's position is the view that:

> it is beyond the capacity of courts to help a child establish or maintain positive relationships to two people who are at cross-purposes with each other; ... by forcing visits, courts are more

> likely to prevent the child from developing a reliable tie to either parent; and ... children who are shaken, disoriented, and confused by the breakup of their family need an opportunity to settle down in the privacy of their reorganized family, with one person in authority upon whom they can rely for answers to their questions and for protection from external interference....
>
> A child develops best if she can trust the adults who are responsible for her to be the arbiters of her care and control as she moves toward the full independence of adulthood, and gradually comes to rely upon herself as her own caregiver. A court undermines that trust when it subjects her custodial parent to special rules about raising her by ordering (even scheduling) visits with the noncustodial parent. In the child's eyes, the court, by directing her to visit against the express wishes of her custodial parent, casts doubt on that parent's authority and capacity to parent. Particularly for the younger child, this undermines her confidence in her parent's omnipotence. It invites the older child to pit one parent against the other rather than to learn to work things out with her custodial parent. The continuity guideline means that the already-stressed relationship between child and custodial parent should not be plagued with the never-ending threat of disruption by the impersonal authority of the court.
>
> We did not and do not oppose visits. We oppose only *forced* visits—court-ordered visits. Indeed, other things being equal, courts, in order to accord with the continuity guideline, could award custody to the parent who is most willing to provide opportunities for the child to see the other parent. * * * [But v]isits that are meaningful for the child can occur only if both the custodial and the noncustodial parents are of a mind to make them work. If parents agree, a court order is both unnecessary and undesirable; if they do not agree, such an order and the threat or actual attempt to enforce it can do the child no good. The child needs a parent who can help her to resolve her wishes to see and not to see the other parent and who can help her to deal with her joys and sorrows following visits, and her hurts when the noncustodial parent refuses to maintain contact or fails to show up.

What practical problems would the Goldstein, Freud, and Solnit approach solve? What practical problems would it create? On balance, is their position persuasive? Why? For critical commentary on Goldstein, Freud, and Solnit's argument that severance of "secondary" attachments serves children's interests, *see* Peggy C. Davis, *The Good Mother: A New Look at Psychological Parent Theory*, 22 N.Y.U. Rev. Law & Soc. Change 295 (1996); Peter Strauss & M.A. Strauss, Book Review, 74 Colum. L. Rev. 968 (1974); Everett Waters & Donna M. Noyes, *Psychological Parenting vs. Attachment Theory: The Child's Best Interests and the Risks in Doing the Right Things for the Wrong Reasons*, 12 N.Y.U. Rev. L. & Soc. Change 505 (1983–84).

3. A nonresidential parent typically has a right to unrestricted visitation with the child unless his or her conduct poses a risk to the child's safety. For example, MICH. COMP. LAWS ANN. § 722.27a requires the court to consider, *inter alia,*

> (c) The reasonable likelihood of abuse or neglect of the child during parenting time.
>
> (d) The reasonable likelihood of abuse of a parent resulting from the exercise of parenting time. * * *
>
> (h) The threatened or actual detention of the child with the intent to retain or conceal the child from the other parent or from a third person who has legal custody. A custodial parent's temporary residence with the child in a domestic violence shelter shall not be construed as evidence of the custodial parent's intent to retain or conceal the child from the other parent.

See also Robert B. Straus, *Supervised Visitation and Family Violence*, 29 FAM. L.Q. 229 (1995).

4. Complete denial of visitation is rare, but does occur. For example, at the end of a highly-publicized custody trial pitting Woody Allen against Mia Farrow, the trial court denied Allen visitation with his adopted teenage son Moses (who did not want to see Allen), authorized supervised "therapeutic" sessions between Allen and his adopted daughter Dylan (who also did not want to see Allen) only after six months and only on condition that the sessions not "interfere with Dylan's individual treatment or be inconsistent with her welfare," and limited visitation with his biological son Satchel to three supervised visits lasting no more than two hours, three times a week. Throughout the litigation Allen openly maintained a sexual relationship with the children's older sister, a college student; he was also accused of sexually abusing Dylan. Although the appellate court found the evidence of sexual abuse "inconclusive," it nonetheless affirmed the trial court's order in all respects. *See* Allen v. Farrow, 197 A.D.2d 327, 611 N.Y.S.2d 859 (1994); Allen v. Farrow, 215 A.D.2d 137, 626 N.Y.S.2d 125 (1995) (upholding subsequent denial of supervised visitation with Dylan based on independent expert's view that "therapeutic visitation" was not in the child's best interests while Allen continued to maintain a sexual relationship with her sister).

MORGAN v. FORETICH

District of Columbia Court of Appeals, 1988.
546 A.2d 407.

STEADMAN, ASSOCIATE JUDGE.

The formal parties to this appeal are the divorced parents of a daughter, *H*, the ultimate real party in interest. She was born in 1982. On November 8, 1984, appellant Morgan was awarded custody of *H* and appellee Foretich was given liberal visitation. Almost continuously since that date, the parties have been in litigation on these issues, with numerous appeals to this court and two published opinions. *See Morgan v. Foretich,* 521 A.2d 248 (D.C.1987) (*Morgan I*), and 528 A.2d 425 (D.C.1987) (*Morgan II*). Now before us is an appeal from an order of August 19, 1987, granting Foretich a two-week summer visitation with *H* and a subsequent order of civil contempt and imprisonment of Morgan for refusal to comply with the August 19 order.

I.

Some of the background facts, through August of 1986, were recited in our previous opinions. In January 1985, within two months of the custody and visitation order of November 8, 1984, Morgan began to make accusations that Foretich was sexually abusing *H* during visitation. Motions were filed by both parties relating to changes in custody and visitation and with respect to evaluation of *H*. These motions were set for hearing before Judge Herbert B. Dixon in November 1985. In his order of December 27, 1985, Judge Dixon denied all these motions with the exception of a minor modification of Foretich's visitation rights.

Matters first came to a head in February 1986, when Morgan refused to allow *H* to visit Foretich in accordance with the court-ordered visitation schedule. Hearings were held in June and July of 1986 on several motions, including Foretich's motions to hold Morgan in contempt and for change of custody and Morgan's motions for temporary suspension of visitation and to compel discovery. On July 17, 1986, Judge Dixon orally announced his finding that Morgan had failed to prove by a preponderance of the evidence that Foretich had abused *H*, and that Morgan had disobeyed the visitation orders without lawful justification or excuse. A series of further hearings and orders then ensued, resulting in a finding of contempt and order of incarceration in August 1986. We stayed the order pending appeal, with various conditions including the posting of a security approved by the court in the amount of $200,000. On appeal, we upheld the closure of the contempt hearings, *Morgan I, supra*, and affirmed the judgment of contempt, *Morgan II, supra*.

Meanwhile, Judge Dixon had ordered that visitation be resumed. When Morgan again failed to comply, Judge Dixon found her in contempt and ordered her incarcerated on February 17, 1987. Morgan was released from jail on February 19, 1987, and on February 24, 1987, visitations resumed for the first time in over a year. From February 24 through April 1, 1987, the visits were supervised and lasted one hour. On April 1, Judge Dixon ordered that the visits be extended to four hours.[2]

On April 6, 1987, Judge Dixon began a series of hearings on a motion by Foretich for a change of custody and termination of Morgan's parental rights and on Morgan's cross motion to suspend visitation, or, in the alternative, to require supervised visitation. Seventeen days of

2. Though Judge Dixon entered an order for unsupervised four-hour visits, Foretich invited H's guardian ad litem to supervise the visits. All of the visits were in fact supervised by the guardian until the court expanded them to overnight visits.

hearings with numerous witnesses were held over the course of the spring and summer, ending on August 21, 1987.

During the course of the Hearings on the motions, Judge Dixon entered several orders continuing to gradually expand the visitation schedule. On April 21, 1987, he ordered the first overnight unsupervised weekend visitations. Pursuant to further orders, *H* spent nine or ten weekends with Foretich. Several emergency stays of the weekend visitation orders sought by Morgan and *H's* guardian were denied by this court. *H's* guardian played some part in most of these weekend visits and submitted reports of her observations to Judge Dixon.

Then on August 19, 1987, with the hearings still not completed, Judge Dixon entered an order providing for an extended visitation from August 22 through September 6, 1987. In his six-page order, he noted, *inter alia*, that since *H* was scheduled to return to school on September 8, "[w]hatever the court's ultimate ruling may be on the pending motions, to further delay the defendant-father's entitlement to summer visitation with his child until that ultimate ruling results in a denial of said summer visitation by default."[3]

Morgan appealed this visitation order that same day. Her emergency motion for stay pending appeal filed the following day was denied by this court on August 21. Morgan failed to comply with the visitation order. She secreted the child and refused to reveal her whereabouts. (To this day, *H* remains hidden.) On August 24, Judge Dixon issued an order to show cause why Morgan should not be held in contempt. On the same day, Morgan moved to have Judge Dixon recuse himself on the ground that he had prejudged both her credibility and the evidence on which her defense rested. She also moved to open her contempt hearing to the public, unseal the record and modify a closure order of April 13.[4]

After a hearing held on August 26, Judge Dixon held Morgan in contempt and ordered her incarcerated, effective August 28. He also ordered that the security posted one year earlier pursuant to this court's order be forfeited at the rate of $5,000 per day. On August 27, Morgan appealed the contempt judgment and sought a stay pending appeal. The stay was denied and Morgan was incarcerated on August 28, where she remains.

II.

A principal issue before us is whether the record supports the trial court's action in ordering a two-week summer visitation. Our standard of review is well-established. Trial court decisions as to visitation rights are reversible only for clear abuse of discretion. By statutory command, a trial court judgment may not be set aside except for errors of law, unless it appears the judgment is "plainly wrong or without evidence to support it." D.C. Code § 17–305(a) (1981). Thus, to the extent that such deci-

3. The order also provided for seven weekend visits during the fall months of 1987.

4. Essentially, that order restricted public disclosure of specific sex abuse allegations in this proceeding or documents, records or images concerning the same.

sions rest on factual foundations, such findings are binding unless clearly erroneous. Such is particularly the case where, as here, the findings rest in significant part on considerations of credibility.

* * *

The critical factual determination challenged by Morgan was that sexual abuse of *H* by her father had not been proven, or, as the court put it, the evidence was "in equipoise." That finding, asserts Morgan, was "plainly wrong."

As indicated in the facts recited above, this issue has been in dispute between the parties since January of 1985. As a result, a trial court file has developed in this case of a size apparently unequaled in a District of Columbia domestic relations proceeding.[5] Morgan asks that the entire record be taken into account, but in particular focuses upon the evidence presented in the 17 days of hearings between April and August of 1987. She notes, of course correctly, that our prior opinion affirming the trial court did not extend to developments subsequent to August 1986.

A review of the record shows that there was probative evidence on both sides of the issue of abuse. The ultimate question, however, is not how we weigh the evidence but rather whether a finder of fact, fully and personally knowledgeable of not only the evidence presented in the April to August hearings but also the entire history of these proceedings from November 1985 forward,[6] would be clearly erroneous in concluding that the alleged sexual abuse had not been proven and would commit a clear abuse of discretion in allowing a two-week visitation. We cannot so conclude.

It is important to keep in mind the posture of the case at the time of the challenged order. The underlying matters before the court were Foretich's motion for change of custody and Morgan's cross-motion to suspend visitation. Evidentiary hearings on those motions were coming to a close. So was the summer, with *H* scheduled to return to school in early September. *H's* relationship with her father, interrupted for over a year by Morgan on grounds found baseless at the time, had been resuming on a gradual basis. The court was satisfied that any prospect of physical or emotional harm beyond that already caused by the litigation was effectively neutralized.[7] With the ultimate issue still open, the court was dealing with the reality that a child's life was moving on.

In this litigation, neither party can conclusively speak for *H*. She has her own champion, a court-appointed guardian. Although the guardian

5. The proceedings in 1985, 1986, and 1987 consist of some 4,000 pages of transcript with approximately 75 witnesses, according to Morgan's own brief.

6. At one point in the proceedings, Judge Dixon observed that with one more change of attorneys, he, the trial judge, would be the longest participant in the litigation short of the parties themselves.

7. The court cited its continuous availability for emergency hearings, Morgan's right to reasonable telephone contact with the child during visitation, monitoring of the visitation by the guardian, and the presence of Foretich's parents or his wife with the child during visitation.

states that she is in clear disagreement with the trial court's order for the extended summer visitation, we think correct her assessment that she "cannot argue that the order was without evidence to support it or an abuse of Judge Dixon's discretion."

III.

Morgan raises four other issues in this appeal. Only one, the challenge to the forfeiture of the posted security, reveals reversible error. See Part IV, *infra*.

1. *Defense of necessity.* Criminal law recognizes the doctrine that an otherwise criminal act is excused "if the harm that would have resulted from compliance with the law would have significantly exceeded the harm actually resulting from the defendants' breach of the law." * * *

In any event, the situation here is far different from that facing one who violates a criminal law. Here there was a specific court order, requiring specific conduct tailored to a specific fact situation—an order which we on appeal had refused to stay. Civil contempt could become meaningless if a lawful defense could rest on the ground that a party took a different view, however, reasonable, of the potential harm in compliance.[8] To the extent that noncompliance may be justified as preserving the opportunity for appellate review, the defier acts at his or her peril in so doing. * * *

2. *Trial judge disqualification.* Subsequent to the entry of the two-week visitation order but prior to the contempt proceeding, Morgan moved to have Judge Dixon recuse himself. This motion was denied. Morgan argues that constitutionally she was entitled to an impartial judge, an argument not in dispute. What is in dispute here is whether she was denied such a judge. Normally, bias must stem from an extrajudicial source, although an extreme manifestation of bias during trial can result in disqualification. We think any such allegation here is without foundation. Morgan points to rulings by the trial court refusing to permit participation in the contempt hearing by an out-of-state member (new to the case) of the major law firm representing her, and to rulings excluding evidence. These may or may not be errors of law, but they hardly constitute strong evidence of bias. No trial court conduct could survive such a test. * * *

3. *Public trial on contempt charges.* A good portion of the proceedings on August 26, the hearing on the contempt show cause order, was open to the public. The hearing was closed only for the segment of Morgan's testimony when she insisted upon reciting allegations as to specific acts of sexual abuse upon *H.* She argues that this limited closure violated her First and Fifth Amendment rights to an open hearing. In so

8. The same may be said of Morgan's argument that the Parental Kidnapping Prevention Act recognizes a defense if the action "is taken to protect the child from imminent physical harm." D.C. Code § 16–1023(a)(1) (1987 Supp.).

doing, she invites us essentially to revisit the issues decided in our prior Morgan opinions. This we decline to do. * * *

IV.

In addition to the civil incarceration of Morgan, the trial court's written order of August 27, 1987 provided:

> That the plaintiff's $200,000.00 bond previously posted following this Court's order of August 5, 1986, shall be and hereby is forfeited at the rate of $5,000.00 per day, excluding Saturdays, Sundays and legal holidays, until the minor child has been taken into the custody of this Court and made available to the defendant for visitation and for placement in accordance with the further order of this Court.

Morgan asserts that the trial court lacked authority to impose this specific condition. We agree.

* * *

V.

A Kikuyu proverb tells us: "When elephants fight it is the grass that suffers." Here, the grass is a little girl who will be six years old this month. For almost a year, she has been deprived of the company of both father and mother. She is the principal figure in a drama of appalling proportions, no matter what the outcome.

The trial court here, as in many family division matters, has the deeply taxing and unenviable responsibility of struggling to deal justly with changing lives. Inherent in the process are new developments and events. One such development occurred at oral argument before us. In her brief to us, Morgan urged, as a "wiser and fairer" alternative, the appointment of a multidisciplinary team of neutral experts to evaluate *H's* case and to recommend an appropriate visitation schedule. The guardian from an early point in her service has consistently championed this step. In our order of May 29, 1987, we expressed our confidence that the trial court would consider the use of a court-appointed expert. Now, before us in oral argument, Foretich announced that he no longer opposed the creation of such a team.

We take no firm position on this alternative or other surfacing issues not yet the subject of an appeal. But time moves on as the impasse continues. Morgan cites to us cases for the proposition that when civil coercion fails to serve its coercive purpose, a contemnor must be released, an argument to be first addressed to the trial court. The long-term custody and visitation questions remain unresolved, apparently in suspension pending the outcome of this appeal and perhaps other matters. The trial court faces the completion of findings on difficult factual issues, which may include a determination of the causes and extent of any physical or emotional stresses borne by *H*. The now lengthy rupture in the gradually increasing visitations of *H* and her father, the apparent object of the trial court's 1987 rulings, seems to change the practical picture facing the court. The Fourth Circuit has recently handed down a decision in a related jury trial proceeding between the parties in the Virginia federal courts holding that the district court had erroneously refused to admit certain evidence probative of possible abuse by Foretich both of *H* and of another daughter. *Morgan v. Foretich*, 846 F.2d 941 (4th Cir.1988). The relevance if any, of that decision and of the other matters mentioned above to further proceedings in the case in our jurisdiction, including a possible reopening of hearings, remains for consideration by the trial court.

Probably neither our courts nor any courts anywhere in the world can deal in a perfect way with matters so intimately linked to a family unit formed and dissolved. We can but try. The little girl *H* grows older day by day. It is she, first and foremost, to whom the courts must seek to render justice as the process moves on.

That portion of the order below forfeiting Morgan's security is reversed. In all other respects, the orders appealed from are affirmed.

Notes and Questions

1. The principal case may be the most extreme visitation dispute ever litigated. By December, 1988, when Dr. Morgan had been jailed for 16 months, she obtained a release through an act of Congress. Following her release, she went to New Zealand to join her daughter. (In 1988, New Zealand had not adopted the Hague Convention.) She remained in New Zealand with her daughter through 1997.

2. A court will rarely hold a custodial parent in contempt of court for failure to permit visitation when the visitation order fails to specify the amount or times of visitation. *See* Ex Parte Brister, 801 S.W.2d 833 (Tex.1990).

3. Can a child be held in contempt? In *In re* Marriage of Marshall, 278 Ill.App.3d 1071, 215 Ill.Dec. 599, 663 N.E.2d 1113 (1996), an Illinois court held two children in civil contempt for refusing to go to North Carolina to visit their father. One of the daughters had testified that she was afraid of her father and that the father said bad things about the mother and her mother's family. The appellate court held that the trial judge had authority to hold the children in contempt:

> In the presence of the trial judge, Heidi and Rachel admitted that they had previously refused to comply with the visitation order and then refused again to comply. Accordingly, they were properly held in direct contempt and dealt with summarily.... [But] we find it necessary to reverse the sanctions imposed and remand this cause for further proceedings.
>
> * * *
>
> Commitment of a minor constitutes a substantial abridgment of personal liberty.

After finding Heidi and Rachel to be in direct civil contempt, the trial judge did not indicate that he considered less restrictive alternatives that might have resulted in visitation. Since the purpose of a civil contempt proceeding is to compel prospective compliance for the benefit of a party to the litigation, a judge should consider all reasonable alternatives for enforcing visitation rights. Such alternatives are not necessarily limited to the contempt proceedings against the minors.

For instance, one possible alternative is contempt proceedings against the custodial parent. * * * If Kathy [the mother] has failed to comply with her duties under the visitation order, the judge could sanction her appropriately. Indeed, the judge may utilize a range of options to compel compliance with the visitation order. The determination as to which alternatives would be appropriate and efficacious is best left to the discretion of the trial court. We merely direct that applicable alternatives should be considered before incarcerating a minor for failing to comply with a visitation order. * * *

4. A parent may typically request injunctive relief to prevent threatened or actual noncompliance with a court order mandating visitation. Some states will also permit the award of money damages based on noncompliance with a visitation directive. *See* ALASKA STAT. § 25.24.300; COLO. REV. STAT. ANN. § 14–10–129.5. Depending on state law, the aggrieved parent may also seek an order requiring: posting of a bond by the custodial parent, compensatory visitation time, modification of the support order, and/or modification of the custody award. Tort or criminal relief may be available as well. A few states have adopted expedited procedures which permit a parent denied visitation an inexpensive and quick means of getting into court. *See* KAN. STAT. ANN. § 23–701.

SECTION 5. CUSTODY DISPUTES BETWEEN A PARENT AND NONPARENT

The United States Supreme Court has long recognized that the "custody, care and nurture of the child reside first in the parents." Prince v. Massachusetts, 321 U.S. 158, 166, 64 S.Ct. 438, 88 L.Ed. 645 (1944); *accord*, Meyer v. Nebraska, 262 U.S. 390, 43 S.Ct. 625, 67 L.Ed. 1042 (1923) (the rights "to marry, establish a home and bring up children" are among "those privileges long recognized at common law as essential to the orderly pursuit of happiness by free men.").

Custody law has traditionally followed the *Prince* approach. State courts have often held that a parent may not be deprived of custody without a showing of abandonment or unfitness. *See, e.g.,* Nielsen v. Nielsen, 207 Neb. 141, 296 N.W.2d 483, 488 (1980); Sheppard v. Sheppard, 230 Kan. 146, 630 P.2d 1121, 1127 (1981), *cert. denied* 455 U.S. 919, 102 S.Ct. 1274, 71 L.Ed.2d 459 (1982).

In recent years, however, this traditional emphasis on parental rights has begun to give way; in a custody contest between parent and nonparent, some courts now apply standards that place more emphasis on the interests of the child and less on the rights of the parent.

PAINTER v. BANNISTER

Supreme Court of Iowa, 1966.
258 Iowa 1390, 140 N.W.2d 152, cert. denied 385 U.S. 949, 87 S.Ct. 317, 17 L.Ed.2d 227 (1966).

STUART, J.

We are here setting the course for Mark Wendell Painter's future. Our decision on the custody of this 7 year old boy will have a marked influence on his whole life. The fact that we are called upon many times a year to determine custody matters does not make the exercising of this awesome responsibility any less difficult. Legal training and experience are of little practical help in solving the complex problems of human relations. However, these problems do arise and under our system of government, the burden of rendering a final decision rests upon us. It is frustrating to know we can only resolve, not solve, these unfortunate situations.

The custody dispute before us in this habeas corpus action is between the father, Harold Painter, and the maternal grandparents, Dwight and Margaret Bannister. Mark's mother and younger sister were killed in an automobile accident on December 6, 1962 near Pullman, Washington. The father, after other arrangements for Mark's care had proved unsatisfactory, asked the Bannisters, to take care of Mark. They went to California and brought Mark to their farm home near Ames in July, 1963. Mr. Painter remarried in November, 1964 and about that time indicated he wanted to take Mark back. The Bannisters refused to let him leave and his action was filed in June, 1965. Since July 1965 he has continued to remain in the Bannister home under an order of this court staying execution of the judgment of the trial court awarding custody to the father until the matter could be determined on appeal. For reasons hereinafter stated, we conclude Mark's better interests will be served if he remains with the Bannisters.

Mark's parents came from highly contrasting backgrounds. His mother was born, raised and educated in Rural Iowa. Her parents are college graduates. Her father is agricultural information editor for the Iowa State University Extension Service. The Bannister home is in the Gilbert Community and is well kept, roomy and comfortable. The Bannisters has served on the school board and regularly teaches a Sunday school class at the Gilbert Congregational Church. Mark's mother graduated from Grinnell College. She then went to work for a newspaper in Anchorage, Alaska, where she met Harold Painter.

Mark's father was born in California. When he was 2 1/2 years old, his parents were divorced and he was placed in a foster home. Although he has kept in contact with his natural parents, he considers his foster parents, the McNelly's as his family. He flunked out of a high school and a trade school because of a lack of interest in academic subjects, rather than any lack of ability. He joined the navy at 17. He did not like it. After receiving an honorable discharge, he took examinations and obtained his high school diploma. He lived with the McNelly's and went to college for 2 1/2 years under the G.I. bill. He quit college to take a job on a small newspaper in Ephrata, Washington in November 1955. In May 1956, he went to work for the newspaper in Anchorage which employed Jeanne Bannister.

Harold and Jeanne were married in April, 1957. Although there is a conflict in the evidence on the point, we are convinced the marriage, overall, was a happy one with many ups and downs as could be expected in the uniting of two such opposites.

We are not confronted with a situation where one of the contesting parties is not a fit or proper person. There is no criticism of either the Bannisters or their home. There is no suggestion in the record that Mr. Painter is morally unfit. It is obvious the Bannisters did not approve of their daughter's marriage to Harold Painter and do not want their grandchild raised under his guidance. The philosophies of life are entirely different. As stated by the psychiatrist who examine Mr. Painter at the request of Bannisters' attorneys: "It is evident that there exists a large difference in ways of life and value systems between the Bannisters and Mr. Painter, but in this case, there is no evidence that psychiatric instability is involved. Rather, these divergent life patterns seem to represent alternative normal adaptations."

It is not our prerogative to determine custody upon our choice of one of two ways of life within normal and proper limits and we will not do so. However, the philosophies are important as they relate to Mark and his particular needs.

The Bannister home provides Mark with a stable, dependable, conventional, middle-class, middlewest background and an opportunity for a college education and profession, if he desires it. It provides a solid foundation and secure atmosphere. In the Painter home, Mark would have more freedom of conduct and thought with an opportunity to develop his individual talents. It would be more exciting and challenging in many respects, but romantic, impractical and unstable.

Little additional recitation of evidence is necessary to support our evaluation of the Bannister home. It might be pointed out, however, that Jeanne's three sisters also received college educations and seem to be happily married to college graduates.

Our conclusion as to the type of home Mr. Painter would offer is based upon his Bohemian approach to finances and life in general. We feel there is much evidence which supports this conclusion. His main ambition is to be a free lance writer and photographer. He has had some articles and picture stories published, but the income from these efforts has been negligible. At the time of the accident, Jeanne was willingly working to support the family so Harold could devote more time to his writing and photography. In the 10 years since he left college, he has changed jobs seven times. He was asked to leave two of them; two he quit because he didn't like the work; two because he wanted to devote more time to writing and the rest for better pay. He was contemplating a move to Berkeley at the time of trial. His attitude toward his career is typified by his own comments concerning a job offer:

> "About the Portland news job, I hope you understand when I say it took guts not to take it; I had to get behind myself and push. It was very, very tempting to accept a good salary and settle down to a steady, easy routine. I approached Portland, with the intention of taking the job, I began to ask what, in the long run, would be the good of this job: 1, it was not *really* what I wanted; 2, Portland is just another big farm town, with none of the stimulation it takes to get my mind sparking. Anyway, I decided Mark and myself would be better off if I went ahead with what I've started and the hell with the rest, sink, swim or starve."

There is general agreement that Mr. Painter needs help with his finances. Both Jeanne and Marilyn, his present wife, handled most of them. Purchases and sales of books, boats, photographic equipment and houses indicate poor financial judgment and an easy come easy go attitude. He dissipated his wife's estate of about $4300, most of which was a gift from her parents and which she had hoped would be used for the children's education.

The psychiatrist classifies him as "a romantic and somewhat of a dreamer." An apt example are the plans he related for himself and Mark in February 1963: "My thought now is to settle Mark and myself in Sausilito, near San Francisco; this is a retreat for wealthy artists, writers, and such aspiring artists and writers as can fork up the rent money. My plan is to do expensive portraits ($150 and up), sell prints ($15 and up) to the tourists who flock in from all over the world * * *."

The house in which Mr. Painter and his present wife live, compared with the well kept Bannister home, exemplifies the contrasting ways of life. In his words "it is a very old and beat up and lovely home * * *". They live in the rear part. The interior is inexpensively but tastefully decorated. The large yard on a hill in the business district of Walnut Creek, California, is of uncut weeds and wild oats. The house "is not painted on the outside because I do not want it painted. I am very fond of the wood on the outside of the house."

The present Mrs. Painter has her master's degree in cinema design and apparently likes and has had considerable contact with children. She is anxious to have Mark in her home. Everything indicates she would provide a leveling influence on Mr. Painter and could ably care for Mark.

Mr. Painter is either an agnostic or atheist and has no concern for formal religious training. He has read a lot of Zen Buddhism and "has been very much influenced by it." Mrs. Painter is Roman Catholic. They plan to send Mark to a Congregational Church near the Catholic Church, on an irregular schedule.

He is a political liberal and got into difficulty in a job at the University of Washington for his support of the activities of the American Civil Liberties Union in the university news bulletin.

There were "two funerals" for his wife. One in the basement of his home in which he alone was present. He conducted the service and wrote her a long letter. The second at a church in Pullman was for the gratification of her friends. He attended in a sport shirt and sweater.

These matters are not related as a criticism of Mr. Painter's conduct, way of life or sense of values. An individual is free to choose his own values, within bounds, which are not exceeded here. They do serve, however, to support our conclusion as to the kind of life Mark would be exposed to in the Painter household. We believe it would be unstable, unconventional, arty, Bohemian, and probably intellectually stimulating.

Were the question simply which household would be the most suitable in which to raise a child, we would have unhesitatingly chosen the Bannister home. We believe security and stability in the home are more important than intellectual stimulation in the proper development of a child. There are, however, several factors which have made us pause.

First, there is the presumption of parental preference, which though weakened in the past several years, exists by statute. We have a great deal of sympathy for a father, who in the difficult period of adjustment following his wife's death, turns to the maternal grandparents for their help and then finds them unwilling to return the child. There is no merit in the Bannister claim that Mr. Painter permanently relinquished custody. It was intended to be a temporary arrangement. A father should be encouraged to look for help with the children, from those who love them without the risk of thereby losing the custody of the children permanently. This fact must receive consideration in cases of this kind. However, as always, the primary consideration is the best interest of the child and if the return of custody to the father is likely to have a seriously disrupting and disturbing effect upon the child's development, this fact must prevail. * * *

Second, Jeanne's will named her husband guardian of her children and if he failed to qualify or ceased to act, named her mother. The parent's wishes are entitled to consideration.

Third, the Bannisters are 60 years old. By the time Mark graduates from high school they will be over 70 years old. Care of young children is a strain on grandparents and Mrs. Bannister's letters indicate as much.

We have considered all of these factors and have concluded that Mark's best interest demands that his custody remain with the Bannisters. Mark was five when he came to their home. The evidence clearly shows he was not well adjusted at that time. He did not distinguish fact from fiction and was inclined to tell "tall tales" emphasizing the big "I". He was very aggressive toward smaller children, cruel to animals, not liked by his classmates and did not seem to know what was acceptable conduct. As stated by one witness: "Mark knew where his freedom was and he didn't know where his boundaries were." In two years he made a great deal of improvement. He now appears to be well disciplined, happy, relatively secure and popular with his classmates, although still subject to more than normal anxiety.

We place a great deal of reliance on the testimony of Dr. Glenn R. Hawks, a child psychologist. The trial court, in effect, disregarded Dr. Hawks' opinions stating: "The court has given full consideration to the good doctor's testimony, but cannot accept it at full face value because of exaggerated statements and the witness' attitude on the stand." We, of course, do not have the advantage of viewing the witness' conduct on the stand, but we have carefully reviewed his testimony and find nothing in the written record to justify such a summary dismissal of the opinions of this eminent child psychologist.

Dr. Hawks is head of the Department of Child Development at Iowa State University. However, there is nothing in the record which suggests that his relationship with the Bannisters is such that his professional opinion would be influenced thereby. Child development is his specialty and he has written many articles and a textbook on the subject. He is recognized nationally, having served on the staff of the 1960 White House Conference on Children and Youth and as consultant on a Ford Foundation program concerning youth in India. He is now education consultant on the project "Head Start". He has taught and lectured at many universities and belongs to many professional associations. He works with the Iowa Children's Home Society in placement problems. Further detailing of his qualifications is unnecessary.

Between June 15th and the time of trial, he spent approximately 25 hours acquiring information about Mark and the Bannisters, including appropriate testing of and "depth interviews" with Mark. Dr. Hawks' testimony covers 70 pages of the record and it is difficult to pinpoint any bit of testimony which precisely summarizes his opinion. He places great emphasis on the "father figure" and discounts the importance of the "biological father." "The father figure is a figure that the child sees as an authority figure, as a helper, he is a nutrient figure, and one who typifies maleness and stands as maleness as far as the child is concerned."

His investigation revealed: " * * * the strength of the father figure before Mark came to the Bannisters is very unclear. Mark is confused about the father figure prior to his contact with Mr. Bannister." Now, "Mark used Mr. Bannister as his father figure. This is very evident. It shows up in the depth interview, and it shows up in the description of Mark's life given by Mark. He has a very warm feeling for Mr. Bannister."

Dr. Hawks concluded that it was not for Mark's best interest to be removed from the Bannister home. He is criticized for reaching this conclusion without investigating the Painted home or finding out more about Mr. Painter's character. He answered:

"I was most concerned about the welfare of the child, not the welfare of Mr. Painter, not about the welfare of the Bannisters. In as much as Mark has already made an adjustment and sees the Bannisters as his parental figures in his psychological makeup. to me this is the most critical factor. Disruption at this point, I think, would be detrimental to the child even tho Mr. Painter might well be a paragon of virtue. I think this would be a kind of thing which would not be in the best interest of the child. I think knowing something about where the child is at the present time is vital. I think something about where he might go, in my way of thinking is essentially untenable to me, and relatively unimportant. It isn't even helpful. The thing I was most concerned about was Mark's view of his own reality in which he presently lives. If this is destroyed I think it will have rather bad effects on Mark. I think then if one were to make a determination whether it would be to the parents' household, or the McNelly household, or X-household, then I think the further study would be appropriate."

Dr. Hawks stated: "I am appalled at the tremendous task Mr. Painter would have if Mark were to return to him because he has got to build the relationship from scratch. There is essentially nothing on which to build at the present time. Mark is aware Mr. Painter is his father, but he is not very clear about what this means. In his own mind the father figure is Mr. Bannister. I think it would take a very strong person with everything in his favor in order to build a relationship as Mr. Painter would have to build at this point with Mark."

It was Dr. Hawks' opinion "the chances are very high (Mark) will go wrong if he is returned to his father." This is based on adoption studies which "establish that the majority of adoptions in children who are changed, from ages six to eight will go bad, if they have had a prior history of instability, some history of prior movement. When I refer to instability I am referring to where there has been no attempt to establish a strong relationship." Although this is not an adoption, the analogy seems appropriate, for Mark who had a history of instability would be removed from the only home in which he has a clearly established "father figure" and placed with his natural father about whom his feelings are unclear.

We know more of Mr. Painter's way of life than Dr. Hawks. We have concluded that it does not offer as great a stability or security as the Bannister home. Throughout his testimony he emphasized Mark's need at this critical time is stability. He has it in the Bannister home.

Other items of Dr. Hawks' testimony which have a bearing on our decision follow. He did not consider the Bannisters' age any way disqualifying. He was of the opinion that Mark could adjust to a change more easily later on, if one became necessary, when he would have better control over his environment.

He believes the presence of other children in the home would have a detrimental effect upon Mark's adjustment whether this occurred in the Bannister home or the Painter home.

The trial court does not say which of Dr. Hawks' statements he felt were exaggerated. We were most surprised at the inconsequential position to which he relegated the "biological father." He concedes "child psychologists are less concerned about natural parents than probably other professional groups are." We are not inclined to so lightly value the role of the natural father, but find much reason for his evaluation of this particular case.

Mark has established a father-son relationship with Mr. Bannister, which he apparently had never had with his natural father. He is happy, well adjusted and progressing nicely in his development. We do not believe it is for Mark's best interest to take him out of this stable atmosphere in the face of warnings of dire consequences from an eminent child psychologist and send him to an uncertain future in his father's home. Regardless of our appreciation of the father's love for his child and his desire to have him with him, we do not believe we have the moral right to gamble with this child's future. He should be encouraged in every way possible to know his father. We are sure there are many ways in which Mr. Painter can enrich Mark's life.

For the reasons stated, we reverse the trial court and remand the case for judgment in accordance herewith. * * *

Notes and Questions

1. Two years after the *Painter* opinion was issued (and following publication of a book by Mark's father entitled, MARK, I LOVE YOU),the grandparents allowed Mark to visit his father in California. The father obtained a California custody order in his favor. Mark wanted to stay with his father and the Bannisters did not appeal the order. *See* CIVIL LIBERTIES No. 258, October 1968, page 12, col. 3. (Had the PKPA been in effect, could Mr. Painter have obtained a custody order in California?)

2. *When Does a Nonparent Have Standing to Petition for Custody?* The first issue a court must address in considering a custody petition by a nonparent is whether the nonparent claimant has standing to bring an action. UMDA § 401(d)(2) gives nonparents standing to file a petition for custody only when the child is not in the physical custody of a parent. Many other states have statutes with similar requirements. (The Bannisters would, of course, have met the UMDA requirement.) In recent years, some legislatures have enacted more liberal standing rules. HAW. REV. STAT. § 571–46(2), for example, authorizes a custody award "to persons other than the father or mother whenever the award serves the best interests of the child." *See also* OR. REV. STAT. § 109.119 (person who has established emotional ties creating a parent-child relationship based on having had physical custody of a child or residing in the same household within the six months preceding filing of action has standing).

Some courts have adopted a liberal approach even without statutory authority. *See, e.g.*, Henrikson v. Gable, 162 Mich.App. 248, 412 N.W.2d 702 (1987); J.A.L. v. E.P.H., 453 Pa.Super. 78, 682 A.2d 1314 (1996); McDonald v. Wrigley, 870 P.2d 777 (Okl.1994). *See generally* Barbara L. Shapiro, *Nontraditional Families in the Courts: The New Extended Family*, J. AMER. ACAD. MATRIMONIAL LAWYERS 117 (1993).

Courts have divided on whether a gay "co-parent" who lived with a child and shared parenting functions with his or her gay partner should have standing to petition for custody or visitation after separation from the partner-parent. Cases holding that the co-parent has no standing include Alison D. v. Virginia M., 77 N.Y.2d 651, 569 N.Y.S.2d 586, 572 N.E.2d 27 (1991); McGuffin v. Overton, 214 Mich.App. 95, 542 N.W.2d 288 (1995) and Nancy S. v. Michele G., 228 Cal.App.3d 831, 279 Cal. Rptr. 212 (1991). Cases holding that a coparent may have standing include In re Custody of H.S.H.-K., 193 Wis.2d 649, 533 N.W.2d 419 (1995); J.A.L. v. E.P.H., 453 Pa.Super. 78, 682 A.2d 1314 (1996); and A.C. v. C.B., 113 N.M. 581, 829 P.2d 660 (N.M.App.1992).

3. *What Custody Standard Should Apply?* There is no consensus on the correct standard to apply in a custody contest between a parent and nonparent. Many states maintain the traditional parental preference rule, under which a nonparent may not be awarded custody unless the parent is unfit or unable to care for the child. *See, e.g.*, McDonald v. Wrigley, 870 P.2d 777 (Okla. 1994) (third parties must show parental unfitness by clear and conclusive evidence to obtain custody). A few states vary the traditional parental presumption by additionally permitting an award of custody to a nonparent in "extraordinary circumstances." *See, e.g.*, Bennett v. Jeffreys, 40 N.Y.2d 543, 387 N.Y.S.2d 821, 356 N.E.2d 277 (1976); Locklin v. Duka, 112 Nev. 1489, 929 P.2d 930 (1996). A larger group of states vary the parental preference by applying the best interests standard when the child has been in the custody of a nonparent and that individual wants to retain custody. *See, e.g.*, Zack v. Fiebert, 235 N.J.Super. 424, 563 A.2d 58 (1989); In re Custody of C.C.R.S., 892 P.2d 246 (Colo.1995). Some states have now abandoned the parental preference rule altogether. In most of these states, the nonparent must make a stronger evidentiary showing to obtain custody than would be required under the best interests test. In California, for example, a nonparent may obtain custody based on finding that "granting custody to a parent would be detrimental to the child and . . . granting custody to the nonparent is required to serve the best interests of the child." CAL. FAM. CODE § 3041. Finally, a very small number of states apply the best interests test in all disputes between a parent and nonparent. Hawaii is perhaps the clearest example. *See, e.g.*, HAW. REV. STAT. § 571–46(2) (custody may be awarded to persons other than a parent whenever the award serves the best interests of the child).

4. The movement away from the parental preference rule reflects a trend toward a functional view of parenthood. Many commentators (and courts) now view a child's "psychological parent" as equally, if not more, deserving of protection than a legal parent. The term "psychological

parent" was coined by Joseph Goldstein, Anna Freud, and Albert Solnit, who defined the psychological parent as the adult "who, on a continuing, day-to-day basis, through interaction, companionship, interplay, and mutuality, fulfills the child's psychological needs for a parent, as well as the child's physical needs." JOSEPH GOLDSTEIN, ET AL, BEYOND THE BEST INTERESTS OF THE CHILD 98 (1973). While Goldstein, Freud, and Solnit's proposals regarding parental visitation rights (p. 684, note 2) have had no discernable effect on statutory standards or case law, their emphasis on a relational, rather than status-based, approach to custody disputes has had a profound and long-lasting impact. Oregon's statute governing standing in a custody dispute, for example, defines a "child-parent relationship" by paraphrasing Goldstein, Freud, and Solnit. Under the statutory standard, a child-parent relationship is one existing "within the six months preceding the filing of an action ... and in which relationship a person having physical custody of a child or residing in the same household as the child supplied ... food, clothing, shelter, ... and provided the child with necessary care, education and discipline, and which relationship continued on a day-to-day basis, through interaction, companionship, interplay and mutuality, that fulfilled the child's psychological needs for a parent as well as the child's physical needs." OR. REV. STAT. § 109.119. Commentary on custody disputes between parent and nonparent relying, at least in part, on the concept of psychological parenting includes Carolyn Wilkes Kaas, *Breaking Up a Family or Putting It Back Together Again: Refining the Preference in Favor of the Parent in Third-Party Custody Cases,* 37 WM. & MARY L. REV. 1045 (1996) (suggesting that when the child has lived with a nonparent for a substantial period of time, the psychological needs of the child are paramount); Nancy D. Polikoff, *This Child Does Have Two Mothers: Redefining Parenthood to Meet the Needs of Children in Lesbian-Mother and Other Nontraditional Families*, 78 GEO. L. J. 459 (1990) (arguing in favor of a functional definition of parenthood); Katharine T. Bartlett, *Rethinking Parenthood as an Exclusive Status: The Need for Legal Alternatives When the Premise of the Nuclear Family Has Failed,* 70 VA. L. REV. (1984).

5. In writing about *Painter*, Anna Freud provides some sense of how an emphasis on psychological parenting would alter traditional custody adjudication:

> In disagreement with the trial judge and in agreement with his expert Dr. Hawks, we discount the importance of the "biological father" as such.... Psychologically speaking, the child's "father" is the adult man to whom the child attaches a particular, psychologically distinctive set of feelings. When this type of emotional tie is disrupted, the child's feelings suffer. When such separations occur during phases of development in which the child is particularly vulnerable, the whole foundation of his personality may be shaken ...
>
> We place less emphasis than Mr. Justice Stuart on benefits such as a "stable dependable background" with educational and profes-

sional opportunities. Important as such external advantages are, we have seen too often that they can be wasted unless they are accompanied by the internal emotional constellations which enable the children to profit from them . . .

It is not possible at this point to foretell whether, after investigation, our advice will be in line with the judgement of the trial court or with Mr. Justice Stuart. What can be promised is that it will be based not on external facts but on internal data. We shall advise that Mark had better stay with his grandparents provided that the following facts can be ascertained:

> that the transfer of his attachment from the parents to the grandparents is fairly complete and promises to be permanent during his childhood; . . . that, given this new attachment, a further change is not advisable . . . ; that the grandparents cherish Mark for his own sake, not only as a replacement for the daughter who was killed, nor as a pawn in the battle with their son-in-law.

Conversely, we shall advise that Mark had better be returned to his father if the following facts emerge:

> that Mr. Painter still retains his place as "father "in Mark's mind and that in spite of separation and new experiences the child's feelings and fantasies continue to revolve around him; that anger about the "desertion" and perhaps blame for the mother's death have not succeeded in turning this relationship into a predominantly hostile one; that the father cherishes Mark for his own sake; that it can be shown that Mr. Painter's using the child for publicity purposes was not due to lack of paternal consideration on his part but happened owing to the bitterness and resentment caused by the fight for possession of his son.

Provided that Mr. Painter, Mr. and Mrs. Bannister, and Mark would allow the clinic two or three weeks' time for investigation, I am confident that we should be able to guide them toward a potentially helpful solution of their difficult problem.

Anna Freud, *Painter v. Bannister: Postscript by a Psychoanalyst*, 7 WRITINGS OF ANNA FREUD 250–55 (1966–70).

6. Some commentators have seen *Painter* as an example of the ease with which the best interests standard can be manipulated to emphasize the personal values of the trial judge. Does application of the psychological parenting concept substantially reduce the risk that a parent will be denied custody of his child because his household is " . . . unconventional, arty, Bohemian, and probably intellectually stimulating" or in some other way offensive to the judge?

Problem 13–3:

Usha K. was born in India. She is an only child whose father died when she was 12. When she was 14 years old she began working full time and attended secretarial school at night so that she might eventually earn enough money to come to this country for a college education. She arrived in the United States at the age of eighteen and began to study agriculture and nutrition. Two years later she obtained an associate degree from the State University system. That same year her mother died in India.

While in New York Usha met an Indian student who apparently agreed to marry her; but when she later became pregnant, he deserted her. She dropped out of school and gave birth to her daughter, Sanjivini. Unwed and temporarily unable to support the child, she agreed to place her in the custody of the Department of Social Services. She refused, however, to surrender the child for adoption and would only consent to temporary foster care. After the child's birth, Usha obtained a job to reimburse the department for medical expenses and to contribute to the support of her daughter. When Sanjivini was about eighteen months old, Usha returned to school after reimbursing the department $800 for her medical expenses. With the aid of a scholarship and part-time employment, she attended a university in Maryland and then in North Carolina, which apparently were the only schools within her means which offered the necessary courses. She still continued to visit her child when able, generally once every two or three months. When her education was completed she returned to New York. At that point Sanjivini was four years old and had lived with her foster parents for two years. Usha requested help from the Department in finding employment; she also asked for the return of her child. The agency worker assigned to the case furnished Usha with the names and addresses of two potential employers selected from the telephone book but did nothing more even though Usha informed her that she had already been denied employment at those locations. She also refused to return Sanjivini in view of Usha's "current financial and residential instability." Because of her immigrant status, Usha was unable to obtain employment in Rockland County where Sanjivini lived. Finally she obtained clerical employment in New York City. She contributed monthly to the child's support and once every other week travelled from New York City to Rockland County to visit the girl. But the Department refused to give her Sanjivini. Instead, when Sanjivini was seven, it filed a petition to award permanent custody to the foster parents, who had by then cared for the child for five years. In its petition, the Department alleged that "while the mother was furthering her own education, the child still needed parents. Mr. and Mrs. Ames [the foster parents] have fulfilled that role and are the child's psychological parents. To return Sanjivini to her mother at this point would pose grave risks to her psychological development." State case law permits an award of custody to a nonparent in a case of parental unfitness, abandonment, or "extraordinary circumstances." What arguments would you make on behalf of Usha K.? the State and Mr. and Mrs. Ames? If you were the judge assigned to the case, what decision would you make and how would you justify it? *See* In re Sanjivini K., 47 N.Y.2d 374, 418

N.Y.S.2d 339, 391 N.E.2d 1316 (1979); Bessette v. Saratoga County Comm'r, 209 A.D.2d 838, 619 N.Y.S.2d 359, 359 (1994).

SECTION 6. NONPARENTAL VISITATION RIGHTS

BEAGLE v. BEAGLE

Supreme Court of Florida, 1996.
678 So.2d 1271.

OVERTON, JUSTICE.

We have for review *Beagle v. Beagle,* 654 So.2d 1260 (Fla. 1st DCA 1995), concerning the sensitive family law issue of grandparental visitation rights. Specifically, we address only the 1993 amendment to § 752.01 of the Florida Statutes. Prior to such modification, the statute at issue allowed the award of grandparental visitation in four other distinct family situations. The constitutionality of those four paragraphs is not at issue in this proceeding. We limit our holding to only those situations in which a child is living with both natural parents, at least one natural parent objects to grandparental visitation, and so relevant matters are pending in the court system. *See* § 752.01(1)(e), Fla. Stat. (1995). In such cases, we find that a judge cannot impose grandparental visitation upon an intact family. We emphasize that our determination today is not a comment on the desirability of interaction between grandparents and their grandchildren. We focus exclusively on whether it is proper for the government, in the absence of a demonstrated harm to the child, to force such interaction against the express wishes of at least one parent in an intact family.

The relevant paragraph is challenged as violative of the privacy guarantees in both the Florida Constitution and the United States Constitution.

* * *

For a full understanding of the challenged paragraph, we set forth subsection one in its entirety with the challenged paragraph underlined.

> (1) The court shall, upon petition filed by a grandparent of a minor child, award reasonable visitation rights of visitation to the grandparent with respect to the child when it is in the best interest of the minor child if:
>
> (a) One or both parents of the child are deceased;
>
> (b) The marriage of the parents of the child has been dissolved;
>
> (c) A parent of the child has deserted the child;
>
> (d) The minor child was born out of wedlock and not later determined to be a child born within wedlock as provided in § 742.091; or

(e) The minor is living with both natural parents who are still married to each other whether or not there is a broken relationship between either or both parents of the minor child and the grandparents, and either or both parents have used their parental authority to prohibit a relationship between the minor child and the grandparents.

§ 752.01(1), Fla. Stat. (1995) (emphasis added).

FACTS

The facts in this case are simple. Roy and Sharron Beagle (the grandparents) filed a petition in the trial court for visitation rights with their granddaughter, Amber Beagle (the child). Dewey and Melissa Beagle (the parents) opposed the award of visitation rights and moved to dismiss the grandparents' petition. At the time of the grandparents' petition, the parents were living together with the child as an intact family. The trial court granted the parents' motion to dismiss, finding that § 752.01(1)(e) violated the parents' right to privacy under article I, § 23, of the Florida Constitution. The district court of appeal reversed.

* * *

OTHER JURISDICTIONS

At the outset, it must be acknowledged that Florida is not the only jurisdiction in which the issue of grandparental visitation rights has been contested. To the contrary, there are divergent views in other jurisdictions as to whether the government can constitutionally infringe upon the rights of parents to raise their children. For instance, in *Brooks v. Parkerson,* 265 Ga. 189, 454 S.E.2d 769, cert. denied, ___ U.S. ___, 116 S.Ct. 377 (1995), the Georgia Supreme Court found that the Georgia Grandparent Visitation Statute was unconstitutional under both the Georgia and federal constitutions. It reasoned that the state cannot interfere with "parental rights to custody and control of children" except in cases where the "health or welfare of a child is threatened." Id. at 773. It then concluded that "even assuming grandparent visitation promotes the health and welfare of the child, the state may only impose that visitation over the parents' objections on a showing that failing to do so would be harmful to the child." Id. The Supreme Court of Tennessee has also addressed this issue in *Hawk v. Hawk,* 855 S.W.2d 573 (Tenn.1993). It found that the Grandparents' Visitation Act was unconstitutional under the Tennessee Constitution. It stated:

> We find, however, that without a substantial danger of harm to the child, a court may not constitutionally impose its own subjective notions of the "best interests of the child" when an intact, nuclear family with fit, married parents is involved.

Id. at 579. It then ruled that "neither the legislature nor a court may properly intervene in parenting decisions absent significant harm to the child from those decisions." *Id.* at 581. The Tennessee high court concluded that a showing of harm must precede any award of grandparental visitation rights. Neither Georgia nor Tennessee have an express right of privacy in their state constitutions.

On the other hand, the Supreme Court of Wyoming, in *Michael v. Hertzler,* 900 P.2d 1144 (Wy.1995), held that a "compelling state interest exists in maintaining the right of association of grandparents and grandchildren." Id. at 1151. While holding that the Wyoming grandparental visitation statute was constitutional, it expressly noted that the statute only applied in situations of divorce, death, or extended residence with a grandparent. Unlike the instant case, the Wyoming statute made no provision for grandparental visitation rights in an intact family. Further, the Supreme Court of Missouri, in *Herndon v. Tuhey,* 857 S.W.2d 203 (Mo.1993), has ruled that its grandparental visitation statute is constitutional under the United States Constitution. The Missouri statute requires a showing that grandparental visitation is in the best interest of the child. Other states have also approved grandparental visitation statutes. In those cases a best interest standard was deemed to be sufficient.

FLORIDA

These cases from other jurisdictions illustrate the constitutional issues created when the government provides for grandparental visitation rights. This issue arises as a result of sociological changes occurring in this country. Our families are increasingly dispersed nationwide. In times past, both the elders and peers within a community could effectuate the internal resolution of this type of dispute. Now, however, there are fewer such natural mechanisms with which to resolve these conflicts. Consequently, governments step in and attempt to establish a process by which to settle these disagreements. The extent to which the government should be involved in settling disputes within the family is a relatively new question in the law. There are, though, certain established principles. We have stated that "this Court and others have recognized a longstanding and fundamental liberty interest of parents in determining the care and upbringing of their children free from the heavy hand of government paternalism." The fundamental liberty interest in parenting is protected by both the Florida and federal constitutions. In Florida, it is specifically protected by our privacy provision. Certainly the imposition, by the State, of grandparental visitation rights implicates the privacy rights of the Florida Constitution. All of the parties concede that a privacy analysis under our constitutional provision is required.

On November 4, 1980, the citizens of Florida amended the Florida Constitution by approving the addition of a strong privacy provision. The specific language of the privacy amendment is as follows:

> Every natural person has the right to be let alone and free from government intrusion into his private life except as otherwise provided herein. This section shall not be construed to limit the public's right of access to public records and meetings as provided by law.

Art. I, § 23, Fla. Const. Only Alaska, California, Florida, Hawaii, and Montana have specifically, through distinct provisions, guaranteed the right to privacy in their state constitutions. In Florida, we have found that our constitutional privacy provision is a guarantee of greater protection than is afforded by the federal constitution.

* * *

With this foundation, we address a very narrow question. Does the State have a compelling state interest in imposing grandparental visitation rights, in an intact family, over the objection of at least one parent? We find that the challenged paragraph, as currently written, does not demonstrate such a compelling state interest. Our standard is stringent. We have previously held that the statute requiring parental consent prior to an abortion did not satisfy the compelling state interest standard. On the other hand, we have approved State interference with the fundamental right of parents to raise their children where the State is acting to protect the children from harm. For example, we have allowed the State to terminate parental rights where a substantial risk of significant harm to a child exists. We have also recognized that the State has a compelling interest in preventing the sexual exploitation of children within the home. Our cases have made it abundantly clear that the State can satisfy the compelling state interest standard when it acts to prevent demonstrable harm to a child.

The challenged paragraph does not require the State to demonstrate a harm to the child prior to the award of grandparental visitation rights. Based upon the privacy provision in the Florida Constitution, we hold that the State may not intrude upon the parents' fundamental right to raise their children except in cases where the child is threatened with harm. While it may be argued that harm or detriment is always an element of a best interest analysis, we must join our sister courts in Tennessee and Georgia in ruling that a best interest test without an explicit requirement of harm cannot pass constitutional muster in this specific context. * * *

We emphasize again that our holding in this case is not intended to change the law in other areas of family law where the best interest of the child is utilized to make a judicial determination. In issuing this decision, we have no intent to disrupt or modify the current requirements for best interest balancing in those other areas of family law proceedings.

Finally, it is not our judicial role to comment on the general wisdom of maintaining intergenerational relationships. We must refrain from expressing our personal thoughts as either grandparents or future grandparents. Instead, we only address whether the State may constitutionally impose grandparental visitation upon an intact family after at least one parent has objected to such visitation. We find that it cannot without first demonstrating a harm to the child.

Notes and Questions

1. Virtually all states have statutes under which grandparents may obtain visitation rights in at least some circumstances; the most com-

monly specified circumstances are a parental divorce, death, or steppar-ent adoption. Many of these statutes date to the 1960s and 70s; they reflect both an increase in the divorce rate and the number of elderly Americans. *See* Elaine D. Ingulli, *Grandparent Visitation Rights: Social Policies and Legal Rights*, 87 W. VA. L. REV. 295 (1985); Richard Victor, Michael Robbins & Scott Bassett, *Statutory Review of Third Party Rights Regarding Custody, Visitation, and Support*, 25 FAM. L.Q. 19 (1991). In explaining the rationale for grandparent visitation, the New Jersey Supreme Court noted that:

> ... It is common human experience that the concern and interest grandparents take in the welfare of their grandchildren far exceeds anything explicable in purely biological terms. A very special relationship often arises and continues between grandparents and grandchildren. The tensions and conflicts which commonly mar relations between parents and children are often absent between those very same parents and their grandchildren. Visits with a grandparent are often a precious part of a child's experience and there are benefits which devolve upon the grandchild from the relationship with his grandparents which he cannot derive from any other relationship. Neither the Legislature nor this Court is blind to human truths which grandparents and grandchildren have always known.
>
> "In view of this, we can only say that it is proper that in the unfortunate case of parental separation or death, grandparents should sometimes have privileges of visitation even over the objections of the adoptive parents. It is not only the ordinary devotion to the grandchild that merits the grandparent's continued right to be with him, but also the fact that in such cases, the continuous love and attention of a grandparent may mitigate the feelings of guilt or rejection, which a child may feel at the death of or separation from a parent, and ease the painful transition."
>
> Mimkon v. Ford, 66 N.J. 426, 332 A.2d 199 (1975).

3. As the *Beagle* court notes, courts have divided on the constitutionality of grandparent visitation in the context of an intact parental household. If the *Beagle* court is correct that grandparent visitation over the objections of parents in an *intact* household constitutes an unconstitutional intrusion upon privacy interests and parental prerogatives, why isn't grandparent visitation over the objections of *separated* parents also unconstitutional? How, if at all, are the privacy interests and parental prerogatives of separated parents different from those of parents in intact families? How, if at all, are the state's and child's interests affected by parental separation? *See* Maner v. Stephenson, 342 Md. 461, 677 A.2d 560 (Md.App.1996).

4. How should a grandparent visitation statute respond to these fact patterns:

a) a father who has lost custody of his children concurs with the children's mother that the paternal grandparents should not visit the children.

b) a father and mother with joint custody concur that grandparents should not visit the children.

c) the parent (and child of the petitioning grandparents) has been deprived of access to the child because of past physical abuse.

d) the grandparents are divorced and *both* want visitation.

Should grandparents be allowed to intervene in a divorce action or should they be required to bring a separate action? Should they have standing to initiate a modification of custody proceeding? *See In re* Marriage of Mitchell, 531 N.W.2d 132 (Iowa 1995).

5. *Stepparent Visitation Rights:* While the common law did not recognize a right to stepparent visitation (any more than it did grandparent visitation), occasionally courts allowed a stepparent visitation where he or she had acted in loco parentis. Today, with 35 million stepparents in the United States, the law is changing. Many states now have statutes which permit stepparent visitation. *See, e.g.,* CAL. FAM. CODE § 3101 (authorizing "reasonable visitation to a stepparent" when "in the best interest of the minor child"). Even in states where there is no such statutory authorization, some courts have granted stepparents visitation based on their inherent equitable powers. *See* Carter v. Brodrick, 644 P.2d 850 (Alaska 1982); Caban v. Healey, 634 N.E.2d 540 (Ind.App. 1994); Evans v. Evans, 302 Md. 334, 488 A.2d 157 (1985); Gribble v. Gribble, 583 P.2d 64 (Utah 1978).

6. *Visitation by Cohabitants and Other Caregivers:* Courts and legislatures have been less receptive to the visitation claims of both heterosexual and homosexual cohabitants. Most courts have denied visitation petitions by cohabitants. *See, e.g.,* Cooper v. Merkel, 470 N.W.2d 253 (S.D.1991) (denying visitation rights to mother's ex-boyfriend who had acted as a father figure and assumed a major role in raising child for seven years); Alison D. v. Virginia M., 77 N.Y.2d 651, 569 N.Y.S.2d 586, 572 N.E.2d 27 (1991) (denying visitation petition of lesbian coparent). Hughes v. Creighton, 165 Ariz. 265, 798 P.2d 403 (Ariz.App.1990); In re Marriage of Gayden, 229 Cal.App.3d 1510, 280 Cal.Rptr. 862 (1991). But, again, the case law is far from uniform, and some courts have permitted visitation by cohabitants under at least some circumstances. *See, e.g.,* Holtzman v. Knott, 193 Wis.2d 649, 533 N.W.2d 419 (1995) ("court has equitable power to hear a petition for visitation when it determines that the petitioner has a parent-like relationship with the child and that a significant triggering event justifies state intervention in the child's relationship with a biological or adoptive parent.") And some state visitation statutes broadly permit visitation petitions by a broad range of persons. *See, e.g.,* CONN. GEN. STAT. § 46b–59 (visitation may be granted to "any person" in accordance with the best interests of the child); ALASKA STAT. § 25.24.250(a) (visitation may be

granted "grandparent or other person if that is in the best interests of the child").

7. Should a child be able to obtain visitation with a sibling or half-sibling? *See* Ken R. ex rel. v. Arthur Z., 546 Pa. 49, 682 A.2d 1267 (1996). A great-grandparent? *See* David M. v. Lisa M., 207 A.D.2d 623, 615 N.Y.S.2d 783 (1994).

Problem 13–4:

Mary married John when her daughter Sara was a year old. For the following year, John played a large role in Sara's daily life, although her biological father, Tom, exercised regular visitation. Shortly after Sara turned two, Mary left John and moved in with Ron, whom she plans to marry after her divorce from John is final. John has petitioned for visitation rights with Sara. Both Mary and Tom oppose his petition; Mary also claims that John is really only interested in maintaining contact with her. The state's nonparent visitation standard is identical to that enunciated by the court in *Holtzman* (note 6). Under the *Holtzman* standard, what facts will be relevant? If John were to obtain visitation rights and Mary marries and later divorces Ron, should Ron also be entitled to visitation with Sara? *See* Klipstein v. Zalewski, 230 N.J.Super. 567, 553 A.2d 1384 (1988).

Problem 13–5:

In 1985, Christine Titchenal and Diane Dexter began an intimate relationship. They purchased a home together, held joint bank accounts, and jointly owned their automobiles. They both contributed financially to their household, and each regarded the other as a life partner. They also decided to have a child together. When their attempts to conceive via a sperm donor failed, they decided to adopt a child. In July 1991, Diane adopted a newborn baby girl, who was named Sarah Ruth Dexter–Titchenal. Christine and Diane described themselves to Sarah and all others as her parents. The child called one parent "Mama Chris" and the other parent "Mama Di." For the first three and one-half years of Sarah's life, Christine cared for the child approximately 65% of the time. Christine did not seek to adopt Sarah because the parties believed that the then-current adoption statute would not allow her to do so. In November 1994, Diane moved out of the couple's home, taking Sarah with her. For the first five months following separation, Sarah stayed with Christine between Wednesday afternoons and Friday evenings. By the spring of 1995, however, Diane had severely curtailed plaintiff's contact with Sarah and had refused her offer of financial assistance; Christine filed a petition for visitation. The state has a grandparent visitation statute, but no other statutory authority for nonparental visitation. The courts have construed the grandparent visitation provision narrowly, but has construed both the adoption and divorce laws quite expansively. *See, e.g.*, In re B.L.V.B., 160 Vt. 368, 628 A.2d 1271 (1993) (construing adoption statute to permit adoption by same-sex partner); Paquette v. Paquette, 146 Vt. 83, 499 A.2d 23 (1985) (construing divorce and separation statutes to empower court to award custody of child to stepparent when circumstances warrant). What arguments would you make on behalf of Christine? Diane? If you were the judge assigned to the case, what decision would you make and how would you justify it? *See* Titchenal v. Dexter, 693 A.2d 682 (Vt.1997).

Problem 13–6:

After Amanda married Doris' son John, Doris began to care for Amanda's baby Christopher (Amanda's son from a prior relationship) while Amanda was at work; typically Doris cared for Christopher between 8:00 a.m. and 6:00 p.m. on weekdays. When Amanda and John had their own child, Jill, Doris continued to care for them both. When Christopher was about four years old, John and Amanda separated. Thereafter, Amanda found other child care arrangements and refused to permit Doris to visit with either Jill or Christopher. State law authorizes a grandparent to petition for visitation "following the death or divorce of the grandparent's child who has given birth to the child who is the subject of the petition." Doris seeks visitation with both Jill and Christopher. What arguments would you make on behalf of Doris? Amanda? If you were the judge assigned to the case, what decision would you make and how would you justify it? *See* In re Hood, 252 Kan. 689, 847 P.2d 1300 (1993).

SECTION 7. MODIFYING A CUSTODY ORDER

Because of the need to protect the best interests of a child, custody and visitation orders are subject to modification throughout the child's minority. But because stability and finality are also important values in child custody litigation, most states permit modification only when there has been a substantial change of circumstances since the original custody and visitation decree. In evaluating whether such a change has occurred, courts typically look at events occurring after the decree was entered and which were unanticipated by the parties. *See, e.g.*, Lizzio v. Jackson, 226 A.D.2d 760, 640 N.Y.S.2d 330 (1996) (asthmatic son's allergy to mother's smoking was not a change of circumstances because mother smoked before the divorce). *But see* In re Marriage of Kiister, 245 Kan. App.2d 199, 777 P.2d 272 (1989) (*all* evidence on the welfare of the child, whether predecree or not, can be considered because child's welfare is paramount); K.J.B. v. C.M.B., 779 S.W.2d 36 (Mo.App.1989) (father's predissolution abusive conduct toward the children was not known to the court at the time of the original custody decree so could be considered in modification).

In a number of states, even a substantial change in circumstances will not provide a basis for modification if a petition is brought too quickly after entry of the original custody decree. In these states, a petitioner for modification within a statutorily specified time period must meet more demanding criteria. Most of these statutory time limits on modification are for one or two years following the last custody order.

See, e.g., DEL. CODE ANN. tit. 13, § 729(c) (two years); MINN. STAT. ANN. § 518.18(a),(b) (one year after order, or within two years from disposition of prior motion).

If the proposed modification would entail a change in physical custody of the child, some states require more than a showing of a substantial change in circumstances. The UMDA § 409(b), for example, specifies that such a modification is permissible only when: (1) the current custodian agrees to the modification; (2) the child has been integrated into the family of the petitioner with consent of the custodial; or (3) the child's present environment seriously endangers his physical, mental, moral, or emotional health, and the harm likely to be caused by a change of environment is outweighed by its advantages.

Some jurisdictions also require less than a showing of a substantial change in circumstances in some cases. In some states, a joint custody order may be modified more easily than a sole custody order. *See, e.g.*, WIS. STAT. ANN. § 767.325(2) (restrictions on modification do not apply when parents have substantially equal physical custody); OKLA. STAT. ANN. tit. 43, § 109(F) (joint custody order modifiable under best interests test). Some states also permit easier modification of an order based on an agreement of the parties. *See, e.g.*, DEL. CODE ANN. tit.13, § 729. And a few jurisdictions do not require a change of circumstances in any modification context. *See, e.g.*, CONN. GEN. STAT. ANN. § 46b–56(b); NEV. REV. STAT. ANN. § 125.510.

A substantial change in circumstances or other threshold showing must typically be established by a preponderance of the evidence before the court will consider whether modification would serve the child's best interests. As the court noted in Wagner v. Wagner, 109 Md.App. 1, 674 A.2d 1 (1996):

> A change of custody resolution is most often a chronological two-step process. First, unless a material change of circumstances if found to exist, the court's inquiry ceases. In this context, the term "material" relates to a change that may affect the welfare of a child. Moreover, the circumstances to which change would apply would be the circumstances known to the trial court when it rendered the prior order. If the actual circumstances extant at that time were not known to the court because evidence relating thereto was not available to the court, then the additional evidence of actual (but previously unknown) circumstances might also be applicable in respect to a court's determination of change. If a material change of circumstance is found to exist, then the court, in resolving the custody issue, considers the best interest of the child as if it were an original custody proceeding. Certainly, the very factors that indicate that a material change in circumstances has occurred may also be extremely relevant at the second phase of the inquiry—that is, in reference to the best interest of the child. If not relevant to the best interest of the child, the changes would not be material in the first instance. Because of the frequency with which it occurs, this two-

step process is sometimes considered concurrently, in one step, i.e., the change in circumstances evidence also satisfies—or does not—the determination of what is in the best interest of the child. Even if it alone does not satisfy the best interest standard, it almost certainly will afford evidentiary support in the resolution of the second step. Thus, both steps may be, and often are, resolved simultaneously.

While a "substantial" or "material" change in circumstances is difficult to define or quantify, courts will ordinarily look for a change that is ongoing and which significantly affects the welfare of the child. For example, a father who alleged in his affidavit that the mother had changed residence several times, was on welfare, and had exposed the children to physically and sexually abusive relationships met his burden of showing a substantial change in circumstances and was permitted to proceed. *In re* Marriage of Morazan, 237 Mont. 294, 772 P.2d 872 (1989). A number of courts have held that significant interference with parental visitation constitutes a substantial change in circumstances. In Ready v. Ready, 906 P.2d 382 (Wyo.1995), for example, the appellate court held that the trial judge had not abused his discretion by modifying a custody decree that awarded sole custody of four children to the mother where the mother had repeatedly violated the visitation order and been found in contempt. The court found that the mother's repeated failure to abide by the district court's orders was a matter which was not foreseen when drafting the original decree and was a sufficient change of circumstances, warranting the trial court's substitution of the father as the custodial parent. *See also* KAN. STAT. ANN. § 60–1616(e) ("Repeated unreasonable denial of or interference with visitation rights granted to a parent ... may be considered a material change of circumstances which justifies modification of a prior order of child custody.")

Many requests for modification arise when one parent wishes to move. In the five-year period from 1985 to 1990, almost half of U.S. residents changed their address. Over 40% who moved went to a different county; half of these moved across state lines. U.S. DEPT. OF COMMERCE, BUREAU OF THE CENSUS, 1990 CENSUS OF POPULATION, GEOGRAPHIC MOBILITY, COMMUTING AND VETERAN STATUS 18 (1993). Families that have experienced divorce move at an even higher rate; one researcher found that almost 40% of divorced mothers moved in the first year after divorce. Even after the first year, divorced women continued to move at a rate of about 20% a year, a rate about a third higher than that of women in intact marriages. Most of these moves resulted from necessity rather than choice, especially in the immediate aftermath of divorce. *See* Sara S. McLanahan, *Family Structure and Stress: A Longitudinal Comparison of Two–Parent and Female–Headed Families*, J. MARRIAGE & FAM. 347 (1984).

LEVINE v. BACON

New Jersey Superior Court, 1997.
297 N.J.Super. 224, 687 A.2d 1057, 1065–66.

MICHELS, P.J.A.D.

[Father, who had primary residential custody of his six year old daughter, remarried, sold his business with a noncompetition clause, and wanted to relocate to Florida for employment and his new wife's health.]

* * * Due to the work demands of Mr. Bacon and the school schedule of Savannah as well as the financial cost of travel, Jessica would lose most of the benefits of the current arrangement, including her relationship with her mother and her sister.

A move to Florida would also adversely affect the defendant's involvement and participation in the critical decisions regarding Jessica. This problem is of great concern to the Court, especially in light of Dr. Orlosky's statement that Jessica has benefitted by the parents' sharing in her development[al] years.

The fact that the plaintiff has already begun to disregard the defendant in several important decisions regarding Jessica is critical in this regard. Such conduct on the part of the plaintiff cannot be expected to improve if the plaintiff and Jessica are separated from the defendant by a distance of 1,500 miles.

The Court must also consider whether the move will adversely affect the visitation rights of the non-custodial parent. At the present time, the defendant visits Jessica two weekends in a row and the Thursday before and after the third weekend, which is the father's weekend. The defendant has the child two weeks a year for vacation, as well as Christmas, Easter, Mother's Day, and alternate holidays.

Under the present arrangement, the visitation is frequent. In place of the current arrangement, the plaintiff proposes the following schedule: Two weeks in July, two weeks in August, one week at Christmas, one week at Easter, and two other trips during the year. When one compares this schedule with the present schedule, it is apparent that the proposed schedule trades their frequency of contact now enjoyed by the defendant and Jessica for the possibility for the mother and daughter sharing larger blocks of time. Other than July and August, however, the rest of the year will be marked by an absence of personal visits for periods of up to two months.

The obvious problem with the proposed schedule is that the personal contact between parent and child and sister and sister will be lost and with that loss most assuredly will come the loss of the current positive relationship between the mother and daughter.

There are additional problems with the proposed schedule as well. The defendant will be unable to afford the cost of the frequent trips to and from Florida, even if she were permitted to use the child support arrearages for the cost of the trips. If, as suggested by the plaintiff, the arrearages were used to purchase the airline tickets, this would only cover the cost of the flights for the first year and, as the plaintiff admitted in his testimony, he is not sure how the defendant would afford the cost of travel if the air fare increased significantly.

There are also time constraints on the defendant and the demands of her new family, including her new daughter, which would make it impossible for her to be able to exercise her visitation during the blocks of time suggested by the plaintiff.

In addition to the foregoing, however, the Court must also consider whether the non-custodial parent could relocate as a means of ensuring the custody arrangement.

In the instant case, the defendant's current husband is a maintenance man at an apartment complex. As part of his consideration, he receives the apartment in which he lives. He also works part time at a local health food store to supplement his income. He made a review of employment advertisements for similar jobs in Florida and was unable to find any positions which offered a residence as part of the consideration.

Under these circumstances, the Court is unable to conclude that a move to Florida by the defendant and her new family is a valid alternative.

For the foregoing reasons the Court finds that although the plaintiff has advanced a good faith reason for the requested move to Florida, the move would not be in the best interest of the child and cannot be accomplished without a significant adverse effect on the defendant's visitation with the child.

Notes and Questions

1. Won't any move have an adverse effect on visitation arrangements between the nonresidential parent and the child? If the court had found a move to be in Jessica's best interests, could (should) the court order the moving parent to pay for the other parent's increased visitation expenses?

2. The states have not reached consensus on the correct approach in a parental relocation case.

a. *Does Parental Relocation Constitute a Substantial Change in Circumstances?* Some jurisdictions treat the relocation of a custodial parent as a substantial change of circumstances warranting reevaluation of the current custody/visitation arrangement. *See, e.g.,* KAN. STAT. ANN. § 60–1620(c); MO. ANN. STAT. § 452.411; Hornbeck v. Hornbeck, 702 P.2d 42 (Okl.1985) (relocation is material change in circumstances if it effectively deprives one parent of visitation). Other courts do not treat relocation as a per se basis for a best interests reexamination of the custody decree. *See, e.g.,* Taylor v. Taylor, 849 S.W.2d 319 (Tenn.1993).

b. *What Standard Must the Relocating Parent Meet to Obtain Permission to Take the Child?* Not only have numerous standards been applied to this issue, but

> "[t]his area of law has been unusually unstable, with some states having recently undergone rather significant shifts in their standards. The clear trend has been that of increasing leniency toward the parent with whom the child has been primarily living. One reason for this trend may be the frustration some appellate courts have experienced with the restrictive way courts have applied prior law."
>
> American Law Institute, Principles of the Law of Family Dissolution § 2.20 Comment d. (Preliminary Draft No. 7 vol. 2, June 9, 1997) (describing standard shifts in some states and variation across states).

The most liberal approach allows the custodial parent and child to move unless the motives for moving are vindictive. *See* Aaby v. Strange, 924 S.W.2d 623 (Tenn.1996). Other states follow the approach of *Levine* and require the relocating parent to establish that the move is in the child's best interests. *See* Pollock v. Pollock, 181 Ariz. 275, 889 P.2d 633 (Ariz.App.1995). For many years New York had the strictest requirements; it required a showing of "exceptional circumstances" necessitating the move and that the move was in the child's best interests. Weiss v. Weiss, 52 N.Y.2d 170, 436 N.Y.S.2d 862, 418 N.E.2d 377 (1981). Using this test, New York courts denied custodial parents permission to move to escape physical abuse by an ex-spouse (Coniglio v. Coniglio, 170 A.D.2d 477, 565 N.Y.S.2d 834 (1991)), to follow a new spouse who had been temporarily transferred by his employer to a different country (Daghir v. Daghir, 56 N.Y.2d 938, 453 N.Y.S.2d 609, 439 N.E.2d 324 (1982)), and in a range of other circumstances. But, in Tropea v. Tropea, 87 N.Y.2d 727, 642 N.Y.S.2d 575, 665 N.E.2d 145 (1996), the New York Court of Appeals abandoned this approach in favor of a standard requiring that "all the relevant facts and circumstances" be balanced. For commentary favoring liberal relocation rules, *see* Carol S. Bruch & Janet M. Bowermaster, *The Relocation of Children and Custodial Parents: Public Policy, Past and Present,* 30 Fam. L. Q. 245 (1996); Anne L. Spitzer, *Moving and Storage of Post-divorce Children: Relocation, the Constitution and the Court*, 1985 Ariz. St. L.J. 1. Commentary favoring stricter standards includes Frank G. Adams, *Child Custody and Parent Relocations: Loving Your Children from a Distance*, 33 Duq. L. Rev. 143 (1994); Meril Sobie, *Whatever Happened to the "Best Interests" Analysis in New York Relocation Cases? A Response*, 15 Pace L. Rev. 685 (1995).

What are the advantages of a liberal approach to relocation? a strict approach? On balance, what approach seems best?

3. *The Right to Travel:* At least one court has held that protection of the custodial parent's constitutionally protected right to travel requires a standard that does not place the burden of proof on the custodial parent. *See, e.g.,* Jaramillo v. Jaramillo, 113 N.M. 57, 823 P.2d

299 (1991). Most courts have rejected the right to travel analysis on the basis that it is custodial status that is at issue rather than freedom to travel. The Indiana Court of Appeals, for example, noted that: "The straightforward answer to [the wife's constitutional] argument is that the court's order does not impose any necessary burden whatever upon *her* right to travel. She remains free to go wherever she may choose. It is the children who must be returned to Indiana." Clark v. Atkins, 489 N.E.2d 90, 100 (Ind.App.1986). Other courts have found that "furtherance of the best interests of a child, by assuring the maximum opportunities for the love, guidance and support of both natural parents, may constitute a compelling state interest worthy of reasonable interference with the right to travel interstate." *In re* Marriage of Cole, 224 Mont. 207, 729 P.2d 1276 (1986).

4. Does a child's newly formed preference to live with the other parent constitute a substantial change of circumstances? What about the child's maturation? A significant increase or decrease in parental income? Remarriage of one or both parents? The birth of additional children? *See* Walker v. Chatfield, 553 N.E.2d 490 (Ind.App.1990) ("mere changes that occur as life goes on do not, standing alone, justify a modification of custody").

Chapter 14

PROPERTY DIVISION AT DIVORCE

SECTION 1. AN OVERVIEW

In Chapter 3, we examined the common law and community property systems that govern property rights during marriage. Now it is time to consider spousal property rights at divorce.

In an earlier era, the same rules that governed property rights during marriage generally governed property rights at divorce. A spouse in a common law state was typically entitled to that property to which he or she held title, plus a share of any assets held in joint tenancy or tenancy by the entireties. In cases where one spouse held title to most of the assets, the common law system often produced inequitable results. For example, in Wirth v. Wirth, 38 A.D.2d 611, 326 N.Y.S.2d 308 (App. Div. 1971), the husband began a "crash" savings program in 1956, telling his wife that the savings were "for the two of us" and "for our latter days." From that point on, the wife's earnings and money from a rental apartment were used to pay the household expenses; most of the husband's salary was invested. All of these investment assets were titled in the husband's name alone, as was the husband's life insurance, his retirement fund, and even the marital home, purchased in 1949 with a downpayment of $6500 supplied by the husband's mother. When husband and wife divorced in 1970, all of these assets remained the husband's property; the wife, who held title to no assets, left the marriage with nothing. The wife appealed, arguing that the husband was able to acquire property in his own name because his legal obligation to support her and their two children was fulfilled out of her earnings rather than his: "What . . . [the wife] seeks," the court noted, "is a community property division in the guise of equitable relief." But such a division was not available in a common law property state. While "[t]here may be a moral judgment that can be made on the basis of respondent's conduct and the imperfectly expressed intention of some possible future benefit to appellant," the court held, " . . . that is not enough to set the court in motion." *Id.* at 613.

Because of inequities like that in *Wirth*, none of the common law states still determine property rights at divorce on the basis of title.

States have adopted different systems, but each must respond to two questions: 1) What property is subject to division at divorce? and 2) What share of that property should each spouse receive? The property system must, in short, provide a basis both for the *definition* and *division* of the marital estate.

On the definitional issue, two basic systems have been adopted. A minority of states follow a "universal community" approach (sometimes, more descriptively called a "hotchpot" or "kitchen sink" system). Under this approach, *all* property owned by either or both spouses at divorce is subject to division. The majority of states follow a "marital property" or "deferred community" approach, under which property is subject to division *only if acquired during the marriage by means other than gift, bequest, or inheritance*. (Other property may not be divided.) This approach, as the tag "deferred community" suggests, is more or less like a community property system except that it comes into play only at the point the marriage terminates through divorce. A few states, sometimes called "hybrid" states, combine these two systems. In these states, marital property alone is subject to division unless the court finds that hardship would result; in such a case, division of separate property is also permitted. Finally, seven community property states follow a community property approach to defining property subject to division at divorce. (The other two community property states, Washington and Wisconsin, are hybrid states.) For a state-by-state summary, *see* J. THOMAS OLDHAM, DIVORCE, SEPARATION AND THE DISTRIBUTION OF PROPERTY § 3.03 (1998).

On the divisional issue, a few states—California, for example—mandate an equal division of the pool of property subject to division. One would expect all community property states to follow this approach; the central concept of community property is, after all, that each spouse is an equal owner of community assets. But some community property states, like most common law states, follow an "equitable distribution" approach, under which the judge is charged with the task of achieving a fair, rather than an equal, division of the marital estate. Most equitable distribution states have statutory factor lists to guide the judge's discretion. Finally, a few states employ a presumption of equal division, from which the judge may deviate if he or she finds (again based on a factor list) that equal division would be inequitable.

As you read the material that follows, it is important to keep in mind that, for a majority of divorcing couples, property division rules are of marginal relevance. The divorce rate for couples living below the poverty line is double that of the general U.S. population; half of all U.S. divorces occur when husband and wife are in their early thirties or younger. *See* Chapter 11. Because of the relative youth and low incomes of the divorce population, many couples have almost nothing to divide. Divorce surveys show that probably half of divorcing couples have a net worth of $30,000 or less. A substantial number have *negative* net worth (*i.e.*, their debts exceed their assets.) *See* Marsha Garrison, *The Econom-*

ic Consequences of Divorce, 32 FAM. & CONCILIATION CTS. REV. 10 (1994) (surveying reports).

The rules detailed in this chapter govern particular types of assets—tort and disability claims, pensions, employment benefits, professional degrees and licenses, business goodwill and the determination of what is separate and what marital. But the typical asset pool is significantly more limited—it includes home equity (encumbered with a substantial mortgage obligation), a car (encumbered by an auto loan), household goods, and a small bank account. Less than 10% of divorcing couples own business assets. LENORE J. WEITZMAN, THE DIVORCE REVOLUTION: THE UNEXPECTED SOCIAL AND ECONOMIC CONSEQUENCES FOR WOMEN AND CHILDREN IN AMERICA 63 (1985). Professional degrees and licenses are sufficiently rare that divorce surveys rarely bother to tabulate the percentage of couples possessing one. And less than half of divorcing couples possess separate property. Marsha Garrison, *Good Intentions Gone Awry: The Impact of New York's Equitable Distribution Law upon Divorce Outcomes*, 57 BROOKLYN L. REV. 621, 660 (1991); WEITZMAN, *supra* at 55. Moreover, the value of individually-owned assets (whether marital or separate) is typically low. In one survey, the median value of the husband's net worth (i.e., the total value of husband's individual property minus his individual debts) was $50. Garrison, *supra*, at 656 tbl. 7.

The scarcity of valuable marital assets at divorce does not, of course, mean that the rules in this chapter are unimportant. Couples with little to divide are disproportionately likely to forgo legal representation; they cannot afford it! Divorcing couples who consult family lawyers are typically wealthier and need legal representatives who are well-versed in the rules governing property distribution at divorce.

SECTION 2. DEFINING AND VALUING MARITAL PROPERTY

A. SEPARATE v. MARITAL: WHEN AND HOW WAS THE PROPERTY ACQUIRED?

In almost all marital property and hybrid states, property interests acquired by one spouse: before marriage; during marriage by gift, bequest, or devise; and after termination of the marriage, are separate property not subject to division at divorce. But courts must still determine when and how the property in question was acquired.

GIHA v. GIHA

Supreme Court of Rhode Island, 1992.
609 A.2d 945.

FAY, CHIEF JUSTICE.

This matter is before the Supreme Court on appeal by the defendant, Nelly Giha (the wife), from a judgment of the Family Court dismissing her complaint for post final judgment relief. The wife urged the Family Court to vacate its final judgment of divorce, arguing that the Massachusetts State Lottery (lottery) prize acquired by the plaintiff, Nagib Giha (the husband), is a marital asset and is subject to equitable distribution. The trial justice dismissed the wife's complaint and determined that the parties' property rights were finally adjudicated upon the issuance of the interlocutory order. For the reasons discussed herein, we reverse that portion of the trial justice's decision concerning the lottery prize.

On October 7, 1987, the husband filed a complaint for divorce on the grounds of irreconcilable differences. The trial began on May 20, 1988. During a recess on the first day of trial the parties reached an agreement for the disposition of their property. Both parties testified that the husband would retain the future income from his medical practice from May 20, 1988, the date of the trial. The parties also agreed to divide equally the net proceeds from the sale of their marital assets. On May 31, 1988, the Family Court entered a decision pending entry of final judgment confirming the parties' agreement reached at trial.

On December 25, 1988, the husband learned that he had won the MEGABUCKS game. His winning lottery ticket was worth approximately $2.4 million, payable over twenty years at $120,000 per year. The husband waited until October 6, 1989, to claim his prize from the Massachusetts State Lottery Commission. He testified that he delayed claiming his prize for health reasons and because he was trying to liquidate his medical practice.

On April 27, 1989, six months prior to the husband's claiming his prize, the Family Court entered its final judgment severing the parties' marriage. The wording of the final judgment was slightly different from the interlocutory order. The final judgment stated that "[c]ommencing as of May 20, 1988, all income of Plaintiff shall be the sole property of Plaintiff."

In December 1990 the wife filed a complaint for post final judgment relief pursuant to Rule 64A of the Rules of Procedure for Domestic Relations. She argued that the husband committed fraud by failing to disclose his lottery prize to her and to the Family Court. The wife asserted that the $2.4 million lottery prize was a marital asset since the husband won the prize during their marriage and that the prize should be divided equally between the parties.

The wife argues that the trial justice erred in dismissing her complaint. She contends that the husband's lottery prize, won prior to the entry of the final judgment, is a marital asset subject to equitable distribution. The husband argues that the equitable-distribution statute contemplates assignment of only those assets that existed at the time of trial. We disagree with the husband's argument.

General Laws 1956 (1988 Reenactment) § 15–5–16.1 governs the distribution of marital assets by the Family Court. The statute is intended "to provide a fair and just assignment of the marital assets * * * on the basis of the joint contribution of the spouses to the marital enterprise." *Stanzler v. Stanzler*, 560 A.2d 342, 345 (R.I.1989). § 15–5–16.1, with the exception of several statutory exemptions, provides for an equitable distribution of all property owned or acquired by either spouse during the marriage.

Although this court has not previously had the opportunity to address the issue presented by this case, we have established that the "parties to a divorce action remain as husband and wife until the entry of the final decree of divorce." *Alix v. Alix*, 497 A.2d 18, 20 (R.I.1985); *see Vanni v. Vanni*, 535 A.2d 1268, 1270 (R.I. 1988); *Centazzo v. Centazzo*, 509 A.2d 995, 998 (R.I.1986). In both *Vanni* and *Centazzo* we concluded that assets acquired by a spouse after the parties had separated or after a complaint for divorce had been filed were subject to equitable distribution. *Vanni*, 535 A.2d at 1270; *Centazzo*, 509 A.2d at 998. "[T]he acquisition of assets after the irremediable breakdown of a marriage or after a valid complaint for divorce is filed *or at any time before final decree for divorce is granted* will not have any effect on the applicability of the equitable-distribution statute." (Emphasis added.) *Vanni*, 535 A.2d at 1270.

In the present case the husband won the lottery prize four months before the Family Court entered its final judgment. The parties remained as husband and wife until the entry of the final judgment in 1989. The mere fact that the husband won the lottery prize after the Family Court issued an interlocutory order does not affect the applicability of the equitable-distribution state. The interlocutory order did not sever either the matrimonial or the economic ties between the husband and the wife. Because the parties' marriage remained in effect throughout the waiting period, so did the property rights each spouse had in the property acquired by the other spouse during that period. Therefore, since the husband won the $2.4 million lottery prize during the existence of the parties' marriage, we conclude that the prize is a marital asset and is subject to the equitable-distribution statute. Because we hold that all property acquired prior to the entry of the final judgment, which property is not excluded in § 15–5–16.1, is subject to equitable distribution, we conclude that the parties to a divorce action have a continuing duty to provide information about changes in their financial condition until the entry of a final judgment of divorce.

In his decision the trial justice noted that "as of the May hearing date, all income received by Dr. Giha thereafter would be his sole property." However, at the time the husband obtained the right to the payment of the lottery prize the interlocutory order was still in effect. The interlocutory order stated that the husband retained only the future income from his medical practice. The $2.4 million lottery prize cannot be classified as income from his medical practice.

The trial justice also suggested that "public policy requires that there must be an end to litigation once the court adjudicates the [parties'] property rights * * * [t]o do otherwise would subject our [judicial] system to chaos by a continual uncertainty of judgments." We disagree with the notion that our decision in the present case will cause "continual uncertainty." Litigation ends, and the parties' property rights in marital assets become final and conclusive upon the issuance of the final judgment. When considering whether to enter a final judgment, the trial justice will determine if the parties have acquired marital assets during the statutory waiting period. If the parties have acquired such marital assets, the trial justice will decide whether to alter the alimony or the equitable assignment established by the interlocutory order. The judge will then enter a final judgment, thereby severing the matrimonial and economic ties of the spouses.

For the reasons stated herein, the wife's appeal is sustained. The judgment appealed from is reversed. For purposes of re-examination of the equitable distribution, the papers in the case are remanded to the Family Court with our decision endorsed thereon.

Notes and Questions

1. Can a stream of income to be received *after* divorce be included in the marital estate? As *Giha* suggests, most courts include such income in the marital estate if the right to receive it was acquired during the marriage without an investment of separate property, the payments do not compensate the recipient spouse for lost post-divorce earning capacity, and post-divorce effort by the recipient spouse is not required to obtain the payments. Issues of apportionment may arise. For example, in Garrett v. Garrett, 140 Ariz. 564, 683 P.2d 1166 (Ariz.App.1983), the court concluded that part of any contingency fee to be received by a lawyer spouse after divorce on cases begun during marriage was marital property; the marital portion was determined by dividing the time the lawyer devoted to the case during marriage by the total time expended. (The problem with this approach, of course, is that it requires knowledge of the total time devoted to the case). *See also* Marriage of Monslow, 259 Kan. 412, 912 P.2d 735 (1996) (awarding nontitled spouse a share of future income from patent developed during marriage).

2. When does the accrual of marital property cease? *Giha* again follows the majority view that marital property continues to accrue until the final divorce decree is entered. But, in some states, marital property ceases to accrue after the date of permanent separation *(see, e.g.*, N.C. GEN. STAT. § 50–20; 23 PA. STAT. § 401; VA. CODE ANN. § 20–107.3) or the date of divorce filing (N.Y. DOM. REL. L. § 236B; FLA. STAT. ANN. § 61.075). What are the advantages and disadvantages of each approach?

3. When should the property be valued? In many urban areas, a contested divorce action can take years to complete. In such a situation, the choice of a date on which to value marital assets will be significant. Most states give the divorce court discretion in selecting a valuation date. *See* In re Cray, 254 Kan. 376, 867 P.2d 291 (1994) (surveying jurisdictions). In most instances, the court will choose a date fairly close to the date of the final decree. *See* MINN. STAT. ANN. § 518.58 [p. 779]; Zern v. Zern, 15 Conn.App. 292, 544 A.2d 244 (1988). This approach

reflects marital partnership theory, under which the marital estate should obtain the benefit of any passive increases in value of the marital estate during the time the divorce action is pending. Accordingly, an "active" increase in the value of the marital estate (that is, one due to the efforts of either or both spouses after the date on which marital property ceases to accrue) should not be treated as marital property. *See* Zelnik v. Zelnik, 169 A.D.2d 317, 573 N.Y.S.2d 261 (1991).

4. Should taxes and sale expenses be deducted from asset values? Spouses sometimes argue that the divorce property valuation should be net of normal sales expenses and tax that would be due were the property to be sold. Most courts have allowed such deductions in cases where a sale is imminent (*see* Oberhansly v. Oberhansly, 16 Fam. L. Rep. (BNA) 1578 (Alaska 1990); Flynn v. Flynn, 402 N.W.2d 111 (Minn.App. 1987)) and rejected it in other cases, based on the speculative nature of a future tax rate, sales expenses, and the sale itself. *See* Marriage of Perino, 224 Ill.App.3d 605, 167 Ill.Dec. 172, 587 N.E.2d 54 (1992); Bayley v. Bayley, 602 A.2d 1152 (Maine 1992); DeHaan v. DeHaan, 572 N.E.2d 1315 (Ind.App.1991); Coviello v. Coviello, 91 Md.App. 638, 605 A.2d 661 (1992); Marriage of Berg, 47 Wash.App. 754, 737 P.2d 680 (1987). (The tax consequences of dividing marital property will be addressed in detail in Chapter 19.)

SHEA v. SHEA

California Court of Appeals, 1980.
111 Cal.App.3d 713, 169 Cal.Rptr. 490.

BROWN, PRESIDING JUSTICE.

Thomas M. Shea appeals an interlocutory judgment dissolving his marriage to Sandra E. Shea. The appeal concerns only the trial court's finding Thomas' veteran's education benefits received during marriage were community property, and the court's method of computing the community interest in the parties' residence.

Thomas served in the United States Navy from January 1969 to January 1973. In May 1973 he began receiving veteran's education benefits (38 U.S.C. § 1651 *et seq.*) which continued with a few interruptions during the summer months when he was not in school, until December 1978. In June 1974, he bought a house, taking title in his own name. He made a down payment of $3,000, paid almost $1,500 in "points" and closing costs, and obtained a loan for the balance of the purchase price. He then began making monthly payments on the loan. Each installment included interest, taxes and insurance, as well as reduction of the loan principal. Sandra and Thomas were married November 27, 1974, and separated May 17, 1979.

At trial Thomas contended the veteran's benefits were his separate property and he sought to introduce evidence showing he had used these funds for most of the house payments made during the marriage. The trial court found the benefits received during marriage were community property and calculated the community interest in the house accordingly. The court did not permit Thomas to offer evidence showing the source of money used for house payments during the marriage. In computing the community interest in the house, the court used the full amount of the monthly payments made during the marriage, instead of the amount by which these payments reduced the principal.

Where one spouse has served in the armed forces before marriage, are veteran's education benefits received during marriage community property?

Congress has enacted a comprehensive program of veteran's education benefits to make service in the armed forces more attractive to prospective recruits and to make educational opportunities available to veterans who otherwise would not be able to afford them, or whose educations have been interrupted by military service (38 U.S.C. § 1651). To receive the benefits, a veteran must meet eligibility requirements, including a minimum of 180 days of service (§ 1652); a veteran must have served at least 18 months on active duty to be eligible to receive benefits for the maximum period of 45 months (§ 1661(a)). A veteran must apply for the benefits, but the Veterans Administration "shall" approve the application unless the veteran or his planned course of study is ineligible (§ 1671). Benefits are payable only while the veteran is enrolled and making satisfactory progress in an approved educational program (§ 1674, 1683, 1772). The benefits are "an educational subsistence allowance to meet, in part, the expenses of the veteran's subsistence, tuition, fees, supplies, books, equipment, and other education costs" (§ 1681), but the statute does not expressly limit the purposes for which the veteran may use the funds. A veteran with dependents receives an increased allowance, based on the number of dependents (§ 1682).

The veteran's educational allowances provided by this statutory scheme are a form of employee benefits, similar in nature to the wide variety of fringe benefits—for example, employer-paid life insurance, tuition reimbursement programs, and pensions—furnished by public and private employers. Like other types of employee benefits, the veteran's education allowance is designed to attract prospective employees, and entitlement to these benefits can be attained only by service with the employer. Consequently, the general principles governing characterization of fringe benefits flowing from the employment relationship determine whether veteran's education benefits are community property.

Under the community property system, each spouse's time, skill, and labor are community assets, and whatever each spouse earns from them during marriage is community property. Fringe benefits are not a gift from the employer but are earned by the employee as part of the compensation for his services. Accordingly, fringe benefits are community property to the extent they are earned by employment during marriage. Conversely, where a fringe benefit is earned by employment before marriage, it is the separate property of the employee even if received after marriage.

Here Thomas' military service occurred entirely before marriage, and his veteran's education benefits are his separate property unless the parties expressly or impliedly agreed these funds would be community property. Since the record contains no evidence of such an agreement, the trial court's finding the benefits community property is not supported by the evidence.

The judgment is reversed.

O'NEILL v. O'NEILL

Kentucky Court of Appeals, 1980.
600 S.W.2d 493.

HOGGE, JUSTICE.

The marriage of Richard and Susan O'Neill has been dissolved. Dr. O'Neill appeals from a portion of the decree of the Fayette circuit court dividing the marital property which he and his former wife acquired during their marriage. Dr. O'Neill contends that the trial court erred by excluding from the marital property certain items which Mrs. O'Neill describes as gifts from Dr. O'Neill.

The issue in this case is whether the trial court erred by failing to consider as marital property certain jewelry and other items of personal property which Dr. O'Neill presented to Mrs. O'Neill on her birthday, at Christmas and other occasions. The items were purchased out of Dr. O'Neill's salary, and included a ring with an appraised value of $35,000.00 and other jewelry with an appraised value of $15,900.00. The circuit court held that these items were gifts to Mrs. O'Neill and should not be included in the marital property.

This issue involves the interpretation of KRS 403.190, which excludes from marital property items acquired by gift.

Under the statute, we start with the premise that all property acquired by either spouse subsequent to marriage is marital property. Without reading the statute further, there is no doubt that the property transferred to Mrs. O'Neill was marital property as it was acquired by her subsequent to marriage. Then the statute excepts from marital property that which is acquired by "gift." The issue, at this point, is whether this property given to Mrs. O'Neill by Dr. O'Neill were "gifts" within the meaning of the statute as intended by the legislature.

In determining this issue, the court's decision would necessarily have to be based on the pertinent facts of each case. In each case, consideration should be given to the source of the money with which the "gift" was purchased, the intent of the donor at that time as to intended use of the property, status of the marriage relationship at the time of the transfer, and whether there was any valid agreement that the transferred property was to be excluded from the marital property.

Further, we note that Dr. O'Neill testified that the jewelry and certain other items were purchased as an investment. He hoped that the purchases would appreciate in value, and that they could be converted into cash in the event money was needed for the children's education. This is evidence of probative value that he intended that the transfer of possession of this property would not divest him of this marital property and that, if necessary, the property could be reconverted into cash, at a future time, at an appreciated price, for a purpose of mutual benefit to the parties, the education of their children. Further, we find no evidence at all that there was any agreement that the property so transferred herein was to be excluded or be treated as the separate property of Mrs. O'Neill. Under these circumstances, we hold that these transfers were not a gift within the meaning of the statute and that the trial court erred in so determining.

As to the "gifts" the judgment of the circuit court is reversed and remanded for further proceedings consistent with this opinion.

Notes and Questions

1. Why did the *Shea* court categorize the veteran's benefits, received during marriage, as separate property? Why did the *O'Neill* court categorize the jewelry, a gift, as marital property? Are the decisions consistent?

2. The categorization of spousal gifts varies. In some states (like Kentucky), categorization depends on the intention of the donor spouse. In others, spousal gifts are always categorized as marital property. *See, e.g.*, N.Y. DOM. REL.L. § 236B(1)(d)(1).

B. SEPARATE v. MARITAL: APPORTIONMENT, COMMINGLING, TRACING, AND TRANSMUTATION

Separate property may become marital property. If, for example, one spouse receives a gift of money during marriage from a parent and deposits it into a bank account where she also deposits her earnings, the gift will likely become hopelessly mixed, or "commingled" with marital assets and, as a result, be treated as marital property. For discussions of commingling, *see* Carol Bruch, *The Definition and Division of Marital Property in California: Towards Parity and Simplicity*, 33 HASTINGS L. J. 769, 782 (1982); J. Thomas Oldham, *Tracing, Commingling and Transmutation*, 23 FAM. L.Q. 219 (1989). Or, if the money is deposited in a joint account, in many states a presumption will arise that the owner intended to make a gift to the marital estate and the funds will be "transmuted" from separate to marital property. *See* Chotiner v. Chotiner, 829 P.2d 829 (Alaska 1992); Robertson v. Robertson, 18 Fam. L. Rep. (BNA) 1110 (Fla. 1991); Verrilli v. Verrilli, 172 A.D.2d 990, 568 N.Y.S.2d 495 (1991).

BROWN v. BROWN

Supreme Court of New York, Appellate Division, 1994.
203 A.D.2d 912, 611 N.Y.S.2d 65.

Before DENMAN, P.M., and BALIO, LAWTON, DOERR and DAVIS, J.J.

* * *

Supreme Court erred in awarding plaintiff 25% of the appreciation in defendant's Investment Management Account at Chase Lincoln First Bank. The account was defendant's separate property and the appreciation in the account during the marriage was not due to defendant's efforts but, rather, was due to the bank's management of the account, market forces, and the 1984 deposit of an inheritance from defendant's father. Consequently, plaintiff has no claim to a share of the appreciation. We modify the judgment, therefore, to reduce plaintiff's distributive award from $96,989.50 to $47,039.50 and otherwise affirm.

COCKRILL v. COCKRILL

Supreme Court of Arizona, 1979.
124 Ariz. 50, 601 P.2d 1334.

GORDON, JUSTICE.

Appellant, Robert Cockrill, and Rose Cockrill, appellee, were married on June 15, 1974. At the time of the marriage, appellant owned, as his separate property, a farming operation known as Cockrill Farms. There seems to be no dispute that the net worth increase of the farm, during the two year and ten month marriage, after some credits, was $79,000. The trial court found that this increase was attributable primarily to the efforts of Mr. Cockrill and was, therefore, community property. Appellant contends that the net worth increase was primarily due to the inherent nature of his separate property, the farm, and was, therefore, also his separate property.

The profits of separate property are either community or separate in accordance with whether they are the result of the individual toil and application of a spouse or the inherent qualities of the business itself.

Seldom will the profits or increase in value of separate property during marriage be exclusively the product of the community's effort or exclusively the product of the inherent nature of the separate property. Instead, as in the instant case, there will be evidence that both factors have contributed to the increased value or profits. In Arizona, these "hybrid profits" have been governed by what can be labeled the "all or none rule." Pursuant to this rule, the profits or increase in value will be either all community property or all separate property depending on whether the increase is primarily due to the toil of the community or primarily the result of the inherent nature of the separate property.

This Court has also become disenchanted with the all or none rule. To implement the all or none rule and determine the primary source of the profits, the portion of the profits that resulted from each source must be calculated. Once this has been done, it is only logical to apportion the profits, or increased value, accordingly. To do otherwise will either deprive the property owner of a reasonable return on the investment or will deprive the community of just compensation for its labor.

We, therefore, also depart from the all or none rule and hold that profits, which result from a combination of separate property and community labor, must be apportioned accordingly.

There are several approaches to the problem of apportionment: "In making such apportionment between separate and community property our courts have developed no precise criterion or fixed standard, but have endeavored to adopt a yardstick which is most appropriate and equitable in a particular situation." *Beam v. Bank of America*, 6 Cal. 3d 12, 18 (1971).

In the case of real estate, the owner of the real property can be awarded its rental value, with the community being entitled to the balance of the income produced from the lands by the labor, skill and management of the parties. Another approach is to determine the reasonable value of the community's services and allocate that amount to the community, and treat the balance as separate property attributable to the inherent nature of the separate estate. [*Van Camp v. Van Camp*, 53 Cal. App. 17, 199 P. 885 (1921).] Finally, the trial court may simply allocate to the separate property a reasonable rate of return on the original capital investment. Any increase above this amount is community property. *Pereira v. Pereira*, 156 Cal. 1, 103 P. 488 (1909).

All of these approaches have merit, with different circumstances, requiring the application of a different method of apportionment. We, therefore, hold that the trial court is not bound by any one method, but may select whichever will achieve substantial justice between the parties.

The judgment of the Superior Court is reversed and the case remanded for the trial court to apportion the profits or increase in value of appellant's separate property between separate and community property.

Notes and Questions

1. Although there are a few exceptions (*see, e.g.*, COLO. REV. STAT. § 14–10–113), most marital property and hybrid states provide, as in *Brown*, that any increase in value of separate property during marriage due to market forces is separate property.

2. In most states, an increase in the value of separate property due to spousal efforts will be categorized as marital. All community property states employ one of the two approaches described in *Cockrill* for determining the value of community property created through spousal effort devoted to a separate asset. Under the *Pereira* approach, the value of the community's interest in the separate asset is computed by adding

a "reasonable" rate of return to the value of the separate asset at the beginning of the marriage; the difference between this sum and the value of the asset at dissolution is community property. Under the *Van Camp* approach, the value of community property interest is determined by computing the reasonable value of the owner-spouse's services to the business during marriage; any salary actually received by the spouse during marriage from the business is deducted from this amount. *See generally* J. Thomas Oldham, *Separate Property Businesses That Increase in Value During Marriage*, 1990 WIS.L.REV. 585. Under either approach, the value of the title-holding spouse's separate property expended for community living expenses is offset against any community claim. *See* Beam v. Bank of America, 6 Cal.3d 12, 98 Cal.Rptr. 137, 490 P.2d 257 (1971).

3. Perhaps because they have had less experience in apportioning separate and marital property, common law states are more variable (and, to be blunt, confused) in their treatment of the *Cockrill* problem. Some require effort by the spouse who is *not* the owner of the separate business to create marital property. *See* N.Y. DOM. REL. L. § 236B; S.C. CODE ANN. § 20–7–473. This position is, of course, inconsistent with the partnership theory (all fruits of marital effort belong to the marriage) that underlies the marital property concept. Such inconsistency may explain the New York Court of Appeal's decision in Price v. Price, 69 N.Y.2d 8, 511 N.Y.S.2d 219, 503 N.E.2d 684 (1986), holding that homemaking services by a non-owner spouse are sufficient to establish a marital claim to business assets that are the separate property of the other spouse; if taken literally, the *Price* directive would mean that the marital estate might have a claim to a separately held business when the owner-spouse had expended no effort in the business whatsoever. *See also* Zelnik v. Zelnik, 169 A.D.2d 317, 573 N.Y.S.2d 261 (1991) (holding that, where any of the increase in value stems from the nonowner spouse's efforts, all of the increase in value during marriage is marital property.) For a general discussion of apportionment problems, *see* Mary M. Wenig, *Increase in Value of Separate Property During Marriage: Examination and Proposals*, 23 FAM. L. Q. 301 (1989); Suzanne Reynolds, *Increases in Separate Property and the Evolving Marital Partnership*, 24 WAKE FOREST L. REV. 239 (1989).

4. In a number of states, spousal effort invested in a separate business will not create marital property unless that effort is substantial. *See* Vallone v. Vallone, 644 S.W.2d 455 (Tex.1982); Marriage of Tatham, 173 Ill.App.3d 1072, 123 Ill.Dec. 576, 527 N.E.2d 1351 (1988); Marriage of Boehlje, 443 N.W.2d 81 (Iowa App.1989).

FRIEBEL v. FRIEBEL

Wisconsin Court of Appeals, 1993.
181 Wis.2d 285, 510 N.W.2d 767.

LAROCQUE, JUDGE.

Diane Friebel appeals a divorce judgment dividing assets in her bank account equally between her and her former husband, Daniel Friebel.

Diane argues that all the assets deposited into her account were exempt from division under § 767.255, Stats. She claims that the court erroneously determined that some of these assets were subject to division at divorce and that property gifted to her was untraceable because it had been commingled with the property subject to division. Because we conclude that the trial court erred in its determination of which assets in the account were gifted to Diane, and because the error affected its tracing inquiry, we reverse and remand to the trial court for further proceedings.

BACKGROUND

Diane and Daniel were married on May 17, 1974. In February of 1987, Diane's father, Douglas Ogilvie, created an irrevocable spendthrift trust naming Diane as the beneficiary. This trust, hereinafter referred to as the main trust, was funded with stocks. By its terms, the trustee had discretion to distribute trust principal, but was required to distribute net income to Diane at least annually. Diane had no right to demand trust corpus. The trustee was required to distribute one-third of the trust corpus to Diane on her fortieth birthday, one-half of the remaining corpus on her forty-fifth birthday and the remaining principal on her fiftieth birthday.

Diane's father also established an irrevocable trust in 1981, naming his wife and all his children, including Diane, as beneficiaries. The trust was funded with $25,000 and real estate. By its terms, the trustee, Valley Bank, had sole discretion to pay any income generated by the trust to beneficiaries. The trust was to pay equal shares of trust principal and undistributed net income to the beneficiaries upon its termination. This trust will be referred to as the real estate trust.

During the marriage, dividend income generated from the stocks in the main trust was distributed to Diane. Diane placed this income in an investment account at Valley Bank. From 1987 through 1991, $295,-522.05 was distributed from the main trust and deposited into Diane's investment account. The real estate trust was dissolved in December 1991, and Diane's share, $31,735.13 was also placed into her investment account. During this same period, Diane's parents gifted $66,000 that she also placed into her investment account.

Throughout the marriage, Diane's investment account, which held only the distributions from the main trust, real estate trust and the cash gifts, also generated income. By the end of 1991, the investment account had earned $11,361.74 interest income, $3,955.36 in realized gains and unrealized gains of $4,084.56. Thus, at the time of the divorce, a total of $412,658.84 in assets had been placed in Diane's investment account.

The trial court determined that the judgment of divorce was granted for the purposes of property division on April 8, 1992. This was before Diane's fortieth birthday. At this date, $153,653.85 remained in Diane's investment account. The main trust had $4,528.80 in undistributed income. There was also a $14,500.74 capital gain realized by the main trust that the trustee had not distributed to Diane as of the date of divorce, although the couple had reported the gain on their 1991 tax return.

In dividing the couple's property, the court faced the problem whether each of the four separate components of Diane's investment account was subject to division. The court concluded that although Diane's interest in the corpus of the main trust was a gift not subject to division, under *Arneson v. Arneson*, 120 Wis.2d 236, 355 N.W.2d 16 (Ct.App.1984), the distributions of trust income were subject to division because they were income generated from gifted property. It concluded that distributions from the real estate trust and the cash gifts were gifts not subject to division. Finally, the court concluded that any income generated by the investment account was also divisible.

The court then addressed whether gifts to Diane had retained their character and identity. While it concluded that the character of the gifts remained unchanged, it concluded that the gifts had not retained their identity. The gifts had become so commingled with the income distributions from the main trust and the income generated by the investment account that identification and valuation of them was purely speculative. Accordingly, the court concluded that the entire investment account was divisible under § 767.255, Stats. The undistributed dividend income totaling $4,528.80 that remained in the main trust was also held to be divisible. The court concluded that the undistributed realized capital gain in the main trust was not subject to division because the trustee had not, nor was required to, distribute it.

DIVISION OF THE INVESTMENT ACCOUNT

Diane argues that the court erroneously determined that her investment account was subject to division under § 767.255, Stats. § 767.255 excludes from division any property acquired by either party prior to or during the marriage by gift, bequest, devise or inheritance, except upon a finding of hardship. Diane argues that all of the assets deposited into that account were gifts to her that were not divisible.

A. Income From Main Trust

We begin by evaluating whether the distributions of income from the main trust were gifts to Diane that were not subject to division. Diane views the trust as the gift and the distributions of income under the terms of the trust as simply the completion of the gift. Daniel, on the other hand, agrees the trust is the gift, but he interprets the gift to be limited to Diane's future interest in the trust corpus. He reasons that the distributions to Diane are income generated from the gifted corpus, which under *Arneson* are divisible upon divorce.

Our courts have interpreted § 767.255, Stats., as exempting from division a gift *and* appreciation in the value of the gift that is due to the general economic conditions of inflation where the nonowning spouse does not contribute to the appreciation in value. *Plachta v. Plachta*, 118 Wis.2d 329, 333, 348 N.W.2d 193, 195 (Ct.App.1984). However, we have treated income generated from a gift differently.

Arneson established that income generated from the gift is distinct from the gift and from appreciation in the value of the gift, and is *not* exempt from division at divorce. *Id.* 120 Wis.2d at 244–45, 355 N.W.2d at 20. In that case, we held that property purchased from income generated by gifted stock was subject to division at divorce. *Id.*; *see also Fowler v. Fowler*, 158 Wis.2d 508, 517, 463 N.W.2d 370, 373 (Ct.App.1990) (inherited stocks exempt from division, but stocks purchased from dividends of inherited stock not exempt).

Arneson's rationale rested on a strict construction of § 767.255, Stats. We viewed income generated by an asset as income not in existence at the time of the gift. We thus noted that such property was *not* acquired by gift, bequest, devise or inheritance and therefore concluded that the income was subject to division. *Arneson*, 120 Wis.2d at 243–44, 355 N.W.2d at 20. However, the asset generating income was stock that had already been acquired by the donee. The donee had legal title to the stock and consequently could have sold, traded or gifted his property interest in it. He had numerous ways to alienate all, or only a portion of, his property interests in his stock.

In contrast, the creation of the trust for Diane vested her with an equitable, but not a legal, title to the trust corpus. Corpus distributions were completely discretionary, and Diane never received any corpus distributions. The spendthrift provisions prevented Diane from alienating her future interest in the corpus. She would not receive a possessory interest in any of the corpus unless she survived to her fortieth birthday, at which point she was to receive one-third of the corpus. We conclude that because Diane had no present or past possessory interest in trust corpus, she had not yet acquired it within the meaning of § 767.255, Stats. Thus, the income generated by the corpus was not generated by property Diane had acquired. Consequently, the distributions of income to her were not generated by acquired gifts, but were themselves gifts.

We note at least one other jurisdiction has adopted a similar rule. Texas courts have held that where a trust grants only an income interest but no power over the corpus, the income is the sole gift of the settlor and thus the beneficiary's separate property. *Buckler v. Buckler*, 424 S.W.2d 514, 515–16 (Tex.Civ.App.1967). However, where a beneficiary has power to reduce the corpus to a present possessory control, any income generated from that portion is community property.

B. *Income From Real Estate Trust*

An examination of the real estate trust and distributions from it yields a similar result. Daniel argues that $12,255.13 of the distribution from that trust was subject to division because it reflected appreciation of the trust resulting from trustee management paid for by income generated by trust corpus. He reasons that because the income generated from the corpus is subject to division and was used to manage the trust to cause its appreciation, the appreciation is divisible. We disagree.

The trust document required payment to the trustee from net income prior to distributions. Distributions were entirely within the discretion of the trustee, and Diane received no distributions prior to the termination of the trust. She was one of only several beneficiaries and, as with the main trust corpus, Diane had no dominion over the real estate trust. We thus conclude, as did the trial court, that the real estate trust distribution was a gift.

C. Cash Gifts and Income From the Investment Account

Neither party challenges the conclusion that the cash gifts Diane received from her parents were gifts that were not divisible at divorce under § 767.255, Stats. The remaining asset in Diane's investment account to be analyzed is the income and capital gains generated by the account. Diane acknowledges that these are not gifts, but argues that they should nevertheless not be subject to division because Valley Bank managed the investment account and neither she nor Daniel exercised any control over it. She contends that her case is analogous to *Wierman v. Wierman*, 130 Wis.2d 425, 387 N.W.2d 744 (1986), where the supreme court held that the increase in value in the wife's business interest resulting from her father's management was not subject to division because neither party actively caused the increase.

We conclude that *Wierman* is not applicable. In *Wierman*, the court noted that the gift did not generate income separate and distinct from itself, but rather was a return of capital and profits. *Id.* at 438, 387 N.W.2d at 750. Thus, *Wierman's* holding applies to income resulting from a return of capital or profits taken on appreciation of capital, but does not apply to income generated by the gift itself. We view the income generated by Diane's investment account to be no different from the dividends generated by stock in *Arneson*. Thus, the $11,361.74 interest income generated by Diane's investment account is income generated from her gifts and is subject to division.

The $3,955.36 in realized gains and unrealized gains of $4,084.56 may stand on different footing. The record is unclear whether these gains represent profits taken on the appreciation of stocks in Diane's investment account. These gains may not be subject to division if they represent appreciation or they may be subject to division under *Arneson*. On remand, the trial court will have to make this finding of fact. However, it is clear that at most $19,401.66 (the interest plus the gains) of the assets deposited into Diane's investment account were properly subject to division.

D. Character and Identity of the Property in the Investment Account

Our cases make clear that while gifted property is not normally subject to division at divorce, if the property has lost its character or identity through commingling with divisible property, then all the property is subject to division. *Trattles v. Trattles*, 126 Wis.2d 219, 376 N.W.2d 379 (Ct.App.1985). Character addresses the manner in which the parties have chosen to title or treat gifted or inherited assets. *Brandt*, 145 Wis.2d at 410, 427 N.W.2d at 132. Changing the property's character can transmute it to divisible property. *Id.* Such changing of title occurs when, for example, a party transfers her gifted property into joint tenancy or uses the property to purchase property for the mutual enjoyment and use of the marriage.

The court concluded that Diane's gifted property retained its character. Daniel does not contest this conclusion. We agree with the court. All of Diane's gifted property, including the distributions from the main trust, were kept in her separately titled investment account. Diane never transferred this property into a joint account. While she used some of these assets to purchase property for the marriage, items that indisputably became subject to division, she never demonstrated any donative intent with regard to the remaining assets in her investment account. Thus, her gifted property retained its character.

Identity addresses whether a gifted or inherited asset has been preserved in some present identifiable form so that it can be meaningfully valued and assigned. *Brandt*, 145 Wis.2d at 411, 427 N.W.2d at 132. Daniel asserts the trial court properly concluded that the gifts to Diane had become so commingled with divisible property as to make valuation of her property completely speculative. Commingling is not per se fatal to the exempt status of a gift; rather, the inquiry is whether the gifted component can be valued.

All the assets deposited into Diane's account were gifts to her except readily determinable income generated by the account. As of the date of divorce, Diane's account received a total of $412,658.84. Thus, at most, five percent, $19,401.66, was divisible property. We conclude that the entire account was not tainted by and so commingled with the five percent of divisible property as to convert the remainder of the account into divisible property.

Diane is willing to concede that all withdrawals were made from her gifted property. She is willing to subtract the full value of divisible property from the remaining $153,653.85 in the investment account and the $4,528.80 of undistributed main trust income that was erroneously determined to be divisible. Her gifted property is easily valued by subtracting the property subject to division from the investment account. Thus, on remand, the court will be required to determine how much of the income generated by the account is divisible and subject the full amount to division. The remaining portion is to be awarded to Diane.

Because the court determined that the entire investment account was subject to division, it did not consider whether Daniel would suffer hardship as a result of its division. On remand, the court may still award some of this to Daniel if it concludes he will suffer hardship under § 767.255, Stats. In addition, the court may determine that this decision affects its prior presumption of equal division and adjust the original division based on equitable considerations embodied in § 767.255.

Notes and Questions

1. According to the appellate court, which portion of the trust assets was divisible? Why? How is the appellate holding different from

that of the trial court? How does each court apply the concept of commingling?

2. Marital property (and hybrid) states have reached conflicting conclusions on the categorization of income from separate property. Much of the time, separate property earns income without spousal effort; market forces, not spousal initiative, determine how much interest a bank account earns and the value of a company's stock dividends. Because marital property represents the fruits of marital partnership and effort, the majority of states have concluded that income from separate property remains separate. *See* Thomas Andrews, *Income from Separate Property: Towards a Theoretical Foundation*, 1993 Law & Contemp. Prob. 171. But the decision to invest in a bank savings account or stocks—or gold, commodities futures, oil wells—may well involve spousal effort. Perhaps for this reason, a minority of states have concluded that the income from separate property received during marriage should be categorized as marital property. *See* Andrews, *supra*; Suzanne Reynolds, *Increases in Separate Property and the Evolving Marital Partnership*, 24 Wake Forest L. Rev. 239 (1989). In these states, an interest-bearing account containing premarital savings may, over time, become a commingled asset.

3. If a spouse incurs expenses to maintain separate property (real estate, for example), any marital income from the separate asset should be calculated on a "net" basis, (i.e., gross income minus expenses). In some states, income from a non-renewable resource (such as a coal mine or oil well) is considered a sale of the resource rather than income. *See* Commissioner of Internal Revenue v. Wilson, 76 F.2d 766 (5th Cir.1935).

4. Wisconsin is a hybrid state. Thus, even if the court finds that the account is not marital property, it may divide it if hardship would otherwise result. How would a "hotchpot" state deal with the issue presented in *Friebel*?

C. ACQUISITIONS OVER TIME

BRANDENBURG v. BRANDENBURG

Kentucky Court of Appeals, 1981.
617 S.W.2d 871.

[The parties here dispute how to calculate the marital claim when a spouse purchases realty before marriage but continues to make payments during marriage with marital funds.]

Gant, Judge.

The guidelines for apportionment between marital and nonmarital property were issued in *Newman v. Newman*, Ky., 597 S.W.2d 137 (1980). The court therein approved the formula utilized by the lower court, saying that the interests of the parties were "the same percentages as their respective contributions to the total equity in the property." In other words, there is to be established a relationship between the nonmarital contribution and the total contribution, and between the marital contribution and the total contribution. These relationships, reduced to percentages, shall be multiplied by the equity in the property at the time of distribution to establish the value of the nonmarital and marital properties.

With this basis established, we provide the following definitions:

Nonmarital contribution (nmc) is defined as the equity in the property at the time of marriage, plus any amount expended after marriage by either spouse from traceable nonmarital funds in the reduction of mortgage principal, and/or the value of improvements made to the property from such nonmarital funds.

Marital contribution (mc) is defined as the amount expended after marriage from other than nonmarital funds in the reduction of mortgage principal, plus the value of all improvements made to the property after marriage from other than nonmarital funds.

Total contribution (tc) is defined as the sum of nonmarital and marital contributions.

Equity (e) is defined as the equity in the property at the time of distribution. This may be either at the date of the decree of dissolution, or, if the property has been sold prior thereto and the proceeds may be properly traced, then the date of the sale shall be the time at which the equity is computed.

[Ed. Note: For the mathematically challenged, equity at the time of marriage can be computed by subtracting the principal balance due on any secured loans (such as a mortgage) from the value of the property at the time of the marriage; equity at the divorce valuation date is computed by subtracting principal balance due on any secured loans from the value of the property on the valuation date.]

The formula to be utilized is:

$$\frac{nmc}{tc} \text{ x } e = \text{nonmarital property}$$

$$\frac{mc}{tc} \text{ x } e = \text{marital property}$$

The contribution of either spouse of other than marital or nonmarital funds shall not be considered in the increase of equity of the property, and any dicta or other language to the contrary in *Robinson v. Robinson*, Ky. App., 569 S.W.2d 178 (1978), is specifically overruled. For example, the contribution of one spouse as homemaker, etc., shall be considered only in affixing the percentage of the marital property to be assigned to that spouse.

ILHARDT PROPERTY

This property was purchased by the husband for $15,900 on December 16, 1968, $900 being the down payment and the husband executing a mortgage of $15,000. Prior to marriage, the husband reduced the mortgage principle by $352.80, the court below finding the value of the property at marriage to be $15,900 and the nonmarital equity to be $1,252.80. After marriage and before sale on July 18, 1975, the mortgage principal was further reduced by $1,176.00. This sum was realized from rents on this property, which rents are marital funds under *Brunson v. Brunson*, Ky.App., 569 S.W.2d 173 (1978). The sale price was $32,500, which was applied in the following manner: $13,471.20 was applied to extinguish the mortgage on this property, leaving a balance of $19,-028.80. Of the latter sum, $13,800 was applied on the husband's mortgage on the Wilmore property, extinguishing that mortgage; $963,43 was applied on the husband's mortgage on the Glen Cove property; $3,717 was paid on a joint mortgage on property with which we are not concerned; and the balance was put by the husband in his lock box.

Applying the formula, we find:

nmc = $1,252.80 (the equity at marriage)

mc = $1,175.00 (mortgage principal reduction during marriage)

tc = $2,428.80

e = $19.028.80

1,252.80 = 51.6% x 19,028.80 = 9,815.25—Value of nonmarital property
2,428.80

1,175.00 = 48.4% x 19,028.80 = 9,213.55—Value of marital property
2,428.80

Notes and Questions

1. Valuable assets, such as cars and houses, are typically purchased through installment payments. Most states follow the *Brandenburg* approach, under which installment payments on a separate asset made with marital funds will create a fractional marital property interest in the separate asset. In a minority of states, installment payments made with marital funds create only a marital lien against the separate asset; at divorce, marital funds must be repaid, without interest, by the title-holding spouse. *See, e.g.*, Hawkins v. Hawkins, 612 S.W.2d 683 (Tex.Civ. App. 1981). For a general discussion of approaches used in different states, *see* J. THOMAS OLDHAM, DIVORCE, SEPARATION AND THE DISTRIBUTION OF PROPERTY, § 7.05 (1998). What are the pros and cons of each approach? Which is more consistent with the partnership theory that underlies the marital property concept? In an age of inflation, which approach is most likely to enhance the marital estate?

2. Under the *Brandenburg* approach, equity derived from payment of indebtedness is not distinguished from equity derived from inflationary appreciation, nor is premarital appreciation distinguished from marital appreciation. The result is that marital equity, as defined by the formula, may bear little relation to the value of marital contributions; during a period of high inflation, the approach will probably yield a marital equity figure that exceeds the value of marital contributions.

What other valuation methods are available? What are the pros and cons of each?

D. INSURANCE PROCEEDS AND TORT CLAIMS

TRAHAN v. TRAHAN

Louisiana Court of Appeals, 1980.
387 So.2d 35.

CUTRER, JUSTICE.

[In this action, the trial court characterized proceeds paid under a homeowner's insurance policy as H's separate property. W appeals.]

The residence in which [H and W] lived was owned by John Trahan before his marriage to Betty Trahan. It was clearly his separate property. While living on the premises certain improvements were made to the residence. Although the extent of the improvements during the marriage is in dispute, it is agreed that a new roof was installed after the marriage.

During the marriage a homeowner's insurance policy covering the residence was purchased in the name of John Trahan. Three or four months later, the home burned and John Trahan received $46,560.00 in insurance proceeds. We conclude that the proceeds from the fire insurance policy were the separate property of John Trahan. The object of the insurance policy was the residence belonging to the separate estate of John Trahan. When that residence burned, the estate, consisting of the residence, was transformed into the insurance proceeds.

We base our conclusion on the case of *Thigpen v. Thigpen*, 91 So.2d 12 (La.1956). in which our Supreme Court faced a similar situation. In that case, the parties, Mr. and Mrs. Thigpen, had a number of disputes regarding their community property settlement which was being settled as a result of a divorce proceeding.

During the existence of a previous marriage, Mr. Thigpen and his wife purchased several buildings. Sometime later, the first wife died and the property then became jointly owned by the deceased wife's heirs and Mr. Thigpen. Later, Mr. Thigpen remarried. Clearly the interest in the property purchased during the existence of his first marriage was separate property of the husband as to the second marriage. During the existence of the second marriage, Thigpen purchased a fire insurance policy to cover the buildings. Shortly thereafter the buildings burned and the loss was replaced with funds from the insurance proceeds. The Supreme Court held that these insurance proceeds did not become community property. The court noted that since the premiums were paid out of the community funds, there may have been a justifiable claim for reimbursement for the wife's contributions to the premiums, but this did not make the proceeds themselves community property.

ANDRLE v. ANDRLE

Texas Court of Appeals, 1988.
751 S.W.2d 955.

ARNOT, J.

This is an appeal from a divorce decree. The sole issue, on appeal, is whether the trial court abused its discretion by divesting appellant of one-half interest in future benefits under a private policy of disability insurance. Because we find the policy is community property, we affirm the judgment of the trial court.

Appellant, Stephen G. Andrle, and appellee, Deanna Lou Andrle, were married on January 15, 1959, and divorced on August 6, 1987. During the marriage, appellant obtained a policy of disability insurance through Western Life Insurance Company. This disability insurance policy was not related to appellant's employment. The premiums for the disability policy were paid with community funds of the parties.

During the marriage, because appellant had suffered disabilities and Western Life had denied coverage, a lawsuit was filed. As a result of the lawsuit, Western Life tendered a lump sum settlement of $38,992.32 and commenced making disability payments to appellant of $1,200.00 per month. From each monthly payment, $400.00 is paid to the attorneys who represented appellant in the lawsuit against Western Life.

Appellant agrees that the lump sum settlement proceeds and the net monthly payments received prior to the divorce were assets of the community estate with each party being entitled to one-half. However, appellant argues that the trial court abused its discretion in awarding appellee one-half interest in the monthly disability insurance proceeds received after the date of divorce, urging these proceeds are his separate property. We disagree.

The disability insurance policy was purchased during the marriage of the parties with community funds. The disability insurance carried by appellant at the time of divorce was a property right that belonged to the community estate. The benefits from a vested property right are community property even though paid after divorce.

Appellant first argues that future payments are mere expectancies and, therefore, not subject to division, citing as authority *Cunningham v. Cunningham*, 183 S.W.2d 985 (Tex.Civ.App.—Dallas 1944, no writ). Unlike the case before us, *Cunningham* was concerned with the division of commissions earned on life insurance policies which may or may not be renewed "Irrespective of the wish or will of either party." The court held that the right to renewals was not a vested property right but merely an expectancy.

Addressing the argument of whether or not rights to disability proceeds were an expectancy, the court in *Mathews* found:

> There are no onerous acts or duties imposed upon appellant by the policies in order to keep the policies in force and the disability

payments continuing. Of course, appellant must not make a miraculous recovery or his payments will cease.

The rights to disability compensation are a property right not a mere expectancy.

Alternatively, appellant argues that the payments are his separate property because the proceeds acquire the character of the thing they replace: namely, his ability to earn money by personal labor. Appellant cites as authority *Rolater v. Rolater*, 198 S.W. 391 (Tex.Civ.App.—Dallas 1917, no writ). In *Rolater*, the wife purchased casualty insurance with her separate funds insuring the house which was her husband's separate property and the contents which were hers. After a loss, a part of the proceeds was used to rebuild her husband's house. When awarded only the amount of the premium she had paid as a charge against her husband's estate, the wife complained that the proceeds of the insurance policy were community property to which she was entitled to half. The court held that, when the house upon the land is destroyed by fire and there exists an insurance policy covering the loss, the proceeds occupy the same status which the house did, the separate estate of the husband. The court reasoned that to hold otherwise would allow one spouse the authority to convert the separate estate of another into the joint property of both for a wholly inadequate consideration without the other's consent.

This reasoning does not apply to the case before us. Appellee did not convert appellant's separate estate into community property. The policy was purchased during the marriage with community funds. The status of property so far as being separate or community property is fixed by facts which existed at inception of the title. Based upon the doctrine of inception of title, it was a vested right of the community.

The judgment of the trial court is affirmed.

Notes and Questions

1. *Andrle* categorizes insurance proceeds based on the character of the premiums used to pay for the policy; *Trahan* categorizes them based on the character of what the policy proceeds will replace. Which approach yields the best results?

2. Most courts follow the *Trahan* approach in categorizing disability benefits to be received after divorce; unless the benefits include a component representing a marital pension or lost marital wages, the benefits are the recipient's separate property. *See, e.g.*, Marriage of Saslow, 40 Cal.3d 848, 221 Cal.Rptr. 546, 710 P.2d 346 (1985); Marriage of Kittleson, 21 Wash.App. 344, 585 P.2d 167 (1978); Fleitz v. Fleitz, 200 A.D.2d 874, 606 N.Y.S.2d 825 (1994).

3. Personal injury awards pose similar issues to those presented by disability benefits. Some divorce statutes specify how damages for a personal injury should be categorized; many do not. When the statute does not specify how such an award should be categorized, the majority

of courts have followed an "analytical" approach, under which an asset may be characterized as separate property even if the statutory definition does not so specify. *See, e.g.*, Ward v. Ward, 453 N.W.2d 729 (Minn.App.1990); Everhardt v. Everhardt, 77 Ohio App.3d 396, 602 N.E.2d 701 (1991). As with disability insurance proceeds, that portion of a personal injury award intended to compensate for lost marital wages may be categorized as marital property even though the pain and suffering component is categorized as separate property. Under the alternate "mechanical" approach, only property specifically defined as separate by the legislature will be categorized as separate. *See, e.g.*, Marriage of Simon, 856 P.2d 47 (Colo. App. 1993); Marriage of Adan, 263 Ill.App.3d 566, 200 Ill.Dec. 439, 635 N.E.2d 778 (1994). So, under this approach, all components of personal injury recoveries received during marriage are considered marital property.

E. PENSION BENEFITS AND OTHER EMPLOYEE COMPENSATION

1. *Basic Terminology*

Pension rights are often the most valuable asset at divorce. Most pension plans are *"defined benefit"* or *"defined contribution"* types.

Under a *defined benefit plan*, the employer agrees to pay an employee who has satisfied the minimum plan requirements (*e.g.*, length of employment, age, etc.) a monthly retirement payment based on a formula set forth in the plan. The formula might, for example, specify that:

Monthly payment = .03 x last monthly salary x number of years of service with the employer.

Under this particular formula, a retiree would receive 90% of his last monthly salary post-retirement if he had worked for the employer for thirty years. With a defined benefit plan, contributions are not made to employees' individual pension accounts; instead, the employer makes deposits to a general retirement fund in an amount estimated to satisfy all retirement obligations. Defined benefit plans typically are funded by the employer.

Defined benefit plan rights are always initially "unvested;" if the employee dies, quits, or is fired before the specified "vesting date," he or she has no rights under the plan. An employee holding unvested pension rights thus possesses only a contingent interest in plan benefits; he or she may ultimately receive full benefits, or no benefits.

Each defined benefit plan specifies a date or event at which the employee's pension benefits will "vest." After vesting, the employee will receive benefits, even if he is fired or quits, as long as he survives until retirement age. Under some, but not all, plans, his estate may be entitled to death benefits should he die before retirement.

When the employee has the right, under the plan, to retire, the benefits will "mature." (Many employees choose to work after the maturity date.) When the employee retires and begins to receive benefits, the pension is "in pay status."

Under a *"defined contribution plan,"* a separate account is maintained for each employee. Contributions, based on a formula (i.e., percentage of salary, percentage of company profits), are periodically made to each employee's account. A defined contribution plan may be funded solely by the employer or by the employer and employee (by payroll deduction). Employee contributions must vest immediately; employer contributions will vest based on a plan schedule. When an employee with a defined contribution plan interest retires, his retirement benefit equals whatever annuity can be purchased with his pension account balance.

Some government pension benefits combine features of a defined contribution and defined benefit plan. The employee makes contributions to a pension account and has the right to withdraw any balance if he or she quits before retirement. If the employee remains at his job until retirement, benefits are calculated under the plan based on a formula rather than the value of the annuity that could be purchased with the account balance.

For a good general reference on pension issues, *see* William Troyan, *Pension Evaluation for Marriage Dissolutions Actions: A Pension Evaluator's Perspective*, 3 VALUATION & DISTRIBUTION OF MARITAL PROPERTY ch. 45 (1986). *See also* William Troyan, *An Update on Pension Evaluation*, 31 FAM. L.Q. 5 (1997).

2. *Apportionment*

TAGGART v. TAGGART

Supreme Court of Texas, 1977.
552 S.W.2d 422.

POPE, JUSTICE.

Ann Taggart instituted this suit against George Taggart for the partition of military retirement benefits that were not divided when the parties were divorced. The trial court, upon a finding that the parties were married during the time that eight-ninths of the retirement benefits accumulated, rendered judgment that plaintiff was entitled to four-ninths of all retirement pay received by her former husband. The court ordered defendant George Taggart to receive plaintiff's share in trust for the plaintiff and make monthly disbursement to her of her share. The court of civil appeals reversed that judgment and rendered judgment that plaintiff take nothing. 540 S.W.2d 823. We reverse the judgment of the court of civil appeals and reform that of the trial court.

On June 5, 1943, George Taggart entered the United States Navy. Ann and George Taggart were married on October 7, 1947, and they were divorced on January 5, 1968. The divorce proceedings made no mention of retirement benefits.

On July 1, 1964, three and one-half years before the divorce, George completed the equivalent of twenty years of active duty. George did not retire but elected to be placed in the Fleet Reserve. As an enlisted man in the regular Navy, he had to complete thirty years of active duty before he was eligible for retirement based on years of service. Mr. Taggart was retired from the Navy on April 1, 1974. Ann Taggart instituted this suit for the recovery of her share of the retirement benefits since April 1, 1974. She did not seek any part of the retainer pay that George Taggart earned for his service in the Fleet Reserve, nor was there any plea of limitations urged in this case.

The court of civil appeals decided this case in August, 1976, at which time the supreme court had granted a writ of error but had not written its opinion in *Cearley v. Cearley*, 544 S.W.2d 661 (Tex.1976). We decided in *Cearley* that retirement benefits are subject to division as vested contingent community property rights even though the present right has not fully matured. We refused to follow the California case of *French v. French*, 17 Cal. 2d 775, 112 P.2d 235 (1941), which treated an unmatured pension right as a nonvested expectancy instead of a vested right. In *Cearley*, we held that military benefits were community property even though the benefits at the time of the divorce "had not matured and were not at the time subject to possession and enjoyment." There is no necessity to again analyze the relevant Texas decisions or the opinion of the California court in *Brown v. Brown*, 15 Cal. 3d 838, 126 Cal. Rptr. 633, 544 P.2d 561 (1976), which rejected the rule of *French v. French*, *supra*, and recognized a present contingent right subject to divestment.

Since *Cearley* controls this case, we hold that Ann Taggart owned as her part of the community estate a share in the contingent right to military benefits even though that right had not matured at the time of the divorce. It appears, however, that the trial court did not make the correct computation of her fractional interest.

The trial court computed Ann Taggart's one-half interest in George Taggart's retirement benefits upon the basis of his twenty years of service as a member of the regular Navy. At the end of the twenty years, he was not entitled to receive any retirement benefits based upon his term of service because he had to serve in the Fleet Reserve for an additional ten years. It was, therefore, his three hundred and sixty months of service that entitled him to the retirement benefits. According to the undisputed evidence Ann and George Taggart's marriage coincided with his service in the Navy for a period of two hundred and forty-six months. The correct computation of Ann Taggart's vested interest is that she was entitled only to one-half of 246/360th's of the retirement pay.

The judgment of the court of civil appeals is reversed; the judgment of the trial court is reformed to adjudge the correct fractional interest to Ann Taggart and as reformed is affirmed.

Notes and Questions

1. Until about two decades ago, divorce courts applied a restrictive definition of "property" that precluded the division of contingent benefits or expectancies such as unvested pension rights. Most courts today follow the *Taggart* approach and permit the division of unvested pension rights. Because a divorcing spouse with an unvested pension right may never receive benefits, some courts apply a "wait and see" or "deferred sharing" approach, like that utilized in *Taggart*.

2. Pension plans often pose apportionment problems. If, as in *Taggart*, the spouse with pension rights accrued those rights before marriage or after marital termination, in a marital property state the rights will be categorized as separate property. The *Taggart* court computed the marital component of the pension by calculating the portion of the employee's career during which the employee was married; because the employee was married for 246 of 360 months of employment, 246/360 of the pension benefits was marital property.

3. A time-based approach to pension apportionment will not make sense unless the pension benefits are based on years of employment. Thus, in In re Marriage of Poppe, 97 Cal.App.3d 1, 158 Cal.Rptr. 500 (1979), the appellate court reversed the trial court's decision to divide the husband's naval reserve pension on a "time" basis when the value of the pension was based on "points" accumulated during naval reserve service. The husband retired with 5,002 points, of which only 1,632 were accumulated during the marriage. The court held that "[i]n this case ... the amount of the pension is not a function of the number of years of service; the number of years of service during the marriage is not a fair gauge of the community contribution; and the court's apportionment of the pension on the basis of the number of "qualifying" years served as compared to the number of years of service during the marriage must be said to be unreasonable, arbitrary and an abuse of discretion." Conversely, in Whorrall v. Whorrall, 691 S.W.2d 32 (Tex.App.1985), the appellate court upheld the trial court's determination that the entire value of an early retirement "special payment" was community property, even though the employee spouse was married during only 65 of his 252 months of employment. The court's determination was based on evidence that the special payment represented a "unique" and "strictly discretionary" incentive designed to coax an unproductive employee into early retirement. "The fact that such payment is purely discretionary," the court held, " ... negates the notion that it is earned or accrued over the employee's tenure."

4. For defined contribution plans, the marital component is typically computed by subtracting premarital contributions (plus interest and dividends) from total contributions. The main complication here is how to treat interest accruing on premarital contributions. Some courts treat all interest accruing during marriage as marital property (*see, e.g.*, Maslen v. Maslen, 121 Idaho 85, 822 P.2d 982 (1991)), while others treat

interest on premarital contributions as the pension owner's separate property. *See, e.g.*, White v. White, 521 N.W.2d 874 (Minn.App.1994).

5. In addition to pension benefits, courts have held that a range of other employment benefits are divisible at divorce:

a. Some courts have held that vacation time earned during marriage may be treated as a divisible asset, particularly when the employee had the option of receiving cash for vacation time. *See* Lesko v. Lesko, 184 Mich.App. 395, 457 N.W.2d 695 (1990); Ryan v. Ryan, 261 N.J.Super. 689, 619 A.2d 692 (1992). In a marital property state, any vacation time accrued but unused before marriage should be subtracted from the employee's accrued vacation time at the end of the marital property accrual period. *See* Everette v. Everette, 620 So.2d 1115 (Fla.App.1993); Cole v. Roberts, 661 So.2d 370 (Fla.App.1995).

b. Stock options and bonuses have generally been held divisible if they represent compensation for marital employment. *See, e.g.*, In re Marriage of Hug, 154 Cal.App.3d 780, 201 Cal.Rptr. 676 (1984); In re Marriage of Nelson, 177 Cal.App.3d 150, 222 Cal.Rptr. 790 (1986).

c. Most courts have concluded that the right to a maintain a term life insurance policy post-divorce is valueless and thus not subject to division. *But see* Marriage of Logan, 191 Cal.App.3d 319, 236 Cal.Rptr. 368 (1987) (term life insurance right could be valuable if employee had become uninsurable during marriage).

Problem 14–1:

William has been married for 14 years; he has worked for Widget Corp. for approximately 21 years. Under the terms of the Widget defined benefit pension plan, employees do not accrue any pension rights until they have five years of service; thereafter, each year of service counts equally. Pension rights vest at 20 years of service. The normal retirement age is 65; William is now 60. If he retires at age 65 (as he currently intends to do), William will receive $1000 per month. What, if any, fraction of the pension is marital? *See* In re Marriage of Joiner, 755 S.W.2d 496 (Tex.App.) reh'g granted, 766 S.W.2d 263 (Tex.App.1988).

Problem 14–2:

George began work at Widget Corp. 30 years ago. Seven years ago he married Mary. During his marriage to Mary, he was promoted to a position that qualified him for a special "executive" pension in addition to his normal defined benefit pension. The defined benefit pension was vested at the time of George and Mary's marriage. Both pensions are based on years of service. George is now 60; normal retirement age is 65. If George retires at age 65 (as he now intends), he will receive $1000 per month in "regular" benefits and $500 per month in "executive" benefits. What, if any, fraction of each pension is marital? *See* Hudson v. Hudson, 763 S.W.2d 603 (Tex.App.1989)

3. *Payment*

JOHNSON v. JOHNSON

Supreme Court of Arizona, 1981.
131 Ariz. 38, 638 P.2d 705.

HOLOHAN, VICE CHIEF JUSTICE.

Appellant, Julia Johnson, filed an appeal from the judgment of the superior court in a dissolution proceeding. The court of appeals modified the judgment. *Johnson v. Johnson*, 131 Ariz. 47, 638 P.2d 714 (1980). Both appellant and appellee, Emery Johnson, filed petitions for review. We granted review. The opinion of the court of appeals is vacated.

The principal issue in this case is the proper method to be used in determining the wife's interest in the husband's retirement plan. During the 15–year marriage of the parties, the husband accumulated vested rights in both a profit sharing plan and a pension plan through his employment with a Tucson law firm. At the time of trial, there was $17,047.14 in the profit sharing plan and $55,380.77 in the pension trust, for a total of $72,427.91. The distribution of the funds under both plans lies within the discretion of an administrative committee. Although the committee has discretion to order early distribution of these funds, in the normal course of events the funds would not become available to the husband until he reaches retirement age, at least fifteen years from now. Because the husband had no right to immediate payment, the trial court discounted the value of the funds at 6% interest for 22 years (the amount of time between the date of the divorce decree and the date when the husband would reach age 65).

VALUATION OF THE WIFE'S COMMUNITY INTEREST IN THE RETIREMENT PLANS

The pension and profit sharing accounts in this case constitute an appreciable portion of the marital estate. Indeed, it is now commonly recognized that pension rights are one of the most valuable of marital assets upon divorce. These pension rights are generally viewed as a form of deferred compensation for services rendered by employees. As such, it is well settled in Arizona and elsewhere that pension rights, whether vested or non-vested, are community property insofar as the rights were acquired during marriage, and are subject to equitable division upon divorce. The difficulty in the present case arises in attempting to determine the exact dollar amount of the wife's community interest in the husband's pension.

A non-employee spouse may be awarded his or her community interest in the employee spouse's pension benefits under either of two methods. The first has been called the "present cash value method," in which the court determines the community interest in the pension, figures the present cash value of that interest, and awards half of that amount to the non-employee spouse in a lump sum, usually in the form of equivalent property; the employee thus receives the entire pension right free of community ties. Under the "reserved jurisdiction methods," the court determines the formula for division at the time of the decree but delays the actual division until payments are received, retaining jurisdiction to award the appropriate percentage of each pension payment if, as, and when, it is paid out.

The present cash value method provides a number of advantages over the reserved jurisdiction method, especially when the anticipated date of retirement is far in the future. The former spouses are spared further entanglement because the litigation is completed, and the problems of continued court supervision and enforcement of the employee's duty to pay the ex-spouse's share are avoided. It is our view that the present cash value method is preferred if the pension rights can be valued accurately and if the marital estate includes sufficient equivalent property to satisfy the claim of the non-employee spouse without undue hardship to the employee spouse.

In this case, the present cash value method is clearly preferable in that the reserved jurisdiction method would require continued court supervision for at least 15 years. Moreover, the Johnsons' marital estate has sufficient other property available to make a current equitable division of all community property including the wife's interest in the pension fund.

The accuracy of any attempt to value a retirement plan is heavily dependent upon the type of plan which confronts the court. The two major kinds of pension plans are "defined contribution" and "defined benefit" plans. Under a defined contribution plan, a specified amount of money is periodically contributed to a fund by the employer, the employee, or both. This fund is invested and the earnings are divided proportionally among all plan participants. At any moment in time, there is a specific amount of money assigned to the account of each participant. These plans are thus analogous to a saving account. The total amount of benefits receivable under such a plan depends upon the success of fund investments. By contrast, under a defined benefit plan, the benefits are specified in advance, usually as a percentage of salary and related to years of service, and no account is kept for the employee. Both the pension and profit sharing programs in the present case are in the nature of defined contribution plans, as shown by the specific amounts that are credited to the husband's account.

With either type of plan, its present cash value must be determined before a present lump-sum satisfaction of the parties' interests can be made. Various actuarial calculations are used to discount the present value of the retirement plan to reflect contingencies affecting the eventual payout, including discounts for mortality, interest, probability of vesting, and probability of continued employment. However, not all of these calculations are applicable to every retirement plan.

Valuation depends in part on the type of plan involved. In a defined contribution plan, employing individual accounts to which contributions are credited, the best estimate of present value is the amount currently credited to the employee's account. An adjustment, however, must be made if the account figure is not vested or if it is not payable when the employee dies prior to reaching retirement age. If those factors are present, then the account balance must be discounted for the probability of vesting and for the probability of survival to retirement.

In the present case the employee's rights in the plans are vested and are not subject to forfeiture if death occurs prior to retirement. Therefore, the discounts for mortality and probability of vesting are inapplicable here. Under a defined contribution plan, the probability of continued employment discount does not significantly alter the present cash value of the plan. The interest discount is also inapplicable because a defined contribution plan is presently earning interest for the employee. The trial court incorrectly discounted the value of the fund because no consideration was given to the fact that the fund was earning interest and would continue to earn interest. There was no need to discount the value of the account because the value of a defined contribution plan, such as that of appellee, is the present amount credited to the account.

Notes and Questions

1. As the *Johnson* court notes, there are two methods of paying the nontitled spouse his or her share of the marital component of a pension:

a. Under the "*reserved jurisdiction*" or "*deferred payment*" approach, the nontitled spouse is paid if and when the titled spouse receives benefits. The primary disadvantage of this approach is delay, a particular problem if the nontitled spouse needs money at the time of divorce. *See* Bulicek v. Bulicek, 59 Wash.App. 630, 800 P.2d 394 (1990). Another problem arises if, post-divorce, the value of the pension increases due to a promotion or merit pay increase. Some courts have held that a former spouse is not entitled to a share of any post-divorce increase in a retirement fund derived from post-divorce effort, education or achievement by the employee spouse; if the value of the pension is increased post-divorce by, for example, a merit raise or an extraordinary promotion, the employee spouse may request the court to adjust the community fraction to credit his or her separate property with that increment. *See, e.g.*, Hare v. Hodgins, 586 So.2d 118 (La.1991); Gemma v. Gemma, 105 Nev. 458, 778 P.2d 429 (1989). Others have rejected this approach and do not permit post-divorce challenges to the pension award even if post-divorce raises or promotions have enhanced its value. *See, e.g.*, Marriage of Judd, 68 Cal.App.3d 515, 137 Cal.Rptr. 318 (1977); Bulicek v. Bulicek, 59 Wash.App. 630, 800 P.2d 394 (1990); Marriage of Hunt, 909 P.2d 525 (Colo.1995); Seifert v. Seifert, 82 N.C.App. 329, 346 S.E.2d 504, 508 (1986). A third group of states avoids the problem by requiring the divorce court to assume that the employee spouse has retired on the date marital property ceases to accrue; post-divorce service must be ignored. *See* Berry v. Berry, 647 S.W.2d 945 (Tex.1983). What are the advantages and disadvantages of each approach? Which seems fairest?

b. Under the "*present value*" approach, the nontitled spouse receives the value of his or her share of the pension at the time of the divorce. This approach has two disadvantages. The first problem is finding funds to pay the nontitled spouse. Because a defined benefit pension interest is not like a bank account from which funds can be immediately withdrawn, the titled spouse must have enough cash to pay the nontitled spouse his or her share or the couple must have other property which can be awarded the nontitled spouse to "offset" the pension. The second problem is computational. As *Johnson* demonstrates, determining the present value of a defined contribution pension is fairly straightforward. If all pension contributions were made during marriage, the present value is the account balance at the cut-off date for marital property accrual. (An offset for future taxes is not generally accepted, probably because the tax rate then applicable is speculative.) If some, but not all, contributions were made during the marriage, apportionment will be necessary. But determining the present value of a defined benefit pension is a more complicated process. The first step is to determine the aggregate value of expected payments by subtracting the employee's expected retirement age from his life expectancy. If the pension is vested but the employee spouse has not yet retired, the aggregate value must be adjusted to reflect the fact that the employee may die before retirement and never collect; if the pension is also unvested, an additional adjustment is required to reflect the fact that the employee may quit or be fired before obtaining a right to receive benefits. Finally, the expected aggregate value of the pension rights must be discounted to "present value." Discounting to present value reflects the fact that the right to receive money in the future is worth less than the right to receive money immediately because of forgone investment opportunities. In light of these complexities, it is fairly easy to see why many family lawyers have close relationships with accountants and actuaries. For a more detailed discussion of present value calculation approach, *see* William Troyan et al., 3 VALUATION & DISTRIBUTION OF MARITAL PROPERTY § 45.23 *et seq.* (1986).

2. A number of courts have held that, when there is enough marital property to "offset" an award of the entire pension to the employee spouse, the present value approach should be utilized. *See, e.g.*, Dewan v. Dewan, 399 Mass. 754, 506 N.E.2d 879 (1987); Bishop v. Bishop, 113 N.C.App. 725, 440 S.E.2d 591 (1994).

3. *The Qualified Domestic Relations Order ("QDRO")*: When courts first began to utilize the deferred payment approach with defined benefit plans, they ordered the employee spouse to pay the other spouse a specified fraction of payments to be received when he or she retired. This approach entailed several disadvantages: it required continuing contact between spouses, thus inviting future disputes; the employee spouse had to pay taxes on the whole pension payment; and the nonemployee spouse could not obtain payment until the employee spouse actually retired. In 1984, Congress enacted legislation permitting a qualified pension plan administrator to pay benefits to an "alternate

payee" in compliance with a "qualified domestic relations order." *See* Retirement Equity Act of 1984, 29 U.S.C.A. § 1056. Such an order may require payment when the employee's rights mature, regardless of when he or she actually retires. All payments made pursuant to a QDRO are taxed to the recipient, not the employee. (If an attorney prepares an order that does not qualify as a QDRO, payments are taxed to the employee, a tax (and malpractice) disaster. *See* Hawkins v. Commissioner, 102 T.C. 61 (1994)).

A QDRO must specify:

1) The name and the last known mailing address of the participant and the name and mailing address of each alternate payee;

2) The amount or percentage of the participant's benefits to be paid to each alternate payee or the manner in which the amount or percentage is to be determined;

3) The number of payments of the period to which the order applies; and

4) Each plan to which the order applies.

A QDRO may not:

5) Provide any type or form of benefit, or any option, not otherwise provided by the plan;

6) Provide any increased benefits (determined on the basis of actuarial value); or

7) Pay benefits to an alternate payee that must be paid to another alternate payee under a previous QDRO.

For a defined contribution plan, a QDRO normally specifies the amount or percentage of benefits the alternate payee is to receive. For a defined benefit plan, a QDRO specifies either a percentage or a formula to be used by the plan administrator to determine the percentage of benefit to be paid. Federal pension plans are not subject to the Retirement Equity Act of 1984. For more on QDROs, *see* GALE S. FINLEY, ASSIGNING RETIREMENT BENEFITS IN DIVORCE: A PRACTICAL GUIDE TO NEGOTIATING AND DRAFTING QDROS (1995).

4. Federal Retirement Benefits

Because federal law "preempts" state law, a state court may not divide a federal pension if division is prohibited by federal law. (Federal preemption does not prohibit an agreement by the parties to divide benefits that would otherwise be indivisible. *See* Owen v. Owen, 14 Va.App. 623, 419 S.E.2d 267 (1992)). Some federal pension systems clearly specify that plan benefits may be divided. All federal civil service retirement benefits, for example, are subject to division at divorce. *See* Naydan v. Naydan, 800 S.W.2d 637 (Tex.App.1990). Some, but not all, railroad retirement benefits are subject to division. *See* 45 U.S.C.A. § 231m; Kamel v. Kamel, 721 S.W.2d 450 (Tex.App.1986). Statutes that do not specify whether benefits are divisible require court interpretation as to Congressional intent; almost all courts, for example, have found that Congress did not intend division of Social Security benefits. *See* Pongonis v. Pongonis, 606 A.2d 1055 (Me.1992); Pleasant v. Pleasant, 97 Md.App. 711, 632 A.2d 202 (1993); In re Marriage of Brane, 21 Kan. App.2d 778, 908 P.2d 625 (1995) (Social Security benefits not divisible, but may be taken into account in dividing other property).

The issue of Congressional intent regarding military retirement benefits has produced a long history of litigation and legislation. In June, 1981, the U.S. Supreme Court held that Congress did not intend that military retirement benefits should be divisible at divorce, and that no offsetting award to compensate the non-employee spouse for the value of the benefits was permissible. McCarty v. McCarty, 453 U.S. 210, 101 S.Ct. 2728, 69 L.Ed.2d 589 (1981). Congress responded to *McCarty* by enacting the Uniform Services Former Spouse's Protection Act (USFS-PA), 10 U.S.C.A. § 1408. USFSPA, which became effective February 1, 1983, permitted, but did not require, divorce courts to award up to 50% of "disposable retired pay" to the spouse of a military employee.

USFSPA did not specify whether it applied retroactively. As a result, it was unclear whether divorce decrees issued pre-*McCarty*, or divorce decrees issued post-*McCarty* and pre-USFSPA, were subject to *McCarty* or the new law. Some states passed laws permitting a divorce court to reopen post-*McCarty*, pre-USFSPA decrees upon motion of the nonemployee spouse within a specified period. *See* CAL. CIV. CODE § 5124; IDAHO CODE § 32–713A. In states that did not enact legislation, some courts permitted reopening of pre-USFSPA decrees (*see* Flynn v. Rogers, 172 Ariz. 62, 834 P.2d 148 (1992)); others did not. *See* Holler v. Holler, 257 Ga. 27, 354 S.E.2d 140 (1987). Still other courts permitted reopening only if the decree was silent regarding pension rights. *See* NEV. REV. STAT. § 121.161; Eddy v. Eddy, 710 S.W.2d 783 (Tex.App.1986).

In 1990, Congress attempted to resolve this debate by adding a provision to USFSPA specifying both that state court orders which reopened pre-*McCarty* decrees would not be honored by the federal government after 1992 and that divorce courts may not reopen a pre-*McCarty* decree unless the decree "treats (or reserves jurisdiction to treat)" the retirement pay as divisible property. Some courts have interpreted this provision to prohibit the reopening of pre-*McCarty* decrees that do not explicitly mention military retirement benefits. *See* Mote v. Corser, 810 S.W.2d 122 (Mo.App.1991); White v. White, 623 So.2d 31 (La.App.1993). Others have held that, at least in a community property jurisdiction, a silent decree implicitly reserves jurisdiction. *See* Walton v. Lee, 888 S.W.2d 604 (Tex.App.1994). In Mansell v. Mansell, 490 U.S. 581, 109 S.Ct. 2023, 104 L.Ed.2d 675 (1989), the Supreme Court held that division of pension benefits falling outside the USFSPA definition of "disposable retired pay" remained impermissible. For a more extensive discussion of military pension division, *see* Mark Sullivan, *Military Pension Division: Crossing the Minefield*, 31 FAM. L.Q. 19 (1997).

In addition to pension benefits, the spouse of a government employee may also qualify for certain privileges after divorce, such as the right to medical coverage and commissary privileges, if the marriage was of sufficient duration. A divorce court may also require the employee spouse to elect a survivor annuity and designate the non-employee as the recipient.

Problem 14–3:

Margaret and John married thirty-five years ago and separated three years ago. John was employed as a pilot with Arrow Airlines from approximately one year after his marriage to Margaret, until about two years before their separation, when he joined a strike called by the Air Line Pilots Association, International (ALPA).

Following the strike, Arrow filed a bankruptcy petition. The bankruptcy court in essence ordered that: (1) the strike be terminated; (2) no recrimination or retaliation be taken against striking pilots; (3) the parties to dismiss all litigation between them pending in federal courts; and (4) striking pilots be given the option of being recalled and reinstated or severance pay.

The severance pay option provided that active pilots on Arrow's seniority list as of the strike date could elect severance pay in exchange for waiving the right to recall and waiving the right to claims against the company connected with the strike. The amount of severance pay was to be computed by multiplying $4,000 times the number of years of active service with Arrow as of the strike date.

John opted for the severance pay option and his severance pay was calculated at $126,800. According to the set schedule, John receives 10 percent in an initial payment this year, 15 percent next year, and the remainder in 20 quarterly payments, with 10 percent interest to be paid on amounts due after the first eight quarterly payments.

John and Margaret worked out a division of their marital estate with the exception of the severance pay, which John claimed was his separate property and Margaret claimed was a community asset.

You are the law clerk of the California divorce court judge who will decide whether the severance pay is divisible. The judge has asked you to research the problem, tell her the right answer, *and* explain the basis for that answer. The following precedents are relevant:

In In re Marriage of Skaden (1977) 19 Cal.3d 679, 139 Cal.Rptr. 615, 566 P.2d 249, the California Supreme Court found termination benefits paid to an insurance agent under an employment agreement to be community property. The benefits consisted of a percentage of insurance premiums collected on insurance policies sold by the agent. The *Skaden* court held the benefits were community property because they were deferred compensation for the agent's previous endeavors.

Following *Skaden*, the issue of whether termination or severance benefits were community or separate property was raised in four published cases: In In re Marriage of Flockhart (1981) 119 Cal.App.3d 240, 173 Cal.Rptr. 818, a federal employee whose job was adversely affected by expansion of Redwood National Park received "weekly lay-off" benefits. The *Flockhart* court held that the benefits were separate property, as they were intended to presently compensate the employee for loss of earnings. *In* In re Marriage of Wright (1983) 140 Cal.App.3d 342, 189 Cal.Rptr. 336, the court also held that the lay-off benefits were separate property as they were designed to ease the employee's transition back into the work force, a need arising from his involuntary termination. In In re Marriage of Kuzmiak (1986) 176 Cal.App.3d 1152, 222 Cal.Rptr. 644, the court reached the same result based on similar facts and the same reasoning. The most recent case to consider the issue is In re Marriage of Horn (1986) 181 Cal.App.3d 540, 226 Cal.Rptr. 666.

In *Horn*, the court concluded that the important issue in cataloging termination or severance benefits is "whether the benefits constitute (a) deferred compensation for past services or (b) present compensation for loss of earnings. If the benefits are deferred compensation for past earnings, the benefits are community property; if they are present compensation for loss of earnings, they are separate property." *Horn* also states that the character of the benefits is to be determined by considering all relevant circumstances.

At issue in *Horn* was the severance pay received by the husband from the National Football League (NFL) on his retirement from football. During the husband's playing days, the management of the NFL and the National Football League Players Association added a severance pay provision to the collective bargaining agreement, which provided that any player with two or more seasons with the NFL was entitled to a lump sum of severance pay, the amount to be based on the player's number of NFL seasons. In finding the severance pay to be community property, the *Horn* court noted these characteristics:

> . . . (a) it is derived from a contract right; (b) it is based on the number of seasons worked; (c) it must be paid back to the NFL if the player returns to professional football within one year of receipt; (d) it will be paid back to him when he again leaves football, but no additional amount will have accrued for the seasons worked after his return; (e) it is given to the player's stated beneficiary or estate if he dies; (f) it is received in a lump sum after a certain period of time has passed following the player's notification to the club of his intent to permanently retire from professional football.

The *Horn* court characterized the severance pay as community property because the husband had an absolute right to it based on his eight seasons with the NFL and the contractual agreement. The court noted that in In re Marriage of Flockhart, *supra*, In re Marriage of Wright, *supra*, and In re Marriage of Kuzmiak, *supra*, there were no absolute rights to receive severance pay; the husband in each case received severance pay only because a loss of work was forced upon him.

The *Horn* court also noted that the three cases did not involve a contractual right to a payment.

1. Margaret and John's lawyers have not yet filed briefs in the case. What arguments would you expect each to make?

2. What decision should the judge reach? Why? *See* In re Marriage of DeShurley, 207 Cal.App.3d 992, 255 Cal.Rptr. 150 (1989); Biddlecom v. Biddlecom, 113 A.D.2d 66, 495 N.Y.S.2d 301 (1985); Ryan v. Ryan, 261 N.J.Super. 689, 619 A.2d 692 (N.J. Super.Ch.Div. 1992).

F. PROFESSIONAL DEGREES AND LICENSES

O'BRIEN v. O'BRIEN

New York Court of Appeals, 1985.
66 N.Y.2d 576, 498 N.Y.S.2d 743, 489 N.E.2d 712.

SIMONS, JUDGE.

In this divorce action, the parties' only assets of any consequence is the husband's newly acquired license to practice medicine. The principal issue presented is whether that license, acquired during their marriage, is marital property subject to equitable distribution under Domestic Relations Law § 236(B)(5).

* * *

Plaintiff and defendant married on April 3, 1971. At the time both were employed as teachers at the same private school. Defendant had a bachelor's degree and a temporary teaching certificate but required 18 months of postgraduate classes at an approximate cost of $3,000, excluding living expenses, to obtain permanent certification in New York. She claimed, and the trial court found, that she had relinquished the opportunity to obtain permanent certification while plaintiff pursued his education. At the time of the marriage, plaintiff had completed only three and one-half years of college but shortly afterward he returned to school at night to earn his bachelor's degree and to complete sufficient premedical courses to enter medical school. In September 1973 the parties moved to Guadalajara, Mexico, where plaintiff became a full-time medical student. While he pursued his studies defendant held several teaching and tutorial positions and contributed her earnings to their joint expenses. The parties returned to New York in December 1976 so that plaintiff could complete the last two semesters of medical school and internship training here. After they returned, defendant resumed her former teaching position and she remained in it at the time this action was commenced. Plaintiff was licensed to practice medicine in October 1980. He commenced this action for divorce two months later. At the time of trial, he was a resident in general surgery.

During the marriage both parties contributed to paying the living and educational expenses and they received additional help from both of their families. They disagreed on the amounts of their respective contributions but it is undisputed that in addition to performing household work and managing the family finances defendant was gainfully employed throughout the marriage, that she contributed all of her earnings to their living and educational expenses and that her financial contributions exceeded those of plaintiff. The trial court found that she had contributed 76% of the parties' income exclusive of a $10,000 student loan obtained by defendant. Finding that plaintiff's medical degree and license are marital property, the court received evidence of its value and ordered a distributive award to defendant.

Defendant presented expert testimony that the present value of plaintiff's medical license was $472,000. Her expert testified that he arrived at this figure by comparing the average income of a college graduate and that of a general surgeon between 1985, when plaintiff's residency would end, and 2012, when he would reach age 65. After considering Federal income taxes, an inflation rate of 10% and a real interest rate of 3% he capitalized the difference in average earnings and reduced the amount to present value. He also gave his opinion that the present value of defendant's contribution to plaintiff's medical education was $103,390. Plaintiff offered no expert testimony on the subject.

The court, after considering the life-style that plaintiff would enjoy from the enhanced earning potential his medical license would bring and defendant's contributions and efforts toward attainment of it, made a distributive award to her of $188,800, representing 40% of the value of the license, and ordered it paid in 11 annual installments of various amounts beginning November 1, 1982, and ending November 1, 1992. The court also directed plaintiff to maintain a life insurance policy on his life for defendant's benefit for the unpaid balance of the award and it ordered plaintiff to pay defendant's counsel fees of $7,000 and her expert witness fee of $1,000. It did not award defendant maintenance.

* * *

The Equitable Distribution Law contemplates only two classes of property: marital property and separate property (Domestic Relations Law § 236[B][1][c], [d]). The former, which is subject to equitable distribution, is defined broadly as "*all* property acquired by either or both spouses during the marriage and before the execution of a separation agreement or the commencement of a matrimonial action, *regardless of the form in which title is held*" (Domestic Relations Law § 236[B][1]][c] [emphasis added]; *see* § 236[B][5][b]m [c]). Plaintiff does not contend that his license is excluded from distribution because it is separate property; rather, he claims that it is not property at all but represents a personal attainment in acquiring knowledge. He rests his argument on decisions in similar cases from other jurisdictions and on his view that a license does not satisfy common-law concepts of property. Neither contention is controlling because decisions in other States rely principally on their own statutes, and the legislative history underlying them, and because the New York Legislature deliberately went beyond traditional property concepts when it formulated the Equitable Distribution Law. Instead, our statute recognizes that spouses have an equitable claim to things of value arising out of the marital relationship and classifies them as subject to distribution by focusing on the marital status of the parties at the time of acquisition. Those things acquired during marriage and subject to distribution have been classified as "marital property" although, as one commentator has observed, they hardly fall within the traditional property concepts because there is no common-law property interest remotely resembling marital property. "It is a statutory creature, is of no meaning whatsoever during the normal course of a marriage and arises full-grown, like Athena, upon the signing of a separation agreement or the commencement of a matrimonial action. [Thus] [i]t is hardly surprising, and not at all relevant, that traditional common law property concepts do not fit in parsing the meaning of 'marital property' " (Florescue, "Market Value," *Professional Licenses and Marital Property: A Dilemma in Search of a Horn*, 1982 N.Y.St.Bar Assn. Fam.L.Rev. 13 [Dec.]) Having classified the "property" subject to distribution the Legislature did not attempt to go further and define it but left it to the courts to determine what interests come within the terms of § 236(B)(1)(C).

We made such a determination in *Majauskas v. Majauskas*, 61 N.Y.2d 481, 474 N.Y.S.2d 699, 463 N.E.2d 15, holding there that vested but unmatured pension rights are marital property subject to equitable distribution. Because pension benefits are not specifically identified as marital property in the statute, we looked to the express reference to pension rights contained in § 236(B)(5)(d)(4), which deals with equitable distribution of marital property, to other provisions of the equitable distribution state and to the legislative intent behind its enactment to determine whether pension rights are marital property or separate property. A similar analysis is appropriate here and leads to the conclusion that marital property encompasses a license to practice medicine to the extent that the license is acquired during marriage.

Section 236 provides that in making an equitable distribution of marital property, "the court shall consider: * * * (6) any equitable claim to, interest in, or direct or indirect contribution made to the acquisition of such marital property by the party not having title, including joint efforts or expenditures and contributions and services as a spouse, parent, wage earner and homemaker, and *to the career or career potential* of the other party [and] * * * (9) the impossibility or difficulty of evaluating any component asset or any interest in a business, corporation or *profession*" (Domestic Relations Law § 236[B][5][d][6], [9] [emphasis added]). Where equitable distribution of marital property is appropriate but "the distribution of an interest in a business, corporation or *profession* would be contrary to law" the court shall make a distributive award in lieu of an actual distribution of the property (Domestic Relations Law § 236[B][5][e] [emphasis added]). The words mean exactly what they say: that an interest in a profession or professional career potential is marital property which may be represented by direct or indirect contributions of the non-title-holding spouse, including financial contributions and nonfinancial contributions made by caring for the home and family.

The history which preceded enactment of the statute confirms this interpretation. Reform of § 236 was advocated because experience had proven that application of the traditional common-law title theory of property had caused inequities upon dissolution of a marriage. The Legislature replaced the existing system with equitable distribution of marital property, an entirely new theory which considered all the circumstances of the case and of the respective parties to the marriage. Equitable distribution was based on the premise that a marriage is, among other things, an economic partnership to which both parties contribute as spouse, parent, wage earner or homemaker. Consistent with this purpose, and implicit in the statutory scheme as a whole, is the view that upon dissolution of the marriage there should be a winding up of the parties' economic affairs and a severance of their economic ties by an equitable distribution of the marital assets. Thus, the concept of alimony, which often served as a means of lifetime support and dependence for one spouse upon the other long after the marriage was over, was replaced with the concept of maintenance which seeks to allow "the recipient spouse an opportunity to achieve [economic] independence".

The determination that a professional license is marital property is also consistent with the conceptual base upon which the statute rests. As this case demonstrates, few undertakings during a marriage better qualify as the type of joint effort that the statute's economic partnership theory is intended to address than contributions toward one spouse's acquisition of a professional license. Working spouses are often required to contribute substantial income as wage earners, sacrifice their own educational or career goals land opportunities for child rearing, perform the bulk of household duties and responsibilities and forego the acquisition of marital assets that could have been accumulated if the professional spouse had been employed rather than occupied with the study and training necessary to acquire a professional license. In this case, nearly all of the parties' nine-year marriage was devoted to the acquisition of plaintiff's medical license and defendant played a major role in that project. She worked continuously during the marriage and contributed all of her earnings to their joint effort, she sacrificed her own educational and career opportunities, and she traveled with plaintiff to Mexico for three and one-half years while he attended medical school there. The Legislature has decided, by its explicit reference in the statute to the contributions represent investments in the economic partnership of the marriage and that the product of the parties' joint efforts, the professional license, should be considered marital property.

* * *

There is no reason in law or logic to restrict the plain language of the statute to existing practices, * * * for it is of little consequence in making an award of marital property, except for the purpose of evaluation, whether the professional spouse has already established a practice or whether he or she has yet to do so. An established practice merely represents the exercise of the privileges conferred upon the professional spouse by the license and the income flowing from that practice represents the receipt of the enhanced earning capacity that licensure allows. That being so, it would be unfair not to consider the license a marital asset.

Plaintiff's principal argument, adopted by the majority below, is that a professional license is not marital property because it does not fit within the traditional view of property as something which has an exchange value on the open market and is capable of sale, assignment or transfer. * * * That a professional license has no market value is irrelevant. Obviously, a license may not be alienated as may other property and for that reason the working spouse's interest in it is limited. The Legislature has recognized that limitation, however, and has provided for an award in lieu of its actual distribution.

Plaintiff also contends that alternative remedies should be employed, such as an award of rehabilitative maintenance or reimbursement for direct financial contributions. The statute does not expressly authorize retrospective maintenance or rehabilitative awards and we have no occasion to decide in this case whether the authority to do so may ever be implied from its provisions. It is sufficient to observe that normally a working spouse should not be restricted to that relief because to do so frustrates the purposes underlying the Equitable Distribution Law. Limiting a working spouse to a maintenance award, either general or rehabilitative, not only is contrary to the economic partnership concept underlying the statute but also retains the uncertain and inequitable economic ties of dependence that the Legislature sought to extinguish by equitable distribution. Maintenance is subject to termination upon the recipient's remarriage and a working spouse may never receive adequate consideration for his or her contribution and may even be penalized for the decision to remarry if that is the only method of compensating the contribution. As one court said so well, "[t]he function of equitable distribution is to recognize that when a marriage ends, each of the spouses, based on the totality of the contributions made to it, has a stake in and right to a share of the marital assets accumulated while it endured, not because that share is needed, but because those assets represent the capital product of what was essentially a partnership entity." (*Wood v. Wood*, 119 Misc.2d 1076, 1079, 465 N.Y.S.2d 475). The Legislature stated its intention to eliminate such inequities by providing that a supporting spouse's "direct or indirect contribution" be recognized, considered and rewarded.

Turning to the question of valuation, it has been suggested that even if a professional license is considered marital property, the working spouse is entitled only to reimbursement of his or her direct financial contributions. * * * If the license is marital property, then the working spouse is entitled to an equitable portion of it, not a return of funds advanced. Its value is the enhanced earning capacity it affords the holder and although fixing the present value of that enhanced earning capacity may present problems, the problems are not insurmountable. Certainly they are no more difficult than computing tort damages for wrongful death or diminished earning capacity resulting from injury and they differ only in degree from the problems presented when valuing a professional practice for purposes of a distributive award, something the courts have not hesitated to do. The trial court retains the flexibility and discretion to structure the distributive award equitably, taking into consideration factors such as the working spouse's need for immediate payment, the licensed spouse's current ability to pay and the income tax consequences of prolonging the period of payment and, once it has received evidence of the present value of the license and the working spouse's contributions toward its acquisition and considered the remaining factors mandated by the statute, it may then make an appropriate distribution of the marital property including a distributive award for the professional license if such an award is warranted. When other marital assets are of sufficient value to provide for the supporting spouse's equitable portion of the marital property, including his or her contributions to the acquisition of the professional license, however, the court retains the discretion to distribute these other marital assets or to make a distributive award in lieu of an actual distribution of the value of the professional spouse's license.

* * *

Accordingly, in view of our holding that plaintiff's license to practice medicine is marital property, the order of the Appellate Division should be modified, with costs to defendant, by reinstating the judgment and the case remitted to the Appellate Division for determination of the facts, including the exercise of that court's discretion, and, as so modified, affirmed. Question certified answered in the negative.

MEYER, JUDGE (concurring).

I concur in Judge Simons' opinion but write separately to point up for consideration by the Legislature the potential for unfairness involved in distributive awards based upon a license of a professional still in training. * * * The implication of Domestic Relations Law § 236(B)(9)(b), which deals with modification of an order or decree as to maintenance or child support, is * * * that a distributive award pursuant to § 236(B)(5)(3), once made, is not subject to change. Yet a professional in training who is not finally committed to a career choice when the distributive award is made may be locked into a particular kind of practice simply because the monetary obligations imposed by the distributive award made on the basis of the trial judge's conclusion (prophecy may be a better word) as to what the career choice will be leaves him or her no alternative.

The present case points up the problem. A medical license is but a step toward the practice ultimately engaged in by its holder, which follows after internship, residency and, for particular specialties, board certification. Here it is undisputed that plaintiff was in a residency for general surgery at the time of the trial, but had the previous year done a residency in internal medicine. Defendant's expert based his opinion on the difference between the average income of a general surgeon and that of a college graduate of plaintiff's age and life expectancy, which the trial judge utilized, impliedly finding that plaintiff would engage in a surgical practice despite plaintiff's testimony that he was dissatisfied with the general surgery program he was in and was attempting to return to the internal medicine training he had been in the previous year. The trial judge had the right, of course, to discredit that testimony, but the point is that equitable distribution was not intended to permit a judge to make a career decision for a licensed spouse still in training. Yet the degree of speculation involved in the award made is emphasized by the testimony of the expert on which it was based. Asked whether his assumptions and calculations were in any way speculative, he replied: "Yes. They're speculative to the extent of, will Dr. O'Brien practice medicine? Will Dr. O'Brien earn more or less than the average surgeon earns? Will Dr. O'Brien live to age sixty-five? Will Dr. O'Brien have a heart attack or will he be injured in an automobile accident? Will he be disabled? I mean, there is a degree of speculation. That speculative aspect is no more to be taken into account, cannot be taken into account, and it's a question, again, Mr. Emanuelli, not for the expert but for the courts to decide. It's not my function nor could it be."

The equitable distribution provisions of the Domestic Relations Law were intended to provide flexibility so that equity could be done. But if the assumption as to career choice on which a distributive award payable over a number of years is based turns out not to be the fact (as, for example, should a general surgery trainee accidentally lose the use of his hand), it should be possible for the court to revise the distributive award to conform to the fact. And there will be no unfairness in so doing if either spouse can seek reconsideration, for the licensed spouse is more likely to seek reconsideration based on real, rather than imagined, cause if he or she knows that the nonlicensed spouse can seek not only reinstatement of the original award, but counsel fees in addition, should the purported circumstance on which a change is made turn out to have been feigned or to be illusory.

Notes and Comments

1. Every other state high court that has considered the issue has rejected the *O'Brien* approach. *See, e.g.,* Nelson v. Nelson, 736 P.2d 1145 (Alaska 1987); Wisner v. Wisner, 129 Ariz. 333, 631 P.2d 115 (App. 1981); In re Marriage of Sullivan, 134 Cal.App.3d 634, 184 Cal.Rptr. 796 (1982); *vacated*, 37 Cal.3d 762, 209 Cal.Rptr. 354, 691 P.2d 1020 (1984) (statute amended to provide for the community to be reimbursed for community contributions to education of a party); In re Marriage of Olar, 747 P.2d 676 (Colo.1987); Hughes v. Hughes, 438 So.2d 146 (Fla.App.1983); In re Marriage of Weinstein, 128 Ill.App.3d 234, 83 Ill.Dec. 425, 470 N.E.2d 551 (1984); Archer v. Archer, 303 Md. 347, 493 A.2d 1074 (1985); Drapek v. Drapek, 399 Mass. 240, 503 N.E.2d 946

(1987); Ruben v. Ruben, 123 N.H. 358, 461 A.2d 733 (1983); Mahoney v. Mahoney, 91 N.J. 488, 453 A.2d 527 (1982); Hodge v. Hodge, 513 Pa. 264, 520 A.2d 15 (1986); Wehrkamp v. Wehrkamp, 357 N.W.2d 264 (S.D.1984); Petersen v. Petersen, 737 P.2d 237 (Utah App.1987). Here are some of the reasons:

a. *Consistency*: Under either a marital or community property regime, post-divorce wages are separate property; *O'Brien* is inconsistent with this approach. Most courts have failed to see a logical basis for distinguishing between cases where enhanced post-divorce wages result from acquisition of a degree or license and cases where enhanced post-divorce wages result from work experience, nondegree training, and promotions obtained during marriage:

> The termination of a marriage represents, if nothing else, the disappointment of expectations, financial and nonfinancial, which were hoped to be achieved by and during the continuation of the relationship. It does not, in our view, represent a commercial loss.
>
> If the plan fails by reason of the termination of the marriage, we do not regard the supporting spouse's consequent loss of expectation by itself as any more compensable or demanding of solicitude than the loss of expectations of any other spouse who, with the hope and anticipation of the endurance of the relationship . . . has invested a portion of his or her life, youth, energy and labor in a failed marriage.
>
> Mahoney v. Mahoney, 182 N.J.Super. 598, 442 A.2d 1062 (App.Div. 1982).

b. *Modifiability*: We do not know where Dr. O'Brien will practice, whether he will in fact pursue his chosen specialty, or how successful he will be. Yet, as Judge Meyer points out in *O'Brien*, property division awards are not modifiable due to changed circumstances. If the court's guess on the value of Dr. O'Brien's degree is inaccurate, no recourse is available to either party.

c. *Valuation*: The *O'Brien* court held that the degree should be valued by comparing the average lifetime earnings of a college graduate and those of a medical doctor practicing in Dr. O'Brien's chosen field of specialization. This approach ignores the fact that those admitted to medical school are a highly credentialed group of college graduates who likely have better than average career prospects whether they attend medical school or not. The *O'Brien* approach thus may substantially overvalue the degree. Further valuation problems arise if the couple divorces after the degree has matured into a professional practice. In many states (including New York) professional goodwill in a practice established during marriage is marital property subject to division. Should the degree "merge" into the practice to avoid double-counting? Must the degree and practice be valued separately? If so, how is it possible to avoid double-counting? The New York Court of Appeals has recently attempted to answer these questions, holding that both the degree and practice are marital property; the court noted that overlapping awards should be avoided, but does not specify a valuation method to ensure such a result. *See* McSparron v. McSparron, 87 N.Y.2d 275, 639 N.Y.S.2d 265, 662 N.E.2d 745 (1995). For a valiant attempt by a trial court to apply the *McSparron* approach, *see* Rochelle G. v. Harold M.G., 170 Misc.2d 808, 649 N.Y.S.2d 632 (1996).

d. *Allocation*: The first Mrs. O'Brien has a claim to $188,000 of Dr. O'Brien's post-divorce earnings, wages that would traditionally be considered marital property of Dr. O'Brien and any second Mrs. O'Brien. Is the $188,000 Dr. O'Brien's separate property with respect to his second spouse? Or is it the property of both marriages? The first approach seems unfair to the second Mrs. O'Brien, the second approach seems unfair to Dr. O'Brien. In New York, a marital property state, income from separate property received during marriage is separate property. *See* Sauer v. Sauer, 91 A.D.2d 1166, 459 N.Y.S.2d 131 (1983). But no New York court has as yet dealt with this allocational issue.

e. *Inflexibility*: Mrs. O'Brien was a very sympathetic plaintiff who not only supported her husband for years, but sacrificed her own career goals and moved to another country, only to be dumped when the degree (but no property to compensate her) was in hand. The *O'Brien* holding, however, applies in all cases in which a degree is earned during marriage, even if there is other property, even if the spouses' living expenses were paid by the educated spouse's parents, even if the claimant spouse has higher earning capacity than the educated spouse, even if the claimant spouse has actively discouraged attainment of the degree.

2. While no other high court has adopted the *O'Brien* approach, in 1993 Oregon enacted a statute that treats "future enhanced earning capacity" as marital property:

> The present value of, and income resulting from, the future enhanced earning capacity of either party shall be considered as property. The presumption of equal contribution to the acquisition of marital property, however, shall not apply to enhanced earning capacity. A spouse asserting an interest in the income resulting from an enhancement of earning capacity of the other spouse must demonstrate that the spouse made a material contribution to the enhancement. Material contribution can be shown by, among other things, having contributed, financially or otherwise, to the education and training that resulted in the enhanced earning capacity. The contribution shall have been substantial and of prolonged duration.

Or. Rev. Stat. § 107.105(1)(f).

How does the Oregon approach differ from that of *O'Brien*? What are the pros and cons of each?

3. As an alternative to treating a professional degree or license as property subject to division, many courts have granted the supporting spouse other remedies, such as a rehabilitative or reimbursement alimony award. *See* Drapek v. Drapek, 399 Mass. 240, 503 N.E.2d 946 (1987); Forristall v. Forristall, 831 P.2d 1017 (Okla. App. 1992). California, for

example, has statutorily adopted a reimbursement approach in the degree cases. CAL. FAM. CODE § 2641 requires reimbursement to the marital community "for community contributions to education or training of a party that substantially enhances the earning capacity of the party. The amount reimbursed shall be with interest at the legal rate, accruing from the end of the calendar year in which the contributions were made." Reimbursement "shall be reduced or modified to the extent circumstances render such a disposition unjust," including, but not limited to, any of the following:

> (1) The community has substantially benefitted from the education, training, or loan incurred for the education or training of the party. There is a rebuttable presumption, affecting the burden of proof, that the community has not substantially benefitted from community contributions to the education or training made less than 10 years before the commencement of the proceeding, and that the community has substantially benefitted from community contributions to the education or training made more than 10 years before the commencement of the proceeding.
>
> (2) The education or training received by the party is offset by the education or training received by the other party for which community contributions have been made.
>
> (3) The education or training enables the party receiving the education or training to engage in gainful employment that substantially reduces the need of the party for support that would otherwise be required.

The statute also excludes educational loans from community liabilities, assigning these debts to the spouse whose education the loan financed. What are the pros and cons of the California approach as compared to *O'Brien*? as compared to the Oregon statute?

4. New York courts have extended the *O'Brien* holding to a wide variety of degrees and licenses. *See, e.g.*, Morimando v. Morimando, 145 A.D.2d 609, 536 N.Y.S.2d 701 (1988) (license and certification as physician's assistant); McGowan v. McGowan, 142 A.D.2d 355, 535 N.Y.S.2d 990 (1988) (Master's degree in teaching); McAlpine v. McAlpine, 176 A.D.2d 285, 574 N.Y.S.2d 385 (1991) (fellowship in Society of Actuaries). Neither *O'Brien* nor the Oregon statute provide any apparent remedy when a spouse goes to graduate school in a discipline that does not increase earning capacity. Is this fair?

5. New York courts have also extended the *O'Brien* holding to the increased value of a celebrity's career occurring during marriage. *See* Golub v. Golub, 139 Misc.2d 440, 527 N.Y.S.2d 946 (1988) (actress Marisa Berensen); Elkus v. Elkus, 169 A.D.2d 134, 572 N.Y.S.2d 901 (1991) (opera singer Fredericke von Stade). Is there any logical basis for treating the career of a celebrity spouse differently from the career of any other spouse? *See* Boyd v. Boyd, 116 Mich.App. 774, 323 N.W.2d 553 (1982) (no). For a discussion of this issue from an economic perspective,

see Allen Parkman, *Human Capital as Property in Celebrity Divorces*, 29 FAM. L.Q. 141 (1995).

6. Some courts have said that the non-educated spouse in the *O'Brien* situation does not support the other with the "expectation of compensation." *See* Sullivan v. Sullivan, 134 Cal.App.3d 634, 184 Cal. Rptr. 796 (1982). But undeniably the spouse would *hope* to share in the fruits from the education. Does this mean that some remedy should be provided?

G. BUSINESS GOODWILL

"Goodwill" refers to the portion of a business's value derived from its reputation. In computing the value of a marital business, almost all courts have concluded that the value of *commercial goodwill*, that associated with the business rather than the owner spouse, should be included in the marital estate. There is less agreement on *personal goodwill* associated with the personal reputation of the owner spouse. Some courts have held that, if earned during marriage, it is a marital asset subject to division. Other courts, troubled by the fact that personal goodwill is an intangible (and often nonrealizable) asset much like earning capacity, have held that it should not be treated as a marital asset. For a general discussion of this problem, *see* THEODORE P. ORENSTEIN & GARY N. SKOLOFF, WHEN A PROFESSIONAL DIVORCES (ABA, 2d ed. 1994). For a general discussion of business valuation methods, *see* Arnold Rutkin, *Valuation of a Closely Held Corporation, Small Business or Professional Practice*, in 2 VALUATION AND DISTRIBUTION OF MARITAL PROPERTY ch. 22 (1998).

PRAHINSKI v. PRAHINSKI

Maryland Court of Appeals, 1990.
321 Md. 227, 582 A.2d 784.

COLE, JUDGE.

In this case we must determine whether the goodwill of a solo law practice is a value includable as marital property for purposes of calculating a monetary award upon divorce.

The facts are neither complicated nor in dispute. Margaret and Leo F. X. Prahinski were married on March 20, 1965. Margaret discontinued her education after her freshman year in college in order to maintain the family home. Leo continued his formal education and eventually obtained a law degree. In 1971, Leo started his own law practice. Margaret became his secretary, and as the law practice grew, so did Margaret's responsibilities in the office. Gradually, the focus of the practice shifted to real estate settlements and Margaret's position evolved into that of office manager.

Leo became involved with another woman in 1983. The parties separated thereafter, and Margaret filed for divorce on November 14, 1986. The Circuit Court for Prince George's County granted an absolute divorce, and on July 10, 1987, the court filed a written order determining what was marital property, providing for distribution of marital assets, and granting both a monetary award and indefinite alimony. Included in the monetary award was one-half of the value of the law practice.

Leo appealed to the Court of Special Appeals claiming that the trial court erred in considering his law practice to be marital property consisting totally of goodwill and dividing the value thereof equally between the parties. Leo also questioned the propriety of setting the amount of alimony at a time far in advance of when the alimony payments were to commence.

The Court of Special Appeals, 75 Md. App. 113, 540 A.2d 833 (1988), held that the value of the practice consisted entirely of the reputation of Leo F. X. Prahinski, Attorney-at-Law, and was therefore personal to him. As such, the value of the practice was not marital property and could not be subject to distribution as part of the monetary award. The intermediate appellate court left open the possibility that goodwill in a solo practice could be marital property if it could be shown that the goodwill was severable from the reputation of the practitioner.

Margaret argues that the value of the practice should be considered marital property, and therefore subject to a monetary award to compensate her for her contributions thereto. She insists that the majority of the work handled by the practice did not require an attorney, and that she contributed the overwhelming majority of the time and effort which made the practice successful. To deny her an equitable share of the goodwill inherent in the practice, she claims, would frustrate the purpose of the monetary award statute, which seeks to adjust the rights of the parties based upon their contributions during the marriage.

Specifically, Margaret contends that goodwill is a form of property which the practice acquired during the marriage; hence it fits the definition of marital property, no matter whose name is on the business. She further urges this Court to adopt the position that the professional goodwill of a sole proprietorship is valuable property to be included in the marital estate.

Leo maintains that his vocation has always been a solo law practice. As such, any intangible value assigned to the business is a result of his personal reputation as an attorney. The only way that goodwill could be considered marital property, he argues, is if the goodwill had a value independent of the continued presence or reputation of the sole practitioner. He contends that he is the only person who can practice under the name "Leo F. X. Prahinski, Attorney-at-law." He claims he could not sell his practice and its intangible assets to anyone; therefore, he concludes that the goodwill is personal to him and should not be considered marital property.

The characterization of goodwill and its relationship to a business is crucial to the determination of this issue. In *Hagan v. Dundore*, 187 Md. 430, 50 A.2d 570 (1947), we examined the sale of a partnership interest. In so doing, we took notice of the definitions of goodwill applied by other jurisdictions. One such definition states: "The goodwill of a business comprises those advantages which may inure to the *purchaser* from holding himself out to the public as succeeding to an enterprise which has been identified in the past with the name and repute of his *predecessor.*" *Id.* at 442, 50 A.2d at 576 (emphasis added). According to this definition, goodwill can exist in those situations in which a business has successive owners, each one benefitting from the management of the business by the preceding owners.

Goodwill exists, however, in businesses that are still in the hands of their founders and which may never be sold. We took notice of such a situation in *Brown v. Benzinger*, 118 Md. 29, 84 A. 79 (1912), where we quoted Lord Eldon's definition of goodwill as "the probability that the old customers will resort to the old place." *Id.* at 35, 84 A. at 81 (quoting *Cruttwell v. Lye*, 34 Eng.Rep. 129, 134 (Ch. 1810)). Such a definition provides for the presence of goodwill in a business even if no monetary value has ever been placed on it.

In *Brown*, the Court was confronted with the sale of a "business conducted by [the vendor] as surgeon chiropodist." 118 Md. at 31, 84 A. at 79. That opinion makes it that as long ago as 1912, this Court considered the goodwill involved in a profession to be different from the goodwill involved in a commercial business. Examining the decisions from other jurisdictions, the *Brown* court noted that in the context of a non-competition agreement in the sale of a business, the goodwill of a professional practice had been held to be personal to the practitioner. The Court specifically observed that there was a distinction between the sale of the goodwill of a trade or business of a commercial character where the location is an important feature of the business, and the sale of an established practice and goodwill of a person engaged in a profession or calling where the income therefrom is the immediate or direct result of his labor and skill and where integrity, skill, ability and other desirable personal qualities follow the person and not the place.

Having recognized the existence of goodwill in the above noted situations, we must now determine whether goodwill can exist in the particular circumstances of the instant case. Although the trial court found that the business was predominantly a title company and treated it as such, both parties' arguments to this Court are based on the Court of Special Appeals' holding that the business was a sole proprietorship, and in particular a solo law practice. It should be noted that neither party is contesting the status of the license to practice law. What is being contested is the existence of goodwill in a practice established once the professional license has been obtained.

Because the question of whether professional goodwill is marital property is one of first impression in Maryland, we found it beneficial to review the decisions of the courts of other states which have addressed the issue. This review revealed three positions. The view most often followed treats goodwill as marital property in all cases. The next largest group considers goodwill to be personal to the practitioner, and therefore not marital property. Finally, a small group of states requires a case-by-case examination to determine how goodwill should be treated. It is interesting to note that the classification of a jurisdiction as a community property state or an equitable distribution state is not determinative of its treatment of goodwill.

The view that the goodwill of a solo practice should be considered as marital property was early on set forth in the California decisions of *Mueller v. Mueller*, 144 Cal.App.2d 245, 301 P.2d 90 (1956) and *Golden v. Golden*, 270 Cal.App.2d 401, 75 Cal.Rptr. 735 (1969).

In *Mueller*, the husband was the sole owner of a dental laboratory which employed six people. The wife sought to have the value of the business divided at the time of the divorce. The husband argued that the goodwill of the business was wholly dependent upon his personal skill and ability. The court examined the business and concluded that the business was too old and too large to be dependent solely upon the owner for its goodwill, 144 Cal.App.2d at 251, 301 P.2d at 95, and held that the value of this business was to be divided between the parties. Furthermore, the *Mueller* court examined the argument that goodwill cannot arise in a professional business depending upon the personal skill and ability of a particular person. Even though unnecessary to its decision, the court stated that this argument was based on the definition of goodwill set forth by Lord Eldon, and the better, more modern, view is that the skill and learning acquired by a professional has intangible value which may be transferred. *Id.* at 251, 301 P.2d at 94–95. This left open the possibility that professional goodwill could also be divided upon divorce.

The court in *Golden* used the opening left by *Mueller* to hold that professional goodwill was marital property. The husband in *Golden* was a sole practicing physician. The wife sought a division of the value of the practice when the couple was divorced. The court, looking to *Mueller*, 270 Cal.App.2d at 405, 75 Cal.Rptr. at 737, set forth the holding that "the better rule is that, in a divorce case, the goodwill of the husband's professional practice as a sole practitioner should be taken into consideration in determining the award to the wife." *Id.*

The *Golden* court distinguished a divorce from the dissolution of a partnership, in which it might be difficult to determine the correct share upon distribution.

> [I]n a matrimonial matter, the practice of the sole practitioner husband will continue, with the same intangible value as it had during the marriage. *Under the principles of community property law, the wife, by virtue of her position of wife, made to that value the same contribution* as does a wife to any of the husband's earnings and accumulations during marriage. She is as much entitled to be recompensed for that contribution as if it were represented by the increased value of stock in a family business.

Id. at 405, 75 Cal.Rptr. at 738 (emphasis added).

Although the California court used community property law to give the wife credit for the increase in the goodwill value during the marriage, the non-monetary contribution aspect of equitable distribution principles tends to accomplish the same result. Note, *Treating Professional Goodwill as Marital Property in Equitable Distribution States*, 58 N.Y.U.L.Rev. 554, 558 (1983).

The New Jersey case of *Dugan v. Dugan*, 92 N.J. 423, 457 A.2d 1 (1983) presents a situation which is quite similar to the instant case, but in that case the court held that the goodwill of a solo law practice was marital property. The husband was an attorney who operated his practice as a wholly-owned professional corporation. New Jersey and Maryland both place the following limitations on the practice of law: (1) sole practitioners cannot sell their law practices, *id.* at 436, 457 A.2d at 8, (2) restrictive covenants prohibiting competition by the transferor of the practice are not allowed, and (3) clients may not be sold between practices. Regarding domestic relations law, both Maryland and New Jersey are equitable distribution states, and neither treats a professional degree or license to practice as property.

The New Jersey court began its analysis by looking at the various definitions of goodwill used in other states. Its conclusion was that goodwill exists and is a legally protected interest. 92 N.J. at 429, 457 A.2d at 4. Next the court examined the relationship between goodwill and "going concern value." Goodwill was found to be closely related to reputation, and the definition settled on by the New Jersey court was that goodwill "is equivalent to the excess of actual earnings over expected earnings based on a normal rate of return on investment." *Id.* at 431, 457 A.2d at 5.

Examining the relationship between goodwill and earning capacity (as that relates to a medical degree), the court found a difference between the two:

> Future earning capacity *per se* is not goodwill. However, when that future earning capacity has been enhanced because reputation leads to probable future patronage from existing and potential clients, goodwill may exist and have value. When that occurs the resulting good will is property subject to equitable distribution.

Id. at 433, 457 A.2d at 6.

Having distinguished goodwill from earning capacity and having found goodwill subject to equitable distribution, the court went on to state its rationale for the decision:

> After divorce, the law practice will continue to benefit from that goodwill as it had during the marriage. Much of the economic value produced during an attorney's marriage will inhere to the goodwill of the law practice. *It would be inequitable to ignore the contribution of the non-attorney spouse to the development of that economic resource.* An individual practitioner's inability to sell a law practice does not eliminate existence of goodwill and its value as an asset to

> be considered in equitable distribution. Obviously, equitable distribution does not require conveyance or transfer of any particular asset. The other spouse, in this case the wife, is entitled to have that asset considered as any other property acquired during the marriage partnership.

Id. at 434, 457 A.2d at 6 (emphasis added).

The view that professional goodwill is personal to the practitioner and is not marital property is articulated by the Texas court in *Nail v. Nail*, 486 S.W.2d 761 (Tex.1972). Despite the fact that Texas, like California, is a community property state, the *Nail* court held that the goodwill built up by a medical practice was personal to the husband doctor. The court determined that the goodwill was based on the husband's personal skill, experience, and reputation. Because the goodwill was not an asset separate and apart from the doctor, it would be extinguished if he died, retired, or became disabled. Because of the personal nature of this asset, it was not considered by the court as an earned or vested property right at the time of the divorce, and did not qualify as property subject to division in a divorce proceeding. *Id.* at 764.

Taylor v. Taylor, 222 Neb. 721, 386 N.W.2d 851 (1986), sets forth the middle ground between the two extremes. The trial court found that the husband's professional medical corporation contained no goodwill which was subject to distribution upon divorce. On appeal, the Nebraska Supreme Court affirmed that finding. In so doing, however, the appellate court noted that in proper circumstances, professional goodwill might exist as a salable or marketable business asset. *Id.* at 732, 386 N.W.2d at 858–59. Whether such a situation existed would be a question of fact. If the goodwill was found to be saleable or marketable, the court could divide that goodwill as a marital asset. The court stated that the essential factor which would determine the goodwill to be personal would be its dependence upon the continued presence of the individual. *Id.* at 731, 386 N.W.2d at 858.

Taylor, therefore, provides for a case-by-case analysis to determine whether goodwill in a particular situation should be considered marital property. Unlike the Texas court, *Taylor* does not rule out the possibility that a professional solo practice might contain such goodwill. And unlike the California cases, it allows for distinctions between those situations where goodwill is truly personal and where it is indeed marital property. It was this rationale which the Court of Special Appeals found persuasive. 75 Md.App. at 133, 540 A.2d at 843.

After reviewing these three alternatives and the rationale of their respective supporting cases, we are of the opinion that the goodwill of a solo law practice is personal to the individual practitioner. Goodwill in such circumstances is not severable from the reputation of the sole practitioner regardless of the contributions made to the practice by the spouse or employees. In order for goodwill to be marital property, it must be an asset having a separate value from the reputation of the practitioner.

We are not convinced that the goodwill of a solo law practice can be separated from the reputation of the attorney. It is the attorney whose name, whether on the door or stationery, is the embodiment of the practice. We are cognizant that in this computer age many law practices, and in Leo's practice in particular, much of the research and "form" work is done by non-lawyers. In the final analysis, however, it is the attorney alone who is responsible for the work that comes out of the office. Rule of Professional Conduct 5.3(c). In the instant case, the responsibility is solely Leo's, and no amount of work done by Margaret will shift the responsibility to her. The attorney's signature or affidavit places his seal of approval on the work being done and makes the attorney liable for its accuracy and authenticity. This professional assurance is what might have convinced some clients to use Leo F. X. Prahinski, Attorney-at-Law, instead of going to a title company to have their settlements completed. The assurance would end should Leo somehow remove himself from the practice. Therefore, the goodwill generated by the attorney is personal to him and is not the kind of asset which can be divided as marital property.

Because the instant case involves the practice of law, special considerations arise which might not be present in other professional practices. In *Brown v. Benzinger*, 118 Md. 29, 84 A. 79 (1912), we quoted with approval from *Yeakley v. Gaston*, 50 Tex.Civ.App. 405, 111 S.W. 768 (1908) where the court said, "the sale of goodwill be a professional carries with it the obligation that he will abstain from practice in the future in the territory from which he binds himself to withdraw." It is clear that an attorney, as distinguished from other professionals, may not covenant to abstain from the practice of law, and therefore, may not sell his or her goodwill.

Other professions do not have the prohibition against the sale of goodwill. *Brown v. Benzinger, supra* (sale of her practice "including goodwill" by a "surgeon chiropodist"); *Warfield v. Booth*, 33 Md. 63 (1870) (sale of a physician's practice including goodwill); *Spaulding v. Benenati*, 57 N.Y.2d 418, 456 N.Y.S.2d 733, 442 N.E.2d 1244 (1982) (goodwill of a dentist is a saleable asset); *Dwight v. Hamilton*, 113 Mass. 175 (1873) (goodwill of a physician is a saleable asset).

Since a lawyer's goodwill is not a saleable asset, it has no commercial value. The methods for valuing the marketable goodwill of a profession or business would not be applicable to an attorney's nonmarketable goodwill. The fact that a lawyer's goodwill cannot be sold by the lawyer is another factor in our determination that it is not marital property.

We have noted, as did the Court of Special Appeals, that the circuit court included the value of the goodwill of the legal practice of Leo F. X. Prahinski as a part of the marital property. The alimony and the monetary award were both calculated with the value being a factor. This was error. Therefore, the entitlements of the spouse must be recalculated.

JUDGMENT OF THE COURT OF SPECIAL APPEALS AFFIRMED.

Notes and Questions

1. *Prahinski* summarizes the various approaches to professional goodwill developed during marriage. What are the pros and cons of each? Which seems the fairest?

2. How a court values a professional practice at divorce varies depending on the position the state has taken toward professional goodwill. Washington, for example, has adopted a relatively expansive definition of divisible goodwill which permits Washington courts to use any of a number of methods to value a practice. In Marriage of Hall, 103 Wash.2d 236, 692 P.2d 175, 179–80 (1984) the court summarized the possible approaches:

> In valuing goodwill five major formulas have been articulated. There are three accounting formulas. Under the straight capitalization accounting method the average net profits of the practitioner are determined and this figure is capitalized at a definite rate, as, for example, 20 percent. This result is considered to be the total value of the business including both tangible and intangible assets. To determine the value of goodwill the book value of the business assets are subtracted from the total value figure.

Average net earnings	$ 60,000
Capitalize at 2	× 5
Total business tangible and intangible assets	300,000
Less current net tangible assets	−30,000
Goodwill	$270,000

> The second accounting formula is the capitalization of excess earnings method. Under the pure capitalization of excess earnings the average net income is determined. From this figure an annual salary of average employee practitioner with like experience is subtracted. The remaining amount is multiplied by a fixed capitalization rate to determine the goodwill.

Average net earnings	$ 60,000
Less comparable net salary	−40,000
Average earnings on intangible assets	20,000
Capitalize at 20%	× 5
Goodwill	$100,000

> The IRS variation of capitalized excess earnings method takes the average net income of the business for the last 5 years and subtracts a reasonable rate of return based on the business' average net tangible assets. From this amount a comparable net salary is subtracted. Finally, this remaining amount is capitalized at a definite rate. The resulting amount is goodwill.

Average net earnings	$ 60,000
Less rate of return on average tangible assets	−2,500
Subtotal	57,500
Less comparable net salary	−40,000
Average Earnings on intangible assets	17,500
Capitalize at 20%	× 5
Goodwill	$ 87,500

The fourth method, the market value approach, sets a value on professional goodwill by establishing what fair price would be obtained in the current open market if the practice were to be sold. This method necessitates that a professional practice has been recently sold, is in the process of being sold or is the subject of a recent offer to purchase. Otherwise, the value may be manipulated by the professional spouse.

The fifth valuation method, the buy/sell agreement method, values goodwill by reliance on a recent actual sale or an unexercised existing option or contractual formula set forth in a partnership agreement or corporate agreement. Since the professional spouse may have been influenced by many factors other than fair market value in negotiating the terms of the agreement, courts relying on this method should inquire into the presence of such factors, as well as the arm's length nature of the transaction.

These five methods are not the exclusive formulas available to trial courts in analyzing the evidence presented. Nor must only one method be used in isolation. One or more methods may be used in conjunction with the *Fleege* factors to achieve a just and fair evaluation of the existence and value of any professional's goodwill.

The danger of using any one method without regard to the *Fleege* factors is apparent in the present case where appellant's expert witnesses used only the capitalized excess earnings approach. Under this approach the experts testified that Phillip had no goodwill. Further testimony, however, indicated that Phillip's comparatively low earnings were a result of office expansion expenses, a deliberate decision to limit hours of practice and failure to compare Phillip with cardiologists in the same age and experience group doing similar procedures in Seattle. Consideration of the appellant's reputation, associations, referrals, location and trade name indicate the existence of goodwill.

This case also exemplifies the need for caution in the use of the buy/sell agreement. The Northwest Cardiology Clinic buy/sell agreement does not include a goodwill factor. When the third doctor became a shareholder, no value was assigned to goodwill. The trial court must, however, inquire whether the omission in the agreement was the result of other factors or deliberations on the part of the shareholders, particularly when the particular agreement is made in close proximity in time to the divorce.

3. States employing a less expansive definition of divisible goodwill may restrict valuation methods accordingly. For example, the Missouri Supreme Court concluded that only goodwill separate from the professional's individual reputation should be divisible; as a result it "state[d] a strong preference" for the fair market value approach to valuation:

> First, the fair market value approach "does not take explicitly into consideration the future earning capacity of the professional goodwill or the post-dissolution efforts of the professional spouse." Comment, *Professional Goodwill in Louisiana: An Analysis of Its Classification, Valuation and Partition*, 43 LA. L. REV. 139, 142 (1982)....
>
> Second, fair market value evidence appears to us to be the most equitable and accurate measure of both the existence and true value of the goodwill of an enterprise. Evidence of a recent actual sale of a similarly situated practice, an offer to purchase the subject or a similar practice, or expert testimony and testimony of members of the subject profession as to the present value of goodwill of a similar practice in the open, relevant, geographical and professional market is the best evidence of value.
>
> Third, the fair market value method is most likely to avoid the "disturbing inequity in compelling a professional practitioner to pay a spouse a share of intangible assets at a judicially determined value that could not be realized by a sale or another method of liquidating value." ...
>
> We reject the use of capitalization formulae as a substitute for fair market value evidence of the value of goodwill in a professional practice. The very purpose of capitalization formulae is to place a present value on the future earnings of the business entity being valued. The formulae draw no distinction between the future earning capacity of the individual and that of the entity in which he or she practices. And as we have said previously, the future earning capacity of the individual professional is not, *per se*, an item of marital property subject to division in a dissolution proceeding.
>
> Hanson v. Hanson, 738 S.W.2d 429, 434–35 (Mo.1987) (citations omitted).

4. The *Hall* approach (note 2, *supra*) would seem to require division of all increased earning capacity acquired during marriage as a result of enhanced reputation. But neither the *Hall* court nor others utilizing an expansive definition of goodwill have in fact gone this far. In *Hall*, for example, both spouses were medical doctors. The husband was a partner in a clinic and had gross yearly earnings of about $52,000. The wife was a professor at the University of Washington Medical School; she earned $42,000 annually and, as a well-known expert in pediatric genetics, had received offers to teach elsewhere, at salaries of up to $60,000

annually. The court concluded that employees, as a matter of law, could not have goodwill; thus the value of the husband's professional reputation was divisible, while the wife's was not. States accepting the expansive Washington/California view of professional goodwill frequently distinguish goodwill from earning capacity in this manner. While most courts have accepted the *Hall* distinction between employees and proprietors, some courts have extended the concept of professional goodwill to celebrities who are not business owners, holding that the increased value of their professional reputation acquired during marriage is divisible. *See* note 5, p. 755.

5. In valuing goodwill, most courts have concluded that a value specified in a partnership agreement (for purposes of buyout), is relevant, but not binding. *See, e.g.*, Burns v. Burns, 84 N.Y.2d 369, 618 N.Y.S.2d 761, 643 N.E.2d 80 (1994). A minority of courts treats the agreement valuation as determinative if made in good faith. *See* McDiarmid v. McDiarmid, 649 A.2d 810 (D.C.App.1994) (citing other cases). Should it matter whether the practice can be sold? If it does matter, should it also matter whether the seller would have to agree not to compete with the practice in order to make a sale?

6. In those states that do not consider "personal" professional goodwill divisible, should "personal" goodwill in other types of businesses be divisible? *See* Rathmell v. Morrison, 732 S.W.2d 6 (Tex.App. 1987) (no); Marriage of Talty, 166 Ill.2d 232, 209 Ill.Dec. 790, 652 N.E.2d 330 (1995) (no).

H. DEBTS

Few state divorce statutes expressly address debts. In a marital property state, premarital and postmarital debts will be the separate obligations of the debtor spouse, while debts incurred during marriage may be assigned to either spouse, regardless of who incurred the debt. *See* Marriage of Stewart, 232 Mont. 40, 757 P.2d 765 (1988). (The divorce court's order does not, of course, affect the right of a creditor to sue the spouse who incurred the debt.)

There is consensus on some recurring cases. Although not typically required under state law, courts generally agree that student loans should be assigned to the spouse who attended school (*see* Tasker v. Tasker, 395 N.W.2d 100 (Minn.App.1986)) and that the spouse who receives property encumbered by a secured debt takes it subject to that debt. (Of course, the value of the debt is subtracted to determine the asset's net value.) *See* Daniels v. Daniels, 726 S.W.2d 705 (Ky.App.1986); Talent v. Talent, 76 N.C.App. 545, 334 S.E.2d 256 (1985). If one spouse incurs a debt when the marriage is breaking down with the intention of depleting the marital estate, it will be allocated to the spouse who incurred it. Debts incurred after separation are typically, but not invariably, assigned to the spouse who incurred the debt. *See* Zecchin v. Zecchin, 149 Mich.App. 723, 386 N.W.2d 652 (1986); Gelb v. Brown, 163 A.D.2d 189, 558 N.Y.S.2d 934 (1990).

There is less agreement on other debt allocation issues. If a spouse incurs an investment loss, should this debt be subtracted from the value of the divisible marital estate? *See* Marriage of Hauge, 145 Wis.2d 600, 427 N.W.2d 154 (Wis.App.1988) (yes). If one spouse was much more frugal than the other during marriage, should this affect how the debts (or property) are divided?

Problem 14–4: Harry and Wilma married in September, 1990. Wilma filed for divorce in September, 1992. Following a reconciliation, the divorce petition was voluntarily dismissed in September, 1993. After the reconciliation failed, Wilma filed another divorce petition in September, 1995; the divorce trial took place in October, 1996. What valuation date should be used for Harry's pension, worth $100,000 in September, 1990; $115,000 in September, 1992; $130,000 in September, 1993; $150,000 in September, 1995; and $172,000 in October, 1996. What factors are relevant?

Problem 14–5:

Ernest and Maggie May were married approximately twelve years ago, when Ernest was 26 and Maggie 22. At the time they married, Maggie had just graduated from college with a B.A. in Early Childhood Education; Ernest had obtained a Ph. D. in Linguistics.

Following their marriage, Ernest and Maggie moved into a home Ernest had purchased with a small inheritance from his grandmother. Ernest took a job as an Assistant Professor of Linguistics; Maggie took a job as a kindergarten teacher. The following year, Ernest and Maggie's first child (Polly) was born. Maggie quit her job and so did Ernest. In his spare time, Ernest started a language school, Lingua Lab.

Two years after Polly's birth, Maggie and Ernest had twins (Jeff and Jane). Ernest worked approximately 40 hours per week at his university job and 15–20 hours at his school. Maggie ran the household and performed virtually all child care tasks until the twins were in kindergarten, when she began to teach again.

Maggie has consulted your law firm for legal advice. She and Ernest have had increasingly bitter arguments over the last couple of years; she wants to terminate the relationship. But she is worried about money and wants to know how much property she would obtain at divorce. Last year, Ernest earned $70,000 from his University position and $35,000 from Lingua Lab; Maggie earns $30,000 per year. She and Ernest own the following assets:

1. Marital home: Purchased by Ernest for $125,000 around the time of his marriage to Maggie with a downpayment ($25,000) inherited from his grandmother. Maggie believes that the house is now worth about $250,000. Ernest is the sole owner of the house. The note has been paid down to a balance owing of $80,000.

2. Lingua Lab: Solely owned by Ernest, Lingua Lab now has two employees in addition to Ernest and serves approximately 500

clients per year. Lingua rents space; its tangible assets (books, desks, computers, etc.) are worth approximately $50,000. Last year, Ernest received a salary of $35,000 from the company's net profits of $50,000. (The other teachers (all part-time), who perform fewer administrative functions than Ernest but teach the same number of classes, earned $25,000 last year.) The remaining $15,000 was used to pay for new computer equipment. Last year's profit picture was typical of the company's profitability over the past few years; in each of the prior five years, Lingua had average net earnings of approximately $50,000. Ernest is the most popular teacher at the school; his classes are always sold out. Maggie thinks that Ernest would have a hard time finding a buyer for the school; he has never received an offer.

3. Pension: Ernest is a participant in a defined contribution plan; his account is currently worth $130,000.

4. Mutual Fund: The shares were originally purchased with money inherited from Ernest's grandmother ($100,000). The account balance ($250,000) represents appreciation and reinvestment of capital gains.

State law permits division of all "marital assets," defined as "property acquired by either spouse during marriage, except for property acquired by gift, inheritance, or bequest." Separate property ("all property acquired by gift, inheritance, or bequest and all property acquired before marriage; income and appreciation from such property; and property acquired in exchange for such property") is not divisible.

What assets are marital property? What assets are separate property? What value (or range of values) would you place on each marital asset?

SECTION 3. DIVIDING THE DIVISIBLE ESTATE

Once the divisible estate has been determined and valued, it must be divided. A few states, like California, require equal division. *See* CAL. FAM. CODE § 2550. A few others, like Arkansas, have established a rebuttable presumption in favor of equal division.

ARK. STAT. ANN. § 9–12–315 Division of property.

(a) At the time a divorce decree is entered:

(1)(A) all marital property shall be distributed one-half (1/2) to each party unless the court finds such a division to be inequitable. In that event the court shall make some other division that the court deems equitable taking into consideration:

(i) The length of the marriage;

(ii) Age, health, and station in life of the parties;

(iii) Occupation of the parties;

(iv) Amount and sources of income;

(v) Vocational skills;

(vi) Employability;

(vii) Estate, liabilities, and needs of each party and opportunity of each for further acquisition of capital assets and income;

(viii) Contribution of each party in acquisition, preservation, or appreciation of marital property, including services as a homemaker; and

(ix) The federal income tax consequences of the court's division of property.

(B) When property is divided pursuant to the foregoing considerations the court must state its basis and reasons for not dividing the marital property equally between the parties, and the basis and reasons should be recited in the order entered in the matter.

Most statutes (or court decisions, if no statute has been enacted) merely instruct the court to divide the marital estate equitably, after considering a number of factors. For a discussion of the various factors applicable in different states, *see Comment*, 50 FORDHAM L. REV. 415 (1981). The Minnesota statute is typical:

MINN. STAT. ANN. § 518.58 Division of marital property

Subdivision 1. Upon a dissolution of a marriage, . . . the court shall make a just and equitable division of the marital property of the parties without regard to marital misconduct, after making findings regarding the division of the property. The court shall base its findings on all relevant factors including the length of the marriage, any prior marriage of a party, the age, health, station, occupation, amount and sources of income, vocational skills, employability, estate, liabilities, needs, opportunity for future acquisition of capital assets, and income of each party. The court shall also consider the contribution of each in the acquisition, preservation, depreciation or appreciation in the amount or value of the marital property, as well as the contribution of a spouse as a homemaker. It shall be conclusively presumed that each spouse made a substantial contribution to the acquisition of income and property while they were living together as husband and wife. The court may also award to either spouse the household goods and furniture of the parties, whether or not acquired during the marriage. The court shall value marital assets for purposes of division between the parties as of the day of the initially scheduled prehearing settlement conference, unless a different date is agreed upon by the parties, or unless the court makes specific findings that another date of valuation is fair and equitable. If there is a substantial change in value of an asset between the date of valuation and the final distribution, the Court may adjust the valuation of that asset as necessary to effect an equitable distribution.

Although many statutes set forth a long list of factors, three central themes—need, contribution and fault—predominate. These themes often lead in conflicting directions. For example, one spouse will often have contributed the majority of the marital assets (although many statutes explicitly recognize nonmonetary contributions), while the other will have greater post-divorce financial need. Which factor should predominate?

In practice, judges appear to tend strongly toward fifty-fifty division. *See* Marsha Garrison, *How Do Judges Decide Divorce Cases? An Empirical Analysis of Discretionary Decision Making*, 74 N.C. L. Rev. 401, 454 tbl. 8 (1996) (judges divided net worth relatively equally in 48% of surveyed New York cases); Suzanne Reynolds, *The Relationship of Property Division and Alimony: The Division of Property to Address Need*, 54 Fordham L. Rev. 827, 854–55 (1988) (judges in six states seldom deviated from equal division except in "extraordinary circumstances.") But when judges do deviate from an equal division, their decisionmaking appears to be relatively unpredictable. In a survey of divorce decision-making by New York judges, Professor Garrison found that indications of the wife's need—poor health, unemployment, low income, low occupational status, and income representing a small fraction of family income were all *negatively* correlated with the wife's percentage award. So were the husband's ownership of a marital business or degree, the percentage of marital property owned by the husband, and the net value of marital assets. The wife's income and the value of the husband's separate property, on the other hand, were *positively* correlated with the wife's percentage award. But the predictive value of these factors was slight; a decision-making model utilizing all of these factors could predict no more than 14% of the variation in net worth outcomes. Garrison, *supra* at 456–64. Outcomes in settled cases were somewhat more predictable, but the important predictive variable was the percentage of property to which each spouse held title—the very factor that equitable property distribution was supposed to make unimportant. *Id.* at 466. The relative unpredictability of outcomes under equitable distribution schemes has led Professor Mary Ann Glendon to call them "discretionary," rather than "equitable," distribution systems. *See* Mary Ann Glendon, The New Family and the New Property 64 (1981).

A 1997 Connecticut divorce generated significant debate about how to divide the marital estate when it is quite large (say, more than $10 million) and was primarily generated by the efforts of one spouse. Some have argued that, in such a situation, the person who generated the wealth should get most of the marital estate, to reward that person for his or her efforts. Others disagree. *See What's a Corporate Wife Worth in Court? Go Figure*, N. Y. Times, Jan. 25, 1998, § 4, p. 7.

GASTINEAU v. GASTINEAU

Supreme Court of New York, Suffolk County, 1991.
151 Misc.2d 813, 573 N.Y.S.2d 819.

LEIS, J.

* * * The Plaintiff, Lisa Gastineau, is represented by counsel. The Defendant, Marcus Gastineau appeared pro se. * * * The parties were married in December of 1979. This action was commenced in September 1986. Consequently, this is a marriage of short duration. The Plaintiff is thirty-one years old and the Defendant is thirty-four. The parties have one child, Brittany, born on 11/6/82. * * * The parties married just after Marc Gastineau had been drafted by the New York Jets to play professional football. The Plaintiff, at that time, was a sophomore at the University of Alabama. The Plaintiff never completed her college education, nor did she work during the course of the marriage.

In 1982, when Britanny was born, the parties purchased a house in Huntington, New York for $99,000.00. In addition to the purchase price, the Plaintiff and Defendant spent another $250,000.00 for landscaping and other renovations. This money came from the Defendant's earnings as a professional football player.

According to the uncontroverted testimony of the Plaintiff, in 1979 (the Defendant's first year in professional football) the Defendant earned a salary of $55,000.00. In his second year, 1980, the Defendant's salary was approximately $75,000.00. In 1981 it was approximately $95,000.00 and in 1982 he earned approximately $250,000.00. The Defendant's tax returns (which were not available for the years 1979 through 1982) indicate that the Defendant earned $423,291.00 in 1983, $488,994.00 in 1984, $858,035.00 in 1985, $595,127.00 in 1986, $953,531.00 in 1987 and in 1988, his last year with the New York Jets, his contract salary was $775,000.00 plus $50,000.00 in bonuses. It must be noted that in most years the Defendant earned monies in excess of his contract salary as a result of promotions, advertisements and bonuses.

In 1985 the parties purchased a home in Scottsdale, Arizona for $550,000.00. During the course of the parties' marriage Plaintiff and Defendant acquired many luxury items including a power boat, a BMW, a Corvette, a Rolls Royce, a Porche, a Mercedes and two motorcycles. They continually had a housekeeper who not only cleaned the house but prepared the parties' meals. In addition, the parties frequently dined out at expensive restaurants. The Plaintiff testified that as a result of this life style she has become accustomed to buying only the most expensive clothes and going to the best of restaurants.

In 1988 the Defendant began an illicit relationship with Brigitte Nielsen. When Ms. Neilsen was diagnosed as having cancer the Defendant testified that he could no longer concentrate on playing football. At that time the Defendant was under contract with the New York Jets at a salary of $775,000.00. He left professional football in October 1988 (breaking his contract) after the sixth game of the 1988 season. The Defendant went to Arizona and remained with Ms. Nielsen while she underwent treatment for cancer.

Regardless of whether the Defendant wanted to be with his girl friend while she underwent treatment for cancer, he had a responsibility to support his wife and child. The Court cannot condone Mr. Gastineau's walking away from a lucrative football contract when the result is that his wife and child are deprived of adequate support.

According to the testimony adduced at trial, there are sixteen games per season in the NFL. Players are paid one-sixteenth of their contract salary at the end of each game. Based on the Defendant's salary for 1988 ($775,000.00), he received $48,437.00 per game. The Defendant played six games in the 1988 season and received approximately $290,622.00 plus $50,000.00 in bonuses. He was entitled to an additional $484,437.00 for the ten games remaining in the season. This Court finds that by walking away from his 1988–89 contract with the NFL the Defendant dissipated a marital asset in the amount of $484,437.00.

Whether or not the Defendant would have been offered a contract by the New York Jets for the 1989/90 football season if he had not broken his 1988/89 contract is pure speculation. In professional football there are no guarantees.... It must also be noted that there has been no testimony offered by the Plaintiff to establish that the Defendant would have been re-signed by the New York Jets for the 1989/90 season had he not broken his contract.

The speculative nature of the Defendant's future in professional football is highlighted by the fact that in 1989 he tried out for the San Diego Chargers, the LA Raiders and the Minnesota Vikings, without success. The New York Jets also refused to offer him a contract. In 1990 the Defendant did acquire a position with the British Colombia Lions in the Canadian Football League at a salary of $75,000.00. He was cut, however, less than half way through the season. The Defendant played five of the 18 scheduled games and was paid approximately $20,000.00. The Defendant's performance in the Canadian Football League lends credence to his claim that he no longer has the capacity to earn the monies that he once made as a professional football player. Under these circumstances the Court is limited to considering the dissipation of a marital asset valued at $484,437.00, to wit: the remaining amount of money that the Defendant was eligible to collect pursuant to his 1988/89 contract.

While Defendant admits that he has name recognition, he claims that his name has a negative rather than a positive connotation. The Defendant testified that because of his antics on the field (such as his victory dance after sacking a quarterback), the fact that he crossed picket lines during the NFL player's strike and because he walked away from his professional football career, his name has no value for promotions or endorsements. There has been no evidence presented to the contrary by the Plaintiff.

The Defendant testified that his chances of obtaining employment with a professional football team are almost nil. Although he is presently attempting to obtain a position at a Jack LaLanne Health Spa he could not provide details as to the potential salary.... Since the Defendant left professional football he has not worked or earned any money (except for the $20,000.00 that he earned when he played football in Canada). According to the Defendant, Ms. Nielsen paid for all of the Defendant's expenses during the period of time that they lived together.

* * *

With all of the money that the Defendant earned throughout the course of his professional football career he has retained only three significant marital assets. (1) The Huntington house, which has been valued at approximately $429,000.00 and has an outstanding mortgage of $150,000.00. (2) A house located in the state of Arizona which was purchased for approximately $550,000.00 and has a $420,000.00 mortgage (which in all probability will be sold at foreclosure [and which the court determines has no net value]); (3) The Defendant's severance pay from the NFL of approximately $83,000.00.

It is clear that the Defendant has also dissipated a marital asset worth approximately $324,573.00 (to wit: $484,437.00 the Defendant was entitled to receive pursuant to his 1988/89 contract tax effected by 33%, reflecting approximate federal and state income tax). Although neither the Plaintiff nor the Defendant attempted to tax effect this dissipated marital asset, it is clear that the Defendant would not have actually received $484,437.00 had he finished the 1988/89 season. The Court therefore, on its own, has tax effected this amount by 33%, approximately what the Defendant would have paid in federal and state taxes had he actually received the $484,437.00....

* * *

It is a guiding principle of equitable distribution that parties are entitled to receive equitable awards which are proportionate to their contributions, whether direct or indirect, to the marriage. In this case, the Plaintiff testified that during the course of the marriage she supervised the renovations made on the Huntington house, traveled with the Defendant wherever he trained and, with the assistance of a full-time nanny, raised and cared for their child.

This is not a long term marriage, and there has been minimal testimony elicited concerning the Plaintiff's direct or indirect contributions to the Defendant's acquisition of marital assets. Although it was the Defendant's own athletic abilities and disciplined training which made it possible for him to obtain and retain his position as a professional football player, equity dictates, under the facts of this case, that the Plaintiff receive one-third of the marital assets. The Defendant's decision to voluntarily terminate his contract with The New York Jets, depriving Plaintiff and the parties' child of the standard of living to which they had become accustomed, his failure to obtain meaningful employment thereafter and the indirect contributions made by the Plaintiff during the course of the marriage warrants an award to the Plaintiff of one third of the parties' marital assets. The court is also mindful of the fact that during the years of the Defendant's greatest productivity, the Plaintiff enjoyed the fruits of Defendant's labors to the fullest, unlike the landmark *O'Brien* case (*O'Brien v. O'Brien*), [p. 756] where a newly licensed professional discarded his wife after she provided years of contributions to the attainment of his medical license.

There are only two marital assets to be considered in granting Plaintiff her one-third distributive award, (1) the Huntington house, and (2) the $324,573.00 dissipated marital asset. The Arizona house has no equity. The Huntington house is valued at $429,000.00. It has a $150,-00.00 mortgage with $15,000.00 owed in back mortgage payments. It thus has an equity of $264,000.00. One third of the equity would entitle the Plaintiff to $87,120.00. when one adds $107,109.00 (1/3 of the $324,573.00 tax effected marital asset which was dissipated), the Plaintiff would be entitled to $194,229.00. This would encompass Plaintiff's 1/3 distributive award of the parties' sole remaining marital asset (the Huntington house) and her 1/3 share of the marital asset dissipated by the Defendant. If one adds this $194,229.00 to the arrears owed by the Defendant on the pendente lite order ($71,707.00) Plaintiff could be awarded the total equity ($264,000.00) in the Huntington house in full satisfaction of her one-third distributive award of the parties' marital assets and still have approximately $1,936.00 remaining as a credit. The Court awards Plaintiff the Huntington house and grants her a Judgment for $1,936.00 for the remaining arrears owed to her.

Notes and Questions

1. *Gastineau* raises a number of questions: Should the court have taken Gastineau's mental condition into account in judging the dissipation issue? If not, why didn't Gastineau dissipate his celebrity status as well as his football contract? And why should the wife receive only one-third of the marital assets?

2. Most states agree that economic fault (dissipation) should be considered at divorce. If, after the marriage has broken down, a spouse destroys, wastes, or sells marital property for less than fair market value, the divorce court will typically divide the marital estate as if the dissipating spouse still owned the property dissipated (or, if the property was sold for less than fair market value, allocate to the dissipating spouse the amount lost by the marital estate). *See* Blackman v. Blackman, 131 A.D.2d 801, 517 N.Y.S.2d 167 (1987); Talent v. Talent, 76 N.C.App. 545, 334 S.E.2d 256 (1985); Dahl v. Dahl, 225 Neb. 501, 406 N.W.2d 639 (1987); Booth v. Booth, 7 Va.App. 22, 371 S.E.2d 569 (1988). Illusory transfers will be disregarded. *See* Marriage of Frederick, 218 Ill.App.3d 533, 161 Ill.Dec. 254, 578 N.E.2d 612 (1991). Common examples of dissipation include gifts to a girlfriend or boyfriend (*see* Zeigler v. Zeigler, 365 Pa.Super. 545, 530 A.2d 445 (1987)) and a sale of marital property for less than adequate consideration when the marriage is

breaking down (*see* Halvorson v. Halvorson, 482 N.W.2d 869 (N.D.1992) (conveyance to children); Marriage of Pahlke, 154 Ill.App.3d 256, 107 Ill.Dec. 407, 507 N.E.2d 71 (1987) (transfer to girlfriend); Kasinski v. Questel, 99 A.D.2d 396, 472 N.Y.S.2d 807 (1984) (transfer to girlfriend); Watson v. Watson, 221 Conn. 698, 607 A.2d 383 (1992)). The dissipation doctrine forces the spouse dissipating property to bear the full amount of the loss; it is intended to deter spouses from behaving badly while the marriage is breaking down.

Should a spouse's loss of marital property on a speculative investment be treated as a case of dissipation? Should it matter whether the investment was made after the marriage has broken down? *See* Booth v. Booth, 7 Va.App. 22, 371 S.E.2d 569 (1988). What about gambling losses? *See* Marriage of Hagshenas, 234 Ill.App.3d 178, 175 Ill.Dec. 506, 600 N.E.2d 437 (1992) (suggesting that gambling losses could constitute dissipation if they are significant in amount and the other spouse objected to the gambling). What about funds spent on alcohol? *See* Marriage of Adams, 183 Ill.App.3d 296, 131 Ill.Dec. 730, 538 N.E.2d 1286 (1989). If a spouse tries to hide marital property and this scheme is discovered, should this affect the division of the marital estate? *See* Sands v. Sands, 442 Mich. 30, 497 N.W.2d 493 (1993) (yes); Belz v. Belz, 667 S.W.2d 240 (Tex.App.1984) (yes). Should the spouse's interest in the hidden property be forfeited? *See Sands, supra* (no). Should this type of behavior produce tort liability? *See Belz, supra* (no).

3. If a spouse controls liquid marital assets of substantial value when the marriage is breaking down and these assets no longer exist at trial, a presumption of dissipation arises in many states. The presumption stems from the common-sense notion that, when a marriage breaks down, a party might well be tempted to hide marital assets. If a spouse can show that the assets were used for reasonable living expenses, this will ordinarily be sufficient to rebut the presumption. *See* Marriage of Randell, 157 Ill.App.3d 892, 110 Ill.Dec. 122, 510 N.E.2d 1153 (1987); Reaney v. Reaney, 505 S.W.2d 338 (Tex.Civ.App. 1974); Contino v. Contino, 140 A.D.2d 662, 529 N.Y.S.2d 14 (1988); Rock v. Rock, 86 Md.App. 598, 587 A.2d 1133 (1991). To determine reasonableness, a court might look to the standard of living before the marital breakdown. *See* Marriage of Stallworth, 192 Cal.App.3d 742, 237 Cal.Rptr. 829 (1987); Marriage of Ryman, 172 Ill.App.3d 599, 122 Ill.Dec. 646, 527 N.E.2d 18 (1988); Zecchin v. Zecchin, 149 Mich.App. 723, 386 N.W.2d 652 (1986).

4. *Noneconomic misconduct:* There is less agreement among the states about the relevance of noneconomic (i.e. marital) misconduct. Professor Ira Ellman conducted a state-by-state survey on the role of marital fault in divorce decision making. In 1996, twenty-three states disallowed consideration of marital misconduct in connection with property division or alimony. Twelve allowed consideration of fault in connection with an alimony award, but not in connection with property division. Fifteen states permitted consideration of marital misconduct in both property division and alimony awards. *See* American Law Institute,

PRINCIPLES OF THE LAW OF FAMILY DISSOLUTION: ANALYSIS AND RECOMMENDATIONS, TENTATIVE DRAFT NO. 2, (MARCH 14, 1996) at 20–23. In New York, marital fault may be considered but only if "outrageous." In interpreting this test, courts have found outrageous conduct in cases of serious criminal misconduct such as attempted murder, kidnapping, rape, and assault, but have found that lesser misconduct does not meet the test. *See* McCann v. McCann, 156 Misc.2d 540, 593 N.Y.S.2d 917, 920–22 (Sup. Ct. 1993) (reviewing cases). What are the pros and cons of each approach? Which, on balance, is the best?

5. *Tort actions as a remedy for spousal misconduct:* Another way to take account of spousal misconduct is through a tort action. Some states have permitted or required joinder of divorce and intraspousal tort actions. *See, e.g.,* Maharam v. Maharam, 123 A.D.2d 165, 510 N.Y.S.2d 104 (1986); Henriksen v. Cameron, 622 A.2d 1135 (Me. 1993); Tevis v. Tevis, 79 N.J. 422, 400 A.2d 1189, 1196 (1979); Weil v. Lammon, 503 So.2d 830, 832 (Ala.1987); Twyman v. Twyman, 855 S.W.2d 619 (Tex. 1993). Others have refused to allow joinder. *See, e.g.,* Heacock v. Heacock, 402 Mass. 21, 520 N.E.2d 151 (1988); Walther v. Walther, 709 P.2d 387, 388 (Utah 1985); Windauer v. O'Connor, 107 Ariz. 267, 485 P.2d 1157 (1971); Simmons v. Simmons, 773 P.2d 602, 605 (Colo.App.1988).

In a state that permits or requires joinder, several issues arise. First, the possibility of double recovery is introduced:

> When a tort action is tried with the divorce ... it is imperative that the court avoid awarding a double recovery. When dividing the marital estate, the court may take into account several factors, including the fault of the parties if pleaded. The trial court may also consider "such factors as the spouses' capacities and abilities, benefits which the party not at fault would have derived from continuation of the marriage, business opportunities, education, relative physical conditions, relative financial condition and obligations, disparity of ages, size of separate estates, and the nature to the property." However, a spouse should not be allowed to recover tort damages and a disproportionate division of the community estate based on the same conduct. Therefore, when a factfinder awards tort damages to a divorcing spouse, the court may not consider the same tortious acts when dividing the marital estate.... [A]n award for tortious conduct does not replace an analysis of the remaining factors to be considered when the trial court divides the marital estate. The court may still award a disproportionate division of property for reasons other than the tortious conduct. To avoid the potential problem of double recovery, the factfinder should consider the damages awarded in the tort action when dividing the parties' property. If a jury is used to render an advisory division of the parties' estate, the judge should limit, by appropriate instruction, the jury's consideration of the alleged tortious acts and later consider the award of damages in determining a just and right division of the marital estate.

Twyman v. Twyman, 855 S.W.2d 619 (1993).

Of course, even if the tort action is tried separately, the prospect of double recovery exists. *See also* S.A.V. v. K.G.V., 708 S.W.2d 651, 653 (Mo.1986) (noting that "to the extent that conduct of the spouses is taken into account in division of marital property, the dissolution decree might be admissible in the subsequent tort action. The same may hold true for the dissolution proceeding if that action follows trial of the tort claim.")

Second, the court must determine which estate is entitled to the damage award. While courts typically distinguish between damages for personal injury (separate) and lost pre-divorce earnings (marital) [*see* notes 2 & 3 p. 742], some courts (unsurprisingly) have held that the tortfeasor should not share in any portion of the the victimized spouse's damages award. *See* Freehe v. Freehe, 81 Wash.2d 183, 500 P.2d 771 (1972).

Finally, in a community property state, the court may also have to decide which estate should bear the loss. Most state statutes do not address this issue; Tex. Fam. Code § 3.203 gives the court discretion to determine which estate, or combination, should bear the loss.

6. *Death Abates Divorce*: The property rights of a surviving spouse (*see* chapter 3) are very different from those of a divorcing spouse. Because a marriage does not terminate until a divorce decree is rendered, in most states the death of one spouse during the pendency of a divorce action will abate the divorce action; the marriage will be treated as dissolving by death rather than divorce. *See* Haviland v. Haviland, 333 Pa.Super. 162, 481 A.2d 1355 (1984); Edgerton v. Edgerton, 203 N.J.Super. 160, 496 A.2d 366 (App.Div.1985).

Should the divorce action be abated if one spouse kills the other? *Compare* Simpson v. Simpson, 473 So.2d 299 (Fla.App.1985) *with* Howsden v. Rolenc, 219 Neb. 16, 360 N.W.2d 680 (1985).

7. *Modification*: As a general rule, a decree dividing property is final and may not be reopened, regardless of how the parties' circumstances change. A decree may be reopened if a party can show extrinsic fraud; intrinsic fraud is not sufficient.

8. *Conflicts of Law*: Most courts today divide property based upon the law of the forum state, regardless of where the property is located (*see* Dority v. Dority, 645 P.2d 56 (Utah 1982)) and where the parties were domiciled when they acquired it (*see* Savelle v. Savelle, 650 So.2d 476 (Miss.1995)); (Ismail v. Ismail, 702 S.W.2d 216 (Tex.App.1985) (applying rule to foreign nationals)). Some courts, however, have applied the law of the situs when dividing foreign realty (*see* Anderson v. Anderson, 449 A.2d 334 (D.C.App.1982)) and at least one court has applied the law of the situs to determine whether foreign personalty could be divided (*see* Marriage of Whelchel, 476 N.W.2d 104 (Iowa App.1991) (applying law of situs to determine divisibility of property and local law to determine actual division)).

9. *Undivided Marital Property*: If marital property is not specifically divided in the divorce decree, the decree must be consulted to see if a general provision of the decree governs. If it does not contain such a provision, common law states have reached different conclusions regarding whether an action to reopen the decree to divide the omitted property is possible. A number have decided that, if a spouse does not challenge the decree within a specified time, the decree is final and may not be reopened. *See* Mitchell v. Meisch, 22 Ark.App. 264, 739 S.W.2d 170 (1987); Boulton v. Boulton, 69 Haw. 1, 730 P.2d 338 (1986). *Cf.* Brink v. Brink, 396 N.W.2d 95 (Minn.App.1986). One court noted that the result might depend upon whether the settlement agreement states that the decree will be reopened if undivided property is discovered. *See* Marriage of Hiner, 669 P.2d 135 (Colo.App.1983). In community property states, each spouse has a vested 50% interest in each marital asset as soon as it is acquired. So, if it is undivided at divorce, the spouses remain tenants in common. *See* Henn v. Henn, 26 Cal.3d 323, 161 Cal.Rptr. 502, 605 P.2d 10 (1980); Bryant v. Sullivan, 148 Ariz. 426, 715 P.2d 282 (Ariz.App.1985).

Problem 14–6:

The state legislature is considering replacing its current property division law (identical to the Minnesota statute on p. 779); the legislature is concerned that "equitable" distribution may, in practice, mean unpredictable and inconsistent distribution. It is also concerned that "equitable distribution may be too complex for most divorcing couples, who have little to divide."

As a replacement for the current system, the legislature is particularly interested in two new ideas. One is the system currently in effect in Germany. This system requires a comparison of each spouse's net worth at marriage and divorce; any gain during the marriage is divided equally. *See* Mary Ann Glendon, The Transformation of Family Law: State, Law, and Family in the United States and Western Europe 217–18 (1989). No American state has adopted a system like this one.

The other system in which the legislature is interested was recently adopted by the American Law Institute; it, again, has currently been adopted by no American state. *See* American Law Institute, Principles of the Law of Family Dissolution: Analysis and Recommendations, Tentative Draft No. 2 (March 14, 1996) (hereinafter "ALI Principles"). For a critical overview of the ALI Principles, *see* J. Thomas Oldham, *ALI Principles of Family Dissolution: Some Comments*, 1997 Ill. L. Rev. 801. This system is more complex.

The ALI definition of marital and separate property is fairly traditional. Marital property includes pension rights earned during marriage (whether vested or unvested), personal injury or disability benefits that replace lost marital wages, and professional goodwill; personal injury or disability benefits that compensate for pain and suffering, earning capacity, and professional degrees and licenses are excluded. Sec. 4.07. Separate property—premarital acquisitions and property acquired during marriage by gift, descent, and devise—includes appreciation of and income from separate property, as well as property acquired after the divorce action is filed.

The ALI approach to division is quite novel, however. Marital property is to be divided equally, except in cases of asset dissipation; also, *separate property gradually becomes marital property.* After a minimum "waiting period" specified in the state statute, a state-specified percentage of separate assets is annually recharacterized as marital; once converted to marital property, separate property is also subject to the equal division rule. For example, a state might specify that 4% of separate property would be recharacterized annually after five years of marriage. Under this approach, all property would be marital property after thirty years of marriage; each spouse (except in a case of dissipation) would obtain fifty percent of all property.

Perhaps because it is an unusual system (hotchpot states permit, but do not require, division of separate assets), the ALI Principles also contain an "opt-out" provision. If one spouse gives the other written notice of his or her intention to maintain separate assets as separate, it is binding from that date forward; the other spouse need not agree.

The drafters of the ALI Principles argue that recharacterization is appropriate because spouses, over time, tend to view all assets as "ours" rather than "yours" and "mine." (They cite no empirical evidence for this proposition.) They also note that the new Uniform Probate Code provisions on spousal rights at death similarly employ an accrual type approach.

You have been asked to evaluate the ALI and German systems in light of the legislature's concerns:

1. How does each differ from a community property approach? a hotchpot approach? an equitable distribution of marital property approach? a presumption of equal division?

2. Which approach will produce the most certain results?

3. Which approach is most responsive to the needs of couples with few marital assets? with many marital assets?

4. Which approach achieves the fairest results?

5. Which approach, on balance, should the legislature adopt?

Chapter 15

SPOUSAL SUPPORT

SECTION 1. AN INTRODUCTION TO SPOUSAL SUPPORT: WHAT IS IT? WHY IS IT AWARDED?

HOMER H. CLARK, JR., THE LAW OF DOMESTIC RELATIONS IN THE UNITED STATES

619–21 (2d ed. 1988).

American law imported the practice of granting alimony as an incident to divorce from the English ecclesiastical law as it existed before the reform of the English court system in 1857. As with other rules borrowed from England, those relating to alimony were applied in a different context. In England the ecclesiastical courts gave only divorces *a mensa et thoro*, authorizing husband and wife to live apart, but not freeing them from the marriage bond. The alimony which was awarded by the ecclesiastical courts under those circumstances merely constituted a recognition and enforcement of the husband's duty to support the wife which continued after the judicial separation. The wife's need was the greater in those days because of the control over her property which the law gave to her husband. This was reflected in the courts' willingness to take into account in fixing the amount of alimony the value of the property which the wife brought into the marriage. Alimony was further made necessary by the lack of employment opportunities for married women. In addition to these factors the English courts gave consideration to the degree of the husband's fault in making the award. Where the wife was at fault, she was entitled to no alimony. Thus even in the English law alimony was not solely measured by the wife's need for support.

* * *

When the English institution of alimony, which served the plain and intelligible purpose of providing support for wives living apart from their husbands, was utilized in America in suits for absolute divorce, however, its purpose became less clear. As a result of absolute divorce the marriage is entirely dissolved. It is harder to justify imposing on the ex-husband a continuing duty to support his former wife than after a divorce a mensa which does not dissolve the marriage. This difficulty is not obviated by labelling alimony a "substitute" for the wife's right to support. Why should there be such a substitute? Would it not be more logical to say that when the marriage is dissolved all rights and duties based upon it end?. . . .

Notwithstanding the logical objection to alimony, as an incident to absolute divorce, it has been granted in the United States from the earliest colonial times to the present. . . . Although nearly all states have statutes authorizing alimony in appropriate cases,[1] there is a lack of agreement on just what purpose alimony serves. In the opinion of some judges alimony continues the support which the wife was entitled to receive while the marriage existed. Others look on alimony as furnishing damages for the husband's wrongful breach of the marriage contract. Still others speak as if it were a penalty imposed on the guilty husband. . . . It is notable that the Uniform Marriage and Divorce Act is framed with the purpose of providing for the spouses by means of a division of property rather than by an award of alimony. Of course it is clear that only a small proportion of divorces involve enough property to be of any benefit to the spouses.

Although the Supreme Court has held that an alimony statute may not discriminate based on gender (Orr v. Orr, 440 U.S. 268, 99 S.Ct. 1102, 59 L.Ed.2d 306 (1979)), the debate on the basis and scope of alimony,[2] now often described as spousal maintenance or support, continues: Should the award serve the primary purpose of providing support for a needy spouse after divorce? If so, should the award be in an amount sufficient merely to lift the recipient out of poverty, or should it be based on the marital standard of living? Alternatively, should the award serve the purpose of compensating a spouse for career damage incurred during marriage due to marital responsibilities, such as child care, that he or she has assumed? Or should it compensate a spouse for expectations that a divorce has shattered? In an era of no-fault divorce, should alimony be denied based on fault? Should it be used to compensate for a "marital wrong"? If so, what fault should suffice and what marital wrongs should be compensated? Should the award be paid for a fixed term or indefinitely (and perhaps for the remainder of the recipient's life)? Should it terminate if either of the parties dies or if the recipient remarries? If the recipient cohabits? In what circumstances should it be possible to change the amount or duration of the award?

Perhaps not surprisingly, no consensus has been reached on any of these questions. One reason for the lack of consensus is simply that

1. Editors note: Since Texas accepted a limited version of post-divorce spousal support in 1995, all U.S. states have permitted the award of alimony.

2. The word alimony comes from the Latin "alimonia," meaning sustenance. See Black's Law Dictionary 67 (5th ed. 1979).

alimony has never had a unitary basis. As Professor Clark notes, the English ecclesiastical courts awarded alimony to protect against need *and* to compensate for property brought into the marriage *and* to punish marital fault. Even with consensus on basic principles, there may not be agreement on how those principles should be applied. Consider these judicial statements on alimony:

> A woman is not a breeding cow to be nurtured during her years of fecundity, then conveniently and economically converted to cheap steaks when past her prime. If a woman is able to do so, she certainly should support herself. If, however, she has spent her productive years as a housewife and mother and has missed the opportunity to compete in the job market and improve her job skills, quite often she becomes, when divorced, simply a "displaced homemaker." In the case at bench we are faced with a woman who, during the last 25 years, has borne 2 children and confined her activities to those of a mother and housewife ... Assuming she does not become blind, her experience as a homemaker qualifies her for either of two positions, charwoman or babysitter. A candidate for a well paying job, she isn't. * * * [In such a case] the husband simply has to face up to the fact that his support responsibilities are going to be of extended duration—perhaps for life. This has nothing to do with feminism, sexism, male chauvinism or any other trendy social ideology. It is ordinary common-sense, basic decency and simple justice.
>
> In re Marriage of Brantner, 67 Cal.App.3d 416, 136 Cal.Rptr. 635 (1977).

> The law should provide both parties with the opportunity to make a new life on this earth. Neither should be shackled by the unnecessary burdens of an unhappy marriage. This is not to suggest that women of no skills, or those who suffer a debilitating infirmity, or who are of advanced age (whatever that may be) should be denied alimony for as long as needed. But such women are the exception, not the rule.
>
> Turner v. Turner, 158 N.J.Super. 313, 385 A.2d 1280 (N.J. Super 1978).

Both the *Brantner* and *Turner* courts appear to agree that need and work skills are key issues in an alimony inquiry. But the *Brantner* court sees need where the alimony claimant is qualified for low-wage employment, while the *Turner* court sees need only where there are "no skills," a "debilitating infirmity," or "advanced age." The two courts also appear to have very different attitudes toward the alimony payor, with one sympathetically focused on the "shackles ... of an unhappy marriage," the other concerned that one spouse may wish to "economically convert [the other] to cheap steaks when past her prime."

State statutes governing post-divorce spousal maintenance do not evidence any more consensus than do judicial opinions. But it is important to keep in mind that there is no state statute under which alimony is awarded frequently or which typically produces awards of high value. The average annual alimony award in 1985 was $3730. U.S. DEP'T OF COMMERCE, BUREAU OF THE CENSUS, CHILD SUPPORT AND ALIMONY, 1985 (CURRENT POPULATION REPORTS, Series P–60, No. 152). State surveys of alimony awards conducted during the 1980s show anywhere from 7% to 30% of divorced women receiving alimony awards. *See* Marsha Garrison, *The Economics of Divorce: Changing Rules, Changing Results* 91 tbl. 3.11 in DIVORCE REFORM AT THE CROSSROADS (Herma H. Kay & Stephen D. Sugarman eds. 1991) (surveying reports). While these surveys also show declines in the proportion of women obtaining alimony between the 1970s and 1980s, approximately 15% of surveyed divorced women reported to the Census Bureau that they had been awarded alimony during the late 1970s and early 1980s, while 17% did so in 1989, the last year the Census Bureau collected alimony data. U.S. BUREAU OF THE CENSUS, CHILD SUPPORT AND ALIMONY, 1989 (Current Population Reports, Series P–60, No. 173 (1990)) (showing alimony rate but not values). Census data from the turn of the century show that 9.3% of divorces included alimony awards. PAUL H. JACOBSON, AMERICAN MARRIAGE AND DIVORCE 127–28 (1959). Debate over alimony principles thus has not substantially altered the relatively low—and constant—*likelihood* of an alimony award.

There has been a recent, marked shift in the typical *duration* of an alimony award. Until the no-fault divorce movement of the 1960s and 70s, the spouse who was at fault in causing the dissolution of the marriage was barred from obtaining alimony; but, once granted, an alimony award typically extended until the recipient's death or remarriage. With the advent of no-fault divorce, some states began to permit a "guilty" spouse to obtain alimony; many states also revised their alimony rules to permit short-term, "rehabilitative" alimony. Divorce surveys suggest that these statutory reforms were typically followed by a substantial reduction—in some states as high as 50%—in the proportion of alimony awards that were awarded permanently (i.e., until death or remarriage). For example, Professor Garrison found that, in the 1970s, about 80% of surveyed New York alimony awards were permanent; less than ten years later, only about 40% were permanent. Marsha Garrison, *Good Intentions Gone Awry: The Impact of New York's Equitable Distribution Law on Divorce Outcomes*, 57 BROOKLYN L. REV. 621, 700 (1991). *See also* Lenore J. Weitzman & Ruth B. Dixon, *The Alimony Myth: Does No-Fault Divorce Make a Difference?*, 14 FAM. L. Q. 141, 161–62 (1980); Heather Wishik, *Economics of Divorce: An Exploratory Study*, 20 FAM. L. Q. 79 (1986); James B. McClindon, *Separate But Unequal: The Economic Disaster of Divorce for Women and Children*, 21 FAM. L. Q. 351 (1987).

Some states have "resolved" the alimony debate by granting judges broad discretionary powers to award and set the duration of alimony based on a broad range of factors; the Pennsylvania alimony statute exemplifies this approach. Other state legislatures have taken a strong position on the alimony question and limited judicial discretion accordingly; the Texas alimony statute provides an example. The Uniform Marriage and Divorce Act takes an intermediate approach.

23 Pa. Cons. Stat. Ann. § 3701. Alimony

(a) General rule.—Where a divorce decree has been entered, the court may allow alimony, as it deems reasonable, to either party only if it finds that alimony is necessary.

(b) Factors relevant.—In determining whether alimony is necessary and in determining the nature, amount, duration and manner of payment of alimony, the court shall consider all relevant factors, including:

(1) The relative earnings and earning capacities of the parties.

(2) The ages and the physical, mental and emotional conditions of the parties.

(3) The sources of income of both parties, including, but not limited to, medical, retirement, insurance or other benefits.

(4) The expectancies and inheritances of the parties.

(5) The duration of the marriage.

(6) The contribution by one party to the education, training or increased earning power of the other party.

(7) The extent to which the earning power, expenses or financial obligations of a party will be affected by reason of serving as the custodian of a minor child.

(8) The standard of living of the parties established during the marriage.

(9) The relative education of the parties and the time necessary to acquire sufficient education or training to enable the party seeking alimony to find appropriate employment.

(10) The relative assets and liabilities of the parties.

(11) The property brought to the marriage by either party.

(12) The contribution of a spouse as homemaker.

(13) The relative needs of the parties.

(14) The marital misconduct of either of the parties during the marriage. The marital misconduct of either of the parties from the date of final separation shall not be considered by the court in its determinations relative to alimony.

(15) The Federal, State and local tax ramifications of the alimony award.

(16) Whether the party seeking alimony lacks sufficient property, including, but not limited to, property distributed under Chapter 35 (relating to property rights), to provide for the party's reasonable needs.

(17) Whether the party seeking alimony is incapable of self-support through appropriate employment.

(c) Duration.—The court in ordering alimony shall determine the duration of the order, which may be for a definite or an indefinite period of time which is reasonable under the circumstances.

Tex. Fam. Code

§ 3.9602. Eligibility for Maintenance

[T]he court may order maintenance for either spouse only if:

(1) the spouse from whom maintenance is sought was convicted of, or received deferred adjudication for, a criminal offense that also constitutes an act of family violence under § 71.01, Family Code, and the offense occurred:

(A) within two years before the date on which a suit for dissolution of the marriage was filed; or

(B) during the pendency of the suit; or

(2) the duration of the marriage was 10 years or longer, the spouse seeking maintenance lacks sufficient property, including property distributed to the spouse under this code, to provide for the spouse's minimum reasonable needs, as limited by § 3.9605, and the spouse seeking maintenance:

(A) is unable to support himself or herself through appropriate employment because of an incapacitating physical or mental disability;

(B) is the custodian of a child who requires substantial care and personal supervision because a physical or mental disability makes it necessary, taking into consideration the needs of the child, that the spouse not be employed outside the home; or

(C) clearly lacks earning ability in the labor market adequate to provide support for the spouse's minimum reasonable needs, as limited by § 3.9605.

§ 3.9605. Duration of Maintenance Order

(a) Except as provided by Subsection (b), a court:

(1) may not enter a maintenance order that remains in effect for more than three years after the date of the order; and

(2) shall limit the duration of a maintenance order to the shortest reasonable period of time that allows the spouse seeking maintenance to meet the spouse's minimum reasonable needs by obtaining appropriate employment or developing an appropriate skill, unless the ability of the spouse to provide for the spouse's minimum reasonable needs through employment is substantially or totally diminished because of:

(A) physical or mental disability;

(B) duties as the custodian of an infant or young child; or

(C) another compelling impediment to gainful employment.

(b) If a spouse seeking maintenance is unable to support himself or herself through appropriate employment because of incapacitating physical or mental disability, the court may order maintenance for an indefinite period for as long as the disability continues. The court may order periodic review of its order, on the request of either party or on its own motion, to determine whether the disability is continuing. The continuation of spousal maintenance under these circumstances is subject to a motion to modify as provided by § 3.9608.

§ 3.9606. Amount of Maintenance

(a) A court may not enter a maintenance order that requires a spouse to pay monthly more than the lessor of:

(1) $2,500; or

(2) 20 percent of the spouse's average monthly gross income.

UNIFORM MARRIAGE AND DIVORCE ACT § 308. MAINTENANCE

9A U.L.A. 347–48 (1987).

(a) In a proceeding for dissolution of marriage, legal separation, or maintenance following a decree of dissolution of the marriage by a court which lacked personal jurisdiction over the absent spouse, the court may grant a maintenance order for either spouse, only if it finds that the spouse seeking maintenance:

(1) lacks sufficient property to provide for his reasonable needs; and

(2) is unable to support himself through appropriate employment or is the custodian of a child whose condition or circumstances make it appropriate that the custodian not be required to seek employment outside the home.

(b) the maintenance order shall be in amounts and for periods of time the court deems just, without regard to marital misconduct, and after considering all relevant factors including:

(1) the financial resources of the party seeking maintenance, including marital property apportioned to him, his ability to meet his needs independently, and the extent to which a provision for support of a child living with the party includes a sum for that party as custodian;

(2) the time necessary to acquire sufficient education or training to enable the party seeking maintenance to find appropriate employment;

(3) the standard of living established during the marriage;

(4) the duration of the marriage;

(5) the age and physical and emotional condition of the spouse seeking maintenance; and

(6) the ability of the spouse from whom maintenance is sought to meet his needs while meeting those of the spouse seeking maintenance.

Problem 15–1:

Harold, age 33, and Winona, age 30, have been married for nine years and have three children, ages 7, 5, and 2. For the first two years of the marriage, Winona worked as a beautician; during these years Harold completed his law school education and worked part-time as a paralegal. Since Harold's graduation from law school, he has been employed as an attorney; Winona has been a full-time homemaker. Her beautician's license lapsed two years ago; she is a high school graduate and has completed one year of college in addition to beautician training. Harold is now employed by the Maxit Corp. at an annual salary of $100,000. Harold has been having an affair with another attorney at Maxit and has asked Winona for a divorce. Harold and Winona own a house, in which they have equity totalling $40,000. They have other liquid assets worth $20,000. Harold has only recently come to work for Maxit and is not yet covered by the company's pension plan. Neither spouse has separate assets. What arguments related to the award of alimony are available to Harold and Winona: a) in Pennsylvania; b) in Texas; c) under the UMDA?

Problem 15–2:

Herman, age 60, and Wendy, age 58, have been married for thirty-four years and have one child, age 30. Herman has for many years been a self-employed businessman; for the past ten years, Wendy has sold real estate part-time. Prior to that time she was a full-time homemaker. She is also actively involved in community affairs, serving as a member of the local school board and as a trustee of the town library. Herman's business is very successful; he has earned, on average, $250,000 per year for the past five years. Wendy, during the same period, has averaged $25,000. Marital assets total approximately 750,000. Harold has separate assets totalling $2,000,000. Both spouses completed two years of college. Both wish to end the marriage due to feelings of incompatibility. What arguments related to the award of alimony are available to Herman and Wendy: a) in Pennsylvania; b) in Texas; c) under the UMDA?

How would your analysis change if marital assets totalled $30,000, neither spouse had separate assets, Herman was an auto mechanic earning $23,000 and Wendy a school custodian earning $5,000?

Problem 15–3:

Harvey and Willa have been married for 10 years; both are 38 years old. Willa earns $120,000 annually; Harvey $40,000. The ratio of their salaries at the time of the marriage was approximately the same. Marital assets total $30,000; there are no children. Both have had affairs and wish to end the marriage. What arguments related to the award of alimony are available to Harvey and Willa: a) in Pennsylvania; b) in Texas; c) under the UMDA?

Problem 15–4:

Henry and Winifred have been married for eight years. Henry is 50 and Winifred is 45. At the time of the marriage, both earned about $50,000 per year. Two years ago, Henry had a heart attack and can no longer work; he receives $700 monthly in Social Security benefits. Winifred is in good health and earns $60,000 annually. Marital assets total $20,000. Winifred wishes to end the marriage. What arguments related to the award of alimony are available to Henry and Winifred: a) in Pennsylvania; b) in Texas; c) under the UMDA?

Notes and Questions

1. Which of the three statutes appears to yield, on average, the "fairest" results?

2. How easy is it to assess: a) the likelihood; b) the duration; and c) the value of alimony under the three statutes?

3. Highly discretionary standards are " ... largely based on the assumption that the infinite variety of circumstances is such that the attempt to lay down general rules is bound to lead to injustice. Justice can only be done by the individualized, ad hoc approach.... " P.S. Atiyah, From Principles to Pragmatism: Changes in the Function of the Judicial Process and the Law 11 (1978). What are the pros and cons of an ad hoc approach to alimony determination?

SECTION 2. FACTORS IN DETERMINING THE AWARD OF ALIMONY

A. NEED

What does "need" mean? Assume that one spouse earns $27,000 annually and the other $10,000, that both are in decent health, and that they have no minor children. Does the lower-earning spouse "need" support?

MORGAN v. MORGAN

Supreme Court Trial Term, New York County, 1975.
81 Misc.2d 616, 366 N.Y.S.2d 977.

Bentley Kassal, Judge.

The parties were married on January 27, 1967 when the husband was in his third year pre-law course at the University of North Carolina and the wife, a sophomore, studying biology, at the Florida State University. Recognizing that both could not simultaneously continue their education and be self-supporting, they agreed it would be preferable for him to finish his undergraduate and law school education while she worked. She commenced working full time, earning a monthly salary of $328.00 until the day before she gave birth to a son, on August 9, 1967. She resumed working a few months later, in January 1968, on a part-time basis, took care of her own and other children, on an exchange basis, and did typing at home for students, as well as her husband's theses. This continued until she and her husband separated in October 1972.

In the interim, Mrs. Morgan has become very proficient at shorthand and typing and also worked as a data analyst. I am satisfied that she is very skilled and, as an executive secretary or technician, could probably command an annual salary of at least $10,000 in normal economy and, very possibly, even in the present employment market.

In February 1973, she returned to the campus to pursue a full time educational career by undertaking a pre-medical course at Hunter College and her grades have been exceptional—a 3.83 general average (out of a 4.0 maximum) and an A score in the organic chemistry course, ranking 5th in a class of 70.

For his part, the husband has progressed well in his profession, having graduated from Columbia Law School after being selected for its Law Journal. His career started, as planned, with a one year stint as a law clerk to a Federal Circuit Judge and he immediately thereafter became an associate at a prominent Wall Street law firm. His starting salary, in August 1972 was $18,000 per annum with $500 increases on November 1, 1972, March 1, 1973, April 1, 1973, a $3,500 increase on November 1, 1973, a $1,500 increase on May 1, 1974 with the most recent increase of $3,000 on November 1, 1974, to a present salary level of $27,500. In all, he has done well and his future appears very promising. * * *

At a time when some call for treating the marriage contract as any other contract, it is particularly appropriate to speak of the wife's duty to mitigate the damages to the husband upon breach. I agree that "when she can, she should also be required to mitigate the husband's burden either by her own financial means or earning potential or both." But it is a corollary to the rule of mitigation that the injured party may also recover for the expenses reasonably incurred in an effort to avoid or reduce the damages. In this case, any possible short-term economic benefit which would result from the wife's returning to a position similar to the one she held over two years ago, is far outweighed by the potential benefit, economic, emotional, and otherwise, of her pursuing her education.

In coming to the conclusion I do, I am seeking to effect a balancing of many factors—the parties' financial status, their obligations, age, station in life and opportunities for development and self-fulfillment. Times have changed, owing not alone to the co-equal status which a married woman shares with her husband, but also to the increase in the number of married women working in gainful occupations.

* * * The provisions of § 236 of the Domestic Relations Law direct, *inter alia*, that the Court consider the "ability of the wife to be self-supporting," as well as "the circumstances of the case and of the respective parties." "Self-supporting," in my judgment, does not imply that the wife shall be compelled to take any position that will be available when her obvious potential in life, in terms of "self-support," will be greatly inhibited.

Cognizance must also be taken of other language in the very same section, namely, "* * * the court *may* direct the husband to *provide suitably* for the support of the wife, *as, in the court's discretion, justice requires,* * * *" (emphasis added). This has been interpreted to vest broad discretion in the court, "unfettered by" literal readings of the law. Obviously two households cannot be maintained as cheaply as one and we therefore encounter the threshold issue of whether the wife—a very capable woman, probably able to earn at least $10,000 annually as a secretary or office worker—shall be compelled to contribute this sum or a fair share thereof, to her own support, at this time, or shall she have an opportunity to achieve a professional education based upon her potential, which will be comparable to the one her husband received as a result of her assistance by working during their marriage.

In my opinion, the answer to this issue is that under these circumstances, the wife is also entitled to equal treatment and a "break" and should not be automatically relegated to a life of being a well-paid, skilled technician laboring with a life-long frustration as to what her future might have been as a doctor, but for her marriage and motherhood.

I am impressed by the fact that the plaintiff does not assume the posture that she wants to be an alimony drone or seek permanent alimony. Rather she had indicated that she only wants support for herself until she finishes medical school in 5 ½ years (1 ½ years more in college and 4 years in medical school) and will try to work when possible.

* * *

Accordingly, I am directing that the defendant shall pay a total sum of $200 weekly for alimony and child support, so long as she does not remarry and continues to be a full-time student, undertaking a premedical or medical course. (I am taking into consideration plaintiff's agreement to work during her vacation periods when not prohibited by school work.) Completion of her medical school training and the awarding of an M.D. degree shall be deemed a sufficient change of circumstances and I am granting leave to the defendant to apply at such time for an appropriate modification to delete the alimony feature of this award.

Notes and Questions

1. On appeal, this sensible judgment was reversed:

"The alimony of $100 per week awarded below was predicated upon plaintiff's ambition to obtain entrance to medical school and receive an M.D. degree. It is not disputed that the plaintiff has present earning ability, which the court below believed might be at least $10,000 per year. A wife's ability to be self-supporting is relevant when determining the amount of support a husband is to provide. Absent a compelling showing that the wife cannot contribute to her own support, courts have "imputed" or deducted a wife's potential earnings from the amount which would otherwise be found payable as alimony by her ex-husband. *While this Court recognizes plaintiff's goal in medicine, this pursuit was never in the contemplation of the parties during marriage and appears to be of recent origin.* The law requires that the alimony award should be predicated upon the present circumstances of the parties. Although the wife's ambition is most commendable, the court below was in error in including in the alimony award monies for the achievement of that goal."

Morgan v. Morgan, 52 A.D.2d 804, 383 N.Y.S.2d 343 (1976) (emphasis added).

2. Does *Morgan* demonstrate that need should not be the sole factor relevant to an alimony award?

MARRIAGE OF HUNTINGTON

California Court of Appeals, 1992.
10 Cal.App.4th 1513, 14 Cal.Rptr.2d 1.

KLINE, PRESIDING JUSTICE.

Ann K. Huntington appeals from a judgment of dissolution of marriage. She urges the trial court adopted an erroneous interpretation of Civil Code § 4801 and abused its discretion in awarding her spousal support of $5,000 a month for a period of only six months....

STATEMENT OF THE CASE

On March 27, 1989, respondent filed a petition for legal separation from appellant; he subsequently filed a petition for dissolution of marriage on April 27, 1989, and an amended petition for dissolution of marriage on July 21, 1989. The parties had been married on August 24, 1985, and separated three years and seven months later on March 28, 1989.

Trial proceeded on October 22, 23, 30 and 31, 1990. The trial court ordered spousal support of $5,000 per month for a period of six months, to permanently terminate thereafter, and ordered the parties to bear their own attorney fees and costs. Appellant had been receiving temporary spousal support of $7,500 per month since May 1, 1989, and her attorney had previously received $19,000 from respondent for attorney fees pursuant to prior court order and stipulation.

STATEMENT OF FACTS

Respondent is a wealthy man with a net worth in excess of $15 million. At the time of the marriage, appellant was 28 years old and respondent 47. Appellant had been working as a dental hygienist, earning about $30,000 a year, but stopped working shortly before the marriage when respondent told her it would not be necessary for her to work. The day before the marriage, the parties entered into a premarital agreement providing for their property to remain separate.

The parties' standard of living during the marriage was extremely high. Respondent owns a home in Tiburon valued at two and a half million dollars, an 18.2–acre property in Tahoe worth three million, and nine cars, and the court found he has a controllable annual cash flow of approximately $500,000 from his investments. Appellant testified that she spent about $6,000 a month on clothes alone. Respondent's attorney stipulated that respondent could pay any reasonable amount of spousal support.

Appellant testified that she did not wish to return to work as a dental hygienist because it was a stressful, "dead-end" job with no advancement, she had lost her contacts, she would be "rusty" if she went back, her license had expired and she would have to take a test to revive it, as well as "brush-up" courses. Additionally, according to literature on the subject, dental hygienists "burn-out" after about five years, which was the length of time respondent had been practicing before the marriage. She had prepared a resume and applied for several other jobs (public relations at a winery, part-time writer for the Independent Journal, record company, cellular telephone company, lobbyist firm) but had not been successful. She testified that she did not think she was ready to go to work immediately because she had been through a lot, had not worked in a long time, and wanted to see what her options were and make the right choice before entering something new.

Appellant presented three expert witnesses who testified that she was not emotionally prepared to immediately begin self-supporting employment.

Appellant next contends the trial court erroneously read Civil Code § 4801. This statute authorizes trial courts to order spousal support "for any period of time, as the court may deem just and reasonable, based on the standard of living established during the marriage." In making its award, the trial court is required to consider nine enumerated factors, several of which explicitly refer to the marital standard of living, as well as any others it deems "just and equitable."[3] The trial court is required

3. The factors the trial court is required to consider under § 4801, subdivision (a), are as follows:

"(1) The extent to which the earning capacity of each spouse is sufficient to maintain the standard of living established during the marriage, taking into account all of the following:

"(A) The marketable skills of the supported spouse; the job market for those skills; the time and expenses required for the supported spouse to acquire the appropriate education or training to develop those skills; and the possible need for retraining or education to acquire other, more marketable skills or employment.

"(B) The extent to which the supported spouse's present or future earning capacity is impaired by periods of unemployment that were incurred during the marriage to permit the supported spouse to devote time to domestic duties.

"(2) The extent to which the supported spouse contributed to the attainment of an

to "make specific factual findings with respect to the standard of living during the marriage, and, at the request of either party, the court shall make appropriate factual determinations with respect to any other circumstances."

In the present case, the court commenced its statement of decision by reference to the factors enumerated in § 4801, its most significant findings being that appellant had a marketable skill she could make use of with little retraining and was young and healthy, that respondent was very wealthy and had not worked during the marriage, and that the marriage was brief and there were no children.[4] With respect to the question of standard of living, the court made specific reference to respondent's Tiburon home, Tahoe estate and cars, and found the marital lifestyle to be "affluent." The court then addressed the issue of appellant's health and ability to work, reviewing the testimony of each of the experts and concluding that appellant suffered from a personality disorder which was exacerbated by the parties' relationship but which was not adequately debilitating to prevent her from working.

Finally, the court expressed its view that the standard of living factor was meant by the Legislature to reflect the common situation in which couples marry with little and over time jointly acquire assets and enjoy a higher standard of living. In that situation the non-working spouse should not be financially prejudiced by divorce. The "same sociological considerations" do not necessarily apply in a marriage of short duration, the court explained, where neither party worked, one was very wealthy and the standard of living derived from inherited

education, training, a career position, or a license by the other spouse.

"(3) The ability to pay of the supporting spouse, taking into account the supporting spouse's earning capacity, earned and unearned income, assets, and standard of living.

"(4) The needs of each party based on the standard of living established during the marriage.

"(5) The obligations and assets, including the separate property, of each.

"(6) The duration of the marriage.

"(7) The ability of the supported spouse to engage in gainful employment without interfering with the interests of dependent children in the custody of the spouse.

"(8) The age and health of the parties.

"(9) The immediate and specific tax consequences to each party.

"(10) Any other factors which it deems just and equitable."

4. The court found appellant had the marketable skill of dental hygienist, for which there was a market within reasonable commuting distance, it would take less than two or three months for appellant to "get up to speed," with no substantial retraining or education required to market her skill, and appellant's period of unemployment had little effect on her current employability and income; issues concerning the supported spouse's contribution to the other spouse's attainment of education or career were irrelevant; respondent had earning capacity, had not worked during the marriage but had assets creating income at a "substantial standard of living" and meeting his needs adequately; respondent had assets approximating $15,000,000 which created an annual available cash flow of approximately $500,000, with fairly small obligations, while appellant "essentially has no assets," owning a vehicle, possibly a condominium in which she did not have much equity, $25,000 or $30,000 saved from the temporary support she had been receiving and something less than $25,000 in assets to be determined when the community property was divided; the marriage lasted three years and seven months; there were no children; respondent's age and health were irrelevant and respondent was of good physical health and in her early to mid-thirties; and tax consequences were "of little meaning" in the case.

money rather than the efforts of either spouse. The court concluded: "In any event, when analyzing the length of the marriage, the lifestyle, the assets of the parties, the marketable skills of [appellant], the availability of her employment, the time in which it would take to get back into the work force and the reasonably full-time employed—that's something she doesn't want to do, but she clearly has the ability to do it—constrains me to make the following orders with regards to spousal support."

Appellant contends that § 4801 does not limit consideration of marital standard of living to situations where the standard of living results from community efforts but requires it to be considered as the starting point in all cases. The trial court's comments, however, make clear that the standard of living *was* considered in determining the spousal support award. The judge simply recognized that the situation of a spouse ending a brief marriage in which the standard of living was determined by the other spouse's separate property assets is different from that of a spouse ending a long-term marriage in which the couple developed a standard of living together. "The marital standard is just one factor to be weighed with all other applicable factors to reach a 'just and reasonable' result." Here, the court properly also considered the duration of the marriage and appellant's ability to become self-supporting in reaching its decision.

Notes and Questions

1. Why should "the situation of a spouse ending a brief marriage in which the standard of living was determined by the other spouse's separate property assets" be treated differently from that "of a spouse ending a long-term marriage in which the couple developed a standard of living together?" What is the court implicitly saying about the alimony entitlement?

2. Professor Garrison found that most alimony decisions made by New York judges could be predicted based on the claimant's income and the duration of the marriage. For unemployed women married more than ten years, the alimony award rate was 83%; for employed women married less than ten years, it was 23%. Eighty-nine per cent of women earning less than 10% of family income were awarded alimony. *See* Marsha Garrison, *How Do Judges Decide Divorce Cases? An Empirical Analysis of Discretionary Decision Making*, 74 N.C.L. Rev. 401, 468–69, tbls. 14–16 (1996). In a related sample of New York cases that were settled during the same time period, only 49% of unemployed women married ten or more years and 58% of women with income representing less than 10% of family income obtained alimony. *Id.* Why would wives who litigate have better alimony prospects than those who settle? One factor may be legal representation. Professor Garrison found that, where both sides in a settled case were represented by counsel, wives obtained alimony in 30% of the cases. No wives received alimony when neither was represented. *See* Marsha Garrison, *Good Intentions Gone Awry: The Impact of New York's Equitable Distribution Law on Divorce Outcomes*, 57 Brooklyn L. Rev. 621, 711, tbl. 48 (1991). (Of course, parties are more

likely to be represented by counsel when they have been married longer and have higher incomes.)

B. MARITAL FAULT

BENDER v. BENDER

Maryland Court of Appeals, 1978.
282 Md. 525, 386 A.2d 772.

DIGGES, JUDGE.

The petitioner does not ask this Court to reverse the decree insofar as it (i) granted her husband a divorce *a vinculo* as a consequence of her adultery, and (ii) denied Mrs. Bender relief on her cross-bill based on allegations of her husband's cruelty and constructive desertion. She does, however, strenuously attack the "fault" approach to alimony in this State, contending that her adulterous conduct after twenty years of marriage should not preclude an award of alimony to her. This is particularly so, the wife asserts, since she is in need of reasonable support—never having worked outside the home and hence having no ability to earn an adequate living—and since her husband, with an amassed fortune of some twenty-four million dollars, could easily afford to provide it.

* * *

We need only add a few facts to those already alluded to in order to convey the flavor of the proceedings below before turning to an explanation of our determinations here. The parties were married in 1956, when Mrs. Bender was seventeen and have five children, two of whom are still minors. The marriage was subject to "some friction and problems" prior to the events in 1976 which provided the husband a basis for filing this divorce suit. The parties ceased having sexual relations as early as September of 1975, and had twice discussed the possibility of divorce, once in 1969, at the wife's suggestion, and again in 1975, this time at her husband's initiation. Nothing came of these discussions, however, and in June of 1976 the husband obtained evidence, through private investigators he had employed, of his wife's adultery. In July he instituted this suit and in August physically removed his wife from their marital abode. The fact of Mrs. Bender's adultery was never controverted, nor did the petitioner contradict Mr. Bender's testimony that she had admitted to him in July, after being confronted with his knowledge of her infidelity, that she had been having an extramarital affair for two or three years. Mrs. Bender appears to have sought to justify her adulterous acts by asserting that her husband had become impotent: she also sought to prove that he had for many years subjected her to abusive treatment and foul language in public. As we have noted, however, the petitioner does not challenge the chancellor's conclusion that the abusive language and physical altercations shown were not of sufficient magnitude to justify granting her an *a mensa* divorce based on either cruelty or constructive desertion.

* * *

Since the petitioner could not have been granted a divorce—and indeed does not here contend otherwise—either on culpatory or nonculpatory grounds, she simply may not have alimony.

Construing the petitioner's argument as a request that we abrogate the rule that a spouse who is not entitled to a divorce is not entitled to alimony, we conclude we are powerless to do so. Mrs. Bender, in support of her plea for alimony, refers to the judicially-determined cause of the demise of her marriage—her adultery—as a "legal fiction," and espouses the view that marriages break down not because of a particular fault on the part of one party, but because of a "myriad of subtle psychological pressures and anxieties created by both parties." While this point of view cannot fail to evoke sympathy in some quarters, particularly in a case such as is revealed by the record before us, we cannot escape the conclusion that the petitioner's views are being advocated in the wrong forum. Divorce, unknown at common law, is entirely a creature of statute, similarly, the authority for allowing alimony in connection with a divorce stems solely from legislative enactment.

* * *

While there may well be cogent reasons for dispensing with notions of fault as a factor in the award of alimony, as with grounds for divorce, it is to the legislature that the petitioner must look if she wishes the law to be rid of the "legal fiction" that either party could be solely responsible for the decay of the marriage, and hence not entitled to alimony.

Notes and Questions

1. The states are about equally divided on whether fault is relevant to an alimony award. In 1995, 25 states barred any consideration of marital fault; 25 permitted its consideration. In most of the states that allow consideration of fault, fault is relevant to the alimony decision, but not determinative. *See* Linda D. Elrod & Robert G. Spector, *A Review of the Year in Family Law: Children's Issues Take Spotlight*, 29 FAM. L.Q. 741, 770, tbl. 1 (1996). Only a few states still bar an alimony award when the claimant spouse has been found guilty of fault causing the dissolution of the marriage. *See, e.g.*, LA. CIV. CODE art. 112; GA. CODE ANN. § 19–6–1.

2. State laws are not always consistent in their treatment of fault as a ground for the divorce and as a basis for alimony. For example, under Florida's no-fault divorce statute, "the court may consider a spouse's adultery in determining the propriety of an alimony award and the amount of alimony, if any, to be awarded." FLA. STATS. § 61.08. Illinois, on the other hand, permits fault to be considered in granting a divorce, but forbids consideration of fault in determining alimony. *See* 750 ILL. COMP. STATS. § 5/503.

Are these statutes appropriately or inappropriately inconsistent? Why?

3. The German Civil Code permits a court to consider making an alimony decision to consider some forms of fault, but not others:

> "A claim for support must be denied, reduced or limited in duration, if the imposition of the obligation—also considering the rights of a child of the obligor and obligee that is in the obligee's custody—would be unconscionable (grossly inequitable) because * * * (2) The obligee is guilty of a crime or of a severe intentional offense against the obligor or against a near relative of the obligor; (3) The obligee has caused his or her own need intentionally or recklessly; (4) The obligee has intentionally or recklessly disregarded significant financial interests of the obligor; (5) For a considerable period of time before the separation, the obligee has grossly violated his or her duty to contribute to the support of the family; (6) The obligee is responsible for obviously serious, clearly unilateral misconduct against the obligor; * * * "

GERMAN CIVIL CODE § 1579.

4. Should the fault of the payor spouse be relevant to an alimony award? In Dyer v. Tsapis, 162 W.Va. 289, 249 S.E.2d 509 (1978), the West Virginia Supreme Court said yes:

> "[The husband was granted a no-fault divorce. At a hearing on alimony, the trial court found that, although the husband's misconduct could not be conclusively proven, the circumstances indicated a 'strong suspicion of guilt' of adultery. The court found the wife's conduct to be blameless. The husband was found guilty of 'inequitable conduct' and ordered to pay $150 per month alimony. The husband brought this action in prohibition on the grounds that no alimony can be awarded unless the party sought to be charged has been found guilty of fault sufficient to support a fault-based divorce.
>
> . . . Once all divorces, like all tort actions, were predicated upon a legal wrong; alimony, like tort damages, served both punitive and compensatory purposes. Now, increasingly, divorces are awarded on no-fault grounds and awards of alimony, like contract damages increasingly emphasize restitution to the exclusion of punishment. The law which once saw marriage as a sacrament now conceptualizes it as roughly analogous to a business partnership. As might be expected in the midst of such change, there is tension between the old and new approaches. On the one hand there is a powerful incentive to punish a wrongdoer and an even more powerful aversion to rewarding one. On the other hand, there is an appreciation of the value of a wife's sacrifice of the opportunity to obtain skills, advancement, and retirement benefits. In addition, a woman of advanced age is likely to experience difficulty in finding another suitable partner. Reluctantly, and possibly because of the difficulty in determining fault in the context of a complex interpersonal relationship, we have shifted the focus of the divorce inquiry from

fault evidence to more dignified and reliable economic evidence. Nonetheless, the more modern approach must be alloyed with the more ancient. It is against a backdrop of confluent policies that we must examine the question before us now.

* * *

"We hold ... that in a divorce action based upon [one year's voluntary separation], a spouse seeking alimony must show the other spouse guilty of inequitable conduct. Although inequitable conduct need not be so serious as to fall into one of the standard fault categories it must be a significant wrong supported by a preponderance of the evidence in the record. In the case before us, while the husband may or may not have committed adultery, his conduct was found to give rise to a strong suspicion of adultery. Conduct of this sort, which would lead persons in the community reasonably to believe that the husband committed adultery, and, therefore, to hold the wife up to ridicule and contempt, could reasonably be considered inequitable by the trial court.

Formerly when a wife established a ground for divorce based on traditional fault she was entitled to damages keyed to her station in life. The husband, however, had reasonably definite notice of those things which he must not do in order to protect himself from this change. What, however, we are attempting to do under the hybrid section of the statute under consideration is not to punish either party, but rather only to avoid unjust enrichment on either side. Therefore, notwithstanding the fact that a wife is blameless, if a divorce is granted on the no-fault ground of voluntary separation and alimony is predicated upon that nebulous notion of inequitable conduct, then the wife has an obligation to mitigate her damages—again an analogy from the contract side of this new confluent stream which merges tort and contract principles (which it should be emphasized again we recognize are applicable *only* by analogy as all parts of an action for divorce are obviously entirely equitable.)

Of course, there will be occasions where the wife is not capable of mitigating the damages and the court should look to all the possible factors and tailor his decree in such a way as to strike a balance among all the competing equities.... While a divorce may now be a simple way out for a spouse who is tired of a marriage, a totally blameless party can never be charged with alimony. When, however, there has been inequitable conduct on the part of the husband and it appears that the wife has been comparatively blameless, the trial court is entitled to award such alimony as justice and the nature of the case demands according to the principles set forth above. Accordingly, the writ of prohibition for which the relator prays is denied."

5. The split among jurisdictions regarding the role of fault in alimony decision making reflects the lack of consensus about alimony's purpose. *If* alimony is compensation for tortious conduct, the wrong-

doing spouse's fault should increase the "damage" award. *If* alimony is compensation for breach of the marital contract, the victimized spouse should be able to recover, but not the wrongdoer spouse. *If* alimony represents accrued economic interests in the marriage relationship, fault should be irrelevant. *If* alimony represents a replacement of lost earnings or pay for unpaid services, fault should be irrelevant. *If* divorce terminates spousal support obligations, then there should be no alimony at all, fault or no fault.

6. Evaluate the following approaches to fault as a factor in alimony decision making:

a. the *Bender* approach;

b. the approach of the German Civil Code (note 3, *supra*);

c. the *Dyer* approach (note 4, *supra*);

d. a bar on consideration of fault by either spouse.

What are the advantages and disadvantages of each approach?

SECTION 3. THE DURATION AND VALUE OF ALIMONY

A. THE DURATION OF ALIMONY

OTIS v. OTIS

Supreme Court of Minnesota, 1980.
299 N.W.2d 114.

TODD, JUSTICE.

Emmanuel and Georgia Contos Otis' marriage was terminated by divorce. Georgia Otis has appealed from that portion of the decree which terminates her maintenance after four years. We affirm.

The parties were married on June 6, 1954. At the time of the marriage, Mrs. Otis was a skilled executive secretary, earning a substantial income. She left her employment to give birth to the parties' only child and has remained absent from the employment market since that time. Mr. Otis has achieved a high degree of success in the business world and is employed by Control Data Corporation as an executive vice president. At the time of the divorce, Mrs. Otis was 45 and Mr. Otis was 46 years of age.

* * *

At the time of the divorce, Mr. Otis received an annual salary in excess of $120,000, plus bonuses. The trial court found that Mrs. Otis was in good health and had held a highly paid secretarial job in the past. Further, the court found that Mrs. Otis, with some additional training, is capable of earning $12,000 to $18,000 per year.

* * *

In addition to the property settlement * * * Mrs. Otis was awarded as "alimony" the sum of $2,000 per month, commencing December 1, 1978, through and until the last day of 1980, and $1,000 per month, commencing on January 1, 1981, through and until the last day of 1982. Thereafter, no further "alimony" must be paid. The only issue presented by this appeal is the correctness of the trial court's order terminating monthly payments to the wife after four years.

* * *

The divorce decree divided the property of the parties as follows:

Mrs. Otis

Household furniture	$ 13,000.00	
Clothing, jewelry, etc.	$ 9,000.00	
Interest in real estate partnership	$ 25,000.00	(cost)
Equity in leased automobile	$ 1,000.00	
Cash	$ 21,400.00	(net)
Equity in homestead	$ 35,000.00	
Control Data stock (2,923 shares)	$121,304.50	
	$225,704.50	

Mr. Otis

Household furniture	$ 13,000.00	
Clothing, jewelry, etc.	$ 2,500.00	
Interest in real estate partnership	$ 25,000.00	(cost)
Porche automobile	$ 10,000.00	
Cash	$ 7,500.00	
Profitsharing plan—cash value	$ 1,300.00	
Life insurance policies—cash value	$ 20,000.00	
Control Data stock (6,827 shares)	$131,320.50	(net)
	$210,620.50	(value)

Mr. Otis was also awarded his substantial interest in his vested pension plan. In addition, he was awarded property in Greece valued at $85,000 which he had inherited.

* * *

The grounds for awarding "maintenance" were established by Minn. Stat. § 518.552 [based on U.M.D.A. § 308. Because this] section is taken in large part from the Uniform Marriage and Divorce Act.... we find commentaries and decisions of other jurisdictions involving this Uniform Act provision and similar provisions instructive.

The basic attitudinal change reflected in the new provision has been summarized as follows:

> In recent years, courts have retreated from traditional attitudes toward spousal support because society no longer perceives the married woman as an economically unproductive creature who is "something better than her husband's dog, a little dearer than his

horse." Traditionally, spousal support was a permanent award because it was assumed that a wife had neither the ability nor the resources to become self-sustaining. However, with the mounting dissolution rate, the advent of no-fault dissolution, and the growth of the women's liberation movement, the focal point of spousal support determinations has shifted from the sex of the recipient to the individual's ability to become financially independent. This change in focus has given rise to the concept of rehabilitative alimony, also called maintenance, spousal support, limited alimony, or step-down spousal support.

Rehabilitative Spousal Support: In Need of a More Comprehensive Approach to Mitigating Dissolution Trauma, 12 U.S.F.L.Rev. 493, 494–95 (1978).

The Missouri Court of Appeals expressed the concerns concisely:

> The most that can be accurately said about the amount to be granted is that it is neither the policy of the law to give the spouse receiving maintenance a lifetime annuity nor to reduce her to menial labor to eke out an existence.

In re Marriage of Schulte, 546 S.W.2d 41, 49 (Mo.App.1977).

The Florida Court of Appeals, which has had various occasions to consider alimony questions, has adopted an approach similar to that of the Uniform Act. The court has recognized the distinction between permanent alimony and rehabilitative alimony (maintenance):

> Under the circumstances, the trial court erred in awarding permanent rather than rehabilitative alimony. As we have previously stated: "The public policy under the new law which the legislature passed and which therefore we must apply seems to be that if the spouse has the capacity to make her own way through the remainder of her life unassisted by the former husband, then the courts cannot require him to pay alimony other than for rehabilitative purposes." (*Roberts v. Roberts*, Fla.App. 1st 1973, 283 So.2d 396, 397); * * *.) The public policy of the State would be utterly frustrated by an award of permanent alimony where it affirmatively appears that the wife has not only the capacity but also the desire to be self-supporting.

Cann v. Cann, 334 So.2d 325, 330 (Fla.App.1976) (citations omitted). More recently that court emphasized, in setting aside a 20–year award of alimony, that rehabilitative alimony must be of reasonable duration:

> Rehabilitative alimony is not a substitute for either unemployment compensation or retirement benefits. The award is clearly an incentive to assist one in reclaiming employment skills outside the home which have atrophied during the marital relationship. It was not meant to remove the recipient from the job market. In *Manning v. Manning*, 353 So.2d 103 (Fla. 1st DCA 1977) we stated that when a wife has completed her maternal role, and provided she is in good health, she should make every effort to rehabilitate herself within a

reasonable time thereafter, and when she has done so, rehabilitative alimony is to be discontinued.

Robinson v. Robinson, 366 So.2d 1210, 1211–12 (Fla.App.1979).

* * *

We are now faced in Minnesota with new legislation which effects a substantial change in the role of the courts in awarding periodic or lump-sum payments to a divorced spouse. Minnesota decisions decided prior to this time provide only minimal help in passing on the validity of trial court awards under the new act. Rather, the focus of this court must now be on a determination of the two basic standards established by the new legislation; namely, we must determine if the spouse seeking maintenance—

> (a) Lacks sufficient property, including marital property apportioned to him, to provide for his reasonable needs, especially during a period of training or education, and
>
> (b) Is unable to support himself through appropriate employment or is the custodian of a child whose condition or circumstances make it appropriate that the custodian not be required to seek employment outside the home.

In construing the Uniform Act provision, the Kentucky Court of Appeals concluded that the statute required satisfaction of the conditions of both subsections. *Inman v. Inman*, 578 S.W.2d 266 (Ky.App.1979). Applying these standards to the findings of the trial court which we are bound to accept in the absence of a transcript, we conclude that the decision of the trial court is not clearly erroneous.

Affirmed.

OTIS, JUSTICE (dissenting) joined by SHERAN, C.J., and WAHL, J.

In this decision, the majority applies a section of the Minnesota session laws, Minn.Stat. § 518.552, (1978) which was not effective until after this case was tried and then holds that it dictates that appellant who has not held a job outside her home for 23 years, may be denied all alimony after only four years have elapsed. In my opinion it is manifestly unjust and inappropriate to deprive a wife of an expectancy on which she had a right to rely after a marriage of 25 years and accordingly I respectfully dissent.

* * *

Nor could appellant have anticipated that in the absence of explicit statutory language, abolishing prior criteria for awarding maintenance, this court would construe the statute to deprive her of rights she might otherwise have expected. It is grossly unfair to assume she would stipulate to a statutory construction which would totally defeat her claims. If the statute works a substantial change in existing practice, then surely it is *ex post facto* with respect to this appellant, not only because her divorce decree was entered prior to the statute's date of effectiveness, but because she was married at a time when the prevailing social custom made her professional career subordinate to her husband's and required that she abandon a career to raise her son and keep house for her husband. This placed him under a corresponding duty to support her to the extent her earning capacity was permanently impaired. An award of permanent alimony is a substitute for his duty of support. Recognizing a wife's contribution to her husband's career, this court has held that the support to which a divorced wife is entitled is not limited to that which will provide her with the bare necessities of life. She can expect a sum which will maintain her at a standard of living commensurate with what she and her husband enjoyed at the time of the dissolution.

The parties were married in June 1954. Today, respondent, is a vice-president of Control Data Corporation, earning more than $120,000 per year. Appellant has not been employed since her son was born, at which time she abandoned a promising career as an executive secretary in order to fulfill the expected, traditional role of wife and hostess for a rising and successful business executive. She performed this role so well that in 1977 she was selected to serve as hostess to the board of directors of Control Data Corporation during a week-long meeting in Greece, which was her homeland and that of her husband. When her husband was being considered for his present position, appellant was herself interviewed to determine whether she could fill the role required of her in her husband's business career. A number of years previously she had been anxious to resume a career of her own. Her husband forbade it stating that he was "not going to have any wife of mine pound a typewriter."

There is no evidentiary support for the trial court's finding that her earning capacity is substantial. There is no showing that at her age, now approximately forty-seven, she can be gainfully employed at her prior occupation after a lapse of more than twenty years.

* * *

As we said in *Bollenbach*, "(the wife's) role in the particular situation of these parties was to expend her youth and intelligence and talents in the home and with her children and in family-related activities of which her husband approved." 285 Minn. 431, 175 N.W.2d at 157. Mrs. Bollenbach also forfeited any opportunity to pursue a career when she was married and we noted it would be unlikely she could find a job "adequate to satisfy the demands of the style of life enjoyed for almost 20 years." Id. at 432, 175 N.W.2d at 157. * * *

Accordingly, I would continue the $2,000 per month payment indefinitely, subject only to a substantial change in circumstances at some later date.

MARRIAGE OF BAKER

California Court of Appeals, 1992.
3 Cal.App.4th 491, 4 Cal.Rptr.2d 553.

KING, ASSOCIATE JUSTICE.

In this case involving a marriage of less than 10 years' duration in which the supported spouse's income from future employment was speculative, we hold that the trial court did not abuse its discretion in refusing to fix a termination date or a future step-down in the amount of spousal support. We also hold that it is premature to consider a claim that the order is erroneous because, without a future change of circumstances, it requires the payment of spousal support for a period far in excess of the length of the marriage. Even if there were no change of circumstances, the court possesses jurisdiction in the future to modify the order if, upon a proper motion, the court finds it would be just and equitable to do so.

FACTS

Marilyn and Daniel Baker were married on January 7, 1978. It was the fourth marriage for Daniel and the second marriage for Marilyn. There were no children of this marriage and neither party had children by any previous marriage. The parties first separated on January 15, 1985, but reconciled in October. The reconciliation failed, and marital status was dissolved in a bifurcated proceeding on December 30, 1988. Marilyn was 51 at the time of the dissolution and Daniel was 50. Both parties were in good health.

Prior to the parties' marriage, Marilyn was briefly employed as a real estate agent. During the marriage, Marilyn was essentially out of the job market. She testified that she gave up her real estate career at Daniel's insistence because he wanted her to be home when he got home, and he did not want her to work on weekends. However, she occasionally used her real estate license to sell property owned by one or both of the parties. Marilyn's earnings were nominal throughout the marriage, ranging from nothing whatsoever in 1981 and 1984 to a high of $31,000 in 1986 earned in connection with the sale of the parties' home.

Prior to and during his marriage to Marilyn, Daniel was an insurance broker in an insurance company in which he had a 20 percent shareholder interest. Daniel's yearly earnings were routinely in excess of $100,000.

The court heard evidence that the lifestyle of the parties was "opulent," including part ownership and use of a $100,000 yacht; vacations to the Bahamas, Hawaii, and Europe; and the use of BMW and Mercedes Benz automobiles. The Lafayette residence in which the parties resided during five years of their marriage was 3,800 square feet on an acre of land and sold for $775,000 in 1985. They employed a housekeeper and a gardener to help maintain the residence. Daniel never placed a limit on Marilyn's expenses, and he gave her more than $50,000 worth of jewelry, including three Rolex watches.

At the time of trial Marilyn was living in a condominium in Lafayette worth approximately $200,000 and driving a Toyota while Daniel was living in a home in Alamo purchased for $550,000 and driving a red BMW, a white BMW and a Jeep Wagoneer. Marilyn had returned to work as a real estate agent, and she believed her long-range future looked good. However, she testified that her income was not sufficient to cover her expenses. Marilyn believed her earning ability was hindered because she had been out of the real estate business for so many years, and during her absence the market had changed and she had lost clients. In addition, the market was experiencing "an incredibly quick slowdown" which would in all likelihood continue. She declined to predict her future earnings because there were too many uncertain economic factors to consider.

The court ordered Daniel to pay Marilyn $2,400 monthly spousal support until "terminated by further order of the court, petitioner or respondent's death, or petitioner's remarriage, whichever first occurs." The spousal support order was based on the court's finding that Marilyn had a gross annual income of $30,000 less $5,619 in unreimbursed business expenses as compared with Daniel's gross annual income of $106,000 less $18,000 in unreimbursed business expenses. The court also continued its prior order requiring Daniel to maintain health insurance for Marilyn. This appeal followed.

Analysis

Daniel submits that the trial court, as a matter of law, should have limited the duration of spousal support by either setting a termination date or providing a "step-down" procedure whereby the level of support would decrease over time. In picturesque language, he claims the trial court's order chained him "to the carcass of this dead marriage for the remainder of his days."

It is within the broad discretion of the trial judge to fix the amount and duration of spousal support. In exercising that discretion, the trial court must evaluate the factors set out in Civil Code § 4801, subdivision (a). These factors as applicable here include: the earning capacity of each spouse; their respective needs; the obligations and assets of each; the duration of the marriage; the time required for the supported spouse to acquire appropriate education, training and employment; the ability of the supported spouse to engage in gainful employment; the age and health of the parties; their standard of living; and any other factors which the court deems just and equitable. "[A]n abuse of discretion is shown—i.e.,—where, considering all the relevant circumstances, the court has 'exceeded the bounds of reason' or it can 'fairly be said' that no judge would reasonably make the same order under the same circumstances."

In determining this was not a case warranting a fixed termination date for spousal support, the trial court made findings which closely parallel the Supreme Court's language and reasoning in *In re Marriage of Morrison,* 20 Cal.3d at page 437, 143 Cal.Rptr. 139, 573 P.2d 41. In that case the Supreme Court found an abuse of discretion when the trial court divested itself of jurisdiction to award future spousal support in a 28–year marriage without any evidence in the record that the wife would be self-supporting. In Morrison, the wife had no significant job skills or work history and had been able to secure only low-paying, part-time employment. Additionally, the record indicated that the wife's ability to obtain full-time employment might be hampered by medical problems. The court emphasized that by terminating jurisdiction, a court "loses forever its power to extend support payments, no matter what circumstances subsequently develop." Consequently, the lesson of *Morrison* is that a court should not "burn its bridges" and fail to retain jurisdiction if the record does not contain evidence of the supported spouse's ability to meet his or her future needs. In a subsequent case, the Supreme Court emphasized that *Morrison* was "particularly applicable to lengthy marriages." (*In re Marriage of Vomacka* (1984) 36 Cal.3d 459, 467, 204 Cal.Rptr. 568, 683 P.2d 248 [marriage of 11 years held to be of sufficient length to bring it within reasoning of *Morrison*].)

Daniel argues there are several reasons why any reliance on the reasoning in *Morrison* is misplaced. Primarily, he emphasizes that the marriage at issue was less than 10 years and thus was not presumptively a long marriage; that the parties were both mature and established adults when they entered into this marriage; that Marilyn could not be considered a "displaced homemaker" who sacrificed her career for her husband and children; and that he had already paid temporary spousal support for more than two years.

* * *

The pertinent facts were that the parties were married for less than 10 years, during which Marilyn was not expected to and did not work outside the home because of the lifestyle of the parties; that after the parties separated she reentered the workforce as a real estate agent but was not producing an income anywhere near what would be sufficient to assimilate the lifestyle enjoyed by the parties during their marriage; and that there was no way to accurately predict her future earnings because the real estate market was volatile and subject to economic factors beyond her control. Meanwhile, Daniel continued to enjoy the same lifestyle enjoyed during the marriage; he had a stable income of long duration; and he had the existing ability to provide such support.... On this record, any order directing Marilyn to be self-supporting on a certain date would be based on "mere hopes or speculative expectations." Consequently, the court was not required to "burn its bridges" by terminating jurisdiction or ordering automatic reductions in spousal support. Such unknown future developments are better left to modification proceedings which have been provided for that very purpose.

* * *

While the number of years the parties were married herein just fell short of the 10 years necessary to qualify for the statutory presumption that the parties' marriage was of "long duration", the 10-year statutory minimum is not absolute. The statute itself points out that "[n]othing in this section precludes a court from determining that a marriage of less than 10 years is a marriage of long duration." Consequently, the trial court could consider the marriage "lengthy" for purposes of concluding that termination of support on a specific date was unwarranted absent evidence Marilyn would be self-supporting by that time.

* * * "Although patterns in marital breakups emerge, each couple has such a diverse mix of circumstances that trial courts must have broad discretion in weighing and balancing the various factors in each particular marriage before making a suitable support award.... Because trial courts have such broad discretion, appellate courts must act with cautious judicial restraint in reviewing these orders." All the decisions relied upon by Daniel found that terminating jurisdiction was within the broad discretion possessed by the trial court in fixing the duration of spousal support. None held that *as a matter of law* it would have been an abuse of discretion, under the same facts, if the court had decided to make an alternative order on the issue of spousal support. For this reason, these cases are of limited usefulness in convincing us that the trial court abused its discretion.

Finally, we come to Daniel's contention that the failure of the trial court to fix a termination date or to provide for a step-down in the amount of spousal support constituted reversible error because it may require the payment of temporary and permanent spousal support for a period far in excess of the length of marriage, if no change in circumstances occur. The propriety of an order modifying spousal support "rests within the trial court's sound discretion." * * * It is gross speculation to assume that circumstances will not change before it would be just and equitable to modify the order for spousal support based upon the order's duration alone.

The judgment is affirmed.

Notes and Questions

1. Why was Mrs. Baker eligible for alimony when Mrs. Morgan and Mrs. Huntington were not?

2. Could Mrs. Otis have obtained permanent alimony under the *Baker* decision? the Texas statute [p. 795]? Could Mrs. Baker have obtained permanent alimony under the *Otis* decision? under the Texas statute [p. 795]?

3. Why didn't the *Baker* court accept the husband's argument that the support order should include a termination date or "step-down" in support?

4. The *Baker* court discusses the presumption that alimony should be awarded indefinitely if the marriage is of "long" duration. What is

different about a long marriage? (And what is a "long" marriage, anyway?) To what extent should the claimant's age and work experience also be taken into account? Which factors should be more important?

5. In studying divorce decision making in New York, Professor Garrison found that permanent alimony was much more common in marriages of at least twenty years duration; 46% of judicial awards to wives in this group were permanent, as compared to 24% in marriages of less than ten years. The likelihood of a permanent award also declined significantly over a ten-year period when the marriage was less than twenty years, while for marriages over twenty years it did not. *See* Marsha Garrison, *How Do Judges Decide Divorce Cases? An Empirical Analysis of Divorce Decision Making*, 74 N.C. L. REV. 401, 471–72 (1996). *See also* Joan B. Krauskopf, *Rehabilitative Alimony: Uses and Abuses of Limited Duration Alimony*, 21 FAM. L. Q. 573, 579–89 (1988) (concluding, based on appellate opinion survey, that "it is likely that marriages over fifteen years will be considered long-term ones and that time limits on alimony needed at the divorce by the long-term, traditional homemaker will not be justified.")

Garrison also investigated the predictability of alimony permanence and found that, for judicial decisions at the trial level, the most significant factors in predicting whether an alimony award was permanent or fixed-term were marital duration and the political party of the judge who made the decision; Republican judges awarded permanent alimony in 40% of the cases they decided while Democratic judges awarded permanent alimony in only 25%. After appeals were taken into account, the most significant predictive factors were marital duration and the year of decision; later decisions were more likely to produce fixed-term awards. Both before and after appeal, decisions on the length of a fixed-term award were completely unpredictable. Garrison, *supra*, at 486–88, 503.

6. The California spousal support statute now provides that "the goal [of alimony] is for the supported party [to become] self-supporting within a reasonable period of time." "Reasonable period of time" is defined to mean one-half the duration of the marriage. CAL. FAM. CODE § 4320. In terms of fairness and predictability, what are the advantages and disadvantages of: a) the traditional approach (i.e., all alimony awards are permanent; b) the *Otis* approach; c) the *Baker* approach; d) the current California statute?

7. Should a court be able to extend the alimony award beyond the time limit set by the trial court if the recipient has failed to become self-supporting? *Compare* Self v. Self, 861 S.W.2d 360 (Tenn.1993) (no) *with* Bentz v. Bentz, 148 Wis.2d 400, 435 N.W.2d 293 (Wis.App. 1988) (yes). If the award may be extended, how does it differ from a permanent award subject to modification based on changed circumstances? *See* Marriage of Heistermann, 234 Cal.App.3d 1195, 286 Cal.Rptr. 127 (1991) (noting that for fixed-term awards the recipient has the burden of showing why the award should continue, while for indefinite awards the obligor must show a change in circumstances).

8. *Otis* discusses the problem of determining how long a spouse should have to develop a career and become self-supporting. A related issue arises when the dependent spouse has a career, but wishes to stay at home with minor children. Sometimes courts have explicitly linked the duration of the alimony award to the period of the children's minority. For example, in Morris v. Morris, 201 Neb. 479, 268 N.W.2d 431 (1978), the court upheld a twelve-year alimony award to a wife under the age of forty who was a college graduate and qualified medical technologist, married for fifteen years. The court noted that:

> "It cannot be realistically doubted that raising four small children is a full-time task. The wife has not been employed outside the household for more than 8 years, and the four children, at the time of the decree here, were 5, 6, 8, and 9 years old. If the alimony payments continue for the full period of 144 months, the youngest child will be approximately 18 years old. The income of the husband is substantial and is likely to continue to rise. It should also be noted that the alimony payments here are deductible by the husband and taxable to the wife."

The Uniform Marriage and Divorce Act provides that alimony may be granted if the spouse is a custodian of a child whose condition or circumstances make it appropriate that the custodian not be required to seek employment outside the home. What circumstances are these? Would the UMDA standard support the result in *Morris*?

9. What social, economic, and legal developments might explain the development of the the short-term, rehabilitative alimony concept and its current use?

B. THE VALUE OF ALIMONY

Alimony statutes seldom specify either a ceiling or a floor for the value of alimony; alimony decisions seldom explain, or justify, the dollar value of an award. The result, in all probability, is a fairly high level of inconsistency. In her study of judicial divorce decision making in New York, Professor Garrison found that, in cases with minor children, adding alimony to the child support award *reduced* the overall predictability of the decision-making process. For cases without minor children, the only factors significantly related to the value of the alimony award were the husband's property (husbands with more valuable assets tended to pay more alimony) and the appellate department in which the case was brought; neither the wife's nor the husband's income was significantly related to alimony value. Garrison, *supra* note 5, at 490–94.

While the dollar value of a specific alimony award is thus hard to predict, one can safely bet that the value of alimony (and child support, if that is relevant) will be inadequate to provide the recipient spouse with a standard of living equal to that of the payor spouse. Every divorce researcher to date has reported that, on average, the post-divorce living standard of former wives (and children in their custody) falls, while that of former husbands (and children in their custody) rises. Most researchers report a living standard decline for divorced wives of around 30%. *See* Marsha Garrison, *The Economic Consequences of Divorce*, 32 FAM. & CONCILIATION CTS. REV. 10, 14 (1994) (surveying reports). Despite the fact that most state "factor lists" include the marital standard of living, alimony case law (to the extent it considers the issue at all) rejects the claim that alimony should enable the supported spouse to enjoy a standard of living equivalent to that of the payor spouse:

> The standard of living achieved by the parties during their marriage is often altered upon termination. While we recognize that "* * * [n]either party should make a profit at the expense of the other * * *," we do not interpret R.C. § 3105.18 to require an alimony award that provides the parties with an equal standard of living or a standard of living equivalent to that established during the marriage. Sustenance alimony is based on need, and the trial court must have latitude to examine all the evidence before it awards an amount that is reasonable and equitable to both parties.
>
> Appellee does not contend that the sustenance alimony awarded is inadequate to meet her living expenses; instead, she argues that it is inequitable and unreasonable not to allow her to share in the higher standard of living that appellant enjoys as his income increases. R.C. § 3105.18(B) lists standard of living as one of eleven factors a trial court is to consider in determining the amount of alimony. Some of the factors enumerated in R.C. 3105.18(B) are more pertinent than others in the process of reaching an equitable property division, while some are more relevant in ascertaining the need for an amount of sustenance alimony. However, all the statutory factors must be considered. The goal is to reach an equitable result. The method by which the goal is achieved cannot be reduced to a mathematical formula. Therefore, we hold that in making a sustenance alimony determination, the court must consider all the factors listed in R.C. § 3105.18(B) and not base its determination upon any one of those factors taken in isolation.
>
> We conclude that the court of appeals erred in its suggestion that an alimony award must establish an equal standard of living for the parties.
>
> Kaechele v. Kaechele, 35 Ohio St.3d 93, 518 N.E.2d 1197, 1200 (1988).

The few statutory standards that give explicit directions on the value of alimony similarly eschew any effort to equalize spousal living standards after divorce. *See* TEX. FAM. CODE § 3.9606 [p. 796] (restricting alimony award (but not child support) to the lesser of $2500 per month or 20% of payor's average monthly gross income). If equalizing post-divorce spousal living standards is not a goal of alimony decision making, what does this tell us about the purposes of alimony?

SECTION 4. THE ALIMONY DEBATE: ARE CURRENT STANDARDS FAIR?

OLSEN v. OLSEN

Supreme Court of Idaho, 1976.
98 Idaho 10, 557 P.2d 604, 606.

SHEPARD, JUSTICE (dissenting).

The parties hereto were divorced following a ten year marriage. Thereafter the appellant faithfully paid his wife for the support of the children of the marriage until they reached majority. Following the divorce and for the ensuing thirty years, he also faithfully, conscientiously and without interruption paid alimony to his former wife. The majority opinion holds that the trial court did not abuse its discretion in finding that the appellant failed to prove a material, permanent and substantial change in the correlative needs and abilities of the parties.

* * *

I believe that the facts of the instant case emphasize the need for re-examination of the entire concept of alimony and the continuing viability of that concept in contemporary society. Put in different words, the question facing the Court is whether a judicially imposed system of involuntary servitude is to be continued wherein one human being is placed in bondage to another for what is effectively the remainder of his natural life.

* * * In my opinion the time has arrived to squarely face the questions and problems of the doctrine of alimony. If society in the past garnered any benefit from this antiquated system of private (versus public) welfare, such is either non-existent in this day and age or at the least is far outweighed by the antagonisms, social dislocations, economic burdens and judicial inefficiency which are involved and result from the perpetuation of the doctrine. The rationales which were once said to justify alimony awards have long since lost their force. Of more importance perhaps is that in consideration of the rapidly evolving status of women there is serious doubt of the constitutional validity of our sexually biased alimony provisions.

* * *

Historically, since 1875 punishment has been the primary rationale for the award of alimony in this state. Our present law, I.C. § 32–706, still predicates awards on an offense of the husband. In the earliest alimony opinions of this Court fault was the dominant concern, although other considerations were noted. * * *

Veiled hints to the contrary, punishment as a dispositive factor has all but been replaced by other more dominant concerns. It was not until 1957 that the judicial branch of government recognized this fact in the case of *Good v. Good*, 79 Idaho 119, 311 P.2d 756 (1957), where the

Court embraced an entirely new rationale for alimony awards. There, the issue was whether or not a wife whose extreme cruelty was the basis for the divorce could receive alimony notwithstanding I.C. § 32–706. Despite the language of that statute predicating alimony upon divorce granted for the husband's offense, the Court concluded that an award of alimony should be upheld where "the wife's fault, though sufficient to justify a divorce to the husband, *is not so grievous*" (emphasis added)(at 130, 311 P.2d at 763).

The Court said in *Good*:

> "Courts have quite universally recognized the inequity and injustice of turning a wife out destitute to become an object of charity in cases where the husband, who obtains the divorce, is amply able to provide for her support, and where she has no means or ability to provide for herself, solely on the ground that she has by her conduct provided the grounds for divorce." 79 Idaho at 125, 311 P.2d at 760.

* * *

That perspective was explained in *Good* as necessary to protect the interest of society in not having a former wife left destitute by the divorce. Yet, how far we have moved from this narrow concern for the interest of society. Somehow the legitimate interest of society in preventing destitute divorcees (unable as contrasted to unwilling to work) from being cast upon the relief rolls has been perverted into an instrument to level economic disparities, both real and imagined, between two people in which there exists no legal relationship. The focus of judicial inquiry is no longer whether the former wife is about to become the object of public charity. Without guidance from this Court and at the sole whim of a trial judge, bound by no ascertainable standard, eternal peonage can be imposed upon a man solely because he was once called a husband.

Since *Good*, "social necessity" has blossomed into a judicial calculus of many and diverse factors and variables. Among the factors and variables which have been discussed are: 1) the fault of the husband; 2) the extent of the wife's needs and her ability to meet those needs; 3) the amount of the community property award; 4) the existence of minor children; 5) the wife's health, age and vocational skills; 6) eligibility for social security; 7) duration of the marriage; and 8) remarriage of either spouse.

* * *

Another rationale for alimony has been that it assuages to some extent the potential trauma of change in the social and financial status of the wife on the occasion of divorce. That reasoning assumes that such disruptions only accrue to the wife and that is clearly not the case. In most divorces, particularly those involving minor children, the wife is awarded the family home and furnishings together with child support. In many cases the husband literally faces bankruptcy and is deprived not only of his marital status but also the greater part of his previous relationship with his children. A good marriage is greater than the sum of its parts and both parties thereto suffer from a division. Alimony only exacerbates the problems by forestalling the recovery of separate identities and rekindling the anguish of the divorce with each periodic payment of alimony. Following a divorce a woman may remarry and usually better her situation through the injection of income from her new husband. On the other hand a divorced man paying alimony and child support is almost automatically barred from remarriage unless willing to risk continued marital discord over which woman he owes more financial loyalty, the one to whom he is married and the law enjoins him to support, or the one to whom he is no longer married but which a judge has required him to support. At the very least he faces financial stress in trying to support two households.

A further rationale is that the wife is entitled to alimony as just compensation for her faithful contribution to the marriage. As in the question of marital fault there is a complete lack of objectivity in forming such facile moral judgment.

The wife may have made the marriage and the household a living hell for her husband and children. She may be a chronic alcoholic who precipitated the break up of the marriage and the family. On the other hand she may have been faithful, loving, tolerant, courteous, kind, obedient, thrifty, industrious and God fearing. We can hardly depend on the parties for an objective evaluation of the wife's contribution to a marriage and any attempted outside evaluation can be nothing but farcical. As John Steinbeck observed in "Cannery Row", people may be very different depending upon the peephole through which they are viewed. There is too little, if any, objective evidence for courts to blandly announce that alimony should be awarded to women because everyone knows that they contribute faithfully to the well-being and stability of the marriage. Beatification and canonization should be granted on an individual rather than a class basis and in any event only by an ecclesiastical court.

* * *

I turn now to the final rationale advanced for the award of alimony to women, i.e., the economic disparity between men and women in our society. I am aware that as a result of overt discrimination or the mere existence of the male dominated culture such disparity to some extent continues to exist. No longer do economic and social differences between men and women in our society provide sufficient basis for the continuation of the award of alimony. As earlier indicated, substantial numbers of women are able to find and hold employment, make investments and accumulate wealth.

* * *

There is not yet absolute economic and social parity between men and women. That does not diminish the significance of the changes which have taken place nor does it alter the clear conclusion that the economic disparities which once served as a rationalization for alimony awards to women have been substantially eroded and no longer provide justification. Obviously, times have changed but the law of alimony has not.

We now have in this state a doctrine created by statute to serve one purpose and molded through legislative erosion and judicial fiat to serve a multitude of purposes. It has no justification in legal history nor any reasoned explanation for its existence. It is assumed to fulfill a necessary function of social economy, but that "necessity" appears suspect at best. As far as I can glean from the law of this jurisdiction, and giving due deference to arguments from other jurisdictions, alimony exists because it has always existed and this alone appears to be its sole justification. Such bears no reasonable relationship to the objective the statute is said to serve and consequently results in an impermissible classification in violation of the equal protection of law guarantees of the Idaho and United States Constitutions.

It is said that there is nothing so dangerous to the status quo as an idea whose time has come. More dangerous yet is the continuance of an idea whose time has past. In voiding I.C. § 32–706 we would not be alone in holding that permanent alimony no longer has any place as a legal concept or doctrine in contemporary society. * * *

In my judgment the time has long since passed when the state and its judiciary should cease its unwarranted, unnecessary, irrational intrusion into the lives of its citizens simply because at one time they occupied a marital status.

In the absence of other factors, we would not countenance the demand of an ex-employee for lifetime support from his ex-employer merely because of the termination of the previously existent employment relationship. How ludicrous would we consider a demand for lifetime support for one who once engaged in a dissolved partnership, the assets of which have been distributed. We would undoubtedly laugh out of court an able bodied person past the age of majority who demanded a judicially mandated lifetime support from another person on the sole basis that a parent-minor child relationship had once existed. I deem it obvious that in all those instances regardless of a plaintive plea that "I gave him (or her) the best years of my life," we would nevertheless rule that when the legal relationship terminated and the accounts were settled each person was required to go his own way freed of liability to the other. In each of these cases we would certainly refuse to institute a system of lifetime peonage and bondage and I doubt not that in the event we complied with such requests we would be speedily overruled by higher authority on constitutional grounds.

Why then do we tolerate, continue and judicially mandate a system of lifetime serfdom upon the dissolution of a marriage relationship? I deem there to be no answer to that question except "that's the way we've always done it." The law of domestic relations requires more than placebos and patent medicines. It is long past time for judicial surgery to excise the doctrine of alimony from the body of the law of domestic relations.

RICHARD POSNER, ECONOMIC ANALYSIS OF LAW

136–37 (3d ed. 1986).

Alimony is analytically quite complex. It appears to serve three distinct economic functions:

1. It is a form of damages for breach of the marital contract. * * *

2. Alimony is a method of repaying the wife (in the traditional marriage) her share of the marital partnership's assets. * * *

3. The last and perhaps most important economic function of alimony is to provide the wife with a form of severance pay or unemployment benefits. In the traditional family, where the wife specializes in household production, any skills that she may have had in market production depreciate and eventually her prime employment possibilities—should the present marriage dissolve—narrow down to the prospect of remarrying and forming a new household where she can ply her trade. Although she could always find some kind of work in the market, the skilled household producer forced to work as a waitress or file clerk is like the lawyer who, unable to find a legal job, becomes a process server.

Because the search for a suitable spouse is often protracted, and because age may depreciate a person's ability (especially if a woman) to form a new marriage that will yield her as much real income as the previous marriage did, it makes sense to provide as a standard term in the marriage contract a form of severance pay or unemployment compensation that will maintain the divorced wife at her previous standard of living during the search for a new husband. Consider an analogy to law practice. By agreeing to work for a law firm that specialized exclusively in negotiating oil-tanker mortgages, a lawyer might make it very difficult for himself, in the event he was ever laid off, to find an equally remunerative position (why?). But that is all the more reason why he might demand, as a condition of working for such a firm, that it agree that should it ever lay him off it will continue his salary until he finds equally remunerative work, even if the search is protracted.

An alternative in both the housewife's and the lawyer's case would be a higher wage to compensate for the risk of prolonged unemployment in the event of layoff. But in the case of marriage, the husband may be incapable of making the necessary transfer payments to the wife, especially during the early years of the marriage, when the household may not have substantial liquid assets. Also, to calculate in advance the appropriate compensation for a risk as difficult to quantify as that of divorce would be costly, especially since the relevant probability is really a schedule of probabilities of divorce in each year of the marriage. This of course is a reason for awarding alimony on a period basis even if the rationale is damages.

Just as severance pay is awarded without regard to whether the employer was at fault in laying off the worker—indeed, often without regard to whether the employee quit or was fired—so alimony, viewed as a form of severance pay, is not dependent on notions of fault. But just as an employee might forfeit his entitlement to severance pay by having quit in breach of his employment contract, so alimony should be denied or reduced (and sometimes it is) if the wife was seriously at fault in procuring dissolution of a marriage. Better, any damages she caused the family by walking out on the marriage could be subtracted from her alimony payments if her share of the marital assets was insufficient to cover them.

Notes and Questions

1. For a detailed discussion of issues presented by the law and economics approach to divorce, *see* Ann Lacquer Estin, *Economics and the Problem of Divorce*, 2 J. INTERDISC. LEGAL STUDIES 517 (1995). *See also* Margaret F. Brinig & Steven M. Crafton, *Marriage and Opportunism*, 23 J. LEG. STUD. 869 (1994); Milton C. Regan, Jr., *Market Discourse and Moral Neutrality in Divorce Law*, 1994 UTAH L. REV. 605.

2. Would the abolition of alimony affect marital roles or the marriage rate? At least one economist argues that the answer is yes:

> * * * Finally, I find that a legal prohibition on alimony reduces the gains from marriage. In states which prohibit alimony, I find both a lower proportion of young women marrying and reduced marital fertility among those who do, even when the variables found to be important in the economic literature on marriage and fertility are held constant. * * * The empirical results in this paper suggest that the alimony system, as administered, acts to compensate wives for their opportunity costs incurred by entering and investing in marriage. This interpretation of the economic function of alimony is directly opposed to the common allegation that alimony is an 'anachronistic' manifestation of the wife's dependency upon her husband. Nevertheless, increasing participation of married women in the labor force and declining marital fertility suggest that the importance of alimony will diminish over time with decreasing levels of household specialization.

Elizabeth Landes, *Economics of Alimony*, 7 J. LEG. STUD. 35 (1978).

To what criticisms are Professor Landes's claims open?

3. While Justice Sheppard opposes alimony primarily because of its potential to impose "lifetime peonage" on divorced husbands, it is also possible to make a case against alimony based on its impact on women:

> ... In the long run, ... I do not believe that we should encourage future couples entering marriage to make choices that will be economically disabling for women, thereby perpetuating their traditional financial dependence upon men and contributing to their inequality with men at divorce. I do not mean to suggest that these

choices are unjustified. For most couples, they are based on the presence of children in the family. The infant's claim to love and nurturance is a compelling one both on moral and developmental grounds. Throughout history, the choice of the mother as the primary nurturing parent has been the most common response to the infant's claim.... But other choices are possible.... Women, like men, should be able to lead productive, independent lives outside the family. Female dependency should no longer be the necessary result of motherhood.

I do not propose that the state attempt to implement this view of family life by enacting laws requiring mothers to work or mandating that fathers spend time at home with their children. But ... since Anglo–American family law has traditionally reflected the social division of function by sex within marriage, it will be necessary to withdraw existing legal supports for that arrangement as a cultural norm....

Herma Hill Kay, *Equality and Difference: A Perspective on No–Fault Divorce and Its Aftermath*, 56 U. CIN. L. REV. 1, 80, 84–85 (1989).

What factual assumptions underlie Professor Kay's view? Justice Sheppard's? Are these assumptions sound?

IRA M. ELLMAN, THE THEORY OF ALIMONY

77 CALIF. L. REV. 1, 17–18, 41–42, 79–80 (1989).

A theory of alimony must explain why spouses should be liable for each other's needs after their marriage has ended. Why should the needy person's former spouse provide support rather than his parents, his children, or society as a whole?

* * *

[Although] the ordinary marriage appears to have many attributes of contract ... the essential problem with a contract analysis should be clear: The wife expects that the marriage itself will compensate her economic sacrifice, by providing not only personal satisfaction but also a share in her husband's financial success.... A formal contract claim would therefore require, as its basis, an allegation that the marriage's termination is due to the husband's breach.... Making such a showing would be difficult.... Indeed, one might well argue that couples divorce precisely because they discover, as specific issues arise after some years of marriage, that in fact there never was a clear contract, that they do not have the same understanding of their mutual commitment....

* * *

If contract does not work, then what principles can we look to in fashioning alimony rules? The question is fundamental, for by shifting away from contract we necessarily shift away from a conception of alimony as a claim based on promise or commitment, to one grounded in some other policy. What should that policy be? Examination of analogous commercial arrangements may be instructive. . . .

* * *

Marriage is usually intended to be a long-term arrangement. The typical commercial arrangement is not; although it may in fact continue over many years, in most cases there is no agreement legally binding the parties over a long term. In some cases, however, parties make a long-term commitment. One reason they do is relevant here: A contracting party might seek a long-term commitment because the relationship requires that party to make an investment that he cannot otherwise justify. . . . For example, the owner of a building might be willing to modify it for a prospective tenant only if that tenant signs a long-term lease; a supplier to IBM might be willing to invest the capital necessary to produce a part only if it is assured that IBM will not change suppliers the next year.

* * *

The traditional marriage bears many similarities to this arrangement. It is a relationship in which the wife makes many initial investments of value only to her husband, investments a self-interested bargainer would make only in return for a long-term commitment. Her investments may be obvious, such as supporting him through a degree or training program, or they may be more subtle, such as providing him with the emotional support or domestic services that allow him to enhance his earning capacity. Her bearing and raising of children, while of value to him, also provides value to her, but—as with the commercial investors—give her no prospects for a return in the open market commensurate with her investment. The traditional marriage thus involves considerable up-front investment by the wife which, like the idiosyncratic improvements in the building or the purchase of equipment needed for the production of a unique part, has little general market value even though it has value to the one person for whom it was made. Like the owner or part supplier, she risks great loss if her husband stops buying.

* * *

. . . [D]ivorce typically burdens the wife more than her husband for two reasons: She has more difficulty finding a new spouse, and she suffers disproportionate financial loss because of her domestic role. . . . Marriage thus poses unavoidable risks for the wife, risks that are different and greater than those assumed by her husband. . . .

* * *

The function of alimony [should be] . . . to reallocate the postdivorce financial consequences of marriage in order to prevent distorting incentives. * * * This conception of alimony differs fundamentally from prevailing law. It casts alimony as an entitlement earned through marital investment, and as a tool to eliminate distorting financial incentives, and not as a way of relieving need.... [It] allows recovery for lost earning capacity when that loss arises from marital investment.... [O]nly financially rational sharing behavior can qualify as such marital investment. Lost earning capacity is thus not compensable if it arises from financially irrational behavior, with.... one major exception [for] losses resulting from the care of children.

* * *

When one spouse cedes a market opportunity in favor of the other spouse's we must provide a remedy. Otherwise, a marital decision made on the assumption that the spouses are a single economic unit will burden the sharing spouse disproportionately when divorce renders them financially separate. In contrast, when one spouse forgoes a market opportunity to accommodate a lifestyle preference, both spouses know that lower income will result. On divorce, the spouse who made the financial sacrifice suffers no additional financial burden as a result, beyond that already incurred during the marriage. Even if the sacrifice was made entirely to accommodate the other spouse's lifestyle desires, the real complaint on divorce is not the economic sacrifice itself, which the spouse would have borne even if the marriage had remained intact. The real complaint is that the marriage did not remain intact despite the economic sacrifice. That complaint, though real, is simply beyond the scope of the alimony remedy, which can never compensate marital partners for the personal loss of marital dissolution.

... If we do not impose a limit, we would have to consider every sacrifice one makes for one's mate, and this would extend to nonfinancial losses as well. Suppose an attorney gives up his prospects for a faculty position to accommodate his wife; would she have to compensate him his lost chance at the professor's life if that was what he really wanted, despite the lower income? Allowing compensation for financial losses incurred for nonfinancial reasons is no less troublesome. If she had a change of heart and sought divorce, would the Duchess of Windsor then owe the Duke for his throne?

Marriage necessarily involves much give and take that the law cannot address or equalize upon divorce. This theory assumes that we can sensibly isolate decisions that a couple rationally expects will enhance their aggregate income, and ensure that in making such a decision neither takes a risk of disproportionate loss if divorce then occurs. Although not repairing every unfair marital loss, this approach yields a principled alimony rule that tends to encourage sharing behavior.

* * *

The difficulties involved in proving lost earning capacity are significant but not fatal. Even crude approximations of theoretically defensible criteria are probably better than intuitive estimates of what is 'fair' under a system lacking established principles of 'fairness' in the first place. Moreover, the establishment of rules clearly specifying the facts that are relevant in judging alimony claims, and the precise impact of these facts on the amount of the claim may itself motivate studies that increase the amount of relevant data. In the end, precision is not obtainable. The determination of alimony claims, even more than most legal questions, will necessarily depend, at least in part, upon the rough justice of trial judge discretion. That is, in fact, one of the lessons of this inquiry. But we are still better off knowing what we should be doing, even if we cannot do it perfectly, than not knowing at all.

JANE RUTHERFORD, DUTY IN DIVORCE: SHARED INCOME AS A PATH TO EQUALITY

58 Fordham L. Rev. 539, 563–64, 573, 578–83, 592 (1990).

* * * Alimony seems to perpetuate the vicious circle of women assuming more household duties because they earn less and then earning less because they have more household duties. Hence, alimony can be viewed as paternalistic for three reasons. First, it encourages women to be dependent instead of self-sufficient. Second, it leaves women under the control of men because women cannot remarry without losing their alimony. Third, it condones the disparity in earning power between men and women because some of that difference will be made up by alimony. Accordingly, even feminists supported courts and legislatures that began to restrict the availability of alimony. . . .

The UMDA reflects this view. . . . § 308 of the UMDA limits maintenance to those "whose circumstances make it appropriate that the custodian not be required to seek employment outside the home." . . .

The earner ethic created a new set of myths about the appropriate recipients of maintenance. . . . The central myth . . . is that families are mere aggregates of separate earners who are not mutually interdependent. . . . [Yet t]ypically, the family divides the labor to increase the total group welfare over time, with the expectation that they will all share in future returns for present sacrifices. . . .

Rather than analyzing the division of labor, the UMDA . . . based alimony on need. A need-based approach has at least three problems. One of the reasons spouses and partners are willing to devote their efforts to such relationships is the belief that they will share in future profits. Although they take the risk that such profits will not materialize, they do not expect to limit their share of actual profits to need. To do so would embrace a more Marxist view: "[f]rom each according to his ability, to each according to his needs!"

Second, limiting one spouse to need while allowing the other one to prosper is inherently unfair; focusing on need leaves spouses in an unequal position because one spouse is limited to the bare essentials while the other enjoys an improved lifestyle.

Finally, there is a stigma associated with need-based alimony. Because only the functionally unemployable are entitled to maintenance on a pure need-based standard, accepting support can lower the spouse's self-esteem. A need-based standard denigrates the needy spouse either in terms of party expectations or lowered self-esteem. We should be striving instead for a system based on sharing and caring. * * *

In order to avoid the problems of need ..., some reformers have focused on a contribution standard.... The contribution theory has two major problems, however. First, it fails to account for expectations. Second, it overcompensates earners and undercompensates homemakers because economic contributions are easier to measure....

Another way to avoid the disparities inherent in the need approach to alimony is to base awards on the pre-divorce standard of living ... [But b]oth spouses cannot maintain their pre-divorce standard of living without new sources of income.... Therefore, requiring a person to support an ex-spouse at the old standard of living is unfair. In theory it could turn the tables and lead to the masculinization of poverty. In reality, it has become an excuse not to award alimony at all. * * *

... [I]t seems more intellectually honest and fairer simply to admit that spouses expect to share income when they are married. Thus we should adopt some form of income sharing.

Income sharing refers to a system in which the incomes of the former couple would be added and divided by the number of people to be supported. Each member of the family would receive an equal share. Income sharing differs from traditional permanent alimony in at least two respects. First, income sharing does not take the form of a fixed award of a specific dollar amount. Indeed, income sharing is not fixed at any given time. Instead, it recognizes the inevitable changes inherent in the passage of time. Rather than fixing a specific award that can only adapt to changed circumstances by court order, income sharing creates a formula that automatically adjusts to changed circumstances. Such income sharing should continue at least until remarriage ...

... [T]he theoretical basis for income sharing is quite different from that of alimony. Income sharing is not based on need, pre-divorce standard of living, prior contributions, or fault. Instead, it represents a conscious effort to achieve equality between spouses who have divided their labors during marriage. If spouses have not divided the labor, either because they were not married long enough, or because they did not have children, then income sharing should not apply.

* * *

Income sharing has four distinct advantages. First, it fosters the kind of sharing and caring that should typify families. Second, income sharing offers a way out of the fault conundrum. Third, income sharing empowers the financially disadvantaged who may be economically trapped in destructive relationships. Fourth, it provides a path to equality that automatically adjusts to reflect the actual market situation of the parties over time ...

Shared income after divorce fosters caring in two ways. First, it reinforces sharing as the model for family life. Law is not only a mechanism to settle disputes. It also sets normative standards for how we ought to behave. If the family is viewed as a shared enterprise for the common good, our rules about income distribution within the family should reflect sharing principles.

* * *

Income sharing may actually foster a more equal division of labor at home. Currently, the UMDA encourages couples to maximize individual profits. This creates an incentive for the party with greater earning ability to shift homemaking tasks to the party who earns less in order to maximize income.

If men and women earned equal amounts in the job market, there would be a greater incentive to share homemaking burdens to avoid jeopardizing either job. Therefore, income sharing provides divorced men with an incentive to help eradicate gender discrimination in the job market. Similarly, there will be a greater incentive to share the burdens of childcare, as the economic burden will be reduced if each contributes enough childcare to enable the former spouse to earn an equal amount of money. Most of the earning disparity between married men and married women can be accounted for by the difference in their family burdens.

* * * Finally, income sharing can address ... changing needs without report to repeated court battles over need and changed circumstances. Changed circumstances will be accounted for simply by continuing to share the couple's available income. Of course, some methods of enforcement will involve the court more than others. A system in which income is withheld at source, as in the case of child support, would require little court involvement or contact between the parties.

* * *

Some might argue that saddling an earner with a non-earning spouse for life is a strict penalty for an improvident marriage. Indeed, the case for income sharing is weakest in childless marriages of young people, who have the time and the opportunity to improve their circumstances, and in cases of those married a short time. Income sharing is a better option in marriages that have lasted for many years because the spouses have relied on each other and therefore restricted their options. This problem can be solved by creating a grace period of three to five years before a childless divorced couple is required to share income.

* * * Income sharing is ... a legal duty, similar to the fiduciary duties of partnership, which society should impose on spouses at divorce. It is a duty not because spouses have agreed to assume it, but because of the mutuality inherent in the division of labor within a marriage. It is a duty required to encourage sharing and equality.

Notes and Questions

1. While alimony based entirely on lost earning capacity is a novel idea, in some states career damage during marriage may be taken into

account in determining whether to award alimony. MINN. STAT. ANN. *See* Gerth v. Gerth, 159 Wis.2d 678, 465 N.W.2d 507, 509 (Wis.App.1990); MINN. STAT. ANN. § 518.552(2)(e).

2. Professors Ellman and Rutherford agree that alimony should not be based on need or some notion of marital contract. The analysis of each emphasizes marriage partners' expectations of sharing and the desirability, from a public policy perspective, of encouraging sharing behavior in marriage. But their proposals for replacing current alimony law are quite different. Why? Is one analysis more persuasive than the other? What are the pros and cons of each approach to the alimony problem?

In evaluating each point of view, make sure that you take into account these issues:

a. Application of Professor Ellman's theory would produce an award representing the capitalized value of lost earning capacity resulting from a financially rational marital investment. Would Mrs. Morgan, Mrs. Otis, and Mrs. Huntington be eligible for alimony if it were so defined? Should they be?

b. If, as Professor Ellman suggests, financially irrational decisions should not be compensable, why should losses arising from child care responsibilities?

c. If Professor Rutherford's income sharing approach were accepted, should it necessarily continue, as she suggests, until income equalization occurred or the recipient remarried? Professor Singer has proposed that income equalization should continue for one-half the duration of the marriage. *See* Jana Singer, *Divorce Reform and Gender Justice*, 67 N.C.L. REV. 1103 (1989); Jana Singer, *Alimony and Efficiency: The Gendered Costs and Benefits of the Economic Justification for Alimony*, 82 GEO. L. J. 2423 (1994). Which approach is best?

d. What post-divorce events should affect an income-sharing award? What if the payor marries someone with substantial needs or has a needy parent? What if one of the spouses decides to take a less stressful (and lower-paying) job or to stay home to raise children? Should the spouses have an obligation to maximize income?

e. Should an income-sharing approach require equality? Professor Sugarman has proposed that a system in which each spouse's interest in the other's earning capacity would be based on marital duration. For example, "one might obtain a 1.5% or 2% interest in the other for every year together, and presumably this interest would survive the remarriage of either party. Such a regime might be subject to minimum vesting rules restricting when the right accrues (such as after three or five years of marriage) and it might possibly be subject to a ceiling (such as 40% or twenty years)." *See* Stephen D. Sugarman, *Dividing Financial Interests at Divorce*, in DIVORCE REFORM AT THE CROSSROADS 159–60 (Stephen D. Sugarman & Herma H. Kay, eds. 1990).

f. If equal income-sharing is desirable, what is the appropriate measure of equality when minor children are involved? Consider this example: if Bill, with an income of $2,000 per month and Ann, with an income of $1,000 per month, divorce and Ann obtains custody of the couple's two minor children, a transfer of $500 per month would be necessary to achieve equal household *incomes*. To achieve equal *living standards* requires a calculation based on one or another "household equivalence scale;" using the widely-utilized U.S. Bureau of Labor Standards scale, a transfer of $1,070 would be necessary to achieve equal *living standards* for the two households. (To read up on household equivalence scales, see p. 889.)

Problem 15–5: Reinventing Alimony

The state legislature is considering replacing its current alimony law (identical to the Pennsylvania statute reprinted at [p. 794]) with standards recently approved by the American Law Institute. *See* AMERICAN LAW INSTITUTE, PRINCIPLES OF THE LAW OF FAMILY DISSOLUTION: ANALYSIS AND RECOMMENDATIONS, TENTATIVE DRAFT NO. 2 (March 14, 1996) (hereinafter "ALI Principles"). For a critical overview of the ALI alimony principles, *see* J. Thomas Oldham, *ALI Principles of Family Dissolution: Some Comments*, 1997 ILL. L. REV. 801 (1997).

Under the ALI Principles, spouses in a "long" [to be defined by each state] marriage would annually accrue an increased percentage-based interest in the other's earning capacity. Post-divorce, the higher-earning spouse would have to pay alimony to the lower-earning spouse in an amount equalling the accrued percentage multiplied by the difference in the spouses' annual earnings. *See* ALI Principles, § 5.05.

Under the Principles, an alimony claim may also arise from the assumption of child care responsibilities. *See* ALI Principles, § 5.06. To establish such a claim, a spouse must show that he or she assumed the majority of the family's child care responsibilities for more than a minimum period and has an earning capacity at divorce that is substantially less than that of the other spouse. The amount of the award is based on the "child care durational factor," determined by multiplying the claimant spouse's years of primary child care by a state-established percentage (say, for example, .015). The higher-earning spouse must pay as alimony that percentage of the earnings difference. So, if the claimant cared for a child for ten years and the relevant state percentage was .015, the claimant would be awarded 15% of the difference between his or her post-divorce earnings and those of the higher-earning spouse.

An award under both §§ 5.05 and 5.06 may be made in the same case. However, the total award may not exceed the state's maximum percentage for an award under § 5.05 alone (say, 40% or 50%). Awards under both §§ 5.05 and 5.06 are modifiable due to post-divorce changes in circumstances. *See* ALI Principles, § 5.09.

Awards under both §§ 5.05 and 5.06 are presumed to be for an indefinite period if the marriage meets specified minimum requirements. Under § 5.05, the requirements are marital duration and age; under § 5.06, the requirements are age and child care duration. Each enacting state is to set the relevant minima. *See* ALI Principles, § 5.07. In a case where the requirements for an indefinite award have not been met, payments under § 5.05 extend for a period determined by multiplying the length of marriage by a state-determined percentage; payments under § 5.06 extend for a period determined by multiplying the child care period by a state-determined percentage.

If an award is unavailable under both §§ 5.05 and 5.06, the Principles suggest that an award should not be made unless: 1) the claimant spouse is unable to recover after divorce the standard of living he or she enjoyed at the time of marriage; and 2) the living standard loss is due to responsibilities assumed by the claimant during marriage. *See* ALI Principles, § 5.16.

The legislature in your state is certain that it would like to reduce alimony-related litigation. It is also sure that it wants to achieve results that are fair. But, legislators have freely admitted to you, many are not quite sure what fairness means in this context. You have been asked to advise the legislature on several issues:

1. What results would the ALI principles produce in the *Morgan, Otis, Baker, and Huntington* cases?

2. What policy goals underlie the ALI Principles? Are there other goals the state should aim to achieve that the Principles do not address? If so, what are they?

3. Would women's groups (NOW, etc.) support or oppose passage of the ALI Principles? What about MUDD ("Men United against Divorce Discrimination") Advocates of "family values"? The State Judges Association?

4. Would adoption of the ALI principles likely produce an increase or decrease in the rate, duration, and level of alimony awards?

5. On balance, should the state adopt the ALI Principles? If not, what approach should the state adopt?

Chapter 16

CHILD SUPPORT

SECTION 1. AN HISTORICAL PERSPECTIVE

WILLIAM BLACKSTONE, COMMENTARIES ON THE LAWS OF ENGLAND, BOOK I

(1765).

1. And, first, the duties of parents to legitimate children: which principally consist in three particulars; their maintenance, their protection, and their education.

The duty of parents to provide for the *maintenance* of their children is a principle of natural law; an obligation, says Puffendorf, laid on them not only by nature herself, but by their own proper act, in bringing them into the world: for they would be in highest manner injurious to their issue, if they only gave the children life, that they might afterwards see them perish. By begetting them therefore they have entered into a voluntary obligation, to endeavour, as far as in them lies, that the life which they have bestowed shall be supported and preserved. And thus the children will have a perfect *right* of receiving maintenance from their parents. And the President Montesquieu has a very just observation upon this head: that the establishment of marriage in all civilized states is built on this natural obligation of the father to provide for his children; for that ascertains and makes known the person who is bound to fulfill this obligation: whereas, in promiscuous and illicit conjunctions, the father is unknown; and the mother finds a thousand obstacles in her way;—shame, remorse, the constraint of her sex, and the rigor of laws,—that stifle her inclinations to perform this duty: and besides, she generally wants ability.

The municipal laws of well-regulated states have taken care to enforce this duty: though providence has done it more effectually than any laws, by implanting in the breast of every parent that * * * insuperable degree of affection, which not even the deformity of person or mind, not even the wickedness, ingratitude, and rebellion of children, can totally suppress or extinguish. * * *

No person is bound to provide a maintenance for his issue, unless where the children are impotent and unable to work, either through infancy, disease, or accident; and then is only obliged to find them with necessaries, the penalty on refusal being no more than 20 s. a month. For the policy of our laws, which are ever watchful to promote industry, did not mean to compel a father to maintain his idle and lazy children in ease and indolence: but thought it unjust to oblige the parent, against his will, to provide them with superfluities, and other indulgences of fortune; imagining they might trust to the impulse of nature, if the children were deserving of such favours.

Blackstone describes the common law approach to child support: Parents were viewed as having a *moral* obligation to support their children, not a legal one. Under the common law, neither the child nor one parent on his behalf could sue to obtain support.

The common law's failure to accord the child an enforceable support right derived, in part, from the legal unity of the family. As we saw in Chapter 3, during Blackstone's day virtually all income and property rights were vested in the male household head; wives had no more entitlement to support than their children. Both had extremely limited inheritance rights; neither could individually maintain a lawsuit, even against an individual outside the family.

Parents in Blackstone's day did have a *public* obligation to support their children, imposed under the Elizabethan Poor Laws (43 Eliz. 1, ch. 2, § vi (1601)) and their colonial counterparts. The Poor Laws instituted both a comprehensive public welfare program and a legal support duty that imposed on parents an obligation to reimburse the state for benefits to their children. This support obligation was not restricted to parents; grandparents were liable for the support of their grandchildren, as were husbands for support of their wives, and adult children for support of their parents. The manner and rate of payment were determined by county Justices of the Peace; default resulted, as Blackstone notes, in a standard penalty of twenty shillings per month. *Id.* at ch. 2, § vi. *See generally* JOYCE O. APPLEBY, ECONOMIC THOUGHT AND IDEOLOGY IN SEVENTEENTH-CENTURY ENGLAND 129–57 (1978); SIDNEY WEBB & BEATRICE WEBB, ENGLISH POOR LAW HISTORY, PART I: THE OLD POOR LAW (1927); Jacobus ten Broek, *California's Dual System of Family Law: Its Origins, Development, and Present Status, Part I*, 16 STAN. L. REV. 258–87 (1964).

The Industrial Revolution brought with it a wave of laws that pierced the legal unity of the family. Statutory divorce laws [Chapter 11], the Married Women's Property Acts [Chapter 3], and the alimony claim [Chapter 15] developed during this period; so did the modern child support obligation. A hundred years after Blackstone wrote, American family law recognized a paternal support obligation that was enforceable on behalf of the child rather than the public, and which applied whether or not the child was in danger of becoming a public charge.

The new child support obligation reflected some, but not all, of the Poor Law concepts that preceded it. Like the public relief applicant, the child who sought support was required to show dependence and worthiness; children who were emancipated from parental control or who refused to obey reasonable parental commands were no more entitled to parental support than were the able-bodied to public funds. In contrast to the Poor Law approach, however, the relief obtainable under the new child support laws was not limited to subsistence. Instead, just as they did in the alimony context, courts held that the child was entitled to support that reflected, insofar as the father's current means permitted, the family's income and prior standard of living. The value of the support obligation was thus left to the discretion of the presiding judge; even when initially fixed, the award was subject to modification based on changes in the child's or father's circumstances. *See generally* HOMER H. CLARK, JR., THE LAW OF DOMESTIC RELATIONS IN THE UNITED STATES 496–507 (1st ed. 1968).

SECTION 2. SUPPORT IN THE INTACT FAMILY

ROE v. DOE

Court of Appeals of New York, 1971.
29 N.Y.2d 188, 324 N.Y.S.2d 71, 272 N.E.2d 567.

SCILEPPI, JUDGE.

It is a sad but telling commentary upon the relationship subsisting between father and daughter that resort to the courts was employed to resolve this domestic problem. The surge of adolescent independence, the breakdown in parental authority and the frustration attending both are indeed matters of common occurrence. Feelings may run high, idle threats may be uttered, but experience teaches us that such hostilities do abate and rapprochements are soon effected. Aware that the law is no interloper in such intrafamily problems, the courts absent any violation of law, refuse to intervene, preferring to leave the parties where they find them, lest they undermine the integrity of the family.

Petitioner is the court-appointed guardian for a 20–year-old student at the University of Louisville who had been fully and generously supported by her father, a prominent New York attorney, until April of 1970. Afforded the opportunity of attending college away from home, and after living in the college dormitory for a time, the daughter, contrary to the father's prior instructions and without his knowledge, took up residence with a female classmate in an off-campus apartment. Upon learning of this deception, the father cut off all further support and instructed her to return to New York.

Ignoring her father's demands, the daughter sold her automobile (an earlier gift from her father) and elected to finish out the school year, living off the proceeds realized upon the sale, some $1,000. During the following summer, the daughter enrolled in summer courses at the university and upon her return to New York chose to reside with the parents of a female classmate on Long Island. The family situation has been tense and somewhat less than stable. The daughter was three years old when her mother died and her father has remarried several times since, most recently in the spring of 1970. Academically, the daughter fared poorly, and was placed on academic probation during her freshman year; though, on a reduced credit work load, she has managed to improve her academic standing over the past year. She has experimented with drugs (LSD and marijuana), apparently without addiction. The girl has been comfortably maintained, and there is no real question about the father's ability to provide. Tuition payments, approximately $1,000 per semester, for the academic year 1970–71, are long past due and petitioner has commenced this support proceeding, alleging that the respondent has refused and neglected to provide fair and reasonable support.

The Family Court entered two separate orders: a temporary order of support (August 21, 1970), requiring the father to remit a tuition payment for the then pending semester and to provide for reasonable medical, dental, eye and psychiatric care; and a final order of support (November 30, 1970), requiring that the father pay $250 per month in support for the period between December 1, 1970 and October 20, 1971, the daughter's twenty-first birthday. Respondent was found to have willfully failed to comply with the temporary order of support and was committed to jail for 30 days, the commitment to be stayed until December 28, 1970 and at that time vacated on condition that he post a cash bond in the sum of $5,750 covering his liability for support. The order of commitment was stayed pending appeal.

On appeal, the Appellate Division modified the temporary order, on the law and the facts and in the exercise of discretion, and directed that the father pay only those university and health bills actually rendered prior to November 30, 1970. The final order of November 30, 1970, requiring that the father pay $250 per month in support for the period between December 1, 1970 and October 20, 1971, the daughter's twenty-first birthday, plus tuition payments through the September, 1971 semester, was reversed on the law and the facts and in the exercise of discretion. As it is our conclusion that where, as in the case at bar, a minor of employable age and in full possession of her faculties, voluntarily and without cause, abandons the parent's home, against the will of the parent and for the purpose of avoiding parental control she forfeits her right to demand support, the order appealed from should be affirmed.

It has always been, and remains a matter of fundamental policy within this State, that a father of a minor child is chargeable with the discipline and support of that child * * * and none would dispute that the obligation cannot be avoided merely became a young enough child is at odds with her parents or has disobeyed their instructions: delinquent behavior of itself, even if unexplained or persistent, does not generally carry with it the termination of the duty of a parent to support.

On the other hand, while the duty to support is a continuing one, the child's right to support and the parent's right to custody and services are reciprocal: the father in return for maintenance and support may establish and impose reasonable regulations for his child. * * * Accordingly, though the question is novel in this State, it has been held, in circumstances such as here, that where by no fault on the parent's part, a child "voluntarily abandons the parent's home for the purpose of seeking its fortune in the world or to avoid parental discipline and restraint [that child] forfeit the claim to support" (C.J.S. Parent and Child § 16, p. 699) * * * To hold otherwise would be to allow, at least in the case before us, a minor of employable age to deliberately flout the legitimate mandates of her father while requiring that the latter support her in her decision to place herself beyond his effective control.

It is the natural right, as well as the legal duty, of a parent to care for, control and protect his child from potential harm, whatever the source and absent a clear showing of misfeasance, abuse or neglect, courts should not interfere with that delicate responsibility. Here, the daughter, asserting her independence, chose to assume a status inconsistent with that of parental control. The Family Court set about establishing its own standards of decorum, and, having determined that those standards were met, sought to substitute its judgment for that of the father. Needless to say, the intrusion was unwarranted.

We do not have before us the case of a father who casts his helpless daughter upon the world, forcing her to fend for herself; nor has the father been arbitrary in his requests that the daughter heed his demands. The obligations of parenthood, under natural and civil law, require of the child "submission to reasonable restraint, and demands habits of propriety, obedience, and conformity to domestic discipline" * * *. True, a minor, rather than submit to what her father considers to be proper discipline, may be induced to abandon the latter's home; but in so doing, however impatient of parental authority, she cannot enlist the aid of the court in frustrating that authority, reasonably exercised, by requiring that her father accede to her demands and underwrite her chosen lifestyle or as here, run the risk of incarceration.

Nor can we say that the father was unreasonable or capricious in his request that the daughter take up residence in the college dormitory or return to New York. In view of her past derelictions, and, to use the Appellate Division's words, "the temptations that abound outside," * * * we can only conclude that it was reasonable for her father to decide that it was in her own best interests that she do so. And the fact that the father doggedly persisted in his demands despite similar evils which may have lurked within the campus residence, or psychiatric advice that the daughter live off campus, cannot be said to amount to a showing of misconduct, neglect or abuse which would justify the Family Court's action. The father has the right, in the absence of caprice, misconduct or neglect, to require that the daughter conform to his reasonable demands. Should she disagree, and at her age that is surely her prerogative, she may elect not to comply; but in so doing, she subjects herself to her father's lawful wrath. Where, as here, she abandons her home, she forfeits her right to support.

The order appealed from should be affirmed.

Notes and Questions

1. Does *Roe* mean that a minor has a "right" to be supported in college by his parents if he follows their reasonable instructions? Would it make a difference if the age of majority were 18 instead of 21? How would *Roe* apply in the case of a divorced parent who had been ordered to pay college expenses? *See* pp. 882–886.

2. If a parent tells his or her child that the child can live at home only if he continues to attend school and the child drops out, may the parent demand that the child leave home? If so, does the parent have a continuing support obligation? *See* Toft v. Frisbie, 122 A.D.2d 456, 504 N.Y.S.2d 844 (1986).

3. The issue of a parent's child support obligation arises both when the child seeks support and when the state seeks reimbursement for benefits provided to the child. Should the same standard apply in both contexts? In Parker v. Stage, 43 N.Y.2d 128, 400 N.Y.S.2d 794, 371 N.E.2d 513 (1977), the New York Court of Appeals applied the *Roe* approach even though the petition was brought by state officials seeking reimbursement for public assistance benefits furnished to the minor:

> * * * [T]he Family Court Judge dismissed the petition on the ground that respondent's daughter, by leaving home to live with her paramour and have his child, had "emancipated herself from her father and his household ... and ... as a result of that emancipation, the respondent is relieved of any obligation to support" her.
>
> The commissioner admits that respondent's daughter ... would be unable to compel him to support her if she had brought the suit on her own behalf [but] ... argues ... that when the suit is brought by a social welfare official ... the duty to support "is absolute upon a showing of sufficient ability on the part of the parent. There is no other qualification or exception in the statute."
>
> * * *
>
> It was once the policy of this State to place the financial burden of supporting needy individuals upon designated relatives, rather than the public, in order to reduce the amount of welfare expenditures. Thus the common-law obligation to support wife and minor children was expanded by statute to include adult children, grandchildren and parents when they would otherwise become public charges.
>
> In recent years however ... [t]he laws were amended to relieve individuals of the obligation to support grandchildren, adult children and parents who were unemployed and destitute. Thereafter the burden passed to the public. In a message accompanying the 1966

bill the Governor noted that ... "Experience has shown that the financial responsibility of a broad class of relatives, imposed by statute, is more often a destructive, rather than cohesive, factor in family unity." Thus the legislative history shows that the current statutory scheme recognizes the need to preserve family unity even though the consequence is to place needy relatives on the public welfare rolls. * * * In addition the Legislature has expressly granted the courts discretionary powers in these cases....

* * *

... Of course the fact that the child is eligible for public assistance may as is evident here, permit her to avoid her father's authority and demands however reasonable they may be. But it does not follow that the parent must then finish what has been begun by underwriting the lifestyle which his daughter chose against his reasonable wishes and repeated counsel. * * *

4. Courts have held that parents, like spouses, are liable for necessaries furnished their minor children. *Compare* Greenspan v. Slate, 12 N.J. 426, 97 A.2d 390 (1953) (requiring parent to pay for medical care for teenage daughter) *with Buckstaff* [p. 137]. Why is the necessaries doctrine of (even) less practical utility to a minor child than to a spouse?

SECTION 3. SUPPORT IN THE SEPARATED FAMILY: WHO PAYS?

A. BIOLOGICAL PARENTS

STRAUB v. B.M.T

Supreme Court of Indiana, 1994.
645 N.E.2d 597.

SHEPARD, CHIEF JUSTICE.

Francine Todd wanted to have a child, but she did not want to be married. She and Edward Straub signed an agreement providing that Edward Straub would not be responsible for supporting any child the two might procreate. B.M.T. was born in the wake of this agreement. When Straub offered this agreement as a defense to a claim for child support, the trial court held it void. When the validity of that agreement was before the Indiana Court of Appeals, it provoked a debate about the public policy surrounding a parent's child support obligation. We conclude that the agreement was void.

I. SUMMARY OF FACT

The facts most favorable to the judgment reveal that in 1986 Francine Todd and Edward Straub engaged in a romantic relationship and sexual relations. In December of that year, Todd informed Straub of her desire to have a child. Straub was a divorcee with five children from a previous marriage, and he expressed resistance to fathering another child. Todd threatened to end the relationship, however, unless he agreed to impregnate her.

Straub handwrote the following statement and told Todd he would attempt to impregnate her if she signed it.

> To whom it may concern
>
> I Francine Todd in sound mind & fore thought have decided not to marry, but would like to have a baby of my own. To support financially & emotionally. I have approached several men who will not be held responsible financially or emotionally, who's [sic] names will be kept secret for life.
>
> Signed Francine E. Todd
> Dec. 15, 1986

Todd signed the statement, and the couple thereafter began having unprotected intercourse. Todd became pregnant in March 1987 and gave birth that November. The birth certificate did not list anyone as the father.

On January 7, 1991, Todd filed a petition asking the trial court to declare Straub the father of the child and require him to pay child support and certain medical expenses. The trial court found Straub to be the father of the child and ordered him to pay support in the sum of $130 per week, arrearages of $20 per week and certain medical expenses.

Straub appealed this decision and the Court of Appeals affirmed. He then petitioned this Court for transfer. Straub raises three issues, but the essence of all three may be stated as follows: whether parent may contract away his or her rights and obligations to a child and/or the child's right to support through a preconception contract for fertilization. We grant transfer and affirm.

II. Some Agreements Concerning Children Are Void

Three rudimentary elements must be present before an agreement may be considered a contract: offer, acceptance of the offer and consideration. *Rodman v. Rodman*, (1878), 64 Ind. 65 (offer and acceptance required); *Berry v. Bates* (1828), 2 Blackf. 118, (promise without consideration is not legally binding). If these components are present, legal obligation results from the bargaining of the parties as found in their language or by implication from other circumstances, as affected by the rules of law. *See, e.g.*, U.C.C. § 1–201(3).

There are instances, however in which an agreement is not an enforceable contract despite proper formation. Where a properly formed agreement contravenes the public policy of Indiana, for instance, courts have traditionally said it is void and unenforceable. Leading commentators frame the principle somewhat differently, saying that in such circumstances there is no contract, because such an agreement produces no legal obligation upon the part of the promisor. *See, e.g.*, John D. Calamari & Joseph M. Perillo, Contracts § 1–11 (3d ed. 1987). It may well be more exact to say that where an agreement violates public policy, no contract is created.

In any event, certain agreements are prohibited outright by statute and thus void. *See, e.g.*, IND.CODE ANN. § 26–2–5–1 (West Supp. 1994) (rendering void provisions which indemnify a promisee against liability for negligence by promisee or his or her independent contractors). There are even court rules outlawing certain agreements. *See, e.g.*, Ind. Professional Conduct Rule 1.5(d)(2) no contingency fees in criminal cases.

More often, though, the question of whether an agreement is void on public policy grounds is a question of law to be determined from the surrounding circumstances of a given case. Where public policy is not explicit, we look to the overall implications of constitutional and statutory enactments, practices of officials and judicial decisions to disclose the public policy of this State. Where there is not a clear manifestation of public policy we will find an agreement void only if it has a tendency to injure the public, is against the public good or is inconsistent with sound policy and good morals.

One well-established public policy of this State is protecting the welfare of children. Expressed by all three branches of Indiana government, this policy is of the utmost importance. In keeping with this public policy, Indiana courts have from time to time voided agreements reached by parents. Agreements which yield up a support opportunity for a child have been especially suspect. We have treated custodial parents who receive child support as trustees of the payments for the use and the benefit of the child. Neither parent has the right to contract away these support benefits. The right to the support lies exclusively with the child. Any agreement purporting to contract away these rights is directly contrary to this State's public policy of protecting the welfare of children, as it narrows the basis for support to one parent. *See* Child Supp.G. 1.

Seeking to avoid the rules that agreements between parents giving up a child's right to support are void, Straub contended during oral argument and in his appellate briefs that he was not a traditional parent but merely a sperm donor for Todd's "artificial insemination." The Indiana legislature has acknowledged the use of artificial insemination, though it has not addressed the support obligation of parents where artificial fertilization leads to the conception of the child. *See* Ind.Code Ann. §§ 16–41–14–1–20. Nonetheless, citizens of this State execute contracts for such fertilization. These contracts have the ability to impact significantly the support responsibility of biological and nonbiological parents. Other jurisdictions have addressed the support issues surrounding artificial fertilization through the adoption of statutes based on the Uniform Parentage Act, 9B U.L.A. (1987)("UPA"), and the Uniform Status of Children of Assisted Conception Act, 9B U.L.A. (Supp.1993) ("USCACA"). The majority of states adopting legislation similar to these acts hold that the donor of semen or ova, provided to a licensed physician for use in the artificial fertilization of a woman, is treated under the law as if he or she were not the natural parent of the child thereby conceived. Otherwise, whether the impregnation occurs through artificial fertilization or intercourse, there *can* be a determination of parentage. *See, e.g., Jhordan C. v. Mary K.* [p. 360].

Statutes based on either the UPA or the USCACA are excellent tools for ensuring that contracts for these services do not violate our public policy of protecting the welfare of children. Such contracts reach the careful balance of enabling childless individuals to bear children while ensuring that the parental responsibilities normally born by the biological parents are assumed by another person or couple.

III. Are Agreements Like This One Enforceable?

While Indiana does not have statutes on assisted conception, common law courts certainly have the ability to fashion and refashion the law of contract, as Judge Conover suggested in his dissenting opinion to the Court of Appeals. *Straub*, 626 N.E.2d, at 854–55.[1] Accordingly, we evaluate the Todd agreement within the parameters of common law as influenced by the emerging contract principles surrounding reproductive technology.

This agreement falls on multiple accounts. First, it looks for all the world as a rather traditional attempt to forego [sic] this child's right to support from *Straub*, which contravenes public policy. We conclude there is no such thing as "artificial insemination by intercourse" as *Straub* contends. The emerging law on contracts for artificial insemination so suggests. *See, e.g.*, USCACA § 1(1), 9B U.L.A. 138 (Supp.1993) ("assisted conception").

Second, consideration for this agreement, received by Straub, was sexual intercourse with Todd. Using sexual intercourse as consideration is itself against public policy. *Glasgo v. Glasgo* (1980), Ind.App., 410 N.E.2d 1325, 1331.

Third, the agreement contains none of the formalities and protections which the legislatures and courts of other jurisdictions have thought necessary to address when enabling childless individuals to bear children.[2] For these reasons, we hold the Todd agreement to be void and unenforceable.

We grant transfer and affirm the trial court.

DeBruler, Justice, dissenting.

1. Judge Conover explained: Thus, in my opinion, the contract in question is valid and enforceable because it is conversant with current public policy. Todd had an absolute right to contract with *Straub* as she did, and is absolutely bound by the obligations she incurred under that contract. Quite simply, she bargained away the right to file a paternity action against *Straub* and to publicly name him as the child's father. *Straub*, 626 N.E.2d, at 855–56 (Conover, J., dissenting).

2. For example, prerequisites such as physician involvement are essential for protecting the health and welfare of the child conceived. *Jhordan C.*, [p. 360] (physician involvement essential to obtain donor's complete medical history which child may later need and creates a formal structure for donation which reduces misunderstandings of the relationship between donor and recipient and donor, recipient and child).

I agree with the majority that one cannot contract away the right of a child to financial support from one of her parents. One cannot contract away one's liability for negligence either, but we do permit people to buy insurance. If an individual's insurance coverage is inadequate then that person must pay. However, we do not void insurance contracts by invoking a public policy of imposing liability for negligence. The proper procedure to make certain that B.M.T. receives adequate support is that suggested by Judge Chezem's opinion in the Court of Appeals. *Straub v. B.M.T. b/n/f/ Todd* (1993), Ind. App., 626 N.E.2d 848, 854. If a person promises to pay the father's share of child support then, if that person is able, he or she should pay.

Notes and Questions

1. *Straub* reflects the general rule that all parents have a child support obligation, regardless of the nature of the parental relationship or understandings between the parents. A waiver of child support in a premarital agreement is unenforceable. *See* UPAA § 3 [p. 204].

2. Support obligations have been imposed even when the parent was himself a child owed support. *See* County of San Luis Obispo v. Nathaniel J., 50 Cal.App.4th 842, 57 Cal.Rptr.2d 843 (1996) (imposing support obligation on 15 year old boy who was a victim of statutory rape).

3. How does the approach advocated by dissenting Judge DeBruler differ from that of the majority? When would Judge DeBruler enforce a child support waiver?

B. STEPPARENTS AND OTHER RESIDENTIAL ADULTS

The increased incidence of divorce and nonmarital parenting has increased the number of "reconstituted" or "blended" families. One commentator has estimated that 33% of children alive in the late 1980s would live with a stepparent by the age of eighteen. Paul C. Glick, *Remarried Families, Stepfamilies and Stepchildren: A Brief Demographic Profile*, 38 FAM. REL. 24 (1989). In 1990, 16% of American children living in married-couple households lived with a parent and stepparent; 92% of these children lived with their mother and a stepfather; 8% with a father and stepmother. U.S. DEP'T OF COMMERCE, BUREAU OF THE CENSUS, STATISTICAL ABSTRACT OF THE UNITED STATES 1995 64, tbl.77 (1996). Indeed, many children with divorced or never-married parents have two stepparents, one resident in the household and one married to the noncustodial parent.

WIESE v. WIESE

Supreme Court of Utah, 1985.
699 P.2d 700.

HOWE, J.

Plaintiff Carl Bruce Wiese appeals from an order of the district court that he pay child support for his stepson.

* * *

Defendant Christine M. Wiese was divorced from her first husband in January of 1973. She knew she was then pregnant, but she did not disclose that fact to the court. She had met the plaintiff about two weeks earlier. They married in August, 1973, shortly before her son was born to "give him a name" and to avoid the cost of adoption procedures. Although both knew that plaintiff was not the father of the boy, plaintiff allowed his name to be so shown on the birth certificate, and he treated the boy as his own during the marriage and supported him.

Plaintiff and defendant lived together for approximately 14 of the 36 months they were married. At the suggestion of the defendant, plaintiff took custody of her son when they were divorced in 1976 in a default proceeding. Plaintiff's attorney prepared the decree of divorce which reflected that the boy was "issue of the marriage" and "child of the parties." (We can only assume that they were prepared in this manner because plaintiff's attorney was not informed of the anomoly and had no reason to believe that the boy was not plaintiff's natural son; but the correctness of that assumption does not affect our holding.) Within three months after the divorce, however, defendant demanded the return of her son because plaintiff had left him in the care of plaintiff's parents while he was away in military training. Plaintiff complied and returned the three-year-old boy in November of 1976. He sent gifts and a savings bond to the boy for the following two Christmases. The parties did not make any child support arrangements, but plaintiff voluntarily sent money for the boy on an irregular basis until January, 1978. His last contact with the boy was a one-day visit in the summer of 1977 when the boy was four years old. * * *

Nearly two and a half years later, defendant caused to be served on plaintiff an order to show cause why he should not pay child support.... [T]he court specifically found that plaintiff was not the father but ordered him to pay child support, holding that plaintiff was equitably estopped from escaping the duty of support. Plaintiff ... appeal[s.]

The legislature of this state has imposed ... [a support] duty on stepparents only during the duration of the marriage ..... We have held that a party asserting equitable estoppel must prove that he detrimentally relied on the actions or representations of the party to be estopped. The trial court found that the boy detrimentally relied on the plaintiff because the latter caused the preparation of the stipulation which was the foundation for the decree of divorce, which decree found that the boy was the "issue of the marriage" and "the minor child of the parties." This representation, the findings continue, placed the child in a "position where it would be substantially impossible to successfully pursue a claim against the biological father."

We cannot agree with the latter finding. No evidence was adduced that it would be "substantially impossible" for the boy to pursue a claim against his biological father. Indeed, the record is totally barren of any evidence that the defendant has ever even approached her first husband (who we assume is the biological father) on the subject of support. We concur with the New Jersey Supreme Court's recent holding that the party asserting equitable estoppel must carry the burden to show that the stepfather's actions have precluded the obtaining of support from the biological father. *Miller v. Miller*, 97 N.J. 154, 478 A.2d 351, 358–359 (1984). In a well-reasoned opinion, the New Jersey Court held that the party alleging equitable estoppel had the burden to prove that the stepfather's conduct established the three prerequisites to equitable estoppel: representation, reliance, and detriment. As to the detriment requirement, the Court held that there must be evidence that the child will suffer because his stepparent's representation or conduct causes him to be cut off from his noncustodial natural parent's support.... The Court emphasized that the natural parent should always be considered the primary source for child support because society and its current laws assume that the natural parent will support his or her child. It concluded that before estoppel could be raised the stepparent "must take positive action interfering with the natural parent's support obligation to be bound." *Id.* at 359.

It is true here that the plaintiff consented to be named as the father on the birth certificate and that he caused the decree of divorce between him and the defendant to reflect that the boy was issue of their marriage. However, that conduct in and of itself is insufficient to establish detriment. In the first place, the trial court made a specific finding that plaintiff was not the father of the boy and erred in not modifying the decree to reflect that finding. Secondly, no legal authority is cited for the proposition that plaintiff's representations to the 1976 divorce court preclude the boy, who was not a party to that action, from obtaining support from his biological father. Other jurisdictions have held that if a child is not a party to a previous action adjudging him the offspring of the parties, the child is not bound by that finding. The fact that the plaintiff treated the boy as his own and supported him is likewise insufficient grounds for imposing the duty of support. *Miller v. Miller, supra.*

We reverse the judgment and order of support entered against the plaintiff without prejudice to the defendant to again bring an order to show cause for support when her efforts to obtain support from the biological father have been concluded. Only at that time can it be determined whether equitable estoppel will lie against the plaintiff.

DURHAM, J., dissenting.

The majority opinion analyzes this case in terms of equitable estoppel and reverses because "detriment" has not been shown. I believe that the appropriate theory to be applied is not equitable estoppel, but judicial estoppel and res judicata, and that the judgment of the lower court should be affirmed.

* * *

In 1976 plaintiff brought a divorce action against defendant. In the complaint, which was signed and sworn by plaintiff (and not by his attorney), plaintiff alleged, "There has been one child born as issue of said marriage, to-wit: CARL JUSTIN WIESE, born 8/31/73." Further, plaintiff alleged in that complaint, "Plaintiff should be awarded the care, custody and control of the minor child of the parties.... " A stipulation and agreement, drawn up by plaintiff and signed by both plaintiff and defendant, provided that plaintiff should be awarded a divorce and custody of the "minor child of the parties." The stipulation was accepted by the court, and a decree of divorce was entered in which plaintiff was awarded custody of the child. Plaintiff then took the child to Arizona. When defendant learned that plaintiff had sent the child back to Utah to stay with plaintiff's parents, she insisted that the child live with her instead. The child has lived with defendant since that time.

* * *

The majority opinion treats this case solely under the rubric of the "duty to support" issue. It relies on cases which limit the application of equitable estoppel in situations where a duty of support is sought to be imposed on a stepparent. In particular, the majority is persuaded by the reasoning in *Miller v. Miller*, 97 N.J. 154, 478 A.2d 351 (1984), that no duty should be imposed in this case. The instant case, however, is distinguishable from *Miller* on a number of grounds. In *Miller*, the stepparent, who never at any time asserted any claim to be the actual or legal father, married the children's mother when the children were six and nine years old. The children in *Miller* had had long-term contact with their natural father, who had supported them up until the time the stepfather insisted on taking over their support. Because it was possible to return to the previous support arrangement, the *Miller* court remanded the case to the trial court to determine whether the children had suffered detriment in relation to their future support. In the instant case, there is no evidence that there has ever been any support provided by the natural father, nor is he legally obligated to provide such support, because all the enforceable legal documents establish that plaintiff is the father of and responsible for the child.

I do not believe, however, that the question of actual detriment to the child is the critical issue in this case.... Plaintiff alleged in his verified complaint that the child was his issue and, on the basis of that complaint, was awarded a divorce and a decree which granted him custody. A judgment was entered which established plaintiff as the father of the child. * * * There are no newly discovered relevant facts which would justify reopening the issue of paternity, since the plaintiff knew at all times that he was not the natural father of the child. * * * If a husband has doubts concerning the paternity of a child born during the marriage, he should raise and resolve that question during the dissolution proceedings ..... To allow former husbands to come into court long after entry of final judgment and challenge the legitimacy of children born during their marriages would be chaotic at best. In my opinion, the trial judge erred in even permitting evidence on the paternity issue in this case. * * *

In addition to the foregoing, I believe that there are other, equitable, reasons to affirm the trial judge's imposition of a support obligation in this case. Plaintiff knew of defendant's pregnancy within hours of defendant's learning that she was pregnant and several months before he decided to marry her. He undertook that marriage and the imminent birth of her child with full knowledge that the child was not his. * * * By the time plaintiff decided that he no longer wanted to be obligated to the child and brought a suit to reestablish paternity, the child was five years old. Under these circumstances, it is wholly inequitable to allow plaintiff to simply walk away from a commitment of this magnitude, voluntarily undertaken and obviously of past benefit to him. * * *

The doctrines of judicial estoppel and res judicata require affirmance in this case, and the equities likewise demand that the trial court's order be upheld.

Notes and Questions

1. At common law, a stepparent relationship created no rights or obligations. Stepchildren were not entitled to support from a stepparent; if the stepparent died intestate, they took nothing. Most states today maintain the common law approach. Some states do impose statutory support obligations on stepparents during their marriage to the child's custodial parent (*see* WASH. REV. CODE ANN. § 26.16.205; DEL. CODE ANN., tit. 13, § 501(b)); Kelley v. Iowa Dept. of Social Services, 197 N.W.2d 192 (Iowa 1972). But given the tradition of noninterference with spending decisions in an intact family, this obligation will seldom be enforceable; it is also terminable at will.

2. *Weise* states the majority view on a stepparent's support obligation. Absent an adoption by the stepparent, only a few courts have imposed support obligations that survive divorce from the child's parent. Some have enforced contracts requiring post-divorce support (*see, e.g.*, L. v. L., 497 S.W.2d 840 (Mo.App.1973); In re Marriage of Dawley, 17 Cal.3d 342, 131 Cal.Rptr. 3, 551 P.2d 323 (1976)). As the *Weise* court notes, a few have used equitable estoppel doctrine to require post-divorce support. *See also* M.H.B. v. H.T.B., 100 N.J. 567, 498 A.2d 775 (1985) and cases collected in Annot., *Stepparent's Postdivorce Duty to Support Stepchild*, 44 A.L.R.4th 521 (1986).

3. Should a post-divorce stepparent support obligation arise: 1) when the natural noncustodial parent has abandoned the child? 2) when the stepparent has discouraged contact between the child and natural parent? 3) when the stepparent is more important to the child than the

natural parent? If stepparents are to have obligations in any of these circumstances, should similar obligations be imposed on cohabitants?

4. Would the imposition of post-divorce support obligations on custodial stepparents significantly affect the remarriage prospects of custodial parents?

5. Federal law requires a custodial stepparent's income to be counted in determining a child's eligibility for federally funded public assistance benefits, regardless of whether the stepparent has a duty to support the child under state law. 42 U.S.C.A. § 602(a)(31). Should the requirement be extended to the income of a cohabitant of the parent? *See generally* Mary Ann Mason & David W. Simon, *The Ambiguous Stepparent: Federal Legislation in Search of a Model*, 29 FAM. L. Q. 445 (1995).

6. In England and Wales, courts have been authorized to order stepparents to pay child support following a divorce from the child's natural parent since 1958. *See* Sarah H. Ramsey & Judith M. Masson, *Stepparent Support of Stepchildren: A Comparative Analysis of Policies and Problems in the American and English Experience*, 36 SYRACUSE L. REV. 659, 689–98 (1985).

7. Consider these comments by Professor Chambers:

> "The major difference between the biological relationship and the step relationship is that most of us hold in our minds a paradigm of what biological parent relationships ought to look like, a clear model for thinking about responsibilities and entitlements ... The stepparent relationship, by contrast, lacks—and, I would argue, cannot possibly obtain—a single paradigm or model of appropriate responsibilities.... Ahrons and Wallish in their study of divorced families cataloged, three years after the divorce, whether the parents had remarried (or recoupled), and whether the new partners brought children of their own into the union and whether the parent and step partner had new children after their union. They found eighteen patterns of family composition among the ninety-eight couples they studied. * * * In his study of children with a residential stepparent, Furstenberg found that children were much less likely to say they felt "quite close" to their stepparent than to say they felt "quite close" to their custodial parent and much less likely to say that they wanted to grow up to be like their stepparent than to say they wanted to be like their custodial parent. In fact, about a third of children living with a stepparent did not mention that person when asked to name the members of their family. Nearly all named their noncustodial parent, even when they saw him or her erratically.
>
> By the same token, about half the stepfathers ... said that the stepchildren were harder to love than their own children, and about half said that it was easier to think of themselves as a friend than as a parent to the stepchildren. Stepparents had difficulty figuring out their appropriate role in disciplining the child and determining how

to show affection for the child. Many stepparents and children remain uninvolved or uncomfortable with each other throughout the years they live together. * * *

We could . . . use laws to announce a particular vision of the stepparent relation, seeking to clarify for stepparents the roles they are expected to perform. But what vision would we choose to impose? Without some new social consensus about either children's needs or adults' responsibilities, is there some new vision we would wish to impose? And, even if we developed some near vision and embodied it in rules—say, rules that treated long-term residential stepparents as equals with biologic parents, eligible for visitation and custody, subject to orders of support—it isn't at all clear what effect such rules would have in lessening the uncertainties about the role that stepparents experience as they enter these relationships."

David L. Chambers, *Stepparents, Biologic Parents, and the Law's Perceptions of "Family" after Divorce*, in DIVORCE REFORM AT THE CROSSROADS 102, 104–06, 126 (Herma H. Kay & Stephen D. Sugarman eds. 1990).

8. *Grandparents*: Some states have enacted statutes providing that a grandparent is responsible for the support of grandchildren born to their children under 18 year of age. *See* S.C. CODE ANN. § 20–7–936. If a child's parent is less than 18 and lives in the same household as the child and the grandparent, federal law requires consideration of grandparent income when determining the eligibility of the child for federal public assistance benefits. 42 U.S.C.A. § 602(a)(39). In Lovelace v. Gross, 80 N.Y.2d 419, 590 N.Y.S.2d 852, 605 N.E.2d 339 (1992) the court rejected a constitutional challenge to this policy.

C. ADULT CHILDREN

WILLIAM BLACKSTONE, COMMENTARIES ON THE LAWS OF ENGLAND, BOOK I

(1765).

3. The *duties* of children to their parents arise from a principle of natural justice and retribution. For to those, who gave us existence, we naturally owe subjection and obedience during our minority, and honour and reverence ever after; they, who protected the weakness of our infancy, are entitled to our protection in the infirmity of their age; they who by sustenance ant education have enabled their offspring to prosper, ought in return to be supported by that offspring, in case they stand in need of assistance. Upon this principle proceed all the duties of children to their parents, which are enjoined by positive laws. * * *

The law does not hold the tie of nature to be dissolved by any misbehaviour of the parent; and therefore a child is equally justifiable in defending the person, or maintaining the cause or suit, of a bad parent, as a good one; and is equally compellable, if of sufficient ability, to maintain and provide for a wicked and unnatural progenitor as for one who has strewn the greatest tenderness and parental piety.

In days not long past, the family constituted a social security microcosm. Parents provided for their children while they were unable to provide for themselves and *vice versa*. The more children parents had, the more they "paid" to their "retirement fund" during their productive period and the greater would be their "pension." Today, the federal social security system has largely supplanted children's contributions as a source of provision for old age. Indeed, the system taxes "children" so heavily on their earnings that many "children" no longer have the financial flexibility to contribute to their parents' retirement. At the same time, laws in many states continue to impose on children responsibility for their indigent parents.

CANNON v. JURAS

Oregon Court of Appeals, 1973.
15 Or.App. 265, 515 P.2d 428.

FOLEY, JUDGE.

Petitioner appeals from a "Final Order" of the Administrator of the Public Welfare Division determining petitioner's liability in the amount of $384 to that agency for public assistance furnished his needy mother. We affirm.

Petitioner claims be is exempt from contribution under ORS § 416.030(2)(c) because he was abandoned or driven from the home as a child. The evidence was that petitioner, when 15 years of age, voluntarily began to work in logging camps. He returned home during his 16th year and found his mother living with a man. Claimant is not sure whether his mother was married to the man at that time or not. The man met petitioner at the door and refused to let him enter. Petitioner's mother was present, did not step forward or make any statement. Petitioner testified:

"ATTORNEY: Okay, and what happened?

"CLAIMANT: And a * * * well he met me at the door. He said that I wasn't welcome there and I said well I'm not going anywhere I'm not welcome and a * * * before that I'd worked in the shipyards and I'd paid the bills there because my mother said that she didn't get any help from her husband, her first husband. And so I had a little disagreement in the shipyards and I went somewhere else and I worked there and I still helped."

Petitioner further testified that he was allowed to return to obtain his belongings but did not again return to his mother's home until he was out of the Army several years later.

The hearing officer concluded that petitioner had emancipated himself and thus was not abandoned or deserted. We need not decide whether petitioner was emancipated. The only evidence of abandonment or desertion was that his mother did not take a stand when the man told him he was not welcome there at the home where his mother was living. We have previously held that

> "* * * expulsion of the child from the home must have been accompanied with a bad purpose or wrongful intent on the part of the mother if petitioner is to be exempt."
>
> *Cheatham v. Jursa*, 11 Or.App. 108, 501 P.2d 988 (1972).

Petitioner presented no evidence to show his mother acted with a bad purpose or wrongful intent. The fact that the mother did not assert herself to overcome the man's refusal to welcome petitioner into the home occupied by herself and the putative stepfather is not a sufficient basis to conclude that she acted with a bad purpose or wrongful intent.

Petitioner's other contentions are without merit. Affirmed.

Notes and Questions

1. Relative responsibility laws have survived a variety of constitutional challenges. *See* Swoap v. Superior Court of Sacramento County, 10 Cal.3d 490, 111 Cal.Rptr. 136, 516 P.2d 840 (1973); Americana Healthcare Center v. Randall, 513 N.W.2d 566 (S.D.1994).

2. The number of states retaining relative responsibility laws requiring adult children to provide for their indigent parent's medical needs dwindled from thirty-six in 1952, to thirty-three in 1971, to twenty-three in 1980. But, in February 1983, the Department of Health and Human Services issued a "transmittal" interpreting Medicaid regulations to permit the states to require adult children to support their parents without violating the Medicaid laws. The number of states with relative responsibility laws thereafter increased. In 1992, twenty-eight states had filial responsibility laws. *See* Catherine D. Byrd, *Relative Responsibility Extended: Requirement of Adult Children to Pay For Their Indigent Parent's Medical Needs*, 22 Fam. L.Q. 87, 89–90 (1988); Terrance A. Kline, *A Rational Role for Filial Responsibility Laws in Modern Society*, 26 Fam.L.Q. 195 (1992).

3. One survey of elderly American parents found that most thought they were entitled to have their health care needs provided by government or private insurance, while only about 10% believed that adult children should provide financial assistance. *See* Alvin Schorr, "Honor Thy Father and Thy Mother . . .": A Second Look at Filial Responsibility and Family Policy 12 (U.S. Dept. of Health & Human Serv., Pub. No. 3–11953 (1980)). But when Singapore recently enacted a law requiring adult children to support their parents, many parents filed suit. *See* Peter Waldman, *In Singapore, Mother of All Lawsuits Is Often Filed by Mom*, Wall Street Journal, Sept. 17, 1996, at A1 col. 4. What facts might explain these two results?

4. Is it fair to require a child who makes social security contributions to reimburse the state for public benefits provided a needy parent? If yes, should there be exceptions? Would the facts of *Cannon* qualify as an exception? Why or why not?

SECTION 4. SUPPORT IN THE SEPARATED FAMILY

A. FROM DISCRETION TO BRIGHT-LINE RULES

UNIFORM MARRIAGE AND DIVORCE ACT § 309

9A U.L.A. 400 (1987).

In a proceeding for dissolution of marriage, legal separation, maintenance, or child support, the court may order either or both parents owing a duty of support to a child of the marriage to pay an amount reasonable or necessary for his support, without regard to marital misconduct, after considering all relevant factors including:

(1) the financial resources of the child; (2) the financial resources of the custodial parent; (3) the standard of living the child would have enjoyed had the marriage not been dissolved; (4) the physical and emotional condition of the child, and his educational needs; and (5) the financial resources and needs of the noncustodial parent.

The UMDA reflects the traditional, highly discretionary approach to determining the value of child support. Under this approach, the support statute sets out factors relevant to the support determination; the court applies those factors and determines the amount of support to be paid.

While the discretionary approach survives intact in alimony and property distribution law, discretion is now much more rigidly cabined in child support determinations. The impetus for this shift has come from the federal government. Beginning in the late 1970s the federal government began both to collect national data on child support and to mandate changes in state child support law. This series of initiatives was motivated by a rising tide of single parenting, children's poverty and welfare dependence—the same concerns that motivated the first support laws. It is thus unsurprising that reforms were initiated by the federal government, which today foots most of the bill for welfare payments to children, instead of the states, which have traditionally made child support law.

Like the Poor Laws, the new rules reflect and reinforce public assistance principles. Thus, just as contemporary welfare law has abandoned individualized assessment of merit and need in favor of standardized eligibility criteria and grants, Congress required numerical guidelines to replace discretionary child support decision making. Like earlier child support innovations, the new initiatives also reflect contemporary cultural and economic norms, norms that have shifted dramatically since the nineteenth century. Reflecting the widespread entry of women into the workforce, the new federal requirements apply exclusively to child support, eroding the prior consistency between child and spousal support principles.

When Congress mandated the development of numerical support guidelines in the mid 1980s, it specified that they:

1) Take into consideration all earnings and income of the absent parent;

2) Be based on specific descriptive and numeric criteria and result in a computation of the support obligation; and

3) Provide for the children's health care needs, through health insurance or other means . . . 45 C.F.R. § 302.56.

But Congress did not specify a particular formula or model. As a result, each state was left to make its own decisions on the values that would guide the development of child support policy and how they would be implemented.

NATIONAL CENTER FOR STATE COURTS, DEVELOPMENT OF GUIDELINES FOR CHILD SUPPORT ORDERS: ADVISORY PANEL RECOMMENDATIONS AND FINAL REPORT

1–3, 4 (September 1987).

In November 1983, the House Ways and Means Committee requested that OCSE establish a national Advisory Panel on Child Support Guidelines and that the project report " . . . include a full and complete summary of the [Advisory Panel's] opinions and recommendations." The Congressional request specified a balanced composition for the Advisory Panel consisting of judicial, legislative, and child support enforcement officials; representatives of custodial and non-custodial parents; a legal scholar; and an economist. . . . [T]he Advisory Panel has prepared recommendations for the development of child support guidelines. . . . :

(1) Both parents share legal responsibility for supporting their children. The economic responsibility should be divided in proportion to their available income.

(2) The subsistence needs of each parent should be taken into account in setting child support, but in virtually no event should the child support obligation be set at zero.

(3) Child support must cover a child's basic needs as a first priority, but, to the extent either parent enjoys a higher than subsistence level standard of living, the child is entitled to share the benefit of that improved standard.

(4) Each child of a given parent has an equal right to share in that parents income, subject to factors such as age of the child, income of

each parent, income of current spouses, and the presence of other dependents.

(5) Each child is entitled to determination of support without respect to the marital status of the parents at the time of the child's birth. Consequently, any guideline should be equally applicable to determining child support related to paternity determinations, separations, and divorces.

(6) Application of a guideline should be sexually non-discriminatory. Specifically, it should be applied without regard to the gender of the custodial parent.

(7) A guideline should not create extraneous negative effects on the major life decisions of either parent. In particular, the guideline should avoid creating economic disincentives for remarriage or labor force participation.

(8) A guideline should encourage the involvement of both parents in the child's upbringing. It should take into account the financial support provided directly by parents in shared physical custody or extended visitation arrangements, recognizing that even a fifty percent sharing of physical custody does not necessarily obviate the child support obligation.

How should these various goals be ordered and effectuated? At the time state legislatures were debating guideline models, three basic approaches garnered the most attention:

1) *Continuity of expenditure*: This approach seeks to ensure that the child receives the same proportion of total parental income that he or she would have received if the parents lived together. It relies on estimates of typical child-related outlay in intact families at different income levels to derive support percentages (calculated either on the basis of gross or net income), which is then prorated between the parents.

2) *Equal outcomes*: This approach (sometimes referred to as a "share the suffering" approach) seeks to ensure that each household in the separated family has the same living standard. It relies on a "household equivalence scale" to calculate the percentage of total family income needed by each family; the value of child support is the noncustodial parent's "excess" income.

3) *Basic needs*: This approach focuses on ensuring that the child's basic needs, calculated from a minimal needs assessment such as the federal poverty thresholds or foster care reimbursement rates, are met. A needs standard, that does not vary by parental income level, is established and child support calculated on that basis. After the support need is established, it is prorated on the basis of parental income.

No one seriously advocated that guidelines should attempt to *maintain* the child's standard of living. Although traditional, discretionary child support standards typically listed "the standard of living the child would have enjoyed had the marriage not been dissolved" (UMDA § 309) as a factor to be considered in determining child support, actual support awards almost invariably fell far short of what would be required to maintain the child's standard of living. One reason for this result is simply that two households cannot live as cheaply as one; thus the federal poverty level for a family of three is approximately 50% less than that of a family of one and a family of two. U.S. DEP'T OF COMMERCE, BUREAU OF THE CENSUS, STATISTICAL ABSTRACT OF THE UNITED STATES 1995 481 tbl. 746. Divorce or separation ensures that some portion of the divided family must experience a living standard loss. Because mothers typically earn less than fathers and obtain custody of the children 80–90% of the time, very large support transfers would typically be required to maintain the children's predivorce living standard.

To use an extreme example, consider the case of Mr. and Mrs. A, who have six minor children and an annual income of $30,000, all earned by Mr. A. If Mrs. A assumes sole custody of the children post-divorce and continues to earn no income, ensuring that the children suffer no living standard loss would require a transfer of $26,763, or 89% of Mr. A's income, leaving him with only $3237 to meet his own needs![1] A law requiring transfers of this magnitude would produce several practical problems. One is enforcement. Researchers report, not surprisingly, that higher support obligations tend to produce a lower percentage of support paid. Even if Mr. A could somehow be forced to pay up, his incentive to keep earning $30,000 per year would be small; why should he work hard to retain only 10%, or even 25%, of his income? Because high support obligations produce significant payment and work disincentives, it is probably unfeasible, in a case like that of the A's, to maintain the child's former standard of living.

In choosing a guideline model, states thus had to address practical concerns as well as issues of fairness. States also had to make a decision on the choice of a guideline model quickly. When Congress mandated advisory support guidelines in 1984, it required states to have mandatory guidelines in place by October 1989 or risk losing federal reimbursement for public assistance benefits to needy children. When the deadline passed, three states had adopted basic needs guidelines and all others had adopted guidelines utilizing the continuity-of-expenditure approach. The continuity-of-expenditure guidelines states have adopted fall into two categories: the "percentage-of-obligor income" model and the "income shares" model. Only one basic needs guideline has been adopted, the so-called "Delaware Melson formula."

1. The support obligation is calculated using "household equivalence scale" contained in the U.S. Bureau of Labor Standards moderate income budgets. For more on household equivalence scales, *see* Burt Barnow, *Economic Studies of Expenditures on Children and Their Relationship to Child Support Guidelines*, at p. 888.

ROBERT WILLIAMS, AN OVERVIEW OF CHILD SUPPORT GUIDELINES IN THE UNITED STATES

IN CHILD SUPPORT GUIDELINES: THE NEXT GENERATION 5–7 (MARGARET CAMPBELL HAYNES ED. 1994).

1. PERCENTAGE-OF-OBLIGOR-INCOME MODEL

The simplest guidelines model determines child support based on a percentage of the obligor's income and number of children. The percentage can be based on either gross income or net (after-tax) income. Perhaps the most well-known guideline of this type is the Wisconsin Percentage of Income Standard, which sets child support based on the following proportions of *gross* income:

One child	17 percent
Two children	25 percent
Three children	29 percent
Four children	31 percent
Five or more children	34 percent

Unlike most other percentage-of-obligor-income models, the Wisconsin Standard includes adjustments for shared and split custody arrangements, as well as serial households.

Minnesota has one of the more prominent examples of a percentage model based on *net* obligor income. Minnesota was the first state to have legislatively established presumptive child support guidelines, which were enacted in 1983. At net income levels above $1,001 per month, these guidelines set child support based on the following percentages of net obligor income:

One child	25 percent
Two children	30 percent
Three children	35 percent
Four children	39 percent
Five children	43 percent
Six children	47 percent
Seven children	50 percent

The child support percentages are lower for obligors with less income. For example, for those with net income of $401–500 per month, the percentage for one child is 14 percent. Minnesota sets a ceiling of $4,000 per month, above which child support is presumptively capped at the same amount as for income of $4,000. Like most other states with percentage models, Minnesota does not have special adjustments for child care, children's extraordinary medical expenses, shared or split custody, or additional dependents.

2. INCOME SHARES MODEL

The Income Shares model is based on the concept that the child should receive the same proportion of parental income that he or she would have received if the parents lived together. A basic child support obligation is computed based on the combined income of the parents (replicating total income in an intact household). This basic obligation comes from a table which is derived from economic estimates of child-rearing expenditures, minus average amounts for health insurance, child care, and child's extraordinary medical expenses. The basic child support obligation is divided between the parents in proportion to their relative incomes. Pro-rated shares of child care and extraordinary medical expenses are added to each parents's basic obligation. If one parent has custody, the amount calculated for that parent is presumed to be spent directly on the child. For the noncustodial parent, the calculated amount establishes the level of child support.

The Income Shares model has been specified in both net and gross income versions, which are designed to yield approximately equivalent results. In some states, the Income Shares model includes separate adjustments for shared physical custody, split custody, and additional dependents. A small number of states with this model also have adjustments for children's educational expenses and visitation-related transportation expenses.[2]

The Income Shares model was developed by the staff of the Child Support Guidelines Project, which was funded by the U.S. Office of Child Support Enforcement and administered by the National Center for State Courts. It utilizes several concepts from the earlier Washington (State) Uniform Child Support Guidelines, but diverges in basing its numerical parameters explicitly on a different and more recent body of economic analysis.

3. Delaware Melson Formula

Initially developed by Judge Elwood F. Melson, Jr. for use in his own courtroom, the Melson formula has been in use statewide in Delaware since 1979, under authority of the Family Court. It was the first presumptive child support standard to be used statewide, predating the Minnesota guidelines by fourteen years.

2. Ed. Note: The Income Shares Guideline requires use of a support table like this one:

Age-Adjusted Child Support for One Child as a Proportion of Net Income*

Ages of Children	$ 0– 5,600	5,601– 10,650	10,651– 16,725	16,726– 28,200	28,201– 39,975	39,976– 51,875	Over 51,875
0–11	22.1	21.9	21.6	20.0	19.5	18.6	16.5
12–17	27.3	27.1	26.7	24.7	24.1	23.0	20.4

After the correct support value has been determined, using the table, it is prorated based on the proportion of total income earned by each parent. For example, if Father's net income is $20,000 per year and Mother's $10,000 and they have one child, age 5, child support would equal 19.5% of $30,000, or $5,850. If Father assumed custody, Mother would pay 33% of that value, or $1,930 per year.

* From Robert G. Williams, Development of Guidelines for Child Support (U.S. Dept. of Health & Human Services Office of Child Support Enforcement (1987) II–78, tbl. 16).

The basic application of the Melson formula can be described as follows:

> *Step 1: Provide for Each Parent's Minimal Self Support Needs.* After determining net income for each parent, a self-support reserve ("primary support allowance") is subtracted from each parent's income. This reserve, currently $550 per month in Delaware, represents the minimum amount required for an adult to meet his or her own subsistence requirements.
>
> *Step 2: Provide for Children's Primary Support Needs.* After determining the amount of each parent's income needed for self-support, remaining income is applied first to the primary support needs of the children, in proportion to the parents' relative incomes. Like the self-support reserve, the primary support amount represents the minimum amount required to maintain a child at a subsistence level. In Delaware, it is currently set at $220 per month for the first child, $165 per month for each of the second and third children and $110 per month for each additional child. Actual costs of work related child care and extraordinary medical expenses are added to the primary support needs of the children.
>
> *Step 3: Determine Standard of Living Allowance (SOLA).* To the extent that the parents have any remaining income available after meeting both the parents' and children's primary support needs, the parents(s) contribute(s) an additional percentage of income towards child support. The percentages currently used in Delaware for the standard of living allowance are: 18 percent for one child, 27 percent for two children, 35 percent for three children, 40 percent for four children, 45 percent for five children, and 50 percent for six or more children.

A total child support obligation for each parent is determined by adding the amounts calculated in steps 2 and 3. The custodial parent is assumed to spend his or her obligation directly on the child. The noncustodial parent's share is payable as child support.

The Melson formula has an adjustment for equally shared joint physical custody and for additional dependents. As noted above, it does provide separately for child care and children's extraordinary medical expenses.

* * *

The Massachusetts and D.C. guidelines are [hybrid models] primarily based on percentages of obligor gross income. However, custodial parent income is counted in the calculation, and reduces the child support amount, to the extent that gross custodial parent income exceeds $15,000 per year in Massachusetts, or, in the District of Columbia, $16,500 per year if there is one child plus $2,000 per year for each additional child.

* * *

Notes and Questions

1. *Implementation Trends*: As of 1996, thirty-three states utilized an income shares guideline, thirteen utilized a "percentage of income" guideline, and four utilized a Melson-type formula. Linda D. Elrod & Robert G. Spector, *A Review of the Year in Family Law: Children's Issues Take Spotlight*, 29 FAM. L. Q.741, 772 tbl. 3 (1996).

2. *Deviation*: Under federal law all state guidelines must establish a *presumptive* award. 42 U.S.C.A. § 667(b)(2) requires that "[t]here shall be a rebuttable presumption ... that the amount of the award which would result from the application of such guidelines is the correct amount of child support to be awarded. A written finding or specific finding on the record that the application of the guidelines would be unjust or inappropriate in a particular case, as determined under criteria established by the State, shall be sufficient to rebut the presumption in that case." *See also* 45 C.F.R. § 302.56(f). Judges are thus free to depart from the guideline if they make written findings describing the basis for a deviation. Many state guidelines contain lists of factors that might justify deviation, including: the child's special needs, an obligation to support children from prior relationships, a large amount of debt, unusually high living expenses, a needy family member, or substantial expenses incurred in connection with visiting the child (which could occur if the custodial parent lives a significant distance from the obligor). Would you order a deviation from the presumptive award in all such instances? When might you order an amount that is larger than the presumptive amount?

Empirical evidence suggests that judges in some states deviate from the presumptive guideline values frequently. State surveys report deviation in anywhere from 10% to more than 60% of cases. *See* David Arnaudo, *Deviation from State Child Support Guidelines*, IN CHILD SUPPORT GUIDELINES: THE NEXT GENERATION 85, 88–94 (Margaret Campbell Haynes ed. 1994) (describing and summarizing research). Most deviation is downward. *Id.* (88% of deviations downward in Kansas survey; 85% in Washington survey; 80% in Colorado survey). What explains this pattern?

3. *Adjustments*: Many guidelines permit adjustment of the basic award.

a) Child care: While the percentage-of-income model does not typically take child care expenses into account in computing the support obligation, income shares guidelines almost invariably treat work-related child care expenses as a mandatory "add-on" to the basic child support obligation. Under this approach, "reasonable" work-related expenses are typically prorated in accordance with the parents' relative proportion of family income; the obligor's portion is added to his basic support obligation. In 1996, 31 states treated child care expenses as an add-on. *See* Linda Henry Elrod, *Adding to the Basic Support Obligation*, in CHILD SUPPORT GUIDELINES: THE NEXT GENERATION 62–71 (Margaret Campbell Haynes ed. 1994). Significant issues relating to childcare include: (1)

whether to factor in the federal tax credit; (2) whether to include child care expenses related to a job search; (3) whether to limit consideration of such expenses (i.e. define "reasonable" costs); and (4) how to take into account direct expenditures for child care by the noncustodial parent.

b) Extraordinary medical expenses: A growing number of state guidelines (33 in 1996) have special provisions relating to extraordinary medical expenses. Some states treat the existence of such expenses as a factor for deviation from the guidelines; others treat them as an add-on (typically those covered by insurance are excluded). *See* Elrod, *supra*. The primary problem with this sort of adjustment is defining extraordinary. "A few states describe the type of services; others set a dollar amount. A few define the type of service or illness as well as the amount. Others leave it totally to the decision maker's discretion." *Id.* at 64.

c) Health Insurance: Federal regulations require state guidelines to provide for children's health care needs, through health insurance or other means. Based on this mandate, many state guidelines provide a credit to the parent who funds health insurance or provide some method of prorating health insurance costs. 1993 federal legislation requires group insurance plans to honor qualified medical child support orders (a "QMCSO") issued by divorce courts. 29 U.S.C.A. § 1169. For a discussion of such orders, *see* Gary A. Shulman, *Qualified Medical Child Support Orders: The New QDRO for Health Care*, 8 AM. J. FAM. L. 49 (1994).

4. *Constitutionality:* Constitutional challenges to child support guidelines have thus far been unsuccessful. *See, e.g.*, Boris v. Blaisdell, 142 Ill.App.3d 1034, 97 Ill.Dec. 186, 492 N.E.2d 622 (1986); Parents Opposed to Punitive Support v. Gardner, 998 F.2d 764 (9th Cir.1993). But when courts, rather than legislatures, have promulgated guidelines, there is case law holding that guidelines must be consistent with existing law. *See* Fitzgerald v. Fitzgerald, 566 A.2d 719 (D.C.App.1989); Schenek v. Schenek, 161 Ariz. 580, 780 P.2d 413 (Ariz.App.1989).

5. *Case Processing*: Although administrative proceedings are sometimes used to prepare orders for judicial approval (*see* Chastain v. Chastain, 932 S.W.2d 396 (Mo.1996)), American child support orders are still typically made by courts. Internationally, the trend is toward administrative case processing due to its lower cost to government and the individuals involved. Some states have also begun to experiment with administrative processing of child support cases; to date, they have survived constitutional attack. *See* State v. Gocha, 555 N.W.2d 683 (Iowa 1996). The success of administrative case processing may depend on the extent of discretion available and the guideline's complexity. In England, for example, administrative processing using a complicated formula produced a high incidence of miscalculated awards, with resulting public criticism. *See* J. Thomas Oldham, *Lessons from the New English and Australian Child Support Systems*, 29 VAND. J. TRANSNATIONAL L. 691 (1996).

6. *State vs. Federal*: Many experts believe that a federal guideline is needed to ensure uniformity and preclude support forum-shopping:

> The advantage of a federal formula related to the father's ability to pay may be substantial. It would provide uniformity (with appropriate adjustments for local factors) and consequently fairness throughout the country, and it would assure that absent fathers are not asked to pay too little or too much. The latter possibility is of equally crucial importance as the former. The total impact of a support order that is pegged too high may be productive of more mischief than if no support order were entered at all. If a support obligation to a first family is imposed that would make it difficult or impossible for the father to meet his other obligations, the net result may be two families on welfare instead of one. This would produce a greater ultimate cost to the taxpayer in terms of welfare dollars spent than if the taxpayer undertook to take care of the first family, not to speak of the social cost of the disarray that would be caused by breaking up the father's new family.
>
> Harry D. Krause, Review of Part X, Child Support, 92d Cong., 2d Sess., Soc.Sec.Am. of 1972, Committee on Finance, U.S. Senate, H.R. 1 (unpublished consultant's paper, pp. 52–53).

7. Child support guidelines are not a uniquely American phenomenon. But the amount of support sought under various national guidelines varies widely:

> The amount of income sought from absent parents obviously has some relation to the level of public support for single-parent families. In countries with minimal public support programs for such families, like Australia and the United States, the percentage chosen is relatively high. In other countries with more substantial public support programs for such families, such as Denmark or Sweden, the percentage chosen has been lower. For example, a Danish absent parent with an avenge income of about $40,000 pays 4% of his gross income as child support for one child. Similarly, in Sweden the average child support order for one child amounts to about 6% of the obligor's gross income. Germany has adopted a level of support somewhere between the levels sought in Australia and those found in Scandinavia. A German obligor is asked to pay between 10–15% of his net income as child support for two children. Oldham, *supra* note 5, at 711.

Problem 16–1:

Wayne and Hillary have one child, Charles (age 6), and are getting divorced. Hillary will assume sole custody of Charles. Wayne's gross monthly income is $1500 per month; his net monthly income is $1000. Hillary's gross monthly income is $800 per month; her net is $600. Hillary has child care expenses totalling $200 per month. Calculate Wayne's support obligation under: a) the Delaware Melson formula; b) the Wisconsin percentage of income model; c) the Minnesota formula; d) the income shares guideline on p. 860 at note 2.

Problem 16–2:

Assume that Wayne will assume sole custody of Charles and that his child care expenses are identical to Hillary's. Calculate Hillary's child care obligation under: a) the Delaware Melson formula; b) the Wisconsin percentage of income model; c) the Minnesota formula; d) the income shares guideline on p. 860 at note 2.

B. DEFINING INCOME

WILLIAM R.T. v. BONNIE R.T.

Supreme Court of Delaware, 1985.
494 A.2d 150.

CHRISTIE, JUSTICE.

* * * We recognize the obligation to support children as the parent's first priority, and that such an obligation limits a parent's ability to purchase assets or to place himself in debt. However, there is no indication in this case that the husband was unwise or premature in terminating his prior employment, or that he otherwise attempted to arrange his finances so as to avoid child support payments. By contrast, in the *Emsley* case, 467 A.2d at 703, the business expenses which were claimed and disallowed were characterized as "[o]perating losses incurred by (the father) in connection with (his) real estate investments" and, therefore, could not be used to reduce the father's support obligation.

Here the separation agreement specifically provides that the Melson Formula is to be employed to calculate the appropriate child support payments. In that formula the net income of each spouse forms a starting point. The Family Court has adopted a definition of net income for use under such circumstances.

This definition mandates that "business expense accounts" be regarded as income, but only to the extent that such accounts provide benefits which the employee would otherwise have to "provide" for himself. Moreover, the definition goes on to provide that "legitimate business expenses" are to be subtracted from income in calculating net income.

In attempting to arrive at an assumed income figure for husband, the Family Court sought to adjust the income figures contained in his financial statements to make them comparable to the "typical employee" who is employed by an unaffiliated employer. In so doing, the judge noted that the "typical employee" is not allowed to deduct expenses such as "depreciation, amortization, automobile operation and expenses, principal and interest on car payments, interest on home mortgage or other debts." As a result, essential corresponding business-related expenses were not deducted from the husband's gross income in arriving at his assumed net income available for child support calculations.

However, to equate the personal expenses mentioned in the definition with business expenses creates an inequitable result not contemplated by the definition of net income. The attempt to account for the husband's business operations on a basis which would put the husband in the same position as an employee was unsuccessful in this case. "Typical employees" simply do not sustain legitimate and essential business expenses similar to some of those here encountered.

The Superior Court judge recognized that the Family Court, in determining net income in child support matters, is not bound by the Internal Revenue Code. The judge noted that the purposes behind the federal and state tax regulations are not the same as those codified in 13 Del.C. § 501 et seq., pertaining to child support.

The state and federal tax laws seek to reflect the taxpayer's income so that a uniform tax may be assessed. However, the Delaware child support statutes and the Melson Formula are concerned with arriving at a net income figure for each spouse, so that a fair amount of child support may be assessed. The calculations as to support payments may be based, in part, on an equitable evaluation of what is sometimes called "cash flow". In any event, some aspects of the tax laws are designed to encourage the growth in business enterprises, whereas the child support laws are necessarily concerned with the welfare of the children. When the two approaches to net income conflict, the Family Court is free to depart from tax law accounting, but in so doing the court must show that the departure is reasonable and fair and practical under all the circumstances.

Therefore, although the Family Court is not bound by the accounting rules which apply under tax laws, the generally accepted principles of proper accounting may not be disregarded by the courts if the net result is likely to be financial ruin and perhaps the complete lose of earning capacity of the spouse obligated to provide child support. Generally accepted accounting practices and practical economic realities are entitled to more weight than they have received in this case. Only if there are practical reasons to depart from these sound accounting practices, is the court free to make reasonable and equitable adjustments in net income in order to designate a fair amount for child support.

In this case the monthly net income figure arrived at by the Family Court does not accurately reflect husband's true financial circumstances or the practicalities of the situation. At least a part of the husband's disallowed expenses and operating costs appear to be reasonable and also essential to his continuing ability to support himself and his children.

An allowance for depreciation recognizes the fact that the assets of husband's business are worth less each year and eventually must be replaced. Furthermore, in this case much of the capital tied up in the initial investment did not belong to the husband in the first place. The startup costs of his business were apparently a necessary part of his scheme to make a living. More importantly, the principal and interest installments which must be paid each month to the business' former owner, represent cash payments which the husband simply does not have available except from his business. It is unsound to consider the cash coming into the husband's business as flowing through to net income without deducting (to the extent that they are reasonable) the items which must be taken from his cash flow in order to maintain his business operation.

Examination of the practical effect of the Family Court's ruling leads this Court to rule that there must be a recalculation of his assumed net income available for child support and of the payment required in the support order.

It is, of course, true that as husband pays off his five-year loan, he may be able to continue to build equity for himself in his business while at the same time he may have limited funds to pay child support. This growing equity may not be fully reflected in the funds which are now deemed to be available for child support and, therefore, it is not entirely inaccurate to picture the husband as diverting money from his children while he is building up his own assets. However, it would not be in the best interest of the minor children to run a substantial risk of destroying the business at this point. If the business does prosper, the husband's net income is likely to increase; this in turn may ultimately be of future benefit to his family. The child support payments he is now required to make must, however, be based on current economic realities.

We reverse the order of Superior Court affirming the Family Court, and we remand the case to Superior Court for further remand to Family Court for a reasonable, fair, and practical recalculation of the amount of child support the husband is required to pay based on a recalculation of the husband's net income in accord with the terms of the Melson Formula. Such recalculation should take present circumstances into account as to future child support. It should also arrive at fair amounts of child support for the various past time periods involved since it is clear that husband's income (and also any assumed income the court may designate) varied during the periods in question.

Notes and Questions

1. As *William R.T.* suggests, guideline definitions of "income" and "net income" are not necessarily consistent with tax law definitions. Courts have generally held that deductibility for tax purposes does not require deductibility for child support purposes. *See e.g.*, Turner v. Turner, 586 A.2d 1182 (Del.1991); In re Sullivan, 243 Mont. 292, 794 P.2d 687 (1990). Should tax law and child support law employ consistent definitions of income and expenses? Why?

2. Should a parent's possession of significant, non-income producing assets affect the support obligation? If so, how?

3. State definitions of income and allowable deductions from income vary. *See* Frazer v. Frazer, 23 Va.App. 358, 477 S.E.2d 290 (1996)

(voluntary contributions to pension plans not deductible under guidelines); In re Long, 921 P.2d 67 (Colo.App.1996) (value of in-kind benefits received in lieu of cash should be added to income under guidelines).

4. What are the pros and cons of using gross income as a basis for calculating child support? net income?

5. Should guidelines apply when the noncustodial parent earns much less than the custodial parent? Why? *See* J. Thomas Oldham, *The Appropriate Child Support Award When the Noncustodial Parent Earns Less Than the Custodial Parent*, 31 HOUS. L. REV. 585 (1994).

C. APPLYING THE GUIDELINES: RECURRING SPECIAL CASES

1. *The Rich Obligor*

MCGINLEY v. HERMAN

California Court of Appeals, 1996.
50 Cal.App.4th 936, 57 Cal.Rptr.2d 921.

MASTERSON, ASSOCIATE JUSTICE.

Children are entitled to share in the standard of living of both parents. To this end a presumption exists that the amount of a child support award is determined pursuant to uniform guidelines. However, the presumption may be rebutted if one of the parents has an "extraordinarily high income." In this case, after finding that the father had an extraordinarily high income, the court awarded child support in an amount that did not relate to the father's standard of living in any meaningful way. We find this award to constitute an abuse of discretion. Accordingly, on the mother's appeal asserting that the amount of support awarded from the father was inadequate, we reverse and remand for a new support determination.

In February 1994, Lori McGinley filed a complaint to establish that Stan Herman is the father of her child, born out of wedlock in January 1993, and for child support. In an accompanying income and expense declaration, McGinley stated that she had a monthly net disposable income of $400 and expenses of $7,627 per month. She sought support from Herman, who she claimed to be "one of the most successful real estate agents in the entire Los Angeles area," in an unspecified amount to be established under the uniform child support guidelines.

In response, Herman admitted paternity and agreed to pay "reasonable child support based on the 18 month old minor child's reasonable needs." He declared that, as a real estate investor, he recently suffered substantial losses due to the downturn in the real estate market and the Northridge earthquake. His income and expense statement indicated an "average cash flow deficit of $42,532." Herman submitted evidence, including the declaration of a certified public accountant, in support of this figure. Herman's evidence placed his "living expenses" at $31,457 a month. Herman also disputed several of McGinley's claimed expenses.

In reply, McGinley submitted the declaration of a certified public account who, based on an examination of Herman's business records, concluded that Herman's net worth was over $11 million, that his living expenses were $80,390 per month, and that he had $116,256 "cash available for support" each month. Utilizing the latter figure, the accountant calculated Herman's monthly support obligation under the uniform guidelines at $14,617. McGinley requested support in this amount.

The only evidence taken at trial concerned McGinley's lifestyle. McGinley testified that she did not graduate from high school. She is not employed and is studying to get a real estate license. She owns a house that she rents out and lives with her child in a 600 square foot apartment which is next to a busy highway. McGinley described the expenses she incurs for the child's preschool, swim lessons, and babysitting. She would like to live somewhere with a backyard in which the child can play.

McGinley argued to the court that, under controlling law, her child was entitled to be supported in a manner that reflected the lifestyle of his father. Herman argued that a monthly award of $1,500, with an additional $500 per month into a blocked account for college expenses, would meet the child's present actual needs, especially since he is not yet in school or involved in other activities.

In making its ruling, the trial court stated that it would be "nonsensical" to award McGinley the guidelines amount of child support based on a "casual relationship that result[ed] in the birth of a child." The court stated that a support figure of $2,000 "came to mind, because we have a lot of cases like this. And that's usually been the real limits that I've seen." The court further stated that, "without a specific finding as to the exact amount, [Herman] has an extraordinarily high earning capacity and/or real income." The court also found that McGinley has a net disposable income of zero.

Based on these and other findings discussed *infra*, the trial court awarded monthly child support of $1,750, with an additional $400 per month for one-half of McGinley's child care expenses, for a total of $2,150.

McGinley contends that the trial court abused its discretion in setting an amount of child support that was inadequate. We find that the trial court's discretion was not exercised along legal lines. We therefore reverse and remand for a new support determination

This case is governed by the Statewide Uniform Child Support Guidelines, which took effect in July 1992 as Civil Code §§ 4720 et seq., and are now set forth as Family Code §§ 4050 et seq. (unless otherwise specified all further section references are to the Fam. Code). Under these guideline, the interests of the child are given "top priority."

(§ 4053, subd. (e).) "Children should share in the standard of living of both parents. Child support may therefore appropriately improve the standard of living of the custodial household to improve the lives of the children." (§ 4053, subd. (f).) The guidelines set forth a complex formula for determining child support based on the circumstances of the parents and child. (§ 4055.) The support amount rendered under the guidelines formula "is intended to be presumptively correct in all cases ..." (§ 4053, subd. (k).) This presumption may, however, be rebutted by evidence of various factors, including that [t]he parent being ordered to pay child support has an extraordinarily high income and the amount determined under the formula would exceed the needs of the children." (§ 4057, subd. (b)(3).)

Long before these principles were incorporated into statute, it was well established that "[a] child, legitimate or illegitimate, is entitled to be supported in a style and condition consonant with the position in society of its parents." "The father's duty of support for his children does not end with the furnishing of mere necessities if he is able to afford more."

McGinley places great reliance on two more recent cases that have applied these principles, albeit before the uniform child support guidelines were enacted—*In re Marriage of Catalano* (1988) 204 Cal.App.3d 543, 251 Cal.Rptr. 370 and *In re Marriage of Hubner* (1988) 205 Cal.App.3d 660, 252 Cal.Rptr. 428. In *Catalano,* the mother sought an increase in child support from $475 to $2,000 per month. The trial court increased the amount to $1,110 and both parents appealed. The father was concededly wealthy, owning at least two residences and numerous automobiles, including a Rolls Royce. The mother's lifestyle had been in decline since separation from the father, resulting in the need for her to invade capital.[3] The court observed that "[a] child's 'need' for more than the bare necessities ... varies with the parents' circumstances. Accordingly, where the supporting parent enjoys a lifestyle that far exceeds that of the custodial parent, child support must to some degree reflect the more opulent lifestyle even though this may, as a practical matter, produce a benefit for the custodial parent." The *Catalano* court found that, under the circumstances presented, "the only tolerable award would be the full $2,000 that [the mother] requested. Anything less would ignore the tremendous disparity between [the child's] lifestyle and that of his father."

In *Hubner*, the mother's net disposable monthly income was $1,000 and the father's was over $43,000. The support guidelines then in effect were discretionary and included a statement of "legislative intent that children share in their parents' standard of living." (Former Civ.Code, § 4724, subd. (a).) Pursuant to a schedule developed under these guide-

3. Evidence was presented in this case that Herman had recently purchased (and sold) a Bentley automobile, and that McGinley was invading capital for living expenses.

lines, the mother asked for child support of not less than $6,000 a month.

The trial court awarded $2,215, finding that " 'the child's standard of living must be based on the reasonable lifestyle of both parents ... [I]t would be inappropriate for the court to make an order which was a disguised form of support for the [mother] herself as opposed to support directed merely toward the child.' " *(In re Marriage of Hubner, supra,* 205 Cal.App.3d at 665, 252 Cal.Rptr. 428.) On appeal, the mother argued that the award was inadequate because it was less than half of the discretionary guideline amount. Without stating what a proper support payment would be, the *Hubner* court held that the support award of $2,215 constituted an abuse of discretion. In explaining its holding the court found that, "at least where the ability of the noncustodial parent to pay a high level of child support is undisputed, and that level is also consistent with the guidelines, the inability of the custodial parent to make a meaningful financial contribution should not significantly affect the level of support ordered."

It would be difficult to imagine any greater discrepancy between a mother's and father's assessment of the father's earnings than exists here. Scant evidence was presented. Thus, we must assume that the trial court considered Herman's income to be the amount reflected in the declaration of McGinley's accountant—i.e., $116,256 a month, or just under $1.4 million a year.

The only basis that we can glean from the record for an award amount of $2,150 is the trial court's comment that this figure "came to mind, because we have a lot of cases like this. And that's usually been the real limits that I've seen." As we view the law, reliance on what has "*usually* been the real limits" is the antithesis of how a trial court should approach what is, by statutory definition, an *extraordinary* situation. The reason that the presumptive guideline amount of support may be rebutted by extraordinarily high earning is set forth in the second clause of the statute: "the amount determined under the formula would exceed the needs of the children." (§ 4057, subd.(b)(3).) Thus, rather than relying on the usual, the trial court must at least approximate at what point the support amount calculated under the formula would exceed the children's needs, and therefore at what point the income of the party paying support becomes extraordinarily high.

We think it no more than common sense that a parent who rebuts the guidelines support presumption because of an extraordinarily high income not be permitted to pay less support than a parent whose income is not extraordinarily high. Because of the lack of meaningful findings in this ease, we have no way of ascertaining the level of income which must have been imputed to Herman in order to yield a figure of $2,150 monthly child support under the guidelines formula. What we can say with certainty is that, if this imputed amount of income were less than the level of income that could properly be considered extraordinarily high, the support award of $2,150 would be prima facie inadequate.

We note that the trial court found that its support award was "consistent with the best interest of the child."

Nonetheless, this conclusionary finding falls far short of providing *reasons* why the level of support that the trial court awarded is consistent with the child's interests as required by § 4056, subdivision (a)(3).

As with our conclusion regarding the finding specified in § 4056, subdivision (a)(1), we do not hold that the trial court's failure to comply with subdivision (a)(3) of the statute is necessarily fatal. However, in this case it would appear that the trial court's assessment of the best interests of the child did not give sufficient consideration to the child's right to share in the standard of living of his extraordinarily high earning father. For example, in *In re Marriage of Hubner, supra*, a support award of $2,215 a month was considered so low as to constitute an abuse of discretion in the case of a father whose annual income was in excess of $500,000. In *Estevez v. Superior Court*, 22 Cal.App.4th 423, 27 Cal.Rptr.2d 470, a monthly support package in excess of $14,000 was provided by a father who conceded that his gross income was over $1.4 million a year.

Utilizing *Hubner* as our guidepost, it is clear that the child support award in this case constituted an abuse of discretion. We will not, however, fathom a guess as to the dollar amounts that define the parameters of this discretion. A proper exercise of discretion in this case would require a statement of the reason(s) why a given amount of support awarded would meet the needs of Herman and McGinley's child. It is not enough to simply say that, because the presumption of the guidelines has been rebutted, the "usual" amount of support should be awarded. Moreover, a satisfactory reason for determining that a support award would be adequate requires at least an approximation of Herman's net disposable monthly income and of the point at which that income became extraordinarily high. Without these findings, the support award might be set in an amount lower than that required of an ordinarily high earner, thus according Herman an undue advantage from his ability to rebut the guidelines presumption based on his extraordinarily high earnings. We remand the matter to the trial court to reassess McGinley's support request under the appropriate criteria.

The order under review is reversed and the matter is remanded for a new support determination. McGinley to recover costs on appeal.

Notes and Questions

1. The *McGinley* court says that "children are entitled to share in the standard of living of both parents" and that the California guidelines do not apply to all income when the noncustodial parent's income is "extraordinarily high." Are these two statements consistent? Why?

2. The federal Department of Health and Human Services has specified that:

> The [Family Support] Act clearly requires guidelines to be used as a rebuttable presumption in any judicial or administrative proceeding for the award of child support. Therefore . . . *States may not simply exempt an entire category of cases with incomes above or below a specific dollar level from application of the guidelines.* 56 Fed. Reg. 22343 (May 15, 1991) (emphasis added).

Does *McGinley* comply with the federal standard? How?

3. What factual and policy assumptions underlie a decision that the rich parent owes a smaller percentage of his income in child support? Are those assumptions sound?

4. Assuming that rich parents should pay a smaller percentage of their income in child support than other parents, how should a court calculate the scope of the obligation?

a) In *McGinley*, the custodial mother alleged that the noncustodial father earned $116,000 per month and asked for "only" $14,617 per month, less than 10% of the obligor's gross income. In a case involving the actor Emilio Estevez, the lawyer for the custodial parent agreed that it would be "absurd" to apply the guidelines where the support would have been $35,000 monthly. *See* Estevez v. Superior Court, 22 Cal. App.4th 423, 27 Cal.Rptr.2d 470, 475 n. 6 (1994). Should these plaintiffs have asked for more? Would it be unreasonable, if the court accepted the evidence submitted that Mr. Herman's monthly living expenses were $80,000, to order monthly child support of $23,000?

b) What expenses are relevant? Should the child support order be fashioned so that the mother could move to a better neighborhood? If so, how much better, and to why type of home—a two bedroom apartment or a nice house? What about private school? a horse? psychotherapy?

c) The *McGinley* trial court initially awarded $2,215 per month, based on a finding that "it would be inappropriate for the court to make an order which was a disguised form of support for the [mother] herself as opposed to support directed merely toward the child." On remand, may the court take benefits conferred on the custodial parent into account? Should such benefits be relevant?

d) The trial court noted the "casual relationship" between the parties as another basis for its award. On remand, may the court take the nature of the relationship into account? Should the type (marital, nonmarital) and duration of the parents' relationship be relevant to relevant the support obligation?

e) If, on remand, the court finds that Herman's net income is negative, but that he owns substantial assets, what should the court do?

Assume that you are the trial court judge to whom the *McGinley* case is remanded and that you find the mother's allegations regarding the father's income and expenses are accurate. What child support will you order? How will you justify your decision?

5. Not all courts have agreed with the *McGinley* approach. For example, in Marriage of Bush, 191 Ill.App.3d 249, 138 Ill.Dec. 423, 547 N.E.2d 590 (1989) the trial court ordered the obligor to pay 20% of his net monthly income of $13,000 in child support for one child. The appellate court held that the award constituted an abuse of discretion given the custodial parent's significant income and the lack of any special needs on the part of the child. On remand, the court ordered the obligor to pay $800 monthly. *See* Marriage of Bush, No. 86D–656 (McClean County Circuit Court 1990).

6. Some high-income obligors, such as athletes, performers, and musicians, tend to have short-lived careers. Can (and should) the court fashion an award that takes account of the possibility of a future income decline? If yes, should the court order payments to a trust for the child on top of payments for current living expenses? *See* In re Paternity of Tukker M.O., 189 Wis.2d 440, 525 N.W.2d 793 (Wis.App.1994).

7. In Australia, which employs a percentage-of-income type support guideline, obligor income in excess of 250% of the average earnings for Australian employees is ignored. What are the pros and cons of this approach as compared to that in *McGinley*? In Texas, child support may not be ordered in an amount higher than the guideline value for an obligor with a $6,000 per month income unless the child has additional "proven needs." TEX. FAM. CODE § 154.126. What are the pros and cons of these approaches as compared to that in *McGinley*?

2. *The Poor Support Obligor*

If a special approach is warranted for a high-income obligor, is one also warranted for the low-income support obligor? No consensus has yet evolved on this issue. The percentage-of-income model applies at all income levels without variation; low-income obligors are not granted special treatment. By contrast, the Melson formula provides a "self-support reserve" based on the federal poverty guidelines for a one-person household; if the support obligor's income falls below the reserve value, the guideline support values do not apply. The original income shares model developed under contract with the federal Office of Child Support Enforcement also features a self-support reserve, and many states with income shares guidelines maintain this approach. *See* Robert G. Williams, *Guidelines for Setting Levels of Child Support*, 21 FAM. L.Q. 281, 305, tbl. 4 (1987). *See also* J. Thomas Oldham, *Lessons from the New English and Australian Child Support Systems,* 29 VAND. J. TRANSNATIONAL L. 691 (1996) (noting that English and Australian support formulae provide for a self-support reserve).

In states where the guideline values do not apply to low-income parents, three basic approaches have been utilized:

> Under one approach, in cases of extremely low income, that is, where income is below the poverty level, the guidelines will presume that an award of $50 per month per child is the appropriate award; as in any other case, the appropriateness of this award can be

rebutted downward. When this method is used in a percentage of income state, for example Tennessee or Texas, the $50 is not stated; rather, the support is calculated by means of the percentage formula.

The Delaware guidelines states the rationale for the first approach:

The judiciary amended the Delaware Child Support Formula to enunciate a minimum monthly support obligation of not less than $50 per child. This amount was selected based on the $50 "disregard" that exists under federal law. Regardless of the support order that is entered, when a family is on AFDC the first $50 in child support paid by the support obligor is passed through to the family. [The $50 "pass-through" has now been repealed.] Therefore, at a very minimum, a noncustodial parent should be required to pay that amount of support which would directly benefit the children, without regard to reimbursement of state and federal costs of welfare. As with the entire formula, it is inappropriate to treat AFDC IV–D, Non–Public Assistance (NPA) IV–D, and Non–IV–D cases differently. As a statewide formula developed and adopted by the Family Court Judiciary, it must be generally applicable to all child support matters coming before the Court.

Under the second approach, an absolute mandatory minimum award, usually $20 to $50, must be made. There can be no downward deviation from this absolute minimum award.

The Rhode Island Guidelines state the rationale for a minimum award:

For obligors with a combined adjusted gross income of less than $500 per month the Guideline support obligation charts are not used, and the Guidelines provide a case-by-case determination of child support (normally within the range of $20 to $50). In such cases, the Court should carefully review the obligor's income and living expenses to determine the maximum amount of child support that can reasonably be ordered without denying the obligor the means of self support at a minimum subsistence level. A specific amount of child support should always be ordered, however, no matter how minimal, to establish the principle of that parent's obligation to provide monetary support to the child.

Under the third approach, the amount of support is left to the discretion of the judge, without any presumptive amount stated.

Laura Morgan, *Child Support and the Anomalous Cases of the High–Income and Low–Income Parent,* 13 Can. J. Fam. L. 161 (1996).

California has adopted yet another approach:

In all cases in which the net disposal income per month of the obligor is less than one thousand dollars ($1,000), the court shall rule on whether a low-income adjustment shall be made. The ruling shall be based on the facts presented to the court, the principles provided in § 4053, and the impact of the contemplated adjustment on the respective net incomes of the obligor and the obligee. Where the court has ruled that a low-income adjustment shall be made, the child support amount otherwise determined under this section shall be reduced by an amount that is no greater than the amount calculated by multiplying the child support amount otherwise determined under this section by a fraction, the numerator of which is 1,000 minus the obligor's net disposable income per month, and the denominator of which is 1,000. If a low-income adjustment is allowed, the court shall state the reasons supporting the adjustment in writing or on the record and shall document the amount of the adjustment and the underlying facts and circumstances.

CAL. FAM. CODE § 4055(7).

One court recently held that, given the federal mandate that states adopt guidelines establishing a *rebuttable* presumption as to the support award, an *absolute* mandatory minimum child support obligation is invalid under the Supremacy Clause. *See* Yeager v. Gilbert, 23 Fam. L. Rep. (BNA) 1585 (Wash. App. 1997).

Notes and Questions

1. Under traditional discretionary child support principles, the available evidence suggests that support awards were regressive, with low-income parents typically paying a significantly higher proportion of their incomes in child support than high-income parents. *See* LENORE J. WEITZMAN, THE DIVORCE REVOLUTION: THE UNEXPECTED SOCIAL AND ECONOMIC CONSEQUENCES FOR WOMEN AND CHILDREN IN AMERICA 462–69 (1985) (California); Marsha Garrison, *Good Intentions Gone Awry: The Impact of New York's Equitable Distribution Law on Divorce Outcomes,* 57 BROOKLYN L.REV. 621, 718 tbl. 53 (1991) (New York); James B. McLindon, *Separate But Unequal: The Economic Disaster of Divorce for Women and Children*, 21 FAM. L.Q. 351, 371–72 (1987) (Connecticut).

Both the Delaware Melson and income-shares model produce regressive results *except* for obligors with incomes below the "self-support" reserve, where both produce much lower rates for below-poverty-level obligors. Under the percentage-of-income model, obligors at all income levels presumptively pay the same percentage of income in child support. What are the pros and cons of each approach?

2. A self-support reserve is inconsistent with the aim of a continuity of expenditure approach, as poor parents in intact families share income with their children to at least the same extent as do wealthier parents. Some studies have found that parents spend approximately the same percentage of household income on their children at all income levels. Others have found that poor parents spend more on their children than their wealthier counterparts. *See, e.g.*, THOMAS ESPENSHADE, INVESTING IN CHILDREN: NEW ESTIMATES OF PARENTAL EXPENDITURES (1984) (finding that poor parents spent 26% of their income on one child, while parents with significantly higher incomes spent 15.2%). It is for this reason that

percentage-of-obligor income guidelines provide for no deviation in the case of low-income parents. *See* Irwin Garfinkel, Assuring Child Support 134 (1992) ("No research suggests that ... the poor spend a smaller proportion of income on their children than middle-income fathers. Indeed, the evidence suggests either that the proportions are about the same or that the poor actually spend a slightly higher percentage.") Given its inconsistency with tradition, the economic research, and the goals of the continuity of expenditure, why would policymakers adopt a policy that imposes low support obligations on poor support obligors?

3. *Joint and Split Custody; "Extra" Visitation*

Guidelines are drafted with the "normal" custody situation, where one parent is the primary caretaker and the other has sporadic access, in mind. Is a different approach needed in other situations?

BAST v. ROSSOFF

New York Supreme Court, 1995.
167 Misc.2d 749, 635 N.Y.S.2d 453.

Friedman, Justice.

This case raises the question of how much child support should be paid when there is "shared" or "joint physical" custody. A review of the New York decisions on the subject reveals that their stated analyses neither answer the question nor provide any guidance. This opinion, therefore, seeks to discern whether there is a rule which should be applied to joint physical custody cases. The court concludes that the application of the Child Support Standards Act percentages is inappropriate in cases of shared physical custody.

These parties were married in September 1986. Their child, Morton Elizabeth, was born March 15, 1989. The parties separated in July 1990. In February 1992, the custody and visitation issues were resolved by stipulation before a justice of the court. The parties agreed that they would have joint custodial decision making. There was also a "shared time allocation." Plaintiff ("Father") is to have his daughter with him from Wednesday evening to Sunday evening during alternate weeks and from Wednesday evening to Thursday morning during the other week. There is no pre-set schedule for vacations; the parties deal with that issue on an ad hoc basis.

* * *

Pursuant to federal mandate every state has adopted child support standards. Yet, the child support statutes of the states show substantial variation in their application to shared custody. Some states have adopted a formula to reduce child support by the time the child spends with the "non custodial" parent once a certain threshold is reached. For example in Colorado the threshold is 92 overnights (Colo.Rev.St. § 14–10–115[8]). Once that 25% threshold is reached there is a pro rata reduction in support by the amount of time spent with the "noncustodial" parent. In California under the current statute there is a complex formula in which the percentage of visitation with each parent is a factor in the amount of support in all cases (Cal.Civ.Code § 4055). Some states have no mechanical formulation but allow adjustments to the support standard amount based on the spending of "substantial amount of the time" with the other parent (see, e.g., Fla.Stat.Ann. § 61.30[11][g]), although in Florida consecutive visitation in excess of 28 days may give rise to a temporary reduction in child support not to exceed 50% (Fla.Stat.Ann. § 61.30[11][g]). In yet other states, such as Massachusetts (Mass. Child Support Guidelines, Part II–D[1]), the guidelines stated that they "are not applicable" to shared custody. That is,"extraordinary visitation" does not impact the support award.

Each of the formulas used by the other states have infirmities. One of the problems with a "threshold" is that small differences in "visitation" may result in vast differences in support. For example, where there is a 25% threshold, an increase of 10%, in visitation from 20% to 30%, may well result in a 45% reduction in support. One commentator has noted that the complex calculations required by pro rata reductions do not produce an equitable result and are not "fundamentally fair" (Florescue, *CSSA Statutes and Their Effect on Practice*, NYLJ, May 11, 1992, p. 2, col. 6).

A pro rata reduction based on visitation time is not necessarily related to a reduction in the costs of support. The formulas often do not take into consideration the generally accepted fact that shared custody does not reduce the costs in either household but actually increases the total child related costs that must be born by both parents. That is, there is no statutory recognition that shared custody necessitates duplication of costs such as housing and clothing and increases the need for transportation expense so that the total required to be expended for the children is generally in excess of the CSSA mandated percentage of the joint income. These increased costs has led one researcher to conclude that joint custody is workable for parties with joint income "in the upper-middle income brackets" but is "out of range for couples with modest income." (Reichler, New York Child Support Manual [1993], 35–3, 35–7). For that reason states such as Colorado increase the basic child support computed under the regular percentage formula by an additional 50% to reflect the increased total costs caused by duplication, before applying the percentage reduction for time in excess of 92 overnights (Colo.Rev.St. § 14–10–115[10][c]).

New York has no similar adjustment built into its CSSA.

Father here argues that the court should apportion the statutory child support by the amount of time he spends with the child. But that approach, of necessity, produces a result that is unjust and inappropriate. If either parent is treated as the primary custodial and a pro rata reduction is applied to support, without consideration of the factors that affect actual costs, the parent receiving support will not be receiving the child support which the Legislature determined to be required. On the other hand this court cannot rationally apply the CSSA basic support percentage to Father's income and require that amount to be paid to Mother, since no doubt, Father incurs substantial expenses during his parenting time. Also the court cannot merely reduce the support to Mother by the percentage of time Father spends with the child. Indeed even a mechanical reduction in support is far from simple. The calculation of the percentage of time spent by each party is not simple. The parties cannot agree on the computation of the percentage of the time Husband is allocated. Father counts Sundays as a "day" for him. He concludes that he has 42.9% of the days. Mother, counting overnights only, allocates 36% of the year to Father. Both computations ignore the time spent during vacations. Without doubt, Father's time with Morton is greater than the "traditional" arrangement of a Wednesday visit and alternate weekends, which works out either to 28.4% or 14.2% of the time depending on whether Wednesday is a sleep over. Also, that does not factor in vacation.... Many other states' statutes use overnights as an objective measurement.

In the vast majority of states, including New York, the "income shares" model of child support was adopted as the theoretical underpinning of the CSSA. That is, child support is determined by the sharing of total support based on the income of each of the parties. Yet the application of a proportional offset reduction, even at a 35% threshold, is clearly unjust and inappropriate. The Income Shares Model uses a proportional offset method (*see* U.S. DEPT. OF HEALTH & HUMAN SERVICE OFFICE OF CHILD SUPPORT ENFORCEMENT, DEVELOPMENT OF GUIDELINES FOR CHILD SUPPORT ORDERS II–67 [Sept.1987]). Under that model support is first computed by application of the guidelines to both parents' income; then those amounts are multiplied by the time the child spends in the other parent's house; then the amounts are offset against each other. It was that formula that the Family Court applied in *Matter of Isaac (Clay)*, NYLJ May 23, 1995, p. 31, col. 5 [Fam.Ct. Monroe Co.]. A simple example shows the strange results. If the parents of one child, in a traditional custodial/non-custodial situation earn, after statutory deductions, $30,000 and $50,000, the non-custodial spouse would owe $8,500 in direct child support. Using the proportional offset method results in reducing that amount by 64%, to $3,060, if the "visitation" is 40%. Even a simple pro rata reduction of support by 40% reduces support by $3,400, to $5,100, with no showing that the costs of the spouse with the greater custodial time have been reduced.

The simple conclusion is that the child support percentages in the CSSA make no sense if "adjusted" for extensive "visitation". This court does not conclude that the Legislature intended the court to apply the support percentages blindly. Rather, where there is extensive time sharing the court must look at the totality of the circumstances in both homes rather than rely on the percentages.

Thus, while this court concludes that while the CSSA "applies" to shared custody, it holds that the basic support percentages should not be used in any shared custody case. The threshold for true shared custody varies by state from 25% to 35%; the maximum figure used appears to be 35% of the overnights. This case meets that standard under Mother's or Father's computation.

Based on the proof at trial Father earned $76,876 and Mother, $83,118. Father's efforts to attribute Mother's parents' gifts to her as additional income is rejected as not supported by the evidence. It appears that Father earns 48% of the total income of the parties.

The analysis of the "factors" in DRL § 204[1–b][f] yields the following results. The child has no resources other than those of her parents; the parents have no substantial assets. Morton has no "special needs". The child would have lived in a substantial upper middle income family if the household were not being dissolved. There are no tax consequences of the payment of child support. Both parents would make substantial non-monetary contributions to the care and well being of the child during the time she is with each of them. Both parents spend substantial time with Morton, but she spends a great deal of time with a nanny who travels from house to house with her. Both parents are attorneys and have no educational needs. As noted the income of the parties is roughly equivalent. The expenses Father incurs "in exercising visitation" are not "extraordinary". Nor does the parties' agreement discuss "extended visitation." There are however expenses. for "routine and essential services" which have traditionally been excluded from consideration under DRL § 240[1–b][f][9].

In a shared custody case it is, however reasonable and appropriate to consider the expenses of the child incurred by each of the parties as one of the "any other factors" referred to in DRL § 240[1–b][f][10], in order to find a number that is just and appropriate. Thus, for example, the court is aware that Father purchased a two bedroom apartment which is larger than his own needs warrant so as to provide space for Morton and her clothing. The court has considered the Net Worth Statements of the parties, which reflect their expenses for Morton, as well as the testimony at the trial. Based on the totality of other circumstances the court fixes the child support to be paid by Father to Mother at $750 per month. Further Father is to bear 48% of costs of child care and 48% of the private school and health care costs for Morton.

Notes and Questions

1. The *Bast* opinion outlines the various possible responses to joint physical custody. The "English" approach is to reduce the obligor's child support on a pro rata basis based on the percentage of time the obligor has possession of the child. Why is the *Bast* court critical of this approach? For a general discussion of support calculation when both parents spend substantial time with the child, *see* Marygold S. Melli & Patricia R. Brown, *The Economics of Shared Custody: Developing an Equitable Formula for Dual Residence*, 31 Hous. L. Rev. 543 (1994).

2. Some states utilize the English pro rata reduction concept but first increase the basic child support obligation. *See* Colo. Rev. Stat.

§ 14–10–115 (50% increase); Marriage of Southwell & Spettel, 119 Or.App. 366, 851 P.2d 599 (1993) (same). Australia utilizes a similar approach. *See* Oldham, *infra* note 5. Does this approach satisfactorily address the *Bast* court's concerns?

3. If child support is to be reduced based on the amount of time the child spends with the non-custodial parent, a definition of "time" is needed. In *Southwell* (note 2, *supra*), the primary custodian argued that time should be computed on the basis of *hours*, while the other parent argued it should be computed based on the number of *overnight stays*. The court, based on the relative ease of calculation and the language of the statute, opted for the overnight stay approach.

4. How should child support be computed when there is "split" custody (i.e., where one parent is primary custodian of at least one child)? *See* Sinclair v. Sinclair, 837 S.W.2d 355 (Mo.App.1992); Simpson v. Simpson, 680 So.2d 1085 (Fla.App.1996); UTAH CODE ANN. §§ 78–45–7.7, 78–45–7.8.

5. In England, for children under fourteen, one component of the support award is aimed at compensating the custodial parent for his or her time and possible career damage incurred as a result of child care responsibilities. What are the pros and cons of this approach? How would it apply in a joint custody situation? *See* J. Thomas Oldham, *Lessons from the New English and Australian Child Support Systems*, 29 VAND. TRANS. L. REV. 691, 730 (1996).

6. Arizona, an income shares state, has adopted the following formula to reduce child support based on visitation. What are the pros and cons of this approach?

(ARIZ. REV. STAT. § 25.320) Adjustment for Costs Associated with Visitation

To adjust for the costs of visitation, first determine the total amount of visitation indicated in a court order or parenting plan or by the expectation or historical practice of the parents. Using the following definitions, add together each period of visitation *within twenty-four hours* to arrive at the total number of visitation days per year.

* * *

After determining the total number of visitation days, refer to the following Visitation Table. The left two columns of the Visitation Table set forth numbers of visitation days in increasingly higher ranges. "Reasonable" visitation or visitation consistent with available county visitation/access guidelines will likely fall within the range of days between 72 and 129. Adjacent to each range is an adjustment percentage. The visitation adjustment is calculated as follows: Locate the total number of visitation days per year in the left columns of the Visitation Table and select the adjustment percentage from the adjacent column. Multiply the Basic Child Support Obligation ... by the appropriate adjustment percentage. The number resulting from this multiplication then is *subtracted* from the proportionate share of the Total Child Support Obligation of the parent who exercises visitation.

VISITATION TABLE		
Number of Visitation Days		Adjustment Percentage
0	3	0
4	20	.012
21	38	.031
39	57	.050
58	72	.068
73	129	.187
130	148	.255
149	166	.289
167	180	.323

D. THE DURATION OF CHILD SUPPORT

1. Termination Due to the Child's Age

Traditionally the age of majority in the United States was 21. Over the past two decades, many states have changed the age of majority to 18. This shift has generated a number of child support issues: Should support continue past 18 if the child has not graduated from high school? Should it continue if the child is disabled or unable to support himself? Should it continue if the child had an expectation of parental support in college?

NEUDECKER v. NEUDECKER

Supreme Court of Indiana, 1991.
577 N.E.2d 960.

DICKSON, JUSTICE.

The parties' 1975 dissolution decree determined that Wendy Neudecker should have custody of the two children and ordered Rolland Neudecker to pay weekly child support. Following a hearing upon Wendy's Petition to Modify Support, the trial court substantially increased the support obligation and required Rolland to pay all costs for the older child to attend college for four years following high school. The Court of Appeals affirmed. Rolland's petition for transfer asserts two issues: 1) abuse of discretion in fixing the support obligation; and 2) constitutionality of Ind.Code § 31–1–11.5–12(b)(*l*) which authorizes support orders to include college expenses. . . .

Rolland contends that the Court of Appeals erred in upholding the constitutionality of Ind.Code § 31–1–11.5–12(b)(*l*). He argues that the statute is unconstitutionally vague, that it impermissibly treats unmarried parents and their children differently from married parents and their children, and that it infringes upon his fundamental child-rearing rights.

It is through subsections 12(a) and 12(b) of Indiana Dissolution of Marriage Act, Ind.Code §§ 31–1–11.5–1 to–28, that the legislature has assigned trial courts the discretionary authority to require either or both parents to contribute to a child's education expenses.

> 12(a). In a [divorce] action ... the court may order either parent or both parents to pay any amount reasonable for support of a child, without regard to marital misconduct, after considering all relevant factors including:
>
> (1) The financial resources of the custodial parent;
>
> (2) The standard of living the child would have enjoyed had the marriage not been dissolved or had the separation not been ordered;
>
> (3) The physical or mental condition of the child and the child's educational needs; and
>
> (4) The financial resources and needs of the noncustodial parent.
>
> 12(b). The child support order may also include, where appropriate:
>
> (1) Sums for the child's education in elementary and secondary schools and at institutions of higher learning, taking into account the child's aptitude and ability and the ability of the parent or parents to meet these expenses;
>
> (2) Special medical hospital or dental expenses necessary to serve the best interest of the child; and
>
> (3) Fees mandated under Title IV–D of the federal Social Security Act.

Rejecting the claim of unconstitutional vagueness, the Court of Appeals noted the rules of interpretation that favor construing statutes as constitutional if reasonably possible, found that the statute provides sufficient guidelines for a trial court to exercise its discretion, and observed that parents "seeking to dissolve their marriages are aware that the trial court may, in its discretion, order them to pay for their children's education." *Neudecker,* 566 N.E.2d at 562. We approve of the determination of this issue by the Court of Appeals.

We likewise agree with the disposition of Rolland's claim that equal protection rights are violated because a divorced parent can be ordered to pay for his child's education, while a married parent may unilaterally refuse to do so.

It is true that there is no absolute legal duty on the part of parents to provide a college education for their children. However, common experience teaches that one of the major concerns of most families is that qualified children be encouraged to pursue a college education in a manner consistent with individual family values. The statutory authorization in dissolution cases to order either or both parents to pay sums for their child's education expenses constitutes a reasonable implementation of the child support criteria that the court must consider the standard of living the child would have enjoyed had the marriage not been dissolved. Ind.Code § 31–1–11.5–12(a)(4). This factor is applicable in support modification proceedings, particularly those in which educational expense is an issue.

When an initial support order or its modification is otherwise appropriate, a party seeking to include therein the required payment of college expense must establish by a preponderance of the evidence that such order is reasonable considering the statutory factors in subsections 12(a) and 12(b). In this regard, the "standard of living the child would have enjoyed had the marriage not been dissolved" means whether and to what extent the parents, if still married, would have contributed to the child's college expenses.

In finding a rational relationship between the child support statutory scheme and the state interest in seeing that children of divorced parents are afforded the same opportunities as children of married parents; the Court of Appeals was correct.

* * *

The expenses of college are not unlike those of orthodontia, music lessons, summer camp, and various other optional undertakings within the discretion of married parents but subject to compulsory payment by inclusion in a child support order in the event of dissolution. The statutes which authorize such orders do not infringe upon fundamental child-rearing rights.

The judgment of the trial court is affirmed.

Notes and Questions

1. *The age of majority*: In all states, child support presumptively terminates at the age of majority. In some, the support obligation ends at the earlier of graduation from high school or age 19. *See* Cal. Fam. Code §§ 3900, 3901; S.D. Cod. Laws Ann. § 25–5–18.1. In others, child support ends at age 18, but can continue if the child is still attending high school. *See* Tenn. Code Ann. § 34–11–102; Tex. Fam. Code § 154.001. A few states continue to impose a support obligation to the age of 21. *See, e.g.*, N.Y. Dom. Rel. L. § 240. Many states extend the support duty past the age of majority if the child becomes disabled before reaching majority. *See* Streb v. Streb, 774 P.2d 798 (Alaska 1989); Ariz. Rev. Stat. Ann. § 25–320; Del. Code Ann., tit. 13, § 501; Nelson v. Nelson, 548 A.2d 109 (D.C.App.1988); Mo. Rev. Stat. § 452.340.4; S.C. Code Ann. § 20–7–90; Tex. Fam. Code § 154.001. *But see* Smith v. Smith, 433 Mich. 606, 447 N.W.2d 715 (1989).

2. *Emancipation*: Emancipation—marriage, joining the armed forces, or other voluntary acts by which the child establishes his or her independence from parental control—will also terminate the support obligation. *But see* In re Fetters, 41 Colo.App. 281, 584 P.2d 104 (1978) (annulment of sixteen year old's marriage revived support obligation); Sakovits v. Sakovits, 178 N.J.Super. 623, 429 A.2d 1091 (1981) ("regard-

less of the fact the child may have been formally declared emancipated, the parents *may* in a given case be called upon to contribute to the college education of such child").

3. *Post-majority college support*: Most courts that have considered the issue of post-majority college support have concluded that a divorce court may constitutionally permit a court to order a separated parent to support his child during college if the legislature has so provided. *See* LeClair v. LeClair, 137 N.H. 213, 624 A.2d 1350 (1993); Kujawinski v. Kujawinski, 71 Ill.2d 563, 17 Ill.Dec. 801, 376 N.E.2d 1382 (1978). The Pennsylvania Supreme Court has disagreed, however, finding it unconstitutional to treat children in intact families and separated families differently, for purposes of a parental obligation to support a child in college. In Curtis v. Kline, 542 Pa. 249, 666 A.2d 265, 269 (1995), the court stated that:

> Act 62 classifies young adults according to the marital status of their parents, establishing for one group an action to obtain a benefit enforceable by court order that is not available to the other group. The relevant category under consideration is children in need of funds for a post-secondary education. The Act divides these persons, similarly situated with respect to their need for assistance, into groups according to the marital status of their parents, i.e., children of divorced/separated/never-married parents and children of intact families.
>
> It will not do to argue that this classification is rationally related to the legitimate governmental purpose of obviating difficulties encountered by those in non-intact families who want parental financial assistance for post-secondary education, because such a statement of the governmental purpose assumes the validity of the classification. Recognizing that within the category of young adults in need of financial help to attend college there are some having a parent or parents unwilling to provide such help, the question remains whether the authority of the state may be selectively applied to empower only those from non-intact families to compel such help. We hold that it may not.

4. In most states, there is no statute defining the court's power to award college support. In some, but not all, of these states courts have determined that a judge may order college support in such instances. Rankin v. Bobo, 410 So.2d 1326 (Miss.1982); Thrasher v. Wilburn, 574 So.2d 839 (Ala.Civ.App.1990). The language of the statute is sometimes key. For example, the Washington Supreme Court held that courts had the power to award post-majority support based on the fact that the legislature had amended the support statute to eliminate any reference to the court's power to award support to "minor" children only. Childers v. Childers, 89 Wash.2d 592, 575 P.2d 201 (1978).

5. Even in states that do not permit judges to order support during college, courts may enforce parental agreements. *See* Bruni v. Bruni, 924 S.W.2d 366 (Tex.1996). At least one court has enforced a provision that

gave the obligor the right to "veto" college choices. *See* Jones v. Jones, 19 Va.App. 265, 450 S.E.2d 762 (1994).

6. Most, but not all, child support statutes establish a maximum age for court-ordered support during college. *Compare* OR. REV. STAT. ANN. tit. 11, § 107.108 (limiting college support to students younger than 21) *with* 750 ILL. COMP. STATS. ANN. § 5/513 (referring to the court's power to award support for "college education or professional training," with no age limit). Which is the better approach?

7. While the duty to support a child generally does not hinge on the quality of the parent-child relationship, some courts have taken this factor into account for older adolescents. *See* Hambrick v. Prestwood, 382 So.2d 474 (Miss.1980); McKay v. KcKay, 644 N.E.2d 164 (Ind.App. 1994) (son's repudiation of his relationship with his father terminated divorced father's duty to contribute toward college expenses). *Compare* Roe v. Doe [p. 838]. *But see* Thrasher v. Wilburn, 574 So.2d 839, 841 (Ala.Civ.App.1990) (lack of contact and a "strained relationship" should not bar the right to support).

What other factors are relevant? Should it matter whether the child is a good, average or poor student? if the child has other resources or loans are available? What if the child obtains admission to an expensive Ivy League college and the parent prefers his attendance at a cheaper state university? In calculating the amount of support, should the court assume that the child will work or obtain loans while attending college?

8. In Hoefers v. Jones, 288 N.J.Super. 590, 672 A.2d 1299 (1994) the court decided that requiring a parent to pay tuition at a religious school did not violate the parent's freedom of religion.

2. *Termination Due to the Death of the Obligor*

"[E]vidence of complete freedom of testation can be found only twice in history, viz., in Republican Rome and in England ..." MAX WEBER, LAW IN ECONOMY AND SOCIETY 137 (Max Rheinstein ed. 1954).

WILLIAM BLACKSTONE, COMMENTARIES ON THE LAWS OF ENGLAND, BOOK I

(1765).

Our law has made no provision to prevent the disinheriting of children by will; leaving every man's property in his own disposal, upon a principle of liberty in this, as well as every other, action: though perhaps it had not been amiss, if the parent had been bound to leave them at the least a necessary subsistence. By the custom of London indeed, (which was formerly universal throughout the kingdom) the children of freemen are entitled to one third of their father's effects, to be equally divided among them; of which he cannot deprive them. And, among persons of any rank or fortune, a competence is generally provided for younger children, and the bulk of the estate settled upon the eldest, by the marriage-articles. Heirs also, and children, are favourites of our courts of justice, and cannot be disinherited by any dubious or ambiguous words; there being required the utmost certainty of the testator's intentions to take away the right of an heir.

Except for Louisiana (which follows the civil law approach), all American states maintain the common law approach described by Blackstone; in these states a parent is free to disinherit his child at will.

The U.S. position is quite aberrant. In civil law countries, children are entitled to a "legitime" share of the parent's estate; only where the child has done something shocking (tried to kill the parent, etc.) is the legitime right forfeited. *See* George Pelletier & Michael Sonnenreich, *A Comparative Analysis of Civil Law of Succession*, 11 Villanova L. Rev. 323 (1966). England has now abandoned the common law rule that a decedent may disinherit children; any needy child, whether a minor or adult, may petition the court for reasonable support from the decedent's estate. *See* R. D. Oughton & E.L.G. Tyler, Tyler's Family Provision (2d ed. 1984). The laws of New Zealand and Australia are similar. *See* John DeGroot & Bruce Nickel, Family Provision in Australia and New Zealand (1993). Indeed, it now appears that in the developed world parents have the right to disinherit needy children only the U.S. and parts of Canada. For criticism of the U.S. approach, *see* Deborah A. Batts, *I Didn't Ask to Be Born: The American System of Disinheritance and a Proposal for Change in a System of Protected Inheritance*, 41 Hast. L.J. 1197 (1990); Ralph C. Brashier, *Disinheritance and the Modern Family*, 45 Case W. Res. L. Rev. 83 (1995).

Despite academic criticism and law reform efforts, most states apply the common law approach to child support as well as inheritance. In these states, the death of the obligor terminates all support obligations. A few states take a different approach. *See* 750 Ill. Comp. Stat. § 5/510 (giving the minor a right to petition the court for an amount from the decedent's estate "as equity may require."); UMDA § 316(c) ("Unless otherwise agreed in writing or expressly provided in the decree, provisions for the support of a child are terminated by emancipation of the child but not by the death of a parent obligated to support the child. When a parent obligated to pay support dies, the amount of support may be modified, revoked, or commuted to a lump sum payment, to the extent just and appropriate in the circumstances.")

SECTION 5. EVALUATING CURRENT GUIDELINES

Problem 16–3:

Federal law requires that each state "must review, and revise, if appropriate, . . . [its child support] guidelines . . . at least once every four years to ensure that their application results in the determination of appropriate child support award amounts." 45 C.F.R. § 302.56(e). In compliance with federal law, the legislature plans this year to thoroughly review the state's current guideline, an income shares model. You are counsel to the legislature's Joint Committee on Family Law, and have been asked to advise the Committee on whether the State's current guideline should be revised. The chairperson wants to consider different models for two reasons: First, an national evaluation of state guidelines in effect in 1990 gave this state's guideline a low mark (a C-). DIANE DODSON & JOAN ENTMACHER, REPORT CARD ON STATE CHILD SUPPORT GUIDELINES 24 (Women's Legal Defense Fund 1994). Second, a recent research report showed that, although most (75%) of awards in the state conform to the guideline values, the introduction of the current guideline in 1989 was associated with only a relatively small average increase in the value of support awards (about 15% overall). Read the material that follows and then advise the chairperson on:

A. How the state is doing compared to other states;

B. Whether revision is warranted and why;

C. If revision is warranted, what issues the legislature must confront in redesigning the current guideline;

D. What advantages and disadvantages the various guideline models offer.

A. ACHIEVING CONTINUITY–OF–EXPENDITURE

Although the federal government in enacting the guideline requirement clearly hoped to raise the level of child support awards, continuity-of-expenditure type guidelines, like our state's, do not explicitly attempt to achieve awards higher than those that resulted from discretionary standards. They aim, purely and simply, at achieving parity between the level of child-related expenditure in intact and separated families. Economist Burt Barnow discusses below problems in measuring child-related expenditure and the extent to which the various guideline types have met the parity goal:

BURT BARNOW, ECONOMIC STUDIES OF EXPENDITURES ON CHILDREN AND THEIR RELATIONSHIP TO CHILD SUPPORT GUIDELINES IN CHILD SUPPORT GUIDELINES: THE NEXT GENERATION 18

(Margaret Campbell Haynes ed. 1994).

A. Problems in Estimating Expenditures on Children

If we could directly observe how a family's budget is allocated among its members, determining average expenditures on children would be straightforward. However, over 90 percent of family expenditures are made either on shared goods, such as housing, or privately consumed goods, such as food, that are not easily attributed to a given family member.... What portion of a family's expenses on a shared good such as housing, should be attributed to the family's children? And what portion of a privately consumed good such as a loaf of bread or a bottle of shampoo should be "charged" to each family member? Only in cases where goods are consumed exclusively by adults (e.g., adult clothing or alcohol) or consumed exclusively by children (e.g., children's clothing or toys) is there a reasonable prospect of sorting out on whose behalf the expenditure was made. * * *

... [A]n easy way to "estimate" expenditures on children is simply to divide the total expenditures of the family by the number of individuals in the family and call the quotient "expenditures per family member." This approach, which is usually called either the per capita or average cost estimator ... solves the problem of attempting to determine what portion of a family's shared goods and privately (but co-mingled) consumed goods should be attributed to the children—it simply assigns each family member an equal share of expenditures.... Unfortunately, the per capita (average cost) procedure has little merit. The most obvious problem is that it does not really correspond to expenditures on children. Rather, it *assumes* that the expenditure patterns are known. The other major problem is that the *marginal* (i.e., extra) expenditures on an additional family member are likely to be less than the *average* expenditures on a family member. Up to some limit, an additional family member can be accommodated without buying a larger house or a larger car. Even if additional expenditures on shared goods become necessary because of the addition of one more person, in many cases the incremental (i.e., marginal) expenditures would be less than the per capita (i.e., average) expenditures on the shared good. That is to say, per capita expenditure "estimates" are likely to overestimate the true level of expenditures on children.

B. The General Approach Used to Estimate Expenditures on Children

The inability to observe directly expenditures made on behalf of a child requires that an indirect approach be used to infer how much families spend on their children. To make such inferences, we introduce the concept of "well-being" or what economists refer to as "utility." [The author describes two different methods of comparing the well-being of differently sized households: the "Engel" estimator relies on the assumption that two families that spend the same proportion of their budget on food have the same level of well-being; the "Rothbarth" estimator relies on the assumption that adults in two households that spend the same amount on goods consumed exclusively by adults have equal levels of well-being. Depending on the choice of estimate, percentage-based estimates of child-related expenditure vary widely ranging, for a one-child family from 11% to 33% and for a two child family from 27% to 49% of total family expenditure. The Engel estimator appears to overestimate expenditures on children, while the Rothbarth estimator appears to underestimate expenditures.] A variety of estimators, which are more sophisticated that either the Engel or Rothbarth estimates have been proposed ... [but] they all suffer from shortcomings. The fundamental dilemma remains: the vast majority of a family's expenditures cannot be attributed directly to any one of the family's members. As a result, very strong assumptions must be made before empirical estimates can proceed, no matter which estimator is chosen.

* * *

... [M]any observers have argued that the noncustodial parent should be required to pay what he or she would have contributed to the child if the family were intact. Bassi et al, conducted simulations based on the guidelines in effect in February 1990 to see if the guidelines met this criterion. The simulations were conducted under three different income scenarios, with combined income set at $25,000, $45,000, and $60,000 for families with two children.... [T]he Engel estimator was used as an upper bound on expenditures on children, and the Rothbarth estimator was used as the lower bound. The major conclusions from these simulations are:

- In most instances the state guidelines generate sufficient child support to fall between the upper and lower bounds of the estimates, although the guidelines tend to fall closer to the lower bound.
- A few of the percentage of income and income shares guidelines resulted in support that would not maintain the noncustodial parent's expenditures on the children. For example, under the specific situations simulated, four of 17 percentage of income state guidelines and two of 31 income shares guidelines generated awards below the maintenance level. The three states using the Melson formula always generated awards that meet the criterion.
- In no case did guidelines generate awards that exceeded the upper bound estimate of the amount required to have the noncustodial parent maintain his or her expenditures on the children.

All three types of guidelines currently in use are capable of producing adequate support levels, as we have defined adequacy, and in most cases they do. The specific child support schedule used is far more important in determining the adequacy of support than the type of guideline used. * * * In choosing among alternative guidelines and/or levels of child support awards, it is crucial to recognize that the dissolution of a family results in lost economies of scale, and thus some loss in well-being. If total income remains the same after dissolution, the central issue in setting child support awards is how the decline in the standard of living should be distributed among the affected parties—the child, the custodial parent, and the noncustodial parent.

To determine if a particular guideline is fair, one must first ascertain the standard of fairness that is to be applied. Thus, states should explicitly consider the fairness criteria they would like to attain. The criterion of requiring the noncustodial parent to spend what he or she would have spent if the family had remained intact appears to be a reasonable lower bound, but states should consider other criteria as well. * * *

B. RAISING PRE-GUIDELINE AWARD VALUES:

No state has reported major increases in child support awards following the introduction of child support guidelines. The largest and most detailed study to date compared pre and post-guidelines support outcomes in Hawaii (a Delaware–Melson state), Colorado (an income-shares state), and Illinois (a percentage-of-income state). Only in Hawaii (which had the lowest pre-guideline award levels) of the three research states did all income groups experience significant increases in the level of child support attributable to the introduction of mandatory guidelines; in one state no income group did. Overall, the introduction was associated with an average increase in monthly award values of 5% in Colorado, 16% in Illinois, and 28% in Hawaii (15% overall). The researchers felt, however, that the estimated increase in Illinois was questionable because it was associated with increases in employment and earnings:

> Further analysis of our case data revealed that much of the increase was due to a reduction in zero-dollar awards among families with unemployed noncustodial and female obligors; following adoption of the guidelines, the proportion of cases with unemployed noncustodial parents without support orders dropped 15 percentage points and the proportion of cases with female obligors without support orders dropped 30 percentage points. By contrast, the incidence of zero-dollar awards among families with employed noncustodial and male obligors remained the same. These findings are supported by a study conducted independent of our research in Arizona. The Arizona study found that the overall level of support for shared custody cases increased 15 percent following adoption of the Arizona Income Shares Guideline and the increase was due entirely to a reduction in zero-dollar awards. This, the author concludes that "child support guidelines have the effect of obligating more parents to pay support, but the level of the child support is not increased." * * * Our study [also] reveals that increases in post guideline award level were unequally distributed among income categories. Combining data from all of the state, we found that low-income single-child maternal custody families experienced a 19 percent increase in award levels following adoption of the guidelines, while middle and upper-income families experienced a 7 percent and 13 percent increase, respectively. Despite the greater increase experienced by low-income families, the average post guideline award is still below the estimated costs of raising a child aid is still inadequate to meet the basic needs of children in this income group. For example, the average percentage of obligor income awarded as

support in single-child, maternal custody low-income families following adoption of the guidelines was 21 percent, while the average percentage of family income expended on childrearing in a single-child, intact low-income household is 26 percent. Moreover, an examination of the actual average monthly award in these families reveals a woefully inadequate amount of $151. Thus, we can conclude that guidelines have increased awards in those cases where the need for improvement was most apparent, but they have not provided a panacea for poverty.

Based on our research, not one guideline appears to produce consistently higher or lower awards. The Income Shares Model produced the highest awards with low-income families, the Melson Formula produced the highest awards in middle-income families, and the Percentage of income Approach produced the highest awards in upper-income families.... None of the interstate differences was statistically significant.

Nancy Thoennes et al, *The Impact of Child Support Guidelines on Award Adequacy, Award Variability, and Case Processing Efficiency*, 25 Fam. L.Q. 325, 342–44 (1991).

C. PREVENTING POVERTY AND STANDARD OF LIVING DISPARITY

The national evaluation of state guidelines that gave our state's guideline a C- rated guidelines on several bases: i) their ability to ensure a "minimum decent living standard" (defined as 150% of the federal poverty threshold for a like-sized family); ii) their ability to protect children from poverty; iii) their impact on the comparative living standards of the two halves of the divided household; and iv) their impact on the uniformity of awards. The median state grade was between a C and C-; 27 states received grades of C- or lower. The best grades (and the only straight A's) were obtained by Connecticut (a hybrid guideline state) and Massachusetts. The Massachusetts guideline (also used in the District of Columbia) received, overall an A-; the Melson formula a C+; the percentage-of-income model a C-; and the income shares model a C-. Income shares states showed the greatest grade variation, with grades ranging from A- (Maryland) to F (South Dakota and Utah). More specifically, the researchers found that:

> Even when mothers were employed, if they had low earnings child support award were too low in many states to permit them to achieve a minimum decent living standard for their children. This was true even when their children's fathers had significantly higher earnings and the families would have been middle income if the parents lived together. For example, in typical family 11, the mother earned $6747 as a service worker and the father earned $23,245. Her wages, a tax credit of $307 and the average child support award under state guidelines would give the mother and children an income 1.35 times the poverty level, which is less than the minimum

decent living standard. However, the father's net income would still be more than twice the poverty threshold for a single person ... This average result translates to a less than a decent standard of living for the mother and children in 47 states. Note, however, that in Connecticut, the District of Columbia, Massachusetts and Washington, 1989–90 child support guidelines were sufficient to bring this family to a minimum decent standard of living ...

* * *

... [C]hildren [also] bore a disproportionate share of the economic impact if their parents lived apart. In the dozen typical families in this study, on average the living standard of children declined by 26% and living standards of non-custodial fathers rose by 34% when parents lived apart and child support was paid according to state guidelines. * * * [C]hildren fared best overall under the Massachusetts/District of Columbia model guidelines.... Under this model, on average, children's households suffered just a 27 per cent decrease in living standards while fathers' households enjoyed an 18 per cent increase.... Children's households fared next best, on average, in states with guidelines based on the Delaware model, averaging a 24 percent decline in living standard while fathers enjoyed a 29 percent increase. The two most commonly used guidelines types—the Income Shares and Wisconsin models—had very similar overall impact on children's relative living standard. On average, in states using guidelines based on the Income Shares model, children's households suffered a 26 percent decline in living standards ... and fathers's households enjoyed a 33 percent increase. Children fared similarly under the Wisconsin model, suffering a 27 percent decline in living standard on average while their fathers enjoyed a 35 per cent increase. * * *

... [T]he Massachusetts/D.C. model performed best overall at ensuring children a minimum decent standard of living when parents live apart [and in reducing the disparity in living standards between the children's and noncustodial households]. The Delaware model performed the next best, and the Income Shares and Wisconsin models next

DIANE DODSON & JOAN ENTMACHER, REPORT CARD ON STATE CHILD SUPPORT GUIDELINES 25, 28–31 (Women's Legal Defense Fund 1994).

D. COMPARING THE MODELS

ROBERT WILLIAMS, AN OVERVIEW OF CHILD SUPPORT GUIDELINES IN THE UNITED STATES, IN CHILD SUPPORT GUIDELINES: THE NEXT GENERATION

8 (Margaret Campbell Haynes ed. 1994).

* * * Following development of the Income Shares model in 1985, a majority of states used that approach in the development of their own guidelines. There are several reasons for this trend. First, there was powerful sentiment that guidelines based on income of both parents would be perceived as being more fair than guidelines based only on the obligor's income. Proponents of the percentage model argue that *both* parents are assumed to contribute to a child's upbringing in the same proportion as the obligor. Although this is a strong argument on the theoretical levy, it does not seem to be convincing at the operational level. Without figuring custodial parent income overtly into the calculation, the noncustodial parent perceives that child support is based on noncustodial parent income alone.

Second, there was considerable appeal in having child support guidelines that are based directly on economic estimates of child-rearing expenditures. Although most states have understood that any single source of such data has weaknesses, they prefer that the guidelines be grounded in a credible body of research.

Third, many states perceived that application of the Income Shares model would be more equitable because it considers a broader range of variables. The most important of these are work-related child care expenses and children's extraordinary medical expenses, but the model also provides adjustments for shared and split custody, additional dependents, and other factors.

AMERICAN LAW INSTITUTE, PRINCIPLES OF THE LAW OF FAMILY DISSOLUTION: ANALYSIS AND RECOMMENDATIONS §§ 3.04, 3.05B

(Preliminary Draft No. 7 vol. I, June, 1997).

i) The Equal Living Standard Model [ELS]. The ELS takes the position that the goal of a child support transfer is to ensure that the supported child enjoys a standard of living that is at least equal to that of the nonresidential support obligor parent. Thus the correct measure of the child support transfer is the amount of money that will enable the residential household to enjoy the same standard of living as a higher income nonresidential parent's household. From the perspective of children, given the income distribution of parents generally, this measure is most likely to protect children from poverty and to enable them to enjoy a relatively high standard of living. From the perspective of the nonresidential parent, this measure makes him the guarantor not only of the child's standard of living, but also of the standard of living of the child's other parent. From the perspective of the residential parent, although this model promises a generous measure of support to the residential parent who earns substantially less than the nonresidential parent, the model creates a substantial work disincentive for the residential parent. Effectively, equalization means that a residential parent must share every dollar earned wit the nonresidential parent. Even social commentators who look with favor on this measure of child support conclude that it would diminish the labor force participation of residential parents by approximately one-third. They also suggest that this may not be a bad thing, because reduced residential parent labor force participation would enable residential parents to devote more time to child-rearing.

ii) The Ordinary Marginal Expenditure Model [OME]. The OME model which includes the American guidelines of all but . . . Massachusetts and the District of Columbia, is based on the notion that the proper measure of a child support obligation derives from the marginal amount that parents spend on children in intact families. . . . This model is surely "fair" to the nonresidential parent. It says: As child support, you do not have to pay any more than you would pay on account of the child if you were sharing a household with the child and the residential parent. It is true that you really have no control over how the child support transfer is spent in the residential household and, even with the best intentions on the part of the residential parent, each dollar you pay will be jointly consumed by all members of the residential household . . . Nevertheless, and this is the important point, the *measure* of your basic child support obligation is merely what you would pay on behalf of the child alone for ordinary consumption (the marginal measure) if you were sharing a home with the child. . . . Thus the model does everything possible, short of entirely abolishing the notion of child support, because of its inevitable joint consumption aspects, to ensure that the measure of a nonresidential parent's child support reflects an obligation to support the child, and no one else. * * *

. . . [T]he model both assumes residential parent labor force participation and is highly supportive of it. This is an important virtue. Any system that creates substantial disincentives for labor force participation, even one that is ostensibly benign and generous, operates against the long-term interests of the very persons it seeks to help.

The marginal measure of child support implicitly enforces the norm of residential parent labor force participation without any need for enforcement measures. If the residential parent declines to work, she and her household suffer. There is no need to impute income to her. The model works well with relatively equal income parents. Effectively, it uses the unusual case, equal parental income, as its paradigm and proposes a broad range of possible adjustments of the garden variety unequal income case.

iii) The Enhanced Marginal Expenditure Model (Enhanced Model). The Enhanced Model begins at the other end, treating income inequality between parents and low residential parent earnings as norms, and then specially adjusting for cases in which the residential parent enjoys substantial gainful earnings. It may be understood as a demographically based model. Its starting place is not aspirational, but is instead abased on social and economic realities.

The Enhanced Model basic measure of child support is not as susceptible to easy definition as are the other two models ... It is composed of two parts: a preliminary assessment, expressed as a percentage of obligor income, and a reduction mechanism. The preliminary assessment is the sum of a percentage of income estimate of marginal child expenditure and a percentage supplement. There is no "correct" percentage for this combined percentage, only a set of possibilities ... The preliminary assessment may exceed even per capita expenditure, which would be 33% in a three-person intact family, and thus must be understood as something more than the most generous estimate of child expenditure. As a result, the Massachusetts formula scores at the very top in evaluations of the capacity of state guidelines to keep children out of poverty, to ensure them a decent standard of living, and to enable them to enjoy a standard of living not grossly inferior to that of a higher income nonresidential parent.

The [Model disregards a state-established portion of the custodial parent's income, in Massachusetts the first $1250 gross monthly plus the cost of day care required by employment. Only] income in excess of this amount serves to reduce the nonresidential parent's support obligation.... When the parents have equal incomes, the Enhanced Model reaches precisely the same result as an ordinary income shares model. When the nonresidential parent is the lower income parent, the Enhanced Model imposes a lower child support obligation than would an ordinary marginal expenditures model. Thus, the enhanced model essentially turns the ordinary marginal child expenditure model on its head ... It avoids the need for most ordinary marginal expenditure model equity "adjustments" by assuming the existence of income inequality and the constraints imposed by children on residential parent labor force participation. The Enhanced Model general case is the demographic norm of income inequality and impeded labor force participation for residential parents, not the aspirational ideal of income equality and full employment.

In terms of adequacy for children, simplicity, and connection with economic reality, the Enhanced Model is attractive. Yet it also has some less appealing aspects. First, from the point of view of the higher income nonresidential parent, the Enhanced Model, while clearly not requiring household standard of living equalization, may impose an obligation that exceeds even per capita child expenditures, so the nonresidential parent may be required, as a measure of child support, to contribute to the support of the residential parent as well.... The support obligor may also feel that he is being asked to subsidize the residential parent's qualitative and quantitative choices about labor force participation. The Enhanced Model addresses this issue by allowing the trier of fact to impute income to a residential parent, but only if she is not caring for a child of the parties under the age of 6.... More importantly, even when the income imputation provision may be invoked ... imputation is meaningful only when the residential parent could earn more than the [monthly set aside]. Thus the provision is likely to reach only the relatively rare residential parent who has substantial earning potential but no inclination to work in the market.... Yet this result may be understood as positive from two perspectives. The labor of low earning women may be better spent on their children than at low wage labor, and the opportunity to combine substantial child support with wages from part-time work and vocational education may profit all concerned in the long term.

On the positive side, the operation of the reduction mechanism of the EM formula should not significantly discourage residential parent labor force participation. The income disregard is sufficiently great that many residential parents will become substantially or fully attached to the labor force before there is any reduction in child support. The Massachusetts version of the Enhanced Model is anecdotally reported to enjoy good public acceptance despite its high child support levels because it is generally perceived to be fair. The design of the Massachusetts formula aptly reflects a popular belief ... that as the income of the residential parent rises, the child support obligation of the nonresidential parent should decline. Finally the Enhanced Model is simple to understand and administer, and the amount due is readily translatable into a percentage of obligor income ...

Chapter 17

SEPARATION AGREEMENTS

SECTION 1. NEGOTIATING AND DRAFTING THE AGREEMENT

A. NEGOTIATING A SETTLEMENT

Because litigation is expensive, time-consuming, and sometimes unpredictable, many divorcing couples, either by themselves or through their attorneys, prefer to negotiate a settlement; experts estimate that no more than 10% of all divorce cases go to trial. Marygold S. Melli, Howard S. Erlanger & Elizabeth Chambliss found that:

> * * * [o]ver the last two decades, many studies, ... have found that the predominant mode of dispute resolution is not litigation, but negotiation. Of the 349 files examined in the first phase of our study, only 32 involved a dispute between the parties that had to be settled by a judge. Several commentators have noted that, given findings such as these, to speak of negotiation as "alternative dispute resolution" is nonsensical. Marc Galanter has argued: "On the contemporary American legal scene the negotiation of disputes is not an alternative to litigation ... [I]t is not some marginal peripheral aspect of legal disputing in America; it is the central core * * * Negotiation is not just the typical outcome; it is also the expected mode of dispute resolution in the minds of the parties and their lawyers."
>
> Marygold M. Melli et al., *The Process of Negotiation: An Exploratory Investigation in The Context of No-fault Divorce*, 40 RUTGERS L. REV. 1133, 1142 (1988).

The aim of settlement negotiations is a result acceptable to all parties. This does not mean that the law is unimportant; negotiations take place in the "shadow" of state laws on child custody, visitation, child support, and marital property.

ROBERT MNOOKIN & LEWIS KORNHAUSER, BARGAINING IN THE SHADOW OF THE LAW: THE CASE OF DIVORCE

88 YALE L.J. 950, 986 (1979)*

* * *

Ideally, a bargaining theory would allow us to predict how alternative legal rules would affect negotiations between particular spouses and the deal, if any, they would strike. Such a theory might be combined with knowledge of how the characteristics that determine bargaining behavior are distributed among divorcing couples. Alternative rules and procedures could then be compared by evaluating the patterns of bargains that would result under each. Unfortunately, no existing theory of bargaining allows confident prediction of how different legal rules and procedures would influence outcomes. * * *

What follows is not a complete theory. Instead, we identify five factors that seem to be importance influences or determinants of the outcomes of bargain, and then offer some observations on the bargaining process. The factors are (1) the preferences of the divorcing parents; (2) the bargain endowments created by legal rules that indicate the particular allocation a court will impose if the parties fail to reach agreement; (3) the degree of uncertainty concerning the legal outcome if the parties go to court, which is linked to the parties' attitudes toward risk; (4) transaction costs and the parties' respective abilities to bear them; and (5) strategic behavior.

* * *

If one accepts the proposition that the primary function of the legal system should be to facilitate private ordering and dispute resolution, then several important questions come into sharp focus. To what extent does the participation of lawyers facilitate dispute resolution? Are there fairer and less costly procedures in which lawyers would play a lesser role?

Many observers are very critical of the way some lawyers behave in divorce negotiations. Lawyers may make negotiations more adversarial and painful, and thereby make it more difficult and costly for the spouses to reach agreement. Indeed lawyers may be more likely than lay people to adopt negotiating strategies involving threats and the strategic misrepresentation of their clients' true preferences in the hope of reaching a more favorable settlement for the client. Ivan Illich has suggested that a broad range of illnesses are "iatrogenic": induced and created by medical treatment and the health industry. The same charge might be made against the legal profession. The participation of lawyers in the divorce process may on balance lead to more disputes and higher costs without improving the fairness of outcomes.

Yet, there are also arguments that lawyers facilitate dispute settlement. Lawyers may make negotiations more rational, minimize the number of disputes, discover outcomes preferable to both parties, increase the opportunities for resolution out of court, and ensure that the outcomes reflect the applicable legal norms. Professor Eisenberg has suggested that a pair of lawyers—each acting for his client—may make the process of negotiation very much like adjudication, in which "rules, precedents, and reasoned elaboration * * * may be expected to determine outcomes." When each disputant is represented, the lawyers "are likely to find themselves allied with each other as well as with the disputants, because of their relative emotional detachment, their interest in resolving the dispute, and, in some cases, their shared professional values. Each * * * therefore tends to take on a Janus-like role, facing the other as an advocate of his principal, and facing his principal as an advocate of that which is reasonable in the other's position."

* * * "Because a lawyer is both a personal advisor and a technical expert, each actor-disputant is likely to accept a settlement his lawyer recommends."

In view of the critical role of lawyers and the disparate functions they may perform, it is startling how little we know about how lawyers actually behave. Obviously, lawyers are not all the same. Their styles and talents differ. Some lawyers are known within the profession as negotiators who strive to find middle ground acceptable to both sides; others are fighters who love the courtroom battle. Research could usefully explore how much specialization there is and, more importantly, the extent to which clients, when they are choosing a lawyer at the time of divorce, have any notion at all of their lawyers' skills or preferences for these various roles. More generally, systematic empirical research might illustrate how often, and in what circumstances, lawyers facilitate dispute settlement at the time of divorce, and how often, and in what circumstances, they hinder it.

At the time Mnookin and Kornhauser wrote, there were few studies of lawyer behavior in divorce cases. Recent research on twenty lawyers and their clients revealed that lawyers typically advise their clients to try to settle rather than litigate. *See* AUSTIN SARAT & WILLIAM L.F. FELSTINER, DIVORCE LAWYERS AND THEIR CLIENTS: POWER AND MEANING IN THE LEGAL PROCESS 56, 108–09, 148 (1995):

> While, at least at the outset, many clients think of the legal process as an arena for a full adversarial contest, most divorce disputes are not resolved in this manner . . . Clients often resist the pro-settlement message of their lawyers and deploy various tactics of resistance to keep alive the possibility of contested hearings or trials. Thus the selling of settlement is a risky business for lawyers. . . . In their interactions with clients divorce lawyers try to manage that

risk in two ways: first, by stressing that the ultimate decision about, and responsibility for, settlement rests with the client; and, second, by describing negotiation as an adversarial process in which lawyers look for an edge and advance their clients' interests even as they seek a consensual outcome.

Lawyers use an array of strategies to try to construct a particular meaning of what is "realistic" and to persuade their clients to adopt a particular definition of what is, in their view, legally possible. Of course, their knowledge of legal rules and process, and the information that they have about specific players, such as other lawyers, judges, and mediators, provide powerful arguments ... In addition to their feel for the legal system and for the dramatis personae, lawyers, particularly specialists in family law, benefit from their experiences in prior cases.

* * * Divorce lawyers realize that when the case for settlement is first proposed to them, may clients cannot be convinced at a single stroke to abandon trial as a mode of disposition and embrace negotiations. They must not only be persuaded that settlement is the more prudent course, they must also be emotionally prepared to engage in negotiations with the very party who has upset their life....

See also J. EWAR WITH S. PARKER, LAW AND THE FAMILY 18–19 (2d ed. 1992) (concluding that U.S. divorce lawyers push disputes towards settlement in part because "lawyers are supreme in the world of settlements whereas in courts they must cede power to the judges.") For more information on negotiation techniques and styles, *see* ROGER FISHER AND WILLIAM URY, GETTING TO YES (2nd ed. 1991); WILLIAM URY, GETTING PAST NO: NEGOTIATING WITH DIFFICULT PEOPLE (1991); GERALD WILLIAMS, LEGAL NEGOTIATION AND SETTLEMENT (1983); Carrie Menkel–Meadow, *Toward Another View of Legal Negotiation: The Structure of Problem Solving*, 31 UCLA L. REV. 754 (1984).

The client's attitude toward the divorce will often color both his willingness to enter into settlement negotiations and his attitude toward settlement proposals. For example, Melli, Erlanger & Chambliss compared settlement agreements containing child support awards based on whether the support obligor was "reluctant" to end the marriage, "impatient" to end the marriage, or "accepting" of the divorce. Reluctant obligors agreed to pay an average of 19% of their income in child support, accepting obligors 24%, and impatient obligors 29%. Similarly, reluctant obligees obtained agreements requiring an average of 30% of the obligor's income to be paid in support, while accepting obligees obtained 24%, and impatient obligees received 19%. *See* Melli et al., *supra*, at 1133.

What steps can (and should) a lawyer take to counsel a client whose emotional state may make him or her inclined to accept an unreasonable offer, or reject a reasonable offer? Are there any malpractice risks here?

B. DRAFTING THE AGREEMENT

Once an agreement has been made, it must be reduced to clear and unambiguous written form. This sounds simple, but it is easier said than done!

STEWART v. STEWART

Missouri Court of Appeals, 1987.
727 S.W.2d 416.

CRIST, JUDGE.

Respondent (father) filed a motion to cite appellant (mother) for contempt for failing to pay him his equity in the marital residence after their youngest son had reached his majority, as provided by their separate agreement and dissolution decree. Father also asked the trial court for its order to sell the residence to satisfy his claim to the equity. Mother filed an answer asking that father be cited for contempt for failing to pay past child support. The trial court denied both motions for contempt, but ordered the sale of the residence with father to get one-half of the equity of such residence as of the time of sale. We reverse and remand with directions.

The seminal issue is whether father was to get one-half the equity at the time of sale, or whether he was to get one-half the equity at the time of dissolution decree on October 22, 1975. The equity in the real estate has increased in value from approximately $12,000 to at least $38,000.

At the time of the divorce, the parties were joint owners of the marital residence. The terms of the dissolution decree referred to a written separation agreement incorporated therein. A portion of the separation agreement provides:

> Party of the First Part (mother) shall be entitled to the Parties' home located at 119 Flesher in Ellisville, Missouri. At the time the Parties' youngest son, Steven Paul Stewart, shall reach the age of majority or be fully emancipated, it shall become the obligation of the Party of the First Part to pay to the Party of the Second Part (father) a sum of money equal to one-half (1/2) of the current equity in the said real estate less all proper expenses of selling said home, taxes and other fees. It is further agreed that the fair market value of said property as of the signing of this Agreement is Twenty Eight Thousand ($28,000) Dollars.

At no time since the dissolution has there been any conveyance of the marital residence, and title continues in both mother and father. Their youngest son became twenty-one years of age on January 28, 1984. Father testified he thought he was to receive one-half of the equity valued at the time of the sale. Mother testified he was to receive one-half the equity, valued at the time of the dissolution decree. There was little evidence on the question of the intention of the parties at the execution of the separation agreement.

Excepting for the words "less all proper expenses of selling said home, taxes and other fees," there can be little question about the intention of the parties at the time of the execution of their agreement. The parties would not have used the term "current equity" or provided that "the fair market value ... as of the signing ... is twenty-eight thousand dollars," unless the equity to be paid to father was to be calculated based upon the value of the home at the time of the dissolution decree.

Mother was to get the marital residence. When their youngest son reached his majority mother had to pay father a sum of money equal to one-half of the equity value at the time of dissolution, which was approximately $12,000. We do not know why the parties chose to add the words "less all proper expenses of selling said home, taxes and other fees," and no reasonable explanation is offered by the parties; but we are not permitted to make an agreement other than that of the parties. In any event, the parties agree that if the property must be sold, each must share the payment of the sale expenses.

The wording of the agreement regarding the proceeds of the marital residence is not ambiguous. The parties are bound by its terms.

The judgment of the trial court that "current equity" was to be measured as of the time mother's obligation to pay had matured rather than the time of the dissolution decree is reversed. The separation agreement shall be interpreted to mean father may receive his "current equity" measured as of the time of the dissolution decree. Mother shall have the right to pay the equity due father in lieu of sale of the marital residence. In all other respects, the judgment of the trial court is affirmed. The trial court is directed to enter an order in accordance with this opinion.

Judgment reversed and remanded.

Notes and Questions

1. What do you think the parties intended by the term "current equity"? How should the agreement have been drafted to avoid ambiguity? Are there other solutions to the problem of dividing the parties' home equity which should have been considered?

2. If a clause in a separation agreement includes a provision that equity shall be divided "upon sale of the property," is division required when foreclosure occurs? *See* Troy Savings Bank v. Calacone, 209 A.D.2d 777, 617 N.Y.S.2d 995 (1994) (yes).

3. In a settlement negotiation, what role should the client play? Should the lawyer initially let the parties try to reach an acceptable settlement on their own? When might this be a bad idea?

SECTION 2. NONDISCLOSURE AND MISREPRESENTATION

HRESKO v. HRESKO

Maryland Court of Appeals, 1990.
83 Md.App. 228, 574 A.2d 24.

ALPERT, JUDGE.

In *Hamilos v. Hamilos*, 297 Md. 99, 465 A.2d 445 (1983), the Court of Appeals held that an enrolled decree will not be vacated even though obtained by use of forged documents, perjured testimony, or any other frauds which are intrinsic to the trial of the case itself. In the present case, this court encounters for the first time the question of whether the fraudulent concealment of assets by one spouse during negotiations leading to a separation and property settlement agreement subsequently incorporated into a divorce decree is intrinsic or extrinsic to the divorce litigation.

During the spring or early summer of 1985, James and Marie Hresko decided to terminate their 24–year marriage. The parties agreed to and signed a separation and property settlement agreement on July 10, 1985. According to terms of the settlement agreement, James (appellant) agreed to pay $400 per month in child support, to pay the total costs of the minor child's college education, and to assume payment of certain family consumer debts. The agreement further provided that Marie (appellee) had the option of buying out appellant's interest in the family home three years from the date of the settlement agreement.

In the summer of 1988, appellee exercised her option to buy out appellant's interest in the family home and on the day of settlement, August 4, 1988, paid appellant $80,000 in cash for his one-half interest. Appellant had assumed that appellee would require a mortgage to purchase his interest in the house and claimed that he was "stunned" when she fulfilled her obligation with cash. He then became convinced that a fraud had been perpetrated against him during the 1985 negotiations that led to the property settlement. This alleged fraud involved the concealment, by appellee, of at least $80,000 in cash at the time of the agreement. As a result of this belief, appellant filed a Motion to Revise Judgment and to Rescind Separation and Property Settlement Agreement, together with a memorandum of law and an affidavit. Appellee responded by filing a motion to dismiss appellant's motion. Judge Cawood held a hearing on appellee's motion on June 7, 1989. After briefly holding the matter sub curia, the judge issued a written opinion on June 13, 1989, granting appellee's motion to dismiss appellant's motion to revise judgment.

In an action to set aside an enrolled judgment or decree, the moving party must initially produce evidence sufficient to show that the judgment in question was the product of fraud, mistake or irregularity.

Furthermore, it has long been black letter law in Maryland that the type of fraud which is required to authorize the reopening of an enrolled judgment is extrinsic fraud and not fraud which is intrinsic to the trial itself.

Appellant contends that appellee concealed from him an unknown, but apparently sizable, sum of money at the time the two parties were negotiating the subject separation and property settlement agreement.

Assuming without deciding that appellant has produced facts and circumstances sufficient to establish fraud, we will address whether this alleged fraud is extrinsic or intrinsic to the trial itself. We hold, based on appellant's claims and verified statements, that appellee's alleged concealment of funds is an example of, at most, intrinsic fraud.

Intrinsic fraud is defined as "[t]hat which pertains to issues involved in the original action or where acts constituting fraud were, or could have been, litigated therein." *Black's Law Dictionary* (5th ed. 1979). Extrinsic fraud, on the other had, is "[f]raud which is collateral to the issues tried in the case where the judgment is rendered." *Id.*

Fraud is extrinsic when it actually prevents an adversarial trial. In determining whether or not extrinsic fraud exists, the question is not whether the fraud operated to cause the trier of fact to reach an unjust conclusion, but whether the fraud prevented the actual dispute from being submitted to the fact finder at all. In *Schwartz v. Merchants Mortgage Co.*, 272 Md. 305, 309, 322 A.2d 544 (1974), the Court of Appeals ... provided examples of what would be considered extrinsic fraud:

> Where the unsuccessful party has been prevented from exhibiting fully his case, by fraud or deception practiced on him by his opponent, as by keeping him away from court, a false promise of a compromise; or where the defendant never had knowledge of the suit, being kept in ignorance by the acts of the plaintiff; or where an attorney fraudulently or without authority assumes to represent a party and connives at his defeat; ... or where the attorney regularly employed corruptly sells out his client's interest in the other side—these, and similar cases which show that there has never been a real contest in the trial or hearing of the case, are reasons for which a new suit may be sustained to set aside and annul the former judgment or decree, and open the case for a new and a fair hearing.
>
> *Schwartz*, 272 Md. at 309, 322 A.2d 544.

Appellant contends that appellee's alleged fraudulent representations were extrinsic to the subsequent divorce action because they took place over two years before its inception and served to prevent appellant from taking advantage of his right to an adversarial proceeding. He argues that appellee's concealment is a "fraud or deception practiced upon the unsuccessful party by his opponent as by keeping him away from court or making a false promise of a compromise."

As stated above, the issue of whether appellee's alleged fraudulent concealment of assets during pre-separation agreement negotiations is intrinsic or extrinsic to the divorce litigation is one of first impression in Maryland courts. Upon looking to other jurisdictions for guidance, we find conflict among our sister states.

California courts have uniformly recognized that the failure of one spouse to disclose the existence of community property assets constitutes extrinsic fraud. *In Re Marriage of Modnick*, 33 Cal.3d 897, 191 Cal.Rptr. 629, 663 P.2d 187 (1983). The principle underlying these cases is that each spouse has an obligation to inform the other spouse of the existence of community property assets. *Id.*, 191 Cal.Rptr. at 633, 663 P.2d at 191. This duty stems in part from the confidential nature of the marital relationship and from the fiduciary relationship that exists between spouses with respect to the control of community property. *Id.*

In *Daffin v. Daffin*, 567 S.W.2d 672 (Mo.App.1978), the Missouri Court of Appeals set aside property provisions of a dissolution of marriage decree. There, equity intervened, not because of the deception that affected the substance of the court's judgment (the concealment of assets) but because of the husband's breach of the relationship of confidence between husband and wife. *See also Compton v. Compton*, 101 Idaho 328, 612 P.2d 1175 (1980)(where Idaho court stated that fiduciary duty extends to parties' negotiations leading to the formation of the property settlement during marriage and requires, at least, a disclosure by both parties of all information within their knowledge regarding the existence of community property).

Other courts have found extrinsic fraud holding, as appellant would have us do, that a spouse's concealment or misrepresentation of assets can be classified as an intentional act by which the one spouse has prevented the other spouse from having a fair submission of the controversy and thus amounts to extrinsic fraud. *Pilati v. Pilati*, 181 Mont. 182, 592 P.2d 1374, 1380 (1979).

Other jurisdictions have reached the opposite result, determining that the fraudulent concealment of assets by one spouse during a property settlement agreement is intrinsic to the divorce litigation. Recently, in *Altman v. Altman*, 150 A.D.2d 304, 542 N.Y.S.2d 7, 9 (1989), the New York Supreme Court, Appellate Division, held that alleged fraud in the negotiations of the separation agreement involves the issue in controversy and is not a deprivation of the opportunity to make a full and fair defense. The court reasoned that the alleged misrepresentations of financial status are in essence no different from any other type of perjury committed in the course of litigation and thus constitute intrinsic fraud.

Similarly, in *Chapman v. Chapman*, 591 S.W.2d 574, 577 (Tex.Civ. App.1979), the Texas court refused to overturn on the basis of fraud a property settlement agreement incorporated into a divorce decree. The court stated that the fraud alleged at most related to untruths which misled the wife into acquiescence and approval an unjust division of property. Because these misrepresentations bore only on issues in the trial (or which could have been at issue in the trial), they, therefore, amounted to no more than intrinsic fraud. *Id. See also Hewett v. Zegarzewski*, 90 N.C.App. 443, 368 S.E.2d 877 (1988)(where court held that allegation that husband had made fraudulent misrepresentations as to his assets in procuring the separation agreement was evidence only of intrinsic fraud).

We are persuaded that these latter cases are the better reasoned ones. Misrepresentations or concealment of assets made in negotiations leading to a voluntary separation and property settlement agreement later incorporated into a divorce decree represent matters intrinsic to the trial itself. In fact, a determination of each party's respective assets, far from being a collateral issue, would seem to be a central issue in a property settlement agreement.

We reject appellant's contention that appellee's misrepresentations are extrinsic to the divorce action because it occurred two years prior to the action and prevented appellant from taking advantage of his right to an adversarial proceeding. The property settlement agreement, which appellant asserts was derived from the fraudulent representations of appellee,[2] was the same agreement that the parties submitted to the court for incorporation into the divorce decree. Appellant had every opportunity to examine these representations through discovery methods or in court. Instead, he chose to file an uncontested answer and permitted the matter to go to judgment.

In *Hamilos, supra*, the Court of Appeals held that an enrolled decree would not be vacated even though obtained by use of perjured testimony. As the trial judge stated in his written opinion and order, "It would be anomalous to give an alleged false statement in a letter (or given orally) greater stature than perjury during the course of the proceedings. If any fraud exists, it is intrinsic to the proceedings, which is not sufficient." We agree.

No "extrinsic fraud" prevented appellant from seeking trial and this court will not, therefore, reopen the decree in the present case. To rule otherwise would be to subject every enrolled divorce decree that includes a property settlement to revision upon discovery of alleged fraud in the inducement of the settlement. Public policy of this state demands an end to litigation once the parties have had an opportunity to present in court a matter for determination, the decision has been rendered, and the litigants afforded every opportunity for review.

Judgment Affirmed; Costs to be Paid by Appellant.

Notes and Questions

1. Courts have not reached consensus on how to handle post-divorce disputes regarding assets not disclosed at divorce. In community

2. We note that the actual settlement agreement made no representations as to the recent assets of either party. Furthermore, Subsection 18.2 of the agreement expressly states that there are no other representations, statements, understandings, promises, either oral or written, which are relied upon by either party.

property states, spouses remain co-owners of community property until the property is divided. *See* Henn v. Henn, 26 Cal.3d 323, 161 Cal.Rptr. 502, 605 P.2d 10 (1980). Common law states divide into the two camps described in *Hresko*. In some states, even if the separation agreement cannot be rescinded when a spouse discovers additional hidden marital assets, the spouse may bring a separate action to divide the discovered property. *See* Gehm v. Gehm, 707 S.W.2d 491 (Mo.App.1986); Marriage of Hiner, 669 P.2d 135 (Colo.App.1983) (court expressly retained jurisdiction in the original decree to divide undisclosed assets subsequently discovered). In others, the provisions of the separation agreement remain in effect.

2. What policies does the *Hresko* approach further? The *Daffin* approach? Which policy, on balance, is the better one?

3. Assuming Maryland has abolished spousal tort immunity, could Mr. Hresko bring an action for fraud?

4. Does footnote 2 suggest that the husband's lawyer should have added another provision to the settlement agreement?

5. What if a spouse misrepresents the value of property, rather than its existence? What if a spouse misrepresents his or her sexual fidelity during marriage and economic concessions are made based on the misrepresentation? *See* Barnes v. Barnes, 231 Va. 39, 340 S.E.2d 803 (1986).

SECTION 3. WHAT TERMS ARE PERMISSIBLE?

A. FAIRNESS

Should a court review the substantive fairness of a separation agreement?

UNIFORM MARRIAGE AND DIVORCE ACT § 306. [Separation Agreement]

(a) To promote amicable settlement of disputes between parties to a marriage attendant upon their separation or the dissolution of their marriage, the parties may enter into a written separation agreement containing provisions for disposition of any property owned by either of them, maintenance of either of them, and support, custody, and visitation of their children.

(b) In a proceeding for dissolution of marriage or for legal separation, the terms of the separation agreement, except those providing for the support, custody, and visitation of children, are binding upon the court unless it finds, after considering the economic circumstances of the parties and any other relevant evidence produced by the parties, on their own motion or on request of the court, that the separation agreement is unconscionable.

(c) If the court finds the separation agreement unconscionable, it may request the parties to submit a revised separation agreement or may make orders for the disposition of property, maintenance, and support.

(d) If the court finds that the separation agreement is not unconscionable as to disposition of property or maintenance, and not unsatisfactory as to support:

(1) unless the separation agreement provide to the contrary, its terms shall be set forth in the decree of dissolution or legal separation and the parties shall he ordered to perform them, or

(2) if the separation agreement provides that its terms shall not be set forth in the decree, the decree shall identify the separation agreement and state that the court has found the terms not unconscionable.

(e) Terms of the agreement set forth in the decree are enforceable by all remedies available for enforcement of a judgment, including contempt, and are enforceable as contract terms.

(f) Except for forms concerning the support, custody, or visitation of children, the decree may expressly preclude or limit modification of terms set forth in the decree if the separation agreement so provides. Otherwise, terms of a separation agreement set forth in the decree are automatically modified by modification of the decree.

OFFICIAL COMMENT

An important aspect of the effort to reduce the adversary trappings of marital dissolution is the attempt, made by § 306, to encourage the parties to reach an amicable disposition of the financial and other incidents of their marriage. This section entirely reverses the older view that property settlement agreements are against public policy because they tend to promote divorce. Rather, when a marriage has broken down irretrievably, public policy will be served by allowing the parties to plan their future by agreeing upon a disposition of their property, their maintenance, and the support, custody, and visitation of their children.

Subsection (b) undergirds the freedom allowed the parties by making clear that the terms of the agreement respecting maintenance and property disposition are binding upon the court unless those terms are found to be unconscionable. The standard of unconscionability is used in commercial law, where its meaning includes protection against one-sidedness, oppression, or unfair surprise (see § 2–302, Uniform Commercial Code), and in contract law * * *. It has been used in cases respecting divorce settlements or awards. Hence the act does not introduce a novel standard unknown to the law. In the context of negotiations between spouses as to the financial incidents of their marriage, the standard includes protection against overreaching, concealment of assets, and sharp dealing not consistent with the obligations of marital partners to deal fairly with each other.

In order to determine whether the agreement is unconscionable, the court may look to the economic circumstances of the parties resulting from the agreement, and any other relevant evidence such as the conditions under which the agreement was made, including the knowledge of the other party. If the court finds the agreement not unconscionable, its terms respecting property division and maintenance may not be altered by the court at the hearing.

The terms of the agreement respecting support, custody, and visitation of children are not binding upon the court even if these terms are not unconscionable. The court should perform its duty to provide for the children by careful examination of the agreement as to these terms in light of the standards established by § 309 for support and by Part IV for custody and visitation. * * *

JAMESON v. JAMESON

Supreme Court of South Dakota, 1976.
90 S.D. 179, 239 N.W.2d 5.

DUNN, CHIEF JUSTICE.

* * * Under the terms of the stipulation and agreement, plaintiff was given custody of the three children. She was to have the home in Sioux Falls and was to receive $1,430 out of the first $2,300 which defendant earned each month. In addition, she was to receive 50% of any of the defendant's earnings which exceeded $2,300 per month. Defendant agreed to pay her income tax, the family's medical expenses, and assume college expenses for each of the three children. Defendant earns approximately $40,000 per year. His present wife, Kay, is a surgical nurse and earns approximately $8,000 per year.

* * *

At trial there was no effort made by defendant [ex-husband] to show a change of circumstances regarding plaintiff [ex-wife] except to insinuate that she should go to work and partially support the family. There is no indication that her role as a homemaker has changed. The children are still at home. She has the usual increasing expenses of a growing family, as well as a general battle with inflation.

The defendant has changed location, but his income is also identical to that at the time of the decree. His wife, Kay, is employed full time and is making a modest income. Defendant alleges in his brief that the change of circumstances is that he now realizes that he cannot carry out the terms of the stipulation and agreement. We do not consider this to be any change of circumstances, much less a change which would justify a modification of the decree at this time. Defendant is getting exactly what he bargained for. Therefore, we hold that the circuit court correctly decided that there had been no change of circumstances.

The real claim is that the defendant signed an unconscionable agreement in the first instance, and the trial court should have relieved him of his bad bargain. This agreement is a harsh one, especially where he agrees to pay plaintiff 50% of any monthly income over $2,300, tax free. After paying taxes at this income level, he would have little if anything left for himself no matter how much additional gross income is received. However, the record indicates that defendant had the advice of an attorney, as well as tax experts, at the time the agreement was signed. He surely should have been aware of the hole he was digging for himself in his effort to rid himself of his marital bonds. His only excuse was that plaintiff would not consent to a divorce until he signed such an agreement, and he indicates that it was a case of blackmail. Plaintiff, however, can scarcely be faulted in her insistence on a standard of living for herself and family that is commensurate with that she could have expected as the wife of a medical doctor. She had not precipitated the marital crisis in any way, and she sought only to salvage what she could from a very unhappy experience. She drove a hard bargain, but the defendant accepted it and it was incorporated into the divorce decree.

Notes and Questions

1. On two visits to the South Dakota Supreme Court, Dr. Jameson obtained little relief. While the Court upheld the trial judge's ruling that Jameson's inability to comply with the judgment was an effective defense against a contempt charge, only minor adjustments were allowed. Dr. Jameson remained liable for (most of) his ex-wife's taxes as well as the full cost of their (by then) adult children's college educations. Jameson v. Jameson, 306 N.W.2d 240 (S.D.1981); Jameson v. Jameson, 332 N.W.2d 721 (S.D.1983).

2. Under the UMDA (and other state statutes employing a similar standard), a court may not rescind or alter a separation agreement without a finding of unconscionability. *See* Wasserman v. Wasserman, 217 A.D.2d 544, 629 N.Y.S.2d 69 (1995); Weber v. Weber, 548 N.W.2d 781 (N.D.1996); Marriage of Franks, 275 Mont. 66, 909 P.2d 712 (1996). *Cf.* Walther v. Walther, 102 Ohio App.3d 378, 657 N.E.2d 332 (1995) (agreement binding unless procured through fraud, overreaching, duress, or undue influence). Under the UMDA, could—should—the trial court have approved the Jamesons' agreement? How would you, as a judge, determine whether a separation agreement is "unconscionable"? *See* In re Marriage of Kirk, 24 Kan.App.2d 31, 941 P.2d 385 (1997) (property values should be specified in agreement to facilitate determination of whether agreement is "just and equitable.")

3. Compare the court's approach in Williams v. Williams, 306 Md. 332, 508 A.2d 985 (1986):

> [T]he husband, without the advice of an attorney, signed a Separation and Property Settlement Agreement ('Agreement') prepared by the wife's attorney. Testimony at trial revealed that the husband executed the agreement in hopes that it would lead to resolution of the marital difficulties and effectuate a reconciliation. The terms of the agreement required the husband to execute a deed ('resulting deed') conveying the marital home to the wife; he did so on September 16, 1982. Further terms of the agreement required

the husband to convey the contents of the marital home and a 1982 Thunderbird automobile to his wife. In addition, the husband agreed to pay indefinitely the mortgage on the marital home, the car loan, and all marital financial obligations. In sum, under the agreement the wife was to receive property valued at approximately $131,000. The husband, on the other hand, would retain property valued at about $1,100. Most significant, we think, is the undisputed fact that the husband's total weekly financial obligations under the agreement would exceed his weekly net salary.

Following execution of the separation agreement by the parties, the wife continued socializing with another man. The husband became suspicious and hired a private detective to observe the wife's social activities. After having been convinced of his wife's infidelity, the husband filed a bill of complaint for divorce on the grounds of adultery and sought to set aside the agreement and resulting deed in the Circuit Court for Harford County on January 10, 1983.

* * *

The legal doctrine * * * applied * * * below is currently labeled "unconscionability." The doctrine is recognized in the Restatement (Second) of Contracts, § 208, which reads:

> 'If a contract or term thereof is unconscionable at the time the contract is made a court may refuse to enforce the contract, or may enforce the remainder of the contract without the unconscionable term, or may so limit the application of any unconscionable term as to avoid any unconscionable result.'

* * *

In the case before us the consideration was grossly inadequate and the burdens on the husband were oppressive to the point that they were impossible to perform. As we have illustrated, [the] fact-findings on these scores are clear and forceful.

* * * Accordingly, it was not error for the trial court to review the agreement at issue and apply in its analysis thereto the doctrine of unconscionability.

Are *Jameson* and *Williams* consistent?

4. Mrs. Jameson would not agree to a divorce unless her husband accepted the disadvantageous terms she proposed. Does this constitute duress? What if one spouse says to the other, "Accept the economic terms I have proposed, or I will contest custody." Is this duress? If yes, should duress be a ground for rescission of the agreement? *Compare* Marriage of Lawrence, 197 Mont. 262, 642 P.2d 1043 (1982) ("custody is frequently a bargaining chip, whether we like it or not") *with* Fanning v. Fanning, 828 S.W.2d 135 (Tex.App.1992) (threat to contest custody is relevant to unconscionability).

5. Under the UMDA, agreements regarding the interests of the spouses are binding (unless unconscionable) while agreements regarding

their children (support, visitation, custody) are not. *See also* RESTATEMENT (SECOND) OF CONTRACTS § 191 (1981) ("A promise affecting the right of custody of a minor child is unenforceable on grounds of public policy unless the disposition as to custody is consistent with the best interest of the child.")

The Restatement and UMDA codify prior law, but is this approach sensible? Custody, support, and visitation will typically be basic and integral factors in the negotiation between the parties inevitably affecting the resolution of interspousal issues; during the marriage, parents may do *anything* they please with their minor children, barring abuse or neglect. Why should they not be equally autonomous on divorce? Specifically, if the mother agrees to a smaller property settlement than she might otherwise have accepted because the husband agrees to let her have custody of the children (thereby imposing long-run child support and, possibly, alimony obligations upon himself), why should the father be able to relitigate the custody issue when he could not if he traded alimony for property? If the family home is relinquished to the wife in exchange for generous visitation arrangements, or if child support was set deliberately low and alimony deliberately high so as to gain a tax advantage, how can a separation agreement be structured to avoid potential problems?

6. Should the same rescission standards apply to separation and premarital agreements? *See* DeLorean v. DeLorean [p. 189]. If not, how can the two situations be distinguished? In which should rescission be more freely available?

B. TERMS ENCOURAGING DIVORCE

RESTATEMENT (SECOND) OF CONTRACTS § 190 (1981)

[p. 195].

Comment to § 190.

b. *Separation agreements*. The policy that limits the parties in modifying the marital relationship does not apply if that relationship has ended. The rule stated in Subsection (1) thus does not apply to a promise that is part of an enforceable separation agreement. To be enforceable, a separation agreement must be made after the parties have separated or when they contemplate immediate separation, so that the marriage has, in effect, already disintegrated. It must also be fair in the circumstances, a matter as to which the court may exercise its continuing discretionary powers. Separation agreements commonly deal with such matters as support and are generally enforceable because the parties could usually accomplish the same result through a judicial separation. They are still subject to the rule stated in Subsection (2) if they tend unreasonably to encourage divorce.

Illustration:

2. A and B who are married but have decided to separate, make a separation agreement that is fair in the circumstances, in which A promises to pay B a stated sum each month in return for B's promise to relinquish all other claims to support. Although the promises of A and B change an essential incident of the marital relationship, their enforcement is not for that reason precluded on grounds of public policy because they are part of a separation agreement.

c. Tending to encourage divorce or separation. When persons contemplating marriage or married persons seek to determine by agreement their rights in the event of a divorce or separation, the rule stated in Subsection (2) comes into play, along with that stated in Subsection (1). See Illustration 2. Because of the public interest in the marriage relationship * * *, a promise that undermines that relationship by tending unreasonably to encourage divorce or separation is unenforceable. Although the parties are free, if they choose, to terminate their relationship under the law providing for divorce or separation, a commitment that tends unreasonably in this direction will not be enforced. Whether a promise tends unreasonably to encourage divorce or separation in a particular case is a question of fact that depends on all the circumstances, including the state of disintegration of the marriage at the time the promise is made. A promise that merely disposes of property rights in the event of divorce or separation does not of itself tend unreasonably to encourage either.

Illustrations:

3. A, who is married to B, promises to pay B $50,000 in return for B's promise to obtain a divorce. The promises of A and B tend unreasonably to encourage divorce and are unenforceable on grounds of public policy. The result does not depend on whether or not there are grounds for divorce or on whether or not B has performed.

4. A, who was married to B but has obtained a divorce that can possibly be set aside for fraud, promises to pay B $50,000 in return for B's promise not to attempt to have the divorce set aside. The promises of both A and B tend unreasonably to encourage divorce and are unenforceable on grounds of public policy. The result does not depend on whether or not B has performed.

5. A, who has begun divorce proceedings against B, promises B that if divorce is granted, alimony shall be fixed at a stated sum, in return for B's agreement to relinquish all other claims to alimony. A court may decide that in view of the disintegration of the marriage relationship, the promises of A and B do not tend unreasonably to encourage divorce and their enforcement is not precluded on grounds of public policy.

Courts distinguish between provisions of an agreement that facilitate divorce and those that induce it. A separation agreement does not induce divorce, because the parties have already separated and the marriage has broken down. Similarly, in Glickman v. Collins, 13 Cal.3d 852, 120 Cal.Rptr. 76, 533 P.2d 204 (1975), the prospective second wife of the husband agreed to guarantee the obligations of the husband to the first wife under the separation agreement; in return, the first wife agreed to facilitate the divorce. The court concluded that, because the marriage of the first wife and the husband had already broken down at the time the agreement was signed and grounds for divorce existed, the agreement was enforceable. By contrast, a court may not enforce an agreement that induces a spouse to facilitate the divorce if the spouses are still cohabiting. *See* Capazzoli v. Holzwasser, 397 Mass. 158, 490 N.E.2d 420 (1986).

SECTION 4. ENFORCEMENT AND MODIFICATION OF THE AGREEMENT

A. MERGER OF THE AGREEMENT INTO THE DECREE

After a settlement agreement is signed, the court will normally enter a divorce decree reflecting the terms of the agreement. This presents the technical, but important, question of whether the contract remains in effect once a decree has been entered. If the contract is still in effect, does modification of the divorce decree inferentially modify the contract as well?

MURPHY v. MURPHY

Delaware Family Court, 1983.
467 A.2d 129

GALLAGHER, JUDGE.

A petition has been filed by petitioner, (father) against respondent (mother) seeking to modify an order entered by this court on June 17, 1982, incorporating into a divorce decree the parties' separation agreement dated October 7, 1981. Under the agreement father is to pay to mother unallocated alimony and child support in the sum of $462 each week. Father now asks that his support obligation be reduced to $250 a week because his income estimations at the time the agreement was entered into were higher than his actual income has turned out to be. Father also suggests that the *Melson* formula, often utilized by this court in determining child support obligations, be utilized by the court if it should produce a lower support figure.

Respondent filed an answer opposing the relief requested by the petition. Although unwilling to relinquish any of her rights under the agreement, mother does admit that father is presently financially unable to meet his obligations under the agreement and indicates a willingness to be satisfied presently with payment of $350 per week support.

Father, in support of his request that the court modify the separation agreement, argues that when the agreement was incorporated into the divorce decree the court gained full power to modify that agreement under 13 Del.C § 1519.

Mother, in response, insists that the agreement retains its contractual nature despite incorporation into the decree. Therefore, according to mother, the court has no power to modify the terms of the agreement.

Under paragraph 7 of the agreement either party may at any time cause the agreement "to be filed of record in any court of competent jurisdiction". By stipulated order dated June 17,1983, the agreement was incorporated into the divorce decree entered herein.

There is a body of well established law defining the powers of, and limitations on, a court in modifying or enforcing a marital agreement. Where the parties have contracted with respect to their rights, privileges and obligations they are bound by their agreement and the court does not have the power either under 18 Del.C. § 1519, or independently, to modify the same. The existence of an agreement treating matters such as child support, custody and visitation will not preclude the court from entering an independent inconsistent order with respect to these matters, the rationale being that since the children were not parties to the agreement neither they nor the court are bound thereby. But even though a court is free to disregard contractual undertakings respecting children it will normally consider those undertakings and, if reasonable, make them the basis for a court order.

But is the situation any different where the divorce or other decree touches upon the agreement itself? Does it matter whether the agreement is merely incorporated into the divorce decree or merged therein?

If the agreement is merely incorporated into the decree it retains, for all intents and purposes, its contractual character, and the decree is limited by the terms of the contract. The purpose of incorporation by reference is to identify and verify the agreement of the parties, provide a basis for *res judicata* and, perhaps, promote enforcement in a foreign forum. But since the court looks exclusively to the agreement for resolution of the parties' post-nuptial rights, privileges and obligations it does not have the power, unless contractually given by the parties, to modify the agreement. In short, incorporation of the agreement into the decree does not empower the court to modify the agreement, pursuant to 13 Del.C. § 1519, as it might alter a judicial disposition because the terms of the order are entirely the product of its contractual genesis. It would also follow that a contempt citation should not issue in the first instance for breach of an agreement incorporated into a decree.

If the court thereafter enters an order inconsistent with any provision of the agreement as regards children such an order does not modify the agreement of the parties. Lindley, *Separation Agreements and Ante-*

Nuptial Contracts, §§ 31–62 (1982). It has been held that in such event suit might then be brought on the contract to recover any monetary differential created by the order. *Knox v. Remick,* 371 Mass. 433, 358 N.E.2d 432 (1976).

But if the agreement is merged into the decree the result is entirely different. In that event the rights, privileges and obligations of the parties under the agreement are displaced by the judgment or decree.... and the court has full power to modify the agreement (now an order) to the extent that it has jurisdiction to do so. Following merger the contract between the parties no longer exists and in its stead there is a judgment or decree under which the rights, privileges and obligations of the parties are to be defined and enforced thereafter. 24 Am. Jur.2d, *Divorce and Separation* § 908 (1966). The contempt citation would alto be available *ab initio.*

Does the fact that the court cannot modify an incorporated separation agreement mean that in every case the court must order the respondent to perform his obligations under the agreement to the letter? The answer is no. The court has the power to award specific performance on such terms and conditions as justice requires even though the performance ordered is not identical with the performance required by the agreement.

I cannot modify the incorporated agreement now before the court to reduce father's support obligation thereunder. I will give mother a judgment for the full amount of support arrears and for counsel fees. I will, nevertheless, order that father pay not less than $325 each week, a lesser sum than the sum specified by the agreement, and so long as he pays the lesser sum ordered by the court he will not be held in contempt for failure to pay the contractual support. Let me emphasize again that the support arrears will continue to accrue and that with respect to those arrears mother can obtain a judgment and execution thereon in the Superior Court.

IT IS SO ORDERED.

Notes and Questions

1. The Delaware Supreme Court has since changed its rule for modifying alimony agreements merged into a decree. *See* Rockwell v. Rockwell, 681 A.2d 1017 (Del.1996) (such obligations should be treated as contractual and generally not modifiable). Still, the *Murphy* approach is applied by a number of courts.

The decision whether to merge the settlement agreement into the decree is surprisingly important in a number of states. If the agreement is only incorporated, not merged, it remains an enforceable contract. In such a case, some courts (like *Murphy)* permit modification of the decree, but not the agreement; the obligor can still be sued on the contract. Other courts will not modify even the decree unless it expressly states that is intended to have validity independent from the agreement. *See* Riffenburg v. Riffenburg, 585 A.2d 627 (R.I.1991).

2. Merger can affect the range of remedies available. A merged agreement can be enforced through a contempt proceeding, while a non-merged agreement can only be enforced through an action for breach of contract. *See* Oedekoven v. Oedekoven, p. 919. Merger thus will be preferable to incorporation for the spouse whose primary concern is child support enforcement. But, if the contractual support obligation exceeds that which a court could impose, incorporation may be preferable. For example, in many states a court may not order post-majority support during college; in some, such an obligation cannot be enforced if the agreement is merged into the decree. *See, e.g.,* Noble v. Fisher, 126 Idaho 885, 894 P.2d 118 (1995).

3. Courts have not reached consensus on what to do if the decree does not expressly state whether the parties intend to merge the agreement into the decree. *See* Doris Brogan, *Divorce Settlement Agreements: The Problem of Merger or Incorporation and the Status of the Agreement in Relation to the Decree*, 67 NEB. L. REV. 235 (1988).

4. Under UMDA § 306(d), the parties to a separation agreement are not required to decide whether to merge the agreement into the decree; those terms set forth in the decree may be enforced by judicial enforcement procedures:

> [This] permit[s] the parties, in drawing the separation agreement, to choose whether its terms shall or shall not be set forth in the decree. In the former event, the provisions of subsection (e), making these terms enforceable through the remedies available for the enforcement of a judgment, but retaining also the enforceability of them as contract terms, apply. This represents a reversal of the policy of the original 1970 Act, which required a choice between "merging" the agreement in the judgment and retaining in character as a contract. Strong representations as to the undesirability of such a choice, in the light of foreign doctrines as to the enforceability of judgment, as compared with contract terms, in this area of the law, made by persons and groups whose expertise entitled them to respect, led the Conference, in 1971, to change its former decision.
>
> There still remains a place for agreements the terms of which are not set forth in the decree, if the parties prefer that it retain the status of a private contract, only. In this instance, the remedies for the enforcement of a judgment will not be available, but the court's determination, in the decree, that the terms are not unconscionable, under the ordinary rules of res adjudicata, will prevent a later successful claim of unconscionability. Such an agreement, unless its terms expressly so permit, will not be modifiable as to economic matters. Other subjects, relating to the children, by subsection (b) do not bind the Court.

Official Comments to § 306.

5. When a settlement agreement is not merged in the decree, does a material breach of the agreement by one party excuse the nonbreaching party from the performance of his or her obligations under the contract and/or under the decree? *See* Herbert v. Herbert, 754 S.W.2d 141 (Tex.1988) (holding that nonbreaching party was excused).

B. ENFORCEMENT BY CONTEMPT

OEDEKOVEN v. OEDEKOVEN

Supreme Court of Wyoming, 1975.
538 P.2d 1292.

RAPER, J.

One serious question, as we see it, arises in this appeal: Is contempt the proper path to travel when a property settlement agreement is only ratified and confirmed by the divorce decree, without incorporating a direction that the parties comply with its terms? There are other significant queries raised by appellant intertwined with that problem which we shall dispose of at the time they are reached. * * *

The rule is plainly stated in 24 Am.Jur.2d (Divorce and Separation) § 921, p. 1049: "Assuming that performance of an act called for by a property settlement may be enforced by a contempt proceeding where the court distinctly orders performance, performance will not be so enforced where the decree is not to be construed as including such an order. Thus, if the decree approves a property settlement but does not order the parties to perform its obligations, the violation of the agreement is not a violation of the decree and is not a contempt of court."

* * *

* * * [M]ere approval of a property settlement agreement is not a command to pay what is due by its terms and so, therefore, there is no order of the court or decree of the court that has been violated. Furthermore, there are hovering in the background constitutional implications that a person may not be imprisoned for debt but we avoid nailing our decision to that reason. The result we then have is when a party to a divorce action, where the court has only approved and ratified the agreement, asserts nonpayment under its conditions, he or she is confined to a claim on contract not enforceable by contempt proceedings. We so hold and consider it fundamental reversible error to hold defendant in contempt with all its overtones of punishment under such circumstances, even in absence of objection. The obligation sought to be enforced is negotiated and contractual and while arising out of marriage, the remedy must conform to the right asserted—one consistent with contract and not a decree enforceable by attachment of the person.

C. WAIVER OF THE RIGHT TO MODIFY

KARON v. KARON

Supreme Court of Minnesota, 1989.
435 N.W.2d 501.

YETKA, JUSTICE.

This case is before the court on the appeal by the petitioner of a decision of the Hennepin County District Court, affirmed by the court of appeals, which modified an award of maintenance originally made pursuant to a stipulation of the parties in which the parties waived any right to future modification of maintenance. We reverse the trial court and reinstate the original terms of the decree of dissolution.

Frima and Howard Karon executed a stipulation in this dissolution action on June 27, 1981, and the trial court incorporated the terms of the stipulation into its judgment ant decree entered August 31, 1981, *nunc pro tunc* to August 28, 1981. The decree awarded temporary maintenance to Frima for a 10–year period. The stipulation, as well as the judgment and decree, states that the parties waived any right to maintenance except as provided therein and that the court was divested of jurisdiction to alter the agreement or maintenance.

On February 7, 1986, the referee recommended and the court held, pursuant to Frima's motion, that it had jurisdiction to modify the dissolution decree pursuant to Minn.Stat. § 518.64 (Supp.1985). On March 11, the court affirmed the referee's recommendation. After a discovery period, the referee recommended and the court ordered that the judgment and decree be modified to increase the amount of maintenance to Frima and made the maintenance award permanent rather than temporary. On April 19, 1987, the court affirmed the referee's order. The court made the increase in maintenance retroactive to October 1, 1986, and an amended judgment and decree was entered on May 14, 1987.

Howard appealed the issue of whether the court had authority to modify the decree while Frima appealed the amount of the modification and the amount of attorney fees awarded. The court of appeals affirmed the trial court. *Karon v. Karon,* 417 N.W.2d 717 (Minn.App.1988). Howard appealed to this court.

Howard F. and Frima M. Karon married on December 21, 1952. Howard commenced a dissolution proceeding in 1979, and the parties executed a stipulation on June 27, 1981. The court entered its judgment and decree on August 28, 1981, incorporating the terms of the stipulation. Both documents provided that Howard would pay Frima $1,200 per month for 6 years and $600 per month for 4 years thereafter. Both documents also stated:

> Except for the aforesaid maintenance, each party waives and is forever barred from receiving any spousal maintenance whatsoever from one another, and this court is divested from having any

jurisdiction whatsoever to award temporary or permanent spousal maintenance to either of the parties.

In late 1985, Frima moved the court for a modification of the maintenance award, requesting permanent maintenance of $3,500 month. Howard challenged the court's authority to modify the maintenance provision, arguing that the parties had waived any alteration of maintenance in the stipulation and that the court had divested itself of jurisdiction to alter the decree. A referee held that Minn.Stat. § 518.64 (Supp. 1985) granted it such authority and ordered that it would hear the modification motion on the merits after a discovery period. The district court affirmed this order.

After the completion of discovery, a referee heard the merits of the motion and ruled that substantial change in circumstances had occurred, warranting a maintenance modification pursuant to § 518.64. The referee determined, however, that Frima had the capacity to earn $1,000 per month and thus increased maintenance to $1,500 per month rather than the $3,500 requested. The referee also made the award permanent because Frima had an uncertain future earning capacity. Finally, the referee awarded Frima $1,000 in attorney fees. The district court affirmed the referee's order.

Howard appealed the jurisdictional decision and the decision on the merits. Frima appealed the decision on the merits and the decision on attorney fees. She claimed that the court had abused its discretion by not awarding the requested amounts.

The court of appeals affirmed the trial court. *Karon*, 417 N.W.2d at 720. This court granted Howard's petition for further review which, like the arguments before the court of appeals, presented only jurisdictional issues. Frima never filed a petition for further review.

The parties have confused and compounded numerous issues, but we believe the question before us is whether one of the adult parties to a stipulation in a dissolution matter made in 1981, which was approved by the trial court and which settled all issues, including maintenance, and which further provided that the parties expressly waived any right to maintenance except as provided in the original agreement, may now reopen the issue of maintenance to seek an increase therein. The trial court allowed reconsideration of the maintenance issue and the court of appeals affirmed. We reverse.

Howard argues that the terms of the original judgment and decree denied the court any further jurisdiction over the issue of maintenance. We agree. The language of the judgment and decree purports to divest jurisdiction. Section 518.64, however, states that the court may modify a maintenance award upon petition of a party. Minn.Stat. § 518.64, subd. 1 (1984). The court must decide, therefore, whether the maintenance issue was res judicata or whether the court correctly modified the maintenance award under § 518.64 regardless of the original order's language.

Initially, the legal doctrines at issue need clarification. Howard, in essence, argues that the form of res judicata known as direct estoppel precludes relitigation of the maintenance issue. Direct estoppel is issue preclusion in a second action on the same claim. Restatement (Second) of Judgment § 27 comment b (1982). The seminal issue, therefore, becomes whether the original decree constituted a final judgment in the dissolution on the maintenance issue. If so, it should have had the res judicata effect of preventing the court from hearing the modification motion. *See Hentschel v. Smith*, 278 Minn. 86, 92, 153 N.W.2d 199, 204 (1967)(consent judgments have estoppel effect). Phrased in other words, we must decide whether the district court properly divested itself of jurisdiction over the issue in 1981. We hold that it did.

It is not the parties to the stipulation who have divested the court of ability to relitigate the issue of maintenance. The court had the authority to refuse to accept the terms of the stipulation in part or *in toto*. The trial court stands in place and on behalf of the citizens of the state as a third party to dissolution actions. It has a duty to protect the interests of both parties and all the citizens of the state to ensure that the stipulation is fair and reasonable to all. The court did so here and approved the stipulation and incorporated the terms therein in its decree. Thus, the decree is final absent fraud.

We have recognized that parties may stipulate to waive all maintenance at the time of the initial decree and that the courts are without authority to award it in the future. Likewise, we have held that if maintenance is awarded and the term has expired, the court is equally without authority to award further maintenance.

We see no valid distinction between the two situations outlined above and the one now before us. Counsel for respondent would have us believe that waiver of a statutory right is without precedent. One can quickly see the fallacy of such an argument. In probate law, for example, heirs frequently enter into stipulations to distribute property or to waive statutory allowances. Antenuptial agreements have become quite common in the past several decades. In criminal law, we have held on numerous occasions that a defendant can waive constitutional rights.

Much of the material filed on behalf of the respondent contains language referring to the economic status of divorced women. While the arguments made in reference to that status are important and should be addresses by both the legislature and the courts, they are not applicable in this case. That is so because the decision would cut both ways if the stipulation were upheld—the husband could not decrease maintenance and would be obligated to pay it for 10 years regardless of any financial setbacks. As a matter of fact, some of the materials submitted to us at oral argument suggest that his financial situation may have already deteriorated since this action was brought.

Amicus for the Family Law Section of the Minnesota State Bar Association stated at oral argument that setting aside the stipulation and decree is insulting and demeaning to women. Counsel who argued on behalf of the association is a woman. She took that position in response to counsel for respondent's implication that women involved in divorce cannot understand or act to protect their rights even when represented by counsel; therefore, the state must protect them in the manner it protects children in the role of parens patriae. Amicus's argument is compelling.

Moreover, what effect would affirmance have on other contracts entered into by married women? Would such a decision supporting the respondent ultimately lead to turning the clock back, outlawing not only antenuptial agreements, but also allowing parties to contest the validity of all instruments ant contracts entered into on behalf of married women? Would we also question the validity or deeds of conveyances and purchase of expensive personal property? Where would the protection end? In short, intelligent adult women, especially when represented by counsel, must be expected to honor their contracts the same as anyone else. Any other holding would result in chaos in the family law field and declining respect for binding agreements as well.

Normally, stipulations are carefully drawn compromises which affect property distribution, real and personal, as well as future income. One may, for example, give or take certain items in order to have another reduced or eliminated. Setting aside one portion of the stipulation may totally warp the effects of other portions of the document. It would be difficult to imagine why anyone would agree to temporary maintenance or even maintenance itself for an indefinite period if the agreement court be later nullified. Why not litigate the matter at the time of the original dissolution proceedings? In the interest of judicial economy, parties should be encouraged to compromise their differences and not to litigate them. It is in the litigation of difficult dissolution matters where much of the acrimony and long-term scars are created, leading to still more litigation.

For any of these reasons, we reverse the modification of the original dissolution decree and remand to the trial court with instructions to enforce the terms of that initial dissolution decree.

Notes and Questions

1. Should a waiver of the right to modify a family law obligation be treated differently from other types of waiver?

2. Why would a party agree to waive the right to modify?

3. The *Karon* dissent expressed concern that the court's decision would prevent the recipient from obtaining increased support even if she became disabled. *See* 435 N.W.2d at 504. Is this an accurate interpretation of the majority decision? If so, did the *Karon* majority reach the wrong result? Can you think of a better approach to limiting modification rights?

4. Would the *Karon* court have reached the same result if the issue were the custodial parent's right to increase child support? What result under UMDA § 306?

5. The *Karon* court enforced the modification waiver when the obligor's income increased. Courts have also enforced a waiver of the right to modify when the obligor's income has decreased. *See* Honore v. Honore, 149 Wis.2d 512, 439 N.W.2d 827 (Wis.App.1989); Josic v. Josic, 78 Ill.App.3d 347, 33 Ill.Dec. 871, 397 N.E.2d 204 (1979).

Problem 17–1:

In 1985, Harry signed a separation agreement in which he agreed to pay Wendy $250 per month in permanent maintenance. Harry did so because he believed, based on the prevailing pattern of judicial decision making, that Wendy stood a good chance of obtaining permanent maintenance should the case go to trial. In 1990, the legislature limited maintenance to a period of 121 months. Can Harry obtain modification of the separation agreement based on the change in the law? *See* In re Marriage of Jones, 22 Kan.App.2d 753, 921 P.2d 839 (1996).

Chapter 18

ALTERNATIVE DISPUTE RESOLUTION

Litigated divorce is like giving a judge a blank pad of paper that you sign your name to and that will decide how your family is going to operate.

Nancy Palmer, Lawyer, ABA Journal, Feb. 1997, at 55.

Discourage litigation ... There will be business enough.

Abraham Lincoln

SECTION 1. INTRODUCTION

Divorce litigation can be expensive and time consuming. It can also escalate hostilities, reduce the possibility of compromise and, in extreme cases, harm both the litigants and their children. One does not have to look too far to find a report like this one:

> PORT St. Joe, Fla., July 28 (AP)—A man in court for an alimony hearing today shot and killed his ex-wife's lawyer, a witness and the judge hearing the case, the authorities said. The man, Clyde Melvin, also wounded his former wife before he was hit by a sheriff's bullet, the officials said. * * * A .357–caliber Magnum and .22–caliber Derringer were found on Mr. Melvin when he was taken into custody.

NEW YORK TIMES, July 29, 1987, at 13, col. 4.

Slow dockets, prohibitive costs, and unpredictable judges have increased enthusiasm for alternatives to the traditional litigation and settlement process. Many experts have noted the need for mechanisms to resolve family disputes without litigation. The ABA, for example, has recommended that:

> [t]he organized bar should encourage court programs that provide mediation of custody, visitation and related issues involving children, and attorneys should recommend mediation and other forms of alternative dispute resolution to their clients where appropriate.
>
> AMERICAN BAR ASSOCIATION PRESIDENTIAL WORKING GROUP ON THE UNMET LEGAL NEEDS OF CHILDREN AND FAMILIES, A NATION AT RISK 58 (1993).

Los Angeles offered the first "alternate dispute resolution" program in the 1930s; its "conciliation" program provided marriage counseling aimed at reconciliation. California later established a conciliation program in each court with principal jurisdiction over divorce cases involving child custody and visitation. Today, almost half the states have some form of court-sponsored conciliation program. In some states, conciliation is voluntary; in others, attendance may be ordered by the court. The content of conciliation programs varies widely. Some programs offer services much like mediation [see § 2]; others offer counseling. Universally, however, the emphasis has shifted from saving marriages to helping couples prepare for divorce and work out divorce settlements. *See* Henry Foster & Doris Jonas Freed, *Divorce Reform: Brakes on Breakdown*, 13 J. FAM. L. 443 (1973–74).

Today, conciliation services have been augmented with a wide variety of alternative dispute resolution (ADR) mechanisms. ADR encompasses mediation, arbitration, and combinations of these techniques. A growing number of states now require lawyers to advise clients of ADR options. The Texas statute is a good example:

TEX. FAM. CODE § 6.404:

> (a) A party to a proceeding under this title shall include in the first pleading filed by the party in the proceeding the following statement:
>
> "I AM AWARE THAT IT IS THE POLICY OF THE STATE OF TEXAS TO PROMOTE THE AMICABLE AND NONJUDICIAL SETTLEMENT OF DISPUTES INVOLVING CHILDREN AND FAMILIES. I AM AWARE OF ALTERNATIVE DISPUTE RESOLUTION METHODS INCLUDING MEDIATION. WHILE I RECOGNIZE THAT ALTERNATIVE DISPUTE RESOLUTION IS AN ALTERNATIVE TO AND NOT A SUBSTITUTE FOR A TRIAL AND THAT THIS CASE MAY BE TRIED IF IT IS NOT SETTLED, I REPRESENT TO THE COURT THAT I WILL ATTEMPT IN GOOD FAITH TO RESOLVE CONTESTED ISSUES IN THIS CASE BY ALTERNATIVE DISPUTE RESOLUTION WITHOUT THE NECESSITY OF COURT INTERVENTION."
>
> (b) The statement required by Subsection (a) must be printed in boldfaced type or capital letters and signed by the party.

See also Colo. Rules of Professional Conduct Rule 2.1 (1993).

SECTION 2. MEDIATION

A. MEDIATION

AMERICAN BAR ASSOCIATION, AMERICAN ARBITRATION ASSOCIATION, SOCIETY OF PROFESSIONALS IN DISPUTE RESOLUTION, MODEL STANDARDS OF CONDUCT OF MEDIATORS

(1995).

Mediation is a process in which an impartial third party—a mediator—facilitates the resolution of a dispute by promoting voluntary agreement (or "self-determination") by the parties to the dispute. A mediator facilitates communications, promotes understanding, focuses the parties on their interests, and seeks creative problem solving to enable the parties to reach their own agreement.

Mediators help the parties collect data, frame issues, establish goals, isolate points of agreement and disagreement, generate options and encourage compromise. The mediator may meet with both spouses individually to establish rapport, or may meet with them both at the same time. Typically, mediation sessions are conducted face-to-face with each party present; in a few jurisdictions, each party's lawyer must also be present.

At the first mediation session, the mediator explains the mediation process, the ground rules for mediation and the mediator's role in the process; he or she will also ask the parties to sign a mediation agreement. The rest of the first session is typically devoted to information gathering. The mediator will want to identify who initiated the divorce, how each spouse has responded to the divorce process, who holds the balance of power within the relationship, and what issues are disputed. Many mediators choose to meet with each party alone after the first mediation session; others do so only when he or she wants to clarify an individual's position.

During its second phase, mediation focuses on identifying the parties' individual goals and alternative ways in which those goals might be met. If custody of the couple's children is in dispute, the mediator can help the parties realistically appraise the parenting abilities of each, the practicality of proposed custody arrangements, and their impact on the child. The mediator typically tries to find a point on which the parties can reach agreement so that they will see the benefits of cooperation; if the process is successful, this may set the stage for continued cooperation.

In its third phase, the parties and mediator ascertain whether they can reach agreement. If agreement is possible, the mediator helps the parties (and their lawyers) work out the details with sufficient precision to avoid future disputes. If agreement is not possible, the parties will proceed to arbitration or litigation. If the parties have reached agreement on some issues but not others, the mediator will draft a memorandum describing the agreement and remaining issues to be arbitrated or litigated.

B. THE MEDIATION PROCESS

JAY FOLBERG, DIVORCE MEDIATION: A WORKABLE ALTERNATIVE

In American Bar Association, Alternative Means of Dispute Resolution 12, 13–15, 41 (Howard Davidson et al. eds., 1982).

The subjects of divorce mediation include, but are not limited to, those that would be resolved by a judge in court, but for the mediated settlement. It can thus be seen as an alternative or, at least, a complement to the court process. Divorce mediation is defined here as a non-therapeutic process by which the parties together, with the assistance of a neutral resource person or persons, attempt to systematically isolate points of agreement and disagreement, explore alternatives and consider compromises for the purpose of reaching a consensual settlement of issues relating to their divorce or separation. Mediation is a process of conflict resolution and management that gives back to the parties the responsibility for making their own decisions about their own lives. It is usually conducted in private without the presence of the parties' attorneys. It has identifiable stages and divisible tasks, but no universal pattern.

In order to better distinguish and isolate mediation from other interventions, we might look at what it is not. It is not, as above defined, a therapeutic process. * * * It is not focused on insight to personal conflict or in changing historically set personality patterns. It is much more an interactive process than an interpsychic one. Mediation is task-directed and goal-oriented. It looks at resolution and results between the parties rather than the internalized causes of conflict behavior. It discourages dependence on the professional provider rather than promoting it. * * *

Mediation is not arbitration. In arbitration, the parties authorize a neutral third person or persons to *decide* upon a binding resolution of the issues. The process used in arbitration is adjudicatory, but is typically less formal than that utilized in court and is usually conducted in private. Other than its informality and privacy, arbitration is much like the judicial process, except the "judge" is chosen or agreed upon by the parties and derives his or her authority from the agreement to arbitrate. In mediation the parties may choose the mediator, but do not authorize the mediator to make the decisions for them. Arbitration may follow mediation, either as a separate proceeding or as part of the same "med-arb" process.

Mediation is not the same as traditional negotiation of divorce disputes. Negotiation is generally a "sounding out" process to aid dispute resolutions but is not accomplished through any established framework and may be pursued through representatives, most often attorneys. Negotiation does not normally utilize a neutral resource person and is premised on an adversary model. Private negotiation may, however, precede mediation, follow unsuccessful mediation, or in some settings go on simultaneously.

Mediation is not conciliation, though the two terms are often used interchangeably. The two can be distinguished by looking at their historical development and application to the field of family law. California first offered court-connected conciliation services in 1939. The initial focus of these services was on providing marriage counseling aimed at effecting a reconciliation of spouses. With the adoption of no-fault divorce and the increase in the divorce rate, the focus of conciliation has shifted from marriage counseling aimed at reconciling parties to separation counseling and evaluation services for purposes of assisting the domestic relations judges in making child custody and visitation orders. Indeed, in California, where mandatory custody mediation is usually performed by conciliation personnel, the distinction between conciliation and mediation has become somewhat obfuscated.

* * *

Divorce mediation has been touted as a replacement for the adversary system and a way of making divorce less painful. Though it may serve as an alternative for those that choose to use it, it is neither a panacea that will create love where there is hate, nor will it totally eliminate the role of the adversary system in divorce. It may, however, reduce acrimony by promoting cooperation and it may lessen the burden of the courts in deciding many cases that can be diverted to less hostile and costly procedures. Divorce mediation does appear to be a rational alternative attracting considerable interest. It is still in its infancy in the United States and, therefore, along with its promises, it has raised substantial issues. The resolution of these issues will require additional empirical research, experience and dialogue.

Notes and Questions

1. When Folberg wrote in 1982, mediation was a relatively new idea. Today, mediation is available in all states; in some, it is mandated for certain types of cases. Mediation is also utilized outside the United States. *See* HILLARY ASTOR AND C. CHINKIN, DISPUTE RESOLUTION IN AUSTRALIA (1992); FAMILY LAW ACT OF 1996, ch. 27; AUSTRALIA FAMILY LAW ACT 1975 (1991 Amendments) 19B(1).

2. Divorce mediation may take place at any point in the litigation process—before filing, after filing and before discovery, after discovery,

after failed negotiations, or post-divorce. Typically, divorce mediation starts after a divorce petition and answer are filed; at that point, it may help resolve discovery problems, focus the parties on unresolved issues, and provide a forum in which to decide issues of temporary support, custody and visitation. Complex equitable distribution and contested custody matters are usually mediated only after extensive discovery.

3. Mediation began as a voluntary alternative for couples wishing to resolve custody and visitation issues amicably, but a growing number of states now mandate pre-trial custody mediation. *See, e.g.*, CAL. FAM. CODE § 3178 (parenting plans, custody, and visitation); FLA. STAT. ANN. § 44.102(b) (custody, visitation or other parental responsibility disputes); IDAHO R. CIV. P. § 16(j)(2); NEV. REV. STAT. ANN. § 3.500 (custody and visitation). Local court rules in several jurisdictions provide that the parties must attend one or two mediation sessions before going to court to litigate custody. Mediation is also now utilized in financial disputes between divorcing couples; in some states, it may even be used in child neglect proceedings.

4. Should the court play the same role in reviewing a mediated agreement that it plays in reviewing a negotiated agreement? *See* In re Marriage of Kirk, 24 Kan.App.2d 31, 941 P.2d 385 (1997) (court has obligation to review agreement of the parties to see if it is valid, just and equitable).

5. Once the parties sign a mediated agreement, is it conclusive on all issues? In Feliciano v. Feliciano, 674 So.2d 937 (Fla.App.1996), the court held that a trial court may set aside provisions of a mediated agreement dealing with child support, custody and visitation, if the agreement is not in the best interest of the children.

6. May a judge order the mediation of future nonemergency disputes? *See* In re Marriage of Aleshire, 273 Ill.App.3d 81, 209 Ill.Dec. 843, 652 N.E.2d 383 (1995):

> We have found no statutory or common law authority for a trial court to order mediation of prospective visitation disputes in the absence of a preliminary finding that the issues in question are proper for mediation. The trial court does have authority to order mediation in certain instances; however, a review of this authority shows that it does not contemplate the ordering of prospective mediation.
>
> Section 607.1 of the Act grants trial courts the authority to order mediation in cases of visitation abuse, but only after the court hears all of the evidence in the case. We interpret the language "after hearing all of the evidence" to mean that the trial court may order mediation only after assessing whether mediation would be useful in resolving a specific dispute before the court. Therefore, § 607.1 does not authorize trial courts to order mediation of prospective visitation disputes.

What are the advantages of voluntary versus court-ordered mediation?

C. MEDIATOR QUALIFICATIONS

Both lawyers and mental health professionals mediate divorce disputes. Lawyers tout their superior knowledge of the law and court processes. Mental health professionals and social workers tout their communication skills and expertise in working with people. Ideally, a mediator should be familiar with both the law and the emotional aspects of divorce.

Most lawyers believe that mediation does not reduce the need for legal assistance. Only a lawyer can provide advice on legal rights and responsibilities, litigation risks and strategy. A lawyer can also assess the client's financial needs and obtain documents (through discovery if necessary) required for an informed decision, give advice about the pros and cons of a settlement proposal, and review documents detailing the parties' agreement.

Lawyers who mediate face unique ethical issues: Does confidentiality or privilege attach to mediation if the mediator is a lawyer? Can the unhappy party subpoena the mediator to testify at trial? Can a lawyer mediator ever represent one of the parties to the mediation in any other forum? Is the lawyer acting as an intermediary? To address some of these problems, the American Bar Association Family Law Section adopted Standards of Practice for Lawyer Mediators in 1984.

STANDARDS OF PRACTICE FOR LAWYER MEDIATORS IN FAMILY DISPUTES

18 Fam. L. Q. 363 (1984).

For the purposes of these standards, family mediation is defined as a process in which a lawyer helps family members resolve their disputes in an informative and consensual manner. This process requires that the mediator be qualified by training, experience, and temperament; that the mediator be impartial; that the participants reach decisions voluntarily; that their decisions be based on sufficient factual data; and that each participant understands the information upon which decisions are reached. While family mediation may be viewed as an alternative means of conflict resolution, it is not a substitute for the benefit of independent legal advice.

* * *

I. Before the actual mediation sessions begin, the mediator shall conduct an orientation session to give an overview of the process and to assess the appropriateness of mediation for the participants.

II. A. At the outset of mediation, the parties should agree in writing not to require the mediator to disclose to any third party any statements made in the course of mediation. The mediator shall inform the participants that the mediator will not voluntarily disclose to any third party any of the information obtained through the mediation process, unless such disclosure is required by law, without the prior consent of the participants. The mediator also shall inform the parties of the limitations of confidentiality such as statutory or judicially mandated reporting.

III. A. The mediator shall not represent either party during or after the mediation process in any legal matters. In the event the mediator has represented one of the parties beforehand, the mediator shall not undertake the mediation.

B. The mediator shall disclose to the participants any biases or strong views relating to the issues to be mediated, both in the orientation session, and also before these issues are discussed in mediation.

* * *

D. The mediator has a duty to ensure that the participants consider fully the best interests of the children, that they understand the consequences of any decision they reach concerning the children.

IV. A. The mediator shall assure that there is full financial disclosure, evaluation and development of relevant factual information in the mediation process, such as each would reasonably receive in the discovery process, or that the parties have sufficient information to intelligently waive the right to such disclosure.

B. In addition to requiring this disclosure, evaluation and development of information, the mediator shall promote the equal understanding of such information before any agreement is reached.

* * *

VI. A. Each of the mediation participants should have independent legal counsel before reaching final agreement. At the beginning of the mediation process, the mediator should inform the participants that each should employ independent legal counsel for advice at the beginning of the process and that the independent legal counsel should be utilized throughout the process and before the participants have reached any accord to which they have made an emotional commitment. In order to promote the integrity of the process, the mediator shall not refer either of the participants to any particular lawyers. When an attorney referral is requested, the parties should be referred to a Bar Association list if available. In the absence of such a list, the mediator may only provide a list of qualified family law attorneys in the community.

D. * * * If the participants, or either of them, choose to proceed without independent counsel, the mediator shall warn them of any risk involved in not being represented, including where appropriate, the possibility that the agreement they submit to a court may be rejected as unreasonable in light of both parties' legal rights or may not be binding on them.

Notes and Questions

1. For discussions of the ethical issues facing lawyers acting as mediators and some of the unanswered questions, *see* Loretta M. Moore, *Lawyer Mediators: Meeting the Ethical Challenges*, 30 FAM. L. Q. 679 (1996); Linda J. Silberman, *Professional Responsibility Problems of Divorce Mediation*, 16 FAM. L. Q. 107 (1982); Richard E. Crouch, *The Dark Side is Still Unexplored*, 4 FAM. ADVOC. 27 (1982).

2. In 1995, the American Bar Association, the American Arbitration Association, and the Society of Professionals in Dispute Resolution jointly issued broad standards which apply to both lawyer and nonlawyer mediators. For a discussion, *see* John D. Feerick, *Standards of Conduct for Mediators*, 79 JUDICATURE 314 (May–June 1996).

3. When mediation first began, almost anyone could hang up a shingle as a mediator. Several states now have established educational and training qualifications for mediators; some require additional specialized training to mediate family disputes. Mediators who receive court referrals often must possess an advanced degree in law, social work, mental health or accounting.

PROBLEM 18–1:

Your client has received a notice that she is required to attend court-ordered custody mediation. What, if any, preparation is advisable? What advice should you give her?

D. THE PROMISE AND RISKS OF MEDIATION

STEPHEN W. SCHLISSEL, A PROPOSAL FOR FINAL AND BINDING ARBITRATION OF INITIAL CUSTODY DETERMINATIONS

26 FAM. L. Q. 71, 74–76 (1992).

* * *

First, "our judicial system continues to intervene in divorce with the same confrontational format that existed prior to the no-fault revolution." The system is premised, in part, on the idea that the court should have ongoing supervision over custody arrangements between the spouses because those arrangements result from an adversarial confrontation between the divorcing parties. The concept seems to be that judicial control is necessary in light of the parties' determination to resort to the judiciary for problem resolution in the first instance. Thus, the courts get their power to control due to the inability of the parents to agree.

* * * Because the present method for resolution of custody disputes is decidedly an adversarial one, the parents are almost required to dig up the dirt on the other. Although the standard most often used in an initial custody determination is the "best interests of the child," each of the parents tries to prove the other less fit. "This adversarial emphasis

is directly contrary to the child's interests in stability of environment and minimum civility and cooperation between his or her parents."

Litigation fosters the process where the parents use the children as bait to get what they want financially and emotionally; it often creates adjustment problems for the children, if not a tug-of-war between their parents. The New York Law Revision Commission has noted these adjustment problems and has stated that:

> The available evidence points almost without equivocation to the conclusion that children are better off if both parents are meaningfully involved in their lives after their separation.... Therefore, the challenge for the custody dispute resolution system is now to organize itself so as to maximize the number of families in which both parents are involved in the child's post-separation life. Available evidence suggests that reliance on adversary litigation controlled by the parents and their lawyers as a primary technique for dispute resolution does not further this goal and, indeed, works against it.
>
> The Commission concluded that the adversarial process exacerbated the harmful effects of divorce on the children.

Second, custody litigation is very costly from the perspective of both the court and the divorcing or separating couple. Matrimonial cases occupy a great deal of scarce judicial time and money. Moreover, a typical divorce case consumes a substantial part of the wealth available to the parties, often reducing each party's future standard of living.

Third, "bitterly contested cases often produce court orders which are resented and violated, leading to repeated rounds of litigation." Many custody cases seem to almost outlive the parents or go on for more years than necessary for the children to reach majority. Litigation is best suited for situations where a judgment must be made concerning present consequences of past behavior. It doesn't work well where the goal is to provide some finality to a dispute, and the parties must thereafter remain in constant contact with each other. "Unlike a settlement in a tort case, where the parties usually never see each other again, parents in a divorce need to maintain a continuing relationship." In domestic relations cases, and especially in custody cases, there are, more often than not, hosts of future problems that must be resolved.

All of the above suggests that we should consider nonlitigation alternatives to resolving custody disputes.

PENELOPE E. BRYAN, KILLING US SOFTLY: DIVORCE MEDIATION AND THE POLITICS OF POWER

40 Buff. L. Rev. 441, 523 (1992).

* * *

Today custody law still favors women and recent reforms in family law create new economic rights for divorcing women. Lawyers negotiating divorce settlements concern themselves with implementing these legal entitlements. Mediation proponents believe the lawyer's focus on rights generates hostility among divorcing parties and unnecessarily infringes upon the couple's right to order their post divorce lives. In contrast, they maintain mediation preserves relationships, empowers the parties, and generates good feelings. Legal rights fade into the shadows of informality.

This shift in focus from rights to relatedness, however, endangers divorcing women and reinforces male dominance. Mediation proponents seductively appeal to women's socialized values by speaking softly of relatedness. Yet mediation exploits wives by denigrating their legal entitlements, stripping them of authority, encouraging unwarranted compromise, isolating them from needed support, and placing them across the table from their more powerful husbands and demanding that they fend for themselves. The process thus perpetuates patriarchy by freeing men to use their power to gain greater control over children, to implant more awareness of male dominance into women's consciousness, and to retain more of the marital financial assets than men would obtain if lawyers negotiated divorce agreements.

* * * At the very least those who structure court affiliated programs, as well as mediators, now should recognize their complicity in the continued oppression of women and their dependent children. * * *

MARTHA FINEMAN, DOMINANT DISCOURSE, PROFESSIONAL LANGUAGE, AND LEGAL CHANGE IN CHILD CUSTODY DECISION MAKING

101 HARV. L. REV. 727, 728, 756 (1988).

* * *

Social workers view divorce as occasioning the birth of an ongoing, albeit different, relationship, with mediators and social workers as its midwives and monitors. "Let's talk about it" seems to be the ideal, and the talk is envisioned as continuing for decades. The continued involvement is not only with each other but with the legal system as well. This ideal is obviously very different from the traditional legal system, which seeks an end or termination of a significant interaction at divorce: a division, distribution, or allocation of the things acquired during marriage—an emancipatory model—and with its "ending," the permission for a "new life" for the participants and the withdrawal of active legal interference in their relationship.

The helping professions' ideal process "avoids" or "reduces" conflict and is typified by mediation. Helping professionals believe that mediation, employing a therapeutic process, is within their exclusive domain because lawyers, unlike social workers, ignore the underlying causes of divorce and give little regard to the "real reason" for the split-up. Therapeutic skills can facilitate acceptance of the divorce and foster a positive approach to the crisis.

Lawyers' skills are downgraded and social workers' and mediators' skills are mystified and reified.

* * *

The adoption of the mediators' image has important substantive implications with significant political and social ramifications. One of the most harmful assumptions underlying social workers' discourse is that a parent who seeks sole custody of a child has some illegitimate motivation. Mediators may acknowledge exceptions to this generalization in situations in which one parent is a drunkard or drug addict or in which a child is abused, but the general assumption is that the parent who is willing to live up to the ideal of shared custody and control is the one with the child's real interests at heart.

Mediation advocates often characterize opposition to shared custody as pathological. The assumption in the social workers' discourse is that the parent who rejects the shared parenting ideal and seeks sole custody of his or her child has an illegitimate motive. A mother who resists sharing her child with her ex-husband is characterized as having "issue overlay"; she protests too much. Such women may be characterized as clinging and overly dependent on the role identification as wife and mother; social workers and mediators assert that these women can be helped through the mediation process only if they are cooperative. Other women are seen as greedy, merely using the children in order to get larger property settlements; it is claimed that an "effective" mediator can block these women from achieving their evil ends. A third stereotype focuses on vindictive mothers who use the children to get back at their ex-husbands; it is perceived that these are the type of women who should be punished by having their children taken away and sole custody awarded to the fathers.

Lost in the rhetoric of the social worker are real concerns. There is little or no appreciation of the many real problems that joint custody and the ideal of sharing and caring can cause. The prospect of a continued relationship with an ex-spouse may be horrifying to contemplate, but the sharing ideal assumes that a relationship between the noncustodial parent and the child cannot proceed without it. Also unsettling is the extent to which allegations of mistreatment, abuse, or neglect on the part of husbands toward either their wives or children are trivialized, masked, or lost amid the psychological rhetoric that reduces mothers' desires to have custody and control of their children to pathology.

We should be deeply skeptical of these views of women and mothers. They are most accurate and the visions they present are deeply misogynous. Most mothers love their children and would not willfully deprive them of contact with a caring and responsible father. In fact, if the children are old enough to assert their own interests, it is unlikely that mothers could deprive them of contact with their fathers even if they wanted to. By making these observations, I do not mean to suggest that abuses never occur, but rather to point out that they are not typical, or even common, and that it is irrational to base custody policy on the deviant rather than the typical post-divorce situation.

Because social workers and others sympathetic to mediation have created and controlled the presentation of both narratives, the real nature of the competition between the legal and therapeutic models has been hidden. Notably, there are no parallel scenarios involving vindictive or greedy husbands in the mediation literature. No alternative narrative, sympathetic to single parent or sole custody and control, has gained any credibility in the literature. Nor do many stories assign different characters to the stock "victim" and "villain" roles.

Further, by branding opposition to mediation and joint custody as the manifestation of a psychological problem to which mediation is itself the solution, mediation rhetoric forecloses any effective expression of women's legitimate concerns. As things now stand, the cries of protest over the imposition of a joint custody or shared parenting solution from mothers who will be assuming primary care for their children (but sharing control) are attributed to the fact that these mothers have not accomplished an "emotional divorce." As soon as they are able to get over "their issues" they will be able to begin "rational problem solving" and will cooperate agreeably.

The social workers' discourse accepts without criticism the superiority of "rational decisionmaking" within the new, reconstructed family structure. Through this method, the "vindictive" woman is thwarted, the "victimized" man allowed to continue to operate as *paternal familius* (in an altered form, of course) by being given "equal rights" without the formal imposition of responsibility. The helping professionals believe this approach remedies the pro-mother imbalance that has existed in custody decisionmaking.

* * *

The mediation movement's strong bias against anything morally "judgmental" has led to an ideological belief that you can compromise anything. This means meeting halfway some propositions that may be not only unspeakable, but plainly irrational.

Notes and Questions

1. Mediation's proponents claim that it can make divorce less painful, promote better communication, and produce more workable custody and visitation arrangements. Note, *The Trend Toward Mandatory Mediation in Custody and Visitation Disputes of Minor Children: An Overview*, 32 J. FAM. L. 491 (1993–1994). While these claims are still largely untested, mediation does appear to produce a high level of user satisfaction. A 1992 study for the National Center for State Courts found that mediation participants typically viewed the process as fair and compared it favorably to traditional settlement negotiations. The majority felt less pressure to agree to provisions to which they objected or to reach a quick resolution, believed that their rights were better protected,

and were more satisfied with their agreements than were couples who negotiated a settlement; mediation also took less time than did the traditional settlement process. SUSAN L. LEILITZ, MULTI-STATE ASSESSMENT OF DIVORCE MEDIATION AND TRADITIONAL PROCESSING (National Center for State Courts, 1992).

2. Some critics of mediation express concern about the lack of public scrutiny in the mediation process. "Mediation may risk second-class private justice that further disadvantages the poor or powerless." Judith L. Maute, *Public Values and Private Justice: A Case for Mediator Accountability*, 4 GEO. J. LEG. ETHICS 503 (1991). *See also* Trina Grillo, *The Mediation Alternative: Process Dangers for Women*, 100 YALE L. J. 1545 (1991). Others argue, by contrast, that mediation offers more public scrutiny than many negotiated settlements:

> Mediation settlement agreements differ from traditional prenuptial and postnuptial agreements. Typically, the parties enter into prenuptial and postnuptial agreements without court supervision. Mediation agreements are reached under court supervision, before a neutral mediator. The mediation rules create an environment intended to produce a final settlement of the issues with safeguards against the elements of fraud, overreaching, etc., in the settlement process.

Trowbridge v. Trowbridge, 674 So.2d 928 (Fla.App.1996).

Which argument is stronger? Why?

3. Some critics argue that cases involving domestic violence are unsuitable for mediation. *See* Fiona Raitt, *Domestic Violence and Divorce Mediation*, 18 J. SOC. WELF. & FAM. L. 11 (1996); Alison E. Gerenscer, *Family Mediation: Screening for Domestic Abuse*, 23 FLA ST. U.L. REV. 43 (1995). But, in one study of mediation, about half of the women reporting domestic violence said they did not feel that it had impaired their ability to communicate with their ex-spouses on an equal basis and only about a third of the women who reported impaired communication also reported feeling that they had less bargaining power than their ex-husbands during mediation. Both men and women who felt a lack of power tended to end mediation without reaching an agreement. *See* JESSICA PEARSON, FINAL REPORT TO THE STATE JUSTICE INSTITUTE: AN EVALUATION OF THE USE OF MANDATORY MEDIATION (OCT. 1991). *See also* ALASKA JUDICIAL COUNCIL, ALASKA CHILD VISITATION MEDIATION PILOT PROJECT (1992) (reporting that 68% of parents requesting mediation of child visitation disputes were found ineligible as a result of domestic violence and that, in many of these cases, women objected to being barred from mediation because they did not expect the violence to continue or believed that mediation would provide a safe context in which to work out their visitation problems.)

4. There is some evidence to support critics, like Professors Bryan and Fineman, who argue that mediation is often disadvantageous to women, particularly in custody contests. A number of state task forces have discovered evidence of coercive behavior by mediators. *See* Junda

Woo, *Mediation Seen as Being Biased Against Women*, WALL ST. J., Aug. 4, 1992, at B1, B5 (describing cases and noting that fourteen research reports have found that women have less bargaining power than men in mediation). Research conducted in New York also revealed that mediation produced more shared or joint custody awards than did the traditional litigation/settlement process. *See* Carol Bohmer and Marilyn Ray, *Effects of Different Dispute Resolution Methods on Women and Children After Divorce*, 28 FAM. L.Q. 223 (1994); Marilyn Ray, *Divorce Settlements: Comparing Outcomes of Three Different Processes for the Resolution of Disputes* (Law & Society Annual Meeting, 1988). Bohmer and Ray found that 84% of the mediated settlements contained some type of joint custody arrangement, as compared to 37% of attorney-negotiated and 47% of judicially-assisted cases. 37% of mediated agreements, 15.8% of attorney-negotiated, and 17.6% of judicially-assisted agreements specified joint *physical* custody. In part as a result of this tendency toward joint custody, mediated agreements were less likely to include a provision for child support. Mediated agreements were also significantly less likely to specify the child's actual post-divorce living arrangements, particularly when the agreement specified joint physical custody. At nine months post-divorce, joint physical residence had been maintained in less than half of the surveyed cases; where a shift occurred, it almost invariably produced de facto mother custody. "The end result," the researchers concluded, "is that more parents who used mediation are caring for children without the benefit of child support than parents who used other mechanisms to resolve their matrimonial disputes." Ray, *supra*, at 6–7; Bohmer & Ray, *supra,* at 227–28, 232. *See also* ELEANOR MACCOBY & ROBERT MNOOKIN, DIVIDING THE CHILD 290 (1992) (based on custody research in California, expressing concern that "on occasion a divorce mediator may push reluctant parents to accept joint physical custody arrangements as a compromise....")

5. Does mediation save time and money? Court-appointed mediators charge anywhere from $35.00 to $100.00 per hour. Private mediator fees are based on their professional fees; thus therapists or counselors might charge $75 to $100 while a lawyer might charge significantly more. Research reports from the United States indicate that mediation is significantly less expensive than traditional litigation, although reports from England are to the contrary. Although mediation clients appear to reach agreement 50% to 85% of the time, it is unclear how many would also have reached agreement through the traditional negotiation process. Nor is it clear whether mediation produces a "better" process or outcome. *See* Joan B. Kelly, *A Decade of Divorce Mediation Research*, 34 FAM. & CONCIL. CTS. REV. 373, 375–76 (1996).

6. For more thorough discussions of the mediation process, *see* JOHN M. HAYNES, THE FUNDAMENTALS OF FAMILY MEDIATION (1996); FORREST S. MOSTEN, THE COMPLETE GUIDE TO MEDIATION (ABA 1997); GARY J. FRIEDMAN, A GUIDE TO DIVORCE MEDIATION: HOW TO REACH A FAIR, LEGAL SETTLEMENT AT A FRACTION OF THE COST (1993).

SECTION 3. ARBITRATION

Arbitration is a consensual process in which the parties to a dispute agree to submit some or all disputed issues to a neutral third party, the arbitrator who makes a final and binding decision. The parties may jointly select the arbitrator. The arbitrator may conduct the hearing in a private informal setting; at the hearing, evidence may be submitted in any form to which the parties agree, without regard to the rules of evidence. The arbitration decision is submitted to the court for confirmation; if it has been property reached, it will be affirmed by the court as part of its judgment.

The roots of arbitration are ancient. Modern arbitration developed in the early twentieth century through judicial and legislative action, particularly in the labor context. The Uniform Arbitration Act, 7 U.L.A. 1 (1985), promulgated in 1955, has been adopted in thirty-four states and the District of Columbia. Today, arbitration is a routine feature of labor law and collective bargaining; it is increasingly common in commercial disputes as well. Arbitration's advocates argue that it should be used more frequently in family law disputes as well.

ALLAN R. KORITZINSKY ET AL., THE BENEFITS OF ARBITRATION

14 Fam. Advoc. 45 (1992).

Arbitration's Benefits

Some of the benefits of arbitration in family law are:

1. *Selection of Decision Maker:* The parties and their attorneys can choose as the arbitrator a family law specialist . . . In many court systems, judges are assigned to family law cases without regard to their background, training, interest, or experience.

2. *Convenient Forum for Hearing:* The arbitration hearing can be scheduled at the convenience of the participants, with none of the interruptions or delays that are so frequent in the courts . . .

3. *Procedural Flexibility:* The parties and their attorneys can agree to . . . [use] telephone [submissions], sworn affidavits, reports, or any other agreed-upon method.

4. *Speedy and Less Costly:* Arbitration is likely to cost significantly less than a trial . . .

5. *Final and Binding*: The parties can stipulate that the decision . . . is final and binding, with limited rights of review and appeal . . .

Arbitration's Detriments

1. *Lack of Discovery:* The parties generally are not protected by discovery rules and have to resort to the courts to compel discovery when items are not produced . . .

2. *Nonapplicability of Evidentiary and Other Rules:* ... To resolve these issues, the parties may provide in the arbitration agreement that some or all of the rules of evidence and other procedural rules apply ... However, this may be counterproductive to the arbitration process itself ...

3. *Nonbinding Nature of Certain Issues:* Court decisions indicate that custody and possibly child support may not be subject to final and binding arbitration, with resulting limited court review and appeal rights ...

4. *Lack of Enforcement:* An arbitrator does not have the power to enforce the arbitration award or enter a decree of divorce ... [but] the Uniform Arbitration Act specifically provides that the decision or award *shall* be confirmed by the court in a judgment or decree unless vacated or changed by that court.

DICK v. DICK

Michigan Court of Appeals, 1995.
210 Mich.App. 576, 534 N.W.2d 185.

PER CURIAM.

Plaintiff, Leslie Dick, appeals from a judgment of divorce that disposed of the property and assets of the parties and awarded custody of their child to defendant, Linda Dick. On appeal as of right, plaintiff challenges the validity of the arbitration procedure to which he had agreed, as well as the substantive determinations of the arbitrator. He contests, in particular, the award of custody of the child to defendant. We affirm....

Plaintiff and defendant had been married approximately 2 1/2 years before plaintiff initiated divorce proceedings. They had one son.

After both sides filed their initial pleadings, they agreed to submit all issues, including the division of property and child custody and support, to binding arbitration. On March 30, 1990, the court entered an order providing for binding arbitration ...

* * *

More than two years later, the arbitrator issued his opinion. The length of the arbitration proceedings is directly related to the acrimonious approach of the parties, especially plaintiff. But for the vexatious litigation tactics employed by the parties throughout the proceedings, this matter could have been resolved in a more expeditious manner. At this point, the parties' divorce proceedings have lasted nearly twice as long as their marriage.

Ultimately, the arbitrator issued a comprehensive, detailed opinion. In determining custody, he made findings of fact regarding the "best interests of the child" factors set forth in M.C.L. § 722.23; M.S.A. § 25.312(3). The circuit court then entered a judgment of divorce that fully incorporated the arbitrator's conclusions.

On appeal, plaintiff first attacks the validity of the arbitration agreement. He asserts that it was void ab initio, because it was tantamount to the appointment of a private judge by the circuit court. Alternatively, he argues that, if deemed valid by our Court, the arbitration agreement is void because Michigan does not recognize binding arbitration in divorce agreements. He stresses that arbitration is not an acceptable procedure for resolving issues of child custody and support. He requests that we vacate the order of divorce and remand the entire case to the trial court for expedited reconsideration before a different circuit judge.

We agree with plaintiff's contention that the circuit court is without authority to appoint a private judge. * * * [But] [w]e hold that the agreement was one for binding arbitration, not one void ab initio as appointing a private judge.

Because the parties invoked binding arbitration, we must consider whether that procedure may be used in divorce proceedings. Moreover, we must determine whether the binding arbitration agreement at issue here is valid.

Both common law and statutory arbitration have well-established histories in Michigan. In recent years, practitioners have made widespread efforts, with some success, to add binding arbitration to the alternative-dispute-resolution methods available to resolve contested divorces. But no state appellate court has resolved the acceptability of binding arbitration in resolving divorce and, particularly, custody issues.

Authority to permit the use of binding arbitration may be found in MCR 3.216. Although the court rule concerns itself with mediation in domestic relations proceedings, it contains a fairly broad grant of authority regarding settlement procedures ... [but] prohibits the court from ordering, on stipulation of the parties, the use of modified mediation or other settlement procedures.

We emphasize that the rule primarily is concerned with mediation rather than binding arbitration. But it does authorize specifically the use of other unenumerated "settlement procedures" to resolve domestic disputes. * * * Moreover, our Court has approved the use of binding mediation to resolve property distribution issues in divorce cases. * * * Because authority exists in both court rule and case law for permitting parties to agree to "other settlement procedures," we hold that binding arbitration is appropriate to resolve property distribution issues.

However, because child custody and support are not property issues, we must examine separately the legal validity of an agreement to submit them to binding arbitration.

The Child Custody Act, M.C.L. § 722.21 *et seq.*; M.S.A. § 25.312(1) *et seq.*, grants circuit courts the power to enter a support order to which the parties have agreed. The amount may deviate from the recommendation under the child support formula, if the requirements of M.C.L. § 722.27(2); M.S.A. § 25.312(7)(2) are met. Subsection 2 permits deviation from the recommendation if application of the recommendation would be unjust and the court has explained the reasons in writing or on the record.

This provision permits us to conclude that child support disputes also may be submitted to arbitration pursuant to the agreement of the parties. However, because the provision deals solely with the question of support, it is insufficient, standing alone, to permit us to analogize that child custody may also be submitted to arbitration.

Further analysis is required to determine whether child custody may be submitted to binding arbitration, especially because it is a matter of first impression in the state.

In our analysis, we must balance: (1) case law that has led to the widely held belief that custody decisions are the exclusive province of the circuit court, (2) the requirements of the Child Custody Act, and (3) the effect of the Uniform Arbitration Act . . .

* * *

[The court recounts several early statements] of our Supreme Court regarding the grave duty of judges to dispose of custody matters require deference and compliance. However, they must be balanced against the language of the Uniform Arbitration Act, which became effective in 1963. M.C.L. § 600.5001; M.S.A. § 27A.5001 provides:

> (1) All persons, except infants and persons of unsound mind, may, by an instrument in writing, submit to the decision of one or more arbitrators, any controversy existing between them, which might be the subject of a civil action, except as herein otherwise provided, and may, in such submission, agree that a judgment of any circuit court shall be rendered upon the award made pursuant to such submission.

We recognize our obligation to read the language of the arbitration statute in light of previously established rules of common law. We acknowledge that well-settled common-law principles are not to be abolished by implication; an ambiguous statute that contravenes common law must be interpreted so as to make the least change in the common law.

Yet, if a statute is clear on its face, judicial construction is not required or permitted. Furthermore, the Legislature is presumed to have intended the meaning it plainly expressed.

The language of the arbitration statute is broad and seemingly all inclusive. It permits all persons to submit any controversy to arbitration upon their agreement. It does not specifically exempt any civil action from binding arbitration. Thus, balancing the Court's instructions to the lower courts regarding custody determinations with the arbitration statute's more recent and broad language, custody disputes are not exempted from arbitration.

Furthermore, we find in no other statute a clear prohibition of arbitration of child custody. The Child Custody Act does not prevent it. Instead, it provides that, where a child custody dispute has been submitted to the circuit court as an original action under the act, the circuit court has the authority to "[t]ake any other action considered to be necessary in a particular child custody dispute." Such language seems to raise a question whether custody disputes may be decided only by the court. There is throughout the act language directing how to proceed where the dispute is handled by the court. For example, M.C.L. § 722.23; M.S.A. § 25.312(3) states:

> As used in this act, "best interests of the child" means the sum total of the following factors *to be considered, evaluated, and determined by the court*.... [Emphasis added.]

Yet, even there, where the function and authority of the court are detailed, use of alternative methods to determine the best interests of the child are not specifically prohibited. Particularly when this portion of the statute is read in conjunction with the broad grant of authority found in M.C.L. § 722.27(1)(f); M.S.A. § 25.312(7)(1)(f), binding arbitration appears to be a legitimate alternative method.

* * *

We do not believe that MCR 3.210(C) precludes binding arbitration. It requires a hearing in a contested case. Yet, if the parties agree to binding arbitration, they effectively move the dispute to a different forum. The court rule does not appear to prohibit such action. The requirement of a hearing, if voluntary nonbinding mediation fails, is equally understandable. If mediation is chosen and fails, the custody dispute remains to be resolved and, save intervention by the courts, there is no other means of resolution. That is not the case if binding arbitration is elected.

Thus, we find no clear prohibition in case law, court rule, or statute against the use of binding arbitration in the resolution of custody disputes. Binding arbitration is an acceptable and appropriate method of dispute resolution in cases where the parties agree to it. Furthermore, the decision of an arbitrator does not prevent a party from seeking to change custody or modify support in the future.

However, our analysis as it relates to the arbitration agreement at issue here is not yet complete. Several provisions of the agreement do not comport with the requirements of the arbitration statute. The agreement denies any appeal of the procedural methods adopted by the arbitrator but permits appeal of the substantive issues to our Court.

The parties have attempted to create a hybrid form of arbitration. However, we find no authority for it. Rather, we conclude that, having invoked binding arbitration, the parties are required to proceed according to the applicable statute and court rule.

According to the court rule, an arbitration award may not be set aside unless (1) the arbitrator or another is guilty of corruption, fraud, or used other undue means; (2) the arbitrator evidenced partiality, corruption, or misconduct prejudicing a party's rights; (3) the arbitrator exceeded the arbitrator's power; or (4) the arbitrator refused to postpone the hearing on a showing of sufficient cause, refused to hear material evidence, or conducted the hearing to prejudice substantially a party's rights. Otherwise, the agreement is to be given broad application. Only limited review by the courts is permitted.

The parties' agreement to appellate review in this case is reminiscent of a mechanism under which the initial ruling is by a private judge, not an arbitrator. We earlier concluded that the parties did not seek to create, and the circuit court lacked the authority to appoint, a private judge. What the parties agreed to is binding arbitration. Thus, they are not entitled to the type of review they attempted to create.

Consequently, we reform the binding arbitration agreement to comport with the requirements of the statutes and the court rules. We strike the clause permitting appeal of substantive matters to our Court and conclude that the agreement may be reviewed only as permitted by court rule. MCR 3.602. There has been no allegation of fraud, duress, or the other factors set forth in MCR 3.602(J). Therefore, we decline to review the agreement further. Affirmed.

Notes and Questions

1. Some courts have disagreed with the *Dick* court's conclusion. While in recent years several states (including Florida, Kansas, Michigan, Missouri, Ohio, Pennsylvania, and Wisconsin) have authorized the use of traditional arbitration in family law cases, others, based on child protection concerns, have been reluctant to allow binding arbitration of child custody and child support matters because of the court's interest in protecting children. *See* Glauber v. Glauber, 192 A.D.2d 94, 600 N.Y.S.2d 740 (1993). Some courts permit the parties to submit their dispute to arbitration, but reserve the power to conduct a de novo review on matters relating to children. *See* Faherty v. Faherty, 97 N.J. 99, 477 A.2d 1257 (1984); Miller v. Miller, 423 Pa.Super. 162, 620 A.2d 1161 (1993); Crutchley v. Crutchley, 306 N.C. 518, 293 S.E.2d 793 (1982).

2. If the arbitration proceeding produces appeals, what is gained by arbitration? Consider Warren Burger, *Isn't There A Better Way*, 68 A.B.A.J. 274, 276 (1982):

> We must, however, be cautious in setting up arbitration procedures to make sure they become a realistic alternative rather than an additional step in an already prolonged process. For this reason, if a system of voluntary arbitration is to be truly effective, it should be final and binding, without a provision for *de novo* trial or review. This principle was recognized centuries ago by Demosthenes, who, in quoting the law, told the people of Athens: "[W]hen [the parties] have mutually selected an arbiter, let them stand fast by his decision and by no means carry on appeal from him to another tribunal; but let the arbiter's [decision] be supreme."

3. For more on arbitration in family law cases, *see* Stephen W. Schlissel, *A Proposal for Final and Binding Arbitration of Initial Custody Determinations*, 26 FAM. L. Q. 71, 74–76 (1992); Melissa D. Philbrick, *Agreements to Arbitrate Post Divorce Child Custody Disputes*, 18 COLUM. J. L. & SOC. PROB. 419 (1985).

4. Mediation-arbitration, "med-arb," in which the parties agree to submit to arbitration whatever they fail to work out in mediation, is one of the newest versions of dispute resolution. *See* FLA. R. CIV. PRO. RULE 1.800 (1994) (court can order any child dispute to arbitration or arbitration in conjunction with mediation, where the court determines that the dispute is of such nature the parties or the court could benefit). Is this preferable to a trial? to mediation or arbitration alone? *See* Barry Bartel, *Med-Arb as a Distinct Method of Dispute Resolution: History, Analysis, and Potential*, 27 WILLIAMETTE L. REV. 661 (1991); William D. Palmer, *Arbitration and Med–Arb: Two "Alternative" Alternate Dispute Resolution Methods,* XXI(3) THE FLORIDA BAR.ASSOCIATION FAMILY LAW COMMENTATOR 1 (1996).

PROBLEM 18–2:

The administrator of your local court is interested in setting up some alternate dispute resolution programs in divorce cases, which represent approximately 30% of the court's very crowded docket. The administrator wants a program that will "resolve cases without using judicial resources, and do it well enough that the litigants won't come back to court later." You have been asked to structure a program. Should it involve mediation, arbitration, or both? In what types of cases does arbitration appear to be preferable to mediation? to judicial decision making? In what types of cases and at what stage of the litigation process will the various forms of ADR be most cost-effective?

Chapter 19

LEGAL CONSEQUENCES OF CHILD SUPPORT, PROPERTY DIVISION AND ALIMONY DISTINGUISHED: TAXATION AND BANKRUPTCY

SECTION 1. BASIC OVERVIEW

Awards of property, alimony, and child support do not have the same legal consequences:

(1) *Federal Income Tax*: Alimony is deductible from the income of the payor and includable in the income of the recipient; a property settlement or child support is not. A property transfer produces no immediate capital gains consequences; a spouse who receives a property distribution incident to divorce takes the transferor's adjusted basis in the property. A "QDRO" pension distribution produces no tax consequences until pension payments are received.

(2) *Federal Gift and Estate Tax*: Transfers between spouses qualify for an unlimited marital deduction; no gift or estate tax liability is incurred.

(3) *Bankruptcy*: Alimony and child support are not dischargeable in bankruptcy; property settlement obligations may, in some instances, be discharged.

(4) *Compromise*: A right to alimony (usually) and property distributions (always) may be compromised, settled or waived; a parental waiver of the child support obligation does not bind the child and thus will not bar a court from reopening the child support issue if the child is in need.

(5) *Modification*: Alimony (unless the separation agreement or divorce decree specifies otherwise) and child support are subject to modification if circumstances change; a property settlement is final and not modifiable.

(6) *Enforcement*: Alimony and child support may be enforced through civil or criminal contempt proceedings; special nonsupport rem-

edies (e.g., wage garnishment, driver's license revocation) are available. A property settlement normally is enforceable only through regular civil enforcement proceedings.

(7) *Termination of obligation*: Alimony usually terminates upon the recipient's remarriage (or possibly, cohabitation); child support usually terminates when the child reaches majority; property settlement obligations are due until paid.

(8) *Effect of Payor or Recipient's Death*: Alimony and child support generally terminate upon the death of either the recipient or the payor; property settlement obligations are enforceable by and against an estate.

So far, so good! We are barely into this Chapter and know most of the law as well as many practical considerations. Before we go on to consider some complexities of alimony, property settlements and child support in this chapter and the next, the basic simplicity of *all* these transactions must be kept in mind: One spouse transfers or promises to transfer value (typically money or property) to other spouse. That is all! A pays or promises to pay money to B.

The wild card in this pack is classification of a transaction as alimony, child support or a property distribution. Appearances can be deceiving: alimony and child support may be paid as lump sums; property may be distributed in short-term or long-term installments. These approaches are not unusual. Property settlements are paid in installments for a variety of reasons, including issues of liquidity, marketability, or taxation; the alimony recipient may bargain to obtain a lump-sum payment in order to avoid future problems with termination or enforcement of the obligation. Worse—and very important—is the fact that what bears one label in one context, may bear another in a different context. The label attached—and whether that label "sticks" in different contexts—will produce a range of legal consequences; the payment's enforceability, taxability, dischargeability in bankruptcy, modifiability, duration and terminability may all be affected.

"Any one may so arrange his affairs [Ed. note: and why not marriages and divorces?] that his taxes shall be as low as possible; he is not bound to choose that pattern which will best pay the Treasury; there is not even a patriotic duty to increase one's taxes." Helvering v. Gregory, 69 F.2d 809, 810 (2d Cir.1934), aff'd 293 U.S. 465, 55 S.Ct. 266, 79 L.Ed. 596 (1935) (Learned Hand, J.).

SECTION 2. TAXATION

A. DURING THE ONGOING MARRIAGE

Although the U.S. tax system once taxed family members as individuals, since 1948 a married couple has been treated as one tax unit. Since

1986, most income of minor children has been taxed at the rate applicable to their parents.[1]

The purpose of this "family tax unit" approach is to avoid "income-splitting" in order to obtain a lower tax rate. Prior to the 1948 spousal tax unit reform, married couples in community property states could assign income of a high-income spouse to a homemaker spouse in order to reduce the rate at which the income was taxed.[2] Couples in community property states could do this because each spouse held a vested one-half interest in wages earned by either during marriage. *See* Poe v. Seaborn, 282 U.S. 101, 51 S.Ct. 58, 75 L.Ed. 239 (1930). Couples in common law states, who had no legal interest in each other's income, could not. Or so held the Supreme Court in Lucas v. Earl, 281 U.S. 111, 50 S.Ct. 241, 74 L.Ed. 731 (1930). *Lucas* caused a sudden brief rush of support for community property; six common law states adopted a community property system between 1939 and 1949. Congress's adoption of the spousal tax unit principle ended this flurry of enthusiasm for community property. *See* Pamela B. Gann, *Abandoning Marital Status as a Factor in Allocating Income Tax Burdens*, 59 TEX. L. REV. 1 (1980); Lawrence Zelenak, *Marriage and the Income Tax*, 67 S. CAL. L. REV. 339 (1994).

While current tax policy avoids the income-splitting problem, it imposes a "marriage penalty" on two-earner married couples. Unmarried couples, who are each taxed individually, can split their income—often qualifying for a lower overall tax rate—while the married couple cannot. The IRS has successfully challenged couples who divorced every December and then married the following January in an attempt to avoid the marriage penalty. On the other hand, when one spouse does not work outside the home, current tax policy produces a "marriage bonus." This bonus is unavailable to unmarried couples, who may not file a joint return even when it would result in a lower level of taxation.

The chart below shows the magnitude of the penalty/bonus at different income levels. It is reprinted from Dorothy Brain, *The Marriage Bonus/Penalty in Black and White*, 65 U. Cin. L. Rev. 787, 790 (1997).

1. The 1986 Tax Reform Act ended most possibilities for income-splitting with minor children. For children under fourteen years of age, only the first $1,000 of unearned income is taxed at the child's own rate, with the rest taxed at the custodial parent's marginal rate. After 1987, the tax rate on trusts for the benefit of a minor child is 28 percent after the first $5,000 of trust income.

2. Assume that the first $25,000 of individual income was taxed at a 20% rate and that additional income at a 40% rate. If one spouse earning $50,000 assigned half of his income to the other, who earned nothing, the couple would pay tax at a rate of 20% on all their income (a total tax of $10,000). On a spousal unit basis, they would pay tax at a rate of 20% on half their income and at a rate of 40% on the other half (for a total tax of $5,000 plus $10,000, or $15,000).

THE MARRIAGE TAX (PENALTY)/BONUS BY INCOME & ALLOCATION BETWEEN SPOUSES/SINGLES (1993)

	INCOME ALLOCATION					
Income	0%/100%	10%/90%	20%/80%	30%/70%	40%/60%	50%/50%
$10,000						(612)
$20,000	728	428	128	(173)	(180)	(180)
$30,000	968	278	(173)	(180)	(180)	(180)
$40,000	2,268	1,148	321	(180)	(180)	(180)
$50,000	3,282	1,882	1,075	425	(226)	(466)
$60,000	3,296	1,602	815	35	(746)	(1,285)
$70,000	3,596	1,568	555	(356)	(1,266)	(1,285)
$80,000	3,896	1,708	428	(746)	(1,285)	(1,285)
$90,000	4,196	1,848	408	(1,032)	(1,285)	(1,285)
$100,000	4,497	1,990	390	(970)	(1,270)	(1,284)
$125,000	4,695	1,590	(411)	(1,195)	(1,570)	(1,857)
$150,000	5,945	1,887	(970)	(1,420)	(1,857)	(1,859)
$200,000	5,990	882	(84)	(3,364)	(4,312)	(4,312)
$500,000	6,164	(4,203)	8,589	(11,642)	(13,442)	(15,024)

B. AT DIVORCE

1. *Timing the Divorce Decree*

The Internal Revenue Service (IRS) determines each taxpayer's marital status as of December 31. If a couple marries on December 30, they are treated as if married for the entire year; if they divorce on December 30, they are treated as if divorced for the entire year. If settlement negotiations are winding up toward the end of the year, the lawyer should consider whether the parties will owe less income tax that year if married or divorced.

2. *Property Division (IRC § 1041)*

Under the Internal Revenue Code, a taxpayer owes tax only if a "taxable event" occurs. Since 1984, a division of property at divorce is not normally a taxable event. This does not mean that a family lawyer can ignore tax issues in negotiating a property division. A spouse who receives property pursuant to a divorce decree takes the transferor spouse's basis. If and when that property is sold, capital gains tax will be assessed on the difference between the net sales price and the seller's basis; low basis property is thus worth less, after tax, than is high basis property. The client who plans to sell appreciated property after divorce needs to be told that there will be tax liability at the time of sale.

Pensions divided at divorce also pose potential tax problems. As you will recall from chapter 14, the value of pension payments are taxed to the recipient if the pension plan is covered by ERISA and *the order requiring the payments is a qualified domestic relations order.* In Hawkins v. Commissioner, 102 T.C 61 (1994), the court determined that a decree awarding a nonemployee spouse $1,000,000 from the employee's pension plan was not a QDRO, so the distribution to the nonemployee was taxed to the employee. Such potential malpractice minefields explain why most family lawyers have divorce decrees involving significant amounts of property reviewed by competent tax counsel.

For sales of a primary residence after May 6, 1997, each divorced spouse may exclude a gain of up to $250,000, as long as the house was the spouse's primary residence for at least two of the last five years, and the spouse had not already used such an exclusion within two years. For sales before divorce, spouses filing a joint return may exclude $500,000. So, for divorcing spouses whose house has appreciated more than $250,-000 who plan to sell the house in the near future, they would be well advised to sell it before divorce and file a joint return for that tax year. (Both spouses need not hold record title to qualify for the $500,000 exclusion.) *See* Margot Slade, *Gainful Way to Splitsville,* N.Y.Times, March 8, 1998, Business Section, p. 10.

3. *Child Support and Alimony (IRC §§ 71 and 215)*

Alimony is deductible from the taxable income of the payor and includable in the taxable income of the recipient; since 1976, the alimony deduction has been available even to taxpayers who do not itemize deductions. Although the "flattening" of tax rates in 1986 has reduced the scope and value of the alimony deduction, tax savings are still possible. In 1997, the highest tax rate for individuals was about 40%. If an obligor is in the 40% marginal tax bracket and the recipient is in the 15% tax bracket, every $100 in alimony costs the obligor $60 after tax, but is worth $85 to the recipient after tax.

In such a high-low rate situation, there are potential advantages to each spouse of substituting a larger amount of alimony for what would otherwise have been paid in child support. There are risks to this strategy, however. The IRS will treat payments to a former spouse as alimony only if those payments meet the requirements of the Internal Revenue Code. To qualify:[3]

1) Payments must be in cash or cash equivalent to or for the benefit of a former spouse;

2) Payments must be required by a

a) written separation agreement;

b) divorce or separate maintenance decree; or

c) other support decree such as an order for temporary support.

3) If the payments are made after a final decree of divorce or legal separation, the payor and payee cannot live in the same household; the parties have a one-month grace period to establish separate households.

3. Alimony payments required under pre-1985 court orders or agreements incident to divorce or separation, are and remain deductible under the *old* rules. Under these rules, payments must be: i) based on the marital or family relationship, ii) paid after the decree, and iii) paid on a "periodic" basis. The payment period must be in excess of 10 years or subject to specific contingencies such as the death of either spouse, the remarriage of the alimony recipient, or a change in the economic status of either spouse. Pre-1985 alimony obligations may be brought under the new rules by specifying in an amendment that the new rules are to apply.

4) The payment obligation must end at the payee's death; the payor cannot be required to make substitute payments to the payee's estate or third parties after the payee's death.

5) The payments must not be "fixed" to a minor child.

See IRC §§ 71, 215.

Payments will be treated as "fixed" to a minor child (even if characterized in the decree as alimony) if:

1) Payments are to be reduced not more than 6 months before or after the date the child is to attain the age of 18, 21, or the local age of majority, or

2) payments are to be reduced on two or more occasions which occur not more than one year before or after a different child of the payor spouse attains a certain age between the ages of 18 and 24, inclusive.

Internal Revenue Service Temp. Reg. § 1.71–1T, Q–18

While lump-sum as well as periodic payments may qualify as alimony, alimony "recapture" provisions may apply if the annual value of alimony paid decreases by more than $15,000 during the first three post-separation years. The recapture provisions are intended to bar spouses from characterizing a property settlement as alimony in order to save taxes. The recapture calculation is done once, in the third year after payments begin. The formula requires a comparison of total alimony paid during Year 2 with total alimony paid in Year 3, then a comparison of total alimony paid in Year 1 with the *average* of total alimony paid in Years 2 and 3, as follows:

1. Subtract [the amount paid in Year 3 plus $15,000] from the amount paid in Year 2 to get R1.

2. Average [the amount paid in Year 2 plus the amount paid in Year 3 minus R1]. Add $15,000 to this amount, and subtract all from the amount paid in Year 1 to get R2.

3. Add R1 and R2 to get the amount of alimony subject to recapture.

Thus, if H pays W $60,000 in Year 1, $30,000 in Year 2, and 0 in Year 3, the formula works this way:

1. $30,000 (Yr 2 alimony)—[$0 (Yr 3 alimony) + $15,000 (allowable variation)] = $15,000 = R1

2. $60,000 (Yr 1 alimony)—[($30,000 + $0–$15,000)/2 + $15,000] = $37,500 = R2

3. $15,000 + $37,500 = $52,500 = Amount recaptured in Year 3.

Or, if W pays H $45,000 in Year 1, $30,000 in Year 2, and $15,000 in Year 3, the formula works this way:

1. $30,000 (Year 2)—$15,000 (allowable yearly variation) = $15,000

2. $15,000 (allowable variation)—$15,000 (Year 3 total) = $0 = R1

3. $45,000 (Year 1 alimony)—[($30,000 + $15,000)/2 + $15,000] = $2,500 = R2

4. $0 + $2,500 = $2,500 = Amount recaptured in Year 3.

Note that the same total sum of money ($90,000) was paid in alimony in both examples. But the amount subject to recapture varied by $50,000 depending on how the payments were structured. Alimony payments thus should be structured to avoid, or at least minimize, recapture.

The recapture provisions apply to *payments*, not obligations. The payor who falls into arrears on his alimony obligations may find that he has lost the tax advantage of the alimony deduction through recapture. Recapture will not apply, however, if: the payments cease due to death of either party or remarriage of the recipient; the payments are made under a temporary support order; or payments are to be made for at least three years in an amount representing a fixed percentage of the income from a business, property, or employment rather than a dollar amount.

4. Medical Expenses, Dependency Exemptions, Child Care and Earned Income Credits

While either parent may claim medical expenses actually paid on behalf of the child (IRC § 213(d)(5)), the Internal Revenue Code generally assigns tax benefits associated with a child to the parent who has custody. *Only* the custodial parent may claim the child care credit, available to some parents with earned income who pay for child care to enable them to work (IRC § 21(d)(5)); *only* the custodial parent may claim the earned income credit (IRC § 32). The custodial parent is also entitled to the dependency exemption *unless* he or she agrees in writing to relinquish the exemption to the other parent; the waiver may be for one or more years. *See* IRC § 152(3). Tax credits for children and education credits are available only to the parent with the dependency exemption.

There has been a good deal of litigation on the power of a divorce court to order the custodial parent to execute a dependency exemption waiver. Most, but not all, state courts have held that the divorce judge does have authority to mandate such a waiver. *Compare* Zogby v. Zogby, 158 A.D.2d 974, 551 N.Y.S.2d 126 (1990) and Serrano v. Serrano, 213 Conn. 1, 566 A.2d 413 (1989) (majority rule) *with* Blanchard v. Blanchard, 261 Ga. 11, 401 S.E.2d 714 (1991) (minority rule). *See also* Benson, *The Power of State Courts to Award the Dependency Exemption at Divorce*, 16 U. Dayton L. Rev. 29 (1990). If the divorce court awards the exemption to the non-custodial parent, but does not order the custodial parent to execute a waiver, it is probably ineffective. *See* Lystad v. Lystad, 916 S.W.2d 617 (Tex.App.1996).

Beginning in 1998, in addition to a dependency *exemption*, a tax *credit* for children will also be available. The credit amount is $400 per qualifying child in 1998; the amount increases to $500 in 1999. If the parents' adjusted gross income exceeds $110,000, the credit is phased out. To be entitled to the tax credit, a parent must be entitled to the dependency exemption. I.R.C. § 24(c)(1)(A).

Legal fees incident to obtaining taxable alimony or other tax benefits are deductible but, since such fees are now categorized among "miscellaneous" itemized deductions, they are deductible only if itemized deductions exceed 2% of the taxpayer's adjusted gross income.

SECTION 3. BANKRUPTCY

HUCKFELDT v. HUCKFELDT

Court of Appeals, Eighth Circuit, 1994.
39 F.3d 829.

LOKEN, CIRCUIT JUDGE.

Roger Huckfeldt appeals the district court judgment affirming the bankruptcy court's dismissal of his petition to liquidate under Chapter 7 of the Bankruptcy Code. The bankruptcy court dismissed the petition on the ground that it was filed in bad faith to frustrate a divorce decree, and the district court confirmed. Concluding that dismissal was warranted under 11 U.S.C. § 707(a), we affirm.

I.

During their twelve years of marriage, Roger and Georgianne Huckfeldt accumulated over $250,000 in debts while Huckfeldt completed college, medical school, and six years of a residency in surgery, and Georgianne completed college and law school. These debts include $166,000 in student loans to Huckfeldt and $47,000 jointly borrowed from Georgianne's parents. The Huckfeldts divorced on March 26, 1992. The divorce decree ordered Huckfeldt to pay his student loans, one-half of the debt to Georgianne's parents, and other enumerated debts totaling some $241,000. The decree ordered Huckfeldt to hold Georgianne harmless for these debts but otherwise denied Georgianne's request for maintenance.

On June 4, 1992, six months before Huckfeldt would complete his residency in surgery, he filed a voluntary Chapter 7 petition, listing assets of $1,250 and liabilities of $546,857. After filing the petition, Huckfeldt accepted a fellowship at Oregon Health Sciences University, a one or two year position paying $45,000 per year, substantially less than the income he could likely earn as a surgeon during the pendency of his Chapter 7 proceeding. Following Huckfeldt's petition, creditors of the debts assigned to him in the divorce decree began pursuing Georgianne for repayment. She filed for bankruptcy protection in March 1993.

In September 1992, Georgianne and her parents ("the Creditors") filed a motion to dismiss Huckfeldt's Chapter 7 petition on the ground that it was filed in bad faith. The Creditors alleged that Huckfeldt had threatened to file for bankruptcy during the divorce proceedings and had commenced this proceeding in defiance of the divorce decree for the purpose of shifting responsibility for assigned debts to Georgianne. The Creditors further alleged that Huckfeldt "has deliberately taken steps to reduce his annual income" to avoid payment of his debts through a

Chapter 7 liquidation. The Creditors argued that this bad faith warranted dismissal under §§ 105, 109, 301, and 707 of the Bankruptcy Code.

After a hearing, the bankruptcy court granted the Creditors' motion to dismiss. After finding that Roger could be earning $110,000 to $120,000 per year, after all expenses except income tax, the court stated:

> It is the purpose of the bankruptcy system to provide a fresh start for the honest but unfortunate debtor. It is not the purpose of the bankruptcy system to eliminate the obligations of a party who is capable of paying same. The Court believes debtor filed this bankruptcy petition in bad faith and with the deliberate intention of unloading debt, particularly that to his spouse, which he could shortly begin to repay. Further this Court believes it was the intent of the debtor to leave his ex-spouse with all the debts and obligations incurred over the twelve years and force her into a bankruptcy situation also....
>
> Accordingly the Court concludes that this case was filed in bad faith and concludes that good faith is a requirement for the filing of a bankruptcy petition no matter what the chapter.

The district court confirmed, expressly holding that § 707(a) of the Code authorizes dismissal for bad faith.

On appeal, Huckfeldt argues that the bankruptcy court committed an error of law in dismissing the Chapter 7 petition because (i) ability to repay debts is not grounds for dismissal under § 707(a), and (ii) his petition could not be dismissed for "substantial abuse" of Chapter 7 under § 707(b), which does focus on ability to pay. Because we uphold the dismissal under § 707(a), we need not consider Huckfeldt's § 707(b) contentions.

II.

Section 707(a) provides that the bankruptcy court may dismiss a Chapter 7 proceeding only after notice and a hearing and only for cause, including—

> (1) unreasonable delay by the debtor that is prejudicial to creditors;
>
> (2) nonpayment of any fees or charges required under chapter 123 of title 28; and
>
> (3) failure of the debtor in a voluntary case to file, within fifteen days or such additional time as the court may allow after the filing of the petition commencing such case, the information required by paragraph (1) of § 521, but only on a motion by the United States trustee.

In authorizing dismissal "for cause," the statute does not define "cause," beyond setting forth three specific examples. Use of the introductory word "including" means that these three types of "cause" are nonexclusive. *See* 11 U.S.C. § 102(3) (" 'includes' and 'including' are not limiting"); *P.C. Pfeiffer Co. v. Ford*, 444 U.S. 69, 77 n. 7, 100 S.Ct. 328,

334 n. 7, 62 L.Ed.2d 225 (1979) ("including" means the enumerated items are part of a larger group).

The legislative history to § 707(a) is meager but does contain one comment that provides the core of Huckfeldt's § 707(a) argument on appeal:

> The section does not contemplate ... that the ability of the debtor to repay his debts in whole or in part constitutes adequate cause for dismissal. To permit dismissal on that ground would be to enact a non-uniform mandatory chapter 13, in lieu of the remedy of bankruptcy.

H.R.Rep. No. 95–595, 95th Cong., 1st Sess. (1977), *reprinted in* 2 Collier on Bankruptcy App. 2, at II–380; S.Rep. No. 95–989, 95th Cong., 2d Sess. (1978), *reprinted in* 3 Collier on Bankruptcy App. 3, at V–94, U.S. Code Cong. & Admin.News 1978, p. 5787. At the urging of consumer lenders, Congress later enacted § 707(b), which permits the dismissal of a petition by a consumer debtor if the requested relief would be a "substantial abuse" of Chapter 7. Ability to pay is the primary inquiry under § 707(b). *See Fonder v. United States*, 974 F.2d 996, 999 (8th Cir.1992); *In re Walton*, 866 F.2d 981, 982–84 (8th Cir.1989).

A. Although Huckfeldt's briefs carefully avoid the issue, the initial question is whether the district court erred in holding that bad faith may be "cause" for dismissal under § 707(a). That is an open issue in this circuit, and few other circuits have considered it. The Sixth Circuit has expressly held that bad faith may be cause for dismissal under § 707(a), but only in "egregious cases." *See In re Zick*, 931 F.2d 1124, 1127, 1129 (6th Cir.1991). The Fifth Circuit in considering whether there was cause to lift the automatic stay in bankruptcy stated:

> Every bankruptcy statute since 1898 has incorporated literally, or by judicial interpretation, a standard of good faith for the commencement, prosecution, and confirmation of bankruptcy proceedings.

In re Little Creek Development Co., 779 F.2d 1068, 1071 (5th Cir.1986). *See generally In re Victory Constr. Co.*, 9 B.R. 549, 551–60 (Bankr. C.D.Cal.1981) (reviewing the historical development of the bad faith doctrine in rehabilitation and reorganization proceedings), *vacated as moot*, 37 B.R. 222 (9th Cir.BAP 1984). But the Fourth Circuit in dictum has suggested that bad faith may only be considered under § 707(b). *See In re Green*, 934 F.2d 568, 571 (4th Cir.1991).

In considering this issue, a number of bankruptcy courts have expressed concern that the open-ended use of bad faith to dismiss Chapter 7 cases is inappropriate. These courts suggest that a different standard of conduct should be applied to debtors willing to surrender all non-exempt assets in a Chapter 7 liquidation proceeding, than to those who seek to reorganize or extend their debts under Chapter 11 or Chapter 13. *See In re Kragness*, 63 B.R. 459, 465 (Bankr.D.Or.1986). They also fear that the bad faith inquiry will be "employed as a loose cannon which is to be pointed in the direction of a debtor whose values do not coincide precisely with those of the court." *In re Latimer*, 82 B.R. 354, 364 (Bankr.E.D.Pa.1988). These are legitimate concerns.

In *In re Khan*, 172 B.R. 613 (Bankr.D.Minn.1994), the court criticized cases such as *In re Zick* for adopting a bad faith exception to Chapter 7 relief without statutory authority, and for basing bad faith decisions under § 707(a) on ability-to-pay factors that should be analyzed exclusively under § 707(b). *Id.*, 172 B.R. at 620–25. Acknowledging that courts do have inherent power to sanction the bad faith litigant, *see Chambers v. NASCO, Inc.*, 501 U.S. 32, 43–46, 111 S.Ct. 2123, 2132–33, 115 L.Ed.2d 27 (1991), the court in *Khan* urged that bad faith under § 707(a) be limited to extreme misconduct falling outside the purview of more specific Code provisions, such as using bankruptcy as a "scorched earth" tactic against a diligent creditor, or using bankruptcy as a refuge from another court's jurisdiction. *Khan*, 172 B.R. at 624–26.

We agree with the narrow, cautious approach to bad faith adopted in *Khan*. Congress has defined the ultimate issue in § 707(a) cases as whether the Chapter 7 petition should be dismissed "for cause." As this case illustrates, some conduct constituting cause to dismiss a Chapter 7 petition may readily be characterized as bad faith. But framing the issue in terms of bad faith may tend to misdirect the inquiry away from the fundamental principles and purposes of Chapter 7. Thus, we think the § 707(a) analysis is better conducted under the statutory standard, "for cause." If the bankruptcy court elects instead to act under the inherent judicial power to punish a bad faith litigant, that action should not be taken under § 707(a).

B. Based upon the legislative history of § 707(a), Huckfeldt argues that the bankruptcy court erred in dismissing his petition based upon his ability to pay. This contention proceeds on a faulty premise. The bankruptcy court expressly stated that it was dismissing because the petition was filed in bad faith, not because Huckfeldt is able to pay some or all of his debts. The court found that Huckfeldt filed the petition for the purpose of frustrating the divorce court decree and forcing his ex-wife into bankruptcy, at a time when his financial prospects made him anything but an "honest but unfortunate debtor" needing Chapter 7 relief. Chief Judge Koger expressly held in a prior case that ability to pay is not cause for dismissal under § 707(a). *See In re Goulding*, 79 B.R. 874, 876 (Bankr.W.D.Mo.1987). We will not assume that he ruled to the contrary here.

C. Huckfeldt filed a Chapter 7 petition to frustrate the divorce court decree and to push his ex-wife into bankruptcy. He then manipulated his immediate earnings to ensure that the Chapter 7 proceeding would achieve these non-economic motives. That conduct meets the narrow standard urged by *Khan*. Indeed, such conduct has long been considered unworthy of bankruptcy protection:

> [T]he petition in this case was not filed for the purpose of a just liquidation by composition with creditors but to defeat the wife from a right of possession in and to the real estate which was to be

> awarded to her under the divorce proceedings. This violates the purpose and intent of the statute . . . and, as said by the Supreme Court of the United States, under that situation, the proceedings will be halted at the outset.

In re Brown, 21 F.Supp. 935, 939 (S.D.Iowa1938). Huckfeldt is not an "honest but unfortunate debtor" entitled to the equitable relief of a Chapter 7 liquidation. His petition was properly dismissed for cause.

The judgment of the district court is affirmed.

HARRELL v. SHARP

Court of Appeals, Eleventh Circuit, 1985.
754 F.2d 902.

R. Lanier Anderson, III, Circuit Judge.

* * * Although the parties dispute the amount of arrearages, the issue they present to this court concerns the dischargeability in bankruptcy of whatever arrearages have accrued.

Debtor filed his Chapter VII petition October 17, 1980. On December 12, 1980, debtor filed a complaint in bankruptcy court to determine the dischargeability of his domestic debts. Specifically, debtor sought to have declared dischargeable the amounts he owed in alimony and child support arrearages because, he contended, such amounts were not "actually in the nature of alimony, maintenance, or support." Debtor also sought to have declared dischargeable his obligation to make payments on behalf of his son past the age of eighteen because, as expressed in his complaint, "such obligations were not and are not actually in the nature of alimony, maintenance, or support," but were "voluntarily assumed and constitute contractual obligations which are discharged by [debtor's] bankruptcy case."

* * *

A debtor may obtain a general discharge under Chapter VII of the Bankruptcy Code from "all debts that arose before the date of the order for relief." 11 U.S.C.A. § 727(b) (West 1979). The Code makes exceptions for certain obligations, however, among which are alimony and support payments. The language in the Code that provides this treatment states that a discharge under § 727 does not discharge a debtor from any debt:

> (5) to a spouse, former spouse, or child of the debtor, for alimony to, maintenance for, or support of such spouse or child, in connection with a separation agreement, divorce decree, or property settlement agreement, but not to the extent that—
>
> (A) such debt is assigned to another entity, voluntarily, by operation of law, or otherwise (other than debts assigned pursuant

to § 402(a)(26) of the Social Security Act [the federal child support enforcement program, see p. 1101]); or

(B) such debt includes a liability designated as alimony, maintenance, or support, unless such liability is actually in the nature of alimony, maintenance, or support;

11 U.S.C.A. § 523(a)(5) (West 1979 & Supp.1984). The effect of the statute, then, is that a given domestic obligation is not dischargeable if it is "actually in the nature of" alimony, maintenance, or support.

A. Post-Majority Payments

Debtor contends that his obligation to pay post-majority educational expenses and child support is dischargeable because he was not required under relevant state law to support his son past the age of majority. * * *

First, the language of § 523(a)(5) does not refer to a particular state law legal duty of support. If Congress had intended dischargeability to be determined by whether an obligation could be imposed under state law, it might have addressed dischargeability in those terms. Congress chose instead to describe as not dischargeable those obligations in the "nature" of support. We believe that in using this general and abstract word, Congress did not intend bankruptcy courts to be bound by particular state law rules.

This conclusion is directly supported by the legislative history of § 523(a)(5). The committee reports that accompanied the new bankruptcy code provide that "what constitutes alimony, maintenance, or support will be determined under the bankruptcy laws, not state law." H.R.Rep. No. 595, 95th Cong., 1st Sess. 364 (1977), U.S.Code Cong. & Admin. News 1978, pp. 5787, 6319. * * *

We are of * * * opinion in the present case, that the nature of debtor's promise to pay educational expenses and child support is not determined by the legal age of majority under state law. The bankruptcy court characterized the agreement to pay educational expenses as in the nature of support, and the only ground on which debtor has challenged that characterization on appeal relates to the state law legal duty as determined by the age of majority. We are persuaded by the language of § 523(a)(5), the legislative history of that section, and the weight of the case law that the absence of a state law duty does not determine that an obligation is dischargeable in bankruptcy.

B. Alimony Arrearages

Debtor argues on appeal that his alimony arrearages are not "actually in the nature of alimony, maintenance, or support" (1) because the payments he did make adequately met his obligation to support defendant as defined under state law; and (2) because, even if federal law applies rather than state law, defendant did not *need* the arrearages as of the time debtor filed his Chapter VII petition, and thus federal law would not classify such amounts as in the nature of support.

We rejected debtor's state law contention * * * above. Thus, we turn directly to debtor's contention that the bankruptcy court should assess a divorced spouse's needs and arrive at the precise amount that the spouse would require for support. In accepting this proposition, the bankruptcy court followed *Warner v. Warner (In re Warner)*, 5 B.R. 434 (Bankr.D.Utah 1980), which held:

> even if the debt was originally imposed on the basis of the need of the spouse or children, the debt cannot be held nondischargeable unless at the time of filing there exists a present need by the spouse or children that the debt be paid.

The court in *Warner* reasoned that the requirement of present need was "necessary to enforce the general purpose of the bankruptcy laws in providing relief for the debtor." Some bankruptcy courts have followed the holding of *Warner*. * * * Other courts have rejected the *Warner* approach. The language of the statute itself, the legislative history and considerations of comity, lead us to the conclusion that the district court in this case was correct in rejecting the reasoning and holding of *Warner*.

* * * The statutory language suggests a simple inquiry as to whether the obligation can legitimately be characterized as support, that is, whether it is in the *nature* of support. The language does not suggest a precise inquiry into financial circumstances to determine precise levels of need or support; nor does the statutory language contemplate an ongoing assessment of need as circumstances change.

The legislative history is to the same effect. It described the process of determining whether an obligation was in the nature of support as being similar to the determination of whether a payment is actually alimony or in reality a property settlement. The House Report that accompanied the Bankruptcy Code reads, in relevant part:

> This provision will, however, make nondischargeable any debts resulting from an agreement by the debtor to hold the debtor's spouse harmless on joint debts, to the extent that the agreement is in payment of alimony, maintenance, or support of the spouse, as determined under bankruptcy law considerations that are similar to considerations of whether a particular agreement to pay money to a spouse is actually alimony or a property settlement.

H.R.Rep. No. 595, 95th Cong., 1st Sess. 364 (1977), U.S.Code Cong. & Admin.News 1978, p. 6319.

Considerations of comity reinforce our interpretation. Debtor's attempt to expand the dischargeability issue into an assessment of the ongoing financial circumstances of the parties to a marital dispute would of necessity embroil federal courts in domestic relations matters which should properly be reserved to the state courts.

We conclude that Congress intended that bankruptcy courts make only a simple inquiry into whether or not the obligation at issue is in the *nature* of support. This inquiry will usually take the form of deciding whether the obligation was in the nature of support as opposed to being in the nature of a property settlement. Thus, there will be no necessity for a precise investigation of the spouse's circumstances to determine the appropriate level of need or support. It will not be relevant that the circumstances of the parties may have changed, e.g., the spouse's need may have been reduced at the time the Chapter VII petition is filed. Thus, limited to its proper role, the bankruptcy court will not duplicate the functions of state domestic relations courts, and its rulings will impinge on state domestic relations issues in the most limited manner possible.

Once the bankruptcy court in this case concluded that the alimony payments were "actually in the nature of alimony," its task was at an end. The obligation was thereby determined to be nondischargeable under § 523(a)(5). The district court correctly rejected the bankruptcy court's subsequent excursion to determine the precise level of the wife's need for support.

For the foregoing reasons, the judgment of the district court is in all respects.

Affirmed.

Notes and Questions

1. As *Harrell* demonstrates, property division obligations have traditionally been dischargeable in bankruptcy while support obligations were not. *See generally* Sheryl L. Scheible, *Bankruptcy and the Modification of Support: Fresh Start, Head Start, or False Start?*, 69 N.C.L. Rev. 577, 578 (1991). 1994 amendments to the Bankruptcy Code have made it more difficult to extinguish property division obligations today. Under § 523(a)(15), such obligations cannot be discharged unless (1) the debtor "does not have the ability to pay such debt from income or property of the debtor not reasonably necessary to be expended for the maintenance or support of the debtor or a dependent of the debtor;" (2) the debtor does not have enough income or property to pay the debt after paying necessary business expenses if the debtor owns a business; or (3) discharging the debt would "result in a benefit to the debtor that outweighs the detrimental consequences to the obligee." 11 U.S.C.A. § 523(a)(15). *See generally* Bernice Donald & Jennie Latta, *The Dischargeability Property Settlement and Hold Harmless Agreements in Bankruptcy*, 31 F.L.Q. 409 (1997).

2. Section 523 of the Bankruptcy Code provides that a claim for "fraud or defalcation while acting in a fiduciary capacity" may not be discharged in bankruptcy. If possible, careful lawyers for obligees will thus try to characterize obligor obligations as those of a trustee. *See* In re Eichelberger, 100 B.R. 861 (Bkrtcy. S.D.Tex. 1989).

3. Section 522 of the Bankruptcy Code provides that a "judicial lien" may be discharged in bankruptcy. Some divorce obligors, relying on this provision, have filed for bankruptcy arguing that a lien imposed by a divorce court to secure an obligation is a dischargeable judicial lien. To date, this argument has generally failed. In Farrey v. Sanderfoot, 500

U.S. 291, 111 S.Ct. 1825, 114 L.Ed.2d 337 (1991), the divorce court awarded a husband (Sanderfoot) the marital home and ordered him to pay his former wife (Farrey) cash to equalize the property division order. To secure the cash award, the decree imposed a lien on the real estate in the amount of the cash award. Sanderfoot filed for bankruptcy, claimed the home as exempt property under the Code's homestead exemption and sought to avoid his former wife's lien as a judicial lien subject to discharge under § 522. The Supreme Court held that the lien was not dischargeable. Section 522 does not apply, the Court held, when the debtor's property interest does not predate the lien. Sanderfoot had conceded that the divorce decree awarded him an entirely new interest in the home rather than simply adding his wife's to the one he already had. Based on that technicality, he lost. Not surprisingly, since *Farrey*, other courts have held that a divorce decree creates a new property interest to which any lien imposed by the decree attaches, rather than attaching a lien to a preexisting interest. *See, e.g.,* In re Catli, 999 F.2d 1405 (9th Cir.1993); Klemme v. Schoneman, 165 Wis.2d 250, 477 N.W.2d 77 (Wis.App.1991); In re Finch, 130 B.R. 753 (D.C.S.Tex. 1991). Section 522 has also been amended to provide that a lien securing a support obligation cannot be avoided. *See generally* Sheryl Scheible Wolf, *Divorce, Bankruptcy, and Metaphysics: Avoidance of Marital Liens under § 522(f) of the Bankruptcy Code*, 31 F.L.Q. 513 (1997).

WHITE v. WHITE

Court of Appeals, Sixth Circuit, 1988.
851 F.2d 170.

WELLFORD, CIRCUIT JUDGE.

The debtor-appellant challenges in this appeal the bankruptcy court's decision to lift an automatic stay to allow divorce proceedings brought by his wife to proceed in state court. The debtor claims an abuse of discretion because lifting the stay divested the bankruptcy court of its alleged exclusive jurisdiction in favor of a state tribunal. We disagree.

Patricia White, appellee, instituted divorce proceedings against her husband John on February 7, 1985 in Ashtabula County, Ohio. The divorce court ordered him to make temporary alimony payments of $800 weekly. When her husband made no payments under this order, Mrs. White moved for the appointment of a receiver for Mr. White's property.

John Paul White countered by instituting Chapter 11 bankruptcy proceedings in the bankruptcy court. For a time he remained in control of the bankruptcy estate, principally his oil and gas business, but later a bankruptcy trustee was appointed to manage the financial affairs of the bankruptcy estate. Debtor still operates the business. The effect of Mr. White's bankruptcy petition was to halt the divorce proceedings because of the automatic stay provisions of 11 U.S.C. § 362.

Mrs. White thereafter moved to lift the stay in order to allow the divorce action to proceed. She seeks permission for the state court to make an appropriate division of the marital estate which, of course, also constitutes the husband's bankruptcy estate. Mrs. White maintains that the state court's previous assumption of jurisdiction over the marital property took precedence over the bankruptcy court, citing *In re Washington*, 623 F.2d 1169 (6th Cir.1980), *cert. denied sub nom. Wasserman v. Washington*, 449 U.S. 1101 (1981). The bankruptcy court granted her motion and lifted the stay so that divorce proceedings, including an apportionment of the marital estate, could be accomplished. In lifting the stay, the court noted that the state court had prior *in rem* jurisdiction. While specifying that it was not allowing the state court to appoint a receiver, the bankruptcy court stated the case could be disposed of in an orderly fashion by first allowing the state court to determine, under state law, how the property should be appropriately divided between the husband and wife.

On appeal, the district court upheld this action despite debtor's challenges to its jurisdictional propriety. The district court decided that the bankruptcy court order at issue did not improperly give up bankruptcy jurisdiction to the divorce court. Further, it noted that if the state court were to overstep its role, the problem could be rectified by actions under 11 U.S.C. § 105(a). Appeal to this court followed.

Appellant argues that the jurisdiction granted the bankruptcy court in 28 U.S.C. § 1334(d) is exclusive and may not be given up in favor of a state court proceeding for any reason. He also claims that *In re Washington, supra*, is no longer valid in light of 1984 amendments to the Bankruptcy Code.

We do not believe *In re Washington* controls the outcome of this case. That decision reversed a bankruptcy court's determination that it could assert jurisdiction over a debtor's property even when a state divorce court already had *in rem* jurisdiction over it. Our decision to award superior jurisdiction to the state court was based on "traditional notions of comity, which require that, as between state and federal courts, jurisdiction must be yielded to the court that first acquires jurisdiction over the property." 623 F.2d at 1172. We traced this holding to a broader doctrine which advocates granting exclusive jurisdiction to the first court asserting *in rem* jurisdiction, when both courts base jurisdiction on control of the same property. *See, e.g., Princess Lida of Thurn and Taxis v. Thompson*, 305 U.S. 456, 466 (1939).

Despite the federalism interests served by such a rule, we agree with debtor's argument that the 1978 and 1984 changes to the Bankruptcy Code were primarily aimed at getting away from the kind of *in rem* jurisdiction set out in *Princess Lida* and *In re Washington*. The jurisdiction granted in 28 U.S.C. § 1334(d) indicates a conscious effort by Congress to grant the bankruptcy court special jurisdiction and to preclude the type of jurisdictional disputes evidenced in those cases.

This interpretation has been followed by other courts presented with similar circumstances. *In re Modern Boats, Inc.*, 775 F.2d 619 (5th Cir.1985) presented the situation in which an admiralty court had obtained *in rem* jurisdiction over the debtor's ship before bankruptcy was declared. Despite this previously-claimed jurisdiction, the bankruptcy court took control of the vessel. The court in *Modern Boats* declared this action to be appropriate because once a bankruptcy petition was filed, the admiralty court was stripped of jurisdiction and it became the exclusive province of the bankruptcy court. *Id.* at 620. The same result was reached in another case where, prior to bankruptcy, the admiralty court had sold a ship and only approval of the sale remained. *See In re Louisiana Ship Management, Inc.*, 761 F.2d 1025 (5th Cir.1985). The outcome in these decisions is premised upon the changes Congress made in bankruptcy court jurisdiction, and we believe we must also follow the intent reflected in the amended language of § 1334(d). The rule in *In re Washington* should therefore no longer apply to give the state court jurisdiction over property simply because it may have been the first court to exercise control over the property.

Whether the bankruptcy court may suspend its jurisdiction, however, is a different question. Lifting the automatic stay as provided in 11 U.S.C. § 362(d) in this case will permit the state court to exercise limited jurisdiction in the kind of matter that is traditionally exclusively reserved for state divorce courts. Bankruptcy courts in other cases have not declined to lift the stay to allow divorce proceedings to conclude. *See In re Johnson*, 51 B.R. 439 (Bankr.E.D.Pa.1985), and *Schulze v. Schulze*, 15 B.R. 106 (Bankr.S.D.Ohio 1981). The Bankruptcy Code does not define a debtor's interest in property; the answer to that question must be made after reference to state law. 4 L. King, *Collier on Bankruptcy* § 541.07 p. 541–29 (15th ed. 1983); *cf. Selby v. Ford Motor Co.*, 590 F.2d 642 (6th Cir.1979) (court looked to Michigan treatment of property rights in deciding bankrupt's interest in trust funds). With regard to the present pending state court divorce proceedings, the bankruptcy court has acted to permit the state court with expertise in such matters to decide questions that are an inherent part of the divorce process.

While the bankruptcy court under § 105(a) may enforce the Code for the benefit of the parties before it, and may seek a just result in light of the interests of creditors and others concerned with the bankruptcy process, we are not sure that it can review or reject the state court's action in allocation of the marital estate once the stay is lifted. This, therefore, represents some abrogation of the bankruptcy court's authority, at least as far as its ability to determine the rights in marital property. Nevertheless, we are persuaded that:

> "It is appropriate for bankruptcy courts to avoid invasions into family law matters 'out of consideration of court economy, judicial restraint, and deference to our state court brethren and their established expertise in such matters.' "

In re MacDonald, 755 F.2d 715, 717 (9th Cir.1985) (quoting *In re Graham*, 14 B.R. 246, 248 (Bankr.W.D.Ky.1981)). *See also Schulze, supra. Schulze* considered the position of the nondebtor spouse and concluded his or her status would be seriously compromised if the bankruptcy proceedings continued while the divorce proceedings were stayed. This was deemed to be "cause" sufficient to lift the stay within the guidelines of § 362(d)(1). 15 B.R. at 108–09. The language of § 362(d) has not been changed by the 1984 amendments to the Code and we believe the bankruptcy court properly deferred to the divorce court's greater expertise on the question of what property belongs to whom.

The 1984 amendments to the Bankruptcy Code have not rendered it a self-contained mechanism to operate entirely without reference to state law. We therefore find no abuse of discretion in the bankruptcy court's decision to defer to the traditional and expert judgment of the divorce court of the State of Ohio for the sole purpose of deciding interests in the marital estate of the debtor husband and wife. The debtor's argument simply proves too much in urging that a bankruptcy court may never give up its jurisdiction for any reason, even for a limited purpose. The provisions for lifting the stay found in § 362(d) should be deemed to apply in these circumstances for the limited purpose of allowing the state court to exercise its exclusive domestic relations authority, including decisions concerning fair allocation of the marital estate.

We find no error, therefore, in the reasoning of Judge Bodoh that, "[U]ntil the court of Common Pleas for Ashtabula County, Ohio, makes a specific determination of the property rights as between the Debtor and his spouse, what is property of the Debtor's estate in this cause is unclear, and the reorganization of Debtor's business cannot proceed in an orderly fashion." The bankruptcy judge proceeded to lift the stay so that the state court might "determine the substantive rights of the parties under applicable, non-bankruptcy domestic relations law and to allow the parties to reach, or the state court to impose, a property settlement based on the state court's inquiry into the need for support and other factors under state law." At the same time, the bankruptcy court indicated its "exclusive jurisdiction over property of the Debtor ... when the state court defines what is the property of the Debtor.... "

As noted above, the district court believed any problems encountered in handing partial resolution of the matter to the divorce courts could be remedied by resort to 11 U.S.C. § 105. We agree that this is an adequate safeguard, and we also suggest that the courts below urge the trustee to appear in the divorce action. By setting out his position as representative of the debtor's creditors, the trustee could make the state court aware that other parties' interests will be affected by the property division, thus possibly facilitating a fairer settlement for all parties concerned.

We affirm the decision to lift the stay under the circumstances here because we are concerned that the Bankruptcy Code could otherwise be abused as a weapon in a marital dispute. We believe the decision to lift the stay in this case was a proper exercise of discretion, but we do not wish to establish a per se rule in every bankruptcy case involving a domestic relations situation that the bankruptcy stay must be lifted. For example, there might be times when the bankruptcy court suspects collusion between the spouses to stage a divorce to avoid payment of the just claims of creditors, and granting a stay in that situation would obviously not serve the ends of bankruptcy or divorce jurisprudence. We simply hold that whether or not to lift the automatic stay in that type of bankruptcy proceeding lies within the reasonable discretion of the bankruptcy court or the district court as the case may be.

We therefore AFFIRM the challenged action in this case.

A Summary. The family lawyer must carefully and precisely assess the tax consequences of a proposed settlement. The tax rules present opportunities for benefits to both parties—but also present a minefield of potential mistakes. For example, in Hoover v. Commissioner, 23 Fam. L. Rep. (BNA) 1104 (6th Cir.1996), the divorce decree labelled payments as alimony, but failed to specify that the obligation would terminate upon the recipient's death. Because it was not clear under Ohio law that alimony automatically terminated if the recipient died, the obligor could not deduct any of the payments. This is not something you want to happen to one of your clients. Think! Read carefully! And get the advice of competent tax counsel.

Other bodies of law, such as bankruptcy, must also be considered. What may look and be treated like an installment property transfer or a mere contractual obligation may, under the bankruptcy laws, be considered in the "nature of" alimony or child support and thus held not to be dischargeable.

Finally, practical concerns must be assessed. If a divorcing woman is thinking of early remarriage, or if her ex-husband is near death, she may be much better off with a small, but final and indefeasible, property settlement than with generous alimony which would terminate on either party's death or her remarriage; where there is an antagonistic and bitter ex-husband, an alimony judgment, with its threat of jail for contempt, may be preferable to a larger installment property settlement; a large, installment-type property settlement from a man in a high-risk (of bankruptcy) business may be worth a lot less than a much more modest (but not dischargeable) alimony obligation.

Chapter 20

MODIFICATION AND ENFORCEMENT OF SUPPORT AWARDS

SECTION 1. MODIFICATION: SOME GENERAL THEMES

Child and indefinite (*i.e.*, permanent) spousal support awards are modifiable; property division and lump-sum alimony awards orders are not. *See* Pittman v. Pittman, 419 So.2d 1376 (Ala.1982). Courts have disagreed on whether rehabilitative spousal support granted for a fixed term may be extended if the recipient does not become economically independent within the prescribed time. *Compare* Self v. Self, 861 S.W.2d 360 (Tenn.1993) *with* Bentz v. Bentz, 148 Wis.2d 400, 435 N.W.2d 293 (Wis.App. 1988).

The traditional basis for modification of a support order is a "substantial (or material) and unforeseeable change in the circumstances of one of the parties." *See* J. Thomas Oldham, *Cohabitation by an Alimony Recipient Revisited*, 20 J. FAM. L. 615 (1982). This is a relatively vague standard; the materials in this chapter describe how courts have interpreted it.

A central problem in modification policy is attaining the right balance between stability and flexibility. Support orders will often remain in effect for a long while. The child who is age 2 at divorce will be entitled to support until age 18 (or 21, depending on state law); the spouse who obtains permanent alimony will be entitled to support until remarriage or the death of either party. Because of their duration, support orders must be flexible; a support order based on the obligor's high income will quickly become unconscionable if he loses his job. But judicial economy and the parties' need for reasonably certain income entitlements also demand stability; we do not want divorced couples to continually relitigate the amount of support owed.

The "substantial change in circumstances" test is an attempt to balance the goals of stability and flexibility. The UMDA comes down more firmly on the side of stability, requiring that, to warrant modification, a change in circumstances must be "so substantial and continuing as to be unconscionable." UMDA § 316. In recent years, child support policy has come down more firmly on the side of flexibility.

When child support orders are initially entered, many parents are young and have relatively low incomes. As time goes by, inflation typically diminishes the value of the initial award, while the noncustodial parent's income typically increases. *See* Elizabeth Phillips & Irwin Garfinkel, *Income Growth Among Nonresident Fathers: Evidence from Wisconsin*, 30 DEMOGRAPHY 227 (1993). In response to this pattern, alimony and child support modification principles have begun to diverge. The federal government now requires review of support orders for children receiving federal public assistance benefits every three years for possible modification. 42 U.S.C. §§ 666(a)(9)(C), 1305.

Some states have gone further in the direction of flexibility than mandated by the federal government. *See* J. Thomas Oldham, *Abating the Feminization of Poverty: Changing the Rules Governing Post–Decree Modification of Child Support Obligations*, 1994 B.Y.U. L. REV. 841. Wisconsin, for example, now permits (but does not require) courts to order child support expressed as a fraction of the obligor's income instead of a dollar value. (Because Wisconsin calculates child support from gross income, the calculation is relatively simple.) This approach has shown some success when the support obligor has stable employment, but has worked less well when the obligor is self-employed. *See* Oldham, *supra*. Minnesota has adopted a system to adjust child support orders for inflation. Every two years, each support obligor receives notice of an increase in the support obligation equal to the annual percentage increase in the cost of living index. The increase is presumptive, and will not be imposed if the obligor can show that the cost of living increase exceeds his or her wage increase during the relevant period. While this approach is simpler to administer than the Wisconsin model, it fails to capture any real increase in the obligor's earnings. Other states have retained the substantial change in circumstances standard, coupled with a presumption that a substantial change in circumstances has occurred if a new support award, based on the current guidelines and the parents' current incomes, deviates from the initial award by more than a specified percentage; specified percentages adopted by states thus far range from ten to thirty percent.

The materials below explore how courts have construed the substantial change in circumstances principle and the rule that spousal support ends at "remarriage."

SECTION 2. MODIFICATION BASED ON A SHIFT IN INCOME

A. THE OBLIGOR'S INCOME

MARRIAGE OF MEEGAN

California Court of Appeals, 1992.
11 Cal.App.4th 156, 13 Cal.Rptr.2d 799.

MOORE, ASSOCIATE JUSTICE.

In a marital dissolution judgment, a husband is ordered to pay monthly spousal support and does so for some years. Thereafter, however, he voluntarily resigns his high-paying job and enters a monastery to pursue a life of religious observance and prayer. In this case of first impression, we must decide whether it was an abuse of discretion for the trial court to grant the husband's request to reduce the spousal support award to zero.

After more than 23 years of marriage, Elizabeth and Patrick Meegan were divorced on May 17, 1988. At the time of the dissolution, Patrick's net disposable income was $4,700 per month. Although the financial records submitted to the court were incomplete, the evidence indicated Elizabeth, who was a nurse, had a monthly net disposable income of $1,900. Patrick was ordered to pay $739 per month spousal support.

In early 1991, Patrick decided to pursue a life of religious observance and prayer. He resigned his job as a sales executive, joined an order of the Catholic church, and entered the Holy Trinity Monastery in St. David, Arizona. He supported himself from his savings and, though he was no longer employed, continued to contribute $875 per month toward his two adult daughters' college educations and expenses. Patrick agreed to pay his 25–year-old daughter $300 per month, and his 19–year-old daughter $425 per month plus $150 a month for her car insurance, until they graduated and found employment.

On March 22, Patrick, then in his mid–50s, filed an order to show cause for modification seeking to terminate his obligation to pay spousal support, stating: "I am no longer employed and I cannot continue my former vocation due to its stress which has caused me depression and my conscience and desire to become a Catholic priest dictate I follow a path of good works and services. In preparation to become a priest, I plan to work at 'Holy Trinity Monestary' *[sic]* for a year of voluntary community work. During the next few years I do not anticipate I will be earning income. I plan to support myself from my separate property from my divorce. I cannot afford to pay spousal support during the time I have no income."

Patrick estimated it would take four and a half to five years to become a permanent member of the religious order, prior to which time he could be asked to leave. He conceded the church might not permit him to become a priest because he had been married previously and would have to obtain an annulment before he could make his vows. At the time of the hearing, he had not started the annulment process. He was not obligated to pay money to the church for his residence at the monastery, and the church supplied his food and drink.

Patrick had $4,873 in checking accounts, $16,379 in a savings account, and stock worth $73,000. He received $4,700 from his pension plan when he resigned his job. In the year prior to the order to show cause (OSC) hearing, Patrick gave $4,000 to the church. Elizabeth testified her income was $28,000 per year at the time of the dissolution and that she had $70,000 in assets, including equity in her home. Patrick contended Elizabeth's income increased 30 percent between the time of the dissolution and the time of the OSC.

The court entered an order reducing the spousal support to zero, ruling: "The judgment of dissolution of marriage ... is modified. Spousal support is reduced to zero ..., with the court reserving jurisdiction over it. In the event [Patrick] obtains employment the spousal support order made in [the] judgment of dissolution of marriage is reinstated upon [Patrick's] receipt of a first paycheck, until a court of competent jurisdiction can evaluate the then existing financial situation in order to make a new order ..."

The court determined Patrick was acting in good faith and did not resign his job to avoid his spousal support obligations. The court also found that Elizabeth had a capacity "to be financially independent without a substantial reduction in her standard of living," and emphasized its decision would have been different if Elizabeth was "unemployable and faced with an impoverished situation as [compared] to being employable and faced with a minimal reduction in standard of living." The court found support should be reduced to zero based upon Patrick's "being no longer income-producing and his rights to a free [ ] alienation of his existing property." The court also stated that Patrick had "the ability to pay until he has no further money. That's patently obvious from the facts presented. The question [is] should the court take from him all capital as a response to this relief presuming that there was a division of community property with some rule of reason as to that division ... some four years ago. The question now is: do I have jurisdiction to take from [Patrick] all that he has, and the answer is no, I do not have that jurisdiction and I will not do that."[1]

Elizabeth contends the trial court abused its discretion by reducing the spousal support to zero and by denying her request to create a lien in

1. The trial court considered numerous hypotheticals and emphasized the importance of this case to the bench and bar. For example, the judge considered a scenario where a wealthy stockbroker from Newport Beach divorces his wife and moves to Utah to rent canoes for $25,000 a year leaving the wife and family destitute. He also considered the possibility of a trial attorney making $250,000 a year deciding to become a judge and earn $80,000 a year. The judge noted that courts have concluded that there are "no rules we could come up with, no pattern ... Every case would be analyzed on an individual basis."

her favor on monies and other property owned by Patrick to secure payment to her of any future spousal support payments ordered made by Patrick.

Spousal support is not a mandatory requirement in dissolution proceedings. (*See* Civ.Code, § 4801.) "Spousal support must be determined according to the needs of both parties and their respective abilities to meet these needs. In this regard, a trial court has broad discretion and an abuse thereof only occurs when it can be said that no judge reasonably could have made the same order."

Similarly, modification of a spousal support order is a matter for the sound exercise of the court's discretion, based upon a showing of a material change of circumstances since the last spousal support order.

In re Marriage of Sinks, 204 Cal.App.3d 586, 251 Cal.Rptr. 379 affirmed the trial court's decision refusing to reduce spousal support. However, the court based its conclusion on the fact that the husband retired from his job in "an attempt to shirk his support obligation." (*Id.* at p. 594, 251 Cal.Rptr. 379.) Because the trial court found the husband's retirement "was improperly motivated," the Court of Appeal did not address the question of first impression raised here. As Elizabeth concedes, the trial court here found Patrick was "well motivated."

Here, the trial court found that Patrick did not quit his job to avoid his spousal support obligation and was acting in good faith. Credibility is a matter within the trial court's discretion. (*In re Marriage of Everett* (1990) 220 Cal.App.3d 846, 861, 269 Cal.Rptr. 917.) The court believed Patrick's testimony that he could not continue his former employment due to stress and depression, and due to the fact that his "conscience and desire to become a Catholic priest dictate [he] follow a path of good works and services in preparation to becoming a priest." The evidence was uncontroverted that he did, in fact, take residence at the monastery, that he was no longer employed, and that he was earning no income. Patrick estimated it would take four and a half to five years for him to become a permanent member of the religious order, at which time he would be required to take a vow of poverty. Deferring to the trial court's findings on these credibility issues, as we must, we conclude there was no abuse of discretion in reducing Elizabeth's spousal support to zero.

Elizabeth also asks us to find that spousal support should be based on Patrick's ability to earn, rather than on his actual earnings. In light of the trial court's determinations, we may not do so. "It has long been the rule the court can consider the payor's earning capacity when determining ... spousal support. However, this rule has been applied only where the parent has demonstrated a willful intention to avoid fulfilling financial obligations through deliberate misconduct." *In re Marriage of Regnery* (1989) 214 Cal.App.3d 1367, 1371, 263 Cal.Rptr. 243. No such facts exist here.

The judgment is affirmed.

HARVEY v. ROBINSON

Supreme Court of Maine, 1995.
665 A.2d 215.

LIPEZ, J.

Cheryl Robinson appeals from a judgment entered in the Superior Court affirming the judgment of the District Court substantially reducing the amount of her former husband's child support payments. Robinson argues that the District Court erred when it approved a reduced level of child support that did not reflect her former husband's current full-time earning capacity. We agree, and accordingly we vacate the judgment.

I.

In a 1988 divorce judgment the District Court determined that Robinson and Harvey's two children, Karen (born 1980) and Sara (born 1981), would reside principally with Robinson and that Harvey would pay to Robinson as child support $345 bi-weekly. In 1991, Harvey made $26,000 as a civilian employee of the National Guard and another $3,500 for weekend Guard service. He had a total income of approximately $35,500 because of additional work with an ambulance service.

In 1992, having completed 20 years of service with the National Guard, Harvey anticipated that he might face involuntary retirement. Rather than waiting to see if this involuntary retirement occurred, Harvey retired from the Guard voluntarily to pursue his long deferred dream of going to college and medical school. He is currently a full-time undergraduate student.

As a result of this decision, Harvey now has a gross income of approximately $13,840. This amount reflects the income from part-time work he is able to do while in school and some educational grant money.

After Harvey left his full-time job with the Guard, he stopped making child support payments. In July 1992 he moved to reduce his support obligation. In November 1992 he cashed in his retirement pension to obtain funds to pay a child support arrearage of $3,400. In December, however, he again stopped making child support payments.

In May 1993, the District Court heard Harvey's motion to reduce his support obligation. Harvey had just completed his first year of undergraduate schooling and was behind approximately $3,800 in his child support payments. Robinson testified that Harvey's failure to make these payments had prevented her from purchasing winter boots and coats for her daughters and had forced them to forego gymnastics, an activity in which they had participated for five or six years. At that time Robinson was employed full-time as a medical secretary earning $21,000 annually. Seven years remained before Harvey would complete medical school, at approximately the same time his younger daughter would no longer be a minor.

Despite Robinson's urging, the court used Harvey's current gross income as a full-time student to calculate the appropriate child support obligation, instead of his earning capacity before beginning college.[2] The court found that Harvey's decision to leave his full-time employment was made in good faith, and, therefore, using $13,840 as Harvey's gross income and $21,000 as Robinson's gross income, established a support payment for Harvey of $60 per week. The court found, however, that it was equitable in this instance, particularly because Harvey had recently purchased a new automobile, to deviate upward from this amount. The court also stated that it was considering the effects on the children of the reduced support payments. Accordingly, it ordered Harvey to pay $80 per week, increasing to $86 per week in December 1993 when his younger daughter reached twelve years of age. Robinson unsuccessfully argued that based on Harvey's earning capacity, his gross income should be $36,000 and his weekly child support payment pursuant to the work sheet should be $213, increasing to $236 in December 1993. The Superior Court affirmed the order and Robinson's appeal followed.

II.

. . . We review for abuse of discretion the court's decision to base a child support award on Harvey's current income as a part-time employee rather than his current earning capacity as a full-time employee, and we "will overturn the trial court's decision only if it results in a plain and unmistakable injustice, so apparent that it is instantly visible without argument." In *Rich v. Narofsky*, 624 A.2d 937, 939 (Me.1993), the mother sought to amend the divorce judgment to modify her support obligation after leaving her full-time job to enroll in college. *Rich*, 624 A.2d at 938. Although she was capable of working part-time while pursuing her studies and full-time during summers, she saw no need to do so. Id. The trial court designated the father as the primary caretaker and relieved the mother of any child support obligations. *Id.* We held that the District Court abused its discretion by eliminating the mother's obligations "without some consideration of her part-time and summer earning capacity." *Id.*

Although Harvey, unlike the mother in *Rich*, is working as many hours as his educational commitments permit, his decision to change his career and pursue a full-time educational program has imposed needless hardships on his children. Harvey's priorities have the same effect on his children as the unwillingness of the mother in *Rich* to use her part-time and summer earning capacity to help support her children.

As justification for its order, the trial court noted that Harvey's decision to pursue a college degree was made in good faith. That is undoubtedly true. There is no suggestion in the record that Harvey

2. The statutory child support guidelines include the following provision on the earning capacity of a party:

> Gross income may include the difference between the amount a party is earning and that party's earning capacity when the party voluntarily becomes or remains unemployed or under employed, if sufficient evidence is introduced concerning the party's current earning capacity. 19 M.R.S.A. § 311(5)(D)(Supp. 1994).

opted for school in an effort to avoid his obligation to his children. Harvey's good faith, however, does not ameliorate the dramatic effect on the children of his decision to give up full-time work. That good faith consideration must be balanced by an evaluation of the effect that Harvey's under employment decision has on the interests of his children. By its nature, an order for child support serves the interests of the child by compelling parents to meet their financial responsibilities to their children. *See* 19 M.R.S.A. § 306 (Supp. 1994).

Although the court acknowledged the effects on the children of reduced child support payments, the court approved that reduction because it accepted Harvey's decision to forego full-time employment in favor of full-time education. The court does not explain how this accommodation to Harvey's preferences serves the interests of the children in any way. Harvey's decision cannot be justified as one that will serve the interests of his children eventually despite their current deprivations. Harvey will complete medical school when his youngest child becomes an adult and he no longer has a legal obligation to support either of his children. This case is markedly different than *Rowland v. Kingman*, 629 A.2d 613 (Me.1993) (cert. denied 114 S. Ct. 884 (1994)), in which we approved a decrease in the amount of child support to be paid by the mother based on our recognition that she had closed her medical practice in Maine in anticipation of her move to Oregon with her children. Her decline in income would only be temporary: "There is evidence in the record that because of the time required to rebuild her practice, Rowland would not be able to immediately achieve her previous level of income." *Id.* at 617. In this case, Harvey has no medical practice to rebuild. His practice is years away, when the children are adults.[3]

In a tacit acknowledgment that the interests of the children matter, Harvey argues that an interests analysis that focuses on money is too narrow:

> This [focus on money] fails completely to consider that children may actually suffer through watching parents stay in bad jobs; the children may suffer if maintaining a certain job keeps the parent from spending time with his/her children; and the children may indeed suffer if they are taught at an early age that having children absolutely bars a parent from continuing his/her education. Certainly more than just money must be considered when ascertaining the best interests of children.

3. The age of Harvey's children and the length of his educational program also distinguish this case from *Rich v. Narofsky*, 624 A.2d 937 (Me.1993). In *Rich*, the two children were 8 and 5 at the time the trial court made its decision. The mother anticipated an educational program of five years. Rich argued on appeal that her enhanced education credentials would permit her to increase her financial support for her children. Harvey's children were 13 and 11 at the time the court made its decision. He had seven years to go in his educational program. He acknowledged that his children would be adults when he finished medical school. He does not argue that his enhanced education credentials will permit him to increase his financial support for his children.

Even if there is some abstract merit in this argument, there is not a testimonial word in the record that supports it.

As further justification for its order, the court noted that Harvey delayed his secondary education so that he could work and earn income while Robinson attended school. Harvey cannot reduce his child support obligations by arguing that it is now his turn to go to college. Robinson pursued her education at a time when the family was intact and her educational endeavors would eventually benefit the family and herself. Harvey's educational endeavors benefit only himself and deprive the children. He has permitted his preferences to override the interests of his children.

Although we recognize the difficult issues posed for the trial court by these cases, the dilemma here was not insoluble. Harvey could work full time and go to school part time. In that way, he could fulfill his support obligation to his children while pursuing his educational interests. If medical school were unattainable through a part time education, he might have to make necessary adjustments to fulfill his parental obligation. The decision to relieve Harvey of that obligation of adequate support "results in a plain or unmistakable injustice, so apparent that it is instantly visible without argument." *Tardif*, 617 A.2d at 1033. This case must be remanded for reconsideration of the child support determination based on Harvey's current earning capacity as a full-time employee.

Judgment vacated.

DANA, J., with whom ROBERTS, J. joins, dissenting.

I respectfully dissent. When determining a party's gross income for purposes of computing child support payments the trial court "may include the difference between the amount a party is earning and that party's earning capacity when the party voluntarily becomes or remains unemployed or underemployed, if sufficient evidence is introduced concerning a party's current earning capacity." 19 M.R.S.A. § 311(5)(D) (Supp. 1994). Consideration of earning capacity as opposed to present income is not mandatory and we should not disturb a court's decision whether to consider earning capacity absent an abuse of discretion. Moreover, we accord "unusual deference" to a court's findings in an order modifying the amount of child support and "will overturn the trial court's decision of such a question only if it results in a plain and unmistakable injustice, so apparent that it is instantly visible without argument." *Tardif v. Cutchin*, 617 A.2d 1032, 1033 (Me.1992).

Unlike determinations of parental rights and responsibilities, determinations of child support payments are not based solely on the standard of the "best interests of the child." *Compare* 19 M.R.S.A. §§ 311–320 (Supp. 1994) *with* 19 M.R.S.A. § 752(5) (Supp. 1994). Following dissolution of marriage, the custodial parent and children cannot be allowed to freeze the other parent in his employment or otherwise preclude him from seeking economic improvement for himself and his family. So long as his employment, educational or investment decisions are undertaken in good faith and not deliberately designed to avoid responsibility for those dependent on him, he should be permitted to attempt to enhance his economic fortunes without penalty.

The trial court carefully considered the motivations behind Harvey's decision to leave his full-time job in order to pursue a college education while maintaining three part-time jobs. The court reached a conclusion that the decision was one based on good faith and not one motivated by a desire to avoid child support payments. There is substantial evidence to support this finding. Moreover, there is no indication that the court did not consider the best interests of the children when it adjusted Harvey's monthly payments to an amount significantly greater than that suggested by the child support payment guidelines.

I find the trial court's action to be within its considerable discretion, and I would affirm the judgment.

Notes and Questions

1. While the court grants downward modification in *Meegan*, an alimony case, and denies it in *Harvey*, a child support case, don't assume that modification outcomes will invariably follow this pattern. Courts often refuse to permit downward modification of an alimony award when the obligor voluntarily reduces his income. *See, e.g.*, Barbarine v. Barbarine, 925 S.W.2d 831 (Ky.App.1996). Should the standard for downward modification be the same for purposes of child support and spousal support?

2. The availability of modification based on a voluntary reduction in income varies substantially from one state to the next. Some courts look primarily at the voluntariness of income reduction, refusing modification whenever the change was in the obligor's control. *See, e.g.,* Shaughnessy v. Shaughnessy, 164 Ariz. 449, 793 P.2d 1116 (Ariz.App. 1990). Some refuse modification whenever there is a negative impact on the payee spouse or child. *See, e.g.*, Moseley v. Moseley, 216 So.2d 852 (La.App.1968). Many take a multifactor approach. *See, e.g.,* Deegan v. Deegan, 254 N.J.Super. 350, 603 A.2d 542 (App.Div. 1992); In re Marriage of Smith, 77 Ill.App.3d 858, 33 Ill.Dec. 332, 396 N.E.2d 859 (1979). All look to the obligor's intentions; if the obligor quits a job for the sole purpose of harming the custodial parent and child, no court would permit modification. *See* Hutto v. Kneipp, 627 So.2d 802 (La.App.1993). What are the pros and cons of these various approaches? Which, on balance, seems preferable? *See generally* Lewis Becker, *Spousal and Child Support and the "Voluntary Reduction of Income" Doctrine*, 29 CONN. L. REV. 647 (1997).

3. Is it possible to harmonize the results in *Meegan* and *Harvey*? If so, on what basis?

4. What, if any, recourse would Mrs. Meegan and Ms. Robinson have had if they had remained married and opposed their husbands' career changes?

5. The *Meegan* court holds that the obligor should not have to exhaust all available resources before the support obligation is suspended. Why? Is this approach fair?

6. Which of these income reductions justify downward modification of support obligations? (Assume in each case that neither the obligee's income nor needs have substantially changed.)

a. A successful dentist, who has long wanted to be a lawyer, plans to attend law school and seeks downward modification of his child support obligation while attending school. His former wife's income has not increased. *See* McKenna v. Steen, 422 So.2d 615 (La. App. 1982)

b. A support obligor is fired from his job for cause (but not because he was trying to reduce his support obligation) and cannot find a comparable job elsewhere. *See* Klahold v. Kroh, 437 Pa.Super. 150, 649 A.2d 701 (1994).

c. A support obligor is involuntarily laid off and finds employment at a considerably lower salary in a different town. After moving, he is recalled to his former job, but declines the opportunity to return. *See* McKinney v. McKinney, 813 S.W.2d 828 (Ky.App. 1991).

d. The support obligor has committed a crime and has been incarcerated. *See* Thomasson v. Johnson, 120 N.M. 512, 903 P.2d 254 (N.M.App.1995); Franzen v. Borders, 521 N.W.2d 626 (Minn. App.1994).

e. The obligor has remarried. His new spouse is offered, and takes, a new job in a distant city at a substantially higher salary; the obligor moves with his new spouse and cannot find employment at a comparable salary.

f. The obligor has an extremely stressful job and "burns out." He takes a less stressful but less remunerative position.

g. Before marriage, husband and wife agree that husband will maintain his current stressful employment as an investment banker for ten years and then pursue his long-term career aim of becoming a minister. Husband and wife divorce after six years of marriage; in year ten, husband quits his job and goes to divinity school.

7. Is there a duty to maximize income in a particular discipline? For example, in Robinson v. Tyson, 319 S.C. 360, 461 S.E.2d 397 (S.C.App.1995) the father was a lawyer who represented poor people. His monthly income was $700, significantly lower than the average income for a lawyer in that area. Could he be considered "underemployed"?

8. Assume the custodial parent chooses not to work outside the home. Is this underemployment? *See* Stanton v. Abbey, 874 S.W.2d 493 (Mo.App.1994). Would the answer be different if the custodial parent was working outside the home for a period but then quits the job to care for children of a new partner?

B. THE RECIPIENT'S INCOME

CARTER v. CARTER

Supreme Court of Utah, 1978.
584 P.2d 904.

CROCKETT, JUSTICE.

In this proceeding, plaintiff Norman G. Carter sought to have his obligation of paying $350 per month alimony to his former wife, defendant Pauline Carter, terminated. Upon a plenary hearing and due consideration of the appropriate factors, the trial court granted his petition only to the extent of reducing the alimony to $100 per month. Plaintiff appeals.

* * * The parties had been married in 1945 and thus, at the time of the divorce in 1976, the marriage had endured for 31 years. They had reared a family of four children, all of whom were of age and independent. At that time, their principal assets were a home worth about $80,000, a mountain cabin worth about $10,000 and household furniture, equipment and other adjunctive assets of the usual character, including an automobile for each.

The plaintiff had worked for ... U.S. Steel in Orem for almost 30 years and his yearly salary was about $18,000 and he also had a Veteran's pension of $300 per month. Defendant Pauline was unemployed, though she was qualified to follow her former vocation as a school teacher. The decree made an equitable distribution of the property (about which no complaint is made in this proceeding) and awarded the defendant alimony of $275 per month while she lived in the family home and until it was sold, and thereafter $350 per month.

Ten months later, the plaintiff filed the instant petition to have the $350 per month alimony eliminated. His counsel stated to the court that they made no contention that plaintiff's income or economic status had diminished since the divorce was granted, but that the ground relied on for termination of alimony was that the defendant Pauline had become employed as a school teacher at a monthly salary of $636.27, and that because of that, together with other fixed income of about $150 per month, she has adequate income for her support and that therefore alimony should be eliminated entirely.

It is not difficult to appreciate that the plaintiff desires to be relieved entirely from the payment of alimony. Neither are we insensitive to the fact that there is some merit to his argument that alimony is primarily to provide support for the recipient. But in adjudicating his petition, it is necessary and proper for the court to consider not only his point of view, but all of the factors bearing on the total problem. This includes the effect its determination will have on each of the parties at present, and also in the future; and moreover, how its ruling will harmonize with the underlying policy of the law and thus affect society generally.

One of the important factors is that it should be the policy of the law to encourage one receiving alimony to seek employment. This purpose would not be served if a wife who manifests sufficient initiative and industry to get a job is penalized by having her alimony cut off entirely. In that connection it is also noteworthy that in this case the defendant is 58 years old; and even though she has present employment with a fairly good salary, there is the likelihood that it may not last very long and she would be left without that income and likewise without alimony.

Another matter of significance is that where parties have been married for many years and reared their family, it is natural to assume that the wife has been occupied mainly with taking care of the home and the family, and thus in comparative isolation from the competitive world, while the husband has been out in it earning a living. He therefore has the advantage of the training, experience and seniority which normally gives him the greater earning potential. Nonetheless, whatever degree of financial success and standard of living they have attained should properly be regarded as a result of their joint efforts. Consistent with this view and in accord with the determination made by the trial court in this matter, it would seem to be manifestly unfair to eliminate the alimony entirely and in effect turn the wife out to fend for herself.

Correlated to the above is the fact that upon consideration of all of the circumstances, the trial court did grant the plaintiff substantial relief by reducing his obligation to pay alimony from $350 to $100 per month.

Notes and Questions

1. What is the probable basis of the trial court's determination that the husband's maintenance obligation should be reduced from $350 to $100, based on his wife's additional monthly income of $636? Given that her income was still substantially lower than her husband's, why didn't the court maintain the husband's obligation?

2. How would the court respond to a petition for increased support by Mrs. Carter based on a $636 monthly income loss? Should its approach to these two fact patterns be consistent?

3. The court notes that it does not want to apply a rule that would deter alimony recipients from finding work. Is the court's approach effective?

SECTION 3. MODIFICATION BASED ON NEW RELATIONSHIPS

A. COHABITATION BY THE ALIMONY RECIPIENT

TAAKE v. TAAKE

Supreme Court of Wisconsin, 1975.
70 Wis.2d 115, 233 N.W.2d 449.

BEILFUSS, JUSTICE.

On October 31, 1966, the plaintiff-respondent, E. Robert Taake, was granted an absolute divorce from the defendant-appellant, Barbara A. Taake, upon the ground of cruel and inhuman treatment. From the findings of fact and judgment on file and a part of the record on appeal, it appears the parties had been married about twelve years. They had three minor children—two of their own and an adopted child. The plaintiff-husband was and still is a physician and surgeon; the defendant-wife was a housewife. The parties resided in Beaver Dam. Pursuant to stipulation of the parties, the court awarded the custody of the children to the wife and required a support money payment of $550 per month by the plaintiff-husband. As a division of estate, the wife was awarded the home of the parties, the household goods, her personal effects and an automobile. In addition, she was awarded alimony in the amount of $200 per month.

On February 6, 1968, based upon a stipulation of the parties, the judgment was amended to provide that the husband have custody of the children, and the provision for support money payments was deleted.

Shortly thereafter the defendant sold the house in Beaver Dam and moved to an apartment complex in Sun Prairie. She lived there for about a year and then moved to an apartment in Madison, where she lived until December, 1971. She worked intermittently as a personnel worker.

During the year 1971 the defendant, Mrs. Taake, met Lyle Fink. Fink was divorced from his wife and was employed as a maintenance painter for the Madison school system. Fink was negotiating for the purchase of a home on School Road in Madison. For a period of four to five weeks prior to actual occupancy of the School Road home, Fink lived with Mrs. Taake in her Madison apartment.

In December of 1971 both Mr. Fink and Mrs. Taake moved into his newly purchased home on School Road and both were still living there at the time of the hearing in this matter in May of 1973. The arrangements were that she was to pay him $25 per month rent and pay for a part of the groceries, and do at least a part of the housework. She had a separate bedroom. Mrs. Taake has been unemployed a part of the time due to alleged emotional problems. Fink suffered an injury while at work, has received some workmen's compensation benefits but is unemployed.

Mrs. Taake admits having occasional sexual relations with Fink and failing to correct persons when they refer to her as Mrs. Fink, although she has not affirmatively identified herself as Fink's wife. Her name does appear as Barbara Fink in a city directory.

Fink testified he considered Mrs. Taake to be his wife but later changed his testimony to the effect that they were very, very good friends. Mrs. Taake and Mr. Fink have not married at any time.

In September of 1972 the respondent, Robert Taake, ceased making the monthly $200 alimony payments and in May of 1973 petitioned the court for an order amending the judgment to terminate alimony.

As stated, the order amending the judgment expunged the alimony arrearages, terminated alimony and barred future alimony.

In a memorandum decision the trial court found that Mrs. Taake and Lyle Fink had a *de facto* marriage relationship and that Mrs. Taake had and was engaging in misconduct of such a nature so as to require a termination of her former husband's obligation to pay her alimony.

The trial court concluded that Mrs. Taake should not be permitted to enjoy both the benefits of her *de facto* marriage relationship with Lyle Fink and the benefit of alimony from her former husband; and that to permit a divorced woman to do so might dissuade her from remarriage. The trial court also concluded that Mrs. Taake's legal misconduct was the kind of misconduct which this court has heretofore recognized as warranting a change or elimination of alimony.

* * *

We acknowledge that a divorced wife owes no duty of sexual fidelity to her former husband. However, her cohabitation with another man can be acknowledged as a change of circumstances affecting her former husband's responsibility to provide alimony for her support. The manner and extent of the cohabitation and circumstances should be considered in determining whether alimony payments are to be changed.

In this case there are several changed circumstances that can be considered. Mrs. Taake was given a substantial division of estate, including the home and household furniture of the parties for the obvious reason that it was going to be used as the home for the minor children. Further, because she was awarded the children, her opportunity for supporting herself was limited. She stipulated that the custody be transferred to the husband and sold the house. These were material changes in the circumstances that the court considered when the original award of alimony was made. Her cohabitation with Lyle Fink was not an occasional indiscretion but continuous cohabitation with arrangements for joint support.

We believe this change of circumstances was sufficient to permit the trial court to expunge the delinquencies in alimony payments and to amend the judgment to delete the provision for alimony. We conclude the trial court did not abuse its discretion in these respects and those parts of the order must be affirmed.

The order also barred any future alimony. This we think goes too far. If, at a subsequent hearing, it appears that Mrs. Taake is not married, is not cohabiting in the manner set forth above, and other circumstances warrant a resumption of alimony in some degree, the court should not be powerless to act. That part of the order barring future alimony must be reversed.

HEFFERNAN, JUSTICE (dissenting).

In Wisconsin it is the rule that, upon divorce, a husband has a continuing obligation to support his former wife in the manner to which she was accustomed. * * *

There may well be good reasons to conclude that, in this day of equal rights, in cases where both parties have the capacity to be self-supporting, the entire concept of alimony should be re-examined. Suffice it to say that alimony serves the public interest where, as here, it is necessary for the maintenance of one party to the divorce and without which the dependent former spouse would become a public charge. It is in the public interest that alimony usually be paid, for without such post-divorce provision for support, there is a substantial likelihood that a divorced spouse would become a public charge.

Bearing in mind this overriding purpose of alimony, what are the facts of this case? Dr. Taake, a Beaver Dam physician, whose ability to pay his divorced wife, the mother of his children, the sum of $200 per month for her support is unquestioned, petitioned the court to be relieved of his legal obligation solely because of his former wife's alleged misconduct.

There was no proof that Dr. Taake could not pay the amount previously decreed, nor was there any proof that Barbara Taake's financial circumstances had changed so that the alimony payments were not necessary for her maintenance.

Rather, the facts indisputably show that, at the time of the hearing, she was ill, was unable to work, and was unable to pay her rent.

The situation of Fink and Barbara Taake is more to be deplored in our society than to be blamed. He is unemployed and is not able to contribute substantially to Barbara's support. In fact, she has been paying him rent. The relationship was one that arose out of mutual economic necessity—a necessity that the record shows continues in respect to Barbara Taake. * * *

It was admitted that Fink and Barbara had intercourse on several occasions, that they lived in the same house, that Barbara on no occasion held herself out as the wife of Fink, but on occasion had failed to correct persons who addressed her as Mrs. Fink. There was evidence that her mail was received under the name of Barbara Taake, no Barbara Fink. No neighbors were called as witnesses to testify that they believed that

Fink and Barbara Taake were apparently living in a marital, rather than in an illicit, relationship.

On the basis of this evidence, however, the trial judge concluded that a *de facto* marriage existed between Fink and Barbara Taake. Under the statutory law of Wisconsin, only a remarriage bars alimony as a matter of law.

* * *

Clearly, the relationship between Barbara Taake and Lyle Fink was not a marriage sanctioned by the law of this state. This state specifically outlaws *de facto* or common law marriages. The law, for obvious public-policy reasons, does not clothe a legally unsanctioned male-female cohabitative relationship with any of the legal protections of a marriage. No legal relationship ever arose between Barbara and Fink except that of landlord and tenant. The trial judge's characterization of the relationship as a *de facto* marriage is without significance except as a shibboleth on which to predicate a desired result. In states where a common law marriage is recognized, it is indeed true that a common law marriage would, if proved, terminate the obligation to pay alimony just as a *de jure* marriage would. The reason for that is, of course, that in a common law marriage there is the manifestation that the relationship is permanent and that each party to it assumes the reciprocal obligations of marriage including the obligation of support and fidelity. * * *

The relationship that the trial judge considered in this case was, however, only a temporary expedient. A true common law marriage requires the common law husband to support the wife, and the need for alimony for a divorced wife would be supplanted by the obligation of the common law husband to support. In such circumstances the divorced husband ought to be relieved of his obligation. In the instant case no obligation was assumed by Fink to support Barbara Taake. The facts that might be pertinent in the event of a common law remarriage do not appear in this case.

The trial judge abused his discretion when he gave the same legal effect to the relationship between the parties as he would have to a legally recognized marriage.

Notes and Questions

1. State rules dealing with the effect of cohabitation on alimony vary. *See, e.g.,* former CAL. CIV. CODE § 4801.5 (West Supp. 1987) (cohabitation creates a "rebuttable presumption, affecting the burden of proof, of decreased need for support"), which was replaced by CAL. FAM. CODE § 4323 (West 1995) (same, except income of supporting spouse's nonmarital partner shall not be considered); N.Y. DOM. REL. L. § 248 (court may modify support payment upon proof that "wife is habitually living with another man and holding herself out as his wife, although not married to such man"); Brister v. Brister, 92 N.M. 711, 594 P.2d 1167 (1979) (support from a "paramour," living with the ex-wife, may be

considered as evidence of changed financial circumstances in determining whether her alimony should be reduced; "[t]he focal point in each case is the recipient's need for support."); 750 ILL. COMP. STAT. § 5/510 (support is to be terminated if the recipient is cohabiting with another on a "resident, continuing conjugal basis.")

2. Evaluate the following fact patterns under the laws of California, New York, Illinois and New Mexico. In cases b, c, and d, assume that the alimony recipient is employed at a low-wage job and earns the same salary as she did when awarded alimony:

a) the *Taake* case;

b) Mrs. Morrison, a recipient of indefinite-term alimony ($1500 per month) now has a sexual relationship with Mr. Adams, who has moved into her home and pays her $800 for "room and board." Mrs. Morrison continues to use the name Morrison; neighbors do not believe that she and Mr. Adams are married. Mr. Adams's annual income is $54,000. *See* Morrison v. Morrison, 139 Or.App. 137, 910 P.2d 1176 (1996)

c) Mrs. Sappington, a recipient of indefinite-term alimony ($750 per month) has for the past two years allowed Mr. Adams to share her home. According to Mrs. Sappington, she charges Adams $120 per month for rent; they share the utilities bills and grocery payments. Mrs. Sappington and Mr. Adams both state that they do not have a sexual relationship and that they have never slept in the same bed. They do, however, typically share meals. Sometimes they go out together. Mr. Adams's annual income is $30,000. Mrs. Sappington continues to use the name Sappington; neighbors do not believe that she and Mr. Adams are married. *See* In re Marriage of Sappington, 106 Ill.2d 456, 88 Ill.Dec. 61, 478 N.E.2d 376 (1985).

d) Mrs. Schroeder, a recipient of indefinite-term alimony, has a sexual relationship with Mr. Adams, and for the past year has allowed him to live in her home. She pays all the household expenses and grocery bills. Mr. Adams pays no rent or utilities; he does pay for occasional entertainment and dining out. He has also done occasional repair work on the house, allows her the use of his car, and gave her a $4200 diamond ring that formerly belonged to his mother. Mr. Adams is currently unemployed and has no income. Mrs. Schroeder sometimes uses the name Mrs. Adams, particularly when she and Mr. Adams have travelled together. The neighbors do not believe that she and Mr. Adams are married. *See* In re Marriage of Schroeder, 192 Cal.App.3d 1154, 238 Cal.Rptr. 12 (1987).

3. In most states, support automatically terminates if the recipient remarries. But consider Grove v. Grove, 280 Or. 341, 571 P.2d 477 (1977):

> We turn now to the question upon which we requested argument: whether spousal support awards should routinely provide that the support payments will terminate upon the remarriage of the sup-

> ported spouse. We hold that they should not. * * * Although this court has expressed the opinion that it was against public policy to permit a woman to look for her support to two different men, that policy has never been held in this state to operate automatically without regard to the particular circumstances. The cases announcing the position that it does not were decided at a time when the husband was considered to have an absolute unilateral obligation to support his wife. We would not now hold otherwise, when legal duties of spousal support are mutual. Public policy does not require that a woman whose first marriage has been dissolved be free to remarry only if her new husband is able to support her. If remarriage by the supported spouse is not, as a matter of law, grounds for automatic termination of spousal support, we cannot approve the general practice of inserting provisions to that effect in support decrees as a matter of routine. Unless there is reason, at the time the decree is entered, to predict a remarriage which will substantially change the circumstances relevant to the support award, the question of the effect of remarriage upon a support decree should await the event and proper application for modification of the decree. * * *

4. If support terminates upon remarriage, without the need for any additional showing of changed circumstances, can a different policy be justified for cohabitation? If yes, should long-term cohabitation be treated like remarriage?

5. If only the financial effects of cohabitation by the alimony recipient are relevant, should cohabitation and an increase in the recipient's salary be treated identically?

6. Should the financial effects (either positive or negative) of cohabitation by the alimony obligor be taken into account? If yes, should the obligor's remarriage be treated the same way? Evaluate Gammell v. Gammell, 90 Cal.App.3d 90, 153 Cal.Rptr. 169 (1979):

> The California courts have held that, while a husband's remarriage does not alone justify reduction of support payments to his former wife, the remarriage with its additional burdens is a factor to be considered. Since a remarriage with its additional burdens is a factor to be considered in modifying support payments, it appears fair and equitable that a remarriage with its additional benefits also ought to be considered. Furthermore, spousal support is determined according to the needs of both parties and the respective ability of the parties to meet those needs. Although the second wife's income in this case is her separate property, as a pragmatic matter this income directly or indirectly reduces the needs of the husband and it directly or indirectly affects the husband's ability to meet the needs of his former wife.

California has now adopted a rule that any income of the obligor's new spouse or cohabitant should be ignored when computing spousal support. *See* Cal. Fam. Code § 4323. Why might California have adopted this rule?

7. Spouses may define the terms under which the alimony obligation will cease in a separation agreement. This approach holds the potential for curing any imprecision in state statutory standards, but realizing that potential is not easy. In O'Connor Brothers Abalone Co. v. Brando, 40 Cal.App.3d 90, 114 Cal.Rptr. 773 (1974), for example, the court was required to interpret this clause in Marlon and Movita Brando's separation agreement:

> (a) Defendant agrees to pay or cause to be paid to Plaintiff, the amount of $1,400.00 per month commencing on the first day of the calendar month next succeeding the month in which this Agreement is executed and continuing for a period of one-hundred fifty-six (156) months, or *until she remarries or dies, whichever occurs sooner. For the purposes of this Agreement, 'remarriage' shall include, without limitation, Plaintiff's appearing to maintain a marital relationship with any person, or any ceremonial marriage entered into by Plaintiff even though the same may later be annulled or otherwise terminated or rendered invalid."* (Emphasis added.)
>
> [Movita argued] that the phrase 'appearing to maintain a marital relationship' means a holding out by Movita that she was in fact married or conduct on her part that would imply a marriage in fact. According to this version, a meretricious relationship, no matter how intimate and enduring, would not terminate the obligation for support payments so long as it was made clear to the world that Movita and her paramour were Not married. This interpretation would place a premium on the persistence with which Movita publicized the illicit nature of the relationship.
>
> . . . Marlon contend[ed] that the Agreement was designed to prevent Movita from maintaining a relationship with a male companion as a result of which the latter appeared to enjoy the usual rewards of marriage without assuming the obligations which flow from a ceremony of marriage. According to Marlon the Agreement means a "marital type" relationship and such interpretation is necessary to avoid what he sought to avoid, i.e., the possibility that Movita's male companion, in sharing Movita's shelter, bed and board, would also benefit from the support payments which Marlon was providing. * * *
>
> The final Agreement evolved from two previously written drafts. The first draft simply used the phrase "until she remarries" without further definition. To this Marlon objected. The second draft defined remarriage as "cohabitation by plaintiff with any person." To this Movita objected. Mr. Garey testified that Movita's attorney indicated that the objection to "cohabitation" was based on a fear that the word might apply to so-called "one night stands."
>
> * * *
>
> Clearly the purpose of the Agreement was not to circumscribe Movita's sexual activity per se as she was free to engage in sexual

> intercourse with other men. The Agreement sought to embrace actual ceremonial marriages on the one hand and on the other, relationships which were not marriages but which had the attributes of marriage such as companionship of substantial duration, the sharing of habitation, eating together and sexual intimacy. The characterization of such a relationship as "marital" does not depend on whether third persons are led to believe the existence of a ceremonial marriage. In fact, public belief that Movita and Ford were actually married would be less demeaning to Marlon than their conduct of "living" together while disavowing an actual marriage.
>
> What is important here from the standpoint of the objectives of the Agreement is that such a relationship creates the strong probability that the male partner will derive benefit from the support payments. And that, in fact, is what occurred here. O'Connor contends in its brief that there was no common financial or economic relationship between Ford and Movita and that this detracts from the "marital" character of the relationship. Interestingly enough, however, in respondent's support of this argument it is admitted that Movita paid for the upkeep of her cars which Ford drove. She paid for the groceries which Ford charged, and she paid for the department store purchases which Ford charged. It appears without contradiction that Movita paid for the maintenance of the house in which they lived.
>
> We interpret the phrase "appearing to maintain a marital relationship" as including the appearance of "living together" under circumstances such as existed here, whether or not there is the appearance of marriage in fact. This appears to us to be the only possible reasonable interpretation of the Agreement.

How could the agreement have been drafted to embody Marlon's point of view? Movita's?

8. Evaluate J. Thomas Oldham, *The Effect of Unmarried Cohabitation by a Former Spouse Upon His or Her Right to Continue to Receive Alimony*, 17 J. FAM. LAW 249, 267–68 (1978–79):

> It is submitted that the optimum approach to unmarried cohabitation by an ex-spouse receiving alimony would be the two-step analysis outlined below. First, a court should consider whether the cohabitants either (i) have lived together for a sufficient length of time and the cohabitant's income is at such a level that it would be equitable, considering the surrounding circumstances, to require the cohabitant to support the ex-spouse, or (ii) whether the alimony recipient has established a de facto remarriage. In connection with the former determination, the length of the marriage, the alimony payor's income, and any other equitable factors should be considered. In connection with the latter determination, all relevant factors, such as the length of the cohabitation and the manner in which the couple conducts their financial affairs, should be considered; the presumption set forth above could be utilized. If it is found that a de

facto remarriage occurred, spousal support should be terminated. If it is decided that it would be fair to require the cohabitant to support the ex-spouse, alimony should be suspended for the duration of cohabitation. If it is determined that it would not be fair to require the cohabitant to support the ex-spouse, and what a de facto remarriage has not occurred, the court should consider whether the cohabitation reduces the support needs of the ex-spouse and reduce or suspend the alimony obligation, as appropriate, if it finds such a reduced need.

Problem 20–1:

You are counsel to the New York State Legislature's Family Law Committee, which is considering a change in its law dealing with the effect of cohabitation on alimony. The Committee has concluded that the current standard is unworkable in an era of widespread cohabitation. Its goal is a statutory standard that "reflects current economic and social realities, treats like situations in a like manner, and resists attempts at evasion and fraud." Draft a statute for the Committee's consideration. Make sure your statute specifies when, if at all, alimony is to be:

(a) cut off fully and permanently;

(b) cut off only to the extent the ex-spouse's financial circumstances have actually changed and only for the duration of the changed circumstances.

B. A STEPPARENT

IN RE MARRIAGE OF NIMMO

Supreme Court of Colorado, 1995.
891 P.2d 1002.

ERICKSON, J.

We granted certiorari to review *In re Marriage of Seanor*, 876 P.2d 44 (Colo.App.1993). The court of appeals concluded the trial court properly denied Nick Nimmo's motion to compel discovery of Margaret E. Nimmo's (now Margaret E. Seanor) (Ms. Seanor's) present spouse's income for purposes of § 14–10–115(7)(a)(I)(A), 6B C.R.S. (1987 & 1994 Supp.).[2] We affirm in part, reverse in part, and return this case to the court of appeals for remand for further proceedings consistent with this opinion.

2. For calculating child support, § 14–10–115(7)(A)(I)(A) provides:

"Gross income" includes income from any source and includes, but is not limited to, income from salaries, wages, including tips calculated pursuant to the federal internal revenue service percentage of gross wages, commissions, bonuses, dividends, severance pay, pensions, interest, trust income, annuities, capital gains, social security benefits, workers' compensation benefits, unemployment insurance benefits, disability insurance benefits, gifts, prizes, and alimony or maintenance received. Gross income does not include child support payments received. § 14–10–115(7)(a)(I)(A), 6B C.R.S.

I

A decree of dissolution of marriage was entered on May 4, 1989. In that decree, the trial court approved and incorporated the parties' separation agreement. Among other things, the agreement granted Ms. Seanor primary physical custody and Nimmo sole legal custody of the parties' two children. The agreement provided that Nimmo would pay maintenance to Ms. Seanor until June 1991. After June 1991, Nimmo would pay child support in accordance with § 14–10–115, 6B C.R.S. (1987 & 1994 Supp.).

In October 1991, Ms. Seanor filed a motion to increase child support payments. In preparation for the hearing, Nimmo submitted interrogatories in November 1991. The interrogatories sought information from Ms. Seanor regarding her income since June 1, 1991. Nimmo's definition of "income" included "all funds available for ... [Ms. Seanor's] use, including gifts." Nimmo wanted a list of "all gifts, including without limitation, jewelry, clothes, entertainment, travel, and restaurant meals provided to ... [Ms. Seanor] or to the children" by Ms. Seanor's present spouse (Mr. Seanor). Nimmo also requested a list of "all amounts paid by Mr. Seanor either directly to ... [Ms. Seanor] or to third parties from which ... [Ms. Seanor] received a benefit...." The interrogatories also sought copies of checking account registers, bank statements, and credit card records.

When Ms. Seanor failed to provide answers to the interrogatories, Nimmo filed a motion to compel discovery. The trial court denied the motion on the grounds that the income and contributions of Mr. Seanor were immaterial to the determination of Nimmo's child support obligation. Also, because Mr. and Ms. Seanor shared checking and savings accounts, granting the motion would constitute an invasion of Mr. Seanor's privacy.

In its order of October 14, 1992, the trial court granted Ms. Seanor's motion to increase Nimmo's child support payments. The trial court found Ms. Seanor had no income. Nimmo was ordered to pay, based on his income, $1,341 per month as child support plus $4,906 in back payments. Nimmo appealed.

The court of appeals found Nimmo's definition of income to be "significantly broader than the definition of income set forth in the child support guidelines." The court of appeals emphasized the common law rule that the income of third parties is not considered when determining income for child support purposes. The court of appeals concluded the child support guidelines did not change the common law rule and held that "the trial court did not abuse its discretion in denying the motion to compel."

II

C.R.C.P. 26(b)(1) allows parties to "obtain discovery regarding any matter, not privileged, which is relevant to the subject matter involved in the pending action.... " Child support obligations are determined by establishing the "combined gross income" which "means the combined monthly adjusted gross incomes of both parents." § 14–10–115(10)(a)(II), 6B C.R.S. (1987 & 1994 Supp.) " 'Adjusted gross income' means gross income less preexisting child support obligations and less alimony or maintenance actually paid by a parent." Id. Using the statutory schedule, child support amounts are extrapolated based on the combined gross income and the number of children due support. *See* § 14–10–115(10)(b), 6B C.R.S. (1987 & 1994 Supp.). Each parent's obligation is determined by dividing the combined gross income "in proportion to their adjusted gross incomes." § 14–10–115(10)(a)(I), 6B C.R.S. (1987).

The statutory definition of " 'gross income' includes income from any source and includes, but is not limited to, income from salaries, wages, ... commissions, bonuses, dividends, severance pay, pensions, interest, trust income, annuities, capital gains, social security benefits, workers' compensation benefits, unemployment insurance benefits, disability insurance benefits, gifts, prizes, and alimony or maintenance received." § 14–10–115(7)(a)(I)(A). For purposes of calculating "gross income," the plain language of the statute "includes all payments from a financial resource, whatever the source thereof." In re *Marriage of Armstrong*, 831 P.2d 501, 503 (Colo.App.1992).

We are aware that various sources of income under the statute are treated differently for tax purposes. However, the statute makes no distinction between sources of income based on the federal or state tax codes. Also, because sources of income are "not limited to" the enumerated items of § 14–10–115(7)(a)(I)(A), domestic relations courts would be required to undergo a complex tax analysis to determine income under the guidelines. Such a tortured analysis thwarts the goals of the guidelines and explains why tax definitions are irrelevant to an interpretation of § 14–10–115.

The court of appeals properly noted that the factors considered in determining child support at common law did not include the financial resources of third-parties. *See also In re Marriage of Conradson*, 43 Colo. App. 432, 604 P.2d 701 (1979) (holding that the financial resources of an aunt with whom the child was living were not to be considered in making a support award); *Garrow v. Garrow*, 152 Colo. 480, 382 P.2d 809 (1963) (concluding that the contributions of third-parties were immaterial to a determination of father's duty of support). The opinion also correctly stated that "by the adoption of the child support guidelines, the General Assembly did not intend to change the common law rule set forth" in *Conradson* and *Garrow*. Based on these principles, the court of appeals concluded the income of Mr. Seanor was not relevant to the determination of child support.

The court of appeals came to the correct conclusion concerning the discovery of Mr. Seanor's income. However, the focus of the court's opinion failed to adequately address the plain language of the child support guidelines. The source of money available to Ms. Seanor is not the relevant factor. Instead, under the guidelines the existence of that money is the relevant inquiry. The guidelines require an examination of the existence of parental income. The source of that income is irrelevant to a determination of child support.

Income may come "from any source," and the definition of "gross income" expressly includes "gifts." § 14–10–115(7)(a)(I)(A). However, the income "could come from relatives, friends, investments, trusts, or the lottery." Because "gifts" are included in calculating income for child support, we must determine whether Nimmo may discover Ms. Seanor's income as defined in § 14–10–115(7)(a)(I)(A). Concluding that Mr. Seanor's income is not relevant does not resolve Nimmo's motion to compel.

III

Colorado's child support guidelines are based on the Income Shares Model. * * * The guidelines were enacted to prevent a drastic decrease in the standard of living of children and custodial parents resulting from divorce. By ensuring child support obligations are proportionate to both parents' combined income, the guidelines attempt to rectify this dramatic decrease in lifestyle. The guidelines were not enacted to prevent an increase in a child's standard of living by denying a child the fruits of one parent's good fortune after a divorce. The standard of living of a child if the parents maintained their marriage is only one factor for the court to consider, which does not lock the child into a single standard of living until emancipation.

IV

We are persuaded by the rule announced in *Barnier v. Wells*, 476 N.W.2d 795 (Minn.Ct.App.1991). In *Barnier*, the court stated "if a gift is regularly received from a dependable source, it may properly be used to determine the amount of a child support obligation." *Id.* at 797. The court found that the father received $833 per month from his father and periodic payments of $5,000 from his grandmother.

The court of appeals found *Barnier* to be inapplicable "since husband did not establish either that ... [Ms. Seanor] received monetary payments or, if so, that such payments were regularly received.... " However, by not allowing Nimmo to discover Ms. Seanor's income "from any source," the court denied Nimmo the ability to "establish ... monetary payments" and "that such payments were regularly received."

Information sought through discovery "need not be admissible at the ... [hearing] if the information sought appears reasonably calculated to lead to the discovery of admissible evidence." C.R.C.P. 26(b)(1). Although Mr. Seanor's income is not discoverable, Nimmo must be able to discover Ms. Seanor's income to properly meet the motion to increase his child support payments. Attempts to discover Ms. Seanor's income "from any source" are "reasonably calculated to lead to the discovery of admissible evidence." Nimmo must be able to obtain information regarding gifts received by Ms. Seanor, so he can attempt to establish that they are "regularly received from a dependable source." *See Barnier*, 476

N.W.2d at 797. Without proper discovery Nimmo cannot establish the *Barnier* requirements.

Pursuant to § 14–10–115(7)(a)(I)(A) Nimmo may not discover the source of Ms. Seanor's income. However, Nimmo may discover the existence of Ms. Seanor's income, "whatever the source thereof." When attempting to establish gift income, a party is subject to the same requirements of proof he or she would face trying to show any other type of income. In a hearing to determine child support, a party must establish with reasonable certainty that the amounts are regularly received from a dependable source. Claims that are too speculative may not be used to determine child support. However, receipt of periodic checks, as in *Barnier*, may be more easily established.

This analysis supports the discovery request for all amounts paid by Mr. Seanor directly to Ms. Seanor. However, it does not extend to amounts paid by Mr. Seanor to third parties for cable television, mortgage payments, car and home repairs, insurance or utilities. The amounts Mr. Seanor may pay to provide himself and his family with certain necessities should not be considered as income to Ms. Seanor. Mr. Seanor is not making a gift of income to Ms. Seanor by paying these expenses. He is satisfying the household's obligations. The fact Ms. Seanor may receive some benefit does not convert the payment into income. It appears this discovery request for the household expenses is an indirect attempt to determine Mr. Seanor's income, which, as previously noted, is irrelevant.

Discovery of the receipt of isolated and irregular tokens would also not be permissible. Mementos or keepsakes do not qualify as "gifts" for purposes of the child support guidelines. These occasional presents fall outside the statute. They are not relevant to a determination of child support because they are not regularly received from a dependable source. Also, the speculative nature of these items, combined with their irrelevance, prevents their discovery.

Accordingly, we affirm the court of appeals decision to not permit the discovery of Mr. Seanor's income and reverse the court of appeals denial of Mr. Nimmo's motion to compel discovery of Ms. Seanor's income. We return this case to the court of appeals for remand to the district court for further proceedings consistent with this opinion.

JUSTICE MULLARKEY concurring in part and dissenting in part.

... Because I would affirm the court of appeals' decision, I respectfully dissent from the partial reversal.

The majority in this case holds that "the source of money available to Ms. Seanor is not the relevant factor," and, in order to determine Ms. Seanor's income, the majority allows discovery of all amounts Mr. Seanor has paid directly to her. It excludes direct payments made by Mr. Seanor to third parties for household expenses. Because I do not believe that such family expenses, whether paid by Ms. Seanor with cash provided to her by Mr. Seanor or paid by Mr. Seanor directly to third parties, are "income" under the Uniform Dissolution of Marriage Act (UDMA), I would hold that none of the information requested in the interrogatories is discoverable.

* * *

In the motion to compel answers to interrogatories, Mr. Nimmo requests [various items paid by Mr. Seanor].

I interpret this motion to request discovery of all the ordinary and necessary household expenses paid by Mr. Seanor for his household which includes Ms. Seanor and Mr. Nimmo's children. In my view, this information is not relevant and therefore not discoverable because: (1) such expenses are not income to Ms. Seanor for purposes of the child support guidelines; (2) the stepparent, Mr. Seanor, has no obligation to support Mr. Nimmo's children; and (3) this discovery request is an impermissible attempt to circumvent the trial court's refusal to impute income to Ms. Seanor because the court found that Ms. Seanor was not intentionally unemployed or underemployed.

In conclusion, I would rule that none of the information requested by Mr. Nimmo is relevant to determining Ms. Seanor's income because the enumerated expenses normally arise from a marital relationship. As such, they cannot be construed as income and are not discoverable. I would also hold that a gift does not have to be regularly received from a dependable source under the UDMA.

Notes and Questions

1. In most states, a stepparent does not have a duty to support a child of his spouse. *See* Chapter 16. Is *Nimmo* consistent with this rule?

2. In light of *Nimmo*, what advice would you give a Colorado child support recipient planning to remarry someone with a substantial income?

3. There is no consensus among the states on whether a new spouse's income may be taken into account in determining the support obligation. Some states permit consideration of the income of a new spouse. *See* McDaniel v. McDaniel, 670 So.2d 767 (La.App.1996); Rodgers v. Rodgers, 110 Nev. 1370, 887 P.2d 269 (1994); Ribner v. Ribner, 290 N.J.Super. 66, 674 A.2d 1021 (App. Div. 1996); Hutchinson v. Hutchinson, 85 Ohio App.3d 173, 619 N.E.2d 466 (1993). Some permit the income of a new spouse to be taken into account if the support obligor seeks downward modification of a support award based on his obligations to subsequent children. *See* Bock v. Bock, 506 N.W.2d 321 (Minn.App. 1993); Johnson v. Johnson, 468 N.W.2d 648 (S.D.1991). But most do not permit consideration of a new spouse's income except in unusual circumstances. *See* Cal. Fam. Code § 4057.5 (not to be considered except in extraordinary cases); Flanagan v. Flanagan, 673 So.2d 894 (Fla.App. 1996); Weber v. Coffey, 230 A.D.2d 865, 646 N.Y.S.2d 382 (1996); Marriage of Hardiman, 133 Or.App. 112, 889 P.2d 1354 (1995); Starck v. Nelson, 878 S.W.2d 302 (Tex.App.1994); Miller v. Miller, 171 Wis.2d 131,

491 N.W.2d 104 (Wis.App.1992). Although the case law is less plentiful, states that forbid consideration of a new spouse's income should logically forbid consideration of a new spouse's needs. *See* State v. Hernandez, 802 S.W.2d 894 (Tex.App.1991).

C. SUBSEQUENT CHILDREN

MILLER v. TASHIE

Supreme Court of Georgia, 1995.
265 Ga. 147, 454 S.E.2d 498.

BENHAM, PRESIDING JUSTICE.

When the parties were divorced, appellee-mother was awarded custody of the one minor child of the parties and appellant-father was ordered to pay a total of $6,400.00 per year in child support. Since that time, these changes have occurred: both parties have remarried; appellant has fathered two more children and has undertaken custody of his child from a marriage preceding his marriage to appellee; and appellant's gross annual income has increased by $7,738.00. Based on those changes, appellant sought a downward modification of his support obligation to the child of his marriage to appellee. The trial court dismissed appellant's petition, holding, in essence, that the increase in appellant's gross income was an absolute bar to modification and that appellant's additional support obligations were not factors which could be considered in determining whether there had been a change in his financial status. Concluding that both those rulings are too broad, we reverse.

1. With regard to the trial court's holding that an increase in the petitioning parent's income is an absolute bar to modification, we note first the general rule that "either parent may seek modification of support based on a change in either of their financial circumstances ..." *Allen v. Georgia Dep't of Human Resources*, 262 Ga. 521, 524 (423 S.E.2d 383) (1992). Nothing in either the statute or the case law limits the right to seek modification to an obligor parent whose income has decreased. OCGA § 19–6–19 "allows revision if the petitioning former spouse shows a change in the income and financial status of either former spouse or in the needs of the child or children." Appellee's reliance on *Wright v. Wright*, 246 Ga. 81 (268 S.E.2d 666) (1980), is misplaced: that case holds only that the trial court did not abuse its discretion in increasing the support obligation of a parent whose income had increased, notwithstanding that the obligor-parent's expenses had increased. There was no holding there that an increase in income would bar a petition for modification or even that such an increase would absolutely preclude a trial court's conclusion that the financial status of the obligor parent had changed in such a way as to warrant reconsideration of the amount of the support obligation. We hold, therefore, that dismissal of the petition on the ground that an increase in appellant's income barred the petition was error.

2. The trial court held that appellant's increased responsibility for the support of children other than the one involved in this case did not constitute a change in his financial status. Appellant and appellee have focused on the issue of whether the factors listed in OCGA § 19–6–15(c)(6) as authorizing variation from guideline amounts require that the trial court take into account obligations to support other children. We look instead to the plain language of OCGA § 19–6–19(a):

> The judgment of a court providing permanent alimony for the support of a child or children ... shall be subject to revision upon petition filed by either former spouse showing a change in the income and financial status of either former spouse or in the needs of the child or children.

The statute requires only a showing of "a change in the income and financial status" of either parent. "In determining a change of the financial condition of a parent, the court should consider every relevant fact ... "*Decker v. Decker*, 256 Ga. 513 (350 S.E.2d 434) (1986).

The proper scope of the trial court's consideration in this case was whether there had been, as alleged by appellant, such a change in the financial status of each parent as would support a reconsideration of the level of appellant's obligation to provide financial support for the parties' child. Focusing solely on the fact that appellant's gross income has increased since the initial child support award was error.

Judgment reversed. All the Justices concur.

Notes and Questions

1. Traditionally, courts have refused to modify a child support obligation based on the support obligor's acquisition of subsequent children; the theory is that the obligor knew his obligations to the first family before the later children were born or adopted. Some courts continue to apply this approach, at least to intact second families. *See, e.g.,* Brown v. Brown, 177 Wis.2d 512, 503 N.W.2d 280 (Wis.App.1993); Fantanzo v. Decker, 161 Misc.2d 529, 614 N.Y.S.2d 671 (Fam. Ct. 1994). But an increasing number of recent decisions take the needs of a second family into account. *See, e.g.,* Martinez v. Martinez, 282 N.J.Super. 332, 660 A.2d 13 (Ch.Div.1995). As in *Miller*, courts in many states may now deviate from the presumptive award under state guidelines based on the needs of a second family. *See* Czaplewski v. Czaplewski, 240 Neb. 629, 483 N.W.2d 751 (1992); Ainsworth v. Ainsworth, 154 Vt. 103, 574 A.2d 772 (1990); Burch v. Burch, 81 Wash.App. 756, 916 P.2d 443 (1996). *See generally* Comment, 20 WM. MITCHELL L.REV. 967 (1994).

2. If you were the trial judge, what decision would you make in *Miller* on remand? In Bock v. Bock, 506 N.W.2d 321 (Minn.App.1993), the trial court was directed to equalize, to the extent possible, support to both families. Is this a desirable approach? If yes, how should equalization be accomplished?

3. In Texas (a percentage of obligor income state), the percentage of income owed by a support obligor is reduced based on the number of his other children:

TEX. FAM. CODE § **154.129**

MULTIPLE FAMILY ADJUSTED GUIDELINES
% OF NET RESOURCES

Number of children before the court

		1	*2*	*3*	*4*	*5*	*6*	*7*
Number of	0	20.00	25.00	30.00	35.00	40.00	40.00	40.00
other	1	17.50	22.50	27.38	32.20	37.33	37.71	38.00
children for	2	16.00	20.63	25.20	30.33	35.43	36.00	36.44
whom the	3	14.75	19.00	24.00	29.00	34.00	34.67	35.20
obligor	4	13.60	18.33	23.14	28.00	32.89	33.60	34.18
has a	5	13.33	17.86	22.50	27.22	32.00	32.73	33.33
duty to	6	13.14	17.50	22.00	26.60	31.27	32.00	32.62
support	7	13.00	17.22	21.60	26.09	30.67	31.38	32.00

What are the pros and cons of this approach?

4. In *Miller*, the court distinguished between "natural" (and presumably adopted) children and stepchildren; it held that the former might justify deviation from the guidelines, but not the latter. Researchers have found that stepparents do in fact contribute to the support of stepchildren, even in states where they have no legal support duty. *See* David Chambers, "*Stepparents, Biologic Parents, and the Law's Perceptions of 'Family' after Divorce*," in DIVORCE REFORM AT THE CROSSROADS 102, 105 (Stephen D. Sugarman & Herma H. Kay, eds., 1990). Given this fact, would it make sense to permit modification of the support obligation if the "natural" parent of the stepchildren is not providing support?

SECTION 4. ENFORCEMENT OF SUPPORT OBLIGATIONS

[The parental support obligation] is so well secured by the strength of natural affection that it seldom [needs] to be enforced by human laws.

Chancellor Kent

Although Chancellor Kent's assertion may well be correct regarding most intact families, it certainly is not correct regarding support obligations pertaining to divorced families. This section outlines the enforcement procedures now available to obtain payment from delinquent support obligors.

A. INCARCERATION

AMERICAN LAW INSTITUTE, MODEL PENAL CODE AND COMMENTARIES

454–58 (1980).

§ 230.5 Persistent Non-support

A person commits a misdemeanor if he persistently fails to provide support which he can provide and which he knows he is legally obliged to provide to a spouse, child or other dependent.

Comment

1. *Antecedent Legislation*. Section 230.5 applies to persistent non-support of a spouse, child, or other dependent. Failure to support a spouse or child did not constitute a crime at common law. However, the law of all American jurisdictions at the time the Model Code provision was drafted contained criminal penalties addressed to desertion or non-support of minor children, and all but three punished desertion or nonsupport of one's wife....

* * *

Imprisonment authorized by legislation in effect when the Model Code was drafted varied from three months to as much as 20 years. Most states had maxima of one year or less. However, the primary objective of the non-support law appeared to be to coerce the accused to support his family, rather than to impose exemplary punishment. Frequently, provision was made for releasing from custody for non-support a defendant who gave assurance of complying with his support obligation. Thus a criminal prosecution for non-support could result in a judicial order that differed from the ordinary civil support order only in the availability of a previously determined sentence of imprisonment that could be invoked if the defendant failed to comply. Used in this way, criminal non-support statutes parallel the usual enforcement mechanisms of a civil order backed by the summary power of the court to punish for contempt.

"With a successful housebuilding business in Burlington, Vt., George J. Chicoine figured to be able to meet the modest $150–a-week child support payments that were due his estranged wife. But he eventually fell $2,550 behind. Brought before Judge Robert W. Larrow, Chicoine claimed he did not have the money. The judge said that there was evidence he had $90,000 stashed away, and ordered him to pay. Chicoine refused. That meant that he was in contempt of the court order, and Judge Larrow threw him into jail. Chicoine has been an inmate ever since—for a total of five years and four months. * * * [H]e conceded that originally 'he had sufficient assets to pay the support payments.' But after he was jailed, a court-appointed trustee liquidated all his property (at prices far below what Chicoine thinks it was worth). In any case, his support debt currently amounts to $40,000 and he says that he is now destitute. * * * Last Christmas Chicoine earned a furlough to see his family, whom he is still close to. That only adds to the irony of his status as something of a celebrity at Vermont's maximum-security prison. Only five men now in Windsor have spent more time imprisoned there, and three of them are murderers." *Debtor's Prison Updated*, TIME, March 5, 1973, at 7, col. 3.

COMMONWEALTH v. POULIOT

Supreme Judicial Court of Massachusetts, 1935.
292 Mass. 229, 198 N.E. 256.

RUGG, C.J.

Manifestly, it is not slavery or involuntary servitude as thus authoritatively defined to sentence this defendant if he fails to perform his duty to support his family. The obligation of a husband and father to maintain his family, if in any way able to do so, is one of the primary responsibilities established by human nature and by civilized society. The statute enforces this duty by appropriate sanctions. A reasonable opportunity is afforded to the defendant by the city to provide for the support of his wife and children. The statutes require that support at the public expense be provided for the poor and indigent residing or found in the several towns. * * * In a period of depression like the present, it is reasonable to require one in the position of the defendant to work under the conditions shown in the case at bar in order to meet his obligation to his family. If occasion arises, the officers of the city can be compelled to perform their functions with respect to the defendant in a lawful way and without oppression.

CHILD SUPPORT RECOVERY ACT OF 1992

18 U.S.C.A. § 228 (West. Supp. 1994).

§ 228. Failure to pay legal child support obligations

(a) Offense.—Whoever willfully fails to pay a past due support obligation with respect to a child who resides in another State shall be punished as provided in subsection (b).

(b) Punishment.—The punishment for an offense under this section is—

(1) in the case of a first offense under this section, a fine under this title, imprisonment for not more than 6 months, or both; and

(2) in any other case, a fine under this title, imprisonment for not more than 2 years, or both.

(c) Restitution.—Upon a conviction under this section, the court shall order restitution under § 3663 in an amount equal to the past due support obligation as it exists at the time of sentencing.

(d) Definitions.—As used in this section—

(1) the term "past due support obligation" means any amount—

(A) determined under a court order or an order of an administrative process pursuant to the law of a State to be due from a person for the support and maintenance of a child or of a child and the parent with whom the child is living; and

(B) that has remained unpaid for a period longer than one year, or is greater than $5,00; and

(2) the term "State" includes the District of Columbia, and any other possession or territory of the United States.

Notes and Questions

1. Federal appeals courts have uniformly rejected arguments that Congress has violated the Tenth Amendment or exceeded its power under the Commerce Clause in enacting the CSRA. *See* U.S. v. Bongiorno, 106 F.3d 1027 (1st Cir.1997); U.S. v. Sage, 92 F.3d 101 (2d Cir.1996), cert. denied ___ U.S. ___, 117 S.Ct. 784, 136 L.Ed.2d 727 (1997); U.S. v. Parker, 108 F.3d 28 (3d Cir.1997); U.S. v. Johnson, 114 F.3d 476 (4th Cir.1997); U.S. v. Bailey, 115 F.3d 1222 (5th Cir.1997); U.S. v. Crawford, 115 F.3d 1397 (8th Cir.1997); U.S. v. Mussari, 95 F.3d 787 (9th Cir. 1996); U.S. v. Hampshire, 95 F.3d 999 (10th Cir.1996).

2. Although researchers have found that the threat of jail is an effective tool in enforcing child support orders (*see* DAVID CHAMBERS, MAKING FATHERS PAY (1979)), most judges are reluctant to put a support obligor in jail. What factors might explain this reluctance?

B. CONTEMPT

HICKS ON BEHALF OF FEIOCK v. FEIOCK

Supreme Court of the United States, 1988.
485 U.S. 624, 108 S.Ct. 1423, 99 L.Ed.2d 721.

JUSTICE WHITE delivered the opinion of the Court.

A parent failed to comply with a valid court order to make child support payments, and defended against subsequent contempt charges by claiming that he was financially unable to make the required payments. The trial court ruled that under state law he is presumed to remain able to comply with the terms of the prior order, and judged him to be in contempt. The state appellate court held that the legislative presumptions applied by the trial court violate the Due Process Clause of the Fourteenth Amendment, which forbids a court from employing certain presumptions that affect the determination of guilt or innocence in criminal proceedings. We must decide whether the Due Process Clause was properly applied in this case.

* * *

II.

Three issues must be decided to resolve this case. First is whether the ability to comply with a court order constitutes an element of the offense of contempt or, instead, inability to comply is an affirmative defense to that charge. Second is whether § 1209.5 requires the alleged contemnor to shoulder the burden of persuasion or merely the burden of production in attempting to establish his inability to comply with the order. Third is whether this contempt proceeding was a criminal proceeding or a civil proceeding, *i.e.*, whether the relief imposed upon respondent was criminal or civil in nature.

Petitioner argues that the state appellate court erred in its determinations on the first two points of state law. * * * Although petitioner marshals a number of sources in support of the contention that the state appellate court misapplied state law on these two points, the California Supreme Court denied review of this case and we are not free in this situation to overturn the state court's conclusions of state law.

The third issue, however, is a different matter: the argument is not merely that the state court misapplied state law, but that the characterization of this proceeding and the relief given as civil or criminal in nature, for purposes of determining the proper applicability of federal constitutional protections, raises a question of federal law rather than state law. This proposition is correct as stated. The fact that this proceeding and the resultant relief were judged to be criminal in nature as a matter of state law is thus not determinative of this issue, and the state appellate court erred insofar as it sustained respondent's challenge to the statute under the Due Process Clause simply because it concluded that this contempt proceeding is "quasi-criminal" as a matter of California law.

III.

A.

The question of how a court determines whether to classify the relief imposed in a given proceeding as civil or criminal in nature, for the purposes of applying the Due Process Clause and other provisions of the Constitution, is one of long standing, and its principles have been settled at least in their broad outlines for many decades. When a State's proceedings are involved, state law provides strong guidance about whether or not the State is exercising its authority "in a nonpunitive, noncriminal manner," and one who challenges the State's classification of the relief imposed as "civil" or "criminal" may be required to show "the clearest proof" that it is not correct as a matter of federal law. Nonetheless, if such a challenge is substantiated, then the labels affixed either to the proceeding or to the relief imposed under state law are not controlling and will not be allowed to defeat the applicable protections of federal constitutional law. This is particularly so in the codified laws of contempt, where the "civil" and "criminal" labels of the law have become increasingly blurred.

Instead, the critical features are the substance of the proceeding and the character of the relief that the proceeding will afford. "If it is for civil contempt the punishment is remedial, and for the benefit of the complainant. But if it is for criminal contempt the sentence is punitive, to vindicate the authority of the court." *Gompers v. Buck's Stove & Range Co.*, 221 U.S. 418, 441, 31 S.Ct. 492, 498, 55 L.Ed. 797 (1911). The character of the relief imposed is thus ascertainable by applying a few straightforward rules. If the relief provided is a sentence of imprisonment, it is remedial if "the defendant stands committed unless and until he performs the affirmative act required by the court's order," and is punitive if "the sentence is limited to imprisonment for a definite period." If the relief provided is a fine, it is remedial when it is paid to the complainant, and punitive when it is paid to the court, though a fine that would be payable to the court is also remedial when the defendant can avoid paying the fine simply by performing the affirmative act required by the court's order. These distinctions lead up to the fundamental proposition that criminal penalties may not be imposed on someone who has not been afforded the protections that the Constitution requires of such criminal proceedings, including the requirement that the offense be proved beyond a reasonable doubt.[3]

* * *

The distinction between relief that is civil in nature and relief that is criminal in nature has been repeated and followed in many cases. An unconditional penalty is criminal in nature because it is "solely and exclusively punitive in character." A conditional penalty, by contrast, is civil because it is specifically designed to compel the doing of some act. "One who is fined, unless by a day certain he [does the act ordered], has it in his power to avoid any penalty. And those who are imprisoned until they obey the order, 'carry the keys of their prison in their own pockets' ".

B.

In repeatedly stating and following the rules set out above, the Court has eschewed any alternative formulation that would make the classification of the relief imposed in a State's proceedings turn simply on what their underlying purposes are perceived to be. Although the purposes that lie behind particular kinds of relief are germane to understanding their character, this Court has never undertaken to psychoanalyze the subjective intent of a State's laws and its courts, not only because that effort would be unseemly and improper, but also because it would be misguided. In contempt cases, both civil and criminal relief has aspects that can be seen as either remedial or punitive or both: when a court imposes fines and punishments on a contemnor, it is not only vindicating its legal authority to enter the initial court order,

3. We have recognized that certain specific constitutional protections, such as the right to trial by jury, are not applicable to those criminal contempts that can be classified as petty offenses, as is true of other petty crimes as well. This is not true, however, of the proposition that guild must be proved beyond a reasonable doubt.

but it also is seeking to give effect to the law's purpose of modifying the contemnor's behavior to conform to the terms required in the order. As was noted in *Gompers*:

> "It is true that either form of [punishment] has also an incidental effect. For if the case is civil and the punishment is purely remedial, there is also a vindication of the court's authority. On the other hand, if the proceeding is for criminal contempt and the [punishment] is solely punitive, to vindicate the authority of the law, the complainant may also derive some incidental benefit from the fact that such punishment tends to prevent a repetition of the disobedience. But such indirect consequences will not change [punishment] which is merely coercive and remedial, into that which is solely punitive in character, or *vice versa*." 221 U.S., at 443, 31 S.Ct., at 498.

For these reasons, this Court has judged that conclusions about the purposes for which relief is imposed are properly drawn from an examination of the character of the relief itself.

There is yet another reason why the overlapping purposes of civil and criminal contempt proceedings have prevented this Court from hinging the classification on this point. If the definition of these proceedings and their resultant relief as civil or criminal is made to depend on the federal courts' view about their underlying purposes, which indeed often are not clearly articulated in any event, then the States will be unable to ascertain with any degree of assurance how their proceedings will be understood as a matter of federal law. The consequences of any such shift in direction would be both serious and unfortunate. Of primary practical importance to the decision in this case is that the States should be given intelligible guidance about how, as a matter of federal constitutional law, they may lawfully employ presumptions and other procedures in their contempt proceedings. It is of great importance to the States that they be able to understand clearly and in advance the tools that are available to them in ensuring swift and certain compliance with valid court orders—not only orders commanding payment of child support, as in this case, but orders that command compliance in the more general area of domestic relations law, and in all other areas of the law as well.

The States have long been able to plan their own procedures around the traditional distinction between civil and criminal remedies. The abandonment of this clear dividing line in favor of a general assessment of the manifold and complex purposes that lie behind a court's action would create novel problems where now there are rarely any—novel problems that could infect many different areas of the law. And certainly the fact that a contemnor has his sentence suspended and is placed on probation cannot be decisive in defining the civil or criminal nature of the relief, for many convicted criminals are treated in exactly this manner for the purpose (among others) of influencing their behavior. What is true of the respondent in this case is also true of any such convicted criminal: as long as he meets the conditions of his informal probation, he will never enter the jail. Nonetheless, if the sentence is a determinate one, then the punishment is criminal in nature, and it may not be imposed unless federal constitutional protections are applied in the contempt proceeding.

IV.

The proper classification of the relief imposed in respondent's contempt proceeding is dispositive of this case. As interpreted by the state court here, § 1209.5 requires respondent to carry the burden of persuasion on an element of the offense, by showing his inability to comply with the court's order to make the required payments. If applied in a criminal proceeding, such a statute would violate the Due Process Clause because it would undercut the State's burden to prove guilt beyond a reasonable doubt. If applied in a civil proceeding, however, this particular statute would be constitutionally valid, and respondent conceded as much at the argument.[4]

The state court found the contempt proceeding to be "quasi-criminal" in nature without discussing the point. There were strong indications that the proceeding was intended to be criminal in nature, such as the notice sent to respondent, which clearly labeled the proceeding as "criminal in nature," Order to Show Cause and Declaration for Contempt (June 12, 1985), App. 21, and the participation of the District Attorney in the case. Though significant, these facts are not dispositive of the issue before us, for if the trial court had imposed only civil coercive remedies, as surely it was authorized to do, then it would be improper to invalidate that result merely because the Due Process Clause, as applied in *criminal* proceedings, was not satisfied.[5] It also bears emphasis that the purposes underlying this proceeding were wholly ambiguous. Respondent was charged with violating nine discrete prior court orders, and the proceeding may have been intended primarily to vindicate the court's authority in the face of his defiance. On the other hand, as often is true when court orders are violated, these charges were part of an ongoing battle to force respondent to conform his conduct to the terms of those orders, and of future orders as well.

Applying the traditional rules for classifying the relief imposed in a given proceeding requires the further resolution of one factual question about the nature of the relief in this case. Respondent was charged with nine separate counts of contempt, and was convicted on five of those counts, all of which arose from his failure to comply with orders to make

4. Our precedents are clear, however, that punishment may not be imposed in a civil contempt proceeding when it is clearly established that the alleged contemnor is unable to comply with the terms of the order.

5. This can also be seen by considering the notice given to the alleged contemnor. This Court has stated that one who is charged with a crime is "entitled to be informed of the nature of the charge against him but to know that it is a charge and not a suit." Yet if the relief ultimately given in such a proceeding is wholly civil in nature, then this requirement would not be applicable. It is also true, of course, that if *both* civil and criminal relief are imposed in the same proceeding, then the "criminal feature of the order is dominant and fixes its character for purposes of review."

payments in past months. He was sentenced to five days in jail on each of the five counts, for a total of 25 days, but his jail sentence was suspended and he was placed on probation for three years. If this were all, then the relief afforded would be criminal in nature.[6] But this is not all. One of the conditions of respondent's probation was that he begin making payments on his accumulated arrearage, and that he continue making these payments at the rate of $50 per month. At that rate, all of the arrearage would be paid before respondent completed his probation period. Not only did the order therefore contemplate that respondent would be required to purge himself of his past violations, but it expressly states that "[i]f any two payments are missed, whether consecutive or not, the entire balance shall become due and payable." What is unclear is whether the ultimate satisfaction of these accumulated prior payments would have purged the determinate sentence imposed on respondent. Since this aspect of the proceeding will vary as a factual matter from one case to another, depending on the precise disposition entered by the trial court, and since the trial court did not specify this aspect of its disposition in this case, it is not surprising that neither party was able to offer a satisfactory explanation of this point at argument. If the relief imposed here is in fact a determinate sentence with a purge clause, then it is civil in nature.

The state court did not pass on this issue because of its erroneous view that it was enough simply to aver that this proceeding is considered "quasi-criminal" as a matter of state law. And, as noted earlier, the court's view on this point, coupled with its view of the Federal Constitution, also led it to reinterpret the state statute, thus softening the impact of the presumption, in order to save its constitutionality. Yet the Due Process Clause does not necessarily prohibit the State from employing this presumption as it was construed by the state court, *if* respondent would purge his contempt judgment by paying off his arrearage. In these circumstances, the proper course for this Court is to vacate the judgment below and remand for further consideration of § 1209.5 free from the compulsion of an erroneous view of federal law. If on remand it is found that respondent would purge his sentence by paying his arrearage, then this proceeding is civil in nature and there was no need for the state

6. That a determinate sentence is suspended and the contemnor put on probation does not make the remedy civil in nature, for a suspended sentence, without more remains a determinate sentence, and a fixed term of probation is itself a punishment that is criminal in nature. A suspended sentence with a term of probation is not equivalent to a conditional sentence that would allow the contemnor to avoid or purge these sanctions. A determinate term of probation puts the contemnor under numerous disabilities that he cannot escape by complying with the dictates of the prior orders, such as: any conditions of probation that the court judges to be reasonable and necessary may be imposed; the term of probation may be revoked and the original sentence (including incarceration) may be reimposed at any time for a variety of reasons without all the safeguards that are ordinarily afforded in criminal proceedings; and the contemnor's probationary status could affect other proceedings against him that may arise in the future (for example, this fact might influence the sentencing determination made in a criminal prosecution for some wholly independent offense).

court to reinterpret its statute to avoid conflict with the Due Process Clause.[7]

We therefore vacate the judgment below and remand for further proceedings consistent with this opinion.

It is so ordered.

JUSTICE KENNEDY took no part in the consideration or decision of this case.

JUSTICE O'CONNOR, with whom THE CHIEF JUSTICE and JUSTICE SCALIA join, dissenting.

This case concerns a contempt proceeding against a parent who repeatedly failed to comply with a valid court order to make child support payments. In my view, the proceeding is civil as a matter of federal law. Therefore, the Due Process Clause of the Fourteenth Amendment does not prevent the trial court from applying a legislative presumption that the parent remained capable of complying with the order until the time of the contempt proceeding.

* * *

It is critical that the only conditions placed on respondent's probation, apart from the requirement that he conduct himself generally in accordance with the law, are that he cure his past failures to comply with the support order and that he continue to comply in the future. The sanction imposed on respondent is unlike ordinary criminal probation because it is collateral to a civil proceeding initiated by a private party, and respondent's sentence is suspended on the condition that he comply with a court order entered for the benefit of that party. this distinguishes respondent's sentence from suspended criminal sentences imposed outside the contempt context.

This Court traditionally has inquired into the substance of contempt proceedings to determine whether they are civil or criminal, paying particular attention to whether the sanction imposed will benefit another party to the proceeding. In this case, the California Superior Court suspended respondent's sentence on the condition that he bring himself into compliance with a court order providing support for his children, represented in the proceeding by petitioner. I conclude that the proceeding in this case should be characterized as one for civil contempt, and I would reverse the judgment below.

7. Even if this relief is judged on remand to be criminal in nature because it does not allow the contemnor to purge the judgment by satisfying the terms of the prior orders, this result does not impose any real handicap on the States in enforcing the terms of their orders, for it will be clear to the States that the presumption established by § 1209.5 can be imposed, consistent with the Due Process Clause, in any proceeding where the relief afforded is civil in nature as defined by this Court's precedents. In addition, the state courts remain free to decide for themselves the state law issues we have taken as having been resolved in this case by the court below, and to judge the lawfulness of statutes that impose similar presumptions under the provisions of their own state constitutions.

Notes and Questions

1. Some states impose more stringent requirements in civil contempt proceedings than those mandated under *Feiock*. Michigan, for example, guarantees the right to a jury trial in a civil contempt proceeding. *See* Mead v. Batchlor, 435 Mich. 480, 460 N.W.2d 493 (Mich. 1990). Some states provide counsel for indigent defendants when a jail sentence is possible. *See* In re Marriage of Stariha, 509 N.E.2d 1117 (Ind. App. 1987).

2. Inability to pay is a defense in a contempt proceeding. Courts narrowly construe this defense, however; a claim that support payments can't be made because of mortgage payments for a new home or car payments for a luxury car will not succeed.

3. Statutes setting forth the maximum penalty for contempt can be misleading, as each violation of the court's order can constitute a separate act of contempt. The support obligor who fails to pay on more than one occasion thus may face multiple charges of contempt. *See* Johnson v. Iowa District Court for Mahaska Cnty., 385 N.W.2d 562 (Iowa 1986).

4. For a detailed discussion of *Feiock*, *see* Note, 22 CREIGHTON L. REV. 163 (1988).

C. INCREASING FEDERAL INVOLVEMENT AND ITS IMPACT ON SUPPORT ENFORCEMENT

In 1975, hoping to significantly reduce the cost of the Aid to Families with Dependent Children (AFDC) program, Congress enacted sweeping legislation to strengthen enforcement of child support obligations across the nation (P.L. 93–647). Since that time, although state authority and state laws remain the primary vehicles for paternity establishment and child support collection, the federal government has been an active stimulator, overseer, and financier of state collection systems.

Under the 1975 legislation, each state enforcement agency—now commonly known as a "IV–D Agency" as a reflection of the section of statute discussing such state agencies—was required to meet standards imposed by the federal Office of Child Support Enforcement (OCSE) as a condition of receiving federal AFDC reimbursement. Under the legislation, state agencies were required, *inter alia,* to: collect data; use the social security numbers of all AFDC applicants as identification; notify the state child support enforcement agency whenever benefits are granted to deserted children; and open its records to support enforcement officials. Public assistance applicants were required to assign their right to uncollected child support to the state and to agree to cooperate in locating the absent parent, establish paternity, obtain a support judgment if none is outstanding, and secure payments. In case of an applicants's unjustified failure to cooperate, AFDC benefits were to be withheld from the applicant. (Since 1996, states have been given discretion to define both "cooperation," and "good cause" for noncooperation, and to determine the penalty for noncooperation (as long as it is not less than 25% of the family's grant).)

The 1975 legislation also required the states to maintain a "parent locator service," equipped to search state and local records for information regarding the whereabouts of absent parents. Using this service, enforcement authorities may call upon the sophisticated, computerized federal parent locator service based in Washington with access to Social Security, Internal Revenue, and other federal information sources. Once the absent (or alleged) parent is located, the state, if necessary and possible, must establish paternity, obtain a support judgment, and enforce the obligation through either in-state or interstate proceedings. All states must cooperate fully with their sister states; access to the federal courts is a last resort. If other efforts have failed, a state may request that OCSE certify to the Internal Revenue Service any outstanding judgments for collection. Past due support is also collectible from state and federal income tax refunds. After collection, the state must disburse child support payments, keeping detailed records and reporting to OCSE. To encourage local participation in child support enforcement, a portion of the proceeds is turned over to the collecting unit of local government.

While the 1975 legislation was aimed at reducing public assistance costs, legislators recognized that preventing the need for public assistance was as important as collecting support for the population already receiving benefits. IV–D services were thus made available to all parents who pay a reasonable fee; by 1994, eight million non-AFDC clients used IV–D services. OFFICE OF CHILD SUPPORT ENFORCEMENT, NINETEENTH ANNUAL REPORT TO CONGRESS (1994).

The Child Support Enforcement Amendments of 1984 (CSEA), P.L. 98–378, 98 Stat. 1205 (1984), required the states to add new enforcement weapons to their arsenal. The law required states to make wage withholding immediate in most new or modified orders using the IV–D system beginning in October 1990 and in most new orders issued after January 1, 1994. It also required the imposition of liens against the property of defaulting support obligors, expedited hearings—judicial or administrative—in support cases, and statutes of limitation permitting the establishment of paternity up to 18 years after the child's birth. The CSEA also allowed credit companies to be informed of unpaid child support in excess of $1,000 and established mechanisms for the deduction of unpaid support from federal and state income tax refunds. Additional requirements enacted as part of the Family Support Act of 1988, P.L. 100–485m, 102 Stat. 234 (1988), included automatic wage withholding for all support orders issued in public assistance cases after 1993, and compelled genetic testing in contested paternity cases; the federal government also promised to pay of 90% of the cost of those genetic tests.

The Personal Responsibility and Work Opportunity Reconciliation Act of 1996 (PWORA), Pub. L. No. 98–378, 98 Stat. 1205 (1996), further extended federal support enforcement requirements. PRWORA mandated a number of innovations in paternity establishment. States were required to provide that a signed voluntary admission of paternity is binding unless challenged within a sixty-day period or in certain other limited circumstances. They were also required to simplify and streamline the process of paternity establishment. The key piece in these new simplified procedures is "up-front" genetic testing without the necessity of filing a paternity action. These procedures complement 1993 legislation that required states to have procedures which establish either a rebuttable or conclusive presumption of paternity based upon genetic test results showing a threshold probability of paternity.

PRWORA also set up additional informational resources for the Parent Locator Services; the Act established a national Directory of New Hires and required that state agencies have access to state and local government records (including vital statistics, tax and revenue records, motor vehicle records, and occupational and professional licenses) as well as certain private records, including customer records of public utilities and cable television companies.

Finally, PRWORA mandated certain "expedited procedures" for handling routine cases. These expedited procedures must permit the state child support agency to undertake routine enforcement procedures (for example, the imposition of a lien on a defaulting obligor's assets) "without the necessity of obtaining an order from any other judicial or administrative tribunal." PWORA § 325. Other expedited case processing mechanisms were also required. *See generally* Paul Legler, *The Coming Revolution in Child Support Policy: Implications of the 1996 Welfare Act*, 30 FAM. L.Q. 519 (1996). Updated information on federal child support initiatives is available on the Office of Child Support Enforcement Home Page [http://www.acf.dhhs.gov/ACFPrograms/CSE/].

Notes and Questions

1. *Wage Garnishment*: Automatic wage withholding in IV–D cases is now required by federal law unless the support obligor can show "good cause." *See* 42 U.S.C.A. § 666. Withholding can be a very useful tool for the custodial parent, as long as the obligor is a stable employee. *See* Irwin Garfinkel & Marieka Klawitter, *The Effect of Routine Income Withholding on Child Support Collections*, 9 J. POLICY ANALYSIS & MGMT. 155, 168 (1990) (finding some improvement in collections). If the employee is self-employed or changes jobs frequently, the remedy is less effective. If the obligor moves to other states or countries, more problems can be encountered.

2. *License Suspension*: One of the newest weapon in the child support enforcement arsenal is license suspension. Under state suspension rules, delinquency for a specified period may cause the obligor to lose any of various state licenses; licenses commonly covered include driver's licenses and professional licenses, such as those required to practice law or medical license. *See* S.D. CODE §§ 32–12–116; 25–7A–56. Early results suggest that these programs may be very effective enforce-

ment tools. For a discussion of the South Dakota results, *see* "South Dakota's Driver's License and Professional License Restriction Program," pages 325–332 of the Tuesday, August 27, 1996 Conference notebook for the National Child Support Enforcement Association. *See also* Michael Holmes, *Millions Culled in Child Support*, HOUSTON CHRONICLE, Sept. 10, 1996, page 20A, col. 2.

Is a child support obligation different from any other type of judgment? Should a person not in compliance with any type of judgment have various licenses suspended? Should a custodial parent who doesn't comply with a visitation order have his or her licenses suspended?

3. *Paternity Establishment*: Lack of a paternity finding continues to be a major factor hampering support enforcement efforts for never-married mothers; in 1991 only about 27% of all never-married parents had a child support order. *See* U.S. DEP'T OF COMMERCE, BUREAU OF THE CENSUS, CHILD SUPPORT FOR CUSTODIAL MOTHERS AND FATHERS: 1991, Current Pop. Rep., Series P60–187 (1995) at 13. In response to the 1984 and 1988 federal mandates, many states have revolutionized the paternity establishment process. Several (for example, Missouri and Oregon) have moved voluntary paternity establishment out of the courts and into the administrative process. Others (for example, Arizona and Massachusetts) now allow paternity to be established by affidavit or signing the birth certificate. Still others (for example, Ohio and Washington) have moved to "in-hospital" paternity establishment. Researchers have found that such changes can significantly improve paternity establishment rates. *See generally* Ann Nichols–Casebolt & Irwin Garfinkel, *Trends in Paternity Adjudications and Child Support Awards*, 72 SOC. SCI. Q. 83, 88, tbl. 1 (showing state-by-state paternity establishment rates ranging from less than 10% to more than 50%). Indeed, one group reports that change as simple as offering the paternity defendant more than one opportunity to consent along with a bifurcated court/administrative process might raise establishment rates by anywhere from 44% to 88%. Freya L. Sonenstein et al., *Promising Approaches to Improving Paternity Establishment Rates at the Local Level*, in CHILD SUPPORT AND CHILD WELL-BEING 52 (Irwin Garfinkel et al., eds. 1994). *See also* Paula Roberts, *Child Support Orders: Problems with Enforcement*, in 4 THE FUTURE OF CHILDREN: CHILDREN AND DIVORCE 107 (Spring, 1994).

4. *Privatization*: States are beginning to experiment with privatizing their child support offices. To date, it appears that private offices could be cheaper and more effective than state enforcement. *See* Child Support Enforcement—Early Results on Comparability of Privatized and Public Offices, Report to the Chairman, Committee on the Budget, U. S. House of Representatives (December 1996).

5. *Efficacy*: The overall effect of the federal innovations in child support enforcement has been to move from a system of private, haphazard enforcement to one where payment is compelled and automatic. With the new innovations mandated by the 1996 legislation, some experts expect that "[c]ollections should soar as a result." Legler, *supra* p. 1008,

at 562. But it is important to keep in mind that two decades of federal effort to improve establishment and collection of child support obligations have thus far failed to materially improve aggregate support outcomes. In 1978—the first year in which the Census Bureau collected national data on child support awards and payments—59% of support-eligible mothers had obtained support orders. About half of those awarded support received full payment. The average value of child support paid ($3865 in 1991 dollars) represented less than half of what economists estimate as typical child-rearing costs and only 13% of average male earnings for that year. U.S. DEP'T OF COMMERCE, BUREAU OF THE CENSUS, CHILD SUPPORT AND ALIMONY: 1978 tbls. A & B (Current Population Reports, Series P–23 No. 106, 1980). In 1991 (the last year for which data is available)—56% of eligible mothers had obtained support orders. About half of those awarded support received full payment. The average value of support paid ($3011 in 1991 dollars) represented less than half of what economists estimate as typical child-rearing costs and only 8% of average male earnings for that year. *See* U.S. DEP'T OF COMMERCE, BUREAU OF THE CENSUS, CHILD SUPPORT FOR CUSTODIAL MOTHERS AND FATHERS: 1991 (CURRENT POP. REP., SERIES P60–187 (1995)). In 1990, approximately $14 billion was collected in child support; if orders had been entered that year against all noncustodial parents consistent with current guidelines and all such orders were paid in full, collections may have been as high as $48 billion. *See* ELAINE SORENSON, NONCUSTODIAL FATHERS: CAN THEY AFFORD TO PAY MORE CHILD SUPPORT? (URBAN INSTITUTE 1994).

6. *Why Don't Obligors Pay?* While some noncustodial parents ordered to pay child support fail to do so because of unemployment or other sources of resource insufficiency, the evidence suggests that many delinquent obligors can pay. We do not have definitive data on the sources of nonpayment, but one recent study provides some evidence. The researchers found that 38% of delinquent obligors said that they hadn't paid because they had no money; 23% because the custodial parent made contact with the children very difficult; 14% because of concerns about their lack of control over how the child support was spent; 13% because they did not want the child; and 12% because they disputed their paternity. Among never-married fathers, lack of money was by far the most common reason for nonpayment; divorced parents more frequently complained about problems with access. *See* Sumati Dubey, *A Study of Reasons for Non–Payment of Child Support by Non–Custodial Parents*, J. SOC. & SOC. WELFARE 115 (Spring 1996). *See also* RON MINCY & ELAINE SORENSON, CHILD SUPPORT REFORM: MOVING THE DEBATE BEYOND DEADBEAT DADS (URBAN INSTITUTE, 1994).

The 1996 welfare reform legislation attempts to facilitate work programs for unemployed fathers (§ 365) and authorizes state IV–D programs to improve the obligor's access to children (§ 469B).

7. *The Limits of Child Support Enforcement*: Even with a fully effective support enforcement system, many children in single-parent families will remain poor because their parents are also poor. *See* Joel Handler, *Women, Families, Work and Poverty: A Cloudy Future*, 6 UCLA

WOMEN'S L. J. 375, 419 (1996) (about 20% of noncustodial fathers are poor). One commentator has estimated that, if all noncustodial parents paid child support based on the guidelines, the AFDC roles would be reduced by 9% and the poverty rate by 5%. *See* Elaine Sorenson, *The Benefits of Increased Child Support Enforcement*, in WELFARE REFORM: AN ANALYSIS OF THE ISSUES 56–57 (Isabel V. Sawhill ed. 1995).

SECTION 5. DEFENSES TO THE OBLIGATION TO PAY SUPPORT

A. LACK OF ACCESS

In some states the duty to pay support is conditioned on a right to access (i.e., visitation). *See, e.g.,* OHIO REV. CODE ANN. § 3109.05; R. I. GEN. LAWS § 15–5–16. A few others authorize courts to consider interference with visitation a ground for support modification. *See,* OR. REV. STAT. ANN. § 107.431. In most states, however, visitation and support are treated as independent obligations; visitation denial does not affect the support obligation (or vice versa). *See* Moffat v. Moffat, 27 Cal.3d 645, 165 Cal.Rptr. 877, 612 P.2d 967 (1980). *See generally* HOMER CLARK, THE LAW OF DOMESTIC RELATIONS IN THE UNITED STATES 682 (2d ed. 1988); Dee Phelps, *Child Support v. Rights to Visitation*, 16 STETSON L. REV. 139 (1986). Under the majority view, an obligor who is being denied visitation should seek enforcement by contempt; the child should not suffer a loss of support due to the actions of the custodial parent.

Some courts have distinguished between frustration of visitation rights and active concealment of the location of the child. In the latter case, some "majority view" states will not permit an action for support arrearages accruing during the period of concealment. *See* Damico v. Damico, 7 Cal.4th 673, 29 Cal.Rptr.2d 787, 872 P.2d 126 (1994) (emphasizing that the child had been concealed until the child became an adult and the obligor made reasonably diligent efforts to try to locate the child); Hoffman v. Foley, 541 So.2d 145 (Fla.App.1989); Williams v. Williams, 109 N.M. 92, 781 P.2d 1170 (N.M.App.1989).

B. ESTOPPEL

Sometimes parents will make an agreement that the obligor will not have to pay support if visitation rights are waived. If a custodial parent then later attempts to collect past due support payments, courts must determine whether he or she is estopped. A few courts have held that the custodial parent is estopped in this situation (*see* Brown v. Brown, 399 So.2d 1083 (Fla.App.1981); Dubroc v. Dubroc, 388 So.2d 377 (La.1980), particularly if the obligor has changed his position in reliance on the agreement (*see* Rodgers v. Rodgers, 505 S.W.2d 138 (Mo.App.1974)). Some courts have barred collection of past due support based on such an agreement, but permitted the custodial parent to retract his or her consent with respect to future payments (*see* Malekos v. Chloe Ann Yin, 655 P.2d 728 (Alaska 1982)). Most courts, however, do not apply estoppel in this situation. *See* Blisset v. Blisset, 123 Ill.2d 161, 121 Ill.Dec. 931, 526 N.E.2d 125 (1988); Hailey v. Holden, 457 So.2d 947 (Miss.1984); Starzinger v. Starzinger, 82 Or.App. 96, 727 P.2d 168 (1986); Peebles v. Disher, 279 S.C. 611, 310 S.E.2d 823 (S.C.App.1983).

C. LACHES

Some courts have permitted a laches defense if the custodial parent has delayed seeking enforcement of past due support payments, particularly if the obligor has been prejudiced by the delay. *See* Wing v. Wing, 464 So.2d 1342 (Fla.App.1985). In most situations, however, it appears that courts will not find prejudice. *See* Connin v. Bailey, 15 Ohio St.3d 34, 472 N.E.2d 328 (1984); Estate of Comiskey, 146 Ill.App.3d 804, 100 Ill.Dec. 364, 497 N.E.2d 342 (1986); Brock v. Cavanaugh, 1 Conn.App. 138, 468 A.2d 1242 (1984). And some courts do not permit a laches defense in a child support obligation proceeding even if prejudice can be shown. *See* Wornkey v. Wornkey, 12 Kan.App.2d 506, 749 P.2d 1045 (1988); Pickett v. Pickett, 470 N.E.2d 751 (Ind.App.1984). *See generally* Annotation, 5 A.L.R.4th 1015 (1981).

The federal government now bars retroactive modification of child support. 42 U.S.C. § 666(a)(9)(C). How will this development affect the ability of the obligor to argue that concealment, laches or estoppel should be a defense to an action for arrearages?

Index

References are to Pages

ABORTION
Generally, 158–61, 268–79, 449–58
Husband's consent or notice, 158–61
Minor's decision, 449–58
Parent's consent to minor's abortion, 458
Parent's notice of minor's abortion, 449–57
Partial birth abortion, 279
Pre–Roe v. Wade legislation, 268–69
Statistics, 279

ADOPTION
Generally, 307–58
Adoptive relationship as marriage impediment, 81–82
Agency's role, 309–10
Anonymity, 308
"Black market babies," 310, 353–58
Consent,
Father's consent, 319–36
Mother's consent, 311–19
Revocation of consent, 318–19
History of, 307–09
Homosexual, 336–43
Incest, 81–82
Independent adoption, 309–10, 355–56
Indian children, 344–45
Interracial adoption, 344–48
Legal effects, 349–53
Religious matching, 348
Revocation, 352–53
Sale of baby, 353–58
Statistics, 309
Wrongful adoption, 353

ADULTERY
Bar to alimony, 805–06
Crime, 28
Ground for divorce, 537
Tort, 153–54

AFFINITY, 77

AGE
See Child Support; Emancipation; Marriage

AGED
Relative responsibility, 852–55

AIDS
Premarital HIV test, 87

ALIENATION OF AFFECTIONS, 153–54

ALIMONY
See also Bankruptcy; Property; Taxation
Generally, 790–835
Adultery as bar, 805–06
ALI standards, 834–35
Cohabitation, effect of, 980–88
Death terminating, 948, 951
Duration, 809–19
Employment of recipient, 804, 978–79
Enforcement, 997–98
Factors, 794–809
Fault as factor, 805–09
Gender neutrality, 791
History, 790–91
Modification, 967–88
Rehabilitative, 793, 809–19
Remarriage, effect of, 985
Statistics, 793
Tax treatment, 951–53
Theoretical basis, 821–35
Waiver in premarital agreement, 207

ALTERNATE DISPUTE RESOLUTION (in divorce)
Arbitration, 940–46
Conciliation, 926
Mediation, 933–39

ALTERNATIVE LIFESTYLES
See Cohabitation (Nonmarital)

ANNULMENT
Generally, 560–62
Consequences, 562
Grounds, 87–92, 561–62
Tax aspects, 560
Validity of void or voidable marriages, 562

ARBITRATION (in divorce)
See Alternate Dispute Resolution

ARTIFICIAL INSEMINATION, 360–69

ASSISTED REPRODUCTION, 359–402

BANKRUPTCY,
Generally, 954–66
Alimony and child support, 947, 958–61
Marital debts, 954–58

BANKRUPTCY,—Cont'd
Property settlement, 947, 961–62

BATTERED SPOUSE
Generally, 168–78
Defense to criminal prosecution, 173–78
Factor in abortion decision making, 160–61
Factor in child custody, 653–58
Violence Against Women Act (VAWA), 39, 177–78

BIGAMY
Crime, 63
Marriage prohibition, 59–65
Putative spouse, 106–09

BILL OF RIGHTS FOR CHILDREN, 413

BIRTH CONTROL
See Abortion; Contraception

BLOOD TESTS
Marriage license, 87
Paternity, 298–300

BREACH OF PROMISE TO MARRY, 254

CAPACITY TO MARRY, 87–90

CHILD ABUSE AND NEGLECT,
Generally, 459–93
Factor in child custody, 658
Medical neglect, 434–46
Prenatal, 471–78
Role of child welfare agencies, 459–61, 469
Statutory standards, 470

CHILD CUSTODY
See also Adoption; Termination of Parental Rights; Visitation Rights
Child's preference, 638
Conflict of laws, 597
Contempt, 686–93
Counsel for child, 632–38
Domestic violence as factor, 653–58
Expert testimony, 658–64
Factors, 638–39
Guardian ad litem, 636
Hague Convention, 617–627
Joint custody, 670–80
Mediation, 933–39
Modification, 712–18
Nonparents, 693–705
Parental Kidnapping Prevention Act, 601–17
Primary caretaker presumption, 664–70
"Psychological parenthood," 701–03
Race of parent, 645–47
Religious practices of parent, 647–53
Sex of parent, 640–44
Sexual orientation of parent as a factor, 652
Statistics on custody litigation, 644
"Tender years" presumption, 640–43
Tort (interference), 693

CHILD CUSTODY—Cont'd
Uniform Child Custody Jurisdiction Act, 597–601, 603–04, 611–17

CHILD SUPPORT
AFDC, 1006–07
ALI Standards, 894–97
Conflict of laws, 588
Contempt of court, 999–1006
Criminal penalties, 997–99
Enforcement, 996–1012
Federal enforcement legislation, 1006–10
Full Faith and Credit for Child Support Orders Act (FFCSOA), 594–97
Guidelines,
Case processing under, 863
Constitutionality of, 863
Defining income under, 865–68
Deviation from, 862
Evaluation of, 887–93
High income of obligor, 868–74
Low income of obligor, 874–76
Models, 857–61
Higher education, 882–86
History, 836–38
Intact family, 838–42
Joint and split custody, 877–81
Majority, 882
Modification, 967–68, 972–77
Obligor's death, 886
Parent locator service, 1007
Relative responsibility, 852–55
Stepparent responsibility, 846–52
Uniform Interstate Family Support Act (UIFSA), 589–94
Uniform Parentage Act, 842–46
Uniform Reciprocal Enforcement of Support Act (URESA), 588

CHILDREN
See Child Custody; Child Support; Parent and Child; Visitation Rights

COHABITATION (NONMARITAL)
Australia (New South Wales), 248–52
Domestic partnership, 253
Factor in child custody decision making, 652
Factor in terminating alimony, 980–88
Statistics, 225–26
Statutory treatment of, 248–53
Sweden, 253
Tax considerations, 246
Validity of agreement, 226–41

COLLUSION (in divorce), 536

COMMON LAW MARRIAGE, 96–106

COMMUNITY PROPERTY
During marriage, 116–27
On death, 127–30
On divorce, 720

References are to Pages

CONDONATION (in divorce), 542–43

CONFLICT OF LAWS
Child custody, 597
Child support, 588
Common law marriage, 98
"Divisible" divorce, 573
Divorce jurisdiction, 571–74
Domicile, 572–73
Foreign divorce, 575–80
Marital property, 587–88
Premarital agreements, 211–12
Residency requirements (divorce), 566–70
"*Sherrer*" rule, 574
Sister state divorce, 571–74

CONNIVANCE (in divorce), 542–43

CONSANGUINITY
See Incest

CONSENT
Adoption, 311–36
Marriage, 87–92
Minor's
  To abortion, 458
  To medical treatment, 434–39

CONSORTIUM (loss of), 154–55

CONTRACEPTION
Minor's access to, 447–49
State regulation of, 266–68

COUNSEL
See Lawyer in Family Law; Right to Counsel

COUNSELING
See Alternate Dispute Resolution, Lawyer in Family Law

CRIMINAL CONVERSATION, 153

CRIMINAL LAW AND THE FAMILY
  See also Battered Spouse, Child Abuse and Neglect, Family Violence
Adultery, 28
Bigamy, 63
Burglary, 165–68
Evidence privilege, 178–83
Failure to support, 997–98
Fornication, 24–30
Rape, 162–64
Sodomy, 28–29

CRUELTY (ground for divorce), 538–42

CUSTODY
See Child Custody

DESERTION, 538

DIVISIBLE DIVORCE, 573

DIVORCE

DIVORCE—Cont'd
  See also Alimony; Alternate Dispute Resolution; Annulment; Child Custody; Child Support; Conflicts of Law; Lawyer in Family Law; Property; Remarriage
"Bed and board," 560
  See also Separate Maintenance
Children, impact on, 41–45, 629–32
Consent divorce,
  Default, uncontested, 536
  Sherrer rule, 574
Constitutional right, 563–65
Defenses
  Connivance, 542–43
  Condonation, 543
  Recrimination, 543–44
Fault grounds,
  Adultery, 537
  Cruelty, 538–41
  Desertion, 537–38
Foreign, 575–80
History, 532–37
Jurisdiction, 571–74
Lawyer's fees, 520–21
Lawyer's role, 494–520
No-fault divorce
  Grounds, 544–51
  Pros and cons, 551–60
  UMDA, 544–45
Residency requirements, 566–70
Right to counsel, 565–66
Statistics, 531–32
United Kingdom, 550

DNA TESTING (in paternity actions), 298–300

DOMICILE
See Conflicts of Law

EMANCIPATION (of children), 408

EQUAL PROTECTION CLAUSE
Illegitimacy, 293–96
Right to marry, 48–58

ETHICS (Lawyer's)
See Lawyer in Family Law

EUGENICS
See Genetics

FAMILY
Constitutional protection of, 9–10
Definition and types, 1–19

FAMILY POLICY
See State and Family

FAMILY VIOLENCE
Battered spouse, 168–72
Battered woman syndrome, 172–79
Effect on children, 657–58
Police protection, 170–71

References are to Pages

FAMILY VIOLENCE—Cont'd
Rape of spouse, 162–64

FEDERAL CHILD SUPPORT LEGISLATION
See Child Support

FEDERAL GOVERNMENT AND FAMILY LAW
See State and Family

FOREIGN DIVORCE
See Conflicts of Law

FORNICATION
See Crime and the Family

FOSTER CARE
See also Adoption; Child Abuse and Neglect; Termination of Parental Rights
Agency practices, 459–61, 469–70
Foster parent's rights, 18–19
Statistics, 492–93

FRAUD
Ground for annulment, 561–62

FULL FAITH AND CREDIT
See Conflicts of Law; Jurisdiction

GENETICS
See also Artificial Insemination
Eugenics, 86–87, 401–02
Incest, 76–82

GRANDPARENTS
Support, 852
Visitation, 705–10

GUARDIANSHIP
See also Child Custody
Of child, 408–09, 632–36
Of spouse, 155–57

HEALTH
Child's medical care, 427–47
Spouse's medical care, 155–58
Qualification for marriage, 86–87

"HEARTBALM" ACTIONS
Alienation of affections, 153–54
Breach of promise to marry, 254
Criminal conversation, 153

HOMOSEXUALITY
Adoption, 336–43
Child custody, 652
Cohabitation, 236, 253
Crime, 28–29
Marriage, 65–76

HUSBAND AND WIFE
See Marriage

ILLEGITIMACY
See also Legitimacy, Paternity
Equal protection, 293–96
Father's parental rights, 319–36, 360–68

IN VITRO FERTILIZATION, 369–79

INCEST, 76–82

INDIAN CHILD WELFARE ACT, 344–45

INFORMAL MARRIAGE
See Cohabitation (Nonmarital); Common Law Marriage

INHERITANCE
Child's rights, 886–87
Spousal right of election, 127–30

JURISDICTION
See also Conflict of Laws
Child custody, 597–611
Child support, 588–97
Divorce, 571–74
Federal, in family law, 30–37
Real estate, out of state, 587–88

LAWYER IN FAMILY LAW
See also Right to Counsel
"Bombers," 517
Conflict of interests, 496–510
Duties to client, 510–16
Duties to opposing parties, 516
Fees, 504–10
Joint representation, 498–503
Malpractice, 521–30
Specialization in family law, 494

LEGITIMACY
Presumption of legitimacy, 279–89
Uniform Parentage Act (UPA), 289–91

LORD HARDWICKE'S ACT, 96–97

LORD MANSFIELD'S RULE, 280

MARITAL CONTRACTS
See Antenuptial Agreements; Postnuptial Agreements; Separation Agreements

MARITAL PRIVACY
See Sexual Privacy

MARITAL PROPERTY
See Property

MARRIAGE
Adoptive relationship as impediment, 81–82
Age, 82–85
Pregnancy, 83
"Battered Spouse Syndrome", 168–178
Capacity, 110–114
Constitutional right to marry, 48–58
Contract or status, 184–188
Criminal law and marriage, 162–183
Evidence, privilege, 178–183
Formalities, 92–96
Impediments, 58–87
License, 92–95
Name of married woman, 147–151
Prohibited, 58–87
Property rights, Chapter 3
Proxy, 93

References are to Pages

MARRIAGE—Cont'd
Putative spouse, 106–109
Rape, of spouse, 162–164
Sham, jest or ulterior motive, 90–92
Solemnization, 92–93
Support obligation, 131–147
Tort law, 152–155
Void, voidable, 58–59

"MARRIAGE PENALTY" (Income Tax), 949–950

MARRIED WOMEN'S PROPERTY ACT, 111–114

MEDIATION AND ARBITRATION
See also Conciliation

MEN'S EQUALITY
See Women's Equality

MEXICAN DIVORCE
Validity in United States, 575–579

MIGRATORY DIVORCE, 571–581
Residency requirements, 566–570

MONOGAMY, 59–65

NAME (Surname)
Married woman, 147–151

"NECESSARIES", 137–142

"NEW LIFESTYLES"
See Cohabitation (Unwed); Communal Associations

PARENT AND CHILD
See also Child Support; Custody; Guardianship; Termination of Parental Rights
Child's duty to support parent, 852–855
Child's emancipation, 882–886
Constitutionally protected relationship, 319–332
Notice to parents of minor child's abortion, 449–459
Parents' consent to minor child's abortion, 449–459
Parents' power to commit child, 428–433
Parents' power to refuse medical treatment, 434–447
Schooling, 418–427

PATERNITY (Ascertainment)
Blood and generic tests, 298–299
DNA fingerprinting, 299
Child's right to establish, 300–304
Court action, 296–297
Father's right to establish, 280–292
Statute of limitations, 304
Uniform Parentage Act, 289–291; 304–305
Uniform Putative and Unknown Fathers Act, 332–333

PENSIONS
Basic terminology, 743–744

PENSIONS—Cont'd
Civil service, 752
Government and military, 744–747; 753–754
Present value approach, 748–751
QDRO, 751–752
Railroad retirement, 752
Reserved jurisdiction approach, 750
Social security, 753
Valuation problems, 751

POLYGAMY
Mormons, 59–65
Moslems, 63

POSTNUPTIAL AGREEMENTS, 216–224

POVERTY
See also Right to Counsel; State and Family
Generally
Alimony, 791–805
Divorce, 503–504
Obstacle to divorce, 563–566

PREGNANCY
Marriage age reduced, 83–85

PRENUPTIAL AGREEMENTS
See Antenuptial Agreements

PRIVACY (Right to)
See Sexual Privacy

PRIVILEGE
See Evidence

PROFESSIONAL LICENSE
As property on divorce, 756–766

PROPERTY
See also Pensions; Taxation
ALI proposal, 788–789
Bankruptcy, 954–966
Common law (separate property systems), 110–111
Community property, 116–127
Conflict of laws, 787
Equitable distribution, 719–721; 778–780
European systems, 788 (Germany), 549–555 (England)
"Goodwill", 766–776
History, 110–111
Homemaker's contribution, 778–780
Inheritance, 127–131
"Marital Property", 719–721
Married Women's Property Act, 111–115
Pension, 743–756
Professional license, 756–766
Uniform Marital Property Act, 117–118

PUTATIVE SPOUSE, 106–109

RACE
As factor in adoption, 344–349
As factor in custody, 645–647
Indian children, 344–345

RACE—Cont'd
Interracial adoption, 344–349
Marriage, 68

RAPE
Of spouse, 162–164

RECONCILIATION AGREEMENT, 222–224

RECRIMINATION, 543–544

RELATIVE RESPONSIBILITY, 852–855

RELIGION
Custody, 647–653

REMARRIAGE
"Means test", 48–58

RESIDENCE
See Conflict of Laws

RIGHT TO COUNSEL
Termination of parental rights, 491

SCHOOLS
Child's rights, 418–427
Parental authority, 418–427

SEPARATE MAINTENANCE
Generally, 560
Divorce from bed and board, 560
Tax aspects, 560

SEPARATION AGREEMENTS
Generally, 898–901
Relationship to divorce decree,915–919
U.M.D.A., 908–910

SEX CHANGE
Capacity to marry, 75–76

SEXUAL DISCRIMINATION
See Women's Equality

SEXUAL PRIVACY
See also Criminal Law and the Family
Abortion, 268–279
Homosexuals, 28–29
In marriage, 19–23
Unmarried persons, 24–30

SINGLE PARENTS
See Cohabitation (Unwed)
Illegitimacy, 293–296

SOCIAL LEGISLATION
See State and Family

SOCIAL SECURITY
See also State and Family
Divorce, 753

SOLEMNIZATION OF MARRIAGE, 87–90

STATE AND FAMILY
See also Termination of Parental Rights
Birth Control, 19–24
Child support enforcement, 996–1012
Family policy, 38–45

STATE AND FAMILY—Cont'd
Federal jurisdiction in family law, 30–37
"Marriage penalty", 949–950
Social functions of family, 1–19
Spousal support, Chapter 15
Tax policy, 947–954

STEP-RELATIONSHIP
Custodial claims, 710
Duty to support child, 846–852

SUPPORT OBLIGATIONS
See also Alimony; Child support
Child's duty to support parent, 852–855
"Necessaries" defined, 137–142
Spouses, 131–142

SURNAME
See Name

SURROGATE MOTHERHOOD, 379–397

SWEDEN
Cohabitation, 253
Marriage and divorce reform, 546

TAXATION
Alimony, 951–953
Annulment, 560–562
Child support, 951–953
Cohabitants, 236
Income tax and family, 947–954
Lawyer's fees, deductible, 954
"Marriage penalty", 949–950
Property distribution, 950–951
Separate maintenance, 560

TERMINATION OF PARENTAL RIGHTS
Generally, 478–483
Adoption terminating parental rights, 507
Right to counsel, 491
Standard of proof, 478–491
Unmarried father, 319–332

UNIFORM PREMARITAL AGREEMENTS ACT, 204–205

UNIFORM CHILD CUSTODY JURISDICTION ACT, 597–601

UNIFORM INTERSTATE SUPPORT ACT, 589–593

UNIFORM MARITAL PROPERTY ACT, 117–118

UNIFORM MARRIAGE AND DIVORCE ACT
Alimony, 796–797
Annulment, 561
Child custody, modification, 713
Child support criteria, 855
Criteria for dissolution, 544–546
Marriage license, 92
Prohibited marriages, 77
Putative spouse, 107
Separation agreement, 908–910

References are to Pages

UNIFORM MARRIAGE AND DIVORCE ACT —Cont'd
Solemnization, 92–93

UNIFORM PARENTAGE ACT
Artificial insemination, 360–369
Paternity action, 297; 304–305

UNIFORM PREMARITAL AGREEMENT ACT, 204–205

UNIFORM PROBATE CODE
Intestacy, 128
Spouse's elective share, 129

UNIFORM PUTATIVE AND UNKNOWN FATHERS ACT, 332–333

UNIFORM RECIPROCAL ENFORCEMENT OF SUPPORT ACT, 588

UNIFORM STATUS OF CHILDREN OF ASSISTED CONCEPTION ACT, 387–390

UNMARRIED FATHER
See Cohabitation (Unwed); Legitimacy; Illegitimacy; Paternity (Ascertainment); Termination of Parental Rights

UNITED KINGDOM
Divorce reform, 549–555

VISITATION RIGHTS
"Best interests of child", 682–686
Enforcement, 692–693
Grandparents, 705–710
Stepparents, 710

VOID AND VOIDABLE MARRIAGES
See also Annulment
In general, 58–59
Putative spouse, 107–109

WOMEN'S EQUALITY
Loss of consortium, 154–155
Married Women's Property Act, 111–113
Name of married woman, 147–151

ZONING
Definition of "family", 1–19

0-314-21123-3

9 780314 211231 90000